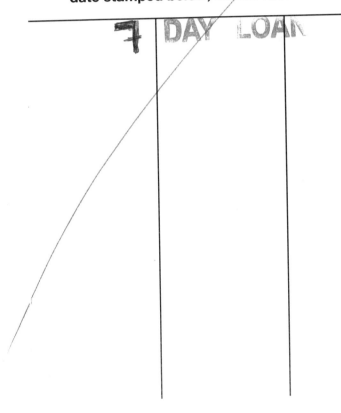

THE LAW AND PRACTICE OF
INTERNATIONAL BANKING

THE LAW AND PRACTICE OF INTERNATIONAL BANKING

CHARLES PROCTOR LLD (B'HAM)

Solicitor of the Supreme Court
England and Wales

Partner, Bird & Bird LLP, London

Honorary Professor of Law,
University of Birmingham

Visiting Professorial Fellow
Centre for Commercial Law Studies
Queen Mary College,
University of London

OXFORD
UNIVERSITY PRESS

OXFORD
UNIVERSITY PRESS

Great Clarendon Street, Oxford OX2 6DP

Oxford University Press is a department of the University of Oxford.
It furthers the University's objective of excellence in research, scholarship,
and education by publishing worldwide in

Oxford New York

Auckland Cape Town Dar es Salaam Hong Kong Karachi
Kuala Lumpur Madrid Melbourne Mexico City Nairobi
New Delhi Shanghai Taipei Toronto

With offices in

Argentina Austria Brazil Chile Czech Republic France Greece
Guatemala Hungary Italy Japan Poland Portugal Singapore
South Korea Switzerland Thailand Turkey Ukraine Vietnam

Oxford is a registered trade mark of Oxford University Press
in the UK and in certain other countries

Published in the United States
by Oxford University Press Inc., New York

British Library Cataloguing-in-Publication Data
Data available

Library of Congress Cataloging-in-Publication Data
Proctor, Charles, LLB
The law and practice of international banking/Charles Proctor.
p. cm.
Includes bibliographical references and index.
ISBN 978–0–19–929186–1 (hardbook: alk. paper) 1. Banks and banking,
International—Law and legislation. I. Title.
K1066.P76 2010
346'.08215—dc22

2010021226

Typeset by Glyph International, Bangalore, India
Printed in Great Britain
on acid-free paper by
CPI Antony Rowe, Chippenham, Wiltshire

ISBN 978–0–19–929186–1

1 3 5 7 9 10 8 6 4 2

For WK

PREFACE

The author of a work on a legal subject has to accept that the subject matter will not remain stagnant during the years of work involved. The stream of new legislation, new cases, new EU regulations and the like will continue unabated as one wrestles with a draft text which is constantly in need of rewriting and stubbornly refuses to mutate into its final form. This is simply an occupational hazard, which the writer must accept with weary resignation.

Yet, even accepting inevitable changes and developments, it remains fair to say that this book differs in many important respects from the text which I originally had in mind. The catastrophe which afflicted the financial markets in 2008 continues to cast a long shadow and has resulted in a mass of regulatory activity in a short time, beginning with temporary legislation for the public ownership of Northern Rock and leading to more comprehensive legislation to deal with problems posed by bank insolvency. Similarly, brief chapters intended to deal with deposit protection and the EU Directive on the reorganisation and winding up of credit institutions expanded as the financial crisis took hold, and acquired a new dimension when the collapse of the Icelandic banking sector mushroomed into a diplomatic, as well as a financial, crisis.

But not all of the new material is the product of these disasters. The EU's Payment Services Directive has been a major project, and was implemented during the course of 2009. The consequences of this initiative are considered in Chapter 5. In addition, the whole subject of Islamic finance has assumed an accelerating importance in the UK's financial markets since exclusively Islamic-based institutions were first authorized here in 2004. It was thus felt appropriate to devote a portion of the text to Shariah-compliant products, the case law to which they have given rise and developments in this market generally.

All of these considerations have resulted in a text which is structured as follows:

(a) Parts (A) and (B) deal with a series of regulatory issues and associated matters such as the reorganization of credit institutions and the protection of depositors;
(b) Parts (C), (D), and (E) deal with contractual and business matters, including the banker-customer relationship, loan, documentary credit and other facilities, and guarantees and security;
(c) Part (F) considers a variety of issues which may cause particular difficulties in an international context, including freezing injunctions, the problems posed by foreign disclosure orders, and the impact of economic sanctions and similar measures; and
(d) Part (G) examines the legal issues arising from the use of Shariah-compliant products, and includes a comparative examination of the case law which has arisen in England, Malaysia and, to a much more limited extent, in other jurisdictions.

A text of this kind is never the sole product of the author's own efforts. I would like to thank Oxford University Press and its personnel, including in particular Rachel Mulally,

Ann Krzyanowska, Bethan Cousins, and Cheryl Prophett for their efforts in bringing this work to fruition. I am especially grateful for their patience as the anticipated delivery date was repeatedly delayed.

As ever, my most grateful thanks go to my wife Martina, who tolerated this project over a period of years and, in addition, gave her time to assist with the research.

This book was completed with reference to the materials available to me as at 31 December 2009 although it has been possible to include reference to a few subsequent items. The views stated in the text are those of the writer alone.

Charles Proctor
London EC4
3 April 2010

CONTENTS—SUMMARY

Contents—Summary

G ISLAMIC FINANCE

Contents—Summary

G ISLAMIC FINANCE

48. Islamic Finance—Principles and Structures 767
49. Islamic Finance Transactions in the Courts 787
50. Corporate and Regulatory Issues 801
51. Harmonization and the Development of the International Islamic Financial Markets 813

Index 821

xi

CONTENTS

A REGULATORY MATTERS

Contents

E GUARANTEES AND SECURITY

26. Guarantees

Contents

G ISLAMIC FINANCE

TABLE OF CASES

TABLES OF LEGISLATION

*Paragraph references in **bold** indicate that the text is reproduced in full*

EUROPEAN LEGISLATION

Regulations

TREATIES AND CONVENTIONS

LIST OF ABBREVIATIONS

AAOIFI	Accounting and Auditing Organisation for Islamic Financial Institutions
BACS	Bankers Automated Clearing Services
Basel II	'International Convergence of Capital Measurement and Capital Standards—A Revised Framework'
BBA	*Al-Bai Bithaman Ajil*
BCBS	Basel Committee on Banking Supervision
BIC	Bank Identifier Code
CEBS	Committee of European Banking Supervisors
CEIOPS	Committee of European Insurance and Occupational Pensions Committee
CESR	Committee of European Securities Regulators
CHAPS	Clearing House Automated Payment System
CPR	Civil Procedure Rules
EEA	European Economic Area
EPC	European Payments Council
ESCB	European System of Central Banks
ESFS	European System of Financial Supervisors
ESRB	European Systemic Risk Board
EURIBOR	Euro interbank offered rate
FATF	Financial Action Task Force
FSA	Financial Services Authority
FSB	Financial Stability Board
FSCS	Financial Services Compensation Scheme
FSMA	Financial Services and Markets Act 2000
G-7	Group of Seven
IBAN	International Bank Account Number
IFSB	Islamic Financial Services Board
ISDA	International Swaps and Derivatives Association
JMLSG	Joint Money Laundering Steering Group
LIBOR	London interbank offered rate
LMA document	Multicurrency Term Facility Agreement (the 'LMA document') published by the Loan Market Association
MiFID	Markets in Financial Instruments Directive 2004/39/EC
OECD	Organisation for Economic Co-operation and Development
OFT	Office of Fair Trading
POCA	Proceeds of Crime Act 2002
PSD	Payment Services Directive
Recast Banking Consolidation Directive	Directive 2006/48/EC of the European Parliament and of the Council relating to the taking up and pursuit of the business of credit institutions (recast) OJ L 177, 30.06.2006, p 1

Regualted Activities	The Financial Services and Markets Act 2000
Order	(Regulated Activities) Order 2001 (SI 2001/544), as amended
Rome I	Regulation (EC) 593/2008 of the European Parliament and of the Council of 17 June 2008 on the law applicable to contractual obligations (Rome I) OJ L 177, 4.7.2008, p 6
RTGS system	real time gross settlement system
SEC	Securities and Exchange Commission
SEPA	Single Euro Payments Area
SOCA	Serious Organised Crime Agency
SWIFT	Society for Worldwide Financial Telecommunications
TARGET	Trans-European Automated Real-time Gross Settlement Express Transfer
TARP	Troubled Asset Relief Programme
UCP	Uniform Customs and Practice for Documentary Credits (ICC Publication no 600)
UNCITRAL	United Nations Commission on International Trade Law

FSA Handbook Abbreviations

BCOBS	Banking: Conduct of Business Sourcebook
BIPRU	Prudential Sourcebook for Banks, Building Societies and Investment Firms
CASS	Client Assets Sourcebook
COBS	Conduct of Business Sourcebook
COMP	Compensation Sourcebook
GENPRU	General Prudential Sourcebook
MAR	Code of Market Conduct
MCOB	Mortgages and Home Finance: Conduct of Business Sourcebook
ML	Money Laundering Sourcebook (no longer in force)
PERG	Perimeter Guidance Manual
PRIN	Principles for Businesses
SUP	Supervisory Sourcebook
SYSC	Senior Management Arrangements, Systems and Controls
UNFCOG	Unfair Contract Terms Guide

Books referred to in abbreviated form

Blair, Walker & Purves	*Financial Services Law* (2nd edn, Oxford University Press, 2009)
Chitty	*Chitty on Contracts* (30th edn, Sweet & Maxwell, 2009)
Dicey, Morris & Collins	*Dicey, Morris & Collins on the Conflict of Laws* (14th edn, Sweet & Maxwell, 2009)
Fisher & Lightwood	*Fisher & Lightwood's Law of Mortgage* (12th edn, LexisNexis Butterworths, 2006)
Jack	*Documentary Credits* (4th edn, Tottel, 2009)

Law of Bank Payments	Brindle and Cox (eds), *Law of Bank Payments* (3rd edn, Sweet & Maxwell, 2004)
Lingard	Timothy Parsons, *Lingard's Bank Security Documents* (4th edn, LexisNexis Butterworths, 2006)
Mann	Proctor, *Mann on the Legal Aspect of Money* (6th edn, Oxford University Press, 2003)
McKnight	*The Law of International Finance* (Oxford University Press, 2008)
Mugasha	*The Law of Multi-Bank Financing: Syndicated Loans and the Secondary Loan Market* (Oxford University Press, 2008)
Paget	Hapgood, *Paget's Law of Banking* (13th edn, LexisNexis Butterworths, 2007)

PART A

REGULATORY MATTERS

Introduction

The first section of this book deals with the regulatory requirements applicable to the establishment and conduct of banking business in the United Kingdom.

The section is arranged as follows:

(a) Chapter 1 considers the regulatory framework applicable to the conduct of deposit-taking business in the United Kingdom;
(b) Chapter 2 examines the very significant impact of EU law in the banking sphere;
(c) Chapter 3 considers the regulatory framework applicable to retail banking and investment business;
(d) Chapter 4 considers the extent to which lending business is subject to regulation in the United Kingdom;
(e) Chapter 5 examines the recently introduced framework for the regulation of the provision of payment services across the EU;
(f) Chapter 6 examines various rules directed towards the prudent management of risk, including capital adequacy and the regulation of large exposures;
(g) Chapter 7 considers the impact of anti-money laundering and anti-terrorist financing legislation on a bank's business; and
(h) Chapter 8 examines the structure of market regulation and the respective institutions involved in that process.

1

THE REGULATION OF DEPOSIT-TAKING BUSINESS

Introduction

The conduct of banking business is regulated in a variety of ways. At the most basic level, **1.01** some form of licence or authorization will always be required before an entity can engage in banking at all.[1] Thereafter, of course, there will be ongoing requirements as to competence of management, adequacy of capital, conduct of business and other matters. In a modern economy in which banking plays such a key role, the existence of these requirements needs no philosophical justification. Indeed, the depth of the financial crisis which gripped the world in the period beginning in 2008 means that political pressure for further regulation of banks and financial institutions will only intensify.[2]

Yet matters are more complex than these broad statements may immediately suggest. For **1.02** example, banking is now an undeniably international business, and the insolvency of an institution will invariably have repercussions beyond its own national boundaries.[3] Yet the framework put in place for banking supervision is in many ways dependent upon purely national, legal structures. One only has to state this proposition to realize that there is in many ways a serious mismatch between the essentially territorial scope of the regulator's powers and the international reach of many banks. Efforts are periodically made—and

---

[1] Although, as will be seen, the mere activity of lending one's own capital to commercial customers (as opposed to consumers) does not require any form of authorization in the United Kingdom.

[2] Some of these developments are considered in Chapter 8 below.

[3] Again, this statement requires no justification but the aspects of the crisis relating to certain Icelandic banks provide an obvious illustration: see the discussion at para 13.13 below.

are currently being made—to bridge this gap. Inevitably, however, domestic political considerations may render this process difficult.

1.03 With these factors in mind, it is proposed to examine the following matters:

(a) the history of the regulation of banking business in the United Kingdom;
(b) deposit-taking as a regulated activity;
(c) the authorization procedure;
(d) the powers of the Financial Services Authority (FSA); and
(e) finally, brief mention will be made of the position of banks incorporated in other parts of the European Economic Area (EEA) but carrying on business or providing services within the United Kingdom.

The History of Banking Regulation in the United Kingdom

Introduction

1.04 Until 1979, there was no domestic legislation that regulated the conduct of banking business in the United Kingdom. Indeed, insofar as banking business comprises the making of loans and advances to customers, the absence of regulation remains a significant feature of the current legislation.[4] Until 1979, the Bank of England operated an informal system of supervision which relied upon an expectation of compliance and the general influence of the central bank in the financial sphere.[5] At that point, however, Parliament passed the Banking Act 1979, which required that the acceptance of deposits from the public should be subject to prior authorization by the Bank of England. The Act was passed in order to give effect to this country's obligations under the First EC Banking Directive, which required a formalized system of authorization and supervision for the banking sector.[6] The regulatory framework was subsequently revised and extended by the Banking Act 1987. The main consequences of the 1987 Act were (i) a streamlining of the authorization process,[7] (ii) the introduction of a 'large exposures' reporting system,[8] and (iii) the Bank of

---

[4] The exceptions to this statement relate principally to mortgage lending and consumer credit, where regulation seeks to compensate for a lack of bargaining power. These aspects will be discussed at paras 4.02–4.54 below. The perhaps somewhat anomalous position stated in the text is in some respects mitigated by the fact that, again subject to exceptions, a person cannot accept a loan (or deposit) from an institution which does not hold an appropriate authorization or whose business does not consist mainly of money lending (see the discussion at para 1.14 below). It should be added that, whilst a bank's lending activities are not *directly* regulated, they are indirectly regulated by a number of means, eg through the rules requiring an institution to hold sufficient capital to meet its risks, rules governing large exposures and similar measures: see generally the discussion in Chapter 6 below.
[5] The history of banking supervision in the United Kingdom is briefly described in the opening remarks of Lord Steyn in *Three Rivers DC v Bank of England* [2001] 2 All ER 513 (HL).
[6] The scope and effect of the First Banking Directive was one of the issues which arose for debate in the *Three Rivers* litigation, and is accordingly discussed in Chapter 14 below.
[7] An institution which wished to accept deposits would henceforth have to be an 'authorized institution'. This replaced the earlier system under the 1979 Act, which provided for a two-tier structure of 'recognized banks' and 'licensed deposit takers'.
[8] On this subject, see paras 6.63–6.68 below.

England was given more 'teeth' in the sense that it had greater powers to demand information and to carry out investigations.

A notable feature of the 1987 Act—especially when compared with the current legisla-   **1.05**
tion—is that the Act regulated *who* could carry on a deposit-taking business but, subject to
minor exceptions—it did not regulate *how* that business should be carried on, in the sense
that there were very limited rules dealing with the conduct of business.

It was at this point of time that the incoming tide of European legislation began to become   **1.06**
more evident. In 1989, the EC Council adopted its Second Council Directive on the coordination of laws, regulations and administrative provisions relating to the taking up and
pursuit of the business of credit institutions,[9] which was implemented in the United
Kingdom by means of the Banking Coordination (Second Council Directive) Regulations
1992.[10] These regulations gave effect to the Community's 'passporting' scheme, under
which it would no longer be necessary for an EC-based institution to be separately authorized in each of the EC Member States in which it had a branch or provided services.
Instead, it would be permitted to establish a branch and undertake local activities in those
other countries in reliance on its home State authorization. Although these particular regulations have now been repealed, the passporting system remains in effect through later
directives and their implementing regulations, and this forms one of the key pillars of
EU banking law.[11] In addition, the Community began to introduce further directives
intended to implement the capital adequacy and other prudential requirements laid down
by the 1988 Capital Accord published by the Basel Committee on Banking Supervision
(Basel I).[12] The further initiatives included the Own Funds Directive,[13] the Solvency Ratio
Directive[14] and two directives dealing with capital adequacy issues.[15] All of these directives
have subsequently been consolidated and amended in the light of further recommendations by the Basel Committee in the field of capital adequacy.[16] So it will be seen that the
early 1990s saw a significant 'Europeanization' of banking law, mainly as a harmonizing
measure with a view to completing the EC's 'single market'.[17]

More recently, however—and in a move which was not dictated by considerations of   **1.07**
Community law—the government determined that the functions of the central bank

---

[9] 89/646/EC, OJ L 386, 30.12.1989.
[10] SI 1992/3218.
[11] For further discussion of this subject, see paras 2.13–2.17 below.
[12] The Basel Committee on Banking Supervision was originally established in 1974. It consisted of the
governors of the central banks of the G10 States, but its membership has recently been expanded. It has no
treaty or other formal, legal basis, but its recommendations have tended to be adopted as minimum standards
for banks which are active in international business.
[13] 89/229/EEC, OJ L 124, 5.5.1989, p 16.
[14] 89/647/EEC, OJ L 386, 30.12.1989, p 14.
[15] 93/6/EEC, OJ L 141, 11.06.1993, p 1 and 98/31EC, OJ L 204, 21.7.1998, p 13.
[16] The later (and current) structure is known as 'Basel II'. On this subject, see generally Chapter 6 below.
[17] The whole subject of EU banking law is considered in more depth in Chapter 2 below. The same
'Europeanization' has also been apparent in the field of investment services: see in particular the Markets in
Financial Instruments Directive which, so far as relevant to banks, is considered at paras 3.26–3.52 below.

should be separated from those of the market regulator,[18] and the task of banking supervision was transferred to the FSA.[19] The decision to transfer banking supervisory functions to the FSA was not, however, a 'stand alone' decision. It formed part of a larger plan to provide for unified supervision of the financial markets as a whole by a single regulator. Given the interdependence of the different segments of the financial markets (banking, insurance, fund management, and other businesses) it was argued that this was an appropriate step, although the wisdom of removing bank supervision from the Bank of England has been questioned by some commentators in the wake of the recent financial crisis.

1.08   The final legislative result of this decision was the Financial Services and Markets Act 2000 (FSMA), most of which came into force on 1 November 2001. It has been pointed out elsewhere[20] that the 2000 Act succeeded in being both a formidable, and yet at the same time inchoate, piece of legislation. It is formidable in the sense that it runs to some 433 sections and 22 schedules; yet it is inchoate in the sense that the Act itself answers few of the practical questions to which the scheme of regulation gives rise on a daily basis. Instead, it confers upon the FSA a broad rule-making power, and it will almost invariably be necessary to refer to those rules in order meaningfully to deal with any issues that may arise. As noted earlier, the legislation deals not merely with banking but also with other aspects of the financial markets. The present discussion will, however, naturally concentrate on issues relevant to the conduct of banking and associated business.

Deposit-Taking as a Regulated Activity

Introduction

1.09   Perhaps the two main activities usually associated with 'banking' are the acceptance of deposits and the lending of funds for business or other purposes.[21] In spite of this general perception, the two aspects of the business are subjected to very different types and levels of supervision. It is thus necessary to examine these two aspects separately. The deposit side of the equation is considered here, whilst the lending side of the equation is considered at a later stage.[22]

---

[18]   It may be added in passing that this decision reflected a growing international trend to entrust monetary policy and market supervision to separate institutions.

[19]   The transfer was effected by s 21 of the Bank of England Act 1998. The same Act also conferred independence upon the Bank of England in determining monetary policy, and established the Monetary Policy Committee for that purpose. Once again, this decision reflected a growing international trend and is consistent with the requirement for central bank independence for institutions forming a part of the European System of Central Banks.

[20]   See Paget, para 1.1.

[21]   Of course, matters are much more complex than this in practice. See, for example, the discussion on payment services in Chapter 5 below and relevant aspects of the Markets In Financial Instruments Directive at paras 3.26–3.52 below. For a recent case considering various aspects of the deposit-taking prohibition, see *Financial Services Authority v Anderson* [2010] EWHC 599 (Ch).

[22]   See Chapter 4 below.

Acceptance of Deposits

Reference has already been made to the broad and inchoate nature of the FSMA. The **1.10** so-called 'general prohibition' contains an excellent illustration of that general proposition. Section 19 provides that 'No person may carry on a regulated activity in the United Kingdom, or purport to do so, unless he is ... an authorised person ... or an exempt person ...'.

It is immediately obvious that the meaning of 'regulated activity' is central to the whole **1.11** scheme of the regulatory system created by the FSMA. This line of enquiry then leads to section 22 of the FSMA, which provides that a 'regulated activity' is '... an activity of a specified kind which is carried on by way of a business and ... relates to an investment of a specified kind ... or ... in the case of an activity of a kind which is also specified for the purposes of this paragraph, is carried on in relation to property of any kind ...'. At first sight, section 22 may not appear to advance matters in a particularly material way, but it does at least confirm that the Act only regulates activities which are carried on as a business; it does not apply to purely 'one-off' transactions or other dealings which cannot be said to be effected in the course of a business. The importance of this point will be discussed later.[23]

The FSMA further defines the activity of deposit-taking by a mere reference to 'accepting **1.12** deposits'.[24] However, for real clarification of the nature of the general prohibition as it relates to deposit-taking, it is necessary to refer to the Regulated Activities Order.[25] In its turn, article 5 of the Regulated Activities Order provides that:

(1) Accepting deposits is a specified kind of activity if—
    (a) money received by way of deposit is lent to others; or
    (b) any other activity of the person accepting the deposit is financed wholly or to a material extent out of the capital of or interest on the money received by way of deposit.
(2) In paragraph (1), 'deposit' means a sum of money, other than one excluded by any of articles 6 to 9A,[26] paid on terms—
    (a) under which it will be repaid, with or without interest or premium, and either on demand or at a time or in circumstances agreed by or on behalf of the person making the payment and the person receiving it; and
    (b) which are not referable to the to the provision of property (other than currency) or services or the giving of security.
(3) For the purposes of paragraph (2), money is paid on terms which are referable to the provision of property or services or the giving of security if, and only if—
    (a) it is paid by way of advance or part payment under a contract for the sale, hire or other provision of property or services, and is repayable only in the event that the property or services is or are not in fact sold, hired or otherwise provided;

---

[23] On the expression 'by way of business', see the Financial Services and Markets Act 2000 (Carrying on Regulated Activities by Way of Business) Order 2001 (SI 2001/1177), as amended. This Order is considered at para 1.15 below.

[24] See FSMA, Sch 2, para 1.

[25] To provide its full title, the Financial Services and Markets Act 2000 (Regulated Activities) Order 2001 (SI 2001/544). As will be apparent from the present discussion, numerous orders have been made in reliance upon the powers delegated to the FSA under the 2000 Act. The Regulated Activities Order may, however, be regarded as the main source of law in the area now under consideration.

[26] The various exceptions and exclusions are discussed at para 1.13 below.

(b) it is paid by way of security for the performance of a contract or by way of security in respect of loss which may result from the non-performance of a contract; or

(c) without prejudice to sub-paragraph (b), it is paid by way of security for the delivery up or return of any property, whether in a particular state of repair or otherwise.

Article 5, when read together with section 19 of the FSMA, thus raises four questions, namely, (i) is a particular sum of money a 'deposit', (ii) if so, is the person concerned 'accepting' deposits for the purposes of article 5, (iii) if so, is he carrying on that activity by way of business, and (iv) if so, is he carrying on that business in the United Kingdom? If all of these questions are answered in the positive, then the relevant activity will be unlawful, unless either the person concerned is authorized or exempt, or the transaction itself is in some way exempt.[27] It is necessary to examine each of these issues in turn.

Deposits

1.13 First of all, when does a payment or transfer of money amount to a 'deposit'? In order to answer this question, it is necessary to examine the terms of the contract between the parties. If the deposit is to be repaid, either on demand or at a future date, with or without interest or premium, then on the face of it the relevant sum will be a 'deposit' for present purposes. A few points of interpretation flow from this apparently simple formulation:

(a) Article 5 requires that the relevant sum must be contractually repayable. It is submitted that this means that the deposit must be repayable in full, that is to say, without any deduction.[28] This view is reinforced by the words 'with or without interest or premium', which suggest that the depositor may receive back more than the amount of his original deposit, but not less.

(b) If the contractual arrangements envisage situations in which the depositor may receive repayment of less than the original principal amount, then the arrangement does not amount to a deposit. In such cases, it must generally be assumed that the payer is assuming greater risk for greater reward, and that there is thus some form of risk or speculative element involved in the deal. Entities offering arrangements of this kind will often require authorization under other provisions of the FSMA,[29] but the arrangement does not fall within the scope of the deposit-taking restriction in article 5.

(c) Similarly, the expression 'repaid' connotes that the deposit must be repaid in money. Consequently, payments made for stored value cards entitling the holder to the use

---

[27] On exempt persons, see para 1.19 below.

[28] This requirement may have to be subject to the minor exception that deductions can be made on account of normal bank charges but, nevertheless, the deposit is still repaid in full in the sense that the customer receives a discharge for liabilities which he would otherwise have to pay directly. Sums deposited with a bank may become subject to a right of set-off in the hands of the bank but, again, it is submitted that this does not alter the fundamental nature of the transaction as a deposit; the customer will still receive full credit for the amounts deposited with the bank, even though it may have the right to refuse their subsequent re-transfer or repayment to the customer. The requirement that a deposit must be repaid in full has caused some difficulty in the authorization of institutions wishing to offer Islamic-compliant products: see the discussion at paras 50.17–50.19 below.

[29] eg on the basis that they are carrying on investment business or managing a collective investment scheme for the purposes of art 53 of the Regulated Activities Order.

of public transport or telephones do not amount to deposits, because the payer is not generally entitled to redeem the card for cash.[30]

(d) A sum of money thus only constitutes a deposit if its initial payment creates a debtor-creditor relationship between the parties, imposing upon the bank an obligation to repay the monies in full regardless of the success of any venture in which the bank may choose to invest those funds.[31] This view is consistent with the general view of the banker-customer relationship.[32]

(e) The exceptions from the definition of 'deposit' set out in article 5(2)(b) (read together with article 5(3)) of the Regulated Activities Order are of some importance in practice. In essence, these provisions exclude any payments which are referable to the provision of goods or services, or the taking of security. Thus, a landlord who takes a dilapidations deposit from his tenant is not accepting a 'deposit' for the purposes of the Regulated Activities Order.[33] Likewise, a broker who accepts cash margin as security for dealings in commodities or financial futures is not accepting a 'deposit', since the payment is referable to the provision of dealing services and is intended as security for the customer's obligations.[34]

(f) Certain payments of money are stated not to constitute deposits even though they might otherwise meet the definition of that term. The list of exempt payments[35] includes:

  (i) sums paid by the Bank of England, the central bank of an EEA State, the European Central Bank, the European Community or certain international financial institutions;

  (ii) sums paid by a person authorized under the FSMA to accept deposits or to carry out insurance business, or by a person whose business consists wholly or to a significant extent in lending money;[36]

  (iii) sums paid by a local authority;

  (iv) sums paid among companies which are members of the same group;

  (v) sums paid among close family members;[37]

  (vi) sums paid to a solicitor in the course of his profession;

---

[30] It should however be noted that issue of e-money is a regulated activity: see the discussion in n 39 below.

[31] Since money is fungible in any event, it is difficult to see how the customer's right to repayment could be linked in this way.

[32] See *Foley v Hill* (1848) HL Cas 28 and the discussion of this point at paras 15.09–15.16 below.

[33] This point is made explicit by art 5(3)(c) of the Order.

[34] See arts 5(3)(a) and (b) of the Order. The point is confirmed by the decision in *SCF Finance Co Ltd v Masri* (No 2) [1987] 1 All ER 175.

[35] For the full list, see arts 6–9A of the Regulated Activities Order.

[36] As a result, a person does not accept deposits for FSMA purposes if he borrows from a bank, insurance company or other money lending entity.

[37] Whilst this clarification is useful, such arrangements would normally fall outside art 5 because they would not have been entered into by way of business. On this subject, see para 1.15 below. The exemption was discussed in *Financial Services Authority v Anderson* [2010] EWHC 599 (Ch) but was of no assistance to the defendants in that case, where loans were raised from a range of individuals only some of whom were close relatives.

(vii) sums paid by way of consideration for the issue of debentures or government securities;[38] and

(viii) sums paid in consideration of an immediate provision of electronic money.[39]

Accepting Deposits

1.14 If the transaction involving the payment of money does amount to a deposit, then it becomes necessary to determine whether the relevant entity is 'accepting deposits' for the purposes of the Regulated Activities Order. It will be recalled that the prohibition only applies where either (i) the monies so received by way of deposit are lent to others or (ii) the business of the person accepting the deposit is financed, wholly or to a material extent out of the capital of, or interest received on, those deposits.[40] If the accepting entity is itself a money lender, then the first criterion will almost inevitably be met, with the result that the entity concerned will be 'accepting deposits' for these purposes. In other cases, it will be necessary to determine whether the second criterion is satisfied, and this may involve difficult assessments of a factual nature. It has to be borne in mind that not all funding received by an entity through the means of debt finance will necessarily constitute a deposit which falls to be taken into account for these purposes. For example, as has been seen,[41] monies received from an authorized institution do not amount to the receipt of deposits by the borrowing entity. Consequently, they would not fall to be treated as deposits in making the necessary assessment.

Carrying on a Business

1.15 If the first two tests have been met, then it will finally be necessary to determine whether the relevant deposits were accepted in the course of a business. This can often be a delicate question in a number of contexts.[42] In the present case, it is specifically provided that a person should not be regarded as accepting deposits if (i) he does not hold himself out as accepting deposits on a day-to-day basis and (ii) any deposits which are accepted are taken only on particular occasions, whether or not involving the issue of securities.[43]

---

[38] Where the debentures constitute short term sterling commercial paper, they will only benefit from this exemption if the subscribers are investment professionals and the face amount of the paper exceeds £100,000—see art 9 of the Regulated Activities Order.

[39] Article 9A of the Regulated Activities Order, as inserted by art 3(2) of the Financial Services and Markets Act 2000 (Regulated Activities) (Amendment) Order 2002 (SI 2002/682). It may be noted that the issue of electronic money involves an obligation on the issuer to make payments (effectively, on behalf of the holder) to retailers which accept the use of the e-money. Consequently, the issuer of the e-money is accepting a deposit which has to be repaid at a later date. This may be contrasted with the position of a stored value card, which involves the provision of services (rather than the repayment of money) and is thus not caught by the legislation now under discussion. Whilst the issue of e-money is specifically stated not to constitute the acceptance of a deposit, issuers are subject to the different regime established by arts 9B–9K of the Regulated Activities Order.

[40] See para 1.12 above.

[41] See para 1.13 above.

[42] For cases decided in different statutory contexts, see *Davies v Sumner* [1984] 1 WLR 1301 (HL) and *R&B Customs Brokers v United Dominions Trust Ltd* [1988] 1 WLR 321 (CA). For a recent illustration of this type of problem, see *Khodari v Tamimi* [2008] EWHC 3065.

[43] Article 2(1) of the Financial Services and Markets Act 2000 (Carrying on Regulated Activities by Way of Business) Order 2001 (SI 2001/1177), as amended. In determining whether deposits are accepted only on

This clarification may be useful in various contexts. For example, a joint venture company which is owned in precisely equal shares[44] may need to raise funds from time to time and will naturally approach its investors to make the necessary cash advances. This will not amount to an acceptance of deposits by the joint venture company, since it does not hold itself out as accepting deposits generally and only does so for the purpose of funding its particular activities.[45]

In the United Kingdom

If all of the above tests have been met, then it is necessary to ask whether the relevant business is being carried on 'in the United Kingdom'. Quite apart from questions of UK statutes and their territoriality, it will be recalled that this requirement explicitly forms a part of the general prohibition.[46] **1.16**

Once again, whether or not a particular business is being carried on in the United Kingdom can be a delicate question. For example, the mere fact that a foreign banker makes occasional trips to the United Kingdom to visit customers in the UK should not lead to the conclusion that his bank is carrying on business in the UK.[47] A bank cannot be deemed to be carrying on business in every country in which it happens to have customers. There will, inevitably, be difficult questions of fact and degree. **1.17**

The FSMA does provide a certain amount of guidance in this area, although it must be said that the effect of these provisions is to 'import' into the United Kingdom business which might otherwise be considered to be carried on outside of the UK. The provisions which are relevant to deposit-taking business are as follows: **1.18**

(a) A UK company which is entitled to carry on deposit-taking business in another EEA State[48] and which carries on that activity in such a State is deemed also to be carrying on that business in the United Kingdom.[49] This slightly convoluted provision reflects the requirement that any entity carrying on activities covered by the Single Market Directives in relation to banking and financial services must be authorized for that purpose in its home State.[50]

'particular occasions', it is necessary to consider (i) the frequency of those occasions and (ii) any characteristics which distinguish those occasions from each other: see art 2(2) of that Order.

[44] ie so that the joint venture company is not a subsidiary of either shareholder and thus does not qualify for the 'group' deposits exemption noted at para 1.13 above.

[45] This analysis is not entirely free from difficulty. In order to satisfy the 'particular occasions' test, it is necessary to have regard to the frequency of the occasions and any characteristics which distinguish them from each other (see art 2(2) of the By Way of Business Order mentioned in n 44 above. If cash advances are requested on a frequent basis and for a variety of different purposes, then it may be more difficult to satisfy the 'particular occasions' test: see *Financial Services Authority v Anderson* [2010] EWHC 599 (Ch).

[46] See FSMA, s 19 reproduced at para 1.10 above.

[47] For the consequences of this type of activity in the context of the EC 'passporting' regime, see paras 2.25–2.28 below.

[48] The expression 'EEA States' comprises the Member States of the European Union plus Iceland, Liechtenstein and Norway.

[49] FSMA, s 418(1).

[50] On the principle of home State supervision in this context, see the discussion of the passporting regime at paras 2.13–2.17 below.

(b) A UK company will be deemed to be carrying on business in the United Kingdom if it is carrying on a regulated activity whose day-to-day management is the responsibility of its registered office or an establishment in this country.[51] Thus, even though a company may be offering deposit-taking services exclusively to persons outside the United Kingdom, it will still require authorization if its operations are 'based' in the UK.

(c) A foreign entity whose head office is abroad but which carries on a regulated activity through an establishment in the United Kingdom will be deemed to be carrying on that business in the United Kingdom even though it has no customers in the UK.[52] In relation to foreign companies, this is essentially a mirror image of the provision described in (b) above.

For these purposes, it will not always be easy to say whether or not a particular entity has an 'establishment' in the UK. That issue is, however, discussed in another context.[53]

Exempt Persons

1.19 If deposits are being accepted in the course of a business carried on in the United Kingdom, then it becomes necessary to consider whether the person accepting the deposits is in some way exempted from the provisions of the FSMA. The Treasury has power to exempt persons (or specified classes of persons) from the scope of the general prohibition created by section 19(1) of the FSMA.[54] The exemptions may be given generally or may relate only to specific transactions or circumstances. A number of institutions and organizations— including municipal banks, credit unions and industrial and provident societies—have been granted exempt status in relation to the prohibition against the acceptance of deposits.[55]

Consequences of Contravention

1.20 Apart from the criminal sanctions for breach of the general prohibition against the unauthorized acceptance of deposits,[56] it should be noted that an agreement entered into by a person in the course of carrying on a regulated business without the appropriate permission from the FSA will be unenforceable against the other party.[57] The other party will generally be entitled to recover both the funds paid by him and appropriate compensation.[58]

1.21 However, whilst the criminal aspect of the above provisions applies to the unlawful acceptance of deposits, the civil consequences do not.[59] It is not immediately clear why this should be the case. If a person places a deposit with an unauthorized person for a return

---

[51] FSMA, s 418(2).
[52] FSMA, s 418(5).
[53] See para 2.28 below.
[54] The power is conferred by FSMA, s 38. The Act itself confers exemption on 'authorized representatives' who carry on a regulated activity under contract with a person who holds a permission for the relevant activity under the terms of the Act: see s 39 of the Act.
[55] See art 4 of the Financial Services and Markets Act 2000 (Exemptions) Order 2001 (SI 2001/1201).
[56] The criminal penalties are set out in FSMA, s 23.
[57] See FSMA, s 26(1). On s 26, see *Brodenik and others v Centaur Services Ltd* (27 July 2006), noted by Blair, Walker and Purves, para 7.14.
[58] FSMA, s 26(2).
[59] See FSMA, s 26(4).

which is below the market rate, he should be entitled to appropriate compensation as well as repayment. It is true that the FSMA allows for an application to court for immediate repayment of the deposit regardless of its stated maturity date,[60] but no specific provision is made for compensation in this particular case.

The Authorization Procedure

If an entity wishes to accept deposits by way of business in the United Kingdom and none **1.22** of the available exemptions apply, then it will be necessary to seek authorization for that purpose in order to avoid a contravention of the FSMA.[61] The required authorization is frequently referred to as a 'Part IV permission', since the details of the authorization process are set out in that Part of the FSMA.[62] Given that the objectives of the authorization process include the protection of consumers and the promotion of confidence in the financial markets,[63] it is unsurprising that the main criteria to be taken into account in assessing such an application revolve around the financial soundness and managerial integrity of the entity concerned.

The starting point in relation to any application for Part IV permission is that the applicant **1.23** must meet the so-called 'threshold conditions' for that purpose.[64] The principal conditions are:

(a) an entity applying for permission to accept deposits must be a body corporate or a partnership;[65]
(b) the applicant must maintain its head office in the UK;[66]
(c) if the applicant is a member of a group of companies or any person directly or indirectly controls more than 20 per cent of the voting rights or capital of the applicant—or the applicant controls 20 per cent of another entity—the FSA must be satisfied that those relationships are not likely to prevent the FSA from effective supervision;[67]
(d) the applicant must have sufficient financial resources for the regulated activities which the entity proposes to carry on;[68] and

---

[60] See FSMA, s 29.

[61] This statement follows from the terms of the general prohibition contained in FSMA, s 19 and to which reference has already been made.

[62] The expression 'Part IV permission' is defined in FSMA, s 40(4).

[63] These objectives are to be taken into account by the FSA in the exercise of all of its statutory functions: see FSMA, s 2(2).

[64] The general requirement is imposed by FSMA, s 41 and the threshold conditions themselves are set out in Sch 6 to that Act.

[65] FSMA, Sch 6, Pt I, para 1(2). Although private individuals are able to apply for authorization from certain types of regulated activities under the FSMA, they are not permitted to apply in relation to the 'accepting deposits' activity.

[66] FSMA, Sch 6, Pt I, para 2.

[67] Where the applicant has close links with an entity established outside the EEA, the FSA must also be satisfied that neither the administrative regulations in force in that country nor any deficiency in their enforcement will prevent the FSA's effective supervision of the applicant. On the points made in this paragraph, see FSMA, Sch 6, Pt I, para 3.

[68] FSMA, Sch 6, Pt I, para 4. This is a general, threshold test, without any specific monetary requirements. The amount would clearly depend on the nature, scope, and extent of the business which the applicant seeks

(e) the applicant must demonstrate that it is a 'fit and proper person' to hold the requested permission, bearing in mind any connections with other persons, the nature of the regulated business to be conducted and the need to ensure that business is conducted soundly and prudently. In practice, this will involve a consideration of the individuals who may be involved in the management of the business (who must be separately approved by the FSA for this purpose) or who may be significant shareholders.[69]

1.24 Compliance with the threshold conditions is a continuing requirement. Consequently, when deciding whether to grant an application for deposit-taking permission, the FSA must satisfy itself that the applicant meets the threshold conditions *and will continue to do so*.[70] The FSA may withdraw the authorization to accept deposits (or, indeed, any other permission) if the relevant entity subsequently fails to meet those conditions or is likely to do so.[71] Thus, for example, when the FSA determined that Kaupthing Singer & Friedlander—a UK authorized institution—no longer satisfied the 'adequate resources' test, it imposed upon that bank a requirement that it should cease to accept any further deposits.[72] Likewise, continued compliance with the 'fit and proper person' test must to a large degree depend on the identity of those who can exercise a significant measure of control over the affairs of the institution, and this may obviously change over time. Accordingly, any person who proposes to acquire or to increase a significant shareholding over an authorized institution should notify the FSA in advance and obtain approval. If the acquisition occurs without prior notification to the FSA and it does not approve the new arrangements, then the FSA may bar the exercise of voting rights and apply to the court for an order that the relevant shares be sold.[73]

1.25 The above discussion has focused on authorization for the acceptance of deposits, since that is the key and distinguishing characteristic of banking business. It should, however, be appreciated that a bank would require further permissions for many of its other activities, including, to name but a few, (i) entering into regulated mortgage contracts,[74] (ii) managing investments,[75] and (iii) advising on investments.[76]

---

to conduct. In determining this test, the FSA can take into account resources available from other members of the same group, and can also have regard to the quality of the applicant's risk management processes.

[69] FSMA, Sch 6, Pt I, para 5.

[70] FSMA, s 41(2). Note that, in giving permission, the FSA may impose such conditions as it believes appropriate, whether as to the applicant's conduct of business, its relationships with other businesses, or otherwise: see FSMA, s 43.

[71] The necessary power (referred to as the FSA's 'Own Initiative' power) is conferred by FSMA, s 45. Permission may also be withdrawn if it is desirable to protect consumers, or if the relevant entity has effectively ceased to carry on any regulated business.

[72] See the FSA's First Supervisory Notice addressed to Kaupthing Singer & Friedlander dated 8 October 2008.

[73] The details of these procedures, including rights of appeal and other matters, are set out in Pt XII of the FSMA. For present purposes, it is the general scheme of the legislation, rather than its detail, which is of relevance. However, notification and FSA approval is required if a person intends to acquire 10 per cent of any institution or to enter into arrangements involving significant influence over its business. For details, see FSMA, s 179.

[74] Regulated Activities Order, art 61, on which see paras 4.43–4.54 below.

[75] Regulated Activities Order, art 37.

[76] Regulated Activities Order, art 53. For a discussion of certain aspects of investment activities carried out by banks for their customers, see paras 3.26–3.52 below.

Powers of the FSA

Reference has already been made to some of the powers of the FSA in the context of the initial authorization of a credit institution, the threshold conditions and the 'fit and proper person' test. However, regulation and supervision are ongoing processes and it is therefore unsurprising that the FSA also enjoys extensive information-gathering and investigatory powers. These are set out in Part XI (sections 165–177) of the FSMA and include the following: **1.26**

(a) Power to require an authorized person to produce information and/or documents specified by the FSA,[77] but the power is limited to material reasonably required by the FSA for the purpose of exercising its functions.[78] The power extends to other entities which are in the same group as the authorized institution.

(b) Power to require an authorized person (or any member of the same group) to provide to the FSA a 'skilled person's' report[79] on any documents produced or required to be produced pursuant to the provisions described in (a) above. It may be noted that it is the duty of any person who has provided services to the relevant authorized person to provide such assistance as the skilled person may reasonably require.[80] This would presumably include accountants, lawyers and others who may have advised the bank on matters connected with the subject matter of the proposed report. However, it would seem that the skilled person could not require the disclosure of any information which is subject to legal professional privilege.[81]

(c) The FSA may appoint one or more competent persons to investigate the nature, conduct, or state of the business conducted by an authorized person, a particular aspect of that business or its ownership or control.[82] The investigatory powers of the competent person extend to group members and to entities which were formerly authorized.[83] Since they may have an impact on the financial health of the authorized person, the investigatory power also extends to any non-regulated business carried on by the authorized person concerned.[84]

(d) The FSA also has a more specific power to appoint a person to carry out an investigation on its behalf if it has grounds for believing that particular criminal offences (including offences such as market abuse or insider trading) may have been committed or if there has been any contravention of certain other rules.[85]

---

[77] FSMA, s 165.

[78] FSMA, s 165(4).

[79] On this power, see FSMA, s 166. The 'skilled person' is nominated by the FSA and the selection will obviously depend upon the particular subject matter at issue. See FSMA, s 166(4).

[80] FSMA, s 166(5).

[81] ie essentially for the reasons given in *R v Special Commissioner, ex p Morgan Grenfell & Co Ltd* [2003] 1 AC 563 (HL).

[82] FSMA, s 167(1). The section confers a like power on the Secretary of State.

[83] FSMA, s 167(2), (3) and (4).

[84] FSMA, s 167(5).

[85] FSMA, s 168. Once again, a parallel power is conferred on the Secretary of State. The investigatory powers may be exercised in relation to suspected misconduct and the possible use of the FSA's own disciplinary powers: see *Financial Services Authority v Westcott* [2003] EWHC 2392 (Comm).

(e) In view of the international nature of the financial markets and the fact that suspected wrongdoing will frequently involve conduct in more than one jurisdiction, the FSA has power to assist an investigation by an overseas regulator[86] by initiating its own investigation in line with the powers described above.[87] Where the request comes from a regulator in another Member State, there may in some cases be a Community law obligation to provide the requested assistance.[88] Subject to that, however, and in deciding whether to provide assistance in this way, the FSA must take into account (i) whether reciprocal assistance would be forthcoming, if requested, (ii) whether the investigation involves activities which would be unlawful or would contravene regulatory requirements in the United Kingdom, (iii) the seriousness of the case and any relevance to the United Kingdom, and (iv) whether it is otherwise in the public interest to provide the requested assistance. The discretion to assist overseas regulators may not, however, be as broad as it first appears. In *R (on the application of Amro International SA) v Financial Services Authority*,[89] the FSA was asked to assist the US Securities and Exchange Commission (SEC) in an ongoing civil action involving fraudulent trading in company stock. The SEC requested documentation from a UK firm of accountants in relation to two entities which were not the target of the SEC allegations, on the basis that this information was required to assist in explaining the relationship between some of the entities which were under investigation. At first instance, the court held that there had been no assertion that the two entities concerned were knowingly involved in share manipulation, nor had it been suggested that the main target of the investigation had any interest in either of these two entities. As a result, the court granted judicial review of the decision to appoint the investigator insofar as it related to these two, specific entities. However, this judgment has recently been reversed on appeal, on the basis that the FSA had properly exercised its powers and was not required to second guess the motives or objectives of the overseas regulator.[90]

(f) Various notice and other procedural requirements apply in relation to the instigation and conduct of the investigations described above.[91] The investigator has power to require the person under investigation to answer questions, to provide information and to produce documents.[92] As a general rule, statements made to an investigator are admissible in court proceedings but this is strictly limited where the target of the investigation is subsequently charged with a criminal offence.[93]

---

[86] 'Overseas regulator' means a corresponding regulator under the EC's Recast Banking Consolidation Directive or a regulator from a third State exercising functions essentially similar to those of the FSA itself: see FSMA, s 195(3).

[87] See FSMA, s 169.

[88] FSMA, s 169(3).

[89] [2009] EWHC 2242 (Admin).

[90] [2010] EWCA Civ 123 (CA).

[91] FSMA, s 170.

[92] See FSMA, ss 171, 172 and 173. In certain cases, s 175 empowers the investigator to require the production of information by third parties. A warrant may be issued to obtain documents and information if a person has failed to provide them on request: FSMA, s 176.

[93] FSMA, s 174.

(g) Unsurprisingly, a person who fails to comply with a documentation or information request made for the purposes of an investigation, or who destroys or falsifies any relevant material, may be guilty of an offence, unless he has a reasonable excuse.[94]

EEA Firms

In accordance with the terms of Community legislation in this sphere, a credit institution[95] **1.27** established in another EEA State[96] and which is authorized by its home State regulator is entitled to be treated as authorized in the United Kingdom to the same extent. The whole subject is dealt with in more detail at a later stage.[97]

---

[94] FSMA, s 177.

[95] In accordance with the terms of Art 1 of the Recast Banking Consolidation Directive, a 'credit institution' is '… an undertaking whose business is to receive deposits or other repayable funds from the public and to grant credits for its own account…'. The Directive is discussed in more detail in Chapter 2 below.

[96] As noted previously, 'EEA State' includes each EU Member State plus Iceland, Liechtenstein and Norway.

[97] See Chapter 2 below.

2

EU BANKING LAW

Introduction

It was noted in the preceding chapter that banking regulation in the United Kingdom is **2.01** now very significantly influenced by Community law. To this extent, the body of law and regulations about to be discussed can properly be described as 'EU Banking Law'. It is proposed to discuss the following subject matter:

(a) the background to the EU Directives in the field of banking law;
(b) the deposit-taking prohibition;
(c) the authorization process;
(d) the relevance of the freedoms created by the EC Treaty;
(e) the right to establish a branch in other Member States;
(f) the right to provide services in other Member States;
(g) the provision of banking services from within an institution's home State;
(h) the free movement of capital and banking services; and
(i) a Commission Interpretative Communication on territoriality questions arising in the field of EU banking law.

Background to the EU Banking Directives

At the very highest level, the object of the Community is to create a common market **2.02** and an economic and monetary union designed to promote, among other things, the harmonious, balanced and sustainable development of economic activities.[1] In order to

---

[1] EC Treaty, Art 2.

achieve these objectives, and so far as relevant in the present context, the common policies and activities of the Community are to include:[2]

(a) the creation of an internal market in which services and capital can move freely and without restriction;
(b) the approximation of laws to allow the proper functioning of the single market; and
(c) the strengthening of consumer protection.

2.03 The EU Banking Directives were thus based upon the principles that individuals and companies should be free to establish branches and to provide their services freely throughout the Community.[3]

2.04 EU banking law is in some respects also bound up with Article 56 of the EC Treaty, which contemplates that all restrictions on the movement of capital and payments shall be prohibited. Free movement of capital and payments must plainly involve a market in which banking services can be freely provided on a cross-border basis throughout the Community.[4]

2.05 The relevant legislation is thus intended to create a 'single market' in financial services. It is, nevertheless, obvious that such freedoms cannot be granted unconditionally in the field of financial services; individuals who entrust their money to financial institutions are clearly unable to make their own assessment of the soundness of that institution or the quality of its management. There must therefore be some assurance that the relevant institutions are adequately regulated and supervised in these respects or, perhaps more relevantly in the light of recent events, that there is an adequate deposit-protection scheme in place.[5] In the past, regulators in each individual Member State would supervise the activities of banks carrying on business within their borders; their jurisdiction would therefore extend both to locally incorporated institutions and to the local branches of banks established in another Member State.[6] But such arrangements clearly constituted an impediment to the exercise of the freedoms contemplated by the EC Treaty.

---

[2] See EC Treaty, Art 3.
[3] EC Treaty, Art 43 provides that '... restrictions on the freedom of establishment of nationals of a Member State shall be prohibited. Such prohibition shall also apply to restrictions on the setting-up of agencies, branches or subsidiaries by nationals of any Member State established in the territory of another Member State ...'. Art 47(2) allows the Council to '... issue directives for the co-ordination of the provisions laid down by law, regulation or administrative action in Member States concerning the taking-up and pursuit of activities as self-employed persons ...'. These provisions were, for example, held to provide a sufficient basis for the directive dealing with the establishment of deposit-guarantee schemes in Case C-233/94, *Germany v European Parliament and EU Council* [1997] ECR I-2405. Likewise, Art 49 of the Treaty states that '... restrictions on freedom to provide services within the Community shall be prohibited in respect of nationals of Member States who are established in a State of the Community other than that of the person for whom the services are intended ...'.
[4] For a fuller discussion of the subject of free movement of capital and payments, see Mann, Money, paras 25.32–25.36.
[5] Some of the issues which arose in this area during the recent 'credit crunch' are considered in Chapter 13 below.
[6] It should be emphasized that the present discussion is limited to institutions which are established within some part of the Community. Banks established outside the Community would continue to be subject to local supervisory requirements in the Member States within which they have a branch.

It would clearly not be possible to dismantle such arrangements overnight. Consequently, **2.06** EU legislation in the field adopted a 'gradualist' approach, and the liberalization of banking services was achieved over an extended period. It may be helpful to provide a brief description and chronology of some of the measures which were introduced for these purposes:

(a) an early Directive[7] addressed the abolition of restrictions on the freedom of establishment and freedom to provide services in respect of banks and other financial institutions;

(b) the First Banking Directive[8] required Member States to introduce a procedure for the licensing and supervision of credit institutions;[9]

(c) the Council Directive on the annual financial statements of banks and other financial institutions;[10]

(d) the 'Own Funds' Directive,[11] requiring that credit institutions should have a certain level of minimum capital;

(e) the Second Banking Directive,[12] which introduced the principle of 'home State' supervision and the concept of the 'passport';

(f) the 'Solvency Ratio' Directive,[13] requiring credit institutions to hold a certain minimum percentage of capital against liabilities;

(g) a Council Directive on the prevention of the use of the financial system for the purpose of money laundering;[14]

(h) a Council Directive[15] on the supervision of credit institutions on a consolidated basis;

(i) the 'Large Exposures' Directive,[16] which required the reporting of exposures to single customers or groups exceeding set levels;

(j) a Council Directive on the capital adequacy of investment firms and credit institutions;[17]

(k) a European Parliament and Council Directive on deposit-guarantee schemes;[18]

---

[7] 73/183/EEC, OJ L 194, 16.7.1973, p 1.

[8] 77/780/EEC, OJ L 322, 17.12.1977, p 30, as amended. It has been noted that this Directive was '... no more than a first step towards the achievement of a common market for credit institutions ...': Case 166/85, *Criminal Proceedings against Bullo and Bonivento* [1987] ECR 1583, para 7.

[9] This Directive was implemented in the United Kingdom by means of the Banking Act 1979. As noted earlier, before that Act came into force, there was no statutory licensing system in operation in this country, but the Bank of England operated an informal approach to supervision.

[10] 86/635/EEC, OJ L 372, 31.12.1986, p 1.

[11] 89/299/EEC, OJ L 124, 5.5.1989, p 1, as amended.

[12] 89/646/EEC, OJ L 386, 30.12.1989, p 1, as amended.

[13] 89/647/EEC, OJ L 386, 30.12.1989, p 14, as amended.

[14] 91/308/EEC, OJ L 166, 28.06.1991, p 77. This Directive has now reached its third version and is considered in Chapter 7 below.

[15] 92/30/EEC, OJ L 110, 28.4.1992, p 52.

[16] 92/121/EEC, OJ L 29, 5.2.1993, p 1, as amended.

[17] 93/6/EEC, OJ L 29, 11.06.1993, p 1.

[18] 94/19/EEC, OJ L 135, 31.05.1994, p 5. This Directive is considered in more depth at paras 13.05–13.08 below.

(l)   a Directive of the European Parliament and the Council in the field of credit institutions[19] which, amongst other things, required a credit institution to have its head office in the Member State in which it is authorized;

(m) a Directive of the European Parliament and the Council relating to the taking up and pursuit of the business of credit institutions (the 'Banking Consolidation Directive');[20] and

(n)   a Directive of the European Parliament and of the Council relating to the taking up and pursuit of the business of credit institutions (the 'Recast Banking Consolidation Directive').[21]

2.07 It will thus be seen that EU Banking Law began by seeking to regulate the licensing system for credit institutions. From there, it sought to ensure that the supervisory system was consistent with treaty provisions guaranteeing the right of establishment and the freedom [22] to provide services. It then sought to harmonize the supervisory requirements further by introducing uniform rules on consolidated supervision and large exposures.

2.08 Fortunately, as noted above, this legislative 'patchwork quilt' was drawn together by the Recast Banking Consolidation Directive, and it is thus possible to refer solely to that Directive for the purposes of the rest of this section.[23]

The Deposit-Taking Prohibition

2.09 Article 5 of the Recast Banking Consolidation Directive requires Member States to '… prohibit persons or undertakings that are not credit institutions from carrying on the business of taking deposits or other repayable funds from the public …'. Certain types of entity (including central banks,[24] governmental authorities, and certain international organizations) are exempted from this general prohibition.

2.10 A few points may be made in relation to this core provision of the Recast Banking Consolidation Directive:

(a)   A 'credit institution' is an undertaking whose business is to receive deposits or other repayable funds from the public and to grant credits for its own account.[25] Article 5, when read

---

[19] 95/26/EC, OJ L 168, 18.07.95, p 7. This Directive is sometimes referred to as the 'BCCI Directive' and was introduced to avoid the difficulties which arose in relation to the supervision of the Bank of Credit and Commerce International SA, which was registered in Luxembourg but had its principal place of business in the United Kingdom.

[20] 2000/12/EC, OJ L 26.05.2000, p 126.

[21] 2006/48/EC, OJ L 177, 14.06.2006, p 1.

[22] In view of the activities carried on by financial institutions, and as already noted, there is an obvious link between the two 'freedoms' mentioned in the text and the free movement of capital. However, the Recast Consolidation Directive is firmly rooted in the 'services' and 'establishment' freedoms: see recital (4) to the Directive, which places emphasis on the 'internal market' perspectives. See also Proctor, 'Taxation, Investments and the Free Movement of Capital' (2001) 8 JIBFL 363, where some of the relevant case law is considered.

[23] It should be noted that this consolidation exercise did not extend to the Directive on deposit-guarantee schemes. That directive is separately considered at paras 13.05–13.08 below.

[24] See Art 2 of the Recast Banking Consolidation Directive.

[25] See the definition of 'credit institution' in Art 4 of the Directive.

together with this definition, may therefore be circular in some respects, although the point is of no practical importance in view of Article 6 of the Recast Banking Consolidation Directive, which requires authorization as a precondition to the ability to accept deposits.[26]

(b) It will be apparent that this central provision of the Recast Banking Consolidation Directive is given effect in the UK by the corresponding provisions of the Regulated Activities Order.[27]

(c) The expression 'deposits or other repayable funds' is not defined in the Recast Banking Consolidation Directive.[28] The Court of Justice has, however, decided that the expression 'repayable funds' embraces not merely 'financial instruments which possess the intrinsic character of repayability',[29] but also funds which are repayable by virtue of an express contractual agreement to that effect.[30] A variety of reasons were offered for the need to adopt a broad approach to this term. First of all, it was clear that the protection of savings constituted one of the objectives of the Community measures taken to coordinate the legal framework applicable to credit institutions.[31] Secondly, in order that consumers are adequately protected by the legislation, it is necessary to ensure that the definition can cover new forms of financial products which are continually being developed by the market.[32]

The Authorization Process

The Recast Banking Consolidation Directive then provides that the national law of Member States must require that credit institutions obtain authorization before commencing their activities,[33] and sets out in broad terms the criteria which must be satisfied before the national authorities may grant such authorization.[34] Briefly, the requirements are as follows:[35]   **2.11**

(a) The institution must possess separate own funds and its initial capital must be at least €5 million.[36]

---

[26] Article 6 is considered in more detail at para 2.11 below.

[27] Article 5 of the Regulated Activities Order has already been considered at para 1.12 above.

[28] This may be contrasted with the provisions of art 5 of the Regulated Activities Order, where the expression is defined in some detail.

[29] The import of this expression, and the features which might distinguish it from a contractual arrangement, may not be immediately obvious. However, the arrangements at issue in the case before the Court of Justice involved the issue of 'trust securities', warrants and other instruments, but the net effect appears to have been a loan to (or deposit with) the issuer.

[30] Case C-366/97, *Criminal Proceedings against Romanelli* [1999] ECR I-855.

[31] See paras 12 and 13 of the judgment, read together with recital (6) to the Consolidation Directive. The theme of consumer protection runs through the few Court of Justice decisions which consider questions of EU banking law (see, in particular, the decision in the *Parodi* case, which is considered at para 2.21 below but, as will be shown, the relevant directives were insufficient to confer rights on individual depositors following the collapse of an institution—see the discussion of the *Peter Paul* case at para 13.05 below.

[32] See para 10 of the judgment in *Romanelli*.

[33] Article 6 of the Recast Banking Consolidation Directive.

[34] See Arts 6–22 of the Recast Banking Consolidation Directive.

[35] The provisions of art 5 of the Regulated Activities Order, discussed at para 1.12 above, do, of course, reflect the corresponding requirements of the Recast Banking Consolidation Directive.

[36] Article 9 of the Recast Banking Consolidation Directive. The Article allows for a lower level of capital (subject to a 'floor' of €1 million) in limited cases and subject to specific safeguards. The credit institution's own funds must not fall below the initial level: see Art 10 of the Directive.

(b) In order to avoid personal dominance over the affairs of a credit institution, there must be at least two individuals who effectively direct the business of the institution. They must be of good repute and must have the experience which is necessary for the performance of their duties.[37]

(c) Authorization can only be granted where the registered and the head office of the institution are both situated within the territory of the Member State from which authorization is sought.[38]

(d) Authorization must be refused if (i) the regulator is not satisfied as to the suitability of the shareholders, having regard to the need for sound and prudent management of credit institutions or (ii) there exist 'close links' between the institution and other persons which may prevent the effective exercise of the supervisory function.[39] For the same reasons, the acquisition of a major shareholding must be subject to prior approval by the national regulator concerned.[40]

(e) An application for authorization must be accompanied by a programme of operations explaining the types of business to be conducted and the organizational structure of the institution.[41] However, the application cannot be refused merely because there are a number of other entities operating in the market and which already offer similar services.[42]

(f) Any authorization which has been granted may subsequently be revoked on various grounds, eg because it obtained the authorization by means of false statements or other irregularities, it no longer holds the necessary minimum capital, no longer fulfils the conditions for authorization, or its solvency has become doubtful.[43]

(g) Finally, no Member State can impose an authorization requirement on credit institutions established in other Member States.[44] This rule follows from the principle of home State supervision, which will be considered at a later stage.[45]

---

[37] Article 11 of the Recast Banking Consolidation Directive. This provision may in some respects be linked to the obligation on national supervisors to ensure that credit institutions licensed by them have adequate administrative, accounting and internal control procedures: see Art 22 of the Recast Consolidation Directive.

[38] Article 11(2) of the Recast Banking Consolidation Directive. This requirement derives from the so-called 'BCCI Directive', to which reference has already been made (see n 20 above). Where the applicant is a member of a group of companies which holds an authorization in another Member State, the relevant national supervisors are required to consult each other on the new application: see Art 15 of the Recast Banking Consolidation Directive.

[39] Article 12 of the Recast Banking Consolidation Directive. The expression 'close links' connotes a parent—subsidiary relationship or a shareholding of 20 per cent—see the definition of that term in Art 4 of the Directive.

[40] Articles 20 and 21 of the Recast Banking Consolidation Directive.

[41] Article 7 of the Recast Banking Consolidation Directive.

[42] See Art 8 of the Recast Banking Consolidation Directive. In other words, the authorization process cannot be used to prevent market overcrowding, or otherwise to deny access to participants which otherwise meet the stated criteria for authorization.

[43] Article 17 of the Recast Banking Consolidation Directive. Art 17(2) requires that reasons for the revocation must be given to the institution concerned.

[44] Article 16 of the Recast Banking Consolidation Directive.

[45] See paras 2.13–2.21 below.

Articles 6–22 of the Recast Banking Consolidation Directive thus provide the broad frame- **2.12**
work for the licensing of credit institutions by the relevant authorities in each Member
State.[46] The ensuing sections of the Directive provide for the mutual recognition of authorizations in other Member States in order to give effect to the Treaty freedoms on establishment and the provision of services; they also deal with the manner in which the ongoing
supervisory functions are to be conducted. A variety of issues arise from these provisions,
and it is proposed to subdivide the subject matter.

The Treaty Freedoms—General Considerations

The starting point for the passporting system is provided by Article 40 of the Recast Banking **2.13**
Consolidation Directive, which establishes the general principle that the prudential
supervision of an institution is the responsibility of the home State regulator. Subject to
certain exceptions, the jurisdiction of the home State in this area is exclusive. As a result,
under the terms of Article 23 of the Recast Banking Consolidation Directive, the national
law of each Member State must allow a credit institution established in another Member
State to carry on listed, banking activities[47] within the territory of the first Member State—
either by means of the establishment of a branch or the provision of services—provided
that the following conditions[48] are met:

(a) the credit institution must hold an authorization granted by the relevant authorities
    in another Member State; and
(b) the activity which that credit institution wishes to carry out in reliance on these
    provisions is covered by its home State authorization.

Similar rights must also be granted to a financial institution which is a subsidiary of another **2.14**
credit institution and which meets certain other formal requirements.[49]

It will thus be apparent that, in terms of general principle, a credit institution is subject to **2.15**
supervision solely by its home State regulator, so that any decisions as to the suitability of
that person to hold a deposit-taking authorization are within the exclusive jurisdiction of

---

[46] It will be apparent that the United Kingdom's domestic authorization requirements as discussed in
Chapter 1 above reflect the wider provisions of the Recast Banking Consolidation Directive.

[47] The banking activities which are the subject of mutual recognition are set out in Annex 1 to the Recast
Banking Consolidation Directive. Although, for the purposes of the present discussion, the focus inevitably
falls on deposit-taking, it should be appreciated that the scope of the listed services is, in fact, much wider than
that. The list includes (i) the acceptance of deposits and other repayable funds, (ii) lending (including consumer and mortgage loans, factoring, and forfaiting), (iii) financial leasing, (iv) money transmission services,
(v) issuing and administering means of payment (including credit cards), (vi) issuing guarantees and similar
instruments (which would include letters of credit), (vii) trading for own account or customers in currencies, futures, money market instruments, and transferable securities, (viii) the provision of certain corporate finance services (including participation in securities and advice on industrial strategy and mergers),
(ix) money broking, (x) portfolio management and advice, (xi) safekeeping and administration of securities,
(xii) credit reference services, and (xiii) custody services.

[48] The United Kingdom has given effect to these requirements by means of FSMA, s 31(1)(b) and Sch 3.

[49] Article 24 of the Recast Banking Consolidation Directive. This is the so-called 'passporting' regime,
designed to assist in the establishment of a single market in financial services. Some aspects of this system were
called into question following the Landsbanki episode in October 2008: see the discussion of the relevant
Treasury Committee Report at para 13.14 below.

that regulator; such decisions may not generally be questioned by the supervisor in the host State.[50] A Member State which sought to impose additional licensing requirements on incoming EEA institutions would plainly thereby commit a breach of its Community law obligations, since such measures would plainly be inconsistent with the rights intended to be conferred by the Recast Banking Consolidation Directive.

The Right to Establish a Branch

2.16 A credit institution which wishes to exercise these rights by establishing a branch may give notice to its home Member State regulator specifying, amongst other things, the Member State in which it wishes to establish that branch and the identity of those who will be responsible for its management. A programme of operations and organizational structure must also be provided.[51] Thereafter, the following procedure applies:

(a) The regulator in the home State must communicate the relevant information to the authorities in the intended host State. The home State regulator may only decline to deliver this information if it has reason to doubt the administrative structure or the financial soundness of the credit institution, having regard to the activities which it proposes to conduct in the host State.[52]

(b) On receipt of that communication, the host State regulator has a two month period in which to prepare for the supervision of the institution and to provide details of the local rules and regulations which are to be applied on the basis of the general good.[53]

(c) On expiry of that two month period (or on receipt of an earlier confirmation from the host State regulator) the credit institution may establish a branch within the territory of the host State.

The Right to Provide Services

2.17 Less stringent rules apply where a credit institution does not wish to establish a full branch, but merely wishes '… to exercise the freedom to provide services by carrying on its activities within the territory of another Member State …'.[54] In such a case, the institution is merely

---

[50] It is important not to lose sight of this essential principle although, in practice, there are a number of important derogations from it. For example, the host State regulator is entitled to enforce local regulations adopted for the general good (Art 32) and the supervision of issues relating to liquidity are ascribed to the host State regulator (Art 41).

[51] On these requirements, see Art 25 of the Recast Banking Consolidation Directive.

[52] The procedures are set out in Art 25 of the Recast Banking Consolidation Directive. If the home State regulator declines to give notice to the host State regulator on the grounds described in the text, then Art 25(4) requires that such decision must be reviewable by a court. The United Kingdom has complied with this obligation by providing for a right of reference to the Financial Services and Markets Tribunal—see FSMA, Sch 3, para 12(b).

[53] Article 26(1) of the Recast Banking Consolidation Directive. Although authorization and supervision are matters for the home State, the manner in which business is actually conducted in the host State (eg the methods adopted to solicit deposits, the content of local advertisements etc) must in any event comply with local rules—the point is perhaps made more explicit in para 13 of Sch 3 to the FSMA, which implements the corresponding provisions of the Recast Banking Consolidation Directive. The ability to impose local rules of this kind under the heading of the 'general good' seems first to have been recognized by the Court of Justice in Case 110/78, *Van Wesemael* [1979] ECR 35.

[54] The expression is taken from Art 28(1) of the Recast Banking Consolidation Directive.

required to notify its home State regulator of the activities which it intends to conduct, and the regulator is required to pass on these details to the host State regulator within one month.[55] In this case, there is no basis upon which the home State regulator can decline to give notice as required by the Directive.[56]

Provision of Services from within the Home State

The last two sections have dealt with the right '… to establish a branch within the territory of another Member State …' and the right '… to provide services … within the territory of another Member State …'. The key expression in each case is, of course, the reference to acting 'within the territory of another Member State'. It is not necessary for an institution to go through the passporting procedures if it is not establishing a branch or providing services within such territories.[57] **2.18**

Whether or not an institution has established a branch in a particular Member State will usually be relatively clear,[58] but it may be less clear whether an entity is providing services within the territory of a Member State.[59] In the view of the present writer, an institution which does not advertise[60] for or actively solicit business from potential customers in a particular jurisdiction, but merely executes such transactions as may be introduced to it,[61] should not be regarded as carrying on activities *within* the Member State in which the customer is established; it is merely providing cross-border services from within its own country of establishment. It follows that the regulator in those Member States should not require the institution to be licensed within their jurisdiction or passported under the procedures described above. **2.19**

In other words, there is a residual, albeit limited, category of banking activity which can be conducted in reliance on the general services 'freedom', without recourse to the provisions of the Consolidation Directive. Member States should only be able to restrict such **2.20**

---

[55] Article 28(2) of the Recast Banking Consolidation Directive.

[56] This point is reflected in para 20 of Sch 3 to the FSMA, insofar as it gives effect to the Recast Banking Consolidation Directive.

[57] This territorial question is by no means limited to the provisions of the Recast Banking Consolidation Directive. In any case in which an authorization requirement applies, it will be necessary to consider whether a particular entity is carrying on regulated activities within the jurisdiction. Modern technology and internet communication has only made this question more difficult to answer in individual cases. Traditionally, it was said that a bank had to be licensed if it was doing business *in* a particular country, but not if it was merely doing business *with* that country. This formulation may not always have been helpful when dealing with the details of particular cases, but it does capture the general notion.

[58] Although difficulties may arise in relation to the use of intermediaries and agents—are they to be regarded as a branch or establishment of the appointor?

[59] It hardly needs to be stated that this expression would have to be given an autonomous meaning for the purposes of the Recast Consolidation Directive, and should not be given separate national meanings in individual Member States.

[60] Indeed, advertising *alone* probably should not have any impact in this area—see the discussion of the Commission Interpretative Communication at paras 2.25–2.28 below.

[61] This may, for example, occur where a bank in the United Kingdom has an established relationship with a group of companies in the UK but, on a request made via the Finance Director in the UK, occasionally accepts deposits or executes other transactions for another group subsidiary incorporated in Germany.

activities on the basis of the 'general good'.[62] They should not be entitled to impose an authorization or passport requirement on institutions established in other Member States and which wish to do business with customers resident within their respective jurisdictions.[63] Particular aspects of this question of territoriality are discussed in more detail at a later stage.[64]

2.21 Finally, it is necessary to consider the decision of the European Court of Justice in *Societe Civile Immobiliere Parodi v Banque H Albert de Bary et Cie.*[65] This decision related to a loan made before the passporting procedure—originally created by the Second Banking Directive—came into force and, as a result, it had to be decided on the basis of the treaty provisions on freedom of establishment. A Dutch bank had made a loan to a French real estate company. The Dutch bank had acted through its office in Amsterdam and it did not have any form of establishment in France. The Dutch bank was authorized in the Netherlands but, in the pre-passporting era, this did not entitle it to any particular form of recognition in France. Although the precise effect of the French laws at issue was disputed, it seems that they prohibited the making of loans to French borrowers unless the lender was authorized in France and had a place of business there. The Court of Justice held that the local authorization requirement could not be imposed on an institution licensed in another Member State for the purpose of granting loans unless (i) the requirement is imposed on every lender in the destination Member State, (ii) the rule is justified on the grounds of the public interest,[66] and (iii) the relevant measure is necessary and proportionate. The requirement to have a local branch in France was directly inconsistent with the Treaty freedom to provide services and was thus unlawful.[67] This was, of course, treated as a case on the freedom to provide cross-border services in the light of the apparently restrictive provisions of French law. In reality, and although the point did not arise against the background of the Treaty framework then at issue, it may be argued that, in fact, the bank was merely providing services from its branch in Amsterdam and, to that extent, the bank was not providing services *in France* at all. Nevertheless, and although it has now in many respects been superseded, the outcome of the *Parodi* case seems to be essentially satisfactory.

---

[62] On the 'general good', see para 2.16 above. The point made in the text does however have wider implications. International banking on any scale would become effectively impossible if a bank had to be authorized or licensed in every jurisdiction in which its customers are resident. So, whilst the present discussion is specifically aimed at the passporting process, similar issues could apply to non-EEA institutions providing services from their home bases to customers located within the EEA.

[63] As noted earlier, this general principle is recorded in Art 16 of the Recast Banking Consolidation Directive.

[64] See the discussion of the Commission Interpretative Communication at paras 2.25–2.28 below.

[65] Case C-212/95, [1997] ECR I-3899.

[66] For example, it may be legitimate to protect local consumers from placing deposits with foreign institutions, but it is less obvious that a borrower of funds from such an institution needs similar protection.

[67] The position would be the same under the current law, save that the host State may require the completion of the passporting procedure as a condition to the entitlement to provide banking services within its jurisdiction.

Free Movement of Capital and Banking Services

The decision in *Parodi* was largely based on the freedom to provide cross-border services, as **2.22** guaranteed by the EC Treaty. Yet banks are intimately associated with the movement of money, and it is thus relevant to consider briefly[68] the Treaty rules on the free movement of capital and the implications of these provisions for banks and legislators.

Article 56 of the Treaty requires that '… all restrictions on the *movement of capital* **2.23** between Member States and between Member States and third countries shall be prohibited …' and that '… all restrictions on *payments* between Member States and between Member States and third countries shall be prohibited …'.[69] These provisions operate to fetter legislative authority in Member States and should thus operate to the favour of banks wishing to promote their cross-border business within the Community. Case law in the European Court of Justice has thrown up some of the consequences of Article 56 for financial institutions. For example:

(a) it has been decided that a Member State cannot discriminate against transactions effected in a currency other than that of the Member State itself. Thus, for example, if a German bank wished to take a mortgage over a property in Austria, Austrian law could not require that the mortgage be expressed in Austrian schillings, since this would expose the bank to an exchange rate risk and hence constitute an obstacle to the free movement of capital across the Community.[70] The effective result of this decision is that lenders must be allowed to take security over assets expressed in the currency of the loan, even if that differs from the currency of the country in which the security is located;[71]

(b) any rule imposed by a Member State prohibiting the acquisition of land by nationals of other Member States—or, by the same token, prohibiting the taking of mortgages over property by lenders based in other Member States—will almost invariably contravene the free movement of capital requirements in Article 56;[72]

(c) it would be unlawful for a Member State to impose stamp or registration taxes exclusively on facilities provided by lenders from other Member States, since this would incentivize borrowers to use local banks and thus act as a brake on the free movement of capital;[73] and

---

[68] For a wider discussion, see Proctor, 'Taxation, Investments and the Free Movement of Capital' (2001) 8 JIBFL 363.

[69] Emphasis supplied. These rules on the free movement of capital and payments are subject to exceptions but it is not necessary to discuss them in the present context. It may be noted that the provisions of Art 56 have direct effect and are thus capable of creating rights which are enforceable in national proceedings: see Case 250/94, *Criminal Proceedings against Sanz de Lera* [1995] ECR I-4821.

[70] This was the effect of the decision in Case 222/97, *Trummer and Mayer* [1999] ECR I-1661. That decision was followed in the very similar factual situation which arose in Case C-464/98, *Westdeutsche Landesbank Girozentrale v Stefan* [2001] ECR I-173.

[71] The case remains relevant even though, as a practical matter, the introduction of the euro has reduced the number of occasions on which the issue could potentially arise.

[72] Case C-302/97, *Konle v Republic of Austria* [1999] ECR I-3099.

[73] Case C-439/97, *Sandoz GmbH v Finanzlandesdirektion fur Wien* [1999] ECR I-7041.

(d) similarly, a Member State could not impose rates of tax on local income received by a foreign lender at rates in excess of those available to a local lender within the Member State concerned.[74]

2.24 Thus, although the single market directives in the sphere of financial services are principally rooted in the Treaty freedoms of establishment and the provision of services, it should be appreciated that the rules on free movement of capital and payments may be of significance in ensuring that banks within the Community are genuinely able to compete on a cross-border basis.

The Commission Interpretative Communication

2.25 Reference has already been made to some of the difficulties posed by territorial questions in the field of the authorization and passporting process.

2.26 The whole subject benefits from a degree of clarification as a result of the EC Commission's Interpretative Communication on the Freedom to provide Services and the Interest of the General Good in the Second Banking Directive.[75] The Interpretative Communication notes the difficulties posed by the reference to providing services '… within the territory of another Member State …', especially given the intangible nature of banking services and the problems involved in identifying the location in which such services are provided. It also notes that these difficulties are exacerbated by the growth of distance/internet banking services.

2.27 In an effort to bring some cohesion to the whole subject, the Interpretative Communication takes the line that a service should be deemed to be provided in the country in which the 'characteristic performance' of the service (ie the essential supply for which payment is due) occurs.[76] The Communication then makes the following, substantive points in relation to the provision of cross-border banking services:

(a) as noted earlier,[77] a bank may have customers in another Member State without necessarily pursuing its banking activities *within the territory* of that Member State;

---

[74] See, for example, Case C-315/02, *Lenz v Finanzlandesdirektion fur Tirol* [2004] ECR I-7063. There have been a number of cases on freedom of establishment and movement of capital in relation to national tax systems, but these are beyond the scope of the present discussion.

[75] 97/C 209/04, EC Commission. The Communication is principally directed to the question whether a credit institution authorized in one Member State should exercise its 'passport' rights before it seeks to provide services in another Member State. But, by the same token, the criteria outlined in the Communication may likewise be applied in determining whether authorization for particular activities is required in the first place (ie because 'passporting' is itself in substance a form of authorization or, perhaps more accurately, a means of extending the geographic reach of that authorization). It should be appreciated that the Communication does not have the force of law and it is understood that not all Member States necessarily subscribe to the guidance contained within it.

[76] The reference to the 'characteristic performance' of the contract is admittedly derived from the Rome Convention on the law applicable to contractual obligations, now replaced by Rome I on the same subject matter. The whole subject of the law applicable to the banker—customer contract is considered in Chapter 40 below.

[77] See para 2.21 above.

(b) as a result, if a UK bank receives a request from a German customer to provide a loan to acquire a commercial property in France, representatives of that bank may (i) visit the customer in Germany to negotiate the facility and (ii) inspect the property in France, without having exercised passport rights in either country. This follows from the fact that the substance of the service—the ultimate making of the loan—will be achieved by means of an advance made by the bank from within the United Kingdom;

(c) thus, where a UK bank receives a request for a facility from a prospective customer in another part of the EU and it accedes to that request, it will not thereby be carrying on business in the customer's country;

(d) if, on the other hand, the transaction is of such a size that the UK bank feels it necessary to send a dedicated member of its staff to the customer's country for an extended period, than the Communication suggests that the 'characteristic performance' of the contract may shift to that country, and a passport notification may therefore be required;

(e) a bank providing distance banking services (eg via the internet) should not be regarded as providing banking services or pursuing its activities in every country in which it has customers and, consequently, such activities should generally be regarded as provided from the banks' head office and, hence, would be covered by its home State authorization;

(f) the mere fact that a bank's advertising or publicity materials may be distributed into, or viewed in, a particular country does not of itself create an inference that the institution intends to carry on business *within* the territory of that country. It may merely be soliciting international customers for its head office within its home State;

(g) importantly from the perspective of the enforceability of banking and loan contracts, the Interpretative Communication takes the view that the notification procedure for banking passports '… pursues a simple objective of exchange of information between supervisory authorities and is not a consumer a protection measure. It should not, in the Commission's view, be a procedural condition affecting the validity of a banking contract …'. Thus, if a UK bank has executed an English law contract with an Italian customer, the English courts should in principle enforce that contract and any argument to the effect that the arrangement was unlawful under Italian law[78] should necessarily fail;[79]

(h) in any event, in relation to the freedom to provide services, the EC Treaty allows that a person providing a service may do so 'temporarily' in another Member State.[80] Whether or not a service is provided on a 'temporary' basis is of course a question of fact, depending on the '… duration, regularity, periodicity and continuity …' of the activities in question.[81] Thus, if an institution is providing its services regularly in a particular

---

[78] ie on the basis that the UK bank was providing financial services in Italy but was not passported into that country.

[79] ie on the basis that the legality and validity of the contract are governed by English law: see the discussion at para 40.12 below.

[80] EC Treaty, Art 60.

[81] Case C-55/94, *Gebhard* [1995] ECR I-4165, as noted in the Interpretative Communication.

Member State, then it would probably cross a boundary line and would have to complete the passporting procedure for that purpose; and

(i) the mere fact that the bank employs intermediaries or agents to secure business within another Member State does not mean that it carries on its business activities *within* that State.

2.28 Insofar as the freedom of establishment is concerned, the Interpretative Communication notes that:

(a) if an institution maintains a permanent presence in a Member State in which it provides services, then it will fall within the scope of the provisions of the EC Treaty on freedom of establishment;[82]

(b) the Court of Justice has ruled that '... a national of a Member State who pursues a professional activity on a stable and continuous basis in another Member State where he holds himself out from an established professional base to, among others, nationals of that State comes under the provisions of the chapter relating to the right of establishment, and not those relating to services ...'.[83] Nevertheless, in the same judgment,[84] the court held that the maintenance of any necessary 'infrastructure' for the provision of services in the host State does not necessarily mean that the institution concerned has created a local establishment. This seems to mean that the maintenance of meeting or similar facilities in another EU Member State for discussions with *existing* clients of a UK bank may not amount to an 'establishment', but the position may be otherwise if the facilities are used as a base for attracting *new* customers in the Member State concerned;

(c) the use of agents or intermediaries in another Member State may also give rise to questions as to whether the institution is maintaining an 'establishment' in that other Member State.[85] In this context, the Court of Justice has held[86] that an institution based in one Member State '... which maintains a permanent presence in [another] Member State ... comes within the scope of the provisions of the Treaty on the right of establishment, even if that presence does not take the form of a branch or agency, but consists merely of an office managed by the undertaking's own staff *or by a person who is independent but authorised to act on a permanent basis for the undertaking, as will be the case with an agency* ...'. Thus, if a bank uses such intermediaries then it may be treated as having an 'establishment' in the country concerned;

(d) a slight difficulty may arise in this context in the context of a bank's 'representative office', which was traditionally understood as an office designed to establish contacts

---

[82] ie as opposed to the freedom to provide services.

[83] See *Gebhard*, n 81 above. Thus, an entity which provides *services* in another Member State via a *permanent establishment* in that Member State is subject to the rules dealing with the right of establishment, and is not entitled to the benefit of rules relating to the provision of services: Case 205/84, *Commission v Germany* [1986] ECR 3375. The case is discussed in the Interpretative Communication.

[84] *Gebhard*, n 81 above.

[85] The question is not dissimilar to the problems which arise in connection with the meaning of 'permanent establishment' as used in double tax treaties and which operate to deprive a taxpayer of a credit where the relevant income is effectively connected with a permanent establishment in the contracting State concerned.

[86] See Case 205/84, *Commission v Germany*, n 83 above. Emphasis supplied.

and maintain relationships with customers but which had no authority to bind its head office to transactions. In principle, it would seem that such offices should not be required to be passported under the Recast Consolidation Directive, since the relevant services are provided from the home Member State. It appears that this position can still be maintained, since the office is not authorized to act on behalf of the head office. Insofar as intermediaries are concerned, this approach is reinforced by the view of the Commission that an intermediary will only be an 'establishment' for these purposes if (i) the intermediary has a permanent mandate, (ii) it is subject to the overall management and control of the head office, and (iii) it has the power to commit the institution to contracts and transactions.[87] As the Interpretative Communication points out, there seems to be nothing in the EC Treaty which prevents a credit institution from *simultaneously* exercising both (i) the right to provide services from its head office and (ii) the right of establishment via the setting up of a branch. Thus, it would be possible for a UK bank to open a branch in France, and yet at the same time provide services to French customers from its Head Office in the United Kingdom. For tax and other reasons, however, it would be necessary to be clear about which contracts are associated with the head office and which are to be ascribed to the local branch.[88]

Conclusions

The present chapter has demonstrated how, over the years, the rules applicable to the authorization and supervision of banking business across the Community have been progressively harmonized. It has also sought to demonstrate that the Treaty provisions on free movement of capital are important to the completion of a single market in financial services, although there is a tendency in practice to focus on the 'establishment' and 'services' freedoms.   **2.29**

The importance of EU banking law will be further demonstrated by the ensuing chapters, which will again show that Community law is of great significance in many other areas relating to financial services.[89]   **2.30**

---

[87] The Interpretative Communication relies for this analysis on Case 14/76 *De Bloos* [1976] ECR 1497, Case 139/80, *Blanckaert & Williams* [1981] ECR 819 and Case 33/78, *Somafer* [1978] ECR 2183.

[88] It may be noted that some of the territorial issues discussed in this section are also relevant to the provision of payment services: see the discussion at paras 5.29–5.33 below.

[89] See in particular Chapters 5 and 7 below, respectively dealing with payment services and anti-money laundering legislation.

3

THE CONDUCT OF RETAIL BANKING AND INVESTMENT BUSINESS

Introduction

For an extended period, the conduct of banks in relation to their retail customers was governed by two voluntary codes, namely, the Banking Code (for personal customers) and the Business Banking Code (for corporate and business customers). These Codes were published and updated from time to time by the British Bankers' Association. **3.01**

This voluntary scheme for the regulation of retail business[1] effectively came to an end on 1 November 2009, when the Banking Conduct of Business section (hereafter 'BCOBS') of the FSA Handbook came into force.[2] The demise of the voluntary scheme was in part a consequence of the newly introduced regime for the regulation of payment services, which came into effect on the same date.[3] Since Community law would result in the application of statutory conduct of business rules to payment services in certain currencies, it made **3.02**

---

[1] Of course, some aspects of retail *lending* business were already subject to statutory regulation: see the discussion of consumer credit and mortgage lending regulation, in Chapter 4 below.

[2] For the consultation and feedback materials leading up to BCOBS, see FSA papers CP08/19, PS09/6, CP09/20 and Handbook Notice 92.

[3] On the details of the Payment Services Regulations, see Chapter 5 below.

sense to apply a uniform regime across the industry, even to services which strictly fell beyond the scope of the Community requirements.[4]

3.03 The principal purpose of the present chapter is to examine the main requirements of BCOBS. It will also briefly examine the requirements applicable to banks in the field of investment services provided to retail clients, to the extent to which these are affected by the EU's Markets in Financial Instruments Directive.

Scope of BCOBS

Application

3.04 First of all, to whom and to what does BCOBS apply? This question is answered by BCOBS 1.

3.05 On the *service user* side, BCOBS applies to a 'banking customer'.[5] This expression is defined in the FSA Handbook Glossary to include a consumer, a micro-enterprise,[6] and a charity with an annual income of less than £1 million. To this extent, the scope of BCOBS runs in parallel with the scope of the Payment Services Regulations.[7]

3.06 On the *service provider* side of the equation, the provisions of BCOBS will only apply to a credit institution insofar as it accepts deposits from relevant banking customers from an establishment in the United Kingdom, and to any connected activities.[8] Thus, whilst the Payment Services Regulations 2009 will apply to service providers authorized or registered under those regulations, such institutions will not be subject to the requirements of BCOBS because their business does not involve the acceptance of deposits in the United Kingdom.[9]

3.07 In relation to the *services* themselves, BCOBS is stated[10] to apply to (i) the regulated activity of accepting deposits in the United Kingdom[11] and (ii) other activities which are 'connected' with that deposit-taking activity. This means that BCOBS applies to current and savings account products, and similar services.

---

[4] It may be noted in passing that the EU has recently introduced a broader directive on the provision of services generally: see Directive 2006/123/EC of the European Parliament and of the Council of 12 December 2006 on services in the internal market, OJ L 376, 27.12.2006, p 36. However, by Art 2(1)(b) of the Directive, its terms do not apply to banking or investment services of the type discussed in this chapter.

[5] See BCOBS 1.1.1R.

[6] For a discussion of the expression 'micro-enterprise', see para 5.44 below.

[7] It should, however, be noted that the 2009 Regulations apply to larger customers as well, although many of the core provisions of those Regulations can be excluded by the express terms of the contract: see the discussion of the 'corporate opt out' in relation to the 2009 Regulations, at para 5.55 below. In contrast, BCOBS is in any event inapplicable to such customers, regardless of the terms of the contract.

[8] BCOBS 1.1.1R.

[9] This point is specifically confirmed by art 9AB of the Regulated Activities Order, as inserted by the 2009 Regulations, Sch 6, para 4.

[10] BCOBS 1.1.1R.

[11] For the definition and parameters of the deposit-taking activity, see art 5 of the Regulated Activities Order, discussed at para 1.12 above.

Although BCOBS 1 is principally concerned with matters of scope and application, **3.08** it nevertheless concludes with a substantive provision which prohibits a bank from excluding or restricting its liability to a customer, unless either (i) it is reasonable for it to do so or (ii) the relevant duty or liability arises in a context which is outside the scope of the regulatory framework.[12]

Communications with Customers

BCOBS 2 deals with communications with customers and financial promotions. The **3.09** introductory comments note that Principle 6 requires a firm to pay due regard to the interests of its customers and to treat them fairly, whilst Principle 7 requires them to pay regard to the needs of their customers for information and the obligation to communicate with them in a manner which is clear, fair and not misleading.[13] It is also stated that the chapter is intended to apply to promotions of retail banking services.[14] The main provisions of BCOBS 2 include:

(a) a duty to ensure that financial promotions relating to deposits are fair, clear and not misleading, having regard to the nature of the information to be conveyed and the category of persons to whom it is directed;[15]

(b) a communication made to a banking customer[16] (i) must include the name of the bank, (ii) must be accurate, (iii) must not emphasize the benefits of a retail banking service without also including a fair and prominent indication of any relevant risks, (iv) must be presented in a way likely to be understood by an average member of the target recipients, and (v) must not disguise, diminish or obscure relevant information, statements of warnings.[17]

---

[12] BCOBS 1.1.6R. An unfair exclusion clause may therefore not only be unenforceable under the terms of legislation discussed at a later stage (see paras 15.38–15.52 below), but any attempt to impose such a restriction or exclusion may constitute a breach of the bank's regulatory obligations. It may, however, be worth repeating that this rule only applies where the customer is a consumer, micro-enterprise, or charity which falls within the definition of 'banking customer' for BCOBS purposes. The provisions of BCOBS 1.1.6R may be seen as a particular expression of the broader obligation to treat customers fairly: see the FSA Handbook, PRIN 6.

[13] BCOBS 2.1.1G. On the high level principles applicable to authorized institutions, see the FSA Handbook (PRIN). In view of the existence of the voluntary codes notes above, PRIN did not formerly apply to deposit-taking business. However, consistently with the introduction of BCOBS, PRIN 3.2.1R has now been extended to include such business.

[14] The glossary to the FSA Handbook defines a 'retail banking service' as '… an arrangement with a banking customer, under which the firm agrees to accept a deposit from a banking customer on terms to be held in an account for that customer and to provide services in relation to that deposit including but not limited to repayment to the customer…'. The expression 'retail banking services' is thus wide enough to encompass the execution of transfer instructions in relation to the deposit—that is, the provision of *payment services* in relation to that deposit for the purposes of the Payment Services Regulations 2009.

[15] BCOBS 2.2.2R and 2.2.2G. It should be emphasized that the duty just described also applies to a much wider range of information and products, but we are here concerned solely with deposit-taking and associated activities involved with the provision of payment services. As para 2.2.4G reminds the reader, the dissemination of certain types of misleading statements may involve the commission of an offence under s 397 of the FSMA.

[16] The restricted scope of this expression should not be overlooked. See n 12 above.

[17] BCOBS 2.3.1R. Guidance on these requirements is contained in BCOBS 2.3.2G–2.3.7G. As that guidance notes, The Credit Institutions (Protection of Deposits) Regulations 1995 (SI 1995/1442) may apply to communications to depositors. In essence, explanatory literature and advertisements for deposits

3.10 It will be seen that the duty described in (a) above relates only to the taking of deposits. However, the duties described in (b) are broader in scope and will thus apply cumulatively with any information requirements or other obligations arising under Parts 5 and 6 of the Payment Services Regulations 2009.[18]

Distance Marketing

3.11 BCOBS 3[19] applies to distance marketing of deposit-taking activities in compliance with the Distance Marking Directive[20] and the E-Commerce Directive.[21] In view of the European derivation of the underlying legislation, it applies not only where the UK bank or branch is providing services to a domestic consumer; it will be equally applicable where the consumer is based in another EEA State.[22]

3.12 In essence, and in compliance with Articles 3(1) and 4(5) of the Distance Marketing Directive, the bank must provide the following information to the consumer before he becomes bound by the distance contract:[23]

(a) information about the service provider, including its name, head office, contact address, registration number and regulatory details;
(b) information about the service, including the main characteristics of the service, the total price including fees, charges and expenses or the basis of their calculation, any special risks (such as market risk) applicable to the product, a statement that past performance is not necessarily a guide to the future, a statement about the possible incidence of taxation or other costs, any closing date applicable to the offer, the arrangements for payment/performance, and any additional costs to the consumer for using a means of distance communication;

---

must include information about the applicable deposit-protection scheme. In addition, regard should be had to the Code of Conduct for the Advertising of Interest Bearing Accounts published by the British Bankers Association/Building Societies Association: see para 2.3.9G.

[18] On Pts 5 and 6 of the 2009 Regulations, see paras 5.42–5.85 below. The point made in the text is confirmed by BCOBS 1.1.4R.

[19] It may be noted that BCOBS 3 reflects the essentially similar requirements set out in COBS 5.

[20] This expression refers to the Directive (2002/65/EC) of the Council and of the Parliament of 23 September 2002 on distance marketing of consumer financial services. The Directive was implemented in the United Kingdom by means of the Financial Services (Distance Marketing) Regulations 2004 (SI 2004/2095).

[21] Directive 2000/31/EC of the European Parliament and of the Council of 8 June 2000 on certain legal aspects of information society services, in particular electronic commerce in the Internal Market, OJ L 178, 17.07.2000, p 1, implemented in the United Kingdom by the Electronic Commerce (EC Directive) Regulations 2002 (SI 2002/2013).

[22] This point is reflected in BCOBS 3.1.1R.

[23] The information requirements from the Distance Marketing Directive are reproduced in BCOBS 3 Annex 1R. In line with recitals 15 and 18 to, and Art 2(a) and (e) of, the Distance Marketing Directive, the FSA Handbook Glossary contains a detailed definition of 'distance contract' for these purposes. A contract is a 'distance contract' if it is concluded with the consumer under an organized distance service provision scheme which makes exclusive use of a means of distance communication (such as the telephone or the internet). An agreement does not amount to a distance contract if it involves face-to-face contact before the agreement becomes binding on the consumer. Of course, BCOBS 3 will only apply if the distance contract relates to business of a kind which itself falls within the scope of BCOBS 1 (see paras 3.04–3.07 above). The Directive and the implementing regulations themselves may apply to any other consumer financial service which falls within their scope.

(c) information about the contract itself, including details of any cancellation rights,[24] the minimum duration of the contract, information on any termination rights and applicable penalties, the law applicable to the initial establishment of the customer relationship,[25] the law applicable to the contract itself[26] and any choice of court, and the language in which contractual communications will be given; and

(d) information about avenues of redress, including details of access to the Financial Services Ombudsman Service[27] and the availability of compensation from the Financial Services Compensation Scheme in the event of the insolvency of the bank.[28]

Without going into the details, it may be noted that there are variations to the list of requirements where the contract involves a payment service which falls within the scope of the Payment Services Regulations 2009.[29] **3.13**

BCOBS 3.2 deals with e-commerce and applies where a bank carries on an electronic commerce activity[30] from within the United Kingdom with a customer within the UK itself or in another EEA State. **3.14**

Once again, the general approach is to require the provision of prescribed information about the bank and the services or products offered by it[31] and details relating to the placing and receipt of orders.[32] In practice, there may be a degree of overlap between the 'distance marketing' requirements of BCOBS 2 and the 'e-commerce' requirements of BCOBS 3, although a bank would of course have to take care to ensure that it complies with the provisions of both chapters, so far as applicable to the particular service at issue. **3.15**

It should be noted that, where the service concerned is a payment service, the requirements of BCOBS 3 will apply in addition to any separate information provisions in Parts 5 and 6 of the Payment Services Regulations 2009.[33] **3.16**

Information Requirements

BCOBS 4 makes provision about information to be provided to retail banking customers. The starting point is the 'appropriate information rule'. A customer must receive the **3.17**

---

[24] On cancellation rights, see the discussion of BCOBS 6, at paras 3.23–3.25 below.

[25] This must be the domestic law of an EEA Member State: see para (16) of BCOBS 3 Annex 1R.

[26] This may be the law of a non-EEA State but, in that event, the bank must ensure that the customer is not deprived of the protection of the rules contained in BCOBS 3: see BCOBS 3.1.17R.

[27] On this service, see the FSA Handbook, DISP.

[28] On this scheme, see paras 13.09–13.10 below.

[29] On these information requirements, see para 3.09 above. On the point made in the text, see BCOBS 3.1.13G.

[30] In accordance with the definition set out in the FSA Handbook Glossary, an 'electronic commerce activity' is an activity which (i) is a regulated activity for the purposes of the Regulated Activities Order and (ii) consists of the provision of an 'information society service'. The latter expression is defined to include any service normally provided for remuneration, at a distance, and by means of electronic equipment for the processing and storage of data at the request of the service recipient.

[31] BCOBS 3.2.2R, reflecting Art 5(1) of the E-Commerce Directive.

[32] BCOBS 3.2.6R, although note that these requirements do not apply where the contract with the customer is concluded *exclusively* by email or other individual forms of communication: see BCOBS 3.2.9R.

[33] On this point, see BCOBS 3.1.2R. On Pts 5 and 6 of the Payment Services Regulations 2009, see paras 5.42–5.85 below.

information necessary to enable him to make decisions on an informed basis and, to that end, the requisite information must be provided to him in good time, in an appropriate medium and in an understandable/comprehensible form.[34]

3.18   BCOBS 4.1 includes a significant amount of guidance to assist in determining whether the appropriate information rule has been met. For example, the guidance suggests that information which is key to the customer's decision-making process should be made available to him directly[35] and in a durable medium before he is bound by the contract.[36] Appropriate information will include details of the bank, its retail banking services, relevant terms and conditions, rates of interest, charges, and other matters.[37] The appropriate level of information may vary according to the likely level of the customer's commitment and the complexity of the product.[38]

3.19   It should be appreciated that the appropriate information rule is not confined to the pre-contractual phase but applies equally throughout the life of the arrangement.[39] Consequently, if a bank proposes to exercise any contractual right[40] to vary the terms of the contract or to vary interest rates/charges to the material disadvantage of the customer, it should notify the customer in good time so that the customer will have an opportunity to exercise his own contractual termination rights, should he wish to do so.[41] Where such a variation applies to interest rates, it may be appropriate to notify the customer of other, alternative products offered by the bank and to advise him of his right to seek equivalent services from other institutions.[42]

3.20   BCOBS 4.2 requires a bank to provide to a customer—free of charge—regular and appropriate statements of account, although this is not necessary in certain specified cases.[43] The guidance to BCOBS 4.2 suggests that a bank should include details of interest rates on its account statements.[44]

3.21   BCOBS 4 is not applicable to the provision of payment services,[45] since there would be a significant degree of overlap and potential conflicts between this chapter and the Payment Services Regulations themselves.

---

[34] BCOBS 4.1.1R.
[35] ie and not merely by reference to information available on a website or other source.
[36] BCOBS 4.1.2G(1) and (2).
[37] BCOBS 4.1.4G.
[38] BCOBS 4.1.5G.
[39] BCOBS 4.1.4G.
[40] In the context of a change in interest rates, the duty to notify the customer only arises if the bank is exercising a power to vary the contract. Consequently, where the interest rate is linked to a tracker or reference rate, an adjustment does not amount to a 'variation' of the contract, nor is the bank exercising any contractual power of variation. Consequently, the obligation to notify the customer would not arise in this case: see FSA Handbook Notice 92, para 4.21.
[41] BCOBS 4.1.2G. However, since this is guidance only, this does not *necessarily* preclude the bank from making a variation which becomes effective before the customer can terminate the contract: see FSA Handbook Notice 92, para 4.24.
[42] BCOBS 4.1.2G.
[43] For the relevant provisions, see BCOBS 4.2.1R.
[44] BCOBS 4.2.2G.
[45] BCOBS 1.1.4R.

Post Sale Requirements

It has already been noted that the 'appropriate information rule' created by BCOBS 4 **3.22**
extends to a duty to provide relevant information throughout the life of the contract (and
not merely at its inception). But the provision of information is but one aspect of the
service which the customer is entitled to expect. This subject is picked up by BCOBS 5,
which creates a number of 'post sale' requirements. The chapter deals with a rather
miscellaneous list of items, but the main requirements include the following:

(a) a duty to provide a retail banking service which is prompt, efficient and fair to the
customer and which has regard to any information communicated to the customer
from time to time.[46] In relation to dealings with small businesses (micro-enterprises),
it is recommended that banks should have regard to 'A Statement of Principles: Banks
and businesses—working together', published by the British Bankers' Association;[47]

(b) banks are required to pay due regard to the interests of their customers and to treat
them fairly.[48] Consistently with this principle, a bank should deal fairly with a customer whom it believes to be in financial difficulty.[49] This guidance would appear to
imply that a bank should make reasonable efforts to find an alternative solution before
it has resort to enforcement or insolvency proceedings;

(c) a bank must provide a prompt and efficient service to assist a customer who wishes to
move to another bank;[50]

(d) a bank must make arrangements to allow customers to trace and access dormant
accounts;[51]

(e) subject to certain limitations and conditions, a bank must reimburse a customer in
respect of any unauthorized payment from his account and must compensate him for
the non-execution or defective execution of his instructions.[52] The relevant liability
provisions are very similar to those set out in Part 6 of the Payment Services Regulations
2009.[53] However, the rules contained in this segment of BCOBS 5 are inapplicable to
services which fall within the scope of the 2009 Regulations.[54] The objective must
therefore be to place the bank's liability regime on a uniform basis for those services to
which the 2009 Regulations apply, and those services to which they do not. The liability rules in BCOBS 5 will thus apply to payments in currencies other than the euro or

---

[46] In other words, the service provided must be consistent with the bank's advertising or publicity:
see BCOBS 5.1.1R.

[47] BCOBS 5.1.3G. This Statement was most recently revised in December 2008. It seeks to provide guidance for the relationship between banks and customers having an annual turnover of less than £1 million. The
principles include (i) a duty to provide clarity in the terms of any facility (including information/monitoring
requirements), (ii) obligations of consultation before action is taken, (iii) the management of complaints, and
(iv) the steps to be taken on the transfer of an account.

[48] See PRIN 6.

[49] BCOBS 5.1.4G.

[50] BCOBS 5.1.5R.

[51] BCOBS 5.1.9R.

[52] BCOBS 5.1.11R–5.1.19R.

[53] On Pt 6 of the 2009 Regulations, see paras 5.54–5.86 below.

[54] See BCOBS 1.1.4R.

sterling, or which are made by cheque.[55] Consequently, subject only to very minor variations, the liability regime in Part 6 of the 2009 Regulations will apply equally to those payment services which fall within the scope of BCOBS.

Cancellation

3.23   BCOBS 6 deals with cancellation rights. The basic position is that a customer can cancel any contract for the provision of retail banking services without penalty within 14 days after the date on which the contract is made.[56] There are various exceptions to this rule. For example, a customer who places a fixed term deposit at an interest rate agreed in advance has no cancellation right.[57]

3.24   If a customer exercises his right of cancellation, he can only be charged a proportionate amount for the services actually provided until the date of termination.[58] Subject to that, the bank must return the customer's funds within 30 days of cancellation.[59]

3.25   It may be noted that BCOBS 6 is not applicable in the context of payment services.[60] The cancellation of payment orders is subject to the terms of the 2009 Regulations themselves.[61]

Investment Services

Introduction

3.26   It is necessary in the present context to consider the position of a bank when it provides investment services or performs investment activities. As in so many areas, this field has been significantly impacted by EU legislation designed to further the single market, namely the Markets in Financial Instruments Directive (MiFID).[62] Member States were required to implement MiFID by 1 November 2007.

3.27   Like the Recast Consolidation Directive discussed earlier,[63] MiFID is a single market measure. It created a similar passporting regime for firms which hold an authorization in their home Member States, and provides for harmonized conduct of business rules.[64]

---

[55] The 2009 Regulations do not apply to payments by means of a cheque or similar instrument: see para 5.11 below.

[56] BCOBS 6.1.1R. The bank must advise the customer of the availability of the cancellation right and the mode of its exercise: BCOBS 6.1.5R.

[57] For this and other cases in which the cancellation right is inapplicable, see BCOBS 6.1.2R.

[58] BCOBS 6.3.2R.

[59] BCOBS 6.4.1R. It must be said that provisions of this type will be of limited relevance in the context of an ordinary current account, where the customer can simply write a cheque to move his funds elsewhere and give notice to close the account in the ordinary way.

[60] BCOBS 1.1.4R.

[61] See reg 55 of the 2009 Regulations, discussed at para 5.58 below.

[62] Directive 2004/39/EC of the European Parliament and of the Council on markets in financial instruments, OJ L145, 30.4.2004, p 1 (MiFID). MiFID replaced the former Investment Services Directive, which was significantly narrower in scope (both in terms of the investments which fell within its scope and the range of services to which it applied).

[63] See Chapter 2 above.

[64] It should be noted that MiFID does not apply to all types of investment business. For example, matters relating to life assurance and pensions will generally fall outside the scope of the Directive and the

Scope of MiFID

It should be appreciated at the outset that MiFID only applies to its fullest extent in rela- **3.28** tion to investment firms and regulated markets.[65] Where investment services or activities are provided or carried out by a credit institution, then MiFID will only apply to the extent discussed below.

MiFID applies to 'investment services and activities', which includes (i) the reception, **3.29** transmission, and execution of orders in relation to financial instruments, (ii) dealing in financial instruments on own account, (iii) portfolio management, (iv) the provision of investment advice, and (v) underwriting and placing financial instruments.[66]

MiFID—Overview

In broad terms, the following provisions of MiFID are applied to banks or credit **3.30** institutions which carry out investment services or activities:

(a) the institution must be a member of the appropriate investor compensation scheme;[67]

(b) the bank must have in place policies, procedures, systems and controls which are appropriate to its business;[68]

(c) the bank must identify and manage conflicts of interest between itself and its clients, and between clients themselves;[69]

(d) the bank must act honestly, fairly and professionally, and in the best interests of its clients. This includes obligations to ensure that marketing material is fair, clear, and not misleading, to ensure that appropriate information is provided to clients, to maintain appropriate records, and to report fully to the client;[70]

(e) the bank must execute orders on terms most favourable to the client;[71]

(f) the bank must implement client order handling rules providing for fair and expeditious execution of client orders relative to the bank's own trading interests;[72]

(g) the bank must make public both the volume and price of transactions in listed securities which are executed outside a regulated market;[73]

---

implementing rules. At the risk of a very broad overgeneralization, however, the FSA has made various efforts to harmonize a number of the rules applicable to both MiFID and non-MiFID business. In order to avoid excessive complexity and detail, the present discussion is based solely on MiFID and associated legislation.

[65] See MiFID, Art 1(1).

[66] For full details, see MiFID, Annex I, Section A. 'Financial Instruments' includes shares, debentures, units in collective investment schemes, options, futures, and similar investments: see MiFID, Annex I, Section C. As noted above, this would not extend to life insurance, pensions, and the like.

[67] MiFID, Art 11.

[68] MiFID, Art 13.

[69] MiFID, Art 18.

[70] MiFID, Art 19.

[71] MiFID, Art 21.

[72] MiFID, Art 22. It should be noted that some of the above requirements do not apply to transactions with 'eligible counterparties': see MiFID, Art 24(1). On eligible counterparties and client classification, see para 3.36 below.

[73] MiFID, Art 28.

(h) banks carrying out investment services and activities in their home Member States are entitled to passport their authorizations and to establish branches/provide services in other Member States without any further requirement for a local permission.[74]

3.31 It may be noted that a number of other provisions of MiFID are expressed to apply to banks.[75] However, the above analysis is directed to the position of banks in the specific context of their dealings with and on behalf of their clients.

3.32 These relatively open-textured requirements were fleshed out by two additional pieces of Community legislation, namely, (i) a Commission regulation implementing MiFID in relation to record-keeping, transaction reporting, market transparency, admission of financial instruments to trading, and other matters[76] and (ii) a Commission directive on organizational requirements and operating conditions for investment firms.[77]

3.33 Having outlined the infrastructure provided by the relevant EU legislation, it may be helpful to examine some of the more detailed requirements by reference to the FSA Handbook, the vehicle for the implementation of many relevant provisions of MiFID in the United Kingdom.[78]

Client's Best Interests

3.34 The MiFID obligation to act honestly, fairly and professionally, and in accordance with the client's best interests has been transposed into the FSA Handbook as a rule,[79] with the result that an individual will be able to seek damages for a breach of this obligation.[80]

3.35 It is true that, separately, banks owe a general duty to treat their customers fairly.[81] However, since this particular requirement is expressed as a principle (and not as a rule), a breach of this requirement would not give rise to a cause of action in the same way.

Client Categorization

3.36 A bank is required to categorize its clients according to pre-set criteria and to notify each client accordingly.[82] The process is designed to ensure that each client receives a level of regulatory protection which is appropriate to his status, knowledge and sophistication in investments matters of the type under consideration. The available categories are:

(a) the *eligible counterparty* category includes banks, investment firms, pension funds, governments, central banks and international organizations. Needless to say, clients of this stature are seen as least in need of regulatory protection. Companies which meet

---

[74] MiFID, Arts 31(1) and 32(1).
[75] For the details, see MiFID, Art 2(2).
[76] Commission Regulation (EC) No 1287/2006 of 10 August 2006, OJ L 241, 2.9.2006, p 1.
[77] Commission Directive 2006/73/EC of 10 August 2006, OJ L 241, 2.9.2006, p 26.
[78] It should be emphasized that the discussion is selective and is intended only to provide an overview of some very detailed provisions.
[79] FSA Handbook, COBS 2.1.1R.
[80] ie in accordance with the statutory right set out in FSMA, s 150.
[81] FSA Handbook, PRIN 6.
[82] FSA Handbook, COBS 3.3.1R.

certain financial criteria may also request classification as an eligible counterparty.[83] However, a client can only be treated as an eligible counterparty in relation to certain types of business, including dealings for its own account, the execution of orders, and certain other arrangements;[84]

(b) a *professional client* again includes banks, investment firms and others, and this categorization will apply to them where they have chosen not to be categorized as eligible counterparties or where the transaction at issue does not constitute eligible counterparty business. Undertakings which meet certain financial or other criteria may also be categorized as professional for this purpose;[85] and

(c) a *retail client* is any client who is neither an eligible counterparty nor a professional client. It may be noted that the expression 'retail customer' is thus not limited to 'consumers' as that term is normally understood,[86] but would include many companies or other bodies which do not meet the sophistication or size for higher categories of client classification. It would also be necessary for private banks and similar institutions to treat their wealthy individual customers as 'retail clients' in most cases, notwithstanding their financial status and experience.[87]

Since the present chapter is intended to focus on retail clients, it is now necessary to review the level of protection afforded to them by MiFID and the FSA Handbook provisions which implement that Directive.[88]   **3.37**

Information Requirements

MiFID requires a firm providing investment services to convey to the client written information about its services and the cost of using them.[89] This requirement finds voice in the COBS chapter of the FSA Handbook. In particular: **3.38**

(a) the total price payable by the client in respect of the relevant service must be disclosed, including all fees, charges, commissions and expenses.[90] In accordance with a recognizable theme, this disclosure must be made in good time before the service is

---

[83] For the details of these matters, see FSA Handbook, COBS 3.6.

[84] See FSA Handbook, COBS 3.6.1R and the definition of 'eligible counterparty business' in the Glossary.

[85] Briefly, an undertaking must meet two of the following tests: (i) it must have a balance sheet of €20 million; (ii) it must have a turnover of €40 million; or (iii) it must possess own funds of €2 million: see MiFID, Annex II and COBS 3.2.5R. Companies which meet lower criteria may also be classified as elective professional clients if they have proven experience in executing transactions in the market concerned: MiFID, Annex II and COBS 3.5.3R.

[86] ie a private individual acting outside the course of his trade or business.

[87] Since many of such clients will often be resident in countries in the Middle East or Far East, it may be appropriate to mention at this juncture that the client classification rules apply to clients of any bank or investment firm which carries on business in the United Kingdom, regardless of the residence or location of the client himself.

[88] For a more detailed and helpful review of this subject, see Blair, Walker and Purves, paras 13.65–13.96. It should be emphasized that some (but not all) of the provisions about to be discussed may be equally applicable to professional clients. However, it is not proposed to undertake a comparative examination.

[89] MiFID, Art 19(3).

[90] FSA Handbook, COBS 6.1.9R.

commenced, so that the client has an adequate opportunity to consider the merits of the proposed arrangements;[91]

(b) the bank must also make full disclosure of the extent to which it is able to give investment advice—for example, whether it will review the whole of the relevant market in order to make recommendations to the client, or whether its advice is limited to one or more selected product providers.[92] The bank cannot proffer its advice as 'independent' if, as is often the case, it will limit its advice to selected product providers which may be associated with the bank itself;[93] and

(c) more broadly, firms are required to prepare and provide information about financial products sold to retail clients.[94] In essence, the bank must provide a description of the nature of the investment and its risks, bearing in mind the status of the client and his retail categorization. This must, where applicable, involve a description of any obligation to provide margin. The dangers of market volatility and the risks involved in leverage (ie borrowing money to fund or maintain the product).[95]

Client Agreements

3.39 The bank must provide a retail client with a written agreement setting out the respective rights and obligations of each of the parties.[96]

3.40 Once again, this must be done in good time before the service begins, except where the arrangements are concluded at the request of the client via a means of distance communication. In that event, the document must be provided immediately after the service starts.[97]

Client Money

3.41 A firm providing investment services is required to make adequate arrangements for the protection of client assets and money, where it is responsible for them.[98]

3.42 This requirement is amplified by the Client Assets Rules, which form a part of the FSA Handbook. These rules will often require the segregation of client money into a separate bank account which ensures that the relevant funds are insulated or 'ring-fenced' in the event of the investment firm.[99] However, since credit institutions are authorized to accept deposits in any event, the requirement for the segregation of client money does not

---

[91] FSA Handbook, COBS 6.1.11R. The rule does not apply where a form of distance communication (such as the internet or telephone) is used at the request of the customer to conclude the contract, in which event the information must be provided immediately after the service begins. More specific remuneration disclosure requirements apply to certain types of 'packaged products': see COBS 5 and 6.

[92] FSA Handbook, COBS 6.2.

[93] FSA Handbook, COBS 6.2.15R.

[94] See generally, FSA Handbook, COBS 13 and 14.

[95] See FSA Handbook, COBS 14.3.2R and Art 31(1) of the implementing Directive noted in para 3.32 above.

[96] FSA Handbook, COBS 8.1.2R.

[97] FSA Handbook, COBS 8.1.3R.

[98] FSA Handbook, PRIN 10.

[99] On segregation and related issues, see FSA Handbook, CASS 7.4.

generally apply where the firm providing the investment services is also an authorized deposit-taker.[100]

Suitability

A 'suitability' requirement applies where the bank is providing either investment advice or discretionary portfolio management services to a retail client.[101] In essence, when providing these services, a bank is required to inform itself about (i) the financial knowledge and experience of the customer in the particular investment sphere, (ii) his financial position, and (iii) his investment objectives. This information is designed to assist the bank in ensuring that its services are properly 'tailored' to meet the client's needs.[102] **3.43**

The suitability requirement is transposed into UK law by the more detailed provisions of the FSA Handbook.[103] Briefly, the bank must obtain from the retail client such information as is necessary to enable it to meet his investment objectives, to ensure that he understands the risks involved with the proposed investment and that he is financially able to bear those risks. The reference to 'investment objectives' includes the purpose of the investment (eg to provide an income or to seek capital growth), the period for which the client wishes to invest and his appetite for risk. Information about the financial situation of the client naturally includes details of the sources and amount of his regular income, his property and assets, and his financial commitments and liabilities.[104] A bank or other investment firm is not permitted to give advice or to administer a portfolio unless the retail client has provided the information necessary to make the suitability assessment.[105] **3.44**

It may be noted that the standards provided by the 'suitability' test may assist in determining whether an investment adviser is liable in negligence for losses suffered by a client after relying on his advice. If the adviser has adhered to and applied the suitability assessment, then that may be evidence that he has not been guilty of any breach of duty. On the other hand if, in the course of the suitability assessment, the client makes it clear that the protection of his family in the event of his death is his key priority, this may be evidence of a breach of duty if the agreed investment package does not include an appropriate level of life insurance.[106] **3.45**

Appropriateness

A bank is required to apply an 'appropriateness' test for non-advised investment services. **3.46**

Where a bank is asked by a retail client to execute a transaction on a non-advised basis, the suitability requirements discussed above will not apply. But the bank is nevertheless

---

[100] Although it should be noted that this is not a compete exemption from all of the client asset provisions. For the details, see FSA Handbook, CASS 7.1.8R and 7.1.9G.

[101] See generally, FSA Handbook, COBS 9.

[102] On this overarching requirement, see MiFID, Art 19(4).

[103] See FSA Handbook, COBS 9.

[104] FSA Handbook, COBS 9.2.2R and 9.2.3R.

[105] FSA Handbook, COBS 9.2.6R.

[106] See, for example, the situation which arose in *Gorham v British Telecommunications plc* [2000] 1 WLR 2129 (CA). See also the discussion of 'mis-selling' claims in *Lloyds TSB General Insurance Holdings Ltd v Lloyds Group Insurance Co Ltd* [2003] UKHL 48.

required to ask the client about his knowledge or experience of the relevant investment in order to assess whether it is appropriate for him.[107] This is, in a sense, a more negative or reactive obligation on the part of the service provider—effectively designed as a 'gate-keeper' to try to ensure that the retail client does not enter into investment transactions which are not in his best interests. Nevertheless, this places an onus on the service provider even in situations in which its advice is not sought.[108]

Conflicts of Interest

3.47 MiFID introduced new requirements on the manner in which banks and other firms manage conflicts of interest which may arise in the course of providing investment services to their clients.[109]

3.48 In brief, a bank is required to take all reasonable steps to identify conflicts of interest:

(a) between the bank itself and its affiliates, and the client; and
(b) between clients themselves,

that arise or may arise in the course of providing investment services and which may adversely affect the interests of their clients.[110] Conflicts of interest may arise in a number of situations, for example, (i) where the bank may make a profit (or avoid a loss) at the expense of a client, (ii) where the bank has an interest in the outcome of a transaction which differs from that of the client, or (iii) where the bank receives an inducement from a person other than the client in providing the service concerned.[111]

3.49 Banks are required to maintain and operate effective organizational and administrative arrangements with a view to preventing conflicts of interest from giving rise to a material risk of damage to client interests.[112] This rule is reinforced by an obligation to establish, maintain and implement a written conflicts of interest policy.[113] MiFID and the implementing rules are relatively prescriptive in terms of the content and operation of the required conflicts policy. For example, the policy must identify the circumstances which may give rise to a conflict of interest in relation to the specific types of services and activities provided or undertaken by the firm.[114] The policy must also specify procedures to be followed in order to prevent or manage conflicts and to ensure that a client's interests are managed separately from those of the bank itself. These procedures may include (i) information barriers (or 'Chinese walls') designed to prevent the sharing of information among individuals working in different parts of the business, and their supervisors, (ii) the elimination of any direct

---

[107] MiFID, Art 19(5) and FSA Handbook, COBS 10.

[108] On this subject, see the discussion of this rule and of 'execution only' transactions in Blair, Walker and Purves, paras 13.85–13. 90.

[109] Recital (25) of the implementing Directive and FSA Handbook, SYSC 10.1.3R.

[110] MiFID Art 18(1) and FSA Handbook, SYSC 10.1.3R and 10.1.4R. It may be noted in passing that this duty is owed equally to professional clients and to eligible counterparties: Recital (25) to the implementing directive and FSA Handbook, SYSC 10.1.2.

[111] For further details, see FSA Handbook, SYSC 10.1.4R.

[112] MiFID, Art 13(3); FSA Handbook, SYSC 10.1.7R.

[113] MiFID, Art 22(1); FSA Handbook, SYSC 10.1.10R. The policy must take into account potential conflicts involving other members of the service provider's group.

[114] In other words, a policy expressed in broad generalities will not suffice.

link between the remuneration of individuals in one department with profits earned in another, where there may be conflicts between the business of the two departments, and (iii) measures to prevent the involvement of individuals in separate services or activities where a conflict may arise as between the two business areas.[115]

Best Execution

MiFID requires firms to take all reasonable steps to obtain the best possible result when executing client orders (unless the client has given specific instructions as to the mode and place of execution).[116]   **3.50**

The 'best possible result' (or 'best execution') requirement is not limited wholly to an obligation to obtain the best price, although that is obviously a relevant factor. The bank may also take into account the costs involved, any particular requirement for speed of execution and the nature and size of the order.[117] Banks and investment firms thus have a certain degree of latitude in determining where the client's interests lie, according to the nature of the financial instrument concerned and the available markets.   **3.51**

In line with the philosophy for the management of conflicts of interest, firms are required to maintain an execution policy setting out the different venues in which the firm executes client orders in relation to particular types of instrument and the factors which will affect the choice in given cases. The firm must obtain the client's specific approval of the its best execution policy and must be able to demonstrate that individual orders have been executed in compliance with its terms.[118]   **3.52**

---

[115] FSA Handbook, SYSC 10.1.11R. Banks are also required to make a formal record of conflicts of interest which have arisen: Art 23 of the implementing Directive and FSA Handbook, SYSC 10.1.6R.
[116] MiFID, Art 21(1); FSA Handbook, COBS 11.2.
[117] Article 44(1) of the implementing directive; FSA Handbook, COBS 11.2.6R.
[118] MiFID, Art 21; FSA Handbook, COBS 11.2.14R and 11.2.29R.

4

THE REGULATION OF LENDING BUSINESS

Introduction

As noted earlier, at least in terms of general perception, the acceptance of deposits is one **4.01** side of the banking coin; lending is the other side. Yet, whilst deposit-taking business has been shown to be quite closely regulated, the opposite is true of lending business. Apart from very specific cases in which the bargaining position of the borrower is seen to be particularly weak, the making of loans and the terms on which they are to be made available is essentially unregulated in the UK.

Consumer Credit

Introduction

The provision of credit to individual borrowers is regulated by the Consumer Credit Act **4.02** 1974 (as amended).[1] It should be appreciated that the scheme is generally limited to loans to natural persons and that the scope of regulation does not apply to corporate loans.[2]

---

[1] It should be appreciated that the whole subject of consumer credit is a highly detailed and technical field. The present discussion is only intended to provide an overview of this complex topic and, in particular, is limited to those areas likely to be of interest to banks (as opposed to others who may be involved in various aspects of the consumer credit business). Detailed consideration of the finer points will be found in the well-known texts, including Goode, *Consumer Credit Law and Practice* (LexisNexis, looseleaf) and Guest and Lloyds, *Encyclopaedia of Consumer Credit Law* (Thomson Reuters, looseleaf).

[2] For a hybrid case, see n 12 below.

The 1974 Act was designed to implement a number of the proposals made by the Crowther Committee on Consumer Credit.[3] The Act replaced something of a patchwork quilt of legislation, including the Pawnbrokers Act 1872 and the Moneylenders Acts 1920 and 1927. The 1974 Act also replaced the Hire Purchase Act 1975, which was itself introduced to deal with the increasing practice of buying cars, household goods, and other items on deferred payment instalments. As noted below, the 1974 Act was amended and updated in various respects by the Consumer Credit Act 2006.[4]

4.03 The 1974 Act was accordingly designed to secure a measure of protection for users of consumer credit who were clearly at a disadvantage in dealing with lenders or other suppliers of credit. In line with the objective of protecting consumers (but not those who were perceived to enjoy greater personal bargaining power), the 1974 Act originally applied only to credit agreements of up to £5,000. Inflationary factors led to the periodic increase of this amount, ultimately to £25,000.[5] The changes introduced by the Consumer Credit Act 2006 have, amongst other things, abolished the concept of a monetary limit. In its place, a new exemption for high net worth individuals has now been introduced.[6]

4.04 In essence, an entity which proposes to carry on a business[7] of providing consumer credit or consumer hire facilities, or certain other, ancillary activities may only do so if it is licensed for that purpose by the Office of Fair Trading (OFT).[8] It thus becomes necessary to examine the types of business which fall within the scope of the 1974 Act.[9]

Regulated Agreements

4.05 The 1974 Act is built around the concept of a 'regulated agreement', in the sense that (i) a provider of credit under a regulated agreement must be appropriately licensed and (ii) there are detailed requirements as to the form and content of a regulated agreement. The pattern of control exercised by the 1974 Act is thus principally exercised through this medium.

---

[3] Cmnd 4596.

[4] The 2006 Act gave effect to an EC Directive on Consumer Credit: Council Directive (EC) No 87/102/EEC of 22 December 1986 for the approximation of the laws, regulations and administrative provisions of the Member States concerning Consumer Credit, OJ L 042, 12.02.1987, p 48, as amended by Council Directive 90/88/EEC of 22 February 1990, OJ L 061, 10.03.1990, p 14 and Council Directive 98/7/EC of 16 February 1998, OJ L 101, 01.04.1998, p 17.

[5] Consumer Credit (Increase of Monetary Limits) (Amendment) Order 1998 (SI 1998/996).

[6] See the discussion at para 4.12 below. The £25,000 limit will, of course, continue to apply to agreements entered into before the 2006 Act was brought into force, and remains applicable to certain business loans (see para 4.11 below).

[7] On the expression 'carrying on a business', see the corresponding discussion in the context of deposit-taking business at para 1.15 above. In the context of the 1974 Act itself, see *Wills v Wood* [1984] CCLR 7. A single or 'one-off' loan will not fall within the scope of the 1974 Act: *Hare v Schurek* [1993] CCLR 47 (CA).

[8] The licensing requirements are discussed in more depth at paras 4.15–4.42 below. The OFT is broadly responsible for (i) the operation of the licensing system, (ii) the supervision and enforcement of the 1974 Act, (iii) the continuing review of developments in the market for consumer credit, and (iv) the publication of information about the 1974 Act: see ss 1 and 4 of the 1974 Act.

[9] It should be noted that the present section considers the subject of consumer credit in an essentially domestic context. Certain issues which may arise where the contract has cross-border aspects are considered in Chapter 41 below.

In principle, an agreement is regulated by the 1974 Act if: **4.06**

(a) the agreement[10] involves the provision of credit;[11]
(b) the debtor is an individual;[12] and
(c) the agreement is not an exempt agreement.[13]

Types of Consumer Credit Agreement

The 1974 Act classifies different types of regulated credit agreement since differences of **4.07** detail apply to the different categories of transaction. Specifically:

(a) 'running account credit' involves an arrangement under which the borrower can draw cash, goods and services up to an overall limit, taking account of amounts paid into the account by the borrower from time to time.[14] Obvious examples of this type of arrangement include a bank overdraft[15] and a credit card;

---

[10] Given the focus of the present work, the emphasis is inevitably on the provision of credit. Other forms of activity relating to consumer credit may also involve the licensing requirement, and these are noted briefly at para 4.18 below.

[11] The expression 'credit' involves any form of financial accommodation—see s 9 of the 1974 Act. This will obviously include loans, overdraft, credit card and similar facilities. Although the definition is broad, the expression 'credit' necessarily connotes an arrangement under which the amount advanced will definitely be repayable. For a case in which this condition was not met, see *Nejad v City Index Ltd* [2001] GCCR 2461 (CA), and see also *McMillan Williams v Range* [2004] GCCR 5041. The cases are noted by Paget, para 2.8. 'Credit' may also be extended if the creditor allows the debtor time to pay pending the outcome of litigation, even though the relevant amounts would otherwise be immediately payable. This is the effect of the House of Lords decision in *Dimond v Lovell* [2002] 1 AC 384. The provision of credit must be made by *agreement* and, consequently, a unilateral delay in payment by the debtor without the consent of the creditor does not engage the terms of the 1974 Act. For a recent judicial consideration of the meaning of the expression 'credit' in this context, see *Maple Leaf Macro Volatility Master Fund v Rouvroy* [2009] All ER (D) 247, aff'd without reference to this point, [2009] All ER(D) 199 (Nov). Of course, in a banking context, this particular point is unlikely to be controversial, since the main purpose of the institution's business is the provision of credit. Nevertheless, there may be the occasional, marginal case. For example, if an institution enters into a sale and leaseback arrangement, this may have the effect of providing a capital sum to the customer but this is achieved by means of providing an asset to the customer in return for a rental stream. Such an arrangement does not involve the provision of 'credit' and the arrangements are therefore outside the scope of the 1974 Act: see *Lavin v Johnson* [2002] EWCA Civ 1138, applying the decision of the Court of Appeal in *Welsh Development Agency v Export Finance Co Ltd* [1992] BCLC 148. This reflects the general reluctance of the English courts to re-characterize transactions because they recognize that parties have a choice as to the structure of their transaction and this should generally be respected: see the observations made in *Wire TV Ltd v Cable Tel Ltd* [1988] CLC 244, at p 258. For a similar discussion in the context of security arrangements, see paras 27.04–27.07 below.

[12] An individual is a natural person. However, the Act extends to partnerships and other unincorporated bodies which include at least one individual as a member—see s 189, read together with s 185(5) of the 1985 Act. Consequently, despite its title, the Consumer Credit Act may extend to facilities provided for business purposes. However, the financial limit of £25,000 will limit the number of such cases to which the Act will, in practice apply.

[13] On exempt agreements, see paras 4.09–4.12 below. It should be noted that the definition involves an 'agreement' for the provision of credit. As will be seen elsewhere (see the discussion of the decision in *Barclays Bank Ltd v W J Simms Son & Cook (Southern) Ltd* [1980] QB 677 at para 17.34 below), the drawing of a cheque on a current account may imply a request for, and an agreement to allow, an overdraft facility to the extent which may be necessary to meet that cheque, and such an arrangement may therefore amount to a 'regulated agreement'. However, where the amounts involved are relatively small and the cheque is simply processed by the bank's systems without human intervention, the drawing of the cheque is probably a breach of the current account agreement, rather than a fresh agreement to provide credit: see examples 17–21 given in Sch 2 to the 1974 Act.

[14] Section 10(1)(a) of the 1974 Act.

[15] The OFT has issued a determination under s 74(1)(b) of the 1974 Act which disapplies the cancellation and documentation rules in Pt V of the 1974 Act provided that the lender has notified the OFT that it

(b) 'fixed sum credit' is any form of credit other than a running account[16] and would include a term loan or a sale of goods on deferred terms;

(c) a 'restricted use credit agreement' is an agreement under which the credit is to be used to finance a purchase of goods or services from the creditor (eg a credit sale agreement), to finance a transaction with a third party (eg pursuant to a credit card agreement), or to refinance existing indebtedness of the borrower.[17] Any other type of consumer credit arrangement is an 'unrestricted use' agreement;

(d) a 'debtor-creditor-supplier' agreement[18] is a regulated agreement which is (i) a restricted use credit agreement to finance a transaction between the debtor and the creditor (eg a credit sale agreement) or (ii) a restricted use agreement to finance a transaction between the debtor and the supplier under pre-existing arrangements between the debtor and the supplier (eg under a credit card agreement);

(e) a 'debtor-creditor' agreement is a regulated agreement (i) to finance a transaction between a debtor and a supplier but which is not a debtor-creditor-supplier agreement (ie because there is no pre-existing arrangement between the supplier and the creditor)[19] or (ii) which is a restricted use credit agreement to refinance existing indebtedness of the borrower;

(f) a 'credit token' agreement is an arrangement under which the creditor or a third party at his request will provide cash, goods or services on credit. Again, credit cards are 'credit tokens' for these purposes.

4.08 It may be important to place a particular agreement in the correct category because different agreements may attract different types of statutory protection. For example, only certain types of agreement attract a cancellation right[20] and a creditor is only responsible for breaches of contract on the part of the supplier in the case of a debtor-creditor-supplier agreement where there are pre-existing arrangements between the creditor and the supplier.[21]

Exempt Agreements

4.09 Certain types of agreements which would otherwise be regulated under the above rules are specifically exempted from the scope of regulation under the 1974 Act. The consequences of these exemptions may vary according to the particular circumstances of the lender. For example, if its *sole* business consists in providing credit under exempt agreements, then it

---

engages in business of this type and prescribed information has been provided to the debtor. On the application of the determination, see *Coutts & Co v Sebestyen* [2005] EWCA Civ 473 (CA).

[16] Section 10(1)(b) of the 1974 Act.

[17] Section 11 of the 1974 Act. An agreement is only a 'restricted use' credit agreement under the 'refinancing' heading if the contract explicitly so states: see *National Westminster Bank plc v Storey & Pallister* [2002] GCCR 2381, noted by Paget at para 2.11.

[18] See s 12 of the 1974 Act.

[19] Section 13(a) of the 1974 Act. A loan made by the customer's own bank to assist in the purchase of a vehicle would fall into this category.

[20] See the discussion at para 4.27 below. It should be noted that this position may change as a result of the Consumer Credit Directive: see paras 4.40–4.42 below.

[21] See the discussion of s 75 of the 1974 Act and the *Lloyds Bank* case at paras 4.30–4.36 below. For a case in which some of the characterizations were considered, see *Goshawk Dedicated (No 2) Ltd v Governor and Company of Bank of Scotland* [2005] EWHC 2906 Ch.

will be outside the scope of regulation altogether. It will thus not require an OFT licence at all, and will not be required to ensure that its agreements meet the statutory requirements as to content and formality.[22]

The main exemption relates to mortgages for the purchase of real estate and/or the con- **4.10** struction of buildings. These transactions are exempt if the lender is carrying on a deposit-taking business for FSMA purposes.[23] This will usually be the case if the borrower (or a close relative) intends to occupy at least 40 per cent of the property as a dwelling.[24] Certain other loans made by banks in relation to property (eg to refinance a prior mortgage or to fund home improvements) are likewise exempt.[25] Subject to these specific exemptions, however, a credit facility provided to an individual will generally amount to a regulated consumer credit agreement even though the repayment obligations may be secured by a mortgage over his principal residence. A similar exemption is extended to investment or 'buy-to-let' property where less than 40 per cent of the land is to be occupied by the borrower or a close relative as his own dwelling.[26]

The second exemption involves loans made to individuals for business purposes. Under **4.11** section 16B of the 1974 Act,[27] a loan exceeding £25,000 made to an individual for business purposes is not a regulated agreement. The difficulty for the bank, of course, is to satisfy itself as to the intended *purpose* of the loan, since this is clearly a matter of the borrower's intention. Section 16B helpfully states that an agreement is presumed to satisfy the 'business' test if the agreement contains a declaration to that effect.[28] In practice, however, this presumption is unlikely to be of great assistance to banks because it falls away if the bank '… knows, or has reasonable cause to suspect, that the agreement is not entered into by the debtor … wholly or predominantly for the purpose of a business carried on, or intended to be carried on, by him …'.[29] Consequently, the bank should carry out a degree of due diligence before seeking to rely on this exemption.

Finally, section 16A of the 1974 Act[30] provides a new exemption for 'high net worth debt- **4.12** ors'. In a very general way, this exemption compensates for the abolition of the £25,000 monetary limit, since facilities for sophisticated customers can still be taken outside the scope of regulation. The exemption is valuable because—unlike those discussed above in relation to business and real estate—the 'high net worth' exemption can be used *regardless of the underlying purposes of the credit*. Nevertheless, the use of the exemption necessarily

---

[22] On these requirements, see paras 4.25–4.29 below.
[23] The exemption also extends to a number of other categories of lenders but the present text is, of course, concerned only with banks. For the details of the exemptions, see s 16 of the 1974 Act.
[24] On mortgage lending as a regulated activity, see paras 4.43–4.54 below.
[25] See the Consumer Credit (Exempt Agreements) Order 1989 (SI 1989/869).
[26] See s 16C of the 1974 Act, as inserted by the Legislative Reform (Consumer Credit) Order 2008 (SI 2008/2826).
[27] As inserted by the 2006 Act.
[28] See s 16B(2) of the 1974 Act. Whether or not a particular activity amounts to a 'business' is, of course, largely a question of fact. However, s 189 of the 1974 Act states that a business includes a trade or profession, but does not include an occasional transaction. Consequently, it seems that the business must have some durability and substance if this exemption is to apply.
[29] See s 16B(3) of the 1974 Act.
[30] As inserted by the 2006 Act. On forthcoming amendments to this provision as a result of the Consumer Credit Directive, see paras 4.40–4.42 below.

implies some investigation into the borrower's financial position and a certain level of documentary compliance is still required. The formalities include the following:[31]

(a) A statement of net worth must be provided[32] to confirm that, during the year to the most recent 31 March, the debtor had either (i) net annual income of at least £150,000 (after allowing for tax and deductions) or (ii) net assets of £500,000 (excluding value/liabilities associated with his primary residence and any life policies or pension plans).

(b) The borrower must sign a statutorily prescribed form of declaration[33] to the effect that (i) he has seen the high net worth statement, (ii) he understands that he is relinquishing the protections which would otherwise be afforded to him under the 1974 Act, (iii) he understands that the court retains its power to adjust the agreement if it is unfair to the debtor,[34] and (iv) he is aware that he should take legal advice if necessary.

The Effect of Regulation

4.13 If a bank or other lender intends to carry on consumer credit business, then the following matters will require consideration:

(a) as already noted, a licensing requirement will apply;

(b) the content of business advertisements will be subject to control;

(c) the terms of consumer credit agreements and the formalities associated with them are likewise subject to detailed regulation;

(d) the 1974 Act regulates certain conduct and liabilities arising during the currency of the contract;

(e) the court has certain powers of intervention; and

(f) it is necessary to note certain recent reforms to consumer credit law as a result of the EC Directive on Consumer Credit.

4.14 Each of these issues will be considered in turn. It should be repeated that the discussion is not intended to provide a detailed overview of the law of consumer credit; it is merely intended to highlight those areas which may be of concern to banks as *providers* of credit.

The Licensing Requirement

4.15 A person who provides credit by means of regulated consumer credit agreements or is otherwise a creditor under such agreements in the course of a business requires a licence from the OFT for that purpose.[35]

---

[31] On these requirements, see regs 2–5 of the Consumer Credit (Exempt Agreements) Order 2007 (SI 2007/1168).

[32] The high net worth statement can be signed by the borrower's accountant or by an institution which holds a deposit-taking permission from the FSA. It seems that this can include the lending bank itself, although it would obviously be in a slight position of conflict and would have to undertake appropriate due diligence before signing such a statement.

[33] The required declaration can be included in the facility agreement itself, in which case no separate declaration document would be required. In view of its purpose, however, the declaration should perhaps be included prominently and, perhaps, in bold type, so that it is not lost among the other provisions of the agreement.

[34] On this power, see paras 4.38–4.39 below.

[35] Section 23 of the 1974 Act. As discussed elsewhere, whether or not a person is carrying on a particular activity as a business is sometimes a difficult question. See para 1.15 above.

In essence, a person who lends money in the course of a business will require a licence under **4.16** the 1974 Act for that purpose unless his lending business comprises *exclusively* of credit facilities which are provided:

(a) to corporate borrowers or similar entities;
(b) to individuals who are high net worth individuals and the use of that exemption is appropriately documented;
(c) for the purchase or improvement of land within the scope of the exemptions discussed above; or
(d) to individuals for business purposes and in excess of £25,000.

It may be noted that EEA institutions which are 'passported' into the United Kingdom[36] **4.17** do not require a licence under the Consumer Credit Act since questions of authorization are a matter for the home State regulator, rather than the FSA.[37] An application from an EEA authorized firm for a consumer credit licence must therefore be refused.[38] However, this does not exempt such institutions from the need to comply with the documentary and other formalities discussed below.

It should be noted in passing that the licensing regime created by the Consumer Credit **4.18** Act 1974 is not limited to *the provision of credit*. Indeed, the categories of available licence now include:[39]

(a) consumer credit;
(b) consumer hire;
(c) credit brokerage;
(d) debt adjusting/debt counselling;
(e) debt collection;
(f) credit reference agencies;
(g) debt administration; and
(h) credit information services.

It will, however, be apparent that banks will be most concerned with the first category of **4.19** licence, namely, consumer credit, and the present chapter is accordingly confined to that category.

As noted earlier, the licensing system is operated by the OFT under Part III of the 1974 **4.20** Act.[40] The criteria for the grant of such a licence as set out in Part III have in some respects been refined by the 2006 Act. In particular:

(a) licences will be issued to cover the various categories of activities outlined above;

---

[36] On the passporting process, see paras 2.13–2.17 above.
[37] On this point, see FSMA, Sch 3, para 15.
[38] See s 27A of the 1974 Act.
[39] For the most recent additions, see s 24A(1) of the 1974 Act.
[40] See ss 21–42 of the 1974 Act. The basic requirement for a licence to carry on consumer credit business is contained in s 21(1).

(b) the applicant[41] must demonstrate to the OFT that he is a fit person to hold the requested licence.[42] This may include an assessment of (i) the applicant's track record in the sphere of consumer credit and the business practices and procedures which the applicant will adopt[43] and (ii) the proposed employees of the business and any offences of a financial character committed by them;[44] and

(c) the business name to be licensed must not be misleading or undesirable.[45]

4.21   The OFT may grant licences unconditionally or subject to terms, and may also vary, suspend or revoke such licences,[46] or impose requirements as to the conduct of business.[47] Appeals against OFT licensing decisions lie to the Consumer Credit Appeals Tribunal.[48] Determinations by the OFT are now subject to appeal to the Consumer Credit Appeal Tribunal.[49] An appeal to the Tribunal operates as a rehearing of the matter under appeal, and the Tribunal may either confirm, quash or vary the original decision or remit it to the OFT for reconsideration.[50]

4.22   A person who enters into a regulated consumer credit agreement as lender in the course of a business and without the appropriate licence commits an offence[51] and the relevant credit agreements will be unenforceable,[52] unless the OFT grants an order that the agreements should be treated as if he were licensed at the relevant time.[53] Obviously, considerations of this kind should not apply to authorized credit institutions in practice.

Advertising

4.23   Part IV of the 1974 Act regulates advertising[54] and solicitations for the purposes of a consumer credit business. Regulation of advertising[55] is largely achieved by means of the

---

[41] The application must, of course, be full and complete. It is an offence to provide false or misleading information in connection with an application or for the purposes of any other provisions of the 1974 Act: see s 7 of the 1974 Act (as inserted by s 51 of the 2006 Act).

[42] See s 25 of the 1974 Act. Note that the OFT is *obliged* to issue a licence if an application is made, the 'fitness' test is met and the business name is unobjectionable. There is no residual discretion or other ground on which a licence may be refused or withheld. As noted below, however, a licence may be granted subject to conditions.

[43] Section 25(1C)(2) of the 1974 Act.

[44] Section 25(1AD) of the 1974 Act.

[45] Section 21(1AD) of the 1974 Act. The name of a finance company may be objectionable if it suggests that it is a member of the supplier's group of companies, when this is not in fact the case: see *Lease Management Services Ltd v Purnell Secretarial Services Ltd* [1994] CCLR 127.

[46] See ss 27–31 of the 1974 Act. A licence may be revoked if the holder ceases to be a fit and proper person for these purposes: see s 32 of the 1974 Act.

[47] Section 33A of the 1974 Act.

[48] Section 56 of the 2006 Act.

[49] See s 40A and Sch A1 to the 1974 Act, as inserted by the 2006 Act.

[50] Schedule A1, para 12 of the 1974 Act. Appeals from the Tribunal may be made (with leave) to the Court of Appeal, but on questions of law only: see s 41A of the 1974 Act.

[51] Section 39 of the 1974 Act.

[52] See s 40(1) of the 2006 Act.

[53] On the power to make this type of order and the criteria to be applied, see s 40(2) of the 1974 Act.

[54] 'Advertisements' includes television, films, the display of notices, the distribution of leaflets or other materials: see s 189 of the 1974 Act. A 'general' advertisement simply giving the name of the advertiser without describing the nature of the business which the company is prepared to undertake may not be an 'advertisement' for the purposes of the 1974 Act: see *Jenkins v Lombard North Central plc* [1984] 1 WLR 407.

[55] The advertising regime does not apply to advertisements which make it clear that the stated facilities are available only to companies or the arrangements otherwise relate to exempt agreements: see s 43(2) and (3) of the 1974 Act.

Consumer Credit (Advertisements) Regulations 2004[56] which contain the type of requirements which are familiar in this context:

(a) A credit advertisement must use plain and intelligible language, be legible (or audible) and must provide the name of the advertiser.[57]

(b) The advertisement must give details of any required security and, where that includes a charge over the debtor's home, must include a clear statement that the home may be repossessed in the event of a default, and other warnings about the need to think carefully before debts are secured in this way.[58]

(c) There are restrictions about references to annual rates of interest and the manner in which these are to be calculated and presented.[59]

(d) The use of certain expressions (such as 'interest free' and 'no deposit') are prohibited unless these reflect the genuine features of the product.[60]

(e) The advertisement must include a variety of further details, including payment instalments, charges and the total amount payable by the debtor.[61]

It may also be noted that it is an offence to canvass for debtor-creditor business off trade premises[62] or to send a circular to a person under the age of 18 inviting him to borrow money or to obtain credit.[63]   **4.24**

Contents of Agreements and Formalities

The 1974 Act deals with the formalities and other matters which must be observed in connection with a regulated consumer credit agreement.   **4.25**

These formalities are of crucial importance because a term of agreement which is inconsistent with a requirement of the 1974 Act will be void.[64] Likewise a failure to meet certain requirements[65] will mean that the contract is 'improperly executed' with the result that the contract is only enforceable with a court order to that effect.[66]   **4.26**

---

[56] SI 2004/1484. On amendments to these requirements as a result of the Consumer Credit Directive, see para 4.42 below.

[57] Regulation 3 of the 2004 Regulations.

[58] Regulation 7 of the 2004 Regulations.

[59] Regulation 8 of the 2004 Regulations.

[60] Regulation 9 of the 2004 Regulations.

[61] See Sch 2 to the 2004 Regulations.

[62] Section 49 of the 1974 Act.

[63] Section 50 of the 1974 Act, on which see *Alliance and Leicester Building Society v Babbs* [1999] GCCR 1657, noted by Paget at para 2.37.

[64] Section 173 of the 1974 Act. A provision is inconsistent with the 1974 Act if it seeks to impose additional duties on the debtor beyond those contemplated by the legislative framework: see s 173(2) of the 1974 Act.

[65] Under s 61 of the 1974 Act, an agreement is not properly executed unless it follows prescribed forms and contains all the terms of the agreement in legible form. The agreement will also not be properly executed if the creditor approaches the debtor at any time during a cancellation period (ie with a view to influencing the debtor's decision in that respect): see s 61(2)(c) of the 1974 Act. It may be noted that similar rules apply to any security given in respect of a regulated agreement, in the sense that prescribed information must be given to the chargor and, failing that, the security will only be enforceable with the aid of a court order: see ss 105 and 106 of the 1974 Act. 'Security' has a broad meaning for these purposes and includes a guarantee given by a third party. In such a case, the guarantor is entitled to a copy of the credit documentation and to receive details of the amounts owing from time to time: see ss 107–111 of the 1974 Act.

[66] On these consequences of an 'improperly executed' agreement, see s 65 of the 1974 Act.

4.27   In a broader sense, a variety of requirements are applied to a regulated consumer credit agreement. For example:

(a)   The Consumer Credit (Disclosure of Information) Regulations 2004[67] require the disclosure of certain pre-contract information, and a failure to comply with those regulations will mean that the agreement is 'improperly executed'. In essence, the lender must provide, in a clear and separate document headed 'Pre-contract information'[68] details of certain statutory protections and remedies available to the debtor.[69]

(b)   An agreement must state the total charge for credit, and the omission of any relevant items will render the contract unenforceable.[70]

(c)   A regulated agreement will generally be cancellable by the debtor.[71]

(d)   A copy of the agreement must be provided to the debtor[72] and a 'cooling off' period applies thereafter during which the debtor has the right to cancel the agreement.[73] Where credit has been extended or funds advanced before the debtor exercises his cancellation option, then the agreement remains effective for the repayment of principal and interest. However, no interest is payable if the debtor repays the principal within 30 days.[74]

4.28   In terms of the contents of the regulated agreement itself, the document will not be properly executed—and, hence, will be unenforceable except with the consent of the court—unless it complies with a series of detailed requirements, including:

(a)   Where the agreement is cancellable, it must contain information about the debtor's right of cancellation and various other matters. The precise nature of the required information varies according to the type of agreement involved[75] but, in relation to facilities provided by banks, this will include matters such as the amount and duration of the credit, timing and amounts of repayment, the applicable interest rate, the total amount payable by the debtor in respect of the credit default charges, and other matters.[76]

---

[67]   SI 2004/1481.

[68]   Regulation 4 of the 2004 Regulations.

[69]   Regulation 3 of the 2004 Regulations, read together with the Consumer Credit (Agreements) Regulations 1983 (SI 1983/1553), as amended.

[70]   See reg 4 of the Consumer Credit (Total Charge for Credit) Regulations 1980 (SI 1980/51) and *London North Securities Ltd v Meadows* [2005] EWCA Civ 956. An agreement will not generally be treated as properly executed (and hence will be unenforceable) if it misstates the amount of the credit: see *Wilson v First County Trust Ltd* [2001] QB 407 (CA).

[71]   There are important exceptions to this rule, eg where the agreement is signed on the bank's business premises, or where the contractual negotiations did not include oral representations made by or on behalf of the creditor. Under s 189 of the 1974 Act 'representation' includes any warranty, statement or undertaking. However, it appears that the statement must be one of fact or opinion which is capable of inducing the debtor to enter into the contract: *Moorgate Services Ltd v Kabir* [1995] CCLR (CA). Where the creditor is a deposit-taker, these rules may overlap with the cancellation rules in the Distance Marketing Directive and the BCOBS chapter of the FSA Handbook—see the discussion in paras 3.11–3.16 above.

[72]   For timing and other details, see s 63 of the 1974 Act.

[73]   On the calculation of the cooling off period, see s 68 of the 1974 Act.

[74]   For the details of these rules, see s 71 of the 1974 Act.

[75]   On the categorization of regulated consumer credit agreements see para 4.07 above.

[76]   See generally the tables of information set out in Sch 1 to the Consumer Credit (Agreements) Regulations 1983 (SI 1983/1553). If the agreement is cancelled, then any security given for the facility is likewise

(b) The agreement must set out all the express terms of the contract.[77]

(c) The document presented to the debtor for signature must be clearly legible.[78]

(d) Copies of the document must be made available to the debtor.[79]

It will thus be apparent that the consequences of non-compliance with the 1974 Act in this   **4.29**
area may be quite draconian for the creditor, in that he may forego the right to recover payment of any monies owing to him,[80] and may lose his security. However, it has been recognized that this reflects the policy of the 1974 Act and that these rules are not inconsistent
with the property rights which are guaranteed by the European Convention on Human
Rights.[81]

Matters arising during the Currency of the Contract

Part IV of the 1974 Act deals with various issues which may arise while a credit agreement   **4.30**
remains in force.

The section which has attracted most judicial (and market) attention in recent times is   **4.31**
section 75. Section 75(1) provides that:

> If the debtor under a debtor-creditor-supplier agreement falling within section 12(b) or
> 12(c) has, in relation to a transaction financed by the agreement, any claim against the sup-
> plier in respect of a misrepresentation or breach of contract, he shall have a like claim against
> the creditor, who, with the supplier, shall be jointly and severally liable to the debtor.

Sections 12(b) and 12(c) respectively refer to restricted and unrestricted use debtor-   **4.32**
creditor-supplier agreements where there are pre-existing arrangements between the creditor and the supplier. The rationale for this provision—as put forward in the Crowther
Report[82]—was that a lender who provided credit to enable third parties to acquire goods
from a particular supplier is connected with that supplier and should be equally liable for
a contravention of the main commercial contract.

The remainder of section 75 deals with various ancillary matters. For example, the creditor   **4.33**
is entitled to an indemnity from the supplier in respect of any amount for which the creditor is made liable under section 75(1),[83] and it is confirmed that the creditor can be liable
to the debtor under section 75(1) even though the debtor may have exceeded his credit

---

ineffective and must be released or returned: see s 106 of the 1974 Act and the decisions in *Wilson v Howard*
[2005] EWCA Civ 147 and *Wilson v Robertsons (London) Ltd* [2006] EWCA Civ 1088.

[77] Section 61(1)(b) of the 1974 Act recognizes the obvious point that the contract cannot set out any terms
which the court may later see fit to imply.

[78] Section 61(1)(c) of the 1974 Act.

[79] For the details of these requirements, see s 63 of the 1974 Act.

[80] Where an agreement is unenforceable by virtue of any the provisions of the 1974 Act, the court cannot
grant relief to the creditor by providing a remedy in restitution, since this would effectively circumvent the
policy of the legislation: *Wilson v First County Trust Ltd (No 2)* [2001] EWCA Civ 633.

[81] On this subject, see *Wilson v First County Trust Ltd* [2004] 1 AC 816 (HL). This decision was reviewed
in some depth in *McGuffick v Royal Bank of Scotland plc* [2009] EWHC 2386 (Comm).

[82] See paras 6.6.20–6.6.30 of the Report.

[83] See s 75(2) of the 1974 Act.

limit or is otherwise in breach of his agreement with the creditor.[84] But, for present purposes, the discussion may focus essentially on section 75(1) itself.

4.34   It is now established that a bank which issues a credit card has a sufficiently close relationship with suppliers who have contracted to accept cards within the scheme and, as a result, there are sufficient 'arrangements' between them to create a debtor-creditor-supplier agreement[85] within section 12(b) or (c) of the 1974 Act, so that the potential liability of the creditor under section 75(1) may in principle be engaged.[86] This will be so because both the bank and the supplier are participants in the 'umbrella' credit card scheme, even though they may be wholly unknown to each other. As a result, the issuing bank is potentially liable to its cardholder in respect of a claim which the cardholder has against the supplier under the commercial contract concerned. Given that the liability is 'joint and several' with that of the supplier, there is no requirement for the cardholder to proceed against the supplier before it asserts its claim against the issuing bank. All of this would be reasonably clear but the waters have in some respects been muddied by the introduction of a new section 75A in to the 1974 Act.[87] Under the terms of that section, the card issuer may be made liable for a claim against the supplier under a linked agreement where there has been a non- or partial delivery of the goods or services, or they do not conform to their contractual description. However, the new liability under section 75A is secondary, in the sense that the debtor can only assert this claim against the creditor '… if the debtor has pursued his remedies against the supplier, which may but does not have to include taking legal proceedings against the supplier, and has failed to obtain the satisfaction to which he is entitled …'. The relationship between these two sections is not entirely clear. Non-delivery of goods and delivery of non-conforming goods will fall within section 75A, but they will also presumably constitute a '… breach of contract …' for the purposes of section 75 itself. Given that section 75 involves primary recourse to the creditor without any need for the time and expense involved in pursuing the suppler, it may be assumed that consumers will prefer to bring their claim under section 75, as opposed to section 75A.

4.35   It was for some time uncertain whether the issuing bank could potentially be liable under section 75(1) in respect of transactions executed outside the United Kingdom—it was argued that the section was not 'extra-territorial' in that sense. Apart from the general presumption against the extra-territorial effect of legislation, section 75(1) refers to a claim for 'misrepresentation or breach of contract' suggesting a contract made in England or governed by English law. However, in *Office of Fair Trading v Lloyds TSB Bank plc*[88] the House of Lords held that the only territorial nexus required for the operation of section 75 was that the credit card agreement itself should be governed by the law of some part of the United Kingdom. The issuing bank could thus be liable under that section even though the

---

[84] Section 75(4) of the 1974 Act.

[85] See the *Lloyds* case, discussed below.

[86] It will be recalled from s 75(1) (reproduced above) that liability under that section can only arise in relation to a debtor-creditor-supplier agreement which falls within the scope of s 12(b) or (c).

[87] Section 75A will be inserted by reg 12 of the Consumer Credit (EC Directive) Regulations 2009. These Regulations are due to come into force on 11 June 2010 but they remain in draft at the time of writing. On the EC's Consumer Credit Directive itself, see the discussion at para 4.40 below.

[88] [2008] UKHL 48 (HL).

underlying supply contract was entered into abroad, expressed in a foreign currency and governed by foreign law. The difficulty is that the issuing bank's statutory right to an indemnity under section 75(2)[89] could not be effective against suppliers outside the United Kingdom.[90] However, a corresponding indemnity could presumably be included as an express contractual term in the overall credit card scheme agreements. Nevertheless, and even though the underlying contract will have been entered into abroad and will relate to foreign goods or services, the English court will always have jurisdiction to make an order against a UK issuing bank since the claim arises from the debtor-creditor-supplier agreement, and not from the purchase contract.[91]

It may be noted that the creditor may also incur liability for statements made by the supplier during 'antecedent negotiations' with the debtor in the context of certain debtor-creditor-supplier agreements.[92]   **4.36**

Finally, it may be noted that various formalities may have to be met before the creditor can take steps to enforce its rights under a regulated agreement. For example, the creditor must give notice to the debtor in relation to any arrears which have arisen[93] and will generally be required to give seven days notice before demanding payment or enforcing a regulated agreement.[94] The lender is also required to provide a copy of the agreement to the debtor on request, together with details of sums paid and payable, and the agreement may not be enforced during any period of default by the lender in respect of its obligations under this provision.[95] A mortgage over land which has been given by way of security for a regulated agreement can only be enforced by means of a court order.[96]   **4.37**

Court's Powers of Intervention

The court has power to reopen the terms of a consumer credit agreement where the relationship between the parties is unfair to the debtor.[97] An agreement may be 'unfair' to the debtor on account of any one or more of the following factors: **4.38**

(a) any of the terms of the credit agreement itself or any related agreement;

---

[89] The bank's right to such an indemnity has been noted above.

[90] The point was noted by the House of Lords in the *Lloyds* case above.

[91] *Jarrett v Royal Bank of Scotland plc* [1999] QB 1 (CA).

[92] See s 56 of the 1974 Act and the cases discussed by Paget, para 2–70 and *Black Horse Ltd v Langford* [2007] EWHC 907. In practice, there may be a degree of overlap between s 56 and the wider liability created by s 75 of the 1974 Act.

[93] Sections 86B and 86C of the 1974 Act.

[94] For the rules on default notices of this kind and the circumstances under which they are required, see ss 87–89 of the 1974 Act.

[95] See s 77 of the 1974 Act. Section 77(4) confirms that the agreement may not be enforced while the lender is in default of his obligations under this provision. However, the rights are not thereby permanently extinguished and may be resumed by the lender following compliance: see *McGuffick v Royal Bank of Scotland plc* [2009] EWHC 2386 (Comm).

[96] See s 126 of the 1974 Act.

[97] See s 140A–D of the 1974 Act, as inserted by the 2006 Act. These provisions replace the court's earlier powers to re-examine 'extortionate credit bargains' under ss 137–140 of the 1974 Act. It may be noted that this power appears to be exercisable in relation to any credit agreement where the debtor is an individual, even if the agreement is otherwise exempt from the provisions of the 1974 Act. On exempt agreements, see paras 4.09–4.12 above.

(b) the way in which the creditor has exercised or enforced any of its rights under the credit agreement or any related agreement; or

(c) any other act or omission of the creditor (whether occurring before or after the contract was made).

4.39 It will be seen that these provisions allow the court a wide power of intervention.[98] Where a court holds the contract to be unfair, it has a range of powers available to it to redress the balance, including a power to make orders for the repayment of amounts transferred by the debtor, and the alteration of the terms of the contract. At the time of writing, there appear to be two cases in which these new powers have been considered but, in each case, the relationship was not found to be unfair and, as a result, the nature of the orders which should be made did not fall for consideration.[99]

Recent Reforms—The Consumer Credit Directive

4.40 The Consumer Credit Directive[100] was adopted by the European Commission in May 2008, and Member States were required to transpose the Directive into national law by June 2010.[101] Since certain aspects of the Directive already form a part of the law of the United Kingdom under existing legislation, it has not been appropriate to adopt a 'copy out' approach to the domestic implementation of the Directive. Instead, existing rules have to be refined and amended to bring them into line with the new Directive or, in a number of cases, existing provisions in the Consumer Credit Act 1974 or secondary legislation were found to be consistent with the requirements of the Directive. The Consumer Credit (EC Directive) Regulations 2009 are designed to give effect to the Directive.[102]

4.41 There is inevitably a mismatch between the scope of the existing UK legislation and the terms of the new Directive itself. For example:

(a) loans to small traders are excluded from the Directive[103], whilst, as has already been seen, certain business loans below £25,000 are regulated under the provisions of the 1974 Act;[104]

---

[98] Under the former, 'extortionate credit bargain' provisions, a court would only intervene if the rate of interest was grossly exorbitant or if the transaction was otherwise contrary to ordinary principles of fair dealing. The new provisions are intended to broaden the types of situation in which the court may grant redress to the debtor.

[99] In *Khodari v Tamimi* [2008] EWHC 3065, a 10 per cent fee charged to an individual to fund his gambling activities was not unfair, because such loans imply a significant degree of risk for the creditor and the transactions were unsecured. In *Maple Leaf Volatility Master Fund v Rouvroy* [2007] EWHC 257 (aff'd without reference to the point, [2009] All ER(D) 199 (Nov)), the court found no evidence of unfairness in a facility designed to assist the debtor in acquiring control of a company.

[100] 2008/48/EC, OJ L 133, 22.5.2008, p 66.

[101] Although the Directive is in part designed for the protection of consumers, it is also designed to avoid distortions in the market for consumer credit as a result of differences in national treatment. In other words, the Directive is a 'single market' measure: see recitals (4)–(9) of the Directive.

[102] These Regulations (hereafter the 'implementing regulations') are due to come into force on 11 June 2010 but they remain in draft at the time of writing. The implementing regulations operate by inserting new sections into the 1974 Act and, where appropriate, by amending some of the secondary legislation made under that Act.

[103] See the definition of 'consumer' in Art 3 of the Directive.

[104] See para 4.11 above.

(b) loans below €200 and above €75,000 are outside the scope of the Directive[105] whilst, as already noted, the 1974 Act now generally applies to consumer loans without any pre-set financial limit;[106] and

(c) interest-free credit arrangements are outside the scope of the Directive,[107] whilst they are within the scope of the 1974 Act.

The key amendments to the existing UK regime[108] include the following: **4.42**

(a) The 'high net worth' exemption[109] required amendment so that it applies only to loans above €75,000.[110]

(b) The Directive prescribes a list of information which must be given to the debtor in good time before he becomes bound by the contract.[111] The information must be provided in the form of a Standard European Consumer Credit Information Sheet (SECCI). This will replace the existing requirements under the Consumer Credit (Disclosure of Information) Regulations 2004,[112] although the list of required information (eg details of the creditor, amount and type of credit, total amount payable, interest rate and charges, and similar matters) is broadly similar in each case.[113]

(c) As noted above,[114] the Consumer Credit (Agreements) Regulations 1983 make certain rules about the form and content of regulated agreements. The Directive will now require the provision of certain additional information within the agreement itself, including, (i) the debtor's right to request an amortization table, (ii) statements as to periods and conditions for the payment of interest, and (iii) termination procedures.[115]

---

[105] See Art 2(c) of the Directive.

[106] See para 4.03 above.

[107] See Art 2(f) of the Directive.

[108] For a discussion of the government's approach to the Directive and the required national legislation, see Department for Business Enterprise and Regulatory Reform, 'Consultation on Proposals for Implementing the Consumer Credit Directive' (April 2009).

[109] This exemption has been discussed at para 4.12 above.

[110] It would be inconsistent with the UK's obligations under the Directive to allow the high net worth exemption to operate below that level, since the Directive does not allow for a corresponding type of exemption at all. The exemption can thus only be applied to credit agreements which are beyond the scope of the Directive in any event. The necessary amendment to the Consumer Credit (Exempt Agreements) Order 2007 is achieved by reg 62 of the implementing regulations. For domestic purposes, the limit of €75,000 has been translated into £60,260.

[111] Article 5 of the Directive and the Consumer Credit (Disclosure of Information) Regulations 2009. These Regulations are due to come into force on 11 June 2010 but they remain in draft at the time of writing.

[112] On these regulations, see para 4.27 above. For the revised text, see the Consumer Credit (Disclosure of Information) Regulations 2009 (see previous footnote).

[113] The form and content of the SECCI is set out in Sch 1 to the Consumer Credit (Disclosure of Information) Regulations 2009 (see n 111 above). Where a lender concludes consumer credit contracts at a distance, the provision of SECCI to the debtor will be deemed to constitute compliance with the pre-contractual notice requirements of the Financial Services (Distance Marketing) Regulations 2004: see Art 5(2) and (3) of the Directive and reg 59 of the implementing regulations, inserting new provisions into the Financial Services (Distance Marketing) Regulations 2004 (SI 2004/2095).

[114] See paras 4.25–4.29 above.

[115] On these points, see Art 10 of the Directive.

(d) Lenders will be required to provide 'adequate explanations' to the borrower to enable them to determine whether the loan meets his needs and is suited to his financial position.[116]

(e) Lenders will be required to assess the creditworthiness of the borrower.[117]

(f) Where a credit agreement falls within the scope of the Directive, the debtor will have a right of cancellation within 14 days of the agreement or the date on which he receives a copy of the applicable terms and conditions.[118] This is wider than the cancellation right available under the current UK regime, which applies only to limited types of contract.[119] Where the debtor exercises his right of cancellation, he must repay the capital and accrued interest within 30 days.[120]

(g) Borrowers will have the right to make partial prepayments of the credit.[121]

(h) Reference has been made above[122] to the calculation of the annual percentage rate (or APR). The details of this calculation will change, although it appears that the differences will not be material.[123]

(i) The Directive will involve significant amendments to the consumer credit advertising regime.[124] In particular, interest rates, charges, and other items must be specified in a clear, concise and prominent means by way of a representative example.[125] Lenders must generally provide that example by reference to a credit value of €1,500. The stated terms must be as good as, or better than, at least 50 per cent of borrowers would receive.[126] The APR must be based on the representative example.[127]

(j) The Directive also contains new provisions dealing with authorized and unauthorized overdrafts.[128] The customer must be provided with details of his credit limit, interest

---

[116] Article 5(6) of the Directive and reg 3 of the implementing regulations (inserting a new s 55A into the 1974 Act).

[117] Article 8 of the Directive and reg 3 of the implementing regulations (inserting a new s 55B into the 1974 Act). Recital (26) to the Directive states that this requirement is not merely directed to the creditor's own interests but also to the consumer's well-being, thus making it clear that part of the object is to ensure a socially responsible attitude to this type of finance.

[118] See Art 14 of the Directive.

[119] See the discussion at para 4.27 above. The wider rights of cancellation or withdrawal are transposed by reg 9 of the implementing regulations (inserting a new s 73A into the 1974 Act).

[120] Article 14(3) of the Directive and reg 9 of the implementing regulations (inserting a new s 73B into the 1974 Act). This differs from the current position under the 1974 Act, where repayment of the capital is required within 30 days but the borrower is absolved from any obligation to pay interest: see the discussion at para 4.27 above.

[121] Article 16 of the Directive. The 1974 Act currently allows for early repayment of the entire credit. Regulation 19 of the implementing regulations (inserting a revised s 94 into the 1974 Act) extends this right to partial prepayment. If the repayment exceeds £8,000 and is made in respect of a fixed rate interest transaction, the lender may be entitled to compensation of up to one per cent of the amount prepaid.

[122] See para 4.23 above.

[123] For the details, see Art 19 and Annex 1 to the Directive.

[124] On the Consumer Credit (Advertisements) Regulations 2004, see paras 4.23–4.24 above.

[125] See Art 4 of the Directive and the Consumer Credit (Advertisements) Regulations 2009. These Regulations are due to come into force on 11 June 2010 but they remain in draft at the time of writing.

[126] It is not immediately obvious how this point could be verified.

[127] For the details, see Art 4(2) of the Directive and reg 15 of the Consumer Credit (Advertisements) Regulations 2009 (n 124 above).

[128] Unauthorized overdrafts are referred to in the Directive as 'overrunning'.

rates and charges.[129] Regular statements of account must be provided.[130] Where the overdraft is unauthorized, the customer must be notified if he has exceeded his credit limit by more than £100 for a period of a month, and must be advised of the applicable interest rates, charges, and penalties.[131]

(k) Finally, the Directive requires the creditor to accept responsibility for breaches of contract by the supplier under any linked commercial agreement.[132]

Mortgage Regulation

Introduction

Residential mortgages or home finance transactions were not originally within the scope **4.43** of the FSA regulatory structure. However, this changed with effect from 31 October 2004, when certain mortgage-related activities were brought within the scope of supervision.

The Scope of Regulation

Paragraph 23 of Schedule 2 to the FSMA (as amended) brings within the scope of regula- **4.44** tion rights under any contract where credit is provided on the security of land. In consider- ing home finance and mortgage transactions, one is instinctively inclined to think of traditional facilities designed to assist an individual to purchase his residence, or to refi- nance such an arrangement. But, as others have pointed out,[133] the expression 'credit' is widely defined by paragraph 23 to include any form of financial accommodation. Thus, if a bank issues a guarantee secured on property belonging to its customer, this could potentially be a regulated mortgage contract because the issue of the guarantee is a form of financial accommodation.

In practice, however, the scope of regulation is cut back by various features of the definition **4.45** of a 'regulated mortgage contract' for the purposes of the Regulated Activities Order. Article 61 of that Order defines such a contract as a credit arrangement secured on land where:

(a) the borrower is an individual (or a trustee for an individual);
(b) the lender carries on its activities by way of business;[134]
(c) the credit is secured on land in the United Kingdom;[135]
(d) the borrower (or a close relative or partner) intends to use at least 40 per cent of the land as a dwelling, or in connection with a dwelling.

---

[129] Articles 6 and 18 of the Directive.
[130] Article 6(1) of the Directive.
[131] Article 18(2) of the Directive.
[132] See Art 15 of the Directive. This provision is mirrored in s 75A of the 2004 Act and has already been discussed at para 4.34 above.
[133] See Blair, Walker and Purves, para 15.16, noting the terms of the FSA's Perimeter Guidance, PERG 4.4.1AG(2).
[134] A one-off secured loan provided by a relative would therefore usually fall outside the scope of regulation.
[135] Note that 'timeshare' accommodation is excluded for these purposes.

4.46 Various features of these criteria may be noted. For example:

(a) the requirement that the borrower must be an individual—or a trustee for an individual—excludes corporate loans from the scope of regulation, even if secured on the borrower's real estate;

(b) there is no positive requirement that the loan must be made for the purpose of purchasing or refinancing the purchase of the residential property which forms the subject matter of the security. Consequently, a loan made to an individual for the purposes of his business may be a regulated mortgage contract for these purposes if it is secured on his residence;[136]

(c) loans to purchase a farm will not, in the ordinary course, be regulated mortgage contracts since (i) less than 40 per cent of the land will be used as a dwelling and (ii) the remainder of the land is not used in connection with the dwelling, but as an independent business;[137] and

(d) a loan to purchase a property for investment purposes will not be a regulated mortgage contract since it will not be used as a dwelling for the borrower himself.[138]

4.47 Since mortgage contracts fall within the scope of the Regulated Activities Order, the following activities—if carried on by way of business—will be 'regulated activities' for the purposes of the FSMA and will thus be subject to the requirement for authorization by the FSA:

(a) arranging,[139] making arrangements with a view to,[140] or advising on[141] a regulated mortgage contract;[142]

(b) entering into a regulated mortgage contract as a lender;[143]

(c) administering a regulated mortgage contract;[144] and

(d) agreeing to carry out any of the above activities.[145]

4.48 In terms of its FSA permissions, the upshot is that a bank will generally need authorization to act as a mortgage lender.[146]

4.49 It may be noted that the regulatory regime applicable to home finance has been further extended in two other respects in order to cater for other developments in the market. In each case, the products concerned involve an outright *transfer* of the land to the financier,

---

[136] The point is made by PERG 4.4.2G. Certain provisions applicable to this type of business loan are discussed below.
[137] PERG 4.4.7G.
[138] For occasional exceptions, see PERG 4.4.8G.
[139] Regulated Activities Order, art 25A(1).
[140] Regulated Activities Order, art 25A(2).
[141] Regulated Activities Order, art 53.
[142] These three activities are collectively defined as 'mortgage mediation activities' for the purposes of the FSA Handbook.
[143] Regulated Activities Order, art 61(1).
[144] Regulated Activities Order, art 61(2).
[145] Regulated Activities Order, art 64.
[146] In view of the focus of this work, it is not proposed to consider the position of mortgage intermediaries or other participants in the process.

as opposed to a loan secured by a mortgage. In the absence of the essential feature of *security,* these products fall outside the definition of a regulated mortgage contract.

The first product is the 'regulated home reversion plan'.[147] This involves the purchase of the **4.50** property by a financier, coupled with a right for the customer to live in the property until death or until other conditions are met. These products allow individuals to remain in their own homes whilst at the same time realizing a capital sum for retirement purposes. Since products of this kind are not generally sold by banks, it is not proposed to consider them further.

Secondly, it was necessary to take account of the growing market for Shariah-compliant **4.51** mortgage products. The nature of these products will be discussed at a later stage.[148] It should be said at the outset that some of these contracts would fall within the definition of a regulated mortgage contract. For example, under a *murabaha* agreement, the bank buys the property itself and then re-sells it to the customer on deferred terms, with the benefit of a charge over the property to secure the later instalments. But other products—such as the *ijara* lease and the diminishing *musharaka*—involve the ownership of the property by the bank itself throughout the period of the financing, with the result that no mortgage can be taken from the customer. Such arrangements have now been brought within the scope of regulation as 'regulated home purchase plans'.[149] Once again, however, such arrangements are only regulated if they relate to an interest in land in the United Kingdom and the customer intends to occupy at least 40 per cent of the property as a dwelling, or a close relative intends to do so. The intention of these provisions is plain—conventional and Shariah-compliant home finance should be regulated on an essentially identical basis, with similar protection being applied to both types of product. A bank which provides Shariah-compliant mortgage products will thus be regulated on the same basis as if it were a conventional provider.

The Nature of the Regulation

Having determined the types of the mortgage/home purchase products which fall within **4.52** the scope of regulation, it is now necessary to consider the nature and effect of the protection conferred on the users of those products.

There are a number of requirements derived from various sources: **4.53**

(a) a mortgage lender must not use or propose the use of any relevant intermediary unless that person is himself authorized or exempt for that purpose under the FSMA regulatory regime.[150] The intention is to ensure that the borrower benefits from appropriate

---

[147] See Regulated Activities Order, art 63B(3).
[148] See generally Chapter 48 below.
[149] Regulated Activities Order, art 63F(2).
[150] MIPRU 5.2.1R. This rule does not prevent the use of law firms for their ordinary services since they are generally outside the scope of the FSMA regulatory regime.

regulatory protection at all relevant stages of the transaction, and does not forfeit that protection as a result of the use of unauthorized intermediaries;[151] and

(b) a firm which engages in mortgage lending must meet a solvency requirement[152] and it must maintain its capital resources in excess of stated minimum requirements.[153] However, it is unnecessary to consider this point further in the present context because these particular requirements are not applicable to banks.[154]

4.54 More detailed conduct of business requirements are contained in the MCOB chapter of the FSA Handbook. It may suffice to note a few brief points:

(a) as noted above, a contract will normally fall within the scope of regulation if at least 40 per cent of the property is to be used as a dwelling. But the only further requirement is that the loan should be secured on such a dwelling, and there is no requirement to the effect that the loan should be used for the purpose of acquiring the property or refinancing its original acquisition. Consequently, a loan made for business purposes[155] may amount to a regulated mortgage contract if it is secured on the main residence of a director or shareholder and he intends to use the proceeds for the purposes of that business. Recognizing this fact, MCOB makes special provision for loans falling within this particular category;

(b) first of all, MCOB applies if the customer is not a 'large business customer'. The definition of that expression[156] means that MCOB only applies if the turnover of the business concerned is less than £1 million;

(c) if a business loan falls within the scope of MCOB on the basis that it is made to a business with an annual turnover of less than £1 million and is secured on a dwelling which meets the 40 per cent occupancy requirement, then the bank has a choice of regulatory approaches. As an initial option, it can simply comply with MCOB in full in any event. This may often be the most convenient approach because—although the full application of MCOB is in many ways more onerous—it may well be more straightforward for the bank to apply a single set of harmonized procedures to all of its mortgage loans, regardless of their purpose. The second alternative open to the bank is to adopt a so-called 'tailored approach' which disapplies some of the MCOB rules to

---

[151] MIPRU 5.1.2G. For discussion of the merits of this approach, see Blair, Walker and Purves, paras 15.39–15.42.

[152] ie it must be able to meet its debts as they fall due.

[153] MIPRU 4.2.3R.

[154] MIPRU 4.1.4R.

[155] Whether or not a loan is made for the purposes of a business will, of course, essentially be a question of fact. It seems that a loan taken out on an already occupied dwelling to facilitate the purchase of a buy-to-let property would be for *investment*, and not for *business*, purposes and would thus not amount to a regulated mortgage contract: see MCOB 1.5.2G.

[156] See the Glossary to the FSA Handbook. In determining whether or not the entity is a 'large business customer', the bank may rely on the annual accounts and other information provided by the customer: see MCOB 1.2.6G.

business loans, although certain further conditions will apply in order to qualify for that approach;[157]

(d) if MCOB applies, then the bank must adopt various business standards and requirements. Apart from the general rule that all financial promotions intended to solicit regulated mortgage business must be clear, fair, and not misleading,[158] the bank is required to make certain points clear to the customer by the use of prescribed expressions, such as 'early repayment charge', 'higher lending charge' and it cannot use other expressions whose meaning may be less clear to the customer;[159]

(e) MCOB also makes detailed rules as to the content of financial promotions for regulated mortgage contracts.[160]

The Lending Code

One of the relatively few remaining strands of voluntary or self-regulation in the financial services sphere is offered by The Lending Code (the Code). **4.55**

The Code was published in November 2009 by the British Bankers' Association, the Building Societies Association, and the UK Cards Association. It applies to loans, current account overdrafts and credit or charge cards provided to consumers, micro-enterprises and charities with an annual income of less than £1 million. The Code does not apply to residential mortgages and certain other types of business.[161] The Code applies to facilities in sterling, but lenders may extend its terms to other currencies on a voluntary basis.[162] **4.56**

Compliance with the Code is monitored by the Lending Standards Board, but the Code obviously does not affect the requirement for lenders to comply with other applicable legislation such as the Consumer Credit Acts and the Payment Services Regulations 2009.[163] **4.57**

The core commitment offered by institutions which subscribe to the Code is to act fairly and reasonably in their dealings with customers. This commitment involves duties on the part of the bank (i) to ensure that promotional material is fair, clear and not misleading, **4.58**

---

[157] For the details, see MCOB 1.2.7. The rule variations applicable to business loans are further described in MCOB 4.9.

[158] This rule is applicable to financial promotions generally but, in the present context, is repeated in MCOB 2.2.6R. The requirement for fairness and clarity is extended to all communications (whether oral or written) with customers throughout the mortgage process, even if they do not strictly fall within the definition of a 'financial promotion': see MCOB 2.2.8G.

[159] MCOB 2.2.3R. A 'higher lending charge' is an additional rate to reflect the fact that the loan exceeds a stated percentage of the property value.

[160] MCOB 3.6. For example, MCOB 3.6.13 R(3) requires the well-known warning to the customer that his home is at risk of repossession if he fails to keep up his mortgage payments. MCOB 3.6 applies to 'non-real time' promotions—ie promotions not involving a personal visit or phone call. 'Real time' promotions involving such personal contact are regulated by MCOB 3.8.

[161] On these points, see paras 1 and 2 of the Code. It will be noted that, in terms of the types of customer to which it applies, the scope of the Lending Code is similar to that of BCOBS: see the discussion of BCOBS, at paras 3.04–3.25 above.

[162] Paragraph 3 of the Code.

[163] On these points, see paras 4 and 6 of the Code. On the Payment Services Regulations 2009, see Chapter 5 below.

and to give customers clear information, (ii) to give clear information about accounts and services, terms and conditions, and interest rates, (iii) to provide regular statements and information about changes to interest rates, charges, and other conditions, (iv) to lend money responsibly, (v) to deal sympathetically and positively with customers in financial difficulties, (vi) to treat customer information as confidential and to provide secure and reliable banking systems, and (vii) to ensure that staff are trained to put the Code into practice.[164]

4.59 The provisions of the Code are relatively detailed and a brief overview must suffice for present purposes:

(a) Section 2 of the Code repeats the requirement that communications should be clear, fair, and not misleading and that customers should be provided with appropriate information at the right time to enable them to make informed decisions.[165] That section then includes a number of rules designed to amplify these obligations and to deal with marketing and advertising issues;

(b) Section 3 deals with the transmission of information to Credit Reference Agencies. This obviously has confidentiality/privacy implications for the customer and the Code provides that information can only be passed to such an agency if the customer is in arrears, has not disputed the amount owing, and has not made an acceptable proposal for repayment following the lender's demand;[166]

(c) Section 4 of the Code requires lenders to make a credit assessment before granting or increasing an overdraft or other loan facility, in order to determine whether the customer will be able to repay it.[167] This exercise is obviously in the interests of the bank itself, but it also represents a part of the core commitment to responsible lending;

(d) Sections 5, 6 and 7 respectively contain provisions dealing with current account overdrafts, credit cards, and loans. As might be expected, these contain a series of provisions about the need to convey certain information to customers about interest rates, charges, and other conditions. Section 7 also contains guidance on personal guarantees and suggests that lenders should not generally take an unlimited guarantee from a private individual;[168]

(e) Section 8 requires that the terms and conditions of any product should be written in clear and intelligible language, and deals with the processes involved in varying those terms and conditions;

(f) Section 9 deals with financial difficulties, and expands on the core commitment to adopt a positive and sympathetic approach to customers in this situation. Nevertheless, debt recovery procedures may be instituted if the customer does not

---

[164] See para 13 of the Code.

[165] Paragraph 15 of the Code. To this extent, it will be noted that the Code mirrors the provisions of BCOBS 4, discussed at paras 3.17–3.21 above.

[166] It will also be necessary to take account of the Information Commissioner's Data Protection Guidance on Filing Defaults with Credit Reference Agencies: see para 38 of the Code.

[167] See para 43 of the Code.

[168] See para 123 of the Code.

cooperate or if his suggested repayment programme is unreasonable in all the circumstances;[169] and

(g) Sections 10 and 11 deal with complaints and compliance monitoring.

As noted above, the Code is observed by subscribing institutions on a voluntary or self-regulatory basis. It may apply alongside statutory forms of regulation which are applicable in the particular circumstances of a given case.   **4.60**

---

[169] See para 162 of the Code.

5

THE REGULATION OF PAYMENT SERVICES

Introduction

In the late 1990's one of the reasons given for the introduction of the euro was the reduction **5.01** of exchange rate risks—and hence, costs—which otherwise burdened enterprises carrying on business across European national boundaries. The single currency would also enhance price transparency and competition. Inevitably, however, some of these benefits would not accrue so long as banks in different countries adopted radically different approaches to the provision of payment services and the cost of cross-border payments across the eurozone significantly exceeded the corresponding costs associated with purely domestic transfers. The absence of direct competition in payment services meant that higher costs were borne by users of those services.

5.02   As a consequence, one of the more recent 'layers' of financial regulation is derived from the EU's Payment Services Directive.[1] The objective is to allow a wider range of participants (including non-banks) in the market for payment services. At the same time, the field of payment services is one of systemic importance in the financial markets. As a result, the desire to enhance competition in this area must be counterbalanced by an appropriate regulatory framework. In addition, the requirements of consumer protection had to be taken into account, with rules requiring clarity and transparency of charging structures. It is, in many respects, of limited value if only cash/note payments are fungible across the eurozone—the same needs to apply to 'cashless' payments.

5.03   Prior to the introduction of the Directive, there was no EU-wide regulatory framework for payment services business. Thus, whilst a 'money transmission service' was one of the activities which could be 'passported' under the terms of the Recast Banking Consolidation Directive,[2] the conduct of that business alone did not of itself require authorization in the United Kingdom under the terms of the Regulated Activities Order.[3] Although the acceptance of funds from the payer was a necessary prelude to the transfer of those funds to a payee, this did not amount to 'accepting deposits' for the purposes of the Regulated Activities Order because the funds were not employed in the business of the service provider—that is, they are not recycled in the form of loans to customers of the service provider. An entity which carried on a business of this kind was thus outside the scope of financial services regulation in the UK.[4]

Implementation of the Payment Services Directive

5.04   As noted, however, this situation has now changed. The Payment Services Directive has now been implemented in the UK by the Payment Services Regulations 2009 (the 2009 Regulations)[5] which were fully effective by 1 November 2009.[6] The FSA has been appointed

---

[1] Directive 2007/64/EC of the European Parliament and of the Council on payment systems in the internal market (OJ L 319, 5.12.2007, p 1). It should be said that both the Directive and the 2009 Regulations noted below are a combination of market supervisory measures and new rules on consumer protection. Nevertheless, in order to provide an overview of the new payment services rules as a whole, it was decided to include a discussion of the entire measure within a single chapter and that this would most appropriately be included in the present regulatory section.

[2] See para 4 of Annex 1 to that Directive.

[3] As will be seen, this position has now changed.

[4] The analysis in the text is derived from those provisions of the Regulated Activities Order dealing with the acceptance of deposits. Article 9AB of the Regulated Activities Order does, however, now specifically and explicitly confirm that funds received for the purpose of providing a payment service are not to be regarded as a 'deposit'. Article 9L makes essentially the same provision in relation to electronic money. These new provisions were imported into the ROA by Pt 2 of Sch 6 to the Payment Services Regulations 2009, which are about to be described.

[5] SI 2009/209. References to the 2009 Regulations are to those regulations as amended (in a variety of relatively minor respects) by the Payment Services (Amendment) Regulations 2009 (SI 2009/2475). For certain transitional provisions which allow an institution to defer applying for authorization, see n 51 below.

[6] For the details of certain provisions which came into effect at an earlier date (eg to enable the FSA to consider applicants for authorization as a payment institution), see reg 1(2) of the 2009 Regulations.

as the competent authority for the purposes of the 2009 Regulations and is thus responsible for the monitoring and enforcement of the Regulations.[7]

The Payment Services Directive is designed to provide a legal framework for a single market in payment services. It also provides for mutual recognition of the authorization process and a 'passporting' process similar to that which applies under the Recast Banking Consideration Directive.[8] The Directive is principally concerned with services relating to the operation of payment accounts (including deposits/withdrawals), the execution of payment transactions, the issue of credit and debit cards, merchant acquiring, money remittance and some mobile phone services.[9] Naturally, these provisions are reflected in the 2009 Regulations. **5.05**

The present chapter examines the following matters which are relevant to the development of the market for payment services under these recent legislative initiatives: **5.06**

(a) it is necessary to define with some precision the meaning of the expression 'payment service' so that the scope and application of the 2009 Regulations can be ascertained;
(b) it is necessary to consider the authorization requirement which may apply if an entity is indeed carrying on a payment services;
(c) the different types of available authorizations and the applicable conditions will be outlined, along with the passporting regime for payment institutions;
(d) the 2009 Regulations create a number of 'conduct of business' requirements for the protection and information of service users;
(e) the 2009 Regulations legislate for the respective rights and obligations of payment institutions and service users;
(f) it is necessary briefly to consider rules on access to payment systems which are designed to ensure a level competitive playing field for the new institutions;
(g) certain powers of the FSA will be noted; and
(h) the parallel development of the Single Euro Payments Area (SEPA) will be described.

It is proposed to consider these issues in turn.[10]

Payment Services

The Definition

First of all, what is meant by the expression 'payment service'? **5.07**

---

[7] On the functions and powers of the FSA, see Pt 7 of the 2009 Regulations. The FSA has published a useful description of its role. See 'The FSA's role under the Payment Services Regulations—Our Approach' (FSA, June 2009, reissued with amendments in October 2009).

[8] On this subject, see paras 2.13–2.17 above.

[9] See the FSA's 'Approach' paper (n 7 above), p 3.

[10] The FSA Handbook (in PERG 15) contains helpful commentary on the 2009 Regulations and on the FSA's view of their precise scope.

The expression comprises the services listed in Part I of Schedule 1 to the 2009 Regulations.[11] In essence, the following activities will constitute 'payment services' if they are carried out '... as a regular occupation or a business activity ...':[12]

(a) services enabling cash to be placed on a payment account[13] and other facilities required for the operation of that account;

(b) services enabling cash withdrawals from a payments account, and associated operations;[14]

(c) the execution of direct debts, standing orders, credit transfers, and payments executed through a payments card or similar device;[15]

(d) issuing payment instruments[16] or acquiring payment transactions;[17]

(e) money remittance services not involving the establishment of payment accounts either for the payer or the payee but which does involve either (i) the receipt of funds from a payer for the sole purpose of transferring a corresponding sum to a payee or a payment service provider on the payee's behalf or (ii) the receipt of funds on behalf of, and to be made available to, the payee.[18] Money transfer companies of the kind which specialize in transferring funds to friends and relatives of the payer in other countries will thus fall under this heading. Payments of this kind will generally be made for no consideration as between the payer and the payee. Where, however, the transfer is intended to meet

---

[11] See the definition of 'payment services' in reg 2 of the 2009 Regulations.

[12] This qualification should be carefully noted. The question whether a particular activity is carried on as business has already been considered in relation to deposit-taking: see the discussion at para 1.15 above. The qualification may be of considerable importance in practice. For example, solicitors will frequently remit money in order to complete transactions on behalf of their clients. But this is done as part of a much wider business activity and the act of remitting the funds will not be seen as a separate or independent form of profitable activity. As a result, it is suggested that solicitors do not provide 'payment services' and, hence, are outside the scope of the 2009 Regulations.

[13] A 'payment account' is an account held in the name of a 'payment service user' which is used for the purpose of executing 'payment transactions'. On the definitions of these expressions, see reg 2 of the 2009 Regulations. From the guidance contained in the FSA Handbook (PERG 15), it appears that an account should only be regarded as a 'payment account' if it is intended to be used for that purpose. Thus, whilst an ordinary current account will almost invariably be a 'payments account' for these purposes, the same will not necessarily apply to a deposit account, which will involve a fixed maturity period and penalty for early termination, and the primary objective is to allow the customer to earn interest.

[14] eg a facility allowing for cash withdrawals from a payments account, whether through an ATM machine or over the counter.

[15] Note that these activities constitute a 'payments service' even if the payment service provider makes available a credit line to enable the transaction to proceed: see paras (c) and (d) of Annex I to the 2009 Regulations. It should also be noted that this provision refers to the *execution* of a payment transaction thus use of a debit or credit card etc. Thus, where a supplier of goods or services accepts payment by means of a credit card, he does not *execute* the payment services, he merely *initiates* it. The same may be said of the buyer in such a case. Consequently, it is the card issuer or merchant acquirer who *processes* the payment which is providing the *payment service* for these purposes. The supplier and buyer in such a case are merely accepting and making payment; neither of them is providing a *service* in relation to that payment. The payer and the payee are both 'payment service users' (and not providers): see the definition in reg 2 of the 2009 Regulations.

[16] 'Payment Instruments' means a personalized device (eg a debit card) or personalized set of procedures (eg instructions for use of an internet account) used by a payment services user to initiate a payment order: see reg 2 of the 2009 Regulations.

[17] 'Payment Transaction' is likewise defined by reg 2 of the 2009 Regulations. Thus, an entity which provides a service ('merchant acquiring') enabling suppliers or sellers to be paid for purchases under credit card transactions may be providing a 'payment service' for the purposes of the 2009 Regulations.

[18] See the definition of 'money remittance' in reg 2 of the 2009 Regulations.

an existing contractual obligation and the recipient payment service provider acts as agent for the payee, so that receipt by the payee's payment service provider constitutes a discharge of the payer's debt, it appears that the payee's service provider is outside the scope of the 2009 Regulations because it is not acting as an intermediary between the creditor and the debtor;[19] and

(e) the execution of payment transactions where the payer gives instructions by phone or by means of a digital/IT device and the payment is made to the telecommunication, IT system, or network operator acting *only* as an intermediary between the payer and the relevant supplier of goods or services.[20] This provision is obviously aimed at payments made by phone[21] or over the internet. Two points may be noted about this provision. First of all, the mere fact that a system conveys a payment instruction is not of itself sufficient to bring the activity within the scope of the 2009 Regulations. This will only occur if the operator is also responsible for the *execution* of the payment transaction. Secondly, if the operator provides some additional service or facility which adds value to the transaction (eg by providing search or distribution facilities), then the operator will not be acting *only* as intermediary and hence will be outside the scope of the 2009 Regulations.[22]

It should be noted that the definition of 'payment services' is apt to include services pro- **5.08** vided in any currency and, consequently, a service provider may require registration or authorization[23] regardless of the fact that he confines his operations to a limited range of currencies. In contrast, most of the information/execution/liability provisions to be dis- cussed at a later stage will only apply where a transaction is executed in euro or an EEA currency. This may in part be explained by the fact that (i) the Payment Services Directive and the 2009 Regulations are designed to support the Single Euro Payments Area (SEPA) project[24] and (ii) it is, in any event, much harder to legislate for execution times for non- EEA currencies, where much may depend on the operation of national payment systems outside the EEA.

The breadth of the services covered by the 2009 Regulations must not, however, be allowed **5.09** to obscure the fact that their scope necessarily has some limits and boundary lines. From the perspective of the payment service provider, the most important limitation seems to be that the 2009 Regulations do not generally apply to foreign exchange business. This view follows from a plain reading of the terms of Schedule 1 to the 2009 Regulations and the fact that the terms of that Schedule rely heavily on the expression 'payment transaction'. That expression is in turn defined by regulation 2 to include the act of '… placing, transferring or withdrawing funds …' and this language does not appear to connote or embrace a foreign exchange transaction. The point may be of significant practical importance because

---

[19] On this point, see the FSA's comments on bill payment firms in the FSA Handbook (PERG 15).

[20] It follows that, where the operator does *not* act *only* as an intermediary between those two parties, its activities will not constitute a 'payment service'. The point is, however, made more explicit by means of a specific exemption in Sch 1, Pt 2(l) of the 2009 Regulations. On Pt 2 generally, see paras 5.11–5.13 below.

[21] Frequently by mobile phone so that an instruction can be given via SMS message.

[22] On this point, see the FSA Handbook (PERG 15) and its commentary on the scope of this provision.

[23] On these processes, see paras 5.20–5.23 below.

[24] On this project, see paras 5.90–5.106 below.

(i) a period of two business days is required to effect a spot foreign exchange transaction and (ii) the 2009 Regulations do not seem to account for the additional time required where a customer instructs his bank to make (say) a euro payment by debiting his sterling account. A possible solution to this particular difficulty is considered in the context of the rules governing the time of receipt of payment orders.[25]

5.10 Some inferential support for the view that foreign exchange facilities are not 'payment services' for present purposes is also provided by regulation 49 of the 2009 Regulations. This provision requires transparency of exchange rates and other charges where the payment service provider offers this type of service. The starting point is that payment transactions must be executed in the currency agreed between the parties. However, regulation 49(2) requires disclosure of exchange rate and charges '... where a currency conversion service is offered *before the initiation of a payment transaction* ...'. Likewise, regulation 27(a)(ii) of the 2009 Regulations[26] allows that a payment institution '...may, *in addition to providing payment services*, engage in ... the provision of operational and closely related ancillary services, including ... foreign exchange services ...'. In each case, the highlighted wording plainly suggests that the foreign exchange transaction should not be regarded as part of the 'payment transaction' for the purposes of the 2009 Regulations.

Exclusions

5.11 It will be apparent that the scope of the definition of 'payment services' is potentially very wide. As a result, the Payment Services Directive catered for a range of exemptions which are reproduced in Part 2 of Schedule 1 to the 2009 Regulations. By way of overview, the list of exemptions includes the following:

(a) payment transactions executed wholly in cash and directly between the payer and the payee, without the intervention of an intermediary.[27] This exemption highlights that the mere fact that a payment is being made as between a debtor and a creditor is not of itself sufficient to bring the 2009 Regulations into operation. It is necessary that another party should be involved who provides a *service* in relation to that payment;

(b) services involving the provision of cash to the payer as part of a wider transaction involving a purchase of goods or services;[28]

(c) money exchange business consisting of cash-to-cash operations where funds are not held on a payment account.[29] Hence, a bureau de change which operates solely on an 'over the counter' basis will be outside the scope of the 2009 Regulations;

(d) transactions designed to place funds at the disposal of the payee by means of a paper-based medium such as a cheque, banker's draft, or postal order;[30]

---

[25] See the discussion of reg 65(4)(c) of the 2009 Regulations at para 5.78 below.
[26] On reg 27 more generally, see para 5.28 below.
[27] Part 2(a) of Sch 1 to the 2009 Regulations.
[28] Part 2(e) of Sch 1. This would include 'cashback' services of the kind provided by supermarkets.
[29] Part 2(f) of Sch 1. As already noted, foreign exchange services are generally outside the scope of the 2009 Regulations in any event: see para 5.09 above.
[30] Part 2(g) of Sch 1 to the 2009 Regulations.

(e) services provided as between payment services providers, settlement agents, central counterparties, clearing houses, and central banks are outside the scope of the 2009 Regulations.[31] This perhaps follows from the fact that the 2009 Regulations are designed for the protection of the ultimate payer and payee—that is, the payment service users. Thus, if a payment service provider has to use the services of a clearing or correspondent bank in order to achieve the required payment, the intermediate payment transactions will be outside the scope of the 2009 Regulations;

(f) an investment firm and certain other types of financial entity may make payments in relation to dividends, distributions, redemptions and other matters. These are ancillary to the firm's main business and are thus exempted from 2009 Regulations;[32]

(g) providers of IT, data processing and similar support services who provide the technical infrastructure for payment services are not themselves responsible for the provision of services to the end users. It is at best, unclear whether they would be caught by the 2009 Regulations, but any doubt is eliminated by a specific exclusion;[33]

(h) services based on payment instruments that can only be used to acquire goods or services on the issuer's premises (eg store cards) are likewise exempted from the scope of the 2009 Regulations;[34]

(i) payment transactions as between payment service providers carried out for their own account fall outside the scope of the 2009 Regulations;[35] and

(j) payment services provided exclusively on an intra-group basis between affiliated companies are likewise exempt.[36]

The above analysis of the Schedule to the 2009 Regulations is important from two perspectives, namely: **5.12**

(a) in determining whether an entity requires authorization as a payment institution; and

(b) if so, in determining which transactions effected by such an institution are subject to the 'conduct of business' rules created by the 2009 Regulations.

In this particular context, it may be noted in passing that the rules dealing with the **5.13** authorization or registration of payment services providers[37] apply to any payment service provider carrying out business in the United Kingdom. In contrast, the 'conduct of business' rules[38] will apply only to payment transactions which are effected in euro or in another EEA currency. Consequently, a provider who does not deal in euro or EEA currencies will require authorization but will not be subject to other significant parts of the

---

[31] Part 2(k) of Sch 1.
[32] Part 2(i) of Sch 1. It is also likely that the payment transactions are not themselves carried on as a 'business activity' and are thus not within the scope of the regulations in any event; compare the discussion in relation to solicitors, in n 12 above.
[33] Part 2(j) of Sch 1.
[34] Part 2(k) of Sch 1.
[35] Part 2(m) of Sch 1.
[36] Part 2(n) of Sch 1.
[37] See paras 5.17–5.19 below.
[38] ie the information requirements discussed in paras 5.40–5.53 below and the liability provisions discussed in para 5.86 below.

2009 Regulations. Given the importance of the euro, this point may often be a matter of purely theoretical interest.

Territoriality

5.14   As in the case of the Banking Consolidation Directive itself, difficult questions of territorial extent may arise.[39]

5.15   Some of these issues will be considered in the specific context of passporting under the Payment Services Directive.[40] However, the present discussion is concerned solely with the position of non-EEA payment institutions but whose services may have some relevant nexus with the UK. Is such an entity within the scope of the 2009 Regulations such that it will be obliged to apply for authorization under them[41] and generally to comply with their requirements?

5.16   In general terms, it appears that an entity incorporated and located outside the EEA should not be regulated as carrying on a payment services business in the UK if it merely provides internet-based services from that location to UK-based customers. Thus, neither the receipt of transfer instructions from a UK customer, nor the execution of any transfer instructions in favour of a UK-based payee, should of themselves result in the provision of a payment service within the United Kingdom.[42]

The Authorization Requirement

5.17   If it is determined that a person is engaging in the provision of payment services in the United Kingdom, what are the consequences that flow from that conclusion?

5.18   The starting point for this particular discussion is provided by regulation 110 of the 2009 Regulations. It is unlawful for a person to provide payment services in the United Kingdom unless it meets one of the following conditions:

(a) it is an authorized payment institution;
(b) it is a small payment institution;[43]
(c) it is an EEA authorized payment institution exercising its passport rights;[44]

---

[39] The territorial extent of the 2009 Regulations is confirmed by reg 110, under which it is an offence to provide a payment service *in the United Kingdom* in the absence of an appropriate authorization or exemption. Reg 110 is considered at n 49 below.

[40] On this subject, see paras 5.29–5.33 below.

[41] On the authorization process, see paras 5.17–5.19 below.

[42] See the FSA Handbook (PERG 15) on this subject. The FSA has noted that the territorial guidance given in the Commission's Interpretative Communication should apply equally in the payment services sphere. On the Interpretative Communication in the context of the Recast Banking Consolidation Directive, see the discussion at paras 2.25–2.28 above.

[43] On this category, see paras 5.26–5.27 below.

[44] On passporting and payment institutions, see paras 5.29–5.33 below.

(d) it is (i) a credit institution,[45] (ii) an electronic money institution,[46] (iii) the Post Office, (iv) the Bank of England, the European Central Bank, or the central bank of any other EEA State;[47] or

(e) it is a government department or local authority.[48]

Criminal penalties apply in the event of a breach of this provision.[49]

Many of these exemptions from regulation 110 require no further explanation, and it **5.19** is thus possible to focus on the categories of 'authorized payment institution' and 'small payment institution'.

Authorized Payment Institutions

Introduction

The initial process for authorization as a payment institution in the United Kingdom is **5.20** driven principally by regulations 5–11 of the 2009 Regulations.[50]

The starting point is an application to the FSA which must include, amongst other details:[51]

(a) a programme of operations and business plan;

(b) evidence that the applicant holds the necessary minimum capital;[52]

---

[45] Including an EEA credit institution exercising passport rights. Money remittance is an activity which can be passported under the terms of Annex 1 of the Recast Banking Consolidation Directive (see para 5.03 above) so that there is obviously no need for further permission in the case of an authorized or passported credit institution.

[46] Including an EEA electronic money institution exercising passport rights.

[47] The exemption for central banks is inapplicable where they are acting in their capacity as monetary authorities or carrying out other functions of a public nature but, in this sphere, they probably would not be providing payment services in any event.

[48] Again, the exemption is inapplicable when carrying out functions of a public nature.

[49] See s 110(2). It is a defence to any prosecution that the accused demonstrates that he took all reasonable precautions and exercised all due diligence to avoid committing the offence. This defence may be available where, for example, (i) the defendant can show that he introduced procedures designed to ensure that only exempt services where provided, but these were disregarded by a staff member, and/or (ii) appropriate (but, in the event, mistaken) legal advice was obtained before the relevant activity was commenced. It is also an offence for an authorized payment institution or a small payment institution to provide payment services which are beyond the scope of its authorization or registration: see reg 17 of the 2009 Regulations.

[50] As the FSA points out in its 'Approach' document (n 7 above), applicants for registration or authorization are likely to include money remittances, mobile network operators offering payment services, non-bank card issuers and merchant acquiring firms.

[51] On these points, see reg 5(1), read together with Sch 2 to the 2009 Regulations. Although the regulations came into effect on 1 November 2009, transitional provisions allow an institution to continue offering payment services up to 1 May 2011 before making an application to the FSA, provided that it was carrying on that business prior to 25 December 2007 (the December 2007 date refers to the publication of the Payment Services Directive in the EU's official Journal when public notice of the measure became formally available) and certain other conditions are met. For the details of these transitional provisions, see reg 122 of the 2009 Regulations.

[52] On the minimum capital for a payment institution, see reg 6(3), considered at paras 5.24–5.25 below.

(c) a description of the arrangements made for the purpose of safeguarding the funds of payment service users;[53]

(d) information and evidence relating to shareholders and directors; and

(e) a description of relevant audit arrangements.

5.21   The FSA is required to grant an application for authorization as a payment institution if all the following conditions are met:[54]

    (i)   the application is complete and otherwise complies with the requirements of regulation 5 of the 2009 Regulations;[55]

    (ii)   the applicant holds the requisite capital;

    (iii)   the applicant is a body corporate established in the United Kingdom and having its registered and head office in the UK;

    (iv)   the applicant has put in place adequate and robust governance, internal control and risk-monitoring procedures;

    (v)   its shareholders and directors are fit and proper persons to be involved in the business;

    (vi)   the applicant's business plan is appropriate and adequate reasons have been dedicated to it;

    (vii)   the provisions made for the safeguarding of funds belonging to payment service users are adequate;

    (viii)   the applicant has complied with any registration requirement under the Money Laundering Regulations 2007;[56]

    (ix)   the FSA is satisfied that any 'close links' which the applicant has with any other party are not likely to impede the FSA's supervision of the applicant.[57]

5.22   The FSA must determine an application for authorization within three months of the date on which it receives the completed application.[58] The FSA may grant an application subject to conditions.[59] If it proposes to refuse an application, then the FSA must give a warning notice to that effect and consider any representations made in response to it. If the FSA decides to refuse the application or to grant it only subject to conditions, the applicant has the right to refer the matter to the Financial Services and Market Tribunal.[60]

5.23   The 2009 Regulations also include provisions for the variation or cancellation of any authorization previously granted.[61]

---

[53] Such arrangements are required under reg 19 of the 2009 Regulations, as to which see paras 5.35–5.39 below.

[54] On this point, see reg 6 of the 2009 Regulations. By the same token, the FSA may refuse the application if any one or none of these conditions is not met.

[55] See para 5.20 above.

[56] The Money Laundering Regulations are discussed in Chapter 7 below. A payment services institution would be required to register with Her Majesty's Revenue & Customs under reg 33 of those regulations.

[57] 'Close links' includes a parent/subsidiary/affiliate relationship and shareholdings of 20 per cent or more: see reg 6(9) of the 2009 Regulations.

[58] Regulation 9(1) of the 2009 Regulations.

[59] Regulation 7(1) of the 2009 Regulations.

[60] On these points, see reg 9(7), 9(8) and 9(9) of the 2009 Regulations.

[61] See regs 10 and 11 of the 2009 Regulations.

Capital Requirements for Payment Institutions

As might be expected, a payment institution is required to have sufficient capital to support **5.24** its operations and to safeguard the users of its services.

The capital requirements are prescribed by regulation 18, read together with Schedule 3 to **5.25** the 2009 Regulations.[62] These provisions can best be described as involved, and a detailed examination is unnecessary for present purposes. It may suffice to provide a very brief overview:

(a) an applicant for authorization must hold initial capital in a range between €20,000 and €125,000, depending on the precise scope of the services which it intends to provide;[63] and

(b) thereafter, a payment institution must hold own funds calculated accounting to one of three possible methods, as directed by the FSA in any particular case.[64] These methods variously depend on the level of payment volumes or the institution's overheads.[65]

Small Payment Institutions

An entity or individual may be registered as a 'small payment institution' if the total amount **5.26** of payment transactions processed by it in the twelve months preceding its application to the FSA does not exceed €3 million.[66] The FSA must register an applicant if it satisfies this threshold requirement and (i) none of the individuals responsible for the management or operation of the business has been convicted of specified money laundering or other financial crimes, (ii) the applicant has made the appropriate registration under the Money Laundering Regulations 2009,[67] and (iii) the applicant's head office or registered office is within the United Kingdom.[68] If the business grows and annual transactions later exceed €3 million, then the applicant must, within 30 days of becoming aware of that fact, either (i) apply for authorization as a 'full' payments institution or (ii) cease to carry on payment services business.[69]

---

[62] These requirements do not apply to a payment institution which is a subsidiary of a credit institution and which is included in its consolidated supervision: see reg 18(2) of the 2009 Regulations. Obviously, there would be no purpose in cresting a 'double layer' of supervision for the payment institution in this type of case.

[63] Part 1 of Sch 3 to the 2009 Regulations. Although the figures are given in euro in order to mirror the terms of the Payment Services Directive itself, the capital may be paid up in sterling or other currencies: see reg 2(2).

[64] Paragraph 11 of Sch 3 to the 2009 Regulations.

[65] See paras 16, 17 and 18 ('Method A', 'Method B' and 'Method C') of Sch 3 to the 2009 Regulations. For the regulator's view of these provisions and a detailed discussion, see the FSA's 'Approach' paper (n 7 above), ch 9.

[66] As noted earlier, the 2009 Regulations came into force on 1 November 2009. However, a person who was lawfully carrying on a small payment services business on 25 December 2007 is allowed to defer applying for registration until 25 December 2010 under transitional provisions contained in reg 123 of the 2009 Regulations.

[67] On this point, see n 56 above.

[68] On these points, see reg 13 of the 2009 Regulations.

[69] This is the effect of reg 15 of the 2009 Regulations.

5.27   The exemption for small operators has the benefit that the applicant is not subject to any minimum capital requirements.[70] Equally, however, some of the benefits available to fully authorized institutions are not available to their smaller brethren. For example, a payment service provider which is registered as a small payment institution cannot exercise any right to passport into other EEA countries.[71]

Ancillary Business

5.28   Authorized and small payment institutions may also provide 'operational and closely related ancillary services', including foreign exchange services, safe keeping, the storage and processing of data, and other activities. They may also carry on any lawful business other than the provision of payment services.[72] Subject to various conditions and safeguards, such an institution may also grant credit to a customer for the purposes of a payment transaction, provided that this is not funded out of monies provided by other service users.[73]

Passporting

5.29   As noted previously, the 2009 Regulations include a passporting regime, allowing UK authorized payment institutions to provide services or to establish a branch in one or more other EEA States.

5.30   Where a UK authorized payment institution proposes to exercise those rights, it must give prior notice of that intention to the FSA and provide details of the services to be provided and of the individuals responsible for their delivery. The FSA must in turn provide that information to the relevant supervisory authority in the host State.[74]

5.31   The FSA may refuse to register, or may cancel any registration previously granted, if it has reasonable grounds to suspect that money laundering is taking place or is being attempted through that branch, or its existence increases the risk of money laundering activity. If the FSA proposes to exercise these powers, then there is a procedure for the giving of a warning notice and the making of representations by the institution concerned.[75] Reciprocal powers are also exercisable in relation to incoming EEA institutions wishing to establish a branch or to provide payment services in the United Kingdom.[76]

---

[70] Regulation 18, which imposes such requirements, applies only to an *authorized* payment institution. It does not apply to an institution which is merely *registered* under the provisions for small payment institutions.

[71] The passporting provisions are discussed at paras 5.29–5.33 below. Again, however, these provisions apply only to *authorized* payment institutions. It is, in any event, perhaps unlikely that a limited business of this type would be looking to exercise passport rights.

[72] For the safeguards which apply in relation to the payment services business itself in such a case, see paras 5.35–5.39 below.

[73] On the points made in this para, see reg 27 of the 2009 Regulations.

[74] On these provisions, see reg 23 of the 2009 Regulations.

[75] On these points, see reg 24 of the 2009 Regulations. Reg 25 also makes provision for supervisory cooperation in relation to passported branches.

[76] It should be noted that any passport granted under these provisions will apply only to *payment services*. Consequently, if the institution wishes to carry on investment or other business, it will need to consider whether further authorizations/passports are required for those purposes.

Reference has already been made to the difficult territorial issues posed by the passporting **5.32** regime in this area.[77] Whether or not it may be necessary to apply for a passport in particular cases can be a difficult question. The answer depends on whether the institution concerned is setting up an establishment (eg a branch) in another EEA State or providing services in such a State. In line with the FSA's guidance,[78] a passport will be required for an establishment or the provision of services in the following instances:

(a) the opening of a branch office will plainly require an 'establishment' notification;

(b) the appointment of an agent in an EEA State will likewise require an 'establishment' passport where the agent has a permanent mandate, is subject to the management and control of the payment institution, and is able to provide services on its behalf; and

(c) the installation of an ATM in another EEA State will require a 'services' passport (assuming that the machine is the institution's only presence in the EEA State concerned).

However, a payment institution does not need to make a passport notification in the **5.33** following cases:

(a) where, from its establishment in the United Kingdom, it executes payment orders or remits money in favour of a payee in another EEA State;

(b) where, through its establishment in the United Kingdom, it acts on instructions received from a service user located in another EEA State; or

(c) where it allows the use of credit or debit cards in other EEA States.[79]

Conduct of Business Requirements

The Payment Services Directive and the 2009 Regulations create a number of conduct **5.34** of business requirements which are designed for both the protection and information of service users. The most important of these rules are considered below.

Segregation Requirements

With a view to safeguarding funds provided by, or destined for transmission to, payment **5.35** service users, regulation 19 of the 2009 Regulations provides a choice of arrangements which must be implemented.

The first alternative[80] is the segregation of funds. The starting point is that an authorized **5.36** payment institution must segregate any funds[81] in respect of any payment transaction exceeding £50 and, if it holds them overnight, must place them in a separate account with

---

[77] See the discussion at paras 5.14–5.16 above.

[78] FSA Handbook, PERG 15.

[79] In other words, the holder of a UK credit card does not act as agent for the issuer in using the card to make payments in other EEA States. This must be correct, since any other conclusion would clearly be unworkable in practice.

[80] As outlined in reg 19(4)–(8) of the 2009 Regulations.

[81] It should be appreciated that this extends to both (i) funds received from the institution's own customers for transmission to third parties and (ii) funds received from another payment service provider for payment to the receiving institution's own customers.

a bank or must invest them in secure assets of a type approved by the FSA.[82] Any separate bank account must be suitably designated so that no third party may acquire an interest in it as a result of garnishee or similar proceedings.[83] The account may only be used for the holding of funds to be employed for the provision of payment services and thus the institution's own working capital cannot be paid into, or withdrawn from, that account.[84]

5.37 The alternative possibility allows the payment services provider to take out an insurance policy or guarantee from an insurance company or bank and which, in the event of insolvency of the service provider, requires the proceeds of the policy or guarantee to be paid into an account which is specifically designated for these purposes.[85]

5.38 The integrity of the cash pool created under either of these alternatives is reinforced by an express provision to the effect that '… No person other than the authorised payment institution may have any interest in or right over the relevant funds …'.[86] A payment institution which executes a fixed and floating charge over the entirety of its assets and undertaking should therefore specifically exclude any such insurance policy/accounts from its scope in order to avoid a contravention of these rules. However, even in the absence of such a precaution, it seems clear that the provisions of the 2009 Regulations would override the security created by the floating charge because:

(a) the language reproduced above is of a mandatory nature and would accordingly prevail against any provision to the contrary effect in any contract or security document;

(b) the objective of the 2009 Regulations is to preserve the assets entrusted to a payment institution by or on behalf of its customers; and

(c) this conclusion is reinforced by regulation 19(11) which, subject to minor exceptions, states that '… the claims of payment service users are to be paid from the asset pool in priority to all other creditors … and … until all the claims of payment service users have been paid, no right of set-off or security right may be exercised in respect of the asset pool …'. In addition, the segregated account is not available for the payment of insolvency expenses, except for the cost of distributing the relevant funds to the payment service users who are entitled to them.[87]

5.39 In addition to the formal segregation requirements, a payment institution must also maintain organizational processes and procedures sufficient to minimize the risk of loss of the asset pool as a result of fraud, misuse, negligence or poor administration.[88]

---

[82] The FSA has for this purpose approved assets of the type referred to in ch 3 of the FSA's Electronic Money Sourcebook.

[83] And so that the account holding bank is aware of the status of these funds and thus cannot attempt to exercise any right of set-off in respect of the liabilities of the payment service provider itself.

[84] This point is in some respects reinforced by reg 28 of the 2009 Regulations, which states that any payment account held by a payment service provider may only be used in relation to payment transactions for service users.

[85] On the points made in this para, see reg 19(9) and (10) of the 2009 Regulations.

[86] See reg 19(7) in relation to a segregated account and reg 19(10) in relation to the proceeds of an insurance policy or guarantee. These funds are referred to as the 'asset pool': see reg 19(15).

[87] Regulation 19(12) of the 2009 Regulations.

[88] See re 19(13) of the 2009 Regulations.

Information Requirements

Part 5 of the 2009 Regulations sets out information (or transparency) requirements for the **5.40** provision of payment services.[89]

It should be noted that there is some overlap between the requirements of the 2009 **5.41** Regulations and those of the Consumer Credit Act 1974 (as amended). Where the Consumer Credit Act provides for an equivalent or a greater degree of protection, the policy of the government was to apply the Consumer Credit Act rules in preference to those of the 2009 Regulations. This is reflected in the detailed provisions of the 2009 Regulations themselves and relevant aspects will be highlighted where appropriate.[90]

Scope of Requirements

It should be appreciated at the outset that the information requirements only apply to **5.42** contracts for the provision of payment services if the following conditions are satisfied:[91]

(a) The services are provided—whether on behalf of the payer or the payee—from an establishment maintained by a payment service provider.[92]

(b) The other payment service provider is also located in an EEA State.

(c) The payment services are carried out in euro or a currency of an EEA State which has not yet adopted the single currency.[93]

---

[89] It should be appreciated that these notification requirements, along with the execution/liability provisions discussed in paras 5.54–5.86 below, apply to all entities which provide payment services. That is, their application is not limited to authorized payment institutions or registered small payment institutions. They extend likewise to credit institutions and others who provide services of this kind.

[90] The Consumer Credit Act 'override' for the purposes of the 2009 Regulations will only apply where the underlying arrangement is a 'regulated agreement' for the purposes of the 1974 Act. On 'regulated agreements', see the discussion at para 5.55 below. Clearly, the override will only be relevant where the payment service provider is not merely providing a payment service but is also allowing credit to the customer for the purposes of that transaction.

[91] See reg 33(1) of the 2009 Regulations.

[92] This will include an EEA authorized payment service provider which has exercised its passport rights into the United Kingdom: see the definition of 'payment service provider' in reg 2 of the 2009 Regulations. The information requirements will also apply to credit institutions as providers of such services, even though they are exempt from the authorization requirement under the 2009 Regulations.

[93] There may be a potential question mark about whether the reference to currencies of an EEA State includes the Swiss franc. Whilst Switzerland is not itself an EEA country, Liechtenstein is an EEA State and uses the Swiss franc as its domestic currency under long standing bilateral arrangements with Switzerland. It is difficult to avoid the conclusion that the Swiss franc is 'the currency' of Liechtenstein and is thus within the scope of the EEA currencies to which the 2009 Regulations apply. It is submitted, however, that the 2009 Regulations can only apply to a Swiss franc payment where the relevant funds are being used or transferred *in their character as the currency of Liechtenstein*. In other words, the payer or the payee would have to be based in Liechtenstein so that the payment transaction has some relevant nexus with that country. Admittedly, this involves implying some limitations into the scope of the 2009 Regulations but it is suggested that the approach just suggested is consistent with their overall scheme. In the writer's view, it would be unreasonable to apply the 2009 Regulations to *all* Swiss franc payments merely because it is used as the currency of Liechtenstein under a bilateral arrangement. But however that may be, it appears that both the Commission and the industry will adopt the view that all Swiss franc payments are within the scope of the Directive, regardless of any nexus (or lack of it) between the transaction and Liechtenstein: see 'Guidance for the Implementation of the Payment Services Directive', European Banking Industry PSD Expert Group, at p 13.

5.43 It should be noted that subparagraph (c) above refers to the requirement that the *payment service* must be provided in euro or an EEA currency. As already noted, the expression 'payment service' involves the transfer of funds from one person to another (or, in some cases, between two accounts of the same person).[94] Consequently, if the transfer of funds is effected in (say) US dollars, then the information requirements in Part 5 of the 2009 Regulations will not apply, even if the payment service user tenders sterling or euro to the payment service provider and requests it to effect the necessary currency conversion. As noted previously,[95] the foreign exchange transaction is not a 'payment service' and accordingly falls outside the scope of the *general* information requirements in Part 5 (although certain *specific* transparency requirements are imposed where a conversion precedes the payment transaction itself).[96]

5.44 It should also be appreciated that the payment service provider and its customer can agree to opt out[97] of the information requirements unless the payment service user is:

(a) a consumer;[98]

(b) a micro-enterprise;[99] or

(c) a charity registered in the United Kingdom whose annual income is less than £1 million.[100]

5.45 Having established the scope and territorial application of the 2009 Regulations, the regulations themselves then draw a distinction between (i) single payment service contracts[101] and (ii) payment transactions executed pursuant to a framework contract.[102]

---

[94] See the discussion of Sch 1 to the 2009 Regulations, at para 5.07 above.

[95] See the discussion at para 5.09 above.

[96] On some of these points, see para 5.53 below, considering the terms of reg 49 of the 2009 Regulations.

[97] Note that the starting point is that the information requirements apply to *all* customers, regardless of their size or sophistication. The provider can only take advantage of the opt out by a specific provision to that effect in its standard terms and conditions.

[98] That is, a private individual acting outside the course of his trade or business: see the definition of 'consumer' in reg 2 of the 2009 Regulations.

[99] In essence, a 'micro-enterprise' is an entity whose annual turnover and/or balance sheet does not exceed €2 million and employs fewer than 10 people, although an institution may not qualify as a micro-enterprise if it is linked to larger entities. For the details, see the definition in reg 2 of the 2009 Regulations and Commission Recommendation 2003/361/EC, which seek to harmonize the meaning of the expression 'micro-enterprise' for a variety of diverse regulatory purposes. A practical difficulty may arise in this context in the sense that the expression 'micro-enterprise' is designed to place small businesses on a par with consumers because, in many respects, their bargaining power may not be significantly greater. Yet the definition could in limited cases catch special purpose vehicles or similar entities which are established for the purpose of a single, structured transaction which involves the placing of a deposit by that entity and, frequently, the creation of a charge over it as security for a limited recourse obligation. However, there will be no ongoing business or other contracts or arrangements. In such a case, it is submitted that an entity of this kind is not an 'enterprise' within the definition because it is not engaged in any *regular* or *recurring* form of economic or business activity: see recital (3) to the Recommendation noted above and Case C-205/03P, *Fenin v Commission* [2006] ECR I-6295 and Case C-97/08 *Akzo Nobel v Commission* (ECR, judgment dated 10 September 2009).

[100] See the definition of 'charity' in reg 2 of the 2009 Regulations.

[101] These are defined by reg 2 as a single (or 'one-off') payment transaction not covered by a framework contract.

[102] The definition of 'framework contract' is considered at para 5.48 below.

Single Payment Service Contracts

The essential information requirements in connection with a 'one off' payment transaction **5.46** are divided into three essential stages, namely, (i) information to be provided before the service contract is concluded, (ii) information to be provided following receipt of the order, and (iii) information to be provided to the payee following execution of the contract. The first two items obviously fall on the payer's service provider, while the final item will fall on the payee's provider. The requirements are as follows:[103]

(a) before the payment service user is bound by the payment service contract,[104] the provider must supply (i) the information or unique identifier which must be provided by the user for the proper execution of the payment order, (ii) the maximum time in which the order will be executed, (iii) the charges to be made by the payment service provider (including a breakdown, where applicable), (iv) where appropriate, the exchange rate to be used for the purposes of the transaction, and (v) any of the information specified in Schedule 4 of the 2009 Regulations as is relevant to the single payment service contract in question;[105]

(b) after receipt of the payment order, the payer's payment service provider must provide to the payer (i) a payment reference identifying the transaction and the identity of the payee, (ii) the amount of the payment transaction expressed in the currency used in the order, (iii) the charges payable by the payer (including a breakdown, where appropriate), (iv) if the exchange rate differs from that previously notified to the payer pursuant to paragraph (a) above, the rate concerned and the amount of the payment following conversion at that rate, and (v) the date on which the order was received, or the value date of the debit;[106] and

(c) immediately following the execution of a payment services transaction, the payee's payment services provider must provide to the payee (i) a reference number identifying the transaction and, where appropriate, details of the payer and any information communicated with the payment transaction,[107] (ii) the amount and currency which has come available to the payee as a result of the transaction, (iii) details of charges payable

---

[103] On the points about to be made, see reg 36 of the 2009 Regulations.

[104] However, the information may be provided immediately after the execution of the transaction if, at the request of the user, the contract is made by phone, internet or other means of distance communication: see reg 36(1)(b) of the 2009 Regulations.

[105] The last item, drawn from reg 36(2)(e), is particularly unhelpful since Sch 4 applies to framework transactions rather than to single payment service contracts. However, based on para 1 of Sch 4, it appears that the additional information may include the name and other details of the provider, including a statement as to its regulatory status. It may also include notification (where applicable) of the customer's rights to use the Financial Ombudsman Service in the event of a dispute: see para 7(b) of Sch 4 and para 8.62 of the FSA's 'Approach' paper referred to in n 7 above.

[106] Regulation 37 of the 2009 Regulations.

[107] As the FSA's 'Approach' paper (n 7 above) points out, the details of the payer of funds must normally be transmitted along with the payment in order to comply with provisions designed to track and forestall terrorist funding: see Regulation (EC) 1781/2006 of the European Parliament and of the Council of 15 November 2006 on information on the payer accompanying the transfer of funds, OJ L 345, 8.12.2006, p 1. However, this does not mean that all of such information should automatically be provided to the payee. For example, considerations of confidentiality may mean that it is appropriate to communicate the name of the payer but inappropriate to provide his bank details: see the discussion at paras 5.104–5.106 below.

by the payee, including a breakdown, (iv) where the payee's service provider has had to convert the remittance on receipt, the amount in the currency of the remittance and the rate of exchange applied, and (v) the value date of the credit.

5.47   There may be occasions when a user enters into a single transaction with payment service provider A under the terms of a framework agreement with payment service provider B, for example, where the holder of a card issued by Bank A—which will have been provided under a framework agreement—uses an ATM of Bank B. In such a case, the necessary information will be provided to the card holder by Bank A under the framework agreement[108] and Bank B is accordingly exempted from that request in relation to the single payment transaction.[109]

Framework Contracts

5.48   A framework contract is '... a contract for payment services which governs the future execution of individual and successive payment transactions and which may contain the obligation and conditions for setting up a payment account ...'.[110] This will accordingly include, for example, agreements governing debit and credit cards and the terms and conditions imposed by a bank for the use of a current account.

5.49   Much of the information to be provided to the payment service user under a framework contract will remain the same, because he will still be concerned with the cost, value, date, and other terms of individual transactions. However, a framework agreement is obviously intended to cover an ongoing relationship and, hence, a further level of detail is required.

5.50   Once again, at the onset of the relationship and, generally before the user becomes bound by the framework contract,[111] the service provider must provide certain listed information to the prospective payment service user.[112] The relevant information may be provided by means of supplying the framework contract in draft, but, in whatever form it is provided, it must include the following information:[113]

(a)   the name, head office, contracting branch or agent and the identity of the regulator of the payment service provider (including registration number);
(b)   a description of the payment service including (i) the main characteristics of the service, (ii) the information or unique identifier[114] which must be provided for the

---

[108]   On this aspect, see para 5.48 below.
[109]   This is the effect of reg 39 of the 2009 Regulations, which is designed to avoid the provision of duplicate information.
[110]   See the definition in reg 2 of the 2009 Regulations.
[111]   There is again an exception to this rule where the contract is made at a distance: see reg 40(1)(b) of the 2009 Regulations.
[112]   Note that, where the framework agreement is a regulated consumer credit agreement, the payment service provider is only required to provide details of interest and exchange rates, and is not required to provide the remainder of the information: see reg 34(b) of the 2009 Regulations. On the override for regulated consumer credit agreements, see para 5.55 below.
[113]   On the points about to be made, see reg 40 and Sch 4 to the 2009 Regulations. The service provider must also provide the same information to the user from time to time if so requested during the life of the framework contract: see reg 41.
[114]   eg a PIN number.

execution of a transaction, (iii) any applicable cut off times, and (iv) the maximum execution period for transactions;[115]

(c) details of applicable charges, interest rates and exchange rates;

(d) details of the means of communication between the parties and the provision of information about transactions;

(e) a description of safeguards and corrective measures, including (i) the steps to be taken by the user to keep safe a payment instrument,[116] (ii) the means of notifying the service provider in the event of loss, (iii) any circumstances under which the provider may stop the use of the instrument,[117] (iv) details of the payer's liability for unauthorized transactions,[118] (v) the method and time limit for the notification of unauthorized transactions and the extent of the provider's liability,[119] (vi) the extent of the provider's liability for non-execution or incorrect execution of a payment order,[120] and (vii) the extent of the service provider's liability for wrongful payments initiated by a payee;[121]

(f) details of (i) the circumstances under which the payment service user will be deemed to have accepted charges to the framework contract made unilaterally by the service provider,[122] (ii) the duration of the framework contract, and (iii) the user's rights of termination;[123] and

(g) in relation to dispute resolution (i) the law applicable to the contract and the courts having jurisdiction and (ii) details of any out of court settlement procedures available to the user and the means of access to them.[124]

5.51 The 2009 Regulations then proceed to deal with variations in, and the termination of, the framework contract. The following points may be noted in this context:[125]

(a) it is, of course, wholly impracticable for a bank or card issuer to seek the specific agreement of customers to every variation of a framework contract. From the perspective of cost and administrative convenience, it is important that a particular service should be provided on uniform terms to all users, and many customers would simply not trouble themselves to reply to any request for consent. The 2009 Regulations naturally recognize this reality and allow for unilateral variation by the service provider;

---

[115] The maximum time allowed for the execution of transactions is considered at para 5.85 below.

[116] eg non-disclosure of PIN numbers to third parties.

[117] The nature of these circumstances are outlined in reg 56 of the 2009 Regulations, on which see para 5.62 below.

[118] The extent of this liability is controlled by reg 62 of the 2009 Regulations, on which see para 5.71 below.

[119] Again, these matters are governed by the 2009 Regulations: see the discussion of reg 59 at para 5.67 below and reg 61 at para 5.70 below.

[120] These issues are governed by regs 75 and 76 of the 2009 Regulations, on which see para 5.86 below.

[121] In practice, this will refer to excessive direct debit payments. In this situation, the liability of the service provider is governed by reg 63 of the 2009 Regulations, on which see para 5.73 below.

[122] This issue is governed by reg 42 of the 2009 Regulations, on which see para 5.51 below.

[123] On the user's rights of termination, see the discussion of reg 43, at para 5.51(f) below.

[124] eg the Financial Ombudsman Service, on which see the FSA Handbook, DISP.

[125] Note that the rules about to be discussed do not apply where the framework contract amounts to a regulated consumer credit agreement, no doubt to avoid duplication of information requirements: see reg 34(a) of the 2009 Regulations.

(b) accordingly, any change in the terms of the framework contract or in any of the information communicated under Schedule 4 of the 2009 Regulations can be varied by notice to the user. The variations must be communicated at least two months before they are to take effect;[126]

(c) changes to the framework contract will become effective at the end of that two month period if (i) the framework contract so provides and (ii) the user has not, before the expiry of the two month period, notified the service provider that he does not agree to such changes.[127] In such a case, the provider must advise the user that (i) the user will be deemed to have accepted the contractual changes in accordance with the terms of that paragraph and (ii) the user has the right to terminate the framework contract with immediate effect and without charge at any time before the contractual variations become effective;[128]

(d) the two month notice period does not apply where (i) the variation relates to a change in interest or exchange rates which is ascertained through a reference source which has been notified to the user and the framework contract allows for an immediate adjustment or (ii) the changes are favourable to the payment service user;[129]

(e) it might be thought that the right of the payment service provider unilaterally to vary the terms of the framework contract is 'unfair' and might therefore be amenable to challenge under the provisions of the Unfair Terms in Consumer Contracts Regulations 1999.[130] However, it is difficult to see how a court could hold the variation clause itself to be unfair, given that a cause which complies with the provisions discussed above now benefits from an implicit legislative imprimatur. In any event, the user is in practice protected because—although the variation clause may itself be valid—the content of any new provision which the service provider seeks to impose in reliance upon it would be amenable to challenge under the 1999 Regulations;[131]

(f) in relation to termination of the framework agreement,[132] (i) the user may terminate at any time, unless the contract provides for an agreed period of notice not exceeding

---

[126] Regulation 41(1) of the 2009 Regulations.

[127] Regulation 41(2) of the 2009 Regulations.

[128] Regulation 42(3) of the 2009 Regulations. Cancellation by the user is not, however, obligatory. Consequently, if he gives notice that he does not accept the proposed variations, then the framework contract would continue on its old terms. This would leave the service provider to exercise its own rights of termination so as to bring the framework contract to an end. However, since it must in its own turn give at least two months' notice of termination (see the discussion of reg 43(4) at subpara (f) below), this could mean that it must continue to apply the old terms to that user for a short period, even after the variation has become effective for other users.

[129] In such cases, the variations may be applied immediately and without prior notice to the user: see reg 42 of the 2009 Regulations. Nevertheless, notice of the change must usually be given to the user as soon as possible after it takes effect, and changes in interest or exchange rates must be applied in a neutral and non-discriminatory manner: see reg 42(5) and 42(6) of the 2009 Regulations. Where the arrangement is a 'regulated agreement' for the purposes of the Consumer Credit Act 1974, reg 42 does not apply: see reg 34 of the 2009 Regulations.

[130] On these regulations, see paras 15.45–15.49 below. The present discussion does, of course, proceed on the basis that the payment service user is a 'consumer' for these purposes.

[131] Although the term is introduced after the original contract, there seems to be nothing in the 1999 Regulations which precludes this view.

[132] On the points about to be made, see reg 43 of the 2009 Regulations. Once again, this provision does not apply where the contract is a regulated agreement for the purposes of the Consumer Credit Act 1974.

one month, (ii) the provider may not levy a charge for termination of a framework contract after it has been in force for twelve months and, if it levies a charge for termination within that twelve-month period, the charge must reasonably reflect the actual costs of termination to the service provider, (iii) the provider may terminate the contract by giving at least two months notice, if the contract entitles him to do so, and (iv) on termination, any charges must be apportioned up to the date of termination and a proportionate refund should be made if necessary;[133]

(g) the payment service user under a framework contract may request details of the maximum execution time and of the charges associated with the transaction;[134]

(h) as in the case of single payment transactions, a payment service user under a framework contract is entitled to receive at the time of the transaction a reference number and details of the amount, charges, applicable exchange rate, and value date of a payment transaction. However, and in line with normal practice, the 2009 Regulations allow the framework contract to stipulate for this information to be provided in a monthly statement instead.[135] The payee's service provider under a framework contract is obliged to provide the corresponding information to the payee but, once again, the framework contract may provide for this to take the form of a monthly statement.[136]

Finally, some of the rules described above[137] do not apply, and the parties are free to contract out of certain other rules,[138] where the relevant payment instrument (i) can only be used to execute individual payment transactions up to €30 (or €60 for transactions within the United Kingdom), (ii) has a spending limit of €150 (or €300 for transactions within the United Kingdom), or (iii) stores funds not exceeding €500 at any given time.[139]   **5.52**

Common Provisions

Although the 2009 Regulations deal with the information requirements applicable to single payment transactions and framework contracts separately, there are certain provisions which are common to both forms of arrangement. Specifically: **5.53**

(a) any information required to be made available under the above rules must be provided (i) in an easily accessible manner, (ii) if the user so requests, on paper or in any other medium which can be stored and reproduced, (iii) in easily understandable language and in a clear and comprehensible form, and (iv) in English or other agreed language;[140]

---

[133] None of these provisions affect the right of a party to assert that the contract is unenforceable, void or discharged, or to take proceedings for any breach of contract: see reg 44(7) of the 2009 Regulations.

[134] Regulation 44 of the 2009 Regulations. Note that the service provider is not obliged to provide this information unless specifically requested.

[135] Regulation 45 of the 2009 Regulation. Once again, in order to avoid duplication of information, only details of the exchange rate have to be provided by the payment service provider where the framework agreement amounts to a regulated consumer credit agreement: see reg 34(c) of the 2009 Regulations.

[136] See reg 46 of the 2009 Regulations.

[137] In particular, regs 40 and 44.

[138] In particular, regs 45 and 46.

[139] For the details of these derogations for low value payment instruments and the terms and conditions to which they are subject, see reg 35 of the 2009 Regulations.

[140] Regulation 47 of the 2009 Regulations.

(b) the payment service provider cannot make a charge for providing the information which it is legally required to provide in accordance with the rules described above. It may charge for the provision of additional information or for the provision of that information on a more frequent basis, but any such charges must be proportionate to the provider's actual costs;[141]

(c) naturally enough, a payment transaction must be executed in the currency agreed between the payment service user and his provider. Where a currency conversion service is offered to the payer, the rate of exchange and associated charges must be disclosed to him;[142] and

(d) where a payee (retailer) in a transaction proposes to make a charge or to offer a discount for the use of any particular payment instrument, he must notify the payer before commencing the payment transaction. The same requirement applies to a payment service provider.[143]

Rights and Obligations of Providers and Users

5.54 The foregoing section dealt with the information required to be provided to the payment service user in connection with payment transactions. Nevertheless, and valuable though these transparency requirements undoubtedly are, they are only a part of the overall picture when considering a payments transaction. Such a transaction has to be authorized, implemented, and completed. In the course of that process, mistakes may occur, and transactions may be effected through lack of authority or fraud.

Part 6 of the 2009 Regulations addresses the respective rights and obligations of the parties in relation to the provision of payment services.

Scope

5.55 The scope of the rules on the respective rights and liabilities of the parties to a payment services transaction essentially mirrors the scope of the transparency provisions discussed in the previous section.

In essence:

(a) Part 6 of the 2009 Regulations applies where (i) the payment services are provided from an establishment of the payment service provider in the United Kingdom, (ii) the payment service providers of both payer and payee are located in the EEA,[144] and (iii) the services are carried out in euro or the currency of another EEA State which has not adopted the euro as its currency;[145]

---

[141] On these points, see reg 48 of the 2009 Regulations.

[142] Regulation 49 of the 2009 Regulations.

[143] See reg 50 of the 2009 Regulations. However, as the FSA's 'Approach' document points out, any discrimination between different forms of payment instrument in the United Kingdom may be unlawful: see n 152 below.

[144] This is subject to the limited exception created by reg 51(2) of the 2009 Regulations, on which see para 5.85(i) below.

[145] See reg 51(1) of the 2009 Regulations.

(b) except where the payment service user is a consumer, a micro-enterprise, or a charity,[146] the parties may contract out of or vary certain of the provisions of Part 6;[147]

(c) where a contract for the provision of payment services amounts to a regulated consumer credit agreement, then certain provisions of the Consumer Credit Act 1974 will apply in substitution for the corresponding provisions of the Regulations;[148] and

(d) certain provisions of Part 6 do not apply to low-value instruments.[149]

Charges for Transactions

Regulation 54 of the 2008 Regulations deals with various matters relating to charges for payment transactions. In particular:

5.56

(a) the payment services provider is only allowed to charge the user for the execution of payment transactions where (i) it is allowed to do so under specified provisions of Part 6, (ii) the charges have been agreed between the parties, and (iii) the charges reasonably correspond to the provider's actual costs;[150]

(b) where the payment transaction does not involve a currency conversion, the payer and the payee must each bear their own payment service provider's charges;[151] and

(c) a payee's payment service provider must not prevent a payee from imposing a charge against or offering a discount to, the payer for using a particular method of payment.[152]

Authorization of Payment Transactions

It is fundamental to any payment transaction that it must have been duly authorized by the payment service user. Any losses flowing from a payment made by the payment service provider without appropriate authority must be borne by the provider itself.[153] So it will be

5.57

---

[146] On the meaning of these expressions, see para 5.44 above.

[147] This flexibility is provided by reg 51(3). The relevant provisions which may be varied or excluded are regs 54(1), 55(2), 60, 62, 63, 64, 67, 75, 76 and 77. Such parties may also agree a different time limit for the notification of unauthorized transactions for the purposes of reg 59(1). Each of these provisions is considered below. For convenience, where a provision may be excluded under these rules, this is referred to as the 'corporate opt out'. It should be noted that this opt out is a flexibility but it will be necessary for the service provider's terms and conditions to exercise that opt out. The relevant provisions will thus remain applicable to *any* customer, unless specifically excluded. When dealing with a dispute involving a large corporate customer, it will thus remain necessary to examine the service provider's standard terms in order to determine the extent to which the relevant opt out has been applied.

[148] For the details, see reg 52 of the 2009 Regulations. Since the 1974 Act could not be used as a basis for detracting from the provisions of the Directive, it will be apparent that the provisions of the 2009 Regulations are only disapplied where the corresponding provisions of the Consumer Credit Act are at least equivalent to, or more onerous than, the excluded terms of the 2009 Regulations themselves.

[149] Regulation 53 of the 2009 Regulations. On the features of a 'low value instrument' see para 5.52 above.

[150] Regulation 54(1) of the 2009 Regulations. The corporate opt out applies to this provision.

[151] Regulation 54(2) of the 2009 Regulations.

[152] Regulation 43(3). As the FSA 'Approach' paper (n 7 above) points out, an agreement to charge different prices for goods purchased with a credit card may be unlawful in the United Kingdom under the Credit Cards (Price Discrimination) Order 1990, but this does not prevent a retailer from unilaterally deciding to impose a charge or offer a discount (see para 8.77 of the paper).

[153] On the service provider's liability for unauthorized transactions falling within the scope of the 2009 Regulations, see para 5.69 below. Similarly, a bank which pays a cheque which has been forged or has

important to determine whether the authority and consent of the customer has been duly given or obtained.

5.58 The 2009 Regulations adopt a relatively formalistic approach to this question, and state that a payment transaction is only to be regarded as duly authorized by the payer if:[154]

(a) the payer has given its consent to that transaction or to the series of transactions of which the relevant payment forms a part;[155] and

(b) the necessary consent (i) may be given before or, if agreed between the payer and the service provider, after the execution of the payment transaction[156] and (ii) must be given in the form, and in accordance with the procedure, agreed between the payer and its service provider.[157]

5.59 In general terms, it is suggested that the necessary 'consent' can be inferred from the very fact that a payment instruction is delivered to the payer's payment service provider. The consent will, however, only be effective for this purpose if it is given in compliance with the terms of the contract between the parties. Thus, if the service provider wishes to accept instructions given by fax, telephone, or email, then it should ensure that the framework contract expressly allows it to do so.

5.60 Similarly, the payment transaction will be treated as unauthorized if the necessary consent is validly withdrawn. Consent may be withdrawn at any time before the payment order becomes irrevocable, or before the next payment in a series of transactions falls due.[158] Although, as noted above, the 2009 Regulations are relatively formalistic in terms of the requirements for the giving of consent, they say nothing about the formalities of its withdrawal. It is thus suggested that this issue should be governed by the terms of the agreement and that the same procedures should apply in each case. However, in a case of doubt as to the validity of any authority, the service provider should be entitled to defer complying with the payment order until the situation has been satisfactorily verified.[159]

---

otherwise paid without due authority cannot debit the customer's account since it has paid beyond the scope of its mandate: see para 17.14 below.

[154] On the points about to be made, see reg 55 of the 2009 Regulations.

[155] The latter formulation would obviously apply in the case of standing order or direct debit.

[156] The payment service user can thus ratify a payment made by the service provider and this will be deemed to be a duly authorized transaction.

[157] Regulation 55(2); the corporate opt out applies to these requirements.

[158] On these points, see reg 55(3) and 55(4) of the 2009 Regulations. On the relevant timing, see the discussion of reg 67 at para 5.80 below.

[159] The provider should incur no liability in respect of any resultant delay because it is an implied term of the contract that a bank can verify its mandate in the case of any doubt or dispute: see the position which arose in *Sierra Leone Telecommunication Limited v Barclays Bank Limited* [1998] 2 All ER 821, noted at para 15.22 below. It is submitted that such a term should likewise be implied into a framework contract or other agreement for the provision of payment services. It is further submitted that such an implied term would not be inconsistent with the terms of the 2009 Regulations themselves, although it will be necessary to return to this issue: see para 5.62 below.

Limits and Use of Payment Instruments

Regulations 56–58 of the 2009 Regulations contain various provisions on the use of **5.61** payment instruments.[160]

Regulation 56 allows for an agreement as to spending limits. It also allows the service pro- **5.62** vider to stop the use of the card on reasonable grounds relating to (i) the security of the card or any suspected unauthorized/fraudulent use[161] or (ii) the ability of the user to meet his obligations in respect of any associated credit line. The service provider must notify the user of the blocking of the card and its reasons for doing so, unless this would contravene anti-money laundering or other legislation, or would compromise the provider's security measures. The service provider must also reinstate or replace the card once the reasons for the block have ceased to exist.

The payment service user is required to use the card in accordance with the applicable terms **5.63** and conditions, to preserve the confidentiality of his PIN or similar security details and to notify the service provider without undue delay in becoming aware of any loss, theft or unauthorized use of the card.[162]

The payment service provider is, inevitably, subject to a rather longer list of obligations in **5.64** this area. In particular,[163] the service provider:

(a) must maintain the confidentiality of the PIN or other security feature;
(b) must not send an unsolicited card, except to replace an expiring card;
(c) must ensure that the payment service user at all times has access to a means to notify the service provider of the theft or misuse of the card;
(d) must, for a period of 18 months after it was made, provide to the user the means of proving that a loss/theft notification was made to the service provider;
(e) must ensure that no further use can be made of the card following a loss/theft notification; and
(f) must bear any losses flowing from the despatch of the card/PIN number to the payment service user.

Misuse of Payment Instruments

Inevitably, the most difficult issues in practice will arise in the context of disputes about **5.65** transactions which are (or which are alleged to be) unauthorized or fraudulent. The 'cloning' of credit cards has led to significant losses through fraud but, at the same time, card issuers will be wary of customers who may be seeking to evade their liability for larger transactions.[164]

---

[160] In the present context, this will apply principally to credit and debt cards.
[161] These provisions in some respects replicate the implied term discussed at para 5.60 above.
[162] Regulation 57 of the 2009 Regulations.
[163] On the points about to be made, see reg 58 of the 2009 Regulations.
[164] The most common complaint will be that a transaction has not been duly authorized by the payment service user, and the present discussion has been prepared on that basis. It should, however, be noted that the provisions about to be discussed apply equally to transactions which were properly authorized but which have been incorrectly executed by the service provider.

5.66 Regulations 59–64 seek to draw a balance between the competing interests of the service user and the service provider although, in the light of the analysis which follows, it is perhaps fair to observe that the weight of these provisions favours the user. It is thus necessary to examine the detailed provisions for the apportionment of liability between the two parties.

Time Limits

5.67 The starting point is that a payment service user can only make a claim against his provider in respect of an unauthorized transaction if he notifies the provider '… without undue delay, and in any event no later than 13 months after the debit date …' on becoming aware of a transaction which was unauthorized or has been incorrectly executed.[165] This provision does not apply where the arrangement is a regulated agreement for the purposes of the Consumer Credit Act 1974 (as amended).[166]

Evidence and Liability for Unauthorized Transactions

5.68 Regulation 60 of the 2009 Regulations[167] places evidential burdens firmly on the payment service provider in the event that the user alleges that a transaction was not authorized by him or that it was not correctly executed.

5.69 Once the user has made such an assertion—and there is no requirement for any further evidence to support it—then it is for the service provider to prove that the transaction was properly authenticated,[168] accurately recorded, entered into the service provider's accounts, and not affected by any technical breakdown or other deficiency. Furthermore, in cases of alleged unauthorized use, the mere fact that the use of the card has been recorded on the systems of the payment service provider is not in itself necessarily sufficient to prove either (i) that the transaction was in fact duly authorized by the user or (ii) that the payer had failed with intent or with gross negligence[169] to notify the issuer of the loss of the card without undue delay.[170] In other words, the mere fact that the card has been misused by a third party does not necessarily lead to the conclusion that the cardholder has been guilty of undue delay in a manner which would deprive him of the remedies now under discussion. However, the use of the word 'necessarily' should be carefully noted. Thus, if a cardholder complains of two unauthorized transactions several weeks apart, the first

---

[165] Regulation 59 of the 2009 Regulations. The expression 'without undue delay' and the permissible duration may be open to debate in particular cases. However, where the service user is receiving regular statements, the actual period allowed for notification ought in practice to be significantly less than 13 months. Note, however, that neither the 'without undue delay' nor the 13 month time limit applies if the service provider has omitted to provide to the user the information required under Pt 5 of the 2009 Regulations: see reg 59(2) and, on Pt 5, see paras 5.40–5.50 above. For larger customers, the corporate opt out applies and it should be possible significantly to reduce the 13 month period without unfairness to the service user.

[166] In that event, s 66 (acceptance of credit tokens), s 83 (liability for misuse of credit facilities) and s 84 (misuse of credit tokens) of the 1974 Act will apply instead.

[167] Note that the corporate opt out applies to reg 60.

[168] ie by reference to the PIN or other security features.

[169] On the significance of this formulation, see para 5.71 below.

[170] ie for the purposes of reg 57 of the 2009 Regulations, considered at para 5.63 above.

transaction could perhaps be seen as evidence that the holder had been guilty of undue delay in notifying the service provider before the second transaction had occurred.[171]

Where (i) a payment transaction was not duly authorized,[172] (ii) any loss or theft of the card **5.70** has been notified to the service provider without undue delay, and (iii) the service provider is unable to prove that the cardholder has acted fraudulently, then the service provider has to accept responsibility for the transaction concerned. It must accordingly make an immediate refund of the amount of the unauthorized payment transaction to the payer and, where necessary, restore the debited account to the balance it would have shown in the absence of that transaction.[173]

These provisions—especially those dealing with the burden of proof—may seem to be **5.71** burdensome from the perspective of the payment service provider. However, regulation 62 does provide for the user to be liable for unauthorized transactions, subject to various conditions and financial limits.[174] In particular:

(a) as noted above, the cardholder or service user is not generally liable for transactions which have not been duly authorized by him. However, by way of exception he is liable for up to £50 for transactions arising from (i) the use of a lost or stolen card or (ii) the misappropriation of the card, where the service user has failed to maintain the confidentiality of the PIN or other security features;[175]

(b) the payer is liable for all losses in respect of unauthorized transactions where (i) he has acted fraudulently or (ii) he has, intentionally or with gross negligence, failed to comply with his obligation to notify the service provider of any loss or theft without undue delay.[176] Fraud will obviously involve—at least in most cases—the deliberate passing of the card and PIN to a third party with the intention of denying liability for resultant transactions. Intentional failure to notify the issuer of the loss of the card means no more than a failure to do so after becoming aware of the loss. Gross negligence in failing to notify is obviously a slightly more difficult concept but perhaps involves a culpable failure to act when aware that the card is missing but without being certain whether it has been lost or stolen;

---

[171] This will be especially the case if the service user receives a statement after the first transaction, but before the second.

[172] See the discussion of reg 55 of the 2009 Regulations, at para 5.58 above.

[173] Thus, if interest or other charges have been debited as a result of the unauthorized transaction, these amounts must likewise be restored. On these points, see reg 61 of the 2009 Regulations. Once again, as in the case of reg 59, this provision does not apply if the arrangement is a regulated agreement for Consumer Credit Act purposes and, in that event, ss 64, 83 and 84 of the 1974 Act will apply instead see n 166 above.

[174] Once again, where the arrangement is a regulated agreement for Consumer Credit Act purposes, ss 66, 83 and 84 of that Act will apply in place of reg 62.

[175] Regulation 62(1) of the 2009 Regulations. 'Misappropriation' presumably refers to a temporary borrowing of a card by an acquaintance who has in some way acquired access to the PIN details. As the FSA points out in its 'Approach' paper (see n 7 above), 'personalized security details' must refer to the PIN or equivalent code, and would not extend to information available from the face of the card itself.

[176] See reg 57 of the 2009 Regulations, discussed at para 5.63 above.

(c) in the absence of fraud, the payer is not liable for any losses incurred in respect of an unauthorized transaction[177] where that loss arises (i) following notification of the theft or loss to the service provider, (ii) where the service provider has failed to provide adequate means for the notification of any theft or loss,[178] or (iii) the card has been used to complete a distance contract.[179]

5.72 Direct debit arrangements pose a slightly different set of problems in the area of unauthorized payments and liability for them. All payments made under a direct debit are 'authorized', in the sense that the account holder will have given a mandate to his bank to debit his account periodically with the amounts requested by the payee, and the authority is normally given without any pre-set financial limit. Yet there is always the risk that the payee will make an excessive claim.[180]

5.73 In essence,[181] a payment service user (the account holder) is entitled to a *full* refund of a direct debit payment if (i) the direct debit did not specify the precise amount to be paid on each payment date[182] and (ii) the amount of the payment '… exceeded the amount that the payer could reasonably have expected taking into account the payer's previous spending patterns, the conditions of the framework contract and the circumstances of the case'.[183] It is not easy to see how a bank can monitor this situation with a view to minimizing its liability, unless it is possible for its systems to generate an alert if a requested payment is a significant percentage above previous payments on the same direct debit.

5.74 It may also be noted that, although the trigger for the operation of this provision is the making of an excessive payment, the obligation to pay a refund relates to the entire payment, and not merely to the excess portion.

5.75 The payer must request the refund within eight weeks of the date of the debit. The bank may request such information as may be necessary to establish that the payment was excessive but, subject to that, the bank must either make the requested refund or state the reasons for its refusal.[184]

---

[177] See reg 62(3) of the 2009 Regulations. This would appear to override the payment service user's liability for up to £50, as discussed in para (a) above.

[178] ie in accordance with its obligation to provide such facilities under reg 58(1)(c) of the 2009 Regulations: see the discussion at para 5.64 above.

[179] ie a payment transaction concluded by telephone or other distance means, where the parties are not physically in each other's presence and PIN or similar details may not be required.

[180] A system to safeguard account holders against errors in payments under these instruments is already operated through the Direct Debit Scheme. But the rules about to be discussed have a broader ambit.

[181] On the provisions about to be discussed, see reg 63 of the 2009 Regulations. The corporate opt out applies to this provision.

[182] As noted above, this condition will invariably be met in the case of a direct debit. Where the instruction to the bank provides for fixed payments, this would be a standing order (rather than a direct debit).

[183] Regulation 63(2) of the 2009 Regulations. Reg 63(3) allows that the framework contract may stipulate for a refund even if these conditions are not met, although it is not immediately obvious why a payment service provider should wish to include such a provision in its standard terms and conditions. The parties may also agree that the right to a refund does not apply where the customer has given authority for the specific payment (although this will rarely be the case in the context of a direct debit arrangement): see reg 63(5) of the 2009 Regulations.

[184] On this point, see reg 64 of the 2009 Regulations.

Execution of Payment Transactions

Regulations 65–68 of the 2009 Regulations contain various provisions on the receipt, **5.76** refusal, and revocation of payment orders. These provisions are of some importance because they assist in determining whether a particular payment transfer was duly authorized, and the date from which permissible execution times are calculated.

First of all, the time of receipt of a payment order is, unsurprisingly, the time when it is **5.77** received by the payment service provider.[185] However, the service provider may stipulate for a 'cut-off' time for receipt of payment orders, and an order received after that time is deemed to be received on the next business day. Likewise, if the payment order is delivered on a non-business day, it is deemed to have been received on the ensuing business day.[186]

It was noted earlier that (i) foreign exchange transactions do not appear to fall within the **5.78** definition of 'payment services' in the 2009 Regulations, (ii) where a foreign exchange transaction is a necessary prelude to the transfer itself, a period of two business days is generally required to complete the preliminary spot transaction, and (iii) the execution periods provided in the 2009 Regulations do not appear to take account of this additional timing requirement.[187] It may be that a solution to this problem is offered by regulation 65(4)(c) of the 2009 Regulations, which provides that '… where the payment service user initiating a payment order agrees with the its payment service provider that execution of the payment order is to take place … on the day on which the payer has put funds at the disposal of the payment service provider, the time of receipt [of the payment order] is deemed to be the day so agreed …' It is submitted that funds are only '..at the disposal of [the] payment service provider …' when it holds the necessary funds in the currency *in which the transfer is required to be made.* If the service user requests the provider to make a payment in euro by debiting a sterling account, then the funds necessary to make the transfer are only at the disposal of the service provider on the day on which it receives the proceeds of the spot foreign exchange transaction. As a result, it is suggested that a bank's standard terms and conditions can provide for an additional two business days for the purposes of such a transaction, without breaching the requirements as to maximum execution times which are discussed below. This is also consistent with the view[188] that a 'payment transaction' for the purposes of the 2009 Regulations refers only to the necessary transfer of funds, and not to any necessary foreign exchange transaction.

As a general rule, if the terms and conditions of the payer's framework agreement have been **5.79** met, the service provider may not refuse to execute a payment order—whether initiated by

---

[185] This rule applies whether the order comes direct from the payer or through the payee under a direct debit arrangement: see reg 65 of the 2009 Regulations.

[186] On these points, see reg 65(2) and (3) of the 2009 Regulations. The relevance of these provisions becomes apparent when considering the allowable period for the execution of the payment transaction: see para 5.85 below. Likewise, if an order is delivered in advance but stipulates for the execution of the transaction on a specific day, then it is deemed to be received on that specified day, so that the execution periods run from the time stipulated by the user: see reg 65(4).

[187] See the discussion at para 5.09 above.

[188] Noted at para 5.09 above.

the payer or by the payee—unless the transaction would be unlawful.[189] If the service provider refuses to execute a payment order, it must notify the user of that fact and of the reasons for its decision.[190] The framework agreement may allow for an administrative or other charge if the refusal proves to be justified.[191]

5.80   Whilst the service provider may in some cases wish to refuse the payment order, the service user may in some cases wish to revoke it. If the order is validly revoked then, if the payment is subsequently made by the service provider, then it will be treated as unauthorized and would have to be refunded under the liability provisions already discussed.[192] The essential rules are as follows:

(a)   generally speaking, the order cannot be revoked after it has been received by the payer's service provider;[193]

(b)   where the payment is to be initiated by the payee, the payer cannot revoke the payment order after transmitting the order giving its consent to the transaction;[194]

(c)   in the case of a direct debit, revocation is only effective if received by the payer's service provider on the business day prior to the due date for payment;[195]

(d)   where the payer has specified a particular day on which the order is to be executed;[196] revocation is again only effective if received by the payer's service provider on the preceding business day;[197]

(e)   effective notice of revocation may be given at a later time if specifically agreed between the payer, his service provider and—where the transfer is initiated by the payee—the payee himself;[198] and

(f)   the framework agreement may allow the service provider to levy a charge for dealing with any revocation.[199]

5.81   In relation to the execution of payment orders, the payee's payment service provider must ensure that the full amount of the requested payment is transferred, and that no charges are deducted. In other words, such charges must be debited to the payer's account, and not to the transaction itself. The payee's service provider must likewise make the full amount of

---

[189] This would usually flow from a suspicion that the funds in the payee's account might represent the proceeds of crime. On this subject, see paras 7.28–7.73 below. On the position stated in the text, see reg 66(5) of the 2009 Regulations.

[190] eg because the payment order does not comply with the requirements of the framework contract, or because the payer's account lacks sufficient funds to make the transfer. It is not necessary to give reasons if it would be unlawful for the provider to do so: see reg 66(4) of the 2009 Regulations. Thus, if the reason for the refusal is a suspicion that the payer's account contains the proceeds of crime, then the service provider need not (indeed, should not) disclose that reason since this might alert the user to a possible money laundering investigation. On this subject, see paras 7.70–7.73 below.

[191] Regulation 66(3) of the 2009 Regulations.

[192] See paras 5.68–5.75 above.

[193] Regulation 67(1) of the 2009 Regulations.

[194] Regulation 67(2) of the 2009 Regulations.

[195] Regulation 67(3) of the 2009 Regulations. In other words, the payer's service provider must have sufficient time to cancel the order before it is processed by its systems.

[196] ie in accordance with reg 65(4), noted at para 5.77 above.

[197] Regulation 67(4) of the 2009 Regulations.

[198] Regulation 67(5) of the 2009 Regulations.

[199] Regulation 67(6) of the 2009 Regulations.

the payment available to the payee although, in this case, the payee and its provider may agree to the debiting of the provider's charges, provided that the full amount of the payment and the deducted charges are stated in the information provided to the payee. If other charges are deducted, then the providers may be required to rectify that situation.[200]

Execution Time and Value Date

Regulations 69–73 of the 2009 Regulations deal with the period of time within which a payment order must be executed and the value date for the benefit of the payee. **5.82**

So far as the payee is concerned, the position is relatively simple. He must be credited with the value of the payment not later than the business day on which the amount of the transaction is in turn credited to the account of his payment service provider, and the funds must be placed at the payee's disposal immediately after that credit has been received.[201] In a similar vein, the debit value date for the payer's account cannot be earlier than the date on which the relevant payment is effected.[202] **5.83**

As is the case for other provisions of the 2009 Regulations, the above rule will apply to a payment transaction in euro or in the currency of another EEA Member State which has not yet adopted the single currency. However, the 'next business day' value dating rule applies only to transactions effected in euro or in sterling.[203] The ambitious timeframe contemplated by that rule is recognized not to be practicable where some other EEA currency is involved.[204] **5.84**

The starting point is that the payer's service provider must ensure that the amount of the payment transaction is credited to the account of the payee's service provider by the end of the business day following the time of receipt of the payment order.[205] However: **5.85**

(a) as a transitional move and to allow time for completion of systems changes, the payer and his payment service provider may agree to extend this period to the third business day following receipt of the payment order. This transitional flexibility will however expire on 1 January 2012;[206]

---

[200] On these points, see reg 68 of the 2009 Regulations.

[201] Regulation 73 of the 2009 Regulations. In other words, the payee's service provider cannot enjoy free use of the payee's funds by deferring the required credit to the payee's own account.

[202] Regulation 73(3) of the 2009 Regulations.

[203] For the details, see reg 69(1) of the 2009 Regulations. The execution time and value date provisions only apply to a payment in sterling if it is executed wholly within the United Kingdom. This follows from an amendment made to reg 69(1)(b) made by reg 9 of The Payment Services (Amendment) Regulations 2009 (SI 2009/2475). Reg 69(2) is a slight curiosity, in that it states that a payment service user can agree with his service provider that those rules will not apply '… in respect of any other transaction … '. But, by virtue of the terms of art 69(1), those rules would not in any event be applicable to other transactions. The slightly confused drafting may flow from an attempt to transpose Art 68 of the PSD itself.

[204] The point is confirmed by the specific provisions of reg 70(4) of the 2009 Regulations, noted at para 5.85(f) below.

[205] Regulation 70(1) of the 2009 Regulations. On the effective time of receipt of the payment order for these purposes, see the discussion at para 5.77 above.

[206] Regulation 70(2) of the 2009 Regulations.

(b) the time limits for the payment are extended by a further business day where a payment transaction is initiated by way of a paper payment order;[207]

(c) where a transaction involves an EEA currency other than sterling or euro and is to be effected wholly within the EEA, then the account of the payee's service provider must be credited by the end of the fourth business day following receipt of the payment order;[208]

(d) the payee's service provider must value date and credit the amount of the payment to the payee's payment account following its receipt of the funds;[209]

(e) where the payee's service provider is to initiate the payment transaction (eg as in the case of a direct debit), it must do so within the time limits agreed with the payee so as to ensure that settlement occurs on the due date;[210]

(f) the above rules presuppose that the payee has an account with the payment service provider to whom the funds are remitted. But this is not, in fact, obligatory and, in that event, the service provider is required to make the funds available to the payee immediately after they have been credited to the service provider's own account.[211] This presumably means that the provider must stand ready to execute a further payment order in favour of an institution at which the payee does hold an account. Since, in the absence of any other agreed payment medium, any creditor generally also has the right to be paid in cash,[212] the payee can also presumably require payment in physical notes. However, the timing requirements set out in the 2009 Regulations would not appear to apply in such a case, since direct cash payments as between debtor and creditor are excluded from their scope;[213]

(g) the above rules have dealt with the receipt of funds on behalf of a payee from the payer pursuant to a payment order. However, as part of the process of ensuring that service users obtain proper value for their funds, it is also necessary that a service provider gives prompt value for funds received from its own client (eg to avoid or minimize interest charges on outward payment orders given at or about the same time as the delivery of the funds themselves). To that end, the 2009 Regulations require that funds provided by a consumer, a micro-enterprise, or a charity must be value dated[214] and made available no later than the close of business on the business day following the receipt of

---

[207] Regulation 70(3) of the 2009 Regulations. The expression 'paper payment order' is not defined by the 2009 Regulations. It cannot include a cheque, since transactions involving 'paper cheques' are wholly excluded from the scope of the 2009 Regulations by para 2(g) of Sch 1. Accordingly, 'paper payment order' must presumably refer to a fax or other physical document which requires some human intervention in order to process the payment—this being the reason for the introduction of an additional business day into the permitted processing cycle.

[208] Regulation 70(4) of the 2009 Regulations.

[209] Regulation 70(5) of the 2009 Regulations. Although not expressly stated, and for consistency with reg 73(1) (considered in subpara (h) below), this obligation presumably arises *immediately* following receipt of the funds.

[210] Regulation 70(6) of the 2009 Regulations.

[211] Regulation 71 of the 2009 Regulations.

[212] See *Libyan Arab Foreign Bank v Bankers Trust Company* [1989] QB 728.

[213] See para 2(a) of Sch 1 to the 2009 Regulations.

[214] Regulation 2 of the 2009 Regulations defines 'value date' as the reference time used by the service provider for the calculation of interest debited from or credited to a payment account.

funds by the service provider itself.[215] The significance of the 'value date' is that an outward remittance of a corresponding amount made on or after the value date cannot give rise to an obligation to pay interest to the service provider. Equally, if the service provider is paying interest on such balances,[216] then that interest must likewise accrue and be calculated on and from the value date;

(h) questions of value dating and availability of funds are, however, most directly addressed by regulation 73, which requires that (i) the credit value date for a payee's payment account must be no later than the business day on which the amount of the payment transaction is credited to the account of the payee's service provider itself[217] and (ii) the service provider of the payee must ensure that the funds are available for drawing and utilization by the payee immediately after those funds have been credited to the account of the service provider.[218] Correspondingly, the debit value date for the payer's account must be no earlier than the time at which the payment transaction is debited to that account;[219] and

(i) by way of exception from the general scheme of this part of the 2009 Regulations, it may be noted that these particular requirements apply to a payee's payment service provider even though the relevant funds are remitted from a service provider located *outside* the EEA.[220]

Liability

Regulations 74–79 of the 2009 Regulations contain various provisions dealing with the liability of the payment service provider in relation to the execution of transactions.   **5.86**

Specifically:

(a) a payment service provider may supply to his user a code (referred to in the 2009 Regulations as a 'unique identifier') for his payment account.[221] Where a transaction is executed in accordance with such a unique identifier, it is deemed to have been correctly executed by the payment service provider, so that it can have no liability to the payer in respect of that transaction.[222] Where the user provides an incorrect unique identifier, the provider is likewise not liable for non-execution or defective execution of the requested transaction.[223] So, if the payer provides an account number and a sort

---

[215] Regulation 72 of the 2009 Regulations.

[216] On the rules applicable to the investment of funds by non-bank payment service providers, see para 5.36 above.

[217] Regulation 73(1) of the 2009 Regulations.

[218] Regulation 73(2) of the 2009 Regulations.

[219] Regulation 73(3) of the 2009 Regulations.

[220] On this point, see reg 51(2) of the 2009 Regulations.

[221] The 'unique identifier' will in practice be (i) the sort code and account number for domestic payments in sterling and (ii) the BIC and IBAN number for a SEPA payment. On BIC and IBAN numbers, and the SEPA project more generally, see para 5.96 below.

[222] Regulation 74(1) of the 2009 Regulations.

[223] On the nature and scope of the service provider's liabilities, see the discussion of regs 75 and 76 below. Note, however, that the relevant information must be provided by the *user* of the service. Where the bank relies on information fraudulently provided by a third party in order to procure the transfer, then the bank will plainly be liable for the resultant losses. For an example of this type of situation, see the decision in *Nemur Varity Pty Ltd v National Australia Bank Ltd* [1999] VSCA 18 (Supreme Court of Victoria).

code, the bank has no liability for transferring funds to that account even if the account number does not correspond to the name of the intended payee.[224] The provider must, however, use his reasonable endeavours to recover any funds which have been disbursed, and may charge a fee for such recovery if the framework agreement so permits;[225]

(b) where a payment transaction is initiated by the payer, his service provider is strictly liable for its execution. The result is that the payment service provider must refund the amount of the transaction to the payer unless it can prove that the amount was actually received by the payee's service provider.[226] In addition to the refund obligation, the payer's service provider must make immediate efforts to trace any payment which appears to have gone astray, and must inform the payer of the outcome;[227]

(c) if, in such a case, it can be proved that the funds reached the account of the payee's service provider, then that service provider must make that amount available to the payee and credit his account accordingly;[228]

(d) the position is a little different where the payment order is initiated by the payee, as in the case of a direct debit. The payee's provider is liable for the correct transmission of the payment order within the time limits necessary to secure payment on the due date.[229] Where required, the payee's service provider must chase up any missing payment and advise the payee of the outcome.[230] If the payee's service provider can demonstrate that it is not liable under these provisions (ie that it sent the correct information to the payer's service provider in order to initiate the payment), then any liability for a failure or defect in the execution of the payment order is placed onto the payer's provider.

---

[224] See the commentary in the FSA 'Approach' paper (n 7 above), at para 8.140.

[225] Regulation 74(2) of the 2009 Regulations. The exoneration of the service provider under reg 74 is not affected by the fact that the user provided additional information which might have avoided the error: see reg 74(3). This reflects the fact that payment systems are computerized and will depend on the accuracy of the basic information as to sort codes etc.

[226] This is the effect of reg 74(1), (3) and (4) of the 2009 Regulations. The refund obligation appears to be absolute and an error or default by a correspondent bank or intermediate service provider does not appear to afford any form of defence. This view is reinforced by the fact that reg 78 creates a right of recourse where the liability of the payment service provider is traceable to an intermediary. This obligation may not be directly enforceable where the relevant intermediary is located outside the United Kingdom, since the contract between the service provider and the intermediary will often be governed by the law of the country in which the intermediary is located. Where the intermediary is located in another EEA State, it may be that a UK service provider could recover the indemnity under the local legislation giving effect to the relevant provisions of the PSD, although this point is not totally clear. The service provider may, in any event, have a claim for breach of contract against the intermediary, quite apart from the statutory indemnity.

[227] Regulation 75(3) of the 2009 Regulations.

[228] Regulation 75(5) of the 2009 Regulations. This apparently anodyne point assumes importance if, for example, having arrived in the account of the payee's service provider, the funds were misappropriated as a result of fraud or were lost as a result of the insolvency of the service provider's bank.

[229] Regulation 76(2) of the 2009 Regulations, read together with reg 70(6). The payee's service provider must also re-transmit the order if necessary, presumably in the event of error or mistake affecting the first attempt: see reg 76(3). There can be no obligation to repeat the request if it is rejected on account of insufficiency of funds: compare *Whitehead v National Westminster Bank Ltd*, The Times, 9 June 1982, noted in Law of Bank Payments, at para 3-004.

[230] Regulation 76(4) of the 2009 Regulations.

In that event, the payer's provider must refund the relevant amount to the payer and restore the payer's account to its previous position;[231]

(e) in addition, a payment service provider (usually, that of the payer) will be liable to its user for any charges or interest for which the user becomes liable as a result of the non-execution or defective execution of a payment transaction.[232] It may be noted that there is no cap on this liability, either as to time or as to amount and, since this is a *statutory* right to compensation, the usual obligation to mitigate losses in a *contractual* context will not apply. Nevertheless, it is submitted that the liability of the payment service provider is limited to the interest and charges suffered by the payer until the date on which he notifies the service provider of the defective or non-execution of the payment order[233] and, since the payer is obliged to notify the provider without undue delay when it becomes aware that the transaction has not been executed, this would appear to provide an effective cap on the *period* of the provider's liability. But the payer may become responsible for significant *rates* of interest as a result of the non-payment, and it seems that there is no cap on the service provider's liability in this sense;

(f) a payment service provider is allowed a right of indemnity against intermediaries responsible for errors which result in an obligation on the provider to reimburse or compensate his user;[234]

(g) finally, it is not generally possible for an obligation to pay money to be terminated by reason of the application of the doctrine of frustration.[235] However, a payment service provider is specifically absolved from liability in the event of *force majeure*, that is, when non-performance of an obligation under the above provisions results from '… abnormal and unforeseeable circumstances beyond the person's control, the consequences of which would have been unavoidable despite all efforts to the contrary …'. In addition, a service provider is excused if he is unable to perform an obligation as a result of some countervailing duty under Community or national law (eg as a result of the provisions of laws dealing with money laundering or terrorist financing).[236]

Access to Payment Systems

As noted earlier, one of the objectives of the 2009 Regulations is to create greater competi- **5.87** tion in the sphere of payment services. However, this objective would obviously be defeated if the new market entrants were unable to gain access to the payment systems and infrastructure which are necessary for the delivery of such services.

---

[231] Regulation 76(5) of the 2009 Regulations.

[232] Regulation 77 of the 2009 Regulations.

[233] Plus, perhaps, the few additional days until a corrected or replacement order is executed and the funds are received by the payee's service provider.

[234] Regulation 78 of the 2009 Regulations. This provision, and some of the difficulties associated with it, have already been noted in a slightly different context at n 226 above.

[235] On this issue, see Proctor, *Mann on the Legal Aspect of Money* (6th edn, OUP, 2005).

[236] On these points, see reg 79 of the 2009 Regulations.

5.88 Accordingly, and subject to certain exclusions,[237] the 2009 Regulations require that rules governing access to payment systems by authorized payment institutions, EEA authorized payment institutions, and small payment institutions (i) must be objective, proportionate, and non-discriminatory and (ii) must not restrict or inhibit access except insofar as that is necessary to safeguard against risks such as settlement, operational, or business risks, or is necessary to protect the financial or operational stability of the system.[238] Since restrictive rules affecting access to payment systems are effectively a competition matter, the Office of Fair Trading has power to launch an investigation where it believes that a rule or condition may contravene this prohibition.[239]

Powers of the FSA

5.89 With the exception of the limited powers of the Office of Fair Trading in relation to payment systems and to which reference has just been made, responsibility for monitoring and enforcing compliance with the 2009 Regulations rests with the FSA.[240] Very briefly, the FSA's powers include the following:

(a) power to require reports from the payment service providers;[241]
(b) power to issue a public censure in the event of a non-compliance with the regulations;[242]
(c) power to impose financial penalties for contraventions;[243] and
(d) power to require the restitution of profits earned as a result of any contravention of the 2009 Regulations.[244]

The Single Euro Payments Area

Introduction

5.90 It hardly needs to be stated that a regulatory initiative of the type contemplated by the Payment Services Directive will only have real effect if it is accompanied by an industry-wide endeavour to realize the broader objectives.

5.91 The industry initiative is known as the 'Single Euro Payments Area' (SEPA) and has been driven by the European Payments Council (EPC). But it is important to understand that this proposal did not materialize out of thin air. The European Union has long sought to

---

[237] The main exclusion relates to systems which are 'designated systems' for the purposes of the Financial Markets and Insolvency (Settlement Finality) Regulations 1999 (SI 1999/2979). This subject is discussed at paras 35.04–35.21 below.
[238] For the details, see reg 97 of the 2009 Regulations.
[239] See generally regs 98–109 of the 2009 Regulations.
[240] Regulation 81 of the 2009 Regulations.
[241] Regulation 82 of the 2009 Regulations.
[242] Regulation 84 of the 2009 Regulations.
[243] Regulation 85 of the 2009 Regulations.
[244] See regs 88–90 of the 2009 Regulations.

foster greater integration in the financial markets.[245] The most high-profile (and the most politically contentious) step in this direction was the introduction of the euro in 1999. Oddly enough, the euro started as a 'cashless' system, in the sense that euro notes and coins did not become available until 2002. Yet, while cash payments in euro became fungible in the sense that euro notes issued by countries of the authorized issuers[246] are accepted across the eurozone without discrimination, the same has not occurred in relation to cashless payments. A unified payment system for large value transfers was created by TARGET and its successor system, TARGET 2.[247] But this is a wholesale system, and does not really touch the consumer, who is confronted by different national payment systems at the *retail* level and practices (eg in the area of settlement, execution times, and the cost of transfers) which could vary very significantly from country to country.[248] If the euro was to achieve its full potential, transfers across the entire eurozone had to be made on the same footing, effectively as if they were purely domestic transfers. Thus, a payer needed to be able to make payments across the entire eurozone from a single bank account, and should not suffer any timing or other disadvantage merely because the recipient of the euro payment happens to be resident in another Member State.[249]

The challenge, therefore, was to create a retail system which would meet these needs and have the capacity to meet the settlement, execution and value date requirements of the Payment Services Directive itself. This challenge was taken up by the banking industry's decision to form the European Payments Council in 2002. The EPC has sought to develop the necessary technical framework and standards for SEPA.   **5.92**

The Aims and Objectives of SEPA

SEPA is intended to be an area in which payments may be made and received in euro,[250] whether within a Member State or across national borders, subject to the same procedures and legal obligations, regardless of the respective locations of the payer and the payee.   **5.93**

At a more political level, SEPA is seen as a project which will enhance European integration and harmonization, which will spur competition and improved/cheaper payment services for users.   **5.94**

With these objectives in mind, it has been said that SEPA consists of: **5.95**

(a) the euro as the single currency;
(b) a single set of euro payment instruments—credit transfers, direct debits and card payments;

---

[245] The 'passporting' system under the Recast Consolidation Directive is but one aspect of this process: see paras 2.13–2.24 above.

[246] That is, the national central banks of the eurozone and the European Central Bank itself.

[247] TARGET 2 is the clearing system for euro payments operated by the European Central Bank.

[248] An early attempt to harmonize the cost of domestic and cross-border payments in euro was made by Regulation (EC) No 2560/2001, of the European Parliament and of the Council of 19 December on cross-border payments in euro: OJ L 344, 28.12.01, p 13: see the discussion at para 5.101 below.

[249] The history and the development of this project is described in 'The Euro Payments Area (SEPA)—An Integrated Retail Payment Market' (European Central Bank, June 2009).

[250] It may be repeated that the SEPA project is confined to the euro, whilst the PSD applies to payments both in the single currency and in other EEA currencies.

(c) efficient processing infrastructure for euro payments;

(d) common technical standards;

(e) common business practices;

(f) a harmonized legal basis;[251] and

(g) ongoing development of new customer services.[252]

The Role of the EPC

5.96 As noted above, the EPC[253] is an industry body intended to drive the implementation of SEPA. It has published a number of rulebooks and guidelines (see below) and operates as a coordinating body for the banking industry in relation to SEPA. The EPC effectively divided its work into three stages, namely:

(a) the design phase, which began in 2004. This involved the creation of new credit transfer and direct debit schemes, together with the framework for SEPA-compliant cards and clearing arrangements;

(b) the second phase—the implementation phase—ran between 2006 and 2007. This phase involved preparations for the actual introduction of new SEPA instruments and standards. National implementation bodies were established in each Member State; and

(c) the migration phase, during which the existing national payment infrastructures will exist alongside the new SEPA arrangements. The objective is to achieve a full transition to SEPA over time and, when this is achieved, non-SEPA compliant payment services will cease to be available.

More specifically:

(a) the SEPA Credit Transfer Scheme for euro payments was launched in January 2008. The scheme creates common standards and facilitates the initiation and straight through processing of euro payments as between scheme participants. The details of the scheme are set out in the EPC's SEPA Credit Transfer Scheme Rulebook and the associated Implementation Guidelines;[254]

(b) the target implementation date for SEPA direct debit schemes was November 2009. This represented the first occasion on which a debit to an account with a bank in country A could be requested by a bank in country B, without the intervention of a correspondent bank in country B. Again, the EPC has published SEPA Direct Debit Scheme Rulebooks and associated Implementation Guidelines;

---

[251] This, of course, is intended to rest on the PSD and its national implementation. Although the Directive was designed with SEPA in mind, it will apply equally to payment transactions effected through existing national systems.

[252] On the various points made in this section, see the European Central Bank publication mentioned in n 249 above.

[253] For more information on the EPC and the documents referred to in this section, see www.europeanpaymentscouncil.eu.

[254] This also involved the introduction of a standard messaging format (ISO 20022XM) for euro transfers. Again this will assist in the move on to an integrated euro payments market.

(c) it has been agreed that the now familiar International Bank Account Number (IBAN) and the Bank Identifier Code (BIC) will be used in the context of SEPA payments; and

(d) turning now to card payments, the EPC has developed a SEPA Cards Framework, designed to ensure that debit and credit cards can be utilized on a pan-European basis.

The Benefits of SEPA

The perceived benefits of SEPA include: **5.97**

(a) the ability to make payments across the entirety of the eurozone from a single bank account, thus avoiding the need to open a local bank account in a number of countries to obtain the benefit of local processing and charging;

(b) since the use of payment cards will become an increasingly efficient process, there will be less need to carry significant amounts of cash;

(c) since payments will be processed on a SEPA-wide basis, this will enable retailers to use any payment processor anywhere within the euro area. This should lead to enhanced competition and lower costs in this sphere;

(d) for the corporate market, SEPA may be particularly helpful in reducing the number of bank accounts which it has to hold, thus reducing costs and saving administrative time;

(e) a single euro payments market will enhance the ability of banks to compete for this type of business across the entire eurozone.

These benefits should be enhanced by the introduction of payment institutions as new and competitive entrants to the market.

Progress with SEPA

As noted above, SEPA is essentially a market-driven project. At the time of writing, it is   **5.98** perhaps fair to say that progress has not been as rapid as might originally have been hoped.[255] Migration from existing national practices and systems to SEPA-compliant products has been slow, perhaps in part because of a desire to defer investment under prevailing economic conditions. As a result, the EC Commission has created a timetable for the completion of the SEPA-migration process, driven by public or State-owned administrations to demonstrate a political commitment to SEPA.

During the course of the implementation process, a concern appears to have been expressed   **5.99** that direct debit mandates may need to be re-executed to ensure that the paying bank retains sufficient authority from its customers.[256] This would obviously be a massive and a wholly impractical step. In any event, at least so far as English law is concerned, it is difficult to see any justifiable basis for this concern. A direct debit mandate is simply an authority from the customer to his bank to meet payment instructions initiated by the payee.

---

[255] On the points about to be made, see Communication from the Commission, 'Completing SEPA—A Roadmap for 2009–2012' (2009).
[256] See p 7 of the Commission Communication mentioned in the preceding footnote.

The document will not normally regulate the mode of payment or even its timing, and this process can be executed in accordance with prevailing banking practices at the time when payment falls due.

Charges for Cross-Border Payments

5.100   The high level objectives of the Payment Services Directive and of SEPA—a single market in payment services across the geographic area covered by the EEA. But, clearly, this objective will only really be achieved in practice if the cost of transferring funds across the entirety of that area is placed on a par with purely domestic transfers within national boundaries. Differential charges in this sphere would inevitably lead to (or preserve) the fragmentation of the single payments area along national lines.

5.101   This principle was originally recognized and given effect in 2001 by the regulation on cross-border payments in euro.[257] This regulation applied only to cross-border payments up to a limit of €50,000. This has now been superseded by a replacement regulation[258] which, in parallel with the Payment Services Directive, came into effect on 1 November 2009. The new regulation applies to cross-border payments in euro or in the national currencies of Member States which have agreed to extend the application of the regulation to their own national currencies.[259] Given that the regulation is directed to charges levied on the ultimate user of the payment services, it does not apply to charges as between payment service providers themselves.[260]

5.102   The regulation applies to electronically processed transactions where the service providers are located in different Member States.[261] The regulation is limited to *electronically* generated orders because paper-based and other orders require different processes and it was felt more difficult to impose a harmonized charging structure for those purposes.[262]

5.103   Article 3 may be regarded as the core provision of the regulation, requiring that charges levied on a payment service user for a payment of up to €50,000 shall be the same for both cross-border and purely domestic transfers.[263] Unlike its predecessor, the regulation applies to payments by way of direct debit.[264] In order to facilitate transactions, provision is made for the use of IBAN and BIC numbers.[265]

---

[257] Regulation (EC) 2560/2001 on cross-border payments in euro, OJ L344, 28.12.2001, p 13.

[258] Regulation (EC) 924/2009 of the European Parliament and of the Council on cross-border payments in the Community and repealing regulation (EC) 2560/2001, OJ L 266, 9.10.2009, p 11. The FSA has been charged with the supervision of compliance by payment service providers: see the Cross-Border Payments in Euro Regulations 2010 (SI 2010/89).

[259] See art 1(2) of the Regulation.

[260] Article 1(3) of the Regulation.

[261] Article 2(1) of the Regulation.

[262] See recital (6) to the Regulation.

[263] Note that the €50,000 limit has been retained, and the regulation is inapplicable to payments above that level. The payment service user is then left to negotiate his own deal in terms of cost. It should also be noted that, if an exchange transaction is required in order to effect the payment, the charges for that transaction are outside the scope of the regulation: see art 3(4).

[264] See regs 7 and 8.

[265] Article 4 of the regulation. On these points, see the discussion of the SEPA project below.

Information on the Payer

Finally, it should be noted that information on the payer must be included or made avail- **5.104** able in relation to any electronic funds transfer or (in some cases) must be made available on request. An EU regulation on this subject[266] requires complete information on the payer, including his name, address and account number or unique identifier.[267]

The requirement for the inclusion of payer information is designed to assist in the fight **5.105** against money laundering and terrorist financing.[268] A payee's payment service provider should query and/or reject a payment which is not accompanied by the necessary informa- tion.[269] It should, however, be appreciated that the payee information is provided *solely* for the purpose of complying with the provisions of the regulation and, apart from the specific anti-money laundering/anti-terrorist finance objectives, the account and other details probably remain confidential to the payer and his service provider and, hence, should not be disclosed to the payee by his service provider.

In terms of territorial scope, the provisions of the regulation apply to any transfer of funds **5.106** which is either initiated or received by a payment service provider established within the Community.[270] These rules will obviously apply cumulatively with the 2009 Regulations and other rules discussed in this chapter.

---

[266] Regulation (EC) 1781/2006 of the European Parliament and of the Council of 15 November 2006 on information on the payer accompanying the transfer of funds, OJ L 345, 8.12.2006, p 1. The regulation does not apply to paper-based instruments such as cheques, or to credit cards, where an audit trail should be available in any event. The regulation has been given further effect in the United Kingdom by the Transfer of Funds (Information on the Payer) Regulations 2007 (SI 2007/3298).

[267] For the details, see arts 4 and 5 of the regulation. Banks are required to retain this information for a period of five years.

[268] The point is made clear both by the recitals to the regulation and by art 1. The wider legislation designed to combat these activities is considered in Chapter 7 below.

[269] Article 9 of the regulation. Insofar as this implies an obligation to return the funds to the remitting bank, this may be problematical because it may alert the payer to the fact that his funds have fallen under suspicion, and yet art 9 also contemplates compliance with applicable anti-money laundering and terrorist financing legislation. It is submitted that a service provider should exercise great care before returning funds in this way since the multiplicity of transfers may itself serve to disguise the origins of the money. However, if the payee's service provider comes under a legal obligation to return the funds in this way, then it cannot thereby incur any liability to the payee for any resultant losses. This may be contrasted with the position which arose in *Tayeb v HSBC Bank plc* [2004] EWHC 1529 (Comm), where the bank exercised its own discretion in returning suspect funds but remained liable to the customer for the funds which had been remitted for his credit. The decision in *Tayeb* is discussed at paras 7.87–7.89 below.

[270] See art 3(1) of the regulation.

6

CAPITAL ADEQUACY, LIQUIDITY, AND LARGE EXPOSURES

Introduction

6.01 Banks occupy a vital position in any modern economy. If anything, this has been emphasized by the depth of the recession which gripped the United Kingdom—and much of the rest of the world—in 2008/2009. The recession was more pronounced in part because the banking industry was in many respects its source, and declining confidence in the stability of such institutions had a major adverse impact on public trust in the financial system as a whole.

6.02 As a result, the rules on the adequacy of the capital resources available to financial institutions, and the risks which they take with that capital, are of more importance than ever. It is perhaps unfortunate that the financial crisis took hold just as the new capital adequacy framework introduced by Basel II was being introduced—this is thought by some to have made the situation worse.[1]

---

[1] The system introduced by Basel II requires the re-assessment of risks and, as the credit quality of a particular borrower or counterparty declines, it becomes necessary to ascribe additional capital to that risk. As a consequence, banks lacked the capital necessary to provide further facilities, with the result that an economy already in crisis was starved of credit.

6.03　But however that may be, capital adequacy rules are assuming greater importance both to banks themselves and—in view of concerns about the stability of the financial system as a whole—to the wider public. The present chapter therefore examines the current capital adequacy framework and associated provisions designed to ensure that a bank's business is managed on a prudent basis. This chapter also examines other closely allied topics which may affect the stability of the banking system namely, liquidity and large exposure requirements.

6.04　Against this background, it is proposed to examine the following matters:

(a)　the broad framework for capital adequacy;
(b)　the origins of the Basel standards;
(c)　the provisions of Basel II;
(d)　the terms of Pillar One of Basel II and the composition of eligible bank capital;
(e)　the calculation of a bank's risk-weighted assets;
(f)　the nature and effect of credit risk mitigation techniques;
(g)　Pillar Two and Supervisory Review;
(h)　Pillar Three and Market Discipline;
(i)　the reform of Basel II;
(j)　liquidity rules;
(k)　limitation and disclosure of large exposures; and
(l)　the conclusions to be drawn from this chapter.

Capital Adequacy—The Broad Framework

6.05　At the highest level of generality, one may perhaps begin this survey by referring to two of the FSA's Principles for Businesses,[2] which set out in very broad terms the bases on which an authorized institution should operate its business. Specifically:

(a)　Principle 3 states that 'A firm must take reasonable care to organise and control its affairs responsibly and effectively, with adequate risk management systems'; and
(b)　Principle 4 requires that 'A firm must maintain adequate financial resources'.

6.06　It seems that these two principles must at least to some extent be linked, since the adequacy of a bank's financial resources can only be measured against the risks which the institution takes and the effectiveness of the systems which it has in place to manage those risks.[3] However that may be, these general principles do not of themselves offer a sufficient basis for the supervision of large and complex financial institutions.

6.07　It thus becomes necessary to turn to the capital adequacy standards themselves, which have largely been driven by the Basel Committee on Banking Supervision.

---

[2] FSA Handbook, PRIN.
[3] This point is implicitly acknowledged by the rules relating the internal ratings-based approach to capital adequacy, which allows for less capital to be held where a bank can demonstrate the sophistication of its risk management processes. On this subject, see paras 6.33–6.39 below.

The Basel Standards

The Basel Committee on Banking Supervision

As noted elsewhere, the Basel Committee on Banking Supervision originally consisted of **6.08** the governors of the central banks of the G10 although its membership has in recent years been expanded to include a number of other countries. The Committee meets at the Bank for International Settlements in Basel, and is an informal grouping in the sense that it does not have its basis in a treaty or agreement between the relevant States. Although therefore lacking any formal or legal authority, the standards which it sets have generally been accepted as appropriate for banks which are active in the cross-border sphere.

The Committee's first major work resulted in the 1975 Basel Concordat on consolidated **6.09** supervision and cooperation between national supervision of international banks.[4] In 1997, it also published its guidelines on an effective supervisory system as 'Core Principles for Effective Banking Supervision'. However, the Committee is best known for its work in the field of capital adequacy.

The Committee's first Capital Accord (hereafter 'Basel I') was the first attempt to create a **6.10** framework of *international* capital standards for banks. Such a framework may be said to have two advantages. First of all, the imposition of minimum standards would help to ensure the stability of the international financial system as a whole. Secondly, it would ensure that banks could not secure a competitive advantage as a result of the imposition of 'softer' capital requirements by its own, home State.

The imposition of minimum capital requirements requires a consideration of various fac- **6.11** tors, including:[5]

(a) What will constitute 'capital'?
(b) What percentage of the bank's risks (assets) should be covered by capital?
(c) How are the bank's assets to be 'valued' in terms of the likelihood of loss or default?

Although Basel II (discussed below) was arguably presented as a radical reform of capital **6.12** adequacy rules for international banks, it should be borne in mind that some of the essential principles remain the same. Specifically:

(a) The rules set out in Basel I as to what constitutes a bank's 'capital' have not changed in any material way.[6]
(b) The percentage of the bank's risks to be covered by a bank's capital was set at a minimum of 8 per cent under both Basel I and Basel II.

---

[4] Although not of direct relevance in the present context, it may be noted that the history and negotiation of the Concordat were considered in some depth in *Three Rivers District Council v Bank of England* [2006] EWHC 816 (Comm), since the very issue of supervisory responsibility was at issue in that case. The decision is discussed in Chapter 14 below.

[5] The items discussed below must clearly be applied on a uniform basis in order to achieve a code which has uniform international application.

[6] However, for current proposals in this area, see 'Reform of Basel II', at paras 6.57–6.58 below.

(c) The key change introduced by Basel II is in the calculation or valuation of the assets which are subject to the capital requirement (a process known as 'risk weighting'). As will be seen, this process has become significantly more complex under Basel II.

6.13 Since the first two items remained significantly the same, they are considered in relation to Basel II, below. But, for comparative purposes, a few points should be made about the risk-weighting provisions under Basel I. The rules in this area came to be criticized as being too simplistic. For example:

(a) exposures to (or guaranteed by) Zone A governments and central banks[7] attracted a zero per cent weighting;

(b) exposures secured by cash collateral/netting arrangements likewise qualified for a zero per cent weighting;

(c) exposures secured by a charge over debt securities issued by Zone A governments/central banks took a 20 per cent weighting;

(d) exposures to residential property were weighted at 50 per cent; and

(e) other exposures—including exposures to corporate borrowers—required a risk weighting of 100 per cent.

6.14 It will immediately be seen that the risk weighting rules were something of a blunt instrument:

(a) A five year facility to a Zone A government would be risk weighted at zero per cent for the entire period of the facility, regardless of any changes in the creditworthiness of that country over that period.

(b) *All* corporate risks attracted a risk weighting of 100 per cent. This rule obviously meant that a bank could not discriminate between well-known corporate names and small borrowers.

(c) In addition, and except in limited cases involving recourse to cash balances, the fact that the bank held security for its facility did not affect the attributable risk weighting.

6.15 On the other hand, banks might be subject to risks which were not taken into account—and for which no capital was therefore needed—under Basel I, for example, market, operational, or interest rate risk.

6.16 With the benefit of this general background, it is thus now possible to turn to the revised framework.

Basel II

Introduction

6.17 The Basel Committee issued its paper, 'International Convergence of Capital Measurement and Capital Standards—A Revised Framework' (Basel II) in June 2004. Countries were

---

[7] 'Zone A' referred to OECD members and certain other countries.

expected to implement the new framework by January 2007, although there was a discretion to extend this for one year.

As in the case of Basel I, the European Union issued directives to Member States to implement Basel II at the national level. This was principally achieved through the Capital Requirements Directive, which was approved in 2005.[8] In the case of the United Kingdom, implementation of the Directive has largely been achieved through the FSA Handbook.[9] **6.18**

As the Basel Committee states in its introduction to Basel II,[10] its fundamental objectives in seeking to revise Basel I were: **6.19**

(a) to develop a framework that would strengthen the soundness and stability of the international banking system;

(b) to maintain sufficient consistency to ensure that capital adequacy would not be a source of competitive inequality among banks; and

(c) to promote the adoption of stronger risk management practices by the banking industry.[11]

In pursuance of these objectives, the Committee notes that it had '… sought to arrive at significantly more risk-sensitive capital requirements that are conceptually sound …'. Whilst recording that it had retained the key elements of Basel I in terms of the definition of eligible capital and the key 8 per cent ratio,[12] it notes that it intends to review the definition of eligible capital in the longer term.[13] The Committee also envisages that further changes may be introduced at a later date to provide for a regulatory approach based on banks' internal risk models, provided that issues about reliability, validation, and competitive equity can be met.[14] **6.20**

By way of general overview, the Basel II framework is based on three key 'Pillars', as follows: **6.21**

(a) The first pillar—titled 'Minimum Capital Adequacy'—sets out the calculation of eligible capital and the quantification of counterparty and other risks which that capital must cover.

---

[8] Insofar as the capital requirements apply to credit institutions, the relevant rules are to be found in the Recast Banking Consolidation Directive, to which reference has already been made.

[9] Principally via the BIPRU and GENPRU sections of the Handbook. For aspects of the rules which fall within the responsibility of the Treasury, see the Capital Requirements Regulations 2006 (SI 2006/3221) and, for proposed amendments dealing with cross-border supervision and other matters, see HM Treasury: 'Implementing Amendments to the Capital Requirements Directive' (December 2009).

[10] See para 4 of the Introduction.

[11] In translation, this means that banks will need less capital if they can demonstrate that they have in place robust and effective risk management techniques. As explained above, these flexibilities were not available under the fairly rigid parameters of Basel I, and the Committee saw this particular change as one of the major benefits of Basel II.

[12] Paragraph 5 of the Introduction to Basel II.

[13] See para 17 of the Introduction. This is a follow-on from the Committee's Press Release 'Instruments eligible for inclusion in Tier 1 capital' (October 1998).

[14] Paragraph 18 of the Introduction. Given the events of 2008–2009, it may be that some time may have to elapse before there is a further loosening of capital adequacy requirements.

(b) The second pillar—titled 'Supervisory Review Process'—addresses prudential super-vision generally and a bank's access to 'higher grades' of review under the Internal Ratings-Based approach.[15]

(c) The third pillar—titled 'Market Discipline'—deals with the requirement for banks to publish information concerning their capital structures and the risks which are inher-ent in their businesses. This is, in a sense, a quid pro quo for the greater flexibility afforded to banks under Basel II as a whole.

6.22 As others have noted,[16] Basel II deals extensively with capital adequacy but does not really address the problems which occurred from 2007 onwards in the context of the 'credit crunch', namely, liquidity and the sources of funds used by a bank to run its business.[17] As will be seen, Basel II also depends to some extent on credit assessments made by rating agencies or in some cases, made by the banks internally. Once again, recent events may mean that the wisdom of that approach may have to come up for reconsideration at an appropriate time.

Pillar One—Eligible Capital

6.23 As noted earlier, the rules as to the required ratio and the ascertainment of eligible capital have not been materially varied from those contained in Basel I. Indeed paragraph 40 of Basel II confirms that the total capital ratio must be not less than 8 per cent, whilst para-graph 41 confirms that, subject to various minor revisions, the definition of eligible regula-tory capital remains as set out in Basel I. But it nevertheless remains to consider how a bank's eligible capital is calculated.

6.24 In this context, it may be helpful to note the following points:

(a) For capital adequacy purposes, the concept of 'capital' is not limited to equity share capital as that expression is generally understood. From a regulatory perspective, 'capi-tal' is represented by the funds or assets which will be available to meet losses and—in the event of liquidation—will thus be distributed to creditors before any payment is made to the bank's shareholders.[18]

(b) In line with this philosophy, Basel I allowed for three 'tiers' of capital[19] which could be taken into account in calculating the 'eligible regulatory capital' side of the equation.[20]

---

[15] The internal ratings-based approach involves more sophisticated and capital-efficient methods of meas-uring a bank's customer exposures. This subject is discussed at paras 6.33–6.39 below.

[16] See, for example, McKnight, para 2.10.1.

[17] On liquidity more generally, see paras 6.59–6.61 below.

[18] On the general characteristics of Tier One capital, see GENPRU 2.2.9G.

[19] Although as will be seen, both Tier Two and Tier Three capital are divided into an 'upper' and a 'lower' tier for these purposes.

[20] The rules as to the calculation and composition of eligible regulatory capital are found in chapter 2 of the Recast Banking Consolidation Directive and these have been transposed by the FSA into GENPRU 2. Annex 2 to GENPRU 2 sets out a useful table which assists in understanding the structure of the capital side of the requirements.

(c) Tier One (or 'core') capital must account for at least 50 per cent of the total regulatory capital requirement. Tier One capital consists of (i) permanent share capital, which generally refers to ordinary shares[21] including any share premium account,[22] (ii) perpetual non-cumulative preference shares,[23] and (iii) innovative Tier One instruments.[24] Certain deductions must be made in calculating Tier One capital.[25]

(d) Tier Two capital is divided into an upper and lower tier, and the upper tier must constitute at least 50 per cent of the total of Tier Two capital.

(e) Upper Tier Two capital consists of (i) perpetual cumulative preference shares,[26] (ii) perpetual subordinated debt and similar securities,[27] (iii) revaluation reserves,[28] and (iv) certain general and surplus provisions.[29]

(f) Lower Tier Two capital includes (i) fixed term preference shares,[30] (ii) long term subordinated debt, and (iii) fixed term subordinated securities.[31]

(g) At this stage of the calculation, certain deductions must be made from the total of Tier One and Tier Two capital, including the value of investments in subsidiaries and associates, securitization positions and the value of any capital instruments issued by other banks or financial institutions.[32]

(h) Upper Tier Three capital consists of short term subordinated debt,[33] whilst lower Tier Three capital is made up of the net interim trading book profit and loss.[34]

---

[21] GENPRU 2.2.83R.

[22] GENPRU 2.2.101R. The share premium account represents any amount received by a bank on an issue of its shares, over and above the nominal value. Company law prohibits the repayment of this account and, for all practical purposes, it is therefore equivalent to ordinary share capital.

[23] ie preference shares in respect of which (i) the right to a dividend is lost if it cannot be paid in any particular year and (ii) the redemption option is exercisable only by the issuer: GENPRU 2.2.109R and GENPRU 2.2.110G.

[24] These particular instruments must exclude any right for the holder to take any form of insolvency proceedings and must not be required to be taken into account in considering the solvency of the issuing institution: GENPRU 2.2.116R. In other words, they must share some of the main characteristics of equity share capital.

[25] eg the value of any of the bank's investments in its own shares, and certain tangible assets: see GENPRU 2.2.155R.

[26] Note that the cumulative element involves a continuing obligation to meet the dividend payment, in contrast to non-cumulative preference shares which are included in Tier One.

[27] On items (i) and (ii), see GENPRU 2.2.159R–GENPRU 2.2.181R.

[28] GENPRU 2.2.185R.

[29] GENPRU 2.2.187R–GENPRU 2.2.193R.

[30] Once again, the shares must only be redeemable at the option of the issuer and it must be a term that the redemption cannot occur before the fifth anniversary of the issue date: GENPRU 2.2.172R.

[31] For the details of the instruments referred to in this paragraph, see GENPRU 2.2.159R–GENPRU 2.2.196R. The relevant contractual provisions in a subordinated debt agreement or instrument will often state that the rights of the creditors will be subordinated '… in the event of a winding up …' of the issuing bank. In order to give effect to the intention of the parties to create a Tier Two capital instrument, the reference to a 'winding up' may have to be read so as to extend to an administration or equivalent process under any relevant foreign law: see *Re Kaupthing Singer & Friedlander Ltd (in administration)* [2010] EWHC 316 (Civ).

[32] For details, see GENPRU 2.2.202R–GENPRU 2.2.233R.

[33] Such debt may only be included if (i) it has an original maturity of at least two years, or a two year notice period and (ii) payments in respect of the instrument are only permitted if the bank would remain in compliance with its solvency ratio: GENPRU 2.2.241R–GENPRU 2.2.245R.

[34] On the calculation of this amount, see GENPRU 2.2.246R–2.2.249R.

(i) Deductions from the resultant figure include (i) the excess trading book position[35] and (ii) free deliveries.[36]

6.25 The figure resulting from this calculation is the bank's *eligible regulatory capital*. The bank is required to monitor its regulating capital *at all times* to ensure that it is in compliance with the Pillar One capital requirements.[37] In broad terms, it is this figure which must constitute at least 8 per cent of the risk-weighted assets.

6.26 Before moving on to related issues, it may be appropriate to make a few general observations about the capital resources rules noted above. First of all, it has already been noted that capital is required to absorb potential losses which may be incurred by the bank. Applying this test, Tier One (or 'core') capital meets the necessary criteria because it is permanent, available to meet losses, ranks for payment after all other debts and liabilities and has no fixed costs, since dividends are payable only out of profits.[38] In contrast, Tier Two capital is not necessarily permanent, and will carry some fixed funding costs, but will usually at least display a medium to long term element. Tier Three capital is a further rung down the ladder, consisting of debt which (although subordinated) has a relatively short maturity, and of trading book profits which will not have been externally verified.[39] Finally, it should be appreciated that the eligible regulatory capital figure is not quite as straightforward as paragraphs (a)–(i) above may seek to suggest. For example, there are various restrictions on the manner in which particular parts or tiers of eligible capital can be used to meet particular requirements.[40] At this point, one descends to a microscopic level of detail which is beyond the scope of this book but, hopefully, this discussion has provided a sufficient overview of the elements which make up the eligible regulatory capital.[41]

6.27 Obviously, having calculated the eligible capital side of the equation, the question is: what is the figure to go on to the risk-weighted assets side? As noted earlier, the basis on which risk-weighted assets are to be calculated is one of the major areas of change introduced by Basel II. The search for a more risk-sensitive approach to the allocation of capital resources has inevitably resulted in a significant degree of complexity.

---

[35] That is, the excess of the bank's net long trading book positions in shares or subordinated debt of other banks or financial institutions: GENPRU 2.2.262–GENPRU 2.2.265.

[36] Free deliveries are described in BIPRU 14.4. They consist of transactions under which one side of a securities transaction (payment or delivery) has occurred in advance of performance of the corresponding obligations by the other party to the trade.

[37] See GENPRU 2.1.9. Note that, in accordance with the terms of the Recast Banking Consolidation Directive (see para 2.11 above) and GENPRU 2.1.48, a bank's capital resources must in any event be at least €5 million. The consequences of the requirement to monitor compliance at all times have already been mentioned: see n 1 above.

[38] See GENPRU 2.2.9G.

[39] On Tier Two and Tier Three capital, see GENPRU 2.2.11 and 2.2.12.

[40] See, for example, the limits on the use of different kinds of capital as set out in GENPRU 2.2.42R–GENPRU 2.2.49R.

[41] On proposed revisions to the composition of the eligible capital calculation, see 'Reform of Basel II' at para 6.56 below.

Risk-Weighted Assets

Introduction

In order to provide for a more sophisticated approach to risk assessment and the calculation **6.28** of risk-weighted assets, Basel II contemplates two main systems for banks:

(a) The Standardized Approach, where risk weightings are to a significant extent based on the assessments of external credit rating agencies such as Moodys or Standard & Poors;[42] and

(b) The Internal Ratings-Based (IRB) Approach, where banks can use their own assessment of borrower/counterparty risk provided that they can persuade the regulator of the quality of their risk management systems.[43] The IRB approach is itself divided into a 'foundation' and 'advanced' approach.[44]

The Standardized Approach

The rules governing the standardized approach to credit risk are found in Articles 78–80, **6.29** Annex II, and Annex VI to the Recast Consolidation Directive, and these have been implemented by the FSA under the terms of BIPRU 3 of the Handbook.

BIPRU 3 begins with the core requirement to which reference has already been made, **6.30** namely that the capital requirement is 8 per cent of a bank's risk-weighted exposure amounts. It then requires the bank to assign each of its exposures to a prescribed series of 'exposure classes', including (i) claims on central governments or central banks, (ii) claims on regional/local authorities, (iii) claims on administrative bodies, (iv) claims on international organizations, (v) claims on financial institutions, (vi) claims on corporates, and (vii) retail claims.[45] Ratings published by approved rating agencies[46] may then be used to calculate the risk weighting applicable to particular exposures.[47]

The core provisions on risk weighting are then set out in BIPRU 3.1. The starting point for **6.31** many of the risk categories noted above[48] is that the risk weighting should be 100 per cent

---

[42] The standardized approach is designed for use by banks involved in less complex forms of lending and underwriting and in practice will therefore probably be used only by smaller institutions.

[43] This subject is discussed at para 6.35 below.

[44] Again, these are discussed at para 6.38 below.

[45] For the full list, see GENPRU 3.2.9R.

[46] Referred to in BIPRU 3 as 'ECAI'—external credit assessment institutions. These organizations must be recognized by the FSA for present purposes: see BIPRU 3.3. One of the misfortunes of Basel II is that it came into force at a time when some of the work undertaken by such agencies was being called into question. For the resultant EU initiative in this area, see the Commission's Proposal for a Regulation of the European Parliament and of the Council on Credit Rating Agencies (COM (2008) 704 final, 12 November 2008). The proposed regulation would create a registration and surveillance framework, address the problems created by conflicts of interest, and require greater transparency. These issues do not, however, directly affect the role assigned to such agencies under the Basel II structure or the FSA Handbook.

[47] See BIPRU 3.3.1R.

[48] See para 6.30 above.

of the value of the exposure. But this is then scaled back if the borrower is rated, with the extent dependent on the precise rating level.[49]

6.32 Some exposures automatically attract a zero per cent risk weighting.[50] In addition, the risk weight of transactions in default may have to be increased up to the level of 150 per cent.[51] This serves further to emphasize that the assessment of capital adequacy is a dynamic process under Basel II and the national legislation which has implemented it, with the result that the amount of capital to be attributed to a particular transaction may fluctuate significantly throughout its life.[52]

The Internal Ratings-Based Approach

6.33 The IRB approach is outlined in BIPRU 4 which, in turn implements Parts 1, 2 and 3 of Annex VIII of the Recast Consolidation Directive.

6.34 In contrast to the position under the standardized approach, the level of the capital requirement for a bank using this approach is based on the bank's own estimate of certain risk parameters.[53]

6.35 The use of an IRB approach is subject to the prior approval of the FSA. That consent will only be forthcoming if the bank's internal systems for the management and rating of credit risk are sound and are implemented with integrity. They must also meet certain minimum standards. In particular:[54]

(a) the bank's rating system must provide for meaningful assessment of obligor/transaction characteristics;[55]

(b) the internal ratings and default/loss estimates used in the calculation of the capital requirements must play an essential role in the credit approval, capital allocation, and corporate governance of the bank;[56]

(c) the bank's rating systems are managed by a credit risk control unit which is appropriately independent and free from undue influence;

---

[49] If the rating indicates a negative outlook, then the amount of the asset to be taken into account for risk weighting purposes may be increased to 150 per cent: see, for example, the table dealing with sovereign risk assessment as part of BIPRU 3.4.2R.

[50] eg exposures to the European Community, the International Monetary Fund and the Bank for International Settlements: BIPRU 3.4.30.

[51] See generally, BIPRU 3.4.96R–BIPRU 3.4.101R.

[52] The practical difficulty is that, as credit quality deteriorates, more capital has to be ascribed to transactions already on a bank's books. This inevitably reduces a bank's ability to take on new business, and thus tends to restrict the ability of banks to provide credit during a recessionary period. The problem has already been noted in general terms: see n 1 above.

[53] Note that it may be possible for a bank to use a combination of the standardized and the IRB approaches—eg where the bank has only a small number of customers in a particular exposure class and it would be unduly burdensome for the bank to implement a rating system for those particular counterparties. For details, see BIPRU 4.2.26R.

[54] On the points to be made, see BIPRU 4.2.2R.

[55] The possible nature, content and effect of such systems is discussed in BIPRU 4.2.5G.

[56] In other words, it is not sufficient that the bank has reliable systems to assess risk; that information must be properly used in the bank's key decision-making fora. Or as the matter is expressed in the guidance in BIPRU 4.2.7G, the IRB approach must be an integral part of the bank's business and should have a substantial influence on its decision-making and actions.

(d) the bank collects and stores all data necessary to provide effective support for its credit risk processes; and

(e) the rating systems are documented and validated.

A firm will only receive FSA approval for the IRB approval if it can show that it has been **6.36** using essentially similar risk management processes for the three year period before the IRB permission is granted.[57]

Once again, a bank using the IRB approach must assign its exposures to particular exposure **6.37** classes, including claims on governments, institutions, corporates and retail customers.[58] There are detailed rules for the valuation of different types of exposure and the level of detail moves beyond the scope of a work of this kind. However, in order to illustrate the operation of the IRB approach in the valuation of exposures, it is proposed to consider in outline the terms of BIPRU 4.4 which applies to exposures to corporates, institutional, and sovereign entities.[59]

The formula for calculation of the risk-weighted exposure amounts for the relevant side of **6.38** the capital adequacy equation is set out in BIPRU 4.4.58.[60] It is fair to say that this formula will be beyond the comprehension of many lawyers, and the present writer will certainly not attempt to explain it. But the 'inputs' into this formula are defined in the Glossary to the FSA Handbook and will be more readily understandable. The nature of these definitions also helps to identify that the relevant provisions are aimed at ascertaining a satisfactory risk weighting, having regard to the likelihood of default and loss. An analysis of these factors also helps to explain the difference between the IRB foundation and the IRB advanced approaches. Thus, the inputs or factors to be taken into account in applying the formula include:

(a) *Probability of Default (PD)*. PD represents the probability of a default by a counterparty over a one year period. A bank using either the IRB foundation or the IRB advanced approach must use its own estimate of PD, ascertained in accordance with the minimum IRB requirements discussed above.[61] The PD for a corporate or institutional exposure must be at least 0.03 per cent and, if the exposure is in default, the PD must be 100 per cent.[62]

(b) *Loss Given Default (LGD)*. This is defined as the ratio of the loss on an exposure due to the default of the counterparty to the amount outstanding at default. Subject to the

---

[57] BIPRU 4.2.11. This mirrors the requirement in Art 84(3) of the Recast Banking Consolidation Directive.

[58] See BIPRU 4.3.2. This list is similar to, although shorter than, the corresponding provisions for the standardized approach, discussed at para 6.29 above.

[59] It will be recalled that 'institutions' refers to banks and other financial institutions. The other categories of risk dealt with in relation to the IRB approach are (i) specialized lending exposures (BIPRU 4.5), (ii) retail exposures (BIPRU 4.6), (iii) equity exposures (BIPRU 4.7), (iv) purchasing receivables (BIPRU 4.8), and (v) securitization (BIPRU 4.9).

[60] Reflecting the Recast Banking Consolidation Directive, Annex VII, Pt I.

[61] See para 6.35 above.

[62] BIPRU 4.4.63R–4.4.66R. PD must be estimated by reference to particular obligor grades from long run averages of one year default rates. For this and other detailed rules about the ascertainment of PD, see BIPRU 4.4.23R–BIPRU 4.4.31R.

availability of credit risk mitigation[63] and certain other details, a bank using the IRB foundation approach is required to apply an LGD value of 45 per cent for senior exposures and 75 per cent for subordinated exposures,[64] whilst a bank using the IRB advanced approach must use its own estimates of LGD.[65]

(c) *Exposure at Default (EAD)*. The exposure value reflects the amount likely to be outstanding in the event of a default by the borrower. For a bank using the IRB foundation approach, the exposure value must be the full amount of a committed facility. However, this is then multiplied by a conversion factor expressed in percentage terms, which thus reduces the overall value.[66] Once again, however, a bank using the IRB advanced approach may use its own estimates of the necessary conversion factors.[67]

6.39 It will thus be seen that the key difference between the IRB foundation and the IRB advanced approaches lies in their respective number of independent 'inputs' into the risk-weighted asset calculation. The IRB foundation approach still depends significantly on factors prescribed by the regulator.

Credit Risk Mitigation

Introduction

6.40 The foregoing parts of this chapter have considered the calculation of eligible regulatory capital and of the risk-weighted assets (or exposure) for which the capital is intended to provide cover.

6.41 However, in good times and in bad, banks will inevitably be seeking to use their capital in the most efficient and effective way. This may enable them to price their transactions more competitively or (alternatively) allow them to make enhanced profits on individual transactions. It has been noted[68] that Basel I provided only very limited instances in which the availability of security or guarantees could be taken into account in reducing capital allocation requirements. This is another area in which Basel II has introduced significant reform. This is perhaps also the area in which lawyers are most likely to be involved, partly because the relevant requirements involve security or guarantees and partly because the capital mitigation effect is only achieved if the relevant arrangements are legally robust.

Most of the rules dealing with credit risk mitigation are to be found in BIPRU 5.[69]

---

[63] Credit risk mitigation is considered at para 6.40 below.

[64] BIPRU 4.4.34R.

[65] BIPRU 4.4.41R; LGD estimates must be calculated over a minimum of five years' data: BIPRU 4.4.54R.

[66] For most credit lines, a factor of 75 per cent applies, but this is reduced to 20 per cent in the case of a commercial credit and to zero per cent for a facility which is unconditionally cancellable: for the details, see BIPRU 4.4.37R.

[67] BIPRU 4.4.45.

[68] See para 6.14 above

[69] BIPRU 5 implements Arts 78, 91–93 and Annex VIII of the Recast Consolidation Directive. As noted below, a few matters which are specific to banks using the IRB approach are covered in BIPRU 4.10. But a number of the principles are common to both the standardized and the IRB approaches.

Common Principles

There are different types of credit mitigation techniques and their precise effect depends **6.42** upon their nature and quality. There are, however, certain common strands:

(a) any technique used to provide credit protection must result in credit protection arrangements which are legally effective and enforceable under the laws of all relevant jurisdictions;[70]
(b) the bank is not allowed to recognize the effect of credit risk mitigation in the calculation of its risk-weighted assets until it has conducted a legal review sufficient for the purposes outlined in paragraph (a) above, and it must periodically conduct such further legal reviews as may be necessary to ensure its continuing enforceability;[71] and
(c) the bank must take all appropriate steps to ensure the effectiveness of the security and to address related risks.[72] Although points of this nature are dealt in more depth in other parts of BIPRU 5, this presumably refers to the need to value the security from time to time, to monitor the financial position of any relevant guarantor and similar matters.

Against that brief background, it is possible to turn to the two forms of credit risk mitiga- **6.43** tion which are permitted for these purposes, namely:

(a) *funded* credit risk mitigation, which depends primarily on the value of a package of security; and
(b) *unfunded* credit risk mitigation, which depends principally on the creditworthiness of a party other than the borrower or counterparty itself.

Funded Credit Protection

Funded credit protection can take one of two main forms: **6.44**

(a) on balance sheet netting of mutual claims and reciprocal cash balances between the bank and the counterparty create effective security and may thus be recognized as an acceptable form of funded credit risk mitigation;[73] and
(b) collateral or security over acceptable forms of assets including (i) cash or cash equivalent instruments, (ii) gold, (iii) government/central bank securities meeting stated credit quality criteria, (iv) debt securities issued by banks, local authorities and certain other entities which meet stated criteria, (v) short term debt securities with an

---

[70] BIPRU 5.2.2. This begs the question of which jurisdictions are 'relevant' for this purpose. In the writer's view, this would probably include (i) the law of the country in which the security (if any) is located, (ii) the law of the country by which the security document is expressed to be governed, and (iii) the law of the country in which the provider of the credit mitigation is incorporated. The first two are necessary to ensure the intrinsic enforceability of the security, whilst the last is necessary to ensure that the security is not liable to be set aside in insolvency proceedings (eg on grounds similar to those discussed in Chapter 39, below). At all events, this is probably the prudent approach to the subject. In practice, it will often be the case that two or more of the relevant jurisdictions will coincide, thus reducing the time, cost and complexity involved in the process.
[71] BIPRU 5.2.3.
[72] BIPRU 5.2.4.
[73] BIPRU 5.3.

acceptable rating, and (vi) equities/convertible bonds listed on a main index.[74] An institution which adopts the comprehensive approach to collateral[75] may also treat as eligible any equities or bonds which are quoted on a recognized stock exchange, and units in collective investment schemes which invest solely in such investments and have a daily price quote.[76] Likewise, a bank adopting the IRB approach can treat commercial real estate as eligible collateral,[77] and may adopt the same approach to receivables linked to a commercial transaction with a maturity value of less than one year.[78]

6.45 The general need for credit risk mitigation techniques to be legally robust has already been noted. In the case of funded credit protection, these general requirements are amplified by a variety of requirements. In particular:[79]:

(a) the security must be enforceable in all relevant jurisdictions notwithstanding the insolvency of the counterparty or any custodian;[80]

(b) the bank must be able to demonstrate to the FSA that it has adequate risk management processes to control any potential risks arising from the security package;

(c) the bank must have the legal right to take possession of the security and to liquidate it following a default;[81]

(d) collateral consisting of debt or other securities issued by an entity related to the counterparty would generally be ineligible for these purposes;[82]

(e) there are further detailed requirements for particular types of collateral.[83]

6.46 Assuming that the bank has taken an eligible form of collateral and has satisfied the various formal requirements noted above, what are the capital consequences for the bank? This, in turn, depends on the bank's approach to collateral issues. In particular:

(a) a bank using the 'simple approach' to collateral[84] must assign a market value to the collateral which must be reviewed at least six monthly and whenever the bank believes

---

[74] BIPRU 5.4.2R.

[75] On the comprehensive approach to collateral, see para 6.46(b) below.

[76] BIPRU 5.4.8R.

[77] BIPRU 4.10.6R. However, and subject to limited exceptions, this only applies where the property itself, and the cash flows from it, are not intended to form the source of repayment.

[78] BIPRU 4.10.14R.

[79] On the requirements about to be discussed, see BIPRU 5.4.11R.

[80] Since most securities are now held in paperless form via one or more intermediary institutions, it is important that the security should not be lost as a result of the insolvency of the custodian.

[81] Some care may be needed as a result of this requirement. For example, negotiations over the form of the security document must not be allowed to detract from the immediate enforceability of the security. Secondly, in some jurisdictions, enforcement may have to occur via a court or similar process. This may mean that the security does not satisfy the 'lender's right to possession' test and that the collateral will accordingly be ineligible for credit risk mitigation purposes.

[82] ie because the insolvency of the counterparty is likely of itself to have an adverse impact on the value of the security.

[83] For example (i) in relation to netting agreements, BIPRU 5.3, requiring that the bank monitors and controls the exposure on a net basis and monitors and controls the associated risks and (ii) in relation to specific requirements for cash collateral, see BIPRU 5.4.

[84] On the 'financial collateral simple method', see BIPRU 5.14.14R–BIPRU 5.4.22R. This method may in any event only be used where the bank has adopted the standard approach to credit risk: BIPRU 5.4.15R.

that there may have been a significant deterioration in value.[85] The risk weight to be assigned to the collateralized exposure is the weight which would be assigned to an exposure to the collateral itself, subject to a minimum weighting of 20 per cent;[86]

(b) a bank using the 'comprehensive approach' to collateral[87] must value the collateral in a manner which takes account of the volatility in the market value of that collateral.[88] A volatility adjustment may also be required if the security consists of cash in a currency other than that in which the exposure is denominated.[89] The fully adjusted exposure value taking into account both the credit risk mitigation effects of the collateral and the volatility adjustments is referred to as E*, and that is the value to be applied to determining the exposure value for risk-weighted asset purposes under the standardized approach;[90]

(c) different rules apply where credit risk mitigation is being applied under the IRB approach.[91] The adjusted exposure value (E*) noted above will frequently not be taken into account directly as risk mitigation but will instead be taken into account in the calculation of loss given default (LGD);[92]

(d) since collateral in the form of real estate and receivables can only be used for credit mitigation by banks using the IRB approach, BIPRU 4.10 also sets out the rules applicable to the recognition of that form of collateral.[93]

Unfunded Credit Mitigation

As the terminology implies, unfunded credit protection depends not upon recourse to an asset by way of security, but upon the undertaking of a third party to pay a specified amount on the default of the borrower or on the occurrence of certain other events.[94]   **6.47**

The recognition of unfunded credit protection for the purpose of calculating risk-weighted assets is subject to a number of requirements: **6.48**

(a) the party providing the necessary undertaking (whether by way of guarantee, credit default swap, or otherwise) must be an 'eligible provider' of such a protection. In practice, this is not much of a limitation since the list of eligible providers includes both banks and financial institutions and any other corporate entity which has a rating with an approved credit agency;[95]

---

[85] BIPRU 5.4.17, read together with BIPRU 5.4.12.

[86] BIPRU 5.4.18R. Thus, if the collateral consists of debt instruments issued by a sovereign state or central bank where the exposure to that entity would have a zero per cent weighting, then that weighting is likewise applied to the collateralized exposure, subject to a 20 per cent floor.

[87] On the 'financial collateral comprehensive method' see BIPRU 5.4.23R–BIPRU 5.4.66R.

[88] For the detailed provisions of volatility adjustments, see BIPRU 5.4.30R–BIPRU 5.4.65R.

[89] BIPRU 5.4.25R.

[90] See BIPRU 5.4.66.

[91] See, generally, BIPRU 4.10.

[92] On this point, see BIPRU 4.10.36R. It is plainly not possible to 'double count' in this respect: see BIPRU 4.10.4R(3). On LGD, see para 6.38 above.

[93] See BIPRU 4.10.6R–BIPRU 4.10.15R.

[94] See the definition of 'unfunded credit protection' in the Glossary to the FSA Handbook.

[95] BIPRU 5.7.1.

(b) once again, the documentation creating the undertaking must be legally enforceable in all relevant jurisdictions. In addition, (i) the credit protection must be direct,[96] (ii) the scope of the credit protection must be clearly defined, and (iii) the credit protection must not include unilateral rights of termination or any right to increase the cost of protection[97] in the event of a deterioration in the borrower's credit quality;[98]

(c) where the undertaking consists of a guarantee, (i) the bank must have the right to pursue the guarantor promptly following default, (ii) prior proceedings against the main borrower must not be a condition to a claim under the guarantee, and (iii) the guarantee must be an explicit and documented obligation assumed by the guarantor;[99]

(d) where the mitigation consists of a credit derivative or credit default swap, the bank will generally have the right to 'put' the relevant debt instrument or obligation onto the writer of the derivative at its face value on the occurrence of stated credit events. For that reason, a credit derivative has an economic effect which is similar to a guarantee, even though the overall structure is different in many respects.[100] In order to qualify as eligible credit protection, the credit events which will trigger the bank's right to exercise its rights must include as a minimum (i) failure to pay, (ii) bankruptcy or insolvency, and (iii) restructuring of the underlying debt obligation.[101]

6.49 What then, is the effect of taking unfunded credit mitigation which meets these criteria? In this context:

(a) under the standardized approach, the risk weighting of the *protection provider* is effectively substituted for the weighting applied to the borrower itself;[102]

(b) under the IRB approach, in the calculation of risk-weighted assets, the PD (probability of default) attributable to the *protection provider* may be substituted for that of the primary obligor.[103]

---

[96] This presumably means that the undertaking must be directly enforceable by the bank. Consequently, a guarantee or credit default swap executed directly in its favour would plainly suffice. However, it is suggested that a document executed in favour of a third party should also be sufficient, provided that notice of the assignment is given to the obligor and the arrangements are legally effective.

[97] It is suggested that this refers to any cost of the protection borne by the bank itself. The provision should not apply if the cost of the protection is borne exclusively by the borrower or obligor.

[98] On the details, see BIPRU 5.7.6R.

[99] On these and other requirements, see BIPRU 5.7.11. These requirements will again have to be taken into account in drafting and negotiating the terms of the guarantees. For example, guarantors occasionally seek to include provisions to the effect that steps must be taken against the borrower before a claim is made under the guarantee, or that the guarantee will only cover the residual amount owing after remedies against the borrower have been exhausted. Provisions of this kind would mean that the guarantee would not constitute eligible credit protection.

[100] For example, and quite apart from other considerations, the credit default swap will be written as between two institutions in the financial market and the underlying borrower will frequently be unaware of the arrangement.

[101] On these and other requirements, see BIPRU 5.7.13R.

[102] See BIPRU 5.7.22R–BIPRU 5.7.25R.

[103] BIPRU 4.10.49R. On PD, see para 6.38 above.

Market Risk

Banks are also required to take account of market risk in calculating their capital ade- **6.50** quacy requirements.[104] This requires banks to ascertain a position risk requirement (PRR) in relation to all of their trading book positions.[105]

In essence, a bank is required to ascribe capital to the risk of loss through fluctuations in inter- **6.51** est rates,[106] equities,[107] commodities,[108] foreign currencies,[109] and options.[110] In the light of the financial market turmoil which began in 2007, it was realized that the 'market risk' rules failed to capture some of the key risks in a bank's trading book. The Basel Committee has thus introduced an incremental capital change for unsecuritized credit products and new 'stress-testing' requirements. The latter stems from the fact that losses in bank's trading books have significantly exceeded the minimum capital requirements under the existing market risk provisions under Pillar I. These rules are due to be implemented by the end of 2010.[111]

Operational Risk

The requirement to apply capital to account for operational risk is a new aspect of the capital **6.52** adequacy regime introduced by Basel II. 'Operational Risk' is defined as the risk of loss result- ing from the inadequate or failed internal processes, people and systems or from external events, including legal risk.[112] The operational risk capital requirements are set out in BIPRU 6.[113]

The capital requirement in this area must be calculated in accordance with: **6.53**

(a) the 'basic indicator' approach;
(b) the 'standardized' approach; or
(c) the advanced measurement approach.[114]

In relation to these three approaches: **6.54**

(a) the basic indicator approach is the most straightforward, and is calculated as 15 per cent of the aggregate of (i) the bank's net interest income and (ii) the bank's net non-interest income;[115]

---

[104] This requirement was not originally a feature of Basel I but was introduced following the issue of a 'Market Risk' revision to Basel I in 1995.
[105] This expression refers to certain instruments held by the bank for its own trading or hedging purposes: see the definition of 'trading book' in BIPRU 1.2.
[106] BIPRU 7.2.
[107] BIPRU 7.3.
[108] BIPRU 7.4.
[109] BIPRU 7.5.
[110] BIPRU 7.6.
[111] On these, points see: 'Revisions to Basel II Market Risk Framework': Basel Committee on Banking Supervision, July 2009, and see also 'Guidelines for computing capital for incremental risk in the trading book', Basel Committee, July 2009.
[112] See the definition of 'operational risk' in the FSA Glossary, tracking the corresponding definition given in Art 4(22) of the Recast Consolidation Directive.
[113] BIPRU 6 implements Arts 102–105 and Annex X of the Recast Banking Consolidation Directive.
[114] BIPRU 6.2.1R.
[115] BIPRU 6.3.2R. The figures are to be calculated on a three year average basis.

(b) the standardized approach can only be used by a bank which has implemented assessment and management systems for operational risk which are closely integrated into the bank's management systems and meet various other criteria.[116] This involves a calculation segregated along business lines, where the indicator percentage varies according to the business line involved (for example, the percentage for corporate finance and trading/sales business is as high as 18 per cent, whilst the corresponding percentage for retail brokerage and asset management is 12 per cent);[117] and

(c) the advanced measurement approach can only be used with permission from the FSA.[118] A bank which can obtain such a permission may base its capital requirement on the bank's own assessment of its operational risks.[119]

Pillar Two—Supervisory Review

6.55 Pillar Two of Basel II creates a requirement for a supervisory review process, under which national regulators are required to verify the sufficiency of a bank's systems and controls for the measurement and management of its exposures. The supervisory process rests on the following provisions:

(a) an ongoing, internal capital assessment by the bank itself. In the United Kingdom, this is referred to as the 'Internal Capital Adequacy Assessment Process' (ICAAP). This requires a continuous review of the bank's financial resources and of the risks to which it is exposed, and includes an obligation to conduct periodic stress testing;

(b) in line with Basel II, the FSA will review[120] the bank's ICAAP processes and may require adjustments to them if necessary.[121] It may also give guidance to a bank on the level of capital which the FSA believes should be required in the circumstances of that particular institution;[122] and

(c) in the event that a bank is unable or is unwilling to bring its capital into line with the FSA's position on that subject, then the ultimate sanction is the variation of that bank's deposit-taking permission so as to compel compliance.[123]

Pillar Three—Market Discipline

6.56 As noted previously, transparency requirements are also introduced by Basel II and from 'Pillar Three'.[124] In essence, in return for the flexibilities afforded to the banks by the capital adequacy rules contained in Basel II—and in order to reinforce the supervisory review

---

[116] For the details, see BIPRU 6.4.1R.
[117] On these points, see BIPRU 6.4.15R.
[118] BIPRU 6.5.1R. A permission will only be granted to a bank which meets certain risk management and other qualitative and quantitative standards: see BIPRU 6.5.5R.
[119] See, for example, BIPRU 6.5.2(g).
[120] The FSA Handbook refers to this process as the supervisory and evaluation process (SREP). See the description of SREP in BIPRU 2.2.9G.
[121] BIPRU 2.2.9G.
[122] BIPRU 2.2.16G–2.2.23G.
[123] On this point, see BIPRU 2.2.15G.
[124] See Arts 68(3), 72, 145–149 and Annex XII to the Recast Banking Consolidation Directive. These rules have been transposed into the United Kingdom by BIPRU 11.

process contemplated by Pillar Two—banks are required to disclose certain details of their internal and technical processes and policies. In particular, a bank must publicize:

(a) its management objectives and policies for each separate category of risk to which the bank is exposed, including details of strategies, processes, reporting, and management systems;[125]
(b) certain accounting details with respect to capital adequacy;[126]
(c) details of the calculation of the bank's capital resources;[127]
(d) information regulating audit risk, dilution risk, market, and operational risk.[128]

As will be apparent, Pillar Three of Basel II involves a series of disclosure rules but does not involve any use or attribution of the bank's capital resources.

Reform of Basel II

As noted elsewhere, one of the misfortunes of Basel II was that it was introduced when the **6.57** world was on the cusp of a major recession, which is seen as having its origins in the financial markets themselves.

As part of an effort to learn the lessons of this disaster and in an effort to buttress capital **6.58** adequacy, the Basel Committee published a consultative document entitled 'Strengthening of the resilience of the banking sector'.[129] The consultative paper includes a number of key comments and proposals:

(a) The paper observes that, under Basel II, 'core' capital consisting of ordinary or common equity shares could constitute as little as two per cent of risk-weighted assets. As a consequence, banks with a very limited tangible equity base were on occasion able to demonstrate strong Tier One ratios. The consultative paper therefore proposes that Tier One capital should consist principally of common equity and retained earnings and, in particular, goodwill is to be excluded. It was felt that the use of 'innovative Tier One instruments' had diluted the quality of Tier One capital and should no longer qualify for these purposes.[130] A limited form of debt instruments may qualify as Tier One 'Additional Going Concern Capital' provided that it is perpetual, fully subordinated, and meets other detailed criteria.
(b) Tier Two capital would be simplified , so that the sole criterion would be that Tier Two capital must be subordinated to deposition and have an original maturity of at least five years.

---

[125] BIPRU 11.5.1R.
[126] BIPRU 11.5.2R.
[127] BIPRU 11.5.3R – BIPRU 11.5.7R.
[128] BIPRU 11.5.8R , 11.5.12R and 11.5.14R. Further requirements applicable to specific methodologies will be found in BIPRU 11.6.
[129] Bank for International Settlements, December 2009.
[130] On these instruments, see para 6.24 above.

(c) Tier Three capital would be abolished, with the result that market risk and operational risk will be subject to international requirements as to the quality and composition of the supporting capital.

(d) These changes would be supported by transparency requirements, under which banks would have to disclose a full reconciliation of regulatory capital elements back to their audited balance sheets and other information designed to reinforce those calculations.

(e) The paper puts forward new proposals for improved and more detailed calculation of counterparty credit risk for capital adequacy purposes; including a requirement for periodic and comprehensive stress testing.

(f) The paper notes that the credit crisis was exacerbated by the accumulation of excessive on-and-off balance sheets leverage within the banking system. The paper therefore proposes the introduction of a leverage ratio, which would limit the build-up of excessive borrowings. The leverage ratio will effectively act as a supplement to the existing Basel II rules, with the result that a bank would have to meet both the risk-weighted assets ratio and the leverage ratio.

(g) It has been noted elsewhere that one of the perceived difficulties with Basel II during the credit crisis was the fact that its risk-sensitivity required further capital to be allocated to deteriorating credit risks, thus constraining the ability of banks to provide credit to the wider economy at a critical time. The proposal looks at the means by which the 'procyclicality' of the risk-weighted assets requirement can be mitigated, possibly by the adjustments to the calculation of the 'PD' (probability of default) component;[131] and

(h) The paper proposes that—outside periods of stress—banks should build up their capital above the required minimum out of retained earnings, so as to provide a buffer against any later downturn. This will effectively reduce or inhibit the ability of banks to pay dividends to shareholders.

6.59 At the time of writing, these reforms remain subject to both consultation and to implementation. There will doubtless be many competing interests at stake but, given the depth and impact of the current financial crisis, the recognition of the need for a higher quality capital base and a distinct restriction on leverage must surely constitute a step in the right direction.

Liquidity

6.60 The capital adequacy rules discussed above examine the extent to which a bank has available to it sufficient resources which are necessary to absorb any losses which arise in the course of its activities. But, in a much wider sense, banks need the cash to fund their activities. Banks may rely on a number of sources for that funding but there is a danger in becoming over reliant on individual sources of finance. This was dramatically illustrated by the problems which confronted Northern Rock in 2007, when the mortgage securitization market—on which it was heavily reliant—ground to a halt as the credit crunch took hold.

---

[131] On PD, see para 6.38 above.

In view of its (now) obvious importance, it may be that the whole subject of liquidity should assume a greater importance in the eyes of an institution's main regulator. Yet, for the present, and in spite of the general principle of home State regulation discussed earlier,[132] Article 41 of the Recast Consolidation Directive provides that '... Host Member States shall, pending further coordination, retain responsibility in cooperation with the competent authorities of the home Member State, for the supervision of the liquidity of the branches of credit institutions ...'. So for the time being, capital adequacy is a home State responsibility, whilst liquidity remains under the jurisdiction of the host State in which each of a credit institution's branches are located.[133] What then are the requirements of the United Kingdom in its capacity as host Member State to EEA institutions?

6.61 It has been noted previously that banks are required to possess adequate capital resources.[134] This principle finds further voice in the requirement that a bank '... must at all times maintain overall financial resources *and liquidity* resources which are adequate, both as to the amount and quality, to ensure that there is no significant risk that its liabilities cannot be met as they fall due ...'.[135] A bank is required to maintain a policy statement as to how it will comply with the liquidity resources requirement.[136]

6.62 A variety of rules may then be drawn from various parts of the FSA Handbook. In particular:

(a) SYSC 11[137] deals specifically with the systems and controls to be put in place to deal with liquidity risk. SYSC repeats the requirement for a bank to have policies in place for the measurement and management of its net funding[138] and obliges a bank to put in place contingency plans to deal with liquidity crises.[139]

(b) In a broader sense, a bank is obliged to have effective processes to identify, manage, monitor, and report the risks to which it is exposed and to have in place appropriate risk management policies. Both these requirements include an assessment of liquidity risk.[140]

(c) As the FSA observes,[141] an important element of banking is 'maturity transformation' that is, using relatively short term customer deposits to make relatively long term loans. As a result, banks run the risk that they will be unable to realize their assets to repay on demand by depositors. But banks must conduct their business in a prudent manner

---

[132] See para 2.13 above.

[133] It should nevertheless be noted that Art 41 specifically contemplates further coordination in this area. Liquidity issues are clearly seen to be both increasingly important and increasingly difficult: see, for example, the Basel Committee papers 'Liquidity Risk and Supervisory Challenges' (February 2008) and 'Principles for Sound Liquidity Risk Management and Supervision' (September 2008).

[134] See para 1.23 above.

[135] GENPRU 1.2.26R. For the reasons given above, this requirement applies to the UK branches of banks authorized by the FSA and to EEA passported firms carrying on business in the UK.

[136] IPRU (BANK) 3.4.3R.

[137] SYSC is the section of the FSA Handbook dealing with systems and controls.

[138] SYSC 11.1.11R.

[139] SYSC 11.1.12R. The contingency plan may include proposals for the disposal of assets or the utilization of committed facilities: see SYSC 11.1.24E.

[140] SYSC 11.1.49, cross-referencing to SYSC 4.1.1R and SYSC 7.1.2R.

[141] IPRU (BANK), 2.1.

and must be able to meet their obligations as they fall due. Those obligations include not only the obligation to repay deposits but also the requirement to meet obligations under committed loan facilities and other expenses of their business. A bank must therefore maintain ample funding capacity and, as far as possible, this should be diversified to avoid over-reliance on volatile markets such as the interbank market.

(d) In monitoring an institution's liquidity, the FSA may apply a 'maturity mismatch' approach, which measures a bank's liquidity by reference to the mismatch between the cash inflows and outflows. The FSA sets recommended guidelines for maximum maturity mismatches,[142] and there are detailed rules as to the inclusion of assets and liabilities in the mismatch calculation.[143]

(e) The FSA has recently consulted on the need to strengthen the supervision of bank liquidity in view of the market difficulties to which reference has already been made.[144] Briefly, the new liquidity policy would consist of five main strands,[145] namely:

  (i) adequate liquidity and self-sufficiency: a bank must have adequate liquidity which is not dependent on other members of the same group;
  (ii) systems and controls: banks will have to establish a liquidity risk management framework to be implemented within the bank;
  (iii) individual liquidity standards: these would be directed towards banks being able to survive liquidity stress of differing magnitudes and duration;
  (iv) group wide and cross-border liquidity management: this would operate as a derogation from the self sufficiency requirement, where appropriate;
  (v) reporting: a new liquidity reporting process and timetable.

Large Exposures

6.63 The rules on large exposures are in many respects separate from the capital adequacy and liquidity frameworks.[146] Nevertheless, avoidance of excessive levels of exposure to single customers is a natural feature of prudent banking, and the rules prohibiting large exposures may thus be said to be consistent with the high level obligations to conduct business with

---

[142] IPRU (BANK), 4.1.

[143] IPRU (BANK), 5.1.

[144] See in particular the FSA Consultation Paper CP 08/2008, 'Strengthening Liquidity Standards' (December 2008) and the follow-up papers CP 09/13, 'Strengthening Liquidity Standards 2: Liquidity Reporting' (April 2009) and CP 09/14, 'Strengthening Liquidity Standards 3: Liquidity Transitional Measures'. Some of the FSA's proposals draw on the Basel Committee's publication 'Liquidity Risk Measurement and Supervisory Challenges' (February 2008), which in turn led to a revised version of the Committee's 'Principles for Sound Liquidity Risk Management and Supervision'. The revised document was published in September 2008 and emphasized, among other things, the need for banks to establish a robust liquidity framework as an integral part of the risk management process. The most recent initiative is a document entitled 'International Framework on liquidity risk measurement, standards and monitoring', published by the Basel Committee on 17 December 2009. This consultation document sets out proposals for global minimum liquidity standards and includes proposals for a uniform approach to liquidity monitoring for institutions operating on a cross-border basis.

[145] See para 1.6 of CP 08/2008.

[146] Although see the discussion (below) on the subject of the concentration risk capital component.

skill, care, and diligence and to take reasonable care to organize and control its affairs responsibly and efficiently, with adequate risk management systems.[147]

The rules on large exposures (or as the FSA Handbook calls them, 'Concentration Risk Requirements') are to be found in BIPRU 10.[148] As the Handbook text explains, a large exposure[149] may involve a loan to a single borrower or it may involve a number of transactions involving different types of financial instruments with several counterparties in the same group of companies. A loss on transactions of this kind could threaten the solvency of the bank itself.[150] **6.64**

BIPRU 10 includes rules requiring the aggregation of exposures to connected clients and counterparties[151] for the purpose of determining the total exposures which may constitute a large exposure[152] and defines a 'large exposure' as total exposure to a counterparty and connected parties which equals or exceeds 10 per cent of the bank's capital resources.[153] A special capital adequacy requirement (called the 'concentration risk capital component') is imposed in relation to risks of this kind.[154] **6.65**

The core rules include the following: **6.66**

(a) a bank must ensure that its exposure to a counterparty, a group of connected clients or its connected counterparties does not exceed 25 per cent of its capital resources;[155]
(b) a bank must not incur large exposures which *in total* exceed 800 per cent of its capital resources;[156] and
(c) if a bank becomes aware that it may breach either of these limits, it must notify the FSA. The FSA would expect to receive such reports only under exceptional circumstances and would expect the reports to include details of (i) how the breach arose and (ii) the bank's remedial proposals.[157]

As noted above, the large exposure rules may appear to be an integral part of prudent bank risk management. Yet the implementation and monitoring of this requirement is an **6.67**

---

[147] See PRIN 2 and PRIN 3.
[148] BIPRU 10 implements Arts 106–117 and para 7 of Annex V to the Recast Banking Consolidation Directive.
[149] Exposures are ascertained in the same way as for risk-weighted assets in the context of the capital adequacy calculation.
[150] BIPRU 10.1.3G.
[151] For these purposes, a 'connected counterparty' is a person who is affiliated with the bank itself, who has a significant influence on the governing body of the bank or who has non-arm's length dealings with it: BIPRU 10.3.8R. Equally, 'connected clients' refers not only to entities with a formal affiliate relationship but also to clients between whom there is no such relationship but '… who are regarded as constituting a single risk because they are so interconnected that, if one of them were to experience financial problems, the other or all of the others would be likely to encounter payment difficulties …': see the definitions of these expressions in the Glossary to the FSA Handbook. The latter part of the test may not always be easy to apply and, as so often, the devil will be in the detail of these provisions.
[152] BIPRU 10.3.5G–BIPRU 10.3.11R.
[153] BIPRU 10.5.1. There are special rules on the calculation of capital resources for specific purpose: see BIPRU 10.5.2R.
[154] For the details, see BIPRU 10.5.16G–BIPRU 10.5.23G.
[155] BIPRU 10.5.6R.
[156] BIPRU 10.5.8R.
[157] 10.5.9R and 10.5.9G.

ongoing obligation and a breach would not necessarily be indicative of recklessness or risk management oversight. For example:

(a) a breach of the limit could occur as a result of one large customer of the bank making a successful takeover of another, so that previously separate exposures have to be aggregated for large exposure purposes;

(b) a breach of the large exposure rules may also occur as a result of events affecting the bank itself. For example, significant losses may have the effect of eroding the bank's capital resources so that, whilst the exposure itself remains unchanged, the limits are exceeded because the capital available to cover the exposure have diminished; and

(c) in view of the definition of 'group of connected clients',[158] the acquisition of a significant shareholding stake in the bank itself could affect its large exposure position. For example, in the context of the government's acquisition of Northern Rock and the recapitalization of banks in 2008 the question arose whether banks with exposures to entities which had the UK Government as a common shareholder should treat those entities as 'a group of connected clients' for large exposure purposes. However, the FSA concluded that such entities should not be considered as 'connected' merely because common ownership could be traced back to the UK Government.[159]

6.68 It will thus be seen that the large exposure regime is not merely an issue which needs to be considered at the initial, credit approval stage. Ongoing monitoring is required and a breach of the large exposure rules can be triggered by events which, at the initial approval stage, are entirely unforeseen. That a breach arises through unfortunate circumstances does not affect the fact that the breach must be remedied although the FSA may allow time for implementation of the necessary action.[160]

Conclusions

6.69 It is difficult to say much by way of general conclusion on the various prudential issues discussed in this chapter, save to remark that:

(a) as noted at various points, it has been the misfortune of Basel II that it came into effect when the world was on the cusp of its most serious recession for many years. A measure that was intended to provide a more risk-sensitive basis for capital adequacy arrived at a time of deteriorating credit qualitatively, thus further constraining the ability of the banks to write new business at a time when credit conditions were already challenging;

(b) some aspects of the framework were found to be inadequate to cover risks which arose in admittedly very extreme circumstances;[161] and

---

[158] See n 151 above.
[159] See FSA Note: Bank Recapitalisation and Connected Exposures under the Large Exposure Regime.
[160] BIPRU 10.5.10G.
[161] See, for example, the discussion of market risk at para 6.50 above.

(c) the difficulties which hit the financial markets in 2008 were borne out of a lack of liquidity—an issue which is not really addressed by the Basel II framework at all.

All of these issues have been, or are in the course of being, addressed. Yet in one sense, the **6.70** discussion illustrates the perennial difficulty with prudential rules of this kind, in that the regulations will always be trying to make provision for crises which have not yet occurred and will display unique features which had not previously occurred to anyone.

7

MONEY LAUNDERING LEGISLATION

Introduction

It is now generally accepted that banks and financial institutions should be active partici- **7.01**
pants in the fight against money laundering.[1] For legal, reputational, and many other reasons, banks are now vigilant to prevent the use of their services and facilities as a means of
laundering or transferring the proceeds of crime.

But what is 'money laundering'? The activity is normally described as a three stage **7.02**
process:

(a) *Placement.* This connotes the introduction of the proceeds of crime into the financial
system or retail economy with a view to concealing their origins (eg, by purchasing
travellers' cheques for cash, or purchasing other currencies through a foreign exchange
dealer).

---

[1] For a helpful discussion of the whole subject, see Blair, Walker & Purves, chapter 10.

(b) *Layering.* Layering may involve a series of wire transfers or other transactions designed to place a further distance between the funds and their criminal origins, thus obscuring any audit trail which might otherwise be available.

(c) *Integration.* This final stage of the process involves the integration of the funds back into the legitimate financial system. This may be done by establishing companies to invest in real estate, shares, or other assets.

7.03 There is sometimes a tendency to think of money laundering in the context of drug trafficking, no doubt because this was the starting point for much of the relevant legislation,[2] and because it is an activity which, in the most obvious sense, generates large amounts of cash whose illegitimacy needs to be concealed. Yet in recent years, the scope of regulation (and criminalization) has been expanded very significantly. These developments have had very far reaching consequences for banks and those who work for them.[3] This is perhaps unsurprising for, as the House of Lords has noted:[4]

> ... in its typical form, money laundering occurs when criminals who profit from their criminal enterprises seek to bring their profits within the legitimate financial sector with a view to disguising their true origin. Their aim is to avoid prosecution for the offences that they committed and confiscation of the proceeds of their offences. Various measures have been taken both internationally and in domestic law aimed at detecting and deterring this activity. They include much closer regulation of the financial sector and the introduction of measures requiring known or suspected money laundering to be reported to the authorities. They also include the enactment of a series of offences to bring the activities of third parties within the reach of the criminal law ...

7.04 The present chapter provides a description of the legislative requirements, and seeks to provide guidance on some of the very difficult issues which can arise in this field. For ease of treatment of this complex area, the present chapter deals solely with the criminal and regulatory issues. However, it should always be borne in mind that a bank which handles the proceeds of criminal activity may in some cases incur liability to the true owner of the funds concerned.[5]

7.05 The subject will be considered under the following headings:

(a) the broad international background to the anti-money laundering initiatives will be considered;

(b) a broad overview of the UK regulatory environment will be provided;

(c) the customer identification ('know your customer') requirements will be considered;

(d) the substantive money laundering offences created by the Proceeds of Crime Act 2002 will be discussed;

---

[2] In relation to the United Kingdom, see originally the Drug Trafficking Act 1986.
[3] Indeed, as will be seen, a new offence has been created for special application to those working in financial institutions and in certain professions. See the discussion of Proceeds of Crime Act 2002, s 330, at para 7.47 below.
[4] *R v Montila* [2004] UKHL 50 (para 3).
[5] This subject is considered at paras 7.83–7.93 below.

(e) the anti-terrorism legislation will be considered;[6] and

(f) certain limited, civil consequences of the anti-money laundering framework will be outlined.

International Background

International Law

At an international level, the main anti-money laundering body is the Financial Action **7.06**
Task Force (FATF). The FATF was established as an intergovernmental organization by the
Group of Seven (G-7) at a summit held in Paris in 1989. The mandate of the FATF is
directed towards the fight against money laundering and terrorist finance[7] in a global environment. To that end, it has published some 40 recommendations and an additional nine
special recommendations.

FATF advises that governments should criminalize money laundering in relation to all seri- **7.07**
ous criminal activity.[8] The FATF's recommendations also include customer due diligence,
record keeping, and reporting of suspicious transactions to a national enforcement authority. As will be seen below, these recommendations find voice in the domestic legislation
enacted in the United Kingdom.

Community Law

The European Community has also seen money laundering as a concern, partly in the **7.08**
context of its single market policy. As a result, it initially introduced a Directive on prevention of the use of the financial system for the purpose of money laundering.[9] The Directive
was limited to criminal activity contrary to the Vienna Convention of 1988, that is to say,
to drug dealing.[10] The scope of this legislation was extended to other forms of serious crime
in 2001 by a second Directive.[11]

The current EC regime is to be found in the Third Money Laundering Directive.[12] **7.09**
The Directive was intended to give effect to the FATF recommendations and to make

---

[6] It may be argued that the anti-terrorism offences fall into a separate category, because they do not necessarily involve the laundering of criminal property in the strictest sense of that expression. Nevertheless, it is
convenient to review these together because the essential structure of the legislation is similar.

[7] Terrorist finance was added to the mandate in 2001.

[8] The recommendation suggests that States should legislate on the basis of the UN Convention against
Illicit Traffic in Narcotic Drugs 1988 (the Vienna Convention) and the UN Convention against Transnational
Organised Crime 2000 (the Palermo Convention).

[9] Council Directive 91/308/EEC of 10 June 1991 on the prevention of the use of the financial system for
the purpose of money laundering OJ L 28.06.1991, p 77.

[10] The Vienna Convention has already been noted: see n 8 above.

[11] See Directive 2001/97/EC of the European Parliament and of the Council amending Council Directive
91/308/EC on the prevention of the use of the financial system for the purpose of money laundering OJ L
344, 28.12.2001, p 76.

[12] Directive 2005/60/EC of the European Parliament and of the Council on the prevention of the use
of the financial system for the purpose of money laundering and terrorist financing, OJ L 309, 25.11.2005,
p 15.

compliance mandatory at a Community level.[13] In particular, Member States are required to criminalize money laundering—including the conversion, transfer, concealment, and possession of criminal property—and the financing of terrorism,[14] and to impose customer due diligence and other obligations on financial institutions and other professionals.[15] The FATF's recommendations for an official reporting procedure were likewise reproduced in chapter III of the Directive.[16] Member States were required to implement this Directive into their national laws by 15 December 2007.

Overview of the United Kingdom Regime

Legislation

7.10 It has already been noted that anti-money laundering legislation has its roots in both international and Community initiatives. The United Kingdom boasts a large financial services sector, and it is therefore unsurprising that the government has taken an active role in promoting the implementation of the standards described above. The current legislation consists principally of:

(a) the Money Laundering Regulations 2007;[17]
(b) the Proceeds of Crime Act 2002; and
(c) the Terrorism Act 2000.[18]

7.11 In line with the FATF recommendations and the Third Money Laundering Directive, the 2007 Regulations are designed to ensure that financial institutions have in place the systems and procedures which will help to minimize the possibility of the laundering of the proceeds of crime through that institution, and to ensure that appropriate reporting processes are in place. Those regulations thus apply principally to banks and other entities whose activities are likely to make them a target for money launderers.

7.12 In contrast, the Proceeds of Crime Act and the Terrorism Act create offences which can be committed by anyone, whether working in a financial institution or not.[19] Generally speaking, these two Acts create offences in connection with the use, possession, or transmission of criminal or terrorist property.[20]

---

[13] See recital (5) to the Directive.
[14] See Art 1 of the Directive.
[15] See Arts 6–19 of the Directive.
[16] Articles 20–27 of the Directive.
[17] SI 2007/2157 (the '2007 Regulations').
[18] References to the Terrorism Act 2000 are to that Act as amended by the Anti-Terrorism, Crime and Security Act 2001.
[19] As mentioned earlier, the notable exception to this statement is the 'regulated sector' offence created by the Proceeds of Crime Act 2002, s 330.
[20] These offences, insofar as relevant to the activities of banks, are considered later in this chapter.

Role of the Financial Services Authority

The Financial Services Authority (FSA) is charged, amongst other things, with the reduc- **7.13**
tion of financial crime.[21] The prevention of money laundering through the financial system
must therefore be seen as one of its key objectives.

Until 2006, the FSA Handbook included specific requirements on money laundering con- **7.14**
trols and procedures at authorized institutions.[22] At that point, however, it was determined
that this should be replaced with 'higher level' requirements relating to the adequacy of a
bank's systems and controls. The relevant provisions are thus now found in the 'Senior
Management Arrangements, Systems and Controls' chapter of the FSA Handbook (SYSC).
A bank must accordingly ensure that it has in place the policies and procedures necessary
to enable it to address the risk that customers may attempt to use its facilities or services for
money laundering purposes. These procedures must be appropriate bearing in mind the
nature and scale of the bank's business, and must be reviewed on a regular basis.[23] The FSA
has in the past imposed significant fines on banks whose anti-money laundering processes
were found to be inadequate, even where there were no grounds to suspect that money
laundering had actually occurred as a consequence of system weaknesses.

Role of Market Associations

Market associations are naturally concerned about legislation of this kind for a number of **7.15**
reasons:

(a) the legislation carries a risk of prosecution for institutions and their staff;
(b) as noted above, compliance failures may be the subject of fines and public censure by
the FSA, and this naturally has adverse reputational consequences;
(c) the implementation of the required compliance procedures has a cost which falls on
institutions, and about which they are apt to complain from time to time; and
(d) in the interests of their members as a whole, such associations—in the present case, the
British Bankers Association—issue guidelines which are intended to represent 'good
practice', so that standards of compliance will assume a degree of uniformity and will
provide a benchmark against which standards can be measured.

It is the last of these features which may be of significance from a purely legal perspective. **7.16**
The legislation recognizes that compliance with guidance issued by such bodies should be
taken into account in determining whether a money laundering offence has been committed in the financial sector concerned.[24] Such guidance is inevitably revised from time to
time and it is unnecessary to attempt a complete review for present purposes. It may be

---

[21] FSMA, s 6.
[22] FSA Handbook, chapter ML.
[23] On these requirements, see FSA Handbook, SYSC 6.3. Compliance by a bank with the guidelines
issued by the JMLSG may tend to suggest that it has also complied with its obligations under SYSC 6.3:
see SYSC 6.3.5G. On the JMLSG Guidelines, see para 7.16 below.
[24] See in particular reg 42(3) of the 2007 Regulations and the 'regulated sector' offences created by the
Proceeds of Crime Act 2002, ss 330(8) and 331(7). Note that such guidelines are only to be taken into
account if they have been approved by the Treasury and have been published to the market. Note also that
compliance is not an absolute defence, but is only to be 'taken into account' by the court.

sufficient to note that the most recent version of the guidance was issued in December 2007 to coincide with the implementation of the Third Money Laundering Directive and that it contains detailed recommendations on the steps which institutions should take for the purposes of (i) identifying and assessing risks, (ii) designing, implementing and monitoring systems of anti-money laundering controls, (iii) standards of customer due diligence, (iv) reporting suspect transactions, and (v) record keeping and related matters.[25]

The Money Laundering Regulations 2007

7.17 The Money Laundering Regulations 2007 came into effect on 15 December 2007. As noted earlier, the regulations are designed to deny money launderers access to the financial system. With this objective in mind, the 2007 Regulations require banks and other financial institutions to comply with four, broad requirements in the context of their business.[26] Failure to comply with these requirements is a criminal offence.[27] These requirements include:

(a) a duty to carry out 'customer due diligence' (CDD) measures;[28]

(b) an obligation to maintain relevant records;[29]

(c) an obligation to introduce and maintain appropriate policies and procedures to counteract money laundering and terrorist financing;[30] and

(d) an obligation to train staff to identify suspect transactions.[31]

Each of these matters will be examined in turn.

Customer Due Diligence

7.18 Clearly, the banking system can more readily be used for money laundering purposes if individuals can provide false names or addresses with impunity. Even if money laundering activity is subsequently discovered, the bank's files will contain no 'audit trail' or other materials which are likely to be useful in the context of the investigation.

7.19 Accordingly, and subject to various exceptions and modifications, regulation 7 requires that an institution must apply CDD measures in various situations. A few points may be noted in this context:

(a) What is 'customer due diligence' for these purposes? In essence, CDD measures involve (i) identifying the customer and verifying his identity with the use of reliable

---

[25] For a more detailed discussion of the guidance, see Blair, Walker & Purves, paras 10.240–10.292.

[26] As a matter of strict law, it should be noted that the 2007 Regulations only apply to the activities of a bank to the extent that these constitute 'relevant business'. However, the definition of that term extends to deposit-taking, lending, investment business, and other activities listed in the Recast Banking Consolidation Directive, which has been considered in Chapter 2 above. As a result, virtually all of a bank's customary business activities will constitute 'relevant business' for the purposes of the Regulations.

[27] See reg 45(1) of the 2007 Regulations. In assessing compliance with these requirements, the court is to take into account any relevant guidance approved by the Treasury in the relevant field: see reg 45(2).

[28] See regs 5–18 of the 2007 Regulations.

[29] Regulation 19 of the 2007 Regulations.

[30] Regulation 20 of the 2007 Regulations.

[31] Regulation 21 of the 2007 Regulations.

documents or data from an independent source, (ii) applying the same process to a beneficial owner of the customer where it is a company, trust, or similar entity,[32] and (iii) obtaining information on the purpose and intended nature of the business relationship.[33] In the case of individuals, this will often take the form of a passport or driving licence to verify identity, and utility or tax bills to confirm the place of residence.

(b) It will be noted that the 2007 Regulations refer to *customer* due diligence. A bank is thus only required to undertake the identification/verification process in relation to its own account holder or client. It will not normally be necessary for the bank to be concerned to verify the identity of other parties involved in a particular transaction.[34]

(c) CDD measures must be applied before a business relationship is established or an occasional (or 'one off') transaction is effected.[35] It may also be necessary to renew or carry out further CDD measures if the bank begins to suspect money laundering at a later stage of the relationship, or doubts the genuineness or sufficiency of the materials previously provided to it for that purpose.[36] A bank is also required to apply further due diligence measures at appropriate times and on a risk-sensitive basis.[37] A bank may elect to undertake this process when customers are buying a new product (eg where a current account customer applies for a mortgage) or where there is a change in ownership of a corporate customer, so that new beneficial owners require verification in accordance with the rules noted in paragraph (a) above.

(d) If the customer fails to provide any required CDD material, then the bank must not carry out any transactions for that customer and should consider whether the refusal to comply suggests that a report should be made under the Proceeds of Crime Act or the Terrorism Act.[38] The requirement that CDD should periodically be renewed may cause particular difficulty in the context of an established relationship. If, again, the customer fails to provide any requested CDD material, then the bank must terminate the existing account relationship. The steps to be taken in that respect are considered separately.[39]

(e) A new requirement first introduced by the 2007 Regulations is a provision for 'ongoing monitoring' of a business relationship. This is stated to involve (i) scrutiny of transactions effected by the client (including his source of funds) to ensure that his activities are not out of the ordinary in the context of the bank's knowledge of the nature and

---

[32] Regulation 6 of the 2007 Regulations provides that a 'beneficial owner' for these purposes is a person with an interest of at least 25 per cent in the entity or trust concerned. His identity should be confirmed and verified in the same way.

[33] On these points, see the definition of 'customer due diligence' in reg 5 of the 2007 Regulations.

[34] Thus, for the purposes of the 2007 Regulations, a bank which is financing the purchase of a property must verify the identity of the buyer, but not the seller. The identity of persons other than the bank's own customer are perhaps more likely to be relevant in determining whether a report ought to be made under the terms of the Proceeds of Crime Act or the Terrorism Act. For a discussion of those aspects, see paras 7.28–7.82 below.

[35] Regulations 7(1)(a) and (b) of the 2007 Regulations, read together with reg 9(2).

[36] Regulations 7(1)(c) and (d) of the 2007 Regulations.

[37] Regulation 7(2) of the 2007 Regulations.

[38] On these reporting requirements, see paras 7.47 and 7.80 below. On the wider points made in the text, see reg 11 of the 2007 Regulations.

[39] See the discussion of the decision in *HSBC Bank plc v Tayeb*, at para 7.87 below.

scale of the customer's business and financial position and (ii) periodic updating of CDD measures.[40]

(f) The CDD measures described above do not generally have to be applied to certain entities where the money laundering risk is perceived to be low. This rule applies where the bank has reasonable grounds for believing that the customer is (i) another credit or financial institution subject to the requirements of the Third Money Laundering Directive, (ii) a credit institution in a non-EEA State but which is supervised for compliance with equivalent requirements, (iii) a company whose securities are listed on a regulated market which imposes transparency and other requirements equivalent to those applicable to EEA exchanges, (iv) a UK public authority, or (v) a public authority within the European Community or whose activities are otherwise transparent.[41]

(g) On the other hand,[42] enhanced CDD measures are required in cases where the prospective money laundering risk is perceived to be greater, for example, (i) where the customer has not been physically present for identification purposes,[43] (ii) where the customer is a bank from a non-EEA State and it is intended to establish a correspondent banking relationship,[44] and (iii) where the customer is a 'politically exposed person'.[45]

(h) The 'net' of compliance with the 2007 Regulations is in some respects extended on an extra-territorial basis. Banks must require their branches and subsidiaries in non-EEA countries to apply equivalent CDD, monitoring and record-keeping measures.[46]

(i) It has already been noted that enhanced due diligence may be required for certain types of correspondent bank relationships. However, relationships of this kind are the subject of an outright ban where the customer is a 'shell bank'.[47] Such an entity will frequently be established in a jurisdiction which seeks to preserve confidentiality and the consequent money laundering risks are obvious.

---

[40] Regulation 8 of the 2007 Regulations.

[41] On these and other, product-specific exemptions, see reg 13 of the 2007 Regulations.

[42] On the points about to be made, see reg 14 of the 2007 Regulations.

[43] In such a case, enhanced CDD may consist of additional documents or other supplementary measures by way of verification, or by ensuring that the first payment is remitted from an account in the customer's own name with another EEA credit institution: see reg 14(2) of the 2007 Regulations. This particular approach may be especially helpful in the context of financial products sold over the internet or by other distance means.

[44] Such arrangements are vulnerable to money laundering risk because the credit institution accepting the business will not be in a position to identify the underlying clients of the customer bank. Enhanced due diligence in this type of case includes a consideration of the reputation of the customer and the quality of its controls in the spheres on money laundering and terrorist financing: see reg 14(3) of the 2007 Regulations.

[45] A 'politically exposed person' is a person who is, or has been within the last 12 months, entrusted with a prominent public function by a foreign State, a Community institution or an international body. The definition extends to close associates and family members of such a person. The concern plainly is that such a person may be seeking to launder the proceeds of corrupt activities. In such a case, the relationship must be approved at a senior level and adequate steps must be taken to verify the source of funds involved in the relationship: see reg 14(4) of the 2007 Regulations.

[46] For the details, see reg 15 of the 2007 Regulations.

[47] A 'shell bank' is also sometimes known as a 'brass plate' bank. It is defined by the 2007 Regulations as a credit institution established in a jurisdiction in which it has no physical presence and which is not part of a larger financial group. For the details, see reg 16 of the 2007 Regulations.

(j) Finally, it may be noted that the Joint Money Laundering Steering Group has issued a set of guidelines (the 'JMLSG Guidelines') which are intended for the guidance of financial institutions in implementing policies and procedures intended to be consistent with the 2007 Regulations. Apart from general guidance, this publication includes product-specific recommendations.

It will thus be appreciated that the CDD requirements apply to any new customer relationship, even though the bank may have no reason whatsoever to suspect its customer of any association with money laundering.. This may be contrasted with the offences created under the Proceeds of Crime Act, which will only apply where a suspicion of money laundering has (or ought to have) arisen. **7.20**

Record Keeping

Money laundering activities can only be effectively countered if the evidence is available for that purpose, so that transactions can be traced through a documentary trail. **7.21**

Consequently, the 2007 Regulations require an institution to maintain both the identification evidence referred to above, together with a record of all transactions carried out for the customer, for a minimum period of five years.[48] **7.22**

Policies and Procedures

A financial institution must establish internal policies and procedures to ensure compliance with the CDD, ongoing monitoring and record keeping requirements and under which employees can report any knowledge or suspicion of money laundering to a Money Laundering Reporting Officer who must be appointed for that purpose.[49] Those procedures must also provide for the identification and monitoring of large or unusual transactions or any other activity which may be indicative of money laundering or terrorist financing. **7.23**

The need to lodge reports of suspected money laundering activity is contained in the Proceeds of Crime Act 2002, and is hence considered later in this chapter. However, the provisions just noted do demonstrate the link between the procedural requirements of the 2007 Regulations and the very serious criminal offences which can be committed under the 2002 Act. **7.24**

Internal Training Procedures

Banks are required to put in place appropriate training procedures[50] so that (i) employees are made aware of the requirements of the 2007 Regulations and the applicable provisions of the Proceeds of Crime Act 2002 and of the Terrorism Act 2000[51] and (ii) employees are able to recognize and deal with transactions which may involve money laundering. **7.25**

---

[48] On the calculation of these periods, and for further details, see reg 19 of the 2007 Regulations.
[49] On the points just made, see reg 20 of the 2007 Regulations.
[50] Regulation 21 of the 2007 Regulations. Training is required to be given to 'relevant employees', which must include those employees who deal with the bank's customers or who are responsible for dealings with deposits or payments.
[51] The relevant provisions of this legislation are considered at paras 7.28–7.82 below.

7.26 The training which is required to enable staff to spot suspect transactions will, of course, vary according to the nature of the institution and the types of product which it offers.

7.27 An employee who has not been provided with adequate training in this sphere may have a defence to a later prosecution for certain money laundering offences.[52]

Proceeds of Crime Act 2002

7.28 The principal money laundering offences are now contained in Part 7 (sections 327–340) of the Proceeds of Crime Act 2002 (POCA).[53] In essence, those provisions create a series of offences which may be committed by those who are in some way involved in the laundering of the proceeds of crime. Equally, however, they create a defence (the 'disclosure defence') for those who have reported their suspicions in the appropriate manner, and a further defence (the 'reasonable excuse' defence) for those who intended to report but have a reasonable excuse for not having done so; they also create a further defence (the 'foreign legality defence') for those who believe that the relevant monies emanate from conduct abroad which did not constitute a criminal offence there. Since the defences to each separate offence are in essentially common form, it is proposed first to consider the substance of each of the offences. The disclosure, reasonable excuse, and 'foreign legality' defence will therefore be considered at a later stage.[54]

7.29 Before moving on to the details, it may be noted in passing that the FSA has power to initiate a prosecution for money laundering offences, at least insofar as the alleged offences have some nexus with the financial markets.[55]

'Criminal Property' and 'Criminal Conduct'

7.30 The POCA provisions which are about to be considered vary in their substance and detail, but they share a common thread; money laundering and related offences are only committed if they relate to 'criminal property'. A review of that term is thus a necessary precursor to a discussion of the substantive offences.

7.31 The starting point is provided by section 340(3) of POCA, which provides that:

Property is criminal property if—

   (a) it constitutes a person's benefit from criminal conduct or it represents such a benefit (in whole or in part and whether directly or indirectly; and
   (b) the alleged offender knows or suspects that it constitutes or represents such a benefit.

---

[52] See, in particular, the 'regulated sector' offence discussed at para 7.47 below.

[53] References to the relevant provisions of POCA include the amendments made to that Act by the Serious Organised Crime and Police Act 2005.

[54] See paras 7.52–7.66 below.

[55] This point was recently decided by the Court of Appeal in *Financial Services Authority v Rollins* [2009] EWCA 1941.

The definition is then explained and expanded in various respects. The following points **7.32** may be noted:

(a) The expression 'property' is defined as '... all property wherever situate ...', including money, real property or any right or interest therein, and any things in action and other intangible and incorporeal property.[56]

(b) As noted in paragraph (a) of the statutory definition, property is 'criminal property' for these purposes if it represents *any* person's benefit[57] from criminal conduct. It remains criminal property regardless of who was responsible for that criminal conduct, and regardless of who benefited from it.[58]

(c) Property is deemed to be 'criminal property' even though it may previously have been passed through a series of transactions (or 'laundered') without detection.[59]

(d) 'Criminal property' includes any pecuniary advantage obtained as a result of or in connection with any criminal conduct.[60]

(e) Whilst the points noted above suggest a very broad definition of 'criminal property', it should not be forgotten that property can only fall within this term if the alleged offender knows or suspects that it represents a person's benefit from criminal conduct.[61] The reference to 'the alleged offender' means the person charged with the offence in which the issue is raised (ie not the person who may have benefited from the criminal conduct at issue). It will be necessary for the prosecution to demonstrate that the defendant at least suspected that the property concerned had a criminal origin.[62]

(f) Furthermore, whilst it is only in practice necessary for the prosecution to prove—in relation to the necessary mental element—that the defendant suspected that the property concerned had criminal origin, it is also necessary for them to prove that the property concerned is *in fact* criminal property. In other words, the bank employee who assists in the transfer of funds in the belief that they are criminal property does not commit an offence if that belief is subsequently found to have been mistaken.[63]

---

[56] POCA, s 340(9).

[57] Perhaps rather obviously, POCA, s 340(5) and 340(9)(a) confirm that a person 'benefits' from conduct if he obtains property as a result of or in connection with the conduct, and that he 'obtains' property if he acquires an interest in it.

[58] POCA, s 340(4). The same section confirms that property may be 'criminal property' even if the conduct giving rise to it occurred before POCA came into force.

[59] This obvious point is derived from the words '... whether directly or indirectly ...' in para (b) of the statutory definition. However, property ceases to be 'criminal property' once it is acquired in good faith by a third party unconnected with the fraud: see *R v Afolabi* [2009] EWCA Crim 2879.

[60] POCA, s 340(6). The expression 'pecuniary advantage' includes the advantage obtained where the payment of a debt is evaded or unlawfully deferred: *R v Smith* [2002] 1 WLR 54. The importance of this provision will become apparent when the position of the proceeds of tax evasion is considered, below.

[61] See para (b) of the statutory definition in POCA, s 340(3).

[62] On the standard of proof in relation to a suspicion in this type of case, see *Hussein v Chong Fook Ham* [1970] AC 942 (PC). In the view of the present writer, a defendant should only be taken to 'suspect' that property has a criminal origin if he receives information or evidence which is suggestive of that fact in relation to the transaction with which he is concerned. General knowledge that tax evasion is rife in a particular country would not be sufficient for these purposes.

[63] This follows from the House of Lords decision in *R v Montila* [2004] UKHL 50. The House reached this decision partly in reliance on the Vienna and Palermo Conventions (see n 8 above), observing that they appeared to contemplate sanctions against individuals who knew they were dealing with the proceeds of crime.

(g) Finally, as noted in the statutory definition, property can only amount to 'criminal property' if it constitutes or represents a benefit from 'criminal conduct'. It thus becomes necessary to consider the meaning of that expression.

7.33   The expression 'criminal conduct' is defined as conduct which either (i) constitutes an offence in any part of the United Kingdom or (ii) would constitute such an offence if it occurred in the United Kingdom.[64]

7.34   This definition is, in some senses, both a benefit and a burden to the bank. It is a burden in the sense that the criminal offences can apply even though the criminal conduct which gave rise to the benefits or property concerned took place wholly outside the United Kingdom. On the other hand, it is a benefit in that the bank does not have any positive obligation to ascertain whether any particular conduct was lawful or unlawful in the jurisdiction in which it took place.[65]

7.35   If one considers the breadth of the definitions of 'criminal property' and 'criminal conduct', one is left with the impression that banks must be vigilant to detect any funds or other assets which may have been obtained or retained unlawfully. No doubt, in the fight against money laundering, the definitions are intentionally broad. It would be a bold lawyer who advised, in any particular case, that particular funds or assets are not 'criminal property'. Nevertheless, it may be helpful to note a few points:

(a) It will have been seen that conduct does not amount to 'criminal conduct' merely because it is an offence abroad; it must constitute an offence in the UK. As a result, funds which have been brought out of a foreign country in breach of its system of exchange control are not 'criminal property' for these purposes, because evasion of exchange controls is not a criminal offence—and hence not 'criminal conduct'—in the United Kingdom.[66] Of course, a bank would have to proceed with caution in taking this view, because a deliberate evasion of exchange controls may suggest that other offences (eg relating to taxation) have also been committed.

(b) If a person obtains a financial advantage as a result of criminal conduct then, as has been seen, he is taken to have obtained criminal property equal to the amount of

---

To permit a prosecution when the Crown could not prove that the property had criminal origins would have extended the effect of the Conventions to an extent which the House of Lords could not support, at least in the absence of very clear words in the relevant statute. On the other hand, it does not seem to be necessary for the prosecution to prove the *specific* offence to which the proceeds relate: see *Mohammad Ahmad v Her Majesty's Advocate* 2009 Scot (D) 10/7, and the earlier decisions there discussed. The position may be different for the 'regulated sector' offence: see the discussion at para 7.47 below.

[64]   POCA, s 340(2).

[65]   This situation does, however, in some senses create an anomaly. For example, a bank could receive, from a foreign customer, any monies which he earned from an activity which was entirely lawful in the country in which the income was generated, yet which would be unlawful in the United Kingdom. The conduct would have to be treated as 'criminal conduct', and the earnings as 'criminal property', even though no criminal offence had been committed by the beneficiary. The position is, however, in many respects, remedied by specific provisions which were inserted into the substantive offences by the Serious Organised Crime and Police Act 2005. These are considered in relation to the individual offences (below).

[66]   The United Kingdom's Exchange Control Act 1947 was suspended in 1979, and has since been repealed.

that advantage.[67] Consequently, a person who evades his liability to taxation in the United Kingdom is in possession of criminal property equal to the amount of the unpaid tax.[68]

(c) As a consequence of the analysis in (b) above, a person who has fraudulently evaded his tax liabilities in a foreign country is likewise in possession of criminal property, because cheating the revenue authorities would amount to 'criminal conduct' if it occurred in the UK.[69] To this it may be objected that courts in the UK have never enforced foreign tax laws; why should an exception be made in the present context? The answer lies in an analysis of the underlying rationale for this rule. The English courts have never allowed foreign States to enforce their tax laws in the UK, for this would be an invasion of the sovereignty of the United Kingdom.[70] This objection cannot stand in the present case, for it is the terms of this country's domestic legislation which requires the courts to have regard to such tax laws;[71] no invasion of this country's sovereignty is therefore involved.[72] Furthermore, it seems that the principle which prevents enforcement of foreign tax laws is mainly of application in the context of a civil claim; it is of doubtful relevance in criminal proceedings.[73]

(d) It should also be appreciated that the potential scope of the expression 'criminal conduct' has been significantly expanded as a result of the Fraud Act 2006. The Act was designed to provide a sound and logical basis for an offence whose boundary lines were not always clear. This has operated to bring certain types of activity within the fraud 'net' which might not previously have belonged there and, given the peculiarly

---

[67] See the discussion of POCA, s 340(2) above.

[68] Evasion of tax liabilities in the UK is, of course, an offence under a number of statutory enactments. In addition, on the common law offence of cheating the public revenue was specifically preserved by s 32(1)(a) of the Theft Act 1968. The offence may be committed by a dishonest failure to declare taxable income: *R v Mavji* (1987) 84 Cr App Rep 34 and *R v Redford* (1988) Cr App Rep 1; see also *R v Mulligan* [1990] STC 220, CA. For a recent case involving a prosecution for this particular offence and in which money laundering issues arose, see *R v May* [2005] EWCA Crim 97.

[69] See the points made in the previous footnote.

[70] The most frequently quoted authority is the House of Lords decision in *Government of India v Taylor* [1955] AC 491.

[71] In addition, it may be noted that the guidance applicable to the banking industry suggests that foreign tax proceeds should be treated on the same footing as other criminal property—see the JMLSG Guidelines, discussed at para 7.16 above.

[72] For arguments to the contrary, see Brindle, 'Beware the Slippery Slope: Can Your Involvement in Trust Design and Tax Planning Constitute Criminal Money Laundering?' (Paper delivered in 1996). There are various difficulties with this approach. For example, the deliberate evasion of tax may constitute a fraud, and it is difficult to see why the English courts should be required to disregard such an offence merely because the victim is a revenue authority; in other words, not every offence committed against a revenue authority can be seen as a purely 'tax' offence. For discussions of these problems, see Alldridge, *Money Laundering Law* (Hart, Oxford, 2003) p 135 and pp 183–191; *Butterworths International Guide to Money Laundering Law & Practice* (Butterworths, 2003), para 2.20. The US Supreme Court—admittedly only by a majority and against a rather different legislative framework—has held that fraudulent evasion of Canadian liquor duties amounts to a predicate offence for the purposes of its federal wire fraud statute although, as the majority were constrained to observe, '... it may seem an odd use of the Federal Government's resources to prosecute a US citizen for smuggling cheap liquor into Canada ...': see *Pasquantino v United States* 544 US 349 (2005).

[73] *R v Chief Metropolitan Stipendiary Magistrate, ex parte Secretary of State for the Home Department (Nuland case)* [1988] 1 WLR 1204, declining to follow the earlier decision in *R v Governor of Pentonville Prison, ex parte Khubchandani* [1980] 71 Cr App Rep 241.

financial nature of the fraud offence, the 2006 Act has particular consequences for banks and banking transactions which merit further consideration.

(e) Section 2 of the Fraud Act creates an offence of fraud by false representation, under which a person commits an offence if (i) he dishonestly makes a false representation and (ii) in doing so, he intends to make a gain (for himself or any other person) or to expose another to a risk of loss. Thus, if a borrower gives a drawdown notice which includes the customary confirmation to the effect that no event of default has occurred, then director signing the certificate will commit an offence if he knows that statement to be untrue and—if the requested advance is made—then the borrower will be in possession of the proceeds of crime to the extent of those proceeds.

(f) In a similar vein, a person will commit an offence if (i) he dishonestly fails to disclose information which he has a legal duty (including a *contractual* duty) to disclose and (ii) he intends thereby to make a gain or to expose another to the risk of loss. Thus, if a loan agreement includes the usual obligation on the borrower to disclose to the bank the occurrence of a default and a director of the borrower withholds that information with the intention of avoiding a possible acceleration of the facility and demand for repayment, then the director concerned will commit an offence and it appears that the retained proceeds of the loan will accordingly constitute 'criminal property' for POCA purposes.

(g) Both of these offences may have significant consequences for banks in the context of their POCA reporting obligations.[74]

7.36 The scope of the property which may constitute 'criminal property' has now been established; the breadth of the definition cannot be doubted. In cases of uncertainty, a bank will clearly have to proceed on the assumption that particular funds or assets do indeed constitute criminal property, especially given that the element of *mens rea* includes or connotes a mere suspicion.[75]

Concealing Criminal Property

7.37 A person commits an offence under section 327 of POCA if he conceals, disguises,[76] converts, or transfers criminal property, or removes it from England and Wales or from Scotland or Northern Ireland.

7.38 In the context of the activities of a bank, an employee could commit the 'transfer' offence if he arranged for the payment of funds out of an account, knowing that such monies represented criminal property.[77] He would also commit the 'removal' offence if he arranged

---

[74] See in particular the discussion of the 'regulated sector' offence at para 7.47 below.

[75] See POCA, s 340(3)(b) noted in para 7.32(e) above.

[76] Concealing or disguising criminal property includes concealing or disguising its nature, source, location, disposition, movement, or ownership, or any rights with respect to it: see s 327(3).

[77] The requirement of knowledge is, of course, essential in a criminal law context in any event. The point is, however reinforced by the definition of 'criminal property', discussed below. As will be seen, a bank employee could commit these offences even though the criminal property belongs to some other party and does not result from criminal activity on the part of the employee concerned.

for the funds to be transferred out of the jurisdiction.[78] The 'converting' offence would be committed by an employee who undertook a foreign exchange transaction in relation to funds which he believed to represent stolen property. The examples could be multiplied. Whilst, on the face of it, the section is most obviously directed to an individual who is directly benefiting from the proceeds of crime, it will be apparent from this discussion that they may equally be committed by a bank employee who is aware of the nature of the funds but elects to carry out customer instructions or transactions in relation to them.

There are specific defences relating to disclosure, a reasonable excuse for non-disclosure, **7.39** and foreign illegality. Since these defences are common to all of the main money laundering offences, they are considered separately at a later stage.[79]

Acquisition, Use, and Possession of Criminal Property

A person commits an offence under section 329 of POCA if he acquires, uses, or has pos- **7.40** session of criminal property. It would, perhaps, be less easy to apply this provision to a bank employee who knows that customer funds may be criminal property, because it is difficult to argue that the employee himself has acquired, used, or possessed criminal property. Rather, the criminal property would be in the possession of the bank itself. However, the point is unlikely to be of much practical importance because, in the absence of disclosure, such an employee who is aware of the criminal provenance of a customer's assets is likely to commit at least one of the offences noted in the present section.

The disclosure defence and the foreign legality defence are again available in this context.[80] **7.41**

Arrangements Relating to Criminal Property

It will be noted that the 'concealing' and 'acquisition' offences described above will only be **7.42** committed by a bank employee who is aware that property represents the proceeds of crime and takes active steps to assist in the laundering process. Such cases will, hopefully, be relatively rare. In practical terms, banks and those who work for them are much more likely to be concerned with the 'arrangements' offence created by section 329 of POCA.

Under the terms of that section, a person commits an offence '... if he enters into or **7.43** becomes concerned in an arrangement which he knows *or suspects* facilitates (by whatever means) the acquisition, retention, use or control of criminal property by or on behalf of another person ...'.

This provision is more obviously aimed at banks and other intermediaries who may **7.44** not themselves directly benefit from criminal property, but who may lend some form of

---

[78] It will be apparent from the present discussion and from a review of the relevant sections that there is a significant degree of potential overlap between the various offences created by Pt 7 of POCA.

[79] See paras 7.52–7.66 below.

[80] A person charged with an offence under this section may also have a defence if he acquired the relevant property for adequate consideration and did not intend to assist another person to carry out criminal conduct: POCA, s 329(3). This particular defence seems unlikely to be of relevance in the context of proceedings against a bank employee.

assistance to those who do.[81] A bank employee who remits funds abroad or who allows a customer to pay his debts from the proceeds of an account will commit an offence under this section if he 'knows or suspects' that the account includes any proceeds of crime. The provision is of concern to banks because the prosecution need only prove suspicion, as opposed to actual knowledge, and the burden of proof on the prosecution is therefore lighter than might otherwise be the case.[82] Nevertheless, the suspicion must be based on a realistic foundation and must go beyond the realm of the purely speculative.[83]

7.45 It is, however, necessary to dwell briefly upon the meaning of an 'arrangement' which 'facilitates' the acquisition, retention, use, or control of criminal property for the purposes of this section, since the existence of such an arrangement is a necessary ingredient of the offence. The following points may be made in this regard:

(a) the word 'arrangement' must be given a narrow construction in the context of section 328.[84] Although the expression itself is somewhat open-textured, the act of entering into or becoming concerned in an arrangement involves a single, identifiable act at an identifiable point of time, and the offence is only committed at that point;[85]

(b) the expression 'arrangement' connotes a degree of deliberate collusion between at least two parties. Consequently, if a bank has been the victim of fraud then the funds thereby acquired by the offender will represent 'criminal property' for the purposes of these provisions. If, however, the bank seeks to recover the funds from the individual concerned by means of legal proceedings, then the institution of those proceedings does not amount to an 'arrangement', because the element of collusion is lacking;[86]

(c) equally, a bank does not become concerned in an 'arrangement' for these purposes if, acting in good faith, it reaches a negotiated settlement of those proceedings;[87]

(d) on the other hand, the expression 'facilitates' is to be given a broad meaning. It is thus only necessary that the defendant is aware, in a general sense, that his involvement in the arrangements will assist another in the retention of criminal property. It is not necessary to show that the defendant intended to assist in retaining the property in a specific form, or that he had a very specific purpose or objective in mind.[88]

7.46 The disclosure defence and the foreign legality defence are again available in this context.

---

[81] Note the reference to facilitating the retention of criminal property 'by or on behalf of another person'.

[82] This point is emphasized by the decision of the Privy Council in *Hussein v Chong Fook Ham* [1970] AC 942 (PC), where suspicion was described as the level of knowledge which is likely to provide the starting point for an investigation.

[83] *R v De Silva* [2006] EWCA Crim 1654.

[84] *Bowman v Fels* [2005] EWCA Civ 226, paras 64–69 (CA). This important decision is mainly of relevance to the conduct of litigation by solicitors where the matter at issue may involve criminal property, but some of the commentary is relevant to the substance of the money laundering offences in a banking context. The decision of the Court of Appeal in this case effectively overruled the earlier decision in *P v P (Ancillary Relief: Proceeds of Crime)* [2003]4 All ER 483.

[85] *Bowman v Fels*, para 67.

[86] Nor, it may be added, is the bank's objective to facilitate '... the acquisition, retention, use or control of criminal property ...' by the fraudster; on the contrary, the bank is seeking to recover that property for the rightful owner. See also *Bowman v Fels*, paras 67 and 68.

[87] On this point, and the policy reasons which underlie this view, see *Bowman v Fels*, paras 99–101.

[88] This seems to be the effect of the decision in *R v McMaster* [1999] 1 Cr App rep 402, approved in *Bowman v Fels*, para 98.

The Regulated Sector Offence

In an effort to secure a greater flow of information about suspect transactions from banks **7.47**
and other financial institutions, a 'regulated sector' offence was introduced by section 330
of POCA.[89]

An offence is committed by an individual under this section if: **7.48**

(a) he knows or suspects, *or has reasonable grounds for knowing or suspecting,*[90] that another
     person is engaged in money laundering;[91]
(b) the information giving rise to his knowledge or suspicion (or, as the case may be, which
     provided reasonable grounds for such knowledge or suspicion) was received by him in
     the course of a business in the regulated sector;
(c) he can identify *either* the person whom he suspects of money laundering *or* the where-
     abouts of any laundered property and he believes, or it is reasonable to expect him
     to believe, that the information in his possession will or may assist in identifying the
     person concerned or in locating any laundered property;[92] and
(d) he does not make the required disclosure as soon as practicable after he received the
     relevant information.

The disclosure defence is separately considered at a later stage.[93] It is thus only necessary for **7.49**
the present to consider the first two elements of this offence, and the particular defences
which may be available.

It will be noted that the scope of the offence is potentially very wide. It may be committed **7.50**
without any positive act on the part of a bank employee, other than the mere receipt of
information in the course of his work.[94] It does not require that the employee be involved
in any transaction of any kind. Indeed, he may decline to accept a proposed transaction on
the basis that he suspects that part of the funding may represent criminal property, yet he
may still commit an offence if he fails to make the required disclosure. It does not even
require that he actually knows or suspects that someone is engaged in money laundering;
an offence is committed if he has reasonable grounds for knowing or suspecting money

---

[89] The offence about to be discussed applies to banks and many other financial institutions, and to lawyers,
accountants and many others: see the definition of 'regulated sector' in Sch 9 to POCA. The present section
only considers the subject from the viewpoint of banking business.

[90] The italicized wording significantly broadens the scope of the offence. Some of the consequences are
discussed below.

[91] For these purposes, 'money laundering' is an act which constitutes an offence under ss 327, 328, or
329 of POCA (considered above). The expression also includes attempt, conspiracy, and other preparatory
offences, and extends to acts committed abroad which would have amounted to such an offence had they
occurred in the UK: see POCA, s 339(11).

[92] This condition was inserted by Serious Organised Crime and Police Act 2005, s 104. The provision
would relieve a bank employee of the need to make a report if the information he held was of such a general
nature that it would not form the basis of a meaningful report which could assist in the fight against money
laundering.

[93] See para 7.52 below.

[94] Since the section creates a criminal offence, this aspect of the provision should be narrowly construed.
Information is only received in the course of work if the employee is in some way engaged on the bank's business. Thus, information casually received in a social environment with work colleagues would not fall to be
taken into account for the purposes of the regulated sector offence.

laundering. This presumably means that he has in his possession such information as would lead a reasonable banker in his position to suspect money laundering activity. The fact that money laundering has not in fact taken place would appear to be an irrelevant factor in determining whether a regulated sector offence has been committed, because it is the mere *suspicion* which lies at the heart of section 330.[95]

7.51 The potentially draconian offence is, however, cut down in certain respects. In particular:

(a) if an employee is prosecuted on the basis that he had reasonable grounds for knowing or suspecting money laundering,[96] then he will have a defence if he has not been provided with appropriate, anti-money laundering training by his employer.[97] That training should, of course, be sufficient to alert the employee to circumstances under which he should be alive to the risks; and

(b) where an employee is prosecuted under this section, the court must take into account the extent to which he complied with any published guidance governing his activities.[98]

The Disclosure Defence

7.52 It has been noted previously that the money laundering offences are each subject to a disclosure defence.[99] Although the details vary in certain detailed respects, this general comment is true of all of the offences discussed thus far, including the regulated sector offence. It is accordingly now necessary to consider the nature of that defence.

7.53 In general terms, it will be apparent that a bank employee who knows or suspects that a person is involved in money laundering may commit an offence if he in any way assists in that endeavour. That rather broad brush statement of the law conceals a number of practical difficulties. In particular, the employee may have grounds for suspicion, yet in fact the property concerned may be entirely legitimate; there can be no guarantee that an employee's suspicions are necessarily well-founded. He will only very rarely have a completely comprehensive view of the customer's assets and activities. The bank may therefore be left in something of a quandary as to the appropriate steps which should be taken once such a suspicion has arisen. Furthermore, the purpose of the legislation is to secure a flow of relevant information to the authorities about real criminal activity.

7.54 Under these circumstances, the legislation creates a 'safe harbour' for employees in the regulated sector; they will not commit an offence if a disclosure of the relevant information is made in accordance with POCA requirements *and* any step which they take is done with the necessary consent. In practical terms, disclosure should always be made in cases in which there are genuine grounds for suspicion, for a bank has only very limited means of

---

[95] See *Mohammad Ahmad v Her Majesty's Advocate* 2009 Scot (D) 10/7. See in particular the discussion at paras 27–38 of the judgment.

[96] ie it is not alleged that he had *actual* knowledge of such activity.

[97] POCA, s 330(7).

[98] On the general relevance of published guidance which has been approved by the Treasury, see para 7.15 above.

[99] See POCA, ss 327(2), 328(2), 329(2) and 330(4).

investigating its concerns and, in any event, that is the function of the investigating authorities.

How, then, may such a disclosure be made?

In the case of a bank employee, disclosure will usually be made to the Money Laundering **7.55** Reporting Officer (MLRO) appointed by his employer institution.[100] A report made by the bank employee to the MLRO in the course of his work and in accordance with the bank's internal procedures will constitute a sufficient disclosure for these purposes.[101] An employee may, however, make a report direct to the Serious Organised Crime Agency (SOCA),[102] even though an internal report would be a sufficient disclosure in his case.[103]

Disclosure alone, however, is not by itself a sufficient defence[104] where the employee may **7.56** be taking some step—such as effecting a transfer of funds—which may have the effect of assisting in the use, retention, or transfer of funds which may be criminal property, or which might otherwise constitute an offence under sections 327, 328, or 329 of POCA. It would clearly be inappropriate if the employee could make the disclosure and then proceed to carry out the (otherwise prohibited act) a few minutes later. Consequently, the act which would otherwise amount to a money laundering offence on the part of the employee concerned and which forms the subject matter of the disclosure can only be effected if he has the 'appropriate consent' for that purpose. The 'appropriate consent' is the consent of the person to whom the disclosure has been made.[105] As has been seen, this will usually be the MLRO in the employer institution, but in limited cases it may be the constable or customs officer to whom the disclosure was made. Where the disclosure has been made to the MLRO, 'appropriate consent' will mean express consent. Where, however, the disclosure has been made to a constable or a customs officer, (i) consent is deemed to have been given if it has not been explicitly refused within seven working days of the disclosure and (ii) even if consent is refused during the initial seven day period, consent is deemed to have been given once a moratorium period of thirty-one days has elapsed from the date of

---

[100] The legislation refers to this individual as the 'nominated officer', but the text will use the term 'MLRO'.

[101] POCA, s 338(5). Section 338(1)(a) states, perhaps rather obviously, that the disclosure must confirm that certain '... property is criminal property ...', but the legislation does not otherwise state precisely what level of disclosure is required for these purposes. However, it is perhaps fair to assume that the statutory reference to 'disclosure' connotes a full, frank and complete disclosure. Consequently, the relevant employee must provide complete details of the information which has come into his possession; otherwise, any consent which he obtains from the MLRO may not sufficiently cover the steps which he proposes to take.

[102] POCA, s 338(1). In practice, disclosures by bank employees are invariably made to the MLRO on an 'internal' basis, since employees will be contractually bound to follow internal procedures in this area.

[103] The legislation adopts this scheme because it is clearly more convenient for the authorities to deal with individuals within the bank who are tasked with POCA compliance, and who will have the experience to decide whether particular situations merit a report. It would also be unreasonable to place on individual employees the burden of reporting direct to the authorities themselves.

[104] By way of exception, disclosure by itself is a defence to the 'regulated sector' offence, because the possession of knowledge, suspicion, or reasonable grounds therefore by themselves constitute the offence, without the need for any further action by the employee or any active participation in a money laundering offence on his part: see POCA, s 330(5). In contrast, the offences created by ss 327, 328, or 329 would always involve some positive act on the part of the employee concerned.

[105] See POCA, s 335(1).

such refusal. There is no provision for the extension of the moratorium period, and accordingly the bank could accede to its customer's instructions on the expiry of that period, even though consent may originally have been refused.[106] The rationale, presumably, is that the period concerned is sufficient for the authorities to act if they believe the case to be sufficiently serious.[107]

7.57 It is perhaps appropriate to add that a disclosure which is made pursuant to the provisions discussed above will not amount to a breach of any duty of confidentiality owed to the customer, whether pursuant to the banker–customer contract, the Data Protection Act, or otherwise.[108]

7.58 An individual does not commit the regulated sector offence if he has a reasonable excuse for the non-disclosure.[109]

The 'Reasonable Excuse' Defence

7.59 In relation to each of the main money laundering offences set out in sections 327, 328, and 329 of POCA, the bank employee concerned does not commit an offence if '… he intended to make such a disclosure but had a reasonable excuse for not doing so …'.[110]

7.60 So far as the writer is aware, there are currently no decisions on the scope of this defence. In order to establish the defence, the employee would have to establish *both* his intention to lodge a report *and* an adequate justification for his failure to do so. It may be that an employee could establish this defence if he could show that he had discussed the matter in general terms with his immediate superiors within the bank, but had been advised that the subject matter did not warrant a report (or, alternatively, that a report on the same subject had already been lodged by another member of staff).

7.61 In contrast, a person charged under the 'regulated sector' offence created by section 330 does not need to show that he intended to make a report. He merely needs to show that he had a reasonable excuse for his failure to make the report.[111] Nevertheless, the factual

---

[106] For the detailed provisions, see POCA, s 335(2)–(6). It should, however, be appreciated that the granting of consent, whether actual or deemed, will only protect the bank from the commission of an offence under the relevant sections of POCA. They will not affect the right of any true owner of the funds to make a civil claim against the bank under the 'constructive trust' principles discussed at paras 18.27–18.31 below.

[107] The provisions just discussed may have civil consequences in the context of the banker–customer relationship: see paras 7.83–7.92 below.

[108] For the details, see POCA, s 337. The effectiveness of this provision was recognized in *Shah v HSBC Private Bank* [2009] All ER (D) 204.

[109] POCA, s 330(6)(b). It is not entirely clear what would constitute a 'reasonable excuse' for these purposes, although presumably a threat of physical violence or intimidation from the customer would suffice, as would reliance on a colleague's assurance that a report had been made, even though that assurance subsequently turns out to be false. It should be noted that this defence differs slightly from the 'reasonable excuse' defence discussed at paras 7.59–7.61 below, where the defence also involves an intention to make a report.

[110] This defence is set out in POCA, ss 327(2)(b), 328(2)(b), and 329(2)(b). The words '… such a disclosure …' do, of course, refer to a disclosure under the rules outlined in the last section. As will be seen, the ingredients of the defence are slightly different where an employee is charged with the 'regulated sector' offence.

[111] POCA, s 330(6)(a). The same defence is available to an MLRO in the regulated sector who is prosecuted for failing to make a report to SOCA: POCA, s 331(6).

circumstances which might justify such a defence must be similar to those which have just been described in the context of the other, principal money laundering offences.

The Foreign Legality Defence

Reference has already been made to the 'foreign legality' defence, which applies in relation to all of the offences discussed thus far.[112] **7.62**

In essence, a person does not commit an offence under those sections if: **7.63**

(a) he knows or believes on reasonable grounds that the relevant criminal conduct occurred outside the United Kingdom; and

(b) the conduct which gave rise to the criminal property[113] (i) did not constitute a criminal offence under the law of the place in which and at the time at which it was committed and (ii) is not of a kind prescribed by an order made by the Secretary of State.[114]

A bank employee would thus not commit an offence under these sections if he knows or reasonably believes that the funds with which he is dealing are derived from activities conducted abroad and which are lawful under the laws of the place concerned. Although such funds strictly remain 'criminal property' for the purposes of POCA, banks in the United Kingdom can lawfully become involved in the transfer of such funds in light of this exemption. **7.64**

The 'De Minimis' Defence

After POCA had been in operation for a period, the government accepted that banks which accept deposits involving minor amounts of money should not generally commit a money laundering offence in relation to relatively small amounts of money, on the basis that the cost of supervising activities in relation to such amounts would exceed the resultant benefit to the detection of money laundering activity. Thus, a deposit-taking institution does not commit an offence of converting or transferring criminal property under section 329 of POCA[115] if the relevant act is carried out in the course of operating an account maintained with it and the value of the criminal property at issue is below the stipulated threshold.[116] **7.65**

---

[112] The defence applies in identical terms to each of the offences discussed above. For the details, see ss 327(2A), 328(3), 329(2A), and 330(7A).

[113] Note that this refers to the original derivation of the property, and not to the fact that it is being laundered through the United Kingdom.

[114] It may seem curious that the Secretary of State has the right to prescribe certain types of conduct committed abroad for these purposes, even though that conduct would not be criminal in the United Kingdom. Certain gambling and financial offences have been prescribed for these purposes: see The Proceeds of Crime (Money Laundering: Exception to Overseas Conduct Defence) Order 2006 (SI 2006/1071).

[115] See POCA, s 327(2C). Note that this defence does not apply to the offences of concealing or disguising criminal property, or the offence of removing such property from the jurisdiction—s 327(1)(a), (b) and (e), read together with s 327(2C). The de minimis exemption would thus not absolve a bank from liability where it was actively involved in money laundering. Furthermore, the defence would not seem to be available where the bank is asked to remit funds outside the country.

[116] The monetary threshold is stipulated by the Secretary of State under POCA, s 339 and is currently set at £250. However, it should be noted that the provision allows for the operation of the account but does not absolve the bank from its 'regulated sector' reporting obligations.

The same defence is available in the context of the 'arrangements' offence[117] and the 'acquisition, use and possession' offence.[118]

7.66 It should, however, be appreciated that this defence is available only to the deposit-taking institution itself. It is not available to a bank employee who may be charged with an offence.

Offences by the MLRO

7.67 It has been seen that the offences created by sections 327–330 of POCA can be committed by any person working within a bank. It has also been shown that the commission of such offences can usually be avoided by means of a full disclosure to the person appointed to act as MLRO within the institution concerned.[119] The reason for the legislative adoption of these reporting lines has already been highlighted,[120] and requires no further justification. Nevertheless, information which rests with the MLRO is clearly of limited value to the investigating authorities. Consequently, the MLRO has to make an assessment of the disclosures made to him, and to decide whether they should be passed on to those authorities.[121]

7.68 The MLRO who works in the regulated sector is thus subject to 'mirror image' offences created by section 331 and 332 of POCA. To summarize those provisions briefly, an MLRO commits an offence if:

(a) he knows or suspects that another person is engaged in money laundering[122] or, in the case of a disclosure made to him pursuant to the 'regulated sector' provision in section 330 of POCA, he knows or suspects, *or has reasonable grounds for knowing or suspecting*[123] that someone is so engaged;

(b) the information which gave rise to the knowledge, suspicion or reasonable grounds (as the case may be) came to him as a result of a disclosure made to him under section 330;

(c) he knows the identity of the money launderer or the whereabouts of the laundered property, or he knows or believes, or it is reasonable to expect him to believe, that the

---

[117] POCA, s 328(5).

[118] POCA, s 329(2C).

[119] Although, in the case of the offences created by ss 327–329, it would also be necessary for the employee to obtain the requisite consent before taking any step which might otherwise constitute an offence.

[120] See n 103 above.

[121] In practice, reports of suspicious transactions are normally passed to the Serious Organised Crime Agency, on forms published by it for that purpose.

[122] As noted previously, 'money laundering' is defined to include any of the offences listed in POCA, ss 327–329, and any associated, inchoate offence. The 'foreign legality' defence is once again available in this context—see s 330(7A).

[123] It will be recalled that an offence is only committed by a bank employee under POCA, ss 327, 328, or 329 if he knowingly becomes involved in a money laundering transaction or arrangement. In contrast, a 'regulated sector' offence can be committed under s 330 if the employee merely knows or suspects, or has reasonable grounds for suspecting, that someone is engaged in money laundering. The *mens rea* element of the offences which can be committed by the MLRO thus 'mirrors' the state of knowledge required of the employee in relation to the underlying offences.

identity of the money launderer or the location of the relevant property can be identified from the information disclosed to him;[124] and

(d) he does not disclose the matter to SOCA as soon as practicable following receipt of the disclosure.[125]

The POCA regime thus relies for its effectiveness on rigorous reporting procedures **7.69** which ultimately lead to the MLRO, providing a point of contact with the investigating authorities themselves.

Tipping off— Regulated Sector

Clearly, if a bank employee suspects that someone is engaged in money laundering and has **7.70** made a disclosure to the bank's MLRO in that respect, it would be unhelpful to any subsequent investigation by the authorities if the existence of the suspicion had been disclosed to the person concerned. Apart from other considerations, this might afford to him an opportunity to transfer funds or to make himself unavailable to the authorities. Confidentiality of the disclosure is therefore paramount. With this in mind, section 333A of POCA[126] creates the offences of 'tipping off' and prejudicing an investigation.

A person commits a 'tipping off' offence under section 333A(1) if (i) he knows that a dis- **7.71** closure has been made to the MLRO or SOCA in accordance with the provisions described above, (ii) he reveals to a third party the fact that such a disclosure has been made, and (iii) information about the relevant disclosure came to him in the course of his employment in the regulated sector.

Likewise, under section 333A(3), an offence is committed if (i) a person discloses to a third **7.72** party the fact that an investigation into money laundering allegations is being carried out, (ii) the disclosure is likely to prejudice the investigation, and (iii) the information came to the relevant person in the course of his employment in the regulated sector.

A few points may be noted in this context: **7.73**

(a) the 'tipping off' or 'prejudicing an investigation' offences may be committed even though only an 'internal' disclosure has been made to the MLRO;

(b) it therefore appears that a bank employee may commit this offence even though the MLRO in his turn decides that the evidence is not sufficient to justify an 'external' report to the authorities;

(c) in relation to the 'prejudicing an investigation' offence, section 333(2) of POCA provided a defence where the employee did not know or suspect that his disclosure was likely to prejudice the investigation. This provision has now been repealed[127] and there

---

[124] Once again, this requirement was inserted by the Serious Organised Crime and Police Act 2005, s 104 so that it is unnecessary to report information which is unlikely to be of material assistance in the context of an investigation.

[125] Since the MLRO sits at the pinnacle of the internal reporting process, he can only obtain the protection of the disclosure defence if he reports the matter via the external reporting procedure, ie to the police.

[126] The provision was inserted by the Terrorism Act 2000 and the Proceeds of Crime Act 2002 (Amendment) Regulations 2007 (SI 2007/3398).

[127] See the 2007 Regulations mentioned in n 126 above.

is now no equivalent provision. However, it would seem that knowledge of potential prejudice to the investigation would remain an essential element of the offence in order to demonstrate the necessary *mens rea*;

(d) the possibility of a later prosecution under the 'tipping off' or 'prejudicing an investigation' provisions illustrates the need for strict confidentiality. Whilst some internal disclosure of the report may be necessary, this should be restricted as far as possible and the bank's procedures should reflect the point;[128] and

(e) certain disclosures will not result in the commission of a 'tipping off' or 'prejudicing the investigation' offences—for example, where the disclosure is made to a fellow employee or to another credit or financial institution within the same group.[129]

Terrorist Financing

Introduction

7.74 Thus far, the present chapter has been principally concerned with the proceeds of crime. For reasons which require no explanation, terrorism has been a major concern for many countries over recent years, and numerous initiatives have been launched against it. In the present context, it is necessary only to consider those aspects which may affect the conduct of banking business.

7.75 It has been recognized that most terrorist actions must be financed by some means, and that funds may have to be transferred internationally in order to achieve those ends. The Terrorism Act 2000 (the 2000 Act) therefore seeks to impede the use of the financial system for those purposes. Notwithstanding the importance of these provisions, it is possible to deal with this subject quite briefly, because the structure of the relevant aspects of the legislation is in many respects similar to the corresponding provisions which have already been discussed in the context of the Proceeds of Crime Act.

'Terrorism' and 'Terrorist Property'

7.76 For the purposes of the 2000 Act, 'terrorism' means[130] any actual or threatened action which is designed to influence the government or to intimidate the public,[131] and which is intended to advance a political, religious, or ideological cause. The action must involve serious violence against a person or serious damage to property, or otherwise must endanger life or create health and safety risks for the public.[132]

---

[128] The recommendation is included in the JMLSG Guidelines (see para 17.15 above).
[129] For these provisions and the relevant conditions, see POCA, ss 333C, 333D, and 333E.
[130] For the details of the definition, see s 1 of the 2000 Act.
[131] References to the 'government' and the 'public' include both the United Kingdom and foreign countries. Likewise, the action prohibited by the section may take place either in the UK or abroad: see s 1(4). The 2000 Act thus criminalizes action taken by foreign nationals outside the UK and which does not involve the government or the public in the United Kingdom. A discussion of the extra-territorial character of criminal legislation is beyond the scope of this work.
[132] Section 1(2) of the 2000 Act. That subsection also confirms that action intended to interfere with computer or other electronic systems may also constitute 'terrorism'.

The 2000 Act prohibits various actions involving 'terrorist property', which is defined[133] to **7.77**
mean:

(a) money or other property likely to be used for the purposes of terrorism, including any
    resources of a proscribed organization;[134]
(b) proceeds—direct or indirect—of the commission of any act of terrorism (including
    any payment or reward for the commission of a terrorist act); and
(c) proceeds of any act carried out for the purposes of terrorism.

The Offences

The 2000 Act does, of course, create numerous offences associated with the commission **7.78**
of terrorist acts and the support of terrorist organizations. In particular, an offence is
committed[135] by any one who:

(a) solicits, receives, or provides funds for terrorist purposes;
(b) uses or possesses money for terrorist purposes;
(c) enters into arrangements involving the provision of funds for terrorist purposes; or
(d) becomes involved in an arrangement which facilitates the retention or control of ter-
    rorist property by another person (whether by means of concealment, removal from
    the jurisdiction, transfer to nominees, or in any other manner).

As will be seen, the offences relevant to the banking sector[136] are linked to the four offences **7.79**
which have just been described.

In this respect, the key offence is created by section 21A of the 2000 Act.[137] Under the terms **7.80**
of that section, an individual commits an offence if:

(a) he knows or suspects, *or has reasonable grounds for knowing or suspecting*, that a person
    has committed one of the four offences outlined above;
(b) the information giving rise to the knowledge or suspicion, or which gives reasonable
    grounds for such knowledge or suspicion, came to him in the course of his work in the
    regulated sector; and
(c) he did not disclose the information to the bank's MLRO as soon as practicable after he
    received it.[138]

The structure of the offence is thus very similar to that adopted for the purposes of the **7.81**
'regulated sector' offence in section 330 of POCA.[139]

---

[133] The definition is to be found in s 14 of the 2000 Act.
[134] The expression 'proscribed organization' refers to organizations which have been proscribed under
the 2000 Act itself or under certain other legislation: see s 11(4) of the 2000 Act. Proscribed organizations
currently include Al-Qaida and the Taleban, amongst many others.
[135] For the offences about to be noted, see ss 15–18 of the 2000 Act.
[136] As in the case of the offence created by POCA, s 330 (see para 7.47 above), the s 21A offence applies
to anyone working in the 'regulated sector': see s 21A(10) and Sch 3A to the 2000 Act. The definition of
'regulated sector' is identical in each case.
[137] The section was inserted into the 2000 Act by Anti-terrorism, Crime and Security Act 2001, s 3.
[138] If a report is ultimately made to the SOCA under these provisions, then the bank is not to be taken to
be in breach of any duties of confidentiality which it may owe to the customer: s 21B of the 2000 Act.
[139] The available defences are likewise similar. For example, no offence is committed if the defendant has a
reasonable excuse for non-disclosure. Furthermore, in assessing whether an offence has been committed, the
court must take into account any relevant guidance issued by market associations or the FSA.

7.82 It is incumbent on banks to have in place appropriate training procedures to ensure that employees can detect transactions which may involve terrorist property.[140]

Civil Consequences of Money Laundering Legislation

7.83 The rules discussed above are mainly concerned with the criminal offences associated with anti-money laundering legislation. But it is apparent that the rules may interfere with the operation of the account of a customer, and it is thus clear that compliance with the legislation may also have civil or contractual consequences. In practice, two types of situation are likely to arise. In one type of case, the bank may have received a transfer for the benefit of its customer and may immediately suspect that the funds represent the proceeds of crime. Alternatively, it may have received the funds in good faith but may later receive information which leads the bank to believe that the funds may be suspect. How should the bank respond in such a case, having regard to its potentially conflicting duties to the customer and the terms of POCA? In addition, how should the bank respond to the inevitable queries from the customer as to non-compliance with his instructions? For convenience of explanation, the three situations will be considered separately.

7.84 In each case, however, it is obvious that the blocking of the customer's account—even for a relatively brief period—may have very serious commercial consequences. He may be unable to meet his debts as they fall due, and his reputation in his business market may suffer very serious damage. The tension between duties under POCA and the obligations to the customer can therefore be particularly acute.

Receipt of Funds

7.85 A bank may suspect that funds remitted to it for credit to a particular client represent the proceeds of crime. That suspicion may arise as soon as the funds are received, for example, because the amount of the credit is unusually large for the customer concerned, because the relevant account has been dormant for a period, or because the payment transaction involves an overseas jurisdiction which may be suspect.

7.86 The bank faces an immediate difficulty at the point of time at which the suspicion arises. The bank suspects that the funds represent 'criminal property' for the purposes of section 340 of POCA. If it transpires that they are in fact the proceeds of crime,[141] then does the bank commit an offence by accepting the funds transfer? The defences to the money laundering offences provided by POCA are designed to facilitate the investigation of crime; they do not affect the civil rights of an innocent party who may be caught up in the investigation.[142]. The bank's position is rendered more complex by the speed at which modern

---

[140] See reg 21 of the Money Laundering Regulations 2007, which has already been considered at para 7.25 above.

[141] This point will have to be proved if the bank is ultimately prosecuted for an offence under POCA: see *R v Montila* [2004] UKHL 50 (HL), to which reference has already been made in para 7.32 above.

[142] The point is made in the *Tayeb* case (para 54) to which more detailed reference will be made below.

payment systems operate, leaving it little time to give detailed consideration to the grounds for its suspicion or to make any further enquiries.[143]

An unhappy situation of precisely this kind fell to be considered in *Tayeb v HSBC Bank* **7.87** *plc.*[144] Mr Tayeb was a Tunisian national who had no place of residence in the UK. In April 2000, he presented himself to HSBC at its branch in Derby, and opened an instant savings account. The account was opened to receive the proceeds of the sale of the domain name '.ly', which was owned by Mr Tayeb and which a Libyan government agency wished to acquire. It seems that the negotiations took several months, and the account thus lay dormant until 21 September 2000. On that day, Mr Tayeb completed the sale of the domain name and a sum approaching £950,000 was remitted to it on behalf of the purchaser by a branch of Barclays Bank.

On the following day, a meeting took place between the bank and the customer to discuss **7.88** the situation. However, the bank remained doubtful about the origins of the funds, and decided to return them to Barclays as the remitting bank. There was some evidence that the return of funds in doubtful circumstances represented established banking practice, but this was rejected by the court and, in any event, it would have required cogent evidence of a practice which overrode the bank's general contractual obligation to collect and receive funds on behalf of its customer.[145]

For present purposes, the key question was—does section 328 of POCA[146] necessarily **7.89** involve the commission of an offence by a bank which receives and retains funds which it believes to be tainted? If so, then it may be argued that the bank has a right to return the funds to the remitting institution in order to avoid the commission of an offence.[147] However, the court rightly rejected this line of argument, holding that there was no 'unavoidable inconsistency' between the contractual requirement to accept funds remitted to the customer's account and the need to comply with section 328 of POCA. The bank could simply accept the funds and block them, pending receipt of the necessary consent from SOCA. The mere retention of the funds in this way would not have involved the bank in the commission of an offence. As a result, the bank was liable to Mr Tayeb for the repayment of his deposit because—having accepted them for credit to his account—it was not then open to the bank unilaterally to cancel its debt by returning the monies to Barclays.

---

[143] On payment systems generally, see Chapter 19 below.

[144] [2004] EWHC 1529 (Comm). The case in fact considered the earlier money laundering legislation contained in the Criminal Justice Act 1988, but the essential principles remain the same.

[145] On the duties of the collecting bank generally, see Chapter 18 below.

[146] The case was, in fact concerned with the forerunner provision contained in Criminal Justice Act 1988, s 93A. Whilst the language of the sections differs in certain respects, those differences do not appear to be material in the present context.

[147] It must be an implied term of the banker–customer contract that a bank is not required to take any step which would involve it in the commission of an offence or, alternatively, the illegality has the effect of suspending the obligation to comply with the customer's instructions so long as the relevant circumstances subsist.

Suspicion Arising in Relation to Funds already Held

7.90   In contrast, a bank may receive funds in good faith and credit them to the customer's account, but a suspicion as to their legitimacy may arise at a later stage. How is the bank to respond in such a situation?

7.91   The most recent decision of relevance in this sphere appears to be *Shah v HSBC Private Bank.*[148] The customer had dealings in Zimbabwe which the bank regarded as a ground for suspicion. The bank accordingly blocked his accounts and reported the matter to SOCA. In fact, the block only lasted for a few days because SOCA provided the necessary consent to operate the accounts. Nevertheless, compliance with payment instructions had been delayed in the interim period, and the customer claimed to have suffered losses as a result. The court held that the customer's claim had no prospect of success because:

(a) once the bank had formed a suspicion, it came under an obligation to notify SOCA. Whether or not the bank had a 'suspicion' was essentially a subjective matter and the customer therefore could not challenge the bank's view on the basis that there were no reasonable grounds for it or on any other basis, unless it could be shown that the bank was acting in bad faith—in other words, that the suspicion was not genuinely held;[149] and

(b) the bank could not be held to be in breach of contract solely as a result of complying with its obligations under POCA. Given the statutory framework and the *subjective* nature of any suspicion, it would not be appropriate to impose any *objective* requirement of reasonableness on the bank in relation to its conduct under POCA. It follows that, in civil proceedings to compel the bank to comply with its contractual obligations, the court will not normally be in a position to compel the disclosure of material which may have given rise to the bank's suspicion.[150]

7.92   This is, of course, a satisfactory outcome so far as the bank is concerned, and ensures that it should not incur any liability to the customer in damages as a result of complying with its POCA obligations.

Dealings with the Customer in Relation to POCA

7.93   As already noted, if a bank elects to block an account on the basis of a suspicion of money laundering, then it must avoid alerting the customer to the fact that a report has been made and to the possibility of an investigation.[151] This is obviously a delicate and difficult situation because, in the normal course, the bank would execute its customer's instructions promptly. However, it is plainly difficult for the bank to explain the position when payments are not being made, or cheques are being 'bounced' when the customer's account is in credit. It is possible for the bank to apply to the court for directions, and a case of this

---

[148]   [2009] All ER (D) 204 (Jan).

[149]   In this respect, the court relied on the earlier decisions to similar effect in *Squirrell Ltd v National Westminster Bank plc* [2005] 1 All ER (Comm) 749 and *K Ltd v National Westminster Bank plc* [2006] 2 All ER (Comm) 655.

[150]   *N2J Ltd v Cater Allen and others* (QBD, 21 February 2006). Note, however, the guidance given for this type of case in *C v S Money Laundering, Discovery of Documents* [1999] 1 WLR 1551.

[151]   See para 7.70 above.

kind came before the Court of Appeal in *Governor and Company of the Bank of Scotland v A Ltd*,[152] where the bank was concerned that funds within an account may represent the proceeds of a fraud on third parties, that the bank might be sued by those parties and that it would be unable to use the relevant evidence in its possession to defend such a claim because this might alert the customer to the investigation. The Court of Appeal noted that, in the absence of any agreement with SOCA, the bank could apply to the court to determine the nature and scope of the information and evidence which could be disclosed as part of the defence. It was, however, inappropriate for the bank to seek or to accept an injunction against itself so as to prohibit the operation of the account.[153] It is respectfully submitted that this decision is of limited assistance to banks and that, in practice, they should simply rely on the existence of a suspicion to block the account, and manage the customer relationship as well as they can pending receipt of the necessary SOCA consent.

---

[152] [2001] 3 All ER 58.
[153] Such an injunction had been offered and accepted at first instance.

8

THE MARKET REGULATORS

Introduction

The preceding chapters in this section have emphasized the role of the FSA in the supervision and regulation of the banking sector. Yet it should not be forgotten that these roles were fulfilled by the Bank of England (the 'Bank') until 1997 and that, notwithstanding the transfer of those particular functions to the FSA,[1] the Bank retains various key roles within the financial system. The Treasury also has a role to play both at the domestic and international levels. **8.01**

It is important to understand the respective roles played by these bodies, and the relationship between them. At an individual level, the FSA, the Bank, and the Treasury each have individual roles of a statutory or official nature. The relationship between the three is, however, agreed and explained in a 'Memorandum of Understanding', which is of significant practical importance and to which reference will be made from time to time.[2] In addition, **8.02**

---

[1] On the transfer of banking supervisory functions to the FSA, see Pt 3, Bank of England Act 1998. The policy decision was made by the incoming Labour Government, partly on the grounds of perceived failings in the supervision of BCCI and Barings.

[2] The Memorandum of Understanding was entered into among the Bank, the FSA and the Treasury in October 1997, as part of the arrangements involving the transfer of supervisory functions from the Bank to the FSA. A revised version was published in May 2006. The Memorandum is intended to establish a framework for cooperation between the three parties in the field of financial stability, and explains their respective responsibilities: see para 1 of the Memorandum. The Memorandum also establishes a Standing Committee

in the current environment of international financial problems, it is also necessary to understand the role played by EU and international bodies in crisis management.

8.03   With these considerations in mind, the present chapter is organized as follows:

(a)   the opening section considers the role of the FSA (including its statutory objectives and powers under the Financial Services and Markets Act 2000);

(b)   the second section explains the role of the Bank of England in the fields of financial stability and monetary policy;

(c)   the next section examines the role of HM Treasury;

(d)   the following section considers the development of regulatory bodies at the European level, largely in response to the credit crunch and the problems to which it gave rise; and

(e)   the final section briefly notes some recent international initiatives.

The Financial Services Authority

History and Functions of the FSA

8.04   The FSA is a company limited by guarantee[3] and has the functions conferred upon it by the Financial Services and Markets Act 2000 (FSMA).[4] The structure and governance of the FSA is in some respects determined by the FSMA.[5] It should be noted that the FSA is not to be regarded as acting on behalf of the Crown,[6] with the result that the Crown cannot incur liability for the FSA's acts or omissions.

8.05   Under the terms of the FSMA as originally framed, the FSA was required to carry out its functions in a manner consistent with four, specific regulatory objectives, namely:

(a)   the maintenance of market confidence in the UK's financial system;

(b)   the promotion of public awareness in the financial system (including awareness of the risks and benefits associated with differing types of investment);

(c)   the protection of consumers to an appropriate extent, having regard to the differing degrees of risk inherent in different types of investment; and

---

on Financial Stability as a forum for discussion of relevant issues: see paras 10–13 of the Memorandum. It should be noted that, at the time of writing, the Memorandum is in the course of revision to reflect the terms of the Financial Services Bill.

[3]   The company was formerly known as The Securities and Investment Board and had been established for the purposes of the Financial Services Act 1986.

[4]   It should be emphasized that the present section provides only a very general overview of the role and powers of the FSA. It does not seek to deal with procedural, governance, or numerous other topics. A detailed and illuminating discussion of these issues is to be found in Blair, Walker and Purves, chs 1 and 2.

[5]   See FSMA, s 1(2) read together with Sch 1 to the Act. Sch 1 provides for a number of matters, including the appointment of a Chairman and governing body (a majority of whom must serve in a non-executive capacity), the review functions of a non-executive committee, the appointment of subcommittees, and the arrangements necessary to monitor and enforce the provisions of the FSMA, and the levying of fees to meet its expenses. It may be noted that, under the terms of para 19 of Sch 1, the FSA is generally not liable for damages in respect of anything done in the context of the discharge of its functions. This form of statutory immunity is considered in another context: see paras 14.05–14.23 below.

[6]   Paragraph 13(1) of Sch 1 to the FSMA.

(d) the reduction of financial crime in connection with activities which are regulated by the Act.[7]

However, under the recently enacted Financial Services Act 2010, these objectives will change significantly.[8] In particular, the FSA effectively assumes a shared responsibility for financial stability.[9] The FSA is required to contribute to the protection and enhancement of the UK's financial stability, taking into account circumstances occurring or arising both within the UK and internationally. The FSA is also required to consult with the Treasury in formulating its strategy in relation to the financial stability objective. At the same time, the FSA is relieved of its obligation to promote public awareness of the risks and benefits of investments. This function will be transferred to a new, financial services consumer body to be established by the FSA.[10]

8.06

Rule-making and Other Powers

The powers of the FSA include the following:

8.07

(a) The power to make so-called 'general rules' applicable to authorized persons and the conduct of their activities.[11] These include rules relating to client money and certain rules relating to collective investment schemes. Many of the rules contained in the FSA Handbook rely on this provision.

(b) The power to make so-called 'specific rules' relating to such matters as financial promotions and money laundering. Some of the rules which have been made in reliance on these powers have already been considered.[12]

(c) The power to issue guidance with respect to the operation of the FSMA or the FSA's functions.[13] Examples include the Perimeter Guidance, to which reference has occasionally been made in earlier chapters.

(d) The power to investigate possible contraventions of the FSMA or the rules made under it, and to take enforcement proceedings.[14]

The FSA Handbook

The practitioner will very frequently be more concerned with the details of the FSA Handbook, rather than the provisions contained in the FSMA itself. This is particularly the

8.08

---

[7] These primary objectives are set out in FSMA, s 2(2) and amplified by s 3–6 of the Act. Section 2 also requires the FSA to have regard to various matters, including the need to promote competition and the principle that a regulatory burden should be proportionate to the benefits which may be derived from it. On the whole subject, see Blair, Walker and Purves, paras 1.47–1.53.

[8] The Financial Services Act is discussed in more detail at paras 8.34–8.37 below.

[9] See s 1 of the Financial Services Act.

[10] See s 6 of the Financial Services Act. This is part of a process designed to ensure that the FSA has a greater focus on prudential and systemic issues: see the discussion at para 8.37 below.

[11] The power is conferred by FSMA, s 138. Regulations may be made affecting both the regulated and unregulated activities of the authorized person, on the basis that losses on the unregulated activities may have an impact on the overall financial stability of an authorized person. In other words, the rules may deal with prudential matters and are not confined to pure conduct of business issues.

[12] In relation to money laundering, see para 7.14 above.

[13] For the details, see FSMA, s 157.

[14] The various powers available to the FSA in this area are contained in FSMA, ss 165–176 and s 284. The procedures are set out in more detail in the DEC and ENF parts of the FSA Handbook.

case given that responsibility for so much of the detail of the regulatory regime has been delegated to the FSA.

8.09   Inevitably, and especially given that the FSA operates as a single market regulator, the Handbook is a substantial resource. It may be helpful briefly to describe the overall structure of the Handbook and its overarching subject headings:

(a) *High Level Standards.* This segment includes the essential principles for business[15] and the obligations of authorized firms under the regulatory system,[16] the threshold or fundamental conditions which a firm must meet in order to qualify for, and to retain, authorization,[17] and various other rules applicable to individuals who are to hold positions of responsibility within the firm;[18]

(b) *Prudential Standards.* This section includes prudential standards for banks and other entities operating under the supervision of the FSA. For example, capital adequacy, credit risk mitigation, and similar matters are addressed,[19] as are the senior management's responsibilities in the context of systems and controls;[20]

(c) *Regulatory Processes.* This segment includes a chapter (SUP) on supervisory matters relating to auditors, notification, reporting, and a chapter (DEPP) dealing with decision-making processes and penalties;

(d) *Redress.* This division includes chapters dealing with the resolution of disputes and complaints handling (DISP) and compensation for losses flowing from dealings with authorized persons (COMP). The latter aspect is in part dealt with in the context of deposit protection arrangements;[21]

(e) *Specialist Sourcebooks.* This section contains a number of sourcebooks on specific areas such as electronic money (ELM) and recognized investment exchanges and clearing houses; (REC) and

(f) *Listing, Prospectus and Disclosure.* This section includes listing rules (LR) and prospectus rules (PR). These are outside the scope of the present work.

8.10   The Handbook also includes guides for certain types of market participants and guides on perimeter matters (PERG), enforcement (ENF) and fair treatment of customers (RPPD).

8.11   Insofar as relevant to banking business, the rules and guidance contained in the FSA Handbook have been discussed in their substantive contexts, in the earlier chapters within this section.

---

[15] See FSA Handbook, PRIN.

[16] eg the duty to conduct business with integrity, to carry on business with due skill and care, to maintain adequate financial resources, and to deal with the regulator in an open and honest way.

[17] eg the adequacy of its financial resources for the purposes of its business, the requirement that the firm should meet a 'fit and proper' test: see FSA Handbook, COND.

[18] See FSA Handbook, chapters FIT (the 'fit and proper' person test for individuals) and APER (code of practice for approved persons).

[19] See FSA Handbook, BIPRU 5. Capital adequacy and credit risk mitigation have been considered generally in Chapter 6 above.

[20] See FSA Handbook, SYSC. Insofar as it relates to money laundering controls, SYSC has already been considered at para 7.14 above.

[21] See Chapter 13 below.

The Bank of England

History and Functions of the Bank

It is only necessary to discuss the history of the Bank in brief terms, in order to place matters **8.12**
in context.

It has already been noted that the FSA is of relatively recent origin. In contrast, the Bank is **8.13**
an institution of considerable antiquity. It was established in 1694 by the grant of a Royal
Charter under the terms of the Bank of England Act of that year,[22] and was originally
founded as a vehicle to raise £1.5 million to finance the war against France.

The Bank is perhaps most generally known for its role as issuer of the nation's banknotes. **8.14**
The Bank Charter Act of 1844 required the Bank to maintain an Issue Department which
was responsible for banknotes and which was to be kept separate from the Bank's more
general business. The issue of notes by private banks was gradually restricted, so that the
Bank eventually enjoyed a monopoly in this sphere.[23]

The Bank was nationalized in 1946 by the transfer of its issued capital stock to the **8.15**
Treasury.[24] The control of interest rates and other matters[25] then rested with the government, because the Treasury was entitled '… from time to time to give such directions to the
Bank as, after consultation with the Governor of the Bank, they think necessary in the
public interest …'.[26] This provision survives but, in view of the autonomy subsequently
given to the Bank in the field of interest rates, the section has been qualified by the insertion of the words '… except in relation to monetary policy …' at the end of the quoted
language.[27]

---

[22] For the legislation which empowered the Crown to establish the Bank see Bank of England Act 1694,
s 19. The Charter of the Corporation of the Governor and Company of the Bank of England was issued under
that Act on 27 July 1694. The provisions of the original Charter remain in force insofar as they conferred
corporate status on the Bank: see Bank of England Act 1946, s 3.

[23] It should, however, be noted that the monopoly does not extend to Scotland and Northern Ireland.
Institutions such as the Royal Bank of Scotland retain the right to issue banknotes, and this subject became
problematical as a result of the financial crisis in 2008. As a result, note issuers in this category were required to
provide appropriate backing or cover for their notes: see Pt 6 of the Banking Act 2009. The details are beyond
the scope of the present work.

[24] See Bank of England Act 1946, s 1.

[25] The Bank has from time to time performed other functions, and continues to do so. For example, it
was responsible for the administration of the Exchange Control Act 1947 until the abolition of that system
in 1979. Once again, however, the Treasury was ultimately in charge of the system and the Bank of England
administered it on the Treasury's behalf. It continues to perform the role of banker to the government, and it
is responsible for the management of the UK's gold and foreign reserves on behalf of HM Treasury. As an EU
central bank, it is a member of the European System of Central Banks, although its role remains relatively limited whilst the United Kingdom itself remains outside the eurozone. These roles will not be explored because
they are only marginally relevant to the subject matter of the present text.

[26] See Bank of England Act 1946, s 4(1).

[27] The additional wording was inserted by Bank of England Act 1998, s 10. It should, however, be noted
that the Treasury continues to enjoy certain 'reserve powers' in the field of monetary policy: see s 19 of the
Act, discussed at para 8.28 below.

8.16 Apart from its roles as issuer of banknotes and in the field of interest rates,[28] the Bank was also responsible for the prudential supervision of the financial sector. For many years, the supervisory system was informal; it was founded upon the Bank of England's role at the heart of the financial system, rather than upon any statutory authority. However, this situation changed, partly because of the need to implement EC banking directives and partly because increasingly sophisticated financial markets required a more formal approach to regulation. The statutory approach to regulation began with the Banking Act 1979, which was superseded by other legislation and, ultimately, by the Financial Services and Markets Act 2000. However, it is unnecessary to consider that subject in detail at this point, since those functions are now exercised by the FSA.[29]

8.17 The Bank now has two roles which it defines as its 'core' functions, namely the stability of the financial system and monetary stability. These two objectives will be considered in turn.

Stability of the Financial System

8.18 It has already been noted above that the FSA is responsible for the supervision of individual banks, investment firms and certain other financial institutions.

8.19 In contrast, the Bank of England bears responsibility for the stability of the financial system *as a whole*. This obligation was not explicitly set out in any of the legislation applicable to the Bank. In earlier times, the point had to be traced through section 2(2) of the Bank of England Act 1998, which provides that the Court of Directors[30] shall be responsible for determining the Bank's objectives and strategy. In pursuance of that provision, the Court had determined that financial stability is one of its core purposes.

8.20 It had defined the financial stability objective as follows:[31]

> Financial stability entails detecting and reducing threats to the financial system as a whole. Such threats are detected through the Bank's surveillance and market intelligence functions. They are reduced by strengthening infrastructure, and by financial and other operations, at home and abroad, including, in exceptional circumstances, acting as lender of last resort.

8.21 These statements are in some respects amplified by the Memorandum of Understanding,[32] which notes that the Bank's role in the maintenance of financial stability includes (i) ensuring the stability of the monetary system through its monetary policy role, (ii) overseeing the

---

[28] Although the Bank was obliged to follow any directions given by the Treasury in the context of interest rates, the implementation of those directions would be achieved through the Bank's financial market operations in setting the rate at which it will lend to financial institutions in the market. This remains the case even though the Bank now enjoys independence in the field of monetary policy.

[29] See generally Chapter 1 above.

[30] The Court of Directors is responsible for the management of the Bank's affairs, other than the formulation of monetary policy which is assigned to the Monetary Policy Committee (see paras 8.24–8.28 below). The Court consists of the Governor, two Deputy Governors and sixteen directors of the Bank: see s 1(2) of the 1998 Act.

[31] See the Bank's Annual Report for the year ended 2007.

[32] On the points about to be made, see para 2 of the Memorandum.

financial infrastructure, with particular responsibility for payment systems,[33] (iii) maintaining a broad overview of the financial system as a whole (including the impact of domestic and international developments), and (iv) undertaking 'lender of last resort' or other support operations.[34]

As in so many other areas, this position changed as a result of the 2008 credit crisis and the governmental response to it. Now, sections 2A, 2B and 2C of the Bank of England Act 1998[35] provide that one of the objectives of the Bank of England shall be to contribute to protecting and enhancing the stability of the financial system in the United Kingdom. The new provisions also establish a Financial Stability Committee which, among other things, is required to make recommendations to the Bank's Court of Directors as to the nature and implementation of the Bank's financial stability strategy, to give advice about particular institutions and the use of the Bank's stabilization powers.[36]   **8.22**

As previously noted,[37] the financial stability objective will effectively become a shared responsibility with the FSA, if the Financial Services Bill is enacted in its current form, although the details of their respective roles will obviously differ (eg the FSA plainly has no authority to act as 'lender of last resort').   **8.23**

Monetary Policy

As noted earlier, the Bank of England now enjoys independence in the conduct of monetary policy.[38] This rather broad statement does, however, require qualification, because the Bank does not enjoy an entirely free hand.   **8.24**

The key statutory objective of the Bank in this field is set out in section 11 of the 1998 Act, which reads: **8.25**

> In relation to monetary policy, the objectives of the Bank of England shall be:
> a) to maintain price stability; and
> b) subject to that, to support the economic policy of Her Majesty's Government, including its objectives for growth and employment.

---

[33] As the Memorandum rightly notes, the Bank acts as banker to commercial banks and stands at the heart of the payments system.

[34] The Bank's role as lender of last resort is designed to ensure that a bank which suffers liquidity problems may seek assistance from the Bank if other financial institutions are unwilling to assist. Liquidity problems may occur because banks will frequently have to commit to long term loans to their borrowers, yet these will have to be funded from relatively short term deposits raised from depositors or via the interbank market. The role is essentially designed as an aid to the preservation of market confidence, but it is generally aimed at problems of liquidity, rather than solvency. On the whole problem, see Blair, Walker and Purves, paras 14.09–14.10; Lastra, *Legal Foundations of International Monetary Stability* (Oxford, 2006) p 113. The provision of financial or liquidity support in crisis situations is subject to various consultation procedures: see paras 13, 14 and 17 of the Memorandum of Understanding.

[35] These provisions were inserted into the 1998 Act by s 238(1) of the Banking Act 2009 and came into force on 1 June 2009.

[36] On the stabilization options created by the Banking Act 2009, see generally Chapter 11 below.

[37] See para 8.06 above.

[38] That is, the establishment of national interest rates through the setting of the rate at which the Bank will itself make funds available to financial institutions.

'Price stability' does, of course refer to the absence of serious levels of inflation within the domestic economy.[39] But how is the acceptable level of inflation to be ascertained? This question is answered by section 12(1) of the 1998 Act, as follows:

> The Treasury may by notice in writing to the Bank specify for the purposes of section 11:
> a) what price stability is to be taken to consist of; or
> b) what the economic policy of Her Majesty's Government is to be taken to be.

8.26 It follows that the *definition* of monetary policy (that is to say, the establishment of an inflation target) is a matter for the Treasury,[40] whilst the *implementation* of that policy is the responsibility of the Bank of England.[41]

8.27 A Monetary Policy Committee is responsible for the formulation of monetary policy within the Bank.[42] The Bank is required to publish a statement about action decided upon at its meetings and, in the interests of transparency, it is also required to publish minutes of its meetings; a quarterly report on monetary policy, inflation developments and other matters is also required.[43]

8.28 Notwithstanding the Bank's independence in the field of monetary policy, it should be noted that the Treasury retains reserve powers to give directions to the Bank with respect to monetary policy if the Treasury is satisfied that the directions are required in the public interest and by extreme economic circumstances.[44]

The Treasury

History and Functions of the Treasury

8.29 The history of the Treasury dates back to the Norman Conquest, whilst the office of the Chancellor of the Exchequer has its origins in the thirteenth century.

8.30 It is perhaps unnecessary to examine the historical evolution of the Treasury for present purposes. It will suffice merely to note that the Treasury is responsible for the formulation and implementation of the United Kingdom's fiscal policy—that is to say, taxation, borrowing, and associated economic policies. The Treasury therefore functions as a ministry for economics and finance.

---

[39] The reference to price stability as the overriding objective mirrors the provisions applicable to the European System of Central Banks under the terms of the EC Treaty; see Art 127 of that Treaty. In monetary terms, price stability is valuable in that it helps to preserve confidence in the value of the currency.

[40] The Treasury is required to set the inflation target on an annual basis, and the relevant notice to the bank is required to be published: see s 12(2) and (3) of the 1998 Act.

[41] This may be contrasted with the position of the European System of Central Banks (ESCB), which is alone responsible for both the definition and the implementation of monetary policy: see Art 127(2) of the EC Treaty. The ESCB thus sets its own inflation target.

[42] The Monetary Policy Committee consists of the Governor and Deputy Governor of the Bank, two members appointed by the Governor after consultation with the Chancellor of the Exchequer and four members appointed by the Chancellor himself. The Bank enjoys immunity from civil liability in the context of its monetary policy functions: see s 244 of the Banking Act 2009.

[43] On these points, see ss 14, 15 and 18 of the 1998 Act.

[44] For the details, see s 19 of the 1998 Act, which also includes various time limits and other safeguards.

Role of the Treasury

The Memorandum of Understanding notes that the Treasury is responsible for '… the **8.31** institutional structure of financial regulation and the legislation which governs it, including the negotiation of EC directives …'. It must also account to Parliament and the government for serious problems and operational disruption affecting the financial system.[45] Whilst the Treasury is not responsible for, or involved in, operational matters relating to the Bank or the FSA, both organizations are required to notify the Treasury of any matters which may have an impact on the Treasury's duties to the government or to Parliament.[46] Thus, the Treasury would naturally expect to be notified where a financial support operation may be required, or where an issue may give rise to problems in the field of foreign relations.[47]

The Treasury also chairs the Standing Committee on Financial Stability. The Committee **8.32** provides a forum for policy discussions and also operates as a medium for the exchange of information. The Committee is also used as the vehicle for handling a serious crisis within the financial sector.[48]

Finally, in circumstances which were hoped to be exceptional but which have proved to be **8.33** depressingly familiar in recent years, there may be a need for a financial support operation where one or more institutions have run into difficulty and this poses a risk of a serious disturbance to the UK economy. Whilst the Treasury, the Bank and the FSA would each have a role to play in such a situation, no such support operation can be carried out except with the authority of the Chancellor of the Exchequer.[49] This subject is discussed in more depth at a later stage.[50]

Current Reforms

Unsurprisingly, the current financial crisis has lead to reform in a number of aspects of the **8.34** regulatory and supervisory process. Some of the reforms which have been introduced relate to the action to be taken when a bank runs into difficulties. These processes are mainly to be found in the Banking Act 2009 and, since these relate to the reorganization or restructuring of a banking business, they are considered at a later stage.[51]

Those aspects of the current reforms which affect the regulatory structure do, how- **8.35** ever, require consideration in the present context. The recently passed Financial Services Act 2010 derives its principal origins from the HM Treasury Review, 'Reforming Financial Markets'.[52]

---

[45] On these points, see para 4 of the Memorandum of Understanding.
[46] See para 5 of the Memorandum of Understanding.
[47] An obvious example in the latter category would include a proposal to withdraw the authorization of the London branch of a major foreign bank.
[48] For further details on these points, see paras 10–13 of the Memorandum of Understanding.
[49] See para 14 of the Memorandum of Understanding.
[50] See the discussion on UK bank rescues in Chapter 11 below.
[51] See Chapter 11 below.
[52] HM Treasury, July 2009. Note, however, that review processes were being undertaken in a number of areas during this period. For example, in March 2009 the FSA published the Turner Review and an associated

8.36 One of the underlying themes of the Treasury Review is that cooperation between the Bank of England and the FSA was insufficient to identify and to mitigate the looming threats to the UK's financial system. The Financial Services Act 2010 picks up on this theme. As already noted above, the Act adds financial stability as an objective of the FSA.[53] In its early form, the legislation would also have established a 'Council for Financial Stability' consisting of the Chancellor of the Exchequer, the chair of the FSA and the Governor of the Bank of England. The Council would have been required to keep under review matters affecting the stability of the UK's financial system and to coordinate any action to be taken to protect or enhance the stability of that system. The draft legislation would have involved an ongoing review of developments—both in the UK and internationally—which may have an impact on UK financial stability and the promotion of international regulatory cooperation. The Treasury would also have been entitled to prepare a statement setting out further objectives and giving further directions with respect to the Financial Stability Council.[54] However, as part of the compromises necessary to secure the passage of this legislation prior to the election in May 2010, these provisions were dropped from the final text. Other provisions of the Bill requiring the FSA to promote international cooperation[55] and allowing for collective financial proceedings against banks[56] also fell victim to the same process.

8.37 The Financial Services Act 2010 then deals with a variety of additional matters. In particular:

(a) in the light of the well-known concerns that bank remuneration structures (including bonus arrangements) encouraged excessive risk taking, the Act allows the Treasury to

---

discussion paper titled 'Regulatory Response to the Global Banking Crisis'. The Review concluded that past regulatory practice had focused too much on matters of form, and that insufficient attention had been paid to the sustainability of business models. As the crisis has shown, the loss of confidence in a single bank can rapidly spread to other institutions and cause contagion. As a result, systemic risk requires a much greater degree of regulatory attention. The Review also argues for a counter-cyclical approach to capital adequacy, requiring banks to build up their capital bases during profitable years to provide a cushion against a downturn. This wide-ranging report also identifies a supervisory gap which proved to be crucial during the credit crunch and the ensuing recession. The FSA concentrated on individual institutions and the Bank of England was engaged in monetary policy analysis, but no one seemed to have responsibility for macro-prudential analysis. As a result, the risks posed by cheap credit, increased personal borrowing and the reliance placed by banks on the wholesale funding markets (as opposed to traditional customer deposits) were not sufficiently understood. For feedback and follow up on the Turner Review, see the FSA's Feedback Statement 09/03 (September 2009). In contrast, the Walker review—'A Review of Corporate Governance in UK Banks and other Financial Entities' (July 2009)—focused on corporate governance issues in banks which may have contributed to the crisis, such as the role of the board and its non-executive directors, the position of institutional shareholders and remunerations structures.

[53] See s 1 of the 2010 Act, noted in para 8.06 above.

[54] On the points just made, see clause 1 of the Financial Services Bill. Clause 2 includes various procedural provisions whilst clause 3 requires the production and publication of an Annual Report. Clause 3(3) of the Bill would, however, allow the omission from the Annual Report of (i) commercially confidential information, (ii) any information which may impede any action taken or to be taken by any relevant authority, and (iii) information which may be prejudicial to the stability of the UK's financial system. One can see the purpose of these exclusions although those of a cynical mindset may wonder how much information of real value will be left over for publication.

[55] See clause 8 of the Bill.

[56] See clauses 18–25 of the Bill.

make regulations for the disclosure of such structures. The FSA is then required to exercise its general rule-making power to compel authorized institutions to formulate and implement a remuneration policy which must be consistent with (i) the effective management of risk and (ii) the Implementation Standards for Principles for Sound Compensation Practices issued by the Financial Stability Board on 25 September 2009;[57]

(b) the FSA is then required to make rules requiring authorized institutions to prepare and keep up to date a 'recovery plan' designed to ensure that the relevant business or part of it can be continued notwithstanding the occurrence of adverse circumstances;[58]

(c) FSA rules must also require authorized institutions to maintain a 'resolution plan'— sometimes referred to as a 'living will'. A resolution plan more explicitly deals with the failure of all or a part of an institution's business. As a result, the resolution plan must include information which would assist with any steps—such as the sale of the relevant assets—which would facilitate anything to be done in consequence to that failure. This would include information that would facilitate planning by the Treasury or the Bank of England in relation to any of their powers under the Banking Act of 2009;[59]

(d) since short selling of shares[60] was perceived to have aggravated the financial market crisis during 2008–9, the 2010 Act confers on the FSA wide powers to ban, or to require the disclosure of, short selling in any listed or traded securities (whether issued by a financial institution or otherwise);[61]

(e) the 2010 Act also confers on the FSA extended powers to suspend the permission granted to an authorized person if it has carried on business in breach of any applicable regulatory requirement,[62] to impose penalties on individuals who perform controlled

---

[57] On the points just made, see ss 4–6 of the 2010 Act.

[58] Section 7 of the 2010 Act, inserting new ss 139A–139F into the FSMA. The nature of the circumstances to be covered by the plan is subject to further elaboration in the relevant FSA rules.

[59] Section 7 of the 2010 Act. Since the various powers under the Banking Act relate to the rescue of insolvent institutions, those provisions are considered in Chapter 11 below.

[60] 'Short selling' is the process by which a seller enters into a transaction in shares and under which he will derive a profit if the market value of the share falls before the delivery date. Commonly, this will involve the sale of shares which the seller does not own at the date of the contract, where the seller hopes to acquire the necessary shares at a lower price during the currency of the contract. If enacted, a statutory definition of short-selling will be included in FSMA, s 131C by virtue of clause 13 of the Financial Services Bill. It may be noted that the 2008 crisis had already justified the introduction of a notification requirement and, subsequently a ban on short-selling in the shares of financial institutions. The ban was justified in the light of the collapse in the value of HBOS shares around the time of its acquisition by Lloyds TSB. These rules were introduced by amendments to the Market Conduct (MAR) chapter of the FSA Handbook. For the details, see the FSA's Short Selling Instrument 2008 (FSA 2008/30) and the Short Selling (No 2) Instrument 2008 (FSA 2008/50).

[61] Section 8 of the 2010 Act inserts new ss 131B–131J into the FSMA for these purposes. These rules are noted since they have their origins in dealings in the shares of financial institutions and are covered in the new Financial Services Bill. However, they are not directly relevant to the conduct of banking business itself and it is thus not proposed to consider them further in the present context.

[62] Section 9 of the 2010 Act, inserting a new s 206A into the FSMA.

functions without FSA approval,[63] and to suspend or impose restrictions on an approved person who has been guilty of misconduct;[64]

(f) the Act allows the FSA to require firms to initiate consumer redress schemes where there has been a widespread regulatory failure which has caused losses which ought to be recovered by consumers;[65] and

(g) the Act includes a requirement for the Financial Services Compensation Scheme to make a contribution to the costs of a bank rescue under the Banking Act of 2009.[66]

The European Framework

8.38 It has been noted previously[67] that European Community law has had a significant influence over the development of the regulatory framework applicable to banking business. Nevertheless, the framework developed under European auspices relied heavily on the national regulators in the so-called 'home' and 'host' States. There was no 'European banking regulator' as such. Instead, there were three financial services committees,[68] namely the Committee of European Banking Supervisors (CEBS), the Committee of European Insurance and Occupational Pensions Committee (CEIOPS) and the Committee of European Securities Regulators (CESR). These Committees produced valuable work in a number of technical fields, but each committee was confined to its own area and had advisory status only.

8.39 However, as happened in the United Kingdom and many other countries, the credit crunch provided a spur to efforts at reform. In November 2008, the European Commission mandated a High Level Group chaired by Jacques de Larosière to put forward proposals on the strengthening of supervisory arrangements for the European financial markets. The Report was published in February 2009[69] and makes a number of points about the causes of the crisis and the regulatory failings which failed to detect the impeding storm. The High Level Group made a series of recommendations which were promptly endorsed by the Commission.[70] This, in turn, was quickly followed by a Communication from the

---

[63] Section 11 of the 2010 Act, inserting a new s 63A into the FSMA.

[64] Section 12 of the 2010 Act, amending s 66 of the FSMA.

[65] Sections 14 and 15 of the 2010 Act.

[66] Sections 16 and 17 of the 2010 Act.

[67] See generally Chapter 2 above.

[68] These were known as the 'Lamfalussy Level 3 Committees'. The name is derived from the Final Report of the Committee of Wise Men on the Regulation of European Securities Markets (Feb 2001). The Committee was chaired by Baron Lamfalussy. The Report made recommendations designed to facilitate the implementation of the Community's Financial Services Action Plan, which in turn was intended to stimulate the creation of a single European capital market. 'Level 3' was intended to stimulate increased cooperation between national supervisors and provided for CESR to issue guidance and non-binding standards. Although the Lamfalussy Report was primarily directed to the securities markets, the same structure and legislative approach was later adopted for the banking and insurance markets. On these processes see, Blair, Walker and Purves, paras 3-22–3-24.

[69] 'The High-Level Group on Financial Supervision in the EU' (Brussels, 25 February 2009).

[70] See 'Communication for the Spring European Council – Driving European Recovery' Brussels, 4 March 2009 COM (2009) 114 final.

Commission on European financial supervision.[71] Amongst other things, and picking up themes from the de Larosière report, the Communication put forward a proposal for a regulatory structure resting on two 'pillars' and involving the creation of a European Systemic Risk Council and a European System of Financial Supervisors. The remit of these two bodies as contemplated by the Communication requires a brief description.

European Systemic Risk Board

The European Systemic Risk Board (ESRB) will consist of the Governors of central banks **8.40** across the community (including the European Central Bank) and various others. National regulatory bodies will attend in an advisory capacity. The ESRB will be responsible for the supervision of the macro-prudential system. It will monitor and assess threats that arise from developments in the financial system as a whole and any associated macro-economic developments.

Where the ESRB detects risks for financial stability it may issue warnings or recommenda- **8.41** tions, which, may be of a general nature or may be directed towards specific Member States. Recommendations would have no legal binding effect but the ESRB will have a discretion to publish its recommendations. Clearly, this is intended to act as an incentive to comply, or as a deterrent to non-compliant Member States.

In a wider, global context, the ESRB would collaborate closely with the International **8.42** Monetary Fund and the Financial Stability Board.[72] The objective would be to establish a 'global risk warning system', within which the EU would enjoy a significant degree of influence.

The ESRB would be accountable to the European Council and the Parliament, making at **8.43** least bi-annual reports to them (although more frequent reports may be required in times of financial crisis). However, and notwithstanding the importance attached to the ESRB, it would be essentially a monitoring and reporting body. It would have no role to play in the actual management of a crisis.

On 23 September 2009, the Commission published a proposal for a regulation on **8.44** Community macro-prudential oversight of the financial system and establishing a European Systemic Risk Board.[73] The proposal essentially mirrors the provisions outlined above, as drawn from the report of the High Level Group.

European System of Financial Supervisors

The second strand of the proposed reforms is the European System of Financial Supervisors **8.45** (ESFS). This would focus on micro-prudential supervision through a framework combining the supervision of firms by national authorities and a centralization of specific tasks at a European level. The Commission Communication states that this should result in

---

[71] Brussels, 27 May 2005, COM (2009) 252 final.
[72] On the Financial Stability Board, see para 8.53 below.
[73] Brussels, 23.09.2009, COM (2009) 499 final.

greater harmonization of rules, as well as more coherence in supervisory practices and enforcement.

8.46   The first element of the ESFS is the national supervisors, such as the FSA, since the day-to-day supervision of financial institutions will remain their responsibility.

8.47   The second element of the ESFS will involve the creation of three new and independent European Supervisory Authorities. These will replace the existing advisory bodies—CGBS, CEIOPS and CESR—to which reference has already been made. In the banking sphere, CEBS would be replaced by the European Banking Authority (EBA). The functions of the EBA would include:

(a)   the promotion of a single set of harmonized rules and binding technical standards in specific regulatory areas, including the preparation of interpretative guidelines to be applied by national supervisors in making individual decisions;

(b)   ensuring consistent application of harmonized EU standards and resolving disputes between national regulators. It is proposed that the EBA would have enforcement powers in relation to compliance although, obviously, this may be a politically contentious issue;

(c)   directly supervising certain types of entities whose activities have a Europe-wide 'reach' (eg credit rating agencies and EU central counterparty clearing houses);

(d)   ensuring a coordinated response in times of crisis by cooperation and exchange of information and assisting national supervisors in making and implementing decisions; and

(e)   undertaking an international role in respect of certain supervisory activities.

8.48   The intended establishment of the EBA was pursued by a Proposal for a Regulation of the European Parliament and of the Council establishing a European Banking Authority.[74] There was some controversy about the Treaty basis for the establishment of agencies of this kind, but the proposal notes that (i) Article 95 of the Treaty provides for the adoption of measures for the approximation of legislation for the establishment and functioning of the internal market and (ii) this has been held to provide sufficient legal authority to establish a new Community body responsible for pushing forward the necessary harmonization processes.[75] The proposed regulation provides for the EBA to have its seat in London.[76] The tasks and powers of the EBA are set out in some detail in Chapter II of the proposed Regulation[77] whilst Chapter III deals with the composition and tasks of the Board of Supervisors and Management Board. Chapter IV[78] confirms that the EBA shall form a part of the ESFS, which is to function as a network of supervisors, whilst Chapter V[79] deals with

---

[74]   Brussels, 23.09.2009 COM (2009) 501 final.

[75]   Case C-217/04 *United Kingdom v European Parliament and the Council (European Network and Information Security Agency)*, at para 44. No doubt, given the financial crisis and related issues, it was unattractive to seek a revision to the Treaty for these purposes and, in any event, more rapid progress was required.

[76]   Article 5.

[77]   Articles 6–24.

[78]   Articles 39–45.

[79]   Articles 46–47.

remedies and appeals. Whilst the intended regulation is detailed in certain respects, it mirrors the earlier reports and proposals which have been discussed above.

The EU Memorandum of Understanding

Reference has already been made to the Memorandum of Understanding between the **8.49** Treasury, the Bank of England, and the FSA governing their respective roles and functions in relation to the UK's financial system.[80]

Given the accepted fact that financial stability is not now a subject which can be monitored **8.50** and controlled on a purely domestic basis, it is unsurprising that a similar memorandum (hereafter, the 'EU Memorandum') has been entered into on an EU level.[81] The main contents of the EU Memorandum may be summarized as follows:

(a) Unlike the UK Memorandum, the EU Memorandum is principally directed towards cooperation between the authorities to deal with cross-border financial crises, although it recognizes that cooperation is likewise necessary 'in normal times' in order to create a situation of preparedness.[82] To that end all parties commit themselves to the establishment of a framework for cooperation, the exchange of information and assessments, the coordination of public communication, and establishment of contingency plans (including stress tests).[83]

(b) The parties agree to a common set of principles to be applied in a cross-border financial crisis,[84] notably (i) the objective of crisis management is to protect the stability of the EU financial system as a whole, not to prevent bank failures,[85] (ii) the management of an institution should be held accountable, shareholders should not be protected and uninsured depositors/creditors must accept losses, (iii) the use of public money to resolve a crisis should not be automatic and should occur only when social benefits are assessed to exceed the costs, and (iv) where the institution has significant cross-border business, rescue costs should be shared among the affected Member States on an equitable basis taking into account the respective supervisory powers of the home and host States.[86]

---

[80] See para 8.02 above.

[81] To give its full title, the 'Memorandum of Understanding on Cooperation between the Financial Supervisory Authorities, Central Banks and Finance Ministries of the European Union on Cross-Border Financial Stability' (1 June 2008). The Memorandum extends and updates an earlier Memorandum agreed in 2005.

[82] See para 1.2 of the EU Memorandum.

[83] See para 1.4 of the EU Memorandum.

[84] See para 6.1 of the EU Memorandum.

[85] On this subject, see the discussion of the 'lender of last resort' function at paras 11.85–11.93 below.

[86] This presumably implies that, since the home State is principally responsible for the supervision of the institution, it should bear a greater proportion of the cost since it should bear greater, supervisory responsibility for the failure. This impression is reinforced by para 1.6 of the EU Memorandum, which states that arrangements for crisis management and crisis resolution will be consistent with the arrangements for supervision and crisis prevention. In this context, it should be noted that whilst the main supervisory burden rests with the home State, the host State remains responsible for liquidity issues (see para 2.15 above). This suggests that the 'lender of last resort' function rests with the host central bank in countries where banks and subsidiaries are located. However, it is made clear elsewhere that primary responsibility for emergency liquidity support

(c) The EU Memorandum sets out procedures for cooperation between the respective parties at a *national* level, including the appointment of the authority which is to act as the national coordinator in a crisis situation, and proposing the establishment of 'Cross-Border Stability Groups' where specific Member States have common stability concerns about a particular financial group.[87]

(d) The EU Memorandum also includes detailed provision for the activation of crisis procedures,[88] information exchange,[89] and the coordination of communications to the public.[90] It is specifically confirmed that the EU Memorandum is not a legally binding document and cannot give rise to damages.[91]

(e) The EU Memorandum includes as Annex 1 a series of Common Practical Guidelines for Crisis Management. Interestingly, in the light of some of the difficulties which were claimed to affect a proposed rescue for Northern Rock[92], paragraph 6 of Annex 1 states that advance consideration should be given to the obligation of listed entities to disclose their difficulties under the EU's Market Abuse Directive,[93] including circumstances where disclosure may be delayed for a limited period of time. The clear inference to be drawn from this is that a delay in disclosure is justified for a period whilst a liquidity support/rescue operation is being considered and arranged.[94]

(f) Annex 1 includes further provisions dealing with crisis notification, assessment and management and, if it does not already exist, for the establishment of a Cross-Border Stability Group for the institution at risk, whilst Annex 2 includes a specimen 'Voluntary Specific Cooperation Agreement' between individual Member States where they have common financial stability concerns around a particular financial institution.

International Developments

8.51 The inter-connectability and mutual dependence of global financial markets—as so dramatically illustrated by the current crisis—means that remedial action at a UK or even at an EU level is not of itself sufficient. Similar action on an international scale has also been required.

8.52 One of the main drivers of this process was the G20 London Summit held on 2 April 2009. The Summit concentrated on the financial crisis and agreed on a range of measures,

---

rests with the home State: see para 30 of Annex 1 to the Memorandum. For a discussion on the 'lender of last resort' (or 'emergency liquidity assistance') function, see paras 11.85–11.93 below.

[87] See para 3 of the EU Memorandum.
[88] See para 4 of the Memorandum.
[89] Paragraph 5 of the Memorandum.
[90] Paragraph 6 of the Memorandum.
[91] Paragraph 10.
[92] On this subject, see paras 11.09–11.19 below.
[93] Directive 2003/6/EC of the European Parliament and of the Council of 28 January 2003 on insider dealing and market manipulation (market abuse) OJ L 96, 12.04.2003, p 16.
[94] The EU Memorandum is dated 5 June 2008 and does, of course, post date the Northern Rock crisis. Earlier versions of the EU Memorandum (particularly the 2005 version) were not made public, so it cannot be said whether they included similar regulatory guidance on this issue.

including strengthened capital standards, improved cross-border crisis management, the establishment of supervisory colleges, the need to ensure appropriate oversight for systemically important institutions, and improved disclosure, reporting, and accounting standards.[95] Some of the work flowing from the Summit has already been discussed in other contexts.[96]

In institutional terms, one of the main outputs of the London Summit was the decision to provide a stronger foundation for the Financial Stability Board (FSB).[97] The FSB has been charged with giving substance to the regulatory objectives established at the Summit, and has issued a series of reports on the progress made to date.[98]   **8.53**

It may also be noted that the FSB has published guidance on the management of cross-border crises, which forms the basis of some of the proposals discussed earlier in this chapter.[99]   **8.54**

Conclusions

It is thus fair to say that the role of the market regulators has come under a fair degree of scrutiny as a result of the credit crunch. This, of course, has occurred in parallel with developments at both a European Community and an international level, which have been discussed above.[100]   **8.55**

As has been shown, this has led to extensive reviews and consequent revisions both to the roles and to the powers of the various market supervisors. It remains to be seen how this process will come out. Of course, the principal difficulty with reforms of this kind is that their adequacy will only genuinely be tested when the next crisis erupts.   **8.56**

---

[95] See the G20 Leaders' 'Declaration on Strengthening the Financial System' (London, 2 April 2009).

[96] See, for example, the discussion of the Basel Committee's proposals on the reform of the capital adequacy regime, at paras 6.57–6.59 above.

[97] Formerly known as the 'Financial Stability Forum'.

[98] See reports issued by the FSB on 7 November 2009: 'Progress since the Pittsburgh Summit in Implementing the G20 Recommendations for Strengthening Financial Stability', 'Exit from Extraordinary Financial Sector Support Measures', 'Guidance to Assess the Systemic Importance of Financial Institutions, Markets and Instruments: Initial Considerations', and 'The Financial Crisis and Information Gaps'.

[99] See 'FSF Principles for Cross-Border Cooperation on Crisis Management' (2 April 2009).

[100] See generally paras 8.38–8.54 above.

PART B

MERGER, REORGANIZATION, AND INSOLVENCY OF BANKS

Introduction

As the recent financial crisis and resultant recession have amply demonstrated, a stable financial system is crucially important to any modern society. But—even if overall stability can be achieved—a stable financial *system* does not necessarily connote that individual financial *institutions* will be static and immutable. To the contrary, the modern era has seen many mergers and the disappearance of banking names which were well known only a few years ago.

In addition, the objective of 'financial stability' cannot merely connote the absence of any difficulties, for that would be a wholly unrealistic expectation. Thus, the proper management of an institution at risk will help to avoid a spread of contagion to other parts of the financial services industry. A problem may therefore remain a local difficulty, rather than developing into a full blown crisis. As the current crisis has shown, this objective may be rather easier to state than to achieve but, nevertheless, this must clearly remain the aspiration.

The choice of title for this section is deliberate. Whilst it is true that bank insolvency has been very much the headline issue in recent times, it must not be forgotten that bank mergers have frequently occurred between sound institutions to further a business strategy, and have not been motivated by solvency concerns. It is thus also necessary to consider mergers and solvent reorganizations, as well as crisis situations.

Against that brief background, the present section considers a variety of issues associated with the merger, reorganization and insolvency of banks. In particular:

(a) Chapter 9 considers Part VII of the Financial Services and Markets Act 2000 (FSMA), which introduced a new regime for the transfer of a banking business, together with broader legislation designed to facilitate cross-border mergers;

(b) Chapter 10 examines the effect of a foreign bank merger insofar as it relates to assets and liabilities situate in the United Kingdom;

(c) Chapter 11 considers recent legislation in the United Kingdom to facilitate the rescue of an institution which has run into difficulty and to deal with issues of systemic stability;

(d) Chapter 12 examines the effect of EU legislation on the cross-border reorganization and winding up of credit institutions;

(e) Chapter 13 reviews deposit protection arrangements which come into operation on the insolvency of a bank; and

(f) Chapter 14 considers the potential liability of a regulator for negligent supervision of a failed institution and for certain other regulatory actions.

9

UK BANK MERGERS AND BUSINESS TRANSFERS

Introduction

Part VII of the FSMA introduced a new procedure to facilitate the transfer of a banking **9.01** business.[1] Before seeking to explain the detail of these provisions, however, it is necessary to consider the rationale for these new rules.

In the past, the intending purchaser of a banking business had three possible means of **9.02** completing that acquisition:

(a) He could acquire the corporate entity which owned that business. There are a number of difficulties with this approach. In particular, directors and shareholders might wish to dispose of part only of the business contained within that entity.[2]

(b) He could take an assignment of the loans, security and other contractual rights which constitute the assets of the business, and he could undertake to perform the obligations associated with it—principally, the repayment of customer deposits. Once again, a number of obstacles stand in the way of this route. First of all, whilst the benefit of any *rights* is in general terms capable of assignment, it has become common in practice to allow major borrowers a say in any proposal for the transfer of their facilities to another

---

[1] For a more detailed discussion of these provisions, see Proctor, 'Bank Restructuring under the Financial Services and Markets Act' (2003) JIBLR 471. See also Moore, 'Banking Business Transfer Schemes under Part VII of FSMA 2000' (2002) 23(7) JIBFL 353. Part VII also deals with the transfer of insurance business but that aspect is, of course, beyond the scope of the present work. Nevertheless, reference will be made to cases decided in an insurance context, where appropriate.

[2] Of course, where the target bank is a public company, then it could be the subject of a takeover offer made in accordance with the provisions of the City Code on Takeovers and Mergers. A discussion of the company law aspects of such an arrangement is beyond the scope of this work.

institution. Perhaps more crucially, it is not possible to transfer *obligations* without the consent of the person entitled to the benefit of that obligation.[3] Consequently, the transfer of deposit obligations to the purchaser could only be fully completed with the consent of each individual customer—an almost impossible task in the context of a banking business of any size.

(c) He could promote a private Act of Parliament to effect the transfer, in terms which would override some of the difficulties noted in (b), above. In practice, however, this route could only be used for 'internal' business transfers within an existing group.[4] A business transfer between different groups would frequently be commercially sensitive and timing is likely to be a critical concern. These considerations would come into conflict with the time required to promote a private Act, and the attendant publicity.[5]

9.03 Against this general background, it is proposed to consider the following topics:

(a) the effect of Part VII;

(b) the scope of Part VII;

(c) procedure under Part VII;

(d) the effect of court sanction; and

(e) the conclusions to be drawn from the overall discussion.

Effect of Part VII

9.04 It was originally intended that the transfer of a banking business should henceforth[6] be capable of completion only by means of a scheme sanctioned under Part VII; in other words, it would no longer be possible to transfer a banking business by means of the web of contractual arrangements described in paragraph (b) above. Thus, section 104 of the FSMA[7] provides that:

> No insurance business transfer scheme or banking business transfer scheme is to have effect unless an order has been made in relation to it under section 111(1).

---

[3] That is to say, deposit liabilities can only be satisfactorily transferred by means of a tripartite novation, whereby the depositor releases the seller from his obligation to repay the deposits in return for a corresponding undertaking from the buyer.

[4] See, for example, the Alliance & Leicester Group Treasury plc (Transfer) Act 2001, the National Australia Group Europe Act 2001 and the Barclays Group Reorganisation Act 2002. It may be noted that para 5(a) of the preamble to the Barclays legislation notes that the reconstruction of the Barclays Group '... could not have been attained without the authority of Parliament *when the Bill for this Act was deposited* ...' (emphasis supplied). This effectively acknowledges that, by the date the Act was *passed* (7 November 2002), the transfer could have been achieved through the use of Pt VII.

[5] It should, however, be said that a requirement for publicity also applies under the Part VII provisions. As a result, the rules about to be described remain most likely to be used in an 'internal' context where the transfer of the business is unlikely to attract any particular comment or criticism.

[6] Subject to the points noted below, Pt VII came into effect on 1 December 2001: see the Financial Services and Markets Act 2000 (Commencement No 7) Order 2001 (SI 2001/3538).

[7] It should be explained that Pt VII of the FSMA consists of ss 104–117 of that Act.

This provision has, however, only been brought into force insofar as it relates to insurance **9.05** transfers.[8] It follows that a scheme for a banking business transfer can either be effected under Part VII of the Act or by any other lawful means, at least until section 104 is fully brought into force in relation to banking schemes.

Whilst parties thus currently retain the ability to achieve such a transfer in a variety of ways, **9.06** the provisions of Part VII do offer a convenient means of completing such an arrangement, and it may be anticipated that this will now generally offer the preferred route.

Scope of Part VII

When and how can the Part VII procedure be used? **9.07**

In certain limited respects—and especially insofar as it provides for court sanction—the legislation draws on the structures adopted for the approval of a scheme of arrangement or reconstruction under Part 26 of the Companies Act 2006.

A Part VII scheme placed before the court must satisfy two essential requirements if the **9.08** court is to have jurisdiction to sanction it. First of all, the business to be transferred must satisfy a 'banking business' definition. Secondly, the transferor must satisfy certain authorization requirements. It is necessary to deal with these points in turn.

Part VII allows the court to sanction a 'banking business transfer scheme'. The parties must **9.09** therefore establish that the arrangements presented to the court do, in fact, qualify for this label. In order to do so,[9] the transfer arrangements must involve a scheme '… under which the *whole or part* of the business to be transferred *includes* the accepting of deposits …' (emphasis supplied). It is necessary to dwell on this fundamental provision before moving on to the other requirements, for in some respects it defines the extent of the court's jurisdiction to sanction a business transfer. In particular:

(a) The business to be transferred must *include* the acceptance of deposits. This seems to imply that the activities to be transferred involve the taking of deposits as an integral part of the business (ie and not merely as an occasional occurrence).[10]

(b) The reference to the *whole or part* of the transferred business consisting of the acceptance of deposits reflects the obvious point that the acceptance of deposits cannot constitute a business on its own. It must be part of a wider business involving the making of loans or some other means by which the deposits are turned to account.[11]

(c) Whilst the transferred business must therefore include deposit taking, this should be seen as a qualifying, rather than a limiting, criterion. The court will also have jurisdiction to order the transfer of the wider activities, provided that they can properly be

---

[8] See art 2(2) of the Financial Services and Markets Act 2000 (Commencement No 7) Order 2001 (SI 2001/3538).

[9] On the points about to be discussed, see FSMA, s 106.

[10] This requirement is, in any event, implicit in the statutory requirements as to the identity of the transferor and the transferee—see below.

[11] Compare the decision in *Re Introductions Ltd* [1970] Ch 199.

described as 'banking business'.[12] Consequently, the court could order the transfer to the transferee of (i) the obligation to repay the deposits, (ii) the benefit of the loan book and associated security, and (iii) the benefit of any asset management agreements, documentary credits, or any other, similar arrangements with the customers of the bank. Ultimately, of course, the scheme document placed before the court should define the business to be transferred, and the court will have to determine whether all of the business so described constitutes 'banking business' within the framework of its jurisdiction. It is to be anticipated that the court will take a broad view of the expression.[13]

9.10   As noted above, the transferor must also meet certain authorization requirements laid down by section 106. Specifically:

(a)   The transferor must be a 'UK authorized person', that is to say, an entity formed in the United Kingdom and which is authorized by the FSA to accept deposits.[14] In such a case, the transferee must intend to carry on that business either in the United Kingdom or elsewhere.

(b)   Alternatively, the transferor must be a person who has permission to accept deposits in this country but who is not authorized to do so by the FSA. In other words, the transferor must be an EC credit institution which has exercised its 'passport' rights to carry on business in the United Kingdom, principally under the supervision of its home State regulator.[15] In such a case, the deposit-taking business must be carried on in the United Kingdom, and the transferee must intend to continue the business in the UK.

9.11   These provisions require brief explanation. Where the scheme is proposed by a UK authorized person as transferor, then courts in the UK can sanction the transfer of the business even though the transferee may intend to continue the business abroad. This may not be as unlikely as it sounds; where the customers of the business are spread around the world, they may not be very concerned if their accounts are to be transferred to another part of the banking group in another part of the globe.[16] Accordingly, where the transferor is a UK authorized person, the court may sanction the business transfer even though it will subsequently be carried on abroad.

9.12   A more limited approach is adopted where the transferor is a 'passported' institution. In such a case, the court's jurisdiction is essentially territorial; it can only sanction the transfer

---

[12]   Note the reference to a business which *includes* the acceptance of deposits. Confirmation of this approach to the interpretation of this provision is offered by the decision of the Court of Session in *The Standard Life Assurance Co* 2007 SCLR 581 (where, however, the court relied on the breadth of the expression 'scheme').

[13]   The court seems to have adopted such an approach in *Re WASA International Insurance Co* [2002] EWHC 2698. It should be noted in passing that Pt VII does not allow the court to sanction business transfers which would be more appropriately handled under legislation on building societies or credit unions, or which constitutes the merger or division of a public company under Pt 27 of the Companies Act 2006: see FSMA, s 106(3).

[14]   See the definition in FSMA, s 106(5).

[15]   On the 'passporting' procedure, see paras 2.13–2.17 above.

[16]   In this context, it should be noted that a banking business is carried on in the United Kingdom if it is managed from the UK and the accounts are maintained in the UK. This conclusion is not affected by the fact that many or most of the customers may be resident elsewhere.

of the business if it is currently carried on in this country and the transferee intends to continue in that fashion. It would plainly be inappropriate for an English court to claim jurisdiction over a transfer by a foreign company of its overseas business.

Procedure under Part VII

If it has been found that the proposed arrangement falls within the definition of a 'banking business transfer scheme' and the transferor has been found to be eligible for the purposes of Part VII, then it becomes necessary to consider the procedures involved in order to obtain the court's sanction. In very broad terms, four sets of conditions must be satisfied.[17] **9.13**

First of all, the application to court to sanction the scheme must be advertised in the London, Edinburgh, and Belfast Gazettes and in two daily newspapers in the United Kingdom.[18] This provides an opportunity to depositors and other customers to obtain a statement setting out the terms and effect of the scheme.[19] These materials will enable them to decide whether to exercise their statutory right of objection to the scheme.[20] **9.14**

Secondly, it must be demonstrated that the transferee institution has adequate financial resources.[21] Since it would be difficult for the court to make such an assessment, the requirement is satisfied by the production of an appropriate certificate from the authority responsible for the supervision of the transferee's business. In the case of a transferee which is a UK authorized institution, this will be the FSA; a transferee from another EU Member State must produce the certificate from its home State regulator; and in any other case, the certificate must be issued by the supervisor in the jurisdiction in which the transferee's head office is situate.[22] **9.15**

---

[17] The various conditions about to be discussed are set out in FSMA, s 111 and the statutory instrument referred to below.

[18] The form of the notice must be approved in advance by the FSA: see art 5(3) of the Financial Services and Markets Act 2000 (Control of Business Transfers) (Requirements on Applicants) Regulations 2001 (SI 2001/3625). Although not expressly stated, it is assumed that the FSA would not approve the notice unless (i) it states the date and place of the hearing set for the application and (ii) refers to the right of interested parties to appear at, and object to, the application under FSMA, s 110 (see below).

[19] On the requirement to prepare such a statement, see art 5(4) of the Financial Services and Markets Act 2000 (Control of Business Transfers) (Requirements on Applicants) Regulations 2001 (SI 2001/3625).

[20] FSMA, s 110 allows for participation in the hearings by (i) the FSA and (ii) any person claiming to be adversely affected by the scheme (including employees of the transferor or the transferee). In practice, it must be unlikely that depositors or other customers will exercise their right to object to a banking business transfer scheme. A disaffected depositor can simply withdraw his money and place it with another institution. A borrower is unlikely to be affected since he is a debtor, rather than a creditor, of the bank.

[21] Although the legislation does not specifically so state, this must mean that the transferee will have adequate financial resources immediately following the transfer, taking account of the additional assets thereby acquired and the additional liabilities thereby assumed.

[22] On these requirements, see FSMA, s 111(2)(a) read together with Pt II of Sch 12 to the Act. It should be noted that additional notice requirements apply where the transferee is authorized in another Member State.

9.16 Thirdly, it must be shown that the transferee has the necessary authorization to carry on the business in the jurisdiction to which it is to be transferred;[23] plainly, it would be inappropriate for the court to sanction the transfer if this would result in the conduct of unlawful banking business in the country concerned. The best evidence will be copies of the relevant licences themselves, accompanied by any appropriate legal opinions.

9.17 Finally, the court must make a more general assessment; it may only sanction the scheme if, in all the circumstances, it considers that it is appropriate to do so.[24] How should the court approach this assessment? Given the context, one might instinctively feel that the protection of depositors should be the major consideration. Yet in practice, this may not be the case; as has been shown, the scheme can only fall for consideration by the court if the regulator of the transferee has certified that it has adequate financial resources. A court cannot realistically look behind such a certificate, nor is it well placed to substitute its own financial assessment for that of the supervisor.[25] The major issue for depositors—the ability of the transferee to repay them—is thus largely foreclosed so far as the court's discretion is concerned.[26] Yet the discretion must have some meaning, and it has been suggested that 'fairness' and the reasonable expectations of customers must guide the exercise of the discretion.[27] With these broad statements in mind, it is suggested that a court may take the following factors into account in exercising its discretion to sanction the scheme:

(a) In deciding whether it is 'appropriate' to sanction the scheme, it is not incumbent on the court to consider whether the objectives could be achieved in a different or better way, since the directors are entitled to select the route they think most appropriate to their business and strategy.[28]

(b) Whilst the position of depositors may have been covered by the 'adequate financial resources' certificate, it must be remembered that the court sanction relates to a broader banking business *as a whole*.[29] Consequently, the criterion of 'fairness' should be

---

[23] FSMA, s 111(2)(b).

[24] FSMA, s 111(3).

[25] The court in *Re Axa Equity & Law Life Assurance Society plc* [2001] 2 BCLC 447 noted that the regulator's views should be given 'great weight' in this context although, for the reasons given in the text, it is hard to see how the court could challenge the regulator's certificate. This situation might change if any depositors exercised their right to challenge the scheme and produced independent accounting evidence casting doubt on the transferee's financial position. But such a challenge would happen only rarely; as pointed out earlier, depositors who were unhappy with the situation could simply move their funds elsewhere, and it is hard to see why they would want to go to the expense of such a challenge. The position could, of course, be very different in the context of an insurance business transfer, where investors may be 'locked in' for an extended period, but it is unnecessary to consider that subject in the present context.

[26] The position is obviously more complex for policy holders, who may be locked into their arrangements for a number of years. It is perhaps for this reason that virtually all of the reported case law deals with insurance companies, rather than banks.

[27] *Re Axa Equity & Law Life Assurance Society plc* [2001] 2 BCLC 447. However, it is inevitably necessary to balance competing interests of different parties (eg shareholders, depositors, and employees), and the fact that one group or a part of it may be disadvantaged does not necessarily mean that the entire scheme should be rejected: *Re Norwich Union Linked Life Assurance Ltd* [2004] EWHC 2802 (Ch).

[28] *Re Axa Equity & Law Life Assurance Society plc* [2001] 2 BCLC 447.

[29] This point has already been made at para 9.09 above.

applied across the whole customer base, including depositors, borrowers, portfolio management clients, and others.[30]

(c) The court may also consider whether the transferee has in place the systems and personnel necessary to administer the loan book, investment portfolios and other business to the same extent as the transferor. It would seem inappropriate to sanction a scheme if this is likely to lead to lower standards of customer service.

(d) Where a banking business carried on by a UK authorized institution is to be transferred to a body which will continue that business abroad,[31] the court will need to exercise special care. In particular, it will need to consider whether the transferee's jurisdiction offers a level of customer protection equivalent to that available in the United Kingdom. For example, does it offer a deposit-protection scheme on terms similar to that provided by the Financial Services Compensation Scheme;[32] does it insist on levels of service equivalent to those required by the relevant sections of the FSA Handbook;[33] will the tax position of depositors or borrowers be affected by the transfer[34] in an adverse way? It is not intended to suggest that the transferee's jurisdiction must offer legal protections and benefits identical to those available in the United Kingdom, but the court must undertake some kind of comparison in order to satisfy itself that customers are not materially disadvantaged.[35]

(e) As already noted, Part VII allows employees to object to a particular scheme. Whether or not they choose to exercise that right, it is thus fair to infer that the interests of employees should be taken into account. Consequently, if the business is to be transferred overseas with the loss of a number of jobs in this country, then this factor may count against approval of the scheme.

(f) If the court finds that the scheme operates fairly as between the various members of the customer base, then the court may give due recognition and weight to the commercial objectives and judgments of the boards of directors of the transferor and the transferee.[36]

---

[30] In other words, since the position of the depositors is essentially covered by the regulatory certificate, the court should focus its attention on other categories of customers who may be affected by the scheme.

[31] It will be recalled that this is one of the types of banking business transfer scheme which can be approved by the court under Pt VII: see para 9.11 above.

[32] On this scheme, see Chapter 13 below.

[33] See, in particular, the discussion of the BCOBS chapter of the FSA Handbook in Chapter 3 above.

[34] For example, a foreign borrower paying interest to a bank in the United Kingdom may be able to pay interest gross under the tax treaty between the United Kingdom and his home country. Clearly, it may be necessary to look at different treaty arrangements if the banking business is transferred outside the UK. This may operate to the disadvantage of the borrower if he has to deduct funds on account of local income tax, and to make a grossing up payment to the lender in the new jurisdiction.

[35] Quite apart from questions of infrastructure and legal protection, simple questions of customer convenience may be relevant. Will the customers in practice be disadvantaged if the business is transferred outside the United Kingdom, on the basis that contact with the account holding branch becomes more difficult? It may be that concerns of this nature should not be overstated, in light of technological developments over recent years.

[36] *Re Axa Equity & Law Life Assurance Society plc* [2001] 2 BCLC 447. The guidance to the exercise of the discretion given in this case (as noted above) has been followed on a number of other occasions. For recent examples, see *Re Equitas Insurance Ltd* [2009] EWHC 1595 (Ch); *Re Commercial Union Life Assurance Co Ltd* [2009] EWHC 2521 (Ch).

Effect of Court Sanction

9.18 Let it now be supposed that the court has found that the scheme placed before it does indeed constitute a 'banking business transfer scheme' for FSMA purposes and that the court, in the exercise of its discretion, has decided that it would be appropriate to sanction the scheme.[37] What are the consequences of that state of affairs? At a fairly high level, it may be said that the transferee bank now carries on the business formerly carried on by the transferor institution. But a general statement of this kind is unlikely to answer the questions of detail which may arise in practice, for a banking business consists of a complex web of contractual, proprietary and security rights. It is thus necessary to ask how the court sanction affects rights and obligations at this level.

9.19 In this context, section 112 of the FSMA allows the court to make an order providing for the following matters:

(a) the transfer to the transferee of the whole or any part of the banking business which forms the subject matter of the order, including '… any property or liabilities …' of the transferor. Such an order may have effect even if the transferor lacks '… the capacity to effect the transfer in question …'. It will be necessary to return to these expressions;

(b) the allotment of shares or debentures intended to constitute the consideration for the transfer;[38]

(c) the continuation against the transferee of legal proceedings relating to the banking business; and

(d) such incidental, consequential and supplementary matters as may be necessary to ensure that the scheme is fully and effectively carried out.[39]

9.20 For present purposes, the issues mentioned in paragraph (a) above are of primary concern. It is proposed to consider the nature of the 'property' and the 'liabilities' which may be transferred by means of the order. The effect of the 'lack of capacity' provision will be considered in the same context.

---

[37] It may be noted that a copy of the order sanctioning a banking business transfer scheme must be sent to the FSA within ten days of the date of the order, although the FSA can extend this time limit: FSMA, s 112(9) and (10).

[38] This serves to highlight the fact that, although the transfer is sanctioned by the court, the directors of both the transferor and the transferee remain subject to a fiduciary obligation to ensure that the transaction is in the best interests of their respective companies, and that appropriate consideration must be paid or received. In the case of an intra-group transfer by an entity incorporated in the UK, particular care must be taken to ensure that the arrangement does not result in an unlawful distribution or reduction of capital in contravention of applicable companies legislation: note the situation which arose in *Aveling Barford Ltd v Perion* [1989] BCLC 626. A fair consideration should therefore be ascertained; in most cases, it will no doubt be left outstanding on an intra-group account (rather than paid in cash), but this will demonstrate that the transferor has not disposed of its assets in contravention of the restrictions described above.

[39] As to matters which may be 'necessary' for the purpose of implementing the scheme, see *Re Norwich Union Linked Life Assurance Ltd* [2004] EWHC 2802 (Ch). It appears from that case that a relatively liberal approach is to be adopted in the interpretation of that expression.

'Property' and 'Liabilities'

The 'property' which may be transferred by means of the court order includes '... property, **9.21**
rights and powers of any description ...'.[40] This enabling provision was clearly written in
the broadest possible terms to facilitate the transfer of all of the assets and rights associated
with a banking business.

It is thus plain that the benefit of the loan book and of any security given for it should vest **9.22**
in the transferee, without any requirement for any further contractual or other document
of any kind.[41] The Land Registry should, therefore, re-register mortgages over real property
in the name of the transferee, solely against production of the court order sanctioning the
scheme. Likewise, if the transferor bank held shares in other companies, those companies
should register the transferee as shareholder on the same basis.[42]

The main liabilities associated with a banking business include (i) deposit obligations to its **9.23**
own customers and (ii) obligations owed to third parties and incurred at the request of
customers (eg liabilities under guarantees, acceptances, documentary credits, and similar
instruments). Whilst the parties will inevitably be principally concerned with liabilities of
a *financial* nature, it should be appreciated that the transfer may comprise all other forms
of liability to which the transferor was subject.[43]

Whilst it is thought that these provisions are generally sufficient to achieve their overall **9.24**
objective, it is appropriate to highlight some potential areas of difficulty:

(a) Insofar as the scheme has the effect of transferring *liabilities* which are governed by
    English law,[44] it is submitted that the court order gives effect to a statutory novation.
    The result is that the transferor is wholly released from the liability concerned, whilst
    the transferee becomes subject to it, in each case without the consent of the person
    entitled to the benefit of that liability. This seems to be true as a matter of principle,
    because an obligation governed by English law can likewise be discharged by English
    law.[45] The approach just described also appears to be consistent with the decision of the
    Judicial Committee of the Privy Council in *Wright v Eckhardt Marine GmbH*,[46] a case
    arising out of the collapse of BCCI. In an effort to deal with some of the difficulties
    flowing from that collapse, Bangladesh introduced a scheme under which the liabilities
    of BCCI's Chittagong branch were transferred to Eastern Bank, a new institution

---

[40] FSMA, s 112(12).
[41] See in particular FSMA, s 112(6).
[42] See FSMA, s 112(7).
[43] eg the transferee will owe duties of confidentiality equivalent to those formerly owed by the transferor:
see FSMA, s 112(13).
[44] In relation to liabilities governed by a foreign system of law, it seems that the beneficiary of the obligation
could simply ignore the effect of the scheme on the basis that English law cannot vary a foreign obligation,
and proceed against the transferor to enforce the liability concerned. See Art 12(1)(c) of Rome I and *Ellis v
M'Henry* (1871) LR 6 CP 228. On the Rome I regulation on the law applicable to contractual obligations,
see generally Chapter 40 below.
[45] For confirmation of this point in the field of private international law, see Art 12(1)(c) of Rome I.
See also the decisions of the House of Lords in *Kuwait Oil Tanker Co SAK v UBS AG* [2003] 3 WLR 14 and
Societe Eram Shipping Co Ltd v Hong Kong and Shanghai Banking Corporation [2003] 3 WLR 21.
[46] [2004] 1 AC 147, a decision on appeal from the Court of Appeal of the Cayman Islands.

formed for these purposes. The rules stated that the liabilities of the Chittagong branch of BCCI '… shall … be the liabilities of the [Eastern] Bank …'. The Privy Council held that, on a natural reading of this language, the Eastern Bank became the debtor in substitution for, and not in addition to, BCCI, and that the transferor institution had therefore been wholly released from liability. It is submitted that the same approach should be adopted in relation to Part VII of the FSMA, with the result that the transferor is wholly released from liabilities transferred pursuant to the scheme. The point may be important in various contexts, for example, in deciding whether a note should be made in the transferor's accounts in relation to any liabilities incurred before the transfer was effected.[47]

(b) The transferee institution will clearly wish to enforce any corporate or personal guarantees given in connection with the loan facilities transferred to it. But in general terms, a change in the identity of the lender will result in the termination of the guarantor's liability, unless the guarantee otherwise so provides.[48] It is thus necessary to ask whether the order made by the court can have the effect of preserving the liability of the guarantor in such cases. The point is not entirely straightforward, in the light of a House of Lords decision to the effect that certain obligations are not transferred by virtue of a scheme of arrangement under the Companies Act.[49] Nevertheless, it is submitted that the lender's rights under a guarantee plainly fall within the scope of the '… property, rights and powers of any description …' which may be transferred under the terms of the court order. This would reflect the obvious intent of the provision when read in its context, and is also consistent with the decision of the Court of Appeal of New Zealand in *Carter Holt Harvey Ltd v McKernan*.[50] In that case, the relevant statutory provision[51] confirmed that '… the amalgamated company succeeds to all the property, rights, powers and privileges … [and] … to all the liabilities and obligations of each of the amalgamating companies …'. The court found that the provision was intended to ensure that the benefits and burdens of the contracts of both of the amalgamating companies were to continue in force for all purposes. As a result, the amalgamated company was entitled to the benefit of, and to enforce, the guarantee which was at issue in that case. It is submitted that this approach is plainly right and that a similar attitude should be adopted in the context of Part VII of the FSMA. It may be

---

[47] Where the transferor remains subject to continuing liabilities governed by a foreign system of law, it is submitted that it is entitled to an implied right of indemnity under the terms of FSMA, s 112(3). However, it may be prudent to include an express indemnity obligation in the scheme document itself.

[48] In practice, standard form bank guarantees will specifically stipulate that the guarantee continues in force in such a case. However, it cannot necessarily be assumed that every guarantee accepted by the transferor will have been completed on standard terms. For an illustration of the problem, see *First National Finance Ltd v Goodman* [1985] BCLC 203.

[49] *Noakes v Doncaster Amalgamated Collieries Ltd* [1940] AC 1014. It is submitted that this case was wrongly decided—a view plainly shared by the New Zealand Court of Appeal in the case about to be discussed. Nevertheless, *Noakes* has not been formally overruled. The case did, however, deal with an employment contract (that is, a contract for personal service) rather than a purely financial obligation of the kind evidenced by a guarantee. This may provide an adequate basis for distinguishing the House of Lords decision in the present context.

[50] [1998] 3 NZLR 403.

[51] New Zealand Companies Act, s 209G dealing with the effect of corporate amalgamations.

noted that, although the decision in *Carter Holt Harvey* does not appear to have been cited to it, an English court adopted this broad approach to Part VII in *Re WASA International Insurance Co.*[52]

(c) In a similar vein, there may be cases in which the transferor has agreed contractual limitations on its power to transfer particular assets. For example, borrowers will frequently require that the lender obtains their consent before transferring the benefit of the loan to a third party. Can a court order under Part VII override such a requirement for consent, so that the borrower's obligations under the facility agreement will be enforceable by the transferee, even though such consent was not obtained? In this context, it must be recalled that the court order '... may ... transfer ... property or liabilities whether or not the [transferor] otherwise has the capacity to effect the same ...'.[53] Consistently with the purposive approach described earlier, it has been held[54] that this provision:

> ... should be construed widely and gives the Court power to sanction ... the transfer of property or liabilities even in cases where those properties or liabilities might otherwise be non-transferable, for example, by reason of express contractual provision. In my view, section 112(2) does therefore provide a distinct and clear difference as between the provisions under the [FSMA] and the equivalent provisions under the Companies Act which were considered in *Noakes* ...

(d) Even if the banking business which forms the subject matter of the transfer is conducted from the United Kingdom, it is very likely that the business will comprise assets situate outside this country. For example, a loan may have been made to a German borrower, on the security of real property within Germany. The application of general principles of private international law would suggest that the court order sanctioning the scheme would not suffice to vest the benefit of the German mortgage in the transferee, for a transfer of land situate within Germany can only be achieved by documentation which complies with local procedures.[55] The tension between the court order and the dominance of the *lex situs* in this field is in some respects recognized by section 112(4) of the FSMA, which provides that 'if any property or liability included in the order is governed by the law of any country or territory outside the United Kingdom, the order may require the [transferor], if the transferee so requires, to take all necessary steps for securing that the transfer to the transferee of the property or liability is fully

---

[52] [2002] EWHC 2698; see also the extract from the judgment quoted in para (b), below. It may be added that the approach described in this paragraph is in harmony with corresponding decisions in other common law jurisdictions: see, for example, *Stanward Corporation v Denison Mines Ltd* (1966) DLR (2d) 674 (Ontario Court of Appeal); *R v Black & Decker Manufacturing Co Ltd* (1974) 43 DLR (3d) 393 (Supreme Court of Canada); *WH McElwain Co v Primavera* 167 NYS 815 (1917) (New York Supreme Court); *Nike Inc v Spencer* 707 P2d 589 (Oregon Court of Appeals).

[53] FSMA, s 112(2)(a). Note the discussion of the corresponding difficulties when the court is called upon to recognize a merger effected under a foreign system of law: see Chapter 10 below.

[54] In *Re Cater Allen Ltd,* unreported, but noted and followed in *Re WASA International Insurance Co* [2002] EWHC 2698. Although the approach adopted in these cases would appear to be correct, it is not without difficulty given the 'capacity' language which has curiously been adopted. It has been held that a 'transfer of engagements' effected by a resolution of a registered society under Industrial and Provident Societies Act 1965, s 51 does indeed have the effect of overriding a contractual restriction against assignment: see *Co-operative Group (CWS) v Stansell Ltd* [2006] EWCA Civ 538 (CA). It is submitted that this approach is both correct and convenient.

[55] For more detailed discussion of this rule, see Dicey, Morris & Collins, para 23R-021.

effective under the law of that country or territory'. This provision appears to confirm that, *as between transferor and transferee*, the English court order has the effect of transferring even those assets and liabilities which are situate abroad. However, it also recognizes the need for further action to be taken in the relevant jurisdiction in order to perfect the transfer as against the relevant counterparty. Pending the perfection of the transfer in the overseas jurisdiction concerned, it seems clear that the transferor is to hold the relevant foreign assets on trust for the transferee.[56] This remains the case even though the property is situate in a jurisdiction which does not itself recognize the concept of the trust, for equity acts *in personam* against the transferor, and not *in rem* against the property.[57] Since the transferor acts as a bare trustee, the transferee could require it to take any necessary proceedings for the enforcement of the foreign security.[58]

(e) It is, of course, vital that any security given to the transferor should continue to be enforceable in the hands of the transferee. In that context, it is necessary to ask whether any security given to the transferor needs to be re-registered against the borrower in order to ensure its continued validity in favour of the transferee under the terms of section 860 of the Companies Act 2006. In principle, this question should be answered in the negative, for section 860 applies only where security is *created* by the chargor company;[59] the section does not (and cannot) operate in relation to a Part VII transfer, to which the company will not even be a party. This approach to the matter would appear to be confirmed by a Canadian decision, even though that case did, of course, involve different statutory language.[60]

(f) It should be noted that the sanction of a banking business transfer scheme operates to transfer the *ownership* of the relevant assets and liabilities to the transferee, but does not otherwise operate to vary or amend the *substance* of the rights and liabilities comprised within the package. This point may have consequences where it is proposed to transfer a banking business currently carried out through a UK branch to an overseas transferee.[61] In general terms, the deposit liabilities of the UK transferor will be governed by English law[62] and, in principle, they should continue to be so governed notwithstanding the sanction of the transfer scheme.[63] This could potentially be a

---

[56] This appears to be the effect of FSMA, s 112(4), although the language of trust law is not employed.

[57] See, for example, *Penn v Lord Baltimore* (1750) Ves Sen 444; *Companhia de Mocambique v British South Africa Co* [1892] 2 QB 358.

[58] ie in accordance with the rule in *Saunders v Vautier* (1841) 4 Beav 115.

[59] For further discussion of the registration requirements applicable under s 860 of the 2006 Act (formerly Companies Act 1985, s 395), see Chapter 27 below.

[60] See *Heidelberg Canada Graphic Equipment v Arthur Andersen Inc* (1992) 7 DLR (2d) 236. The decision is based upon the specific language of the Ontario Personal Property Securities Act 1990, although it is submitted that the same logic should apply in the context of s 860 of the 2006 Act.

[61] It will be recalled that such a transfer can be sanctioned under FSMA, s 106(2)(a).

[62] Bank accounts and deposit liabilities are, as a general rule, governed by the law of the place in which the relevant bank branch is situate: see *Joachimson v Swiss Bank Corporation* [1921] 3 KB 118; *Attock Cement Co Ltd v Romanian Bank for Foreign Trade* [1989] 1 All ER 1189; *American Training Services Inc v Commerce Union Bank* 415 F Supp 1101 (1976), aff'd 612 F 2d 580 (1979), and other cases discussed in a private international law context in Chapter 40 below.

[63] Any change in the system of law governing the banker–customer contract can only be effected with the consent of the customer: Rome I, Art 3(2).

matter of great inconvenience and expense from the perspective of the transferee institution. For example, the law of the transferee's jurisdiction may require it to withhold local tax from interest payable to the depositor. Yet the deduction and payment of a foreign tax will not amount to a discharge of an obligation governed by English law, with the result that the transferee may have to pay interest gross to the depositor and pay the tax as well.[64] It may be that the court could be persuaded to include in its order a provision to the effect that transferred rights governed by English law would henceforth be subject to the laws of the transferee's jurisdiction, on the basis that this is an '… incidental, consequential [or] supplementary …' matter which is necessary to ensure '… that the scheme is fully and effectively carried out …'. It has been seen that the court has power to make orders of this kind,[65] but it must be doubtful whether the court can use this provision to override the requirement for the explicit consent of the customer to a change in the law applicable to the relationship.[66] Even if the court's power could be used for that purpose, it must be very doubtful that the court should, as a matter of discretion, make an order which may have a fundamental impact on the nature of the customer's rights. Part VII of the FSMA is designed to facilitate a transfer of rights and obligations, not a variation in their substantive content.

(g) One question which could in theory arise relates to the banker's right of set-off.[67] For example, suppose that a customer happens to have an overdraft facility with the transferor bank but has a credit balance on accounts with the transferee. When the right to demand repayment of the overdraft vests in the transferee by virtue of the court order, does this also entitle the transferee to exercise a right of set-off over the deposit account when, plainly, no such right would have existed prior to the effective date of the transfer order? Although there seems to be no direct authority on this point, it seems that the banker-customer contract should be regarded as a single, indivisible relationship, even though a particular aspect of that relationship may have come into existence as a result of a court order (rather than by agreement). Consequently, the transferee bank should enjoy the usual right of set-off as soon as the overdraft liability is vested in it.

The Cross-Border Mergers Regulations 2007

Although they were not specifically designed to facilitate bank mergers, it may be helpful **9.25** to note for completeness the terms of the Companies (Cross-Border Mergers) Regulations 2007 (the 'Cross-Border Mergers Regulations').[68] The Regulations came into effect on 15 December 2007 and were designed to implement an EU Directive on the same subject matter.[69]

---

[64] For a comparable situation, see *Indian and General Investment Trust Ltd v Borax Consolidated Ltd* [1920] 1 KB 539.

[65] ie under FSMA, s 112(1)(d).

[66] ie under Rome I, Art 3(2).

[67] On this right generally, see Chapter 36 below.

[68] SI 2007/2974.

[69] Directive 2005/56/EC of the European Parliament and of the Council on cross-border mergers of limited liability companies, OJ L 310, 25.11.2005, p 1.

9.26   In essence, a UK company and a company established in another EEA State can merge under the new procedures, either by acquisition (where one party acquires the other in consideration of an issue of shares in the transferee) or by amalgamation (where the assets and liabilities of the two companies concerned are acquired by a new entity in return for an issue of shares in that entity).[70] An English court can issue an order certifying that the English company has met the conditions for a cross-border merger for the purposes of the EU Directive. The prerequisites to such an order include the preparation of a draft scheme and reports from the directors and appropriate experts. The court may summon meetings of shareholders and creditors to approve the proposed merger arrangements. The English court order can be made provided that a corresponding order has also been made in the EEA State in which the other entity is incorporated.[71] Provision is also made for for employee participation in the case of larger companies.[72]

9.27   The completion of a cross-border merger involves the vesting of the respective assets and liabilities in the transferee company, the dissolution of the transferor entity without a process of liquidation, and the issue of shares in the transferee entity as required.[73] It may be noted that the Cross-Border Merger Regulations contemplate a merger of the *entire* assets and undertakings of the companies concerned; there is no provision for a *partial* merger.

9.28   Additional formalities would plainly apply if one of the merging entities were a UK authorized person, and it would be necessary to obtain FSA approval in advance to any acquisition or change of control.[74] The court should clearly decline to sanction the merger unless it is shown that the required approval has been obtained.

Conclusions

9.29   Notwithstanding some of the difficulties and other issues raised above, it seems that Part VII of the FSMA offers a convenient means of dealing with the transfer of a banking business, and will be of particular assistance in the context of intra-group reorganizations. This view is reinforced by the court's apparent willingness to adopt a purposive and robust approach to the new provisions. Whilst Part VII inevitably suffers from certain limitations, it should be observed that the most difficult issues arise in the field of cross-border transfers involving interaction with foreign systems of law. It is fair to observe that territorial problems of this character could not be solved even when reorganizations of this kind were effected by means of a private Act of Parliament.

---

[70] For more detail on these points, see the definitions of 'merger by absorption', 'merger by absorption of a wholly-owned subsidiary' and 'merger by formation of a new company' in reg 2 of the Cross-Border Mergers Regulations.

[71] On the various points just made, see regs 6–16 of the Cross-Border Merger Regulations.

[72] See Pt 4 of the Cross-Border Merger Regulations.

[73] On these points, see reg 17 of the Cross-Border Merger Regulations.

[74] See the discussion at para 1.23 above.

The Cross-Border Merger Regulations offer a useful means of merging two entities albeit **9.30** that this route is available only where the counterparty to the merger is established in an EEA State. It should be appreciated that this particular legislation was not specifically aimed at financial institutions and additional complexities will apply in that context. It may therefore be that these regulations will not be a popular means of achieving mergers in that market.

10

FOREIGN BANK MERGERS

Introduction

As noted in the previous chapter, mergers between banks have been a common feature of **10.01** the financial scene over recent years. Some of these have been motivated by the desire to establish global and prosperous institutions, others simply by the desire to survive. The statutory procedure available in the United Kingdom for completing such mergers has been considered in the previous chapter. It is, of course, obvious that an order made by an English court must be recognized in England, especially insofar as it deals with the impact of the transfer on the assets and liabilities of the entities concerned.

By contrast, the present chapter examines the consequences of foreign bank mergers **10.02** achieved under the law of another country but which may have consequences in England (eg because the affected banks are parties to contracts governed by English law and/or have assets or liabilities in England). A reading of that sentence will make it clear that the present chapter must, again, deal with a number of issues of private international law.[1]

It should be appreciated that the present chapter refers to 'mergers' in the sense in which **10.03** that expression is generally understood, that is to say, with arrangements which involve the transfer by one entity (the 'transferor') of the whole or substantially the whole of its business to another entity (the 'transferee')[2] *by operation of law by means of a court order or through a legislative medium*. Arrangements merely involving the *contractual* sale of individual assets

---

[1] Where a merger or reorganization involves an entity incorporated in an EEA State, it will be necessary to consider whether a duty to recognize the relevant arrangement arises under the EU Directive and implementing regulations discussed in Chapter 12 below.

[2] Usually, the transfer will be effected in consideration of an issue of shares in the transferee, so that the former shareholders in the transferor will become shareholders in the enlarged, transferee entity. In some cases, the businesses of two entities may both be transferred to a new company which has been formed for that purpose. In that event, the new company would be the 'transferee' for the purposes of the present discussion. Indeed, this was the position in one of the leading cases on the subject (*National Bank of Greece and Athens SA v Metliss*, which will be considered below).

or a portfolio of assets are subject to different rules, and the validity of the transfer of each individual asset will generally be judged by reference to the law of the country in which the various assets are legally situate.[3] Likewise, a 'merger' achieved through a takeover offer by one institution for another does not raise the same issues since there is merely a transfer of shares in the target institution. There is no direct impact on the underlying contractual relationships of the target bank with its own customers.

10.04 In practical terms, five sets of questions may potentially arise after a bank has completed a transfer or merger arrangement under a foreign law, namely:

(a) Will the English courts recognize the effect of the merger as far as the transferee is concerned?

(b) Will the transferee entity be entitled to the benefit of the loans and other assets transferred to it under the terms of the relevant foreign law, and be bound by obligations (including guarantees, outstanding floating rate notes and other instruments) issued or assumed by the transferor prior to the merger?

(c) What will be the consequences of the merger for the transferor?

(d) What will be the consequences for counterparties to transactions with the transferor?

(e) What are the consequences of The Companies (Cross-Border Mergers) Regulations 2007?

Each of these questions will be considered separately.

Recognition of the Merger

10.05 On what basis can the English courts recognize the effect of a foreign court order[4] which gives effect to a merger by transferring the entire business and undertaking of the transferor to the transferee? The Rome I regulation on the law applicable to contractual obligations[5] offers no assistance in this sphere, because (i) the merger will not have been achieved by contract[6] and (ii) the regulation does not in any event apply to questions which are governed by the law of companies.[7]

---

[3] A partial merger may fall in between these two extremes. On that aspect, see para 10.15 below.

[4] It is assumed for present purposes that the foreign merger is achieved by a court order in the jurisdiction in which the relevant banks are incorporated. However, the comments made in this section would apply equally if the merger had been achieved by means of legislation enacted in that jurisdiction.

[5] On Rome I, see generally Chapter 40 below.

[6] ie in the sense that there is no contract between the transferor, transferee, and the underlying customer pursuant to which the underlying assets are transferred. Although the House of Lords was able to overcome these difficulties in *Metliss* (discussed below), Viscount Simmonds noted (at p 521) that '… I am not aware of any case … in which, in the courts of this country, a plaintiff has, without a plea of novation or statutory assignment, recovered a sum due under a contract from one who was not a party to that contract …'. Lord Keith also remarked (at p 530) that there were '… material differences between a succession and a novation. In succession no question of contract arises. In both cases, it is true, the creditor will have lost the personal credit of the debtor on which he may be assumed to have relied. On the other hand, he will not have lost, in a universal succession, the security of the debtor's assets which will have passed to the successor and be available for the creditor, whereas in a novation no transfer of assets need take place at all. The extinction of a corporation under statute or decree and the passing of all its rights and liabilities to a successor exhibits, in my view, all the features of a universal succession … in the present case, the new bank has been declared the universal successor of the old banks. The result is to fix on it the status and liabilities of a universal successor …'.

[7] See Rome I, Art 1(2)(f).

It is necessary to start with the basic proposition[8] that '… the existence … of a foreign **10.06** corporation duly created … under the law of a foreign country is recognised in England …'. Pausing there, one might immediately think that this rule has no relevance in this context, for the existence of the transferee as a corporate entity is not in dispute. The question is: have the transferor's assets and liabilities been effectively vested in the transferee, and that question should more obviously be directed to the law of the respective countries in which those assets are situate.[9]

Yet, thankfully, this is not the position at which the English courts have arrived, for it would **10.07** be very inconvenient to have to consider the laws of all of such jurisdictions. Instead, the courts treat a merger as an occurrence affecting the *corporate status* of a foreign entity, rather than as a matter merely concerning the *transfer or acquisition of assets*. As a result of this exercise in characterization, the validity and effect of the merger fall to be governed by the law of the country of incorporation, and under whose laws the merger will have been carried out.[10] Generally speaking, the foreign merger court order or law will state that the transferee acquires all of the transferee's assets, and becomes subject to all of the transferee's liabilities, at the point of time at which the merger takes effect. As a rule, the English courts will recognize a foreign merger if the legal system under which it was effected provides for universal succession (*successio in universum jus*) to the assets and liabilities of the predecessor entity. Both the principle itself and certain limitations to it are clearly borne out by the leading decisions of the House of Lords in the so-called 'Greek Bond' cases.

In the first case, *National Bank of Greece and Athens SA v Metliss*,[11] the Greek Government **10.08** decided to merge two Greek banks, namely, the National Bank of Greece (NBG) and the National Bank of Athens (NBA). Under a decree passed in 1953, these two entities were both dissolved but the entirety of their respective assets and liabilities were vested in a new entity formed for that purpose and known as the National Bank of Greece and Athens (NBGA).

NBG had previously executed a guarantee in respect of bonds issued by a Greek issuer; **10.09** default had been made both by the issuer and by NBG itself. It was difficult for the holder to achieve any recovery, since NBG had no presence in London and, in any event, a Greek moratorium law would have prevented the Greek courts from giving judgment in favour of the bondholders. However, NBA did have a London branch and, upon the merger, this became a branch of NBGA. A holder therefore took proceedings against NBGA in England.

---

[8] See Dicey, Morris & Collins, paragraph 30R-009 and the cases there cited.
[9] This particular rule of private international law is considered in relation to the validity and effect of foreign security granted to a lender: see generally the discussion of security rights in relation to foreign assets in Chapters 27–34 below.
[10] If the transferor and transferee are incorporated in different jurisdictions, then it seems that the merger should only be recognized in England if it has been sanctioned by the appropriate procedures in both countries: although the point did not directly arise, see *Global Container Lines Ltd v Bonyad Shipping Co* [1999] 1 Lloyds Rep 287 (where a Delaware corporation was substituted as a party to litigation in place of its Bahamian predecessor).
[11] [1958] AC 509 (HL).

10.10   The House of Lords rightly noted that this was in many respects a remarkable case, for the holder was seeking to enforce a guarantee against a person who was not an original party to it and had not subsequently become a party by means of a novation.[12] Nevertheless, the House of Lords held that the amalgamation and its effects were to be governed by Greek law in accordance with the principles outlined above. Since NBGA was subject to the liabilities imposed by the guarantee in accordance with the law of its country of incorporation,[13] that state of affairs would be recognized by the English courts and judgment was given for the bondholder.[14] This principle has been applied on a number of subsequent occasions.[15]

10.11   The law of the country of incorporation can therefore provide for a universal succession which the English courts must recognize on the basis that corporate matters of this kind must be governed by the laws of the home State. However, it should be appreciated that the role of the merger law is closely circumscribed. For example, whilst the law of the place of incorporation may be determinative in the sense that a merger achieved under that law will be recognized, nevertheless the intrinsic validity of the rights and obligations thereby transferred will continue to be governed by the law applicable to them.[16]

10.12   This point is well illustrated by the companion decision of the House of Lords in *Adams v National Bank of Greece SA*.[17] Following the decision in *Metliss* (above), the Greek Government in 1956 introduced new legislation which provided that the obligations of NBG with respect to the relevant guarantees were not part of the assets, liabilities and undertakings transferred to NBGA pursuant to the original decree. The new legislation was stated to be retrospective to the date of the original decree. As a result, NBGA claimed that it was not subject to those guarantee liabilities, and refused to make payment. This ingenious attempt to avoid payment on the bonds once again failed before the House of Lords. The 1956 Greek legislation was again framed as a law affecting the corporate status of NBGA, no doubt anticipating that, following the decision in *Metliss*, the English courts would feel obliged to give effect to the 1956 legislation in accordance with its terms and to hold that NBGA was not (or was no longer) liable on the guarantees. Indeed, this line of argument succeeded before the Court of Appeal, but their decision was reversed by the

---

[12]   See the extracts from the House of Lords decision reproduced in n 6 above.

[13]   To express matters in a different way, Greek law gave birth to NBGA, and Greek law thus governed the features and characteristics which it bore at the time of its birth.

[14]   The House of Lords also held that, since the moratorium was a creature of Greek law, it could not be invoked to prevent the holder from obtaining judgment on a guarantee governed by English law.

[15]   See, for example, *Toprak Enerji v Sale Tilney Technology plc* [1994] 1 WLR 840; *Industrie Chimiche Italia Centrale v Alexander G Tsavliris & Sons Maritime Co* [1996] 1 WLR 777; *Eurosteel Ltd v Stinnes AG* [2000] 1 All ER (Comm) 964, where the court remarked that '… the whole point of universal succession is that the successor is treated as the same person as the person to whom he succeeds …'. In earlier times, it was occasionally noted that the English courts would recognize a 'universal succession' achieved under a foreign law even though no equivalent process was known to English domestic law. The latter part of this statement is probably no longer accurate: see, for example, the Cross-Border Merger Regulations discussed at para 9.25 above.

[16]   This statement does, of course, assume that the obligation at issue is governed by English law. It has already been shown that English law is then to be applied in dealing with matters touching the interpretation, performance, and discharge of the obligation: see Rome I, Art 12.

[17]   [1961] AC 255 (HL). By the time of the second proceedings, NBGA had changed its name to 'National Bank of Greece SA'.

House of Lords. The decision of the House of Lords rests on a number of grounds, but the main point rests in the characterization of the 1956 law.[18] If one looks at the substance of the matter, the 1956 law did not deal with the corporate status of NBGA; rather, it sought to discharge NBGA from a guarantee obligation to which it had been made subject as a result of the original amalgamation law. Once the 1956 law had been classified as legislation dealing with the discharge of contractual obligations, then the law could have no further relevance to the proceedings. The guarantee was governed by English law, and questions touching the performance or discharge of that obligation were thus governed exclusively by English law.[19] As far as English law was concerned, the guarantee remained valid and effective. The bondholders were thus entitled to judgment.

It should also be emphasized that—as happened in *Metliss*—the effect of the foreign merger law is recognized both in relation to rights and liabilities governed by English law and in relation to assets which are situate in England. It is perfectly acceptable that the foreign merger law should operate in this way for, at least in formal terms, the law is operating in relation to the foreign corporation, and not in relation to the assets and liabilities themselves.[20] **10.13**

It is necessary to sound one note of caution, in that the precise scope and effect of the merger—for example, as to assets which are or are not included in the transfer—must also be determined by reference to the law of the place of incorporation.[21] **10.14**

For the reasons given below, these decisions are helpful to creditors and others dealing with a foreign bank which becomes subject to a merger process. It should, however, be appreciated that these rules have only been held to apply in cases of 'universal succession', that is, where the transferee acquires the *whole* of the assets, liabilities, and undertaking of the transferor. What would be the position if an English court were asked to recognize a succession involving only *part* of the assets and liabilities of the transferor? In the apparent absence of direct authority on this specific point, it is suggested that: **10.15**

(a) provided that the transfer is achieved by way of succession (and not by way of a contractual novation), then it seems that the arrangement should still be characterized as a matter affecting the corporate status of the transferee. In the absence of a contract with

---

[18] The question of characterization, or classification, of a foreign law for private international law purposes is an initial question for the court, and is to be determined by reference to English principles (rather than by reference to the foreign law at issue). This rather intricate subject is dealt with in some detail in Dicey, Morris & Collins, ch 2. In essence, however, it is necessary to decide whether a particular foreign law should be classified as a corporate law or as a law dealing with the performance or discharge of a contract. Issues of corporate law are governed by the law of the company's home jurisdiction, whilst questions of performance are governed by the law applicable to the contract. Different results may therefore follow from the ultimate classification. The decision in *Adams* itself is a clear illustration of the importance of the classification of conflict questions.
[19] See now Rome I, Art 12.
[20] As a result, the general rule to the effect that title to assets situate in England cannot be transferred by virtue of foreign legislation has no application in the present context. On that general rule, see *Bank voor Handel en Scheepvart NV v Slatford* [1953] 1 QB 248.
[21] ie and not by English law, because it is the merger which affects the corporate status of the parties: see *Pfizer Ltd and another v Dainippon Sumitomo Ltd and another* [2006] All ER (D) 172. This decision is discussed in more detail in n 31 below.

the debtors and creditors of the transferor, it is hard to see what other classification can be adopted;

(b) given that matters of corporate status are governed by the law of the place of incorporation, it would appear that cases of partial succession should be treated on the same basis as universal arrangements;

(c) whilst there are some observations in *Adams* to the effect that a *partial* amalgamation should not be recognized,[22] these remarks seem to be focused on the possibility of abuse—for example, where an attempt is being made to divorce assets from their corresponding liabilities in order to defraud or defeat creditors. It is of course to be hoped that such cases would be rare[23] but, by way of exception, the court could plainly decline to recognize such a merger on public policy grounds. The mere *possibility* that a partial succession could be used as a vehicle of fraud does not offer a compelling basis to refuse recognition to other potential mergers effected for bona fide commercial reasons. In other words, considerations of public policy should only be applied on a case-specific basis;[24] and

(d) considerations of comity may also influence the court's attitude. For example, it has already been noted that the English courts can sanction the transfer of a banking business under Part VII of the FSMA[25] and it is quite possible that this will be equivalent to a partial merger. It would obviously be the hope that, to the greatest extent possible, foreign courts would recognize the effect of such orders on assets within their jurisdiction. Reciprocity may help to secure that objective.

10.16   For these reasons, it would appear to be appropriate for an English court to recognize a partial merger which occurs under a foreign system of law and can properly be regarded as a corporate reorganization, rather than a mere transfer of assets.

---

[22] Lord Reid observed (at p 283) that English law might not recognize a 'selective' amalgamation, which imposed on the successor '… some but not all of the obligations of the old bank …'.

[23] It may be hoped that the relevant foreign legislation would normally provide a right for the creditors to object to a proposed merger, so that any attempt to defraud creditors would be discovered before the merger could even be effected. It would be particularly difficult to achieve such an objective in the case of a bank merger, where greater publicity may be expected and regulatory approvals will be required.

[24] In this context, it may be appropriate briefly to cross-refer to the Icelandic crisis of 2008, which is discussed in more depth in the context of cross-border reorganization of banks (para 12.11 below) and deposit-guarantee schemes (para 13.13 below). As there noted, the loan and other assets of 'Old Landsbanki' were transferred to 'New Landsbanki' together with Old Landsbanki's liabilities in respect of domestic deposits accepted within Iceland. However, liability for deposits accepted abroad was not transferred, with the apparent result that foreign depositors were deprived of recourse to assets which would otherwise have been available to meet their claims. It appears that Old Landsbanki was to be compensated by the issue of a bond by New Landsbanki, which would compensate it for the assets transferred (the issue of this bond is noted in *Jeffries International Ltd v Landsbanki Islands HF* [2009] EWHC 894 (Comm)). If the value and terms of the bond were found to be appropriate having regard to the assets transferred, then it would seem that the arrangements should be recognized in accordance with the principles discussed above. However, if the consideration for the transfer were found to be manifestly inadequate such that the creditors of Old Landsbanki were plainly disadvantaged, then this would perhaps lead an English court to the conclusion that the merger should not be recognized on public policy grounds. This example is, however, used purely for illustrative purposes in this context. Given that Iceland is an EEA State, it is probable (although not certain) that the reorganization would have to be recognized by the English courts under the Directive and implementing regulations considered in Chapter 12 below.

[25] See Chapter 9 above.

The Transferred Assets and Liabilities

Recognition of foreign bank mergers in the manner described above has a variety of consequences in practice. The rules are convenient from both an asset and a liability perspective.   **10.17**

Dealing firstly with the liability perspective, a person who has lent money to, or has the benefit of some other obligation formerly owed by, the transferor will have the benefit of a corresponding claim against the transferee, without any requirement for any further documentation or other action on his part. If it becomes necessary to enforce the obligation, he will merely need to obtain a legal opinion or other evidence to the effect that the transferee has succeeded to all of the assets and liabilities of the transferor. He will often be relieved of even this formality for, in the normal case a multinational bank involved in this type of merger will have issued press announcements publicizing the merger, explaining its effects and its undoubted benefits for the customers of the bank. The bank will thus not normally seek to defend proceedings on the technical basis that a particular obligation was not comprised in the transfer. Even if such an attempt were made, it may well fail on the grounds that the transferee, having gone to great lengths to make the public aware of the consequences of the merger, will be estopped from pleading the detailed provisions of the foreign law as a defence.[26]   **10.18**

It should be added that the liabilities to which a foreign merger may apply are not limited to purely *financial* obligations. For example, if the London branch of the transferor owed a duty of confidentiality to a customer before the merger took effect, the transferee will continue to owe the same obligation, and it will apply to information received both before and after the merger. In other words, the merger will usually transfer the *entirety* of the contractual rights and obligations.   **10.19**

Turning now to the asset perspective, the English courts will recognize that the assets of the transferor have been duly vested in the transferee by virtue of the foreign merger law. Once again, no specific or further formality is necessary to ensure that the court reaches that conclusion; if it becomes necessary to take proceedings against a debtor, then the bank will again merely need to produce evidence that the foreign merger law has had the effect of vesting the benefit of the relevant debt in the transferee.[27] Once again, however, if the debtor continues to have dealings with the merged bank after becoming aware of the change of status, he may well be estopped from asserting that, in fact, his liability was not carried over by the merger.   **10.20**

---

[26] Estoppel will usually be a matter of procedure which will be governed by English law as the law of the forum. The fact that the merger will itself be subject to the laws of a foreign jurisdiction would thus not prejudice the plea of estoppel.

[27] In practice, however, the transferee will take various steps to safeguard its position. It will usually notify customers about the transfer by means of a standard letter. In addition, it may take steps to substitute its name for that of the transferee on public registers, especially where these record outstanding security (eg the Land Registry).

10.21 It should however be appreciated that, whilst these rules may lead to recognition of a transfer of rights and obligations, they will not operate to alter the terms of pre-existing contracts nor will they deprive them of their effect. For example, if the transferor has issued bonds governed by English law which include a prohibition against a merger, then the completion of such a merger will constitute a default under those bonds.[28] Likewise, if those bonds contain a minimum net worth undertaking, a default will occur if the effect of the merger is to dilute net worth below the required minimum level. Equally, if the transferor has undertaken not to dispose of substantially the whole of its undertaking, a breach of this provision would occur as soon as the merger takes effect.[29] In other words, the fact that a foreign merger is recognized under the *Metliss* principle does not excuse the transferor or the transferee from compliance with pre-existing contractual undertakings affecting the conduct of their businesses.

Consequences for the Transferor

10.22 What are the consequences of the completion of the merger for the transferor entity? Plainly, since the English courts will recognize the foreign merger, this must mean that the transferor will no longer be regarded as the owner of its pre-merger assets, nor will it be regarded as subject to any of its pre-merger liabilities. So far as the English courts are concerned, any attempt to take possession of those assets, or to enforce those liabilities, against the transferor would necessarily fail.

10.23 It is sometimes suggested that the concept of universal succession necessarily connotes that the transferor must be dissolved in consequence of the merger. Whilst the amalgamating banks in *Metliss* and *Adams* were indeed dissolved under the relevant Greek decree, there is no indication that this is a necessary requirement for recognition of the succession in England. It is submitted that it is not, because (i) the matter is a question of corporate status which is governed by the law of the place of incorporation (and not by English law) and (ii) a requirement for the dissolution of the transferor would necessarily lead to the conclusion that only a *universal* succession could be recognized and, for reasons given earlier,[30] this would not seem to be justifiable.

Consequences for Transaction Counterparties

10.24 In large measure, the consequences of the bank merger for transaction counterparties will mirror those referred to above. In other words, the counterparty will henceforth owe his obligations to the transferee and will have to look to the transferee for the performance of the corresponding obligations. He will no longer be able to look to, or otherwise be concerned with, the transferor.

---

[28] As noted in relation to the *Adams* decision, above, a foreign law cannot operate to vary or discharge an obligation governed by English law.

[29] On undertakings prohibiting mergers and disposals, and net worth covenants, see Chapter 20 below.

[30] See the discussion of 'partial' successions, at para 10.15 above.

Nevertheless, it remains to consider whether the counterparty may have any right of complaint or action for breach of contract as a consequence of the merger. In this respect, it has been noted earlier[31] that the foreign law which effects the merger cannot vary or discharge contracts governed by English law.[32] This point will be of limited importance for the ordinary current account holder but may assume significance in relation to major borrowers who may have negotiated provisions restricting assignments by the lending bank.[33]   **10.25**

The precise effect of such provisions will, of course, be a matter of interpretation of the particular document concerned. But an example of the issue may perhaps be offered by reference to the assignment provisions used in the standard documentation published by the Loan Market Association.[34] In broad terms, a lender is permitted to '… *assign* any of its rights or *transfer* by novation any of its rights and obligations …' under the facility agreement to another lender. However, '… the consent of the [Borrower] is required for an assignment or transfer …', although such consent '… must not be unreasonably withheld or delayed …'.   **10.26**

As noted above, a foreign merger law cannot override these provisions, which are governed by English law. In consequence, it becomes necessary to determine whether the completion of such a merger would create a requirement for consent under these provisions.[35] It is submitted that they do not, because references to an *assignment* or *transfer* connote a *contractual* disposal of the entitlement to the loan. But, as has been shown,[36] it is of the very essence of the foreign merger that it is recognized as a matter of corporate succession, and not as a result of any contractual arrangement. It follows that a lender who enters into a   **10.27**

---

[31] See the discussion of the *Adams* decision in para 10.12 above. In this sense, the court in *Pfizer Ltd and another v Dainippon Sumitomo Pharma Co Ltd and another* [2006] All ER (D) 172 may have fallen into error. A contract governed by English law stated that '… This Agreement shall not be assignable by either party without the prior consent of the other …'. The Japanese party to the agreement undertook a merger which took effect by way of universal succession and, according to the judgment (see para 10), the question arose whether the Japanese merger 'overrode' the English law prohibition against assignment, and that this was essentially a question of Japanese law. It is respectfully submitted that this approach to the matter was misconceived, because Japanese law cannot vary or discharge an obligation governed by English law. The true questions were (i) as a matter of *Japanese law*, did the merger have the effect of transferring the benefit of the contract to the surviving entity and (ii) if so, did that arrangement infringe the *English law* prohibition against assignment, properly construed? For the reasons given in the text, the second question should be answered in the negative.

[32] To this extent, the position of a foreign merger in England necessarily differs from that which has been effected under a domestic statutory procedure: compare the discussion (at para 9.24 above) of the decision in *Co-operative Group (CWS) v Stansell Ltd* [2006] EWCA Civ 538 (CA).

[33] The growth of the debt trading markets has made major corporate borrowers sensitive to the possibility that their debt might be sold, and they may insist on continuing to do business with the institution which they originally selected.

[34] Emphasis supplied. This documentation, which is usually used only for transactions with major corporate borrowers, is discussed in more detail in Chapter 20 below.

[35] Whilst this may appear to be a small point, it can assume great significance in practice. For example, disclosure of the merger proposals to customers may be difficult until a public announcement is made, and this may be very late in the process. Equally, banks cannot run the risk that the intended merger might be derailed as a result of a refusal of consent by a few major customers.

[36] See the discussion of the *Metliss* decision at para 10.08 above.

merger arrangement would not thereby contravene the contractual provisions reproduced above.[37]

The Cross-Border Mergers Regulations

10.28   Reference has already been made to the Cross-Border Mergers Regulations and to the EU Directive on cross-border mergers.[38] Although the Cross-Border Mergers Regulations themselves contemplate a merger involving at least one UK company, the EU Directive obviously applies to mergers between entities established in any EEA State, regardless of any specific UK nexus.

10.29   Given the UK's membership of the EU and the obvious expectation that other EEA States would recognize cross-border mergers involving a UK company, it seems plain that English courts should, on a reciprocal basis, recognize mergers between other EEA companies effected pursuant to corresponding domestic legislation. The English courts should, correspondingly, recognize the impact of such a merger on assets and liabilities located in England. It would appear that the essential outcomes of this process should be broadly similar to those produced by an application of the private international law principles discussed earlier in this chapter.[39]

Conclusions

10.30   It appears from the foregoing discussion that bank mergers effected under a foreign system of law will be entitled to recognition in England. The English courts will accordingly give effect to the merger insofar as it effects a transfer of property and contractual rights and obligations.

10.31   Although one should not overgeneralize, it is striking that the private international law rules on foreign mergers lead to legal consequences essentially similar to those which apply to a transfer effected under English law.[40] This is so even though very different sets of rules have to be applied in each case.

10.32   This is a happy result. In terms of London's position as a leading financial centre, it would be unfortunate if domestic and foreign bank mergers had radically different effects in relation to assets situate in England or contracts governed by English law.

---

[37] This impression is reinforced by one of the general clauses in the Loan Market Association standard agreement, to the effect that references to any party to the agreement shall be taken to include '… its successors in title, permitted assigns and permitted transferees …'. The distinct reference to 'successors in title' suggests that they are not to be regarded as 'assignees' or 'transferees' for the purposes of the provisions reproduced in the main text.

[38] See paras 9.25–9.28 above.

[39] And, of course, reliance on those principles will continue to be necessary where non-EEA companies are involved.

[40] ie pursuant to a transfer of the kind described in Chapter 9 above.

11

BANK RESCUES AND FINANCIAL STABILITY IN THE UNITED KINGDOM

Introduction

For many years, there were no special or specific statutory arrangements in place in the United Kingdom to deal with bank restructuring or insolvencies.[1] Such difficulties had generally been handled by the Bank of England, acting in concert with market participants. **11.01**

This relatively informal approach to bank failures became harder to sustain for a variety of reasons. First of all, bank regulation had to be placed on a statutory footing in order to enable the United Kingdom to comply with its obligations under various EC Banking Directives.[2] **11.02**

---

[1] Banks were subject to the rules applicable to all companies in these spheres. The insolvency of Barings Bank in 1995 was accordingly conducted in accordance with the ordinary rules applicable to the administration process under the Insolvency Act 1986.

[2] For discussion of EU-inspired banking legislation and its dominance in the regulatory field, see the discussion in Chapter 2 above.

Secondly, the growing complexity of the financial markets made it difficult to assess an institution's liabilities and this, in turn, made it harder to identify a buyer or to take other appropriate action on a very rapid basis. The inability to assess likely losses from Japanese derivatives trading pending contract maturity dates was one of the factors which prevented an immediate rescue of Barings Bank when its problems came to light in early 1995. Rescue efforts therefore failed despite interest from various quarters.[3]

11.03 Yet, ultimately, it was not the increasing drive towards the harmonization of EU financial services law which produced a legislative framework for bank insolvencies in the United Kingdom.[4] Rather, it was the essentially domestic collapse of Northern Rock in the autumn of 2007—coupled with the embarrassment of the first bank run for over a century and the ultimate decision to issue a Treasury guarantee in respect of the bank's liabilities[5]—which finally persuaded the government of the need for bespoke insolvency legislation in this particular area. The legislative agenda was further accelerated by a severe sharpening of the financial crisis in the autumn of 2008 and the difficulties faced by much larger institutions at that time.

11.04 Against this brief background, it is proposed to consider the subject matter of this chapter under the following headings:

(a) the collapse of Northern Rock;
(b) the bespoke legislation—the Banking (Special Provisions) Act 2008—introduced to deal with the nationalization of Northern Rock;
(c) the ensuing difficulties encountered by larger institutions;
(d) the Banking Act 2009;
(e) the terms of the government's asset protection scheme; and
(f) the Bank of England's role as 'lender of last resort'.

Collapse of Northern Rock

11.05 Although, unfortunately, it has transpired that Northern Rock was by no means the only casualty of the United Kingdom's banking crisis, it was certainly the first victim. It therefore seems appropriate to consider that situation as a starting point.[6]

11.06 As is well known, the credit crisis began with worries over problems in the US subprime mortgage market.[7] This in turn constituted a threat to the global financial system, in part because of the vast scale of that market and in part because a significant proportion of the

---

[3] The rather different circumstances surrounding the closure of the Bank of Credit and Commerce International SA are considered in Chapter 14 below, in the context of supervisory responsibility for bank failures.

[4] As will be noted in Chapter 12 below, the European Union had seen the need for legislation in this particular area, but the rules which it promulgated were of relatively limited scope.

[5] The details are discussed at paras 11.09–11.15 below.

[6] For a useful discussion, see Blair, Walker & Purves, paras 14.220–14.240.

[7] The cynical observer may think that the term 'subprime' is both something of a euphemism and a significant understatement.

mortgages were 'repackaged' and sold internationally to participants in the asset-backed securities (ABS) sector. The securitized debt thus created was sold as collateralized debt obligations (CDOs) to financial institutions and their (supposedly) off balance sheet investment vehicles. These superficially attractive assets collapsed in value when the scale of default in the subprime sector became apparent. The resultant losses reported by major financial institutions led to a drying up of credit both in the United Kingdom and in may other countries. Although Northern Rock itself appears to have no material exposure to the US subprime market, the effective closure of the wholesale funding markets was disastrous for Northern Rock, since it relied on those markets to cover approximately 80 per cent of its lending business.

As a result, Northern Rock had to approach the Bank of England for emergency liquidity support.[8] This support was granted on 14 September 2007,[9] but this did not stem the tide of depositors seeking to move their money. As time went on, it became apparent that confidence in Northern Rock had completely evaporated, and that—pending identification of an alternative and longer term solution—the business could only continue under the cover of a guarantee from HM Treasury. This recognition seems to have dawned gradually, because the Treasury began on 17 September 2007 by merely guaranteeing all existing deposits. This was extended to cover returning customers and wholesale deposits on 20 September and new deposits were given the benefit of the guarantee on 9 October 2007.[10]   **11.07**

The Treasury had hoped to find a private sector solution to the Northern Rock situation, but it was unable to structure a transaction with interested parties which could include a sufficient return to the government, bearing in mind the levels of risk borne by the taxpayer through direct funding and guarantees.[11] It was accordingly felt to be necessary to take Northern Rock into public ownership. This was achieved via emergency legislation, to which it is now necessary to turn.   **11.08**

Banking (Special Provisions) Act 2008

The Scheme of the Legislation

It is only necessary to comment briefly on this legislation because it has been superseded by the longer term measures described below.[12]   **11.09**

The Banking (Special Provisions) Act 2008 received Royal Assent on 21 February of that year. On its face, it allows the Treasury to bring any UK deposit-taker into public   **11.10**

---

[8] On this support, provided in the Bank's role of lender of the last resort, see paras 11.85–11.93 below.

[9] See the News Release, 'Liquidity Support Facility for Northern Rock' issued on 14 September 2007 by HM Treasury, the Bank of England and the FSA.

[10] For the details of the guarantee, see HM Treasury Press Releases on Northern Rock dated 20 September, 9 October and 18 December 2007. These developments are also described in the Court of Appeal judgment in *SRM Global Master Fund LP v The Commissioners of Her Majesty's Treasury* [2009] EWHC 227 (Admin) discussed in paras 11.16–11.19 below.

[11] See the HM Treasury Statement on Northern Rock, 17 February 2008.

[12] The 2008 Act was in any event to expire on 21 February 2009, the anniversary of its original enactment: see s 2(8) of that Act.

ownership if it appears desirable to do so in order to maintain the stability of the UK financial system and/or to protect the public interest where the Treasury has provided financial assistance to a deposit-taker for the purpose of preserving the stability of that system.[13]

11.11 The 2008 Act allowed the Treasury to make an order which transfers securities in the UK deposit-taker to the Bank of England, a nominee of the Treasury, or certain other persons.[14] An order under this provision was made by the Treasury vesting the Northern Rock shares in the Treasury Solicitor, and dealing with de-listing and other ancillary matters.[15] The Act also allowed, in addition and by way of alternative, for the transfer of the property, rights and liabilities of (rather than the shares in) an authorized UK deposit-taker.[16] A 'dual' approach was adopted in the case of Bradford & Bingley plc, where the shares in the company were transferred to the Treasury[17] but much of the retail banking business and certain other liabilities were transferred to Abbey National plc.[18]

11.12 It may be noted that the transfer of shares achieved by means of this legislation was effected '… free from all trusts, liabilities and encumbrances …', with the result that the security rights of any chargee of the relevant securities were also extinguished.[19] This provision was plainly necessary to ensure that the nationalization was fully effective.

11.13 The Treasury was also required to make an order setting out a scheme for the determination of compensation payable to shareholders whose securities had been mandatorily transferred under the Act.[20] Controversially, however, the 2008 Act required the assessment of compensation to be made on the basis that all financial assistance given by the Treasury and the Bank of England[21] had been permanently withdrawn, and that no further assistance would be provided.[22] This situation was compounded by the terms of the compensation

---

[13] Banking (Special Provisions) Act 2008, s 2. On its face, the Act could apply to any UK deposit-taker but, at the time, the Treasury made it clear that the Act was directed only to Northern Rock: see Treasury Statement of 17 February 2008. The provisions of the Act were, however, subsequently used for another rescue operation in relation to Bradford & Bingley plc: see para 11.11 below. They were also used to make orders transferring the retail deposit business of Kaupthing Singer & Friedlander to ING (see Kaupthing Singer & Friedlander Transfer of Certain Rights and Liabilities Order 2008 (SI 2008/2674)) and of the retail deposit business of Heritable Bank, likewise to ING (see The Transfer of Rights and Liabilities to ING Order 2008 (SI 2008/2666)). It should be noted that Kaupthing Singer & Friedlander (KSF) and Heritable Bank were respectively subsidiaries of Kaupthing Bank and Landsbanki Islands hf, Icelandic banks which became insolvent in October 2008. KSF and Heritable were, however, both UK-passported subsidiaries which fell within the UK regulatory framework, and could accordingly be dealt with on the same statutory basis as Northern Rock and Bradford & Bingley. However, Landsbanki itself had a branch in London but operated as a EEA authorized institution. This gave rise to a rather different set of problems, and these are discussed at para 12.11 below.

[14] See s 3, read together with Sch 1, of the 2008 Act.

[15] See the Northern Rock plc Transfer Order 2008 (SI 2008/432).

[16] See ss 6 and 8 of the 2008 Act.

[17] See art 3 of the Bradford & Bingley plc Transfer of Security and Property etc Order 2008 (SI 2008/2456).

[18] See art 16, read together with Sch 2, of the Order mentioned in the previous footnote.

[19] See, for example, art 2 of the Northern Rock plc Transfer Order 2008 (SI 2008/432).

[20] See s 5 of the 2008 Act.

[21] The guarantees and other support given by the Treasury and the Bank of England in respect of Northern Rock have already been recorded: see para 11.07 above.

[22] See s 5(4) of the 2008 Act.

scheme itself, which provided that the valuation also had to be prepared on the bases that Northern Rock (i) was unable to continue as a going concern and (ii) had gone into administration.[23] These provisions would, of course, only serve to depress the ultimate valuation. Whilst some shareholders had asserted that a proper valuation would result in a payment of some £4.00 per share, it appeared likely that any ultimate award was likely to be zero or at best negligible.[24]

It may be noted in passing that, at various points of the process to rescue Northern Rock, **11.14** it was necessary to determine whether the support provided by the Treasury constituted a 'State Aid' prohibited by Article 87 of the EC Treaty.[25] Important though this subject is, these matters do not raise issues of a purely banking character and, accordingly, a detailed discussion is beyond the scope of the present work.

The most recent development in relation to Northern Rock has been the restructuring of **11.15** its business into two entities, so that its back mortgage book is managed separately from its other business. The new arrangements took effect from 1 January 2010.[26]

Challenges to the Legislation

It may be noted that the statutory rules for the nationalization of Northern Rock and the **11.16** calculation of compensation have been the subject of a challenge by shareholders in *SRM Global Master Fund LP v Her Majesty's Treasury*.[27] The challenge rested on the argument that the compensation principles contravene the right to property enshrined in Article 1 of the First Protocol to the European Convention on Human Rights. That provision states that:

> Every natural or legal person is entitled to the peaceful enjoyment of his possessions. No person shall be deprived of his possessions except in the public interest and subject to the conditions provided for by law and the general principles of international law. The preceding provisions shall not, however, in any way impair the right of a State to enforce such laws as it deems necessary to control the use of property in accordance with the general interest or to secure the payment of taxes or other contributions, or penalties.

The effect of this article is that the action taken by the government in nationalizing **11.17** Northern Rock must be proportionate to the objective and, although not explicitly stated,

---

[23] See art 6 of the Northern Rock Compensation Scheme Order 2008 (SI 2008/718). The powers of the appointed valuer were extended in certain respects by the Northern Rock plc Compensation Scheme (Amendment) Order 2009 (SI 2009/791).

[24] At the time of writing, the valuer has expressed a 'provisional view' to the effect that no compensation will be payable.

[25] Subject to numerous exceptions and various approval processes, Art 87 provides that '… any aid granted by a Member State or through State resources in any form whatsoever which distorts or threatens to distort competition by favouring certain undertakings or the production of certain goods …' is to be regarded as incompatible with the single market.

[26] See the Northern Rock plc Transfer Order 2009 (SI 2009/3226). Since Northern Rock was originally taken into public ownership under the Banking (Special Provisions) Act 2008, the new Order was made under that Act, even though it has otherwise been superseded by the Banking Act 2009 (see paras 11.24–11.79 below).

[27] [2009] EWCA Civ 788 (CA), affirming [2009] EWHC 227 (Admin).

nationalization implies an obligation to pay compensation at a level and in a manner which provides a fair balance between the public and private interests at stake.[28]

11.18 The shareholder claimants did not dispute that the nationalization of Northern Rock was '… in the public interest' for the purposes of the property provision of the Convention, nor did they dispute that the nationalization had occurred '… subject to the conditions provided for by law …', bearing in mind the enabling provisions of the 2008 Act and the instruments made under it. They merely asserted that the requirement to disregard the availability of Treasury and Bank of England support, effectively meant that Northern Rock's assets had to be valued on a 'fire sale' basis. Yet, as the Court of Appeal noted,[29] Northern Rock had no legitimate expectation that official support would be provided or extended. Under these circumstances, the compensation formula could not be characterized as lacking any reasonable basis for the purposes of the protection of property provision.[30]

11.19 From the point of view of the government and the taxpayer (if not from the perspective of Northern Rock shareholders) this is plainly an appropriate outcome. As will be discussed later, the 'lender of last resort' facilities[31] provided by the Bank of England are designed to support the stability of the financial system *as a whole*. They are not intended for the benefit of individual institutions or shareholders. It would therefore be unreasonable for shareholders to receive compensation based on the assumption that official support would be available. Such support had originally been provided because the Northern Rock situation presented threats of a systemic nature and because it had no other sources of funding, bearing in mind its heavy reliance on wholesale markets which had effectively closed down. But there was no binding obligation on the Bank of England to continue providing such support.

Other Financial Crisis Events

11.20 As is well known, the events of autumn 2008 were not confined to the relatively smaller institutions to which reference has already been made.

11.21 In particular, the Royal Bank of Scotland had to arrange a £15 billion capital raising underwritten by HM Treasury, plus a further Treasury subscription for £5 billion preference shares in order to reinforce the Bank's Tier One capital base.[32] Likewise, the HBOS Group was the subject of an agreed acquisition by Lloyd's TSB Bank.

---

[28] See, for example, *James v United Kingdom* (1986) EHHR 123. The requirement of compensation for the expropriation of assets is one of the 'general principles of international law' for the purposes of this provision. For a discussion of the whole subject, see Lester & Pannick, *Human Rights Law and Practice*, paras 4.19.1–4.19.29.

[29] See para 67 of the judgment.

[30] At the time of writing, it is understood that the shareholders intend to pursue the matter to the European Court of Human Rights.

[31] For discussion of the lender of last resort function, see paras 11.85–11.94 below.

[32] The details are set out in the company's announcement 'Royal Bank of Scotland Group plc—Capital Raising' (13 October 2008).

All of these arrangements relied essentially on existing company law structures, rather than **11.22** new legislation of specific relevance to the banking industry. But the Treasury invested some £20 billion in the Royal Bank of Scotland and £17 billion in Lloyds Banking Group as part of a bank recapitalization plan announced by the government in October 2008. The scheme was designed to provide short term liquidity, to strengthen capital ratios and to ensure that institutions could continue lending to the wider economy. The price of government investment included support for homeowners in difficulty with their mortgages and restrictions on remuneration and dividend policies.[33]

The government also established the Asset Protection Agency as an Executive Agency of **11.23** HM Treasury. As matters turned out, the Royal Bank of Scotland was the only participant of this scheme, which effectively provided for a further capital investment by the Treasury and a Treasury guarantee (or insurance policy) in relation to an agreed pool of distressed assets.[34]

Banking Act 2009

Introduction

At the time of writing, the various measures taken during the course of 2008–2009 seem **11.24** to have enjoyed a reasonable degree of success in stabilizing the financial markets, even if new lending activities remain depressed, with the inevitable consequences for the wider economy. But the very fact that the government took steps to 'stand behind' the financial system has itself restored a measure of confidence. But however that may be, one of the problems which became apparent as a result of the crisis was the absence of a tailored legal framework to deal specifically with the problems of a troubled bank.[35] After all, banks play a special role in holding the nation's savings and making their regular payments. A breakdown in the system therefore has major consequences and a legal framework is required which allows rapid action to be taken.[36]

---

[33] See, for example, HM Treasury Notice, 'Treasury Statement on Financial Support to the Banking Industry' (13 October 2008).

[34] For the details, see HM Treasury, 'Royal Bank of Scotland: Details of Asset Protection Scheme and Launch of the Asset Protection Agency' (December 2009). Other governments also had to institute plans with the same objective, if not the same design. Most notably, the US Government provided its Troubled Asset Relief Programme (TARP) under the terms of its Emergency Economic Stabilisation Act 2008. The Act allows the US Treasury to purchase and insure up to US$700 billion of troubled assets, including residential or commercial mortgages or instruments related to them (eg collateralized debt obligations). An institution which takes advantage of TARP must also issue equity warrants or other securities to the Treasury entitling it to profit from any later upturn in the stock value of the institution concerned.

[35] It should however, be noted that the origins of the work on this Act date back to 2007, before the financial crisis took hold.

[36] This situation may be contrasted with the United States, where specialized regimes have been in place for a number of years: see, for example the Federal Deposit Insurance Corporation Act (insolvent banks), the Securities Investment Protection Act (broker-dealers) and the Commodities Exchange Act (for commodities brokers).

11.25 This took the form of the Banking Act 2009, which in many respects expands on the structure of the 2008 Act, discussed above. It may be that the very existence of a robust regime to deal with failing banks will of itself help to buttress confidence in the UK's financial markets.[37]

Scope and Content of the Act

11.26 The Banking Act 2009 is arranged as follows:

(a) Part I of the Act deals with the new 'stabilization options'. It occupies the first 89 sections of the Act and deals with the different routes available in this area. The stabilization options, together with the bank insolvency and bank administration procedures referred to below, are collectively referred to as the 'special resolution regime';[38]

(b) Part II of the Act creates a 'bank insolvency procedure', under the terms of which an insolvent bank is ultimately wound up;

(c) Part III creates a 'bank administration procedure' to be used where part of the business of the bank is to be sold to a commercial purchaser or transferred to a 'bridge bank';

(d) Part IV of the Act deals with a number of changes to the Financial Services Compensation Scheme for the purposes of the 2009 Act;

(e) Part V makes various provisions about interbank payment systems and their oversight by the Bank of England;

(f) Part VI contains various provisions about the private issue of banknotes by authorized issuing institutions; and

(g) Part VII deals with various miscellaneous items, including the payment of any expenditure incurred by the Treasury under the Act, and insolvency regulations for investment banks.

11.27 The 2009 Act applies to banks holding deposit-taking permissions from the FSA and accordingly does not extend to EEA authorized or to other foreign institutions.[39]

11.28 The ensuing discussion describes selected aspects of the new Act and the secondary legislation made pursuant to it. It is also necessary to consider the impact of some of the new rules for creditors and counterparties who may be dealing with UK banks and may thus be subject to the terms of the 2009 Act in the event of the insolvency of the UK party. At the outset, however, it is necessary to review a few overriding considerations of a general nature.

General Considerations

11.29 As noted above, the special resolution regime is in effect a 'menu' of options for dealing with a bank in difficulty.

---

[37] At least, this was the expectation of the government; see HM Treasury Press Release, 'New Banking Act comes into effect' (23 February 2009).

[38] See s 1(2) of the 2009 Act.

[39] On this point, see s 2 of the 2009 Act.

This type of situation has to be dealt with jointly by the Tripartite Authorities (ie the **11.30** Treasury, the Bank of England, and the FSA). In deciding whether and if so, how, to exercise their powers under the special resolution regime, those authorities are required to take account of certain 'special resolution objectives' set out in the 2009 Act[40] which are stated to include the following:

(a) Objective 1 is to enhance and protect the stability of the UK's financial system;[41]
(b) Objective 2 is to protect and enhance public confidence in the stability of the UK banking system;
(c) Objective 3 is to protect deposits;
(d) Objective 4 is to protect public funds; and
(e) Objective 5 is to avoid interfering with property in contravention of the property rights granted under the Human Rights Act 1988.

The order in which these objectives are listed is stated to be of no significance, and they are **11.31** to be balanced appropriately in individual situations.[42]

The starting point for any of the stability procedures lies with the FSA, in the sense that no **11.32** stability powers can be exercised unless the FSA is satisfied that the institution concerned is failing, or is likely to fail, to meet the threshold test, and is not likely to remedy that situation through its own efforts.[43] There are also specific conditions for particular options, but these will be considered below where appropriate. In addition, sections 5 and 6 of the 2009 Act required the Treasury, following consultation with other bodies, to publish a Code of Practice on the use of the special resolution regimes, including guidance on the how the objectives were to be understood and achieved, and how choices between different regimes would be made. This was published by the Treasury at the time when the 2009 Act came into force.[44]

The Code of Practice amplifies the five objectives referred to above. For example, the Code **11.33** states that:

(a) The reference in objective 1 to the stability of the UK financial system is a wide-ranging expression which includes the stable functioning of payment and settlement systems and other institutions and systems supplying financial services and markets.[45] In deciding whether or not to use the special resolution regime, the Tripartite Authorities must have regard to the wider systemic risk posed by the actual or potential failure of a particular institution.[46]
(b) The reference in objective 2 to public confidence in the stability of the banking system is of particular importance because banks do not hold sufficient liquid assets to meet

---

[40] See s 4(2) and 4(4) of the 2009 Act.
[41] This includes, in particular, a reference to the continuity of the banking services: see s 4(9) of the 2009 Act.
[42] See s 4(10) of the 2009 Act.
[43] See s 7 of the 2009 Act. On the threshold conditions and, in particular the requirement for the adequacy of financial resources, see para 1.23 above.
[44] See HM Treasury, 'Banking Act 2009 Special Resolution Regime: Code of Practice' (February 2009).
[45] See para 3.4. of the Code of Practice.
[46] See para 3.6 of the Code of Practice.

all of their deposit liabilities at any given time. Public confidence thus refers to the expectation that deposits will be paid in accordance with their terms, that normal banking services will continue to be available and that, in the event of a failure, there are systems in place to protect the depositors.[47]

(c) The 'protection of depositors' objective recognizes the need for the protection of depositors in a failed institution.[48]

(d) The 'protection of public funds' objective refers to the obvious fact that taxpayers have an interest in the effective use of public funds.[49]

(e) The 'avoiding interfering with property rights' objective refers to the property rights of the institution itself, its shareholders and creditors.[50] Although not explicitly stated in the Code, this implies that a fair compensation scheme should be put in place for shareholders whose assets are expropriated, although it may of course be difficult to establish a fair price in this type of situation.[51]

11.34 After the special resolution regime has been adopted in any particular case, the Tripartite Authorities will publish a statement as to the manner in which they have used those powers and the manner in which the various objectives have been balanced against each other.[52]

11.35 The Code of Practice also explains the respective roles of the Tripartite Authorities in relation to the special resolution regime. Although the resolution of the failed bank will obviously involve close collaboration, each of the Tripartite Authorities will have lead responsibility in relation to particular aspects. For example, the FSA will determine whether the institution is failing to meet its threshold conditions, and that it is not likely that the institution will be able itself to remedy the position.[53] The FSA would also be responsible for the deposit-taking permission of any 'bridge bank'[54] and the supervision of an institution undergoing a special resolution process. On the other hand, the selection of the process to be used and its implementation will generally rest with the Bank of England, as will responsibility for emergency liquidity support.[55] The Treasury will be responsible for issues relating to public funds and the wider public interest.[56]

11.36 Beyond these general points, the Code deals with various matters applicable to particular types of procedure or other specific aspects. These points will be considered below in their appropriate contexts.

---

[47] See paras 3.8–3.10 of the Code.

[48] eg through the arrangements administered by the Financial Services Compensation Scheme. On this scheme, see Chapter 13 below. On the points made in the text, see paras 3.11–3.13 of the Code.

[49] See para 3.14 of the Code.

[50] See para 3.15 of the Code.

[51] See the discussion of the *SRM Global Master Fund* case, at para 11.16 above.

[52] See paras 3.17–3.22 of the Code.

[53] See s 7 of the 2009 Act. This is in line with the existing obligations of the FSA. On the threshold conditions (including the obligation to maintain adequate financial resources), see para 1.23 above.

[54] On 'bridge banks' see para 11.40 below.

[55] On emergency liquidity support or the Bank of England's role as lender of the last resort, see paras 11.85–11.94 below.

[56] On these points, see paras 4.1–4.7 of the Code of Practice.

The Stabilization Options

The three 'stabilization options' which form the first 'limb' of the special resolution regime **11.37** include the following:

(a) transfer of the failing bank to a private sector purchaser;
(b) transfer of the bank to a 'bridge bank' and
(c) transfer of the bank to temporary public ownership.

Transfer to a Private Sector Purchaser

The first stabilization option involves the sale of all or part of the bank's business to a **11.38** commercial purchaser, and the Bank of England may make share or property transfer instruments in order to give effect to that sale.[57]

Before the Bank of England can exercise the power to transfer shares or property in this way, **11.39** (i) the FSA must have determined that the general condition stated in section 7 of the 2009 Act (ie inability to meet the threshold conditions) has been met,[58] (ii) the Bank, after consulting the FSA and the Treasury, must be satisfied that the exercise of the power is necessary,[59] having regard to the stability of the UK financial system, the need to maintain public confidence in the banking system, or the protection of depositors, and (iii) if the Treasury has previously provided financial assistance[60] to the bank concerned, the Treasury must also have recommended the transfer to a commercial purchaser on the basis that it is necessary to protect the public interest and the Bank must believe that a commercial sale is the best means of providing that protection.[61]

Transfer to a Bridge Bank

The second stabilization option involves the transfer of all or part of the business of the **11.40** failing bank to a company which is wholly owned by the Bank of England (defined as a 'bridge bank'). This may involve a property transfer order, since the Bank would not be acquiring the shares of the failing institution.[62]

Once again, the Bank of England may only exercise these powers if the conditions noted in **11.41** sections 7 and 8 of the 2009 Act have been met.[63]

---

[57] See s 11 of the Act. On share transfer instruments and property transfer instruments, see paras 11.45–11.50 below.

[58] On s 7 of the 2009 Act, see para 11.32 above.

[59] It should be noted that the word 'necessary' alone is used. There is no alternative formulation such as 'expedient' or 'desirable'. The test is, therefore, a relatively stringent one: see para 5.14 of the Code of Practice.

[60] Apart from direct funding, financial assistance would also include guarantees given to depositors (eg as in the case of Northern Rock) indemnities or similar arrangements: see the definition of 'financial assistance' in s 257 of the Act.

[61] On these conditions, see s 8 of the 2009 Act.

[62] On these points, see s 12(1) and (2) of the 2009 Act.

[63] See para 11.32 above, substituting a reference to the bridge bank for the commercial purchaser.

11.42   The Code of Practice includes various statements about the management and control of a bridge bank.[64] As its name implies a bridge bank is intended to offer a short term solution, until a market sale can be completed. The primary objective of a bridge bank is accordingly to achieve such a sale.[65] It is recorded that the bridge bank will require the requisite deposit-taking and other authorities under the terms of the FSMA and that the bridge bank will be subject to FSA supervision throughout.[66] Where a market solution is unlikely to be found immediately and the bridge bank is therefore likely to remain in existence for a period of time, the Bank of England is required to put in place governance structures designed to ensure that the shareholder relationship operates at arms length and the Bank of England is concerned only with strategic matters.[67]

Temporary Public Ownership

11.43   The third stabilization option is to take the failing institution into temporary public ownership.[68] This power may only be exercised if the Treasury after consulting the FSA and the Bank of England, is satisfied that this step is necessary to resolve or reduce a serious threat to the stability of the UK financial system *or* the exercise of the power is necessary to protect the public interest, where the Treasury has previously provided financial assistance in relation to that bank for the purpose of reducing or resolving such a serious threat.[69]

11.44   Where an institution is taken into public ownership, it will be the intention to return the business to the private sector in a manner which maintains financial stability, protects depositors, and promotes competition.[70] If the institution is likely to remain in public ownership for an extended period, then the Treasury will set out the objectives as to how the bank should be operated, and the board must produce a business plan setting out commercial funding, risk management, and competitive strategies.[71]

Share Transfer Orders

11.45   Where one of the stabilization options is to be achieved by a transfer of shares in the institution (as opposed to a transfer of its property, assets, and liabilities), then the Act contains detailed provisions as to the transfer arrangements. Where the transfer is to be effected by the Bank of England under the 'commercial purchaser' or 'bridge bank' option, then the Bank may make a 'share transfer instrument'.[72] Where the institution is to be taken into temporary public ownership then the Treasury may make a 'share transfer order' in favour of a nominee of the Treasury or a company wholly owned by it.[73] The only material distinction between the two types of legal act appears to be the identity of the party by whom

---

[64]   Such statements were required pursuant to s 11(3) of the 2009 Act.
[65]   For further details, see paras 8.1–8.6 of the Code of Practice.
[66]   See para 8.10 of the Code.
[67]   See paras 8.11–8.21 of the Code.
[68]   Section 13 of the 2009 Act.
[69]   On these specific conditions, see s 9 of the 2009 Act.
[70]   Paragraph 9 of the Code.
[71]   Paragraphs 9.7 and 9.8 of the Code.
[72]   Section 11(2)(a) of the 2009 Act.
[73]   Section 13(2) of the 2009 Act.

it is made. The detailed provisions are set out in sections 14–32 of the 2009 Act and include the following:

(a) A share transfer order or instrument may relate to any or all securities issued by an institution including shares, debentures, subscription warrant, and other securities and may make other associated provisions in connection with the transfer.[74]

(b) A transfer of shares in a failing institution takes effect by virtue of that document (ie there is no requirement for a consensual stock transfer document in common form).[75] The transfer takes effect regardless of the provisions of any law or other restriction, or any requirement for a third party consent, and the order or instrument may provide for the transfer to extinguish any trust security subscription or other rights associated with the transferred security and may also provide for their de-listing.[76]

(c) A share transfer instrument or order may enable the Bank of England or the Treasury (as the case may be) to appoint or remove directors and vary or terminate director's service contracts.[77]

(d) The share transfer order or instrument may also negative the consequences of termination rights to which creditors of the institution may otherwise be entitled. Typically, for example, lenders in the instrument may have a contractual right to terminate their facilities and to demand repayment in the event of a change in control,[78] and the mandatory transfer of shares to the Treasury or the Bank of England would plainly trigger this type of clause.[79] The difficulty with this type of statutory provision is that it can only vary the application of contracts which are governed by the law of some part of the United Kingdom.[80] There may therefore be some difficulty if, for example, the failing institution has entered into a credit agreement governed (say) by New York law, since such a provision would in principle remain effective notwithstanding the terms of the 2009 Act. It is true that an English court may well give effect to the statutory provisions *regardless* of the governing law, on the basis that they are intended to constitute overriding mandatory provisions of the laws of the United Kingdom.[81] Nevertheless, a New York court would almost certainly give judgment and allow enforcement of the resultant payment obligations against any US dollar accounts which the institution holds with a New York bank. There seems to be no way to forestall such action, which is an inevitable consequence of the territorial nature of the UK legislation.

---

[74] See ss 14–16 of the 2009 Act. Although referred to as a 'share transfer' instrument or order it should be noted that these arrangements can also be applied to debt securities. The point may be important because a claim for the face value of the debt instrument would be replaced by a claim for compensation in accordance with the rules discussed at paras 11.64–11.66 below.

[75] However, a share transfer instrument or order may provide for the execution of associated documents and require the registration of the transfers: s 21 of the 2009 Act.

[76] On these points, see ss 18 and 19 of the 2009 Act.

[77] Section 20 of the 2009 Act.

[78] For a discussion of this type of provision, see para 20.23 below.

[79] The statutory provision is rather more detailed than just described: see s 22 of the 2009 Act.

[80] This follows from Art 12 of Rome I, which is considered more generally in Chapter 40 below.

[81] Such laws may be applied by an English court regardless of the governing law. An 'overriding mandatory provision' is a legal provision which is regarded by a country as '… crucial … for safeguarding its political, social or economic organisation …': see Art 9 of Rome I. The background to the 2009 Act suggests that it contains provisions of social and economic importance which would fall within this definition.

(e) Where the Bank of England makes a share transfer instrument (ie in favour of a commercial purchaser), it must advise the institution concerned and the other Tripartite Authorities, and must advertise the instrument on its website and in the press.[82]

(f) Where the Treasury makes a share transfer order (ie under the 'temporary public ownership' route) it must likewise notify the other Tripartite Authorities and publicise the order.[83]

(g) Where a bank has been taken into temporary public ownership the Treasury may later execute an 'onward transfer' presumably in favour of a commercial purchaser when the bank's difficulties have been resolved.[84]

(h) The Treasury may also restore the shares in the bank to the original owners by means of a 'reverse share transfer'. Again, this would presumably only occur when the bank's difficulties have been resolved and the Treasury has recouped its costs plus a return.[85]

(i) Where the shares in an institution have been transferred to a bridge bank by means of a share transfer instrument made by the Bank of England, the Bank has 'mirror image' powers to make an order transferring those shares to a commercial purchaser or back to the original owners.[86]

11.46 Subject to the comments made above, these statutory powers appear to be relatively straightforward and to draw on the experience gained from the Banking (Special Provisions) Act 2008.[87] The powers are drawn widely to maximize both the authorities' freedom of action in a crisis situation and the prospects of a private sector solution.

11.47 However, if an immediate private sector purchaser is found, the transaction may *optionally* be effected by a transfer of all or part of the assets and liabilities of the bank[88] and, if the 'bridge bank' route is to be used, then the transfer *must* be achieved by means of a business (rather than a share) transfer.[89]

11.48 It is thus now necessary to turn to the arrangements for the transfer of all or part of a bank's property, assets and liabilities which, as will be seen, do give rise to various issues of a more complex nature.

---

[82] Section 24 of the 2009 Act.

[83] Section 25 of the 2009 Act.

[84] This process is available because the use of a statutory procedure (rather than an ordinary form of share transfer) will give greater legal certainty to the prospective buyer.

[85] On the 'reverse share transfer' procedure and associated consultation requirements, see s 29 of the 2009 Act. The range of powers provided by ss 28 and 29 of the 2009 Act is intended to maximize the prospects of an onward sale and a market-based solution to the institution's problems: see generally the points made in Part 6 of the Code of Practice.

[86] See ss 30 and 31 of the 2009 Act. Again, consultation procedures apply before such an instrument can be made.

[87] See the discussion of this Act at paras 11.09–11.15 above.

[88] See s 11(2)(b) of the 2009 Act.

[89] See ss 12(1) and 12(2) of the 2009 Act. Note that the 'temporary public ownership' option can only be achieved by means of a share transfer order: see s 12(2) of the Act, noted at para 11.40 above.

Property Transfer Instruments

A 'property transfer instrument' is, unsurprisingly, an instrument by which all or part of the   **11.49**
property, rights, and liabilities of an institution are transferred to another person.[90]

The following points may be noted in relation to property transfer instruments: **11.50**

(a) A transfer of property, assets, and liabilities takes effect by virtue of the instrument
itself.[91] Thus, for example, loan agreements signed by the affected institution may
include a restriction on assignment or transfer by the borrower[92] but will take effect
notwithstanding such restrictions.

(b) Once again, the broadest possible powers are given and a property transfer instrument
may transfer all or any specified property, rights, and liabilities of the institution,
including (i) contractual and statutory rights and liabilities, (ii) property outside the
United Kingdom, and (iii) rights and liabilities arising under or governed by a foreign
system of law.[93] The 2009 Act recognizes that items (ii) and (iii) may be problematical
given that—as already noted above—a foreign system of law will not generally recognize the effect of UK legislation which purports to transfer property within that foreign
jurisdiction. Accordingly, the Act provides that the transferor and the transferee must
take any steps necessary to effect the transfer under the relevant foreign law and, pending such completion, the transferor (i) must hold the relevant property or right for the
benefit of the transferee and (ii) must discharge any relevant liabilities on behalf of, and
at the expense of the transferee.[94] However, the prospects for automatic recognition of
a property transfer instrument may not be quite so dim as at first appears. Under the
heading 'Continuity', section 36 allows that a property transfer order (i) may be treated
as a 'succession' and (ii) for the transferee to be treated as the same person as the transferor.[95] These provisions imply that—although a transfer of all or even only some of
the assets, rights, and liabilities is involved—the transfer is a matter affecting the *corporate status* (rather than merely the assets and liabilities) of the transferor and the transferee. In view of this, there must be a realistic prospect of a foreign court recognizing
the effect of a property transfer instrument on the local property within its jurisdiction,

---

[90] See s 33 of the 2009 Act. Since, as noted above, the 'private purchaser' and the 'bridge bank' options
are the only options for which the business (or property) can be used and both of these processes are initiated
by the Bank of England, there is no general requirement for a corresponding 'order' procedure to be used
by the Treasury—contrast the position with share transfer orders/instruments discussed above. Instead, the
provision for the Treasury to make 'property transfer orders' are limited to cases in which the Treasury has
previously made a share transfer order to take a bank into temporary public ownership: see the discussion of
s 45 of the 2009 Act, below.
[91] ie no further documentation is required to record or complete the transfer, or to make it effective, and
the transfer takes effect notwithstanding any legal or contractual provision to the contrary: see s 34(2) and
(3) of the 2009 Act.
[92] On restrictions of this kind, see paras 22.05–22.16 below. There may be difficulties with the application
of this provision if any relevant agreements are governed by a system of law outside the United Kingdom:
compare the discussion at paras 10.24–10.26 above.
[93] See s 35 of the 2009 Act.
[94] See s 39 of the 2009 Act.
[95] See in particular s 36(1), (2) and (3) of the 2009 Act.

and without any local law formality being completed.[96] Indeed, recognition may be mandatory before the courts of other EEA States because the partial property transfer order is likely to constitute a 'reorganization measure' for the purposes of the EU Directive on reorganization and winding up of credit institutions.[97]

(c) Once again, a transfer or expropriation of all or part of the property and assets of the failing bank may give rise to an event of default under loan agreements or similar documents executed by the bank.[98] It is therefore provided that events of this nature will not give rise to a right to terminate the relevant agreement or demand immediate repayment.[99]

(d) The Bank of England is required to notify the FSA and the Treasury of any property transfer instrument and to ensure appropriate publicity.[100]

(e) As in the case of share transfers, provision is made for an 'onward property transfer' to vest the relevant assets and liabilities into a third party purchaser, or to restore them back to the institution concerned.[101] As noted above,[102] the power of the Treasury to make a property transfer order is limited to those cases in which a bank has already been taken into temporary public ownership by means of a share transfer order. This power[103] will generally be used where a complete or partial solution to the problems has been achieved by means of the identification of a commercial purchaser.[104]

Partial Property Transfers

11.51   It is perhaps fair to say that the commercial effects of property transfer instruments/orders will be essentially similar to share transfer instruments/orders, where the property transfer orders relate to the entirety of the relevant bank's assets and undertaking. However, as the Code of Practice acknowledges,[105] it is most likely that the power to make partial property transfers will be used to separate 'good' assets from 'bad' (or 'toxic') assets. This may happen in a variety of ways. For example, the 'good' assets—consisting of the profitable divisions of the business—may be transferred to a commercial purchaser or a bridge bank, leaving behind a 'residual bank' with the 'bad' assets.[106] Alternatively, the 'bad' assets may be

---

[96] On the recognition of corporate successions in this way, see the discussions at para 9.24 above (in relation to transfers under Part VII of the FSMA) and at paras 10.05–10.16 above (in relation to the recognition of foreign bank mergers).

[97] On this Directive and on the mutual recognition of reorganization measures, see Chapter 12 below.

[98] On non-disposal provisions, see para 20.37(c) below and, on expropriation defaults, see para 20.38(h) below. Given that the transfer will be effected pursuant to a statutory order made by the Bank of England (as opposed to a voluntary transfer) it is perhaps the expropriation clause which would be more appropriate to cover this type of situation.

[99] See s 38 of the 2009 Act. Again, the relevant provisions are rather more complex than the summary in the text.

[100] See s 41 of the 2009 Act.

[101] See ss 43 and 44 of the 2009 Act.

[102] See n 90 above.

[103] For the details, see s 45 of the 2009 Act.

[104] Once again, there is provision for 'reverse property transfer orders' to restore the assets to the original institution: see s 46 of the 2009 Act.

[105] See in particular paras 7.2 and 7.3 of the Code and part 7 of the Code more generally.

[106] Although the Code does not explicitly so state, the 'bad' bank would then separately have to be subjected to one of the stabilization options or put into the bank administration/insolvency procedures.

transferred to a bridge bank, leaving the troubled institution solvent and able to continue its remaining business in the usual way.

The Code recognizes that partial property transfers may prejudice market participants— **11.52** for example, by separating out of a bank the assets on which a counterparty has relied, while leaving the associated liabilities with the bank itself.[107] This possibility could have had serious market repercussions, in that foreign institutions would become reluctant to deal with UK banks in the light of this possibility. The 2009 Act and secondary legislation made under it, accordingly seeks to provide safeguards designed to avoid this unhappy eventuality.

To take a simple and perhaps exaggerated example of the difficulties, a counterparty may **11.53** have entered into arrangements with a failing bank under which the bank may incur liabilities against a cash deposit with the counterparty. This may amount to effective funded credit risk mitigation so that no capital has to be ascribed to the counterparty's exposure to the bank.[108] If a partial property order had the effect of 'splitting' this transaction such that the liabilities remained owing to the 'bad bank' but the deposit with the counterparty became owing instead to the 'good bank', then the effect of the credit protection is entirely lost. This would create legal uncertainty and be unfair to the counterparty, since it will originally have entered into the transaction in reliance on the effective security afforded to it by the set-off arrangements. It thus appeared likely that foreign institutions would be deterred from entering into transactions with UK banks (or, at least, would review the pricing at which they were prepared to do so) because of the risks and uncertainty created by the new special resolution regime. This would have rendered UK banks less competitive by increasing their costs. This seems to have been no mere theoretical concern. For example, the British Bankers Association was moved to comment that:[109]

> We are aware of a number of large international banks that have raised with the Tripartite Authorities their belief that, unless concerns expressed by the banking industry and the legal profession are taken on board, then they would need to unwind current positions with UK banks to the tune of hundreds of billions of pounds, which would have an immediate disruptive effect on key UK financial markets.

Whilst it was thus necessary to create a special resolution regime which created maximum **11.54** flexibility for the authorities in a crisis, it was thus equally necessary to ensure that the regime did not prejudice competitiveness of UK banks.

To that end the Treasury is permitted by order to restrict the making of partial property **11.55** transfers, or otherwise to regulate their content and effect.[110] More particularly, the Treasury may make orders restricting the making of partial property transfers where this would affect certain 'protected interests' of creditors or counterparties. 'Protected interests'

---

[107] This problem could, of course, cut both ways. The failing bank itself may have enjoyed the benefit of set-off rights against a particular customer, but these rights would be lost if the liability is left with the failing institution but the correlative asset is transferred to a commercial purchaser or to a bridge bank.
[108] On funded credit risk mitigation for these purposes, see the discussion at paras 6.44–6.46 above.
[109] See British Bankers Association, 'Banking Bill: Lord's Briefing' (12 December 2008).
[110] For the details, see s 47 of the 2009 Act.

includes (i) security interests, (ii) title transfer collateral arrangements,[111] (iii) set-off arrangements, and (iv) netting arrangements.[112]

11.56 In reliance on these powers, the Treasury made the Banking Act 2009 (Restriction of Partial Property Transfers) Order 2009.[113] The Order applies in any situation in which a partial property transfer instrument or order is made by the Bank of England or the Treasury under the powers described earlier.[114] The Order achieves its objectives through the following central provisions:

(a) A partial property transfer order may not provide for the transfer of some, but not all, of protected rights and liabilities[115] under a set-off arrangement, a netting arrangement, or a title transfer financial collateral arrangement.[116]

(b) In a similar vein, Article 5 of the Partial Property Transfers Order provides that a partial property transfer order may not transfer (i) any property or rights against which a liability is secured, unless the correlative liability is also transferred and (ii) any liability, unless the assets which have been charged by way of security are also transferred. In other words, where a party (be it the bank or the counterparty) has given security for a liability, both the liability and the security must be transferred together, or not at all. One of the difficulties flowing from this approach is that a UK company can grant a floating charge over the whole (or substantially the whole) of its assets and undertaking.[117] This could create a serious obstacle to the implementation of a partial property transfer instrument or order since the entirety of the bank's undertaking would have to

---

[111] These are effectively equivalent to security arrangements so far as the creditor is concerned. On these arrangements, see the discussion at paras 35.22–35.31 below.

[112] On netting arrangements and their validity under English law, see the discussion of those arrangements under the Financial Collateral Regulations at para 35.29 below.

[113] SI 2009/322, hereafter the 'Partial Property Transfers Order'. For the consultation process leading up to the Order, see in particular, HM Treasury, 'Special Resolution Regime: safeguards for partial property transfers' (November 2008). For a detailed discussion of the issues raised, see Financial Markets Law Committee, 'Issue 133—Banking Reform, Depositor Protection—the Special Resolution Regime: Safeguards for Partial Property Transfers' (January 2009).

[114] See para 11.49 above. On the point made in the text, see art 2 of the Partial Property Transfers Order.

[115] In essence 'protected rights and liabilities' include the right to set-off, the right to net, and rights under a title transfer collateral arrangement: see art 3(3) of the Partial Property Transfers Order. Note that these rights are principally designed to protect transactions between institutions, and deposits and liabilities relating to retail transactions are specifically excluded.

[116] On title transfer financial collateral arrangements, see paras 35.22–35.31 below, although the expression is also specifically defined in s 48(1)(b) of the 2009 Act. 'Set-off' arrangements are arrangements under which two or more debts, claims or obligations can be set-off against each other. The reference to an 'arrangement' suggests a contractual or consensual right of set-off: see s 48(1)(c) of the 2009 Act. Consequently, *statutory* rights of set-off (eg as arise under r 4.90 of the Insolvency Rules 1986) would not be 'protected rights' for these purposes since they do not arise pursuant to an *arrangement*. Obviously, however, if the right and correlative liability could be 'split' between two entities as a result of a Partial Property Transfer Order, then the intended right of set-off would be lost. 'Netting arrangements' are arrangements under which a number of claims or obligations can be converted into a net claim or obligation: see s 48(1)(d) of the 2009 Act. Thus, for example, where the UK bank has entered into a series of derivatives contracts with a counterparty, there will usually be a single governing agreement under which, following a default by the UK bank, all of the contracts will be valued and a single net sum will be payable by one party. Once again, if the series of contracts could be split between two institutions as a result of a partial property transfer, then the overall netting rights would be distorted.

[117] On security of this type, see paras 28.06–28.13 below.

'follow' the liability secured by such a floating charge. This difficulty was considered, but ultimately not directly addressed, during the consultation process for the Order[118] on the pragmatic basis that banks rarely create floating charges in practice.[119]

(c) Article 6 likewise provides for the integrity of 'capital market arrangements', that is to say, the property, rights, and liabilities of such an arrangement must be kept intact within the same institution. The expression 'capital market arrangements' includes securitization products, covered bonds, and collaterized debt obligations, where a number of inter-related contracts are 'packaged' together to create the ultimate product.[120]

(d) Article 7 of the Partial Property Transfers Order also provides that an order may also not modify or render unenforceable (i) market contracts entered into on a recognized investment exchange or covered by a recognized clearing house or (ii) the rules of such organizations dealing with the default or likely default of a contractual counterparty.

In addition, the Order contains further restrictions on reverse transfer orders[121] and the **11.57** operation of termination rights under contracts.[122] The Order also acknowledges the possibility that a partial property transfer or instrument may later be found to have contravened the terms of the Order, possibly through oversight or because relevant information was not available when the order or instrument was made. The Order provides that any such partial property transfer will be void and includes arrangements to remedy the situation.[123]

The 'No Creditor Worse Off' Order

As has been shown, the Partial Property Transfers Order is designed to protect the expecta- **11.58** tions of creditors who have taken a security or equivalent arrangement from their UK bank counterparty.

But even in the absence of taking security, a creditor elects to deal with a bank on an unse- **11.59** cured (or 'clean') basis because he has an understanding of the bank's asset and business position, and has taken his risk on that basis. Again, his expectations may be defeated by a partial property transfer and the splitting of the assets and liabilities into a 'good' and 'bad' bank. Once again, concerns of this kind might deter foreign institutions from dealing with UK banks, or may affect their pricing process.

---

[118] See paras 3.1–3.10 of the consultation paper referred to in n 44 above.
[119] The difficulty with this approach, of course, is that counterparties could start to press UK banks to provide floating charges because that would offer the counterparty the maximum possible protection against the potential operation of the special resolution regime. If this became problematical, it would be open to the FSA to prohibit the grant of floating charges by banks, and it is specifically provided that security created by a UK bank in breach of the FSA Handbook or otherwise than in accordance with that bank's deposit-taking permission will not qualify for the special creditor protection just described: see art 5(5) of the Order.
[120] For the details of the definition, art 6(5) of the Partial Property Transfers Order refers to the definition in para 1 of Sch 2A to the Insolvency Act 1986 (as inserted by the Enterprise Act 2002). In essence, the arrangements must relate to instruments which are listed, rated or traded.
[121] See art 8 of the Order. On reverse orders of this kind, see para 11.45(h) above.
[122] Article 9 of the Order.
[123] For the details, see arts 10–12 of the Order.

11.60   The Treasury has sought to address this separate but closely related issue by means of the Banking Act 2009 (Third Party Compensation Arrangements for Partial Property Transfers) Regulations 2009.[124]

11.61   Where the Treasury makes an order for the assessment of compensation payable to shareholders in a bank,[125] it must also make a 'third party compensation order' where the arrangements involve a partial property transfer. In essence, a third party compensation order must provide for the appointment of an independent valuer to determine whether any pre-transfer creditors should receive compensation and, if so, how much.[126] The valuer is required to assess:[127]

(a)   the amount which pre-transfer creditors would have received if the bank had gone into an insolvency proceeding;

(b)   the amount which creditors are receiving in consequence of the partial property transfer.

11.62   If the valuer determines that any pre-transfer creditor is less favourably treated as a result of the partial property transfer (ie as compared to the treatment he would have received in ordinary insolvency proceedings), then he must determine the compensation payable by reference to that differential and on the basis of fair and equitable treatment.

11.63   The valuation must be made on the assumption that the bank would otherwise have gone into an insolvency process specified by the Treasury[128] and on the bases that (i) the bank would have entered insolvency proceedings at the time when the partial property transfer order was made, (ii) no other action would have been taken in relation to the bank under the special resolution regime, and (iii) no financial assistance would have been provided to the bank by the Treasury or the Bank of England after the date on which the partial property transfer order or instrument was made.[129] The independent valuer may order interim payments, having regard to the desirable objective of ensuring that creditors receive prompt compensation.[130]

Compensation for Transferors

11.64   The above commentary dealt with the protection of secured creditors and others who have had dealings with a failed bank. But it is also necessary to take account of the interests of the shareholders whose securities have been expropriated, not least because their property rights are guaranteed by the Human Rights Act 1998 and the European Convention on Human Rights.[131]

---

[124]   SI 2009/319. These were often referred to as the 'No Creditor Worse Off' regulations.

[125]   An order of this kind must generally be made where one of the stabilization options is used. For a discussion of the compensation aspects, see para 11.64 below.

[126]   See reg 4 of the Order.

[127]   On the point about to be made, see reg 5 of the Order.

[128]   See reg 6 of the Order.

[129]   On these points, see reg 7 of the Order. The required assumption that the bank would receive no further official financial assistance was one of the points of dispute in relation to Northern Rock: see the discussion of the decision in *SRM Global Master Fund*, at paras 11.16–11.19 above.

[130]   On this point, see reg 8 of the Order.

[131]   See the discussion on this aspect of the decision in the *SRM Global Master Fund* case, at paras 11.16–11.19 above.

11.65 Two types of compensation schemes may be established for the benefit of transferors[132] whose shares are expropriated[133] namely:

(a) a compensation scheme order; or
(b) a resolution fund order.

11.66 Compensation orders were made under the Banking (Special Provisions) Act 2008 in relation to Northern Rock and this order has already been discussed.[134] The general principles thus do not need to be repeated. It should, however, be explained that a 'resolution fund order' is designed to provide the failing bank or its shareholders with a financial interest in the resolution process, for example, by means of a share calculated by reference to the ultimate process of sale of the assets of the institution. Once again, an independent valuer must be appointed and the Treasury may specify the applicable valuation principles.

Continuing Obligations and Other Matters

11.67 It may be noted that the remaining segments of Part I of the 2009 Act include a variety of miscellaneous provisions which may briefly be summarized as follows:

(a) A bank whose assets are transferred under a property transfer order must provide such services and facilities as may be necessary to enable the transferee to operate that business effectively.[135] Especially where the transferee is a bridge bank, it will need to operate from the premises of the failed institution and will need access to its systems and its personnel, who will have knowledge of the history and conduct of the transferred business, and this provision is designed to ensure the necessary level of cooperation.[136]
(b) A share transfer order or instrument or a property transfer instrument may include provisions about the bank's pension scheme, and may modify or apportion rights and liabilities arising under that scheme.[137]
(c) The Treasury may make regulations modifying the tax consequences of the exercise of a stabilization power.[138]
(d) The Treasury enjoys a very broad power to amend the law to enable the stabilization powers to be used effectively, having regard to the special resolution objectives.[139] The Code of Practice emphasizes that this power must be used strictly to further the use of the stabilization options, and cannot be used for wider public policy purposes. It also notes that the exercise of the power will be subject to parliamentary scrutiny.[140]

---

[132] Reference is generally made to shareholders whose securities are acquired but a compensation order may also be made in favour of the failing bank where the property transfer powers are used.
[133] On the points about to be made, see ss 49–62 of the 2009 Act.
[134] See paras 11.16–11.19 above.
[135] Section 63 of the 2009 Act.
[136] Similar provisions apply to other members of the bank's group where the share transfer route has been used: see s 66 of the 2009 Act.
[137] Section 7 of the 2009 Act.
[138] Section 76 of the Act.
[139] See s 75 of the 2009 Act. Subject to the various constraints, such legislation may even be made on a retrospective basis: see s 75(3). The special resolution objectives have already been discussed at para 11.30 above.
[140] See s 75(7) and (8) and see generally paras 6.18–6.23 of the Code of Practice.

(e) The Treasury has power to give notice to the Bank of England in relation to the exercise of the stabilization powers in order to avoid any contravention of any of the UK's international obligations.[141] It is anticipated that this would refer principally to EU rules on State aid.

11.68 Finally, it may be noted that the new regime created by the 2009 Act was in fact first tested in relation to the Dunfermline Building Society, where (i) the retail and wholesale business was transferred to the Nationwide Building Society; (ii) the social housing loan book was transferred to a bridge bank, and (iii) the remaining 'high risk' assets of the society were placed into a building society administration.[142] The entire process was completed in a short time frame and, to that extent, the enabling provisions of the 2009 legislation may be judged a success.

Bank Insolvency

11.69 Part II of the 2009 Act[143] provides for a new procedure known as 'bank insolvency'. In many respects, this process does not differ greatly from an ordinary liquidation process, save that the primary objective of the bank liquidator is to arrange for the bank's eligible depositors to have their accounts transferred to a reliable institution or, failing that to receive their compensation from the Financial Services Compensation Scheme.[144]

11.70 A 'bank insolvency order' is an order appointing an insolvency practitioner as the liquidator of the bank.[145] An application for such an order must be made to the court on notice to the bank, and the application may be made by the Bank of England, the FSA or the Secretary of State.[146] The application may only be made on the basis that (i) the bank is (or is likely to become) unable to pay its debts,[147] (ii) winding up of the bank would be in the public interest, or (iii) the winding up of the bank would be 'fair'.[148] At this point, the division of official responsibilities becomes a little more complex, in that:

(a) the Bank of England may apply for a bank insolvency order only if (i) the Bank is satisfied that the institution has eligible depositors,[149] (ii) the Bank is satisfied that

---

[141] Sections 76 and 77 of the 2009 Act.

[142] See Treasury Press Release, 'Dunfermline Building Society', 30 March 2009.

[143] Sections 90–135 of the 2009 Act.

[144] On this objective, see s 90(2)(c) of the 2009 Act. 'Eligible depositors' means depositors eligible for compensation under the Financial Services Compensation Scheme: see s 93(3) of the 2009 Act and, on the Financial Services Compensation Scheme, see paras 13.09–13.12 below.

[145] See s 94 of the 2009 Act. A bank liquidator is treated as an officer of the court: see s 106 of the 2009 Act.

[146] Section 95 of the 2009 Act.

[147] This expression includes the usual tests of balance sheet insolvency and inability to pay debts as they fall due, as formulated under s 123 of the Insolvency Act 1986. In addition, however, a bank which is in default on an obligation to pay any amount under an agreement which forms a part of its regulated business will also be treated as unable to pay its debts for these purposes: see s 93(4) of the 2009 Act.

[148] Section 96(1) of the 2009 Act. The expression 'fair' is intended to be effectively equivalent to the expression 'just and equitable' as used in the grounds for winding up of a company under s 122(1)(g) of the Insolvency Act 1986: see s 93(8) of the 2009 Act.

[149] Thus a specialized bank which accepted only deposits from large corporate customers could not be the subject of an application for this type of order since its depositors are not 'eligible' for the purposes of the

the winding up of the institution would be fair, or that the institution is, or is likely to become unable, to pay its debts,[150] and (iii) the FSA has notified the Bank of England that the institution is failing, or is likely to fail to satisfy the threshold conditions for its authorizations and that it is unlikely that it will be able to remedy that situation;[151]

(b) the FSA is entitled to apply for a bank insolvency order on essentially the same grounds;[152] and

(c) the Secretary of State may apply for a bank insolvency order if satisfied that (i) the institution has eligible depositors and (ii) the winding up of the institution would be in the public interest.

The High Court may grant a bank insolvency order if it is satisfied that the requisite grounds are made out.[153] **11.71**

Following his appointment, a bank liquidator has two objectives. First of all, he is required to work with the Financial Services Compensation Scheme (FSCS) to ensure that as soon as practicable, liabilities in respect of eligible deposits are transferred to another financial institution or that the relevant depositors receive payment from the FSCS.[154] This second objective is to wind up the affairs of the bank so as to achieve the best possible result for the bank's creditors as a whole. The protection of eligible depositors takes priority but the liquidator is required to begin working towards both objectives from the date of his appointment.[155] **11.72**

Apart from ensuring the orderly winding up of a failed institution, these provisions are designed in part to prevent a crisis or 'run' on a bank by ordinary depositors because they will have the assurance that the deposit liabilities will either be taken up by a sound institution or will be paid out by the FSCS. **11.73**

The 2009 Act then contains a number of detailed provisions on the liquidation process. For example, a liquidation committee must be established whose initial members will be nominated by the Bank of England, the FSA, and the FSCS. The liquidation committee must in particular be kept advised on progress towards the 'eligible depositor protection' objective described earlier. Once that objective has been achieved, then new members of the liquidation committee must be appointed to represent the general body of creditors, **11.74**

Financial Services Compensation Scheme. On eligibility criteria generally, see para 13.10 below. However, note that the 'eligible depositors' requirement is a qualifying, rather than a limiting criterion. Thus, if an institution has *some* eligible depositors, a bank insolvency order can be made against it even though the vast majority of its depositors are 'non-eligible'

[150] As will be seen below, the 'public interest' ground is reserved to the Secretary of State.

[151] Section 96(2) of the 2009 Act. On the threshold conditions for authorization, see para 1.23 above.

[152] Section 96(3) of the 2009 Act.

[153] Section 97 of the 2009 Act.

[154] As to the choice between seeking another institution to take on the deposits, or having recourse to the FSCS, the liquidator is required to follow the recommendation of the liquidation committee described below: on the point in the text, see s 102 of the 2009 Act.

[155] On these points, see s 99 of the 2009 Act. For these purposes, the 'creditors' of an institution would include all 'non-eligible' depositors.

and the 'official' members of the committee are replaced since the main purpose of their presence will have been achieved.[156] The 2009 Act then deals with the general powers of the bank liquidator and the application (with modifications, where appropriate) of the Insolvency Act 1986 to the bank insolvency process[157] and the steps to be taken on termination of the process.[158]

Bank Administration

11.75   Part 3 of the 2009 Act[159] introduces a new procedure called 'bank administration'. The process is in many respects similar to an ordinary administration process under the Insolvency Act 1986 but it is generally to be used only where the Bank of England has exercised its powers to transfer *part* of the business of a failing bank to a commercial purchaser or to a bridge bank.[160] The administrator is then appointed in respect of the 'non-transferred' or 'residual' part of the bank, and he is required to provide to the commercial purchaser or bridge bank the services or facilities which are necessary to enable the commercial purchaser or the bridge bank to operate the transferred business effectively.[161]

11.76   The Bank of England is the only eligible applicant for a bank administrator order, and such an application may only be made if (i) the Bank has made or intends to make a property transfer instrument in respect of part of the institution's business in favour of a private sector purchaser or a bridge bank and (ii) the Bank is satisfied that the residual bank is unable to pay its debts, or is likely to become unable to do so as a result of the Bank making the partial property transfer instrument. The court may grant the bank administration order if satisfied that these grounds are made out.[162]

11.77   Once again, a bank administrator has two objectives. The first is to support the commercial purchaser or bridge bank (as the case may be). The second is the normal process of administration. The first objective takes priority but the bank administrator must start working towards both objectives from the time of his appointment.[163] The administrator must prepare a statement of his proposals for achieving the statutory objectives, to be agreed with the Bank of England.[164] The first objective involves cooperation with any request from the Bank of England for the residual of the bank to provide services and facilities to the private

---

[156] On these points and for further details of the liquidation committee and its process, see ss 101–102 of the 2009 Act.

[157] Section 103–112 of the 2009 Act.

[158] Sections 113–135 of the 2009 Act. The bank liquidator may propose a company voluntary arrangement or an administration process for the benefit of the general body of creditors as a whole or may propose a final winding up.

[159] Sections 136–168 of the 2009 Act.

[160] On transfers to a commercial purchaser, see s 11 of the 2009 Act, described at para 11.38 above. On transfers to a bridge bank, see s 12 of the 2009 Act, considered at para 11.40 above.

[161] On these points, see s 136 of the 2009 Act.

[162] On these points, see ss142–144 of the 2009 Act. As in the case of an ordinary administration, a bank administrator is an officer of the court: see s 146 of the 2009 Act.

[163] Section 137 of the 2009 Act.

[164] For the detailed process, see s 147 of the Act.

sector purchaser or bridge bank as the case may be.[165] The first objective comes to an end if the relevant services are no longer required.[166] In relation to the second objective, the obligations of the bank administrator resemble those of an ordinary administrator under the Insolvency Act 1986. Briefly, he must seek to rescue the residual bank as a going concern, unless it is not reasonably practicable to achieve that aim. In that event, he must seek to achieve a better result for the bank's creditors as a whole than could be achieved by a winding up. Where, however, the partial property transfer was in favour of a bridge bank,[167] then the administrator is constrained in that he can only realize assets if the Bank of England has agreed to their disposal or has confirmed that the primary objective (services and facilities) has been fully achieved.[168] Given that the bridge bank and the residual bank will formerly have been a part of the same business, there are detailed provisions for the sharing of financial and other information, and access to the books and records of the residual bank.[169]

A bank administrator generally has the same rights and powers as an administrator **11.78** appointed under the Insolvency Act 1986. Thus, for example, there will be a moratorium on legal proceedings and other enforcement processes against the bank once the application for the order has been made.[170]

Investment Banks

It will be recalled that the rules discussed in the preceding sections apply principally to UK **11.79** institutions which hold a deposit-taking permission. However, the insolvency of Lehman Brothers International Europe—a UK subsidiary of Lehman Brothers—has demonstrated that the insolvency of a merchant bank—which does not hold a deposit-taking permission—can nevertheless cause serious disruption of a systemic character. The 2009 Act allows the Treasury to make 'investment bank insolvency regulations' which may modify insolvency law applicable to investment banks and to establish new or amended liquidation/administration procedures to apply to investment banks.[171] For these purposes, an 'investment bank' is defined as an entity incorporated in the United Kingdom and which holds permission from the FSA to carry on the regulated activities of dealing in investments as principal or agent or safeguarding and administering investments, and which holds assets on behalf of its clients.[172] The clear intention is that investment banks should be subjected to a liquidation or administrative procedure similar to that created for banks.[173]

---

[165] See s 138(3) and (4) of the 2009 Act. As noted previously, the services and facilities may include use of premises and computer systems, and access to employees with knowledge of transactions/customer relationships.

[166] See s 139 of the 2009 Act.

[167] ie so that the transferred business is effectively owned by the Bank of England.

[168] See s 140 of the 2009 Act. The purpose of the last provision is to ensure that the administrator cannot dispose of assets if the result would be to prejudice the cooperation which the bank administrator is statutorily required to extend to the bridge bank.

[169] See s 148 of the 2009 Act. The Act also includes detailed provisions about the multiple and subsequent property transfer instruments: see ss 149–152 of the 2009 Act.

[170] See s 145 of the 2009 Act.

[171] Section 233 of the 2009 Act.

[172] Section 232 of the 2009 Act.

[173] See in particular, s 233 of the 2009 Act.

For investment banks, one of the priorities will be the protection of client assets (as opposed to the repayment of eligible deposits).[174]

11.80 At the time of writing, no draft regulations have been prepared for these purposes but detailed work has been undertaken on the outlines of the proposed scheme.[175]

Interbank Payment Systems

11.81 Part 5 of the 2009 Act provides for the Bank of England to exercise oversight of payment systems. Reliable payment systems are important not only to the financial markets but also to their customers in the wider economy as a whole, and the intention of Part 5 is to provide for the effective supervision of those payment systems where a disruption may have consequences for the stability of the UK's financial system as a whole.

11.82 Part 5 is thus directed towards 'interbank payment systems'. That expression is designed to include arrangements designed to facilitate or control the transfer of money between participating financial institutions.[176]

11.83 The Treasury may by means of a 'recognition order' specify that a particular interbank payment system is a recognized system for Part 5 purposes.[177] The Treasury may only make such an order if satisfied that any deficiencies in its design or disruption of its operations would be likely to threaten the stability of the UK financial system or have serious consequences for business or other interests throughout the United Kingdom. The Treasury must make that assessment on the basis of the number, size and nature of the transactions processed through that system, and various other factors.[178]

11.84 The Bank of England has various powers in relation to recognized interbank payment systems:

(a) the Bank may publish principles to be observed in the operation of recognized systems, and may publish applicable codes of practice;[179];
(b) the Bank may require the system operator to establish rules for the operation of the system, and to change those rules to achieve a stated objective;[180]

---

[174] See s 233(3) of the 2009 Act.

[175] See HM Treasury, 'Establishing resolution arrangements for investment banks' (December 2009).

[176] Section 182 of the 2009 Act. A system may be an 'interbank payment system' for these purposes even though it operates wholly or partly in relation to persons or places outside the United Kingdom: s 182(5).

[177] Section 184 of the 2009 Act. Since the effect of recognition is to impose obligations, this is a unilateral power of the Treasury and there is no requirement that a system should apply for recognition.

[178] See s 185 of the 2009 Act. Various consultation processes apply before a recognition order can be made: see s 186 of the 2009 Act. On the whole process, see HM Treasury, 'The recognition process for interbank payment systems – a guidance note' (August 2009). The Bank of England has also issued 'The Bank of England's Oversight of Interbank Payment Systems under the Banking Act 2009' (September 2009), which explains the Bank's approach to its statutory responsibilities under Pt 5 of the 2009 Act.

[179] Sections 188–189 of the 2009 Act.

[180] Section 190(1) of the 2009 Act.

(c) the Bank has power to give directions to the operator of the system requiring or prohibiting the taking of specified action, or setting standards for the operation of the system;[181]

(d) the Bank is required to consult with the FSA in relation to the exercise of its powers in relation to any interbank payment system which is also a recognized investment exchange or recognized clearing house for the purposes of the FSMA;[182]

(e) the Bank also has various enforcement powers to inquire into the operation of a recognized system, for example, by the appointment of an inspector or commissioning an independent report,[183] and to order a recognized system to pay a penalty in respect of relevant compliance failures.[184] Ultimately, if the Bank of England believes that a compliance failure threatens the stability of the UK financial system or confidence in it, or has serious consequences for business, or other interests throughout the United Kingdom, then it may order the operator temporarily or permanently to cease operating all or part of the activities of that system.[185]

Emergency Liquidity Assistance

The Nature of the Assistance

The discussion in the foregoing segments of this chapter may create the impression that banks are either fully solvent and operational, or that they must be subject to a formal stabilization or insolvency procedure. **11.85**

In practice, of course, matters are not quite so straightforward. As with any other commercial or industrial company, a bank may run into difficulties, whether through poor management, misfortune or through any other cause. But there is a key difference. Where an ordinary company runs into cash flow difficulties, it may employ a variety of techniques to try to nurse itself through that period. One of the principal techniques is simply to borrow from one's own creditors, either by negotiating extended periods for payment or, perhaps more frequently, by simply delaying settlement on the basis that the creditor/supplier is dependent on the business flow and will not make too much fuss about the situation. **11.86**

Of course, this approach to cash flow problems would be unthinkable for a bank. Its very credibility rests on payment when it falls due. So the remedies or fixes which are available to an industrial company are simply not open to a bank. So, what are the avenues available to a bank which may be solvent—in the sense that its assets exceed its liabilities—but which is suffering from a shortage of liquidity which impedes its ability to meet its debts as they arise and is unable to raise the necessary funds from commercial sources?[186] **11.87**

---

[181] Section 191 of the 2009 Act. The Treasury must be notified before any such directions are given.
[182] Section 192 of the 2009 Act.
[183] Sections 193–198 of the 2009 Act.
[184] Section 198 of the 2009 Act.
[185] Section 199 of the 2009 Act.
[186] Of course, as the recent financial crisis has shown, the difference between insolvency and illiquidity may be a narrow one but, as will be seen, the distinction runs through the whole concept of emergency liquidity assistance.

11.88   The answer lies in 'Emergency Liquidity Assistance' facilities provided by the Bank of England.[187] There seems to be no formal, legal right for an institution in difficulties to receive this type of support, which thus rests entirely within the discretion of the Bank of England.[188] The issue is—under what circumstances will such assistance be provided?

11.89   It has been said that the following are the 'fundamental principles' for emergency liquidity assistance:[189]

(a) as already noted, emergency liquidity assistance should be granted by the Bank of England only to banks which are illiquid but which are not insolvent;[190]

(b) the funding should be subject to a penal rate of interest;[191]

(c) collateral must be provided for the facility; and

(d) the funding must be discretionary and there should be no market expectation that this will be available.[192]

11.90   To these points, it may be added that the purpose of emergency assistance is not to prevent the failure of an individual bank or to reassure its shareholders. That may well be a by-product of the assistance, but the overall objective is to avoid or mitigate risks in the financial system *as a whole*.[193]

Recent Use of Emergency Liquidity Assistance

11.91   Unsurprisingly, the recent crisis has given rise to a number of occasions on which the Bank of England's role as provider of Emergency Liquidity Assistance (or as 'lender of last resort') has come into sharp relief.

11.92   The provision of such assistance to Northern Rock at the beginning of the crisis has already been noted.[194] In addition, emergency liquidity assistance of up to £36.6 billion and £25.4 billion was provided to the Royal Bank of Scotland and to HBOS during the last few

---

[187] Emergency liquidity assistance is a common feature of central banking around the world. Reference used to be made to the Bank of England's role as 'lender of last resort', and the two expressions are effectively interchangeable for present purposes.

[188] The absence of any legal obligation to provide emergency liquidity assistance may have been of some importance in the *SRM Global Master Fund* case, noted at paras 11.16–11.19 above.

[189] See Delston and Campbell, 'Emergency Liquidity Financing by Central Banks: System Protection or Bank Bailout?' IMF Legal Department and IMF Institute Seminar on Current Developments in Monetary and Financial Law, May 2002, p 2.

[190] The authors of the paper mentioned in n 189 above do however, proceed to note that '… in practice, illiquidity almost always means insolvency …'.

[191] This may be necessary for a variety of reasons. First of all, since public funds are involved, the central bank is under a duty to obtain the best possible return, and the benefits of providing the assistance should accrue to the taxpayer, not to the shareholders of the institution concerned. Finally, a proper commercial return may be necessary to avoid any infringement of the 'State aid' rules in Art 82 of the EC Treaty.

[192] Were that the case, then this would create a moral hazard that banks will engage in excessive risk-taking, knowing that any resultant problems can be cured with the help of the central bank.

[193] See George, 'The Pursuit of Financial Stability' (1994) *Bank of England Quarterly Bulletin* 63, and the discussion of *SRM Global Master Fund* decision, at paras 11.16–11.19 above. In effect, that decision confirmed the view that a financial institution has no right or expectation that it will receive emergency liquidity assistance, and it was therefore appropriate that this factor should be left out of account in calculating shareholder compensation.

[194] See para 11.07 above.

months of 2008. The existence of those facilities remained confidential until November 2009, when the Bank of England determined that the secrecy of those arrangements was no longer necessary.[195]

Legal Aspects of Emergency Liquidity Assistance

The United States and many other countries have developed a formal legal framework for the provision of liquidity assistance by their central banks.[196] However, there seems to be no directly corresponding statutory framework in the United Kingdom. However, if a statutory basis is required, it may perhaps be found in section 2A of the Banking Act 1998[197] which provides that, '… An objective of the Bank shall be to contribute to the stability of the financial system of the United Kingdom …' and that, in pursuit of that objective, '… the Bank shall aim to work with the other relevant bodies (including the Treasury and the Financial Services Authority) …'. As noted above, the avowed purpose of emergency liquidity assistance is to preserve the stability of the financial system as a whole (and not merely the rescue of an individual institution). The provision of such assistance would therefore seem to be entirely consistent with the objective set out in section 2A of the 2009 Act. The Bank's obligation to work with the other Tripartite Authorities finds voice in paragraphs 14–16 of the Memorandum of Understanding between those parties,[198] which provide for emergency support operations '… in the case of a genuine threat to the stability of the financial system to avoid a serious disturbance in the UK economy …'. It may thus be said that—at least since the above statutory provisions were introduced pursuant to the Banking Act 2009—there is a sufficient legal basis for the provision of emergency liquidity assistance by the Bank of England. It may thus also be said that a previously relatively informal process has now been placed on a firmer statutory footing. **11.93**

But this is not the sole statutory development in this sphere. The move towards greater statutory formality perhaps highlighted that a decision by the Bank of England to refuse or to withdraw liquidity assistance could have very significant consequences both for the institution itself and for its shareholders. In order to avoid any possible liability for damages in this area,[199] the Bank of England has been granted immunity from any liability in respect of any act or omission in its capacity as a monetary authority—that is to say, in acting as the central bank of the United Kingdom or in connection with its function of protecting or enhancing the stability of the UK's financial system.[200] As a result, decisions made by the Bank of England in relation to the provision of liquidity support could not generally give rise to a liability to institutions or shareholders in relation to any resultant loses. **11.94**

---

[195] See HM Treasury, 'Statement on Emergency Liquidity Assistance' (25 November 2008).
[196] See generally Delston and Campbell (n 189 above).
[197] As inserted by s 238(1) of the Banking Act 2009.
[198] On the Memorandum of Understanding between the Tripartite Authorities, see generally Chapter 8 above.
[199] And perhaps to deter legal proceedings of the type discussed in Chapter 14 below in relation to the collapse of BCCI.
[200] Section 244 of the 2009 Act. The immunity does not extend to actions taken in bad faith or in contravention of s 6(1) of the Human Rights Act 1998. Both the immunity itself and the derogations from it are very similar to the corresponding provisions for the protection of the FSA under the FSMA. For a discussion of those provisions, see paras 14.05–14.11 below.

Other Forms of Assistance to the Financial Markets

11.95 It should be noted in closing on this subject that the emergency liquidity assistance/lender of last resort function has been considered because this has been a long-accepted role of central banks and will no doubt continue to be so. It should, however, be noted that various bespoke facilities were also introduced by both the Bank of England and the Treasury. Briefly, these included the following:

(a) The Bank of England's Special Liquidity Scheme, which allowed banks to swap high quality, mortgage-backed, and other securities in exchange for UK Treasury Bills. Although the risk of loss on the mortgages and other securities rests with the banks, this structure allowed them to swap illiquid assets for highly liquid government securities, and to raise cash in that way;[201]

(b) The Bank of England's Asset Purchase Facility, also designed to increase market liquidity by allowing the banks to purchase high quality assets through the use of Treasury bills, or through the creation of bank money;[202]

(c) The Treasury's Asset Protection Scheme, which was announced in February 2009[203] which ultimately found expression in the Banking Act 2009;[204]

(d) The Treasury's general scheme for asset-backed securities under which the government sought to enhance liquidity by giving a guarantee in respect of residential mortgage-backed securities;[205] and

(e) The Treasury's Credit Guarantee Scheme, under which the government assisted the fund-raising capacity of institutions by guaranteeing certificates of deposit, commercial paper and senior unsecured bonds, and notes having a maturity period of up to three years.[206]

Conclusions

11.96 It hardly needs to be stated that the events of 2007–2009 were unfortunate, both from the perspective of the United Kingdom's financial markets and the wider economy as a whole. However, it has at least served to focus attention on the need for a bespoke insolvency regime for banks as a means of buttressing the stability of the UK's financial system. It is apparent that a vast amount of detailed work was undertaken on the Banking Act 2009 and associated, secondary legislation. The new rules seem to represent a fair attempt to draw a

---

[201] See Bank of England News Release, 'Special Liquidity Scheme' (21 April 2008) and the Information and Market Notice Papers issued by the Bank on the same day.

[202] See the Bank of England Market Notice, 'Asset Purchase Facility—Corporate Bond Secondary Market Scheme' (22 December 2009), and associated notices referred therein.

[203] See HM Treasury Press Release, 'Asset Protection Scheme and Increased Lending' (26 February 2009).

[204] See the discussion at para 11.23 above.

[205] See Debt Management Office, 'Market Notice: Outline of UK Government's 2009 Asset Backed Securities Guarantee Scheme' (22 April 2009) extending a scheme created in the previous year.

[206] See Debt Management Office, 'Market Notice: The UK Government's 2008 Credit Guarantee Scheme' (13 October 2008).

balance between the competing interests of the creditors and shareholders of the institution, and the taxpayer. There is thus far only limited experience of the operation of the Banking Act 2009. It remains to be seen how matters will work out in practice although, for obvious reasons, it may be hoped that the 2009 Act does not have to be tested on too many occasions.

12

CROSS-BORDER REORGANIZATION AND WINDING UP OF BANKS

Introduction

It has been noted previously[1] that banks incorporated in an EEA Member State derive their **12.01** authorization from the supervisory body in that Member State, and that such authorization is effectively to be recognized throughout the Community.[2] Whilst certain 'passporting' formalities apply and the host State regulator performs limited functions in the regulatory area,[3] it is the authority established in the home Member State which is generally responsible for the supervision of the activities of that bank throughout the Community. It will also be seen that, likewise, the establishment of a deposit-protection scheme is the responsibility of the home State, and that the benefit of such a scheme must be available to all depositors with branches of that institution throughout the Community.[4]

Under these circumstances, and given the emphasis placed on the responsibility of the **12.02** home State for credit institutions authorized by it, it is perhaps logical that control over a bank's affairs should continue through to legal and other proceedings which flow from the failure of an institution or any financial difficulties which may afflict it.

---

[1] See the discussion in Chapter 2 above.
[2] See the discussion of the 'passporting' system at paras 2.13–2.21 above.
[3] The host State regulator performs certain functions in the fields of liquidity and conduct of business: see para 2.15 above.
[4] On the whole subject of deposit protection schemes, see Chapter 13 below.

12.03   The Directive of the European Parliament and of the Council on the Reorganisation and Winding up of Credit Institutions[5] seeks to give voice to these principles. To a lesser degree, it also seeks to legislate for the problems which may arise when a non-EEA institution with branches within the Community runs into difficulties. But it must not be forgotten that the Directive is essentially an EEA measure and that it may be necessary for the English courts to deal with the assets or liabilties of an entity established outside the EEA.

12.04   With these considerations in mind, this chapter will cover the following subject matter:

(a)   the scope of the Directive;

(b)   the impact of the Directive in the context of the reorganization or winding up of an EU credit institution; and

(c)   the consequences of the Directive in relation to the insolvency of institutions established outside the EEA; and

(d)   in a non-EEA context, it is appropriate briefly to consider the assistance which the English courts may provide to the liquidator or receiver of a foreign financial institution.

Scope of the Directive

12.05   As the Directive notes,[6] under the terms of the Consolidated Banking Directive, '… a credit institution and its branches form a single entity subject to the supervision of the competent authorities of the State where authorisation valid throughout the Community was granted … It would be particularly undesirable to relinquish such unity between an institution and its branches where it is necessary to adopt reorganisation measures or open winding up proceedings …'. This follows from the fact that '… The important role played by the competent authorities of the home Member State before winding-up proceedings are opened may continue during the process of winding up so that these proceedings can be properly carried out …'.

12.06   In essence, therefore, the Directive does not seek to influence the content of the substantive or procedural law applicable to the winding up.[7] Rather, it seeks to preserve and extend the principle of home State supremacy over the authorization process to proceedings involving the reorganization or liquidation of a bank. Likewise, the principle that other Member States should recognize the authorization granted in the home Member State is extended to include an obligation to recognize the effect of reorganization and winding-up proceedings in that Member State. As a corollary, it prohibits host Member States from

---

[5]   Directive 2001/24/EC of the European Parliament and of the Council of 4 April 2001 on the winding up of credit institutions, OJ L 125/15, 05.05.2001. The Directive has been implemented in the United Kingdom by means of the Credit Institutions (Reorganisation and Winding Up) Regulations 2004 (SI 2004/1045), hereafter the '2004 Regulations'. Note that certain detailed amendments were made by the Credit Institutions (Reorganisation and Winding Up) (Amendment) Regulations 2007 (SI 2007/830).

[6]   See paras 3, 4 and 15 of the preamble.

[7]   For this general principle and certain exceptions to it which will have to be discussed below, see para 23 of the preamble.

commencing insolvency procedures against institutions authorized in other Member States.

It should be noted that the Directive applies only in the following situations:[8]   **12.07**

(a) where a credit institution is subject to 'reorganization measures', that is to say, '... measures which are intended to preserve or restore the financial situation of a credit institution and which could affect third parties' pre-existing rights, including measures involving the possibility of a suspension of payments, suspension of enforcement measures or reduction of claims ...'; and

(b) where a credit institution is subject to 'winding-up proceedings', that is to say, '... collective proceedings opened and monitored by the administrative or judicial authorities of a Member State with the aim of realising assets under the supervision of those authorities, including where the proceedings are terminated by a composition or other, similar measure ...'.

In other words, the Directive deals with cases in which an institution is subject to some   **12.08** form of legal or statutory process[9] designed either to avert or to deal with the consequences of insolvency.[10] There is, therefore, no inconsistency between the terms of the Directive and the 2004 Regulations (on the one hand) and the provisions facilitating transfers of banking businesses contained in Part VII of the FSMA (on the other hand).[11] The latter provisions can be invoked only where the transferee of a banking business is solvent[12] and, in any event, they deal with a transfer of some or all of the assets of a bank, as opposed to matters directly affecting the solvency of the institution as a whole.

For the purposes of illustration, the ensuing parts of this section examine the effect of the   **12.09** Directive in the event that a UK institution becomes subject to reorganization or winding-up proceedings. However, courts in the United Kingdom would clearly be bound by reciprocal obligations in the event of proceedings involving an EEA institution which has a presence in the UK.[13]

---

[8] On the definitions about to be given, see Art 2 of the Directive.

[9] That some form of legal procedure must be involved for the Directive to apply is inherent both in the scheme of the Directive as a whole and in the terminology employed in the definitions: note the use of the word 'measures' in the context of a reorganization, and the word 'proceedings' in the context of winding up. As a result, a multilateral renegotiation with creditors would not amount to a 'reorganization' within the Directive. On the other hand, an administration would amount to a reorganization for these purposes, because the procedure is laid down by statute; this is so even though a court order is not always a necessary prerequisite for the use of this procedure. The subject is further discussed later in this chapter.

[10] A reading of the preamble to the Directive makes it clear that a reorganization is an attempt to deal with the financial problems besetting a credit institution, and that winding up may be a necessary sequel. For further discussion of the expressions 'reorganization measures' and 'winding up proceedings', see Moss and Wessels, *EU Banking and Insurance Insolvency* (OUP, 2006), paras 1.83–1.90.

[11] Part VII of the FSMA has already been considered in Chapter 9 above.

[12] This is the effect of s 111(2)(a) of the FSMA, requiring that an 'adequate financial resources' certificate must be provided: see para 9.15 above.

[13] See, for example, paras 3 and 5 of the 2004 Regulations.

Impact of the Directive on EEA Credit Institutions

12.10 What, then, are the consequences if an EEA credit institution is subjected to a procedure which falls within the scope of the Directive? These may perhaps be best illustrated by using the example of a United Kingdom institution which has become insolvent, and examining the relevant provisions separately in the context of a reorganization and a winding-up procedure.

Reorganization

12.11 If a bank established and authorized in the United Kingdom goes into bank adminis-tration,[14] then it seems clear that this would amount to a 'reorganization' for the purposes of the Directive, because:

(a) the administration process is a 'measure' which is designed to rescue the bank con-cerned; and

(b) the measure affects third parties' pre-existing rights, for example, by suspending the enforcement rights which secured creditors would otherwise enjoy, and prohibiting the institution of legal proceedings.[15]

12.12 It was noted above that a bank administration order will be a 'reorganization' measure for the purposes of the Directive. This will clearly be the case if the purpose of the administra-tion '… is to rescue the residual bank as a going concern …' within section 140(1)(a) of the Banking Act 2009. However, it may be argued that a bank administration designed to achieve 'a better result for the residual bank's creditors as a whole than would be likely if the residual bank were wound up without first being put into administration' (see section 140(1)(b) of the Banking Act 2009) should be treated as a winding-up proceeding (rather than a reorganization) for the purposes of the Directive. For the present, this point must be regarded as open, although it would only assume limited importance in a minority of cases since the obligation to recognize the authority of the home Member State is broadly the same in the context of both a reorganization and a winding up.

12.13 In *Jeffries International Ltd v Landsbanki Islands hf*,[16] it seems to have been accepted by all parties that the declaration of a moratorium by an Icelandic court pursuant to emergency legislation introduced in that country amounted to a 'reorganization measure' for these purposes, even though it did not form part of a wider process to place the bank in any form of insolvency proceeding. However, the point was not central to the decision because, by the time of the hearing, the moratorium had been withdrawn in any event.[17] It seems

---

[14] It will be recalled that this process is used where part of the business of a failing bank has been transferred to a commercial purchaser or a bridge bank, and the remainder of the institution is to be put into the new process known as 'bank administration' created by Part 3 of the Banking Act 2009: see the discussion of this process at paras 11.75–11.78 above.

[15] On this subject, see para 43 of Sch B1 to the Insolvency Act 1986, as applied to the bank administration procedure by s 145(6) of the Banking Act 2009.

[16] [2009] EWHC 894 (Comm).

[17] Note that the Financial Markets Law Committee took the view that the moratorium would have to be applied throughout the EEA States because it amounted to a reorganization measure for the purposes of

possible (although not certain) that the measures taken by the Icelandic Government to split the business between 'Old Landsbanki' and 'New Landsbanki' would also have to be recognized and applied in the UK as a 'reorganization measure' for the purposes of the Directive, even though those arrangements were perceived to be to be to the disadvantage of UK depositors since deposits with Icelandic branches were transferred to 'New Landsbanki', whilst foreign deposits were left with the old entity.[18] The main reservation to this view is that the restructuring may be contrary to the ban on national discrimination, especially bearing in mind that: (i) recital (12) to the Directive contemplates equality of treatment; and (ii) recital (21) and Article 16 of the Directive specifically require non-discrimination between creditors in the home Member State and those based in other Member States (although, admittedly, the substantive provision is directly applicable only in the case of a winding up, and not in the context of a reorganization). It is true that an English court cannot directly impeach the validity of an act by the *Community* itself[19] but—Community law aside—there seems to be no reason why the English courts could not decline, on public policy grounds, to recognize a legislative act of another State on the basis that it is inconsistent with the treaty obligations of that State to the UK.[20] In terms of Community law itself, it is also difficult to believe that the framers of the EU Directive could have intended to compel Member States to give effect to domestic legislative measures of other Member States which contravene a core tenet of Community law—in other words, recognition of the measure would surely itself be contrary to *Community* public policy? For the present, however, the point must perhaps be regarded as unclear since, as far as the writer is aware, no court has yet declined to recognize legislation of another EU Member State on grounds of its inconsistency with the EC Treaty.[21]

The primary EU law consequences of the commencement of the bank administration in relation to the UK credit institution are set out in Article 3 of the Directive and include the following: **12.14**

(a) the procedures applicable to the bank administration procedure in the United Kingdom must be applied in courts throughout the European Economic Area without further formality and even though the domestic law of the particular Member State may not have a similar procedure. The relevant insolvency measure should apply both to the relevant UK branches of the EEA credit institution, any of its property and assets, and to any of its liabilities;[22]

---

the Directive: see Financial Markets Law Committee, 'Issue 141—The Landsbanki Freezing Order 2008' (May 2009), para 3.38.

[18] See the description of those restructuring arrangements in *Jeffries International Ltd v Landsbanki Islands hf* [2009] EWHC 894 (Comm).

[19] See Case C-314/85, *Foto-Frost v Hauptzollamt Lubeck-Ost* [1987] ECR 4199.

[20] See, for example, the situation which arose in *Royal Hellenic Government v Vergottis* (1945) Lloyds Rep 292. A mere court decision to this effect would not appear to offend the Community rule against the imposition of countermeasures, discussed at para 13.20 below.

[21] For discussion of the deposit protection aspects of the Landsbanki episode, see paras 13.13–13.23 below.

[22] Article 3(1) of the Directive, as implemented by para 5 of the 2004 Regulations. Note that the obligation of recognition does not of itself extend to reorganization or winding-up proceedings affecting the subsidiaries of a credit institution.

(b) subject to points made in (c) below and subject also to the preservation of certain security and similar rights,[23] this means that an administration order made in relation to a UK credit institution has extra-territorial effect and must accordingly be applied by courts throughout the EEA. This state of affairs is necessary to give effect to the notion of the responsibility of the home State, which has already been discussed;

(c) if another EEA State determines that it must take local steps to implement a UK reorganization, then it must notify the FSA to that effect.[24]

12.15   The general principle to drawn from these provisions is that the procedural and substantive law applicable to a reorganization of a credit institution is that of the home Member State.[25] This represents, in many respects, something of a radical step, not least because questions of procedure are almost invariably governed by the domestic law of the State in which the proceedings are taking place and, as a corollary, a court does not usually apply the procedural laws of a foreign State. In practice, this principle is not quite the radical departure which it at first appears to be, because a number of exceptions are made where the law of some other State is to be applied in particular cases.[26] Nevertheless, in the example given above, a court sitting in another Member State would have to give effect to the rule that a creditor cannot take proceedings to enforce his debt against a credit institution in administration without the consent of an English court.[27] Likewise, that court would have to recognize that execution proceedings against the institution's assets—even though situate within the territory of the host State—could not be enforced for so long as the administration remains in effect.[28] These examples serve to illustrate the extra-territorial 'reach' for reorganization measures which flows from the application of the Directive.

Winding Up

12.16   The provisions dealing with winding-up proceedings affecting a credit institution are similar, although not identical, to those discussed above in the context of a reorganization. This is understandable, given that the common objective is to concentrate powers (and responsibilities) into the hands of the home Member State.

12.17   As a result, the administrative or judicial authorities of the home State have the sole power to adjudicate upon winding-up proceedings against a credit institution; any decision to that effect must be recognized in other Member States without further formality.[29]

---

[23] On this subject, see 'Common Provisions', below.

[24] Article 5 of the Directive. As Moss and Wessels (n 10 above) point out at para 2.25, the English version of the Directive is misleading because it suggests an independent right for the host State to take reorganization measures in relation to an institution established in another EEA Member State. However, this would be inconsistent both with the general principle of the Directive and the explicit terms of Art 3.

[25] The point is recognized by para 23 of the preamble to the Directive and repeated in Art 3(2).

[26] See the discussion under 'Common Provisions', below.

[27] That is to say, the rule applicable in a bank administration referred to in para 11.78 above.

[28] That is to say, the rule set out in para 44 of Sch B1 to the Insolvency Act 1986, as applied to bank administrations by s 145(6) of the Banking Act 2009.

[29] See Art 9 of the Directive, which also provides for notification to the authorities of the home State. Consistently with points made earlier in this chapter, this provision relates to winding up proceedings referable to insolvency of the institution concerned. Voluntary winding up proceedings are governed by Art 11 of the Directive.

Once again, the domestic law and procedures applicable to the winding up of the institu- **12.18** tion in its home State must be applied.[30] Accordingly, in the example currently under discussion, English law would govern the following matters arising in connection with the winding up of a UK credit institution, even if the relevant issue arises for decision before the courts of another EEA State:[31]

(a) the extent of the liquidator's powers;
(b) the conditions under which rights of set-off may be invoked;[32]
(c) the effect of winding-up proceedings on contracts to which the credit institution is a party;[33]
(d) the admissibility of proofs of debt and the procedures involved in their verification;[34]
(e) rules governing the realization of assets and the distribution of funds among the creditors; and
(f) the rules relating to voidness, voidability, or unenforceability of legal acts detrimental to creditors.[35]

Equally, if a court in the United Kingdom has to consider a matter falling in any of the **12.19** above categories with reference to a credit institution established in another EEA State, it should apply the laws of that jurisdiction on the same basis.

Although these principles are subject to a number of exceptions, it should be said that the **12.20** institution of multiple legal proceedings against a bank in the different jurisdictions in which it has branches is likely to produce a distortive effect. In the absence of legislation of the kind now under discussion, creditors in Member States with relatively prosperous branches would be likely to make a significant recovery, to the detriment of creditors in less fortunate countries. Consequently, the Directive requirement that the home Member State

---

[30] See Art 10(1) of the Directive. The principle should be read subject to the various exceptions and other points noted under 'Common Provisions', below.

[31] The list of examples about to be given is drawn from Art 10(2) of the Directive. It should be appreciated that the list is non-exhaustive and does not limit the general principle stated in Art 10(1).

[32] Set-off in insolvency is generally regarded as a matter of procedure which is thus to be governed by the law applicable to the winding up. As a result, a debtor of the institution who was also a depositor would be entitled to set off his debt against the deposit, provided that the requirement of 'mutuality' and other conditions set out in r 4.90 of the Insolvency Rules 1986 are met; on this rule, see para 36.07 below. This principle is, however, subject to the important reservation that a debtor may also claim a right of set-off to the extent allowed by the law applicable to the debt owing to the credit institution: see the discussion of Art 23 of the Directive, under 'Common Provisions', below.

[33] Thus, in the winding up of a credit institution incorporated in the United Kingdom, the ability of the liquidator to disclaim onerous property would be governed by s 178 of the Insolvency Act 1986, even though the contracts are governed by a foreign system of law and/or relate to assets situate outside the United Kingdom.

[34] All creditors throughout the Community are to be allowed to lodge claims and are entitled to equal treatment: see Art 16 of the Directive.

[35] Thus, where a transaction is alleged to be detrimental to creditors, it can only be set aside by the court if it constitutes a preference, transaction at an undervalue or other objectionable form of arrangement within the terms of ss 238–246 of the Insolvency Act 1986. This remains the case even if the arrangement is governed by the legal system of another Member State or relates to an asset situate in such a Member State, although this statement must be read subject to an exception provided by Art 30 of the Directive.

should have exclusive jurisdiction in winding-up proceedings is more likely to lead to equal treatment among the body of creditors as a whole.[36]

12.21 The winding up of a credit institution necessarily involves the revocation of its deposit-taking licence, although this does not prevent the liquidator from taking any steps necessary for the purposes of the winding up.[37]

12.22 The Directive also contains a number of provisions for the publication of information to creditors in the context of a winding up.[38]

Common Provisions

12.23 As noted above, the reorganization or winding up of a credit institution will be governed by the law of its home Member State.

12.24 As may be imagined, however, it is not possible to apply such a rigid rule in all circumstances, for it may operate to deprive creditors of vested rights under other systems of law, or may operate to deprive a weaker contracting party of rights to which he would otherwise be entitled. In addition, a bank will have customers and assets in numerous jurisdictions, and it is plain that such a simplistic rule could not be applied without qualification. For present purposes, it must suffice to provide a brief summary of some of the more important exceptions which are recognized by the terms of the Directive itself:

(a) the consequences of reorganization and winding-up proceedings on employment contracts will be governed by the law applicable to the employment contract;[39]

(b) the consequences of those events for a lease or other real property right are governed by the law of the Member State in which the land is situate;[40]

(c) proprietary and security rights will generally be governed by the law of the place in which the assets are situate when the relevant proceedings are started;[41]

(d) a creditor of the institution may continue to assert rights of set-off which are permitted by the law which governs the credit institution's cross-claim against that creditor.[42] A few points may be noted about this provision. First of all, it is designed to ensure that legitimate expectations are met. For example, if a UK customer has both a loan and a deposit account with the London branch of a French institution, he would expect to enjoy a right of set-off, and this should not be defeated by the institution of

---

[36] Equality of treatment is one of the objectives of the Directive: see para (16) of the preamble.

[37] See Art 12 of the Directive.

[38] See in particular Arts 13 and 14 of the Directive.

[39] Article 20(a) of the Directive, mirrored in para 23 of the 2004 Regulations. The provision is obviously designed for the protection of staff employed outside the home State.

[40] Article 20(b) of the Directive. Rights relating to ships will be governed by the law of the Member State in which it is registered: Art 20(c).

[41] Article 21 of the Directive, reflected in para 26 of the 2004 Regulations. This provision does not, however, preclude the credit institution from asserting that the relevant security interest is void, voidable, or unenforceable: see Art 21(4) of the Directive.

[42] Article 23 of the Directive, mirrored by para 28 of the 2004 Regulations. As with many of the principles listed in paras (a)–(f), this rule reflects established principles of private international law. See, for example, *Re Bank of Credit and Commerce International SA (No 10)* [1996] 4 All ER 796. Once again, note that the preservation of rights of set-off does not preclude any action designed to assert that one of the relevant obligations is void, voidable or unenforceable: see Art 23(2) of the Directive.

reorganization or winding-up proceedings in France. Secondly, there may be occasions when cross-claims arise under different contracts governed by different systems of law. In such a case, the set-off is only allowed if it is permitted by the law which governs the credit institution's own claim against the counterparty (and, in the absence of any express limitation, it seems that this provision would apply even if the claim is governed by the law of a non-EEA State). Finally, there is a question mark as to the content of '… the law applicable to the credit institution's claim …' for these purposes. Whilst the point is not clear, it is suggested that this refers to the applicable law as ascertained pursuant to Rome I.[43] The result would be that where, say, a French bank is subject to winding up proceedings in France, rights of set-off among contracts concluded by its London branch under English law would be determined by reference to the ordinary principles of English commercial law. However, the expression '… law applicable to the credit institution's claim …' would not operate to bring into effect any *statutory* rights of set-off provided by English law,[44] since those rights should have no application in the context of a foreign winding up;

(e) the enforcement of proprietary rights against registered shares or bonds held in a clearing system will be governed by the law of the Member State in which the register or system is located;[45]

(f) it is also necessary to protect transactions in financial instruments which are effected on regulated markets. Accordingly, netting and repurchase agreements,[46] and transactions effected on regulated markets, continue to be governed by the law applicable to them, notwithstanding the commencement of reorganization or winding-up proceedings.[47]

It should, however, be appreciated that the above list is not exhaustive. For example, financial collateral would continue to be effective in accordance with the law applicable to the relevant arrangements.[48] Equally, the provisions of the Directive which give primacy to the law of the home State would not operate to displace the rules on settlement finality in payment and securities settlement systems.[49]   **12.25**

Regulatory Issues

There are, in addition, a number of regulatory provisions designed to facilitate compliance with the overall objectives and purposes of the Directive. These include (i) an obligation to consult with the FSA if a UK authorized credit institution is contemplating a voluntary winding up,[50] (ii) an obligation on a court to notify the FSA if it makes any kind   **12.26**

---

[43] On the Rome I regulation on the law applicable to contractual obligations, see generally Chapter 40 below.

[44] Most notably, r 4.90 of the Insolvency Rules 1986, to which reference has already been made at para 12.16 above.

[45] This is the effect of Art 24 of the Directive and para 33 of the 2004 Regulations.

[46] On these agreements, see para 36.29 below.

[47] See Arts 25, 26 and 27 of the Directive. For the corresponding UK provisions, see paras 29, 34 and 35 of the 2004 Regulations.

[48] Financial collateral arrangements are considered in Chapter 35 below.

[49] On settlement and finality, see paras 35.04–35.21 below.

[50] Paragraph 8 of the 2004 Regulations.

of insolvency decision against a credit institution, (iii) an obligation on the FSA to notify any relevant UK proceedings to regulators in other EEA States in which the affected institution has a branch,[51] (iv) an obligation on the FSA to withdraw an institution's deposit-taking permission as soon as reasonably practicable after being notified of an insolvency decision or the appointment of a liquidator or administrator under the terms of the Insolvency Act 1986,[52] and (v) an obligation of confidentiality in relation to information received by the FSA from an EEA regulator in relation to the insolvency or reorganization of an institution supervised by it.[53]

Third Country Institutions

12.27   In the present context, of course, the expression 'third country institution' refers to a bank whose head office is established outside the EEA.

12.28   The provisions of the Directive apply to the reorganization or winding up of a third country institution only where that institution has branches in two or more Member States.[54] If the institution has a branch only in a single Member State, then there is no Community dimension to its reorganization or liquidation for—as between Member States—only that State could have jurisdiction over the institution in the context of its insolvency.[55]

12.29   In cases in which the Directive applies to a third country institution, it does not seem appropriate to give priority to one Member State over another in the context of a local reorganization or winding up procedure. Consequently, each Member State retains its jurisdiction over local branches. The Directive merely requires that the authorities in a Member State which proposes to take any action in this sphere should notify the authorities in other Member States, and that they should endeavour to coordinate their actions.[56] Where a third country institution has a branch in the United Kingdom but not in any other Member State, the Directive has no application and the reorganization or liquidation of the local branch will proceed according to the domestic laws of the United Kingdom. Even where the Directive does apply, the proceedings will be governed by the domestic laws of the United Kingdom, subject only to the obligations of notification and coordination noted above.

---

[51] Paragraph 10 of the 2004 Regulations.

[52] Paragraph 11 of the 2004 Regulations. Note that the obligation to withdraw the deposit-taking permission arises if an administrator is appointed under the Insolvency Act 1986. Accordingly, the obligation to withdraw the permission will not arise under this paragraph in relation to a bank administration order, since such an order is made under the Banking Act 2009 (as opposed to the Insolvency Act 1986).

[53] Paragraph 18 of the 2004 Regulations.

[54] See Art 1(2) of the Directive.

[55] For the same reason, the Directive would not apply where an institution incorporated in a Member State has no branches outside that country, for there would be no jurisdictional conflict or EEA dimension.

[56] See Art 8 (reorganization) and Art 19 (winding up).

Court Assistance for Foreign Liquidators

It remains briefly to consider the powers of an English court to lend assistance to liquida-   **12.30**
tors of foreign banks who are seeking to recover assets situate in England. Three aspects
may be noted for present purposes, namely (i) the Cross-Border Insolvency Regulations
2006, (ii) section 426 of the Insolvency Act 1986, and (iii) the general powers of the
court.

Cross-Border Insolvency Regulations 2006

The Cross-Border Insolvency Regulations 2006[57] give effect to the Model Law on Cross-   **12.31**
Border Insolvency as adopted by the United Nations Commission on International Trade
Law on 30 May 1997. The 2006 Regulations allow an English court to recognize a foreign
liquidation proceeding and to make various orders designed to assist the liquidator.
Recognition may be extended to a liquidator appointed in proceedings in the country in
which the insolvent bank has its centre of main interests[58] or in proceedings instituted in a
country in which the bank has a branch or establishment.[59]

It should, however, be appreciated that recognition can only be extended to an official   **12.32**
appointed under '… a collective judicial or administrative proceeding in a foreign State …
pursuant to a law relating to insolvency in which proceeding the assets and affairs of the
debtor are subject to control or supervision by a foreign court, for the purpose of reorganisation or liquidation …'.[60] There is, consequently, no scope to extend recognition to a
receiver of assets appointed to protect defrauded investors in a particular jurisdiction,
because the relevant laws will not relate to insolvency or to the liquidation or reorganization of the institution.[61] Subject to that, however, the English court is required to recognize
the relevant foreign proceeding if certain formal requirements are met.[62]

Once a recognition order has been made, then legal proceedings and the execution of judg-   **12.33**
ments against the debtor are stayed, although this does not prevent the enforcement of

---

[57] SI 2006/1030. The 2006 regulations are considered in the context of their application to banks, but the
regulations apply to a much wider range of entities. It should be noted that, to avoid overlap with the rules
discussed earlier in this chapter, the Cross-Border Insolvency Rules cannot be applied in relation to banks
established within the EU or which are 'third country' institutions (see paras 12.27–12.29 above) for the purposes of the EU Directive on the reorganization and winding up of credit institutions: see paras 2(j) and 2(k)
of the 2006 Regulations. Those rules can, however, be applied to banks falling outside that scope.
[58] Referred to in the 2006 Regulations as a 'foreign main proceedings': see para 7(j) of the Model Law
as reproduced and revised in Sch 1 to the 2006 Regulations. The 'centre of main interests' of a company is
presumed to be the country in which the insolvent bank has its registered office: see para 16(3) of Sch 1 to
the 2006 Regulations. The presumption can only be rebutted by factors which are both objective and ascertainable: see *Re Stanford International Bank Ltd* [2010] EWCA Civ 137 (CA), applying the decision of the
European Court of Justice in Case C-341/04 *Re Eurofoods IFSC Ltd* [2006] ECR I-3813.
[59] Referred to in the 2006 Regulations as a 'foreign non-main proceeding': see para 7(k) of the Model Law
as reproduced and revised in Sch 1 to the 2006 Regulations.
[60] See the definition of 'foreign proceeding' in para 2(i), Sch 1 to the 2006 Regulations.
[61] This consideration prevented the recognition of the US official in *Re Stanford International Bank Ltd*
[2010] EWHC Civ 137 (CA).
[62] See art 17 of the Model Law, as reproduced and revised in Sch 1 to the 2006 Regulations.

pre-existing security rights.[63] Broadly speaking, the effect of recognition would be to prevent predatory actions by unsecured creditors, thus helping to preserve the principle of *pari passu* distribution in the main liquidation.

12.34 The English court may make an order for the transfer of monies realized by an English liquidator of a local branch of the debtor to the liquidator in the foreign main proceeding, provided that the interests of English creditors will be adequately protected in those proceedings.[64]

12.35 It follows that the procedures made available through the Cross-Border Insolvency Regulations may be used to assist the liquidator of a non-EEA bank by protecting the assets of its English branch and ensuring that they are made available for distribution to the general body of creditors pursuant to the main liquidation proceedings.

Section 426 of the Insolvency Act 1986

12.36 Section 426(4) of the Insolvency Act 1986 provides that '… The courts having jurisdiction in relation to insolvency law in any part of the United Kingdom shall assist the courts having the corresponding jurisdiction in any other part of the United Kingdom or any relevant country or territory …'.[65] Where an English court receives a request for assistance from a court in a relevant jurisdiction, the English court can effectively extend the benefit of local insolvency laws to the foreign proceeding[66] although it has a discretion in this regard and, in deciding whether to accede to any particular request, it must have regard to considerations of private international law.[67]

12.37 The court may make an order under section 426 for the transfer of funds by the liquidator of the English branch to the liquidator in the main proceedings even though the law in the relevant place will not ensure a pro rata distribution to all unsecured creditors.[68] Where section 426 applies, the absence of any constraint on this point may mean that the section will be a more effective ally for the foreign liquidator.

---

[63] For the details, see arts 20–24 of the Model Law.

[64] See art 21(2) of the Model Law, as applied in *Re Swissair Schweizerische Luftverkehr-Aktiengesellschaft* [2009] BIPR 1505.

[65] A 'relevant country or territory' for these purposes includes the Channel Islands and the Isle of Man, and any other country designated for these purposes: see s 426(11). Designation orders have been made principally in relation to Commonwealth countries, and the scope of s 426 is limited accordingly.

[66] Section 426(5) of the Insolvency Act 1986. This would mean, for example, that the English court could allow for transactions to be challenged on the basis that they constituted a preference within the scope of s 239 of the Insolvency Act 1986.

[67] Thus, for example, the English court might decline assistance if the principal beneficiary of the proceedings would be a foreign revenue authority, since this would imply the enforcement of the sovereign powers of the foreign State within the United Kingdom. This would contravene the principle laid down by the House of Lords in *Government of India v Taylor* [1955] AC 491 (HL). An illustration of this rule in the context of insolvency proceedings is offered by *QRS I ApS v Frandsen* [1999] 1 WLR 269, on which see Proctor, 'Foreign Taxes in English Proceedings' (1999) 7 JIBFL 292.

[68] It seems that a requirement for equal treatment is not implicit in s 426, For the main authority on this section, see *Re HIH Casualty and General Insurance Ltd* [2008] 1 WLR 852 (HL).

General Powers of the Court

Quite apart from the statutory rules discussed above, it has been decided that an English **12.38** court has power to direct the English liquidator of a foreign company to remit assets in his hands to the liquidator of the company in its main proceedings.

However, before taking that course, it is incumbent in the English court to satisfy itself that **12.39** unsecured creditors will receive *pari passu* treatment in the main liquidation proceedings.[69] This would be a matter to be proved by expert evidence. Creditors of the English branch who wished to preserve their separate access to the assets of that branch would thus have to demonstrate that they would suffer adverse and discriminatory treatment if their claims fell to be administered as part of the main liquidation.

Conclusions

The insolvency or impending insolvency of any company will tend to precipitate a quest **12.40** for assets, with creditors seeking to secure their own individual positions so far as possible. As the run on Northern Rock in the autumn of 2007 and subsequent events in 2008 so clearly demonstrated, credit institutions are particularly vulnerable to a loss of confidence, and the difficulties are clearly exacerbated in the context of a multinational institution.

Difficulties of this kind lead to a competition among creditors which may tend to disrupt **12.41** the principle of equal treatment among creditors. The Directive thus represents a welcome attempt to bring some degree of order to situations in which chaos would otherwise prevail. Yet it is necessary to reflect and respect certain individual arrangements (eg involving security and rights of set-off), with the result that the overall scheme of the Directive is subject to a number of detailed exceptions. At least in the United Kingdom, the Directive still awaits detailed judicial consideration.

---

[69] For an example in a banking context, see *Re Bank of Credit and Commerce International SA (No 10)* [1997] Ch 213, and see also the discussion in *Re Swissair Schweizerische Luftverkehr-Aktiengesellschaft* [2009] BPIR 1505.

13

DEPOSIT PROTECTION SCHEMES

Introduction

Until 2007, it was perhaps possible to say that the outright failure of a major banking institution was, thankfully, a relatively rare occurrence. Subsequent events have, however, deprived both the United Kingdom and the rest of the world of such easy complacency. Northern Rock was not of itself generally considered to be a major financial institution, yet its failure was in many ways catastrophic for the stability (or perceived stability) of the United Kingdom's financial system and, as matters turned out, it was a harbinger of much worse events to come. The system suffered from a 'domino effect', so that problems were not confined to particular institutions but infected even the largest banks. **13.01**

Significant failures in the United Kingdom during the 1990s included the Bank of Credit and Commerce International SA[1] and Barings. Failures towards the end of the most recently completed decade have included Royal Bank of Scotland, HBOS and a clutch of other, less well-known, institutions. Ordinary depositors with such institutions will rarely have the financial expertise, the time or the inclination to examine the financial standing of their bank; at least under normal circumstances, they will assume that it is reliable. As a result, it has long been felt appropriate that provision should be made for the protection of certain classes of depositors in the event of a failure. The same principle applied to building societies, insurance companies and others within the financial markets and, as will be seen, they are all now covered by a unified compensation scheme. For present purposes, however, it is obviously appropriate to focus on the position of depositors, rather than other types of claimants. **13.02**

---

[1] Some of the legal fallout from this particular failure will be discussed in Chapter 14 below.

13.03 It has also been noted previously that EU law now has a very significant influence in the field of banking regulation. This applies equally to the specialized field of deposit protection and it will thus again be necessary to consider the European angle.

13.04 Against this brief introductory background, the present chapter will consider the following matters:

(a) EU law requirements in the field of deposit protection;
(b) the implementation of those requirements in the United Kingdom by means of the Financial Services Compensation Scheme;
(c) the revisions to the powers and role of that scheme made pursuant to Part 4 of the Banking Act 2009; and
(d) the legal aspects of the recent diplomatic rift between the United Kingdom and Iceland, following from deposit protection arrangements applicable to the UK branch of an Icelandic bank.

EU Law and Deposit Protection

13.05 EU law in this field is primarily governed by a 1994 Directive on deposit-guarantee schemes.[2] It is necessary briefly to examine the terms of this Directive, in part because the protection of depositors is not its sole objective. The following points may be noted in this regard:

(a) The Directive recognizes the importance of deposit-guarantee schemes in general terms, and provides that such schemes should be funded by the banking industry itself, apparently on the basis that the failure of one institution may lead to a run on other banks which are otherwise sound.[3] It thus requires Member States to ensure that deposit-protection schemes are introduced and officially recognized within their respective territories,[4] but specifically prohibits schemes which consist of a guarantee given by a Member State or one of its regional authorities.[5] The nature and scope of the required schemes was, however, significantly influenced by other developments in European law.

(b) In particular, whilst the desire to protect depositors lies at the heart of the Directive, that was by no means its 'stand alone' objective. Rather, there was a desire to promote cross-border banking business within the Community, and the existence of deposit protection arrangements was in many ways simply one of the features which was necessary to further the larger objective. This impression is reinforced by the fact that the

---

[2] Directive 94/19/EC of the European Parliament and the Council of 30 May 1994 on deposit-guarantee schemes OJ L 135, 31/05/94, p 5. The Directive includes various detailed, transitional provisions which are now 'spent', and will thus not be discussed.
[3] See para 4 of the preamble to the Directive. The validity of this particular assumption has been amply justified by the current financial crisis.
[4] Article 3 of the Directive.
[5] Article 3(1) of the Directive. In practice, the current crisis has forced many EU Governments to provide ad hoc guarantees for a number of institutions (see the discussion of the UK guarantees in relation to Northern Rock (at para 11.08 above) and Landsbanki (at para 13.13 below). However, these emergency arrangements have not displaced the operation of the established guarantee schemes.

Directive was made in reliance on the 'single market' provisions now contained in Article 57 of the EC Treaty.[6]

(c) The Second Banking Directive had already introduced the principle of 'home State supervision' within the Community.[7] A British institution was supervised by the authorities in the United Kingdom. Regulators in other parts of the Community were responsible for issues such as conduct of business and the monitoring of liquidity.[8] As a result, it was appropriate that the scope of the deposit-protection scheme should mirror this situation, and the scheme established in the home State should thus cover deposits placed with other branches of the same institution in other Community countries.[9]

(d) Whilst the promotion of cross-border banking services within the Community suggested that deposit protection should apply to all deposits placed with banks within the Community, it was felt that guarantee schemes should be essentially uniform. They should not be used as an 'instrument of competition', such that banks supervised in a Member State offering a higher level of cover could thereby attract deposits away from institutions established in other Member States. This, it was felt, could lead to 'market disturbances' which could be harmful.[10]

(e) Moving to a greater level of detail, the Directive sets out the terms on which a deposit-protection scheme is to be operated and the rights which must be conferred on depositors.[11] Since these provisions are reflected in the United Kingdom scheme, they will be considered below. Before leaving the European aspect, however, it may be noted that the Landesgericht (Regional Court) at Bonn has held that the Directive entailed the grant of rights to individuals,[12] that a failure to transpose the Directive into national law constituted a serious breach of Community law, and that there was a direct causal link between Germany's failure to implement the Directive and losses suffered by depositors on the failure of a local bank.[13] Consequently, a depositor who suffered loss as a result of non-implementation could recover from the State by way of damages an

---

[6] It may be noted in passing that the validity of the Directive was challenged by Germany on the grounds that Art 57 did not offer a sufficient Treaty basis for it, but this argument was rejected by the European Court of Justice: see Case C-233/94, *Germany v European Parliament and EU Council* [1997] ECR 1-2405.

[7] This principle is now to be found in the Recast Consolidation Directive and has been discussed in general terms at paras 2.13–2.22 above.

[8] On the responsibilities of the 'host State regulator' in relation to liquidity, see para 6.60 above.

[9] On this requirement, see Art 4(1) of the Directive.

[10] On these points, see para 14 of the preamble to the Directive.

[11] It may be noted that, where a bank established outside the Community has a branch within a Member State, it is incumbent upon that Member State to ensure that the branch falls within the scope of a deposit protection scheme equivalent to that contemplated by the Directive. Otherwise, it must require that branch to join the local scheme: Art 6(1) of the Directive.

[12] This point is apparent from Art 7(6) of the Directive, which requires Member States to '… ensure that the depositors' rights to compensation may be the subject of an action by the depositor against the deposit-guarantee scheme …'.

[13] These three conditions must be met for a Member State to incur liability to individuals for failure to implement a Directive. For some of the leading cases on this subject, see cases C-6/90 and C-9/90, *Francovich & Bonifaci v Italy* [1991] ECR I-5357, as explained in later cases including Joined Cases C-46/93 and 46/93, *Brasserie du Pecheur SA v Federal Republic of Germany; R v Secretary of State for Transport, ex p Factortame Ltd* [1996] I-1029 and Joined Cases C-178/94, C-179/94 and C-188/94 to C-190/94, *Dillenkofer and others v Federal Republic of Germany* [1996] ECR I-4845.

amount equal to the minimum amount which he would otherwise have received in accordance with the terms of the required scheme.[14] The adequacy of a particular deposit-guarantee scheme must therefore always be judged against the terms of the Directive.

13.06　As with so many of the other limbs of financial regulation, however, the Directive was found to be inadequate in the face of the unprecedented storms which battered the financial markets in 2008. This led to an amending Directive in March 2009.[15] As the 2009 Directive notes, the 1994 Directive '... already provides for basic coverage for depositors. However, the ongoing financial turmoil necessitates an improvement to that coverage ...'.[16] In addition, the 2009 Directive noted that both the extended payout period and the 90 per cent limitation on deposit coverage had been found to be counter-productive, in that they had undermined public confidence in the financial system.[17] For essentially similar reasons, the €20,000 minimum limit on deposit-guarantee schemes was inadequate to cover a significant proportion of bank deposits across the Community.[18]

13.07　Against that background, the main changes introduced by the 2009 Directive included the following:

(a) Member States are required to ensure that the coverage for the aggregate deposits of each depositor is at least €50,000;[19]

(b) the minimum cover is required to be increased to €100,000 by 31 December 2010, and the minimum levels may now be increased in line with the level of inflation across the EU;[20] and

(c) verified claims are required to be paid within 20 working days of a court order or regulatory decision as to the insolvency of the institution concerned.[21]

13.08　In other words, the 2009 Directive recognizes that a guarantee scheme must cover 100 per cent of significant deposits and assure rapid payout. A robust and effective scheme of this kind will help to reassure ordinary depositors and, hence, reduce the danger of the type of 'run' which occurred in relation to Northern Rock.

---

[14] The decision of the Landesgericht in this respect is recorded in the decision of the European Court of Justice in Case C-222/02 *Peter Paul and others v Bundesrepublik Deutschland* [2004] ECR I-9425, although the German Government had not asked the Court of Justice to review that particular aspect of the decision.

[15] Directive 2009/14/EC of the European Parliament and of the Council amending Directive 94/19/EC on deposit-guarantee schemes as regards the coverage level and the payout delay, OJ L 68, 13.3.2009, p 3 (hereafter 'the 2009 Directive').

[16] Recital (2) to the 2009 Directive.

[17] See recitals (10) and (15) to the 2009 Directive.

[18] See recital (3) to the 2009 Directive.

[19] Article 3 of the 2009 Directive, amending Art 7(1) of the 1994 Directive. Member States outside the eurozone are required by that provision to apply the national currency equivalent figure.

[20] See the provision referred to in the previous footnote.

[21] Article 6 of the 2009 Directive, amending Art 10 of the 1994 Directive.

The Financial Services Compensation Scheme

At present, the United Kingdom's obligations under the Directive are implemented by means of Part 15 of the Financial Services and Markets Act 2000.[22] **13.09**

The core elements of the scheme may be briefly described, as follows: **13.10**

(a) The Financial Services Authority is required to establish a Financial Services Compensation Scheme to compensate depositors with authorized institutions which arc unable, or likely to be unable, to satisfy claims for the repayment of deposits. The scheme must provide for the assessment and payment of any claims made against the scheme, and for the raising of levies from authorized institutions to meet the cost of paying compensation.[23]

(b) The scheme is to be administered by a scheme manager which is required to be constituted, and to act, independently of the FSA itself.[24] The scheme manager is the Financial Services Compensation Scheme Limited (FSCS). The FSCS is required to administer the scheme in accordance with the rules set out in the FSA's COMP Sourcebook and in a manner which is procedurally fair and in compliance with the terms of the European Convention on Human Rights.[25] It is required to pay compensation to an eligible depositor with a credit institution which is unable to meet its obligations, and to fund that activity by making a levy on institutions within the scheme.[26]

(c) The scheme generally applies to UK authorized deposit-taking institutions. EEA banks are largely excluded from the scheme because the 1994 Directive requires that deposits accepted by them in other EEA States should be covered by their home State scheme.[27]

(d) The 'trigger point' for the payment of compensation under the scheme is the making of a court order which suspends the payment of protected claims by that institution[28] or a regulatory determination by the FSA that the bank is unable, or is likely to become unable, to meet protected claims against it.[29] At that point, an eligible claimant can apply to the FSCS for compensation.

(e) The FSA Handbook allows the FSCS to make payment to an 'eligible claimant'. That expression is defined in a negative way, in the sense that a long list of *excluded* claimants

---

[22] They were originally implemented by the Credit Institutions (Protection of Depositors) Regulations 1995 (SI 1995/442), which were made pursuant to s 2(2) of the European Communities Act 1972. Subject only to minor reservations, these Regulations have now been repealed. For recent additions to Part 15, see the discussion of Part 4 of the Banking Act 2009, at paras 13.11–13.12 below.
[23] FSMA, s 213.
[24] FSMA, s 212.
[25] FSA Handbook, COMP 2.2.1R.
[26] FSA Handbook, COMP 2.2.2G. The FSA Handbook (FEES 6) includes detailed provisions on the calculation of the levies to be made by the FSCS for these purposes.
[27] For an exception to this rule, see the discussion of the 'top up' scheme, below.
[28] 'Protected claims' are those which fall within the scope of the scheme.
[29] In other words, the institution has been found to be 'in default' for the purposes of COMP 6.3.1R–6.3.3R.

is provided.[30] The net effect is that only retail customers and small businesses are eligible for the protection offered by the scheme.

(f) As noted earlier, a deposit claim against an incoming EEA institution is not covered by the UK scheme unless that entity has 'top up' cover. As the name implies, this allows a credit institution from another EEA State to enhance the deposit protection cover applicable to deposits accepted in the *United Kingdom*. If the cover which is provided by the institution's home State scheme is less than that provided by the UK scheme, then the EEA institution may participate in the FSCS to cover the differential.[31] In such a case, the home State compensation scheme should pay out up to its limit, with the FSCS being liable for the excess over that limit up to the maximum level of the FSCS compensation.[32] That, at least, was the position in theory. As noted elsewhere, Landsbanki was an EEA authorized institution which was backed by Iceland's deposit-protection scheme and had participated in the 'top up' arrangements just described. However, the apparent inability of Iceland's deposit protection fund to meet the initial payment led to a significant diplomatic rift between the United Kingdom and Iceland.[33]

(g) The FSCS generally has a period of up to three months to determine a compensation claim made to it.[34] However, where the claim relates to a protected deposit, the FSCS will have to pay the necessary compensation to the depositors within 20 working days of the date on which it has been calculated.[35]

(h) The maximum amount payable by the FSCS in respect of any individual claim is £50,000 or €50,000, whichever is greater as at the date of default or the due date of the deposit.[36]

(i) Where the scheme manager has made a payment to a depositor, it acquires a right of reimbursement from the defaulting institution, thus effectively 'stepping into the shoes' of the disappointed depositor.[37]

---

[30] The excluded list comprises governments, local authorities, international organizations, other financial institutions, and directors or managers of the entity in default: see COMP 4.2.2R.

[31] See FSA Handbook, COMP 14.1. The statutory authority for those arrangements is provided by FSMA, ss 213(10) and 214(5) and the Financial Services and Markets Act 2000 (Compensation Scheme: Electing Participants) Regulations, 2001 (SI 2001/1783).

[32] FSA Handbook, COMP 14.1.6 (G). On the financial limit for the FSCS arrangements, see para (h) below.

[33] This incident is described at para 13.14 below.

[34] FSA Handbook, COMP 9.2.1R.

[35] This requirement will come into effect on 31 December 2010: see para 2.2.10R of the Compensation Sourcebook (Deposit Guarantee Schemes Amendment Directive) Instrument 2009 (FSA 2009/29) giving effect to the revised Art 10(1) of the Deposit Guarantee Directive: see para 13.07 above.

[36] COMP 10.2.3R. As noted earlier, the amended 1994 Directive requires a minimum cover of €50,000 and this provision ensures that the United Kingdom is not placed in breach of this obligation as a result of exchange movements.

[37] FSMA, s 215 read together with the rules made thereunder in the FSA Handbook. In particular, COMP 7.2 requires the scheme manager to insist on an assignment of the depositor's claims as a condition of paying compensation. It may be noted that documentation difficulties in this area gave rise to the well-known decision on contractual interpretation in *Investors' Compensation Scheme v West Bromwich Building Society* [1998] 1 All ER 98 (HL) which, however, ultimately upheld the validity of the assignment. The right of subrogation is consistent with Art 11 of the Deposit Guarantee Directive.

(j) The scheme only covers claims made by 'depositors', that is to say, by the customers who originally placed the deposits in question. It is thus not possible to 'enlarge' the claim to compensation by assigning interests in a large deposit to a number of different people, with the intention that they should each lodge a separate claim against the scheme.[38]

(k) Finally, it should be noted that the scheme is not merely a discretionary arrangement which pays out on proof of hardship or other subjective criteria. An individual who proves that he satisfies the criteria for compensation has a legally enforceable right to that payment, regardless of his other personal circumstances.[39]

Part 4 of the Banking Act 2009

It will be apparent from some of the discussion elsewhere in this text that the FSCS has **13.11** played a very significant role in seeking to restore some semblance of stability to the financial markets in the turbulent conditions of 2008 and its immediate aftermath.

Part 4 of the Banking Act 2009 contains various provisions designed to sharpen both the **13.12** powers and the responsibilities of the FSCS in the light of the experience gained during that period. For the most part, the detailed provisions of Part 4 of the 2009 Act operate by way of amendments to Part 15 of the FSMA, which has already been discussed, and provides for further secondary legislation to be made by the Treasury. Not all of that legislation is available at the time of writing but the following salient points may be noted in relation to Part 4:

(a) regulations may allow the FSCS to make levies for contingency funding;[40]

(b) it is confirmed that the Treasury may require the FSCS to make payments to depositors where a stabilization power has been exercised in relation to the relevant credit institution, and that such payments shall be treated as made pursuant to the scheme;[41] and

(c) rules may be made allowing the FSCS to treat an eligible claimant as having lodged a claim, even though he may not yet have done so.[42]

---

[38] This is the effect of the House of Lords decision in *Deposit Protection Board v Dalia and another* [1994] 2 All ER 577 (HL).

[39] The right to compensation must be legally enforceable in order to comply with Arts 7(6) and 13 of the Deposit-Guarantee Directive. In the United Kingdom, decisions of the FSCS are accordingly subject to judicial review: see *R (on the application of Geologistics Ltd) v Financial Services Compensation Scheme* [2003] EWCA Civ 1905.

[40] Section 170 of the 2009 Act, inserting a new s 214A of the FSMA.

[41] ie and may thus be recovered from participating institutions by means of levies: see s 171 of the 2009 Act, inserting a new s 214B of the FSMA. Detailed rules under this section were made at short notice to enable the Treasury to deal with the position of the Dunfermline Building Society: see the Financial Services and Markets Act 2000 (Contribution to Costs of Special Resolution Regime) Regulations 2009 (SI 2009/807). However, the Treasury subsequently consulted on the content of the Regulations: see HM Treasury: 'Special Resolution Regime: the FSMA (Contribution to Costs of Special Resolution Regime) Regulations 2009', July, 2009.

[42] Section 174 of the 2009 Act, adding further provisions into s 214 of the FSMA. This apparently odd provision allows the FSCS to arrange an urgent transfer of deposit obligations to a third party bank even before depositors have had time (or much time) to react to the situation, thus helping to preserve confidence in the financial system: see, for example, the 2008 transfer orders referred to at para 11.10 above.

The object of these provisions is clearly to enable the FSCS to play a greater and more urgent role in the context of any future crisis.

The Landsbanki Freezing Arrangements

The Background

13.13 The importance of a robust and effective deposit-protection scheme has been clearly highlighted by the prevailing financial crisis. But the insolvency of the major Icelandic banks in 2008 elevated their importance to the international plane, and caused a significant diplomatic crisis between Iceland and the United Kingdom. This episode has already been noted both in relation to the recognition of foreign bank mergers and in relation to the EU Directive on the reorganization and winding up of credit institutions.[43] However, since that incident arose directly in the context of deposit guarantee arrangements, it is appropriate to examine the issue in slightly more depth at this juncture.

13.14 The essential background was as follows:

(a) partly as a result of the collapse of Lehman Brothers in September 2008,[44] the three major Icelandic banks found themselves in serious financial difficulty;

(b) in response to these problems, the Icelandic authorities promulgated and passed on 6 October 2008 an Act on the Authority for Treasury Disbursements under Unusual Financial Circumstances;[45]

(c) on the following day, the Icelandic Financial Supervisory Authority (referred to as the 'FME') took control of Landsbanki Islands hf by appointing a receivership (or resolution) committee under the terms of the Emergency Act;

(d) on that day, the FME announced that all *domestic* deposits of Landsbanki were fully guaranteed by the Icelandic Government. However, no mention was made of the fate of depositors with the UK branch of Landsbanki, which had offered an internet deposit product called 'Icesave'. Some £4.5 billion of deposits were outstanding at the UK branch at the time of the failure;[46]

(e) by virtue of the deposit protection arrangements described earlier,[47] Icesave deposits with the UK branch of Landsbanki were covered up to €20,887 by the Icelandic deposit insurance scheme as created in accordance with the EU Directive on deposit-guarantee schemes. However, Landsbanki had opted into the 'top up' cover provided

---

[43] See, respectively, the discussions at paras 10.15 and 12.13 above.
[44] For a discussion of this and other aspects of the Icelandic banking collapse, see House of Commons Treasury Committee, 'Banking Crisis: The impact of the failure of the Icelandic banks' (4 April 2009).
[45] Act No 125/2008, hereafter the 'Emergency Act'.
[46] See the Treasury Committee Report at n 44 above, para 35. On the same day, the FSA determined that Heritable Bank—Landsbanki subsidiary—no longer had the financial resources to meet its obligations. However, Heritable Bank was incorporated in the United Kingdom, was supervised by the FSA and fell squarely within the terms of the UK's own FSCS. On the action taken with respect to Heritable Bank, see para 11.10 above. In contrast, Landsbanki itself operated in the UK as a branch of the Icelandic bank itself, with the consequences described below in terms of its deposit protection position.
[47] See para 13.05 above.

by the FSCS, which meant that the UK scheme was liable for an excess amount to bring the total recovery in respect of each insured deposit up to £50,000;

(f) however, on 8 October, the Icelandic finance minister apparently intimated to the Chancellor of the Exchequer that Iceland '… have no intention of honouring their obligations …' to UK depositors with Landsbanki and, according to the Chancellor, the Icelandic deposit protection scheme was bereft of cash;[48]

(g) given the exceptional circumstances of the time, the Chancellor of the Exchequer announced that he would guarantee retail deposits with Icesave;[49]

(h) in view of this guarantee, and presumably in order to maximize the potential recovery of the Treasury's outlay from the UK assets of Landsbanki, steps were taken to freeze those assets pending further developments and greater clarity of the intentions of the Icelandic Government in relation to this matter;

(i) unfortunately, the crisis was exacerbated by the enabling legislation used as a basis for the freeze, namely, the Anti-Terrorism, Crime and Security Act 2001 (the 2001 Act), which allows the Treasury to make an asset freezing order if it reasonably believes that '… action to the detriment of the United Kingdom's economy (or part of it) has been or is likely to be taken by a person or persons …', and the relevant person is '… the government of a country or territory outside the United Kingdom …'. In this context, the '… action to the detriment of the United Kingdom's economy (or part of it) …' was presumably the alleged intention of the Icelandic Government not to honour the deposit guarantee obligations to UK depositors in Icesave and/or the proposal to transfer the assets and domestic deposit obligations of 'Old Landsbanki' to a 'New Landsbanki', whilst leaving the liabilities to UK depositors in the old entity;[50]

(j) a freezing order made under the 2001 Act is '… an order which prohibits persons from making funds available to or for the benefit of a person or persons specified in the Order …';[51]

(k) the Landsbanki Freezing Order 2008[52] came into force on 8 October 2008 and froze both funds held by Landsbanki itself and funds held on its behalf by its receivership

---

[48] On this episode, see the Treasury Committee Report at n 44 above, para 38. It should be appreciated that the precise train of events and the inferences to be drawn form the situation are matters of some controversy: see para 45 of the Report.

[49] HC Deb, 8 October 2008, col 279.

[50] See para 12.13 above.

[51] See Anti-Terrorism, Crime and Security Act 2001, s 5. The provisions of the 2001 Act and their use by the government were perhaps more directed to the 'security', rather than the 'anti-terrorism' aspects of the 2001 Act. Nevertheless, the use of legislation with this title caused offence within Iceland, and the Treasury Committee Report (n 43 above) suggested that it might be better to put in place separate pieces of legislation to deal with the distinct types of situation: see para 51 of the Report.

[52] SI 2008/2688. The order was amended on 21 October 2008: see the Landsbanki Freezing (Amendment) Order 2008 (SI 2008/2766) and, following settlement discussions between the two governments, was revoked on 15 June 2009: see the Landsbanki Freezing (Revocation) order 2009 (SI 2009/1392). In the meantime, a series of General Licences were issued between 9 October 2008 and 11 February 2009 which were designed to allow the London branch to continue its commercial lending business with UK customers, on the basis that the UK assets were 'ring fenced' from the rest of the bank. Freezing orders of this type can cause a number of detailed but serious practical problems for banks. For a useful discussion of these issues, see Financial Markets Law Panel, 'Issue 141: Landsbanki Freezing Order 2008' (May 2009).

Chapter 13. Deposit Protection Schemes

committee, the Government of Iceland, the Central Bank of Iceland, and the FME.[53] In view of the inevitable territorial limitation of the Order, an offence under it could only be committed by a person in the United Kingdom, or by a British citizen, or a UK company (whether acting within or outside the United Kingdom).

13.15 Against this admittedly truncated version of the facts, it is possible to consider some of the legal questions arising from the action taken both by Iceland and the United Kingdom and, indeed, some of the wider issues which arise from this episode.

The Legal Issues—Action taken by Iceland

13.16 It is necessary at the outset to consider the extent of Iceland's responsibility and legal liability for the various steps noted above. In essence, there appear to be two main lines of argument to the effect that Iceland has a liability in respect of the failure of its deposit protection scheme. The first relates to a liability under the 1994 Directive itself, whilst the second concerns the wider Community law principle of non-discrimination. These may be considered in turn.

13.17 The following points may be noted in relation to the 1994 Directive:

(a) The UK (and other, non-Icelandic) depositors should in principle be able to claim their minimum compensation from the Icelandic deposit guarantee fund. However, as is well known, that fund lacks the necessary resources to meet these claims. Where do the depositors go from there? Specifically, is there a route or means by which a legal claim against the Icelandic Government itself can be established?

(b) The Government of Iceland was responsible for the implementation of the 1994 Directive under its national law. In accordance with well-established principles of Community law, Iceland could incur a liability to compensate depositors if the 1994 Directive was intended to confer rights upon them, the Icelandic Government had been guilty of a serious breach of Community law in failing to implement the Directive and the losses suffered by the depositors are directly traceable to that failure. It seems clear from the decision in *Peter Paul and others v Bundesrepublik Deutschland* that a depositor who, following a bank collapse, has no claim on a compensation scheme due to non-implementation—or inadequate implementation—of the 1994 Directive will be able to satisfy these tests quite easily.[54] In the *Peter Paul* case, however, it does not seem seriously to have been disputed that Germany had failed to implement the 1994 Directive. In contrast, Iceland had taken steps to comply with its obligations under the

---

[53] See art 4 of the Order. Although the Icelandic authorities were only affected by the Order insofar as they held funds for Landsbanki, the very fact that they were named in the Order at all plainly added fuel to the diplomatic fire.

[54] See the discussion of the decision of the Court of Justice in this case and the leading authorities on Member State liability for non-implementation of directives set out in para 13.05 above. Given that Iceland is an EEA (rather than an EC) Member State, it may be appropriate to add that the Community law principles on State liability have been applied equally in the context of the EEA Agreement itself: see Case E-4/01 *Karlsson* [2002] EFTA Ct Rep 240 (see in particular paras 25 and 37–48 of the judgment), as more recently reflected in a case involving the implementation of a directive relating to compulsory insurance for motor vehicles: see Case E-8/07 *Nguyen v Norway* (20 June 2008).

274

directive through the passage of Act 98/1999 on the Deposit Guarantees and Investor Compensation Scheme, and the creation of a fund bearing the same name.

(c) Article 6 of the 1998 Act[55] required that the deposit department of the fund should hold one per cent of the average amount of the guaranteed deposits held by commercial banks over the preceding year. In addition, commercial banks were required to make further payments to the fund as necessary, but such demands for contributions could not exceed ten per cent of the total assets of the fund. Furthermore, if the assets of the fund were insufficient to meet its liabilities, then article 10 of the law allowed it to take out a loan for that purpose '… if it sees compelling reasons to do so …'. It may thus be argued that the 1999 Act fails to achieve the result dictated by the Directive—namely, that depositors must be legally and unconditionally guaranteed the minimum refund of up to €20,000. To that extent, it may be said that Iceland has failed to implement a scheme which is compliant with the 1994 Directive and that it should accordingly be liable to Icesave depositors to that extent.

(d) On the other hand, it could be said that the statutory provision dealing with the possible insolvency of the scheme is simply a recognition of reality. In this context, it must be borne in mind that the 1994 Directive contemplates that guarantee schemes will be funded by the banking industry[56] and, furthermore, that the provisions of the Directive '… may not result in the Member States or their competent authorities being made liable in respect of depositors if they have ensured that one or more schemes guaranteeing deposits or credit institutions themselves and ensuring the compensation or protection of depositors under the conditions prescribed in this Directive have been introduced and officially recognised …'. This may be read as suggesting that the responsibility of a Member State is at an end once it has implemented a compliant scheme and that, having done so, it is not required to 'back-stop' the scheme with government funds. In other words, there is no implied sovereign guarantee of such funds. Nevertheless, the question remains whether the introduction of a scheme which may not have had sufficient capacity to call for contributions can be said to comply with the requirements of the 1994 Directive.

13.18 The second line of complaint rests on the argument that the Icelandic reorganization of Landsbanki has placed depositors with Icelandic branches in a better position than depositors with other EEA offices of the bank. In this context:

(a) it is argued that the reorganization discriminates on the grounds of nationality;

(b) Article 4 of the EEA Agreement[57] provides that '… within the scope of application of this Agreement … any discrimination on grounds of nationality shall be prohibited …'.

(c) In relation to the first test, this would appear to be met because the dispute plainly falls '… within the scope of application of [the EEA] Agreement because the obligation to provide a deposit protection scheme to encompass both Icelandic and EEA

---

[55] The writer has, of course, relied on an English translation.

[56] Recital (23) to the Directive records that '… the cost of financing such schemes must be borne in principle by credit institutions themselves …'.

[57] The provision replicates Art 12 of the EC Treaty.

depositors arises directly from the exercise by Landsbanki of its rights on the freedom of establishment and the provision of services.[58]

(d) As to the second test, the case law of the Court of Justice establishes that discrimination between nationals of different EEA Member States can be justified only if it is based on objective considerations which are independent of the nationality of the individuals concerned and the extent of any discrimination is proportionate to the stated objective.[59]

(e) Although the arguments may no doubt develop, it is not easy to see an objective basis for the preferential treatment of depositors with branches within Iceland[60] in the face of a requirement for a deposit protection scheme which is intended to cover depositors on an EEA-wide basis.

The Legal Issues—Action taken by the United Kingdom

13.19 It is necessary now to consider some of the legal and technical issues arising from the action taken by the Treasury in relation to Landsbanki and the Icelandic Government. These questions are no mere matters of theory, for the Icelandic Government originally agreed to support possible legal action against the UK authorities.[61] However, it appears that the Icelandic Government received advice to the effect that there was '… scant possibility that the Icelandic Government would have the [Landsbanki] Freezing Order invalidated by a UK court …' and that '… there was no probability of the Icelandic State being awarded compensation by a UK court as a result of the Freezing Order …'. Partly because of this, and perhaps partly because a settlement was being negotiated, the threat of this type of legal proceeding receded, although apparently a challenge before the European Court of Human Rights remains in prospect.[62] It is no doubt true that section 4 of the 2001 Act (as reproduced above) gives a breadth of authority to the government which the English courts would be reluctant to investigate, although it should be noted that the section requires the government to have a 'reasonable belief' that the action of the other person is detrimental to the economy of the United Kingdom before it can make a freezing order, and this might form an admittedly very slim basis for a challenge.[63] However, without wishing to go into excessive detail or to attempt to express a concluded view on an admittedly complex area where, in any event, not all of the relevant information may yet be in the public domain, it may be worth considering whether the matter could be examined from different angles and from an international law perspective.

---

[58] The EEA Agreement contains provisions on the right of establishment (Arts 31–35) and the freedom to provide services (Arts 36–39) which convey the same substance as the corresponding provisions in the EC Treaty itself.

[59] On this point, see Case C-148/02 *Garcia Avello v Belgium* [2003] ECR I-1613.

[60] And, in the nature of things, the vast majority of such customers will be of Icelandic nationality.

[61] See the Treasury Committee Report (n 44 above), para 46.

[62] See 'Statement from the Icelandic Government concerning Legal Proceedings against UK Authorities' (Prime Minister's Office, 1 June 2009). The prospect of the anticipated settlement has subsequently also receded (see para 13.22 below), and the legal issues may therefore nevertheless remain extant.

[63] On formulations of this kind, see the well-known dissenting speech of Lord Atkin in *Liversidge v Anderson* [1942] AC 206 (HL), later approved in cases such as *IRC v Rossminster Ltd* [1980] AC 452 (HL). However, the present section will not attempt a detailed, administrative law analysis.

The following points may be made in this context: **13.20**

(a) as noted above, it appears that the Landsbanki Freezing Order was made on the basis that the Icelandic Government had intimated that it could not fulfil the obligations which it owed to the United Kingdom in respect of the deposit-guarantee scheme arrangements;[64]

(b) it would therefore seem that the Order was intended as a countermeasure against Iceland's alleged repudiation of its obligations to the United Kingdom under the Agreement on the European Economic Area ('EEA Agreement'), from which the EU deposit protection directive derives its force as between the UK and Iceland;[65]

(c) the starting point must be that the decision by the United Kingdom to freeze the assets of Landsbanki—including any of its assets in the hands of the Icelandic Government or its authorities—was itself a breach of the EEA Agreement, in the sense that it interfered with the exercise of Landsbanki's right of establishment in the United Kingdom under Articles 31–35 of the EEA Treaty and, in a broader sense, inhibited Landsbanki in the exercise of its 'passport' rights under the rules discussed at an earlier stage;[66]

(d) in general terms, a countermeasure is an action which would of itself normally be a breach of an international obligation to another State, but which is effectively excused because it is a justifiable response to a breach of an international obligation committed by the target State itself.[67] In essence, a countermeasure will only be justified if (i) it is taken in response to a previous international wrong by the target State, (ii) the State imposing the countermeasures must have called on the target State to desist or to make reparation for the wrong, (iii) the purpose of the countermeasures must be to secure compliance (ie and not to escalate tensions), and (iv) the countermeasures must be proportionate to the original wrong.[68] In principle, it could be argued that these tests had been met in the context of the Landsbanki Freezing Order. In particular, it could not be said that the measure was disproportionate, since it only targeted assets of the UK branch of Landsbanki and did not seek to impede assets beneficially owned by the Government of Iceland or any of its authorities;

---

[64] See the discussion at para 13.14 above. It is proposed to proceed on the basis stated in the text, even though the background seems to be disputed. If it is argued that the Order was designed to prevent the reorganization of Landsbanki into 'Old' and 'New' entities as discussed earlier—or at least to mitigate the impact of that reorganization for UK depositors—then it is probably fair to say that this would not provide an adequate legal basis because the United Kingdom had a treaty obligation to recognize and give effect to Iceland's steps for the reorganization of Landsbanki: see the discussion of the EU Directive on reorganization and winding up of credit institutions in Chapter 12 above and, in particular, the comments in paras 12.12–12.13.

[65] The EU Directive was incorporated into the EEA Agreement by a Decision of the European Economic Area Joint Committee no 18/94, amending Annex IX (Financial Services) to the EEA Agreement OJ L 325, 17.12.94, p 70 and became binding on Iceland accordingly.

[66] See the discussion at paras 2.13–2.22 above. The United Kingdom (acting through the FSA) had various reserve powers in its role as the host State, and it may be argued that the proper course was for it to exercise those powers, rather than to have resort to a freezing order.

[67] On countermeasures generally, see Crawford, *The International Law Commission's Articles on State Responsibility: Introduction, Text and Commentaries* (Cambridge University Press, 2002), articles 49–54 and associated discussion.

[68] See the materials cited in the preceding footnote and the decision of the International Court of Justice in *Gabcikovo-Nagymaros Project* ICJ Rep 1997, p 7.

(e) nevertheless, it is open to States to renounce the right to take countermeasures in favour of some other form of dispute resolution. They are often found to have done so, especially in the context of multilateral treaties and, in such a case, the imposition of countermeasures would clearly amount to a breach of an international obligation on the part of the State which imposes them. This has been found to be the case in the context of the EC Treaty, where the Court of Justice has held on a number of occasions that the imposition of such measures is inconsistent with Community law;[69]

(f) although the EEA Agreement differs in a number of respects from the EC Treaty, it may be possible to draw the same inferences, because the EEA Agreement includes its own surveillance and dispute resolution procedures which may exclude the possibility of unilateral countermeasures;[70]

(g) separately, it was noted above that a referral to the European Court of Human rights was in contemplation.[71] Presumably, any challenge to the Landsbanki Freezing Order would have to be based on Article I of the First Protocol to the European Convention on Human Rights, which guarantees to natural and legal persons '... the peaceful enjoyment of his possessions. No one shall be deprived of his possessions except in the public interest and subject to the conditions provided for by law and by the general principles of international law ...'. Again, without seeking to express a concluded view, various issues would arise from this formulation. First of all, it is not entirely clear whether the freeze over UK assets of Landsbanki amounted to a 'deprivation' for these purposes, since it was always assumed that those assets would be applied in repaying pre-existing obligations of the London branch. Secondly, for the reasons given above, it is not clear that the measures were imposed in a manner consistent with general principles of international law. Thirdly, however, it must be noted that the second paragraph of Article 1 of the First Protocol allows a State '... to enforce such laws as it deems necessary to control the use of property in accordance with the general interest ...'. Given that the assets of Landsbanki were frozen (rather than expropriated) pending clarification of Iceland's intentions in relation to the deposit-guarantee scheme and that the freeze was designed for the protection of UK creditors, it may be that the arrangements could be justified under the 'general interest' heading.

13.21 Although it is impossible to express a firm view on the above matters, the episode does demonstrate that the EU's deposit guarantee arrangements were not only inadequate to ensure the objective of a rapid payout to qualifying depositors, but they also provided fertile ground for an inter-State diplomatic dispute.

---

[69] 'A Member State may not unilaterally adopt, on its own authority, corrective or protective measures designed to obviate any breach by another Member State of rules of Community law': see Case C-5/94, *R v Ministry of Agriculture, Fisheries and Food, ex parte Hedley Lomas (Ireland) Ltd* [1996] ECR I-2553 at para 20, citing Joined cases 90/63 and 91/63, *Commission v Luxembourg and Belgium* [1964] ECR 625 and Case C 232/78, *Commission v France* [1979] ECR 2729.

[70] See Arts 108–111 of the EEA Agreement. It is true that Arts 112–114 of the Agreement provide for 'Safeguard Measures', but these are referable to broader economic circumstances and not to a breach of the Agreement by one of the parties.

[71] See para 13.19 above.

The Current Position

It should be noted that the above discussion rests purely on Iceland's responsibilities for the minimum cover required under the 1994 Directive and associated materials.[72] However, in order to put matters into context, it is appropriate to note a few developments which have occurred outside the narrow scope of that legislation. First of all, it is understood that the Icelandic Government originally intimated[73] that it would '... support the Depositors' and Investors' Guarantee Fund in raising the necessary funds, so that the Fund would be able to meet the minimum compensation limits in the event of a failure of Landsbanki and its UK branch ...', but it is not proposed to express a view on the legal consequences of that assurance. In addition, in December 2009, the Icelandic legislature approved a new law which treated the payments made to Icesave depositors as a loan from the UK Government, and set out an agreed repayment schedule.[74] However, in the face of public protests, the President refused to sign the legislation and, in compliance with the terms of the national constitution, the proposal was submitted to a national referendum. The nation voted against the plan in March 2010, and the issue is accordingly unresolved at the time of writing.

13.22

The Wider Issues

Quite apart from the diplomatic rift to which reference has just been made, the difficulties encountered by Iceland have highlighted various issues which go to the heart of the deposit protection arrangements contemplated by the EC Directive on this subject. It is quite probably the case that a large number of UK individuals who placed funds with Icesave either had not realized that they were relying on Iceland's deposit protection arrangements or, if they did, that they did not understand the implications of that situation. The difficulties which arose as between the United Kingdom and Iceland might well have been avoided (or at least, been mitigated) if the UK operations of Landsbanki had been required to be a full participant in the UK's Financial Services Compensation Scheme. This would have reinforced both the position of UK depositors and confidence in the UK's financial system generally.[75]

13.23

---

[72] It should be said that UK local authorities which were Icesave depositors have claimed a special position of preference under the relevant Icelandic legislation. This issue has been left out of account for the purposes of the present discussion.

[73] Letter from Icelandic Ministry of Business Affairs to HM Treasury, 5 October 2008.

[74] The law made similar provisions with respect to the Government of the Netherlands, where Landsbanki also had a branch. The attempts at settlement followed the conclusion of some so-called 'Agreed Guidelines' dated 14 November 2008. This, in turn, led to agreements with the United Kingdom and the Netherlands dated 5 June 2009, under which the Icelandic Deposit and Guarantee Fund would treat its liability in respect of the insured deposits as a loan from the UK and the Netherlands, under the guarantee of the Icelandic Government.

[75] The need for reform in this area appears to be acknowledged by the FSA: see, for example, the Treasury Committee Report (n 44 above), para 111. In some respects, the issue goes to the heart of the passporting system as a whole because host State concerns over the stability of foreign braches are not limited purely to the fate of *insured* deposits.

Conclusions

13.24 There seems to be no dispute that adequate deposit protection arrangements are an integral part of the structures designed to reinforce confidence in the stability of a national banking system. Any scope for dispute on that issue has surely been eliminated by the unprecedented financial collapse witnessed over the last two years. The role of the Financial Services Compensation Scheme is being developed to meet that need and to reassure depositors that they will receive rapid compensation, should the need ever arise.

13.25 However, the United Kingdom–Iceland episode has demonstrated the dangers for a host State in relying on deposit protection schemes operated by a home State supervisor in times of acute crisis. In such a situation, it is perhaps inevitable that the home State authorities will look first to the protection of their home depositors (and voters), and obligations to foreign depositors may well appear to be distant priority. Further review of the operation of the EU system for deposit protection therefore seems to be an urgent necessity.

14

THE LIABILITY OF THE REGULATOR

Introduction

14.01 Can the financial market regulator incur liability to depositors who lose money as a result of the failure of a supervised institution?

14.02 The whole subject is of some importance, not least to the regulator, but also to depositors; as recent years have painfully illustrated, the losses which may flow from a bank collapse can be massive. It was for this reason that the Bank of England's success in defending the well-known proceedings brought against it in respect of the collapse of BCCI is of great significance to regulators generally.[1]

14.03 In view of the scale of the potential losses to the public purse in the event of an adverse finding, it is perhaps unsurprising that the legislator will frequently confer some form of immunity on the regulator from claims in tort, with the intention of foreclosing any proceedings to establish a claim of this kind. It is perhaps equally unsurprising that the Core Principles for Effective Banking Supervision place an early priority on legal protection for the supervisor in the performance of his functions.[2] The precise nature and scope of such immunities will depend upon the interpretation of the relevant provisions, but their intended effect is—obviously—to deprive the depositor of any remedy which it might otherwise have

---

[1] *Three Rivers DC v Bank of England* [2006] All ER(D) 175. For a useful recent discussion of the whole subject, see Huplas, Quintin and Taylor, 'The Accountability of Financial Sector Supervisors: Principles and Practice' (International Monetary Fund Working Paper 05/5, 1 March 2005). For a South African perspective, see de Jager, 'Three Rivers District Council v Governor and Company of the Bank of England: A Red Flag or a Red Herring for Supervisors in South Africa?' (2001) 13 SA Merc LJ 531.

[2] The Core Principles are published by the Basel Committee on Banking Supervision and are intended to provide a framework for sound standards of supervisory practice. The requirement for supervisory legal protection is set out in Principle One.

against the supervisor.[3] It is necessary to consider (i) whether such immunities are subject to challenge on any basis and (ii) the extent to which a regulator may be subject to any residual bases of liability.

14.04   Under these circumstances, it is proposed to consider:

(a) the consistency of immunity provisions with Community law;

(b) the consistency of immunity provisions with the European Convention on Human Rights;

(c) the scope and effect of immunity provisions; and

(d) the cases on regulatory immunity which have arisen in common law jurisdictions.[4]

Immunity Provisions and Community Law

14.05   Although the relevant case law is not vast, it is perhaps unsurprising that the body of law which can now appropriately be termed 'EU Banking Law' has given rise to a certain amount of litigation, both before the national courts of Member States and the European Court of Justice itself. The litigation is of some interest, since it considers the extent to which various aspects of EU Banking Law have direct effect within the Member States and the extent to which those States may incur a liability in damages to individuals as a result of (alleged) non-implementation of the relevant measures.

14.06   It has already been shown[5] that EU Banking Law was essentially a 'single market' measure, designed to ensure that banking services could more readily be offered across the Community, thus promoting competition in this sphere. As has been seen, the First Banking Directive introduced a requirement that all credit institutions should require authorization under national law to conduct business. Certain harmonized, minimum requirements had to be applied for that purpose. Once this had been achieved, it was possible to introduce the Second Banking Directive, which provided for mutual recognition of banking licences and for the principle of home State supervision.

14.07   It has already been seen that the Deposit Guarantee Directive created rights for individuals and that they could recover damages against a Member State which failed to implement its requirements.[6] But did the Second Banking Directive create an enforceable right to adequate supervision of institutions, such that a statutory immunity clause[7] had to be

---

[3] Both the *Peter Paul* Case and the *Three Rivers* case (discussed below) involved an immunity provision of this kind. It may be added for completeness that the Bank of England has recently been given immunity in the context of its monetary policy and financial stability roles (see s 244 of the Banking Act 2009) and that the Financial Services Compensation Scheme also enjoys immunity under s 222 of the FSMA. All of these immunities are expressed in essentially similar terms and are subject to the same exceptions. It is accordingly proposed to focus on the liability of the supervisor since, in the nature of things, it is the most obvious target in the event of an attack by disgruntled depositors.

[4] The matters discussed in the present section are considered in more detail by Proctor, 'Regulatory Liability for Bank Failures—The Peter Paul Case' (2005) 1 *European Banking and Financial Law Journal* 73.

[5] See generally the discussion of EU banking law in Chapter 2 above.

[6] See the discussion at para 13.05 above.

[7] The provision at issue in these proceedings—art 6(4) of the German Law on Credit Institutions—stated that the supervisory authority carried out its functions *only* in the public interest. This clearly implies that the supervisor owes no private law duties to individual depositors.

disregarded if it was inconsistent with that right? The insolvency of a licensed credit institution in Germany (BVH Bank) provided the European Court of Justice with the opportunity to consider this subject in *Peter Paul and others v Bundesrepublik Deutschland.*[8]

Of course, the validity of the immunity clause could only be called into question if the **14.08** Second Banking Directive did indeed create an effective and enforceable right to adequate supervision of credit institutions. It is immediately apparent that this was a significant obstacle to the depositors' case, because a Member State can only incur a liability to damages based on its failure to implement a Directive if (i) the result prescribed by the Directive entailed the grant of clearly defined rights on individuals, (ii) the non-implementation of the Directive is sufficiently serious, and (iii) there is a direct causal link between the non-implementation and the loss suffered by the claimant.[9]

If the depositors' arguments were correct, then the effective immunity from legal proceed- **14.09** ings conferred by German law[10] could not stand, because the Community law requirement for a private law remedy would have to take precedence over it. In that event, the depositors would be entitled to compensation if they could prove some negligence or default on the part of the supervisor. The claimants accordingly argued that the First and Second Banking Directives precluded a national rule to the effect that the supervisory function was carried out only in the public interest. They failed because the directives were based on Article 47(2) of the EC Treaty and were designed as harmonization measures to facilitate the completion of the internal market in the field of financial services. The Directives did not confer on depositors any express right to damages in the event of defective supervision, nor was any such right to be inferred. The court noted that the domestic laws of many Member States prohibited recourse to the supervisor, on the basis that banking supervision was a complex field involving a plurality of interests, including in particular the overall stability of the financial system.[11] Under these circumstances, Community law could not offer a basis on which to strike down the regulator's immunity.

It is of some interest to compare the decision of the Court of Justice in the *Peter Paul* case **14.10** with an earlier decision of the House of Lords, on the identical point, in the proceedings arising out of the collapse of BCCI.[12] The claimants in that case were attempting to avoid the effect of section 1(4) of the Banking Act 1987, which conferred immunity on the Bank

---

[8] Case C-222/02, [2004] ECR I-9425.

[9] See in particular cases C-6/90 and C-9/90, *Francovich & Bonifaci v Republic of Italy* [1991] ECR I-5357, as explained in later cases including Joined Cases C-46/93, *Brasserie du Pecheur SA v Federal Republic of Germany; R v Secretary of State for Transport, ex p Factortame Ltd* [1996] ECR I-1029 and Joined Cases C-178/94, C-179/94, and C-188/94 to C-190/94, *Dillenkofer and others v Federal Republic of Germany* [1996] ECR I 4845.

[10] The immunity flowed from art 6(4) of the German Law on Credit Institutions, which provided that the bank supervisory authority had to carry out its duties solely in the public interest. This provision thus negated the existence of any enforceable private law duties owed to individual depositors.

[11] See para 44 of the judgment.

[12] *Three Rivers District Council v Bank of England* [2001] 3 All ER 1. It may be noted that, whilst the German courts referred the point to the European Court of Justice, the House of Lords elected to decide the point itself, on the basis that it was *acte clair*. Under the circumstances, it is perhaps fortunate that the two tribunals arrived at the same conclusion.

of England in the performance of its statutory functions, unless bad faith could be proved.[13] The House of Lords held that a right to adequate supervision could not be derived from the terms of the First Banking Directive, partly because it did not prescribe specific duties or standards of supervision, and partly because the existence of such rights was not a necessary consequence of the harmonization objectives. Consequently, the immunity provision could not be struck down or disregarded on the basis that it contravened a directly enforceable Community law right.

14.11   Given the weight of authority offered by the decisions of the Court of Justice and the House of Lords, it can be asserted with confidence that Community law does not confer any rights on depositors who lose money as a result of the collapse of a credit institution.[14]

Immunity Provisions and the European Convention on Human Rights

14.12   The European Convention on Human Rights was, in various respects, incorporated into the domestic law of the United Kingdom by the Human Rights Act 1998. The Convention is designed to ensure, amongst other things, that individuals are not unlawfully deprived of their property and that their rights are protected in both criminal and civil proceedings.

14.13   Can a court justifiably disregard a statutory immunity on the basis of its inconsistency with the Convention? In order to consider this question, it is convenient to make the assessment by reference to the immunity conferred on the Financial Services Authority. In some respects, the current legislation answers this question itself.[15] Paragraph 19 of Schedule 1 to the FSMA reads as follows:

> (1) Neither the Authority nor any person who is, or is acting as, a member, officer or member of staff of the Authority is to be liable in damages for anything done or omitted in the discharge, or purported discharge, of the Authority's functions.
>
> (2) Neither the investigator appointed under paragraph 7 nor a person appointed to conduct an investigation on his behalf under paragraph 8(8) is to be liable in damages for

---

[13] The section read, 'Neither the bank nor any person who is a member of its Court of Directors or who is, or is acting as, an officer or servant of the Bank shall be liable in damages for anything done or omitted in the discharge or purported discharge of the functions of the Bank unless it is shown that the act or omission was in bad faith'. The section has now been replaced by the corresponding immunity in favour of the Financial Services Authority. The relevant provisions are considered at para 14.13 below.

[14] The one exception to this statement is that the Deposit Guarantee Directive does confer rights on depositors, so that they are entitled to hold a Member State responsible for losses suffered as a result of non-implementation of that Directive. This aspect of the *Peter Paul* decision has already been discussed at para 13.05 above.

[15] It is perhaps of some significance that the provisions about to be reproduced appear under the heading 'Exemption from liability in damages' (ie as opposed to 'Immunity' or similar expression). Although the heading may not be conclusive in characterizing the nature of the provisions which appear beneath it, the draftsman was clearly conscious of the distinction between the substantive and procedural questions which are about to be considered.

anything done or omitted in the discharge, or purported discharge, of his functions in relation to the investigation of a complaint.[16]

(3) Neither sub-paragraph (1) nor sub-paragraph (2) applies—

    a) if the act or omission is shown to have been in bad faith; or

    b) so as to prevent an award of damages made in respect of an act or omission on the ground that the act or omission was unlawful as a result of section 6(1) of the Human Rights Act 1998.

Section 6(1) of the Human Rights Act 1998 provides that, 'It is unlawful for a public **14.14** authority to act in a way which is incompatible with a Convention right', and the Convention rights include the right to a fair hearing of a civil dispute in accordance with Article 6(1) of the Convention.[17]

Now, paragraph 19(3)(b) is directed to an act or omission by the FSA or an investigator **14.15** which contravenes a Convention right. It is quite possible that the provision is really directed to the need for fairness in relation to the investigation of complaints. Nevertheless, it is necessary to consider whether the exemption from damages conferred upon the FSA is consistent with the depositor's right to a fair trial, in the sense that it imposes upon him an additional burden of proof. The importance of this point—both to the depositor and to the regulator—is obvious.

In general terms, it seems clear that Article 6(1) of the Convention is designed only to **14.16** secure fairness in a procedural sense; the provision is not intended to dictate the content of the substantive law of the Convention States.[18] Of course, it is easy to state this type of distinction, but much more difficult to apply it in practice. It is perhaps also easy to assert that the expressions 'procedural' and 'substantive' must be given an autonomous meaning for Convention purposes.[19] In law, the expression 'immunity' tends to connote an advantage of a procedural nature, such that the beneficiary of the immunity is not amenable to the jurisdiction of the court at all, regardless of the merits of the case. Yet the use of the expression may be misleading in the present context, because a statutory provision which defines the civil rights of the parties, or a court decision to the effect that it is not fair,

---

[16] Paragraphs 7 and 8 of Sch 1 deal with the investigation of complaints made against the FSA itself. Paragraph 19(2) is therefore of only limited relevance in the present context, but it is reproduced because it may have an impact upon the interpretation of the remainder of the paragraph—see the discussion in the text.

[17] For the definition of 'Convention right', see s 1 of the 1998 Act. For the purposes of s 6 of the Act, the expression 'public authority' includes a court or tribunal. The first sentence of Art 6(1) of the Convention itself reads: 'In the determination of his civil rights and obligations, everyone is entitled to a fair and public hearing within a reasonable time by an independent and impartial tribunal established by law'. A claim in tort against a public authority is a 'civil right' for the purposes of the Convention even thought the proceedings arise out of the exercise of governmental authority: see Lester and Pannick, The European Convention on Human Rights, para 4.6.5.

[18] The point is made by Lester & Pannick, The European Convention on Human Rights, para 4.6.5.

[19] *Konig v Germany* (1978) 2 EHRR 170, followed by the House of Lords in *R (On the application of Alconbury Developments Limited) v Secretary of State for the Environment, Transport and Regions* [2003] 2 AC 295.

just, and reasonable to impose a duty of care in a particular case, deal with questions of substantive law, rather than procedural matters.[20]

14.17   In the view of the present writer, the immunity/exemption from liability conferred upon the FSA must be viewed in the context of the FSMA as a whole. The Act creates a framework for the supervision of financial institutions in the United Kingdom; in doing so, it seeks to define the functions which the Authority is to fulfil and the extent of both the rights and obligations to which it is subject for those purposes. It would thus be pointless to regard paragraph 19(1) as a procedural immunity; the FSA is not thereby exempted from a liability which others could incur, for no one else is entitled to carry out the functions of financial market supervision in this country.[21]

14.18   Perhaps more crucially, however, courts sitting in common law jurisdictions have tended to hold that the market supervisor owes his duties to the public as a whole, and that the imposition of a private law duty of care in such a case would thus be inappropriate.[22] A decision of this kind is clearly to be regarded as a matter of substantive law, which thus falls entirely outside the scope of Article 6(1) of the Convention.[23]

14.19   Even if, however, the views expressed in the last two paragraphs are incorrect and the protection afforded to the FSA by paragraph 19(1) is to be regarded as a procedural provision,[24] it may still not infringe Article 6(1) of the Convention; certain limitations on access to the courts are permissible, provided that they pursue a legitimate aim, are proportionate and are legally certain.[25] In this context, it is appropriate to draw a parallel with the decision in *Ashingdane v United Kingdom*.[26] In that case, government employees were exempted from liability to detained mental patients in their custody, unless the claimant could prove bad faith or a lack of reasonable care. This provision was not inconsistent with Article 6(1). The provision pursued the legitimate objective of protecting hospital staff from vexatious

---

[20] On this subject, see the remarks of Lord Browne-Wilkinson in *X and others v Bedfordshire County Council* [1995] 2 AC 633.

[21] Although the point was not directly addressed, the House of Lords seems to have regarded the supervisor's statutory immunity as a matter of substantive law, rather than merely a procedural benefit: see the remarks of Lord Steyn in *Three Rivers District Council v Bank of England (No 3)* [2001] 3 All ER 513, at p 529.

[22] For a discussion of these decisions, see paras 14.24–14.34 below.

[23] The decision of the European Court of Human Rights *in Osman v United Kingdom* (1998) EHRR 245 (paras 131–140) is to contrary effect, However, it seems that the Court now adheres firmly to the position that Art 6(1) applies only to procedural rules which impede free access to the process of the courts: *Z v United Kingdom* (2002) 34 EHRR 97. See also Rosamund English, 'The Decline and Fall of Osman' (2001) 151 NLJ 973.

[24] In one case—*Capital Bank International Limited v Eastern Caribbean Central Bank* (10 March 2003)—the Eastern Caribbean Court of Appeal accepted that the statutory immunities from suit conferred upon the central bank could not be absolute because they may to some extent be inconsistent with the claimant's right to a fair trial under constitutional provisions equivalent to Art 6(1) of the Convention. It is implicit in this view that the statutory immunities are of a procedural character and are thus vulnerable to attack under Art 6(1). However, the authority of this decision is limited because the central bank appears to have conceded the point.

[25] On this subject, see Lester and Pannick, The European Convention on Human Rights, para 4.6.18, and materials there cited.

[26] (1985) 7 EHRR 528, paras 57–60. The court did not decide whether the statutory provision at issue in that case was substantive or procedural because the provision would not have infringed Art 6(1) even if it fell within the procedural category. The decision in this case has been followed on a number of occasions.

litigation; the provision was proportionate to the objective because it did not operate as a complete bar to court proceedings; it merely added an additional requirement to prove bad faith or want of reasonable care. Reasoning of this kind should also be applied in relation to the immunities of a financial market supervisor, because:

(a) the proper regulation of the financial markets is plainly a desirable objective, and the efficient conduct of that function justifies wide-ranging immunity from liability;[27]

(b) the regulator works with limited resources and it would not be in the public interest for those resources to be diverted to the defence of vexatious litigation;

(c) the regulator will always require a breadth of discretion in supervising the market and extremely difficult decisions may have to be made at short notice;

(d) given that the regulator's responsibility for a bank failure will be at best secondary,[28] it is unreasonable to expect the regulator to carry the full burden of the resultant losses; and

(e) the provision is proportionate, because it does not impose a total ban on proceedings against the regulator, and damages can still be won if the hurdle of bad faith can be overcome.

It follows that the Authority's exemption from liability is not open to challenge under Article 6(1) of the European Convention on Human Rights.

The Effect of an Immunity Provision

The foregoing sections have examined the general consistency of regulatory immunity with other legal norms. It has been seen that immunity provisions should survive any such scrutiny. Yet it must not be forgotten that an immunity provision will require interpretation in order to ascertain whether it applies to the particular acts which form the subject matter of the proceedings at hand.   **14.20**

This point is perhaps obvious but it assumed a certain importance in *Gulf Insurance Limited v Central Bank of Trinidad and Tobago*.[29] In brief, the government and the central bank had become concerned about the stability of certain institutions in Trinidad and Tobago. As a result, a new section 44D was inserted into the Central Bank Act which enabled the central bank to take action in relation to an institution which was, or which was likely to become, insolvent. In such a case, the central bank was authorized to '... acquire or sell or otherwise deal with the property, assets and undertaking of, or any shareholding in, the institution at a price to be determined by an independent valuer ...'. The central bank determined that three institutions were in serious financial difficulties and, in an   **14.21**

---

[27] In *Capital Bank International Limited v Eastern Caribbean Central Bank* (10 March 2003), the Eastern Caribbean Court of Appeal held that wide immunities were justified when dealing with governmental functions such as the protection of the currency and the supervision of the financial sector. In this respect, the court relied heavily on the decision in *Fayed v United Kingdom* (1994) 18 EHRR 393.

[28] Primary responsibility for a bank collapse must be taken to rest with its management, rather than the regulator.

[29] [2005] All ER (D) 153 (PC). It is unfortunate that the point discussed in the text was not considered in more depth in the Privy Council's judgment.

effort to forestall a bank run, it made an order transferring the business and assets of all three institutions to a specially incorporated entity. Unfortunately, the order effecting the transfer did not include any provision for a valuation, with the result that the central bank had acted beyond the powers conferred on it by section 44D. In principle, therefore, the central bank was liable to the three institutions in conversion as a result of ordering an ultra vires transfer.

14.22 It thus became necessary to consider whether the central bank was protected from this liability by the immunity clause in the Central Bank Act. Section 44H provided that '… the Bank, its directors and officers … are not subject to any action, claim or demand by, or any liability to, any person in respect of anything done or omitted to be done in good faith and without negligence in the performance, or in connection with the performance, of functions conferred on the Bank under this Part …'. The Privy Council held that this provision was inapplicable to the particular circumstances of the case because:

(a) the specific language of the section ('… in the performance or in connection with the performance of functions conferred on the Bank under this Part …') could not be extended to cover acts which *purported* to be in performance of the statutory powers but which were in fact ultra vires. This suggests, if only by inference, that the immunity conferred on the FSA[30] ('… the Authority is [not] to be liable in damages for anything done or omitted in the discharge, or the *purported* discharge, of the Authority's functions …') would be sufficient to protect the FSA if it was acting in the performance of its functions but in fact overstepped the boundary of its statutory powers;[31] and

(b) since immunity clauses would operate to deprive individuals of remedies which would otherwise be available to them, '… provisions of this kind should be restrictively construed. They should not be treated as a licence for unlawful expropriation without compensation, provided only that the acts are done in good faith and without negligence …'.[32]

14.23 Whatever the merits of this decision, it is plain that the supervisor should seek the broadest possible immunity for any action which it might find it necessary to take—at least insofar as such a provision is consistent with the need for an adequate level of public accountability.

---

[30] The terms of this immunity have already been noted: see para 14.13 above.

[31] Although this point appears to follow from the *Gulf Insurance* decision, it is submitted that the distinction is unattractive. Expressions such as 'the *purported* discharge' (as found in the FSMA) and '*in connection with* the performance of functions' (as found in Trinidad and Tobago's Central Bank Act) should be given a similar meaning. The objective is the same in each case—namely to protect the regulator from liability if he is trying to carry out his duties in good faith.

[32] See para 53 of the judgment. Nevertheless, it is not obvious why the claimants should have claimed damages rather than merely obtaining an order that the valuation should be carried out. It should also be noted that a restrictive approach to the interpretation of immunity clauses had previously found favour with the Eastern Caribbean Court of Appeal: see *Capital Bank International Ltd v Eastern Caribbean Central Bank* (10 March 2003).

Regulatory Liability

Since neither Community law nor the European Convention on Human Rights offer any **14.24**
basis for a right of recourse against the supervisor following the collapse of a credit institution, it must follow that the extent of the supervisor's liability is governed exclusively by
reference to the relevant domestic legal system. If there is a statutory immunity clause
which covers the particular situation then the regulator will be free of any liability. As has
been seen, however, immunity provisions will rarely be unqualified for it cannot be appropriate to protect public bodies against the consequences of their own dishonesty or bad
faith. Furthermore, some jurisdictions may not provide for an explicit statutory immunity.[33] As a result, it remains instructive to consider those few cases in which depositors or
investors have sought recourse against the market supervisor.

As a matter of general principle, the regulator could incur liability to the depositors in this **14.25**
type of case if (i) the regulator owes a duty of care to the claimant, or to a class of persons
which includes the claimant, (ii) the regulator is in breach of that duty, and (iii) the claimant has suffered loss as a result of that breach.

It is the existence of a duty of care which proves to be most problematical in cases against **14.26**
public authorities, such as a market supervisor. In the first instance, it may be appropriate
to ask whether the defendant has assumed any form of special responsibility to the claimant, such that a duty of care may arise.[34] In the absence of that feature then, when confronted with a new category of claim in negligence, the court must determine whether it is
'… fair, just and reasonable that the law should impose a duty of care of a given scope upon
the one party for the benefit of the other …'.[35] Furthermore, it is generally accepted that
'… the law should develop novel categories of negligence incrementally and by analogy
with established categories, rather than by a massive extension of a prima facie duty of care
restrained only by indefinable considerations which ought to negative, or to reduce or limit
the scope of the duty or the class of person to whom it is owed …'.[36] There can thus be no
doubt that questions of policy are very much to the fore in cases brought against public
authorities.

It is fair to say that, in most cases of this kind, the claimant has failed to establish the exis- **14.27**
tence of a duty of care, and the cases have therefore frequently failed at this first hurdle. In
general terms, the courts have noted that the authority concerned has to operate within a

---

[33] This was the position in Hong Kong at the time of the proceedings in *Yuen Kun-Yeu v Attorney General
for Hong Kong* [1988] AC 175 (PC), discussed below.
[34] This basis for the imposition of a duty of care was perhaps most clearly explained in a case dealing with
bank references: *Hedley Byrne & Co v Heller & Partners* [1964] AC 465, as applied in *Henderson v Merrett
Syndicates* [1995] 2 AC 145 and many other cases.
[35] *Caparo Industries plc v Dickman* [1990] 2 AC 605. It seems clear that the 'assumption of responsibility'
test and the 'fair, just, and reasonable' tests are independent bases upon which a duty of care may be imposed.
Consequently, if one of the tests is met, there is no need to demonstrate that the second is also met; see the
judgment of Lord Goff in *Henderson v Merrett Syndicates* [1995] 2 AC 145.
[36] *Sutherland Shire Council v Heyman* (1985) 157 CLR 424,481. The quotation was approved in
the *Caparo* case (see n 35 above); see also *Marc Rich & Co AG v Bishop Rock Marine Co Ltd* [1996] AC 211,
at p 236.

statutory framework which defines its functions and duties for the benefit of the public as a whole,[37] and have concluded that the imposition of an additional, private law duty of care would be inconsistent with those duties or would not be fair, just and reasonable in the circumstances.[38]

14.28 Principles of this kind have been applied in two decisions of the Judicial Committee of the Privy Council which dealt directly with the liability of the supervisor following the collapse of a financial institution. In the first case,[39] the Hong Kong authorities had granted a deposit-taking licence to The American and Panama Finance Co under the terms of an Ordinance made '… to regulate the taking of money on deposit and to make provision for the protection of persons who deposit money and for the regulation of deposit taking business for monetary policy purposes …'. The company collapsed, and depositors sought recourse against the regulator on the basis that it should have realized that the company was speculating with the moneys deposited with it. The claims were, however, struck out, on the basis that the Ordinance did not create a specific, private law duty of care; nor would it have been appropriate to impose such a duty, because the regulator had to balance a number of competing interests in exercising his powers (eg the possibility that the fortunes of the company could be revived and the need to maintain confidence in the markets as a whole). The issue of a licence did not amount to an 'official seal of approval' and did not imply any governmental warranty or guarantee as to the soundness of the institution.[40]

14.29 In the second case,[41] the Savings and Investment Bank had been authorized to accept deposits by the Treasurer and the Finance Board, Isle of Man. When the bank collapsed in 1982, the depositors sought recourse to the regulator. Once again, the claim was struck out, largely because the public functions of the supervisor did not imply—indeed, they were inconsistent with—the existence of a private law duty of care. Significantly, however, the Privy Council added a further reason for its decision, namely that the regulator only had a secondary degree of control over the bank's business and that it would be inappropriate to

---

[37] It does not seem to have been argued that the fact that the regulator has been established by statute with specific responsibility for the supervision of the financial markets constitutes an 'assumption of responsibility' to depositors or investors. Such a line of argument would almost certainly fail.

[38] Examples of this approach are offered by *D v East Berkshire Community Health NHS Trust* [2005] UKHL 24 (social worker investigating a possible case of child abuse did not owe a duty of care to parents who came under suspicion as a result of the enquiry); *Brooks v Metropolitan Police Commissioner* [2005] UKHL 24 (police owe no duty of care to afford particular protection to a victim of crime); *Elguzouli-Daf v Commissioner of Police* [1995] QB 335 (prosecuting authorities owe no duty of care to those whom they decide to prosecute).

[39] *Yuen Kun-Yeu v Attorney General of Hong Kong* [1988] AC 175. As the court observed in *SRM Global Master Fund LP v The Commissioners of Her Majesty's Treasury* [2009] EWHC 227 (Admin) at para 114, the decision in *Yuen Kun-Yeu* established that the regulator owed no duty of care to an institution's depositors and, a fortiori, it owes no duty to its shareholders. This remark was specifically approved by the Court of Appeal in *SRM Global Master Fund v Her Majesty's Treasury* [2009] EWCA Civ 788 (CA), para 80. For a decision to similar effect, see *Hall v Bank of England* [2000] All ER (D) 570 (CA), noted at para 14.34 below.

[40] The Privy Council was clearly alive to the policy issues in this case. It was noted (at p 198) that a decision to hold the regulator liable '… would surely be applicable to a wide range of regulatory agencies, not only in the financial field but also, for example, to the factory inspectorate and social workers, to name but a few …'.

[41] *Davis v Ratcliffe* [1990] 1 WLR 82.

impose a duty of care which would effectively cover the claimant against the default of a third party.

The Supreme Court of Canada, in a compelling judgment, reached a similar conclusion in **14.30** relation to the collapse of Eron Mortgage Corporation, an entity which had been authorized to accept funds from the public under the Mortgage Brokers Act of British Columbia.[42] In this case, the regulator had allegedly been aware of irregularities at Eron for several months before its licence was suspended; depositors instituted proceedings against the Registrar of Mortgage Brokers on the basis that, had he acted with greater dispatch, at least some of their losses would have been avoided. In the absence of a direct precedent in Canada, the court analysed the matter from first principles, noting that a claim in negligence could only be established if the claimants could satisfy both (i) a foreseeability test and (ii) a proximity test.[43] The first test could easily be met; if the regulator was negligent in performing his supervisory duties, then it was clear that the depositors could suffer losses as a result. However, the proximity test could not be met; this test involves a 'close and direct' relationship between claimant and defendant. No such relationship could be proved because the regulatory function sought to support the existence of orderly financial markets. The public nature of this duty precluded the existence of a private law duty of care to depositors with particular institutions.[44]

It is submitted that principles of this kind would apply equally in the context of a claim **14.31** against the FSA as supervisor of the financial markets in the United Kingdom. The functions of the Authority include the protection of consumers but this factor would be insufficient to create private law duties of care in their favour, because the Authority is also required to pursue a number of other objectives of a more public nature, including the fostering of confidence in the financial markets, the promotion of public awareness of the risks and benefits of financial dealings and the reduction of financial crime.[45]

These obstacles are already formidable, and would make it difficult for the disappointed **14.32** depositor to establish a right to damages even in an ordinary negligence claim. But, as has already been seen, the position of the depositors is made even more difficult by the statutory immunity conferred upon the FSA.[46] A claim against the FSA in its capacity as supervisor of the financial markets can succeed only if the claimant can demonstrate bad faith. In practical terms, this means that the depositors can only succeed if they can establish the tort of 'misfeasance in public office'.

---

[42] *Cooper v Hobart* [2001] 3 SCR 79, followed by the same court in *Edwards v The Law Society* [2001] 3 SCR 562. Note, however, that the Canadian Supreme Court has recently seemed more willing to impose liability for public acts: see *Hill v Hamilton-Wentworth Regional Police Services Board* 2007 SCC 41.

[43] It may be noted that this formulation is derived from the House of Lords decision in *Anns v Merton Borough Council* [1977] 2 All ER 492, which was ultimately overruled by the House in *Murphy v Brentwood District Council* [1990] 2 All ER 908. However, the decision in *Anns* continues to find favour in a number of other common law jurisdictions—see, for example, the discussion in *Invercargill Council v Hamlin* [1996] 1 All ER 756.

[44] New Zealand offers a decision to essentially similar effect, albeit decided in a slightly different context: *Fleming v Securities Commission* [1995] 2 NZLR 514.

[45] Sections 2–6 of the FSMA.

[46] See para 19 of Sch 1 to the FSMA. The provision has already been noted at para 14.13 above, and it has already been concluded that there is no valid basis for a challenge to a statutory immunity of this kind.

14.33   This particular tort[47] was the subject of careful examination by the House of Lords in the well-known litigation brought by depositors against the Bank of England and arising out of the collapse of the Bank of Credit and Commerce International SA.[48] The House indicated that the following were the ingredients of the tort:

(a) the defendant must be a public official or body;

(b) the acts alleged to amount to misfeasance must involve the exercise of a public function;

(c) the defendant must have acted in bad faith (that is to say, he must have acted in a way which was designed to injure a particular person or class of persons, or he must have known that he was acting beyond the scope of his powers and that this was likely to cause loss to the claimant);

(d) the defendant must owe a duty of care to the claimant;[49] and

(e) in order to recover damages, there must of course be a causal link between the breach of duty and the loss suffered by the claimant (or, to put matters another way, the loss must not be too remote).

14.34   As an evidential matter, it is clear that the proof of bad faith will inevitably pose the greatest problem for the claimant.[50] This was the rock on which the depositors' claim in the BCCI case was destined to founder. Whilst the claimants withdrew their proceedings when they were part-heard, the decision on the question of costs[51] made it clear that the necessary evidence of dishonesty was wanting. A less well-known case brought against the Bank of England as supervisor alleged that the shareholders of a supervised institution had suffered loss because the Bank had failed to exercise its powers to intervene in the management of the business. The case was struck out on the basis that a mere failure to act would not normally amount to misfeasance and, in any event, there was no evidence of dishonesty necessary to support the charge of misfeasance.[52]

Conclusions

14.35   It seems to follow from this discussion that depositors in a failed institution will only rarely be able to obtain redress from the supervisor. The combination of the statutory immunity and the need to prove bad faith will normally prove to be an insurmountable hurdle.

14.36   Nevertheless, as demonstrated by the decision in the *Gulf Insurance* case, a regulator which acts beyond the scope of its statutory powers will not necessarily be protected, even if it has acted in good faith.

---

[47] For a detailed discussion with some comparative materials see Andenas and Fairgrieve, 'Misfeasance in Public Office, Governmental Liability and European Influence' (2002) 51 ICLQ 757.

[48] See *Three Rivers District Council v Bank of England* [2001] 2 All ER 513, approving an earlier formulation in *Melton Medes v Securities and Investment Board* [1995] 3 All ER 880.

[49] This will not usually pose too much difficulty, since everyone has the right not to be injured by a deliberate abuse of public power.

[50] Allegations of dishonesty and bad faith are invariably subjected to a heavy burden of proof.

[51] *Three Rivers District Council v Bank of England* [2006] All ER (D) 175.

[52] *Hall v Bank of England* [2000] All ER (D) 570.

As the recent financial crisis has demonstrated, governments may ultimately feel compelled **14.37** to support failing banks or to guarantee their deposits in order to maintain the stability of the financial system and the wider economy as a whole. However, the available case law suggests that this will almost always remain a matter of policy, as opposed to legal obligation.

Part C

THE BANKER-CUSTOMER RELATIONSHIP

Introduction

The present section deals with the general nature of the relationship which subsists between the banker and its customer. In particular, it considers the account relationship and the scope of the respective obligations arising with respect to an ordinary bank account.

Some of the more specialized types of service offered by a bank are considered in Part (D) below, whilst guarantees and security given to cover bank facilities are discussed in Part (E).

Against that general background, the present section is arranged as follows:

(a) Chapter 15 considers the nature of the basic contractual relationship between the bank and its customer;
(b) Chapter 16 examines the general law relating to cheques;
(c) Chapter 17 considers the position of the bank in its capacity as a paying bank, the consequences of a payment in excess of the mandate, and certain other statutory protections available to it;
(d) Chapter 18 outlines the remedies of the bank in its capacity as a collecting bank, in receiving credits to the account on behalf of the customer, including protective statutory provisions; and
(e) Chapter 19 considers certain legal implications of electronic funds transfers.

15

THE BANKER-CUSTOMER CONTRACT

Introduction

The present chapter outlines the fundamental nature of the banker-customer contract, in **15.01** the sense in which it is focused around the account relationship. It will accordingly consider the following matters:

(a) the meaning of 'banker' and 'customer';
(b) the general nature of the banker-customer relationship;
(c) the terms of the banker-customer contract;
(d) the customer's duties to the bank; and
(e) the regulation of the contractual terms of the banker-customer relationship.

The Banker and the Customer

Introduction

The respective rights and obligations of the parties under a banker-customer relationship **15.02** can plainly only come into existence under arrangements involving a 'banker' on the one hand and a 'customer' on the other. It is therefore necessary at the outset briefly to examine the meaning of these two expressions.

'Banker'

15.03 Before the conduct of deposit-taking business was first subjected to formal regulation by the Banking Act 1979, it had been held that the characteristics of 'banking business' included (i) the conduct of current accounts, (ii) the payment of cheques, and (iii) the collection of cheques.[1] In practice, these three activities are intimately connected, and it is difficult to see how an institution could carry out some, but not all, of these activities.[2] Since a business of this kind involves the acceptance of deposits from the public and now requires authorization or permission,[3] the expression 'bank' will for all practical purposes refer to an institution which holds such an authorization. It follows that an institution which merely engages in the business of lending its own money will not be treated as a 'bank' for these purposes,[4] with the result that the various terms which would be implied into a banker-customer contract will not come into operation.

15.04 Although it is true that the definition of 'banker' for contractual purposes was developed in an era which pre-dates modern regulatory structures, for all practical purposes the banker-customer relationship can now only come into existence where the bank party is authorized to accept deposits for Financial Services and Markets Act (FSMA) purposes.

'Customer'

15.05 In contrast, there does not seem to be any satisfactory definition of 'customer' for these purposes. Logic does, however, suggest that he must be a person who is using the services which constitute 'banking business', as described above; in other words, he must hold a current account with a bank which he uses for the payment and collection of cheques, or at the very least he must be in serious discussions with a view to the establishment of such an account.[5] As a result, the duration of the relationship between the parties is not a material factor in determining whether the banker-customer contract has come into existence; a person thus becomes a customer at the latest when his current account is opened,[6] and, possibly, even earlier than that. The fact that a cheque book is issued to a particular individual is, of course, a very strong—perhaps conclusive—indication that he is to be regarded

---

[1] *United Dominions Trust Ltd v Kirkwood* [1966] 2 QB 431. In earlier times, a 'banker' was perhaps less happily described as a person whose business is trafficking in money of others for the purposes of profit: *Re Shields Estate* [1901] 1 IR 173 at p 198 (Ireland).

[2] It is submitted that this is so notwithstanding the doubts expressed by Diplock LJ in *Kirkwood* (above) at p 447.

[3] On this subject, see generally Chapter 1 above.

[4] This conclusion was reached in *United Dominions Trust v Kirkwood* [1966] 2 QB 431 and was followed in *Hafton Properties Ltd v McHugh* (1986) 59 TC 420. See also *Re Roe's Legal Charge* [1982] 2 Lloyds Rep 370.

[5] Under the terms of the FSMA, s 138(7) 'customers' are persons '... who use, have used *or are or may be contemplating using* ...' any of the services offered by an authorized institution (emphasis supplied). This definition is obviously intended to assist in the interpretation of the FSMA itself, but it may also be of assistance in a more general context. It tends to support the view, expressed in various cases, that a person may be a 'customer' even before the account is established: see, for example, *Woods v Martins Bank Ltd* [1959] 1 QB 55, *Warren Metals Ltd v Colonial Catering Co Ltd* [1975] 1 NZLR 273, and other cases cited by Paget, para 6.6.

[6] *Taxation Commissioners v English, Scottish and Australian Bank Ltd* [1920] AC 683 (PC). This discarded an earlier view to the effect that continuity of the arrangements over a period of time is one of the essential indicia of the relationship: see, for example, *Matthews v Williams Brown & Co* (1894) 10 TLR 386.

as a customer of the bank concerned.[7] This remains the case even though the account is overdrawn.[8] There is no restriction on the type of person who may be a 'customer' for these purposes, and a bank which uses the services of another bank can rely on its own status as a 'customer', even though it is itself a member of the banking fraternity.[9]

15.06 Whilst the cases referred to in the previous paragraph provide an indication of the types of case in which an individual should be treated as a customer, it is submitted that these cases should be treated as descriptive or non-exclusive, rather than definitive. In particular, they tend to concentrate on the existence of a running (or current) account, the use of a cheque book and similar matters. Whilst the running account will perhaps always remain a useful indicator, the cheque book as a means of payment is rapidly diminishing in importance. In addition, banks may provide various other services which do not involve a running account, but where the counterparty may legitimately claim the benefit of confidentiality and other protections which the law affords to a 'customer'. For example:

(a) a person who merely opens a deposit account with a view to accumulating interest over an extended period will not have a running account of the type discussed above. Nevertheless, he will have an extended financial relationship with the bank, and it would seem that he should be regarded as a 'customer' for these purposes;[10] and

(b) a company may merely borrow a fixed period term loan from a particular bank, without holding a current account or conducting any other business with that bank. This may occur in the syndicated loan market,[11] where the bank is participating in a facility arranged by a group of institutions. Under these arrangements, payments are passed through the agent bank and the company would not be involved in the operation of separate accounts with the individual lenders. In such a case, the bank may receive confidential information about the borrower in the course of a lending relationship which forms an integral part of its business. Although there is no current account, it seems that the borrower should be treated as a customer and thus be entitled to the benefit of the obligation of confidentiality. This is so notwithstanding the absence of a running account in the traditional form.[12]

15.07 Nevertheless, it is clear that not every transaction between a bank and a member of the public will confer the status of 'customer' on the person concerned. For example, it would appear that a person does not become a 'customer' merely because he occasionally calls into

---

[7] *Great Western Railway Co v London and County Banking Co Ltd* [1901] AC 414 (HL).
[8] *Clarke v London and County Banking Co* [1897] 1 QB 552.
[9] *Importers Co Ltd v Westminster Bank Ltd* [1927] 2 KB 297 (CA). It should be noted that it is the bank itself which is the 'customer' of the clearing bank in such a case. The person on whose behalf the first bank is acting does not become a customer of the clearing bank in such a case because, apart from other considerations, there is no contractual relationship between them: *Aschkenasy v Midland Bank Ltd* (1934) 50 TLR 209.
[10] A suggestion to this effect was made in *Great Western Railway Co v London and County Banking Co Ltd* [1901] AC 414, at p 421.
[11] On syndicated loans, see Chapter 21 below.
[12] In the two examples just given, it would no doubt be the practice of banks to treat the counterparty as its 'customer' and to extend to it the benefit of the duty of confidentiality. Even if they were ultimately found not to be customers in the strict sense, it may be that sensitive information provided by borrowers would be impressed with a duty of confidentiality for other reasons: on this subject, see generally the discussion of the banker's duty of secrecy in Chapter 42 below.

a particular bank branch to effect foreign exchange transactions for travel purposes. Likewise, an individual may in fact be a customer of a branch, but particular transactions may fall outside the scope of that relationship.[13]

15.08 It should be noted that, in spite of the advances in technology which allow for ready access of customer details at any branch, banking law continues to treat the relationship as focused on the particular account holding branch.[14] Although this may appear to be a somewhat dated approach, the identification of the account holding branch is of particular importance where questions of private international law may arise.[15]

The Nature of the Relationship

15.09 It is often repeated that the relationship between a bank and its customer is of a contractual nature and is that of debtor and creditor. The bank is the debtor of the customer to the extent of the credit balance on the customer's account, since the bank is obliged to repay that sum to or to the order of the customer when it falls due—usually, on demand.

15.10 Although the case proceeded on points of pleading which seem unfamiliar and remote to the modern reader, the debtor-creditor nature of the account relationship is clearly articulated in *Foley v Hill*,[16] where a customer sought to recover a large balance by means of proceedings *in equity*. The question was—did the court have jurisdiction to entertain such a suit? In that regard, Lord Brougham observed:[17]

> Now, as to the banker: is his position with respect to his customers that of a trustee ... Is it that of a principal with respect to an agent? Or that of a principal with respect to a factor? ... I am now speaking of the common position of a banker, which consists of the common case of receiving money from his customer on condition of paying it back when asked for, or when drawn upon, or of receiving money from other parties to the credit of the customer, upon like conditions to be drawn out by the customer or, in common parlance, the money being repaid when asked for, because the party who receives the money has the use of it as his own, and in the using of which his trade consists, and but for which no banker could exist, especially a banker which pays interest. But even a banker who does not pay interest could not possibly carry on his trade if he were to hold the money, and to pay it back, as a mere depositary of the principal. But he receives it, to the knowledge of the customer, for the express purpose of using it as his own, which, if he were a trustee, he could not do without a breach of trust ... I cannot at all confound the situation of a banker with that of a trustee, and conclude that the banker is a debtor of the customer with a fiduciary character ...

---

[13] The point is perhaps unlikely to arise in practice with any great frequency. However, see the discussion in Paget, para 6.6, based upon the decision in *EB Savory & Co Ltd v Lloyds Bank Ltd* [1932] 2 KB 122 (CA), [1933] AC 201 (HL).

[14] See, for example, the discussion of this subject in *Burnett v Westminster Bank Ltd* [1966] 1 QB 742. In particular, a demand at the account holding branch is a condition precedent to the bank's legal obligation to repay, even though it may in its discretion allow drawings at other branches: see the discussion of *Joachimson v Swiss Bank Corporation* [1921] 3 KB 110 (CA), at para 15.20 below).

[15] On this subject, see generally Chapter 41 below.

[16] (1848) 2 HL Cas 28 (HL). It may be added that the bank becomes a debtor to its customer when it receives the credit for his account. The bank has no unilateral right to cancel its debt by returning the funds to the remitting bank: see *Tayeb v HSBC Bank plc* [2004] All ER (Comm) 1024, discussed in a different context at paras 7.87–7.89 above.

[17] At p 43.

Similarly, it was observed that:[18]   **15.11**

> Money, when paid into a bank, ceases altogether to be the money of the principal ... it is then the money of the banker, who is bound to return an equivalent by paying a similar sum to that deposited with him when asked for it ...

Whilst the House of Lords proceeded to note that the banker could be an agent or trustee   **15.12** in specific cases—for example, where items were deposited with it for safe keeping—the relationship arising on the account was purely that of debtor and creditor and no further obligations of a fiduciary character could be superadded.[19]

Thus, where a bank receives a remittance to be credited to the account of the customer, it   **15.13** in fact receives the money *for itself* and becomes indebted to its customer for the corresponding sum; it does not receive those sums as *agent or trustee* for the customer.[20] The matter was well expressed in *Royal Bank of Scotland v Skinner*,[21] where the court noted that, '... The banker is not, in the general case, the custodian of the money. When the money is paid in, despite the popular belief, it is simply consumed by the banker, who gives an obligation of equivalent amount ...'.

The essence of the decision in *Foley v Hill* has been followed on numerous occasions, and   **15.14** its authority in this area is undoubted—perhaps because any attempt to superimpose a fiduciary relationship on the account arrangements would render ordinary banking business virtually impossible in practice.[22]

It may be added that the establishment of a banker-customer relationship does not *of itself*   **15.15** create a duty of care in tort.[23]

The above discussion serves to emphasize that, in ordinary circumstances, the account   **15.16** relationship between the bank and its customer will be of a contractual, debtor-creditor nature, unencumbered by extraneous duties of a tortious or fiduciary nature.[24]

---

[18] At p 35. It may be noted that the judgment contains a number of other formulations to essentially similar effect.
[19] As a result, the House of Lords determined in *Foley v Hill* that the customer should have proceeded at law on the debt, rather than in equity. It should be noted that, where the bank makes a payment to a third party at the behest of the customer, it is acting as agent for the customer in effecting that payment and owes fiduciary duties accordingly: see generally Chapter 17 below.
[20] *Midland Bank Ltd v Conway Corporation* [1965] 2 All ER 972, discussed by Paget at para 7.1.
[21] 1931 SLT 382, at p 384. See also *Jeffers v Northern Bank* [2004] NIQB 81.
[22] The decision in *Foley v Hill* has been applied in a variety of contexts. For example, it has been held that the monies deposited by a customer under a 'hawala' transaction with a view to a transfer of funds to a relative in Pakistan were subject to a debtor-creditor relationship and that the recipient or intermediary (the 'hawalder') does not become a trustee of those amounts: see *SA v WI* [2007] EWHC 2025 (Admin), following the earlier decision to similar effect in *Re H* [2003] EWHC 3551. The principle has also been applied to confirm that—in the absence of any special, statutory priorities—all deposit obligations of an insolvent institution will rank *pari passu* in the winding up: see *Space Investments Ltd v Canadian Imperial Bank of Commerce Trust Co (Bahamas) Ltd* [1986] 3 All ER 75 (PC). The decision has also been applied by courts in Australia: see, for example, the decision in *Bank of New South Wales v Laing* [1954] AC 135 (PC).
[23] *Stanley Drilling Co Pty Ltd v Australia and New Zealand Banking Group Ltd* [2003] WASC 63 (Supreme Court of Western Australia); *Williams & Glyns Bank Ltd v Barnes* [1982] Com LR 205, at p 208. Such duties may, however, arise at a later stage, as the relationship is developed: see generally Chapters 17 and 18 below.
[24] Although see the agency point mentioned in n 19 above. There are also various additional obligations which are implied into the contract and which in some respects embellish the basic debtor-creditor position.

The Terms of the Banker-Customer Contract

Introduction

15.17 It used to be the case that the relationship between the bank and its customer depended principally on a series of implied terms developed by the courts over the years, as and when disputes had arisen. The main documentary evidence of the relationship would be the form of mandate, which requested the opening of the account and included specimen signatures on which the bank was authorized to act. But the documentation would include very little by way of express contractual terms.

15.18 That state of affairs has now changed, in part because of greater demands for transparency and fair dealing, and for the customer to be properly informed about the service which he is to purchase, and its cost. Nevertheless, where a bank sets out the terms of the banker-customer relationship in express terms, these will not normally depart in any significant way from the implied terms which have been worked out by the courts over the years. To offer worse contractual terms may attract criticism and may well be unproductive, since such provisions may be vulnerable to challenge under the legislation discussed at a later stage.[25] Equally, there is probably little purpose in seeking to offer improved contractual protection to the customer, since he will generally make his decisions essentially on the basis of financial cost.

15.19 This position was until recently reflected in both the Banking Code and the Business Banking Code, which were expressed to be voluntary codes of practice adopted by banks in the context of their dealings with customers but which in large measure reflected some of the contractual terms to be discussed later in this chapter.[26] These codes have now been replaced by the BCOBS section of the FSA Handbook, which imposes various standards in relation to dealings with retail customers.[27]

The Terms of the Contract

15.20 The nature and terms of the banker-customer contract were discussed by the Court of Appeal in *Joachimson v Swiss Bank Corporation*.[28] In that case, a German firm maintained an account with the London branch of the bank. The firm became an enemy alien on the outbreak of war in August 1914, with the result that the account could not be operated for the duration of the conflict. Thereafter, the firm started proceedings to recover the credit balance on the account. The Court of Appeal held that the claim against the bank could not arise until a demand had been made at the branch at which the account was held.

For the best known twentieth century case which confirmed the relationship of debtor and creditor and which considers the nature of the terms to be implied into the contract, see *Joachimson v Swiss Bank Corporation* [1921] 3 KB 110 (CA). The case is discussed at para 15.20 below.

[25] See paras 15.38–15.52 below.
[26] The Codes were published by the British Bankers Association and others. On these Codes, see Paget, para 7.2.
[27] This subject has already been discussed at para 3.02 above.
[28] [1921] 3 KB 110 (CA).

This central proposition has been applied on a number of occasions.[29] One of the important practical consequences of this rule is that the customer's debt claim against the bank does not arise until the demand is made, with the result that the limitation period for the issue of proceedings only runs from the date of the demand (ie and not from the earlier date on which the funds were deposited and the customer thus acquired the *right* to make a demand).[30] Although the core decision in *Joachimson* was thus confined to a relatively short point, the Court of Appeal took the opportunity for a broader examination of the banker-customer contract. In particular, the court noted that:

(a) the obligations of the bank include (i) to receive funds and to collect cheques for the customer, (ii) to repay the account balance on demand at the account-holding branch during normal banking hours, (iii) to honour the customer's written orders against the account, and (iv) whilst the bank has the right unilaterally to terminate the relationship by repaying the credit balance to the customer at any time, it will give reasonable notice before doing so in order to permit the clearance of outstanding cheques;[31] and

(b) for his part, the customer is required to exercise reasonable care in drawing cheques or other instruments, so as to minimize the possibility of fraudulent alteration.[32]

Given that the bank is a service provider engaging in its business activities with a view to profit, it is perhaps unsurprising that its obligations to the customer are of a relatively more detailed nature. For example, the bank owes various duties to its customer in making payments out of his account, and in collecting items for its credit. These obligations are considered at a later stage.[33] Likewise, a bank owes a general duty of confidentiality to its customers. This duty gives rise to particular problems where a cross-border element is involved and, accordingly, the duty is considered in the context of a series of private international law issues.[34] **15.21**

It is perhaps not possible to provide a comprehensive list of a bank's broader duties, not least because it may voluntarily assume obligations which would not otherwise arise, and cases of that kind will obviously be highly fact-specific. It is, however, possible to provide by way **15.22**

---

[29] See, for example, *Reksten v Severo Sibirsko* [1933] 1 KB 47; *Arab Bank Ltd v Barclays Bank DC&O* [1954] AC 495 (HL). In relation to the application of this rule in Australia, see *Bank of New South Wales v Laing* [1954] AC 135 (PC); *Bank of New South Wales Savings Bank v Fremantle Auto Centre Pty Ltd* [1973] WAR 161.

[30] The Court of Appeal also observed that the issue of a writ may itself constitute a sufficient demand for these purposes. More recently, it has been held that, where multiple demands are made, the limitation period of six years runs from the date of the first demand, so that the customer cannot unilaterally extend the limitation period by making further demands: see *Bank of Baroda v Mohamed* [1999] 1 Lloyds Rep (Bank) 14 (CA), *National Bank of Commerce v National Westminster Bank plc* [1990] 2 Lloyds Rep 514 and *Das v Barclays Bank plc* [2006] EWHC 817 (QB). The cases are noted by Paget, para 18.6.

[31] The bank's right to close an account in this way has recently been confirmed in *National Commercial Bank of Jamaica v Olint Corp Ltd* [2009] UKPC 16 (PC).

[32] This duty is discussed in more detail at paras 15.25–15.28 below.

[33] See Chapter 17 below (paying bank) and Chapter 18 below (collecting bank).

[34] The duty of confidentiality is principally derived from the well-known decision in *Tournier v National Provincial and Union Bank of England* [1924] 1 KB 461 (CA). See the discussion of this subject in Chapter 42 below.

of illustration a brief overview of a few cases in which the extent of (and limits on) the bank's duties have been considered:[35]

(a) a bank is under no general obligation to consider or to advise upon the special tax position of a customer or the wisdom of a course of action which he proposes to take, unless specifically requested to do so;[36]

(b) a bank is not required, on its own initiative, to advise a customer that it now offers new types of deposit product which may offer terms more favourable than the arrangements currently used by that customer;[37]

(c) whilst a bank is under a duty to give reasonable notice to the customer before exercising its right to terminate the relationship, it does not owe a corresponding duty to give reasonable notice of a decision to withhold margin finance on futures transactions;[38]

(d) a bank has the right to defer compliance with the customer's instructions whilst there is some genuine doubt as to their validity or effect;[39]

(e) since a bank's primary relationship is with its own customer, it will generally owe no duty of care to the intended beneficiary of an intended payment in the event of its non-execution, although it may of course incur a liability to its own customer for the consequences of its own failure to act on instructions;[40] and

(f) likewise, a collecting bank owes no general duty to protect a drawee bank from the theft and fraudulent alteration of a cheque.[41]

The Customer's Duties to the Bank

Introduction

15.23 As noted above, it may not be possible to place a definitive limit on the scope of the obligations imposed on the bank under the terms of the banker-customer contract.

15.24 In contrast, the nature and scope of the obligations of the customer seem to be subject to relatively well-defined boundaries, and it is accordingly possible to deal with them comprehensively at this juncture. This section will accordingly consider (i) the customer's duty of care in drawing cheques, (ii) the customer's duty of disclosure in relation to forgeries, and (iii) the possible existence of other duties. In considering these duties, it should be borne in mind that, in the normal course, a bank which pays a cheque must itself bear the risk of forgery since, in meeting such an instrument, the bank pays without the authority of its customer.

---

[35] On these decisions and for further case law, see Paget, paras 7.7–7.9.

[36] This appears to be the effect of *Schioler v National Westminster Bank Ltd* [1970] 2 QB 719, although the case is a little more complex than that. See also *Murphy v HSBC Bank plc* [2004] EWHC 467 (Ch).

[37] *Suriya & Douglas v Midland Bank plc* [1999] 1 All ER 612 (CA).

[38] *Socomex Ltd v Banque Bruxelles Lambert SA* [1996] 1 Lloyds Rep 156.

[39] See *Sierra Leone Telecommunications Ltd v Barclays Bank plc* [1998] 2 All ER 821.

[40] *Wells v First National Commercial Bank* [1988] PNLR 552 (CA). The general point is discussed in more detail at para 17.62 below.

[41] *Yorkshire Bank plc v Lloyds Bank plc* [1999] 2 All ER (Comm) 153. The case is discussed at para 18.32 below.

The Drawing of Cheques

The customer owes a duty to exercise reasonable care in the drawing of cheques so as to **15.25** minimize the danger of forgery and, if he fails to do so, then the subsequent payment of the forged instrument will be binding on the customer and his account. This is the result of the House of Lords decision in *London Joint Stock Bank v Macmillan and Arthur*,[42] where a trusted clerk presented a cheque to his employer for signature. The employer did not notice that the amount in words was not stated and that only the sum of '£2.0.0' was written into the numbers block. After procuring the signature, the clerk expertly altered the '£2.0.0' to '£120.0.0' and completed the amount in words. The employer had clearly failed to exercise reasonable and ordinary care in signing the cheque, and its action against the bank for reinstatement of its account by the excess debit accordingly failed.[43]

The rule in *Macmillan* is well established and has been followed in other common law **15.26** jurisdictions.[44] Disputes about the existence, nature and scope of the duty are thus now unlikely to arise, but litigation is more likely to focus on the factual background to determine whether, on the particular facts, a breach of the duty has indeed occurred. The following points may be noted:

(a) the fact that the customer delegates the preparation of cheques to a trusted employee does not detract from the customer's own obligation to use care in the drawing of cheques. Thus, in *Macmillan* itself, the customer was found to be in breach of the duty even though it had no reason to mistrust the clerk concerned;

(b) the standard of 'reasonable care' may vary over time. In 1931, it was decided that a customer was not in breach of the duty merely because he had not blocked out the 'payee' line of the cheque after the name of the intended payee, thus enabling a dishonest solicitor to insert his own firm's name and to convert the cheque to his own use.[45] However, the practice of inserting manuscript lines after the payee's name is now widespread and well established, and it is highly likely that a similar case would be differently decided today.

The *Macmillan* duty is specifically limited to the act of drawing the cheque itself, and the **15.27** court will be very reluctant to extend the scope of that duty.[46] However, it is not uncommon for customers to give instructions to their banks by letter or other means, and it may

---

[42] [1918] AC 777.

[43] The rule described in this paragraph is usually described as a 'duty' to the bank. Yet this may in some respects be a misnomer. There would not seem to be any case in which the bank could itself recover an award of damages for breach of the duty. Failure by the customer to observe a proper standard of care merely means that the resultant debit to the customer's account will be upheld. There would not appear to be any further or other loss which the bank could recover by way of damages for the breach of the 'duty'.

[44] In *Commonwealth Trading Bank of Australia v Sydney Wide Stores Pty Ltd* (1981) 148 CLR 304, the High Court of Australia elected to follow *Macmillan*, noting that the decision had been applied in *Will v Bank of Montreal* (1931) 3 DLR 526 (Canada), *National Bank of New Zealand Ltd v Walpole* [1975] 2 NZLR 7 (New Zealand), *Standard Bank of South Africa Ltd v Kaplan* (1922) CPD 214 (South Africa) and *Reiter v Western State Bank of St Paul* (1953) 42 Am LR (2d) 1064 (USA).

[45] *Slingsby v District Bank* [1932] 1 KB 544 (CA).

[46] See the discussion at para 15.35 below.

well be that a duty to take care in the preparation and signature of such instructions would arise in that context as well.[47]

15.28 From the bank's perspective, a note of caution must be sounded in relation to the *Macmillan* rule, in that the bank can only rely on it if the customer's failure to take reasonable care was causative of the bank's action in paying the cheque. The bank may not be able to rely on this rule if the alterations are of an amateur nature and should therefore have been detected, or there are other circumstances which ought to have placed the bank on enquiry.[48]

Duty to Disclose Known Forgery

15.29 If a customer becomes aware that his cheques have been forged, he comes under an obligation to notify the bank immediately. If he complies with this duty, then he may be able to compel the bank to reinstate his accounts with the amounts wrongfully debited. However, if he fails to do so, then he will be estopped from seeking such reinstatement because (i) his continuing silence in the face of his knowledge amounts to a representation that there is no difficulty with respect to the account, (ii) the bank will rely on that implied representation to his detriment, and (iii) as a result of the breach of the customer's duty, the bank may lose its right to seek reimbursement from the person responsible for the forgeries.

15.30 These duties are derived from the House of Lords decision in *Greenwood v Martin's Bank Ltd*,[49] where a husband discovered that his wife had been forging his cheques. She dishonestly misrepresented to him the reasons for her forgery and, at her request, he deferred notifying the bank of the situation. Sometime later, mistakenly believing that he had by then advised the bank, the wife committed suicide. The husband subsequently started proceedings against the bank in order to secure the reinstatement of his account by an amount equal to the forged cheques. Although the husband's non-disclosure had not resulted in the payment of the cheques—they had been paid before the husband himself had discovered the forgery—the estoppel nevertheless operated to defeat the husband's claim because his delay had deprived the bank of a possible right of recourse against the wife.[50] However, it may now be that the estoppel operates only to the extent that the bank has genuinely been deprived of an effective right of recourse to the forger, so that some assessment of the bank's realistic prospects of recovery would be required.[51]

15.31 Whether or not the customer has knowledge of the forgeries so as to trigger the duty of disclosure will plainly be a factual question, but it appears that the test refers to *actual* knowledge, as opposed to constructive knowledge or an awareness of circumstances that might prompt further inquiry. Thus, a request by the bank to the customer to look into the size of its overdraft might have prompted inquiries which would have led to the discovery

---

[47] See *Burnett v Westminster Bank Ltd* [1966] 1 QB 742 and the decision in *Pertamina Energy Trading*, considered at para 15.37 below.

[48] eg a very large cheque payable to 'cash': see *Varker v Commercial Bank of Sydney Ltd* [1972] NSWLR 967.

[49] [1933] AC 51 (HL).

[50] See also *Brown v Westminster Bank Ltd* [1969] 2 Lloyds Rep 387.

[51] See *National Westminster Bank plc v Somer International (UK) Ltd* [2002] 1 All ER 198 (CA), discussed by Paget, para 19.8.

of the fraud, but this does not amount to 'knowledge' for the purposes of triggering the duty to disclose.[52] An argument to the effect that the customer had an implied contractual duty to report to the bank a fraud which ought to have been discovered by a reasonable person in possession of the same information was specifically rejected in *Patel v Standard Chartered Bank*.[53]

Whether or not disclosure has been duly made will obviously also be a factual question, but disclosure to a person authorized to receive it on behalf of the bank should usually be sufficient.[54] The customer is presumably under a duty to provide the bank with all relevant information which he holds in relation to the forgery, so as to assist the bank in exercising its rights of recourse against the forger.   **15.32**

It may be that the duty of disclosure is not confined purely to *forgery* as such, but may also extend to any other situation in which the customer becomes aware that his account is being operated in an improper or unauthorized manner.[55]   **15.33**

It should be appreciated that the *Greenwood* duty effectively involves a misrepresentation made by silence. Plainly, however, an express representation made by the customer to the effect that cheques or other instruments are genuine may also create a similar estoppel which will prevent the customer form pleading the forgery to secure the reinstatement of his account.[56]   **15.34**

Other Duties

Over the years, banks have sought to argue that customers owe wider duties to protect the bank against the consequences of forgery or fraud relating to their accounts. The courts, however, have been noticeably reluctant to extend the duties of the customer in this sphere.   **15.35**

The most notable case is *Tai Hing Cotton Mills Ltd v Liu Chong Hing Bank Ltd*,[57] where an accounts clerk fraudulently obtained over HK\$5 million by drawing over 300 cheques over a six year period under a forged signature. The bank argued that the customer owed a general duty to manage its business in a manner designed to minimize the risk that forged cheques would be presented for payment. The Privy Council specifically refused to extend the scope of the customer's duties in this way and reiterated that the customer's duty under *Macmillan* was limited to the act of drawing the cheques themselves. Furthermore, although the fraud took place over an extended period and could thus have been mitigated had the customer checked its bank statements, its failure to do so did not constitute a   **15.36**

---

[52] *Price Meats Ltd v Barclays Bank plc* [2002] 2 All ER (Comm) 346.
[53] [2001] All ER (D) 66 (Apr).
[54] See the unusual situation which arose in *Ogilvie v West Australian Mortgage and Agency Corp Ltd* [1896] 257 (PC).
[55] eg because one of the joint signatories on a corporate account has persuaded the bank to accept an unauthorized amendment to the mandate which allows him to operate the account as a sole signatory: see the situation which arose in *West v Commercial Bank of Australia* (1935) 55 CLR 319.
[56] See *Bank of England v Vagliano Bros* [1891] AC 107 (HL); *Brown v Westminster Bank Ltd* [1964] 2 Lloyds Rep 187.
[57] [1986] AC 80 (PC).

defence for the bank because the customer owed no positive duty to review its statements in this way.[58]

15.37 It should be noted that courts in other jurisdictions have likewise concluded that the duties of the customer are limited to the *Macmillan* and *Greenwood* duties which have already been discussed above.[59] However, formulations of this kind are limited to the *implied* duties of the customer. In principle, there is nothing to prevent the extension of the implied duties by means of *express* terms of the contract. This was specifically acknowledged by the Privy Council in *Tai Hing* (above), where it was noted[60] that the banks '... can increase the severity of their terms of business ...'. Thus, the Singapore Court of Appeal in *Pertamina Energy Trading Ltd v Credit Suisse*[61] held that an express provision to the effect that the customer must examine his bank statements and that they will become binding on him unless any discrepancy is notified within 14 days is valid and effective as between the parties. This decision seems in part to be motivated by the fact that the *Macmillan* duty in relation to cheques does seem to be quite narrow in terms of the scope of its application, because transfer instructions are now frequently given by other means. Given that they will be contained in the bank's standard terms of business, provisions of the type just described will be amenable to challenge under unfair contract terms and similar legislation.[62] However, under the Unfair Contract Terms Act as applied in Singapore, the Court of Appeal in *Pertamina Energy Trading* held that—provided that the clause was clearly defined and expressed—such a provision was not an unenforceable exclusion clause because it amounted to a fair allocation of risk as between the bank and its customer.[63] Indeed, the Singapore courts have held a 'discrepancy' provision of this kind to be binding on an individual (non-corporate) customer.[64] It must be regarded as unclear whether the English courts would adopt the same approach to terms of this kind but, so far as the writer is aware, provisions of the type discussed in this paragraph have not generally been adopted by the banking industry in the United Kingdom.

Regulation of the Banker-Customer Contract

Introduction

15.38 A wide variety of regulatory issues were considered in Part (A) of this book. In contrast, the present discussion has a rather narrower focus and is directed towards a consideration of the

---

[58] For an application of this rule in relation to forged cheques, see *Price Meats Ltd v Barclays Bank plc* [2000] 2 All ER (Comm) 346 and, for a recent discussion of the rule in relation to the unauthorized use of a credit card, see *Duncan v American Express Services Europe Ltd* 2009 SCLR 200 (Court of Session, Inner House).

[59] See *National Bank of Australia Ltd v Hokit Pty Ltd* (1996) 39 NSWLR 377 (New South Wales Court of Appeal) and *Canadian Pacific Hotels Ltd v Bank of Montreal* (1987) 40 DLR (4th) 385.

[60] At p 59.

[61] [2006] SGCA 27 (Court of Appeal, Singapore).

[62] On the application of this legislation to the banker-customer contract, see paras 15.38–15.44 above.

[63] *Pertamina Energy Trading*, at para 60, approving the earlier decision in *Consmat Singapore (Pte) Ltd v Bank of America NT & SA* [1992] 2 SLR 828 (High Court, Singapore).

[64] *Elis Tjoa v United Overseas Bank Ltd* [2003] 1 SLR 747.

legislative impact on an ordinary banker-customer contract. It is proposed briefly to examine three aspects of regulation in this area, namely:

(a) the Unfair Contract Terms Act 1977;
(b) the Unfair Terms in Consumer Contracts Regulations 1999; and
(c) the guidance issued by the Financial Services Authority in this particular sphere.

Unfair Contract Terms Act 1977

Two immediate points should be made about the Unfair Contract Terms Act 1977: **15.39**

(a) the Act does not, in fact, seek to regulate all contractual terms which might be regarded as 'unfair'. Rather, it seeks to restrict the application of exemption clauses; and
(b) again, despite its title, the Act is not restricted to contracts but also regulates notices or other provisions which seek to exclude or restrict liability in negligence.

So far as a bank is concerned, the main effects of this Act are as follows: **15.40**

(a) the bank cannot exclude or restrict its liability for breach of contract[65] or for negligence except to the extent to which the relevant term satisfies the requirement of 'reasonableness';[66]
(b) except insofar as it satisfies the requirement of reasonableness, the bank's written standard terms of business cannot (i) exclude or restrict liability for its own breach of contract or (ii) entitle the bank to render a performance which differs substantially from that reasonably expected of him, or to render no performance at all;[67]
(c) the contract cannot compel a consumer to indemnify the bank against any liability which it may incur in negligence or for breach of contract, unless the terms satisfies the reasonableness test;[68] and
(d) a term will only satisfy the reasonableness test if it was a fair and reasonable term to include in the contract bearing in mind the circumstances known to the parties at the time the contract was made. The burden of proving the reasonableness of the term will rest on the bank as the party seeking to rely on it.[69]

There do not appear to be any cases in England which have considered the application of **15.41** the 1977 Act in the specific context of the banker-customer contract, although the decision of the Singapore Court of Appeal in *Pertamina Energy Trading* considers the application of the Act to express terms to the detriment of the consumer.[70] It must therefore suffice to note a few general points.

---

[65] It may be noted that references to a breach of contract include a breach of an *implied* term see s 1(a) of the 1977 Act. This may be of importance given that a significant part of the banker-customer contract may be reliant on implied terms: see the discussion at para 15.17 above.

[66] Section 2(2) of the Unfair Contract Terms Act 1977.

[67] Section 3 of the 1977 Act.

[68] Section 4 of the 1977 Act.

[69] On these points, see s 11 of the 1977 Act. Schedule 2 to the Act contains various guidelines on the application of the reasonableness test.

[70] The decision in *Pertamina Energy Trading* has been considered at para 15.37 above.

15.42 First of all, it is quite likely that exclusion clauses which significantly detract from the core features of the banker-customer contract would be subjected to careful scrutiny and would be very likely to fail the 'reasonableness' test.[71] However, the standard terms of business used by banks in this country tend to track the duties established by the case law, so the point is perhaps unlikely to arise in practice.

15.43 Secondly, it will be noted later that both a paying bank and a collecting bank act as agent for the customer in paying/collecting cheques, and that they are entitled to an indemnity from the customer for liabilities which they may incur in their capacity as such an agent. It would in theory be possible to challenge the implied right of indemnity on the basis that it amounts to an 'unreasonable indemnity clause' for the purposes of section 4 of the 1977 Act.[72] Nevertheless, it would seem that the implied right of indemnity for the agent is both well established and justifiable in this type of case and a challenge based on section 4 of the 1977 Act would thus be unlikely to succeed.

15.44 Finally, modern concerns about fair treatment of consumers and the wider regulation of banking business perhaps help to explain the absence of case law on the application of the 1977 Act to the banker-customer contract.

Unfair Terms in Consumer Contracts Regulations 1999

15.45 The Unfair Terms in Consumer Contract Regulations 1999 (the 1999 Regulations)[73] apply more broadly to contractual provisions which may be seen as 'unfair'. The regulations are, in that sense, of wider application than the 1977 Act. On the other hand, the 1999 Regulations are of narrower scope, in the sense that they apply only to contracts involving 'consumers'.[74]

15.46 Regulation 5 of the 1999 Regulations provides that a term which has not been individually negotiated is to be regarded as unfair if, contrary to the requirements of good faith, it causes a significant imbalance in the rights and obligations of the parties to the contract, to the detriment of the consumer.[75] A term of this kind which is found to be unfair[76] will not be

---

[71] It is for this reason that it is not certain whether the English courts would adopt the reasoning put forward by the Singapore Court of Appeal in *Pertamina Energy Trading*.

[72] It is not completely clear whether the 1977 Act can apply to an *implied* term of the contract, although s 1(a) of the Act would inferentially support such an approach. The point would, in any event arise if the implied right to an indemnity were reproduced by the bank as an express provision in its standard terms of business.

[73] SI 1999/2083.

[74] That is, to natural persons acting outside the scope of their trade, business or profession: see reg 3(1) of the 1999 Regulations. In contrast, the 1977 Act may apply in any situation where one party is dealing on its standard terms of business, even though the customer may be a corporate entity. Note, however, that a person can be a 'consumer' for the purposes of the 1999 Regulations if he uses the proceeds of a loan to finance the purchase of shop premises, part of which are to be used as a residence: see *Evans v Cherry Tree Finance Ltd* [2008] EWCA Civ 331.

[75] On this formulation, see *Director General of Fair Trading v First National Bank plc* [2002] 1 AC 481 (HL), holding that a provision for the continued payment of interest at the contractual rate following default was not 'unfair' for the purposes of the 1999 Regulations. This decision was followed in the *Abbey National* case, discussed below.

[76] The 'unfairness' assessment is made with reference to the nature of the services and the circumstances subsisting at the time the contract is made: reg 6(1) of the 1999 Regulations.

binding on the consumer, although the contract continues in effect if it is capable of doing so without the unfair term.[77]

Importantly, however, the 1999 Regulations are essentially aimed at the peripheral terms **15.47** of the contract which may be of detriment to the consumer, and not with the central commercial bargain. This point is made by regulation 6(2), which provides that:

> In so far as it is in plain and intelligible language, the assessment of fairness of a term shall not relate:
> (a) to the definition of the main subject matter of the contract; or
> (b) to the adequacy of the price or remuneration as against the goods or services supplied in exchange.

This provision was central to the recent decision of the Supreme Court in the 'bank charges' **15.48** litigation, *Office of Fair Trading v Abbey National plc*.[78] In that case, the question was whether a bank's standard terms providing for the payment of charges (or additional charges) to be levied against a customer in the event that an unauthorized overdraft arose on his account were amenable to the 'fairness' assessment under the 1999 Regulations, or whether they fell within the scope of regulation 6(2) and were accordingly immune from that process. The Supreme Court held that the charges on excess overdrafts and certain other items were a fundamental part of the bank's charging structure—not least because some 30 per cent of their revenue stream from current account services was derived from that source. This was so even though only a small minority of customers actually paid the disputed charges. The Supreme Court—reversing the courts below—accordingly held that the charging arrangements fell within the scope of regulation 6(2)(b) and could not be subjected to the 'fairness' assessment. It therefore appears that some other basis may have to be found if the challenge to bank charges is to be continued or, perhaps, a revision to the 1999 Regulations could provide the necessary grounds.[79]

It remains to add that the 1999 Regulations have been raised in relation to an action against **15.49** a guarantor under a standard form of guarantee. This aspect of the matter is accordingly considered at a later stage.[80]

FSA Guidance

The final level of regulation in relation to unfair contract terms is provided by the Unfair **15.50** Contract Terms Guide (UNFCOG), which forms a part of the FSA Handbook. The guidance given in UNFCOG is principally directed to the 1999 Regulations (rather than the Unfair Contract Terms Act 1977).

The FSA is a qualifying body under the terms of the 1999 Regulations and, accordingly, **15.51** it is entitled to issue guidance and perform various other functions in relation to those

---

[77] Regulation 8 of the 1999 Regulations.
[78] [2010] 1 All ER 667 (Supreme Court).
[79] See the remarks of Lord Walker at para 52 of the judgment.
[80] See para 26.41 below.

regulations.[81] In line with this role, the FSA has issued a Statement of Good Practice.[82] The Statement includes a useful discussion of some of the key aspects of the 1999 Regulations and the FSA's attitude to their enforcement.

15.52   Moving to a greater level of detail, the Statement notes that a contract which enables the bank '... to alter the terms of the contract unilaterally without a valid reason which is specified in the contract ...' is likely to be treated as 'unfair' for the purposes of the 1999 Regulations.[83] Provisions of this kind are important to banks, since their contracts frequently contain unilateral rights of variation in favour of the bank. The Statement of Good Practice suggests that such a right will have a 'valid reason' if it is designed to allow the bank to respond to regulatory or legal changes, or to implement variations in the Bank of England base rate or other, applicable market rates.[84] In the view of the FSA, a right to vary interest rates is subject to the 'fairness' assessment under the 1999 Regulations because it is not a part of the core terms of the contract.[85]

---

[81]   On these points, see FSA Handbook, UNFCOG 1.2.3(G).

[82]   'Fairness of Terms in Consumer Contracts: Statement of Good Practice' (May 2005). The document forms appendix I to UNFCOG 2.

[83]   On the language reproduced in the text, see para 1(k), Sch 2 to the 1999 Regulations.

[84]   See para 3.7 of the Statement of Good Practice. Notice of such a change should also be given to the customer, although the required period of notice may depend on the type of variation at issue: see para 3.12 of the Statement.

[85]   See para 4.5 of the Statement of Good Practice. This view may now require reconsideration in view of the Supreme Court's decision in the *Abbey National* case: see para 15.48 above.

16

CHEQUES

Introduction

The rules relating to cheques are invariably considered to be an integral feature of bank- **16.01**
ing law. Yet, as in many fields, technology is overtaking paper, and the use of cheques is
therefore of diminishing practical importance.

There are numerous reasons for this decline. Partly for reasons of security, commercial **16.02**
customers making larger payments will prefer to make larger payments by direct funds
transfer. Personal customers will frequently pay by credit or debit card rather than by
cheque, and regular, periodic payments will be dealt with by means of standing order and
direct debit. Employees, likewise, will be paid by direct transfer to their bank accounts.
Many other factors could also be cited. As will be seen, legislation has also effectively
rendered cheques non-transferable, with the result that fewer parties can become involved
in a cheque transaction. This, in turn, has significantly reduced the number of potential
complexities and disputes associated with such instruments.

The banking industry in the United Kingdom has now determined that the precipitous **16.03**
decline in cheque use must be carefully managed, with a view to phasing out the cheque
altogether. It would clearly be impracticable and ineffective from a cost perspective if the
cheque were allowed to suffer a slow and gradual death. Accordingly, in December 2009,
the Payments Council Board determined that the central cheque clearing system should
close by 31 October 2018. This will be subject to a final review in 2016 to ensure that the
2018 target date remains feasible at that point. In the interim, alternative methods of payment will have to be promoted for all users.[1] Whether or not the current target date is met,

---

[1] The Payments Council is an industry body which sets strategy for the UK payments industry. On the
decision mentioned in the text, see Payments Council, '2018 target date set for closure of central cheque
clearing' (16 December 2018) and, for the report leading up to this decision, see the Council's publication,

it seems clear that the cheque now has a relatively limited lifespan within the United Kingdom payments industry. It must follow that the use of electronic payment instruments will increase and the Payment Services Regulations 2009 will thus acquire even greater significance as cheque use is managed down.[2]

16.04 The present chapter, and the ensuing chapters dealing with the functions of the paying and collecting bank, are thus likely to be of diminishing importance. Nevertheless, the use of cheques currently remains significant and it therefore remains necessary to consider the rules applicable to these instruments. In addition, some of the general principles applicable to the roles of the paying and collecting banks will apply equally to remitting and receiving banks in the context of other types of transfer. The factors noted in the last two paragraphs do, however, justify a relatively brief discussion of the subject matter.[3]

16.05 The subject matter will be considered in the following order:

(a) the definition of bills of exchange and cheques;
(b) the impact of the Cheques Act 1992;
(c) the legal effects of payment by cheque; and
(d) the terms of the UK's cheque guarantee scheme.

Definitions

Bills of Exchange

16.06 As will be seen, a cheque is a form of a bill of exchange. It is therefore necessary to begin with the definition of a bill of exchange.[4]

16.07 Under the terms of section 3(1) of the Bills of Exchange Act 1882 ('the 1882 Act'), a bill of exchange is:

> an unconditional order in writing addressed by one person to another, signed by the person giving it, requiring the person to whom it is addressed to pay on demand, or at a fixed or determinable future, a sum certain in money to or to the order of a specified person or to bearer.

16.08 A few points arise from this definition:

(a) An order can only be 'unconditional' for these purposes if the obligation to pay is not subject to the occurrence of a contingency[5] and the order is intended to constitute a

---

'The Future of Cheques in the UK' (December 2009). The closure decision clearly has a wide-ranging impact and is to be subjected to parliamentary inquiry: see 'Payments Council comments on the Treasury Select Committee's inquiry into cheque closure decision', 12 February 2010.

[2] The Payment Services Regulations have been considered in depth in Chapter 5 above.

[3] For a more detailed discussion, see Paget, chapter 15.

[4] It is not felt necessary to deal with bills of exchange in depth for present purposes, given the general decline in the use of cheques. The definitive works on the subject are *Chalmers & Guest on Bills of Exchange and Cheques* (17th edn, Sweet & Maxwell, 2009); *Byles on Bills of Exchange and Cheques* (28th edn, Sweet & Maxwell, 2007).

[5] Section 11 of the 1882 Act. An instruction to pay subject to the signature of a receipt is accordingly not a cheque: see *Bavins Junr & Sims v London & South Western Bank Ltd* [1900] 1 QB 270 (CA). However, the fact

general obligation of the person to whom it is addressed.[6] A bill (or a cheque) will still be unconditional for these purposes even though the instrument is expressed to expire if not presented for payment within a reasonable time.[7]

(b) A bill must be addressed by one person to another. The drawer and the drawee of the bill must therefore be different persons.[8] As a result, a draft drawn by a branch of a bank on its own head office is not a bill or a cheque,[9] notwithstanding a decision to the contrary.[10] Likewise, an instrument payable to 'cash' is not a 'cheque' for formal purposes, because 'cash' is plainly not a personal payee. However, the document may still constitute a valid authority to the bank to make payment, with the result that the bank is entitled to debit the customer's account with the amount concerned.[11]

(c) A bill must be payable on demand or at a fixed or determinable future date. A bill is deemed to be payable on demand if it contains no reference to the time for payment.[12]

(d) The order must involve '… a sum certain in money …'.

(e) Although the point is not dealt with in the definition reproduced above, the person to whom the order is addressed (the 'drawee') does not become liable to comply with the order unless he accepts the obligation by signing the bill.[13]

(f) If the instrument is incomplete then the recipient may be entitled to complete it and the drawer may be estopped from denying the validity and content of the instrument as against the paying bank and other parties.[14]

Cheques

A cheque[15] is '… a bill of exchange drawn on a banker payable on demand …'. **16.09**

A cheque is thus a bill of exchange but must also comply with the two additional requirements noted above. The order must be addressed to a bank,[16] and must be payable

---

that the instrument is intended to be conditional as between drawer and drawee does not affect the status of the instrument as a cheque, provided that the condition is not intended to apply to the paying bank: *Nathan v Ogdens Ltd* [1905] 94 LT 120.

[6] That is to say, the obligation to pay cannot be limited to a particular source of funds: s 3(3) of the 1882 Act.

[7] Section 74 of the 1882 Act; *Thairlwall v Great Northern Railway Co* [1910] 2 KB 509. For other cases on this subject, see Paget, para 15.3, note 5.

[8] For the position where the payee is fictitious or does not exist, see Paget, para 15.7 discussing the decisions in *Vagliano Bros v Bank of England* [1891] AC 90 (HL), *Clutton v Attenborough & Son* [1897] AC 90 (HL), *Vinden v Hughes* [1905] 1 KB 795 and *North and South Wales Bank Ltd v Macbeth* [1908] AC 137 (HL).

[9] For these purposes, a bank is regarded as a single corporate entity, even though carrying on business from a number of branches: see *Prince v Oriental Bank Corporation* (1889). Especially in a cross-border context, different branches of a bank are in certain cases treated as separate units: see generally Chapter 40 below.

[10] *Ross v London County Westminster and Parr's Bank Ltd* [1919] 1 KB 678.

[11] *North and South Insurance Corp Ltd v National Provincial Bank Ltd* [1936] 1 KB 328.

[12] Section 10 of the 1882 Act.

[13] On this point, see s 23 of the 1882 Act.

[14] Section 20 of the 1882 Act; *London Joint Stock Bank Ltd v MacMillan and Arthur* [1918] AC 777 (HL). This subject is discussed in more detail in the context of the customer's duties under the banker-customer contract: see para 15.25 above.

[15] Section 73 of the 1882 Act.

[16] This means a company or partnership which carries on the business of banking: s 2 of the 1882 Act. 'Bank' for these purposes connotes an institution which runs current accounts for its customers by accepting

on demand.[17] These conditions will obviously be met in the context of cheques issued in the ordinary course.

16.10 A cheque will not ordinarily have been 'accepted' by a bank in the sense that it has assumed liability for the payment thereof, and the issue of cheque forms does not amount to acceptance.[18]

16.11 An instrument remains a cheque even though it has been post-dated.[19]

16.12 In theory, the drawer of a cheque is entitled to receive notice of dishonour if the cheque is not met, and is discharged if such notice is not duly given. The point will not usually arise, because notice is not required if the drawer has insufficient funds or has himself countermanded payment.[20]

Impact of the Cheques Act 1992

16.13 As noted earlier, a cheque is really a specialized or particular form of bill of exchange. As a result, a cheque made payable to bearer was in principle transferable by delivery; and a cheque made payable to or to the order of a named payee was transferable by way of indorsement.

16.14 The difficulty with this position is that the transferability of a cheque effectively facilitated fraud. A cheque could be stolen in the course of post and, with the aid of a forged indorsement, paid into the account of a person not entitled to the proceeds. In such cases, a bank which paid the cheque in good faith and in the ordinary course of business remained entitled to debit the customer's account.[21] The customer would no doubt be required to pay his creditor again, and was thus left to bear the loss.

16.15 A relatively simple solution to this particular problem was to render cheques non-transferable. This has been achieved by the provisions of the Cheques Act 1992 and the almost invariable practice of banks to take advantage of the protection thereby created. The Act inserted a new section 81A(1) into the 1882 Act, which reads as follows:

> Where cheque is crossed and bears on its face the words 'account payee' or 'a/c payee', either with or without the addition of the word 'only', the cheque shall not be transferable, but shall be valid only as between the parties thereto.

---

deposits and honouring cheques: *United Dominions Trust Ltd v Kirkwood* [1966] 2 QB 431. The case has already been noted at para 15.03 above and, as there stated, in modern times a 'bank' will be an institution holding permission to accept deposits for the purposes of the FSMA.

[17] As noted above, an instrument will be taken to be payable on demand if no date is specified.

[18] That is the pre-printing of the bank's name on the cheque does not amount to a 'signature' by way of acceptance for the purposes of s 23 of the 1882 Act.

[19] Section 13(2) of the 1882 Act. See also the decisions in *Royal Bank of Scotland v Tottenham* [1894] 2 QB 715 (CA); *Hodgson & Lee Pty Ltd v Mardonius Pty Ltd* (1986) 5 NSWLR 496 and other cases discussed by Paget, para 15.13.

[20] Section 50(2)(c) of the 1882 Act; see also the discussion at para 18.10 below.

[21] See section 80 of the 1882 Act. For further details, see para 17.52 below.

Clearly, if a cheque cannot be transferred (ie subject to equities) then neither can it be **16.16** negotiated (ie transferred free from such equities). Accordingly, the effect of such a crossing is that only the originally named payee can be entitled to receive payment of the cheque.[22] As pointed out by other writers,[23] the major banks now invariably issue cheques with a pre-printed 'account payee' crossing. If required, the drawer could open the crossing by deleting these words and initialling the amendments, so that the cheques thereby becomes negotiable; but this must happen very rarely. A person who writes a cheque intends to pay the payee, not an indorsee or some other third party.

The result is that the particular avenue of fraud noted above is now foreclosed, for the pay- **16.17** ing bank should pay only the named payee (and not an indorsee).[24] A person who steals a cheque would thus only be able to make use of it if he can alter the name of the payee in a manner which escapes detection, or if he can fraudulently open an account in the name of the original payee.[25] If a thief does succeed in cashing such a cheque, then the drawer will usually have to pay his creditor again, since his debt under the underlying commercial contract will remain undischarged. The possible liability of the paying and the collecting bank is considered elsewhere.[26]

Payment by Cheque

Introduction

Rules dealing with the effect of payment by cheque are essentially a matter between the **16.18** drawer and the payee of the cheque, and the bank will only rarely need to become involved in the terms of the underlying commercial contract between the parties or its requirements as to the time or manner of payment.[27] Yet a brief discussion of this subject seems to be a necessary and appropriate part of this chapter.

Acceptance of a Cheque

In 1899, it was observed that there was no custom which created an obligation on a credi- **16.19** tor to accept a cheque in payment, even though it was common practice to do so.[28]

---

[22] *Smith v Lloyds TSB Bank Group plc* [2001] QB 541.

[23] See, for example, Paget, para 15.24.

[24] In view of this situation, it is not proposed to consider the other provisions of the 1882 Act relating to crossings, negotiability, and transferability. On this subject, see Paget paras 15.14–15.32.

[25] The first route obviously requires a significant degree of expertise. The second is rendered more difficult by the requirement for banks to verify the identity of individuals seeking to open accounts in order to comply with the Money Laundering Regulations 2007. On this subject, see para 7.19 above. Of course, the reality is that criminal attention has shifted away from the cheque itself to the forgery of the necessary identification materials. However, this may be a more difficult task so it may be that the Act has achieved its objective to that extent.

[26] See Chapters 17 and 18 below.

[27] Exceptionally, a bank may have to concern itself with the terms of that contract where it needs to rely on subrogation to the creditor under the terms of the *Liggett* defence discussed at para 17.19 below.

[28] *Johnstone v Boyes* [1899] 2 Ch 73, followed by the New Zealand Court of Appeal in *Stembridge v Morrison* (1913) 33 NZLR 621.

This remains the case unless there is some express or implied contractual obligation on the creditor to accept a cheque, or he elects to do so.[29]

16.20 Nevertheless, notwithstanding the strict legal position, a creditor will frequently accept a cheque when proffered to him by the debtor. What are the legal consequences of that state of affairs? The following points may be noted in this regard:

(a) the cheque is accepted as 'provisional' payment—ie in the sense that payment and the discharge of the underlying obligation are conditional on the cheque subsequently being met by the drawee bank. In reality, 'payment' does not occur as a result of the delivery of the cheque, since no effective monetary value changes hands at that point;

(b) if the cheque is later honoured by the paying bank, the payment relates back to the date on which the cheque was accepted, with the result that no right to interest can accrue during the intervening period, nor can the creditor terminate the underlying contract on the basis of non-payment, even though he may not be in possession of cleared funds as at the relevant contractual deadline;[30]

(c) if the creditor accepts the cheque, this will effectively suspend any right to sue for the underlying debt pending clearance of the instrument, since the creditor cannot accept the cheque on the one hand and yet sue for the unpaid debt on the other whilst the cheque is in the course of clearing;[31] and

(d) it should be noted that a cheque is intended, so far as possible, to represent the equivalent of cash in the hands of the payee, with the result that the payee is usually entitled to judgment for the face amount of the instrument regardless of any counterclaim or other rights asserted by the drawer.[32]

Cheque Guarantee Scheme

16.21 As noted above, a bank does not add its signature to a cheque and thus does not accept any responsibility for its payment vis-à-vis the payee.[33]

16.22 This rule is indisputable but it was commercially inconvenient to retailers, who could not safely accept cheques in payment for goods and services provided at the point of sale.[34]

---

[29] Compare the remarks of the Supreme Court of New Zealand in *Otago Station Estates Ltd v Parker* [2005] NZSC 16 at para 27, where the court observed that '… a contractual requirement for the making of a payment must, as a matter of law, be performed by means of legal tender, bank cheque or other cleared funds unless the payee by words or conduct indicates a preparedness to accept a personal cheque …'.

[30] For authorities on this point, see *Felix Hadley & Co v Hadley* [1898] 2 Ch 680; *Homes v Smith* [2000] Lloyds Rep Bank 139; *ENE Kos 1 Ltd v Petroleo Brasiliero SA* [2010] 1 All ER 1099 (CA).

[31] *Re Hone* [1951] Ch 85; *ED & F Man Ltd v Nigerian Sweets & Confectionary Co Ltd* [1977] 2 Lloyds Rep 50; *Coltrane v Day* [2003] 1 WLR 1379. The provisional nature of a payment by cheque is also recognized in the United States: see *Ornstein v Hickerson* 40 F Supp 305 (1941).

[32] *Nova (Jersey) Knit Ltd v Kammgarn Spinnerei GmbH* [1977] 2 All ER 463 (HL). The payee may also be entitled to damages, either under the terms of the underlying contract or under the cheque itself. If the cheque is drawn on a foreign bank, the right to damages as a result of its dishonour may be governed by the law applicable to the cheque itself: see *Karafarin Bank v Gholam Reza Mansoury Dara* [2009] EWHC 3265 (Comm).

[33] Of course, as against its own customer, the bank is obliged to meet the cheque if the customer has funds available or the cheque is within the agreed overdraft limit: see para 17.04 below.

[34] The point is of diminishing importance because of the growth in the use of debit and credit cards.

The banks therefore agreed to issue cheque guarantee cards which the account holder could use to back his cheques. Provided that the terms of the scheme and the conditions of the card were met, the bank effectively undertook that the cheque would not be dishonoured. As a result, so far as the retailer is concerned, it is the credit of the bank and the satisfaction of its conditions which are relevant; he is relieved of any concern with the credit of the drawer of the cheque.[35]

The ability of the retailer to rely on the bank's guarantee is, of course, dependent upon the **16.23** formation of a contract between the retailer and the bank itself. This contract comes into existence because (i) the bank, by issuing the card to its customer, vests him with authority to present the card to a retailer on behalf of the bank itself, (ii) the presentation of the card constitutes an offer on behalf of the bank to guarantee the payment of the cheque drawn in favour of the retailer, and (iii) the retailer accepts that offer by supplying goods or services in reliance on the cheque and the supporting card.[36] The issuing bank will usually reserve the right to withdraw the card and, if it writes to the customer to do so, then the customer ceases to have the necessary authority to present the card by way of an offer to the retailer;[37] if, however, the bank fails to secure the return of the card, then the customer retains ostensible authority and the retailer may continue to rely on the terms of the guarantee.[38] Any counterclaim by the drawer of the cheque must be litigated separately and at a later stage.

The terms of the guarantee are contained in the UK Domestic Cheque Guarantee Card **16.24** Scheme. These may be varied from time to time, but the essence of the conditions is as follows:

(a) the bank will guarantee the payment of a cheque in a single transaction up to the limit stated on the card;[39]

(b) the cheque must correspond with the card, in that the customer name and sort code must be identical;

(c) the cheque must be signed in the presence of the retailer;[40] and

(d) the card number must be written on the back of the cheque for verification purposes.

The bank's 'guarantee' has rightly been described as an undertaking not to dishonour the **16.25** cheque for lack of funds on the account.[41] As a necessary corollary, a customer who uses the card under these circumstances must be taken to have requested his bank to provide an overdraft facility to cover the necessary payment.

---

[35] *R v Kassim* [1992] AC 9, 19D.

[36] For an analysis of the various contractual relationships involved, see *First Sport Ltd v Barclays Bank plc* [1993] 3 All ER 789.

[37] *Metropolitan Police Commissioner v Charles* [1977] AC 177.

[38] At all events, it seems right that the bank should bear the risk of loss in cases of this kind.

[39] The reference to a single transaction is designed to ensure that the limit stipulated on the card cannot be circumvented by drawing a series of cheques for the same transaction. If such a case comes to light, then the bank must honour one cheque but could dishonour the others.

[40] This provision is designed to reduce the incidence of fraud.

[41] *Re Charge Card Services Ltd* [1987] Ch 150.

Cheque Clearing

16.26 It is appropriate briefly to explain the clearing cycle for sterling cheques under the system currently operated by the Cheque and Credit Clearing Company. The process will usually operate as follows:[42]

(a) the payee will present the cheque to his own bank for collection. The date on which this is done is referred to as 'D'. The value of the cheque will often be shown on the account with immediate effect, although they will not be available for withdrawal at that point. Details of the amount of the cheque, the drawer and other key details are sent electronically to the paying bank, and the physical cheque will be sent on some time later;

(b) on D+2, the payee should receive value for the cheque, in that any overdraft will be effectively reduced on that day and his obligation to pay interest should be adjusted accordingly. On that day, the Cheque and Credit Clearing Company will calculate the total value of cheques drawn on all of the clearing banks and a net settlement is made via their accounts at the Bank of England;

(c) on D+4, the funds are cleared for withdrawal, in that the creditor can now use those funds to make other payments or transfers;

(d) on D+6, the payee has absolute certainty of funds. If the credit to his account has not been reversed by this time,[43] then the credit entry cannot later be reversed unless the account holder has been party to a fraud in connection with that payment. This stage of the cycle is referred to as 'clearing for fate'.

16.27 It should be appreciated that this cycle has little to do with the contractual relationship between the debtor and creditor or the time of payment as between them. As discussed elsewhere,[44] if the cheque is ultimately cleared then the payment relates back to the date on which the instrument was originally accepted by the creditor.

---

[42] On the process about to be described, see '2-4-6 Changes to Cheque Clearing' (Cheque and Credit Clearing Company).
[43] eg as a result of dishonour or countermand.
[44] See paras 16.18–16.20 above.

17

DUTIES OF THE PAYING BANK

Introduction

17.01 Chapter 15 above considered the general nature of the relationship between the bank and its customer, whilst Chapter 16 above reviewed the law relating to cheques.

17.02 The present chapter moves to a slightly higher degree of detail by considering the position of the bank in its capacity as a paying bank, that is, in meeting cheques and in making payments at the request and for the account of the customer. Given that the banking industry in the United Kingdom has now taken a decision to manage the reduction in cheque use with a view to closing the clearing system in 2018,[1] it may be anticipated that problems of the type discussed in this chapter will occur less frequently.

17.03 The present chapter is divided into five main sections, as follows:

(a) the obligation of the bank to make payment;
(b) the nature and consequences of an unauthorized payment;
(c) various statutory protections available to an institution in its capacity as a paying bank;
(d) payment by mistake; and

---

[1] On this decision, see para 16.03 above.

(e) the extent to which the paying bank may incur liabilities to third parties in the course of performing its functions.

The Duty to Pay

The General Nature of the Obligation

17.04   As noted previously,[2] a bank which receives funds for the account of its customer thereby becomes indebted to the customer for a sum equivalent to that amount on demand made by the customer.[3] Accordingly, subject to any rights of set-off which it may wish to exercise and to any statutory impediment,[4] the bank is obliged to make payments on the instructions of the customer provided that (i) the customer has sufficient funds available for the purpose of the payment,[5] (ii) the payment instruction is regular and unambiguous in form,[6] and (iii) the bank's authority to meet the payment order has not been terminated.[7]

The Bank's Duty in Executing Payment Instructions

17.05   Although the general nature of the relationship is that of debtor and creditor, this transmutes into a principal–agent relationship where the bank meets the customer's cheques or other instructions in order to make a payment to a third party.[8] The bank owes fiduciary duties and a duty of care to the customer in carrying out his instructions, although the mode of achieving the customer's objectives (eg as to the selection of the payment system to be used) appears to rest with the bank itself.[9]

Termination of the Bank's Authority to Pay

17.06   The authority of the bank to pay a cheque comes to an end when the bank receives notice of the customer's death[10] but, plainly, it obtains a good discharge for cheques honoured

---

[2] See the discussion of the decision in *Foley v Hill* at para 15.10 above.

[3] On the need for a demand, see *Joachimson v Swiss Bank Corporation* [1921] 3 KB 110 (CA), discussed at para 15.20 above.

[4] See, for example, the obligations imposed on the bank pursuant to the Proceeds of Crime Act 2002, as discussed at paras 7.28–7.73 above.

[5] This would include any amount available on any uncancelled overdraft facility, as well as any positive credit balance. Note that sufficiency of funds is to be determined as at the time when the bank is required to make the payment. The bank is not required to monitor the account to see whether individual payments could be made at a later date: see *Whitehead v National Westminster Bank*, The Times, 19 June 1982. The case is noted by Paget, para 18.8. In addition, the bank is entitled to take account only of items which have been finally cleared to the account, and may disregard items which have only been provisionally credited. On the cheque clearing process, see para 16.26 above.

[6] It is, accordingly, an implied term of the banker-customer contract that, in cases of doubt, the bank may defer complying with a payment instruction whilst it verifies the authenticity or propriety of the instruction: see, for example, the situation which arose in *Sierra Leone Telecommunications Ltd v Barclays Bank plc* [1998] 2 All ER 821. However, this rule can only apply if the bank has some genuine ground for querying the instruction: *Bank of England v Vagliano Bros* [1891] AC 107 (HL).

[7] Paget, para 18.2.

[8] Paget, para 18.3 noting *Westminster Bank v Hilton* (1926) 43 TLR 124.

[9] *Dovey v Bank of New Zealand* [2000] NZLR 641 (New Zealand Court of Appeal).

[10] Bills of Exchange Act 1882, s 75.

between the date of death and the date on which the bank receives notice of that occurrence.

17.07 Likewise, a cheque must not be met following an express countermand from the customer.[11] The countermand must come to the actual attention of the bank before it makes payment.[12] It has formerly been held that the notice of countermand must be received at the account holding branch,[13] but it may be that modern communications might suggest a relaxation of this rule.

17.08 As noted above, the bank is under a duty to the customer to make payment in accordance with his clear and unambiguous instructions. As a corollary, the termination of that authority must likewise be clear and unambiguous. A telephone instruction may often be unclear, with the result that the bank would incur no liability for paying the cheque.[14] In England, it has been held that a telegraphed countermand instruction was insufficiently clear when just one of the digits on the quoted cheque number was mistaken.[15] In contrast, Canadian courts have held that errors of detail in the countermand notice will not affect its essential validity provided that the relevant cheque is adequately identified.[16]

17.09 An authority to pay may also come to an end on the insolvency of a company. For example, when a company is placed into the process of administration pursuant to the terms of the Insolvency Act 1986 (as amended), the administrator has power to take possession of the company's property.[17] Likewise, in the event of a liquidation, the powers of the directors will come to an end.[18] Consequently, when the bank receives notice of such events,[19] it should regard the existing mandate as terminated and thenceforth deal with the relevant insolvency official.

17.10 A bank which pays a cheque in disregard of an effective countermand or other termination of authority plainly pays without the customer's authority, and cannot debit the customer's account unless it can show some other defence.[20]

Failure to Comply with Payment Instructions

17.11 A bank which wrongfully[21] refuses to meet a payment instruction out of an available credit balance or overdraft facility will thereby incur a liability to pay damages to the customer for

---

[11] Bills of Exchange Act 1882, s 75.

[12] *Curtice v London City & Midland Bank Ltd* [1908] 1 KB 293.

[13] *London Provincial and South-Western Bank Ltd v Buzzard* (1918) 35 TLR 142, noted by Paget, para 18.15.

[14] See, for example, *Commonwealth Trading Bank v Remo Auto Sales Pty Ltd* [1967] VR 790.

[15] *Westminster Bank Ltd v Hilton* (1926) 136 LT 315.

[16] *Giordano v Royal Bank of Canada* [1973] 3 Ont Rep 771; *Remfor Industries Ltd v Bank of Montreal* (1978) 90 DLR (3d) 316.

[17] Insolvency Act 1986, Sch B1, para 1.

[18] Insolvency Act 1986, s 103.

[19] Appropriate supporting evidence will also be required, such as the court order confirming the relevant appointment.

[20] See, for example, the discussion of *B Liggett (Liverpool) Ltd v Barclays Bank Ltd* [1928] 1 KB 48, at para 17.19 below.

[21] Whether the refusal is wrongful is a question that may require detailed analysis. For example, was the bank released from its immediate obligation to meet a cheque because of a suspicion of money laundering

breach of the banker-customer contract. The claim will usually be for general damages for loss of reputation and resultant impaired credit or business standing.[22] It is conceivable that special damages[23] might be recoverable for loss of bargain where the customer has notified the bank of an impending transaction and impressed upon it the importance of payment being made on time. However, there does not appear to be any reported case in which this particular type of situation has arisen.

17.12   Where a cheque is dishonoured, it will usually be returned to the collecting bank marked 'refer to drawer', 'insufficient funds' or similar expression. These words will obviously lower the drawer's reputation in the mind of the collecting bank and are therefore capable of being defamatory.[24] In practice, a claim for breach of the banker's duty to pay and a claim in defamation are likely to shade into each other, since neither claim can succeed if the bank was justified in refusing payment.

Nature and Consequences of Unauthorized Payment

Introduction

17.13   As noted in other contexts, a bank is the debtor of its customer to the extent of the credit balance on the account, and will plainly incur liability to the customer in the event of wrongful non-payment. This applies equally where the bank fails to meet an instruction in favour of a third party. In the latter case, the bank also acts as agent for the customer in making the requested payment, and is entitled to an agent's indemnity in the usual way.

17.14   By the same token, the bank is only entitled to that indemnity if it has paid in compliance with the terms of the mandate (ie within the scope of its actual authority). There are various situations in which a bank may be deemed to have paid without authority. In such cases, the bank will usually have to reinstate the account accordingly although, as will be seen, it does not *invariably* follow that the bank will be liable to the customer in this way.

17.15   There are various alternative scenarios which require consideration.

Payment beyond the Scope of the Mandate

17.16   The bank's standard form of account mandate will usually include a specimen of the customer's signature upon which the bank will be authorized to rely in accepting instructions for the operation of the account. Where the customer is a corporate body, the mandate frequently takes the form of a board resolution approving the opening of the account and naming the relevant signatories on behalf of the company. As a precaution, two signatures may be required on payment instruments and special arrangements may apply where the

---

(see generally paras 7.83–7.93 above) or was the bank justified in delaying payment because of legitimate doubts over the adequacy of the authority (see n 6 above).

[22] In relation to a business customer, see *Wilson v United Counties Bank Ltd* [1920] AC 102 (HL) and, in relation to private customers, see *Kpohraror v Woolwich Building Society* [1996] 4 All ER 119.

[23] ie damages representing losses specifically within the contemplation of the parties for the purposes of the second limb of the rule in *Hadley v Baxendale* (1854) 9 Exch 341.

[24] *Davidson v Barclays Bank Ltd* [1940] 1 All ER 316; *Baker v Australia and New Zealand Bank Ltd* [1958] NZLR 907 and the wider discussion in Paget, para 18.20.

cheque is above a stated monetary limit. There is no set formula and the terms of the mandate are a matter for agreement between the bank and the customer.

As a general rule, a bank which pays a cheque not covered by the mandate does so with- **17.17** out authority and must therefore restore the account. There are, however, two important exceptions to this rule.

First of all, it must be remembered that, whilst the mandate will be the *usual* source of **17.18** authority, it is not necessarily the *sole* source. In one case, the bank paid a cheque against a single signature when two were required under the terms of the mandate. Notwithstanding this irregularity, the bank was given leave to defend the customer's claim for the reinstatement of its account because there was evidence that the payment had been specifically approved by the company's directors—in other words, that the signatory had *actual* authority to bind the company to the instrument, even though it was outside the terms of the formal mandate itself.[25] For these purposes, it may be sufficient that all of the directors were aware of, and approved, the payment; it is not necessary that a formal board resolution should have been passed to that end.[26] It should be appreciated that the mandate itself is not varied in this type of case. The bank is merely able to avoid liability for reinstatement of the account on the basis that—regardless of the terms of the mandate—the signatory enjoyed the actual authority of the company to draw the cheque.[27] It is thus conceivable that a bank might mistakenly pay a series of cheques outside the scope of the mandate, but will still have to reimburse those particular items where a specific authority cannot be traced.

The second exception is more likely to be of importance in practice. Since a bank has a **17.19** general authority to pay the customer's debts on its behalf, the bank is entitled in equity to the benefit of any payment so made, even if it strictly falls outside the scope of the mandate. This rule is derived from the well-known decision in *B Liggett (Liverpool) Ltd v Barclays Bank Ltd*[28] where, once again, the bank had paid against a single signature where the mandate required two signatories. Nevertheless, the proceeds of the unauthorized cheque had been used to pay a creditor of the customer, and its liabilities had been reduced by an amount equal to the payment concerned. The customer was therefore no worse off as a result of the mistake made by the bank. In effect, the bank was subrogated to the creditor whom it had paid on behalf of the customer. The equitable principle applies whether the payment is made out of a credit balance or by means of an overdraft.[29] Given the equitable basis and purpose of the *Liggett* defence, it appears that it would be available even in relation to cheques which had been countermanded by the customer prior to their payment by

---

[25] *Symonds (HJ) & Co Ltd v Barclays Bank plc* [2003] EWHC 1249 (Comm).
[26] See *London International Trust Ltd v Barclays Bank Ltd* [1980] 1 Lloyds Rep 241.
[27] This will largely be a matter of good fortune so far as the bank is concerned, since it will not have known of the position at the time of mistakenly paying the cheque, and it will be dependent on appropriate evidence emerging at a later stage.
[28] [1928] 1 KB 48.
[29] This point was made in *Liggett* itself.

the bank.[30] The principle has subsequently been discussed and approved in later cases[31] and has also been applied in other common law jurisdictions.[32]

Forged Signatures

17.20 Under section 24 of the Bills of Exchange Act 1882, '… where a signature on a bill is forged or placed thereon without the authority of the person whose signature it purports to be, the forged or unauthorised signature is wholly inoperative …' unless the party concerned is estopped from pleading the forgery or lack of authority.

17.21 Forgery involves the creation of a false instrument, with the intention of representing it to be genuine and procuring a third party to do or omit a particular act on that basis.[33] In disputed cases, expert handwriting evidence may be required to determine whether the signature is indeed a forgery. But the legal definition of a forgery will not normally be in issue.

17.22 Want of authority perhaps poses a greater degree of difficulty, and it may not always be easy to distinguish between forgery and a mere lack of authority.[34] However, if an otherwise authorized signatory of the company uses his authority to draw a cheque on behalf of the company with a fraudulent purpose in view, then it seems that the cheque should be treated as a forgery, rather than merely as unauthorized.[35]

17.23 As noted above, the customer may be estopped from pleading the relevant forgery or want of authority. This may occur where the customer is in breach of his own duties to the bank in the drawing of cheques and the reporting of forgery. These aspects of the customer's duties to the bank have been discussed at an earlier stage.[36]

---

[30] The *Liggett* defence does, however pre-suppose that a debt of the customer has been discharged, and a countermand of the instrument may suggest that the underlying debt is disputed. It may be that the application of the *Liggett* defence has to be limited in certain respects, since it would be unfair to the customer if the bank's mistaken payment deprived the customer of the right to dispute the debt. Given that the defence operates by way of subrogation, in the sense that the bank steps into the shoes of the creditor, it may be that the customer can raise against the bank any set-off or counterclaim which he could have invoked against the original creditor. With this difficulty in mind, it has been suggested that the customer should only be barred from recovering the unauthorized payment if this would amount to unjust enrichment on his part: see *Crantrave Ltd v Lloyds Bank plc* [2000] 3 WLR 877. This serves further to emphasize the equitable nature of the *Liggett* defence.

[31] See *Lloyds Bank Ltd v Chartered Bank of India, Australia and China* [1929] 1 KB 40 (CA); *Crantrave Ltd v Lloyds Bank plc* [2000] 3 WLR 877.

[32] See, for example, the Australian decision in *Christianos v Westpac Banking Corp* (1991) WAR 336 and the New Zealand decision in *Westpac Banking Corp v Rae* [1992] 1 NZLR 338.

[33] Forgery and Counterfeiting Act 1981, s 1 considered by Paget at para 19.5.

[34] The distinction may be of some practical importance. For example, it appears that a *forged* signature cannot be ratified by the customer. On the other hand, an *unauthorized* signature is capable of ratification if the customer has full knowledge of the relevant facts at the time of ratification: see *English Scottish & Australian Bank Ltd v Beatty* [1931] QSR 291 (Supreme Court of Queensland).

[35] This was the approach adopted in a case of this kind in *Kreditbank Cassel GmbH v Schenkers Ltd* [1927] 1 KB 826 (CA).

[36] See paras 15.25–15.34 above.

Misappropriation by an Authorized Signatory

Misappropriation of funds by an authorized signatory raises a slightly different set of prob-   **17.24**
lems. The signatures on a payment instruction may be genuine and, on their face, accord
with the terms of the mandate. A mechanistic approach to the mandate would mean that
the bank is discharged when paying cheques under these circumstances.

But a bank cannot ignore its wider knowledge of the customer or circumstances which give   **17.25**
rise to suspicion. The authorized signatories on a corporate account act as agents for their
principal (the customer), and the bank cannot simply ignore evidence that the agents are
using their authority to defraud the principal. The earlier cases in this area suggested that
the bank may have to look behind the mandate and to make appropriate inquiries into the
true intentions of the customer, as opposed to merely relying on the mandate.[37] As noted
previously, the bank is allowed to defer making payment whilst it makes inquiries of this
kind, but this clearly comes into conflict with the bank's duty to pay on demand.[38]

This conundrum fell for consideration in *Barclays Bank plc v Quincecare Ltd*,[39] where the   **17.26**
chairman of the customer instructed the bank to transfer some £340,000 to a firm of solicitors who acted for him personally. He then asked that firm to remit the funds to an account
in the United States, from where they were stolen by the chairman. Since the funds represented the proceeds of a loan made by Barclays to the customer, the bank then sued both
the customer and the guarantor for repayment. The company defended the claim on the
basis that the transfer to the solicitors should have raised doubts in the mind of a reasonable
banker and that, in failing to make inquiries, the bank had been negligent.

The court noted that, in paying cheques to third parties out of funds standing to the credit   **17.27**
of the customer's account, the bank was acting as agent of the customer. The bank accordingly owed fiduciary duties to the customer and was also bound to use reasonable skill and
care in the execution of the customer's instructions.[40] However, these duties were subordinate to the bank's primary duty to make payments against a valid and proper order. Since,
in the absence of contrary indications, the bank was generally entitled to trust the individuals with whom it dealt, it was entitled to implement the requested transfer because there
were no circumstances to place it on inquiry. It followed that the bank was entitled to
recover the loan, notwithstanding the subsequent misappropriation of the proceeds.

---

[37]   This was the effect of the decisions in *Selangor United Rubber Estates Ltd v Cradock (No 3)* [1968] 2 All
ER 1073 and *Karak Rubber Co Ltd v Burdon (No 2)* [1979] 1 All ER 1210. These decisions were applied in
subsequent cases: see, for example, *Rowlandson v National Westminster Bank Ltd* [1978] 3 All ER 370. The
decisions were criticized (see, for example, Paget, para 19.10) and, as will be seen, they are no longer regarded
as good law in England. The decisions have nevertheless been followed in other common law jurisdictions:
see, for example, *Grover Raffin Construction Ltd v Bank of Nova Scotia* [1976] Lloyds Rep 373 (Canada); *Ryan
v Bank of New South Wales* [1978] VR 555 (Victoria); *Esanda Finance Corp Ltd v Reyes* [2001] NSWSC 234
(New South Wales Supreme Court); *Glover v Blumer* [2008] ACTCA 1 (Court of Appeal, Australian Capital
Territory).
[38]   See the discussion at n 6 above.
[39]   [1992] 4 All ER 363.
[40]   The court regarded the latter duty as an implied term of the contract, rather than as a duty owed in
tort.

17.28 The decision in *Quincecare* was shortly thereafter followed by the Court of Appeal in *Lipkin Gorman v Karpnale Ltd.*[41] In *Lipkin Gorman*, a firm of solicitors maintained a client account with a bank under the terms of a mandate which allowed a sole partner to sign cheques on the account. One of the partners was an habitual gambler, and this was known to the bank since he had a personal account at the same branch. Indeed, the branch manager had met with the partner to discuss the difficult status of his personal account and his gambling activities had been specifically raised. Despite this knowledge, some £220,000 was drawn from the firm's client account over a period and in reliance on the sole signature of the partner concerned. The funds were applied in the purchase of gambling chips.

17.29 The Court of Appeal found that the bank was not liable for breach of its obligation to use reasonable skill and care in operating the account. The court noted that a single phone call to the senior partner of the solicitors' firm would have put an end to the fraud, but the bank had not been negligent in failing to make that call because:

(a) the bank's knowledge of the relevant partner's gambling habit was derived from its position as personal banker to the partner concerned and, in view of the banker's duty of confidentiality[42] it was not open to the bank to discuss these details with the firm.[43] It is respectfully submitted that this is the wrong approach to the matter. Cheques were being drawn on the firm's client account and it was thus open to the bank to query these transactions with the firm. The bank could simply have drawn the number and size of the cheques to the firm's attention, without making any reference to the gambling issue; and

(b) the required standard of care was measured by reference to a 'reasonable and honest banker'. Would such a banker, in possession of the information held by the bank itself, believe that the customer was being defrauded by its authorized signatory? In this context, the court observed[44] that practising solicitors were generally seen as respectable clients and there was no particular reason to think that the partner might be dishonest. It would be unrealistic to place a burden of monitoring the client account, searching for evidence that a partner might be abusing his signing authority. In abstract terms, this formulation may well be accurate but it seems to bear limited relationship to the facts of the case, where the bank had knowledge of the salient facts but failed to draw the necessary conclusions.

17.30 The bank in *Lipkin Gorman* may thus have been rather fortunate. The Court of Appeal specifically disapproved the decisions in *Selangor United Rubber Estates* and *Karak Rubber* but, perhaps in its desire to move away from that line of authority, had veered a little too far in the opposite direction. Unlike *Quincecare*, where no trust account was involved, the

---

[41] [1992] 4 All ER 409 (CA). Reference is made to the Court of Appeal judgment because this deals with the liability of the bank which held the account concerned. The claimant subsequently pursued its appeal against Karpnale Ltd (The Playboy Club) to the House of Lords: [1992] 4 All ER 512, but they did not appeal against the Appeal Court's finding in favour of the bank.

[42] On this duty, see generally Chapter 42 below.

[43] See p 422 of the judgment.

[44] At p 444.

bank in *Lipkin Gorman* clearly knew that the funds standing to the credit of the client account were held in trust for the benefit of third parties.

Separately, the Court of Appeal noted that the solicitors' firm had discovered the partner's **17.31** dishonesty when he had submitted incorrect travel expense claims earlier in the year, but had taken no action. Since that failure amounted to contributory negligence on the part of the firm, the bank would not in any event have been liable for cheques drawn after the partner's dishonesty had become apparent.

It may be added that the above discussion is specifically confined to a potential liability to **17.32** the *customer*. Possible liabilities to third parties are considered at a later stage.[45]

The Recovery of Payments Made

Although not strictly a 'duty' of the paying bank, it is nevertheless relevant to consider some **17.33** of the other consequences of an unauthorized payment. As between the bank and the customer, it has been noted that the customer's account cannot be debited (or must be reinstated) with the value of any payments which prove to have been made on the basis of a forged instruction, or which are paid in error after a cheque has been validly countermanded. Such a payment may also occur if the bank makes an error as to the true status of the customer's account (eg where it pays a cheque in the belief that all items on the account are cleared, but a provisional item is later reversed). But, in such a case, the bank will be out of pocket and a third party will have received the benefit of the payment or transfer. In very general terms, it may therefore be said that the recipient has been unjustly enriched at the expense of the bank. Under what circumstances can the bank recover such a payment?

It is fair to say that the law in this area seems to have developed in a rather haphazard fash- **17.34** ion.[46] In essence, the bank will be seeking to make a recovery of the payment on the basis this was induced by the bank's own mistake. It no longer matters whether the mistake relates to a question of fact or a matter of law.[47] The ability of the bank to recover the payment from the third party under these circumstances was considered by the court in *Barclays Bank Ltd v W J Simms, Son & Cooke (Southern) Ltd*[48], where a bank officer overlooked a countermand instruction and made payment to the payee of the stopped cheque. The court illustrated the position by reference to two, contrasting situations:

(a) where the bank mistakenly believes that there is a sufficient credit balance or overdraft facility to meet the cheque; and
(b) where the bank has overlooked a countermand instruction (ie the situation in *Simms* itself).

In the first example, the court observed that (i) the customer, by drawing the cheque, **17.35** impliedly requests an overdraft facility on the bank's standard terms and of the amount necessary to meet the cheque and (ii) the bank, in meeting the cheque, impliedly assents to

---

[45] See para 17.58 below.
[46] See the discussion in Paget, para 19.14.
[47] *Kleinwort Benson Ltd v Lincoln City Council* [1999] 2 AC 349 (HL).
[48] [1980] QB 677.

the customer's request. Although it may be something of a legal fiction, the result is that the bank has recourse to the customer for the impliedly agreed overdraft. The payment made by the bank to the third party is therefore made as agent for the customer and discharges the customer's obligation to the creditor concerned. Since the creditor's claim as against the customer is irrevocably discharged by the payment, he has not been unjustly enriched and can thus retain the benefit of that sum. Although this was not necessary for the decision in *Simms*, the very same issue subsequently arose in *Lloyds Bank plc v Independent Insurance Co Ltd*,[49] where the bank mistakenly believed that a large credit to the customer's account was final and thus made a payment to Independent Insurance on that basis. The credit was in fact provisional and was later reversed. Adopting the *Simms* approach, the customer's debt to the insurer was discharged and it would thus not be unfair for the insurer to retain those proceeds. The bank's inability to recover the payment in this type of case seems to rest on the fact that the bank has ostensible authority to pay on behalf of the customer and the payment—albeit mistaken—thus discharges the underlying debt.

17.36 In the second situation (payment of a countermanded cheque), the bank does not have the customer's actual authority to pay and, consequently, the mistaken payment by the bank does *not* have the effect of discharging the underlying commercial obligation of the customer. Since the recipient creditor retains his cause of action against the customer, there is nothing inequitable in ordering repayment to the bank. This approach to the matter is objectionable on various grounds. First of all, it disregards the fact that the bank will have ostensible (if not actual) authority to discharge the customer's debt on his behalf. Secondly, when the payee is advised that the cheque has been cleared and unconditionally credited to his account, it is reasonable for him to assume that the payment is final, but the decision undermines that finality.[50]

17.37 The bank may be precluded from recovering the mistaken payment if the creditor has changed his position in reliance on the receipt of the funds. The mere spending of the funds by the payee will not of itself amount to a 'change of position' for these purposes. Where, however, the recipient spent the money on the basis of an explicit confirmation from the bank that the relevant amounts did indeed represent her entitlement, then the 'change of position' defence was held to be made out.[51] Similarly, if the recipient foregoes other benefits—such as social security claims—available to him in reliance on the amounts received into his account, the bank's claim may likewise fail on 'change of position' grounds.[52]

---

[49] [1999] 1 Lloyds Rep (Bank) 1 (CA).

[50] In spite of these reservations, the decision has been applied in Australia: see *Commonwealth Bank of Australia Ltd v Younis* [1979] 1 NSWLR 444 and *Bank of New South Wales v Murphett* [1983] 1 VR 489 (Supreme Court of Victoria). New Zealand courts have adopted a similar approach to this subject: see *Southland Savings Bank v Anderson* [1974] 1 NZLR 118 and *Davies Ltd v Bank of New South Wales* [1981] NZLR 262.

[51] *Lloyds Bank Ltd v The Hon Cecily K Brooks* (1950) 6 LDAB 161. It may be noted in passing that the burden of proof is on the recipient of the mistaken payment to demonstrate that he has changed his position in reliance on the payment and is thus entitled to resist the claim for repayment on that basis. In the case of other negotiable instruments, it seems only to be necessary to show that the recipient's position *could* be prejudiced: see *Cocks v Masterman* (1829) 9 B&C 902, *London and River Plate Bank v Bank of Liverpool* [1896] 1 QB 7 and the discussion in Paget, para 19.30.

[52] *Avon County Council v Howlett* [1983] 1 WLR 605.

Equally, an intermediary who receives funds and accounts to his principal before receiving notice of the error will plainly have changed his position in reliance on the receipt, and the mistaken payment will again be irrecoverable.[53] The 'change of position' defence will however only 'bite' when the funds are released from the intermediary to his client.[54]

It should be appreciated that, in making payment on a cheque, the paying bank does not **17.38** owe any duty to the payee nor does it impliedly represent that the customer's signature is genuine. The paying bank's claim for repayment from the payee in this type of case is thus not precluded by any alleged negligence on its part, nor by any estoppel based on the actions taken by the bank itself in meeting the cheque.[55]

Finally, it should be noted that the bank's right to recover the mistaken payment is essen- **17.39** tially an equitable claim based on unjust enrichment. The court in *Chase Manhattan Bank NA v Israel-British Bank (London) Ltd*[56] held that a claim for recovery of a mistaken double payment might amount to a proprietary or trust claim, with the result that the claimant might be entitled to a preferential recovery in the insolvency of the recipient, at least pro- vided that it was possible to trace and identify the relevant funds. However, this line of reasoning was rejected in *Westdeutsche Landesbank Girozentrale v Islington Borough Council*,[57] where the House of Lords confirmed the *personal* nature of the remedy and held that no fiduciary relationship came into existence as a result of the mistaken payment.

Statutory Protection of the Paying Bank

Introduction

The present section considers the circumstances under which the bank will be deemed to **17.40** have made due payment of a cheque so that it is entitled to debit its customer's account accordingly. Questions about the due payment of the cheque are most likely to arise in two cases, namely, (i) where the cheque is stolen in the course of post or by a dishonest employee of the payer or the payee, and he succeeds in opening an account in the name of the payee for the purpose of paying the cheque or (ii) where the payee alters the cheque to obtain payment of a greater amount. A particular case could also involve a combination of both features. The present treatment takes into account the fact that, in the vast majority of cases, cheques are no longer transferable or negotiable, and the question of paying a cheque under a forged indorsement will now hardly ever arise in practice.[58] This section

---

[53] *ANZ Banking Group Ltd v Westpac Banking Corp* (1988) 164 CLR 662 (High Court of Australia); *State Bank of New South Wales v Swiss Bank Corporation* (1995) 39 NSWLR 350; *Imperial Bank of Canada v Bank of Hamilton* [1903] AC 49 (PC).

[54] *Admiralty Commissioners v National Provincial and Union Bank of England* (1922) 127 LT 452; *National Westminster Bank Ltd v Barclays Bank Ltd* [1975] QB 654.

[55] See *National Westminster Bank Ltd v Barclays Bank International Ltd* [1975] QB 654, applying the Privy Council decision in *Imperial Bank of Canada v Bank of Hamilton* [1903] AC 49. The case is discussed by Paget, paras 19.22–19.25.

[56] [1978] 3 All ER 1025.

[57] [1996] AC 669 (HL).

[58] Those issues may, however, continue to arise in relation to other forms of bills of exchange. For a discussion, see Paget, ch 20.

accordingly considers briefly the concept of 'payment in due course', and various statutory provisions designed for the protection of the paying bank.

Payment in Due Course

17.41 The starting point for this discussion is to be found in section 59 of the Bills of Exchange Act 1882, which provides that:

(a) a cheque is discharged by 'payment in due course' by the bank upon which it is drawn; and

(b) 'payment in due course' means payment on or after the date of the cheque to the holder in good faith and without notice that his title to the cheque is defective.

17.42 The difficulty with this provision is that, under modern systems for cheque clearance, the paying bank will merely receive an electronic message providing the computer-read data from the foot of the cheque and the amount to be paid.[59] It will frequently not receive the original cheque until after payment has been made. The paying bank thus does not know the identity of the 'holder' for the purposes of section 59, nor can it physically examine the cheque to determine whether the holder's title may be defective.

Material Alteration to the Cheque

17.43 Under section 64, Bills of Exchange Act 1882, a cheque which is materially altered without the assent of the drawer is avoided. A 'material alteration' includes an alteration in the date of the instrument or the sum payable.[60] There is a further proviso which operates in favour of a holder in due course where the alteration is not apparent from the face of the instrument. However, this will not be relevant in the case of a non-transferable cheque because no one can become a holder in due course.[61] Given that the effect of section 64 is to avoid the instrument, it cannot constitute a sufficient authority to the bank to debit the customer's account, and the bank accordingly takes the risk of cheques which have been altered in this way.[62]

Incomplete Cheques

17.44 If a customer signs an incomplete cheque form, the person to whom it is delivered has authority to complete the amount of the cheque and the bank will obtain a good discharge by the payment of such an instrument.[63] The recipient can thus insert such amount and such payee (including himself) as he deems appropriate.[64]

---

[59] Bills of Exchange Act 1882, s 74B as inserted by the Deregulation (Bills of Exchange) Order 1996 (SI 1996/2993). Section 74B gives the paying bank the option to require production of the physical cheque instead but, subject to that, its obligations as a paying banker remain the same even against electronic presentation.

[60] Bills of Exchange Act 1882, s 64(2).

[61] The payee of a cheque is not a holder in due course for these purposes.

[62] *Smith v Lloyds TSB Group plc* [2001] QB 541 (CA).

[63] Bills of Exchange Act 1882, s 20.

[64] *Garrard v Lewis* (1882) 10 QBD 30; *Gerald MacDonald & Co v Nash & Co* [1924] AC 625 (HL).

It is plain that the bank should be able to pay such an instrument in the ordinary course and **17.45** obtain a good discharge, since it will have no knowledge of dealings with the cheque prior to its presentation for payment.[65]

Forged and Unauthorized Indorsements

Section 60 of the Bills of Exchange Act 1882 provides that, where a bank pays a cheque **17.46** payable to order in good faith and in the ordinary course of business, it will be deemed to have paid the instrument in due course even though the indorsement of the payee or a subsequent indorsee is forged or unauthorized.[66]

The expression 'payable to order' as used in section 60 clearly implies that the document at **17.47** issue must be a negotiable instrument.[67] The immediate difficulty with this formulation is that nearly all cheques will now be non-transferable and, as an inevitable consequence, non-negotiable. The protection of section 60 is therefore now unlikely to be relevant in many cases dealing with cheques (as opposed to other forms of bills of exchange).

In cases where the section is invoked, the paying bank must show that it acted: **17.48**

(a) in good faith;[68] and
(b) in the ordinary course of business, that is to say, in the recognized course of banking business.[69]

If these tests are met, then the bank will be taken to have paid the instrument in due course **17.49** even though payment is made to a holder under a forged indorsement.[70]

The provisions described above deal with the position of the paying bank in relation to **17.50** indorsements on cheques. Insofar as these provisions remain relevant in the present context, it is reasonable that the bank should be protected in paying the cheque in these situations, since it will often have no relationship with, or knowledge of, the indorsers and cannot possibly know whether those signatures have been forged or are otherwise unauthorized.

In contrast, the ensuing provisions may protect the bank in the 'ordinary' case of a credit to **17.51** the account of the payee of a cheque.

Section 80 of the Bills of Exchange Act 1882

Where a bank pays a cheque—including a non-transferable cheque—drawn on it in good **17.52** faith and without negligence to a banker or to another bank as its agent for collection, the

---

[65] See *London Joint Stock Bank v Macmillan and Arthur* [1918] AC 777 (HL) and the discussion of that case at para 15.25 above.
[66] The difference between a forged and an unauthorized indorsement has already been considered at paras 17.21–17.22 above.
[67] See, for example, the discussion in Paget, para 20.16.
[68] A bank acts in good faith if it acts honestly, even though it may have acted negligently: Bills of Exchange Act 1882, s 90.
[69] See Paget, para 20.18 and cases there noted.
[70] Stamp Act 1853, s 19 contains a similar provision dealing with indorsements on a cheque, but without any stipulation as to payment in the ordinary course of business. Once again, the section appears to be confined to instruments which are negotiable: see Paget, paras 20.22–20.27.

bank is treated as if it had made payment to the true owner (ie as if it had made payment in due course). The drawer of the cheque is placed in the same position in relation to the discharge of his debt if the instrument has come into the hands of the payee.[71]

17.53 As noted above, this protection is given to the paying bank because it will not usually be able independently to verify that the collecting bank is acting on behalf of the true owner.[72] Nevertheless, in order to avail itself of this protection, the bank will have to show that it acted in good faith[73] and without negligence. By section 81A(2) of the Bills of Exchange Act 1882, a bank is not to be regarded as negligent by reason only that it does not concern itself with indorsements on a non-transferable cheque. In other words, the bank can simply ignore any purported indorsements because they will be of no legal effect in relation to an instrument of this kind. The paying bank can thus work on the assumption that the collecting bank is acting on behalf of the named payee and not on behalf of any purported indorsee. If, in fact, the collecting bank is seeking payment on behalf of an indorsee then the collecting bank may itself incur a liability to the payee of the cheque but this will not affect the discharge of the paying bank.[74]

17.54 If the requirements of section 80 are met then, as noted above, the paying bank is deemed to have paid in due course as if payment had been made to the true owner, whether or not that is in fact the case.

Section 1 of the Cheques Act 1957

17.55 Section 1(1) of the Cheques Act 1957 provides that:

> Where a banker in good faith and in the ordinary course of business pays a cheque drawn on him which is not indorsed or is irregularly indorsed, he does not, in doing so, incur any liability by reason only of the absence of, or irregularity in, indorsement, and he is deemed to have paid in due course.

17.56 Section 1(2) of the 1957 Act contains a similar provision with respect to certain other forms of payment instrument.

17.57 Before the 1957 Act was passed, it was prudent banking practice to require cheques to be indorsed prior to payment.[75] This was plainly inconvenient and section 1 now allows the bank to pay a cheque which is not indorsed and to obtain a good discharge, provided that it pays in good faith and in the ordinary course of business.[76]

---

[71] Bills of Exchange Act 1882, s 80 and see *Charles v Blackwell* (1877) 2 CPD 151.
[72] See para 17.50 above.
[73] See Bills of Exchange Act 1882, s 90 noted at para 17.48 above.
[74] See also the discussion in Paget, para 20.30.
[75] Paget, para 20.23.
[76] These two expressions have already been noted at para 17.48 above. It is true that the section also allows for payment where the cheque is irregularly indorsed. However, this will not normally arise given that virtually all cheques will now be non-transferable.

Liability to Third Parties

Introduction

The earlier parts of this chapter have been primarily concerned with the duties of a paying **17.58**
bank vis-à-vis its own customer. Although the paying bank is entitled to the benefit of the
various statutory protections which have been considered, the essential starting point of
that relationship is *contractual*. In contrast, the bank will not be in a contractual relationship either with the payee or with any other third parties who may be affected by its actions.
Consequently, a third party seeking recourse to a paying bank for any action taken by it will
need to have recourse to alternative causes of action. The available routes appear to lie in
conversion, negligence, and a possible, claim based on 'dishonest assistance' in a breach of
trust.[77]

Conversion

A paying bank which pays the proceeds of a cheque to a person other than the true owner **17.59**
of the instrument will thereby incur a liability to the true owner. However, this may beg an
obvious question, namely, who is the 'true owner' of the cheque? If a cheque is negotiable
and is indorsed generally by the payee, then payment to the indorsee will suffice because he
will be the true owner of the instrument.[78]

In practical terms, a paying bank will incur a liability in conversion only in exceptional **17.60**
circumstances. Once the cheque has been paid, it becomes the property of the paying bank
and, provided that the bank has or is deemed to have paid in due course in accordance with
any of the statutory protections discussed above, then it can come under no liability to the
true owner.[79]

A paying bank which pays out on an instrument which has been materially altered by the **17.61**
substitution of a new payee cannot debit the customer's account.[80] However, whilst the
bank can in theory also be made liable to the original payee of the cheque, the damages
will be nominal because the material alteration voids the cheque, thus converting it from a
valuable instrument into a worthless piece of paper.[81]

Negligence

There would seem to be no basis on which a paying bank could be said to owe a duty of care **17.62**
to the payee of a cheque in deciding whether or not the instrument should be paid. There
would seem to be two main reasons for this view. First of all, in receiving the request for
payment, the bank cannot be said to be assuming any form of duty or responsibility in

---

[77] The present section is intended to provide an overview of the possible heads of liability. For further
discussion and case law, see Paget, ch 21.
[78] *Smith v Union Bank of London* (1875) 1 QB 31 (CA).
[79] Paget, para 21.3, discussing the decision in *Charles v Blackwell* (1877) 2 CPD 151 (CA).
[80] See the discussion at para 17.24 above.
[81] See Bills of Exchange Act 1882, s 64 (noted at para 17.43 above) and the decision in *Smith v Lloyds TSB Bank plc* [2001] 1 All ER 424 (CA).

favour of the payee. Secondly, in acting as paying bank, the institution acts as agent for its own customer and owes fiduciary duties to him as principal. The imposition of a duty of care in this type of case might therefore come into conflict with the bank's equitable duties to its own customer.[82]

17.63 A claim of this kind would accordingly seem destined to fail unless it could be shown that the bank had expressly or by its conduct assumed a duty in favour of the payee. This is very unlikely to occur in practice.[83]

'Dishonest Assistance'

17.64 A bank which dishonestly assists in the misappropriation of money by a trustee or other fiduciary (such as a director or agent) may incur a liability to the beneficiaries or principal as a consequence. It is sometimes said that the bank incurs a liability as a 'constructive trustee' because it has facilitated the fiduciary's fraudulent design. This captures the spirit, if perhaps not the detail, of the rationale for the bank's liability in this type of case.

17.65 The *locus classicus* on dishonest assistance and its ingredients is now provided by the Privy Council in *Royal Brunei Airlines Sdn Bhd v Tan*,[84] although the case did not arise in a banking context. In that case, the defendant was a director of a travel agency and he helped the company to withhold funds from the airline and to divert those funds to other purposes. The agency became insolvent, so the airline sought to recover its losses from the directors of the travel agency personally. In holding that it could succeed, the Privy Council observed that:

(a) a person who knowingly and dishonestly assists in the commission of a breach of trust or similar fiduciary duty may be liable to compensate the beneficiaries of that duty for their loss. The fact that the trustee has not been dishonest (eg because he has been fraudulently misled) is not in point, because the secondary liability of the person providing the assistance is founded upon his *own* dishonesty, and not that of any other person;

(b) the defendant must have taken some steps which may be said to assist in the breach of trust or other duty. In the case of a paying bank, this would usually consist in honouring cheques drawn by the fiduciary for the purposes of the fraudulent design; and

(c) the assisting party can only be made liable if he acted dishonestly, so mere knowledge of a fraudulent design on the part of the trustee would be insufficient to impose liability on the assisting party.

---

[82] On this subject, see Paget, para 25.15, noting *National Westminster Bank Ltd v Barclays Bank International Ltd* [1975] QB 654 and *Dublin Port and Docks Board v Bank of Ireland* [1976] IR 118. The absence of any duty to a payee of a funds transfer was confirmed by the Court of Appeal in *Wells v First National Commercial Bank* [1998] PNLR 552 (see para 19.31 below), and there seems no reason to doubt that the same principle would apply to a cheque.

[83] It may be noted that a paying bank does not incur any contractual liability to the payee of a cheque, since there is no privity of contract between them: see *Calico Printers Association v Barclays Bank Ltd* (1931) 36 Com Cas 71. This may remain the case even when the collecting bank seeks from the paying bank a specific assurance that the cheque will be paid on presentation: see *Grosvenor Casinos Ltd v National Bank of Abu Dhabi* [2008] EWHC 511 (Comm).

[84] [1995] AC 378 (PC).

In a banking context, the need to prove dishonesty is likely to be a very significant impediment to any claim. However, it is this aspect of the *Royal Brunei* decision which has given rise to the most difficulty and debate. It seems clear that there must be some objective standard of dishonesty, perhaps to be ascertained by reference to accepted standards of conduct in the particular market concerned. In *Twinsectra Ltd v Yardley*,[85] the House of Lords held that a dual test must be satisfied, namely, (i) the conduct of the defendant must be objectively dishonest and (ii) he must himself have realized that he was being dishonest by reference to that objective standard. The requirement to prove *subjective* dishonesty, in addition to the *objective* test, has not met with universal approval,[86] and the Privy Council has explained that the subjective test merely requires that the defendant must have realized that his conduct was dishonest, and that no independent inquiry into his actual state of mind was required.[87] By way of further elucidation of these tests, it was recently held that the requirement of objective dishonesty could not be met if differing views as to the dishonesty of the relevant course of conduct could reasonably be held.[88]   **17.66**

At all events, it will be necessary for the claimant at least to prove that, when the paying   **17.67**
bank honoured the relevant instruments, it was aware that (i) the signatory was a fiduciary, (ii) it was aware that the fiduciary was acting in a manner designed to defraud his beneficiary or principal, and (iii) the bank dishonestly intended to assist in that design. Unusual and convincing evidence will be required to establish a claim of this kind.

---

[85] [2002] 1 AC 164 (HL).
[86] See Paget, para 21.11, noting the decision in *US International Marketing Ltd v National Bank of New Zealand* [2004] 1 NZLR 589.
[87] *Barlow Clowes International Ltd v Eurotrust International Ltd* [2006] 1 All ER 333 (PC).
[88] *Starglade Properties Ltd v Nash* [2009] EWHC 148 (Ch).

18

DUTIES OF THE COLLECTING BANK

Introduction

The last chapter dealt with the duties and potential liabilities of a bank in its capacity as a **18.01** paying bank in meeting the customer's cheques and other payment instructions. In contrast, the present chapter examines the bank's position in collecting cheques and other items for the credit of the customer. It is appropriate to repeat the point made in the introduction to the last chapter, namely that a target date of 2018 has been set for the closure of central cheque clearing, with the intention that it should be superseded by other forms of payment instrument by that time. The issues noted in this chapter are thus likely to be of diminishing importance, and the commentary has been prepared on that basis.[1]

The subject matter of this chapter is arranged as follows: **18.02**

(a) the collection and clearance of cheques;
(b) statutory protections available to the collecting bank; and
(c) the potential liability of the collecting bank to third parties.

---

[1] Alternative means of payment such as payment instruments governed by the Payment Services Regulations 2009 (on which see Chapter 5 above) and electronic funds transfers (on which see Chapter 19 below) will assume increasing importance as a result of the management of the decline in the use of cheques.

Collection of Cheques

Introduction

18.03 The previous chapter dealt with the position of the paying bank on the footing that cheques are now almost invariably non-transferable, and the present chapter will adopt the same approach with respect to the position of the collecting bank.[2]

18.04 This first part of this chapter will consider:

(a) the role and position of the collecting bank;
(b) the collection of cheques; and
(c) the requirement for notice of dishonour.

Role and Position of the Collecting Bank

18.05 It was noted earlier[3] that a paying bank acts as agent for its customer in making payments to third parties on its behalf. The same applies to the collecting bank, in that it acts as agent for its customer in seeking payment from the drawee bank on the customer's behalf. Consequently, in the absence of fault on its part, the collecting bank is entitled to the usual agent's indemnity. For example, if a cheque which is provisionally credited to the customer's account is later dishonoured by the paying bank, then it can reverse the relevant entry and debit the customer's account accordingly.[4]

18.06 Whilst the roles of the paying and collecting bank are obviously different, the essential legal analysis is the same in both cases. The bank acts as an agent and owes fiduciary duties to the customer, but will also be entitled to an indemnity for any losses or liabilities which it incurs in the proper conduct of its respective role.

18.07 It may be added that—just as the paying bank is under a duty to meet its customer's payment orders—a collecting bank is under a duty to collect items presented to it and to credit them to the customer's account. Subject to any possible challenge on the basis of the Unfair Terms in Consumer Contracts Regulations 1999,[5] the precise date on which the proceeds of the cheque are actually credited to the customer's account will be determined by reference to the bank's standard terms of business.[6] The point is of importance because the credit will reduce the level of the customer's overdraft facility from the effective date of the credit, and the earliest possible date is therefore obviously in the best interests of the customer.

---

[2] Material and case law dealing with cheques which remain transferable or negotiable is to be found in Paget, ch 22.

[3] See para 17.05 above.

[4] The provisional credit does not imply any form of representation to the customer that the cheque has already been honoured.

[5] On these regulations, see paras 15.45–15.49 above.

[6] On this point, see *Emerald Meats (London) Ltd v AIB Group (UK) plc* [2002] EWCA Civ 460 (CA), following *Lloyds Bank plc v Voller* [2000] 2 All ER (Comm) 978.

The Collection of Cheques

As noted previously, a cheque is defined by section 73 of the Bills of Exchange Act 1882 **18.08**
as '… a bill of exchange drawn on a banker payable on demand …' The cheque must be
presented for payment within a reasonable time after its issue.[7] Of course, this usually
presents no difficulty since the payee can generally be expected to present the cheque
promptly so as to obtain the benefit of the payment.

Presentment of cheques for payment is normally achieved through the clearing system **18.09**
operated by the Cheque and Credit Clearing Company Ltd.[8] In addition, a cheque may
now be presented to the drawee bank by notifying the amount of the cheque, its serial
number, the drawer's account number, and the sort code. The drawee bank has the option
of requiring physical presentation of the cheque instead. Where electronic or similar means
of communication are used, the obligation of the collecting bank remains identical to that
which would apply to a paper instrument.[9]

Notice of Dishonour

Where a cheque is dishonoured by non-payment, the collecting bank must give notice of **18.10**
dishonour to his customer, although this is excused where dishonour is due to countermand by the drawer.[10] If the bank has provisionally credited the customer's account with
the amount of the cheque, it will be entitled to reverse that entry and to charge interest on
the customer's account as if the payment had never been received.[11]

Statutory Protections Available to the Collecting Bank

Various statutory provisions formerly required consideration in the context of the role of **18.11**
the collecting bank. However, as noted previously,[12] virtually all modern cheques are non-
transferable and subject as stated below, this has had a significant impact on the availability
of the statutory protections.[13] By way of brief overview:[14]

(a) section 2 of the Cheques Act 1957 provides that a bank which gives value for a cheque
     payable to order and delivered to it for collection[15] has the same rights as if the cheque
     had been indorsed to it. In other words, a collecting bank which has given value could

---

[7] Bills of Exchange Act 1882, s 45(2).

[8] On the impending closure of this system, see para 16.03 above.

[9] On the points made in this paragraph, see Bills of Exchange Act 1882, s 74B as inserted by the
Deregulation (Bills of Exchange) Order 1996 (SI 1996/2993).

[10] Bills of Exchange Act 1882, ss 48, 49 and 50(2)(c) and the discussion in Paget, para 22.10. On the time
for giving notice of dishonour, see s 49 of the 1882 Act and the case law cited by Paget, para 22.12.

[11] This follows from the fact that the collecting bank acts as agent of his customer and is accordingly
entitled to a full indemnity: see *Gordon v Capital and Counties Bank* [1903] AC 240 (HL) and the discussion
in Paget, para 22.13.

[12] See para 16.15 above, discussing the Cheques Act 1992 and the insertion of s 81A into the Bills of
Exchange Act 1882.

[13] This may well have been unintentional: see Law of Bank Payments at para 7-008.

[14] For further discussion and case law, see Paget, para 22.16.

[15] The section only operated if the bank held the cheque in its capacity as a collecting bank: see *Westminster
Bank Ltd v Zang* [1966] AC 182 (HL).

become a holder and have the right to sue the drawer on the cheque accordingly. However, for the reasons noted above, most cheques are not payable to order and any indorsement would be ineffective. Consequently, the protection of this section will no longer be available to the collecting bank in the ordinary case;

(b) section 27(3) of the Bills of Exchange Act 1882 provides that, where a bank has a lien on a cheque, it is deemed to be a holder for value to the extent of the lien. Once again, however, only the payee of a non-transferable cheque can be the 'holder' of it, with the result that a collecting bank could no longer avail itself of this provision.

18.12 As a general rule, therefore, a collecting bank can no longer acquire an action against the drawer of a cheque which has been dishonoured and for which the bank has given value.

18.13 In contrast, section 4 of the Cheques Act 1957 remains a valuable source of protection for the collecting bank and was specifically updated by the terms of the Cheques Act 1992. The revised version of section 4, so far as relevant to the present commentary, reads as follows:

> (1) Where a banker, in good faith and without negligence—
>   (a) receives payment for a customer of an instrument to which this section applies; or
>   (b) having credited a customer's account with the amount of such an instrument, receives payment thereof for himself,
> and the customer has no title, or a defective title, to the instrument, the banker does not incur any liability to the true owner of the instrument by reason only of having received payment thereof;
> (2) This section applies to the following instruments, namely:
>   (a) cheques (including cheques which under section 81A(1) of the Bills of Exchange Act 1882 or otherwise are not transferable);
>   (b) any document issued by a customer of a banker which, though not a bill of exchange, is intended to enable a person to obtain payment from that banker of the sum mentioned in the document;
>   (c) ...
> (3) A banker is not to be treated for the purposes of this section as having been negligent by reason only of his failure to concern himself with the absence of, or irregularity in, indorsement of an instrument.

18.14 Since the section provides a defence to a claim in conversion for which the bank would otherwise be liable, the onus is on the bank to demonstrate that it acted in good faith and without negligence for the purposes of the section.[16] What, then, are the standards of conduct needed to meet the statutory threshold?

18.15 The standard of 'without negligence' is to be derived from the ordinary practice of bankers[17] in seeking to protect both their own business and their customers against the possibility of fraud.[18] The standard will inevitably change as banking practice moves on. A good example

---

[16] Paget, para 24.8, noting the decision in *Lloyds Bank Ltd v E B Savory Ltd* [1933] AC 201 (HL).

[17] *Lloyds Bank Ltd v Chartered Bank of India Australia and China* [1929] 1 KB 40 (CA); *Taxation Commissioners v English Scottish and Australian Bank* [1920] AC 683 (HL). Note that, the bank may also be able to raise a defence of contributory negligence against the true owner of the cheque: Banking Act 1979, s 47.

[18] *Lloyds Bank Ltd v E B Savory Ltd* [1933] AC 201 (HL).

of this position is offered by the decision in *Marfani & Co Ltd v Midland Bank Ltd*,[19] where the Court of Appeal held that:

(a) a bank which had taken a reference from an apparently reputable source had acted in accordance with good banking practice; and
(b) the bank's failure to verify the identity of an applicant for an account (eg by examining his passport) was not thereby guilty of negligence.

It is fair to say that neither element of this decision would apply today. It is now very **18.16** unusual for a bank to seek a reference before opening an ordinary current account, and the verification of identity has become invariable practice as a consequence of anti-money laundering legislation.[20] Nevertheless, the court approached the matter from the perspective of prevailing banking practice, and the decision thus remains appropriate in general principle, if outdated on the facts.

A bank is not obliged to examine the detailed background to each cheque presented to it. **18.17** In one case, a bank was held to have acted 'without negligence' when it collected an instrument payable by a company in favour of one of its own employees, where the bank had no reason to know of that relationship and there was nothing else in the circumstances which gave rise to suspicion.[21] It has been said that,[22] '... the test of negligence is whether the transaction of paying in any given cheque, coupled with the circumstances antecedent and precedent, was so out of the ordinary that it ought to have aroused doubts in the banker's mind and caused them to make inquiry ...'. In line with this standard, a bank which collects a cheque signed under a power of attorney and drawn in favour of the attorney himself will probably be regarded as negligent.[23] In the rare cases where a cheque remains transferable, a bank is probably also negligent if it collects a cheque drawn in favour of a company but indorsed in favour of an individual;[24] why should a company be dealing with cheques received by it in such a manner?

Equally, a bank which agrees to collect a cheque as agent for another institution may be **18.18** liable in conversion to the true owner of a cheque, subject to any defence which may be available to it under section 4 of the 1957 Act. In *Honourable Society of the Middle Temple v Lloyds Bank plc*,[25] a cheque drawn by the Middle Temple in favour of an insurer was stolen and indorsed, and subsequently found its way to a Turkish bank, which in turn asked Lloyds to collect it as agent for that bank. It was found that Lloyds could not avail themselves of the 'no negligence' defence in section 4 because (i) it was the practice of UK banks to advise foreign banks that the Cheques Act 1992 had rendered UK cheques non-transferable, but Lloyds itself had failed to take that step and (ii) there were various features

---

[19] [1968] 2 All ER 573 (CA).
[20] On the Money Laundering Regulations 2007, see paras 7.17–7.27 above.
[21] *Orbit Mining and Trading Co Ltd v Westminster Bank Ltd* [1962] 3 All ER 565.
[22] *Commissioners of State Savings Bank of Victoria v Permewan Wright & Co Ltd* (1915) 19 CLR 457 (High Court of Australia) adapting a similar formulation adopted in the *Taxation Commissioners* case (n 17 above).
[23] *Midland Bank Ltd v Reckitt* [1933] AC 1 (HL), noted by Paget, para 24.20.
[24] *United Australia Bank Ltd v Barclays Bank Ltd* [1941] AC 1. See also *Ross v London County, Westminster and Parr's Bank Ltd* [1919] 1 KB 678.
[25] [1999] 1 All ER (Comm) 193

of the case which placed Lloyds on inquiry. For example, the Turkish bank had never used the services of Lloyds before, and the indorsement on the cheque was handwritten, without a company stamp.[26]

18.19   The case law and the required standards of care in this area have most recently been examined by the Court of Appeal in *Architects of Wine Ltd v Barclays Bank plc*.[27] In that case, the bank had an account for a customer known as 'Architects of Wine (UK) Ltd'. The bank accepted for credit to the account some 400 cheques which seem to have merely been made payable to 'Architects of Wine Ltd'. Unknown to the bank, this was a Cayman Islands affiliate of its UK customer. Following the insolvency of the Cayman Islands entity, its liquidator sought to recover the value of the cheques in an action against Barclays as collecting bank. The Court of Appeal recognized that cheques with abbreviated names were frequently credited to the payee's account and that banking business would be significantly impeded if a pedantic approach had to be adopted in relation to every cheque. The court accordingly held that the bank had a reasonable prospect of establishing that it had acted 'without negligence' for the purposes of section 4 of the 1957 Act, on the basis that its actions reflected the normal practice of bankers. The bank was accordingly given leave to defend the action.

18.20   The more recent case law described above suggests that the courts are aware that the 'no negligence' test needs to be measured by reference to prevailing banking practices, and that a fair balance needs to be drawn between the protection of the true owner and the ability of a bank to process cheque clearing at a proper speed.

Liability of the Collecting Bank to Third Parties

Introduction

18.21   The present section considers the various bases on which a collecting bank may incur liability to the true owner of a cheque if he collects payment for someone who is not entitled to it. There are four possible causes of action, namely, (i) conversion, (ii) monies had and received, (iii) knowing receipt, and (iv) negligence.[28]

Conversion

18.22   Conversion involves a wrongful interference with goods in a manner which is inconsistent with the true owner's possession or right to possession. A cheque amounts to 'goods' for the purposes of this tort. It should be noted that conversion is a tort of strict liability and no element of intention on the part of the defendant has to be proved.[29] It will, however, be

---

[26] It may be noted in this context that the bank did have occasion physically to examine the cheque. The decision was followed in *Linklaters v HSBC Bank plc* [2003] 2 Lloyds Rep 545.

[27] [2007] EWCA Civ 239 (CA).

[28] This is the categorization adopted by Paget, ch 23, where further discussion and case law in this area will be found.

[29] On these points, see Paget, para 23.2, discussing Torts (Interference with Goods) Act 1977, s 1(a) and the decisions in *Morison v London County and Westminster Bank Ltd* [1914] 3 KB 356 (CA) and *Lloyds Bank Ltd v Chartered Bank of India Australia and China* [1929] 1 KB 40 (CA).

necessary for the claimant to prove that he had a right to possession of the cheque since, otherwise, the defendant bank cannot have interfered with that right. Consequently, it may be difficult for a person other than the payee of a cheque to establish a claim for conversion, even though he may otherwise have had an interest in its proceeds.[30]

The tort of conversion has to apply to something in physical form, but the law treats the **18.23** physical piece of paper on which the cheque is written as having a value equal to its face amount so that (i) a cheque is capable of conversion and (ii) damages for conversion will be the face amount of the instrument.[31] However, if the cheque has no value—for example, because it has been avoided as a result of a material alteration[32]—then damages must be nominal because the cheque is not good for its face amount.[33]

If the bank has collected the relevant cheque in good faith and without negligence, then it **18.24** may in any event have a good defence to an action in conversion under section 4 of the Cheques Act 1957.[34]

Monies Had and Received

An action for money had and received will often arise independently of the nature of the **18.25** instrument at issue, because it is simply a claim for restitution based on unjust enrichment.[35] The action may apply where a claim in conversion is not available to the claimant, although it remains necessary for the claimant to establish a good title to the funds concerned.[36]

So far as a bank is concerned, an action of this kind will only rarely succeed in a manner **18.26** which will require the bank to meet the claim from its own resources. If the claim is notified to the bank before it has paid away the relevant sums, then it will simply be able to debit the customer's account with the amount concerned for, by definition, the customer will not have had valid title to those monies. In addition, having collected the relevant funds as agent for the customer, the bank will be entitled to an indemnity for any liability arising in that connection.[37] On the other hand, the action will fail if the funds have been fully paid out to the bank's customer and nothing remains to the credit of the account. In such a case, the bank will have changed its position to its detriment in reliance on the receipt of

---

[30] See the situations which arose in *Robinson v Midland Bank Ltd* (1925) 41 TLR 402 and *Surrey Asset Finance Ltd v National Westminster Bank plc* [2001] EWCA Civ 60 (CA). The cases are noted by Paget, para 23.4. Whether or not a payee has a right to possession of a cheque issued pursuant to a contract which is void or voidable can be a difficult question; see the discussion in Paget, paras 23.5–23.8.

[31] See the *Chartered Bank* case, mentioned in n 29 above.

[32] See Bills of Exchange Act 1882, s 64 discussed at para 17.43 above.

[33] *Smith v Lloyds TSB Group plc* [2000] 2 All ER (Comm) 693.

[34] This section has been discussed at para 18.13 above.

[35] *Westdeutsche Landesbank Girozentrale v Islington London Borough Council* [1996] AC 669 (HL).

[36] Thus, depositors with an unauthorized institution could not recover their money from the receiving bank because it was the intention of the depositors that title to the funds should pass to the unauthorized institution: see *Box v Barclays Bank plc* [1998] Lloyds Rep Bank 185, discussed by Paget at para 23.19.

[37] This was the situation which arose in *Bavins Junior and Sims v London and South Western Bank Ltd* [1900] 1 QB 270.

the funds.[38] It appears that the change of position defence remains available even if it can be shown that the collecting bank may have acted negligently in paying out the funds concerned.[39]

'Knowing Receipt'

18.27   The Privy Council decision in *Royal Brunei Airlines Sdn Bhd v Tan*[40] has already been noted in relation to the potential liabilities of the paying bank.[41] It was pointed out that a paying bank may incur liability to (say) the beneficiaries of a trust or a principal if it dishonestly assists in a fraudulent design to their detriment. A similar claim could in theory be asserted against the collecting bank but, in either case, the need to prove dishonesty will be a significant hurdle in the way of the claimant.

18.28   Given that a collecting bank will be a recipient of the disputed funds, it may be more attractive to proceed against the collecting bank under the heading of 'knowing receipt', if only because proof of positive and intentional dishonesty is not required.

18.29   What, then, are the necessary ingredients of a 'knowing receipt' claim against a collecting bank? They appear to include the following:

(a)   the bank must receive trust property (eg via a trustee, directors of a company, agent, or other fiduciary);

(b)   the bank must have dealt with that property in a manner inconsistent with the trust or other fiduciary relationship;[42] and

(c)   it is necessary to prove an appropriate degree of knowledge on the part of the collecting bank. However, the precise degree of knowledge is unclear. It has been said that constructive notice of the breach of trust may be sufficient, but that the courts may be reluctant to find that constructive notice is established in commercial cases.[43] In another case, it has been suggested that it is sufficient to establish that it would be unconscionable for the recipient to retain the benefit of the payment.[44]

18.30   Various defences may be available to the collecting bank when confronted with a 'knowing receipt' claim. First of all, a bank receives funds as agent for its customer and, if it pays those monies away at the behest of the customer before receiving notice of any impropriety or mistake,[45] then it may be able to rely on the defence of 'ministerial receipt'. However, this

---

[38] *Transvaal and Delagoa Bay Investment Co Ltd v Atkinson* [1954] 1 All ER 579, noted by Paget, para 23.21.

[39] *Dextra Bank & Trust Co Ltd v Bank of Jamaica* [2002] 1 All ER (Comm) 193.

[40] [1995] 2 AC 378.

[41] See the discussion at para 17.65 above.

[42] Clearly, it is the state of the bank's knowledge at the time at which it pays out the money that is crucial, since that is the point at which the beneficiaries or principal suffers loss: see *Baden Delvaux and Lecuit v Societe Generale pour Favoriser le Developpement du Commerce et de l'Industrie en France SA* [1987] BCLC 161.

[43] *El Ajou v Dollar Land Holdings Ltd* [1993] 3 All ER 717 (reversed on a different point, [1994] 2 All ER 683), *Eagle Trust plc v SBC Securities Ltd* [1992] 4 All ER 488 and other cases noted by Paget, para 23.28.

[44] *Bank of Credit and Commerce International (Overseas) Ltd v Akindele* [2001] Ch 437 (CA).

[45] Of course, if the bank is still in possession of the funds when it receives that notice, then its primary duty would be to return the funds to the true owner: see *British American Continental Bank v British Bank for Foreign Trade* [1926] 1 KB 328; *Gower v Lloyds and National Provincial Foreign Bank Ltd* [1938] 1 All ER 766 and the discussion in Paget, para 23.30.

defence may cease to be available if, having received the funds as agent, the bank uses the funds to reduce the customer's overdraft, since the bank then goes beyond a pure agency function and holds the funds for its own benefit.[46]

Equally, if the bank has changed its position to its detriment in reliance on the receipt of the funds and before it received notice of the beneficiary's claims, then it may be inequitable to require him to refund those monies.[47]   **18.31**

Negligence

It has recently been decided that a collecting bank does not owe any duty to the drawer of   **18.32**
a cheque collected by it for the account of a customer.[48] The decision was motivated by a number of factors, in particular (i) the bank had not assumed any duty of care to the drawer, (ii) the imposition of such a duty might lead to a conflict with the contractual duties owed by the collecting bank to its own customer, and (iii) the collecting bank has no contact with a drawer of a cheque until it receives the instrument for payment. It has also been decided that a collecting bank does not owe a duty to protect the drawee bank against losses flowing from the theft and fraudulent alteration of a cheque. In *Yorkshire Bank plc v Lloyds Bank plc*,[49] a cheque drawn on Yorkshire Bank came into the possession of Lloyds but was stolen. The cheque was fraudulently altered and subsequently paid by Yorkshire Bank. It could not debit its customer's account and it accordingly sued Lloyds to recover its loss. However, the claim failed because the collecting bank owes no duty to the drawee bank to organize its business in such a way as to minimize the risk of presentation of a stolen or altered cheque.[50]

It follows that, in the absence of extremely unusual circumstances, the collecting bank will   **18.33**
incur no liability to the drawer of a cheque or to the drawee bank if the funds are misappropriated as a result of a fraud coordinated by the collecting bank's own customer, or as a result of the loss or theft of the cheque.[51]

---

[46] *Agip (Africa) Ltd v Jackson* [1990] Ch 265.
[47] *British American Continental Bank* (n 45 above); *Lipkin Gorman v Karpnale Ltd* [1991] 2 AC 548 (HL).
[48] *Abou-Ramah v Abacha* [2005] 1 All ER (Comm) 247.
[49] [1999] 2 All ER (Comm) 153.
[50] In this respect, the court relied to some extent on the decision in *Tai Hing Cotton Mills Ltd v Liu Chong Hing Bank Ltd* [1986] AC 80 (PC). The case has already been considered at para 15.36 above.
[51] This was the situation in the *Abacha* case itself.

19

ELECTRONIC FUNDS TRANSFERS

Introduction

There are various means of effecting a payment between a debtor and a creditor.　**19.01**

The first method—unrelated to questions of banking law—is the physical delivery of notes and coins. This remains the common mode of settlement for smaller transactions and is perfectly satisfactory for that purpose. However, the risk of theft, robbery or loss makes this process unacceptable for significant transfers.

The second method involves the use of a cheque, which plainly does involve the interposi-　**19.02** tion of the banking system between the debtor and the creditor. Whilst plainly preferable to the use of cash in large amounts, cheques nevertheless still suffer from a variety of disadvantages. The skilful forger can alter a cheque and obtain payment; even in the absence of any criminal intervention, the creditor is kept out of his funds for a period while the cheque is in the course of clearance.

The final alternative is a payment by means of a transfer from the payee's account to　**19.03** an account of the creditor. This is sometimes referred to as a giro or 'cashless' transfer. The present chapter is concerned with payment via this means.[1]

With these considerations in mind, the present chapter is arranged as follows:　**19.04**

(a)　electronic funds transfers systems;
(b)　the legal nature of electronic funds transfers;
(c)　the legal consequences of a payment by means of an electronic transfer; and
(d)　liabilities to third parties.

---

[1]　For a detailed and valuable discussion of the whole area, see Law of Bank Payments, ch 3.

Electronic Funds Transfer Systems

Introduction

19.05 An electronic funds transfer (EFT) may be defined as any transfer of funds initiated or processed by electronic means.[2]

19.06 Systems for the electronic transfer of funds take advantage of modern technology and thus avoid the costs and risks (such as transport, theft, and fraudulent alteration) associated with the transfer of physical cash and the use of cheques or other paper based forms of instruction.

19.07 The importance of these systems should not be underestimated; very substantial sums are transferred by this means every year. With this in mind, it may be helpful briefly to describe some of the main systems.

BACS

19.08 BACS (Bankers Automated Clearing Services) was established as the UK's first electronic clearing system in 1968. BACS deals with a very large volume of transactions which are normally of a relatively low value. BACS is an industry-based association which is owned by a number of leading banks and building societies. Its two principal services are BACS Direct Credit, which enables organizations to initiate payment transactions in favour of payees, and Direct Debit, which allows for the collection of funds from the payer's account at the initiation of the payee.

19.09 Perhaps in part because the system has operated successfully and in part because it deals with smaller value payments, the use of BACS does not of itself appear to have generated any litigation in this country.

CHAPS

19.10 CHAPS (Clearing House Automated Payment System) was established in 1984 and generally handles higher value payments or, as described in its own materials,[3] 'systemically important and time dependent payments'. CHAPS deals with some 130,000 payments with an aggregate value of some £300 billion on a daily basis. CHAPS operates a real time gross settlement system (RTGS system) in sterling.[4] The reliability of the CHAPS system

---

[2] This is the definition adopted by Paget, para 17.3. As there pointed out, there is no generally accepted definition of the term. The US Electronic Funds Transfer Act 1978 (Title XX of the Financial Institutions Regulatory Control Act) also adopts a definition which focuses on the *origination* (as opposed to the *processing*) of a transaction by electronic means. The 1978 Act is designed to the respective rights and obligations of the consumer and the financial institution in respect of an electronic funds transfer. The objectives of this Act are therefore in some respect similar to the Payment Services Regulations 2009 (discussed in Chapter 5 above), although the form and content is rather different. On the whole subject, see Geva, *The Law of Electronic Funds Transfers* (Matthew Bender, Looseleaf) and Geva, *Bank Collections and Payment Transactions—Comparative Study of Legal Aspects* (Oxford University Press, 2001).

[3] See materials on CHAPS available at www.chapsco.co.uk.

[4] CHAPS also formerly offered a euro clearing service for some nine years from the introduction of the single currency. However, the ability to use the TARGET system (see para 19.12 below), the realization that

is underpinned by an undertaking that payments are to be unconditional, irrevocable, and guaranteed. Credits are 'irrevocable' in that a payment through the system cannot be recalled on the insolvency of the payer.[5] Payments are 'guaranteed' in the sense that the recipient bank will receive a credit to its account with the Bank of England, which sits at the heart of the United Kingdom's payment system. Consequently, the credit is effectively represented by 'central bank money'. The significance of 'real time' is precisely what it says; the transaction is processed in full and immediately on receipt.[6] The sequence of events will be broadly as follows:

(a) the paying bank will initiate the transfer by sending a computer-generated message to the Bank of England, setting out the amount and details of the account of the payee bank;

(b) the Bank of England will settle the transaction by debiting the paying bank and crediting the account of the payee bank;

(c) the Bank of England will then send a notification to the paying bank, confirming settlement of the transaction;

(d) on receipt of that confirmation, the paying bank will send a computer-generated message to the payee bank;[7] and

(e) the payee bank's system will then automatically generate and transmit an acknowledgement of receipt to the paying bank.

The operation of CHAPS was neatly and carefully described in a judicial context by **19.11** Colman J in *Tayeb v HSBC Bank plc*,[8] where he commented as follows:

> CHAPS Sterling commenced operation as a same day value electronic credit transfer system in 1984 ... In 1996, CHAPS Sterling converted to a real time gross settlement system. This means that payments clear during the day on which they are made, within a short period after the payer's bank issues the payment instruction, rather than by netting off against all other relevant payments at the end of the day.

> The immediate clearing of such payments is an extremely important advantage of CHAPS because it enables transactions involving the transfer of property, including foreign exchange and securities, to be completed on the same day. There is, as between a transferee bank and its transferee account holder, normally a crediting of the customer's account immediately following electronic acknowledgement in respect of the transfer.

---

the United Kingdom was unlikely to join the eurozone in the medium term and declining payment volumes prompted a decision to close the euro clearing system in May 2008: see 'CHAPS euro system to close after nine years of service' (APACS press release, 15 May 2008).

[5] In this context, see the discussion on settlement finality at paras 35.04–35.21 below.

[6] This may be contrasted with other systems, where the various mutual transactions between banks are reckoned up at close of banking hours and settlement is effected on a 'net' basis. In other words, an RTGS provides *intra-day* settlement finality, whereas other systems only provide *end of day* finality.

[7] It will be noted that the payee bank has no involvement in the process at all until after its account with the Bank of England has received the credit.

[8] [2004] All ER (Comm) 1024. The extracts about to be quoted are taken from paras 10–14 of the judgment. References to a 'LAK' mean a 'logical acknowledgement', which informs the debtor's bank that payment has been received and credited to the account of the payee. The substance of the dispute in *Tayeb* is discussed at para 19.23 (f) below.

Both HSBC and Barclays were CHAPS settlement members and as such were bound by the CHAPS rules ... It is important to note that payments under the system were required to be ... an irrevocable, guaranteed unconditional sterling payment for settlement in real time across members' settlement accounts at the Bank of England ...

Further, by sending a LAK each member agreed, after authentication, to give same day value to its payee customer.

The CHAPS system works in the following manner: CHAPS settlement members are provided with special computer software known as gateways. The gateways handle all communications between participating banks and security. The gateways are linked to and accessible from the member's own computer systems and they can communicate with the gateways of other participants over telecommunication links. A critical feature of CHAPS is that every payment is settled across the payer's bank's and the payee's bank's accounts at the Bank of England before any instruction is sent to the payee's bank. The sequence of events is as follows:

(1) the payer's bank initiates a payment transaction on its computer system;
(2) the payer's bank's computer causes a settlement request to be sent to the Bank of England. This includes details of the payee's bank and account number;
(3) if there are sufficient funds in the payer's bank's account at the Bank of England, the payment is settled by the Bank of England debiting the payer's bank's account and crediting the payee's bank's account;
(4) the Bank of England sends a confirmation of settlement to the payer's bank's account;
(5) on receipt of confirmation from the Bank of England, the payer's bank's gateway automatically sends a payment message to the payee's bank;
(6) on receipt of the payment message, the payee's bank immediately transmits a LAK to the payer's bank. This follows authentication ...
(7) mechanisms exist to ensure that interbank settlement can take place even where there is a temporary shortage of liquidity. However, in every such case, settlement occurs before the payee's bank receives notification of the payment ...

TARGET

19.12 TARGET[9] is the payment system operated by the European Central Bank for large value payments to be settled in the course of interbank operations.

19.13 It is, once again, a real time gross settlement system for the single currency. TARGET is, however, different from a purely national payments system, since it is designed to serve the entire eurozone. TARGET therefore consists of two levels, namely, (i) a national RTGS system in each individual eurozone Member State and (ii) an interlinking arrangement

---

[9] In full, Trans-European Automated Real-time Gross Settlement Express Transfer. The current system is formally known as 'TARGET 2' following the introduction of a modified system in 2007 which, among other things, was designed to cater for the expansion of the eurozone and the consequent increase in payment volumes.

which provides the interface with the system operated by the European Central Bank itself.[10]

Legal Nature of EFT

As noted above, payment by means of an electronic transfer[11] involves the following steps: **19.14**

(a) The customer seeking to make a payment (the debtor) will instruct his own bank to transfer the required amount to a specified account of the intended payee (the creditor).
(b) The debtor's bank will debit the relevant amount to the customer's account.
(c) The debtor's bank will then credit the payee's bank via one of the recognized payment systems.[12]
(d) Upon receipt of advice, the creditor's bank will credit the payee's account with the amounts so received.[13]

It will be seen that the use of the expression 'transfer' is thus in some respects misleading, in   **19.15** the sense that funds are not really transferred at all. The debtor-creditor relationship of the payer and his bank is adjusted by deducting the amount of the payment, whilst the corresponding relationship between the payee and its bank is increased to the same extent.[14] Corresponding debits and credits are made between accounts held by the two settlement banks with the Bank of England.[15]

What is the correct legal analysis of these arrangements? The payer suffers the cancellation   **19.16** of his rights as creditor as against his own bank by an amount equal to the value of the transfer instruction. Equally, the payee benefits from a corresponding increase in his claim against his own bank. But—notwithstanding the terminology which is invariably used— this does not amount to a 'transfer' of funds in a legal sense. There is no assignment if the credit balance of the payer, and the payee does not acquire any rights as against the payer's bank.[16]

---

[10] For further details of TARGET and other eurozone settlement systems, see 'A Single Currency—An Integrated Market Infrastructure' (European Central Bank). The main competitor to TARGET for large value cross-border payments is the euro clearing system operated by the Euro Banking Association. On this system, see Law of Bank Payments, para 3-045.

[11] A wholesale system is a system operated between institutions and which cannot be directly accessed by the ordinary customer.

[12] On these payment systems, see the discussion earlier in this chapter.

[13] It may be noted that the creditor's bank may credit his account on receipt of advice from the debtor's bank, even if it has not then received the corresponding funding from the debtor's bank. As between debtor and creditor, however, the debtor's obligation is to procure a credit to the creditor's account. Once this has been done, the debtor has performed his obligation regardless of the position as between the two banks.

[14] On the debtor-creditor nature of the banker-customer relationship, see *Foley v Hill* (1848) HL Cas 28, discussed at para 15.10 above.

[15] See the discussion of CHAPS, at para 19.10 above.

[16] As Staughton J correctly noted in *Libyan Arab Foreign Bank v Bankers Trust Co* [1989] QB 728, 750, 'Transfer may be a somewhat misleading word, since the original obligation is not assigned ... a new obligation by a new debtor is created ...'.

19.17   Given that no 'transfer' of property in the true sense is involved, the House of Lords held that an individual who dishonestly procured a transfer of funds by means of a false mortgage application was not guilty of 'obtaining *property belonging to another* by deception' for the purposes of section 15(1) of the Theft Act 1968.[17] The deception resulted in a credit to the borrower's (or his solicitor's) account, but this created a new chose in action represented by the debt owing by the borrower's/solicitor's bank. Since this chose had never belonged to anyone else, it could not be said to represent property which had been 'obtained' from another person.[18]

19.18   It must equally follow that, at least in the ordinary course, a request by a debtor to his bank to pay the necessary sums to the account of the creditor will not normally have the effect of creating a trust over the funds in the debtor's account. The instruction does not involve any intention on the part of the debtor to create a trust. Consequently, if the debtor becomes insolvent and the payment is not made to the creditor,[19] the creditor will not be able to establish a claim as beneficiary to the funds standing to the credit of the debtor's account at the time the transfer instruction was given.[20]

19.19   The above analysis leads to the view that the paying bank acts as agent for the payer in making the payment but does not thereby incur any liability either to the payee or to his bank.[21]

Legal Consequences of an EFT Payment

19.20   It might be anticipated that the introduction of new systems of payment would give rise to novel legal issues. A few of these points may be noted, along with the cases which have helped to resolve some of these difficulties.

---

[17] *R v Preddy* [1996] AC 815 (HL). So far as the criminal law is concerned, the loophole was closed by introducing a new offence of obtaining a money transfer by deception under the terms of section 15A of the Theft Act 1968. That section was in turn overtaken by the introduction of a more general offence of fraud: see the Fraud Act 2006. On this subject, see Paget, para 17.18.

[18] It is submitted that—even though a strict interpretation is required in the context of a criminal statute—the House of Lords took an unduly narrow view of the position. If the money had been handed over in the form of banknotes, then the offence would clearly have been made out, and it is not obvious that the defendant should be better placed merely because the banking system had been used to effect payment. Equally, the bank which had been defrauded would have been able to trace the funds or property into which they had been invested. Furthermore, there is no doubt that the lender had been deprived of his funds and the borrower had, as a direct consequence, derived a precisely corresponding benefit. The fact that these results flowed from a series of debits and credits on various bank accounts should not detract from the fact that the borrower had thereby obtained the property of the lender.

[19] eg because the insolvency prompts the bank to exercise a right of set-off against the funds which would otherwise have been used for the payment.

[20] The difficulties of establishing such a claim where the debtor has become insolvent are demonstrated by a number of case: see, for example, *Triffit Nurseries v Salads Etcetera Ltd (in administrative receivership)* [2001] 1 All ER (Comm) 737; *Moriarty v Anderson* [2008] EWHC 2205 (Ch). On the other hand, the decision in *Re Kayford Ltd (in liquidation)* [1975] 1 All ER 604 should be noted, but in that case there was a clear and expressed intention to create a trust over the bank account in question.

[21] In other words, the duties of the paying bank and the collecting bank are owed solely to their respective customers: see the discussions in Chapters 17 and 18 above.

Agreement of Creditor

First of all, the creditor must have agreed to receive payment via electronic means, because **19.21** there is no general rule of law which entitles a debtor to discharge his indebtedness through the use of an electronic system. Despite the ever-increasing importance of alternative means of payment, the law still only formally requires a creditor to accept payment in banknotes and coin.[22] This position may appear anomalous under modern conditions, yet it remains defensible in certain respects.[23] But in a commercial context, reality and an awareness of the risks involved in other forms of payment[24] dictate that an agreement to receive payment by this means will be readily inferred in practice. Thus, in one case, an obligation to pay 'in cash' was construed as a duty to transfer immediately available funds to the creditor's account.[25] Thus, if the creditor provides its bank account details to the debtor in order to make an initial payment, the court is likely to infer that the same account can be used for all subsequent payments to be made in the course of the same relationship, at least until the creditor gives contrary instructions.

Authorization of Payee's Bank

In accordance with ordinary principles of agency law, a payment made by a debtor to his **19.22** creditor's bank account will only operate to discharge the debt if the creditor's bank has authority to receive the payment on the creditor's behalf. A series of points may be made in relation to this apparently straightforward principle:

(a) if the debtor makes payment to a bank which is not authorized to receive it on behalf of the creditor, then the debtor can be made to pay again and may suffer the resultant loss if it cannot recover the erroneous payment from the first bank (eg because it has become insolvent). In this context, it is the creditor himself who must clothe the bank with its authority, and the debtor must not rely purely upon a representation from the creditor's bank itself to that effect.[26] The mere fact that, to the knowledge of the debtor, the creditor has an account with a particular bank does not of itself clothe that bank with authority to receive payment for the creditor;[27]

(b) even where the creditor has provided his bank account details to the debtor for the purposes of making transfers under the commercial contract, questions may arise as to the precise scope of the bank's authority;

---

[22] On this subject, see Mann, para 2.26, noting the Currency and Bank Notes Act 1954 and the Coinage Act 1971 (as amended by the Currency Act 1983). See also Paget, para 17.5.

[23] If a creditor is compelled to accept payment through an electronic transfer, then this compels him to take a credit risk on the recipient institution; he should only be obliged to take such a risk if he has agreed to do so.

[24] eg the risk of loss or theft in the case of cash and the delays which may be involved in the acceptance of cheques.

[25] *Tenax Steamship Co Ltd v The Brimnes (Owners)* [1975] QB 929 (CA).

[26] See the situation which arose in *Cleveland Manufacturing Ltd v Muslim Commercial Bank Ltd* [1981] 2 Lloyds Rep 9.

[27] *Commissioners of Customs and Excise v National Westminster Bank plc* [2002] EWHC 2002 (Ch) where the absence of apparent authority was reinforced by a specific request not to use the particular account in question.

(c) in some cases, the bank may have authority to accept the payment in discharge of the underlying obligation, in which case its acceptance of funds would amount to a waiver of any prior breaches of the commercial agreement. For example, in *Central Estates (Belgravia) Ltd v Woolgar* (No 2),[28] a notice had been served on a tenant with a view to forfeiture of his lease but, as a result of an internal error, the managing agent accepted a subsequent payment of rental on behalf of the landlord. This was held to constitute an unequivocal recognition of the continued existence of the lease notwithstanding the prior breaches, with the result that they could no longer be relied upon in forfeiture proceedings;

(d) whilst the *Central Estates* case is perhaps a useful illustration of the issue, it should be borne in mind that a managing agent enjoys authority not merely to accept rent but to manage its client's property on its behalf, and it will usually have a significant level of knowledge concerning the portfolio and its tenants. But this will not usually be the case with the receiving bank, whose sole task will be to receive the remittance, credit it to the account and advise the customer. As a consequence, it seems that a bank nominated by the creditor will have authority to accept a *tender* made by or on behalf of the debtor, but will not have authority to accept the *payment*. The significance of this distinction is apparent from the decision in *Mardorf Peach & Co Ltd v Attica Sea Carriers Corporation of Liberia (The Laconia)*.[29] In that case, a payment of charterhire fell due on a Sunday and it was accepted that, in the circumstances, payment should have been made to the owner's bank on the preceding Friday. In fact, the payment was made to that bank on the following Monday. On being advised by their bank that the payment had been received,[30] the owners instructed their bank to return the payment, and then served notice terminating the charter on the basis that the payment had been made after the due date. The charterers argued that the acceptance of the payment by the owner's bank had the effect of waiving the lateness of the payment, but the House of Lords rejected that contention. The bank had no knowledge of the terms of the charter and had not accepted the payment with knowledge of the default, nor had the owners clothed the bank with authority to accept a payment in a manner which might affect the underlying contractual relationship. Accordingly, since the owners had rejected the payment as soon as they became aware of it, the late payment default had not been waived and the withdrawal of the vessel was accordingly valid and effective. In other words, the authority of the owner's bank was limited to the *receipt of the tender* and did not extend to *acceptance of the payment*;

(e) it follows that a payment to a bank which has neither actual nor apparent authority to accept the funds on behalf of the creditor will be wholly ineffective so far as the commercial contract between the debtor and the creditor is concerned. However, even if the nominated bank does have authority to receive those funds on behalf of the

---

[28] [1972] 1 WLR 1048.

[29] [1972] 1 WLR 1048 (HL).

[30] Of course, had the owners been guilty of serious delay in rejecting the payment or had treated the funds as their own, then they may be taken to have accepted the tender themselves: see *TSB Bank of Scotland plc v Welwyn Hatfield District Council* [1993] 2 Bank LR 267.

creditor, the precise scope of that authority may require careful analysis in order to determine the implications of such a transfer for the underlying commercial contract.

The Nature of the Payment

When a creditor agrees to accept payment by means of a bank transfer, he is effectively **19.23** agreeing that the debtor can discharge his obligation by procuring that the creditor's own bank becomes indebted to him for a corresponding sum. Payment in this sense must therefore be complete at the point of time at which the creditor's bank becomes a substitute debtor.[31] A few points must be noted in this regard:

(a) Payment must usually be in full, complete, and unconditional, in the sense that the creditor's bank must assume a payment obligation to the creditor which is in all respects identical to the one previously owed by the debtor himself. Anything short of this will not usually amount to payment for the purposes of the underlying commercial agreement. The point is well illustrated by the decision of the House of Lords in *The Chikuma*.[32] The charterparty provided for payment to be received at the owner's Italian bank by 22 January. The funds had indeed arrived by that date but the Italian correspondent institution used by the charterer's bank had added a stipulation for value on 26 January. Under Italian banking practices, this meant that the owners could only access the money on 22 January by paying a penalty or fee. The result was that the full amount was not unconditionally available to the owners on 22 January, and payment had thus not been made in accordance with the terms of the charter.

(b) The point of time at which the debtor substitution occurs may be important for the reasons discussed above, but it may not always be easy to identify. The mere fact that the debtor has requested his bank to make the payment to the creditor's bank cannot of itself amount to payment, even if the debtor has sufficient available funds and there is no obvious impediment to the implementation of that instruction.[33] Likewise, a request by the debtor's bank to the creditor's bank to credit the account of the payee as necessary will not amount to payment, because there is at that point no complete guarantee that the instruction will be implemented, and it remains revocable up to that point.[34]

(c) It is sometimes said that payment is only complete once the payee's account has actually been credited with the amount of the payment. Whilst perhaps superficially attractive and providing a simple test to ascertain the precise time of payment, it should be borne in mind that the creditor's bank acts as agent for the creditor, and the question whether or when the debt was discharged by the debtor should not depend solely on the discretion of the creditor's agent. As a result, the rule appears to be that the payment[35] is complete at the point of time at which the creditor's bank decides that it will

---

[31] See Law of Bank Payments, para 30-093.
[32] [1981] 1 All ER 652 (HL). The date by which payment is due will be a matter governed by the underlying commercial contract. For an example, see *The Zographia* [1976] 2 Lloyds Rep 382.
[33] *The Effy* [1972] 1 Lloyds Rep 18.
[34] *Tenax Steamship Co Ltd v The Brimnes (Owners)* [1975] QB 929 (CA).
[35] In view of the comments in para 19.22 above, it may be more accurate to refer to the *tender* of the payment, rather than the payment itself.

credit the funds received to the account of the payee. The fact that the computer entries and other steps necessary to complete that process are undertaken at a later time will not affect the position.[36] Completion of the payment is not conditional on notice of the payment being given to the creditor.[37]

(d) A decision to credit the payee's account does not necessarily have to be made during ordinary banking hours and, as a consequence, the creditor may be well advised to wait until midnight before taking the firm position that payment has not been received.[38]

(e) The necessary corollary of the 'debtor substitution' concept noted above is that the discharge of the debt owing by the commercial debtor must substantially coincide with the point at which the corresponding obligations of the creditor's bank to the creditor become unconditional and irrevocable. Thus, in *Momm v Barclays Bank International Ltd*[39] Barclays had decided to credit the account of Herstatt Bank with funds for value on 26 June 1974. Having put this process in motion, Barclays heard that Herstatt had gone into liquidation at 4.15 pm on 26 June. It accordingly reversed the entries on the following morning. The court held that the payment was complete when the decision to credit the account was made, and it was not thereafter open to Barclays to reverse that decision without the authority of Herstatt.

(f) Likewise, in *Tayeb v HSBC Bank plc*,[40] the court noted that a bank which opened an account for a customer was bound to receive CHAPS transfers to its credit. Payments through this system were intended to be irreversible and, once received by the bank, constituted the bank a debtor of the customer to a corresponding amount. Consequently, the bank could not then unilaterally return the funds to the remitter, since this would amount to a unilateral cancellation of the debt which the bank had already incurred.[41]

(g) On the other side of the coin, it seems that the debtor's instruction to his bank to make the necessary payments will become irrevocable once the bank has initiated the necessary process for payment through the relevant system.[42]

International Payments

19.24 International funds transfers involve a higher degree of complexity. This is partly due to the involvement of two or more systems of law and partly because (for example) a UK bank

---

[36] *The Brimnes*, n 34 above.
[37] See Law of Bank Payments, para 3-094, discussing the decisions in *Eyles v Ellis* (1827) 4 Bing 112 and *Rekstin v Severo Sibirsko AO* [1933] 1 KB 47 (CA).
[38] See *Afovos Shipping Co SA v Pagnan* [1983] 1 All ER 449 (HL); *The Lutetian* [1982] 2 Lloyds Rep 140; *Amman Aviation Pty Ltd v Commonwealth of Australia* [1990] FCA 55 (Federal Court of Australia). It is by no means out of the question that 'payment' (in the sense of a decision to credit the payee's account) could be made after banking hours. For example, the debtor's bank may itself have an account with the creditor's bank and may simply instruct the creditor's bank to debit that account as necessary. No movement of funds through an interbank payment system would be necessary for that purpose.
[39] [1977] QB 790.
[40] [2004] All ER (Comm) 1024. The decision has already been noted in the context of CHAPS (see para 19.10 above) and in the context of the Proceeds of Crime Act 2002 (see para 7.87 above).
[41] The court held that the debt came into being when the LAK was generated.
[42] See *Delbreuck & Co v Manufacturers Hanover Trust Co* 609 F2d 1047 (1979), another case arising from the collapse of Herstatt Bank.

which is asked to make a US dollar payment for a customer will have to use the services of a correspondent bank in New York,[43] because the payment will ultimately have to be cleared through that country. Difficulties can obviously arise if the payment system in a particular country ceases to be available for particular transfers for legal or other reasons. In such a case, English law will be reluctant to come to the conclusion that the payment has become unlawful or impossible. This, in turn, has led the English courts to the curious position that—if all else fails—Eurodollar deposits must be repaid in physical cash. In *Libyan Arab Foreign Bank v Bankers Trust Co*,[44] the Libyan Bank was a customer of Bankers Trust in both London and New York and maintained accounts with both branches. The United States imposed sanctions against Libya, which froze all assets held by Libyan entities with US institutions, whether in the US or through their overseas branches. The Libyan bank then demanded payment of some US$131 million which was held in the London account. Bankers Trust sought to defend the claim on two main grounds:

(a) It was argued that the agreement between the parties was governed by New York law. Had this point been established, then the obligation to repay the deposit would have been suspended under the terms of the law applicable to it. The English court would thus have been unable to give judgment against the bank. However, and although the arrangements involved periodic transfers between the two accounts, the court held (rightly, it is submitted) that the contract was governed by English law insofar as it related to the London accounts,[45] and New York law insofar as it related to the head office accounts. Subject to the point made in (b) below, the US blocking orders could not excuse payment under the deposit arrangements governed by English law;

(b) Even on the footing that the London deposit contract was governed by English law, it was said that the contract could not be enforced because the acts required to that end would be illegal in the place of performance[46]—a credit in US dollars ultimately had to be reflected by a movement between accounts through the dollar clearing system in New York. This argument was rejected on the grounds that the depositor retained a right to payment in cash,[47] that the bank could have shipped US$131,000,000 from

---

[43] It is an implied term of the contract that a bank may use the services of a correspondent bank to effect a foreign currency or international payment: see *Royal Products Ltd v Midland Bank Ltd* [1981] 2 Lloyds Rep 194.

[44] [1989] QB 728.

[45] The banker-customer contract is generally governed by the law of the place in which the account holding branch is located. On this point, see generally Chapter 40 below.

[46] Authority for this proposition is provided by the decision in *Ralli Bros v Compania Naviera Sota y Aznar* [1920] 2 KB 287 (CA). *Ralli* is similar to the decision in the *Libyan Arab* case, in the sense that illegality supervened after the contract had been made, but the same rule applies even where performance would be unlawful in the relevant place as at the time the contract is made: see Paget, para 17.12, citing *Toprak Mahsulleri Ofisi v Finagrain Cie Commerciale Agricole et Financiere SA* [1979] 2 Lloyds Rep 98 (CA) and *Ispahani v Bank Melli Iran* [1998] Lloyds Rep Bank 133 (CA). The principle appears to form a part of English domestic law (rather than its private international law), with the result that it would not apply to contracts governed by a foreign system of law: see Mann, para 16.38. The present writer has argued in a different context that the rule should be reconsidered, at least insofar as it relates to obligations of a monetary character: see Mann, para 16.38.

[47] Under English private international law, an undertaking to pay an amount in foreign currency connotes an obligation to pay in whatever constitutes legal tender under the laws of the issuing country: see Mann, para 9.03, and cases there cited. Once again, this rule would be subject to any contrary agreement to accept payment by other means.

New York to London without contravening the blocking order[48] and that under these circumstances the place of performance was London. It is submitted that the court should have upheld the invariable practice that Eurodollars obligations are settled solely by means of credits[49] (and not in cash), but held that the bank's obligation was to procure a credit to another account in London. The place of performance was thus London and it would have been immaterial that some preparatory action may have been required in New York. The court further held that, but for its decision to order payment in dollar notes, it could have required payment in sterling. A debtor obliged to pay a foreign currency debt in England has the option to pay in that currency or in sterling, and he should be compelled to pay in sterling if payment in the foreign currency is impossible. Whilst this result would have been preferable to a decision in favour of the defendant bank, the application of this principle is not free from difficulty. The option to pay in sterling (and, correspondingly, its obligation to do so) is subject to contrary agreement. International banks dealing in Eurodollar deposits would expect to be paid in the currency of the deposit, because the application of the sterling option may give rise to exchange losses.[50]

19.25   Whilst the ultimate outcome of the *Libyan Arab* proceedings is satisfactory,[51] it is submitted that it was arrived at via the wrong route. The obligation of the bank was to procure that the funds should be credited to an account nominated by the depositor. Whilst the English courts would not have ordered that the funds should be credited to an account in New York on the basis that payment would be unlawful there,[52] it could have ordered that the funds be credited to an account in London. This would have been consistent with the practice of the Eurocurrency markets[53] and would have avoided the rather artificial (and questionable) view that the depositor had the right to require repayment of such deposits in cash.[54]

Liabilities to Third Parties

19.26   It was noted earlier in the context of cheques that the obligations of the paying bank and the collecting bank are owed principally to their own respective customers, and not to other parties to the payment transaction.[55]

---

[48] This, in itself, is a highly questionable proposition, given the scope and objectives of the order itself.
[49] A term to this effect could have been implied on the basis of market practice.
[50] It is true that the rate of exchange to be applied is governed by the law applicable to the contract, but rates of exchange are constantly fluctuating, even on an intra-day basis. Given the amounts at issue in the *Libyan Arab* case, even very small fluctuations could have resulted in significant losses.
[51] Had the court given judgment for the bank, then this would have effectively allowed to the United States a degree of extraterritorial influence over the activities of banks in London. In other words, the English courts would have been used to enforce the sovereign authority of the United States within the territory of the United Kingdom, contrary to the principle explained in *Government of India v Taylor* [1955] AC 491 (HL) and the numerous cases which have followed it.
[52] ie on the basis of the *Ralli Bros* principle discussed above.
[53] Although it was not applied by the court, that practice is correctly described in the evidence of Dr Marcia Stigum, which is discussed in the *Libyan Arab* judgment.
[54] Certain problems associated with cross-border payments are considered further in Part (F) below.
[55] See Chapter 17 above (paying bank) and Chapter 18 above (collecting bank).

This position appears to be the same in relation to other types of funds transfer. In *Wells v* **19.27**
National Commercial Bank,[56] the bank had been instructed to make a large payment in
favour of the claimant, but the bank failed to do so. The claimant's attempt to hold the
paying bank liable for that failure was struck out by the Court of Appeal on the basis that
there was no contract between the paying bank and the payee and the paying bank had not
assumed any duty of care or other responsibility in favour of the claimant.

---

[56] [1998] PNLR 552 (CA).

PART D

THE BANK AS SERVICE PROVIDER

Introduction

The last section considered the general relationship between the bank and its customer. The discussion was based around the basic and best-understood contract, focused on the current account, the payment of cheques, and other payment services.

The present section examines the bank's role as a service provider in more depth, examining some of the more sophisticated types of business which banks may undertake with their customers.

For these purposes, the present section is arranged as follows:

(a) Chapter 20 considers the role of the bank as a lender;
(b) Chapter 21 examines the structure of syndicated (or multi-bank) facilities;
(c) Chapter 22 examines the various means by which loan assets may be traded or sold;
(d) Chapter 23 provides a brief overview of swaps and derivatives;
(e) Chapter 24 considers documentary credits (including bank guarantees and performance bonds); and
(f) Chapter 25 examines certain possible sources of bank liability which may arise in the context of the sale of complex products.

20

THE BANK AS A LENDER

Introduction

Banks can provide loan facilities and other accommodation to their customers in a variety of ways. **20.01**

The best known forms of facility include the overdraft and the term loan. A bank may also provide accommodation by assuming an obligation to a third party for the benefit of the customer (eg by issuing a guarantee, performance bond or letter of credit). The present chapter, however, concentrates on loan facilities.[1] Having considered single bank facilities, the next chapter will examine the additional terms required in the context of a syndicated transaction. **20.02**

Against this background, this chapter will consider: **20.03**

(a) overdraft facilities; and
(b) term loan facilities.

---

[1] Bonds, guarantees, and similar facilities are considered in Chapter 24 below.

Overdraft Facilities

Operation

20.04 An overdraft facility[2] entitles a customer to draw on his current account beyond his credit balance and up to a stipulated limit.[3] This may be achieved by drawing cheques or giving any other form of payment instruction to the bank.

Cancellation

20.05 Subject to any contrary agreement,[4] an overdraft facility can be cancelled by the bank on notice to that effect to the customer. Nevertheless, the bank remains liable to meet cheques up to the pre-agreed overdraft limit, to the extent to which those cheques were drawn *before* the notice of cancellation was given.[5]

Demand

20.06 Upon cancellation of the facility, the bank may make a demand for immediate repayment of all moneys owing in respect of the overdraft.[6]

20.07 In this context, 'immediate repayment' means what is says. The customer is allowed time to go and collect or remit the necessary funds (eg from an account which is in credit with another bank). But there is no grace period during which the customer can negotiate and raise a facility from another bank.[7]

---

[2] The present discussion assumes that the overdraft is created by agreement (as opposed to an unauthorized overdraft). Note that an overdraft facility is, for the purposes of the Consumer Credit Act 1974, an agreement for the provision of running account credit. However, overdraft facilities are generally excluded from the terms of the 1974 Act by virtue of rulings made by the Office of Fair Trading: see, for example, the discussion in Paget at paras 2.58–2.59.

[3] An overdraft is therefore merely one form of a loan of money: see Paget, para 11.16, citing *Re Hone (a bankrupt)* [1950] 2 All ER 716.

[4] A contrary agreement of this kind will be very rare in practice.

[5] *Williams & Glyns Bank Ltd v Barnes* [1981] Com LR 205.

[6] At least, the right to make a demand for immediate repayment will be the usual position. But it must not be overlooked that the right is essentially a matter of contract. Thus, if a bank makes available an overdraft facility on 'usual banking terms' for the specific purpose of meeting obligations under bills of exchange, it may be an implied term of the contract that the facility is kept open until the bills have matured and been paid, so that the usual right of demand is overridden: see *Williams & Glyns Bank Ltd v Barnes* [1981] Com LR 205. For a case in which the facility letter provided that the overdraft should be available for 12 months but also stated that it was repayable on demand, see *Titford Property Co Ltd v Cannon Street Acceptances Ltd* (1975, unreported). The court held that the 12 month period prevailed because this was consistent with the underlying purpose of the transaction, but this would inevitably be a matter of interpretation in each case. Thus, in *Lloyds Bank plc v Lampert* [1999] 1 All ER (Comm) 161 (CA), a statement that the bank had the right to make demand 'in accordance with normal banking practice' did not have the effect of cutting down the bank's discretion to make a demand at any time. The decision in this case has recently been followed in *Hall v Royal Bank of Scotland plc* (Commercial Court, 2 December 2009), where it was also noted that the bank did not owe a duty of care to the customer in deciding whether and when to make demand.

[7] This is the effect of *R A Cripps & Son Ltd v Wickenden* [1973] 1 WLR 944. This decision has been followed on a number of occasions: see *Bank of Baroda v Panessar* [1987] Ch 335, *Williams & Glyns Bank Ltd v Barnes* [1981] Com LR 205 and *Bank of Ireland v AMCD (Property Holdings) Ltd* [2001] 2 All ER (Comm) 894. In the *Cripps* case, it was found to be reasonable to appoint a receiver just two hours after the demand,

Interest

The rate of interest chargeable on an overdraft will again principally be a matter of contract **20.08**
and will usually be stipulated in the facility letter itself. In the absence of an express provision, interest will be payable as a matter of banking custom.[8] An agreement to pay interest
may also be inferred if the customer has previously allowed debit interest to be deducted
from his account without objection[9] and indeed may be inferred from the very fact that the
customer requests an overdraft.[10]

The rate of interest will usually be computed by reference to a base or other benchmark rate **20.09**
quoted by the lender, and will be expressed to be variable according to changes in that
published rate. The bank's right to vary the rate must be exercised honestly and in good
faith, but there is no legal obligation to exercise the variation right in line with broader
market movements.[11]

Interest on an overdraft accrues on a daily basis on the outstanding debit balance on the **20.10**
account. This formulation obviously begs the question as to the level of the daily balance
and precisely when incoming payments should be credited to the customer's account so as
to reduce the effective interest liability. In this context, the bank is required to credit the
proceeds of cheques in accordance with its normal practices and this may be the day following the actual receipt of the funds by the bank itself.[12] However, where the incoming payment is received by means of a funds transfer, same day value must now generally be given
in compliance with the Payment Services Regulations 2009.[13]

Finally, it is accepted that—as a matter of general banking custom—the bank is contractually entitled to compound interest periodically, so that interest is charged on the accrued **20.11**
interest itself.[14] It has been accepted that a bank can compound interest at three monthly

---

partly because the borrower did not have the necessary funds available from any source. It may be observed
that the Canadian courts have been more indulgent towards borrowers. For example, in *Whonnock Industries
Ltd v National Bank of Canada* (1987) 42 DLR (4th) 1, the court said that a reasonable time for payment may
connote a period of a few days. An award of exemplary damages has also been upheld where the bank required
repayment by 3.00 pm on the day of the demand: *Royal Bank of Canada v W. Got Associates Electric Ltd* [1993]
3 SCR 408 (Supreme Court of Canada).

[8] *Gwyn v Godby* (1812) 4 Taunt 346.
[9] *Re Marquis of Anglesey* [1901] Ch 548.
[10] *Lloyds Bank plc v Voller* [2000] 2 All ER (Comm) 978 (CA).
[11] *Paragon Finance v Nash* [2001] 2 All ER 1025 (CA). On the same issue, see *Rahman v Sterling Credit Ltd*
[2002] EWHC 3008 (Ch), *Paragon Finance Ltd v Pender* [2005] EWCA Civ 760 and *Broadwick Financial
Services Ltd v Spencer* [2002] 1 All ER (Comm) 446. The decision in *Tricity Finance Ltd v Paton* [1989] 1 All
ER 918 (which denied the existence of any form of implied fetter on the broad contractual discretion even in
the context of a regulated agreement under the Consumer Credit Act 1974) should no longer be followed.
[12] *Emerald Meats (London) Ltd v AIB Group plc* [2002] EWCA Civ 460 (CA).
[13] On the Payment Services Regulations 2009 and the point made in the text, see para 5.83 above.
The 2009 Regulations do not apply to paper-based payments such as cheques, and thus do not affect the
Emerald Meats decision mentioned in the last footnote.
[14] *National Bank of Greece SA v Pinios Shipping Co* [1990] 1 AC 637 (HL).

intervals,[15] but this does not necessarily preclude more frequent compounding.[16] The right to compound interest continues even after the demand has been made, up to the date of repayment.[17]

Term Loans

Nature and Operation

20.12   As its name suggests, a term loan is made for a specific period of time. For a private individual, a loan secured by a mortgage on real estate will be the most obvious example.

20.13   In the corporate field, many more examples may be offered. For example, a term loan may be appropriate to fund the acquisition of a new business, or the acquisition or construction of a new property. In each of these cases, the borrower will clearly need a period of time to turn such an investment to account, and it would obviously be preferable to obtain a term commitment from the bank; the relevant assets are illiquid and the borrower would not be in a position to respond to an immediate demand for repayment if the transaction were funded by way of overdraft.

20.14   Equally, however, a bank cannot commit to maintain a facility for five years, come what may. There must be some flexibility to require repayment in the event of a material change in circumstances.[18]

20.15   The present section will accordingly consider the provisions which may commonly be found in a term loan agreement, and which have been developed with a view to reconciling these conflicting objectives.[19]

---

[15] *Kitchen v HSBC Bank plc* [2000] 1 All ER (Comm) 787.

[16] The contract at issue in *Multiservice Bookbinding Ltd v Marden* [1979] Ch 84 provided for the compounding of interest at 21 day intervals, and the court did not interfere with this provision.

[17] *Pinios Shipping*, n 14 above.

[18] On this subject, see the discussion on events of default at para 20.38 below.

[19] The list of clauses about to be discussed is selective, rather than comprehensive, but is designed to provide an overview of the key provisions. It should be appreciated that the precise terms of the loan agreement will always depend heavily on the purpose and terms of the particular transaction. For convenience of illustration, reference will be made to clauses found in the standard Multicurrency Term Facility Agreement (the 'LMA document') published by the Loan Market Association on its website (www.loan-market-assoc.com). Although this particular issue does not merit detailed consideration for present purposes, it may be noted that the specimen agreements published by the Loan Market Association have gained wide acceptance in the UK debt markets, and that this may have legal consequences. For example, although such agreements will usually be prepared on behalf of the lenders and may be regarded as 'standard', they probably do not constitute the lenders' 'standard terms of business' for the purposes of the Unfair Contract Terms Act 1977, s 3(1) (on which see generally paras 15.38–15.44 above), with the result that the provisions of the 1977 Act could not be applied to the terms of such an agreement. Even if this is incorrect, any relevant terms should probably be treated as 'reasonable' (and, hence, enforceable) for the purposes of the Act since major corporate borrowers would be familiar with the accepted market terms. In other words, the borrower '... knew or ought reasonably to have known of the existence of the term ...' for the purposes of para (c), Sch 2 to the Act. Although arising in a slightly different context, lenders could perhaps draw some comfort from the refusal of a US Federal Court to apply the *contra proferentem* rule of interpretation in the context of a contract prepared by a trade association (the Savings and Loan League) in *Carondelet Savings & Loan Association v Citizens Savings & Loan Association* 604 F2d 464 (7th Cir, 1979).

The Facility/Purpose

After any necessary introductory provisions and a list of definitions, the agreement will **20.16** provide a description of the facility[20] and its purpose.[21] Where the facility is to be applied to the purchase of a particular property or other asset, the lender will in practice be concerned to ensure that the proceeds are in fact so applied since the asset will usually constitute its main security for the repayment of the facility. Nevertheless, the lender is not under any formal obligation to monitor the proper application of the funds[22] and, having drawn advances, the borrower is unconditionally obliged to repay them in accordance with the terms of the agreement.[23]

Conditions Precedent

The agreement will contain a list of conditions precedent to the availability of the facility.[24] **20.17** These will fall into various categories:

(a) Conditions precedent to the *first* utilization of the facility. When the borrower signs and hands over a loan agreement, the bank merely receives a document with a signature on it. For obvious reasons, this is not of itself sufficient. Before the bank parts with any of its money, it will require evidence that the document constitutes a valid and binding obligation of the borrower, which can be enforced if necessary. It will thus require the borrower's constitutional documents and a board resolution to demonstrate that the transaction has been approved by all necessary internal procedures.[25] It may also require legal opinions to confirm the validity of the documentation, especially where the borrower or any other obligors are incorporated outside the United Kingdom. Depending on the terms and purpose of the transaction, the bank may also require a series of other documents before it is prepared to proceed (eg a guarantee from the borrower's parent

---

[20] See LMA document, clause 2. For present purposes, it is assumed that the facility takes the form of a fixed term loan. It may, however, take the form of a revolving credit, where the borrower has the right to draw and repay advances at the end of interest periods. This greater flexibility is often more appropriate to facilities which are to be used for working capital purposes. In other cases, the facility may not even provide for the availability of cash at all; it may, for example, allow for the issue of guarantees or documentary credits for the account of the customer. On instruments of that kind, see Chapter 24 below. Regardless of the precise structure of the facility, many of the provisions discussed below would nevertheless remain in broadly identical form.

[21] See LMA document, clause 3.

[22] A point confirmed by the LMA document, clause 3.2. Thus, the borrower remains liable for repayment even though he uses the loan for unauthorized purposes, such as the promotion of a gambling habit: see the situation which arose in *Politharis v Westpac Banking Corporation* [2009] SASC 96 (Supreme Court of Western Australia).

[23] Since the application of the proceeds of the facility for a non-permitted purpose would be a breach of the borrower's obligations under the agreement, the lender could demand immediate repayment of all outstanding advances as soon as it becomes aware of the breach: see Events of Default at para 20.38 below.

[24] In the LMA document, the conditions precedent to utilization are found in clause 4, read together with schedule 2.

[25] This will be the position in practice, although the bank may enjoy the protection of ss 40 and 41 of the Companies Act 2006 if it fails to take these precautions. These sections allow an outsider dealing with the company in good faith to assume that its directors are duly authorized and that the exercise of their powers is not subject to any limitation under the company's constitution.

company; security over any property or other assets which are to be acquired with the assistance of the loan).

(b) Conditions precedent to *individual* utilizations. Additional documentary conditions may apply for each individual utilization under the facility.[26] For example, if the loan is intended to fund the construction of a building, the agreement is likely to require an architect's certificate confirming that a specified amount of money has been expended to that end. This provides comfort to the bank that the proceeds of its facility are being applied to the intended purpose, and that the value of the project has been or will be enhanced by an amount equal to the amounts drawn.

(c) General conditions precedent. In addition to the conditions noted above (which are usually of a documentary character), the agreement will also stipulate that an advance may only be made if the representations set out in the agreement continue to be true and no event of default has occurred.[27]

Utilization

20.18 If the various conditions precedent noted above have been satisfied, then the borrower will be entitled to draw advances from the bank up to the stated facility limit. Utilization provisions will typically deal with the following matters:[28]

(a) the period of notice required for drawdown (typically, one business day for sterling and two business days for other currencies);

(b) the mode of drawdown (eg whether the loan is to be drawn in a single amount or by multiple drawings);

(c) if multiple drawings are allowed, the agreement may provide for drawings in minimum amounts of (say) £500,000 so that the bank does not have the administrative burden of dealing with numerous small advances;

(d) the availability period for utilization. Any undrawn portion of the facility will cease to be available for utilization at the end of that period.

Currencies

20.19 If drawings in different currencies are allowed, then the permitted currencies ('optional currencies') will be listed.[29] In addition, since the overall facility limit will necessarily be expressed in one currency (the 'base currency'), it may be necessary to include some fairly detailed provisions so that the outstanding amount of currency advances will be compared to the facility limit at prevailing exchange rates. Repayments may be required if the base currency has weakened as against the optional currencies[30] since, otherwise, the amounts

---

[26] A term loan may be drawn in a single lump sum but it may also be used in tranches: see Utilization below.

[27] Representations and events of default are discussed later in this section.

[28] See LMA document, clause 5.

[29] Optional currency provisions are set out in clause 6 of the LMA document. Optional currencies frequently include any freely transferable and convertible currency.

[30] Obviously, the facility limit is established in order to limit the bank's exposure to the borrower to the stated amount. As will be seen from the analysis in the text, however, a multicurrency facility of this kind involves the additional risk that the borrower may default when currency movements have resulted in an exposure which exceeds the basic facility limit.

outstanding under the agreement may exceed the approved credit limit as expressed in the base currency.

Repayment

The loan will obviously have a fixed or maximum period, and must be repaid at the end of it.[31] The loan may either be repayable in one lump sum (a so-called 'bullet' repayment) or by a series of instalments leading up to the final repayment date.

20.20

Prepayment

In general terms, where a borrower takes up a loan for (say) a five year period, it thereby commits to pay the bank an interest return for the entire period. This may be burdensome for the borrower if (for example) the asset acquired with the loan is unexpectedly re-sold within a short period. It is therefore generally accepted that the borrower should have a right to prepay the facility.

20.21

It used to be customary to impose a prepayment fee (usually a flat percentage of the principal amount prepaid). This is now less common, although a fee is sometimes required if the borrower intends to refinance the transaction with another bank, or if the transaction is prepaid at a particularly early stage. This compensates the first lender for the loss of the transaction even though the borrower still has a funding requirement, and for the loss of interest revenue over the anticipated remaining period of the loan. A fee of this kind should not be open to challenge on the basis that it is excessive and therefore subject to the rules on contractual penalties. This follows from the fact that the prepayment is voluntary and, hence, is not intended to penalize the borrower for any breach of his contractual obligations.[32]

20.22

Prepayment will also be mandatory in certain cases. For example:

20.23

(a) *Illegality.* The agreement will provide that a bank is excused from its obligations if their performance becomes illegal under the laws of any relevant jurisdiction.[33] It may be asked why such a provision is necessary, given that supervening illegality has the effect of excusing performance, or at least of suspending the obligation until performance becomes lawful.[34] The answer lies in the multinational nature of banking. For example, the London branch of a US bank may agree to provide a facility to a sovereign borrower under an agreement governed by English law. As a result of a rupture in diplomatic relations, the US subsequently introduces sanctions which render it unlawful to lend money to that country. The difficulty for the bank is that the introduction of a US law

---

[31] See LMA document, clause 7.

[32] See the decision of the Court of Appeal in *Campbell Discount Co Ltd v Bridge* [1961] 1 QB 445. The decision of the House of Lords in the same case ([1982] AC 600) proceeded on the basis that there had indeed been a breach of contract. If a termination sum is payable following acceleration by the lender, then this will flow from a default by the borrower and the law on penalty clauses could then be engaged: see *London Trust Ltd v Hurrell* [1955] 1 WLR 391. Termination penalties are applied in certain specialist financing markets but are not common. It is more usual to provide for penalty or default interest in such cases. On provisions of this kind, see paras 20.26 and 20.27 below.

[33] See LMA document, clause 8.1.

[34] On the whole subject, see Chitty, ch 16.

cannot vary or discharge a lending obligation which is governed by English law, and its obligation to lend would thus remain enforceable in the UK.[35] The standard illegality clause will thus expressly excuse the bank from its obligations if performance becomes illegal under the law of the country in which its lending branch is located or the law of the country in which its head office is situate. The borrower will also be required to prepay the facility at the end of the then current interest period.[36]

(b) *Change of control.* The facility agreement will usually provide for mandatory prepayment—or at least, a lender's right to require prepayment—in the event of a change of control of the borrower. There are two main reasons for this provision. First of all, the identity of the owners and controllers of the borrower will have been a material factor in the bank's original credit decision —for example, because the parent company has the financial capacity and/or technical know-how to support the borrower's business. More mundanely, the acquisition may cause difficulty for the lending bank if the acquirer is already a customer of the bank, since the aggregation of all of the relevant outstanding facilities may place the bank in breach of its large exposure limit.[37] It should be said that, in the past, directors of listed companies occasionally argued that they could not agree to a trigger clause of this kind, on the basis that it could deprive the shareholders of the benefit of a takeover offer which might otherwise be forthcoming. Acceptance of the clause would thus constitute a breach of fiduciary duty on the part of the directors. This argument is no longer heard and it is submitted that it was always misconceived. If the facility as a whole is in the interests of the company, then it must likewise be in its interests to agree to such provisions as are necessary to finalize the facility agreement. Furthermore, as noted above, the bank has a legitimate interest in the identity of the ultimate owner of the business. It must be said, however, that if a bank continues to accept payments under the facility after it has become aware of a change of control to which it has not formally consented, then it may be taken to have waived the relevant default.[38]

(c) *Cash sweep.* Where the business is generating cash in excess of its current requirements, the agreement may require the surplus to be applied in prepayment of the facility.

Interest

20.24 Interest may be calculated in a variety of ways. Where the loan is made in sterling, interest may be expressed by reference to the bank's base lending rate. For larger transactions, LIBOR[39] or EURIBOR[40] are likely to be used. These rates essentially represent the bank's

---

[35] Compare the situation which arose in *Libyan Arab Foreign Bank v Bankers Trust Company* [1989] QB 728. The case is noted at para 19.24 above.

[36] For the relevant provisions, see LMA document, clause 8.2.

[37] On large exposures, see paras 6.63–6.68 above.

[38] Compare the situation which arose in *Leofilis v Lonsdale Sports Ltd* [2008] EWHC 640 (CA).

[39] London interbank offered rate, the rate at which banks deposit funds with each other in the London market. The rate may refer to deposits in any currency.

[40] The rate quoted for euro deposits in the European interbank market. In practice, both LIBOR and EURIBOR will be determined by reference to a rate displayed on a screen-based information service. If the screen rates are unavailable for some reason, then the agreement will contain alternative provisions for the calculation of the interest rate (eg by reference to the bank's actual cost of raising the funds). For the relevant provisions, see LMA document, clause 11.

cost of funding the loan and, consequently, the interest payable by the borrower will be a margin[41] in excess of those rates. In each case, the agreement will also stipulate the periods by reference to which interest will be calculated—usually, one, three, or six months, at the choice of the borrower.[42]

The margin chargeable on the loan may be variable, or subject to a 'ratchet'. For example, **20.25** the margin may be reduced if the borrower meets certain profit or other financial targets, which would imply that the credit risk on the borrower has improved.

It is also customary for the interest calculation to include an element in respect of addi- **20.26** tional costs incurred by the lender in providing the advances.[43] Additional costs will include the cost of complying with any special deposit or similar requirements of the Bank of England, the FSA, or any other relevant regulatory authority.[44]

The agreement will also provide for 'default interest', that is to say, an additional rate of **20.27** interest on sums which are paid after their due date. This will typically be one or two per cent above the basic interest rate. It has occasionally been argued that such clauses are penalties,[45] and that they are therefore unenforceable since they do not represent a reasonable pre-estimate of the losses incurred by the bank as a result of the payment default. It has, however, been decided that a one per cent default margin fairly reflects the increased risk of loss to which the bank is exposed as a result of non-payment.[46] This decision is helpful to the bank in confirming the enforceability of this type of provision. It is, however, limited to a default rate of one per cent, and there is no guarantee that the court would adopt a similar attitude to a higher rate, although it is submitted that the court should generally uphold the agreed rate in commercial cases, unless it is unconscionable, oppressive, or extortionate.[47] In addition, the decision is limited to cases involving *non-payment and to the amount*

---

[41] ie the profit margin earned by the bank over and above its own cost of funding the outstanding amounts.

[42] A variety of factors will influence the borrower's choice. Apart from the differential between one, three, and six month rates, the borrower may choose the longest possible period if it believes that rates are likely to rise in the short term. Equally, if it believes that rates may fall imminently, it will choose a shorter period so that it will be able to take advantage of the rate reduction as soon as it comes into effect.

[43] The interest calculation is therefore expressed to be the aggregate of (i) the margin, (ii) LIBOR (or EURIBOR), and (iii) a percentage rate reflecting the additional costs: see LMA document, clause 9.1.

[44] See LMA document, schedule 4.

[45] On contractual penalties generally, see Chitty, paras 26-109–26-133.

[46] *Lordsvale Finance Ltd v Bank of Zambia* [1996] 3 All ER 156. It should be noted that the court did not regard the default interest provision as a penalty clause in the strict sense of that term. For US authority to similar effect, see *Citibank NA v Nyland and the Republic of the Philippines* 878 F 2d 620 (2nd Cir, 1989). Since interest accrues on a daily basis and involves payment by time for the use of money, a provision for payment of all interest which may become owing under a 20 year facility even on early acceleration will inevitably amount to a penalty, since no attempt will have been made to relate the liquidated damages provision to the actual loss likely to have been suffered by the lender: see *County Leasing Ltd v East* [2007] EWHC 2907. For a case in which a loan facility was renegotiated to include more burdensome default interest provisions on late payment and which were accordingly held to be a penalty, see *Donegal International Ltd v Republic of Zambia* [2007] All ER (D) 184.

[47] On this basis, the Hong Kong Admiralty Court upheld a default margin of two per cent in *Re Mandarin Containers Ltd* [2004] HKLRD 554. In Australia, a default rate of nine per cent has been held to be a penalty in the absence of any evidence that this was likely to be a fair representation of the loss suffered by the lender on default: see *Bell v Pacific View (Qld) Pty Ltd* [2006] QSC 199 (Supreme Court of Queensland).

which is unpaid. Consequently, it may not necessarily be enforced in the context of an agreement which provides for default interest to accrue on the *entire* loan, even though only one instalment may be in arrears. In the writer's view, such a provision ought to be enforceable because the right to compensation flows from the increased credit risk flowing from the default, rather than the mere fact that a particular instalment is overdue.[48]

Fees/Expenses

20.28 Apart from the interest margin, the bank will also usually derive two forms of fee income from the facility.[49] These will comprise:

(a) An arrangement fee. This fee will usually be payable on signature of the facility agreement and, aside from any profit element, is designed to cover the costs incurred by the bank in structuring the facility, undertaking due diligence into the borrower's financial position, negotiating the facility documentation, and other matters.

(b) A commitment fee. This fee will be calculated on the undrawn portion of the facility, so that the bank is compensated for the cost of keeping funding available to meet its obligations on receipt of a utilization request from the borrower.[50]

The borrower will also be required to meet any out of pocket expenses incurred in connection with the facility (eg legal and valuation fees) and any enforcement proceedings which may become necessary.[51]

Tax Gross-up

20.29 It is obviously essential to the lender to receive payment of interest in full on the due date. But tax legislation may have an impact on this expectation. In the United Kingdom, a borrower obliged to pay yearly interest[52] is required to retain out of that interest, and to account to the revenue authorities for, an amount equal to basic rate tax on the interest payment.[53] Although the withholding requirement is imposed on the *borrower*, the duty is imposed to ensure the collection of tax owing by the *lender* in respect of that income receipt. Since the deduction is required by law, this would ordinarily discharge the interest obligation to

---

[48] Some agreements may even provide for default interest to accrue once *any* event of default has occurred, even though no payments are in arrears. As will be seen below, a number of events of default do not involve non-payment. Since the decision in *Lordsvale Finance* (above) justifies the enhanced level of interest by reference to the increased possibility of loss, it seems likely that the decision would apply equally in this type of case, provided that the default rate is otherwise reasonable.

[49] See LMA document, clause 12.

[50] In other words, the bank earns interest on the amounts drawn, and commitment fee on the amounts undrawn. If the bank has committed to make funding available, then this will usually have a cost to the bank in the sense that it must allocate capital to that commitment. It is thus unable to use that capital by lending to others, and has to forego other opportunities which might be offered to it. The commitment fee compensates the bank for that state of affairs. On the allocation of capital and the requirements of Basel II, see generally Chapter 6 above.

[51] See LMA document, clause 17. At least insofar as legal fees are concerned, there seems to be no implied term to the effect that these will be reasonable although the point will often be negotiated into the agreement by way of an express provision: see *Bank of New York Mellon v GV Films Ltd* [2009] EWHC 3315 (Comm).

[52] In view of the expression 'yearly interest', the withholding obligation would not apply in relation to very short term facilities.

[53] Income Tax Act 2007, s 874.

the extent of the deduction, but that position would obviously be unacceptable to the lender. In practice, the difficulty will not often arise because the withholding requirement does not apply where the lender is a bank.[54] Nevertheless, standard documentation will include a tax gross-up clause, requiring the borrower to pay such additional sums as may be necessary to ensure that the bank receives the full amount of interest even after the tax deduction has been made. Provisions of this kind[55] may require careful consideration in various situations. For example:

(a) Where the lending bank is itself established outside the United Kingdom and is making the facility available from outside the UK. In that event, the duty to withhold amounts on account of UK taxation is, in principle, applicable. In practice, however, the problem may be eliminated or mitigated if the lender is resident in a jurisdiction with the United Kingdom which reduces the level of withholding required.[56]

(b) Where the borrower is established outside the United Kingdom, the borrower may be under an obligation to withhold on account of taxation imposed in that country.[57] It is true that a withholding made under a foreign law will not discharge an obligation governed by English law,[58] with the result that the borrower will have to pay twice. However, the lender will in practice wish to deal with the issue by means of express contractual terms.

20.30 It has been noted above that any withholding is made on account of the lender's own liability to taxation. Accordingly, if the lender receives both the benefit of a grossed up payment and a subsequent credit against its own tax liability, then it will have received a double benefit at the expense of the borrower. The lender will therefore usually agree to refund an 'excess' benefit received by it, although there may be a significant time-lag since the credit will only accrue when the lender's tax affairs for the relevant year have been finalized.[59]

Increased Costs

20.31 Occasionally, as a result of a change in law or regulation during the lifetime of the facility, a bank may suffer an increased cost in making the loan available. This may follow from a change in capital adequacy requirements, a new requirement to place special deposits with a central bank, or similar matters. As has already been shown, where such requirements are in force as at the date of the loan agreement, they will usually be covered by the terms of the document and will form a part of the interest calculation,[60] but the risk of any future changes in such requirements is placed on the borrower.[61] An example of the application of

---

[54] On this exemption, see Income Tax Act 2007, s 879.
[55] For an example, see LMA document, clause 13.2.
[56] A certain amount of form filling and process will be required: see LMA document, clause 13.2.
[57] The rationale for the withholding is that the interest has its source in the borrower's country since it is borne by an entity resident there. As a result, the foreign lender is in principle liable to local tax on that interest. But if the borrower pays the interest in full, then the tax authority will be unable to recover it abroad since no country will actively enforce the tax laws of another: see the general principle as explained in *Government of India v Taylor* [1955] AC 491 (HL).
[58] See the decision in *Indian and General Investment Trust Ltd v Borax Consolidated Ltd* [1920] KB 539.
[59] For an example of this type of provision, see LMA document, clause 13.4.
[60] See the discussion at para 20.24 above.
[61] See LMA document, clause 14.

this type of provision is offered by the implementation of Basel II via the Capital Requirements Directive.[62] The new framework required a more risk-focused approach to capital adequacy, with the inevitable result that more capital would have to be ascribed to facilities made available to riskier borrowers. The cost of funding the additional capital could be recovered from the borrower under the standard increased costs clause. As a matter of practice and in the interests of their customer relationships, however, it is understood that banks did not generally seek to invoke this clause in relation to Basel II costs.

Indemnities

20.32 A standard facility agreement will contain a series of indemnities against various costs, losses, and expenses which the lender may incur in making, maintaining, and enforcing the loan. Very briefly, these may include the following:

(a) *Currency indemnity.* There may be cases in which the lender recovers payment in a currency other than that in which the facility was originally denominated. This may occur where it is necessary to take proceedings outside England—for example, because the borrower is incorporated abroad or and/or the security is situate outside England. In such a situation, the lender may plainly suffer an exchange loss—especially where the applicable exchange rate is fixed as at the date of judgment and payment is only received at a later date. The borrower will—in addition to paying the judgment—be required to indemnify the bank against such losses.[63] To this arrangement, it may be objected that the judgment constitutes a complete satisfaction of the cause of action; how, therefore, can the borrower be required to make further payments? It is suggested that the indemnity constitutes a separate cause of action which may be enforced independently of the other payment obligations under the agreement[64] and, in any event, a foreign judgment on the primary payment obligations would not discharge an indemnity obligation governed by English law. Difficulties of this kind will now arise only rarely since the English courts—and courts in many countries which follow its jurisprudence—will now give judgment in the currency in which the relevant loan obligations are expressed.[65]

(b) *Other indemnities.* The borrower will be required to meet, and to indemnify the lender against, other costs and losses which the lender may incur during the course of the facility,[66] including (i) the costs arising as a result of the occurrence of an event of default,[67] (ii) losses resulting from any failure by the borrower to make any payment on

---

[62] On the whole subject, see Chapter 6 above.

[63] For a standard provision, see LMA document, clause 15.1.

[64] The drafters of the LMA document appear to have had this point in mind, since they describe the indemnity as an 'independent obligation': see LMA document, clause 15(a).

[65] This follows from the decision in *Miliangos v George Frank (Textiles) Ltd* [1976] AC 443 (HL). On the whole subject and for further case law, see Proctor, 'Changes in Monetary Values and the Assessment of Damages' in Saidov & Cunnington, *Contract Damages—Domestic and International Perspectives* (Hart Publishing, 2008) ch 19.

[66] On the indemnities about to be discussed, see LMA document, clause 15.2.

[67] This could include the costs of any enquiries necessary to substantiate the existence of any such default.

the due date,[68] and (iii) losses incurred by the lender as a result of making arrangements to fund an advance which is not in fact made on the intended utilization date.[69]

Representations

The agreement will contain a number of representations and warranties on the part of the   **20.33** borrower. Notwithstanding the terminology, these clauses are not 'representations' in the sense that they are made to induce the lender to enter into the contract, and may thus create a right to rescind the agreement if they are found to be untrue.[70] Some of these may be tailored to the specific transaction but many may be regarded as 'standard'. These will include statements to the following effect:[71]

(a) *Due incorporation*. The borrower will represent that it is duly incorporated and validly existing under the laws of its country of incorporation. This is, in some respects, a pointless representation, since the bank cannot acquire an action for misrepresentation against an entity which does not exist.[72] Nevertheless, one has to begin somewhere and this statement does perhaps at least present a logical starting point.[73] Although the point will not often arise in practice, it may be noted that the English courts were formerly unable to entertain proceedings involving companies established in foreign States not recognized by the United Kingdom. However, subject to various conditions, such an entity may now be party to proceedings in England, whether as claimant or defendant.[74]

(b) *Binding obligations*. The borrower will represent that the obligations assumed by it under the agreement and any security documents are legal, valid and binding. This provision must have limited value because, apart from other considerations, the lender would hardly place great reliance on the borrower's statement to this effect. However, it may be that the borrower would thereby be estopped from pleading that particular aspects of the documentation were not binding on it.

(c) *Corporate capacity and authority*. This representation will confirm that (i) the borrower has the corporate capacity under its memorandum of association (or equivalent document) to enable it to borrow the loan, (ii) the borrowing of the loan will not result in

---

[68] This may include the cost to the lender of funding the unpaid amount during the period of the default. However, some care is required in this field because the indemnity and its purpose in some respects overlap with the default interest clause discussed at para 20.27 above. The lender plainly cannot achieve a 'double recovery' in respect of the same loss.

[69] This may occur, for example, if the lender contracts the necessary interbank funding but an event of default occurs so that the conditions precedent to the advance are not met: see para 20.17 above.

[70] This point is impliedly acknowledged by the introductory language of clause 19 of the LMA document, which states that the representations are made '… on the date of this Agreement …' (ie rather than as a prelude to it). If any of the representations are later found to be untrue, the remedy is to be found in the agreement itself: see para 20.38(d) below.

[71] For the details of such representations, see LMA document, clause 19.

[72] Although, for whatever value it might have, the lender would have an action against the signatories of the agreement for breach of warranty of authority.

[73] In practice, the bank will verify this point—and the other representations as to 'legal' matters discussed below—by making its own enquiries and relying on appropriate legal opinions.

[74] See the Foreign Corporations Act 1991.

any breach of any borrowing limit imposed upon it,[75] and (iii) all internal steps (including the passing of any necessary board resolutions) required to sanction the execution of the documentation have been duly taken. The bank will wish to verify these statements so as to avoid any dispute about the binding nature of the facility documentation, and to avoid any need to rely upon the rules set out in sections 40–42 of the Companies Act 2006.[76] However, the representations may have some additional value in that the borrower may be estopped from denying their accuracy at a later stage.[77]

(d) *No conflict.* The borrower will confirm that the utilization of the facility does not conflict with any regulations applicable to it or any contract to which it is a party. For example, the borrower may also have other facilities in place and the lender would need to know that the new transaction does not breach borrowing restrictions or other undertakings which may be included in those documents. The immediate creation of defaults in favour of other lenders obviously serves no positive purpose.

(e) *All official consents obtained.* The borrower will confirm that it has obtained all governmental consents required to authorize the borrowing and repayment of the loan and the performance of all of the borrower's obligations under the facility documentation. In general terms, no consents are required for a corporate borrower to borrow money in the United Kingdom. Official consents may, however, be important in a variety of contexts. For example, (i) when dealing with an overseas borrower, it will be necessary to check whether any approvals are required in its country of incorporation and (ii) consents may be required in order to carry into effect the objectives of the facility, for example, to acquire a regulated entity[78] or to construct the building for which the loan is to be made.[79]

(f) *No default.* The borrower will confirm that no event of default is outstanding under the facility agreement and that it is not in default under any other loan agreements or other contracts to which it is a party.

(g) *Accuracy of financial statements and other information.* In making its credit assessment and fixing the terms upon which it is prepared to make the facility available, the bank will have relied upon information and materials provided by the borrower. The borrower will therefore have to confirm that (i) its latest audited financial statements provide a true and fair view of its financial position, (ii) there has been no material adverse change in its financial position since the date to which those statements were made up, and (iii) all other information provided to the bank was accurate and remains accurate as at the date of the loan agreement.

---

[75] A limit on overall corporate borrowings—frequently expressed as a multiple of paid up share capital and reserves—may sometimes be found in the company's articles of association. Contractual restrictions may be found in facility documents for other loans raised by the borrower.

[76] On these provisions, see n 25 above.

[77] It should be emphasized that this is very much a tentative view, given that it would be the invariable practice of a bank (or its advisers) to ensure that the necessary resolutions had been passed.

[78] In relation to an entity regulated by the FSA, see the 'change of control' rules discussed at para 1.23 above. In the case of loan transactions intended to fund a substantial takeover bid, approvals from competition authorities may be required. Examples of this kind could be multiplied.

[79] LMA document, clause 19 includes various other 'legal' representations, eg that the documentation is admissible in evidence and not subject to any stamp duty or filing requirements.

(h) *Pari passu.* The borrower will represent that its obligations rank *pari passu* with its obligations to other lenders.[80] This seems to mean simply that, in a winding up, the creditors would be paid equally and rateably. In the case of a loan to an English corporate borrower, this requirement would usually be met as a matter of law, and the subject calls for no further comment in that context.[81] The clause is, however, frequently found in loan agreements to sovereign borrowers, where no framework for liquidation exists. It is thus much more difficult to ascertain the precise meaning of that clause in this particular context. Some creditors have sought to argue that the clause obliges the sovereign borrower to pay *all* of its creditors equally and rateably at all times, although it is submitted that this line of argument is both impracticable and unsupportable.[82]

(i) *No litigation.* The borrower will confirm that no material litigation is pending or threatened against it which could have a material and adverse impact on its business or its ability to perform its obligations under the facility agreement. Again, any such litigation may be an important factor in determining whether the facility should be made available in the first place.

(j) *Repetition.* The agreement will provide for a number of representations to be repeated on each drawdown date and at the beginning of each interest period. The point is that, since these representations and warranties are seen to be the basis on which the facility is made available, the relevant statements should remain true and accurate throughout the life of the facility, and not merely as at the date of execution of the agreement.

Information Undertakings

The lender will obviously wish to monitor its credit risk throughout the life of the facility. In the event of a deterioration in the borrower's financial position, it will wish to be able to take prompt action, perhaps by declaring a default or by seeking to renegotiate the terms of the transaction. The monitoring process clearly depends on a free flow of information and, to that end, the facility agreement[83] will contain provisions to the following effect: **20.34**

(a) *Financial statements.* The borrower will be required to deliver to the lender copies of (i) its audited financial statements, usually within a period of 90–180 days after the end of the relevant financial year[84] and (ii) its semi-annual, unaudited financial statements, usually within 30–60 days of the end of the relevant period.[85]

---

[80] The agreement would frequently also contain a representation to similar effect. However, the point is dealt with here to avoid duplication.

[81] The clause perhaps has its origins in loans to borrowers in some countries where different types of debt may have differing levels of priority in the event of insolvency.

[82] A detailed assessment of the *pari passu* clause in the sovereign context is beyond the scope of this discussion. For further material, see Proctor, 'Sovereign Debt Litigation and the Courts—Some Recent Developments' (2003) 8 JIBFL 302, (2003) 9 JIBFL 351 and (2003) 10 JIBFL 379.

[83] See LMA document, clause 20.

[84] The facility agreement will usually require that the audited statements must be prepared by reference to generally accepted accounting principles which must be consistently applied: see LMA document, clause 20.3.

[85] Depending on the borrower's business and the nature of the credit, quarterly and even monthly financial information may also be required.

(b) *Compliance certificate.* If the facility agreement includes financial undertakings,[86] then the borrower will usually also be required periodically to deliver a certificate confirming that it is in compliance with those undertakings (or, as appropriate, stating the extent of any breach), and setting out the relevant calculations.

(c) *Other information.* The bank will wish to have parity of information with other stakeholders in the business, and the borrower will thus be obliged to provide to the bank copies of all documents circulated to its other creditors or shareholders from time to time. It will, in addition, be required to provide details of any material litigation as soon as it becomes aware of it, together with such other business or financial information as the lender may require.[87]

(d) *Notification of default.* If the borrower fails to make a payment when due under the facility agreement, then the lender will naturally be aware of that fact. However, other defaults may occur of which the lender is not immediately aware—for example, a cross-default under another agreement to which the borrower is a party.[88] Accordingly, the agreement will require the borrower to notify the lender of any default as soon as it becomes aware of it.

Financial Undertakings

20.35 When the lender originally agreed to make the facility available, it will have made an assessment of the borrower's financial position and—where applicable—of the particular asset or transaction which forms the subject matter of the particular facility. The assessment may have depended on a variety of factors, including (i) the level of the borrower's current indebtedness, (ii) its performance in terms of profit generation, (iii) the value of the asset to be acquired compared to the amount of the loan, and (iv) the revenues to be generated by the new asset. This assessment will have created expectations as to the borrower's future performance. But there would clearly be difficulty if these expectations are disappointed just a few months into a facility of (say) five years. For this reason, the facility agreement will often contain financial undertakings designed to monitor the borrower's overall performance and/or the value of the asset acquired with the facility proceeds. In other words, the undertakings will be designed to ensure that the financial and business profile of the borrower remains broadly similar throughout the life of the facility. These undertakings may include the following:

(a) a net worth undertaking, requiring the borrower to ensure that its net worth (or consolidated net worth) does not fall below a stipulated figure;

(b) an interest cover covenant, requiring the borrower to maintain a level of earnings which satisfactorily exceeds its interest obligations under the facility agreement;

(c) an undertaking limiting the borrower's capital expenditure in any given period; and

(d) a loan to value ratio, creating an event of default if the value of any relevant property exceeds a pre-set percentage of the facility.

---

[86] See para 20.35 below.
[87] See LMA document, clause 20.4.
[88] On cross-default provisions, see para 20.38(c) below.

Undertakings of this kind rely heavily on detailed definitions which must be in line with **20.36** the borrower's accounting policies and practices.[89]

General Undertakings

A broader set of undertakings will also be included, regulating the overall conduct of the **20.37** borrower's business. These will generally include the following:[90]

(a) *Authorizations and compliance.* The borrower will undertake to maintain any authorizations necessary to perform its obligations under the facility agreement, and to comply with all laws to which its business is subject.[91]

(b) *Negative pledge.* The borrower will undertake not to create any security over its assets. This clause will be of particular importance to a lender which has not itself taken security, for it would not wish a subsequent lender to obtain priority over it. The clause is perhaps of less importance where the lender is to take a full fixed and floating charge over the borrower's assets, although even then a restriction on the creation of security over the assets caught by the floating charge will remain important.[92] The negative pledge is thus a 'standard' provision both in the contexts of secured and unsecured financing.

(c) *Non-disposal.* The borrower will undertake not to dispose of any of its assets, except in the ordinary course of business and for proper consideration. The bank will have undertaken its credit assessment based upon a review of the assets of the company, and it would not wish to allow the borrower a free hand to dispose of its core assets. The bank would thus wish to approve any such proposals on a case-by-case basis.[93]

(d) *No merger.* The borrower will undertake not to enter into any amalgamation or merger. Clearly, the bank should have a veto over any such arrangement since it may significantly affect the borrower's asset and liability profile.

(e) *Conduct of business.* The borrower will frequently undertake not to change the essential nature of its business.[94]

---

[89] For specimen provisions, see the document entitled 'Financial Covenant Provisions', produced by the LMA for use in conjunction with its primary documents.

[90] See LMA document, clause 22. It was noted above—both in relation to the representations and the financial undertakings—that the objective of these provisions was to ensure that the borrower remains essentially the same entity throughout the life of the facility. The same general objective, and the preservation of the borrower's business, asset and credit profile, also forms the subject matter of the provisions which are about to be discussed.

[91] Failure to comply with the first part of this undertaking may render it difficult for the borrower to make payments under the agreement, whilst failure to comply with the second part of the provision may result in unanticipated liabilities which could burden the borrower's business.

[92] On floating charges generally, see paras 28.06–28.13 below.

[93] It should be appreciated that a borrower will seek to negotiate exceptions to this restriction, in order to preserve its own freedom of action so far as possible. The ultimate outcome depends upon the relative bargaining strength of the parties, but this does not undermine the general objective of the clause as described in the text. Similar considerations will apply to the negative pledge clause (above).

[94] As noted above, the non-disposal, negative pledge, non-merger and change of business clauses may be regarded as key features of the package of undertakings. The bank will have agreed to lend to an entity which owns the borrowers' assets free of any encumbrance, and which carries on the business then conducted by the borrower. It has assumed a credit risk and priced the transaction on that basis. These undertakings seek to ensure that, so far as possible, these assumptions will remain valid over the entire period of the facility.

Events of Default/Acceleration

20.38   As noted earlier, whilst a bank may commit itself to provide a long term facility, it plainly cannot do so on an unconditional basis. It must have the right to demand repayment if the borrower runs into difficulty. The question is, under what circumstances can such a demand be made? As with all such matters, the relevant provisions will be subject to heavy negotiation and some clauses may have to be tailored to the particular risks and circumstances of the transaction. But standard documentation will usually include the following:[95]

(a) *Non-payment.* The failure to pay monies owing under the loan agreement when due is an obvious sign of financial difficulty on the borrower's part. Consequently, this will always constitute an event of default, although a short grace period may be given to cater for administrative or other oversights.

(b) *Financial undertakings.* As noted above, the financial undertakings will have been included as a continuing measure of the health of the borrower's business. Consequently, a breach of these undertakings will usually constitute an immediate default.

(c) *Failure to perform other obligations.* As noted above, the agreement will contain a number of other undertakings designed to support the credit. Consequently, a breach of the non-disposal or negative pledge clauses is likely to constitute an immediate event of default. A breach of other clauses (eg late delivery of financial statements) is likely to be less critical, and a grace period will usually apply to enable the borrower to remedy the breach.[96]

(d) *Breach of representations.* Some of the representations and warranties discussed above are likely to be repeated periodically throughout the life of the loan.[97] If they become untrue with reference to the facts and circumstances subsisting at the time of repetition, then this will likewise constitute an event of default. Although invariably seen as a 'standard' provision, this clause is of limited value in practice; any matters which are seen as particularly critical from a credit perspective are likely to be dealt with by a specific default clause.

(e) *Cross-default.* If the borrower fails to pay any monies due to any of its other lenders, then this will also constitute an event of default. The rationale is that other lenders might then be able to take action to enforce their debts and thereby obtain an effective priority over the bank. The ability of the bank to treat such action as a default under its own document thus in some respects may be seen as an extension of the *pari passu* undertaking discussed above. Even if other creditors are not currently taking enforcement action, the existence of an event of default may enable the bank to

---

[95] See LMA document, clause 23. It should be borne in mind that it is one thing for the lender to *have* the right to terminate and accelerate the facility; it is quite another for the bank to *exercise* that right. In practice, the borrower will hardly ever have the funds available to repay the facility in full under the circumstances described below. The lender will therefore use the existence of a default as a means of negotiating an improved package—eg by increasing the margin, or obtaining further security.

[96] Whether or not a breach has been remedied and, if so, within the applicable timeframe, is plainly a factual matter and will thus not always be a suitable issue for proceedings for a summary judgment: see *Bank of New York Mellon v GV Films Ltd* [2009] EWHC 3315 (Comm).

[97] Usually on the dates on which an advance is requested and on the dates on which a payment of interest is due.

renegotiate the terms of the loan in order to reflect the increased risk resulting from the default.

(f) *Insolvency.* The commencement of proceedings relating to the insolvency of the borrower will invariably be an event of default, thus enabling the bank to accelerate the facility—and, hence, to enforce its security—at the earliest possible stage in the process. For these purposes, the contract will usually also treat the commencement of negotiations for a general debt rescheduling as an insolvency situation, even though no legal or formal steps have been taken with a view to any form of insolvency order. For these purposes, a 'restructuring' of indebtedness may include a group reorganization which has the effect of transferring assets away from the debtor companies;[98]

(g) *Execution proceedings.* If another creditor takes attachment or other proceedings by way of execution of a judgment, then this will be a clear sign of the borrower's difficulties. The consequences in terms of the facility agreement must thus be broadly equivalent to insolvency proceedings (above).

(h) *Expropriation.* Likewise, the expropriation of assets by the State will often mean that the borrower will thenceforth lack the resources to meet its obligations to the lender, and this type of action will thus also be stated to constitute an event of default.[99]

(i) *Material adverse change.* An event of default will occur if, in the opinion of the bank, there occurs a material adverse change in the borrower's financial position which may affect the borrower's ability to perform its payment obligations under the loan agreement.[100] Although banks insist on clauses of this kind, they prefer not to rely upon them, especially if alternative defaults are available. There is a degree of risk involved in reliance on such a clause, not least because the 'materiality' of a particular event inevitably involves a degree of subjective appreciation. The available case law is at present relatively limited.[101]

---

[98] See *Bank of New York Mellon v GV Films Ltd* [2009] EWHC 3315 (Comm) for an illustration of this type of situation. A scheme of this kind may also constitute a breach of the 'non-disposal of assets' undertaking discussed at para 20.37(c) above.

[99] It may be noted that an outright expropriation will not necessarily amount to a disposal by the borrower itself, and will hence not be caught by the non-disposal undertaking mentioned at para 20.37(c) above.

[100] Two general points may be made about this clause. First of all, borrowers used to argue against it because the document would already contain detailed defaults dealing with a wide range of situations. Why should the borrower agree to an additional clause which effectively gave the bank a power unilaterally to determine that the borrower's position had deteriorated, and to demand payment accordingly? However that may be, the clause has now become part of the standard architecture of agreements of this kind. Secondly, whilst borrowers now frequently accept that a clause of some kind is necessary, the detailed language may be the subject of debate. It is frequently a requirement that the bank acts reasonably and/or after consultation with the borrower.

[101] For a case in which the court held that a borrower had no reasonable prospect of establishing that a lender had acted improperly in issuing a default notice on the basis of a 'material adverse change' clause, see *BNP Paribas v Yukos Oil Company* [2005] EWHC 1321 (Ch). A clause of this kind was also discussed by the House of Lords in the *Concord* case (below), although the point arose in a slightly different context. Courts in the United States have placed the burden of proving the occurrence of a material adverse change firmly on the party alleging it, and the burden has not easily been discharged. For cases which arose in an equity (rather than a debt) situation, see *In re IBP Shareholders Litigation* 789 A 2d 14 (Delaware, 2001) and *Hexion Speciality Chemicals v Huntsman Corp*, WL 4457544 (Delaware, 2008). For a useful discussion of these clauses and their implications, see Julien and Lamontagne-DeFriez, 'Material Adverse Change and Syndicated Bank Financing' (2004) JIBLR 172 and (2004) JIBLR 193.

(j) *Acceleration.* If an event of default occurs, then the bank will have various options open to it. If the loan is not fully drawn, then it may terminate its obligation to advance the remaining commitment. It may also demand repayment of all monies owing, together with accrued interest. If the borrower is unable to pay, then the bank can enforce any security which it may hold or take any other proceedings which it may deem appropriate. It should, however, be appreciated that these steps will usually only be taken in extreme circumstances. In practice, the bank will use the existence of the default to manage its exposure in other ways (eg by seeking an increase in the interest rate, by requiring the borrower to execute additional security over its assets, or to undertake a programme of asset disposals with the proceeds being applied in reduction of the loan). A bank must in any event be aware of the potential consequences if it seeks to exercise an acceleration right and it later transpires that it was not, in fact, entitled to do so. In this context, it is necessary to distinguish between two situations. First of all, where the loan is fully drawn, the bank should incur no liability for serving an invalid acceleration notice. Whilst the notice itself is void, the delivery of it is simply ineffective, and no further legal consequences flow from it. There is no implied term in a contract to the effect that a bank will not serve a notice when it is not entitled to do so and, given that the relationship is contractual, there is no basis for imposing a duty of care in tort. Consequently, there is no legal 'peg' on which to hang the borrower's claim for damages in this type of situation.[102] On the other hand, if the (ultimately ineffective) notice purports to cancel the bank's obligation to make *future* advances under the agreement, then the bank will be in breach of its express obligation to fund those advances at the request of the borrower, and would be liable in damages accordingly.[103]

Payment Mechanics

20.39　The agreement will provide for the transfer of funds to a nominated account of the borrower (in the case of advances) and the bank (in the case of payments of interest, principal, and other amounts).

20.40　Provisions of this kind will avoid any suggestion that payments may be made (or required to be made) in cash.[104]

Set-off

20.41　The agreement will provide for the borrower to make all payments under the agreement free of any set-off, counterclaim, or other deduction.[105] In other words, the borrower must pay in full and cannot seek to withhold amounts due on the basis that it has some alleged cross-claim against the bank.

---

[102] It may be noted that these losses could be significant. For example, news of the acceleration may render it difficult for the borrower to obtain credit from other sources, or may increase its cost of funding.

[103] On the liability points just made, see *Concord Trust v Law Debenture Trust Corp* [2005] UKHL 27 (HL).

[104] The parties would hardly ever raise such a point but see the situation which arose in *Libyan Arab Foreign Bank v Bankers Trust Company* [1989] QB 728. The case is considered at paras 45.32–45.37 below.

[105] LMA document, para 29.6.

The effect of this clause is that a borrower cannot hold back payments on the basis of mis- **20.42**
representations said to have been made by the bank in the period leading up to the execution of the loan agreement. To the extent to which any such provision may be subject to
the terms of the Misrepresentation Act 1967 or the Unfair Contract Terms Act 1977, it
appears to be reasonable for the bank to expect payment to be made in full and the clause
should therefore survive any attack made in reliance on those sections.[106] Indeed, 'no set-
off' provisions of this kind will often be enforceable even where the borrower has purchased
securities issued by the lender which will admittedly give rise to a future claim.[107]

Assignments and Transfers

Facility agreements will contain various provisions designed to allow for the transfer of the **20.43**
lenders' commitment to the transaction. Since this particular subject is bound up with the
whole question of secondary debt trading, the topic is considered separately at a later
stage.[108]

Governing Law

At least where a loan agreement has cross-border elements, the document will specifically **20.44**
select English law as the law as the law applicable to the contract.[109]

In the absence of very unusual circumstances, this provision will be valid and binding on **20.45**
the parties. As a result, questions touching the essential validity, interpretation and performance of the contract will fall to be determined in accordance with English law
principles.[110]

Jurisdiction

The jurisdiction clause contained within the LMA document[111] provides that, in the first **20.46**
instance, the English courts are the most appropriate forum for the resolution of any dispute, but that the lender may nevertheless take proceedings before the courts of any other
country which has jurisdiction.

The underlying intent of these provisions may be summarized as follows: **20.47**

(a) if the borrower wishes to take proceedings against the bank for breach of its obligations under the contract, then it must do so in England. This is not an unreasonable
position, given that (i) the contract is governed by English law (ii) the bank will
be performing its obligations through a branch located within the jurisdiction, and

---

[106] This follows from the decision in *Skipskredittforeningen v Emperor Navigation* [1998] 1 Lloyds Rep 66.
See also *Continental Illinois National Bank and Trust Co of Chicago v Papanicolaou* [1986] 2 Lloyds Rep 441.
Compare the situation which arose in *WRM Group Ltd v Wood* [1998] CLC 189 (CA). The position may be
different where the borrower is a consumer, but the present chapter is concerned with commercial loans.
[107] For a recent illustration of this point, see *Re Kaupthing Singer & Friedlander Ltd (in administration)*
[2009] EWHC 740 (Ch).
[108] See paras 22.05–22.16 below.
[109] See LMA document, clause 38.
[110] ie in accordance with the rules of private international law considered in Chapter 40 below.
[111] See LMA document, clause 38.2.

(iii) the branch will have assets within this jurisdiction to meet any judgment awarded against it;

(b) as against the borrower, the starting point is that proceedings will also take place in England. However, the lender must reserve the right to proceed against the borrower in any jurisdiction in which it has assets, and in which a judgment is therefore most likely to be of effective value;[112]

(c) this eminently sensible commercial position is, unfortunately, to some extent undermined by a decision of the European Court of Justice[113] which held that the court explicitly selected by the parties must stay proceedings if one of the parties has already taken the matter before a court in another country. The selected court may then only proceed with the matter if the latter court determines that it has no jurisdiction. This decision, which has been reluctantly applied in England,[114] places a premium on litigation tactics over the substance or merits of the case.

Conclusions

20.48   The present chapter has considered, in general terms, the contents of a typical facility agreement. The detailed terms—including in particular any financial undertakings—will very much depend on the nature of the transaction and the relative bargaining strength of the parties. But the development of 'market standard' agreements has clearly been a significant benefit to all parties, reducing the time and resultant cost involved in negotiating transactions of this kind.

---

[112] In some cases, the bank may wish first to obtain judgment in England, and then seek to register and enforce that judgment in other relevant jurisdictions. This is a large subject which lies beyond the scope of the present work. For a full discussion, see Dicey, Morris and Collins, chs 10–16.

[113] Case C-116/02, *Erich Gasser GmbH v MISAT Srl* [2003] ECR I-14693. The decision flows from Arts 23 and 27 of Council Regulation (EC) No 44/2001 on jurisdiction and the recognition and enforcement of judgments in civil and commercial matters.

[114] See, in particular, *JP Morgan Europe Ltd v PrimaCom* [2005] EWHC 508.

21

SYNDICATED LOANS

Introduction

The previous chapter dealt with loan facilities made available by a single lender.[1] Many **21.01** transactions may, however, be of such a size that, in the interests of prudence, a single bank would not wish to make available on its own.[2] In such cases the bank may have to syndicate the loan by inviting a number of institutions to participate in the transaction as well.[3]

---

[1] As in the last chapter, for convenience of illustration, reference will be made to the provisions of the Multicurrency Term Facility Agreement (the 'LMA document') published on the website of the Loan Market Association.

[2] Indeed, in some cases, the bank may not be permitted to undertake the entire transaction. See the discussion on large exposures and concentration risk at paras 6.62–6.67 above. There may, however, be other considerations which may lead to the syndication of a loan transaction. For example, the borrower may have relationships with a number of other institutions, and may thus wish to ensure that they each have a share of the new business; or it may wish to establish a wider range of banking relationships. Completion of a large, syndicated transaction may also enhance the borrower's standing in the financial markets generally, thus enhancing its access to those markets on future occasions.

[3] In some cases, it may be equally possible for the borrower to raise a series of bilateral facilities, rather than a syndicated loan. However, the syndicated structure may be much more convenient, especially where all of the lenders are to share in a common security package: see the security trust structure discussed at paras 21.43–21.50 below.

21.02 For the most part, this will not really affect the terms of the facility agreement so far as the borrower is concerned. Subject to the comments made later in this chapter, the terms governing the utilization of the loan, the package of undertakings, and the events of default will remain essentially the same, even though a number of banks may be involved. The various standard provisions discussed in the last chapter will therefore apply equally in the context of a syndicated transaction. This is, of course, only logical. As explained in that chapter, the purpose of these provisions is to ensure that the borrower and the credit risk remain the same—so far as practicable—throughout the life of the facility. Concerns of this kind remain the same even though the facility has been syndicated.

21.03 Nevertheless, the presence of a number of lenders does serve considerably to complicate—and, hence, to lengthen—the documentation. In some respects, this follows from the fact that a number of institutions acquire rights and assume obligations to the borrower under the terms of a single document. For the most part, however, the additional provisions to be found in a syndicated loan agreement are designed to govern the relationship between the banks themselves, and to deal with consequential administrative matters.[4]

21.04 An additional layer of legal complexity is also introduced by the role of the various parties.[5] Whilst most banks will participate in the facility as lenders, one bank will have organized the facility in its capacity as arranger by inviting the participation of other institutions as lenders. Another bank (or possibly the same one) will assume the role of agent and will be responsible for the administration of the facility after the documentation has been signed. These additional relationships and functions clearly have legal consequences for the various parties involved.

21.05 With these considerations in mind, the present chapter is arranged as follows:

(a) the role and liability of the arranger will be considered;
(b) the role of the agent will be considered;
(c) the legal nature of the relationships between the individual banks and the borrower will be discussed;[6]
(d) the relationships between the banks themselves will be discussed; and
(e) the particular structure adopted for any security arrangements will be described.

The Arranger

Duration and Nature of the Role

21.06 The commencement and duration of the arranger's role[7] are, of course, closely linked to the functions which it is required to undertake (see below). However, as the title implies, the

---

[4] eg such as the making and distribution of payments.

[5] It must therefore be appreciated that a syndicated loan creates a web of separate contractual relationships among the various parties.

[6] For a very useful and detailed work dedicated to this topic, see Mugasha, *The Law of Multi-Bank Financing* (Oxford University Press, 2008), hereafter 'Mugasha'.

[7] The duration of the arranger's role is, perhaps, of relatively limited legal significance. However, the point is made so that the roles of the agent and the arranger can be contrasted in this respect.

essential task of the arranger is to bring matters to a position where a number of institutions have given a formal commitment to participate in the facility, that is to say, they have executed a formal loan agreement which legally obliges them to provide the facility, subject to the terms and conditions set out in that document. The arranger's role may thus be said to commence once it receives a mandate from the borrower, authorizing it to act as arranger and to take the various steps which are necessary to that end.[8]

The arranger's *functions* may be said to come to an end when the agreement is executed by all parties, in that it will have completed the task for which it was mandated. However, it may remain subject to liabilities arising out of that role. As a result, it will be a party to the facility agreement so that it may seek to take advantage of the various exculpatory clauses included for its benefit.[9] It will also be noted that the *contractual* obligations of the arranger are derived from the terms of the mandate and are thus owed exclusively to the borrower.[10] Whilst the arranger will be a party to the facility agreement for the reasons already noted, the standard LMA document imposes no obligations on it in favour of either the borrower or the other lenders. **21.07**

Functions of the Arranger

As noted above, the essential role of the arranger is to invite other institutions to participate in the proposed facility. **21.08**

This may involve a variety of functions. The process will usually start with the negotiation of a set of outline terms which the arranger believes will be acceptable to the market and will thus attract a level of commitments from participants.[11] **21.09**

The borrower and the arranger will then produce an information memorandum or similar package, which will be distributed to potential lenders and assist them in determining whether or not they wish to participate in the facility and (if so) what level of financial commitment they are prepared to provide. The information memorandum will thus contain details of the borrower, its business and financial position, the amount of the proposed loan, the detailed financial terms, and the purpose for which it is to be provided. The information memorandum will frequently go further than this, providing an analysis of any particular risks and any steps which have been taken in an effort to mitigate them. **21.10**

---

[8] The arranger will, of course, receive a fee for its efforts. In most cases, the mandate will include a description of the essential terms of the proposed facility and authorize the arranger to syndicate the transaction on a 'best efforts' basis. This means that the arranger will take appropriate steps to market transactions to institutions which may have an interest in that type of business, but will not incur any liability to the borrower if it proves impossible to raise the required funds. In some cases, the arranger may also underwrite the facility, in the sense that it undertakes to provide the funding itself if it cannot find participants to the required level. Needless to say, the detailed terms and conditions of such a mandate are considerably more complex and the underwriting arrangements will have a significant cost so far as the borrower is concerned.

[9] See paras 22.21–22.25 below.

[10] The extent to which the arranger may incur liability *in tort* to the participants is considered below.

[11] It may be that this aspect of the process involves an element of an advisory role. However, since the advice will relate to market conditions and sentiment—all of which may change at short notice—it is perhaps unlikely that the arranger could incur any liability to the borrower in respect of such advice.

Liability of the Arranger

21.11   As has been shown, the arranger in some respects acts as a 'salesman' for the facility, seeking loan participations from other institutions in the market. To what extent may the arranger incur liability if it transpires that the information memorandum was incomplete or mis-leading, or if it has fallen short of accepted market standards[12] in the preparation of that document? Apart from the preparation of the information memorandum and any associ-ated materials, are there any other circumstances under which the arranger may incur lia-bility to the syndicate? Of course, questions of this kind will only become 'live' if it becomes apparent that the borrower itself will be unable to repay the facility.[13] But, should the worst happen, will the arranger be liable to meet losses suffered by facility participants who relied on the information memorandum in making a commitment to the loan?

21.12   Before considering the possible heads of liability, it is perhaps appropriate to deal with one threshold matter. Whether one speaks in terms of an action in contract or in tort, it will be necessary for the participant to show that he relied on the misleading information in mak-ing his decision to join the loan. In other words, there must be a sufficient nexus between the alleged breach and the loss. This will, of course, be a matter of evidence but in practice this will be a significant obstacle to any claim against the arranger, however the claim may be pleaded. The recipient of the information memorandum will itself be a sophisticated financial institution, with the resources and market knowledge to make its own assessment of the borrower and the underlying transaction. In any event, and regardless of the underly-ing factual matrix, it will be unattractive for the applicant bank to start proceedings on the footing that it did not make its own independent analysis of the deal. It will thus in practice be difficult for it to plead unequivocal reliance on the memorandum as the reason for its commitment to the deal.

21.13   Leaving aside this practical caveat, it has been suggested[14] that there are three possible bases of arranger liability under these circumstances, namely, (i) misrepresentation, (ii) negli-gence, and (iii) breach of fiduciary duty. The following observations may be made in this regard:

(a) *Misrepresentation.* As noted above, the information memorandum is circulated by the arranger on behalf of the borrower. Consequently, the arranger will not normally be liable for misrepresentations contained in the information memorandum, since an

---

[12] Any institution acting as an arranger will, of course, seek to ensure the accuracy and completeness of information which it circulates to the market. It needs to preserve its reputation for future transactions, and the dissemination of misleading information may have regulatory consequences: see for example, FSA Handbook, MAR.

[13] If the borrower is able to meet its obligations, then the lenders would not generally suffer any loss. In some cases, it might just be arguable that, had the correct information been given, the lenders would only have committed to the transaction at a higher interest margin, and the excess figure would then be recoverable from the arranger. Such a case would, however, be highly fact-sensitive and the case would, in practice, be very difficult to run. It may be added that, whilst the information memorandum is actually prepared and circulated by the arranger, the document remains the responsibility of the borrower—a fact emphasized by the provision found in the facility agreement and allowing for acceleration of the loan if the memorandum is found to have been materially misleading: see para 20.33(g) above.

[14] See Mugasha, paras 3.64 et seq.

agent is not responsible for statements made by his principal, or made by the agent on behalf of the principal and within the scope of his authority. To the extent to which the arranger may itself be said to have made any misrepresentation *as principal*, it must be remembered that the statement induces the lender to enter into a contract with the borrower, and not with the arranger itself.[15] Under these circumstances, it seems that the arranger would only be liable for misrepresentation if (i) to the knowledge of the arranger, the relevant statement was made fraudulently or (ii) the relevant statement creates a collateral contract between the lender and the arranger.[16] Fraud is unlikely to be an issue in this type of case, since individuals within an institution are unlikely to go so far in order to sell down a facility, and the mere act of circulating an information memorandum should not suffice to create a collateral contract between the arranger and the recipient. The Court of Appeal has recently held that the distribution of the memorandum does not imply a warranty on the part of the arranger to the effect that it had no knowledge of any facts which would or might render parts of the information contained in it untrue.[17] Liability under this heading is therefore unlikely to arise in practice.[18]

(b) *Negligence*. The question of liability in negligence can only arise if the arranger owes a duty of care to recipients of the information memorandum who choose to take a participation in the facility. For that purpose, there must be some assumption of responsibility by the arranger in the knowledge that the recipient will rely on the information provided to it in making its credit decision.[19] There are two reasons why such liability will not generally arise in this type of case. First of all, the recipient bank will be a financial institution capable of making its own analysis of the borrower and its status. Secondly, the information memorandum will specifically disclaim any liability on the part of the arranger and, in the context of arrangements between financial institutions, such disclaimers would appear to be valid.[20] In *IFE Fund SA v Goldman Sachs International*,[21] the Court of Appeal held that such a disclaimer made it clear that the arranger did not assume a liability or duty of care in favour of the recipient, and that the court should not strain to identify a duty of care in a transaction between sophisticated parties where the documentation specifically sought to exclude such a

---

[15] The arranger will generally be a party to the facility document, but any statement will have been designed to induce the lender to contract with the borrower itself.

[16] ie the lender enters into the contract with the borrower in consideration of the information and assurances provided by the arranger. On misrepresentations by third parties, see Chitty, para 6-021.

[17] *IFE Fund SA v Goldman Sachs International* [2006] EWHC (Comm) 2282 (CA). The decision does however suggest that the arranger makes an implied representation of 'good faith', in the sense that it is not knowingly in possession of details which show that the information memorandum is inaccurate. The point did not directly arise for decision in that case.

[18] In some jurisdictions, statutory rules dealing with improper trade practices may have an impact on the arranger's liability: see Mugasha, para 3-113, discussing the decision of the Supreme Court of Victoria in *Natwest Australia Bank Ltd v Tricontinental Corp Ltd* (26 July 1993).

[19] *Hedley Byrne & Co Ltd v Heller & Partners Ltd* [1964] AC 465 (HL); *Caparo Industries plc v Dickman* [1990] 2 AC 605.

[20] *Hedley Byrne*, above.

[21] [2006] EWHC (Comm) 2287 (CA).

relationship. Once again, therefore, it seems that the arranger should not normally be liable to loan participants under this heading.

(c) *Breach of Fiduciary Duty.* In circulating an information memorandum, the arranger is effectively trying to induce other participants in the market to subscribe for a share of the proposed facility. Especially bearing in mind that the arranger is—to the knowledge of the recipient—mandated by the prospective borrower, there should be no scope for implying a fiduciary duty or similar obligation of good faith owed by the arranger to the prospective participant.[22] It is true that, in some cases, courts have expressed the view that a fiduciary relationship may exist between the arranger and the syndicate member[23] but, as others have pointed out,[24] the court seems to have applied general principles of law without examining in depth the nature of the particular market.[25] Once again, it is therefore submitted that the court should not find or imply any fiduciary duty owed by the arranger to the recipient of the memorandum.[26]

21.14 In the ordinary course, therefore, the arranger should not incur any liability to a loan participant merely because the information memorandum contains information which is later found to be untrue and on which the recipient places reliance.[27] As noted earlier, the arranger will usually be a party to the syndicated facility agreement and this will include a number of exculpatory provisions with respect both to the information memorandum and any other material generated in connection with the facility.[28] Since the arranger's role will have been completed as at the time of signature of the loan agreement, it is by no means clear that it provides any consideration for the benefit of these protective clauses.[29] However, the point will not normally be of great practical importance because the information memorandum will itself have contained similar provisions, which will have been known to the participants when they decided to commit to the transaction.

---

[22] How can one act on behalf of one party, and yet owe a fiduciary duty to the other? Such a view would expose the arranger to undue conflicts of interest.

[23] *UBAF Ltd v European American Banking Corp* [1984] QB 713 (CA).

[24] Mugasha, para 3-124.

[25] The syndicated facility agreement will usually state explicitly that the arranger owes no fiduciary duties: see LMA document, clause 24.6(b).

[26] For an article written from an Australian perspective and which broadly shares this view, see Skene, 'Syndicated Loans: Arranger and Participant Bank Fiduciary Theory' [2005] JIBLR 269. It may be added that the circulation of the information memorandum is effected on behalf of the borrower. It is thus impossible to infer any form of advisory relationship between the arranger and the recipient. This view seems to be right as a matter of principle but it is reinforced by a recent decision which suggests that advisory obligations will not readily be implied in this type of situation: see *JP Morgan Chase v Springwell Navigation Corporation* [2008] EWHC (Comm) 1186. The case is considered in more detail in Chapter 25 below.

[27] Of course, if the arranger knew that the information was untrue when the memorandum was circulated, then it may be that the arranger has acted fraudulently, and different considerations will then apply. As noted earlier, however, such cases will be rare in practice. For a financial markets case in which fraud was established, see *Smith New Court Securities Ltd v Scrimgeour Vickers Ltd* [1997] AC 254 (HL). This case helpfully deals with the measure of damages in this type of situation, but did not involve either a syndicated loan or the circulation of an information memorandum.

[28] Clause 26.14 of the LMA document includes confirmation by the lenders that they have made their own assessment of the borrower and of the facility, and of the accuracy and adequacy of the materials contained in the information memorandum.

[29] In some respects, the court in *Sumitomo Bank, Ltd v Banque Bruxelles Lambert SA* [1997] 1 Lloyds Rep 487 proceeded on the footing that the contractual protections available to an arranger did not cover conduct prior to the execution of the facility agreement. The decision is considered below.

Yet not every case will be 'ordinary course'. Litigation in this type of area is highly fact-**21.15** sensitive, and there may be instances where the arranger will be held responsible for information provided to the syndicate in the pre-contractual period. An example is offered by the decision in *Sumitomo Bank, Ltd v Banque Bruxelles Lambert SA*,[30] where a group of banks were invited to participate in a property facility. Since the loan to value ratio exceeded that which banks would normally accept, the excess amount was to be covered by a mortgage indemnity guarantee policy. The arranger indicated to the participants that it would be responsible for organizing the policy but, when a claim ultimately fell to be made, the insurer denied liability on the basis that the required full disclosure had not been made at the outset. The arranger was held to be liable for the syndicate's losses, on the basis that (i) it had assured the participants that the policy would be put in place, (ii) this necessarily implied that the arranger would take steps to ensure the validity of the policy, (iii) in practical terms, the arranger was the only party who could ensure that full disclosure was made, and (iv) it realized that the syndicate would be relying on it to ensure that the policy was put in place. This situation can readily be distinguished from the 'ordinary course' situations discussed above, on the following bases:

(a) the information provided by the arranger related to steps which it was itself to take in ensuring that the facility was correctly secured, and these assurances were not related to or dependent upon information provided by the borrower;
(b) it was reasonable for the participants to rely on the expectation that the arranger would act competently in putting the policy arrangements in place; and
(c) in the circumstances, the standard contractual protections did not apply to cover pre-contractual negligence.

The Agent

Duration and Nature of the Role

It has been noted above that the arranger's role comes to an end when the facility agreement **21.16** has been signed. In contrast, the role of the agent is to administer the agreed facility. Consequently, its role is derived from the facility agreement itself, and thus only comes into formal effect once that agreement has been executed by the parties.

The role of the agent thus runs in parallel with the loan agreement itself. It will continue to **21.17** be obliged to perform those functions until the loan has been repaid in full.[31]

Since the role of the agent is derived from the facility agreement, it follows that it owes **21.18** obligations of a *contractual* nature both to the borrower and to the banks themselves.[32]

---

[30] [1997] 1 Lloyds Rep 487. On this case, see Sequeira, 'Syndicated Loans—Let the Arranger Beware!' [1997] 3 JIBFL 117.
[31] It should be noted that a particular agent has the right to resign, but there must be an institution which acts as agent throughout the life of the loan: see LMA document, clause 26.11(e).
[32] As noted above, the parties to the facility agreement will include the borrower, the lending banks, the arranger, and the agent. However, the agent does not usually assume any material obligations in favour of the arranger (they are not infrequently the same institution in any event).

Functions of the Agent

21.19 The core function of the agent is to act as a 'conduit' between the borrower and the banks, both for payments and for the provision of information.[33] This is partly a matter of administrative convenience, but it also helps to ensure that the banks have an equality of information on developments affecting the facility or the financial position of the borrower. Moving to a greater level of detail:

(a) the agent receives funding requests from the borrower and, if the conditions of the agreement have been met, will request the necessary funds from each of the banks;[34]

(b) the lenders will remit those funds to an account of the agent on the drawdown date, and the agent will in turn transfer those monies to the account nominated by the borrower;[35]

(c) when the borrower makes a repayment, it is required to do so through an account of the agent. It is then the responsibility of the agent to distribute that sum proportionately among all of the participating banks;[36]

(d) the agent receives financial and other materials from the borrower, and is required to distribute them to the individual syndicate members;

(e) generally, the agent is required to exercise—or refrain from exercising—its other functions on the instructions of a majority of the lenders.[37] The agent will even be entitled to amend the terms of the loan and security documentation on the basis of a majority vote, although certain items (eg the interest rate, the repayment date and other core commercial terms) will be 'entrenched', and unanimous lender consent will be required in relation to those provisions.[38]

---

[33] Notwithstanding the 'conduit' nature of the role, it should be appreciated that the agent is appointed to act as agent for the lenders—it is not an agent for the borrower. The significance of this point is explained in n 35 below.

[34] LMA document, clause 5. On the extent of the obligations of individual banks to contribute to advances, see para 21.27.below.

[35] It should be noted that, so far as the borrower is concerned, the process of payment to it is only complete when the funds actually reach the borrower's nominated account. Consequently, if the agent receives funds from the lenders but fails to pass them on to the borrower (eg because the agent goes into administration on that day) then payment *to the borrower* has not been made, and it could require the lenders to advance the funds to it again. Payment *to the agent* does not discharge the lenders' obligations, because it acts as agent for the lenders (and not for the borrower). As a result, payment to the agent does not equate to payment to the borrower. Of course, if the funds reach the borrower's bank then the lenders' obligations are discharged. From that point, the borrower takes the risk that the funds are lost through the failure or default of its own bank.

[36] On payment mechanics generally, see LMA document, clause 29. Since the agent has been appointed as agent of the banks to receive this payment, it follows that the borrower's payment obligation is discharged once the funds reach the agent's account. Consequently, if the agent fails to account to the lenders, the borrower cannot be made to pay a second time. It should be noted that the obligation of the agent is to distribute funds received pro rata to the participations of the individual banks. This is designed to ensure that the risks and rewards of the facility are shared according to the percentage interests of the banks. This has occasionally been referred to as the 'equal misery' provision and it is further reflected in the 'pro rata sharing clause', which is considered later in this section in the context of the relationship between the individual lending banks (see paras 21.28–21.39 below).

[37] This will frequently be a group of lenders who account for 66.66 per cent of the loan.

[38] On these points, see LMA document, clause 35.

It will therefore be apparent that the respective roles and functions of the arranger and the **21.20** agent are quite different. The arranger's task is to *sell* the loan asset; the agent's task is to *administer* that asset on behalf of the lenders. To carry the distinction further, the arranger's functions are *pre-contractual*, whilst the agency role only comes into being *after the contract has been signed*. The two functions are thus also distinct in terms of time. It is thus unsurprising that the circumstances under which an agent may incur liability to the syndicate members differs significantly from those discussed earlier in relation to the arranger.

Liability of the Agent—Gross Negligence and Wilful Misconduct

As noted above, the agent will owe duties of a *contractual* nature both to the borrower **21.21** and to the lenders. Those contractual obligations will involve the due performance of the functions assigned to it under the terms of the loan agreement itself. Nevertheless, the existence of contractual obligations does not necessarily exclude the existence of a concurrent liability in tort.[39]

In practice, the terms of the facility agreement will limit the liability of the agent (both in **21.22** contract and in tort) to cases in which any losses incurred by the lenders have been directly caused by the agent's '... gross negligence or wilful misconduct ...'.[40] Provisions of this kind have become 'market standard', and there is no reason to doubt the essential validity of this particular exclusion clause.[41] By the same token, since the facility agent is acting at the request and on behalf of the lenders, the documentation will entitle it to an indemnity against any losses which it may suffer, again provided that these losses do not flow from the agent's own gross negligence or wilful misconduct.[42] It follows that, both in terms of exculpation and its right to indemnity, the meaning of the expressions 'gross negligence' and 'wilful misconduct' will be critical and those terms therefore merit a brief review.[43]

The expression 'gross negligence' has been described cleverly—but not especially helpfully— **21.23** as the same thing as ordinary negligence but '... with a vituperative epithet ...',[44] and it has been doubted whether there is any material difference between 'negligence' and 'gross negligence'.[45] Yet the House of Lords has said that the meaning of a contract must be ascertained objectively, by determining '... the meaning which the document would convey to a reasonable person having all the background knowledge which would reasonably have been available to the parties in the situation in which they were at the time of the

---

[39] On this point, see *Henderson v Merrett Syndicates* [1994] 3 All ER 506 (HL).
[40] See LMA document, clause 26.9(a).
[41] This impression is reinforced by the Court of Appeal decision in *IFE Fund SA v Goldman Sachs International* (see n 17 above) upholding the validity of similar exculpatory provisions in the information memorandum. It may be added that the fees paid for the performance of the agency function are in practice relatively modest, and this may reinforce the impression that it is not intended to undertake wide-ranging and substantive liability to the syndicate members. However, it is, of course, one thing to say that the clause is valid, but it is quite another to determine its scope, meaning and effect. These issues are considered below.
[42] See LMA document, clause 26.10.
[43] On the same subject, see Mugasha, paras 9.58–9.61.
[44] See *Wilson v Brett* (1843) 11 M&W 113.
[45] *Pentecost v London District Auditor* [1951] 2 KB 759; *Armitage v Nurse* [1998] Ch 241 (CA).

contract …'.[46] Applying that test, it is surely inappropriate simply to disregard the word
'gross'; it is plain that, by using it, the parties intended to refer to something more than
ordinary negligence. It may be that the difference between 'negligence' and 'gross negligence' will often be difficult to discern in practical situations, but that does not absolve the
court from its obligation to give effect to the terminology which the parties have chosen to
use. The law is, in any event, accustomed to fine distinctions and questions of degree.

21.24 Happily, more recent case law acknowledges this position. A US court has specifically confirmed that 'negligence' and 'gross negligence' involve different degrees of culpability—a
point which, apart from the English case law, would be linguistically obvious. In the case
concerned,[47] an agent's bank failure to consult counsel on the need to register a security
interest was careless but, under the particular circumstances,[48] did not amount to 'gross
negligence'. The English courts have picked up this baton, again holding that gross negligence 'exceeds' negligence, and involves either conduct undertaken in the knowledge of the
likely risks, or serious disregard of (or indifference to) an obvious risk.[49]

21.25 On the other hand, 'wilful misconduct' connotes a deliberate (rather than merely careless)
step, taken in the knowledge that the step is wrongful.[50] The use of the word 'wilful' includes
the notion that the step is known to be wrongful at the time it is taken, rather than with the
benefit of hindsight.[51]

Other Sources of Liability and Protections

21.26 Leaving aside the specific provisions dealing with gross negligence and wilful misconduct,
it is appropriate to highlight a few miscellaneous points relating to the liability and protection of the agent:

> (a) an agent who takes action on the instructions of the majority lenders[52] will generally
> be protected from any liability for any loss suffered by a lending bank as a consequence
> of that action.[53] This will remain the case even though the bank concerned may have

---

[46] See *Investors Compensation Scheme Ltd v West Bromwich Building Society* [1998] 1 WLR 896, at p 912.
The proper construction of contract terms is, of course, a very large one. For an authoritative discussion,
see Chitty, para 12-041 et seq.

[47] *Chemical Bank v Security Pacific National Bank* 20 F 3d 375 (9th Cir, 1994).

[48] A security interest had already been registered in favour of the agent in a separate facility, and it had not
been appreciated that a further registration was required for the subsequent, syndicated transaction.

[49] See *Red Sea Tankers v Papachristidis* [1997] 1 Lloyds Rep 547. For an English case in which the Court
of Appeal had to consider the German law concept of gross negligence, see *Tradigrain SA v Intertek Testing
Services Canada Ltd* [2007] All ER (D) 376 (CA). See also *Great Scottish & Western Rail Co v British Railways
Board*, (10 February 2000, CA), noted by Mugasha, para 9.59.

[50] *Lewis v Great Western Railway* Co (1887) 3 QBD 195 (CA).

[51] *Chemical Bank v Security Pacific National Bank* 20 F 3d 375 (9th Cir, 1994).

[52] As noted earlier, 'Majority Lenders' is normally stated to be lenders holding 66.66 per cent of the
participations, although this is a matter for agreement.

[53] See LMA document, clause 26.7. It is implicit in these provisions that the agent will obtain its mandate
from the syndicate by making a full disclosure of the issues at stake and the reasons or need for the proposed
action. The agent obviously could not rely on an authority obtained on the back of an incomplete disclosure
to its principals.

voted against that action because—obviously—the agent has to be able to obtain binding instructions from some quarter, and the majority lenders are the obvious source;[54]

(b) an agent is generally obliged to avoid placing itself in a position in which its own interests conflict with those of its principal.[55] In order to counteract any suggestion that the agent is prohibited from other dealings with the borrower or has to account for any resultant profit, the LMA document—recognizing market realities—specifically states that the agent may conduct other business with the borrower.[56]

(c) it has been suggested that an agent bank which takes security for its own separate facility—thus diluting the assets available to the unsecured syndicate—is liable to the syndicate members for resultant losses because the taking of such security constitutes a breach of the agent's fiduciary duty.[57] Now, it may be that the use of the language of 'agency' tends to confuse matters but, in any event, agency relationships are not homogeneous; the precise nature and extent of the respective rights and obligations of the parties depend both on the terms of the contract itself and the practices of the market concerned. In essence, the agent is appointed solely to perform the tasks imposed upon it by the facility agreement itself. It is suggested that the court should take great care in imposing wider duties of good faith falling outside the scope of the agreement—especially in a case of this kind where it is invariably accepted that the agent may have other business relationships with the borrower;[58]

(d) a similar, excessively broad brush approach taints the decision of the US court in *Chemical Bank v Security Pacific National Bank*,[59] where the court simply held that acceptance of an appointment as agent necessarily involved an assumption of fiduciary duties to the principal. This may well be so, although it places terminology ahead of substance and fails to recognize that different markets will have different expectations. The court held that an agent bank which mistakenly failed to register a security interest thereby incurred liability to the syndicate for breach of its fiduciary duty, on the basis that it had acted negligently and in breach of its contract. It is submitted that this confuses a number of different heads of liability which might have benefited from individual treatment. Nevertheless, the point did not ultimately matter because the court

---

[54] Certain 'core' actions affecting the amounts owing under the agreement, the maturity dates, and the interest margin are reserved matters which would require the consent of all of the lenders: see LMA document, clause 35.

[55] Although, on the application of general agency principles in this particular context, see para 21.22 above.

[56] LMA document, clause 24.

[57] *NZI Securities Ltd v Unity Group Ltd*, (High Court of New Zealand, 11 February 1992), discussed by Mugasha, para 3–125.

[58] It may well be that the problem which arose in the *NZI Securities* case (see previous footnote) could satisfactorily be viewed from another angle. As has been shown (see para 20.37(b).above), facility agreements will generally include a negative pledge clause which will prohibit the creation of security in favour of third parties. If the agreement in *NZI Securities* contained no such provision, or the security given to the agent in its separate capacity fell within the allowable exceptions, then it is hard to see why there should be any objection to the arrangement. If, on the other hand, the security offended the negative pledge clause (and the agent would obviously have been aware of that fact), then it could have been made liable in tort for inducing or conspiring with the borrower to breach the terms of the syndicated agreement. It would not have been necessary to have recourse to any supposed fiduciary duty for that purpose.

[59] 20 F 3d 375 (9th Cir, 1994).

found that the agent, whilst in breach of some duty, had not been guilty of 'gross negligence' and was thus protected by the provisions which have been discussed above;[60]

(e) another US decision holds (rightly, it is submitted) that the existence or absence of a fiduciary relationship is to be determined by reference to the terms of the contract, and that no such relationship should be inferred in a commercial transaction between parties of similar bargaining power and experience where no such relationship is expressly created;[61]

(f) in summary, it is submitted that the extent of the agent's liability should be determined by reference to its functions and any relevant protections under the facility agreement itself. It is not generally appropriate for the court to look for broader fiduciary duties in cases of this kind.

Relationship between Individual Banks and the Borrower

21.27 As in the case of a single bank loan, the essence of the relationship between a syndicate bank and the company remains that of lender and borrower. How does the grouping of the banks as a syndicate affect this relationship? The key points of difference are as follows:

(a) Crucially, each bank is only liable for the advance of funds to the borrower up to its own agreed participation limit.[62] A bank is not responsible for the failure of another institution to perform its obligations.[63] Although the situation rarely arises in practice, it should be appreciated that the borrower is taking a performance risk on a group of banks.[64] The point could be important where the loan is to be used to fund an acquisition, for failure by a single, relatively minor participant could leave the borrower unable to complete the commercial transaction, even though all of the other lenders have complied with their funding obligations.

(b) Each bank is able independently[65] to take steps to enforce payment of the monies *which have already fallen due* to it. This point will usually be made apparent by the terms of the facility agreement itself, which will specifically state that the rights of the lenders are several and, hence, an individual lender can take proceedings against the borrower in respect of sums due to it without being required to join in the facility agent or the other lenders for this purpose.[66] Yet some care is still required. In an unusual case, the New York Court of Appeals has recently held that the delegation of

---

[60] See the discussion of the 'gross negligence' aspects of this decision at para 21.24. above.

[61] See *First Citizens' Federal Savings and Loan Association v Worthern Bank and Trust Co* 919 F2d 510 (9th Cir, 1990), distinguishing *Women's Federal Savings and Loan Association v Nevada National Bank* 811 F 2d 1255 (9th Cir, 1987). The two decisions are considered by Mugasha, para 3.128.

[62] This must necessarily be the case, since the lending bank will have obtained credit approval only for its agreed participation limit.

[63] In other words, the obligations of the lenders are several, and not joint. This important point is confirmed by LMA document, clause 2.2(a).

[64] It should be said, however, that the global financial market crisis which set in during the course of 2008 has sharpened market awareness of this particular consideration.

[65] ie without any reference to, or consent of, the agent or the other lenders. This point is confirmed by LMA document, clause 2.2(b).

[66] See, for example, LMA document, clause 2.2.

enforcement rights to the agent, coupled with the absence of a clause allowing individual lenders to take separate action for overdue amounts, must lead to the conclusion that the lenders contemplated 'collective action' by way of enforcement and that individual proceedings were thus inadmissible.[67] Even if it is somewhat unpopular from the debtor's perspective, the correct view appears to be that—in the absence of a specific prohibition—syndicate members can sue for the monies due to them even if the other lenders decline to take proceedings under the same circumstances.[68]

(c) The formulation in paragraph (b) above does, however, beg a significant question namely, to what extent are the amounts owing in respect of the facility actually due for payment? In this context, it should be appreciated that an individual bank cannot *cancel or accelerate* the facility. That right will usually be exercisable only by the agent on the instructions of a majority group of lenders.[69] The majority may, equally, direct the agent to refrain from exercising any discretion which may be vested in it with respect to the acceleration of the loan.[70]

(d) It should be appreciated that the enforcement rights listed in (b) above are limited in certain practical terms. For example, whilst an individual bank may take legal proceedings with a view to seeking payment and could serve a statutory demand with a view to the presentation of a winding-up petition,[71] it cannot enforce any security over the borrower's assets.[72] That security is held by the agent as trustee, and the individual syndicate banks only have a beneficial interest in the security arrangements. Enforcement proceedings must therefore be initiated in the name of the agent, and the agent will

---

[67] *Beal Savings Bank v Viola Sommer* 8 NY 3d 318 (2007). It is submitted that the dissenting judgment of Smith J is to be preferred, in the sense that it would probably more closely reflect market expectation. At all events, the case highlights the need for careful preparation of the required facility documentation. It may be noted that the Court of Appeals cited with approval the earlier decision in *Credit Francais International v Sociedad Financiera de Comercio SA* 490 NYS 2d 670 (1985). This decision—based on the notion that the lenders had surrendered their individual rights in return for the benefit of the 'joint venture' arrangement created by the syndicated facility agreement—has been roundly and rightly criticized: see, for example, Asiedu-Akrofi, 'Sustaining Lender Commitment to Sovereign Debtors' (1992) 30 Col J Transnat'l Law 13.

[68] See *AI Credit Corp v Government of Jamaica* 666 F Supp 629 (SDNY, 1987). An alternative approach is to imply into the syndicated loan agreement a term allowing for individual lender enforcement in relation to sums which have fallen due. There must be a strong argument that considerations of business efficacy justify such a term. It is unreasonable to suppose that an institution in the business of providing debt finance would enter into arrangements under which it could only pursue recovery proceedings if the majority lenders agreed with it.

[69] On this point, see LMA document, clause 23.13. As previously noted, the requisite majority is usually stated to be 66.66 per cent in loan value of the syndicate members. The principle of majority control runs through many aspects of the facility agreement. For example, amendments to the documentation and approval of consents and waivers usually require majority approval: see LMA document, clause 35.1. Certain key provisions of the facility agreement (such as those dealing with the interest rate, repayment dates, and similar matters) are 'entrenched', and can only be amended if every lender so agrees: see LMA document, clause 35.2.

[70] See *New Bank of New England v Toronto-Dominion Bank* 768F Supp 1017 (SDNY, 1991).

[71] A creditor to whom at least £750 is owing may present a demand for that sum and, if it remains unpaid after 21 days, it is assumed that the company is insolvent; as a result, the creditor concerned is entitled to seek the compulsory winding up of the company. On this procedure, see Insolvency Act 1986, s 122.

[72] Thus, for example, an individual syndicate lender in this position could not appoint an administrator of the borrower, because that right is exercisable only by a creditor who holds a qualifying floating charge. On this procedure, see Insolvency Act 1986, Sch B1 (as amended).

normally only take that step if the majority lenders so determine.[73] In other words, the individual syndicate member can enforce those rights which are referable to its status as an unpaid (and unsecured) creditor, but it cannot directly enforce any rights associated with the security package.

Relationship between the Individual Banks

Introduction

21.28 As noted above, a syndicated facility is in many ways merely a convenient means of documenting a series of bilateral loans, all of which are made available for the same purpose. But, in practice, it is impossible to avoid the reality that the banks have all been invited to participate in what is effectively a single facility. The present section accordingly examines the consequences of that state of affairs for the contractual relationship among the lenders themselves.

Several Obligations

21.29 As noted earlier, an individual syndicate bank is not liable for the performance of the obligations of any other syndicate bank. In other words, the obligations of the lenders are several, rather than joint. In this sense, the legal relationship between the lending banks is of a relatively limited nature.[74]

Consents, Instructions, and Waivers; Majority Rule

21.30 There are, however, certain cases in which the action of some lenders may affect the interests of others. For example, and as already noted above, the majority lenders may decide to give a waiver or consent under the terms of the facility agreement.[75] They may also elect to accelerate the facility following the occurrence of a default and determine whether (and if so, when) any security is to be enforced. Under the terms of the agreement, any such action will be binding on other lenders notwithstanding that they voted against it.[76] Under a bilateral facility, the lending bank would have a veto on such matters; in a syndicated loan, it merely has a vote on them.

21.31 Yet it is necessary to go further than this. To what extent does a lender have to take into account the interests of other syndicate members in deciding how to vote on a particular matter? It seems plain that the lender owes no fiduciary duty to the borrower in exercising its powers, since their interests will often be diametrically opposed.[77] But do the banks owe any duties as between themselves? The relationship among the banks is that of co-lenders

---

[73] On this point, see para 21.19 above and *Re Enron Corp* 2005 WL 356985 (SDNY, 15 February 2005).

[74] In many ways, this conclusion is appropriate because the banks have entered into the facility in order to make loans to the borrower, and not for the purpose of entering into relationships with other banks.

[75] See LMA document, clause 35.1 and para 21.19(e) above. This comment is subject to the 'entrenched rights' referred to in that paragraph.

[76] On this point, see LMA document, clause 26.7(b).

[77] On the relationship between the lenders and the borrower, see para 21.27 above.

and, once again, there is no basis for implying any form of fiduciary duty in this context. As a starting point, therefore, a lender is entitled to look solely to its own interests in deciding how to vote on any particular matter. Yet, as in almost any context, the court will be astute to prevent the misuse of powers or obvious cases of bad faith.[78] Thus, in earlier cases dealing with the voting powers of bondholders, the court observed that those powers may be exercised in the interests of the bondholder himself, even though he may have particular interests which differ from those of the other bondholders; the court would only intervene to prevent 'unfairness or oppression'.[79] Clearly, a vote to prioritize or divert payments to the majority bondholders will be oppressive, because it is designed to advantage the majority at the expense of the minority.[80]

In more recent years, the type of dispute which formerly arose under debenture stock trust deeds has crossed over into the syndicated loan market. There have been instances which have illustrated the conflict between the 'majority rule' and the 'entrenched rights', to which reference has already been made. For example, a US case illustrates the point that the individual, entrenched right of each lender to veto an extension of the maturity date of the loan may be of limited value if the majority lenders retain the right to direct (or prevent) the enforcement of the security or collateral package by the agent or security trustee.[81] **21.32**

The English courts have been confronted with a similar problem in recent times. In *Redwood Master Fund v TD Bank Europe Ltd*,[82] a syndicated facility had been made available to a borrower in three separate tranches (labelled facility A, B, and C). Facility A was a revolving credit facility which had not been drawn at the relevant time. Apart from relatively minor amounts, facilities B and C were fully drawn. The borrower ran into difficulties and applied for waivers of breaches of financial undertakings.[83] The majority voting procedures allowed lenders holding 66.66 per cent of the overall facilities to grant waivers of this kind.[84] The necessary majority voted for a waiver of the default on the basis of the borrower's undertaking to pay down a part of facility B by drawing the necessary funds on facility A. Perhaps unsurprisingly, the facility B lenders voted in favour of this arrangement; the necessary majority was easily obtained because facility B was by far the largest segment of the overall facilities. Equally unsurprisingly, however, the facility A lenders viewed this prospect with rather less enthusiasm. Their currently undrawn position would be utilized solely for the purpose of paying lenders in another part of the syndicate. The A lenders thus brought proceedings for a declaration that they were not bound by the terms of the waiver letter on the basis that the majority were required to use their powers for the benefit of the syndicate **21.33**

---

[78] For a helpful discussion on these issues and some of the cases about to be noted, see Rawlings, 'The Management of Loan Syndicates and the Rights of Individual Lenders' [2009] JIBLR 179.

[79] *Goodfellow v Nelson Line (Liverpool) Ltd* [1912] Ch 324.

[80] *Re New York Taxi Cab Co* [1913] 1 Ch 1.

[81] See the situation which arose in *First National Bank of Louisville v Continental Illinois National Bank and Trust Co of Chicago* 933 F 2d 466 (7th Cir, 1991).

[82] [2002] EWHC 2703 (Ch).

[83] On undertakings of this kind, see paras 20.35–20.36 above.

[84] ie facilities A, B and C in the aggregate. There was no provision for voting by reference to the individual classes of lender.

group as a whole or, at least, could not use them to the specific disadvantage of a distinct lender group. The court rejected this line of argument, holding that it was impossible to imply terms of this kind into a lengthy facility agreement which had been professionally prepared and negotiated. More generally, the court held that it should only interfere with decisions taken under 'majority rule' provisions of this kind if the relevant action was manifestly discriminatory or oppressive towards the minority lenders. The evidence would have to show that the majority had been acting in bad faith and seeking to use their powers for an improper purpose. In the light of these tests, minority lenders who seek to challenge majority decisions will thus have something of a hill to climb. In particular, it seems that the fact that one group of lenders is disadvantaged will not be a sufficient ground of challenge if the overall proposal is clearly for the benefit of the lending group as a whole.

Pro Rata Sharing

21.34 The pro rata sharing clause[85] supports the central principle that the syndicate lenders should share equally the risks and rewards of the facility—occasionally referred to as the 'equal misery' principle. In essence, the clause provides that, in the event that a bank receives a payment from the borrower which is in excess of its pro rata share of that payment, then it must account to the agent for that sum so that it can be paid proportionately to all syndicate members. The clause is intended to reinforce the application of the equal risk/equal reward principle to which reference has already been made.[86] It is necessary to ask why a pro rata sharing clause should be required at all. The borrower's obligation is to make all payments to the agent, which is in turn responsible for ensuring that those sums are distributed proportionately among the syndicate banks.[87] Why, then, are further provisions necessary in order to reinforce the equality principle?

21.35 The answer lies in various episodes which have affected the syndicated loan markets over the years. For example, during the Iran hostage crisis in 1979,[88] the Government of Iran ignored its obligation to direct repayments through the agent. Instead, they made payments direct to all of their European bank lenders, but they withheld payment from US-based lenders. This action was, of course, politically motivated but it resulted in a violation of the equal risk/equal reward principle. A similar situation arose in 1982, when Argentina invaded the Falkland Islands, a British Dependent Territory. Once again, the Argentine Government made payments direct to US and continental lenders, but bypassed the process for payment via the agent and withheld payment from UK banks. The pro rata sharing clause was thus developed and refined in response to these crises, in an effort to ensure that banks bore the risks proportionately, regardless of the country in which they happened to be based.[89]

---

[85] See the version of the clause set out in clause 28 of the LMA document. For further discussion of the pro rata sharing clause and the principles which underlie it, see Mugasha, paras 5.106–5.115.

[86] See n 36 above.

[87] See para 21.19 above.

[88] The crisis involved the kidnapping of staff at the US Embassy in Tehran.

[89] Whilst the 'equal risk/equal reward' principle is well-established in the syndicated loan markets, it may well be asked whether it should apply in this type of situation. Individual banks are always exposed to political

It will thus be apparent that the pro rata sharing clause owes its origins and subsequent **21.36** development to crises of a political nature involving sovereign borrowers. Nevertheless, the issue may arise in the context of ordinary corporate loans. Suppose, for example, that a corporate borrower goes into insolvent liquidation. It has an outstanding syndicated loan with a group of five banks. However, one of those banks holds substantial deposits from the borrower. Accordingly, that bank exercises a right of set-off against those deposits to repay its portion of the syndicated facility. It seems clear that the proceeds of the set-off would have to be shared with the other syndicate members under the terms of the pro rata sharing clause, because the relevant bank has received an amount in excess of its proportionate share of that payment.[90] There may also be cases in which one bank is able to recover on its security, whilst another is not. Cases of this kind will be rare, given that the security is generally created in favour of the agent[91] for the benefit of all lenders. Nevertheless, this did occur in one case,[92] and it is possible to conceive of its application in others.[93]

Whilst these principles appear to be clear, their application in a particular case may not be **21.37** quite so straightforward. In particular, the clause only comes into operation if an individual syndicate member receives a direct payment in respect of monies owing to it under the relevant facility agreement. But some lenders[94] may have amounts owing to them under separate, bilateral facilities or even under separate, syndicated facilities. If such a lender receives a payment direct from the borrower, it will have to redistribute those monies for the benefit of the other syndicate lenders if it has received those monies *in respect of the particular syndicated facility concerned*. But money is a fungible commodity, so how will this be proved? If a payment of an amount equal to a principal and interest instalment is received by that lender on the due date under the syndicated agreement, then that will obviously be very strong evidence that the payment relates to that agreement and the pro rata sharing clause would have to be applied accordingly.

If, however, the receipt cannot be allocated in this way—for example, because the payment **21.38** is received as a result of the lender's unilateral decision to exercise a right of set-off—then can the lender appropriate the receipt to its own, bilateral facilities and thus retain the full benefit of it for its own account? Or is it under an obligation to prefer the syndicated deal,

---

risks of this kind, and it is by no means clear why they should enjoy any protection from them simply because they participate in syndicated facilities involving lenders from other countries.

[90] If the bank concerned also had separate, bilateral facilities outstanding with the same borrower, then it seems clear that it could apply the proceeds of the deposits against those bilateral facilities. There is nothing in the LMA document which obliges a bank to exercise a right of set-off under these circumstances and, if it elects to do so, there is no obligation to apply the proceeds against the syndicated loan in preference to the bilateral facilities.

[91] In this capacity, usually referred to as the 'security trustee'.

[92] *Chemical Bank v Security Pacific National Bank* 20 F 3d 375 (1994). Security Pacific had accepted in that case that it had to share the proceeds of a security interest which it held for itself, even though an intended security interest in favour of the other lenders had not been perfected.

[93] For example, see the discussion of 'parallel debt' clauses at paras 21.48–21.50 below. If the courts of any foreign jurisdiction found that the security was only valid in relation to monies owing to the agent in its personal capacity, then it would have to share the proceeds with the other lenders, whose security had proved to be void.

[94] This applies particularly to the arranger, who will often have the closest relationship with the borrower.

and thus bring those funds into account under the pro rata sharing clause? In the absence of an express provision dealing with this matter,[95] then the lender could only be obliged to give priority to the syndicated transaction if it were possible to imply into the agreement a clause to that effect. However, it is submitted that there is no consideration of 'business efficacy' which is necessary to create such an implication. If anything, the LMA document implies to the contrary,[96] and it is thus necessary to conclude that the lender is free to prioritize its own bilateral facilities in applying the proceeds of any set-off.

21.39 As a final point, it has already been noted[97] that individual banks may take proceedings to enforce their own debt claims as against the borrower. Since that exercise involves both risk and expense for the bank concerned, it would be unreasonable to expect that bank to share the fruits of that litigation with other lenders who chose not to participate in the proceedings. The syndicated facility agreement should accordingly exclude the obligation to share receipts in this type of situation.[98]

Liability and Regulatory Aspects

21.40 It remains to consider two issues relating to risk and regulatory liability which may arise in the context of participation in a syndicated loan, namely, (i) the risk that a lending bank may be responsible for the obligations of another lender which fails or refuses to advance funds under the agreement and (ii) the possibility that the structure might constitute a 'collective investment scheme' for the purposes of the Financial Services and Markets Act 2000 (FSMA) and, hence, would become subject to a variety of regulatory requirements.

21.41 As to the first, liability point:

(a) It has already been noted that a syndicated loan agreement will provide that the obligations of the lenders are several and not joint, and that syndicate members should not have any liability for a failure or non-compliance by another syndicate member. Is there any basis on which the effect of such a contractual provision could be disregarded?

(b) It is fundamental to the lenders in a syndicated loan facility that they are responsible only for the provision of funds up to their pre-agreed commitment. They will, after all, have obtained the necessary internal credit approval on that basis. But courts in the United States have stressed the collective or 'joint venture' nature of syndicated loans.[99] It is thus necessary to consider whether a disaffected borrower could sue other

---

[95] The LMA document does not explicitly deal with the subject.
[96] Clause 26.5 of the LMA document confirms that the agent and the arranger are free to enter into other business transactions with the borrower, If this is true of the parties which may—arguably—owe fiduciary duties to the lender, then it must equally be true of the general body of the participants, where no such duty can arise.
[97] See para 21.27 above.
[98] For a provision to this effect, see LMA document, clause 28.5(b).
[99] See, for example, *Credit Francais International SA v Sociedad Financiera de Comercio* 490 NYS 2d 670 (1985).

syndicate banks on the basis that they are responsible for the failure of one of their number to provide its share of the facility.

(c) So far as English law is concerned, the only basis of such possible liability appears to be the Partnership Act 1890, on the footing that the syndicated loan agreement constitutes a partnership among the lenders. Section 1 of the 1890 Act provides that partnership '... is the relation which subsists between persons carrying on business in common with a view of profit ...'. Where such a relationship exists, then each member of the partnership '... is jointly liable with the other partners ... for all debts and obligations of the firm incurred while he is a partner ...'.[100]

(d) It might conceivably be argued that the syndicate members are carrying on business in common and with a view to profit, on the basis that they share both the risks and rewards of the arrangements on a proportionate basis.

(e) Nevertheless, whilst the banks will be sharing the gross margins and fees on a proportionate basis, they will not be sharing profits on the same basis, since the actual profit on the transaction of each individual institution will vary according to its particular circumstances.[101] As a result, an ordinary syndicated loan should not result in the creation of a partnership since '... the sharing of gross returns does not of itself create a partnership ...'.[102]

(f) Matters may become a little more involved where—as is commonly the case—the interest margin varies according to the profitability of the borrower's business.[103] The linking of the interest return to the underlying profits certainly creates at least an impression that the banks are acting in partnership with the borrower itself. But this will not be treated as a partnership at law because (i) the lenders are not carrying on a business *in common* with the borrower and (ii) it is specifically provided that '... receipt of a payment contingent on or varying with the profits of a business ...' does not of itself render a person a partner in that particular business.[104]

(g) In any event, there is nothing in the 1890 Act which prohibits a specific agreement to the effect that individual partners are only to be liable among themselves to a particular extent or manner. Accordingly, the borrower's usual acknowledgement that the obligations of the lenders are several and that they will not be responsible for the default of the other lenders[105] should, in principle, be legally valid and effective.

(h) It follows that, in ordinary circumstances, a syndicate lender is not responsible for the performance of the obligations of any other lender.

---

[100] Section 9 of the 1890 Act.

[101] For example, some institutions will suffer higher funding costs than others, with the result that their profit on the deal will be lower to that extent.

[102] Section 2(2) of the 1890 Act.

[103] This type of 'margin ratchet' can operate in one of two ways. First of all, the margin could increase if profits increase, as a reward to the banks in supporting the success of the business. Alternatively, the margin could reduce, on the basis that the higher level of profitability reduces the risk to the lenders.

[104] Section 2(3) of the 1890 Act.

[105] See LMA document, clause 2.2(a).

21.42 As to the second, regulatory issue:

(a) Part XVIII (sections 235–283) of the FSMA regulates 'collective investment schemes' in a variety of ways. In particular, it restricts the circulation of promotional material, even by persons who hold authorization from the FSMA.[106] Furthermore, a person who establishes or operates a collective investment scheme must hold authorization from the Financial Services Authority for that purpose.[107] These rules would have obvious consequences, in that the arrangers need to circulate an information memorandum in order to identify participants for the facility, and the facility agent plainly acts as administrator of the arrangements. It is therefore necessary to determine whether a syndicated loan transaction does indeed amount to a 'collective investment scheme' for these purposes.

(b) It is accordingly necessary to ask (i) what is a collective investment scheme and (ii) does a syndicated loan agreement have the characteristics of such a scheme?

(c) By virtue of section 235(1) of the FSMA, a collective investment scheme is constituted by

> ... any arrangements with respect to property of any description, including money, the purpose or effect of which is to enable persons taking part in the arrangements (whether by becoming owners of the property or any part of it, or otherwise) to participate in or receive profits or income arising from the acquisition, holding, management or disposal of the property or sums paid out of such profits or income ...

On the face of it, this definition is wide enough to embrace a syndicated loan.

(d) However, an arrangement only amounts to a collective investment scheme if '... the persons who are to participate do not have day-to-day control over the management of the property, whether or not they have the right to be consulted or to give directions ...'.[108] In the writer's view, this condition is not met because—apart from administrative duties—the facility agent will in practice have very limited discretion as to the management of the loan or any decisions to be taken in connection with it. It will have to consult all of the lenders and will have to act in accordance with their directions.[109] It is true that, in some cases, the agent will be required to act on the instructions of the majority lenders, but this would not appear to detract from the fact that the lenders have effective day-to-day control over their own individual participations in the loan.[110]

(e) Quite apart from this, the arrangements will only constitute a collective investment scheme if either (i) the contributions of the participants and the profits or income out of which they are to be paid are pooled or (ii) the property is managed as a whole by or on behalf of the operator of the scheme.[111] It is doubtful whether either of these tests is met. The facility agreement will make it clear that the amounts owing to the individual investors are separate and independent debts, and this should negate any inference of

---

[106] FSMA, s 238.
[107] Financial Services and Markets Act 2000 (Regulated Activities) Order 2001 (SI 2001/544), art 51.
[108] FSMA, s 235(2).
[109] See para 21.19(e) above.
[110] Compare the remarks in Blair, Walker and Purves, para 17.18.
[111] FSMA, s 235(3).

'pooling'.[112] As to the second element, the requirement that the property should be 'managed' by the operator of the scheme connotes a degree of discretion in its management. The essentially administrative duties of the facility agent would not appear to cross this threshold test.

(f) As a result, a syndicated loan does not amount to a collective investment scheme and is thus not subject to the corresponding regulatory provisions of the FSMA.[113]

Security Arrangements

The Security Trust Structure

When a bank makes a facility available to a borrower, it will often take a guarantee from other group companies, and may also take security over the assets of the obligor group. This poses no difficulty where the guarantee and security arrangements are of an essentially bilateral nature.[114] Two issues do, however, arise where the transaction is to be made available by a syndicate of lenders: **21.43**

(a) it is cumbersome and inconvenient for a group of lenders to take security over the same assets. The concept of security created in favour of a number of entities does not sit well with English law; and

(b) the secondary loan market has been very active in recent years, and it is important to banks and other financial institutions that they should be able to trade their loan participations.[115] Whilst it is possible to assign the benefit of a fully drawn loan and the associated security, this is an untidy process in the context of a syndicated transaction. Furthermore, if the credit is of a revolving nature,[116] an assignment is not possible insofar as the lender remains obliged to make future advances. In such a case, a novation would be required; in substance, this amounts to a new facility and accordingly it

---

[112] Although it must be said that the pro rata sharing provisions and the general notion that risks and rewards are to be shared on a proportionate basis does convey an element of 'pooling'. In addition, the court will not be bound by individual terms in the facility agreement but will examine the matter on a broader basis: see Blair, Walker and Purves, para 17.19, citing *Enviro Systems Renewable Resources Pty Ltd v ASIC* (2001) ASCR 762.

[113] It should be added that it is a matter of some importance to be able to reach this conclusion on the basis of the main provisions contained within s 235 itself. The overall scheme of the legislation is to create the widest possible definition of 'collective investment scheme', and then to cut back the definition by exemption in appropriate cases. But the Schedule to the Financial Services and Markets Act 2000 (Collective Investment Schemes) Order 2002 (SI 2001/1062, as amended) contains no exemptions which would be directly applicable in this type of case. For example, (i) the exemption in para 5 (Debt issues) of Sch 1 applies only where debentures or similar instruments are issued, and this is not generally the case in the context of a syndicated loan and (ii) although it is possible that para 9 (Schemes entered into for commercial purposes wholly or mainly related to existing business) of Sch 1 may potentially apply to syndicated loans, it was clearly not designed for that purpose.

[114] On guarantee and security arrangements generally, see Part (E) below.

[115] There are various reasons for this development. First of all, banks may wish to free up the capital ascribed to the facility in order that they may pursue other opportunities. Secondly, loans in default can be sold at a discount, thus disposing of problem assets and crystallizing (and perhaps limiting) the relevant loss. On the subject generally, see Chapter 22 below.

[116] A revolving credit may be drawn and repaid by the borrower, and the bank may thus remain under an obligation to make further advances until the termination date of the facility.

would be necessary for the borrower to execute fresh security in favour of the incoming lender. The cost and inconvenience of this exercise would be significant, especially if a particular facility is heavily traded.

21.44 These difficulties have been circumvented by the use of a security trust structure. Any security associated with the facility is executed in favour of the agent as trustee[117] for the banks which are members of the syndicate from time to time.

21.45 An institution which wishes to sell its participation in the loan may execute a form of transfer certificate.[118] The effect of this arrangement is to transfer to the new lender (i) the outgoing lender's title to the loan, (ii) the outgoing lender's obligation to make further advances, and (iii) the outgoing lender's interest in the security trust.[119] Since the new lender acquires an interest in the security which is already established under a fully constituted trust, there is no need for the borrower to execute new security documents.

21.46 The agent bank will hold the security on trust for the lending group. It will usually be required to enforce the security if the set majority of the syndicate banks require it to do so.[120] Individual banks cannot enforce their share of the security since, as noted earlier, the individual banks are not the owners of it; their interest is held in their capacity as beneficiaries under a trust.[121]

21.47 In the normal course, and for the reasons given above, the facility agent will usually enter into any security documents under the label 'security trustee'. But some care is required in distinguishing between these two roles because, where the agent is acting as a trustee, the banks will be beneficiaries under the trust but will not have any positive obligations to the borrower in that particular capacity. On the other hand, where the facility agent is genuinely acting as agent for the banks, then any obligation contained in the relevant documents will be binding on the banks as principals. The capacity in which the agent acts for particular purposes will depend upon an analysis of the individual clauses of

---

[117] Although the agent bank will act as a trustee in this capacity, in practice some of the more onerous fiduciary duties imposed on a trustee will be excluded by the documentation: see, for example, LMA document, clause 26.4.

[118] On this procedure and the form of the certificate, see LMA document, clause 24 and schedule 5. Clause 24 also deals with the terms of the contractual relationship between the incoming and outgoing lenders. In essence, the clause provides that the new lender has been responsible for its own credit assessment, and the outgoing lender gives no warranties as to the quality of the loan asset. The protections given to the selling lender are thus very similar to those afforded to the arranger of a syndicated loan: see para 21.14 above.

[119] In other words, the transfer of the benefit of the existing loans and the obligation to make further advances is novated in favour of the incoming lender. It is, perhaps, not strictly accurate to speak of the 'transfer' of the outgoing lender's interest in the security package to the new lender, even though this may be the practical effect. In fact, the outgoing lender simply ceases to be a beneficiary under the trust, because it no longer falls within the defined class of beneficiaries. By the same token, the new lender, having acquired a loan participation, will now fall within the defined class. There is thus no assignment of a beneficial interest; rather, the former interest is extinguished and a new one is created in its place.

[120] See, for example, LMA document, clause 26.7.

[121] For confirmation of this point, see *Re Enron Corp* 2005 WL 356985 (SDNY, 15 February 2005), where the attempt by the syndicate participants directly to enforce security failed on the basis that a security agent had been appointed and there was no contractual provision allowing for enforcement by any other party.

the agreement concerned. It has, for example, been held that the security assets and their proceeds may be held as a trustee, whilst contractual restrictions on assignment may be entered into as agent for—and, hence, will be binding on, the individual syndicate members.[122]

Parallel Debt Clauses

The difficulty with the security trust structure lies in the fact that the trust device is not **21.48** recognized in a number of civil law jurisdictions,[123] and this may pose difficulty where any of the charged assets are situate in such a jurisdiction.[124]

The practical consequences of this state of affairs are highly significant; a charge created in **21.49** favour of the security trustee could not secure a debt owing to other syndicate members, who would be treated as third parties for these purposes. This difficulty is frequently addressed by so-called 'parallel debt' provisions, which state that the amount outstanding under the facility agreement will be deemed to be owing to the security trustee, but that debt will be reduced by an amount equal to the payments actually received by the syndicate members under the facility agreement. The clause is designed to ensure that the security trustee can enforce the foreign security for the full amount owing to the syndicate, even though they are not parties to the relevant security document. A specimen of such a clause might read as follows:

a) The borrower and each of the lenders agree that the security trustee shall be the joint creditor (together with the relevant lender) of each and every obligation of the borrower towards each of the lenders under the facility agreement, and that accordingly the security trustee will have its own independent right to demand performance by the borrower of those obligations (the 'Parallel Debt'). However, a discharge of any such obligation to one of the security trustee or the lender shall, to the same extent, discharge the corresponding obligation owing to the other.
b) Without limiting the security trustee's rights under (a) above, the security trustee agrees that it will not exercise any rights as joint creditor in respect of the Parallel Debt unless it has consulted with the relevant lender as to the action which it proposes to take.
c) In relation to the Parallel Debt, the security trustee acts in its own name and not as trustee, and none of its claims in respect of the Parallel Debt shall be held on trust for any other party. The security granted to the security trustee under the [foreign security documents] to secure the Parallel Debt is granted to the security trustee in its own capacity as creditor of the Parallel Debt.

It hardly needs to be stated that the 'deeming' provisions contained in the parallel **21.50** debt clause are highly artificial. They seek to create a series of debt relationships which,

---

[122] *British Energy Power and Trading Ltd v Credit Suisse* [2008] EWCA Civ 53 (CA).
[123] On the Hague Convention on the Recognition of Trusts, see Dicey, Morris & Collins, para 29-014 et seq. The Convention has entered into force in various jurisdictions, particularly in Europe. Nevertheless, the Convention is not of widespread application and, accordingly, a detailed discussion lies beyond the scope of this work.
[124] eg land which is physically located in that country, or shares issued by a company incorporated there. On the whole subject, see the discussion of the respective forms of security in Part (E) below.

otherwise, would not exist and which bear limited similarity to the realities of the underlying factual situation. If the borrower becomes insolvent, then the extent to which the parallel debt clause suffices to cover all of the debt owing to the entire syndicate would arise. The point would almost certainly fall to be determined by reference to the law of the country in which the charged assets are situate.[125]

---

[125] It is true that the document creating the parallel debt provision would itself often be governed by English law. However, the validity of a charge over foreign property is governed by the *lex situs*, and that principle must surely also extend to the amount which can be treated as validly secured against the assets concerned.

22

TRADING LOAN ASSETS

Introduction

The preceding chapters have considered both bilateral and syndicated loans and the man- **22.01** ner in which they are arranged, structured, and documented. In contrast, the present section examines the various means of acquiring or disposing of loan commitments through secondary market activity.

Over recent years, the ability to trade loan assets has become increasingly important to **22.02** banks and other institutions. There are a number of reasons for these developments.

In particular, a bank may find that it has insufficient capital to write new business, either **22.03** generally or with the particular borrower concerned.[1] Or it may feel that a particular facility which has gone into default is likely to absorb a great deal of time for limited return. It may therefore wish simply to be rid of the commitment, realize whatever value it may have and move on. The buyers, on the other side of such transactions, may be institutions which wish to acquire experience of the particular borrower with a view to exploring further opportunities or, in the case of defaulted debt, may be a so-called 'vulture fund' which specializes in acquiring such assets and turning them to account.[2]

The present chapter considers the various techniques which have been developed to allow **22.04** for such trading, and their respective advantages and disadvantages.

---

[1] Capital adequacy requirements have been discussed generally in Chapter 6 above. A bank may have insufficient capital to take on further business with a particular customer in view of the 'large exposure' rules considered at paras 6.63–6.68 above.

[2] On institutions of this kind, see further para 22.07 below.

Restrictions on Assignments and Transfers

22.05   It is necessary at the outset to consider the extent to which assignments or transfers of loan participations are permissible, and the extent to which the borrower controls that process and the identity of those who may acquire its debt. Loan agreements have long contained clauses dealing with the assignment or transfer of the lender's rights and obligations under the contract. The provision was for many years regarded as a 'standard' provision and attracted little attention, largely because banks were unlikely to sell the business relationship.

22.06   This relaxed attitude changed with the establishment and explosive growth of the secondary debt markets; lenders and borrowers alike began to focus on the clause and the impact on the relationship. As noted above, lenders wanted the ability to trade their assets, partly as a means of disposing of defaulted debt, and partly as a means of freeing up capital for more profitable opportunities. Borrowers, for their part, realized that they wanted more control over the identity of their creditors because, if they run into difficulties, the quality of their relationship with the lender may be a critical factor in riding out the crisis. Furthermore, whilst the amount owing by the borrower would not increase as a result of the transfer, it must be remembered that the relationship goes beyond a pure debtor-creditor contract. So long as the facility remains outstanding, the lender has a degree of control over the borrower's activities,[3] and the borrower may occasionally wish to seek waivers or consents for particular purposes. It will therefore wish to know that it will be seeking the necessary flexibility from an institution with which it has an established and satisfactory working relationship.

22.07   What, then, is the compromise between these two extremes? The LMA document[4] provides that a lender may assign its rights and obligations to a transferee provided that the transferee is a financial institution regularly engaged in purchasing or investing in loans, securities, or other financial assets.[5] In addition, the consent of the borrower is required for any transfer, but (i) the required consent cannot be unreasonably withheld or delayed and (ii) the consent is deemed to have been given if the borrower fails to respond within five business days.[6] A few points may be made in relation to this provision and assignments generally:

   (a)   As is well known, an assignment which breaches an express prohibition in the underlying contract is not binding on the debtor.[7] However, the nature of the prohibition has to be construed in each individual case. It has been held that, unless the provision explicitly states otherwise, the *proceeds* of a contract may be assigned, even if the

---

[3] See the undertakings and various other provisions discussed earlier in this chapter.
[4] See LMA document, clause 24.
[5] See LMA document, clause 24.1.
[6] See LMA document, clause 24.2.
[7] *Helstan Securities Ltd v Hertfordshire County Council* [1978] 3 All ER 262.

contract *as a whole* may not.[8] Nevertheless, it must be doubtful whether this interpretation should be applied to a loan contract, the main object of which is to secure the right to repayment and payment of interest. In such a case, an assignment of the *proceeds* is, in substance, virtually an assignment of the contract *as a whole*.

(b) Where the clause provides for assignment subject to the borrower's consent and stipulates that consent must not be unreasonably withheld, an assignment is only valid if the consent has been requested and either (i) consent has been given in accordance with the terms of the contract or (ii) the court has declared that the withholding of consent was unreasonable.[9]

(c) As noted above, the standard clause provides for assignments to 'financial institutions' and other defined categories of transferee. Whether or not a particular entity is a 'financial institution' obviously depends on the nature of its business, and the point became contentious when so-called 'vulture funds' purchased sovereign debt with a view to profiting from the restructuring processes for governmental debt.[10] In this context, the English courts have recently held that a financial institution includes a business which provides capital to the financial markets. In other words, the expression is significantly broader that a 'bank', as traditionally understood.[11]

(d) Where consent is deemed to be given after a certain period (ie to prevent the borrower from 'dragging its feet'), it is necessary to comply strictly with the terms of such a provision. Thus, a transfer effected before the expiry of the designated time period will be void, and that invalidity will 'infect' any subsequent transfers made in reliance on it.[12]

(e) The clause also allows for disclosure of information to a potential transferee, by way of exception to the normal duty of confidentiality.[13] However, as noted elsewhere, confidential information relating to the borrower must be handled with great care.[14]

On the basis that the facility agreement does not contain any prohibition against assign- **22.08** ments or transfers, or that any necessary borrower consents have been obtained, how can the lender complete the proposed transaction? There are various options open to the parties, according to the circumstances of the particular case.

---

[8] *Linden Garden Trust Ltd v Lenestsa Sludge Disposals Ltd* [1994] 1 AC 85. The whole subject is complex and there is a considerable body of case law. For a full discussion, see Chitty, ch 19.

[9] *Hendry v Chartsearch Ltd* [1998] CLC 1382.

[10] 'Vulture funds' are entities which seek to purchase defaulted debt at heavily discounted prices with a view to recovering profits through negotiation or litigation. Insofar as these activities have targeted sovereign debt of poorer countries, they have generated a certain amount of political concern. For an attempt to rein in their activities, see the Developing Country Debt (Restriction of Recovery) Bill, introduced into the House of Commons as a private member's bill in May 2009. A similar, 'Stop the Vulture Funds Act' was introduced in Congress in August 2008. For a detailed discussion of some of the case law (both in England and New York) on the acquisition of such debt by secondary market purchasers, see Proctor, 'Sovereign Debt Restructuring and the Courts—Some Recent Developments' (2003) 8 JIBFL 302, (2003) 9 JIBFL 351, and (2003) 10 JIBFL 379. For a review of some of the case law specifically involving Zambia, see Proctor, 'Vulture Funds and Sovereign Debt—The Zambian Experience' (2007) 4 *Journal of South African Law* 629.

[11] *Argo Fund Ltd v Essar Steel Ltd* [2006] 2 All ER (Comm) 104 (CA).

[12] *Barbados Trust Co Ltd v Bank of Zambia* [2007] EWCA Civ 148.

[13] See LMA document, clause 24.7.

[14] See generally Chapter 42 below.

Assignment

22.09 An assignment involves the transfer of a chose in action from its existing owner to a new owner, such that the latter obtains title to the chose concerned.[15]

22.10 The transaction concerned will constitute a *legal* assignment[16] of the loan if four conditions are satisfied:

(a) the assignment is in writing;
(b) the assignment is absolute (ie and not merely by way of security);
(c) the assignment relates to the whole of the loan, and not merely to a proportion of it; and
(d) notice of the assignment is given to the borrower.

22.11 If these conditions are met, then the assignee acquires the exclusive right to give a good discharge for the debt[17] and to exercise '… all legal and other remedies for the same …'.[18] This would seem to imply two things:

(a) if the loan agreement has been transferred by means of a legal assignment, then the assignee is entitled to enforce and security for the loan even though this was not specifically referred to in the assignment document itself;[19] and
(b) given that the assignee has acquired full title to the debt and has become its 'owner', it may exercise any rights of set-off which it may have in view of obligations separately owing by the assignee to the borrower itself (eg in respect of deposits held by the assignee).

22.12 The assignment will only take effect as an *equitable* assignment if one of the four conditions listed above is not met. Usually, this will be the case because the assignment relates only to a part of the debt or loan.[20] Such an assignment may give rise to a number of issues, especially in the context of a transaction which started life as a purely bilateral facility. In particular:

(a) Which of the two lenders is entitled to decide to accelerate the loan following the occurrence of an event of default? Or can each lender do so independently of the other? Where the original loan was a bilateral arrangement, it will not include provisions to cater for this type of situation.[21]
(b) Can the assignee elect to enforce any security? This question must probably be answered in the negative, since the original lender will remain the holder of record of the security and will remain interested in it.

---

[15] See *Norman v Federal Commissioner for Taxation* (1963) 109 CLR 9 (High Court of Australia), noted by Mugasha at para 8.16.

[16] ie for the purposes of Law of Property Act 1925, s 136.

[17] 'Exclusive', in the sense that the borrower can no longer discharge his debt by payment to the original lender/assignor.

[18] See Law of Property Act 1925, s 136(1)(b).

[19] In practice, of course, the assignment would normally include specific reference to the transfer of the security. As a result, the writer has not been able to identify any specific authority for this proposition.

[20] In such a case, the assignee will have to join in the primary lender in order to take proceedings for the recovery of the debt, since the primary lender remains its owner at law: *Re Steel Wing Co* [1921] 1 Ch 349.

[21] On majority voting provisions in the context of syndicated loans, see para 21.30 above.

The above analysis suggests that a legal assignment may be an appropriate vehicle for an **22.13** assignment of the entirety of the loan and associated security package. But the assignment route will frequently be untidy and unsatisfactory where a partial transfer is contemplated.

Novation

As has been seen, an assignment is an essentially bipartite arrangement between the lender **22.14** and the intending purchaser of the whole or part of his interest in the loan. The borrower may be asked to consent to the arrangement, and he may be given notice of it when it has been completed. But the borrower is not a necessary party to the assignment itself.

A novation, in contrast, is a tripartite agreement to which the original lender, the purchaser **22.15** and the borrower will all be party. Such an arrangement may be particularly desirable for the original lender where the loan is not yet fully drawn, and it wishes to be formally absolved by the borrower from any obligation to make further advances,[22] with that obligation instead being assumed by the incoming lender. In terms of a contractual analysis, a novation involves an agreement by the borrower to release the original lender from its obligation to provide further loans, in consideration of a promise by the incoming lender to perform the corresponding obligations. In addition, the existing lender releases the borrower from its repayment obligations, in consideration of the borrower assuming equivalent obligations in favour of the incoming lender.[23]

A novation agreement will thus be a convenient route for all parties to achieve a loan trans- **22.16** fer although, once again, the procedure will be untidy in the context of a partial transfer of a bilateral facility. Where the incoming institution is taking over a *secured* loan facility, it should be noted that the novation of that security would have to be registered at Companies House under section 860(1) of the Companies Act 2006, because the novation in fact has the effect of creating a new security interest for the purposes of that section.[24]

Participation Arrangements

Introduction

The present section considers a slightly different means of acquiring an interest in a loan **22.17** transaction, without becoming a 'lender of record' so far as the borrower is concerned.[25]

---

[22] Quite apart from the fact that the original lender will not wish to take the risk that the transferee institution may fail to perform the obligation to make future advances, the commitment may require the attribution of capital under the terms of Basel II: see generally the discussion in Chapter 6 above.

[23] A novation agreement is thus an excellent illustration of the rule that, whilst consideration must move *from* the promisee, it need not move *to* the promisor: see Chitty, para 3-039.

[24] This follows from the fact that the old debt owing to the original lender is discharged, and a new debt owing in favour of the new lender is created, pursuant to the novation agreement: see the discussion in the text. Of course, a new registration process will only be required if the security falls within the various categories listed in s 860(7) of the 2006 Act. On the whole subject, see Chapter 27 below.

[25] For a very illuminating discussion of the whole subject and a wider discussion of the North American case law considered below, see Mugasha, ch 6. For discussion of the English law approach in the same area, see ch 1 of the same text.

In essence, the original lender remains the contracting party with the borrower, whilst the participant[26] enters into a contractual relationship with the primary lender to assume a portion of the risk associated with the underlying facility.

22.18 Why should the intending buyer and seller decide to structure their transaction in this way, when it would seem much simpler to effect an outright assignment and transfer? There may be a variety of reasons for this approach. First of all, as noted above, the facility agreement may allow for outright transfers only in limited situations or to limited categories of transferee, and the proposed transaction may not satisfy the relevant criteria. Or the facility agreement may stipulate for loan commitments to be transferred in multiples of (say) £10 million, but the buyer only wants to acquire £5 million. Transactions involving security can also pose particular difficulty, especially where the facility is not fully drawn and remains available for utilization. In such a case, the existing security will often not extend to advances made by the transferee, with the result that new security documentation would have to be executed. This is obviously highly inconvenient for all parties and introduces an extra layer of expense to the transaction.[27] Finally, the lender may have a wider relationship with the borrower, and does not wish it to know that it has taken steps to reduce its exposure.

22.19 There are two ways in which participation techniques may be used to reduce a lender's exposure to a particular transaction.

Funded Participations

22.20 Under the terms of a funded participation agreement:[28]

(a) the participant will agree to place deposits with the principal lender reflecting the proportion and amount of his intended share in the facility;

(b) the deposits will be 'limited recourse', in the sense that both the deposits themselves and the interest thereon will be paid by the principal lender only against receipt of the corresponding amounts from the borrower itself; and

(c) if the loan facility is only partly drawn down as at the date of the participation agreement, the participant will agree to place the necessary additional deposits as and when further utilization requests are received from the borrower.

---

[26] Commonly, and perhaps more accurately, referred to as the 'sub-participant'. It may be added that structures of this kind were at one time popular precisely because they avoided outright transfers of the debt, because *ad valorem* stamp duty applied to such assignments. The duty no longer applies in this context.

[27] Perhaps oddly, this problem is more pronounced in the case of simple, bilateral facilities. In the case of a more complex, syndicated facility, the security is held on trust and the new lender automatically joins the class of beneficiaries: see the discussion at para 21.45 above.

[28] For specimen forms of risk participation agreements, see the various precedent documents available via the website of the Loan Market Association. US courts have tended to stress the *contractual* nature of the participation agreement: see Mugasha, para 6.08, citing *First Bank of WaKeeney v Peoples' State Bank* 758 P 2d 236 (1985), *First National Bank of Belleville v Clay-Hensley Commission Co* 525 NE 2d 217 (1988) and *Hibernia National Bank v FDIC* 619 F Supp 1341 (1985). Yet, as will be apparent from the discussion below, they have often strayed outside the agreement itself in order to define the nature of the relationship between the primary lender and the participant.

The economic effect of these arrangements is virtually identical to the outright sale and **22.21** purchase of the loan commitment. But the arrangement remains 'behind the curtain' so far as the borrower is concerned. There are various consequences of this state of affairs. For example, as against the borrower, the principal lender remains obliged to fund future advances, even though the participant defaults on its corresponding obligations under the participation agreement. Likewise, the borrower obtains a full and final discharge of his obligations by making payment to the primary lender. If the lender fails to account to the participant for its appropriate share, that is of no concern to the borrower. He is not a party to the participation agreement and will often be entirely unaware of its existence; he is therefore plainly unaffected by these arrangements. This slightly odd structure also means that a degree of caution is required for the participant. For example, if the loan is secured and the participant is relying on valuations of the charged assets, it may be that the valuer will not owe any duty of care to the participant and hence will not be liable to him in the event that the valuation proves to have been negligent.[29]

What are the other legal characteristics and consequences of a funded participation **22.22** agreement? A few observations may be made:

(a) it will often be the case that the principal lender must be a *bank*, in the sense that it must be authorized to accept deposits.[30] Although, as noted above, the economic effects of a funded participation are similar to a sale and purchase of the relevant share of the loan, the fact remains that the arrangement is structured as a deposit, even if only repayable on certain contingencies. It may therefore be unlawful for other types of institution to enter into such an agreement as the 'seller'.

(b) The participation agreement creates a limited recourse structure, in the sense that the deposits and interest on them flow back to the participant in tandem with the payments received from the ultimate borrower in respect of the loan concerned.[31] Yet the principal lender does not have the right to apply those deposits against repayment of the loan following a default by the borrower. It merely has the right to retain the deposits pending receipts from the borrower which, in the worst case, may never occur. As a consequence, the participant should not be taken to have created a charge over the deposits and it should be unnecessary to consider the possible application of the registration requirements set out in section 860 of the Companies Act 2006.[32]

(c) Although the cash deposits do not constitute 'security' in the formal sense, it nevertheless remains the case that the right of the principal lender to retain the deposits is legally

---

[29] For a case in which this point was discussed, but not decided, see *Helmsley Acceptances Ltd v Lambert Smith Hampton* [2010] EWCA Civ 356 (CA).

[30] On the need for FSA authorization to accept deposits, and the various available exemptions, see generally Chapter 1 above.

[31] Whether or not an amount has been received from the borrower *in respect of the participated loan* will not always be a straightforward issue, especially where the primary lender has a wider banking relationship with the borrower. Where the payments are made by the borrower on the due dates under the relevant facility agreement, it will be fairly clear that the borrower has exercised its right of appropriation towards that facility, but the position may be different where the primary lender has realized funds as a result of exercising a right of set-off. Compare the discussion in relation to pro rata sharing clauses at para 21.34 above.

[32] On these requirements, and their application to security over bank deposits, see Chapter 31 below.

robust. As a result, it appears that this type of arrangement would constitute satis-factory credit risk mitigation for capital adequacy purposes.[33] The exposure to the borrower could therefore be zero-weighted for those purposes.

(d) It has already been noted that the participation agreement has no impact on the rela-tionship between the borrower and the principal lender itself. But it remains to con-sider the nature of the relationship between the lender and the participant. The participation agreement will invariably disclaim any form of fiduciary relationship[34] between those two parties and will state that the relationship between them is merely that of debtor and creditor.[35] Provisions of this kind are probably legally effective, in the sense that there is no declaration of trust in relation to the underlying loan asset and, hence, no transfer of the beneficial interest in the loan to the participant. Nevertheless, the absence of a *fiduciary* relationship[36] does not negate the existence of obligations of a purely *contractual* nature. What is the scope and extent of such obligations?

(e) The participation agreement will generally regulate such matters by means of express terms. But even in the absence of such provisions, it is probably an implied term of the agreement that the principal lender will consult the participant on the action to be taken following a default, and will administer the facility with the same degree of care which it would apply if it had retained the entire exposure for its own benefit and risk. If the participation relates to the entirety of the loan (as opposed merely to a set per-centage), then these implied terms may go even further. Under these circumstances, it may be an implied term that the principal lender will administer the facility in accor-dance with the directions of the participant.[37]

(f) The extent of the principal lender's authority to agree modifications of the loan agree-ment without the consent of the participant will again be regulated by the terms of their agreement. Where the primary lender is entrusted with the 'servicing' of the loan, it is likely that it will have the authority to negotiate commercially reasonable exten-sions or amendments to the facility agreement following a default.[38] But this will plainly depend upon a reading of the participation agreement as a whole.

(g) Having discussed the form and content of the participation agreement, it is now neces-sary to examine some of the competing theories as to the legal nature and effect of these arrangements.

(h) The legal characterization of a participation agreement is a matter of some difficulty, not least because of the terminology which is occasionally employed. For example, it is

---

[33] On credit risk mitigation under Basel II, see paras 6.40–6.49 above.

[34] Compare the discussion of the role of the facility agent in a syndicated loan, at para 21.16 above.

[35] ie as opposed to an agent/principal or a trustee/beneficiary relationship.

[36] It should be emphasized that the absence of a fiduciary relationship reflects the writer's views in this area, but North American case law challenges these views. On the competing theories, see subparas (h) and (i) below.

[37] In each of these cases, it is suggested that the implied terms would meet the 'business efficacy' or 'officious bystander' test which are so often quoted as the touchstone for implied contractual terms.

[38] *Carondelet Savings & Loan Association v Citizens Savings & Loan Association* 604 F.2d 464 (7th Cir, 1979). This case also proceeds on the (apparently unchallenged) assumption that the primary lender owes fiduciary duties to the participant. It is unlikely that this aspect of the decision would be followed in England—see the decision of the Privy Council discussed at subpara (f) below.

common to speak of the 'sale' and 'purchase' of a loan participation, even though the actual structure is that of a limited recourse deposit. So what is the true nature of the relationship? Is it that of seller/buyer, or creditor and limited recourse debtor? North American decisions have tended to find that a participation agreement constitutes an (uncompleted) assignment, so that a trustee/beneficiary relationship is created between the primary lender and the participant.[39] This analysis has a superficial attraction, in that the participant may regard itself as having acquired an interest in the loan. The result would be that, in the event of the insolvency of the primary lender, its administrator or liquidator would receive payments pursuant to the underlying loan on trust for the participant, who would then be entitled to the those monies in preference to the general body of unsecured creditors of the primary lender.[40] This approach to the matter is supported by the decision in *Savings Bank of Rockland v FDIC*,[41] where the court held that a loan participation creates an 'ownership interest' in the underlying loan for the participant. This was based on the 'sale and purchase' language employed by the parties and on considerations of equity, which implied that the 'purchasing' participant should receive the proceeds of the underlying loan, in preference to the unsecured creditors of the primary lender.[42] On the other hand, US authority in favour of the 'creditor-limited recourse debtor' approach is rather sparse.[43] Yet it is submitted that the sale and purchase/trust analysis will frequently be unsatisfactory. As noted above, the participation agreement will specifically state that the participant does not acquire a proprietary interest in the loan, and that no fiduciary relationship comes into being. The sale/trust approach therefore necessarily involves the court in disregarding the express terms of an agreement which will usually have been negotiated between commercial parties of equal bargaining strength. Furthermore, as noted earlier, a participation agreement will frequently be used precisely because an outright sale and purchase (or assignment) of the loan is not possible. The sale and purchase/trust characterization, whilst superficially attractive, will thus often involve an approach which is at odds with the parties' original intentions, and there is no obvious policy reason for re-characterizing such a transaction in order to give the participant a preference in the primary lender's insolvency—to the detriment of the general body of unsecured creditors.

(i) The analysis in the preceding paragraph attempted to support the 'debtor-creditor' approach by reference to the express terms of the contractual relationship between the participant and the primary lender, and the potential consequences of the primary lender's insolvency. But the choice of the correct analysis also has other consequences.

---

[39] *Re Canadian Commercial Bank (No 2)* [1986] 5 WWR 531. See also *Re Canadian Commercial Bank (No 3)* (1987) 46 DLR (4th) 518.

[40] For US cases which have relied on the sale/trust analysis, see *Seattle First National Bank v FDIC* 619 F Supp 1351 (1985) and *Women's Federal Savings & Loan Association v Nevada National Bank* 811 F 2d 1255 (9th Cir, 1987). Other cases have used a combination of assignment/agency arguments to reach a similar conclusion: see *Franklin v Commissioner of Internal Revenue* 683 F 2d 125 (5th Cir, 1982) and other materials cited by Mugasha, para 6.15.

[41] 668 F Supp 799 (SDNY), noted by Mugasha, para 6.16.

[42] If the participant does acquire a beneficial interest in the proceeds of repayment of the underlying loan, then the trust would presumably likewise extend to the benefit of any security held by the primary lender.

[43] See *Re Woodson Co, Fireman's Fund Insurance v Grover* 813 F 2d 266 (9th Cir, 1987), discussed by Mugasha, para 6.22.

For example, if the primary lender remains the true owner of the entire loan,[44] then it can exercise set-off rights against any deposits it holds from the borrower, up to the full, face amount of the loan. But the bank cannot set off its deposit liability against an asset which it no longer owns. Thus, on the 'debtor-creditor' approach, the bank can exercise set-off rights up to the full amount of the loan but, on the 'sale and purchase/trust' approach, the primary bank can only set off against deposits up to the limit of its retained portion of the loan.[45] In particular, if the borrower has gone into liquidation, then the mutuality which is an essential feature of set-off would be lacking, because the deposit would be owing by the bank in its own right, whilst the relevant portion of the loan would be owing to it in its capacity as a trustee for the participant, with the result that set-off would not be permitted to that extent.[46]

(j)   In order to preserve the confidentiality of the participation arrangements, the agreement will often provide that the participant may not make contact with, or take any proceedings against, the primary borrower. Once again, it appears that such provisions should be binding as between the lender and the participant. Yet it is necessary to note the decision of the US Court of Appeals for the Second Circuit in *Commercial Bank of Kuwait v Rafidain Bank and Central Bank of Iraq*.[47] In that case, lending banks had entered into facility agreements with Rafidain Bank and had subsequently laid off portions of the risk to other banks (including the Commercial Bank of Kuwait) via participation agreements. The Commercial Bank of Kuwait then sought to sue Rafidain for non-payment, even though there was no privity of contract between them and Rafidain had not even been aware of the involvement of that particular institution. The facility and participation agreements were expressed to be governed by English law. The court held that (i) the lead banks entered into the facility agreements as agent for the intending participants and (ii) under English law, an undisclosed principal has the right to sue on the main contract.[48] It is submitted that the first proposition is highly questionable since, apart from other considerations, this approach will frequently involve both an unjustified re-characterization of the arrangements and the disregard of express contractual terms agreed between the parties.[49] In this particular case, the lead banks appear to have entered into the facility agreement some weeks before the participation agreement was signed. The lead banks will have received fees and other remuneration commensurate with the size of the facility and its resultant risks; they will have entered into those arrangements as principal vis-à-vis Rafidain. The subcontracting of part of the risk via the participation agreement will not have been intended to create a

---

[44]   ie as will be the case under the 'debtor-creditor' analysis, but not if the 'sale and purchase/trust' analysis is applied.

[45]   In either case, the proceeds of the set-off would be treated as a payment or recovery in respect of the loan, and the primary lender would usually be obliged to share the benefit of that payment with the participant under the terms of the agreement.

[46]   On set-off in the course of a liquidation and the requirement for the respective debts to arise from mutual dealings, see Insolvency Rules 1986, r 4.90. For a different view to that which appears in the text, see Mugasha, para 6.44.

[47]   15 F 3d 238 (2nd Cir, 1994).

[48]   The court relied on the decisions in *Tehran-Europe Co v ST Belton (Tractors) Ltd* [1968] 2 QB 545 and *Moto Vespa SA v MAT (Britannia Express) Ltd* [1979] 1 Lloyds Rep 175.

[49]   Compare the discussion in subpara (d) above.

principal-agent relationship between the principal lender and the participant. Although the decision was purportedly based on English law as the governing law of the agreement at issue, it must be unlikely that the English courts would adopt an equivalent analysis;

(k) It is submitted that *so far as English law* is concerned, the correct approach[50] to all these matters is illustrated by the decision of the Privy Council in *Lloyds TSB Bank plc v Clarke (Liquidator of Socimer International Bank Ltd) and Chase Manhattan Bank Luxembourg SA*.[51] In that case—which arrived at the Privy Council from the Court of Appeal of the Bahamas—Socimer International Bank had granted a participation in various instruments derived from a bond issue. Socimer received payments which were referable to those bonds but went into liquidation before making the corresponding payments to its participant. The Privy Council held that the participant had acquired no beneficial interest in the underlying debt and thus ranked as an unsecured creditor in the liquidation of Socimer. Whilst it was true that the characterization and effect of an arrangement was a matter of law and not merely a question of the 'label' employed by the parties,[52] the agreement was nevertheless clear in terms of the nature of the relationship which the parties had intended to create. Clause 2 of the agreement contained the standard provision to the effect that '… the relationship between the [primary lender] and the [participant] shall be a debtor-creditor relationship. The [participant] shall have no rights of ownership in the Notes. Nor will the [primary lender] act as agent or trustee for the [participant] …'. As the Privy Council pointed out,[53] a bank can share the risk on a particular transaction in a variety of ways. Some methods may involve the transfer of ownership, whilst some do not. It is thus necessary to refer to the document itself to ascertain the parties' intentions in this regard, and clause 2 could not have been clearer. It is true that the judgment is also influenced by the fact that the primary lender was contractually obliged to pay to the participant an amount 'equal to' amounts received from the borrower, and this suggested that the payment to be made by the primary lender was *calculated by reference to* the sums received from the borrower. The primary lender was thus not required to *account* for monies received, which might have suggested a trustee or agency relationship. But the independence of the loan and the participation arrangements is further emphasized by

---

[50] It may be appropriate to emphasize at this point that the correct approach will always depend to a large extent on the precise terms of the documentation agreed between the parties. The present discussion assumes that the agreements are in a relatively standard format. It must also be said that the forms of agreement in common use in the United States, whilst disclaiming any relationship of trust or agency, do categorize the parties' relationship as that of *seller and buyer* and state that the buyer is to acquire an 'undivided interest' in the loan. The result seems to be that the two lending institutions become tenants in common with respect to the loan. See generally Mugasha, ch 6.

[51] [2002] 2 All ER (Comm) 992. Although the point does not appear to have been central to the decision, it should be noted that the advice of the Privy Council in this case was cited with evident approval in *Altman v Australia and New Zealand Banking Group Ltd* [2002] EWHC 2488 (Comm). It is also approved by McKnight, para 12.8.4.

[52] Compare the issues which arose in relation to the characterization of fixed and floating charges over book debts in *Agnew v IRC* [2001] 2 AC 714 (PC) and *Re Spectrum Plus Ltd* [2005] 2 AC 680 (HL), discussed at para 30.04 below.

[53] See paras 21–23 of the decision.

the fact that the two items will be maintained on separate accounts, and the deposit is never in fact applied against the loan even in the event of a payment default by the borrower.[54] Finally, the Privy Council held that there was nothing inequitable in requiring the participant to rank *pari passu* with the general body of unsecured creditors because, under the terms of the agreement, the participant had not acquired any proprietary rights and the underlying loan was not the specific source of repayment. In other words, the structure demonstrated that the participant had agreed to take not only the credit risk of the underlying borrower, but that of the primary lender as well.

22.23   It will be apparent from the above discussion that the legal nature of funded participation agreements has attracted significant judicial attention in the United States and Canada, but there appears to be limited relevant case law which has arisen from English proceedings. Nevertheless, and for the reasons given above, it is suggested that the English courts should adopt a fundamentally different approach. The decision of the Privy Council in the *Socimer International Bank*[55] case demonstrates the correct approach to these arrangements.

Risk Participations

22.24   A risk participation agreement[56] also involves a laying off of credit risk, but the means by which it is achieved are rather different.

22.25   In essence, a risk participation agreement amounts to a guarantee of the borrower's obligations in favour of the lending bank. Consequently, the risk participant will receive a guarantee fee in return for that arrangement.[57] The following points may be noted:

(a)   since the participant does not place any deposits with the primary lender, this structure can be used regardless of the authorized status of the lender.[58] All payments made by the participant will be outright payments made in response to a demand under the guarantee contained in the participation agreement;

(b)   if the lender subsequently makes recoveries in respect of the relevant amounts paid by the risk participant, then it must make the corresponding refunds;

(c)   in contrast to the position in the *Rafidain Bank* case,[59] it cannot be argued that the lender is acting as agent for the participant in entering into the facility agreement, since the participant is not providing any funds, either directly or indirectly, to the ultimate borrower. It is merely giving a guarantee to the main lender;

---

[54]   See the discussion at para 22.22(b) above.

[55]   See para 22.22(f) above. It must be said, however, that the extensive North American case law does not seem to have been drawn to the Privy Council's attention in this case.

[56]   For a specimen of such an agreement, see the precedents available on the website of the Loan Market Association.

[57]   This will usually be a portion of the margin charged on the loan. The lender's obligation to pay this fee will usually be limited recourse, in the sense that it will only be payable out of interest payments actually received from the borrower.

[58]   Contrast the 'deposit-taking' issue which arises in the context of a funded participation agreement: see para 22.22(a) above.

[59]   See the discussion at para 22.22(k) above.

(d) since the arrangement constitutes a guarantee,[60] it will be necessary for the agreement to comply with the provisions of section 4 of the Statute of Frauds 1677;[61]

(e) although the risk participant is effectively in the position of a guarantor, it cannot claim a right of subrogation so as to take proceedings directly against the borrower or to enforce security held by the primary lender. This follows from the fact that the guarantee has been issued at the request of the lender, rather than that of the borrower;[62] and

(f) in calculating its risk-weighted assets for capital adequacy purposes, the lender may take account of the credit rating of the risk participant, rather than the borrower itself.[63]

Credit Default Swaps

Credit default swaps are a relatively recent innovation in the financial markets. They are **22.26** documented on the basis of standard form materials produced by the International Swaps and Derivatives Association. They are, in economic terms, similar to a risk participation agreement, under which the primary lender retains the ownership of the loan asset and the cash flow arising from it, but foregoes a part of the income in return for an underwriting of part of the risk.[64] There is a difference, however, in that a risk participation agreement is invariably linked to a facility which the primary lender currently holds on its books. In contrast, a credit default swap may be used as a purely speculative instrument.[65]

The essential features of a credit default swap include the following: **22.27**

(a) The agreement will identify one or more 'reference entities' to which the swap relates.[66] The reference entities are those borrowers or issuers whose performance is guaranteed by the writer of the swap (the 'protection seller') in favour of the holder or prospective holder of the assets to be guaranteed.

(b) The protection seller will obviously receive a premium in return for the cover, which may be payable as a 'one-off' sum at the outset of the transaction or may be payable periodically throughout the life of the cover.

(c) The cover will be triggered when the reference entity concerned goes into a contractually specified default. These will usually include a payment default, the commencement of a general debt restructuring or the initiation of insolvency proceedings.

---

[60] There seems to be no basis on which a risk participation could be re-characterized as something other than a guarantee. Contrast the discussion at para 22.22(h) above, in the context of funded participations.

[61] On these provisions, see para 26.19 below.

[62] The right of subrogation is an equitable remedy which depends on a request made by the borrower itself: see *Owen v Tate* [1976] 1 QB 402.

[63] On this subject, see paras 6.40–6.49 above.

[64] On credit default swaps generally, see McKnight, para 11.2.6.

[65] On some of the consequences of this factor, see para 22.28 below. The use of these instruments for speculative purposes does not render them void as a gaming or wagering contract: see FSMA, s 335.

[66] Again, in contrast to a risk participation agreement which will relate to a single borrower and a single transaction, a credit default swap will often cover the obligations of a portfolio of debtor entities.

(d) At this point, the protection buyer will usually be entitled to serve a notice and demand payment of the stated sum from the protection seller, against the tender of 'deliverable obligations'. The deliverable obligations will usually include bonds, loans, or other debt instruments issued or guaranteed by the reference entity. The contractual definition of 'deliverable obligations' will usually be fairly generic, on the basis that the protection buyer does not wish to commit himself to holding any particular obligations of the reference entity for the entire duration of the swap. Indeed, as noted above, he may not hold any such obligations as at the date of the execution of the credit default swap. Of course, generic definitions have their dangers, in that it will always be necessary to decide whether specific securities satisfy the relevant characteristics. For example, and for obvious reasons, the agreement will usually specify that the reference entity's obligations in respect of the relevant instrument must be 'not contingent', in the sense that the obligation to pay must be ascertained, unconditional, and not subject to any condition precedent. Expressions of this type must be interpreted with a commercial mindset and in the light of the objectives of the agreement. Thus, in the case of bonds exchangeable into shares of the issuer where the conversion option was exercisable at the option of the holder, the instrument constituted a 'deliverable obligation' because the protection sellers' title to payment could only be defeated by its own decision to exercise the option. The payment obligation was thus not 'contingent' in any meaningful respect, and the protection seller was thus obliged to accept the tender of those bonds under the swap.[67]

(e) If a specified default occurs in relation to the reference entity, then the protection buyer who acted on a speculative basis will have to enter the market to acquire securities or loans of that entity, so that it may present them to the protection seller and derive the profit represented by the excess of (i) the principal amount of such securities as payable under the credit default swap and (ii) the market cost of the relevant assets. In the case of a very serious default, the market value of obligations of the reference entity will obviously be depressed. Nevertheless, one of the ironies created by the use of credit default swaps is that their value may actually increase in this situation, because the occurrence of the default creates a demand for such instruments from protection buyers.

(f) As an alternative, the agreement may provide for payment of a cash settlement sum, without any need for delivery of any relevant debt obligations. The settlement sum will generally represent the difference between the principal amount of the reference obligations and their ascertained market value.

22.28 The market in credit default swaps or derivatives received something of a negative press during the 2008 financial crisis, with some parties alleging that the weight of such transactions exacerbated the prevailing difficulties. A discussion of issues of this kind obviously lies beyond the scope of this work.

---

[67] See *Nomura International plc v Credit Suisse First Boston International* [2002] EWHC 160 (Comm).

23

SWAPS AND DERIVATIVES

Introduction

The present chapter considers swaps and derivatives, and the principal focus will be on **23.01** interest rate and currency swaps.[1] These are but two types of a much wider product range within the derivatives market.[2] But other forms of derivatives tend to be encountered in rather more specialized contexts, whilst interest rate and currency swaps may be used by the full range of commercial customers for purposes closely allied with their core businesses.

By way of examples: **23.02**

(a) A company which purchases an office block is likely to know the level of contractually committed rental receipts over the next few years and, hence, will know the affordable interest rate. But most loans bear interest at a floating rate, and increases in that rate over the lifetime of the loan will defeat the borrower's carefully laid plans. In order to protect itself against that eventuality, the company will enter into a swap which ensures that its interest payment obligations are fixed at an acceptable level throughout the period of the loan facility.

(b) A UK company may have a long term export contract with a US buyer, and the buyer insists that the price is to be denominated in US dollars. The UK company obviously meets its expenses in sterling and, in order to ensure that its sterling income is not diminished as a result of the possible depreciation of the US dollar over the life of the contract, it enters into a long term swap contract to exchange the US dollars for sterling at a pre-determined and fixed rate.

---

[1] The whole subject is one of some complexity and the volume of case law in the area continues to increase. The present discussion is intentionally brief.

[2] The expression 'derivatives' is used because the products are 'derived' from an underlying instrument, index, market rate, or transaction.

23.03   These are cases in which the swap contract is genuinely designed to hedge against changes in interest rates or in the value of other assets. Contracts of this kind may, however, be entered into for purely the purposes of speculation on the relevant markets. They may therefore be used as an instrument designed to realize a profit in its own right, as well as for hedging or 'insurance' purposes.

23.04   Finally, it may be added that most derivatives transactions are entered into bilaterally, either between financial institutions or between a financial institution and its customer. The result is that the respective parties are free to negotiate the detailed terms of the transaction, but they are also taking a performance risk on each other. This is referred to as the 'over the counter' or 'OTC' market. Transactions may also be effected through an exchange. In such cases, the contract must be one of the standard products traded through the relevant exchange, with the result that the only element of the deal which is open for negotiation is the pricing itself. On the other hand, contracts effected through an exchange are guaranteed by the relevant clearing house, with the result that counterparty risk is very significantly reduced.[3] The present chapter is accordingly concerned exclusively with OTC contracts, partly because they are more likely to give rise to problems in practice and partly because they are more relevant in a specifically banking context.

23.05   It should be noted that most swap transactions are agreed on the basis of standard form documentation prepared and periodically updated by the International Swaps and Derivatives Association (ISDA).[4] These documents contain significant detail on calculations, default, termination, and a series of other matters. However, the present chapter is confined to a discussion of general and selected principles.

23.06   Against this brief background, it is proposed to consider the following matters:

(a) interest rate swaps;
(b) currency swaps;
(c) default and termination;
(d) the netting of multiple contracts on default; and
(e) certain defences available to a swap counterparty on the basis of its contractual capacity.[5]

Interest Rate Swaps

23.07   An interest rate swap transforms a floating rate interest obligation into a fixed rate obligation (or vice versa, according to the requirements of the buyer).

23.08   Thus, in the example of the property company given above, the company may be obliged to borrow the necessary loan for (say) a five year period at a rate referable to the London

---

[3] On this subject, see McKnight, para 11.3.
[4] For information, see the Association's website at www.isda.org.
[5] It should be said that a wider range of defences may be available, eg on the basis that the product was 'mis-sold' by the financial institution. However, since these defences may extend to other sophisticated structures and are not limited to swaps, they will be considered in Chapter 25 below.

interbank offered rate (LIBOR). That rate may obviously vary very significantly over a five year period. In contrast, the rental income may remain fixed for the corresponding period.[6] The level of the rental cash flows means that a fixed interest cost of five per cent will be sustainable, but any increase in LIBOR above that level is likely to result in an inability to service the interest payments and, hence, a default.

In order to protect itself against that eventuality, the borrower enters into a swap agreement with a bank under which: **23.09**

(a) the bank pays floating rate interest to the borrower, calculated by reference to the principal amount of the loan and payable on dates corresponding to the relevant interest due dates under the borrower's facility agreement; and

(b) the borrower pays to the bank fixed rate interest at five per cent per annum on the same payment dates.

It will usually be the case that a single, net payment will be made by the relevant party, according to which party is in debit on each payment date. But the result will be that the borrower's interest cost will be fixed at five per cent for the entire life of the facility; any excess over the five per cent level will be covered by the corresponding payments received from the bank under the swap. **23.10**

The advantages of such an arrangement for the borrower are obvious. Yet there may also be drawbacks. For example: **23.11**

(a) If the property is sold during the five year period of the loan and swap, there will generally be no unilateral right for the borrower to terminate the swap agreement. The swap will thus remain in effect for its original tenor and the borrower will therefore either have to continue the payments under the swap or it will have to negotiate a settlement figure with the bank to close out (or terminate) the swap on an agreed basis.

(b) If the borrower defaults under the swap,[7] then its counterparty will have the right to terminate the swap agreement and to claim compensation for its losses. The ISDA documentation contains various options for the calculation of these amounts but, in essence, the counterparty is entitled to recover the cost of procuring an equivalent contract for the remaining period of the swap. If rates have moved against the borrower (ie because LIBOR has moved significantly below five per cent), then the premium payable by the counterparty to secure such a contract may be very significant. In such a case, the existence of the swap may create additional difficulties for the borrower, in that it will be in default under both the loan agreement and the swap at the same time.

It is implicit in the above discussion that long term loans are made on floating rate terms, largely because interbank funding tends to be available only on a short term basis. A borrower who is fortunate enough to be able to secure fixed rate funding should not, however, **23.12**

---

[6] Even if there are rent reviews, these will only take place occasionally and, in any event, they will reflect the market value of the lease, rather than variations in LIBOR.

[7] This may occur if, for example, a major office tenant defaults on its own lease, so that the cash flows necessary to service the swap are not available to the borrower.

thereby assume that he is entirely free of the disadvantages associated with an interest rate swap, since a commercial borrower may be taken to be aware that the bank itself may have to enter into hedging arrangements in order to provide such a loan in the first instance. Thus, if a fixed rate loan agreement requires the borrower to indemnify the lender against '... all costs, charges and expenses ...' associated with an early prepayment of the loan, the lender may argue that it is entitled to be reimbursed the cost of unwinding the corresponding swap arrangement. Such an argument did, however, fail in *Bank of Scotland v Dunedin Property Investment Co Ltd*,[8] largely on the basis that the bank had entered into the swap for its own protection without discussing its proposed terms with the borrower. A lender who wishes to enter into such arrangements and to recover any unwinding costs from the borrower will accordingly need to make that position very clear to the borrower and ensure that the loan agreement includes plain wording to that effect.[9]

Currency Swaps

23.13   A currency swap works on essentially the same principles and will usually be contracted on the basis of similar documentation. In the example of the UK exporter given above, the buyer of the swap would agree to pay over to its bank the fixed US dollar amounts expected to be received from the US buyer in return for pounds sterling at the pre-agreed rate. Of course, the obligation to pay the US dollar amounts will be a primary obligation of the UK customer, and it may thus be placed in difficulty if the US buyer defaults on the timely payment of the dollar instalments.

23.14   The general comments made above in relation to the commercial consequences of default and termination of interest rate swaps will apply equally in the context of currency swaps.[10] In essence, the commercial user is left with two problems. Not only does he have to deal with the buyer's default, he also has to find the necessary cash flow in the relevant currency in order to service his own obligations under the currency swap.

Default and Termination

23.15   Reference has already been made to some of the practical problems which may arise when a swap contract is terminated. It is now proposed briefly to consider the circumstances under which this may occur and the consequences which may ensue.

---

[8] [1999] SLT 470.

[9] It should be appreciated that this question turned on the interpretation of the contract. No question of foreseeability of the loss or the rule in *Hadley v Baxendale* (1854) 9 Exch 341 arose, since the borrower was contractually entitled to prepay the loan. Hence, in the absence of a breach of contract, no question of damages arose.

[10] As mentioned above, the present discussion has been confined to interest rate and currency swaps, largely because these are most likely to be encountered by the ordinary, non-specialist commercial customer. But it should be appreciated that hedging transactions may be used in a much wider variety of commercial transactions—eg in relation to the price of oil, electricity, gas, and other commodities. For an example, see *Enron Australia Finance Pty Ltd v TXU Electricity Ltd* [2003] NSWSC 1169 (New South Wales Supreme Court), noted by McKnight, para 11.2.3.

As noted earlier, currency and interest rate swaps are almost invariably recorded by means **23.16** of standard documentation produced by ISDA. A typical suite of documentation will include the following:

(a) an ISDA Master Agreement.[11] This document contains a broad and standard framework under which the parties may from time to time enter into individual transactions;

(b) a Schedule to the Master Agreement. This document tailors some of the general, Master Agreement terms to the specific situation of the parties (eg by stating whether particular defaults occur only if they relate to the particular contractual counterparty, or whether they will also be triggered if the relevant adverse event occurs in relation to an affiliate of that party, whether the occurrence of monetary defaults on other transactions is subject to minimum financial thresholds, and similar matters);

(c) a Trade Confirmation. This will set out the financial terms of a particular transaction (eg the notional principal amount by reference to which the parties obligations are to be computed, which party is to pay the fixed/floating rate, the duration of the swap, and other matters); and

(d) Credit Support Documents. These documents will create security over any collateral which either party is required to provide if he is 'out of the money' on the outstanding contracts made under these arrangements.[12]

Of course, as with any other transaction, there will be no special difficulty so long as both **23.17** parties are solvent and complying with their obligations.[13] But the real problems can arise when a party is unable to pay or cannot provide any necessary collateral under the credit support documents.

Against that background, the essential features of the ISDA Master Agreement which may **23.18** give rise to default or termination include the following:

(a) first of all, each party is contractually obliged to make the payments ascribed to it under the trade confirmation for any transaction, provided that the other party is not in default and no early termination of the transaction has been designated.[14] Where a series of cross-payments are to be made on the same day, these may be made on a 'net' basis;[15]

---

[11] The present chapter refers to the 2002 version of the Master Agreement.
[12] ie he would be liable to make a payment to the other party under the provisions described below if all of the contracts were terminated.
[13] Naturally, there may occasionally be disputes as to the meaning and effect of those obligations but, as will be seen, most of the litigation inevitably flows from the (alleged) occurrence of a default on the side of one of the parties.
[14] See section 2(a) of the ISDA Master Agreement. On the application of this provision where one of the parties has become insolvent, see *Enron Australia Finance Pty Ltd (in liquidation) v Yallourn Energy Pty Ltd* [2005] NSWSC 316 (New South Wales Supreme Court). For a discussion of some of the difficulties posed by this provision, see Daley, 'Defining the limits of section 2(a)(iii)' (2009) 11 JIBFL 647.
[15] ISDA Master Agreement, section 2(c). Thus, in the case of an interest rate swap, the party owing the higher amount on the relevant day will simply pay the excess amount, and the party owing the lesser amount will pay nothing.

(b) the parties make a series of representations to each other (eg as to corporate status, power to enter into swap transactions, absence of material litigation, and various other matters) which may be repeated periodically throughout the life of a transaction and which may accordingly trigger a default if they prove to be untrue at any relevant time;[16]

(c) the parties undertake with each other to provide certain information required under the terms of the ISDA schedule and confirmation,[17] to maintain official authorizations necessary for the swap and to comply with any laws applicable to its performance;[18]

(d) having created the framework for the parties' essential contractual obligations under swap transactions, the ISDA Master Agreement then proceeds to set out the circumstances under which a default may occur in relation to one of the parties. The listed defaults include (i) non-payment under a swap, (ii) breach of other obligations or repudiation of the swap, (iii) cross-default under other contracts, and (iv) the instigation of insolvency proceedings;[19]

(e) in addition to default provisions, the Master Agreement also prescribes a series of 'termination events' which are generally not the fault of either party and which therefore attract a different treatment. These include illegality and *force majeure* events which may prevent payments from being made under the swap, and tax changes which may have implications for the cash flows under the swap and oblige one party to make 'grossing up' payments;[20]

(f) as might be expected, the occurrence of an event of default or a termination event entitles the other party to terminate outstanding transactions, although the details of the right and its consequences may differ according to the particular nature of the event at issue;[21]

(g) in the event of default or termination, the obligations of the parties to make further, scheduled payments in respect of outstanding transactions will come to an end.[22] In the case of an event of default affecting one of the parties, the innocent party can determine the 'close out amount' which effectively represents the current value of the outstanding transactions in the market or the cost of acquiring replacement arrangements for the remaining period of the swap. Those transactions are then finally settled by means of a single payment of the close out amount.[23] The ISDA Master Agreement specifically provides that the calculation of the close out figure is intended to amount to proper compensation and is not intended to operate as a penalty, and the courts have recently held that these arrangements are indeed valid and enforceable and are not

---

[16] See section 3 of the ISDA Master Agreement. On representations of this kind in the context of loan agreements, see the discussion at para 20.33 above.

[17] This will frequently include audited accounts and other periodic financial information.

[18] See ISDA Master Agreement, section 4.

[19] See ISDA Master Agreement, section 5(a). On defaults of this kind, see para 20.38(f) above.

[20] See ISDA Master Agreement, section 5(b). On tax provisions of this kind, see the discussion at para 20.29 above.

[21] See section 6(a) (events of default) and section 6(b) (termination events) of the ISDA Master Agreement.

[22] ISDA Master Agreement, section 6(c).

[23] Multiple contracts are thus 'netted' for these purposes. On this process, see paras 23.20–23.22 below.

affected by the rules against penalties.[24] However, as a safeguard, the ISDA Master Agreement requires the party calculating the close-out amount to act in good faith, and it will not meet this requirement if it seeks to influence the judgments of the market participants which it approaches for the purpose of obtaining the necessary price quotations,[25] and some care may be required if the terminating party is to place any reliance on its own, internal dealers as part of the process for obtaining the required quotations.[26] Nevertheless, if the relevant party acts in good faith in obtaining the necessary quotations, the court is likely to uphold the resultant calculation unless the counterparty can demonstrate that the figure is plainly misconceived.[27]

Based on the above discussion, it seems that the contractual provisions of the ISDA Master **23.19** Agreement allowing a party to terminate and close-out contracts following the occurrence of a default or termination event will be valid and binding, at least provided that the occurrence of the relevant event can be proved and the party arranging the necessary close-out calculation acts in good faith. This nevertheless leaves open the possibility that a party may purport to exercise termination rights when they are not in fact available to it, either because the relevant events do not fall squarely within the scope of the provision on which reliance is placed, a relevant grace period has not fully expired, or for some other reason. So far as English law is concerned, the giving of an ineffective termination notice should not of itself involve a liability in damages on the part of that party.[28] However, in a case involving equity margin contracts, an Australian court has held a counterparty liable in damages for exercising termination rights when the necessary formalities required as a condition precedent had not been fully observed.[29] In that case, the right to damages perhaps flows from the fact that, following wrongful termination, the counterparty also took steps to liquidate the collateral which had been provided to it.

Netting of Multiple Contracts

It is common for counterparties to enter into numerous swap transactions with each other **23.20** pursuant to a single ISDA Master Agreement, and to work on the basis that their exposure to the other party is effectively a single, net figure. Is that a justifiable approach, having regard to the possibility of the insolvency of the counterparty?

---

[24] See ISDA Master Agreement, section 6(e)(v) and the decision in *BNP Paribas v Wockhardt EU Operations (Suisse) AG* [2009] All ER (D) 76 (Dec). This decision seems to be appropriate given that the close-out amounts are intended to represent the cost of obtaining a substitute and equivalent contract in the market for the remaining period of the original swap transaction: see the definition of 'close-out amount' in section 14 of the ISDA Master Agreement.

[25] *High Risk Opportunities HUB Fund Ltd v Credit Lyonnais*, New York Supreme Court, 7 July 2005, a case arising from the collapse of the Russian rouble in 1998.

[26] *Socimer International Bank Ltd v Standard Bank of London Ltd* [2008] EWCA Civ 116.

[27] It is suggested that this is the inference to be drawn from the decision in *Flame SA v Primera Maritime (Hellas) Ltd* [2009] EWHC 1973 (Comm); see in particular the remarks at para 40 of the judgment.

[28] See the House of Lords decision in *Concord Trust*, considered at para 20.38(j) above.

[29] *Morgan and others v BNP Paribas Equities (Australia) Ltd* [2006] NSWCA 197 (New South Wales Court of Appeal).

23.21   One of the key tenets of UK insolvency law is that the available assets of the entity should be distributed among creditors on a *pari passu* basis. It is true that rights of set-off (ie effectively, the right for debtors to settle on a 'net' basis in a liquidation) were created by rule 4.90 of the Insolvency Rules 1986,[30] but it was not clear whether the set-off could be extended to cover amounts owing as a result of one party's unilateral calculation of the value (or cost) of the contract. If this type of provision produced a more favourable treatment for a particular creditor, then it would be unenforceable on public policy grounds.[31] However, as noted in a different context,[32] rule 4.90 of the Insolvency Rules 1986 allows for the set-off of an amount representing a proper valuation of a contingent claim, and the close-out netting provisions simply provide a convenient means by which that amount can be calculated. In any event, netting arrangements which subsist within the context of a 'financial collateral arrangement' are now afforded special statutory protection.[33]

23.22   In addition, arrangements designed to deprive a company of the benefit of assets in the event of its insolvency may likewise be contrary to public policy on the basis that this, too, will deprive the creditors of assets which would otherwise be available to them and, hence, disrupt the application of the *pari passu* principle. However, whilst the termination provisions do indeed deprive the insolvent party of the benefit of the contract for the future, the asset is appropriately valued at the point of insolvency and, in any event, the provision could operate to the detriment of either party. For those reasons, termination and close-out provisions should not be susceptible to challenge on this public policy ground.[34] This view has been reinforced by the recent decision of the Court of Appeal in *Perpetual Trustee Co Ltd v BNY Corporate Services Ltd*,[35] where the court was invited to apply this 'anti-deprivation' rule in the context of complex, structured collateralized debt obligations. The rule has nineteenth century origins and the court clearly felt it inappropriate to be applying an open-textured principle of this kind when the Insolvency Act 1986 contains a comprehensive framework for those transactions which are to be vulnerable in the event of insolvency.[36] The approach adopted by the court tends to reinforce the view that the anti-deprivation rule will not be applied to financial market products of the type now under discussion.

Defences

23.23   Some of the difficulties which may arise when taking guarantees from local authorities will be noted at a later stage.[37] However, swap contracts have given rise to particular difficulty

---

[30]   On r 4.90, see para 36.07 below.
[31]   ie by virtue of the decision in *British Eagle International Airlines Ltd v Compagnie Nationale Air France* [1975] WLR 758 (HL), which holds arrangements to be unenforceable to the extent to which they would conflict with the mandatory rules for the distribution of assets on insolvency.
[32]   See the discussion of r 4.90 at para 36.07 below.
[33]   On this subject, see Chapter 35 below.
[34]   *Money Markets International Stockbrokers Ltd v London Stock Exchange Ltd* [2002] 1 WLR 1150. For more detailed discussion of the public policy issues, see McKnight, para 11.12.1.
[35]   Court of Appeal, 6 November 2009.
[36]   The relevant provisions are discussed in Chapter 39 below.
[37]   See para 26.54 below.

where the counterparty is such an authority, and it is therefore proposed briefly to consider that subject in the present context.

The main and best known decision is that of the House of Lords in *Hazell v Hammersmith* **23.24** *and Fulham LBC*,[38] where the council had entered into a large number of swap contracts with a notional principal amount of some £600 million. The district auditor contended that the swaps were beyond the powers of the council and, hence, void. The swap counterparties relied on section 111(1) of the Local Government Act 1972, which provides that '… a local authority shall have power to do anything (whether or not involving the expenditure, borrowing or lending of money or the acquisition or disposal of any property or rights) which is calculated to facilitate, or is conducive or incidental to, the discharge of any of their functions …'. Unsurprisingly, the 1972 Act makes no explicit mention of swap contracts, since they only really came into vogue in the 1980s. Consequently, it was necessary to rely on an 'ancillary' or 'incidental' powers provision of the type just reproduced.

The House of Lords rejected the argument that the swap transactions fell within the scope **23.25** of section 111(1). Although local authorities had power to borrow money and, hence, could do anything designed to facilitate that objective, the execution of swap contracts did not fall within the section. Apart from other considerations, swaps were often entered into separately and independently from the council's borrowing agreements. The swap contracts could therefore not be justified because councils were required to adhere strictly to the functions conferred on them by Schedule 13 to the 1972 Act. Speculative transactions fell beyond the scope of those powers and could not be supported as 'incidental' to the council's activities merely because they might prove to be profitable.

The swap counterparties did, however, later receive some consolation in that the House of **23.26** Lords held that they could recover from the local authorities the value of payments made to them under the void contracts. This was so even though the payments had been made on the basis of an error of law (ie on the mistaken assumption that the swap contracts were valid effective).[39] Consequently, a local authority which received benefits under such a contract was required to disgorge those funds to its swap counterparty.

It hardly needs to be stated that the litigation described above achieved a relatively high **23.27** profile in financial circles at the time, since banks suffered significant losses on transactions which they had perhaps assumed to represent 'quasi-sovereign' risk. The litigation also served to sharpen market awareness of 'legal risk' as an important part of the credit assessment process.

---

[38] [1992] 2 AC 1 (HL).

[39] On this point, see *Kleinwort Benson Ltd v Lincoln City Council* [1999] 2 AC 349 (HL). This overturned an earlier, longstanding rule that payments could only be recovered if made under a mistake of fact (as opposed to a mistake of law). For subsequent litigation on the right of restitution holding that the right subsists in common law and is not based on an implied trust or other form of fiduciary obligation, see *Westdeutsche Landesbank Girozentrale v Islington LBC* [1996] AC 669 and, for a further decision to similar effect, see *Guinness Mahon & Co Ltd v Kensington and Chelsea RBC* [1998] 2 All ER 272. Insofar as the *Westdeutsche* case holds that the claimant can only recover simple (as opposed to compound) interest, this is no longer good law: see *Sempra Metals Ltd v Her Majesty's Commissioners of Inland Revenue* [2007] UKHL 34 (HL).

23.28   Yet, regardless of lessons which may be thought to have been learnt, problem areas do have a habit of recurring. In the present context, this is exemplified by the recent decision in *Haugesund Kommune v Depfa ACS Bank*,[40] which relates to swap transactions executed by a local authority in Norway. The case involved contracts concluded on the standard ISDA documentation, but the net commercial effect was that the local authority received an upfront payment in return for a later, larger payment. Effectively, the upfront payment represented the net present value of franchise payments which the authority expected to receive in relation to power generation.[41] Since the case involved a foreign authority, questions touching its powers and contractual capacity plainly had to be determined by reference to Norwegian (rather than English) law. The Norwegian legislation which regulated local authorities of this kind allowed them to raise loans only for restricted purposes and, if the swap arrangement constituted a 'loan', it would be beyond the powers of the authority in the instant case.[42] On the basis that a 'loan' connotes the right to borrow or use money in consideration of an obligation to return it at a later date, the court found that the swap agreement clearly constituted a 'loan' for these purposes.[43] It necessarily followed that the swaps were beyond the capacity of the authority and were accordingly void. Nevertheless, as the court pointed out, this was something of a Pyrrhic victory since the bank was entitled to restitution of the sums paid to the authority at an earlier stage.[44]

Conclusions

23.29   The above discussion has considered the nature of swap transactions and the types of issues which may require review following the occurrence of a default. It has also highlighted the need for care in selecting counterparties, since swap transactions may not be within the powers of certain types of entity. It may be that further case law in this area will become available as a result of the current turmoil in the financial markets.

---

[40] [2009] All ER (D) 34 (Sep).

[41] The transaction was referred to as a 'zero coupon swap'.

[42] It may be added that, as a necessary consequence, the question whether the transaction constituted a 'loan' for these purposes would also fall to be determined by reference to Norwegian law. However, it was accepted that the analysis would in any event be the same under both systems of law: see para 69 of the judgment.

[43] See para 72 of the judgment.

[44] See para 82 of the judgment. In another case, a German counterparty to a swap transaction also sought to rely on an ultra vires point and argued, accordingly, that it would be more appropriate for the proceedings to be heard in Germany. Although the particular point at issue would depend on German law, the fundamental question was whether the English law swap agreement was valid and enforceable against that party, and the court accordingly dismissed the preliminary jurisdictional objection: see *JP Morgan Chase Bank NA v Berliner Verkehrsbetriebe Anstalt des Öffentlichen Rechts* [2009] EWHC 1627 (Comm).

24

BANK GUARANTEES, PERFORMANCE BONDS, AND DOCUMENTARY CREDITS

Introduction

Much of the preceding material in this book has been concerned with the relationship between the bank and its customer. In broad terms these materials have considered the purely *bilateral* obligations which arise from the lending of money and the provision of security. **24.01**

In contrast, the present section considers transactions of a *trilateral* nature where the bank, acting at the request of its customer, issues a guarantee or assumes a similar obligation to a third party. Although conveniently described as a trilateral relationship, these **24.02** arrangements do in fact create a series of separate contracts between the various parties, and a proper analysis thus requires a careful distinction between each of those contracts.[1]

24.03 For convenience, the present chapter is arranged as follows:

(a) bank guarantees;
(b) performance bonds;
(c) documentary credits;
(d) security under a commercial credit;
(e) standby credits;
(f) the fraud exception; and
(g) certain private international law issues.

Bank Guarantees

24.04 A bank guarantee is no more than a guarantee issued by a bank to a third party in respect of an obligation owed by the bank's customer to that third party. It should, however, be noted that a bank guarantee is normally issued to cover a *fixed* or *liquidated* obligation of the customer—for example, in respect of a loan made by the third party to the customer. This serves to distinguish a bank guarantee from a performance bond, which is issued to secure the performance of a *non-monetary* obligation of the customer.[2]

24.05 Since the document issued by the bank constitutes a guarantee, it will follow that many of the points discussed later in the context of guarantees generally will be equally applicable in the present context.[3] For present purposes, it is thus only necessary to explain those areas in which the general rules applicable to guarantees will not apply or will be varied for some reason. The following points may be briefly noted in this context:

(a) First of all, as a matter of practice, a bank guarantee must always be carefully limited both in terms of the maximum amount which may be demanded under the guarantee and the date on which the guarantee is to expire.[4] These limitations are important as a matter of prudence but clarity in this area is also necessary in the light of the issuing bank's capital adequacy requirements.[5] The bank must be clear about the amount of its

---

[1] It should be noted that, in some cases, further parties may become involved, eg the confirming bank in the case of a letter of credit.

[2] On this aspect of performance bonds, see para 24.07 below. Whilst a performance bond will obviously involve the payment of money by the issuing bank, this will constitute liquidated damages, rather than the payment of a pre-existing debt of the customer.

[3] On guarantees generally, see Chapter 26 below.

[4] It may be noted in passing that the beneficiary of the guarantee must strictly comply with any time limit which is imposed. The court has no power to grant an extension or otherwise to assist the beneficiary who is a day (or even just a few minutes) overdue in making his demand: see *Lorne Stewart plc v Hermes Kreditversicherung AG* [2001] All ER (D) 286. It may be added that bank guarantees and similar documents will frequently contain a provision requiring the beneficiary to return the guarantee on expiry. This is perhaps a matter of good housekeeping, but the beneficiary's failure to return the document clearly has no impact on the extent of the bank's obligations under the guarantee.

[5] On this subject, see Chapter 6 above.

exposure and the date on which it may be removed from the capital adequacy calculation.

(b) Since the bank will usually determine or negotiate the precise form of the guarantee, there will usually be no scope to challenge the terms of the guarantee on the basis that they are unfair, because the bank will not be dealing on the standard terms of the beneficiary of the guarantee.[6]

(c) The issue of guarantees by banks is a part of their normal business and (it is hardly necessary to add) a fee will be charged to the customer for the issue of such a document. In view of these considerations, a third party who accepts such a guarantee will usually be under no duty to enquire into the bank's reasons for issuing the guarantee, nor will it usually be on notice of any possible breach of duty by the bank's directors in authorizing the issue of such a guarantee. In other words, the third party can effectively accept a bank guarantee at face value.[7]

(d) It will not usually be necessary for the third party to require the production of a board resolution or similar corporate documents to evidence the due execution of the guarantee on behalf of the bank. In larger transactions, a bank may make available a list of authorized signatories, with specimen signatures and the limits of their authority. Provided that the execution of the guarantee conforms to the signatory list, the issuing bank will be estopped from asserting a want of internal authority or other defect in the execution of the document.[8] The execution of bank guarantees for smaller amounts may fall within the scope of the apparent authority of a branch manager or similar official.

(e) The bank guarantee will usually stipulate that the bank must make payment against receipt of a proper demand from the beneficiary. The bank will thus usually be unable to refuse to meet a demand unless there is strong evidence for believing that the demand is fraudulent.[9]

(f) When the bank has made payment under the guarantee, it will be subrogated to the third party's claim against the customer. In practice, however, the bank will require an express form of counter-indemnity from the customer, confirming the obligation of reimbursement and waiving any defences to which the customer might otherwise be entitled.

As a final point, it may be noted that some banks prefer to employ the mechanism of a standby letter of credit when asked to cover an obligation of a customer. This practice started with US-based banks, which were subject to regulatory constraints in the issue of guarantees. There is, however, a certain convenience to the practice and it has been more **24.06**

---

[6] On this subject, see the discussion of the Unfair Contract Terms Act 1977 in its application to guarantees, at paras 26.38–26.43 below.

[7] This may be contrasted with the 'commercial benefit' issues which may arise where guarantees are given in other contexts: see paras 26.49–26.53 below.

[8] In large or unusual transactions, however, it may be incumbent on the beneficiary to ensure that the guarantee has been approved at an appropriate senior level since it may be difficult to establish that particular officials had the necessary apparent authority for that purpose: see the situation which arose in *Sea Emerald SA v Prominvestbank* [2008] All ER (D) 75.

[9] In this sense, a bank guarantee may be similar to a performance bond or a documentary letter of credit: on this point and the autonomy principle generally, see para 24.24 below.

widely adopted, especially in the context of cross-border transactions.[10] The whole subject is considered later in this section.[11]

Performance Bonds

Introduction

24.07   As noted above, a performance bond—alternatively labelled a 'demand guarantee'—will usually be issued in respect of a non-monetary obligation of the customer.[12] The 'performance' to which the document refers will frequently be the performance of a construction contract of some kind—often a major project such as a power station or an hotel. If the customer fails to complete the construction work—for example, because of its own insolvency—then delays will occur and the beneficiary will be put to the expense of finding another contractor to complete the project. A demand under the performance bond will assist the beneficiary in meeting the additional costs which will inevitably be involved in such a process.

Nature of a Performance Bond

24.08   Performance bonds/demand guarantees are sometimes issued subject to the terms of the Uniform Rules for Demand Guarantees (URDG).[13]

24.09   Article 2 of the URDG provides a definition of a 'demand guarantee' which includes the following criteria:

(a) the expression includes any guarantee, bond, or other payment undertaking given by a bank in writing to a beneficiary;
(b) the undertaking must involve an obligation on the part of the issuer to pay to the beneficiary a specified sum of money against presentation of conforming documents (such as an architect's certificate or an arbitration award);

---

[10]   In particular, a bank guarantee remains a secondary obligation which is dependent upon the validity of the primary obligation. Whilst defences of this kind can be waived by the express terms of the guarantee, a standby letter of credit constitutes a primary obligation of the issuer and is thus not subject to technical defences of this kind. A standby letter of credit is thus a simpler document and is in many respects a straightforward undertaking to pay on demand.

[11]   On standby letters of credit, see paras 24.56–24.60 below.

[12]   For discussion of the various forms of performance bond, see para 24.10 below.

[13]   The Uniform Rules on Demand Guarantees, ICC Publication No 458 (October 1992). As pointed out in Jack, para 12.90, the URDG does not seem to have won general acceptance (although they were adopted by the World Bank and were endorsed by the United Nations Commission on International Trade Law (UNCITRAL)) and, as a result, they have not been the subject of any significant judicial analysis. References to the UDRG may be found in *Wahda Bank v Arab Bank plc* [1996] 1 Lloyds Rep 470 and *Uzinterimpex v Standard Bank plc* [2008] 2 Lloyds Rep 456. The URDG have recently been revised and the new text comes into force on 1 July 2010 (the new publication is URDG 758). Amongst other things, the new version is designed to clarify the nature of a compliant presentation. It may be hoped that the new text will become more established.

(c) the undertaking must be given at the request and under the liability of a party (who will usually be the contractor in a construction context) or by a bank acting on behalf of that party.[14]

In spite of the use of expressions such as 'performance bond' and 'demand guarantee', it **24.10** should be appreciated that the issuing bank is not really guaranteeing performance by the contractor at all, at least in the strictest sense of that term. It merely undertakes to make available to the beneficiary a stipulated sum on demand. As a result, a demand guarantee is not a 'guarantee' in the sense of a secondary obligation, with all of the weaknesses which that status implies.[15] Rather, it is a primary obligation to make payment to the beneficiary against a proper demand. It is a self-standing contract which is independent of the underlying construction contract to which it relates, and is thus to be treated as separate from it. This is the so-called 'autonomy principle' which runs through the law relating to documentary credits and is also considered at a later stage.[16] Nevertheless, some of the issues relevant to the principle in the context of performance bonds may be noted at this stage:

(a) In order for the autonomy principle to apply to a particular instrument, it must be clear that the instrument concerned was intended to constitute a performance bond or demand guarantee of the type now under discussion—ie that it is payable on demand or against the production of the specified documentation, without reference to the underlying commercial contract or the extent of any breach which may have occurred. This point is obvious but it necessarily raises a question of characterization, which must be determined by reference to the commercial intention of the parties as derived from the terms of the document itself. If an instrument issued by a bank relating to an underlying contract requires payment to be made on demand by the beneficiary, then the document is likely to be a bond/guarantee for these purposes. This conclusion will be reinforced if the obvious commercial purpose of the instrument is to provide the beneficiary with a set sum of money immediately upon the occurrence of a default by a contractor.[17] It has been suggested by one of the leading writers that a first demand guarantee/performance bond would not usually contain all of the protective clauses

---

[14] The second part of the formulation covers cross-border contracts, where the contractor in the United Kingdom asks his London bank to issue the bond, but the employer will only accept an obligation of a bank in its home country. In such a case, the latter bank issues the required performance bond against a counter-indemnity from the London bank, which in turn takes a counter-indemnity from the contactor/customer. This chain of obligations is similar to that which arises in the context of a confirmed letter of credit: see para 24.19(e) below.

[15] On this subject, see the discussion at para 26.72 below in relation to the various defences available to a guarantor.

[16] See para 24.24 below. In the context of demand guarantees, the application of the autonomy principle is confirmed by article 2(B) of URDG, which states that '… Guarantees by their nature are separate transactions from the contract(s) or tender conditions on which they may be based, and the Guarantors are in no way concerned with or bound by such contract(s) or tender conditions, despite the inclusion of a reference to them in the Guarantee. The duty of the Guarantor under a Guarantee is to pay the sum or sums therein stated on the presentation of a written demand for payment and other documents specified in the Guarantee which appear on their face to be in accordance with the terms of the Guarantee'. For a case dealing with the autonomy principle in the specific context of performance bonds, see *TTI Team Telecom International Ltd v Hutchison 3G UK Ltd* [2003] 1 All ER (Comm) 914.

[17] Paget, para 34.4; *Siporex Trade SA v Banque Indosuez* [1986] 2 Lloyds Rep 146.

which are usually found in a guarantee,[18] but it is submitted that this indicator is only of limited value. Standard protective provisions of this kind are frequently inserted out of pure (or excessive) caution, and should not necessarily be seen as a reliable guide as to the characterization of the instrument which the parties had in mind.[19]

(b) The correct characterization of a document will of course depend principally upon the intentions of the parties as drawn from the language which they have employed. Thus, if the parties have specifically referred to the document as a 'performance bond', and there is an engagement to pay up to a set sum on demand against the occurrence of stated circumstances, then the bond will usually be payable against a demand which certifies that the relevant circumstances have indeed occurred. This approach is consistent with the autonomy principle, ie that the issuing bank should not be concerned with the underlying contractual relationship between the customer and the beneficiary and any dispute which may have arisen in relation to it. Instruments of this kind are often described as 'on demand bonds' and are payable against written demand and production of any supporting documentation required under the terms of the bond itself, without reference to the underlying commercial contract or any circumstances affecting it.[20]

(c) But not every bond is intended to be of the 'on demand' variety. Some bonds will be intended to be guarantees, in the sense that they are a secondary obligation which cannot be entirely divorced from the underlying commercial contract to which it relates. The distinction between the two types of instrument has occasionally given rise to some difficulty, not least in the context of the conditions which must be met for a valid demand, when it must be paid and precisely how much is payable. This may follow from the fact that these instruments do not necessarily follow a standard form, and they are often carefully negotiated because the contractor is aware of the highly damaging consequences of a demand. The resultant compromise is not always consistent with a desire for clarity. A leading example of the confusion which may arise is offered by the House of Lords decision in *Trafalgar House Ltd v General Surety Co Ltd*,[21] which considered a form of bond in common use in the construction industry. The House of Lords held that the wording of the document amounted to a guarantee of the contractor's obligation to pay damages, but did not amount to a bond which was payable simply against a demand for its face amount (ie it was not an 'on demand' bond). Following earlier decisions,[22] the House held that the document amounted merely to

---

[18] Paget, para 34.4(iv). This argument has some attraction because, as noted earlier, demand guarantees/performance bonds are intended to be primary (as opposed to secondary) obligations, and the protective clauses should therefore be unnecessary in this context.

[19] See, for example, *Gold Coast Ltd v Caja de Ahorros del Mediterraneo* [2003] 1 All ER (Comm) 142; *Frank Maas (UK) Ltd v Habib Bank AG Zurich* [2001] Lloyds Rep Bank 496.

[20] For examples of wording which has been held to create an 'on demand' bond (as opposed to a secondary guarantee), see *Esal Commodities Ltd v Oriental Credit Ltd* [1985] 2 Lloyds Rep 546, *Siporex Trade SA v Banque Indosuez* [1986] 2 Lloyds Rep 146; *IE Contractors Ltd v Lloyds Bank plc* [1990] 2 Lloyds Rep 496 and *Gold Coast Ltd v Caja de Ahorros del Mediterraneo* [2003] 1 All ER (Comm) 142. These cases are considered by Jack, paras 12.56–12.60.

[21] [1996] AC 199 (HL).

[22] See, in particular, *Workington Harbour & Dock Board v Trade Indemnity Co Ltd (No 1)* [1937] AC 1 (HL) and *Workington Harbour & Dock Board v Trade Indemnity Co Ltd* (No 2) [1938] 2 All ER 101 (HL).

a guarantee of the contractor's duty to pay damages on a failure to perform the contract. The result was that the beneficiary of the bond had to prove his loss, and the guarantor was liable only to the same extent as the contractor itself. Consequently, the issuer of the bond could avail itself of any defences or counterclaims available to the contractor itself. Indeed, the secondary nature of the bond means that the issuer can also invoke any of the general defences available to a guarantor,[23] and it may accordingly claim to have been fully discharged from the bond if the primary contract has been varied to its disadvantage and without its consent. These problems are well illustrated by the decision in *Marubeni Hong Kong and South China Ltd v Government of Mongolia*,[24] where the central bank of Mongolia undertook to pay any amounts '… if not paid [by the buyer] when the same shall become due …'. This language suggested a secondary guarantee, rather than an on demand bond. Since the instalment payments had been rescheduled without the consent of the central bank, the Court of Appeal held that the guarantor had been discharged from its guarantee. This position will not invariably be helpful to the beneficiary of the bond because, quite apart from the scope for disputes over both the liability of the contractor and the quantum of the claim, the beneficiary does not have access to an immediate cash sum to enable him to complete the project. It will also be necessary for him to ensure that the issuer of the bond is kept advised of variations or other matters affecting the principal contract. These are plainly matters of significant inconvenience but, nevertheless, the *Government of Mongolia* decision plainly illustrates the importance of the correct characterization of the instrument at hand. The solution, of course, lies in the wording of the document itself. If the instrument is intended to be an 'on demand' bond, then it should be made clear that payment is due solely against the beneficiary's demand and confirmation that a default has occurred under the primary contract.[25]

(d) In practice, it will always be desirable to make it clear whether the beneficiary must produce objective evidence of the breach giving rise to the demand (eg an architect's certificate) or whether it is sufficient merely for the beneficiary itself to certify that a breach has occurred.[26] If no objective evidence of the breach is required, then it is perhaps likely that the court will construe the bond/guarantee as requiring an explicit statement by the beneficiary to the effect that a default has occurred.[27] Where the URDG applies, the demand must include particulars of the relevant breach of the underlying contract.[28] This may operate as a restraint against doubtful claims, since a

---

[23] On these defences, see para 26.72 below.

[24] [2005] EWCA Civ 395.

[25] A beneficiary may also be well advised to ensure that the words 'On Demand Bond' appear in the heading to the instrument.

[26] For a case of this kind, see *Esal (Commodities) Ltd and Reltor Ltd v Oriental Credit and Wells Fargo Bank Ltd* [1985] 2 Lloyds Rep 546 (CA). The point is of particular importance to the issuing bank; if it pays out against an invalid demand, then it will not usually be entitled to an indemnity from its customer.

[27] See Paget, para 34.5, noting *Esal Commodities* (above) *and IE Contractors Ltd v Lloyds Bank plc and Rafidain Bank* [1990] 2 Lloyds Rep 496. For a case in which the written demand was held to be inadequate because a breach of the underlying commercial contract was not specifically asserted, see *Frank Maas (UK) Ltd v Habib Bank AG Zurich* [2001] Lloyds Rep Bank 496.

[28] This rule appears to apply even if the bond itself is otherwise silent on the point.

false representation to obtain payment will involve the commission of a criminal offence in England.[29]

(e) In one of the leading cases on the subject, the Court of Appeal has held that an on demand performance bond is effectively equivalent to a promissory note payable on demand.[30] It is submitted that this is an appropriate analogy, because the issuer is obliged to pay solely against a compliant demand.[31] In the absence of cogent evidence of fraud,[32] the issuer is not concerned with any dispute relating to the underlying transaction, and is not entitled to delay payment merely because it has been notified of such a dispute.

(f) As in the case of a bank guarantee, the issuing bank will seek a counter-indemnity from its customer to cover any payments made under the bond.[33] It should, however, be appreciated that the payment made under the bond is intended to provide security to the beneficiary for any losses and expenses which it may incur as a result of the contractor's default. The payment is not intended to constitute a payment of liquidated damages in respect of the breach.[34] Consequently, if the amount of the bond is insufficient to compensate the employer for his actual loss, then he will be entitled to recover the excess from the contractor. Equally, if the amount paid under the bond exceeds the employer's losses, then the contractor can likewise recover the balance.[35] The autonomy principle applies, in the sense that payment must be made against a compliant demand, but this does not affect the right of the contracting parties to a later adjustment when the actual loss suffered by the employer has been quantified.

(g) Where documentation is required to be produced in support of a claim, it seems that the issuing bank must examine the documents with reasonable care to ensure that the documentation conforms to the requirements of the instrument.[36]

(h) The form of wording required to be used in any demand under the bond requires careful consideration. In one case, for example, the beneficiary was entitled to certify that a breach of the underlying contract had occurred and that '… accordingly the claimant is entitled to receive payment …'. It was held that this merely meant that the beneficiary was entitled to payment under the bond. The wording did not connote any assurance that the loss suffered by the beneficiary was in fact equal to the amount of the demand.[37]

---

[29] See Fraud Act 2006, s 2.

[30] *Edward Owen Engineering Ltd v Barclays Bank International Ltd* [1978] QB 976 (CA).

[31] See URDG, article 2(B), reproduced in n 16 above.

[32] On the consequences of a potentially fraudulent demand under any form of documentary credit, see paras 24.61–24.68 below.

[33] On this point, see para 24.05(f) above.

[34] This must necessarily be so, for the bond will usually cover the entire period of the contract and may cover virtually any breach of which the contractor may be guilty. The actual loss suffered by the employer would depend upon a variety of circumstances, including the stage of the contract at which the breach occurs.

[35] On these points, see *Comdel Commodities Ltd v Siporex Trade SA* [1997] 1 Lloyds Rep 424 (CA); *Cargill International SA v Bangladesh Sugar and Food Industries Corp* [1998] 2 All ER 406.

[36] The standard of care should be similar to that which applies in the context of letters of credit: see paras 24.30–24.40 below. On the point made in the text, see the discussion in Paget, para 34.6.

[37] See *Enka Insaat Ve Sanayi AS v Banca Popolare dell'Alto Adige SpA* [2009] All ER (D) 61 (Oct).

Types of Performance Bond

Having considered the legal nature and characteristics of a performance bond, it may be **24.11** helpful briefly to outline some of the commercial circumstances in which bonds of this type may be used.

It has already been noted that bonds may be issued to guarantee performance by a contrac- **24.12** tor of its obligations under a construction contract. But the use of bonds is not confined to that particular type of situation. For example:

(a) A buyer of goods may require his seller to issue a bond to guarantee the performance of the contract—for example, to provide a source of compensation in the event that the goods are not delivered or are substandard in terms of the contract specification.[38]

(b) A bid bond may be required when a major contract is put out for tender. The bond is in effect a form of 'earnest' to demonstrate that the party lodging the tender is serious about winning the contract. The bid bond will usually be callable if (i) having won the tender, the contractor fails to enter into the full contract documentation within a set time limit following the award or (ii) the contractor fails to deliver the full performance bond required in respect of the contract itself.

(c) Occasionally, it may be agreed that a buyer or developer will make an up front payment to his seller or contractor to assist in funding the initial stages of the contract, and to provide a degree of security to the payee. But the buyer or developer is obviously taking a risk in letting go of his money in advance of any counter-performance. He may there-fore require an advance payment bond to guarantee the repayment of that money in the event of non-performance by the seller or contractor.[39]

(d) Construction contracts will often provide for the retention of a proportion of stage payments to be made to the contractor, largely to provide a measure of security to the developer pending final completion of the contract. The developer may allow the release of these retentions against the provision of a retention money bond by the contractor's bank.

Documentary Credits

Introduction

The expression 'commercial credit' will be used to describe a documentary credit, or letter **24.13** of credit, which is intended to assure to the seller the payment of the purchase price of goods despatched to a buyer. This expression is adopted to distinguish a 'standby credit', which, in contrast, is usually issued to guarantee payment of a contractual payment obligation owing by the customer.[40]

---

[38] For an example of this type of arrangement, see *RD Harbottle (Mercantile) Ltd v National Westminster Bank Ltd* [1978] QB 146.

[39] For examples of this kind of bond, see Jack, para 12.50, citing *Howe Richardson Scale Ltd v Polimex-Cekop* [1978] 1 Lloyds Rep 161, *Gulf Bank KSC v Mitsubishi Heavy Industries Ltd (No 2)* [1994] 2 Lloyds rep 145 and *Uzinterimpex JSC v Standard Bank plc* [2008] 2 Lloyds Rep 456.

[40] On standby credits, see paras 24.56–24.60 below.

24.14 Before moving into the details, however, it may be helpful to provide a practical illustration of the use and purposes of a letter of credit. Suppose that a New Zealand seller has negotiated a sale of goods to an English buyer. The goods have to be despatched by sea and the New Zealand seller wants to paid as soon as the goods are en route. The seller cannot take the risk that the buyer becomes insolvent, or simply refuses to meet its payment obligations; lengthy legal proceedings against a recalcitrant buyer on the other side of the world will be an unattractive and costly prospect for the seller. On the other hand, the English buyer will not wish to pay in advance, for he, too, will then take the risk that the New Zealand seller becomes insolvent or otherwise simply fails or refuses to despatch the goods. The solution to this conundrum is offered by a letter of credit. It operates as follows:

(a) the English buyer will request its bank in this country to open a letter of credit in favour of the New Zealand seller;

(b) the English buyer will undertake to reimburse his bank for amounts paid out under the credit, and may be required to provide advance cash cover to the bank by way of security for that obligation;

(c) the letter of credit will constitute the undertaking of the English buyer's bank to pay the price of the goods against presentation of the bill of lading and other documents stipulated in the terms of the credit itself;[41] and

(d) the seller will, however, usually require the benefit of a payment obligation from an institution in its own country. In order to meet this requirement, the English bank will request its correspondent bank in New Zealand to add its confirmation. By doing so, the correspondent bank will undertake an obligation to pay the credit against presentation of compliant documents.[42]

24.15 The use of the letter of credit has thus helped to resolve the concerns of both buyer and seller. The buyer knows that payment will only be made once the goods have been shipped, whilst the buyer has an assurance of payment from an independent source. But the use of a documentary credit has the effect of introducing new parties and new contracts into the overall transaction.

Definition

24.16 Commercial credits are invariably governed by the Uniform Customs and Practice for Documentary Credits (UCP), issued by the International Chamber of Commerce. The current version (UCP 600) came into effect on 1 July 2007.[43]

---

[41] On the bank's undertaking, see para 24.17 below.

[42] On the effect of the confirmation and the reimbursement obligation of the issuing bank, see para 24.19(e) below.

[43] It will be necessary to refer to the rules contained in the UCP throughout this section. The rules are intended to provide a uniform, international framework for documentary letters of credit. However, they will have effect in relation to any particular documentary credit only because they are expressly incorporated into the terms of that contract. The interpretation and application of those rules will therefore depend upon the domestic law which governs the point at issue. On the subject of the law applicable to a credit, see paras 24.72–24.87 below.

Article 2 of the UCP defines a 'credit' as '… any arrangement, however named or described, **24.17** that is irrevocable and thereby constitutes a definitive undertaking of the issuing bank to honour a complying presentation …'. The same article provides that a bank's undertaking to 'honour' a complying presentation involves a duty:

a) to pay at sight if the credit is available by sight payment;
b) to incur a deferred payment undertaking and pay at maturity if the credit is available by deferred payment; or
c) to accept a bill of exchange drawn by the beneficiary and pay at maturity, if the credit is available by acceptance.

It will be seen that the specimen transaction described above falls within the scope of **24.18** part (a) of this definition.

Contracts, the Parties, and their Obligations

It will be apparent from the foregoing paragraphs that a commercial credit may involve a **24.19** number of different parties. It is important to understand both the identity and role of each party, and the nature of the contracts by which they will be bound.[44]

(a) *The seller.* The seller is, of course, the party agreeing to supply goods at a particular price, and he will have entered into a contract with the buyer for that purpose. He requires a commercial credit to be opened in his favour in order to assure the prompt and full payment of the purchase price. He is thus also referred to as the 'beneficiary' of the credit. The beneficiary of the credit has no obligations to the issuing or the confirming bank. It merely holds the benefit of a promise to pay, conditionally against presentation of compliant documents.[45]

(b) *The buyer.* The buyer is, of course, the party seeking to purchase goods from the seller. This involves a payment obligation on the buyer's part. In view of the seller's requirement for security of payment, the buyer will have to approach his bank and request it to issue the required commercial credit. For this reason, the buyer is also referred to as the 'applicant' for the credit.[46] He will undertake to the bank to reimburse it for any amounts paid out under the credit. This point is not dealt with in the UCP, but will be covered by a separate contract between the applicant and the issuing bank.

---

[44] For a discussion of some of these relationships in the context of a confirmed letter of credit, see *United City Merchants (Investments) Ltd v Royal Bank of Canada* [1983] 1 AC 168 (HL).

[45] The absence of any positive obligations on the part of the beneficiary has meant that it is difficult to identify any consideration given by the beneficiary. It cannot be said that the delivery of the documents to obtain payment under the credit constitutes consideration. It is true that, whilst the beneficiary must generally provide consideration, there is no requirement that it should move in favour of the issuing bank. The generally accepted view appears to be that letters of credit offer an exception to the usual requirement for contracts to be supported by consideration. This view is derived from *Hamzeh Malas & Sons v British Imex Industries Ltd* [1958] 2 QB 127 and *Discount Records Ltd v Barclays Bank Ltd* [1975] 1 WLR 315. For a discussion of this and other cases, see Jack, paras 5.8–5.16.

[46] It may be noted in passing that the UCP deals with the contractual relationships of many of the parties, but it does not address the relationship between the applicant and the issuing bank. This is accordingly dealt with by the bank's own standard documentation. This will include an undertaking by the applicant to reimburse the bank for payments made by the bank under the credit, and the provision of any cash cover which the bank may require for these purposes.

(c) *The issuing bank.* The issuing bank is the bank which opens the credit at the request of the buyer/applicant, who will almost invariably be an existing customer of the bank. Subject to compliance with the terms of the credit (including submission of any required shipping/insurance/other documentation), the bank undertakes to perform the obligations imposed on it under the terms of the credit.[47] Perhaps with an eye on the difficulties of demonstrating consideration for a credit, it is specifically provided that the issuing bank's obligations become binding as at the time of the issue of the credit, thus seeking to foreclose any argument that the issuing bank can revoke the credit prior to presentation of the documentation.[48] The obligation of the issuing bank is to 'honour' the credit in accordance with the rules described above.

(d) *The advising bank.* The role of the advising bank[49] is to notify the beneficiary that it has received the credit from the issuing bank. The advising bank will usually be a bank within the seller's/beneficiary's country and the main comfort offered to the beneficiary lies in the obligation of the advising bank to take reasonable steps to verify the authenticity of the credit.[50] The advising bank assumes no other responsibility with respect to the credit.

(e) *The confirming bank.* A confirming bank will also likewise usually be based in the seller's country. At the request of the issuing bank, the confirming bank adds its 'confirmation' to the credit, thereby signifying that it accepts responsibility for payment of the credit.[51] The issuing bank is then responsible for the reimbursement of the payment made by the confirming bank.

(f) *The nominated bank.* A nominated bank has authority from the issuing bank to pay, to incur a deferred payment undertaking, to accept drafts or to negotiate the credit.[52]

Types of Commercial Credit

24.20 Having considered the parties involved, it is appropriate to consider the types of commercial credit which may be opened.[53] These fall into four main categories.

---

[47] UCP, article 7.

[48] UCP, article 7(b).

[49] For the details, see UCP, article 9.

[50] For obvious reasons, it is important to the beneficiary that the document should be genuine. If the beneficiary relied on the credit and it later transpired that the advising bank had not taken reasonable steps to verify a credit which subsequently proved to be a forgery, then presumably the advising bank would be liable to the beneficiary in damages for the losses thereby suffered. The point will arise only rarely in practice given that credits are normally transmitted by secure means. In the unlikely event that the advising bank is not satisfied with the authenticity of the credit, then it may either (i) decline to advise the credit at all (in which case it must notify the bank which appears to have issued the credit) or (ii) it may nevertheless advise the credit but inform the beneficiary that it has been unable to verify it.

[51] Under UCP, article 8(b), the confirming bank assumes to the beneficiary obligations which replicate those of the issuing bank. Again, these obligations are effective when the confirmation is notified to the beneficiary. A bank can be a 'confirming bank' for these purposes if it is *authorized* (rather than *directed*) to add its confirmation, and even though it is stipulated that the beneficiary must agree to meet the associated cost: see *Fortis Bank and Stemcor UK Ltd v Indian Overseas Bank* [2009] EWHC 2303 (Comm).

[52] UCP, article 12. A bank which honours or negotiates a compliant presentation is entitled to reimbursement from the issuing bank: see the discussion in the *Stemcor* case (n 51 above), paras 62–64.

[53] It should be noted that any form of documentary credit is irrevocable unless its terms clearly indicate that it is intended to be revocable: UCP, article 6(c). It would hardly be necessary to mention this obvious point but for the fact that earlier versions of the UCP provided for the opposite rule. For obvious reasons, a revocable credit is of little value to the beneficiary; for an illustration of the weaknesses, see *Cape Asbestos Co*

(a) *Sight credits.* This is the simplest form of credit, in that the beneficiary is entitled to payment as soon as the issuing bank (or, if the credit is confirmed, the confirming bank) accepts the documentation presented to it in conformity with the credit. The beneficiary is often required to present a sight draft drawn on the issuing or confirming bank, but this is not accepted in a formal sense and therefore merely serves as a notice of demand.

(b) *Deferred payment credits.* A deferred payment credit entitles the beneficiary to payment a set number of days after compliant documentation has been presented to the issuing or confirming bank. Although no drafts are required to be drawn under a deferred payment credit, the commercial effect of the two types of credit is very similar. Both an accepted bill and a deferred payment obligation on the part of a bank can be discounted, so that the beneficiary receives immediate value. A bank which confirms this type of credit will often discount its own payment obligation in this way, but it should be aware that the scope of its mandate only entitles it to pay at maturity, so that it takes the risk that, during the intervening period, a fraud may come to light and the issuing bank may then refuse to reimburse it. This problem will not arise where the confirming bank has accepted bills in accordance with its mandate, for the bill will be enforceable by a holder who is not party to the fraud.[54] Furthermore, where the credit is governed by UCP 600, this position has effectively been reversed because the issuing bank's obligation to reimburse the confirming bank now applies even though the bank has prepaid or purchased the drafts accepted under the credit.[55]

(c) *Acceptance credits.* An acceptance credit requires the issuing bank to accept a bill of exchange and to pay it on the stipulated future date. As noted earlier,[56] the acceptor of a bill of exchange is primarily responsible for its payment. The drawer of the bill is not—by reason only of drawing the bill—liable to reimburse the acceptor for the amount paid by it under the bill at maturity.[57] In any event, the drawer of the bill will be looking to receive payment for goods sold, so it would plainly be inappropriate for him to have any liability on the bill. As a result, it is specifically confirmed that bills accepted under this type of credit are without recourse to the drawer.[58] It has been pointed out by others that the UCP does not explicitly require the bank to deliver the accepted bill to the beneficiary.[59] Whilst this is true, it is submitted that, at least so far as English law is concerned, the bank is under an obligation to deliver the bill because the contract created by an acceptance is only complete when the accepted bill is delivered to the beneficiary who takes it as a holder.[60] However that may be, no

---

Ltd v Lloyds Bank Ltd [1921] WN 274, discussed by Jack, para 2.7. It was invariable practice to include the word 'irrevocable' in the credit itself, but nevertheless the point created a trap for the unwary. Happily, this issue can no longer arise.

[54] The position is discussed in *Banco Santander SA v Bayfern Ltd* [2000] 1 All ER (Comm) 776. The case is considered by Proctor in 'Confirmed Letters of Credit—A New Twist' (2000) 4 JIBFL 109.

[55] See UCP, article 12(b) and the discussion in Jack, paras 9.46–9.47.

[56] See para 24.16 above.

[57] There is no provision in the Bills of Exchange Act 1882 which imposes such liability on the drawer. Where a bill is used as a means of raising finance (ie as opposed to a means of payment), the facility agreement itself will contain a contractual obligation to that effect, but that is a different type of arrangement.

[58] UCP, article 8(a)(ii).

[59] Paget, para 35.11.

[60] On this point, see Bills of Exchange Act 1882, s 21.

difficulty will usually arise in this regard, because the very objective of this type of credit is to allow the beneficiary to discount the bill with another bank, thus obtaining the present value of the moneys otherwise due to him at a later date.

(d) *Negotiation credits.* Negotiation means the giving of value for drafts or documents by a bank authorized to negotiate.[61] A credit will often allow for any bank in a particular country to negotiate the credit.

Issuing Commercial Credits

24.21 It is generally felt that commercial credits best serve their purpose when they are straight-forward, uncomplicated documents where the conditions to payment are clear and com-prehensible.[62] Instructions for the issue of credits should be complete and precise, and also requires banks to discourage the use of excessive detail.

24.22 Perhaps inevitably, matters are not so straightforward in practice. Given that a commercial credit is designed to secure payment against evidence that the relevant goods exist, are insured, and have been despatched, the credit should be sufficient if it requires presentation of the invoice, an insurance document, and a bill of lading or other transport document. Yet in practice, numerous additional conditions may be stipulated.[63] Where these condi-tions do not stipulate for the production of documents, banks involved in the transaction are required to ignore those conditions.[64] Further, a bank which receives incomplete or unclear instructions to advise or confirm a credit should seek clarification from the issuing bank before it does so.[65] There may, however, be cases in which time is of the essence and, even in the modern era of rapid communication, it will not always be feasible for the advis-ing/confirming bank to seek clarification. In such a case, it is submitted that the issuing bank must take the risks which flow from its own inability to provide clear instructions,[66] and it should thus generally be obliged to reimburse a confirming bank which has acted reasonably in paying out against the documentation presented to it by the beneficiary.[67]

24.23 The requirement for clarity of terminology applies equally where amendments are made to the terms of the credit at a later stage.[68]

---

[61] UCP, article 2.

[62] In terms of process, a credit may be issued by means of a letter or through the secure messaging service provided by SWIFT. Given that the seller of goods will be a commercial organization which will not nor-mally have access to SWIFT, it will usually be necessary for the credit to be advised to the buyer via a bank in his country. A SWIFT message will usually be the operative instrument and can be relied on by advising or confirming banks: see UCP, article 11(a).

[63] On this practice, see the discussion in Paget, para 35.20.

[64] See UCP, article 14(h). The English courts had previously held that a bank was entitled to call for reason-able documentary proof that such a condition had been met: see, for example, *Banque de l'Indochine et de Suez SA v J H Rayner (Mincing Lane) Ltd* [1983] QB 711 (CA).

[65] *European Asian Bank v Punjab and Sind Bank (No 2)* [1983] 1 WLR 642 and the discussion in Jack, paras 4.6–4.8.

[66] In other words, the risks which flow from its own inability to comply with UCP, article 5(a).

[67] Some support for this view may be found in *Credit Agricole Indosuez v Muslim Commercial Bank Ltd* [2000] 1 All ER (Comm) 172 (CA).

[68] On amendments to a credit, see UCP, article 10 and, on some of the anomalies to which this provision may give rise, see Paget, para 35.25.

Application of Autonomy Principle

The autonomy principle has already been discussed in relation to performance bonds.[69] **24.24**
The general principle likewise applies to documentary credits.[70] The point is of such
importance that it receives specific confirmation in articles 4 and 5 of the UCP, which
provide for the following matters:

(a) documentary credits are separate from the sales or other contracts on which they are
based;

(b) issuing banks are in no way concerned with or bound by the terms of such contracts,
even if they are referred to in the credit itself;[71]

(c) the undertaking of the issuing bank to pay, accept drafts, or fulfil any obligation assumed
by it under the credit is not subject to claims or defences by the applicant resulting from
his relationships with the issuing bank itself [72] or with the beneficiary;[73]

(d) the beneficiary can in no case avail himself of the contractual relationships existing between the banks involved in the transaction, or between the applicant and the
issuing bank;[74] and

(e) all parties to a credit deal in documents, and not in the underlying goods, services or
other transactions to which those documents relate.[75] Leaving aside the fraud exception, this provision serves to focus permissible areas of dispute on the documentation
presented under the credit and the extent of compliance with its terms—thus once
again emphasizing the autonomy of the credit itself. Disputes are thus most likely to
arise where (i) the issuing bank refuses payment, on the basis that the documents
presented to it do not conform to the terms of the credit or (ii) payment is made on
the credit but the applicant disputes its obligation to reimburse, on the basis that the
documents did not meet the terms of the credit.[76] This has generated a significant
amount of litigation, which is considered at a later stage.[77]

---

[69] See the discussion at para 24.10 above.

[70] The rationale for the rule has been considered in a number of the cases which have already been noted in this
sphere. From the perspective of the issuing bank, it is clearly unable to get involved in disputes relating to the underlying contract. For the beneficiary, the value of the credit or bond is in some respects lost if payment can be delayed
by reference to a dispute with the buyer/contractor. This leaves the applicant/seller exposed to an inappropriate call
under the credit or bond, but this is a risk which he will be required to take in order to win the contract concerned.

[71] Although article 4 does not explicitly say so, it seems clear that a bank would not be bound by the terms
of the underlying contract even if it had received a copy as part of its internal authorization process. Any other
conclusion would be inconsistent with the autonomy principle. More generally, it is difficult to see why the
rights of the beneficiary under the credit should be in any way modified or affected merely because the applicant had provided a copy of the contract to the issuing bank.

[72] In many respects, this point is obvious. The issuing bank has undertaken specific obligations in favour
of the beneficiary; it cannot detract from those obligations by reference to a contract made between itself and
the applicant, to which the beneficiary will not have been party and which he will not usually have seen.

[73] The inability of the issuing bank (subject only to the fraud exception) to raise defences relating to the
underlying commercial transaction represents the real core of the autonomy principle.

[74] UCP, article 4(a).

[75] UCP, article 5. The requirement that parties deal specifically with the documents stipulated in the credit
itself once again serves to insulate the credit from the underlying transaction.

[76] In other words, the issuing bank has paid the credit in a manner which exceeded the authority conferred
upon it by the applicant.

[77] See paras 24.30–23.40 below. The success of the autonomy principle is perhaps well illustrated by the
fact that most of the case law arising in this sphere has flowed from either (i) the fraud exception or (ii) disputes
over the sufficiency of documents presented under the credit.

24.25 Given that documentary credits are used to facilitate international trade, it is perhaps unsurprising that courts around the world have been conscious of the need to adopt a uniform approach to these instruments. The autonomy principle has thus been recognized in England,[78] in the United States,[79] in Canada,[80] in Australia,[81] and in South Africa.[82]

Transfer and Assignment of Credits

24.26 The beneficiary of a credit, with a view to fulfilling his delivery obligation to his buyer, may wish to effectively 'split' the credit, so that a portion of the price is made available to the end supplier, whilst the profit portion remains available for drawing by the original beneficiary. This is an efficient way to proceed, in that the beneficiary does not have to make separate financing arrangements for the benefit of his end-supplier. Multiple transfers may be permissible if a series of end-suppliers are involved.

24.27 In essence, it will be seen that the first beneficiary of the credit is a 'middleman', taking his profit from identifying a source of supply not known or available to the ultimate buyer. The arrangements are efficient because the single, originating credit provides the source of payment for all of the parties involved in the underlying commercial transaction. But it will be important to the first beneficiary that his original source of supply, the price paid and his profit margin remain confidential.[83] It is therefore an implied term of the contract between the issuing bank and the first beneficiary that the issuing bank will maintain the confidentiality of invoices and other materials identifying the end-supplier. Accordingly, where the issuing bank mistakenly provided copies of the end-supplier's invoices to the applicant for the credit (ie the buyer)—with the result that the buyer cut out the middleman and dealt directly with the end-supplier—the first beneficiary was entitled to damages in respect of the lost profit for the likely remaining period of the business relationship.[84]

24.28 It should be noted that, where the credit is expressed to be 'transferable' for these purposes, this does not create a positive *right* for the first beneficiary to transfer all or part of the credit. It merely allows the beneficiary to *request* such a transfer, and it appears that the issuing

---

[78] There are numerous authorities, but the leading House of Lords decision is *United City Merchants (Investments) Ltd v Royal Bank of Canada* [1983] 1 AC 168.

[79] See the New York decision in *Semetex Corp v UBAF Arab American Bank* (1995) 4 Bank LR 73.

[80] See the decision of the Canadian Supreme Court in *Bank of Nova Scotia v Angelica Whitewear* [1987] SCR 59, noted by Jack at para 1.34.

[81] *Wood Hall Ltd v Pipeline Authority* (1979) 141 CLR 443. However, subsequent decisions such as *Olex Focas Pty Ltd v Skodaexport Co Ltd* [1997] ATPR (Digest) 46–163 and *Boral Formwork v Action Makers* [2003] NSWC 713 have suggested that a court may restrain a demand by the beneficiary if the requirement for payment would be 'unconscionable', and this obviously detracts from the independence of the credit. On this subject, and for helpful comparative reviews, see Dixon, 'As good as cash? The Diminution of the Autonomy Principle' (2004) 32(6) *Australian Business Law Review* 391 and Gao and Buckley, 'A Comparative Analysis of the Standard of Fraud required under the Fraud Rule in Letter of Credit Law', (2003) 13 Duke J of Comp & Int'l Law 293.

[82] *Loomcraft Fabrics v Nedbank Ltd* 1996 (1) SA 812(A).

[83] Where the credit is transferred in this way, the transferee acquires the right to present his invoice and supporting documents to the issuing bank, and to obtain payment direct for his portion of the credit: see UCP, article 38(h).

[84] On this implied term and the calculation of damages, see *Jackson v Royal Bank of Scotland plc* [2005] 1 WLR 377 (HL).

bank has an absolute discretion to decline such a request.[85] In that event, the first benefi-ciary may seek to open a 'back to back' credit in favour of his own end supplier. However, this will obviously involve additional expense and his bank may in any event be unwilling to open such a credit unless it is entirely satisfied that payments under the first credit will be forthcoming when due.[86] Consequently, although a credit may be stated on its face to be transferable, the beneficiary will in practice still need to rely on the flexibility and coop-eration of the issuing bank.

Separately, it is also possible to assign the proceeds of a letter of credit.[87] In contrast to an **24.29** outright transfer, the assignment of a credit relates only to its proceeds.[88] Accordingly, the assignee does not acquire any right himself to draw under the credit. The assignee merely acquires the right to receive payment from the issuing bank when due, and its rights as assignee are therefore subject to any defences to payment (such as set-off, fraud) which the issuing bank could raise against the assignor/beneficiary.[89] It would obviously be advisable for the assignee to give notice to the issuing bank and other parties to the credit (eg the confirming bank), and it is accepted that such a notice may validly be given even though the obligation to make payment under the credit remains wholly contingent until compliant documentation is presented to the issuing bank.[90]

Documents Presented under a Commercial Credit

Introduction

It has been noted previously that, in the context of a commercial credit, the parties deal in **24.30** documents, rather than in goods. This principle denies to the applicant/buyer the right to raise disputes relating to the underlying commercial contract as a defence to a reimburse-ment claim made by the issuing bank. As has been seen, there are sound commercial rea-sons for this rule. It does, however, mean that the applicant must ensure that the terms of the credit offer to him such protection as he is able to secure.[91] In particular, the terms of the credit must be clear as to the nature and content of the documentation which the ben-eficiary must present in order to obtain payment. Equally, the issuing bank must ensure that it pays only against documentation which complies with the terms of the credit, for it can only claim reimbursement from the applicant if it has paid in accordance with its mandate.

---

[85] UCP, article 38(a) and see the situation which arose in *Bank Negara Indonesia 1946 v Lariza (Singapore) Pte Ltd* [1988] 1 AC 583 (PC).

[86] See the discussion in Jack, para 10.7.

[87] This could be done by way of security for some other obligation of the beneficiary of the credit.

[88] On this point, see UCP, article 39. There is no need for the credit expressly to state that the proceeds are capable of assignment.

[89] See, for example, the decision in *Banco Santander v Bayfern Ltd* (noted at para 24.20(b) above) and the discussion in Jack, paras 10.41–10.41.

[90] *Marathon Electrical Manufacturing Corp v Mashreqbank* [1997] 2 BCLC 460.

[91] From the perspective of the buyer, clarity is also important since he is relying on the credit as his source of payment.

24.31 Under these circumstances, it is perhaps unsurprising that—leaving aside the fraud exception[92]—many disputes involving commercial credits revolve around the documents presented in order to obtain payment.

Strict Compliance

24.32 The starting point is that the documents presented by the beneficiary must strictly conform to the terms of the credit. This flows in part from the requirement to deal in documents, and in part from the bank's obligation to act only in accordance with the terms of its mandate or the authority of the applicant. The need for this rule becomes even clearer when one considers the position of a confirming bank, which may have no knowledge at all either of the applicant or of the underlying commercial transaction and the need for a 'mechanistic' approach to the credit becomes more obvious. It is, in any event not open to an issuing or confirming bank to rewrite the authority conferred by the applicant for the credit. The bank has either acted within the scope of its authority, or it has not. As a result, a bank has no discretion to accept documents which might have equivalent effect or appear to do the same job as those stipulated in the credit. The bank has insufficient knowledge of the underlying transaction and is not authorized to make judgments of this kind.[93]

24.33 Whether or not a particular document conforms to the terms of the credit will, of course, depend both upon the terms of the credit itself and the nature of the document purportedly presented in compliance with its terms.[94] Nevertheless, the need for a 'mechanistic' approach to document checking,[95] coupled with the limited time available to the issuing/confirming bank for that purpose,[96] has given rise to a few general principles:

(a) article 13 of the UCP requires the issuing or confirming bank to examine the documents presented to it to ascertain whether they appear *on their face* to comply with the terms of the credit;[97]

---

[92] On this exception, see paras 24.61–24.68 below.

[93] On this subject, see *Equitable Trust Co of New York v Dawson Partners Ltd* (1927) 27 Ll L Rep 49, at p 52; *Banque de l'Indochine et de Suez v JH Rayner (Mincing Lane) Ltd* [1983] 1 QB 711; *Glencore International AG v Bank of China* [1996] 1 Lloyds Rep 135 (CA). For additional cases, see Paget, para 36.1. It should be noted that the doctrine of strict compliance has been developed by the courts, and the expression has not been adopted in the UCP itself.

[94] Thus, if the applicant has specified the content of the required document in detail, then it must be assumed that he had good reason for doing so, and the issuing bank must take care to ensure that the strict requirements are met. It should be appreciated that it is the terms of the credit, rather than the broader commercial background, which is relevant to this exercise since the terms of the credit will generally be the limit of the bank's participation in the transaction. For a case which emphasizes this point and illustrates the court's approach to a 'discrepancy' analysis, see *Fortis Bank SA and Stemcor Ltd v Indian Overseas Bank* [2009] EWHC 2303 (Comm).

[95] This point should not, however, be overstated. It must be borne in mind that a commercial credit is intended to constitute a means of payment, and that standards of documentary compliance are to be governed by international banking practice as reflected in the UCP itself; see the discussion below and the decision in *Glencore International AG v Bank of China* [1996] 1 Lloyds Rep 135 (CA). In other words, the bank must apply judgment and experience in assessing the extent to which the documents comply with the requirements of the credit. See also the materials and commentary noted by Paget, para 36.2.

[96] On the time available to the bank for the purpose of checking documents presented to it, see para 24.45 below.

[97] See also article 2 of the UCP, which states that a 'complying presentation' is to be determined with reference to the UCP itself, the terms of the credit and international standard banking practice. On international standard

(b) if the items of information given in the various documents are found to be in conflict with each other, then this will not amount to a compliant presentation;[98]

(c) the bank is not required to make any judgment as to the value of a particular document or its legal effect, nor is it required to consider whether the applicant should have stipulated for other or further documents;[99]

(d) the UCP places great emphasis on the commercial invoice, transport documents, and insurance documents. As a consequence of the importance placed on these materials, the doctrine of strict compliance should be applied with some rigour, but this may not be the case with other, ancillary documents specified in the credit;[100]

(e) the issuing bank is entitled to reject documents which do not obviously conform to the credit, or where further enquiry would be necessary to confirm the adequacy of the document for the purposes of the credit;[101] and

(f) a bank may nevertheless accept documents which do not strictly conform to the credit but where there is no possible ground on which the discrepancy could be seen as material to the applicant, or where the only discrepancy flows from what is plainly a typing or other error;[102]

(g) as noted above, the bank is merely required to check that the documents *on their face* conform to the terms of the credit. Apart from that specific and limited obligation, the bank accepts no responsibility for the adequacy or effectiveness of the material presented to it under the credit,[103] and they are not obliged to examine the detailed terms and conditions of such documents;[104]

(h) in view of the autonomy of the credit and the need to deal in documents, not goods, the bank should not seek to 'look behind' the documents presented to it or to inquire into any underlying factual issues. The bank's contractual obligation to the beneficiary is to pay against conforming documents, so enquiries of that nature would go beyond the bank's remit.[105] Thus, if a credit provides for payment against documents referring to 'coromandel groundnuts', the bank should not pay against invoices referring to 'machine-shelled groundnut kernels', even though enquiries with those in the trade

---

banking practice, see ICC publication 645, 'International Standard Banking Practice for the Examination of Documents under Documentary Credits'. The precise legal status of this document may not be entirely clear: see Jack, paras 8.11–8.14.

[98] UCP, article 14(d). Thus, for example, the commercial invoice and the bill of lading should refer to goods of the same type and quantity. Note, however, that the contents of any document presented to the bank but not required under the terms of the credit are to be disregarded for these purposes: see UCP, article 14(g).

[99] See *British Imex Industries Ltd v Midland Bank Ltd* [1957] 2 Lloyds Rep 591, *Commercial Banking Co of Sydney Ltd v Jalsard* [1973] AC 279 (HL).

[100] *Kydon Compania Naviera v National Westminster Bank Ltd* [1981] 1 Lloyds Rep 68.

[101] *M Golodetz & Co Inc v Czarnikow-Rionda Co Inc* [1980] 1 WLR 495.

[102] See, for example, *Netherlands Trading Society v Wayne and Haylitt Co* (1952) 6 LDAB 320; *Gian Singh & Co Ltd v Banque de l'Indochine* [1974] 1 WLR 1234 (HL); *Forestal Mimosa Ltd v Oriental Credit Ltd* [1986] 2 All ER 400.

[103] UCP, article 34.

[104] UCP, article 20(a)(v), reflecting the decision in *British Imex Industries Ltd v Midland Bank Ltd* [1958] 1 QB 542.

[105] See *United City Merchants (Investments) Ltd v Royal Bank of Canada* [1983] 1 AC 168 (HL); *Westpac Banking Corp v South Carolina National Bank* [1986] 1 Lloyds Rep 311 (PC).

reveal that these are merely two identical names for the same product; the bank has no authority to pay against those invoices, and should simply reject them as discrepant;[106]

(i) in a similar vein, banks should disregard conditions which relate to factual matters and are not of a documentary character;[107]

(j) if a beneficiary allows that the credit may only be drawn against a document provided by the issuing bank itself confirming compliance with the underlying contract, then this remains a documentary condition and the beneficiary is effectively left to rely on the issuing bank.[108]

Transport Documents

24.34 Articles 19–25 of the UCP deal with various different forms of transport document, including bills of lading, multimodal transport documents and air transport documents. These contain a number of provisions which outline the required terms of such documents and the conditions under which the issuing bank must accept them. It is not proposed to deal with these provisions in depth,[109] but one general point must be noted.

24.35 A transport document presented to obtain payment under a commercial credit must be 'clean', that is to say, it must bear no clause or notation which states that the goods or packaging are defective.[110] A bill of lading which casts doubt on the suitability of perishable goods will not be a 'clean' document for these purposes.[111]

Insurance Documents

24.36 Article 28 of the UCP deals with insurance documents.[112]

Subject to the terms of the credit, insurance documents must have been issued and signed by the insurer and cover must commence no later than the date of loading. Cover must be expressed in the currency of the credit and must be at least equal to 110 per cent of the CIF/CIP value of the goods.[113] The credit should stipulate the risks to be covered but, if it does not, then the bank will accept a policy which relates to the goods and otherwise conforms to the requirements of the UCP. Since a bank deals in documents, it may claim reimbursement from the applicant even though it has accepted a policy which subsequently proves to be forged.[114]

---

[106] *JH Rayner & Co Ltd v Hambros Bank Ltd* [1943] KB 37 (CA).

[107] UCP, article 14(h) and, on this provision, see the decision of the Singapore Court in *Korea Exchange Bank v Standard Chartered Bank* [2006] SLR 565. The case is considered by Jack, para 8.25.

[108] Such a condition cannot be avoided on the basis of UCP, article 14(h): see *Oliver v Dubai Kenya Bank Ltd* [2007] EWHC 2165 (Comm). Plainly, a beneficiary should not accept a credit in these terms. He should ensure that the documents listed in the credit are those which the beneficiary is in a position to obtain.

[109] For discussion of these provisions, see Paget, ch 36.

[110] On this subject, see UCP, article 27.

[111] *Westminster Bank Ltd v Banca Nazionale di Credito* (1928) 31 Ll L Rep 306. See Jack, paras 8.124–8.126.

[112] It should be appreciated that the need for insurance cover should be stipulated in the commercial credit itself.

[113] UCP, article 28(f).

[114] *Gian Singh & Co Ltd v Banque de l'Indochine* [1974] 2 All ER 754.

Commercial Invoices

A commercial invoice presented under the terms of a commercial credit must have been **24.37** issued by the beneficiary and must be addressed to the applicant. If the quantity specified in an invoice exceeds that stated in the credit, then the bank has discretion to accept or reject it.[115]

As noted earlier, the commercial invoice must comply strictly with the terms of the credit **24.38** itself. Given that the commercial invoice is issued by the beneficiary of the credit, one would not have expected this to cause too much difficulty; the beneficiary simply has to copy the relevant terms of the credit onto his invoice. The beneficiary may find itself unable to claim payment if his invoice uses an alternative formulation, even though the different expressions used in the credit and the invoice have an identical meaning in the trade.[116]

Original Documents

In order to obtain payment, the beneficiary must generally present originals of the docu- **24.39** ments stipulated in the credit.

Article 17(b) of the UCP also requires banks to accept a carbon copy, photocopy, or com- **24.40** puter generated copy as an original, '… provided that it is marked as original and, where necessary, appears to be signed …'. It should be appreciated that article 17(b) does not detract from the rule that a bank must accept an original document; it merely extends the range of documents which must be regarded as 'original'. Consequently, where a document is itself the original, then article 17(b) has no application and it is thus unnecessary to mark the document as an 'original' for these purposes.[117]

Presentation and Examination of Documents

Presentation of Documents

In view of the matters discussed earlier in this chapter, it will be obvious that the examina- **24.41** tion of the documentation presented under a commercial credit is a key function.

The beneficiary must present documents for payment at the place stipulated in the credit. **24.42** Banks must accept documents presented to them during banking hours on or before the expiry date of the credit.[118]

---

[115] On these points, see UCP, article 18.

[116] *JH Rayner & Co Ltd v Hambros Bank Ltd* [1943] KB 37 (CA), and other cases noted by Paget, para 36.29.

[117] UCP, article 17(a); *Kredietbank Antwerp v Midland Bank plc* [1999] 1 All ER (Comm) 801 (CA). To this extent, the decision overrules the earlier decision in *Glencore International AG v Bank of China* [1996] 1 Lloyds Rep 135 (CA), which appeared to hold that even an original document itself had to be marked as an 'original' for the purposes of article [20(b)]. The *Kredietbank* decision was followed in *Credit Industriel et Commercial v China Merchants Bank* [2002] 2 All ER (Comm) 427. On the whole subject of original documents, see the ICC's Policy Statement of 12 July 1999, discussed by Paget, para 36.35.

[118] On these points, see UCP, articles 29 and 33.

Examination of Documents

24.43 Banks are required to examine documents presented to them with reasonable care. If the documents appear, on their face, to comply with the terms of the credit, then they must be accepted by the bank as complying with the terms of the credit.[119] The bank's action in accepting those documents cannot subsequently be impugned merely because (i) it transpires that one of the documents presented under the credit was forged[120] or (ii) the bank could have discovered inconsistencies between the various documents presented under the credit by undertaking mathematical calculations.[121]

24.44 If documents are presented which are not required under the terms of the credit, then the bank should decline to examine them and return them to the beneficiary.[122] The consequence must be that the bank is unaffected by the contents of any such document, even though a consideration of it might have affected the bank's decision to accept other documents presented to it under the credit. Conversely, where a credit stipulates a factual condition but does not describe the document required to be presented in order to prove it, then the condition should be disregarded.[123]

24.45 It used to be the case that banks were required to examine documents within a reasonable time, but in any event within seven banking days of their receipt.[124] However, under the current rules, the bank has a maximum period of five banking days to determine whether the presentation is compliant.[125]

24.46 If the issuing bank decides that the documents do not conform to the terms of the credit, then it may approach the applicant for a waiver of any discrepancies.[126]

24.47 Otherwise, the issuing bank must give notice to the beneficiary stating that it has refused the documents and listing all of the discrepancies on which the bank relies for that purpose.[127] The bank must unconditionally reject the documents and state that it holds them at the disposal of, or return them to, the beneficiary. If it fails to reject the documents in accordance with the UCP, then it will be deemed to have accepted them.[128] If documents

---

[119] UCP, article 14(a). This is consistent with the principle that the parties deal in documents, and not in goods.

[120] *Gian Singh & Co Ltd v Banque de l'Indochine* [1974] 2 All ER 754.

[121] *Credit Industriel et Commercial v China Merchants Bank* [2002] 2 All ER (Comm) 427.

[122] UCP, article 14(g).

[123] UCP, article 14(h).

[124] On this formulation and its application to banks in the United Kingdom, see *Bankers Trust Co v State Bank of India* [1991] 2 Lloyds Rep 443.

[125] UCP, article 14(b).

[126] UCP, article 16(b). The issuing bank would presumably only make this approach if it believes the documentation to be substantially (if not strictly) in compliance with the terms of the credit. If the applicant waives the discrepancy, then the bank will be paying within the scope of its mandate and will thus be entitled to reimbursement.

[127] UCP, article 16(c). The notice must be given within five banking days of receiving the documents: UCP, article 16(d).

[128] See, for example, the discussion in Paget, para 37.12. The documents must either be returned to the beneficiary or the notice of rejection must contain an unconditional statement that the documents are held at the beneficiary's disposal. The relevant notice was held to be unconditional in *Rabobank Nederland v Sumitomo Bank Ltd* [1988] 2 Lloyds Rep 250. However, the notice was held to be conditional (and thus defective) in

are rejected by the issuing bank, then it remains open to the beneficiary to re-present the documents prior to the expiry of the credit, if he is able to remedy the discrepancies within the time which remains available to him for that purpose.[129]

A confirming bank may occasionally make payment 'under reserve'. This may be done **24.48** where discrepancies may have been identified and the confirming bank is thus unable to make payment to the beneficiary on an unconditional basis. The payment is thus made on condition that the beneficiary will refund the payment if the issuing bank itself rejects the documentation. Generally speaking, it is the *fact* of rejection by the applicant which will give rise to the obligation to repay the proceeds. Whether the applicant was *justified* in such rejection will usually not be in point for these purposes so that the obligation to refund the proceeds of the credit will arise as soon as the issuing bank notifies the beneficiary of rejection by the applicant.[130]

Security under a Commercial Credit

As noted above, a beneficiary who wishes to obtain payment under a commercial credit will **24.49** need to present to the issuing bank documents of title to the goods for that purpose.

Since the issuing bank receives the documents with the authority of the buyer, the bank has **24.50** a security interest over those documents in the form of a pledge.[131] This form of security will be of importance to the bank if it has not been able to take full cash security as a condition of issuing the credit—for example, where the applicant is a 'middleman' and is purchasing the goods with a view to their immediate resale. He will be reliant on the receipt of the ultimate sale proceeds in order to comply with his reimbursement obligation. How, then, does the pledge operate and what is the extent of the security thereby afforded to the issuing bank in the event of the applicant's insolvency after the credit has been paid but before the resale/reimbursement has been achieved? In the absence of other security, the issuing bank will need to look to the purchased goods or their proceeds of sale. How does its security operate in practice?

Bankers Trust Co v State Bank of India [1991] 2 Lloyds Rep 443 and *Credit Industriel et Commercial v China Merchants Bank* [2002] 2 All ER (Comm) 427.

[129] The issuing bank would not, however, be prevented from raising any further discrepancies in the documents originally presented to it, unless it had by its conduct estopped itself from doing so. On this point, see *Kydon Compania Naviera v National Westminster Bank Ltd* [1981] 1 Lloyds Rep 68, *Floating Dock Ltd v Hong Kong and Shanghai Banking Corporation* [1986] 1 Lloyds Rep 65, and other cases noted by Paget, para 37.18.
[130] On this procedure and the points made in the text, see *Banque de l'Indochine et de Suez SA v JH Rayner (Mincing Lane) Ltd* [1983] QB 711 (CA) and, for further discussion of this case, see Jack, paras 5.81 and 5.85.
[131] See, for example, *Ross T Smyth & Co. Ltd v TD Bailey Son & Co* [1940] 3 All ER 60 and other cases cited by Paget at para 37.20. Although questions of security are addressed more generally in Part (E) below, it was felt more convenient to deal with pledges and trust receipts at this point since they principally arise in the context of commercial credits.

Pledge of Goods

24.51 Under English law, a 'pledge' generally involves the *physical* delivery to, and possession of, the relevant goods by, the pledge. But it has long been recognized that—by way of exception to the general rule—the delivery of a negotiable bill of lading operates as a transfer of property in the goods themselves and thus amounts to constructive possession of the goods in the hands of the recipient.[132] When the bill of lading comes into the possession of the bank, it will therefore obtain a security interest over the goods because that represents the intention of the parties. In practice, of course, this should be specifically confirmed in the contractual documentation. Since it relies on a pledge or possession (rather than a charge), an arrangement of this kind does not require registration under section 860 of the Companies Act 2006.[133]

24.52 When the seller delivers the bill of lading and other documents to the issuing, advising, or confirming bank, title to the goods accordingly passes to the buyer. However, the bank enjoys a possessory title which remains effective until it receives reimbursement in respect of the credit.[134] If the goods are delivered to a warehouse, the issuing bank should procure an acknowledgement of its title from the warehouseman to secure its title.[135]

24.53 The pledge implies a power of sale,[136] and the bank may exercise that power of sale as and when reimbursement becomes due or on notice to the applicant.[137]

24.54 Whilst the pledge of goods is a convenient mode of creating security under a letter of credit transaction, it should be appreciated that this is only effective where the document of title is negotiable, so that its delivery is sufficient to confer a possessory title on the bank. In practice, the category of relevant documents is limited to a bill of lading and, hence, the security will only be available where the goods are to be transported by ship. The increasing use of other modes of transport means that a negotiable document of title will not become available as part of the process, and the security arrangements described above cannot come into operation.[138]

Trust Receipts

24.55 It has been seen that the delivery of the bill of lading constitutes a pledge of the goods in favour of the issuing bank. But, of itself, this is only half of the story. In order to reimburse the credit, the buyer will need to resell the goods in their turn. In order to be able to do so,

---

[132] *Official Assignee of Madras v Mercantile Bank of India* [1935] AC 53 (PC). See generally the discussion in Jack, paras 11.3–11.15.
[133] On this subject, see generally Chapter 27 below.
[134] See *Sale Continuation Ltd v Austin Taylor & Co Ltd* [1968] 2 QB 849 and *The Stone Gemini* [1999] 2 Lloyds Rep 255 (Federal Court of Australia). The cases are noted by Jack, para 11.4.
[135] *Rafsanjan Pistachio Producers Cooperative v Bank Leumi (UK) plc* [1992] 1 Lloyds Rep 513; *Niru Battery Manufacturing Co v Milestone Trading Ltd* [2002] 2 All ER (Comm) 705.
[136] *The Odessa* [1916] 1 AC 145 (PC).
[137] *Deverges v Sandeman Clark & Co* [1902] 1 Ch 579, noted by Jack, para 11.7.
[138] For an argument to the effect that the issuing bank, having paid the seller, may be subrogated to the seller's title to the goods and thus obtain his title via that route, see Jack, para 11.5. The difficulty with this argument is that the bank has paid the price on behalf of the buyer (and not as guarantor or in some similar capacity), so that the legal basis for a right of subrogation seems obscure.

it will plainly need possession of the goods. How can this be achieved without prejudicing the bank's security position pending final completion of the sale? The answer lies in the mechanism of the trust receipt, under which the documents of title are released to the customer as agent for the bank, and on the basis that the proceeds of sale will be remitted to the bank and, pending such remittance, will be held on trust for the bank. The initial pledge is continued by this means and the release of the bill of lading hence does not prejudice the bank's security.[139] In other words, the usual rule that surrender of the document of title equates to a surrender of the security does not apply where the pledgor receives that document as agent for the bank and for the specific purpose of selling the goods.[140] A few points may be noted in this context:

(a) as noted above, a pledge is not a form of security requiring registration under section 860 of the Companies Act 2006. The trust receipt likewise does not require registration because it does not amount to the *creation* of a charge for the purposes of that section; it merely *continues* a pre-existing security interest;[141]

(b) the obligation of the customer to account for the proceeds of sale does not constitute a registrable charge over book debts,[142] since the customer is simply undertaking to account for the proceeds of sale of goods over which the bank holds an existing security interest;[143]

(c) the result is that, if the customer becomes insolvent the bank is entitled to the proceeds of sale as against the liquidator or administrator;[144]

(d) the trust receipt mechanism does to some extent rely on the integrity of the customer. If he receives the proceeds of sale and misapplies them, then there will be nothing on which the bank's security can 'bite'. The goods will have been sold and, since the customer had the bank's authority to dispose of the goods, the security over them will have been discharged, at any rate in favour of a buyer who acted in good faith.[145] Likewise, if the customer wrongfully re-pledges the bill of lading in favour of another bank which acts in good faith, then the title of the latter bank will prevail;[146]

(e) as others have observed,[147] the reasoning which seeks to preserve the bank's security from the point at which the bill of lading has been received under the credit until it receives the proceeds of sale is subtle, but delivers a commercially convenient outcome. Nevertheless, it must be repeated that this applies only where the relevant document of

---

[139] *North Western Bank Ltd v Poynter Son and Macdonalds* [1895] AC 56 (HL); *Official Assignee of Madras v Mercantile Bank of India Ltd* [1935] AC 53 (PC); Jack, para 11.11.

[140] This technique is useful but it should be remembered that it is only available where the document of title is itself negotiable—ie a bill of lading.

[141] The trust receipt thus does not amount to a bill of sale (that is, a charge over chattels which remain in the physical possession of the chargor) and, hence, does not require registration under Companies Act 2006, s 860(7)(b). On these points, see *Re David Allester Ltd* [1922] 2 Ch 211.

[142] On the requirement for registration of security over book debts, see Companies Act 2006, s 870(7)(f). The provision is considered at para 30.07 below.

[143] *Re David Allester Ltd* [1922] 2 Ch 211.

[144] See the *North Western Bank* and *Mercantile Bank of India* cases, referred to in n 139 above.

[145] See Factors Act 1889, s 2 and *Lloyds Bank Ltd v Bank of America NT & SA* [1938] 2 KB 147.

[146] See the situation which arose in *Midland Bank Ltd v Eastcheap Dried Fruit Co* [1962] 1 Lloyds Rep 359.

[147] See Paget, para 31.8.

title is recognized to be negotiable. Otherwise, an attempt to claim the goods themselves as against a liquidator is likely to fail on the basis that the security has not been registered as a bill of sale,[148] and any attempt to claim the proceeds of sale is also likely to fail on the basis that this aspect of the security involves an unregistered charge over book debts.[149]

Standby Credits

Introduction

24.56 Standby credits are in many respects a hybrid or cross between a commercial credit and an on demand bond. They have their origins in the United States, where national banks are precluded by regulation from issuing guarantees. The device of the standby credit was thus developed to enable banks to provide cover for their customers' obligations in favour of third parties.[150] With the seemingly customary inevitability, the practice extended to other countries, not least because branches of US banks operating abroad were still bound by this restriction. The standby credit thus became familiar to non-US customers dealing with such branches.

24.57 The structure of a standby credit is very similar to an ordinary commercial credit. The terminology is similar ('applicant', 'issuing bank', 'beneficiary', etc), and a standby credit can be confirmed by a correspondent bank where required. The key distinction between the two types of instrument lies in the nature of the obligations covered by the credit and, in consequence, the nature of the documents to be presented under it. A standby credit will usually cover the obligations of the customer in respect of a loan or similar financial transaction and, as a consequence, the only document to be presented under the credit is a simple demand confirming the occurrence of the default and the amount payable. In this respect, the standby credit resembles the 'on demand' bond discussed earlier in this section.[151]

---

[148] ie in the case of a corporate customer, under Companies Act 2006, s 860(7)(b).

[149] See Companies Act 2006, s 860(7)(f) and the decision in *Ladenburg & Co v Goodwin Ferreira & Co Ltd* [1912] 3 KB 275.

[150] That standby letters of credit are not caught by the prohibition against the giving of guarantees was confirmed by the decision in *Barclays Bank DCO v Mercantile National Bank* 481 F 2d 1224 (New York Court of Appeals, 1973). In that case, Mercantile had confirmed a standby letter of credit and sought to avoid its obligations on the footing that this was equivalent to a guarantee of the underlying customer and, hence, prohibited by the regulations. The court rejected this argument, largely on the basis that—in contrast to a 'guarantee' as generally understood—the confirmation of the standby credit involved the assumption of a *primary* obligation to the beneficiary. Essentially similar reasoning was adopted in *Republic National Bank of Dallas v Northwest National Bank of Fort Worth* 578 SW 2d 109 (Tex, 1978), where the court observed that the issuing bank is obliged to pay under the credit itself, without reference to the underlying contract. There are, however, limits to this approach and it appears that it must be clear that the autonomy principle applies to the instrument concerned. Thus, in *Wichita Eagle & Beacon Publishing v Pacific National Bank* 493 F 2d 1285 (9th Cir, 1984), the document at issue purported to be a standby credit but payment under it involved an investigation by the issuing bank into the factual basis for the demand. This feature meant that the purported standby credit in fact had the characteristics of a guarantee, and was unenforceable accordingly.

[151] See paras 24.07–24.12 above.

Nature of the Standby Credit

Given its similarity to both a commercial credit and an on demand bond, as a result, the **24.58** standby credit will be regarded as an autonomous obligation and, in the absence of fraud, the court will not be concerned with disputes relating to the underlying contract or obligation—they will be concerned only with the contractual obligations imposed on the bank by the terms of the standby credit itself.[152]

The autonomy of the credit and, hence, its particular value to the beneficiary, were illus- **24.59** trated in various cases involving 'names' at Lloyds of London, who were required to provide a standby credit to cover their underwriting capacity. There were disputes about alleged breaches of the underlying agreements by Lloyds, counterclaims and similar matters, but the banks were unable to demonstrate that the existence of those disputes meant that the calls under the credits were fraudulent. Consequently, Lloyds was entitled to judgment for the amount of the standby credits.[153]

That the court is concerned solely with the contract before it—the standby credit—and **24.60** not with the underlying contract is neatly illustrated by the factual background to the decision in *Sepoong Engineering Construction Co Ltd v Formula One Management Ltd.*[154] Sepoong had procured the issue of a standby credit which was confirmed by National Westminster Bank in London and which covered payment of a stated amount to Formula One in the event that a Grand Prix race did not take place in South Korea. That event did not take place and Formula One as beneficiary made a demand under the credit. It was alleged that Formula One had agreed with Sepoong not to make a call under the credit, but that was disputed and, in any event, the alleged agreement would have been made between the two parties to the underlying contract—and not between the parties to the credit itself. Since the alleged/disputed agreement did not render the demand fraudulent, there was no basis to prevent a demand.

The Fraud Exception

It has already been noted above that performance bonds and documentary credits are to be **24.61** regarded as autonomous obligations. The issuing bank must make payment against compliance with the terms of the bond or credit itself, without reference to any extraneous factors.

Yet fraud must be an exception to any rule of this kind. A performance bond is issued in **24.62** order to enable the beneficiary to protect his legitimate business interests, not in order to provide him with a source of ready cash when the notion happens to appeal to him. Likewise, as a commercial matter, a documentary credit is intended to secure to the seller

---

[152] On these points, see the decision in *Kvaerner John Brown Ltd v Midland Bank plc* [1998] CLC 446.
[153] The litigation in England, Canada, and Australia is noted by Jack at para 12.19: see *Society of Lloyds v Canadian Imperial Bank of Commerce* [1993] 2 Lloyds Rep 579 (England), *Bank of Montreal v Mitchell* (1997) 143 DLR (4th) 697 (Canada), *Royal Bank of Canada v Darlington* (1995) 54 ACWS (3d) 738 (Canada) and *Commonwealth Bank of Australia v White* (22 October 1999, unreported, Supreme Court of Victoria).
[154] [2000] 1 Lloyds Rep 602.

the payment of the price of goods which have been delivered in accordance with the terms of the underlying contract. Consequently, the issuing bank cannot be compelled to pay (indeed, must not pay) if it has grounds for believing that the demand is fraudulent, or if any of the documentation presented in support of the demand is itself fraudulent. This rule is, perhaps, fairly obvious, and it has been applied by the courts on a number of occasions in relation to the various different forms of bonds and guarantees.[155]

24.63   Yet if the high principle is easily stated, the practical position is altogether more complex. In the typical case involving a performance bond, the contractor and the employer will be engaged in a dispute over compliance with the underlying contract. When the demand on the bond is made, it is good practice for the issuing bank to notify the contractor of its receipt. The contractor will then claim that the call is unjustified and hence fraudulent, and request the bank to withhold payment. The form of the bond will usually require payment within a few business days following receipt of the demand, and time will be running out. The bank faces a choice between:

(a) making payment in response to the demand, and finding itself unable to recover the amount of that payment from the customer;[156] or

(b) refusing payment and finding itself on the receiving end of proceedings from the beneficiary, with the reputational damage which may ensue.

24.64   How should a bank respond when confronted with this type of dilemma? It will not usually be in a position to form any judgment about the competing claims of the contractor and the employer. These cases will never be easy because the bank faces a direct conflict of interest between the position of its own customer and that of a third party. It is suggested that a bank should adopt the following guidelines when deciding upon its course of action:

(a) it must be remembered that performance bonds are designed to assure to the beneficiary a reliable and prompt source of cash in the event that the contractor fails to meet its obligations. Consequently, the starting point should be that payment is required to be made in accordance with the terms of the bond itself;

(b) 'fraud' connotes dishonesty, in the sense that the beneficiary has made the demand in the knowledge that it was unjustified.[157] The fact that the beneficiary may dispute the

---

[155] See, for example, *Sztejn v J Henry Schroder Banking Corporation* 31 NYS 2d 631 (1941); *Edward Owen Engineering Ltd v Barclays Bank International Ltd* [1978] QB 159 (CA); *United City Merchants (Investments) Ltd v Royal Bank of Canada* [1983] AC 168 (HL). It should be appreciated that the present discussion is concerned principally with a fraudulent *demand* under the credit, and presupposes that the credit is an otherwise valid instrument. If the *original issue* of the credit was procured by fraud *to which the beneficiary was himself a party*, then the bank may have the right to avoid or rescind the credit in the ordinary way: see *Solo Industries UK Ltd v Canara Bank* [2001] EWCA Civ 1059 (CA). It should also be appreciated that letters of credit are subject to the general principles of contract law. Thus, for example, if a regime of sanctions is imposed following the issue of the credit and which prevents payment under it, then those arrangements will render performance unlawful and the court would not enforce payment against the bank: see *Shanning International Ltd v Lloyds TSB Bank plc* [2000] All ER (D) 731 (CA).

[156] The customer/contractor will have undertaken to reimburse the bank for moneys paid out in respect of the bond, but it must be implicit in the arrangements that a claim should not be paid if there is substantial reason to believe that it is fraudulent.

[157] *United Trading Corporation SA v Allied Arab Bank* [1985] 2 Lloyds Rep 554. But in an international commercial context, a requirement to prove positive *dishonesty*—in the sense of deceit flowing from fraudulent

validity of the demand does not by any means lead to the conclusion that the demand is fraudulent. Consequently, the mere existence of a dispute as to the existence of a breach of the underlying contract would not of itself justify a refusal of payment;[158]

(c) the bank must pay out on the bond unless it has received clear and cogent evidence of fraud.[159] Various formulations have been used to express this requirement, but it seems that the available evidence must be unequivocal, such that the circumstances demonstrate obvious fraud and admit of no other conclusion.[160]

(d) if the customer does produce evidence of apparent fraud, then the beneficiary must be allowed an opportunity to produce evidence to the contrary.[161] This is not to suggest that the bank must make a final judgment about the evidence, for it is plainly not in a position to do so. Rather, the bank must simply place itself in a position where it can decide whether the evidence of fraud is genuinely clear and cogent.

(e) the bank should only invoke the fraud exception if it is satisfied that the evidence would amount to sufficient evidence of fraud in any later proceedings. Furthermore, the evidence must relate to the specific transaction at hand; it is not enough that generalized allegations of fraud have been made against the beneficiary by other parties, even if in a related context;[162]

(f) in the light of the considerations noted above, the bank should be very wary of invoking the fraud exception. It should be remembered that the autonomy principle exists in part because an issuing bank is not in any position to form any judgments about any dispute which may have arisen in respect of the underlying contract. Under those circumstances, how can the bank feel well placed to form a judgment about the state of mind of one of the parties?

(g) it must be appreciated that fraud may take a variety of forms. In the case of a demand for payment under a bond or a standby credit, the alleged fraud will be essentially a question of intention on the part of the beneficiary, and it will usually be impractical for a bank to make enquiries in that direction. In contrast, fraud may more readily be established in the case of a commercial credit, where documentation presented under the credit may have been forged. If, for example, the buyer alleges that shipping or insurance documents have been forged or altered, then this can be checked with the third party responsible for the document concerned;

---

misrepresentation—may be setting the bar a little too high. In a commercial situation, the test for fraud is not outright dishonesty (as in the case of a criminal prosecution), but *deception*, which suggests that it may be slightly easier to prove fraud in the context now under consideration: see *Kensington International Ltd v Seaton Insurance Co* (Court of Appeal, 16 December 2009).

[158]   This is consistent with the autonomy principle, above.

[159]   The uncorroborated statement of the customer alone is not sufficient: *Bolivinter Oil SA v Chase Manhattan Bank* [1984] 1 Lloyds Rep 251. Cogent evidence will always be required and it may be necessary to allow the beneficiary an opportunity of explanation: see *United Trading Corp SA v Allied Arab Bank Ltd* [1985] 2 Lloyds Rep 554n (CA).

[160]   *Edward Owen (Engineering) Ltd v Barclays Bank International Ltd* [1978] 1 QB 159 (CA). The decision contains guidance for the issuing bank which is requested by the applicant to refuse payment under the credit.

[161]   See, for example, *Bolivinter Oil SA v Chase Manhattan Bank* [1984] 1 Lloyds Rep 251.

[162]   This conclusion seems to be justified by reference to *Society of Lloyds v Canadian Imperial Bank of Commerce* [1993] 2 Lloyds Rep 579.

(h) it seems that the beneficiary must be the perpetrator of the fraud, or at least be aware that the document presented under a commercial credit is irregular in some way, usually by containing material misrepresentations which are designed to induce the issuing bank to make payment under the credit when it would not otherwise be obliged to do so.[163] Thus, where a document has been produced by a third party for some fraudulent purpose of which the beneficiary is unaware at the time of presentation, then the beneficiary is entitled to receive payment if the document on its face complies with the terms of the credit;[164]

(i) in the normal course, the fraud must be directed against the issuing bank or the buyer. This will usually be obvious, for the beneficiary of the bond or credit will be seeking to obtain an improper payment, to the detriment of the other parties to the transaction. In a very limited class of cases, however, the fraud may be directed against the wider public (eg where a standby credit forms a part of a wider transaction designed to give a misleadingly positive view of the financial position of a company). It seems that a fraud of this kind may likewise justify a refusal of payment under a credit;[165] and

(j) if the bank incurs an obligation (usually by accepting drafts under a commercial credit) or otherwise pays in accordance with its mandate[166] out before receiving any evidence of fraud, then it is clearly entitled to an indemnity from the customer even if evidence subsequently comes to light.[167] However, if the bank has refused to pay but evidence of fraud has only come to light *after* the date on which payment should have been made, the court will decline to enforce the bond on the grounds that the court cannot be an accessory to fraud.[168]

24.65 Under these circumstances, the applicant for the credit may explore two possible avenues to prevent payment by the issuing bank.

24.66 First of all, if he knows that a demand is pending, he may seek an injunction to prevent the presentation of that demand by the beneficiary. In one case,[169] the Court of Appeal granted such an injunction but it is submitted that this approach is wrong in principle. The question

---

[163] In such a case, the beneficiary clearly cannot avail himself of the fraud in order to obtain payment: see *United City Merchants (Investments) Ltd v Royal Bank of Canada* [1983] 1 AC 168 (HL).

[164] Apart from other considerations, this is necessary to support the autonomy principle: *Montrod Ltd v Grundkotter Fleischvertreibs GmbH* [2002] 1 WLR 1975 (CA).

[165] See the decision in *Mahonia Ltd v JP Morgan Chase Bank* [2003] 2 Lloyds Rep 91 and, on this decision, see Proctor, 'Enron, Letters of Credit and the Autonomy Principle' (2004) 6 JIBFL 204. For subsequent proceedings in which the beneficiary obtained judgment on the credit, see *Mahonia Ltd v West LB AG* [2004] All ER (D) 10 (Aug). This type of fraud will usually only arise in the context of a standby credit used to support a wider transaction involving significant sums of money (as occurred in the *Mahonia* litigation itself).

[166] Note the qualification that payment must be made in accordance with the terms of the mandate. This is perhaps an obvious point but its consequences in particular circumstances were highlighted by the decision in *Banco Santander SA v Bayfern Ltd* [2000] 1 All ER (Comm) 776. The case is considered at para 24.20(b) above.

[167] *United Trading Corporation SA v Chase Manhattan Bank* [1984] 1 Lloyds Rep 554; *European Asian Bank AG v Punjab and Sind Bank* [1983] 2 All ER 508.

[168] *Mahonia Ltd v J P Morgan Chase Bank* (n 165 above).

[169] *Themehelp Ltd v West* [1966] QB 84. For further discussion of this case, see Paget, para 34.12. Generally speaking, a court will not imply into the commercial contract a term that the beneficiary will not make a call on the bond unless it is properly justifiable: see *State Trading Corp of India v ED & F Man (Sugar) Ltd* [1981] Com LR 235 (CA).

of fraud does not arise until a demand is made and, if it is, the principles discussed above can be applied. Furthermore, in practice, the grant of an injunction at this point appears to be premature.

Secondly, and more usually, the applicant may seek an injunction against the bank itself in **24.67** order to restrain payment.[170] In order to obtain such an injunction, the customer must establish that there is an arguable case that the fraud exception applies (ie that fraud is the only realistic inference from the available evidence) and that the balance of convenience favours the issue of an injunction. Once again, given the autonomy principle, the importance of the integrity of demand guarantees and other factors noted above, the court should be very slow to grant an injunction of this kind. The 'balance of convenience' argument will often also present insuperable problems, for payment by the issuing bank should not prejudice the customer. If, at a later trial, it is shown that the evidence of fraud should have persuaded the bank not to pay out on the bond, then the bank will be unable to recover the amount of that payment from the customer.[171]

If the issuing bank elects to pay the credit in any event, then it will usually be entitled to **24.68** immediate reimbursement by the applicant. The applicant will only be able to avoid that position if he can show that, despite the action taken by the bank, there was indeed cogent evidence of fraud and it ought not to have paid.[172]

Damages for Failure to Pay under a Credit

A bank may incur a liability to pay damages to the beneficiary for breach of its obligation **24.69** to make payment under a guarantee, performance bond, or documentary credit. A liability may arise for a number of reasons, for example, because the bank has acted on an allegation of fraud based on insufficient evidence, or because it has rejected documents which are later found to have complied with the terms of the credit. What is the extent of the issuing bank's liability in such a case?

First of all, it seems that the credit creates a conditional debt obligation on the part of the **24.70** issuing bank. That obligation becomes unconditional against presentation of a demand

---

[170] In practice, an application of this kind will be made by the customer after the bank has indicated that any evidence of fraud produced by the customer is insufficient to justify a refusal of payment to the beneficiary. The bank will generally have no objection to this procedure; if the court elects to issue an injunction which renders payment unlawful pending any further order, then the bank can suffer no liability to the beneficiary or reputational damage in consequence of the non-payment.

[171] On the points made in this paragraph, see *Bolivinter Oil SA v Chase Manhattan Bank* [1984] 1 Lloyds Rep 251; *Czarnikow-Rionda Sugar Trading Inc v Standard Bank London Ltd* [1999] 1 All ER (Comm) 890. The application for such an injunction has failed in a number of other cases: see, for example, *Harbottle (Mercantile) Ltd v National Westminster Bank Ltd* [1978] QB 146; *Group Jose Re v Walbrook Insurance Co Ltd* [1996] 1 Lloyds Rep 345 (CA).

[172] *Turkiye Is Bankasi AS v Bank of China* [1998] 1 Lloyds rep 250 (CA); *Banque Saudi Fransi v Lear Siegler Services Inc* [2006] All ER (D) 333 (Jul), on which see Stephen, 'The Fraud Exception' (2006) 156 NLJ 1634. For a similar case in which the language employed in the bond made it unclear whether a demand under the bond (and, hence, a claim under the counter-indemnity) was permitted in particular circumstances, see *Rainy Sky v Kookmin Bank* [2009] EWHC 2624 (Comm), where, however, the beneficiary was ultimately successful.

and any other documents stipulated by the documentary credit or other instrument. A debt is a fixed obligation and no question of mitigation of damage could be applied to that aspect of the beneficiary's claim. If the issuing bank has failed to pay when obliged to do so, then judgment for the amount due under the credit would normally follow as a matter of course.[173]

24.71 It is then necessary to determine the extent of any further damages to which the beneficiary may be entitled. In principle, the beneficiary is entitled to damages reflecting the losses flowing ordinarily from the breach, and any additional damages flowing from circumstances within the contemplation of the issuing bank and the beneficiary at the time when the credit is opened or the instrument is issued.[174] Since the obligation is of a monetary character, the beneficiary would be entitled to recover damages representing interest on the amounts unpaid, and this would be compounded where appropriate.[175]

Private International Law Issues

Introduction

24.72 As has already been noted, commercial credits are used to facilitate international trade and hence, by their very nature, they are likely to give rise to questions of private international law.[176] It is true that the UCP seeks to bring a degree of uniformity to worldwide practice in this sphere, but the fact remains that the contracts contemplated by a commercial credit cannot exist in a vacuum; in the final analysis, they rely for their legal effectiveness on a domestic legal system.

24.73 As a result, it is often important to identify the system of law applicable to particular obligations under a credit.[177] The issue is often complicated by the fact that a credit will involve a number of different parties in multiple jurisdictions, and each individual relationship may be governed by different systems of law.[178] The present section examines the law applicable to each relationship. For ease of illustration the factual example noted earlier[179] (New Zealand Seller/English buyer/English issuing bank/New Zealand confirming bank) will be used in this section.

---

[173] The beneficiary is not, however, entitled to recover the price of goods twice. Consequently, if the buyer has independently paid the price in the meantime, then the seller will be unable to recover the corresponding sum from the issuing bank.

[174] This test is derived from the decision in *Hadley v Baxendale* (1854) 9 Exch 341.

[175] On this point, see *Sempra Metals Ltd v Her Majesty's Commissioners of Inland Revenue* [2008] 1 AC 561 (HL).

[176] Although this section will focus principally on commercial credits, the same general rules will likewise apply in the context of standby credits.

[177] The earlier discussion in this section has, of course, proceeded on the footing that the credit is governed by English law.

[178] It is true that it is open to the parties to particular contracts on a letter of credit to include an express selection of the law which is to govern their contract: see Rome I, Art 3(1). But in the ordinary case, the parties will seek to produce a brief and clear document, unencumbered by legal technicality. The present section thus proceeds on the assumption that no express choice is included.

[179] See para 24.14 above.

English Buyer—English Issuing Bank

The initial contract between the UK buyer and his bank will set matters in motion, and **24.74** provides the first link in the documentary credit chain. The buyer will ask his bank to issue the letter of credit against an undertaking by the buyer to reimburse the bank with any amounts paid out under the credit.

It will often be the case that no private international law issue will arise as between the **24.75** applicant for the credit and the issuing bank. They will often both be based in the same jurisdiction and it will be plain that the arrangements between the parties are governed by English law. In other words, there will be no '… situation involving a conflict of laws …' which brings Rome I into operation.[180] The obligation of the bank to issue the credit, and the customer's reimbursement obligation, will plainly be governed by English law.

Even if the buyer were in fact based in another jurisdiction but was using the services of a **24.76** bank branch in England English law would still apply. Rome I would clearly come into operation at this point but, in the absence of an express choice of law, '… a contract for the provision of services shall be governed by the law of the country where the service provider has his habitual residence …'[181] and, for these purposes, the 'habitual residence' of the service provider is the country in which the relevant branch is located.[182] It also seems clear that, in agreeing to open the credit, the issuing bank is providing a 'service' for the purposes of this provision.

Questions touching the interpretation and legal effect of the contract between the buyer **24.77** (applicant for the credit) and the issuing bank will thus fall to be determined by reference to English law.

Issuing Bank—Seller

As was noted earlier, by issuing the credit in favour of the New Zealand seller, the bank **24.78** undertakes to make payment against the stipulated documentation.[183] But what is the governing law of that undertaking?

Plainly, the provisions of Rome I come into operation in this context, because there is **24.79** clearly a '… situation involving the conflict of laws …' for the purposes of that instrument. But the analysis given in the preceding paragraphs cannot apply, for the issuing bank is not providing a 'service' to the seller of the goods. It merely gives an undertaking to pay if the terms of the credit are satisfied. Such an undertaking does not fall within any of the specific categories of contracts for which specific rules are provided by Article 4(1) of Rome I.[184] Consequently, it is necessary to have recourse to Article 4(2), which provides that the contract will be governed by the law of the place in which the party required to perform the obligations which are characteristic of the contract has his habitual residence. Since the issue of the letter of credit is a unilateral act on the part of the bank and the beneficiary

---

[180] See Rome I, Art 1. On Rome I more generally, see Chapter 40 below.
[181] Rome I, Art 4(1)(b).
[182] Rome I, Art 19(2).
[183] See para 24.19(c) above.
[184] On Art 4(1) of Rome I, see paras 40.09–40.10 below.

does not assume any obligations at all, this necessarily points to the issuing bank as the 'characteristic obligor'.

24.80 But does this position vary if, as in the present example, the credit is advised or confirmed[185] by a bank in the seller's country? In both of these two cases, the necessary documentation will be presented to a bank in the seller's country. In the case of an advised credit, the seller/beneficiary will still rely on the issuing bank itself for the payment undertaking; in the case of a confirmed credit, the seller beneficiary will have recourse to two banks but his first port of call will usually be the confirming bank. The entire purpose of requesting the credit to be advised/confirmed in the beneficiary's home country is to enable him to present documentation under the credit in that country.[186] It is thus reasonable to infer that questions touching the standard of compliance and the validity of the presentation should be governed by the law of the place in which presentation is to be made. This desirable objective[187] can only be achieved if the issuing bank's obligations to the beneficiary are governed by the law of that country.

24.81 But how can this objective be achieved? As noted above, the application of the 'characteristic obligations' test will normally lead back to the laws of the country in which the relevant branch of the issuing bank is located. The only possible answer lies in Article 4(3) of Rome I, which provides that '... where it is clear from all the circumstances of the case that the contract is manifestly more closely connected with a country other than that indicated in [Articles 4(1) or 4(2)], the law of that other country shall apply ...'. In *Bank of Baroda v Vysya Bank Ltd*,[188] the equivalent provision in the Rome Convention[189] was applied in order to override the earlier provisions, and to hold that the obligations of an issuing bank in India were governed by English law, because it had arranged for the credit to be advised and confirmed in London. The contract was thus most closely connected with England. Nevertheless, a note of caution must be introduced. Rome I differs from its predecessor, in that the basic presumptions in Articles 4(1) and 4(2) can only now be disregarded if the contract is *manifestly* more closely connected with another country.[190] Plainly, this is designed to reinforce the basic presumptions, and an English court which has to consider

---

[185] On advised and confirmed letters of credit, see para 24.19(d) and (e) above.

[186] Under English private international law as in effect before the Rome Convention/Rome I were brought into effect, see *Offshore International SA v Banco Central SA* [1976] 3 All ER 749. A Spanish bank had opened a US dollar letter of credit in favour of a US-based entity. The credit was advised to the beneficiary by a New York bank, but was not confirmed. The credit was held to be governed by New York law, since payment could only be obtained by presenting the necessary documentation in that State. In the case of a confirmed credit, this reasoning would become even more compelling because the contractual nexus with New York becomes even stronger.

[187] It is especially desirable that the obligations of the issuing and confirming bank are governed by the same system of law and, as will be seen, the obligations of the confirming bank are governed by the law of the country in which the confirming branch is situate. Otherwise, one could in theory face a situation in which the presentation is valid as against the confirming bank, but not as against the issuing bank (or vice versa).

[188] [1994] 2 Lloyds Rep 87. The decision in the *Vysya Bank* case was substantially applied in *Marconi Communications International Ltd v PT Pan Indonesian Bank Ltd TBK* [2005] 2 All ER (Comm) 325. In that case, a letter of credit issued and confirmed by Indonesian banks was nevertheless held to be governed by English law because the requisite documentation was to be presented to an advising bank in London, which would also act as negotiating bank.

[189] See Rome Convention, Art 4(5).

[190] The word 'manifestly' is absent from Art 4(5) of the Rome Convention.

the issue within the framework of Rome I will thus have to reconsider the *Vysya Bank* decision in the light of the revised provision. Nevertheless, it is submitted that the court should arrive at the same conclusion. The beneficiary will have requested (and the bank will have agreed) that the credit be advised/confirmed in the beneficiary's country for convenience and to provide a link with the banking laws and practices in that country. Strict application of the presumptions would therefore defeat the legitimate expectations of the parties.

Confirming Bank—Seller

In the worked example, the New Zealand bank will advise the credit to the seller and add its confirmation. It may well be argued that no conflict of laws issue arises in this context. Both the beneficiary of the credit and the confirming bank are based in New Zealand, and the contract created by the confirmation would fall to be performed there. On this basis, the confirmation is plainly governed by the laws of New Zealand and the provisions of Rome I would not become relevant. **24.82**

Even if Rome I is relevant, it will be necessary to have recourse to the 'characteristic obligations' test in Article 4(2).[191] The confirmation only creates obligations to be performed by a bank acting through its branch in New Zealand. Once again, therefore, it is plain that this contract would be governed by the laws of New Zealand.[192] **24.83**

Issuing Bank—Confirming Bank

The English issuing bank has requested the New Zealand confirming bank to add its confirmation to the credit. In acceding to this request, it would appear that the confirming bank is providing a 'service' to the issuing bank, and the contract between the two banks would thus be governed by the laws of New Zealand.[193] Even if that is not correct, it seems clear that it is the New Zealand bank's agreement to add its confirmation and to pay the beneficiary which is 'characteristic' of the contract. On this basis, the contract would again be governed by the laws of New Zealand.[194] **24.84**

Matters may be a little more straightforward where the instrument concerned is a performance bond or similar document, since this will normally be issued direct by the issuing bank to the beneficiary. In the absence of an express selection of the applicable law in such an instrument, it seems likely that the bond will be governed by the law of the country in which the issuing branch is located.[195] **24.85**

---

[191] The starting presumptions given in Art 4(1) will not be relevant, in this context, essentially for the reasons given in the context of the issuing bank-seller relationship (see para 24.81 above).

[192] This conclusion is again supported by the decision in the *Vysya Bank* case: see para 24.81 above.

[193] ie in accordance with Art 4(1)(b) of Rome I, which provides that a contract for the supply of services is governed by the law of the country in which the service provider is habitually resident.

[194] ie in accordance with Rome I, Art 4(2).

[195] ie again, because it is the obligations of the issuing bank which characterize the contract: see Rome I, Art 4(2). For an earlier case to similar effect, see *Attock Cement Co Ltd v Romanian Bank for Foreign Trade* [1989] 1 All ER 1189 (CA), and see also *Turkiye Is Bankasi v Bank of China* [1993] 1 Lloyds Rep 132 (CA).

The Impact of the Applicable Law

24.86 It has been noted earlier that a uniformity of approach is essential if letters of credit are to fulfil their intended functions in the sphere of international trade.

24.87 Yet it must not be overlooked that the contracts created through a letter of credit transaction must necessarily exist within a framework of domestic law. Those frameworks will differ in their detail and may accordingly produce different results against the background of an identical factual matrix. It may be helpful to give a few examples to illustrate how the decision as to the applicable law may affect outcomes in particular cases:

(a) In *Mannesman Handel AG v Kaunlaran Shipping Corp*,[196] a Swiss bank had opened a credit in favour of a German seller. It subsequently refused to pay out on the credit on the basis that the documents presented to it were non-compliant. The credit was governed by Swiss law and the bank would normally be justified in rejecting the documentation. However, the issuing bank had itself received the benefit of a payment made to it by another bank on the strength of the same documents. Swiss law requires a party to perform its contractual obligations in good faith. On the facts of the particular case, a refusal to pay out would have been contrary to the good faith requirement. Consequently, the issuing bank was ordered to pay out under the credit, notwithstanding the discrepancy. It is not entirely clear that the same result would have followed if the credit had been governed by English law.

(b) In *Power Curber International Ltd v National Bank of Kuwait SAK*,[197] the National Bank of Kuwait had opened a credit in favour of Power Curber. The credit was advised to the beneficiary by a bank in North Carolina, and the necessary documents had to be delivered to the advising bank in order to request payment. Shortly before the credit became payable, an order of a court in Kuwait prevented the issuing bank from making payment. It was decided that the obligations of the issuing bank were governed by the laws of North Carolina, because that was the place in which documents were to be presented under the credit, and payment was to be made.[198] Had the credit been governed by the laws of Kuwait, then the outcome would clearly have been different and the issuing bank would not have been compelled to pay.

---

[196] [1993] 1 Lloyds Rep 89.

[197] [1981] 3 All ER 607.

[198] Compare the discussion at para 24.81 above. The case was decided under the common law rules which pre-date the Rome Convention.

25

SOURCES OF BANK LIABILTY

Introduction

Mention has been made in other parts of this work about the liabilities which a bank **25.01** may incur in the course of its business. This includes the liabilities of an institution in its roles as a paying or collecting bank.[1] But those liabilities arise in the ordinary course of the business of a commercial bank as a clearing institution.

In contrast, the present chapter examines claims which may be made against banks as sellers **25.02** of sophisticated and complex products, such as collateralized debt obligations, credit default swaps,[2] and similar instruments. By their very nature, these instruments will be sold to larger corporate customers with considerable financial resources.[3] However, especially against the backdrop of the prevailing financial crisis, some of these instruments have or may result in significant liabilities for buyers. For example, the implications of the so-called 'credit crunch' in the context of credit default swaps are obvious. Some corporate buyers may accordingly now be inclined to argue that their treasury or finance departments lacked the detailed knowledge required for a full understanding of these products and that, as a result, reliance was placed on the seller to provide an explanation of the merits of the arrangements.

---

[1] See Chapters 17 and 18 above. Possible liabilities arising in the course of the arrangement of syndicated loans are particular to that market, and have accordingly been considered in Chapter 21 above. It should be appreciated that liabilities of that type are likely to be incurred (if at all) to other members of the syndicate. The present chapter is concerned with potential liabilities to the bank's direct customer or client.

[2] On credit default swaps generally, see paras 22.26–22.28 above.

[3] The present chapter is therefore not concerned with particular rights or remedies which may be available to consumers. That subject is considered at various other points: see, for example, the discussion in Chapter 3 above.

25.03 It should be said at the outset that claims of this kind are likely to be highly fact-sensitive. Evidence as to who said what, to whom, under what circumstances, and for what purpose is likely to be crucial, as is the nature of the relationship between the parties and any expert evidence as to prevailing market practice at the relevant time.

25.04 Having said that, it is quite likely that the buyer's or the customer's claim will be formulated under a permutation of the following headings:

(a) a breach of a contractual duty to advise;

(b) negligent misstatement; or

(c) breach of fiduciary duty.

25.05 Since these headings were all pleaded in a recent case, it may be helpful to use that decision as a backdrop for the present discussion. It will then be possible to consider cases in which the bank is involved as an investment manager or adviser (as opposed to the seller of the product concerned).

The Springwell Navigation Case

Factual Background

25.06 In *JP Morgan Chase v Springwell Navigation Corp*,[4] Springwell was an investment vehicle for a wealthy, Greek ship-owning family. Springwell was essentially used to invest spare cash generated from the shipping business, until such time as it was required for reinvestment in the family's main business. During the 1990s Springwell, via its relationship with a particular individual at Chase, built up a very substantial portfolio in 'GKO-linked notes', a derivative instrument issued by a Chase entity and linked to a Russian investment which suffered huge losses as a result of Russia's default on its external debt in 1998. Springwell claimed to have suffered additional losses because the investment portfolio was highly leveraged, thus forcing Springwell to sell in a falling market in order to meet margin calls. Springwell thus alleged a breach of contractual and other duties on the part of Chase.

Claims in Contract and Tort

25.07 In the absence of a written contract under which a party agrees to provide investment advice, the court proceeded on the footing that the contractual and tortious questions were likely to be similar. Whether a contract can be implied from the circumstances is likely to depend on whether the alleged investment adviser had in fact assumed a responsibility to advise (see below). The existence of contractual and tortious duties may thus tend to shade into each other.[5]

---

[4] [2008] EWHC 1186 (Comm), a decision of Gloster J. It should be emphasized that the evidence and factual background to this case are very complex, and the present section attempts only a brief summary. For a useful discussion, see Ryan and Yong, 'Springwell—are the English Courts the Venue of Last Resort for Complex Investor Claims?' (2009) 1 JIBLR 54.

[5] See *Henderson v Merrett Syndicates* [1995] 2 AC 145 (HL).

The original documentation establishing the relationship between Springwell and Chase **25.08** consisted of an ordinary bank mandate and account opening form. It was plainly impossible to read into those early arrangements any duty to advise Springwell on its investment strategy. Later contracts for the acquisition of specific investments generally stated that Chase had not given advice on the product concerned. Under these circumstances, it was not possible to infer the existence of an implied advisory contract. Apart from anything else, this would be inconsistent with the explicit terms of the materials before the court. On that basis, it becomes necessary to frame the question in tort; had Chase assumed a responsibility to advise Springwell in this way?

The starting point for liability in tort for economic loss is the well-known decision in **25.09** *Hedley Byrne & Co Ltd v Heller & Partners Ltd,*[6] as more recently examined and explained in *Commissioners for Customs & Excise v Barclays Bank plc.*[7] A variety of tests may be applied. For example, did the defendant assume an advisory responsibility to the claimant, and did the latter rely on him? Was the loss reasonably foreseeable, and is it fair, just, and reasonable to impose a duty of care in the particular circumstances of the case?[8] Ultimately, Springwell relied on the introduction of a particular individual in 1987 as an expert in emerging products to imply an obligation to provide general market or investment advice. That individual was effectively a salesman on behalf of Chase, and the evidence appears to have negated any suggestion that Springwell was intended to rely on him for advice, or that it did in fact do so. He had not been introduced as an adviser, nor was any advisory agreement signed to mark his introduction to the relationship. This conclusion was reinforced by the fact that—to Springwell's knowledge—the relevant individual specialized in particular types of emerging market products but had no broader, advisory experience.[9] Furthermore, the individuals within Springwell were themselves experienced businessmen and investors. They frequently made decisions which went against the ideas proposed by the individual concerned, thus demonstrating that they were not relying on his advice or recommendations. In any event, if an advisory relationship is to arise, there must be some clarity and certainty about the scope and nature of the advice which is to be given.[10] This approach is consistent with the broader view that a bank does not generally owe a duty to advise the customer on the merits of any transaction which the customer is to enter into with the bank or (more usually) with a third party with the assistance of funding provided by the bank,[11] unless the bank has expressly or impliedly assumed an advisory obligation.[12]

---

[6] [1964] AC 465 (HL).

[7] [2006] 4 All ER 256 (HL). This case concerns liability in tort for failure to observe the terms of a freezing injunction. The case is accordingly considered in more depth at para 43.34 below.

[8] See the discussion in *Springwell,* at para 48.

[9] See para 104 of the judgment.

[10] See para 100 of the judgment.

[11] See, for example, *National Commercial Bank (Jamaica) Ltd v Hew* [2003] UKPC 51 (PC). In a recent case, the court adopted the same view in the context of a sale and purchase of a derivatives product, noting that (i) the bank had acted on an 'execution only' basis, (ii) the bank owed no duty of care to advise the customer on the suitability of the product, and (iii) to the extent to which the usual disclaimer clause fell within the scope of the Unfair Contract Terms Act 1977, they satisfied the test of reasonableness: see *Titan Steel Wheels Ltd v Royal Bank of Scotland plc* [2010] EWHC 2111 (Comm).

[12] For cases in which this has occurred, see *Woods v Martins Bank Ltd* [1959] 1 QB 55; *Cornish v Midland Bank Ltd* [1985] 3 All ER 513 (CA) and *Verity and Spindler v Lloyds Bank plc* [1995] CLC 1557. Even if the

Contractual Disclaimers

25.10 When Chase and Springwell entered into individual transactions, the documentation stated, in a variety of ways, that Springwell was a sophisticated and experienced investor, had made its own decisions as to the merits of the particular deal and was not relying on any advice or recommendations made by Chase.

25.11 Was there any basis on which Springwell could pursue its claims despite these provisions? The court found that these were not 'exclusion clauses' which had to satisfy the 'reasonableness' test in section 3 of the Unfair Contract Terms Act 1977,[13] since they did not seek to exclude or restrict a liability which Chase would otherwise owe to Springwell. They merely sought to define the nature of the relationship; Chase was providing trading and banking services, but it was not providing investment advisory services. As a result, Chase was entitled to rely on provisions of this kind.[14]

Misrepresentation

25.12 Springwell argued that Chase had misrepresented the suitability of the GKO-linked notes for Springwell's investment purpose, and had also made misrepresentations about the state of the Russian economy. Once again, however, arguments of this kind were effectively precluded by the contractual documentation, which confirmed that Chase was not assuming any formal responsibility for statements of fact or opinion.

Breach of Fiduciary Duty

25.13 The claimant in *Springwell* also sought to argue that the bank owed a fiduciary or equitable duty to act in the best interests of the client, and that this formed the basis on which an award of damages could be made. But, given that the court had already rejected the contention that an ordinary (non-fiduciary) advisory relationship had come into existence, there was no basis on which any form of fiduciary relationship could be implied.[15]

---

bank does assume an advisory role, it does not thereby become responsible for the periodic review or updating of that advice: see *Fennoscandia Ltd v Clarke* [1999] 1 All ER (Comm) 365 (CA). But the cases in which an advisory duty has been found to exist have generally involved financially inexperienced customers where it may have been reasonable to expect them to rely on the bank's views. As the court noted in *Springwell*, this is unlikely to arise in relation to a sophisticated client.

[13] On this Act, see para 15.39 above.

[14] It appears that courts in the United States will adopt a similar approach in upholding provisions of this kind: see, for example, *Banco Espirito Santo de Investimento SA v Citibank NA*, 2003, SDNY, 2nd Cir.

[15] See para 573 of the judgment. In *Hospital Products Ltd v United States Surgical Corporation* [1984] HCA 64, the High Court of Australia observed, at para 70, that contractual and fiduciary obligations can subsist within the same relationship. In such a case, however, the contractual relationship enjoys primacy and '… the fiduciary relationship, if it is to exist at all, must accommodate itself to the terms of the contract so that it is consistent with, and conforms to, them. The fiduciary relationship cannot be superimposed upon the contract in such a way as to alter the operation which the contract was intended to have according to its true construction …'. This approach was approved by the Privy Council in *Kelly v Cooper* [1994] 1 BCLC 395 (PC).

It may be noted that US courts have likewise been reluctant to impose a fiduciary rela- **25.14**
tionship between the bank and its client in the context of a sale of a complex financial
product.[16]

Conclusions

As noted above, mis-selling claims of this kind will always be highly fact-sensitive. But it **25.15**
seems fair to infer from *Springwell* that—at least when dealing with sophisticated
investors—the courts will respect contractual documentation which seeks to define the
nature and scope of the relationship and will not seek to impose duties of care or a duty to
advise which runs counter to such provisions. The point is of some practical importance,
because the contractual provisions discussed in that case are in common use throughout
the financial markets.

Other Cases

Other, recent cases have tended to adopt a broadly similar line. For example, in *Peekay* **25.16**
Intermark Ltd v Australia and New Zealand Bank Group,[17] a trader mistakenly advised his
customer that a derivative instrument to be issued by his bank would confer on the
customer a proprietary interest in the securities on which such an instrument was based.
He also omitted to mention that the customer would have no influence over the enforcement process in the event of a default. However, the correct information was contained
in the formal documentation later executed by the customer (albeit without reading it).
The terms of the contract thus overrode the effect of any misrepresentation. In any event,
having signed the agreement, the customer was estopped from arguing that it had worked
on the basis of the incorrect information. Furthermore, applying the reasoning in *Springwell*,
a trader is not an investment adviser and the customer could not have relied upon him
as such.

Earlier cases had likewise held that a sophisticated client could not set aside a complex **25.17**
financial product on the basis that the bank had misrepresented its effect, in part because
ordinary sales banter should not be regarded as a 'representation' in any event.[18] Courts in
the United States have also tended to the view that statements made in the context of transactions of this kind are more likely simply to describe the product, and are not intended to
amount to formal representations on which the client is entitled to rely.[19]

---

[16] See, for example, the court's refusal to infer such a relationship in *Power & Telephone Supply Co v Sun
Trust Bank* 447 F 3d 923 (6th Cir, 2006).
[17] [2006] EWCA Civ 386. For a helpful review of this case, see Gooding, 'Selling Investment Products to
Sophisticated Clients: Reflections on Peekay v ANZ' (2006) 11 JIBLR 628.
[18] *PT Dharmala Sakti Sejahtara v Bankers Trust Co* [1996] CLC 518.
[19] See, for example, *Kwiatkowski v Bear Sterns Co Inc* 306 F 2d 1293 (2nd Cir, 2002).

Advisory and Management Arrangements

25.18 The above discussion has noted cases in which the bank was acting as a seller of a financial product, where the bank and its customer were therefore acting on a principal-to-principal basis.

25.19 As might be expected, the position differs where the bank is acting as an adviser or manager in relation to the client's own portfolio of investments. In such a case, the bank will plainly owe a duty to act with reasonable care.[20] That duty, and the extent of (non) compliance with it, will be measured by reference to the mandate and objectives which the customer has given to the bank. For example, a bank responsible for the discretionary management of its client's portfolio and which invests in highly speculative instruments will incur liability to a client who has indicated the importance of preserving his capital and thus looks for a conservative strategy. But, on exactly the same facts, it may not be liable to a client who is investing spare cash which he can afford to lose and has asked the bank to adopt a strategy for high and short term capital growth.

25.20 Of course, whatever cause of action is pleaded, it will be necessary for the client to demonstrate that the relevant breach of contract or duty is causative of his losses—he cannot recover from his investment manager/adviser simply because the market has turned against his own investment strategy. Thus, for example, if the adviser recommends that the client should accept losses in order to facilitate the diversification of the portfolio, then the adviser cannot be liable if the portfolio continues to decline in value after the client has specifically rejected that advice.[21] Equally, if the client is himself a sophisticated investor, it may be more difficult for him to demonstrate that he relied on the bank's advice.[22]

Conclusions

25.21 It seems to follow from the above discussion that a sophisticated client will frequently encounter difficulty in establishing recourse to a bank which has sold him a complex financial product, at least provided that the bank has not specifically misrepresented the position to him and he receives documentation which contains a fair and accurate description of the product before he became committed to the transaction. The same general comment will apply to investment advisory relationships and, even if the bank is found to be in breach of a contractual or other duty, the client may still have to overcome obstacles to demonstrate that such advice was the proximate cause of his loss.

---

[20] This will be an implied term of the advisory/management contract, even if it is not explicitly stated.

[21] See the situation which arose in *Valse Holdings SA v Merrill Lynch International Bank Ltd* [2004] All ER (D) 70 (Nov).

[22] *Valse Holdings*, above.

PART E

GUARANTEES AND SECURITY

Introduction

The present section is intended to provide an overview of the law relating to guarantees and security which a bank may take in order to provide additional cover for facilities provided to borrowers.

The section is arranged as follows:

(a) Chapter 26 contains a discussion of the law relating to guarantees, including the formalities applicable to a guarantee, the defences potentially available to a guarantor, and various other matters;

(b) Chapters 27 to 34 deal with particular types of security, such as charges over book debts, shares, real estate, ship, and aircraft;

(c) Chapters 35 to 39 examine various statutory and other rules which may have the effect of avoiding or vitiating the bank's security.

26

GUARANTEES

Introduction

The present chapter is designed to provide a brief overview of the law of guarantees as it **26.01** applies in a banking context.

The selection of topics considered in this chapter is as follows:

(a) the purpose, definition and characteristics of a guarantee;
(b) the formal requirements applicable to the creation of a guarantee;
(c) the distinction between a guarantee and an indemnity;

(d) the interpretation of, and liability under, a guarantee;

(e) the application of legislation on unfair contract terms;

(f) the rules applicable to individual and corporate capacity;

(g) the duties of the bank to the guarantor;

(h) the discharge of the guarantor;

(i) certain vitiating factors;

(j) termination by the guarantor; and

(k) the rights of the guarantor following payment.

Purpose, Definition, and Characteristics

Purpose

26.02 First of all, what is the purpose of taking a guarantee?

The main answer to this question is obvious. The lending bank is looking for additional recourse in the event that the primary borrower is unable to repay. Yet the requirement may flow from the manner in which the customer chooses to organize its business. If a company maintains all of its assets under a single corporate 'roof', then that entity will be the borrower and no guarantees will be needed. If, on the other hand, a parent company chooses to organize its businesses and assets through a variety of subsidiaries, then its creditworthiness may depend on a group, cross-guarantee structure.

26.03 There may even be cases where it is favourable to the borrower itself to provide a guarantee from its parent company. For example, a particular subsidiary may be regarded as sufficiently creditworthy on its own. But, if the parent has a higher credit rating, then the provision of a parent guarantee may mean that the bank is able to dedicate a reduced amount of its capital to the transaction. This, in turn, may mean that the cost of the facilities can be reduced, to the benefit of the borrower.[1]

Definition

26.04 A guarantee may be defined as a contract by which one person (the 'guarantor') agrees to answer for a liability of another person (the 'borrower' or 'principal debtor') to a third person (the 'creditor').[2]

26.05 It has been more fully defined as[3] '... an accessory contract by which the promisor undertakes to be answerable to the promisee for the debt, default or miscarriage of another person, whose primary liability to the promisee must exist or be contemplated ...'.

---

[1] On this subject, see the discussion of unfunded credit mitigation, at paras 6.46–6.48 above.

[2] See Chitty, para 44–001. A similar definition is adopted in Paget, para 33.2. See also the language employed in Statute of Frauds 1677, s 4, (discussed at para 26.19 below).

[3] Halsbury's Laws of England, *Guarantee and Indemnity*, para 101.

Characteristics

In view of the definitions given above, a guarantee necessarily connotes an overall arrange- **26.06** ment between three parties, even if established by separate contracts. A guarantee involves one party assuming responsibility for a debt in the event that a primary obligor fails to perform. Consequently, the principal debtor cannot stand as surety for his own obligations,[4] nor can the creditor stand as the guarantor for the moneys owing to him.[5]

But what are the other characteristics of a guarantee? The classification of the obligation **26.07** may be important for, as will be seen, a guarantee is only enforceable if it has been reduced to writing,[6] and a guarantor may be able to avail himself of defences which are peculiar to the contract of guarantee.[7] Whether or not a contract falls to be characterized as a guarantee does not depend solely upon the use of terminology,[8] it depends upon the substance of the obligations which the parties intended to undertake.[9] It would thus appear that a contract should be classified as a guarantee if it is apparent from its terms that, in favour of the creditor, the obligor intended to assume responsibility for the performance of an obligation of the principal debtor in the event of a default.[10]

It should also be appreciated that an arrangement may be a guarantee if the party concerned **26.08** provides assets by way of third party security, where the lender's recourse is limited to the security package and the chargor gives no personal undertaking to pay.[11]

Various consequences flow from this characterization. A guarantor does not merely under- **26.09** take to perform an obligation in place of the principal debtor if necessary; in effect, he undertakes to procure that the primary obligor will perform.[12] As a result, a guarantor of a principal sum will often have to cover interest flowing from the debtor's breach, even if the document does not expressly render the guarantor liable for such amounts.[13]

---

[4] *Lakeman v Mounstephen* (1874) LR 7 HL 17, although see the particular situation which arose in *Heisler v Anglo-Dal Ltd* [1954] 2 All ER 770.

[5] *Re Hoyle* [1893] 1 Ch 84.

[6] See the discussion of Statute of Frauds 1677, s 4 at para 26.19 below.

[7] This subject is discussed at para 26.69 below.

[8] Indeed, terminology can be positively misleading. For example, in the context of the sale of goods, the expression 'guarantee' is frequently used but, in law, a warranty is intended: see Halsbury, *Guarantee and Indemnity*, para 101.

[9] This point is very clearly illustrated by the decision of the House of Lords in *Actionstrength Ltd v International Glass Engineering Ltd* [2003] 2 All ER 615, where the parties may not even have regarded their arrangement as a guarantee, or even turned their minds to the legal nature or characterization of their arrangement. This case is considered further at para 26.26 below.

[10] See *Moschi v Lep Air Services Ltd* [1973] AC 331 (HL); Paget, para 33.2.

[11] Or, alternatively, where the obligation to pay is limited recourse in terms of the assets concerned. On this subject, see *Deutsche Bank v Ibrahim* [1992] 1 Bank LR 267 and other cases noted by Paget, para 33.27.

[12] On this point, see Chitty at para 44-001, citing *Moschi v Lep Air Services Ltd* [1973] AC 331 (HL); *Trafalgar House Construction (Regions) Ltd v General Surety & Guarantee Co Ltd* [1996] 1 AC 199 (CA) and *Sunbird Plaza Pty Ltd v Maloney* (1998) 166 CLR 245 (High Court of Australia). An undertaking to procure payment by the primary debtor constitutes a 'guarantee': see *Technology Partnership plc v Afro-Asian Satellite Communications (UK) Ltd* [1998] EWCA Civ 1520, a case on the Statute of Frauds 1677 (below).

[13] ie the interest will represent damages for the guarantor's failure to procure performance by the primary debtor. The point will usually be theoretical since standard forms of bank guarantees will invariably extend specifically to interest and any other sums owing by the debtor.

Formalities

Introduction

26.10 It has already been noted that a guarantee is a form of contract. As a result, an arrangement will only constitute an enforceable guarantee if it satisfies the general requirements for a valid and binding contract. It is not proposed to examine all of these requirements in detail,[14] rather, it is intended to deal with those issues which can be of particular difficulty in the context of guarantees given to banks.

26.11 As will be seen, guarantees are subject to additional requirements over and above those applicable to ordinary contracts.

Offer and Acceptance

26.12 The existence of an offer and its acceptance are fundamental to the existence of a contract.

26.13 In the context of a guarantee given to a bank, the executed guarantee will usually be delivered to the bank, thus constituting the offer. The receipt and retention by the bank of the document proffered to it may constitute the acceptance; alternatively, acceptance may occur when funds are advanced in reliance on the guarantee.[15]

Consideration

26.14 If a guarantee is to be contractually binding, then the bank must give consideration for the guarantor's promise.[16] In most cases, this requirement is satisfied because, in return for the guarantee, the bank will agree to advance funds to the borrower.[17] In other cases, a guarantee may be given in consideration of the bank deferring a demand for repayment against a borrower who has run into financial difficulties.[18]

26.15 As a matter of practice, standard forms of bank guarantee provide for execution as a deed, thus obviating the need to prove consideration in a more positive way.[19]

---

[14] For full discussion of that subject, see Chitty, ch 2–4.

[15] The exact point of time at which acceptance occurs would depend upon the precise factual background. The issue could be of some importance in practice, because the offer can be withdrawn at any time prior to its acceptance.

[16] Whilst it is necessary that consideration should exist, it is not necessary that it should be explicitly stated in the guarantee itself: Mercantile Law Amendment Act 1856, s 3.

[17] Note that the consideration must move *from* the bank, but it need not move *to* the guarantor: see Chitty, para 3-039.

[18] If a guarantee is given at the request of the bank in this type of situation, then it may be inferred that the guarantee is given in order to avert an immediate demand: *Greenham Ready Mixed Concrete Ltd v CAS (Industrial Developments) Ltd* (1965) 109 Sol Jo 209.

[19] In such a case, a guarantee given by an individual must comply with the requirements of s 1(3)(a) of the Law of Property (Miscellaneous Provisions) Act 1989. The provision requires the execution of the document by the guarantor, the signature of a witness and delivery as a deed. In the case of a company, the document must be duly executed under the common seal of the company, or it may be executed by two directors, or one director and the secretary. For details of the execution formalities, see Companies Act 2006, ss 43–47. Some care is, however, needed in procuring the execution of a guarantee by way of deed, since it has been

Intention to Create Legal Relations

A guarantee is only legally binding if the parties intended to create a legally enforceable **26.16**
relationship.[20] Standard forms of documentation will be used which will make it plain
that a formal relationship is contemplated; the loan agreement or facility letter will make it
clear that the guarantee is a condition precedent to the obligation to lend, thus emphasizing the importance attached to its legally binding character as a part of the overall
transaction.

Inevitably, however, difficulties may arise where the (alleged) guarantee is given in 'non- **26.17**
standard' circumstances. In such a case, it may be necessary to examine carefully the terms
of the document and the circumstances surrounding its conclusion. In this respect, 'letters
of comfort' are sometimes encountered, which do not contain the language usually seen in
standard guarantee documentation. Such letters do not explicitly guarantee the payment
obligations owing to the bank; they will instead contain obligations of a much more nebu-
lous nature (eg '… it is our normal policy to ensure that our subsidiaries have adequate
resources to meet their obligations as they arise …'). If a letter of comfort was given in lieu
of a guarantee for specific reasons (eg because a full guarantee would have required exchange
control approval in the obligor's jurisdiction), then the court is likely to conclude that the
parties did not intend to create a legally binding guarantee.[21] It does, however, remain open
to the court to conclude that the parties intended to create a contractual obligation of some

stated that the signature and witness attestation must all form a part of the same physical document: *R (on
the application of Mercury Tax Group and another) v Her Majesty's Revenue and Customs* [2008] EWHC 2721,
para 40. This may appear uncontroversial for this requirement will invariably be met in the case of standard
form bank guarantees. However, where—as is common practice in the context of international transactions—the guarantor sends a signing page to be attached to the final text, the decision in *Mercury* suggests
that the guarantor should specifically acknowledge the content of the final text. If the execution version is
subsequently altered, the guarantee will remain binding if it can be shown that this was to correct an error or
the guarantor intended the signing page to be applied to the revised text: *Koeningsblatt v Sweet* [1923] 2 Ch
314 (CA); *New Hart Builders Ltd v Brindley* [1975] 2 Ch 342.

[20] Thus, for example, if the parties refer in desultory fashion to the giving of a guarantee in the preliminary
heads of terms for their transaction but the fully negotiated agreement contains no reference to it, then the
court is likely to hold that no guarantee was intended to be given solely as a result of the passing reference
to such an arrangement in the heads of terms: see *Carlton Communications plc v Granada Media plc* [2002]
EWHC 1650 (Comm).
[21] In *Kleinwort Benson Ltd v Malaysia Mining Corporation Berhad* [1989] 1 WLR 379 (CA), the comfort
letter stated that it was the policy of the Malaysian parent company '… to ensure that the business of MMC
Metals Limited is at all times in a position to meet its liabilities to you under the above arrangements …'.
It was held that this did not create a legally binding obligation, in part because a full guarantee would have
required the approval of the central bank under the Malaysian Exchange Control Act. The absence of such
consent suggested that no legally binding commitment was intended, since it could not be presumed that
the parent intended to act unlawfully with respect to its own, national monetary laws. In Australia, however,
very similar wording ('… we take this opportunity to confirm that it is our practice to ensure that our affiliate
will at all times be in a position to meet its financial obligations as they fall due …') was held to constitute a
guarantee: see *Banque Bruxelles Lambert SA v Australian National Industries Ltd* (1989) 21 NSWLR 502. It is
suggested that the absence of exchange control considerations was a key consideration in the latter case, leaving the court free to take a broader view of the parties' commercial intentions. For an English case in which
the court appeared willing to enforce the terms of a comfort letter, see *Chemco Leasing SpA v Rediffusion plc*
[1987] 1 FTLR 201. In the event, however, the court declined enforcement on the basis that the lender had
not complied with some of the conditions set out in the comfort letter.

form, albeit falling short of a guarantee in its fullest sense. For example, if a parent company undertakes to notify the lending bank of any proposal to dispose of the borrowing subsidiary, it may be liable in damages if it fails to comply with that undertaking, since the lender may have continued to provide funding on a false premise. In other words, the choice does not lie between a fully enforceable guarantee and a void document; a range of legally valid obligations can exist in the area between those two extremes.[22]

26.18   In the writer's experience, letters of comfort in the loose sense described above are less frequently encountered in modern banking practice.[23] There may be technical reasons for this state of affairs; for example, if the lending bank wishes to account for the risk-weighted asset by reference to the guarantor's credit standing, then the guarantee must be an enforceable and unequivocal document.[24] But quite apart from that, banks will be disinclined to accept such diluted undertakings in an era of tight credit conditions.

Requirement of Writing

26.19   Most contracts can be made orally and without any requirement for the contract to be reduced to writing; the agreement will remain enforceable provided that its terms can be proved by evidence and the other criteria for the creation of an enforceable contract have been met. In the case of a contract of guarantee, however, this rule is varied by the surviving provisions of the Statute of Frauds 1677. Section 4 provides that:

> … no action shall be brought … whereby to charge the defendant upon any special promise to answer for the debt, default or miscarriage of another person … unless the agreement upon which such action shall be brought, or some memorandum or note thereof, shall be in writing and signed by the party to be charged therewith or some other person thereunto by him lawfully authorised …[25]

26.20   The Statute does not state that the guarantee is void, but merely provides that it cannot be enforced in the absence of written evidence and a signature by the guarantor or his agent.[26] The provision is thus apparently of a procedural character,[27] with the result that the

---

[22] There may even be occasions when the lending institution itself may wish to argue that the arrangement is not a full guarantee but is a more diluted—albeit legally effective—undertaking. This might occur where the arrangement has not been reduced to writing or has not been executed by or on behalf of the party concerned. Such an arrangement would not be legally enforceable as a guarantee in view of its lack of compliance with s 4 of the Statute of Frauds 1677 (on which see para 26.19 below).

[23] Although it arose in a non-banking context, it may be noted that an argument that a particular undertaking amounted merely to a letter of comfort (or moral obligation) was rejected in *Associated British Ports v Ferryways NV* [2009] All ER (D) 198.

[24] On risk-weighted assets and credit risk mitigation under Basel II, see paras 6.40–6.49 above.

[25] The section applies not only to the guarantee itself but also to an agreement under which a party undertakes to provide such a guarantee: *Compagnie Generale d'Industrie et de Participation v Myson Group Ltd* (1984) 134 NLJ 788.

[26] See *Maddison v Alderson* (1883) 8 App Cas 467. In a development which cannot possibly have been within the contemplation of the 1677 legislature, it has been held that an individual's name *automatically* reproduced in his email address is not a 'signature' for the purposes of s 4, although a manually typed name is more likely to be sufficient: see *Mehta v J Pereira Fernandes SA* [2006] EWCA 813 (Ch).

[27] Provisions to the effect that a contract shall be 'void' suggest a rule of substantive law which should in principle be applied wherever the contract is governed by English law. Expressions such as 'unenforceable' or 'no action shall be brought' suggest a rule of procedure, to be applied by the English courts regardless of the

principle has been applied by the English courts in cases involving a guarantee governed by a foreign system of law.[28] The importance of this point in a cross-border context has, however, been diminished by Rome I, which allows that the existence of a contract can be proved by reference to the laws of various different countries with which the contract has a connection; the matter is thus no longer assigned exclusively to the procedural law of the forum.[29]

Nevertheless, the fact that the guarantee may be unenforceable (as opposed to absolutely **26.21** void) may have practical consequences. For example, if the guarantor is also a depositor with the beneficiary bank, then the bank may be able to exercise a right of set-off. When the guarantor sues for the repayment of the deposit, the bank could plead the obligation under the guarantee by way of defence. This would not offend section 4, since the bank is not 'bringing an action' for the purposes of that provision.

But it remains necessary to ask: what will constitute a sufficient 'memorandum' for the **26.22** purposes of section 4 of the 1677 Act? It seems clear that the requisite signature must be appended to a document which sets out all of the core terms of the guarantee[30] so that, as a minimum, the memorandum must identify the principal debtor and the arrangements in respect of which the guarantee is given. It must also make clear the guarantor's intention to answer for the relevant obligations in the event of the borrower's default. Extrinsic evidence cannot be admitted to fill in the gaps in an otherwise inadequate memorandum, since this would defeat the objectives of section 4. Nevertheless, such evidence may be admissible to explain the terms of the memorandum against its factual background. Thus, if the section 4 memorandum refers to 'proposed leasing arrangements' between the principal debtor and the financier, then other evidence can be admitted to identify the arrangements to which the memorandum was intended to refer.[31]

---

law applicable to the contract in issue. However, it is impossible to lay down firm rules in this area, since much will depend on the circumstances, the detailed statutory language and the policy objectives of the legislation concerned.

[28] See *Leroux v Brown* (1852) 12 CB 801 and other cases discussed in Dicey, Morris and Collins, para 7-018. Notwithstanding the discussion in the text, it should be said that the characterization of s 4 as a procedural provision is by no means certain, and the decision in *Leroux v Brown* has been doubted.

[29] See Art 11 of Rome I and the materials mentioned in the previous footnote. Of course, Rome I only applies if a conflict of law issue arises for the purposes of Article (1) of the regulation. It cannot assist where the guarantee is of a purely domestic nature. If an attempt is made to enforce a foreign law guarantee in an English court under circumstances where the guarantee is valid under its applicable law but would be unenforceable on the basis of section 4, the court would have to decide whether section 4 is intended to be an overriding mandatory provision of the forum which must be given effect in any event in accordance with Art 9(1) of Rome I. It may also be argued that, as a rule of procedure, s 4 is applicable to all court proceedings in England, regardless of the law applicable to the contract. It is not proposed to pre-empt these complex issues.

[30] See *The Anemone* [1987] 1 Lloyds Rep 546 and other authorities cited by Paget, para 33.3.

[31] Mercantile Law Amendment Act 1856, s 3; *Perrylease Ltd v Imecar AG* [1988] 1 WLR 463. For further cases on this principle, see *Beckett v Nurse* [1948] 1 KB 535 (CA); *Elias v George Sakely & Co (Barbados) Ltd* [1983] 1 AC 646 (PC).

Guarantees and Indemnities

Introduction

26.23 Although the issue now arises only occasionally in modern banking practice, it is necessary to make a few observations on the distinction between a guarantee and an indemnity.[32] The distinction between the two types of arrangement has been described[33] as follows:

> An indemnity is a contract by one party to keep the other harmless against loss, but a contract of guarantee is a contract to answer for the debt, default or miscarriage of another …

Distinction between Guarantees and Indemnities

26.24 The above quotation highlights the reason for the peculiar quirk in English law created by section 4 of the Statute of Frauds 1677.[34] In order to enforce an indemnity, it is merely necessary for the claimant to show that he has suffered a loss falling within the scope of the indemnity agreement. It is unnecessary to attribute that loss to the default of a third party and section 4 accordingly has no application to such an arrangement. An oral indemnity is thus enforceable on the same footing as any other contract.[35] A guarantee is, however, necessarily a secondary obligation, and its enforcement depends upon the existence of an unsatisfied obligation on the part of the primary debtor. Accordingly:

(a) as already noted, a guarantee is only enforceable if reduced to writing and signed by or on behalf of the guarantor;

(b) the obligations created by a guarantee (strictly so called) can only be enforceable if the guaranteed party has indeed been guilty of a default in respect of the underlying obligation concerned. Consequently, if that obligation is not enforceable, then there is no 'default' to which the guarantee can apply or which can justify a call under it,[36] a debtor cannot default on an obligation which does not legally exist. Equally, if the underlying obligation has been fully discharged by the primary debtor in accordance with its

---

[32] In *Yeoman Credit Ltd v Latter* [1961] 2 All ER 294, at p 299, the issue was rightly described as '… a most barren controversy. It dates back, of course, to the Statute of Frauds 1677, and has raised many hair-splitting distinctions of exactly that kind which brings the law into hatred, ridicule and contempt by the public …'.

[33] *Yeoman Credit Ltd v Latter* [1961] 2 All ER 294, p 296. In *Stadium Finance Co Ltd v Helm*, (1965) 109 Sol Jo 471 (CA), the distinction was said not to be a pure matter of construction but depended on the 'whole burden' of the agreement—was there a primary obligation and a secondary obligation, or were there two primary obligations?

[34] The relevant wording of s 4 has been reproduced in para 26.19 above.

[35] It should be noted that, since the indemnity is designed to hold the beneficiary harmless against losses flowing from a particular source, it is incumbent on the beneficiary to prove his loss: see *The Fanti* [1992] AC 1 (HL). To this extent, an indemnity is similar to a guarantee in the sense that the beneficiary's claim is in damages, rather than debt: compare the discussion of *Moschi v Lep Air Services Ltd* at para 26.07 above.

[36] See *Coutts & Co v Browne-Lecky* [1946] 2 All ER 207; *Yeoman Credit Ltd v Latter* [1961] 2 All ER 294 (CA). Both of these cases involved primary debtors who were under the age of majority, and whose obligations under the primary contract were unenforceable. The guarantee in *Browne-Lecky* was unenforceable because, under s 1 of the Infants Relief Act 1874, a loan made to a minor was void. The position of the guarantor in such a case may now be different, because s 1 of the 1874 Act has been repealed and s 1 of the Minors Contracts Act 1987 now provides that a guarantee is not to be unenforceable solely on the ground that the principal debtor is a minor. On this subject, see Chitty, para 8-045.

terms, then the guarantor will likewise be fully discharged without further act or payment on his part;[37] and

(c) the distinction can be of further importance in that the special defences available to a guarantor[38] are not generally available in relation to a contract of indemnity.

Standard forms of bank guarantee will attempt to create both a guarantee and an indem- **26.25** nity, and will confirm that the guarantor assumes the role of principal debtor and thus remains liable notwithstanding the unenforceability of the underlying debt obligation.[39] In principle, such provisions should be enforceable because the character of the agreement—ie whether it should be classified as a guarantee or indemnity or as a primary or secondary obligation—depends on the true construction of the words used.[40] Nevertheless, banks should remain astute to ensure that guarantees comply with section 4 of the 1677 Act,[41] because a court may hold that 'principal debtor' and 'indemnity' language are merely subsidiary clauses in a document whose overall effect is intended to be that of a contract of guarantee.[42]

The durability of this antiquated section has recently been confirmed by various recent **26.26** decisions. In particular, the House of Lords has decided that the principle of estoppel cannot be invoked against a guarantor so as to prevent him from relying on the protection intended to be afforded to him by this provision.[43] Attempts to enforce guarantees have also failed in various cases as a result of the section.[44]

The *procedural* nature of the provision does give rise to some potentially difficult questions, **26.27** because the offending guarantee remains a valid obligation, even though it is not enforceable by action. Consequently, if the guarantor happened to have an account with the lending bank, the lender may be able to make demand and to debit the account with amounts owing under the guarantee even though it does not comply with section 4. If the guarantor sued for repayment of his deposit, then the bank may plead its right of set-off by way

---

[37] The Court of Appeal found it necessary to decide this apparently obvious point in *Western Credit Ltd v Alberry* [1964] 2 All ER 938.

[38] See the discussion at para 26.67 below and the decision in *Associated British Ports v Ferryways NV* [2009] EWCA Civ 189 (CA).

[39] It has been held that 'primary obligor' wording of this kind is sufficient to render the guarantor liable as principle debtor, so that he cannot raise defences which may be available to the borrower himself: see *ILG Capital LLC v Van der Merwe* [2008] All ER (D) 297 (May).

[40] *Moschi v Lep Air Services Ltd* [1973] AC 331 (HL); *Associated British Ports v Ferryways NV* [2009] EWCA Civ 189 (CA).

[41] The 'email signature' decision in *Mehta v J Pereira Fernandes AS* [2006] EWHC 813 (Ch) (see n 26 above) provides a salutary lesson in this respect.

[42] For an illustration of this approach, see *State Bank of India v Kaur* [1995] NPC 43 (CA).

[43] *Actionstrength Ltd v International Glass Engineering SpA* [2003] 2 All ER 615. If the guarantor could be estopped from pleading s 4, then the purpose of the provision would be defeated since a guarantee could be enforced even though it did not comply with the requirements or policy of the section.

[44] See, for example, *Zabihi v Janzemini* [2008] EWHC 2910, para 64 and *Masood v Zahoor* [2008] EWHC 1034 (Ch), para 251. See also *Pitts v Jones* [2008] 1 All ER 941 (CA), which includes a discussion of the approach which the court should adopt in seeking to distinguish between a guarantee and an indemnity. In the event, the arrangement at issue in that case was found to constitute a guarantee which could not be enforced for want of compliance with s 4 of the 1677 Act.

of defence. This would not seem to offend section 4, since the proceedings have not been instituted by the bank.[45]

Interpretation and Liability

Introduction

26.28   It has been noted earlier that, historically, the courts have tended to be protective of guarantors. It has also been shown that standard forms of bank guarantee will seek to deprive the guarantor of that protection in many cases. This state of affairs gives rise to various issues, namely, (i) how will the court approach the interpretation of guarantees, (ii) the nature and extent of the guaranteed liabilities, (iii) the essential validity of a guarantee, and (iv) the nature of the guarantor's liability.

Interpretation

26.29   A guarantee is a form of contract and is thus subject to the ordinary rules applicable to the interpretation of commercial agreements. The document must therefore be construed as a whole, having regard to the circumstances known to the parties at the time of its conclusion.[46] The key question will usually be: what is the nature and extent of the indebtedness which is covered by the guarantee? Two points may be briefly noted:

(a)   standard forms of bank guarantee will often provide for the guarantor to cover all of the obligations from time to time owing by the primary debtor.[47] It should be made clear that the guarantee extends to obligations owed jointly with others and (if such be the intention) that it extends to obligations which the primary obligor himself owes as surety for the debts of another;[48] and

(b)   if the guarantee relates to the indebtedness of the primary obligor in respect of 'banking facilities', it is submitted that this should include obligations in respect of bonds, guarantees, bills of exchange, and similar instruments issued or accepted by the bank, as well as overdrafts and other advances.[49]

26.30   This straightforward approach to contractual interpretation must nevertheless be treated with care in the context of guarantees given to banks. There are two, related reasons for this cautionary statement. First of all, the court's approach to questions of interpretation will inevitably be coloured by the traditionally protective attitude towards guarantors. Secondly,

---

[45] Section 4 appears to contemplate that it should apply only where the proceedings are instituted by the creditor. It does not appear to prevent the use of the guarantee obligation by way of defence, set-off or counterclaim.

[46] See *Prenn v Simmonds* [1971] 1 WLR 1381, *Perrylease Ltd v Imecar AG* [1988] 1 WLR 463, *Bank of Scotland v Wright* [1991] BCLC 244, *Investors Compensation Scheme Ltd v West Bromwich Building Society* [1998] 1 WLR 896 and other cases cited by Paget at para 33.15. On the rules of contractual interpretation generally, see Chitty, paras 12-041–12-094.

[47] In the case of a personal customer, however, banks will now stipulate for a specific financial limit. This practice was originally adopted to comply with para 11 of the Banking Code, on which see Chapter 4 above.

[48] See the situation which arose in *Bank of Scotland v Wright* [1991] BCLC 244.

[49] The expression was also held to extend to foreign exchange facilities in *Bank of India v Transcontinental Commodity Merchants Ltd* [1982] 1 Lloyds Rep 506 (CA).

bank guarantees are almost invariably provided on the bank's own standard form, with the result that any ambiguities in the meaning of the document should usually be resolved in favour of the guarantor.[50] But in spite of these considerations, courts have admitted evidence to clarify both the scope of the liabilities intended to be covered by a guarantee, and the existence of any preconditions to the enforcement of the document.[51]

It must be said that—in commenting on the correct approach to the interpretation of guarantees—there is an obvious tension between the assertion that ordinary contractual principles of interpretation apply and the court's defensive approach to the position of a guarantor. There are, however, signs that the courts are seeking to place the contract of guarantee on the same footing as any other commercial contract, and are moving away from the broader desire to protect a guarantor. In the broader commercial context, the courts will now look to ascertain the common aim or intention of the parties against the background of the information available to the parties at the time the agreement was made.[52] Thus, where a company director gave a guarantee covering 'the whole debt' of his company, the natural meaning of this language to a person familiar with the background would have extended to both past and future indebtedness, and would not have been restricted to liabilities arising from future transactions only.[53] **26.31**

The Guaranteed Liabilities

It will also be necessary to determine precisely the nature and extent of the obligations which the guarantor has agreed to cover. This will not usually cause any great difficulty where—as is commonly the case—the guarantee relates to '… all sums from time to time owing by the principal debtor on any account whatsoever …'. **26.32**

But the point will not always be so straightforward, and banks need to exercise some care in this field. The problem is well illustrated by the decision in *Triodos Bank NV v Dobbs*.[54] The bank had entered into two loan agreements in 1996 with a company called Acorn Televillages Limited. Mr Dobbs was a director of Acorn and gave a guarantee of certain monies owing '… under or pursuant to …' those loan agreements. The bank subsequently entered into new loan agreements (described as 'replacements') with Acorn in 1998. **26.33**

---

[50] See, for example, *Amalgamated Investment and Property Co Ltd v Texas Commerce International Bank Ltd* [1982] QB 84; *Eastern Counties Building Society v Russell* [1947] 2 All ER 734 (CA). In spite of this principle, the court will view a guarantee as a whole with a view to ascertaining its intended scope and extent: *Bank of Scotland v Wright* [1991] BCLC 244. In attempting to protect the guarantor, the court should not strain to avoid the clear meaning of the guarantee: see *Tam Wing Chuan v Bank of Credit and Commerce International Ltd* [1996] 2 BCLC 693.

[51] See *Coghlan v SH Lock (Australia) Ltd* [1987] 3 BCC 183, *Perrylease Ltd v Imecar AG* [1988] 1 WLR 463, *Associated Japanese Bank (International) Ltd v Credit du Nord SA* [1988] 3 All ER 902, and other cases cited in the Encyclopaedia of Banking Law, para 2054.

[52] ie in accordance with the broader approach endorsed by the House of Lords in *Investors Compensation Board Ltd v West Bromwich Building Society* [1998] 1 All ER 98.

[53] See *Static Control Components (Europe) Ltd v Egan* [2004] EWHC Civ 392. See also the construction issues which arose in the context of the guarantee in *Dumford Trading AG v OAO Alantrybflot* [2005] EWHC Civ 24.

[54] [2005] EWCA Civ 630 (CA). For a case in which a bank lost the benefit of a director's personal guarantee of his company's borrowings because of apparent confusion between the parties, see *Lloyds TSB Bank plc v Hayward* [2005] EWCA Civ 466.

The agreements were further replaced in 1999 and the overall amount available for utilization was significantly increased. Unfortunately, the bank omitted to take fresh guarantees from Mr Dobbs. The Court of Appeal seems to have taken the view that the 1996 guarantee would have extended to any 'amendments or variations' to the original facility agreements. However, the court then went on to observe:[55]

> The question is then whether what is said to be an amendment or variation is correctly so called. To my mind, an agreement which truly 'replaces' the original loan agreement would not rightly be called an amendment or variation to the original agreement, since it will be a new agreement. This will be particularly true in the context of a guarantee which obliges the guarantor to pay sums falling due 'under or pursuant to' an earlier agreement. For this purpose, it does not matter whether the old agreement is discharged in the sense of the loan being fully repaid and a new agreement then made (in the technical sense of their being a novation) or whether there is a replacement agreement which is, for the future, treated as governing the parties' relationships. The new governing agreement is not the agreement 'under or pursuant to' which there falls due the money which the guarantor has guaranteed to pay…

26.34 It is also necessary to emphasize that (i) the identity of the intending guarantor must be clear and (ii) the guaranteed liabilities must be the liabilities of the person identified in the guarantee as the principal or primary debtor. Again, these questions of identification may appear to be obvious point but confusion can occur, especially in relation to groups of companies which may have very similar names.[56] A problem of misnomer arose in *Dumford Trading AG v OAO Alantrybflot*.[57] In that case, ZAO Alantrybflot was a subsidiary of OAO Alantrybflot.[58] The guarantee at issue had named one entity as the guarantor but then referred to the registered office of the other company. As a result of this confusion, it was unclear which entity was intended to be the guarantor. That issue had to be tried on the facts and the claimant was thus unable to obtain summary judgment. Needless to say, difficulties of this kind can result in delays in enforcement which, in turn may often lead to a lower recovery.

Essential Validity

26.35 Like any other contract, the essential validity of a guarantee can be attacked on a variety of grounds, including fraud, mistake, and undue influence.[59] There is, however, one particular point which will generally be specific to a guarantee.

26.36 If it is sought to set aside the guarantee on the basis that the bank has misled the guarantor as to the financial status of the main borrower, then that action can only be maintained if

---

[55] At para 9 of the judgment.
[56] To avoid this problem and also to minimize confusion which may be caused by later changes of corporate names, it is good practice to include the registered numbers of the various entities involved.
[57] [2005] EWHC Civ 24.
[58] The relevant entities were incorporated in Russia. According to the judgment, 'OAO' denotes a public company, whilst 'ZAO' refers to a private company.
[59] See the discussion of the decision in *Etridge* and companion cases at para 32.44 below.

the representation[60] was reduced to writing. Section 6 of the Statute of Frauds Amendment Act 1826[61] reads as follows:

> No action shall be brought whereby to charge any person upon or by reason of any representation or assurance made or given concerning or relating to the character, conduct, credit, ability, trade or dealings of any other person, to the intent or purpose that such other person may obtain credit, money or goods, unless such representation or assurance be made in writing, signed by the party to be charged therewith.

Nature of the Guarantor's Liability

It is one thing to say that a guarantee is valid and legally binding and has the legal effect **26.37** contended for by the creditor in a particular case. It is quite another to decide exactly how much is due under the guarantee. Two points may be noted in this regard:

(a) first of all, and perhaps somewhat strangely, it has been held that a claim under a guarantee is a claim in *damages*, rather than in *debt*. This follows from the fact that the guarantor effectively undertakes to ensure that the principal obligor will perform his payment obligations and the creditor's claim is in the nature of a claim for damages for failing to procure that performance.[62] This would mean that the creditor would have to take steps to mitigate his loss so as to minimize his claim under the guarantee. Yet it seems to be accepted that the claim in damages must equate to the amounts which have gone unpaid by the primary obligor; and

(b) the bank must prove the amount owing under the guarantee in support of its claim. The guarantee is a separate contract from the underlying agreement and the lender thus cannot rely on a judgment against the borrower as evidence of the liability of the guarantor.[63] In practice, the guarantor should be joined into the main proceedings against the primary obligor, wherever possible. In addition, the standard guarantee clause to the effect that the records maintained by the bank as to the level of the borrower's indebtedness will be conclusive as against the guarantor will usually be valid and binding, at least in the absence of manifest error.[64]

---

[60] Although the provision about to be discussed is drawn from the Statute of Frauds Amendment Act 1826, it appears that the provision would apply to any form of representation made by the bank, whether innocent, negligent, or fraudulent.

[61] For a decision relating to this section, see *UBAF Ltd v European American Banking Corp* [1984] 2 All ER 226 (CA).

[62] See *Moschi v Lep Air Services Ltd* [1973] AC 331 (HL). It is submitted that this analysis suffers from an air of unreality. Where the guarantor is a subsidiary of the principal debtor, or is a bank providing a guarantee for a fee, it will not be in a position to 'ensure' that the primary debtor does anything. The reality is that the guarantor is accepting liability for the debt of a third party. There is no reason why this should not be treated as a debt of the guarantor, albeit subject to the contingency of a default by the main borrower.

[63] See, for example, *Sabah Shipyard (Pakistan) Ltd v Islamic Republic of Pakistan* [2007] EWHC 2602 (Comm).

[64] See *Van der Merwe v IIG Capital LLC* [2008] EWCA Civ 542.

Unfair Contract Terms

Introduction

26.38   As noted elsewhere,[65] the relationship between a bank and its customer may be signifi-cantly affected by both the Unfair Contract Terms Act 1977 and the Unfair Terms in Consumer Contracts Regulations 1999.[66]

26.39   It is not proposed to repeat that discussion here, but it is appropriate briefly to consider the implications of that legislation in the specific context of guarantees taken by banks to cover the obligations of their customers.

26.40   It has already been noted[67] that a guarantee is a species of contract. Consequently, guaran-tees are in principle within the scope of both the 1977 Act and the 1999 Regulations. What are the practical implications of this position?

Unfair Contract Terms Act 1977

26.41   As noted elsewhere,[68] the primary effect of the 1977 Act in the context of the banker-customer relationship is to prevent the bank from excluding or restricting liability for its own breach where the customer is dealing as a consumer or where the bank is dealing on its own standard terms of business. This position is qualified, in the sense that such terms will remain enforceable if they satisfy a 'reasonableness' test. As a matter of principle, the 1977 Act will apply to guarantees given to a bank—even if given by corporate entities—on the footing that they will generally be given on the bank's own standard form. Nevertheless, it must be borne in mind that a guarantee is essentially a unilateral undertaking by the guar-antor to answer for the default of the principal debtor. The bank will not normally under-take any obligations to the guarantor under the terms of the document and, in the absence of any such obligations, the possibility of clauses restricting the bank's liability for its own breach of contract will not generally arise. For example, standard form guarantees will seek to preserve the guarantor's liability notwithstanding variations to the principal agreement, time given to the debtor or other matters.[69] But provisions of this kind do not exclude or restrict a liability to which the bank would otherwise be subject. So, viewed from this per-spective, it is difficult to see how the provisions of the 1977 Act can in practice apply to a standard form of bank guarantee.

26.42   Yet the 1977 Act does apply in other respects. Any provision which restricts the exercise of the guarantor's rights under the guarantee may also be amenable to attack under the

---

[65] See paras 15.38–15.52 above.
[66] SI 1999/2083.
[67] See para 26.04 above.
[68] See paras 15.38–15.52 above.
[69] On matters of this kind, see the discussion at para 26.67.below. Note that the 1977 Act applies where (i) one party deals as a consumer *or* (ii) the parties deal on the bank's standard terms. The 1977 Act may there-fore apply to a bank even in the context of its dealings with corporate customers. This should be contrasted with the1999 Regulations discussed below, which apply only to consumers.

1977 Act.[70] By way of example, guarantors have occasionally asserted that they have a claim or counterclaim against the bank—for example, on the footing that the bank has a liability in damages to the guarantor in respect of the transaction. Guarantees will invariably contain provisions requiring guarantors to make payment on demand and free of any set-off or counterclaim,[71] and guarantors have argued that this provision should not be enforceable under the 1977 Act because it deprives the guarantor of defences or procedures which would otherwise be available to him. This defence has been rejected, on the basis that the bank has a legitimate commercial interest in receiving immediate payment without waiting for the cross-claim to be litigated.[72]

Guarantors have also sought to argue that the 'no set-off' clause is unreasonable in the sense **26.43** that it may require the guarantor to pay even though it asserts that it has a claim in damages for misrepresentation made by the bank with a view to inducing the guarantor to execute the document in the first instance. The reasonableness (or otherwise) of such a provision must be tested with respect to the circumstances as at the time of execution of the contract, and not with reference to the particular circumstances which subsequently arose. On this basis, and although written in very wide terms, a 'no set-off' clause was held to be reasonable in *Skipskredittforeningen v Emperor Navigation*,[73] and the lender was able to obtain summary judgment notwithstanding an alleged claim in respect of misrepresentations made by the bank. The same result followed in *Continental Illinois National Bank and Trust Co of Chicago v Papanicolaou*,[74] where the court held that, in a commercial case, a guarantee of this kind was intended to be equivalent to a letter of credit and—except in cases of fraud or other exceptional circumstances—should not be subjected to counterclaims or similar defences.

Unfair Terms in Consumer Contracts Regulations 1999

The Unfair Terms in Consumer Contracts Regulations 1999 ('the 1999 Regulations')[75] **26.44** approach the issue from a slightly different perspective. The following points may be noted:

(a) the scope of the 1999 Regulations is in some respects wider than the 1977 Act. The 1999 Regulations are not restricted to exclusion clauses. Instead, the regulations

---

[70] See s 13 of the Act, which extends the meaning of 'exclude or restrict' a liability to embrace provisions which (i) exclude or restrict any right or remedy in respect of a liability, (ii) render the enforcement of a liability subject to onerous conditions, or (iii) exclude or restrict rules of procedure.

[71] On provisions of this type, see the discussion in relation to loan or facility agreements at para 20.42 above.

[72] For a decision specifically in relation to a 'no set-off' clause in a guarantee, see *Barclays Bank plc v Kufner* [2008] EWHC 2319 (Comm). In *Stuart Gill Ltd v Horatio Myer & Co Ltd* [1992] QB 600 (CA), it was held that a clause was unreasonable insofar as it prevented set-off in respect of a claim arising with respect to the goods and services for which the relevant payment was claimed. It would be more difficult to apply this reasoning to a purely financial contract and, in any event, a bank undertakes no obligations to the guarantor under a standard form guarantee. As a result, it is suggested that the decision in *Stuart Gill* could not be applied in this particular context. This view derives some support from the decision in *Bank of Scotland v Reuben Singh* (unreported, 17 June 2005).

[73] [1997] 2 BCLC 398. In theory, the clause prohibited set-off even in respect of fraud by the bank, but this was held to be immaterial since fraud would have been outside the contemplation of the parties in any event. For a further case discussing (but not deciding) the extent of a guarantor's right of set-off under these circumstances, see *National Westminster Bank plc v Bowles* [2006] All ER (D) 447 (Jul).

[74] [1986] 2 Lloyds Rep 441 (CA).

[75] SI 1999/2038.

provide that standard form contractual terms are not binding on a consumer[76] to the extent to which they are 'unfair'. A term is 'unfair' if, contrary to the principle of good faith, there is an imbalance in the rights and obligations of the parties, to the disadvantage of the consumer;[77]

(b) a term which is deemed to be 'unfair' is not binding on the consumer, although the remainder of the contract may remain in force;[78]

(c) however, provided that they are written in plain and intelligible language, the court cannot undertake a 'fairness' assessment in relation to (i) the main subject matter of the contract or (ii) the adequacy of the remuneration as against the services supplied in exchange. Thus, the court cannot review the primary guarantee provisions, nor can it enquire as to the adequacy of the consideration received by the guarantor. This is perhaps a fortunate position, in that the guarantor will not generally receive any payment for the giving of the guarantee and, even if he does, he will not receive it from the bank.[79] As a result—subject to the 'plain intelligible language' requirement—an inquiry into the fairness of the terms of the principal terms of a guarantee will generally be foreclosed;

(d) yet this is not the end of the matter and further issues may arise in relation to ancillary clauses which are designed to support the validity of the guarantee. For example, as will be seen,[80] the bank owes various duties to the guarantor, and it is common practice to exclude those duties by means of the express terms of the standard form guarantee itself. It seems clear that such provisions would be amenable to challenge under the 1999 Regulations, to the extent to which they are applicable to the guarantee;

(e) this, in turn, begs a further question which flows from the secondary nature of a guarantee. Do the 1999 Regulations apply merely because the guarantor is acting outside the course of his trade or business? Or must the primary obligor likewise be incurred as a consumer if the regulations are to apply to the guarantee? Article 4(1) of the 1999 Regulations states that they are to apply '… in relation to unfair terms in contracts concluded between a seller or a supplier and a consumer …'. It had previously been decided that the 1999 Regulations should therefore not apply to a guarantee at all, because the bank is not selling or supplying services *to the guarantor*; it is merely receiving the benefit of a unilateral undertaking from him.[81] However, in *Barclays Bank plc v Kufner*,[82] this line of argument was rejected but it was also held that the 1999 Regulations

---

[76] ie a person acting outside the scope of his trade, business or profession: art 3(1) of the 1999 Regulations.

[77] Article 8 of the 1999 Regulations. Schedule 2 to the regulations sets out a list of factors which must be taken into account in determining whether a term is 'unfair' for these purposes. Many of these factors will be inapplicable to guarantees in view of their essentially unilateral nature. Provisions which may potentially be applicable to consumer financial contracts have already been noted at paras 15.38–15.52 above.

[78] Regulation 9 of the 1999 Regulations.

[79] As noted at para 26.14 above, the bank provides *consideration* for the guarantee in the technical sense, but this consideration is not *received* by the guarantor.

[80] See paras 26.55–26.68 below.

[81] This view was adopted in *Bank of Scotland v Reuben Singh* (unreported, 17 June 2005), followed in *Williamson v Bank of Scotland* [2006] EWHC 1289 (Ch) and *Manches v Freer* [2006] All ER (D) 428.

[82] [2008] EWHC 2319 (Comm), relying on a decision of the European Court of Justice in case C-45/96, *Bayerische Hypotheken- und Wechselbank AG v Dietzinger* [1998] 1 WLR 1035, albeit decided in a slightly different context.

apply only where the underlying facility is itself entered into by a consumer. It is submitted that *Kufner* is consistent with the scheme of the legislation and is to be preferred to the earlier authorities;

(f) even apart from the restrictive approach correctly adopted in *Kufner*, it should be remembered that a guarantor—even though a private individual—will frequently not himself be a 'consumer' for the purposes of the 1999 Regulations in any event. A director/shareholder who guarantees his company's overdraft will frequently be acting in the course of a business carried on by him, with the result that the 1999 Regulations cannot apply in any event.[83] But marginal cases may arise. For example, if a husband guarantees a loan to his wife to acquire a residence for them, then both are acting as consumers and the 1999 Regulations will apply to the husband's guarantee. Matters become more marginal if the loan is to be used by the wife to purchase shares or similar assets. Assuming that these are intended to be personal investments and are not acquired as part of a trade or business carried on by the wife, then both she and her husband will be acting as consumers and the 1999 Regulations will apply to the husband's guarantee.[84]

Capacity to Guarantee

Introduction

This section will consider the special defences which may be available to individuals, companies, and other entities which provide a guarantee in respect of the obligations of another person. It should be emphasized that some of the defences about to be discussed may be of general application and may thus be available in a number of other contexts. However, guarantees pose special problems because they are unilateral instruments and it will frequently be obvious to the recipient lender that the guarantor derives no immediate or obvious benefit from the arrangement. **26.45**

Individuals

An individual who has attained the age of 18 enjoys contractual capacity[85] and is thus able to provide a guarantee to a bank. **26.46**

The courts have, however, traditionally regarded the giving of a guarantee as an onerous obligation, especially where private individuals are involved. There is always the danger that such a guarantee has been procured as a result of undue influence applied by the intending borrower; and that danger naturally increases where the guarantee is given by the borrower's wife or in any other case in which the borrower and guarantor are involved in a **26.47**

---

[83] This alternative line of reasoning was explored in *Kufner*, above.
[84] Cf *Standard Bank Ltd v Apostolakis* [2003] IL Pr 766.
[85] See Family Law Reform Act 1969, s 1(1). In formal terms, capacity can thereafter only be called into question if the guarantor was of unsound mind, or was insufficiently sober to understand the implications of the transaction at hand; on these aspects of contractual capacity, see Chitty, ch 8.

non-commercial relationship.[86] In cases of this kind, the bank is put on inquiry and is effectively required to assume that the borrower has brought improper influence to bear, unless it has taken adequate steps to ensure that the guarantor has received adequate and independent legal advice on the effect of the guarantee.

26.48   In practice, this type of issue has tended to arise in the context of an agreement by a wife or partner to provide security over the matrimonial home to support facilities provided to the husband's business. As a result, this subject is considered in more depth in the context of real estate security.[87] But it should be borne in mind that identical principles will apply where a spouse, partner, or other family member is asked to provide a guarantee, whether with or without security.

Companies

26.49   The contractual capacity of a company to provide a guarantee is governed by the terms of its memorandum of association. However, the giving of guarantees will be treated as one of the objects of the company, unless its ability to do so is expressly restricted by the terms of the memorandum.[88] The procedural steps required to sanction the execution of a guarantee will in turn be governed by the articles of association.[89]

26.50   In practical terms, however, any limitations imposed by these documents are now principally of concern as between the directors of the company and its shareholders;[90] outsiders—including banks—dealing with a company have now been largely insulated from the effect of these rules by sections 39, 40, and 41 of the Companies Act 2006 ('the 2006 Act').[91] These provisions accordingly require some explanation.

26.51   First of all, by virtue of section 39 of the Companies Act 2006, the validity of a guarantee cannot be called into question on the ground that the constitution of the company did not confer the necessary capacity to undertake such an obligation. It follows that it is no longer incumbent upon lenders to examine the detailed terms of the memorandum of association to determine whether the proposed guarantee falls within the scope of the express objects of the company or, under more modern circumstances, to determine whether the provision of the guarantee is specifically restricted by that document.[92] Banks and practitioners are thus relieved of a process which was frequently both tedious and pointless, and occasionally involved matters of fine interpretation. It should be added that section 39 will apply to

---

[86] This delicate turn of phrase was employed by Lord Nicholls in *Royal Bank of Scotland plc v Etridge (No 2)* [2001] UKHL 44 (para 87). The case is considered in more detail, below.

[87] See para 32.44 below.

[88] Companies Act 2006, s 31.

[89] Companies Act 2006, s 18.

[90] The memorandum and articles of association constitute a contract as between the company itself and its members: see Companies Act 2006, s 33.

[91] As a matter of detail, it should be noted that some of the provisions about to be discussed will not apply where the company concerned is a charity: see Companies Act 2006, s 42.

[92] See Companies Act 2006, s 31, to which reference has already been made.

protect the lending bank even if it has actual notice that the guarantee is beyond the contractual capacity of the company.[93]

Secondly, in favour of a bank dealing with a guarantor company *in good faith,* the power **26.52** of the board of directors to bind the company, or to authorize others to do so, is deemed to be free of any limitation under the company's constitution.[94] Once again, the bank is relieved of any obligation to examine the articles of association of the guarantor because it '… is not bound to enquire as to any limitation on the powers of the directors to bind the company …'.[95] As a result, the bank is not concerned with borrowing limits[96] and other internal restrictions on the powers of the board; nor is the bank obliged to ensure that any quorum requirements have been met, although it seems that there must have been at least some attempt—however legally defective—to hold a meeting to sanction the transaction or to authorize someone else to do so.[97] The requirement of good faith must, however, be carefully noted—especially in the present context. The bank is presumed to have acted in good faith in accepting a guarantee from the company concerned, and that presumption is not rebutted merely because the bank has actual knowledge of a relevant limitation on the directors' powers under the terms of its constitution.[98] Nevertheless, the presumption may be rebutted on other grounds, and it appears that the bank needs to exercise particular caution in the case of a corporate guarantee. The directors of a company are bound to exercise their powers in good faith for the benefit of the company itself;[99] by its very nature, however, a guarantee is given for the benefit of someone other than the company itself, because it is intended to facilitate borrowings by another entity. Under these circumstances, a bank which accepts a corporate guarantee is placed on notice of a possible irregularity, and it may be unable to satisfy the 'good faith' requirement unless it takes steps to satisfy itself that the guarantor company does indeed derive a benefit from the transaction at hand, or that it is

---

[93] eg whether because it has in fact examined the memorandum or because the directors have advised it of the position.

[94] Companies Act 2006, s 40(1). References to limitations deriving from the company's constitution include any such restrictions as may be found in any resolution of the company or any shareholders' agreement: s 40(3) of the 2006 Act.

[95] Section 40(2)(b)(i) of the 2006 Act. Once again, it is submitted that the bank can hold the company to the transaction even though it knew that the guarantee fell within the scope of some limitation applicable to the exercise of the directors' power to give guarantees. If the bank is not under a duty to make enquiries in the first place, it should not be disadvantaged by the fact that it had chosen to make such enquiries or had otherwise discovered the relevant limitation.

[96] A limit on borrowings will usually include a limit on the level of guarantees which may be given for the benefit of subsidiaries and others. For companies which adopted articles of association in the form of Table A to the Companies Act 1948, a borrowing limit equal to the company's capital and reserves applied—see art 79 of Table A.

[97] *Smith v Henniker-Major* [2002] BCC 544 (CA). A failure to give adequate notice to all of the directors of the company as a result of a mistaken interpretation of the relevant provisions of the articles of association will thus not affect an outside party dealing with the company in good faith, since the provision constitutes a '… limitation on the powers of the directors …' for these purposes: see *Ford v Polymer Vision Ltd* (Blackburn J, 6 May 2009).

[98] Companies Act 2006, s 40(b)(ii) and (iii).

[99] For reasons which will become apparent, it is necessary to emphasize that the directors must exercise their powers for the benefit of their particular company, and not for the benefit of the wider group of which the company forms a part. It should be noted that the duties of directors are now to some extent codified by ss 170–181 of the Companies Act 2006.

otherwise consistent with the directors' fiduciary duties.[100] The following points may be noted in this context:

(a) A parent company has an obvious interest in the commercial success of its subsidiaries and the availability of facilities to fund their activities. Consequently, where a parent provides a guarantee in such a case, the bank must generally be taken to have acted in good faith if it has verified the parent-subsidiary relationship. In the normal course, no further enquiries should be necessary for this purpose and the bank could rely on section 40 of the 2006 Act to hold the parent company to its guarantee.

(b) The position may, however, be different where a successful subsidiary is requested to provide an 'upstream' guarantee in respect of borrowings by its parent company. This may be justifiable where the parent company acts as treasurer to the group as a whole. The subsidiary will have access to the guaranteed funding and the cost of funding will be lower as a result of the provision of group guarantees.

(c) Yet it is necessary to exercise caution in such cases. For example, a commercially successful subsidiary which does not itself require additional funding may be asked to provide a guarantee in respect of a loan to its struggling parent company. A bank which accepts a subsidiary guarantee under such circumstances cannot necessarily be said to have acted in good faith, for it is on notice of a possible breach of duty by the directors of the guarantor. The bank may thus be unable to rely on section 40 to preserve the validity of the guarantee in such a case.[101] Nevertheless, even if the bank had accepted the guarantee without any enquiry, the guarantee would be binding if it was in fact given in the best interests of the company.[102]

(d) A guarantee given by a company in respect of the liabilities of an unconnected company necessarily places a duty of enquiry on the bank, and the 'good faith' test cannot be satisfied unless that duty is adequately discharged.[103] Likewise, if the bank knows that the guarantee is given for an improper corporate purpose, it will not be able to hold the company to the guarantee.[104]

---

[100] Although the case did not arise in a banking context and the statutory provisions were only briefly noted, the point made in the text is well illustrated by the House of Lords decision in *Criterion Properties plc v Stratford Properties LLC* [2004] UKHL 28.

[101] In this type of situation, it would be necessary to have recourse to more traditional procedures. The bank would have to ensure that company has power to provide the guarantee under the terms of its memorandum, and that all internal procedures required to sanction the transaction under the articles of association had been duly carried out. It would then have to obtain from the holding company a waiver of any breach of fiduciary duty involved in the execution of the guarantee, although it should be noted that any such waiver may only be effective if the subsidiary remains solvent notwithstanding the obligations assumed pursuant to the guarantee: on this subject, see *Rolled Steel Products (Holdings) Ltd v British Steel Corporation* [1986] Ch 246. In other words, if the statutory protections are not available for some reason, then the bank must take steps to satisfy itself that the directors are not in fact acting in breach of their fiduciary duties.

[102] In other words, the guarantee can only be impugned if (i) the directors did in fact provide the guarantee in breach of their duties *and* (ii) the bank was aware of the facts which gave rise to such breach: see, for example, *Charterbridge Corporation Ltd v Lloyds Bank Ltd* [1970] Ch 62, where a guarantee and security given to cover the liabilities of a fellow group member was upheld.

[103] *Rolled Steel Products (Holdings) Limited v British Steel Corporation* [1986] Ch 246.

[104] *Re Introductions Ltd* [1970] Ch 199.

(e) The presumption that the bank has acted in good faith is not displaced merely because the bank is aware of a division among the directors as to the intended guarantee.[105]

(f) If the bank has acted in good faith in taking the guarantee,[106] then a guarantee will be binding on the company so long as it is executed by a director who has actual or ostensible authority to do so.[107]

The points outlined above deal with the powers of the directors to bind the company to contracts with third parties. They may therefore conveniently be seen as a branch of the law of agency; the directors have apparent authority to enter into transactions with others, but a third party cannot rely on that authority if he is on notice that the directors are exercising their powers improperly.[108]   **26.53**

Other Entities

Care is also required when accepting guarantees from other forms of legal entity or business organization. Possible areas of difficulty include the following: **26.54**

(a) as already noted, the statutory protections discussed above may not be available where the company is a charity;[109]

(b) a member of a partnership does not have implied authority to execute a guarantee on behalf of a partnership.[110] Consequently, the lender should satisfy itself that the signatory has actual authority under or pursuant to the partnership agreement or, alternatively, should procure the signature of all partners;

(c) the powers of local authorities are prescribed exclusively by statute and the courts have adopted a very restrictive view of their capacity to provide guarantees;[111] and

(d) the powers of treaty organizations to provide guarantees will be governed exclusively by the treaty concerned and the statutes of the organization in question.

Duties of the Bank to the Guarantor

Introduction

It has been noted above that the courts have tended to regard a guarantee as an onerous contract, and have thus tended to adopt a protective attitude towards the guarantor. It thus   **26.55**

---

[105] *Ford v Polymer Vision Ltd* (Blackburn J, 6 May 2009), para 92.
[106] eg by making such inquiries as may be necessary to satisfy itself that no breach of fiduciary duty is involved.
[107] *Criterion Properties plc v Stratford Properties LLC* [2004] UKHL 28, discussed and applied in *Ford v Polymer Vision Ltd* (Blackburn J, 6 May 2009).
[108] On apparent authority and the position of the third party dealing with the company, see Chitty, paras 31-054–31-081. On the application of the principle in the present context, see Paget, para 10.5. For a recent case in which a claimant sought to rely on the ostensible authority of the chief executive of a Korean company to execute guarantees in respect of a shipbuilding contract, see *Rimpacific Navigation Inc v Daehan Shipbuilding Co Ltd* [200] EWHC 2941 (Comm).
[109] See Companies Act 2006, s 42.
[110] See *Alliance Bank Ltd v Kearsley* (1871) LR 6 CP 433.
[111] *Credit Suisse v Allerdale Borough Council* [1996] 2 Lloyds Rep 241 (CA); *Credit Suisse v Waltham Forest London Borough Council* [1996] 4 All ER 176 (CA). The guarantees given in each of these cases were held to be void on the basis that they fell beyond the authority's powers. Note also the *vires* issues which arose in relation to swap contracts entered into by local authorities: see the discussion at paras 23.23–23.28 above.

becomes necessary to consider whether the bank proposing to accept a guarantee owes any specific duties to the guarantor, for example, to ensure that he understands the effect of the guarantee and the commercial circumstances surrounding it.

26.56 It has already been seen that a bank should ensure that a guarantor in a non-commercial relationship with the borrower should be required to obtain independent legal advice, and that the bank may be required to satisfy itself that the directors of a corporate guarantor are acting in the interests of the company.[112] Yet it must be emphasized that these are not positive *duties* which the bank owes to the guarantor; rather, they are steps designed to ensure the validity of the guarantee. They are thus intended for the protection of the bank itself, not for the protection of the guarantor. Does the bank have any further or wider obligations to the prospective guarantor?

A Duty to Advise?

26.57 At the outset, it should be appreciated that a bank is not under any duty to offer advice to a prospective guarantor about the merits of giving the requested guarantee.[113] Apart from other considerations, this would create a direct conflict of interest since the bank will itself be the beneficiary of the arrangement.

26.58 Thus, whilst the bank will obviously make its own credit decision about the merits of the underlying transaction, this will be solely for its own protection. Credit approval for a particular facility will therefore not imply any positive advice or recommendation to the prospective guarantor.[114]

A Duty of Good Faith?

26.59 The relationship between the bank and the guarantor is not one of utmost good faith.[115] The bank is thus under no *general* duty to disclose to the guarantor any information in the possession of the bank and which might be relevant to the obligations which the guarantor is about to assume. Consequently, if the guarantor agrees to provide an 'all moneys' guarantee, it is not incumbent upon the bank to disclose either the extent of the customer's present borrowings, his overdraft limit or the existence of any other obligations which might fall within the scope of the 'all moneys' guarantee.[116] Acceptance of responsibility for such sums is inherent in the nature of a guarantee of this kind. Likewise, the bank is not obliged to disclose the fact that it has reservations about the borrower's own credit standing.[117]

---

[112] See the discussion at para 26.49 above.

[113] *Barclays Bank plc v Khaira* [1992] 1 WLR 623; *Union Bank of Finland v Lelakis* [1995] CLC 27, and other cases noted by Paget, para 28.22.

[114] *National Commercial Bank (Jamaica) Ltd v Hew* [2003] UKPC 51 (PC).

[115] The point has most recently been re-affirmed by the House of Lords in *Royal Bank of Scotland plc v Etridge (No 2)* [2001] UKHL 44, para 185.

[116] See, for example, *Union Bank of Australia Ltd v Puddy* [1949] VLR 242, *Goodwin v National Bank of Australasia* (1968) 117 CLR 173, *Westpac Banking Corporation v Robinson* (1993) 30 NSWLR 668 and other cases cited in Paget, para 33.13.

[117] *Commercial Bank of Australia Ltd v Amadio* (1983) 151 CLR 447. It may be said that such reservations will often be implicit in the request for the guarantee.

A Duty of Disclosure?

The bank is, however, subject to a more limited duty of disclosure, in that it must advise the **26.60**
guarantor of any particular circumstances which may be regarded as outside the normal
course and which may have an impact on the essential nature of the arrangements between
the bank and the guarantor. In one case,[118] the bank failed to disclose to the sureties that
the loan to the principal customer matured on the day on which the loan stock pledged
by the sureties was to mature, thus rendering it virtually certain that the bank would have
first recourse to the loan stock, to the detriment of the sureties. The security arrangements
were set aside in view of the non-disclosure of this vital point which materially affected the
fundamental nature of the underlying transaction and which would quite probably have
led the guarantors to act differently. Furthermore, if the bank believes that the guarantor
may have been misled into offering the guarantee, then the bank must disclose the true
state of affairs. It will, otherwise, be unable to enforce the guarantee, for it will have become
party to a scheme to defraud the guarantor.[119]

Of course, if the bank does elect to provide information about the borrower's financial **26.61**
position and the risks which the guarantor is about to assume, then it must take steps to
ensure the accuracy of that information; otherwise, the guarantor may be able to rescind
the guarantee on grounds of misrepresentation.[120]

Once the guarantee has been given, there is no obligation on the bank to advise the guaran- **26.62**
tor of any irregularities which subsequently come to light, such as fraud on the part of the
borrower.[121]

A Duty to take Other Security?

There may be situations in which it is anticipated that the bank will be taking additional **26.63**
guarantees and security in addition to the assurance to be provided by the particular
guarantor.

If the bank fails to complete the remainder of the anticipated security package, then this **26.64**
may deprive the guarantor of an expected right of subrogation or contribution.[122] On the
other hand, it has been decided that a bank does not owe an equitable duty to the guarantor
to perfect other security which it intended to take from the primary debtor.[123]

There may appear to be an element of inconsistency between these two views but, in any **26.65**
event, a standard guarantee will usually explicitly state that it remains effective notwithstanding any failure to take other security, so that defences of this nature will be contractually excluded.

---

[118] *Levett v Barclays Bank plc* [1995] 1 WLR 1260.
[119] See Paget, para 33.12, citing *Goad v Canadian Imperial Bank of Commerce* (1968) 67 DLR (2d) 189
and *Credit Lyonnais Bank Nederland v Export Credits Guarantee Department* [1996] 1 Lloyds Rep 200 (CA).
In similar vein, see *National Westminster Bank plc v Kotonou* [2006] All ER (D) 325 (May).
[120] See generally the provisions of the Misrepresentation Act 1967; *Barton v County NatWest Bank Ltd*
[1999] Lloyds Rep Bank 408.
[121] Paget, para 33.13, and cases there cited.
[122] On the rights of subrogation and contribution, see paras 26.84–26.85 below.
[123] See *Barclays Bank v Kufner* [2008] EWHC 2319 (Comm).

A Duty of Realization?

26.66 A guarantee will often be given as part of a larger package designed to secure the repayment of the facility. For example, the bank will often take a fixed and floating charge over the assets of the primary borrower.

26.67 Generally speaking, standard forms of bank guarantee will allow the bank to take proceedings against the guarantor before it takes any steps to enforce any of the other aspects of its security package. Of course, if the guarantor discharges the entirety of the debt in response to a demand, then it will take over the bank's security by virtue of its right of subrogation.[124] Realization of the security is then for the risk and benefit of the guarantor itself. But what is the position if the guarantor does not or cannot afford to discharge the underlying indebtedness in this way? The bank itself will be left in charge of the process of enforcement. It will be seen[125] that the lending bank owes duties to the primary debtor or mortgagor in enforcing its security. Does it owe similar duties to a guarantor of the same facility?

26.68 It has recently been confirmed in *Barclays Bank plc v Kingston*[126] that the lender in such a case does indeed owe an equitable duty of care to ensure that reasonable steps are taken to realize the security at a proper value. Given that the guarantor would have expected its potential liability to be mitigated by the value of the security, the court may perhaps be reluctant to hold this duty has been excluded by the terms of the guarantee itself.[127]

Discharge of the Guarantor

Introduction

26.69 Once a lending bank has made facilities available to a borrower, the parties are free to vary the terms of the arrangements in any way. For example, the bank may agree to increase or to extend the facilities or to release any security originally provided over the borrower's assets. It is, however, obvious that any such action may have an impact on the position of any guarantor. An increase in the amount of the facilities clearly increases the guarantor's exposure;[128] the release of security may deprive the guarantor of his right of subrogation to securities held by the bank; and the release of co-guarantors may deprive a guarantor of his rights of contribution.[129]

---

[124] On the guarantor's right of subrogation, see paras 26.84–26.85 below.

[125] See para 32.31 below.

[126] [2006] 1 All ER (Comm) 519.

[127] The point was made in the *Kingston* case, above. For earlier cases confirming the existence of this equitable duty, see *Standard Chartered Bank v Walker* [1982] 3 All ER 938, *American Express International Bank Corp v Hurley* [1985] 3 All ER 564 and *Skipton Building Society v Stott* [2000] 1 All ER (Comm) 257 (CA). In other cases—eg *Barclays Bank Ltd v Thienel* (1978) 247 EG 385 and *Burgess v Auger* [1998] 2 BCLC 478—it had been decided that no such duty was owed to a guarantor who had made no payment. But these decisions cannot stand in the face of the authorities just mentioned.

[128] At any rate, this is the case if the guarantee is given on an 'all monies' basis, and is not capped at a particular financial limit.

[129] The guarantor's rights of subrogation and contribution are briefly discussed at paras 26.84–26.85 below.

Discharge by Payment

Before moving to the more technical defences which may be available to a guarantor, it is **26.70** necessary to consider the more obvious and more common mode of discharge—namely, payment by the principal debtor itself. Provided that such a payment is not clawed back in the insolvency of the debtor itself,[130] then this must constitute a complete discharge of the guarantor. He has, after all, only agreed to answer for the debtor's *default*. Thus, if the primary debtor has exercised contractual rights to terminate his liability under the underlying contract and has complied with any conditions necessary to that end, then the guarantor will himself be discharged even though, as a result of the termination, the beneficiary has not earned his anticipated profit on the deal. The guarantor was not assuring to the beneficiary his expected return; he was merely guaranteeing that the debtor would pay whatever he was obliged to pay.[131]

It may not always be easy to determine whether the principal obligation has been dis- **26.71** charged for these purposes. For example, payment may occur as a result of an exercise of a right of set-off by the principal debtor, although this may to some extent depend on the terms of the main contract.[132] However, the mere fact that the debtor may have a counterclaim for unliquidated damages against the lender will not of itself afford any form of defence to a guarantor.[133]

Discharge of the Guarantor

As the above analysis demonstrates, there is a tension between the bank's desire to deal flex- **26.72** ibly with its borrower and the need to ensure that the guarantor is not unfairly prejudiced. How does the law resolve these tensions? What steps can banks take to minimize the risk that guarantees will inadvertently be discharged? A few points may be noted in this context:

(a) A guarantor may be discharged if the bank agrees to allow to the borrower additional time for payment.[134] At first sight, this may seem curious given that a call on the guarantee is thereby likewise deferred. However, it must be borne in mind that the borrower's financial position might deteriorate further during the extended period, thus devaluing the guarantor's rights of subrogation. It should also be appreciated that a bank does not agree to give time to the debtor merely because it defers enforcement as against the borrower itself or other security.[135]

---

[130] On preferences, see para 39.06 below.

[131] For a decision which illustrates this point, see *Western Credit Ltd v Alberry* [1964] 2 All ER 938 (CA). In discussions with the guarantor, the bank must take care not to give assurances that it will not vary the underlying facility agreement, since this may override the protective contractual clause noted in the text: see *Lloyds TSB Bank plc v Haywood* [2005] All ER (D) 384 (Apr).

[132] *Hyundai Shipbuilding and Heavy Industries Ltd v Pournaras* [1978] 2 Lloyds Rep 502; *The Maistros* [1984] 1 Lloyds Rep 646.

[133] *National Westminster Bank plc v Skelton* [1993] 1 All ER 242 and *Ashley Guarantee PLC v Zacaria* [1993] 1 WLR 62. These cases are noted by McKnight, para 16.10.3.

[134] *Mahant Singh v U Ba Yi* [1939] AC 601; *Associated British Ports v Ferryways NV* [2009] EWCA Civ 189 (CA).

[135] See *China and South Sea Bank Ltd v Tan* [1990] 1 AC 536.

(b) Material amendments to the terms of the underlying facility may also discharge the guarantor, since they may alter the nature of the risk which the guarantor had agreed to assume.[136] Such amendments would not usually affect the validity of an 'all moneys' guarantee for, by its very nature, the guarantor has agreed to accept responsibility for every obligation of the borrower to the bank, however they may arise.[137] But considerable care may be required where the guarantee is limited to monies due under specified facility agreements. Standard guarantees will always provide that the bank can agree to variations or amendments of those agreements without affecting the liability of the guarantor, but there may be cases in which the underlying deal is varied to such an extent that the original debt is extinguished and replaced by a new obligation which falls outside the scope of the guarantee. Difficult questions of degree will be involved, and the prudent course will be to obtain the explicit consent of the guarantor in each case.[138]

(c) The release of any security held for the borrowers' obligations and the release of any co-guarantor will respectively prejudice the guarantor's rights of subrogation and contribution, and may thus discharge the guarantor, at least to the extent of the value of the security thereby foregone.[139] For the same reasons, the bank's failure to take any additional guarantees and security contemplated at the time of the transaction may likewise provide a defence to the guarantor.[140] Again, the guarantee form will seek to exclude defences of this kind.

---

[136] *Holme v Brunskill* (1878) 3 QBD 495. Courts in Australia have formulated this test rather more strictly, holding that '… any departure by the creditor from the suretyship contract which is not obviously and without enquiry insubstantial, will discharge the surety from liability, whether it injures him or not …': *Anker Ltd v National Westminster Finance Australia Ltd* [1987] 162 CLR 549, at p 588. It is open to a guarantor to agree otherwise, but the wording must be clear and must cover the circumstances which have arisen. Thus, where a clause stated that the guarantor '… will not be released from any obligations by reason only of any extension of time granted or any other act or omission by the [lender] favouring the [borrower] …' this language was not broad enough to cover the lender's agreement to increase the overall amount of the facilities and the guarantor was discharged accordingly: see *Valstar v Silversmith* [2009] NSWCA 80 (New South Wales Court of Appeal).

[137] *Bank of Scotland plc v Makris and O'Sullivan* (Ch D, 15 May 2009).

[138] The difficulties experienced by the bank in *Triodos Bank v Dobbs* [2005] EWCA Civ 630 (CA) (see para 26.30 above) provide a salutary reminder of the need to secure the guarantor's consent for these purposes. See also *Silverburn Finance (UK) Ltd v Salt* [2001] 2 All ER (Comm) 438 (CA), where the guarantee in question applied to a factoring agreement. It was found to have terminated when the factoring agreement came to an end, and thus could not be invoked in relation to a subsequent factoring agreement between the same parties. Whether or not the guarantors have agreed to a variation in a particular case may be a difficult factual question. Company directors may be taken to have agreed to an extension of their personal guarantees if, in their capacity as directors, they sign a letter agreeing to an increase in the facility and that letter stipulates that the personal guarantees should apply: see *Moat Financial Services Ltd v Wilkinson* [2005] EWCA Civ 1253. However, a restructuring of the underlying indebtedness will not always discharge the guarantor: see *Wittman (UK) Ltd v Willdav Engineering SA* [2007] EWCA Civ 824 (CA). Cases of this kind will inevitably tend to be highly fact-sensitive.

[139] *Mercantile Bank of Sydney v Taylor* [1893] AC 317 (PC); *Liverpool Corn Trade Association Ltd v Hurst* [1936] 2 All ER 309; *Skipton Building Society v Scott* [2001] QB 261; *Barclays Bank plc v Kufner* [2008] All ER (D) 102.

[140] See *James Graham & Co (Timber) Ltd v Southgate Sands* [1986] QB 80 (CA). If the guarantor was not aware of the proposal to take other guarantees and security and had thus not placed any reliance on those arrangements when deciding to execute his own guarantee, then it seems that any subsequent release

(d) Conduct which amounts to bad faith vis-à-vis the guarantor will likewise discharge the guarantee,[141] and clearly no contractual provision could protect the bank against the consequences of its own bad faith. The expression 'bad faith' does, however, need to be treated with some care because, as noted earlier, the guarantee is not a contract of utmost good faith. Consequently, a bank does not act in bad faith merely because it holds or releases security of which the guarantor was unaware, or because it seeks to enforce the guarantee in priority to any other remedies which may be open to it.[142]

Standard forms of bank guarantee will seek to deprive the guarantor of the benefit of **26.73** many of the defences which might otherwise be available and will seek to preserve the validity of the guarantee under all circumstances. Subject to legislation dealing with unfair terms and consumer protection where applicable, it seems that the courts will generally uphold provisions of this kind.[143]

Vitiating Factors

The possibility that a security arrangement may be impugned in a subsequent insolvency **26.74** of the grantor is considered in general terms at a later stage.[144] However, as in so many other contexts, guarantees raise particular problems and it is necessary to make a few special observations.[145] In the event of the insolvency of the guarantor, it may become necessary to consider whether the validity of the guarantee can be challenged by the administrator or liquidator, or by any of the guarantor's other creditors.

In some cases, the guarantee may be challenged on the basis that it was void or voidable **26.75** from the outset; some of these grounds have already been considered;[146] those arguments are available even while the company is a going concern.[147] However, the Insolvency Act 1986 provides additional grounds which may be invoked solely because of the insolvency of the guarantor. These grounds may be noted briefly since the relevant statutory provisions are considered in more depth elsewhere in this work.[148]

---

of those additional securities should not affect the guarantor's liability—see *Mount v Barker Austin* [1998] PNLR 493 (CA), noted by Paget, para 33.5.

[141] *Bank of India v Trans Continental Commodity Merchants Ltd* [1983] 2 Lloyds Rep 298 (CA).
[142] This seems to follow from the decision in *Mount v Barker Austin* (n 139 above).
[143] For a recent example, see *Barclays Bank plc v Kufner* [2008] All ER (D) 102.
[144] See generally Chapter 39 below.
[145] The comments about to be made would apply equally to any security given for the obligations of a third party, whether or not supported by a guarantee.
[146] See paras 26.46–26.54 above.
[147] For example, a shareholder could challenge a guarantee given by the company on the basis that it was, to the knowledge of the lender, given in breach of the directors' fiduciary duties. A situation of this kind arose in *Criterion Properties plc v Stratford Properties LLC* [2004] UKHL 28.
[148] See Chapter 39 below. Whilst the present discussion is framed by reference to the rules applicable to corporate insolvency, it should be noted that similar provisions apply to individuals: see Insolvency Act 1986, ss 339–343.

Preference

26.76   If a company gives a preference to a creditor during the six month period prior to the commencement of administration or liquidation proceedings, then the transaction may be set aside as a preference.[149]

26.77   A 'preference' is given to a person if:[150]

(a)   the recipient is one of the company's creditors; and

(b)   the company does some act which has the effect of putting that creditor in a better position than he would otherwise have enjoyed in the event of the insolvency of the company.

26.78   In the normal course, it is submitted that the 'preference' provision cannot be applied to a guarantee which is given by a company in the period leading up to insolvency. This follows from a reading of the requirement described in paragraph (a) above; the bank is not a creditor *at the time* the guarantee is given; it only becomes a creditor *as a result of* the execution of the guarantee.[151] This technical point is, however, likely to be of limited practical importance because a guarantee could also be challenged on the alternative ground about to be discussed.

Transactions at an Undervalue

26.79   A guarantee given to a bank may be set aside if it was given during the two year period prior to insolvency and constitutes a 'transaction at an undervalue'. That term is defined to include any transaction for which the company receives no consideration or for which it receives consideration which is significantly less valuable than the benefit conferred on the other party.[152] In the case of a guarantee, this may be a particularly difficult analysis since, as noted elsewhere,[153] the guarantor receives the consideration necessary to support a contract in technical terms, but it does not directly receive consideration which can readily be 'valued' for the purposes of this provision. However, it is submitted that the guarantor does receive consideration equal to the value of the underlying loan facility where the guarantee is given to support a loan to its subsidiary, at least where the subsidiary is wholly-owned. In such a case, the guarantee is given simply because the holding company chooses to carry on its business through subsidiaries (rather than directly) and, in any event, the guarantor receives the full economic benefit of the loan facility concerned.

26.80   If the guarantee cannot be defended on the basis of the sufficiency of the consideration, then it may nevertheless be valid if either (i) the company was solvent when the guarantee was given[154] or (ii) the company entered into the transaction in good faith for the purpose

---

[149]   This is the combined effect of the Insolvency Act 1986, ss 239 and 240. A longer time period applies where there is some group or other connection between the debtor and creditor, but this will not normally arise in the context of an ordinary banking relationship.

[150]   The following definition is derived from the Insolvency Act 1986, s 239(4).

[151]   For more detailed discussion of the 'preference' provision in a banking context, see Paget, para 14.24.

[152]   This is the combined effect of the Insolvency Act 1986, ss 238 and 240. For more detailed discussion of this provision and for decided cases, see Paget, para 14.23.

[153]   See para 26.14 above.

[154]   This follows from the definition of 'relevant time' in the Insolvency Act 1986, s 240.

of carrying on its business, and there were reasonable grounds for believing that the guarantee would benefit the company.[155] The first situation is self-explanatory. The second situation could conceivably arise where, for example, the guarantee is given in an effort to support one of the guarantor's major customers, in an effort to save it from insolvency and, hence, to preserve the cash flows derived from that source.

Termination by the Guarantor

Introduction

A person or company that provides a guarantee may not wish to be bound by it in perpetuity. For example, a holding company may dispose of a subsidiary to a third party and it will naturally no longer wish to stand as guarantor for its bank facilities following the sale. The lender will frequently agree to the termination of the guarantee as part of the sale arrangements, or its facilities may be refinanced by the purchaser's bank. But, in the absence of a solution of this kind, does the guarantor enjoy any unilateral rights of termination? **26.81**

Express and Implied Termination Rights

Standard forms of bank guarantee will often confer upon the guarantor a right of termination, subject to an appropriate period of notice. The guarantor will, of course, remain liable for obligations incurred by the borrower before the notice period expires. Where a director or shareholder of a company has given a guarantee in that capacity, the bank is not obliged to assume that the guarantee is to be terminated merely because it is aware that the individual concerned has ceased to have an interest in the borrowing entity.[156] It thus remains important to give express notice of termination in such a case. **26.82**

In the absence of a specific, contractual right of termination, it seems that the guarantor has an implied right to terminate his obligations under a continuing guarantee with reference to any future borrowings by the principal debtor.[157] **26.83**

Rights of the Guarantor following Payment

Rights of the Guarantor

If the guarantor is compelled to make payment, he will have the right to recover these amounts by way of indemnity from the primary borrower—at least if the guarantee **26.84**

---

[155] Insolvency Act 1986, s 238(5).
[156] See, for example, the situation which arose in *First National Finance Corporation v Goodman* [1983] BCLC 203 (CA).
[157] *Silverburn Finance (UK) Ltd v Salt* [2001] 2 All ER (Comm) 438 (CA). Note, however, that the decision applies to guarantees given on a continuing basis to cover transactions from time to time entered into by the borrower with the financier. The implied right of termination should not apply to a guarantee given in respect of a particular and ascertained facility, since the guarantor will have contracted to cover that facility in full.

was given at the borrower's request.[158] Likewise, one of multiple guarantors who has discharged the debt will be entitled to a proportionate contribution from his fellow guarantors.[159]

26.85 Rights of the kind just described usually subsist as between the borrower and the guarantor themselves. They will, therefore, generally be of limited concern from the perspective of the lending bank itself. However, the lender will wish to ensure that the guarantor waives any such right of recovery from the primary debtor until the lender itself has been repaid in full. This will be of particular importance where the borrower has become insolvent because the effect of a proof by the guarantor will be to dilute the assets available to other creditors (including the bank itself). The terms of the guarantee will generally prohibit the submission of such a proof until the bank debt has been fully redeemed. Clauses of this kind are, in principle, valid and binding on the guarantor.[160] However, their effect may vary in the competing circumstances of particular cases.[161]

Obligations of the Bank

26.86 The bank cannot, however, entirely ignore the position of the guarantor after a demand has been made against him. The right of subrogation also implies that the guarantor may 'step into the shoes' of the lender and take over its rights in respect of the debt which he has paid.

26.87 The lender must therefore take care to ensure that, in such a case, the security is not released but is instead made available to the guarantor. Of course, the lender will not wish to find itself in competition with the guarantor and, for that reason, standard forms of bank guarantee will defer the exercise of the right of subrogation until the lender has been repaid in full. For that purpose, a guarantee should always cover the entirety of the underlying debt, even if there is to be a financial cap on the guarantor's total liability. If, instead, the lender merely takes a guarantee of *part* of the debt, then the guarantor's right of subrogation will apply when he has paid that amount, even though the balance of the debt remains outstanding. For this reason, a guarantee which is to be subject to any form of financial limit must be prepared with some care.[162]

---

[158] Subrogation is an equitable right and will generally arise only if the transaction was entered into at the behest of the principal debtor: see *Owen v Tate* [1976] QB 402.

[159] These rights of subrogation and contribution are derived from equitable principles but see also Mercantile Law Amendment Act 1856, s 5.

[160] See *Re SSSL Realisations (2002) Ltd v AIG Europe (UK) Ltd* [2006] Ch 610. The court specifically held that an undertaking of this kind did not contravene s 107 of the Insolvency Act 1986 (dealing with the distribution of a company's property) or r 4.181 of the Insolvency Rules 1986. There was therefore no basis on which such clauses could be disregarded on public policy grounds.

[161] In *Cattles plc v Welcome Financial Services Ltd* [2009] EWHC 3027, the court held that a clause of the type described in the text was effective to preclude the guarantor from competing with the lenders (see in particular para 55 of the judgment). However, at around the same time (and admittedly on the basis of different documentation) another court reached a different conclusion in *Mills and others v HSBC Trustee (CI) Ltd* [2009] EWHC 3377 (Ch). It is understood that the latter decision is under appeal at the time of writing.

[162] This apparently bizarre distinction follows from the decision in *Re Sass* [1896] 2 QB 12, on which see *Goode on Legal Problems of Credit and Security* (4th edn, Louise Gullifer, 2008) para 8–18.

Conflict of Law Issues

In a case involving a cross-border situation, it may be necessary to consider questions of **26.88** private international law. In particular, where (say) a guarantee is given by a German parent company in respect of the obligations of a French subsidiary to an English bank,[163] will the obligations of the German guarantor be determined by reference to German, French, or English law?

This issue will be governed by the EC regulation on the law applicable to contractual obli- **26.89** gations, which is considered in more detail at a later stage.[164] However, it seems appropriate to make a few general comments about the system of law which will govern a guarantee in such a case:

(a) the parties are free to select the system of law which is to govern the contract of guarantee.[165] In the normal course, it will not be necessary to pursue the matter further because standard form documents used by the bank will include an express selection of English law as the applicable law;

(b) there may, however, be occasions when the guarantee is provided by the German guarantor on its own terms and in the format preferred by it, and the bargaining power of the German parent is such that the bank is prepared to accept this arrangement. In such a case, if the guarantee includes an express selection of German law, then no further enquiry will be required from a private international law perspective. The obligations of the guarantor will be governed by German law, as will any question as to whether those obligations have been duly performed or have been terminated or discharged for any reason;[166]

(c) matters become a little more difficult if the guarantee contains no express choice of law. As will be discussed at a later stage,[167] Article 4(1) of Rome I contains a list of rules dealing with the law applicable to particular categories of contracts. However, contracts of guarantee do not fall within that list. As a result, it is necessary to have recourse to more general rules;

(d) in such a case, the starting point is that the contract is governed by the law of the country in which the party required to effect the 'characteristic performance' of the contract has his habitual residence.[168] This test naturally points to German law, since the performance which is 'characteristic' of a guarantee is payment by the guarantor. In any event, the bank has no positive obligations under a guarantee and thus is not responsible for 'performance' under it at all;

---

[163] It is assumed for present purposes that—as would usually be the case, the agreement between the French borrower and the English bank is governed by English law.

[164] See Chapter 40 below.

[165] See Art 3 of Rome I.

[166] On these points, see Art 12 of Rome I.

[167] See para 40.09 below.

[168] Article 4(2) of Rome I.

(e) nevertheless, Article 4(3) of Rome I provides that '… where it is clear from all the circumstances of the case that the contract is manifestly more closely connected with a country other than [Germany], the law of that other country shall apply …';

(f) in general terms, it is suggested that Article 4(3) should be applied in this type of case. The guarantee is not a 'stand alone' or independent contract. It only derives its commercial meaning and substantive effect from the fact that the borrower is raising money from an English bank under English law. Under these circumstances, it is suggested that the German parent guarantee is '… manifestly more closely connected …' with England and hence should be governed by English law.[169]

---

[169] For an earlier case which adopted this approach under the pre-existing rules of private international law, see *Broken Hill Pty Ltd v Xenakis* [1982] 2 Lloyds Rep 304.

27

SECURITY—CHARACTERIZATION, FORMALITIES, AND REGISTRATION

Introduction

27.01 The present section will outline the various forms of security which are available to a bank in respect of facilities made available to customers. Before moving to examine individual types of security, however, it is proposed to outline some general issues by way of introduction.

Contractual Nature of Security

27.02 In general terms, it must be borne in mind that, so far as English law is concerned, the creation of security is of an essentially *contractual* character. It is important to retain sight of this fundamental feature, even though it is overlaid and obscured by numerous statutory provisions designed for the protection of creditors. The result is that security documents must be construed with a view to ascertaining the intention of the parties from the words which they have used. The security will thus extend to the class of assets agreed between the parties, as evidenced by the relevant document. The nature and extent of that class is to be ascertained by ordinary processes of contractual interpretation.

27.03 The contractual nature of security also means that the arrangement must be supported by consideration although, in practice, the point is often avoided by requiring that the security document should be executed as a deed.[1]

---

[1] It should, however, be appreciated that security which is given for no 'real' consideration in the sense of new money advanced at the time the security is given—may later be vulnerable to attack as a transaction at an undervalue under s 238 of the Insolvency Act 1986: see para 39.04 below. Execution as a deed will be required in certain cases in any event—eg where the security package comprises real estate.

What is a Security Interest?

27.04 When should a particular arrangement be characterized as a security interest? This may seem to be a highly theoretical question, especially to the practising lawyer. Yet the nature of a transaction as a security interest or as a charge can be a matter of some moment in a variety of contexts. For example:

(a) as will be seen, a 'charge' created by a company requires registration under section 860 of the Companies Act 2006, and it will become void against creditors and insolvency officials if this requirement is not met. It thus becomes necessary to consider whether a particular arrangement amounts to a 'charge' for these purposes;

(b) an equity of redemption only arises in relation to any assets if they are subject to a charge. Thus, if X has transferred assets to Y for cash, X can reclaim the asset if the cash transfer was intended to be a secured loan, but not if the transaction was intended as an outright sale and purchase of the assets concerned. These statements may seem to be obvious but modern financing techniques have occasionally clouded the distinction between the two types of transaction. The distinction matters because, as noted above, the correct characterization of a transaction may affect the application of registration or other requirements.

27.05 By way of examples:

(a) A executes a transfer of freehold property in favour of B. B immediately executes a lease of the property back to A, and grants him an option to repurchase the property in five years time. Is this a genuine sale and purchase transaction—in which case no security registration requirements can apply—or is it in reality a loan secured on the property, to which registration requirements would apply?

(b) A enters into an agreement with B under which A agrees to transfer securities to B to cover A's mark-to-market exposure under a derivatives contract.[2] This arrangement is plainly designed to cover B against potential losses in the event of a subsequent payment default by A. Nevertheless, the transfer of the securities is expressed to be unconditional, and B is free to use those securities in the course of its own business. In the event that the mark-to-market exposure is reduced or eliminated, B's obligation is to return to A *equivalent securities* of the same, fungible class. Again, is the purported outright transfer genuine, or does the arrangement really amount to the creation of a security interest?

27.06 Obviously, the correct approach to these transactions is important to both parties, but especially to the side which has parted with his money and is relying on the legal efficacy of the arrangements.[3] The English courts generally favour the certainty of transactions and—at least in the absence of fraud or some other form of evasion[4]—have shown themselves to be reluctant to recharacterize transactions. They have usually taken the view that

---

[2] On these contracts, see Chapter 23 above.

[3] The risk that a court may hold that the legal effect of a transaction differs from the structure or documentation used by the parties is generally referred to as 'recharacterization risk'.

[4] Even then, the transaction may still be enforceable at the suit of a party not involved in the deception: see *Snook v London and West Riding Investments Ltd* [1965] QB 786.

parties should be able to structure their transactions in the manner selected by them in the confidence that their expectations will be met. Nevertheless, cases involving proprietary or security issues have an unpleasant habit of coming to the fore when one of the parties has become insolvent, with the result that the position of unsecured creditors or other third parties may be affected by the outcome.

Even in such situations, however, it is fair to say that the English courts have been reluctant to recharacterize transactions so that they have the legal consequences of an unregistered security interest. By way of examples: **27.07**

(a) In *Re George Inglefield Ltd*,[5] a furniture dealer sold the benefit of hire purchase agreements to a finance company. Payment by the hirers was effectively guaranteed by the furniture, which accepted bills drawn on it by the financier for the discounted value of the receivables. Despite the personal liability of the dealer itself, the court found that the transaction was a genuine sale of the receivables; it was not a disguised loan and (unregistered) charge over the book debts. The decision was influenced by the fact that the dealer had no right to pay off the financier and to demand the re-transfer of the receivables.[6] Nevertheless, whilst it is possible to sell receivables, it is equally possible to create security over them. Thus, the court must look to the overall language and effect of the documentation to determine the intention of the parties. Accordingly, where the documents included language such as '... as security for its obligations hereunder ...', '... such security ...' and similar expressions, the structure was found to be a charge rather than an outright sale, with the result that it was void for want of registration.[7]

(b) A transaction will not be recharacterized merely because the parties have structured it in a manner designed to avoid impediments standing in the way of the route which they may otherwise have originally intended. For example, in one case,[8] financiers had intended to make a loan of £30,000 against a charge over rolling stock. However, it was then discovered that the proposed facility would result in a breach of the borrowing restrictions applicable under the private Act of Parliament which had incorporated the borrower. The transaction was accordingly structured as a 'sale and leaseback', so that

---

⁵ [1932] All ER Rep 244 (CA).

⁶ ie the transaction did not include an equity of redemption, which is a key feature of a security arrangement. The factoring of debts in this way is a common method of financing and the arrangements have been categorized as a genuine sale (as opposed to a disguised, secured loan) on a number of occasions. See, for example, *Olds Discount Co Ltd v John Playfair Ltd* [1938] 3 All ER 275; *Olds Discount Co Ltd v Cohen* [1938] 3 All ER 281n; *Lloyds & Scottish Finance Ltd v Cyril Lord Carpet Sales Ltd* [1992] BCLC 609 (HL); *Welsh Development Agency v Export Finance Co Ltd* [1992] BCLC 148 (CA). A clause designed to retain title to goods pending payment to the seller may be effective for so long as the goods remain in the physical possession of the buyer (see *Clough Mill Ltd v Martin* [1985] BCLC 64). However, to the extent that the retention seeks to extend to the proceeds of sale of those goods, the relevant contractual provision is likely to be characterized as a charge over book debts, and will be void if unregistered: see, for example, *E Pfeiffer Weinkellerei-Weinkauf GmbH & Co v Arbuthnot Factors Ltd* [1987] BCLC 522; *Tatung (UK) Ltd v Galex Telesure Ltd* (1988) 5 BCC 325; *Re Weldtech Ltd* [1991] BCLC 393; *Compaq Computers Ltd v Abercorn Group Ltd* [1993] BCLC 602.

⁷ *Orion Finance Ltd v Crown Financial Management Ltd* [1996] 2 BCLC 78. For a further case in which a disputed assignment was held to be by way of security, see *Coakley v Argent Credit Corporation plc*, 4 June 1998 (Ch).

⁸ *Yorkshire Railway Wagon Co v Maclure* (1882) 1 CLD 309.

the obligations of the company would not be 'borrowings' for the purposes of the statutory calculation. The rolling stock was transferred to the financiers, the company still received £30,000 and the payments under the lease were structured such that the financial return to the financiers was identical; the company had the right to repurchase the rolling stock for £1.00 at the end of the lease term. The economic effect of the transaction was thus effectively identical to the original (and abortive) secured loan. The company defaulted and, when sued on their personal guarantees, the directors argued that the underlying transaction was a sham. The court rejected this argument on the basis that there had been no attempt to disguise the true nature of the transaction. The fact that the arrangements could not lawfully be implemented as a secured loan did not necessarily prevent them from being implemented on an alternative basis.[9]

(c) There may be cases where a provision in the 'small print' of a contract creates a security interest where the parties have not really turned their minds to the matter. For example, in *Smith (Administrator of Cosslett (Contractors) Ltd v Bridgend County Council*,[10] a standard form construction contract allowed the employer council, in the event of an insolvency of the contractor '… at any time [to] sell any of the constructional plant, temporary works and unused goods and materials and apply the proceeds of sale in or towards the satisfaction of any sums due or which may become due to [it] from the contractor under the contract …'. Although this was a remote clause in a standard contract, it was hard to see '… how a right to sell an asset belonging to a debtor and appropriate the proceeds in payment of a debt can be anything other than a charge …'.[11] The security was construed as a floating charge, because it referred to classes of assets which would be turning over during the course of the contract ('unused goods and materials'), and the language of the contract did not suggest a fixed charge even in the context of larger or more permanent items which might remain on site for the entire contract period.[12]

(d) In many collateral and security documents in use in the financial markets, provision is made for the 'security' to be provided by means of an *outright transfer* of bonds or other securities.[13] There will be no equity of redemption in the normal sense—the collateral-taker will merely be obliged to return 'equivalent' securities at a later stage. It has recently been argued before the Federal Court of Australia in *Beconwood Securities Pty Ltd v Australia and New Zealand Banking Group*[14] that such an arrangement involves a security interest. Unusually, the argument was not advanced by an unsecured creditor

---

[9] As Lord Devlin remarked in *Chow Yoong Hong v Choong Fah Rubber Manufactory* [1962] AC 209 (at p 216), '… there are many ways of raising cash besides borrowing—if it is not in form a loan it is not to the point to say that its object was to raise money for one of them or that the parties would have produced the same result by borrowing and lending money …'.

[10] [2001] UKHL 58.

[11] See para 41 of the judgment.

[12] The House applied the decision in *Agnew v Commissioner of Inland Revenue* [2001] AC 714 (PC). The decision is further noted at para 30.04 below.

[13] See, for example, the form of collateral title transfer documents produced by the International Swaps and Derivatives Association.

[14] [2008] FCA 594.

against the liquidator (as would be the normal case), but by the alleged provider of the security itself (although, as will become apparent, the court did not accept that status). The reason was that the transferee of the of the of the securities had become insolvent, and the transferor sought to argue that (i) the original transfer had been by way of security and (ii) upon payment of the monies owing to the transferee, the transferor would be entitled to the return of its securities by virtue of its equity of redemption, with the result that the body of unsecured creditors would have no claim on these assets. However, the assertion that the arrangements amounted to a security interest were simply not tenable. The original transfer of the securities had been effected under a securities lending agreement, where the *outright* transfer of title was a vital feature, since the transferee wished to use the securities as a means of settling its own delivery obligations in favour of third parties. This objective could not be met if the transferee's status were effectively 'downgraded' from that of an owner to a mere chargee. The terminology and commercial objectives of the agreement, coupled with the obligation to redeliver *equivalent* (rather than *identical*) securities reinforced the view that no charge or security arrangement was intended.[15]

(e) The foregoing remarks dealt with the danger that a transaction intended by the parties to take effect as a particular structure (eg sale/purchase, sale/leaseback) might be recharacterized as a security arrangement and hence found to be void for want of registration or other formality. But recharacterization can occur even within a transaction that is intended to take effect as security, with results that can also be catastrophic for the financier. For example, the parties may have intended to create security over assets by way of *fixed* charge, under circumstances where no registration would be required[16] but, if the charge is later recharacterized as a floating security, then it would be void for want of registration. In recent times, this narrower form of recharacterization risk has arisen in the context of security over receivables, and it is accordingly discussed later in that particular context.[17]

The Scope and Extent of the Security

It is common to focus on the nature of security as it applies to particular assets, applicable **27.08** registration requirements and similar matters. But it is also sometimes necessary to focus on the precise *extent* of the security, ie what is the extent of the indebtedness which has the benefit of the security?

---

[15] As the Federal Court pointed out, the US Supreme Court has adopted the same approach in giving effect to the intention of the parties: see *Provost v United States* 269 US 443 (1926). The simple position is that the stock lender receives a fee for the loan of the securities and takes the risk that the borrower will be unable to redeliver equivalent securities on the contracted date. In essence, the stock lender takes a risk which, in credit and economic terms, are very similar to those which apply in the context of an ordinary, monetary loan. For another case which has sought to adhere to the intention of the parties rather than attempt a recharacterization exercise, see *Granite Partners LP v Bear Sterns & Co Inc* 175 F Supp 275 (SDNY, 1998). The US courts have also been sensitive to the need to uphold market standard documentation in the manner expected by market participants in order to avoid prejudice to the proper functioning of those markets: see, for example, *Re County of Orange* 31 F Supp 2d 768 (1998 CD Cal).

[16] See, for example, the discussion of fixed charges over shares at para 29.22 below and note also the discussion in the *Re Cosslett* case, above (n 10).

[17] See the discussion in Chapter 30 below.

27.09   In the normal course, this will not cause great difficulty; a standard debenture or other security document will secure all monies from time to time owing by the customer.[18] But there may be occasions when the security is limited to a particular facility. This will inevitably be the case with syndicated transactions,[19] where the security package will cover only that particular facility and will not be intended to be available for separate and independent loans made available to the borrower on a bilateral basis by the individual syndicate members. But this necessary limitation of the security can cause practical difficulties. Unforeseen events may mean that the underlying facility has to be varied or extended, or additional funds have to be provided to assist the borrower with cash flow problems. The difficulty is: to what extent will the security continue to apply notwithstanding such variations or amendments?

27.10   Lawyers responsible for the preparation of such security documents are, of course, alive to these problems and—seeking to take advantage of the contractual and, hence, flexible nature of English security arrangements—will seek to provide that the security document extends to any additional or supplemental documentation executed between the parties with respect to the same facility. Yet provisions of this kind cannot operate without limit, since they have the potential to operate to the detriment of unsecured creditors in the event of a later insolvency.

27.11   A provision to the effect that the security document will also extend to the facility agreement 'as from time to time varied, extended, amended or replaced' will be sufficient—and hence the original security will continue to be effective—if the maturity date of the underlying facility is extended, or if the interest rate is increased by an amount appropriate to reflect the borrower's deteriorating credit quality. It may even be that amendments to the facility agreement providing for a modest level of additional advances may also be covered, at least provided that these are made for purposes consistent with the original facility itself. But if the facility agreement is amended to provide extra funding for other purposes, then it is doubtful that the security would extend to the additional amounts so made available. Questions of degree will no doubt be involved in each case.

27.12   The difficulties involved in seeking to extend security documents to cover future amendments and variations have recently been illustrated in *Public Trustee of Queensland v Octaviar Ltd.*[20] In that case, a guarantee and supporting charge was given by Octaviar to secure '… all monies, obligations and liabilities of any kind that are or may in the future become due, owing or payable, whether actually, contingently or prospectively by [Octaviar] in relation to any Transaction Document …'. The expression 'Transaction Document' referred to (i) an A$250 million facility agreement executed between the lender and Octaviar Castle Pty Ltd, a subsidiary of Octaviar and (ii) any document designated by the parties as a 'Transaction Document' for the purposes of the facility agreement. Octaviar had previously provided a guarantee ('YVE guarantee') to the same lender in respect of a

---

[18] Note, however, the question of interpretation which arose in *Bank of Scotland v Wright* [1991] BCLC 244, noted at para 26.27 above in the context of guarantees.
[19] On syndicated facilities generally, see Chapter 21 above.
[20] [2009] QSC 37 (Supreme Court of Queensland).

facility granted to another of its subsidiaries, Young Village Estates (YVE), but no specific security had been granted in relation to the YVE guarantee. The facilities granted to Octaviar Castle and to YVE were clearly intended to be separate transactions, at least as at the date of their inception. However, no doubt in the light of a deteriorating financial situation, Octaviar and the other relevant parties executed an agreement to the effect that the YVE guarantee should also be regarded as a 'Transaction Document' and, hence, brought within the scope of the charge originally given by Octaviar in respect of the Octaviar Castle facility.

On the construction of the documentation, the Queensland Supreme Court held that it was open to the parties to agree that the YVE guarantee would be a 'Transaction Document', and there was no sufficient reason to limit this expression to documents associated with the Octaviar castle facility itself. However, the agreement designating the YVE guarantee as a Transaction Document had the effect of increasing the amount secured or creating a new security interest over the assets concerned. Given that the relevant agreement had not been filed, the attempt to extend the charge to cover the YVE guarantee was ineffective as against a liquidator or administrator of Octaviar. It should be said that this decision depended to a significant extent on the specific language of the registration provisions contained in the Australian Corporations Act, and that these differ in material respects from the corresponding English rules.[21] It should also be said that the first instance decision was subsequently overturned by the Queensland Court of Appeal, on the basis that the relevant provisions of the legislation were directed to variations in the terms of the charge itself, and not at increases in liability which were imposed consistently with the original provisions of the charge.[22] Nevertheless, this particular saga illustrates the need for great care in ensuring that the security document does indeed extend to all of the liabilities which are intended to be secured, and that a cautious drafting approach is required. **27.13**

The prudent course for the lenders in such a case is to take a further security document to cover the increased or extended facility, thus placing the issue beyond doubt. The difficulty is that this may not always be practicable or may involve negotiations with holders of other security and who may have different interests. **27.14**

Formalities

On the whole, modern commercial law sets its face against excessive formal requirements, preferring instead to ascertain the intentions of the parties and to give effect to them where appropriate. It is for this reason that, for the most part, English law will enforce contracts which have been concluded orally, provided that the necessary evidence is available.[23] **27.15**

This relatively relaxed approach is both acceptable and justifiable when dealing with arrangements of a purely contractual character as between the parties concerned. However, the creation of security clearly has an impact on third parties; the effect of a security interest **27.16**

---

[21] On these rules, see paras 27.18–27.44 below.

[22] *Re Octaviar Ltd (No 7)* [2009] QCA 282. At the time of writing, it is understood that a further appeal may be in contemplation. On this case, see Anderson, 'Overturning Octaviar: one big anticlimax?' (2010) 25(6) *Australian Banking and Finance Law Bulletin*.

[23] For a notable exception, see Statute of Frauds 1677, s 4 insofar as it relates to guarantees. The subject has been discussed at para 26.19 above.

is to establish rights of a *proprietary* nature, which will plainly have an impact on the rights of other creditors in the event of insolvency.

27.17   It is therefore entirely natural that the law should impose a greater degree of formality in this particular sphere. The formalities may be divided into two categories, namely:

(a) *Requirements of writing.* In many cases, a security interest will only be effective if created in writing. Regardless of particular statutory requirements, this is a natural precaution in any event, but the applicable rules will be noted against each category of security.[24]

(b) *Registration or notice requirements.* The essential validity of security as against third parties may be made dependent on the completion of registration requirements, so that third parties dealing with the chargor may have the opportunity to discover the existence of the security. Once again, the requirements applicable to each particular category of security will be considered in the relevant section, although some general commentary is also set out below.

Part 25 of the Companies Act 2006

27.18   Although registration requirements are discussed in relation to particular categories of security, the regime applicable to the registration of charges by companies applies in a number of contexts and it is therefore felt appropriate to include some general commentary on this subject.[25] The application of the section to particular types of security will then be considered under the appropriate heading, below.

27.19   It should, of course, be appreciated that the relevant provisions apply only to *companies*. They are extended to security given by limited liability partnerships—a form of body corporate,[26] but they do not apply to security created by individuals or general partnerships.

27.20   A new statutory framework for the registration of charges was introduced by sections 860–894 (Part 25) of the Companies Act 2006.[27] This replaces Part XII (sections 395–409) of the Companies Act 1985 ('the 1985 Act'). Subject to a few minor exceptions, the new

---

[24] Where, as in the case of transactions involving land, there is a requirement for execution of the relevant instrument as a deed, it has been suggested that s 1(3) of the Law of Property (Miscellaneous Provisions) Act 1989 requires a deed to be executed in its full text, and that the mortgagor cannot simply leave executed, blank pages in the possession of his advisors for use at the completion: see *R (on the application of Mercury Tax Group and another) v HM Revenue and Customs Commissioners* [2008] EWHC 2721. This view appears to proceed on the basis that s 1(3) would thereby offer a safeguard against fraud. Earlier authority suggests that a signed contract can be altered or completed at a later stage provided that the amendment or completion is authorized by the parties concerned: see *Koeningsblatt v Sweet* [1923] 2 Ch 314; *United Dominions Trust Ltd v Western* [1976] QB 513. However that may be, it may be appropriate to adopt a cautious approach to the execution of documents and insist that they should be executed in their final and completed form.

[25] It may be noted that the system for registration of company charges is due for review and consultation in early 2010.

[26] ie by the Limited Liability Partnership Regulations 2001 (SI 2001/1090), Sch 2.

[27] These provisions were brought into force with effect from 1 October 2009: see art 3 of the Companies Act 2006 (Commencement No 8, Transitional Provisions and Savings) Order 2008 (SI 2860/2008).

regime mirrors the corresponding provisions of the 1985 Act, and most of the variations reflect a change in drafting approach.[28]

The starting point is section 860(1), which reads: **27.21**

> A company that creates a charge to which this section relates must deliver the prescribed particulars of the charge, together with the instrument (if any) by which the charge is created or evidenced, to the registrar for registration before the end of the period allowed for registration.

The company is thus principally responsible for completion of the registration process   **27.22** and, in the event of a default, both the company and the relevant officers are liable to a fine. However, any person with an interest in the charge may also complete the process and, in practice, the lender will assume this responsibility since it has the greatest interest in ensuring compliance.[29]

A few points may be made in relation to section 860(1):   **27.23**

(a) The section only applies where a company 'creates' a charge to which the registration requirements apply. This implies that only voluntary arrangements entered into by a company will require delivery to the Registrar. A lien or other form of security arising by operation of law (rather than by way of contract) is thus outside the scope of the registration regime.

(b) An instrument will only require registration if it constitutes a 'charge' for the purposes of section 860(1). This question of characterization will have to be determined by reference to the definitions of that expression which have been adopted by the courts from time to time. For example, a charge has been defined as[30] '... a security whereby real or personal property is appropriated for the discharge of a debt or other obligation, but which does not pass either an absolute or a special property in the subject matter of the security to the creditor, nor any right to possession. In the event of non-payment of the debt, the creditor's right of realisation is by judicial process ...'. This definition has been judicially approved[31] and perhaps offers a suitable starting point for these purposes. It is, however, necessary to note a few reservations. First of all, the definition was adopted specifically in the context of an *equitable* charge. Section 860(1) is clearly intended to be broader than this and is intended to catch legal mortgages as well.[32] Secondly, the emphasis placed on judicial process as a means of enforcement[33] will not

---

[28] It may be noted that ss 860–877 deal with charges created by companies established in England and Wales, and in Northern Ireland, whilst the reminder of Part 25 deals with security created by Scottish companies. On security created by foreign companies, see Companies Act 2006, s 1052 considered at paras 27.33–27.44 below.

[29] On these points, see Companies Act 2006, s 830(3) and (4).

[30] Fisher & Lightwood, para 6.1.

[31] *Swiss Bank Corp v Lloyds Bank Ltd* [1982] AC 584 (CA).

[32] This clearly follows from the fact that a charge over land requires registration pursuant to s 860.

[33] The emphasis on the need for judicial enforcement proceedings is present in other cases: see, for example, *National Provincial and Union Bank of England v Charnley* [1924] 1 KB 431, approved in *Re Bank of Credit and Commerce International SA (No 8)* [1998] AC 214. However, in *Re Charge Card Services Ltd* [1987] Ch 150, emphasis was instead placed on the creditor's general 'right to resort' to the property, rather than judicial proceedings.

always be appropriate. For example, a charge over a bank deposit will be enforced by the simple act of appropriation. A charge over receivables will be enforced by giving notice of the charge to the debtors (if that has not previously been done) and collecting payment from them. Taking all of these factors into account it is submitted that the expression 'charge' as used in section 860(1) is apt to refer to any voluntary arrangement[34] designed to provide to the lender priority over particular assets of the chargor in the event of its insolvency and which includes powers of realization, appropriation, or sale, whether by virtue of the terms of the arrangement or by law. Marginal cases will inevitably arise. For example, if a bank takes a contractual right of set-off over deposits, this may well amount to a charge because it seeks to ring fence certain assets of the customer in the event of its insolvency and allows the bank a right of appropriation by way of enforcement.[35] On the other hand, if the customer merely agrees that certain deposits will not be repayable until a particular facility has been discharged, then the bank has no right of appropriation, but merely a right of retention. Such a structure (commonly referred to as a 'flawed asset' arrangement) therefore lacks one of the key indicia of a 'charge' and hence should not require registration under section 860(1).[36]

(c) It should be noted that the section requires the delivery of 'the instrument' by which the charge is created, ie the original must be delivered and a copy will not suffice.[37]

(d) The 'period allowed for registration' of a charge is (i) 21 days calculated from the day *after* the date on which the charge was created[38] or (ii) where the charge is created outside the United Kingdom, 21 days beginning with the day *after the day* on which the instrument or evidence of the charge could, in due course of post and if despatched with due diligence have been received in the United Kingdom.[39]

(e) Although some of these particular issues will be considered at a later stage, it may be helpful at this juncture to record that the registration requirements do not apply to every form of security created by a company. They apply only to charges within the following categories:

  i. a charge on land or any interest in land, including land situate outside the United Kingdom;[40]

---

[34] On the need for the arrangement to be voluntary, see sub-para (a) above. The word 'arrangement' is used advisedly because there is no necessary requirement that the charge should be created in writing: note the requirement in s 860(1) for the delivery of '… the prescribed particulars of the charge, together with the instrument (*if any*) by which the charge is created …' (emphasis supplied). However, security in unwritten form will be very rare in practice, and security over land must be created in writing in any event.

[35] Such a set-off arrangement may not necessarily be subject to registration on the basis that the security does not fall within the prescribed categories. On rights of set-off generally, see Chapter 36 below.

[36] A right to retain an asset and use it for a particular purpose (but without any power of sale or realization) does not amount to a charge: Fisher & Lightwood, para 6.1. See also the recent decision in *Online Catering Ltd v Acton* [2010] EWCA Civ (CA).

[37] For limited exceptions to this rule, see subpara (n) below.

[38] Under s 395 of the Companies Act 1985, it appeared that the date of creation was included within the 21 day period.

[39] On these points, see Companies Act 2006, s 870. It seems that the time concession made by the second part of this formulation can be used wherever the charge is executed/created abroad, even if the security interest itself relates to property in the United Kingdom.

[40] The registration requirement is specifically extended to foreign land by Companies Act 2006, s 861(2).

ii. a charge which, if executed by an individual, would require registration under the Bills of Sale Acts 1878–1890;[41]

iii. a charge for the purpose of securing an issue of debentures;

iv. a charge on uncalled share capital of the company;

v. a charge on calls made but not paid;

vi. a charge on book debts of the company;

vii. a floating charge on the company's property or undertaking;

viii. a charge on a ship (or share in a ship) or an aircraft; and

ix. a charge on goodwill or any intellectual property.[42]

(f) There are some notable omissions from this list. In particular, a fixed charge[43] over shares in subsidiaries would not require registration. As a result, creditors of a holding company which has charged its interests in its subsidiaries could find that none of the group assets are even indirectly available to them, and yet details of that security will not have appeared on the company's register.

(g) A common feature of statutory requirements for the registration of security is that they are designed for the protection of other creditors of the chargor, and not for the protection of the chargor itself. This principle is reflected in section 874, which renders an unregistered[44] charge void against the liquidator, administrator, and creditors of the chargor. It is implicit in this formulation that the security remains valid as against the chargor company itself,[45] and the chargee may enforce its security in accordance with its terms until a liquidator, administrator, or creditor intervenes.[46]

(h) Whilst the section may render the *security* void in stated circumstances, it does not vitiate the contractual obligation to repay money which was intended to be secured by the charge. Indeed, section 874(3) confirms that the avoidance of the charge '… is without prejudice to any contract or obligation for repayment of the money secured by the charge; and when a charge becomes void under this section, the money secured by it becomes immediately payable …'. The acceleration of the obligation is presumably designed as an incentive to the company to comply with its obligation to

---

[41] In essence, this refers to a mortgage over chattels which remain in the physical possession of the chargor. On bills of sale created by companies, see *Online Catering Ltd v Acton* [2010] EWCA Civ 58 (CA), where the earlier authorities are discussed.

[42] 'Intellectual property' means (i) any patent, trade mark, registered design, copyright, or design rights, and (ii) any licence in respect of any such rights: see s 861(4) of the 2006 Act.

[43] The reference to a *fixed* charge should be carefully noted. If the relevant security were a *floating* charge then it would require registration under that separate heading.

[44] Expressions such as 'registration' and 'unregistered' are used for convenience. It should, however, be appreciated that there is no positive obligation on the company or the chargee to procure that the charge is actually *registered*; s 860(1) merely imposes an obligation to deliver the charge (together with the prescribed particulars) for registration within the 21 day time limit. If that has been done, then s 860(1) cannot apply to strike down the security even if, for some reason, the security is not subsequently entered on the register. The point may assume some importance if, for example, the Registrar declines to enter the security onto the company's register on the ground that the security is not one which falls within the categories of registrable charge listed in s 860(7) (see generally below). The secured creditor will be protected even though a court subsequently holds that the Registrar's view was incorrect.

[45] A point confirmed by the judgments in *Re Monolithic Buildings Ltd* [1915] 1 Ch 643 (CA).

[46] This point may appear to be largely theoretical, since the availability of security usually only becomes material at the point of insolvency. However, the point could become relevant in other circumstances, eg where the borrower is solvent but is refusing to perform some of its other obligations under the facility agreement.

register the charge.[47] Although the point does not seem to have been decided, it is submitted that this provision does not operate to accelerate the date on which a *non-monetary* obligation is required to be performed, nor would it require the chargor to make immediate payment in respect of a *monetary* obligation which is subject to a contingency.[48]

(i) It should be noted that the 21 day period for registration of the charge runs from the date after the date on which the charge was *created*. This expression does not necessarily coincide with the date which has been inserted into the document and, of course, there may be cases in which a document which is intended to create security has been delivered—perhaps through oversight—without any date written on it at all. It is submitted that a charge is 'created' for these purposes when it is delivered to the chargee (or to an agent acting on his behalf) with the intention that it should take effect by way of security.[49] Thus, if the company executes and dates the charge on 1 January but only delivers it to the chargee on 1 February, then the 21 day period for registration should end at midnight on 22 February.[50] On the face of it, of course, the document would have been delivered out of time, and it would be necessary to furnish evidence[51] to the Registrar to demonstrate that the charge was, in fact, 'created' on 1 February.[52]

(j) The court has a discretion to extend the 21 day period if (i) non-registration was due to inadvertence and does not prejudice creditors or (ii) it is otherwise just and equitable to do so.[53] The discretion can be exercised even though the chargor has become insolvent, although permission to register the charge will not normally be given if a winding-up petition has been presented.[54]

(k) It should be appreciated that registration under section 860(1) only prevents a security from becoming void as against the liquidator, administrator, and creditors. So far as the secured lender is concerned, registration under this section has no further purpose or

---

[47] Section 399 of the 2006 Act confirms that it is the obligation of the company to procure compliance with the registration formalities, no doubt because the section is intended for the protection of the company's own creditors. In practice, however, the lender has an obvious interest in completion of the registration procedure, and so the lender or its advisers will frequently assume this responsibility. Section 860(2) recognizes this reality and provides that any person having an interest in the charge may likewise deal with the process of registration; since the duty to lodge particulars falls primarily on the company, and other person who carries out that task may recover the lodgement fees from the company: s 860(3).

[48] This may occur where, for example, the bank issues a performance bond at the request of the company, and the company's obligation to reimburse the bank is secured by a charge over the company's assets. It is submitted that the quoted language from s 874(3) is apt to convert a *future* obligation into a *present* one, but it does not convert a *contingent* obligation into an *immediate* obligation where the relevant contingency (in this case, a demand against the bank under the performance bond) has not occurred.

[49] This position would coincide with the rules applicable to the delivery of a deed.

[50] As noted above, the period allowed for registration runs from the day *after* the creation of the charge.

[51] In practice, this would usually take the form of a statutory declaration stating the factual background described in this paragraph.

[52] In the ordinary case, the Registrar will assume that the instrument was 'created' on the date stated in the document itself, for he will have no other evidence on which to proceed.

[53] Companies Act 2006, s 873, providing for rectification of the charges register.

[54] *Re RM Arnold & Co Ltd* [1984] BCLC 535. For further discussion and authorities, see Parsons, *Lingard's Bank Security Documents* (4th edn, LexisNexis Butterworths, 2006) para 3.09.

advantage. Thus, if the security document itself is invalid for some reason, registration under section 860(1) will not serve to validate it.[55]

(l) Section 860(1) relates only to a charge *created* by a company, which connotes a voluntary act on its part. Hence, a lien arising by operation of law or a statutory security arrangement would not fall within the scope of section 860(1).

(m) If the creation of the security must be a voluntary act in order to attract the requirements of section 860, it should be appreciated that this does not necessarily involve the execution of a security document.[56] Such arrangements nevertheless require registration under section 860.[57]

(n) Whilst section 860(1) is stated to apply only to companies incorporated in England and Wales, it is expressed to apply to any assets of the company listed in section 860(7). The latter subsection is not subject to any territorial limitation and will thus apply to assets situate outside the United Kingdom.[58] As a result, any security over foreign assets which has not been registered in this country will equally be void against the liquidator, administrator and creditors of the chargor in accordance with the rules described above. It may, however, be noted that the security will—if otherwise valid—be regarded as effective in England even though it has not been registered or perfected under the relevant local law.[59] This point is of some significance and is discussed in other contexts, below;

(o) On occasion, a company may acquire property which is subject to a pre-existing charge, without requiring that security to be released on the completion of the purchase.[60] In such a case, the acquiring company must lodge the charge document and the required particulars within the requisite 21 day period following completion of the acquisition.[61] It should be noted, however, that failure to register the charge in this particular case does not render the security void against a liquidator or any other person.[62] No doubt this would be unfairly prejudicial to the creditor, who may not always be aware that the charged asset has been transferred.[63]

---

[55] The point was made in *R v Registrar of Companies, ex p Central Bank of India* [1986] 1 All ER 105 (CA).

[56] For example, (i) an assignment of book debts may be created orally, (ii) in some cases, security can be created by a mere deposit of title documents, and (iii) the security may be created under a foreign system of law under which no requirement for signed documentation arises: see *Sun Tai Cheung Credits Ltd v AG for Hong Kong* [1987] 1 WLR 948 (PC).

[57] Note that the obligation under s 860 is to '… deliver the prescribed particulars of the charge, together with the instrument *(if any)* by which the charge is created or evidenced …'.

[58] The point is confirmed by s 866(1) of the Act, which provides that a verified copy (rather than the original) of the charge document may be delivered where the charge is *both* (i) created outside the United Kingdom and (ii) relates to property situate outside the United Kingdom.

[59] See s 866(2) of the 2006 Act.

[60] In practice, this is perhaps most likely to occur where the property is transferred by a company to another company within the same group.

[61] Companies Act 2006, s 862.

[62] Section 874 renders security void as against liquidators and others for want of registration under s 860 *only*. That consequence is not extended to a failure to comply with the requirements of s 862.

[63] Some assets, such as land, are difficult to transfer without the lender's knowledge, but in principle it seems right that the creditor should be protected in this type of case.

(p) In some 'financial market' cases in which the registration requirements would otherwise apply, their application is excluded by specific rules relating to financial collateral.[64]

(q) Provisions dealing with the operation of the system of registration are to be found in section 869 of the 2006 Act. The Registrar is required to maintain a register of the charges delivered to him under the provisions described above, and to make it available for public inspection. He is also required to issue a certificate of registration in respect of each charge registered by him, and that certificate is conclusive evidence that the statutory registration requirements have been duly met.[65] This provision is commercially convenient (at least to lenders) for it means that honest mistakes made in the completion of the prescribed particulars will not vitiate the security or limit its scope; any such challenge is foreclosed by the issue of the certificate,[66] even if the amount secured by the charge is incorrectly reproduced in the prescribed particulars.[67] This principle would appear only to give way in the face of fraud on the part of the person presenting the particulars for registration.[68] More recent cases have tended to re-confirm the difficulties of challenging or 'going behind' a certificate of registration.[69]

Foreign Assets

27.24 It should be noted that the registration requirements discussed above generally apply because the chargor company is incorporated in the United Kingdom.[70] Given that the place of incorporation operates as the jurisdictional nexus, the duty to register security applies regardless of the geographical location of the assets to which the security applies. This is logical because a person searching the charges register of a UK company would be concerned to know about security subsisting over assets anywhere in the world.[71]

27.25 Where appropriate, comments will be made about foreign elements in the later parts of this section which address security over specific asset classes. But a few broader and more general comments may be helpful at this stage.

27.26 First of all, where the chargor is incorporated in the United Kingdom, there is no territorial limitation on the application of the registration requirements. This is made clear in a variety of ways. It is explicitly stated that a charge over land is subject to registration wherever

---

[64] On these rules, see paras 36.22–36.31 below.

[65] See s 869 (5) and (6) of the 2006 Act.

[66] *Re CL Nye Ltd* [1971] Ch 442 (CA).

[67] *Re Mechanisations (Eaglescliffe) Ltd* [1966] Ch 20. A certificate cannot be challenged even if it was issued following an application for late registration in accordance with the procedure described at para 27.23(i) above: *Exeter Trust Ltd v Screenways Ltd* [1991] BCC 477 (CA).

[68] See the commentary in *Sun Tai Cheung Credits Ltd v AG of Hong Kong* [1987] 1 WLR 948 (PC). This could conceivably occur, for example, if the charge had been dated (and created on) '1 December' but the creditor altered this to '10 December' in order to enable him to lodge the particulars and the charge on 23 December.

[69] See, for example, *Exeter Trust Ltd v Screenways Ltd* [1991] BCC 477 (CA); *Re Top Marques Car Rental Ltd* [2006] EWHC 109 (Ch).

[70] The rules applicable to foreign companies are considered at paras 27.33–27.44 below.

[71] At the risk of a simplistic comparison, the company's financial statements will show the company's assets on a worldwide basis. It is therefore legitimate to expect easy access to details of the extent to which those assets have been encumbered in favour of third parties.

the land happens to be situate.[72] More generally, section 866 of the 2006 Act deals with certain procedural matters where the charged assets are situate abroad, thus reinforcing the impression that the registration requirements apply to assets worldwide.[73] Thus, a floating charge created by an English company must be registered even though all of its assets are outside the United Kingdom when the charge is created. Likewise, a mortgage over a ship or aircraft will require registration under section 860, regardless of its location at the time of the execution of the charge, the Port of Registry, or any other matter.

Secondly, registration will be required irrespective of the law applicable to the document **27.27** which creates the security.[74] This point may seem obvious, since section 860(1) merely refers generally to a 'charge', without discrimination as to the law applicable to the arrangement. Yet this, in turn, creates questions of its own—when does a foreign law document create a 'charge' for these purposes? A question of characterization is necessarily involved. Whether or not the document constitutes a 'charge' must strictly be a matter of English law, since it is necessary to give meaning to that expression in the context of an English statute. The meaning of 'charge' has already been discussed.[75] It would thus be necessary to examine the nature of the rights and remedies conferred by the foreign security and consider whether these 'match' the criteria (priority and realization) which have been noted.[76] If they do, then the arrangement will require registration under section 860(1) of the 2006 Act if the arrangement falls within the scope of the arrangements listed in section 860(7). In this context, it should be noted that a charge over foreign assets which has not been perfected in accordance with local requirements will almost invariably be treated by the English courts as a floating, rather than a fixed security, because the failure to observe local formalities will mean that the lender has not obtained the degree of control over the assets which is emblematic of a fixed charge.[77] The result is that the charge will be effective as against the chargor whilst it is a going concern, but will be void as against a liquidator, administrator or creditor.[78]

Thirdly, it should be appreciated that the English courts will enforce an English law charge **27.28** over property situate abroad, even though the security may be unrecognized or invalid under the law of the country in which the asset is situate. In practice, this point will most often arise in the context of a floating charge over the entire assets and undertaking of the chargor and it happens to hold significant overseas assets at the point of insolvency. The willingness of the English courts to enforce the security in such a case follows from the

---

[72] See para 27.23(e) above.
[73] Section 866 of the 2006 Act is considered in more detail at para 27.31 below.
[74] This point is made here since it will primarily be of relevance to foreign assets, but this will not invariably be the case. For example, a UK company might create a charge over its receivables by means of a New York law assignment executed in favour of its American financier. Some of the receivables may be situate in the United Kingdom. But even if they are not, the foreign law document will still constitute a charge over book debts and will hence require registration under s 860(7)(f) of the 2006 Act.
[75] See para 27.04 above.
[76] For a case in which the problems of categorization of a foreign security instrument for these purposes were discussed (but not resolved) in the context of a factoring agreement governed by French law, see *Cofacredit SA v Morris* [2006] EWHC 353 (Ch), para 120.
[77] See the discussion of the decision in *Re Spectrum Plus Ltd*, at para 30.04 below.
[78] ie in accordance with the rules discussed at para 27.21(g) above.

equitable nature of the floating charge. The English courts will enforce such a charge against the chargor *in personam*. Thus, in *British South Africa Co v De Beers Consolidated Mines Ltd*,[79] the court observed that:

> An English debenture purporting to charge by way of floating security all the English company's property and assets does amount, where the English company possesses land abroad, to an agreement to charge that land, and is a valid equitable security according to English law; and the debenture holders, upon any winding up of that company would rank as secured creditors in respect of the foreign land, and upon a winding up in England they would be paid in full out of the proceeds of sale of that land, before any distribution of the proceeds of it was made among ordinary unsecured creditors. The law on this point is correctly stated in Palmers Company Law 5th Edn p 236: 'Even without complying with the formalities required by the local law in relation to transfers or mortgages, it is competent to a company to create an effective charge on property belonging to it in a foreign country, for the court, in virtue of its Chancery jurisdiction *in personam*, enforces equities in relation to foreign land where the mortgagor is within the jurisdiction … and in determining whether there is an equity the court regards English, not foreign, law and if according to English law there is an equity, e.g., if for valuable consideration a company agrees to give a charge on foreign property, the court will enforce it, although the equity may be one not recognised by the *lex loci rei sitae*…'.

27.29 This statement has been accepted on subsequent occasions. Thus, where an English company executed a floating charge over all of its assets, the proceeds of sale of a property in Scotland fell within the scope of the floating charge even though the security had not been perfected in Scotland and even though the very concept of a floating charge was not at that time recognized in Scotland.[80]

27.30 In every case, the practical difficulty for the secured creditor will lie in the *realization* of the charged asset. He will be unable directly to enforce his security in the foreign country if it has not been registered, or otherwise does not comply with the formalities prescribed by the local law.[81] As a result, he only has an effective claim against the *proceeds of sale* of the property when they are received by the administrator or liquidator in the United Kingdom.[82] The existence and the amount of those proceeds will be diminished by action taken by creditors against the property through local proceedings, since the local courts will ignore the security interest. Furthermore, the English courts will not attempt to restrain unsecured creditors from taking any such proceedings, since it would be inappropriate to do so in the face of the jurisdiction of the local court over the land concerned.[83]

27.31 It will thus always remain appropriate to register the security locally, wherever possible. The 2006 Act recognizes that foreign formalities may apply in this type of case and contains provisions designed to facilitate those processes:

---

[79] [1910] Ch 354 at p 387, aff'd [1910] 2 Ch 502 (CA), reversed on unrelated grounds, [1912] AC 52 (HL).
[80] *Re Anchor Line (Henderson Bros) Ltd* [1937] 2 All ER 823.
[81] See *Luckins v Highway Motel (Caernarvon) Pty Ltd* (1975) 133 CLR 164, noted by Dicey, Morris & Collins, para 30–123.
[82] This reinforces the impression that equity is enforcing the security against the company *in personam*, rather than directly *in rem*.
[83] *Re Maudslay, Sons & Field Ltd* [1900] 1 Ch 602.

(a) where a charge is executed outside the United Kingdom and comprises property abroad, it is sufficient to deliver a certified copy of the charge to the Registrar, as opposed to the original instrument.[84] Furthermore, in such a case, the 21 day period for delivery of the charge is extended to allow for a period in the course of post;[85] and

(b) where a charge relates to property outside the United Kingdom but is executed in the UK, it can be delivered for registration under section 860(1) even though further steps may be necessary to validate that security under the law of the country in which the asset is situate.[86]

As a final point, it will be obvious that the failure to comply with applicable foreign registra- **27.32**
tion requirements or other formalities will not be taken into account by the English courts in this context. The equitable charge arises under English law by virtue of the chargor's promise to give the security. The validity of that charge thus cannot be challenged by reference to any other system of law.

Foreign Companies

It was noted earlier that the registration requirements applicable to English companies **27.33**
apply to security created over any of its assets, whether situate in the United Kingdom or abroad. Since the provision applies to all assets of such a company, wherever found, one is in practice released from the need to consider in which country particular assets are deemed to be situate.[87]

This happy state of affairs changes when considering the position of companies incorpo- **27.34**
rated outside the United Kingdom. The relevant statutory provisions have a slightly unhappy history, which it is necessary briefly to describe. Under section 409 (now repealed) of the Companies Act 1985, the requirements as to registration of charges applied apply equally '… to charges on property in England and Wales which are created, and to charges on property which is acquired by, a company (whether a company within the meaning of this Act or not) which has an established place of business in England and Wales …'.

This formulation gave rise to two main questions, namely: **27.35**

(a) When will a company incorporated abroad be taken to have '… an established place of business in England and Wales …'?

(b) When is property deemed to be found *in* England and Wales?

The existence of an established place of business is, in practice a mixed question of law and **27.36**
fact which can raise significant difficulties. An overseas company is obliged to register particulars of its branch or place of business in the United Kingdom under provisions now

---

[84] Section 866(1) of the 2006 Act.

[85] Section 870(1) of the 2006 Act, already noted at para 27.23(d) above.

[86] Section 866(2) of the 2006 Act. This rule is, of course, only logical, for the Companies Registry could scarcely be expected to concern itself with foreign law formalities or compliance with them.

[87] At least, this is the case in the context of the s 860 registration requirements. It will often be necessary to identify the *situs* of particular assets in order to determine which system of law determines the essential validity of the security interest. The point is discussed in relation to the various individual categories of security, below.

contained in section 1052 of the Companies Act 2006.[88] But the duty to register charges created by foreign companies under section 409 was linked to the *existence* of a place of business in the UK, and not to its *registration*. This led to a 'mis-match' which could be confusing for secured creditors, in that there could be an obligation to register such security even though the chargor had failed to register the existence of its branch in the United Kingdom at Companies House. As a result, security executed by a Bermudian company with a place of business in England was held to be void against a liquidator for want of registration, even though the chargor had not registered its branch in this country: see the well-known decision in *Slavenbergs Bank NV v Intercontinental Natural Resources Ltd.*[89] As a result of this decision, it became the practice to deliver to the Registrar particulars of all charges created by foreign companies and affecting assets in England and Wales. The charge could not judge whether the chargor might later be judged to have an established place of business here, and delivery of the requisite particulars was therefore obviously the prudent course. Since many such chargors had not registered a branch or place of business here, this was highly inconvenient for the Registrar since he had no file against which the particulars could be lodged. This was ultimately dealt with by the establishment of the so-called 'Slavenberg Register', which maintained a record of the particulars so delivered.

27.37 Happily, this area of difficulty is now resolved by the Companies Act 2006. Section 1045 empowers the Secretary of State to make regulations requiring an 'overseas company'[90] to deliver certain particulars about a branch or place of business established in the United Kingdom. He is also empowered to make regulations '... about the registration of specified charges over property in the United Kingdom of a registered overseas company ...'. The regulations made under these provisions are the Overseas Companies (Execution of Documents and Registration of Charges) Regulations 2009[91] and Part 3 (articles 8–28) deal specifically with the registration of charges. Since the rules about registration of charges now apply only if the foreign company has itself registered a branch or place of business here,[92] the 'mis-match' described above and highlighted by the *Slavenberg* decision can no longer arise. The following points may be noted in this respect:

(a) It will now only be necessary to register a charge over UK property created by a foreign company if it has registered a branch or place of business in this country.[93]

---

[88] The corresponding provisions were formerly found in Part XXIII of the 1985 Act.
[89] [1980] 1 All ER 955. For an Australian case addressing a similar problem (although now reversed by legislation), see *Luckins v Highway Motel (Caernarvon) Pty Ltd* (1975) 133 CLR 164.
[90] ie any company incorporated outside the United Kingdom: s 1044.
[91] SI 2009/1917 (hereafter the 'Overseas Companies Charges Regulations' or the '2009 Regulations').
[92] Part 3 of the Regulations applies only to a foreign company which has registered particulars in respect of one or more UK establishments and has not subsequently de-registered all of those establishments: see art 8(2) of the Overseas Companies Charges Regulations. A foreign company is only treated as registered once the relevant details have become available for inspection at Companies House: Overseas Companies Charges Regulations, art 8(3). This provision is presumably designed for the protection of chargees where the foreign company is in the course of filing particulars of an establishment in this country but these have not found their way onto the public file when the charge is created.
[93] The existence of such registration can be verified by the usual search at Companies House. It should be emphasized that the statement in the text is directed specifically to the registration requirements in s 860 of the 2006 Act. Other requirements attributable to security over specific assets (eg such as land) will apply regardless of the chargor's own registration status in the UK.

(b) A charge created by a registered overseas company requires registration if (i) it falls within the categories of charge that are registrable in the case of an English company,[94] (ii) the relevant property is situate in the United Kingdom on the date on which the charge is created, and (iii) it remains so situate on the expiry of the period allowed for registration of the charge.[95] Consequently, the validity of a charge over *foreign* property is not prejudiced merely because that property is subsequently brought into the United Kingdom.[96]

(c) As in the case of charges created by UK companies, the period for registration is 21 days, starting from the day following the creation of the charge.[97]

(d) It may be noted that the registration requirement is disapplied if, at the end of the period allowed for registration, the relevant asset is no longer situate in the United Kingdom.[98] Thus, if a foreign buyer acquires equipment from a UK supplier with property passing to the buyer in the UK at the point of sale, it will not be necessary to register any security created to finance the acquisition merely because the equipment remains in the UK for a few days prior to export. It would seem that the registration regime is disapplied in such a situation because the security arrangement is probably initiated by the foreign buyer and has no meaningful or permanent connection with the buyer's registered branch in the United Kingdom.

(e) A failure of registration—where it is required—has the usual consequence that the security becomes void against a liquidator, administrator, or creditor of the chargor.[99]

(f) Security created by a foreign company which has not lodged particulars under the Overseas Companies Regulations 2009 will remain valid notwithstanding any insolvency or similar proceeding, because no registration requirement applies to such security either under the Companies Act itself or under the 2009 Regulations.[100] This statement will remain true even though the foreign chargor does indeed have an establishment in the United Kingdom and ought to have delivered particulars in respect of it in accordance with the 2009 Regulations.

The second question—the location of an asset—may continue to arise. For example, an overseas company may have registered its branch in the United Kingdom and may also have created security. That security may thus become void against a liquidator, administrator, or creditor of the overseas company by parallel application of section 860 of the **27.38**

---

[94] ie it falls within one of the categories listed in s 860(7) of the 2006 Act, as discussed at para 27.23(e) above.

[95] On this novel provision, see the discussion in subpara (d) below. Authority for the points noted in this paragraph is to be found in art 9(1)(f) of the 2009 Regulations.

[96] This may be contrasted with the position which arose in *Slavenberg* (above), where a charge was held to become void for want of registration where the goods concerned were brought into England at a later date.

[97] Overseas Companies Charges Regulations 2009, art 12(1). Where, as will often be the case, the charge is created outside the United Kingdom, the 21 day period is extended to account for the course of post: art 12(2).

[98] Overseas Companies Charges Regulations 2009, art 10(4).

[99] Overseas Companies Charges Regulations 2009, art 19(1).

[100] This comment will apply from 1 October 2009, which is the effective date of the 2009 Regulations. Where security has been created prior to that date, the issues posed by the *Slavenberg* decision will continue to apply, because the validity of the security must be judged by reference to the law in force as at the date of its creation.

2006 Act.[101] However, this consequence will only follow if the charged asset constitutes '… property in the United Kingdom …' both at the time the security is created[102] and at the expiry of the period allowed for registration.[103]

27.39 The legislation is also alive to this issue and the regulations made by the Secretary of State in relation to foreign companies could include provision as to '… the circumstances in which property is to be regarded, for the purposes of the regulations, as being, or not being, in the United Kingdom …'.[104] This enabling provision was originally followed through by article 49 of the original draft 2009 Regulations, which broadly stated that property '… shall be regarded as situated in the United Kingdom …'[105] in the following cases:

(a) property registered in a land registry within the United Kingdom;

(b) a ship or aircraft maintained on the applicable UK register;

(c) intellectual property registered on the UK designs register, the Register of Trade Marks or the Patents Register;

(d) tangible chattels, equipment or other assets which are physically situate in the United Kingdom at the point of time at which the charge is created;[106] and

(e) intangible property[107] if, at the time the charge is created, the property is governed by the law of any part of the United Kingdom. This formulation was not entirely happy. For example, a debt may be 'governed' by English law in the sense that the respective rights and obligations of the creditor and debtor fall to be determined by English law as the law applicable to the relevant contract.[108] Alternatively, the debt may be 'governed' by English law in the sense that it is owing by a debtor who is resident in the United Kingdom such that the debt is situate in this country for private international law purposes.[109] There is no necessary requirement that these two systems of governing law should coincide; it is perfectly feasible for a debtor resident in France to owe a debt to a German creditor under a contract governed by English law. However, given the context, it seems clear that the provision was intended to be directed to the *situs* of the debt, rather than its applicable law. Whether or not a debt is 'governed' by English law for these purposes would accordingly be determined by reference to the place in which the debtor is resident.

---

[101] See art 19(1) of the 2009 Regulations, to which reference has already been made.

[102] See art 9(1)(b) of the 2009 Regulations, noted above.

[103] See art 10(4) of the 2009 Regulations, noted above.

[104] Companies Act 2006, s 1052(2)(b).

[105] The wording is reproduced because it suggests that the list provided by art 49 is intended to be exclusive, in the sense that any asset not falling within the art 49 criteria must be regarded as property outside the United Kingdom and, hence, outside the scope of the registration regime applicable to charges created by registered overseas companies.

[106] Although, as noted at subpara (d) above, the registration regime would not apply in such a case if the relevant asset has been removed from the United Kingdom before the end of the period allowed for registration.

[107] The expression is defined to mean any intangible or incorporeal property, including any thing in action, or any corresponding property under a foreign law.

[108] ie in accordance with the terms of Rome I: see the analysis in Chapter 40 below.

[109] Compare the analysis at para 27.28 above.

However that may be, these provisions were ultimately omitted from the final version of **27.40**
the Overseas Companies Regulations 2009, which means that the court will be left to
determine whether assets are to be regarded as situated in the United Kingdom for these
purposes. It will no doubt apply the usual conflict of law principles governing the *situs* of
property.[110]

It remains to consider the attitude which the English courts should adopt when consider- **27.41**
ing a security interest created by a foreign company over assets situate in England where any
necessary English formalities have been met so that the security is in principle valid in this
country, but the company has failed to comply with applicable registration requirements
in its home jurisdiction.[111] Although there seems to be no case law which directly decides
these issues, it is submitted that the position is as follows:

(a) If the security document is governed by English law,[112] then the English courts should
    enforce that security at the behest of the creditor, regardless of non-compliance with
    formalities in the chargor's jurisdiction of incorporation.[113] Some inferential support
    for this view may be drawn from the decision in *Arthur D Little Ltd (in administration)
    v Ableco Finance LLC*[114] where a Scottish company had executed a charge over shares
    in its English subsidiary pursuant to a security document governed by English law. The
    charge had not been registered in Scotland and it was argued that (i) the security took
    effect as a floating charge and (ii) the English court should hold the charge to be void
    against the administrator on the basis that it had not been registered under the corre-
    sponding registration requirements relating to companies incorporated in Scotland.
    The court seems to have worked on the basis that a foreign law registration require-
    ment would not affect the validity of a charge over English property and governed by
    English law.[115]
(b) Where the security is governed by the laws of the chargor's home jurisdiction and that
    law invalidates the security as a result of non-compliance with registration formalities,
    then the English courts should likewise hold the security to be void. This reflects the
    fact that an arrangement which is invalid under its applicable law will be treated as
    invalid in England to the same extent.[116]

---

[110] On the whole subject, see generally Dicey Morris & Collins, Part Five. The relevant rules are also
discussed later in this section, in the context of the individual types of asset concerned.

[111] This is in some respects the converse of the situation which arose in the *British South Africa* case,
discussed at para 27.28 above.

[112] This must be the case if, for example, the lender is to have valid security over land in England.

[113] This follows from the fact that foreign laws cannot generally affect questions of title to assets situate in
the UK: see *Bank voor Handel en Scheepvaart NV v Administrator of Hungarian Property* [1954] AC 584 (HL);
Williams & Humbert Ltd v W&H Trade Marks (Jersey) Ltd [1986] AC 368 (HL).

[114] [2002] 2 BCLC 799.

[115] In the event, the provisions for registration of charges created by Scottish companies were held to form
a part of the law of England as well as Scotland and, hence, were not a registration requirement imposed by a
'foreign' law for these purposes. However, that line of reasoning plainly could not be applied to jurisdictions
outside the United Kingdom.

[116] See Art 10 of Rome I.

Summary of Registration Requirements—Foreign Companies

27.42   What can be said by way of summary? In dealing with security created by an overseas company, it may be said that the registration of such security at Companies House will be required for the purposes of article 51 of the 2009 Regulations where:

(a)   the company concerned has itself registered a UK establishment under the provisions of those Regulations;[117]

(b)   the charged property consists of or includes assets within the United Kingdom;

(c)   those assets are situate within the United Kingdom at the time of creation of the charge; and

(d)   those assets remain situate in the United Kingdom when the 21 day period allowed for registration expires.

27.43   If any one of these tests is not met, then the registration requirement will not apply.[118] It should be appreciated that the registration requirements are also disapplied in certain specific contexts, principally in relation to financial market transactions.[119]

27.44   Finally, it appears that a failure to comply with registration requirements applicable to the chargor in its jurisdiction of incorporation will only have the effect of invalidating security in England if the security document is also governed by the law of that country.[120]

---

[117] From 1 October 2009, the Slavenberg register has ceased to operate and it is thus no longer necessary or even possible to deliver particulars of a charge in relation to a foreign company which has not itself delivered branch details in accordance with the 2009 Regulations. Even under the revised regime, however, some difficulties may remain. For example, where a foreign company is registered in a country which uses a different form of alphabet, its correct translation into English may be a matter of debate and there may be alternative formulations which would be equally acceptable. In such a case, it may not be possible for the charge to be completely certain whether or not the foreign company has registered a branch in England (although inquiry with the chargor ought to resolve the issue). In marginal cases of this kind, there may remain some merit in delivering the charge and the prescribed particulars to the Registrar, if only out of an abundance of caution.

[118] Although it should again be emphasized that registration requirements applicable to the particular *asset*—such as land—will continue to apply.

[119] See Chapter 35 below.

[120] See the discussion at para 27.41(b) above.

28

TYPES OF SECURITY

Introduction

The foregoing chapter has set the scene in establishing the framework for the registration 28.01 of security over corporate assets. But, as there noted, the registration process merely prevents an otherwise valid security from becoming void against the liquidator, administrators, and creditors of the chargor. It does not otherwise dictate the nature, form or content of the security interest created as between the parties, nor does it determine whether or not a security is intrinsically valid in the first place.

It therefore remains to consider three points, namely: 28.02

(a) What is the nature of the security which the borrower creates?
(b) What are the specific characteristics of security created over particular types of asset?
(c) In the case of competing layers of security on the same asset, which lender is entitled to priority?

Fixed Charges

A valid and effective fixed charge over an asset assures to the charge the benefit of the entire 28.03 proceeds of sale following enforcement, subject only to such marketing and other incidental costs as may be associated with that process. It creates a greater degree of security for the creditor, for the security conferred by a merely floating charge is subject to the rights of certain preferential creditors and may also be subject to dilution to create a prescribed pool of funds for the unsecured creditors.[1] The distinction can therefore be one of some importance.

28.04 What, then, are the indicia of a fixed charge? The language of the security document will provide a starting point, but the mere fact that the parties have referred to a 'fixed charge' will by no means be conclusive.[2] Recent case law[3] suggests that the lender must enjoy a sufficient degree of control over the charged assets.[4] What amounts to a sufficient degree of control must in large measure depend upon the nature of the asset and the type of supervision which may be exercised.

28.05 Nevertheless, since they are now a relatively common occurrence, it is perhaps appropriate to comment on the effect of security substitution clauses, which allow a borrower either (i) to require the release of any security which exceeds a pre-set security ratio or (ii) to withdraw assets for the security package on the basis that they are replaced by other assets meeting stated valuation and other stated criteria.[5] The lender still has a degree of control over the security and such arrangements do not amount to an authority to the borrower to deal with its assets in the ordinary course of business.[6]

Floating Charges

Definition

28.06 The most frequently cited description[7] of a floating charge is that provided by Romer LJ in *Re Yorkshire Woolcombers Association Ltd*,[8] where he identified the three core characteristics as follows:

---

[1] On these points, see para 28.20 below.

[2] On the other hand, if the parties use the expression 'floating charge', then this would seem to be conclusive that the creditor intended to content himself with a floating charge, or the lesser form of security. In such a case, there would seem to be no reason for the court to 'look behind' the language employed by the parties.

[3] See, in particular, *Agnew v Commissioner of Inland Revenue* [2001] 710 (PC) and *Re Spectrum Plus Ltd* [2005] 2 AC 680 (HL). These cases arose specifically in the context of fixed charges over book debts, and they are therefore considered in more depth at para 30.04 below.

[4] At the risk of a very significant over-simplification, this in many ways means that the arrangement must not be a floating charge which involves a sufficient authority for the chargor to deal with the assets in the ordinary course of its business: see para 28.06 below.

[5] Such provisions are often seen in the context of real estate finance, or security over portfolios of listed or rated securities.

[6] See Lingard, para 9.3, citing *Re Queen's Moat Houses plc* [2004] NPC 67. It seems that this analysis would remain valid notwithstanding the later decision of the House of Lords in *Re Spectrum Plus Ltd* [2005] 2 AC 680, although the point is not beyond debate.

[7] The word 'description' is used rather than 'definition'. It has been observed that the nature of a floating charge does not lend itself to an exhaustive definition: see *Re Brightlife Ltd* [1986] 3 All ER 673, at p 677. The present discussion naturally focuses on the *security* aspects of a floating charge. But it should be appreciated that the distinction between a fixed and a floating charge may have other consequences. For example, a building society may be able to create a *fixed* charge over its assets but a security interest classified as a *floating* charge (whether involving all of the assets of the society or part only) will be void: see Building Societies Act 1986, s 9B (as inserted by Building Societies Act 1997, s 11). Equally, a fixed charge over shares and certain other assets will not be subject to registration under Companies Act 2006, s 680(7), but if the arrangement is characterized as a *floating* charge, then registration would be required under s 860(7)(g). On that subject, see para 28.10 below. In addition, a floating charge is subject to various preferential and other claims: see paras 28.14–28.23 below.

[8] [1903] 2 Ch 284 at p 295 (CA).

(a) it is a charge on a class of assets[9] of the company;[10]

(b) that class of assets is one which would be changing from time to time in the ordinary course of business;[11] and

(c) the charge contemplates that the company may continue its business in the ordinary course until the lender takes some step to crystallize or enforce the security. As a result, the company can continue to sell its stock in the ordinary course, and buyers will thus obtain a good title to the stock, free of any security interest. To express matters in a different way, the company retains authority to deal with its assets *in the ordinary course of business*[12] so long as the operation of the charge remains suspended. Or, in other words, the charge retains a degree of control over the assets to the extent necessary to negative the existence of a fixed charge.[13]

When the case reached the House of Lords, it was noted that a floating charge moves with **28.07** the class of assets to which it relates until some event occurs or the lender takes some action which causes the charge to crystallize and to fasten on the assets to which it relates.[14] A floating charge thus applies to a fluctuating class of assets, but the company retains control of the assets so that it can continue to carry on its business in the ordinary way. To express matters in a different way, a floating charge is an equitable security which remains dormant until the creditor takes action to enforce it.[15] The chargor thus remains in control of the charged assets so that it can continue to operate its business as a going concern.

As already noted, it is this element of control which, in recent times has received a **28.08** greater degree of emphasis from the courts; if a chargee wishes to establish the existence of a fixed security, then he must show that the chargor lacks this element of control which is indicative of a floating charge.[16]

---

[9] In practice, security documents will frequently seek to take a floating charge over the entire assets and undertaking of the company, in addition to a list of specific, fixed charge assets.

[10] Although some writers have occasionally put forward a different view, it is generally thought that a floating charge can only be created by a limited company.

[11] The obvious example would be the stock in trade and finished goods of a manufacturing company.

[12] This limitation should be carefully noted—the chargor's authority is by no means unfettered, although it should be said that the expression 'ordinary course of business' was given a fairly extended meaning in *Ashborder BV v Green Gas Power Ltd* [2004] EWHC 1517 (Ch).

[13] See the discussion at n 4 above. The fact that the right to deal with the assets may in some way be restricted does not necessarily mean that the chargor has insufficient control over them for these purposes: see *Re Cosslett (Contractors) Ltd* [1998] Ch 495 (CA).

[14] *Illingworth v Houldsworth* [1904] AC 355 (HL). A floating charge was vividly described (at p 358) as '… ambulatory and shifting in its nature, hovering over and so to speak floating with the property which it is intended to affect …'.

[15] *Government Stock and Other Securities Investment Co Ltd v Manila Railway Co* [1897] AC 81. The security nevertheless comes into existence at the point of time when the security is created—the charge does not amount to a contract to create security at a future date or as at the point of crystallization: *Evans v Rival Granite Quarries Ltd* [1910] 2 KB 979.

[16] *Agnew v Commissioner for Inland Revenue* [2001] 2 AC 21 (PC); *Re Spectrum Plus Ltd* [2005] 2 AC 680 (HL). As a result of these decisions, it has been suggested (eg by Lingard, para 8.56) that cases such as *Re Atlantic Computers plc* [1992] Ch 505 and *Arthur D Little (in administration) v Ableco Finance LLC* [2002] EWHC 701 (Ch) may require reconsideration because they were based primarily upon the view that the key characteristic of a floating charge was its ambulatory nature.

28.09 Given that the security only finally attaches to the company's assets at the point of enforcement, and that the borrower remains in control of its assets up to that point,[17] it may readily be imagined that there is scope for conflict between the holder of the floating charge and other creditors—both secured and unsecured—dealing with the company. These questions of priority are more conveniently dealt with at a later stage.[18]

Importance of the Characterization

28.10 Why is the characterization of a charge as 'fixed' or 'floating' important?

The most obvious consequence is that a floating charge is subject to various priority and other matters which may have the effect of diluting the value of the security and, as already noted, those issues will be considered at a later stage. However, there may also be other consequences. For example:

(a) As noted above, a charge over shares will not generally be a form of security which requires registration under section 860 of the Companies Act 2006,[19] because it does not fall within the list of assets or arrangements set out in section 860(7) of that Act. However, if the charge over shares in fact takes effect as a *floating* security, then the document will become subject to registration under section 860(7)(g). There may therefore be cases in which the lender has not registered his security and it will be of first importance for him to demonstrate that his charge is fixed (rather than floating) in character.[20]

(b) If the security takes effect as a floating charge, then an administrator will have authority to sell the relevant assets in the course of the performance of his duties. If, however, the security operates as a fixed charge, then the consent of the creditor or the court will be required for that purpose.[21]

Crystallization

28.11 A floating charge usually crystallizes and becomes attached to the chargor's assets on the appointment of an administrative receiver, in the limited cases in which such an appointment remains possible.[22] The commencement of winding up also results in crystallization, because the borrower's authority to deal with the charged assets in the ordinary course of business must plainly terminate at that point, even if the winding up is on a

---

[17] Again, note the contrast with the fixed charge which attaches to the asset from the date of creation and, form that date, the lender must exercise a sufficient degree of control.

[18] See paras 28.14–28.35 below.

[19] See the discussion at paras 29.22–29.24 above.

[20] For an example of this type of problem in relation to a charge over shares, see *Arthur D Little Ltd (in administration) v Ableco Finance LLC* [2002] 2 BCLC 799.

[21] See Insolvency Act 1986, s 15(2).

[22] On the few cases in which it remains possible to appoint an administrative receiver, see Insolvency Act 1986, ss 72A–72G, as inserted by the Enterprise Act 2002, s250(1). The exceptions include (i) security created in respect of capital markets transactions in excess of £50 million, (ii) security given by a project company in respect of a public-private partnership, (iii) security given by certain railway and utility companies and urban regeneration projects, and (iv) certain financial collateral arrangements of the kind described in Chapter 36 below.

voluntary basis.[23] It would appear that crystallization should also occur when the company ceases to carry on its business as a going concern,[24] for the chargor's authority to deal with the assets is limited to that objective. At least in the absence of some express contractual term, however, the appointment of an administrator under the terms of the Insolvency Act 1986 will not lead to the crystallization of the security since, in many cases, the very object of his appointment is to continue the company's business.[25]

Crystallization has the effect of converting the formerly floating security into a fixed, equi-   **28.12**
table charge.[26] Crystallization has no real benefit for the charge in terms of his statutory position, because his security will continue to be categorized as 'floating' and, hence, will remain subject to those provisions of the Insolvency Act dealing with preferential creditors, the prescribed pool of assets for unsecured creditors, and similar matters.[27]

In other respects, however, the point of time at which crystallization occurs may be of some   **28.13**
importance. For example since, as noted above, crystallization has the effect of creating a fixed equitable charge over the formerly floating charge assets, the crystallized charge will take priority over any security subsequently created by the company.[28] The precise point of time at which crystallization occurs may thus occasionally be a matter of some moment as between competing chargees. As a result, and in an effort to bolster the position of the floating charge holder, it became the practice to provide for automatic crystallization of the floating charge if certain events occurred (eg if the chargor attempted to create a first rank-ing security over any of the relevant assets). Alternatively, the lender may be entitled to give notice of crystallization if it believed any of the security to be in jeopardy (eg as a result of impending action by other creditors). Such case law as is available suggests that provisions of this kind are valid as between chargor and charge, and that crystallization under such provisions will also be effective as against other creditors who have notice of them.[29]

Priorities

Introduction

Given that a floating charge 'hovers' over the assets of the chargor company and that the   **28.14**
charge does not take control of the assets concerned—thus giving the chargor the ability

---

[23] *Re Compton & Co Ltd* [1914] 1 Ch 954.
[24] See *Government Stock and other Securities Investment Co Ltd v Manila Railway Co* [1897] AC 81 (HL) and *Robson v Smith* [1895] 2 Ch 118.
[25] In any event, a provision in a floating charge to the effect that crystallization will occur when a morato-rium is sought or obtained is void: see Insolvency Act 1986, Sch A1, para 43.
[26] *NW Robbie & Co Ltd v Witney Warehouses Co Ltd* [1963] 3 All ER 613.
[27] For the purposes of the Insolvency Act 1986, a charge *originally created* as a floating charge will continue to be treated as such, notwithstanding crystallization: see the definition of 'floating charge' in Insolvency Act 1986, s 251.
[28] Save that, in accordance with ordinary principles, a mortgagee who takes a legal charge in good faith, for value and without notice of the crystallization will enjoy priority: see Ellinger, p 792, citing *Business Computers Ltd v Anglo-African Leasing Ltd* [1977] 2 All ER 741.
[29] See *Re Brightlife Ltd* [1987] Ch 200, approving the New Zealand decision in *Re Manurewa Transport Ltd* [1971] NZLR 909, and the discussion in Lingard, para 9.28.

and authority to trade in its assets in the ordinary course—it is perhaps unsurprising that its status as a first ranking security is somewhat tenuous when compared to a fixed charge.

Categories of Priority Claims

28.15 It is therefore necessary to consider the extent to which the priority of a floating security is diluted in the event of an insolvency of the chargor. Such dilution occurs in essentially three ways. The first form of dilution is created by various statutory provisions designed to strike a balance between the charge and employees/unsecured creditors of the chargor. The second category involves the resolution of priority issues with holders of other charges (whether fixed or floating). The final set of issues arises from claims by unsecured creditors who may have asserted their rights in the period leading up to the formal insolvency process. Each of these categories will be considered in turn.

Statutory Priorities

28.16 The starting point for the statutory regime of priorities is provided by sections 40 and 175 of the Insolvency Act 1986.

28.17 Section 40 applies where a receiver is appointed in respect of a charge which, as created, was a floating charge.[30] In such a case, the funds coming into the hands of the receiver with reference to the floating charge are to be applied first in payment of preferential debts,[31] in priority to payments to the holder of the floating charge. Likewise, where a company is in liquidation, preferential debts incurred before the crystallization of the floating charge will also enjoy priority.[32]

28.18 Where a bank holds a standard form debenture over the entire assets and undertaking of an insolvent borrower, it will thus be necessary to distinguish carefully between fixed and floating charge assets, since only the floating charge assets are available to meet preferential debts.[33] As has already been noted,[34] the distinction is not always a straightforward matter.

28.19 What, then is the nature of the claims which may enjoy a statutory priority over a floating charge?

The Prescribed Part

28.20 One of the innovations introduced by the Enterprise Act 2002 was the creation of the so-called 'prescribed part', a portion of the assets to be set aside for the unsecured creditors out of assets which would otherwise be available to the holder of the floating charge. Where a company has gone into liquidation, administration, or receivership, under section 176A

---

[30] In consequence of the use of the words 'as created', the section will apply even if the floating charge has subsequently crystallized.

[31] On the definition of 'preferential debts', see Insolvency Act 1986, s 396 and Sch 6.

[32] Insolvency Act 1986, s 175(2); *Re Christonette International Ltd* [1992] 3 All ER 225.

[33] On this point, see *Lewis Merthyr Consolidated Collieries Ltd* [1929] 1 Ch 498 and *Re GL Saunders Ltd* [1986] 1 WLR 215.

[34] See paras 28.03–28.10 above.

of the Insolvency Act 1986,[35] the relevant insolvency official must set aside a prescribed part of the floating charge assets[36] for the benefit of unsecured creditors. The court may order that the 'prescribed part' rules need not be applied where the cost involved in the process would be disproportionate to the benefits.[37]

It should be appreciated that the prescribed part is intended for the benefit of creditors who **28.21** have been unsecured throughout. Hence, if the assets are insufficient to pay the floating charge holder himself, he cannot claim a share of the prescribed part as an unsecured creditor.[38]

Occupational Pension Schemes

Amounts owing by the company in respect of contributions to its occupational pension **28.22** scheme constitute a preferential debt and are thus payable in priority to a floating charge. There is no specified limit or cap on the amount which qualifies for priority under this heading.[39]

Employees

Amounts due to employees in respect of remuneration owing for the four month period **28.23** leading up to insolvency, together with accrued holiday pay for any employees who are dismissed, likewise rank in priority to a floating charge.[40] A lender who funds payments which would otherwise qualify for this priority (eg by making a loan to the administrator for that purpose) is effectively subrogated to the employees and thus enjoys the same, preferential creditor status in respect of those amounts.[41]

Priority as against other Secured Creditors

As will be seen,[42] fixed charges usually rank in priority according to the date of their **28.24** creation. However, since the floating security only attaches to assets at the point of enforcement, it is perhaps unsurprising that this rule does not extend to floating charges.

As a result, and whilst successive *floating* charges will rank according to the order of the date **28.25** of their creation,[43] a fixed charge would rank in priority to a floating charge even though the fixed charge was executed at a later date.[44] The application of this rule would, of course, very seriously undermine the value of the floating charge as a security interest. As a result,

---

[35] As inserted by Enterprise Act 2002, s 252.
[36] On the calculation of the prescribed part, see The Insolvency Act (Prescribed Part) Order 2003 (SI 2003/2097). The maximum amount of the prescribed part is £600,000.
[37] Insolvency Act 1986, s 176A(5). This power would presumably be exercised where the deficiency is so great that each unsecured creditor would receive only a very nominal recovery.
[38] See *Re Airbase (UK) Ltd* [2008] EWHC 124 (Ch).
[39] Insolvency Act 1986, s 386, read together with para 8 of Sch 6 to that Act.
[40] Insolvency Act 1986, s 386, read together with paras 9 and 10 of Sch 6.
[41] Insolvency Act 1986, s 386, read together with para 11 of Sch 6.
[42] See, for example, the discussion in relation to competing security over shares at para 29.25 below and, in relation to mortgages over land, at paras 32.37–32.38 below.
[43] *Re Benjamin Cope & Sons Ltd* [1914] 1 Ch 800.
[44] *Wheatley v Silkstone and Haigh Moor Coal Co* (1885) 29 Ch D 715.

standard forms of debenture will prohibit the creation of any further security over assets which are subject to the floating charge. Since a disposal of assets can likewise be detrimental to the interests of the chargee, they will also prohibit such disposals, except in relation to the sale of stock in trade in the ordinary course of business.

28.26   Provisions of this kind are effective as between the parties, but how are they to be made effective against a subsequent chargee? In practice, details of the restrictions are usually included on the form lodged with the Registrar of Companies under section 860 of the Companies Act 2006.[45] If the subsequent chargee has actual or constructive notice of the restriction, then it will be unconscionable for him to claim priority and the fixed charge will be postponed to the interests of the floating charge.[46] Whilst the mere registration of the required particulars of charge does not constitute constructive notice to *any* person dealing with the company,[47] it is submitted that this does amount to notice to any person who might reasonably be expected to undertake a search of the register.[48] This category would plainly include any person intending to lend money to the company on the security of its assets; any security taken by such a person would thus be postponed to a prior floating charge, provided that notice of the restriction against the creation of further security had been included on the forms lodged with the Registrar.[49] Indeed, it is submitted that a lender who discovers (or ought to have discovered) the existence of an existing floating charge through his search at Companies House is put on notice that there may be a restriction against the creation of any later security, largely because the existence of such restrictions in the modern context is virtually a matter of course; the subsequent, fixed chargee should not be able to benefit from turning a blind eye to a state of affairs which ought to have been obvious, given the information available to him.[50]

Priority as against Unsecured Creditors

28.27   The object of taking security is, of course, to obtain priority over unsecured creditors. Nevertheless, the particular nature of the floating charge does mean that the holder of the security can find himself in competition with unsecured creditors who have attempted to take enforcement action against the company.

Rights of Set-off

28.28   A floating charge generally has no impact upon any rights of set-off enjoyed by third parties dealing with the company.

---

[45]   On registration under s 860, see para 27.18 above.

[46]   *Wilson v Kelland* [1910] 2 Ch 306; *English and Scottish Mercantile Investment Co Ltd v Brunton* [1892] 2 QB 700 (CA).

[47]   *Manchester Trust Ltd v Furness Withy & Co Ltd* [1895] 2 QB 539.

[48]   Lingard, para 9.15.

[49]   The present discussion ignores the effect of Companies Act 1985, s 711A (inserted by the Companies Act 1989) because this provision has not been brought into force.

[50]   In order to reach such a conclusion, a court would have to circumvent the decision in *Wilson v Kelland* [1910] 2 Ch 306, where the court held that registration of the charge involved notice of its *existence* but not notice of its *contents*. In the modern context, this approach seems unrealistic, especially where the chargee is a bank whose own standard forms of floating charge would include precisely the kind of restrictions at issue.

The debtor will thus not have notice that the debt due from him to the company has been **28.29** the subject of an assignment or charge to the holder of the floating security, and he will accordingly be able to continue to exercise any rights of set-off which he may have in respect of transactions effected before he receives actual notice that the floating charge has crystallized.[51] As a consequence, rights of set-off arising in the normal course of business will take priority over the security created by a floating charge. The position is essentially similar even where the document seeks to create a fixed charge over book debts,[52] at any rate until the debtor receives actual notice of the security.

Liens

A lien will usually arise where assets of the company are delivered to a third party for the **28.30** provision of a service, such as repair or storage. The third party will be under no obligation to redeliver the asset until the relevant charges have been paid.

Once again, a lien created or arising[53] before a floating charge has crystallized will take **28.31** priority over the charge, in the sense that the third party cannot be required to return the asset until charges have been paid. This is so even though the floating charge had been created before the lien arose. This is a reasonable result, in that warehousemen, repairers, and others who are likely to become the beneficiaries of such liens cannot reasonably be expected to search their customer's register at Companies House, and so would not be affected by constructive notice of the floating charge. Even if they were aware of the existence of the charge, there is no reason why they should be affected by it unless they also have actual knowledge of its crystallization.

Execution Creditors

Priority as between an execution creditor and the holder of a floating charge depends upon **28.32** the date on which the floating charge crystallizes.[54]

If an execution creditor has seized goods and completed the sale—or accepted a payment **28.33** in lieu of sale—before crystallization of the floating charge, then the execution creditor may retain the proceeds.[55] If, however, goods have been seized but remain unsold at the point of crystallization, then the chargee may claim those goods in priority to the execution creditor.[56]

---

[51] *Biggerstaff v Rowatt's Wharf Ltd* [1896] 2 Ch 93 (CA); *Business Computers Ltd v Anglo-African Leasing Ltd* [1977] 2 All ER 741

[52] On this subject, see Chapter 30 below.

[53] A possessory lien arises when the person claiming it has provided services in relation to the goods entrusted to him, whilst a contractual lien is created on the date on which the parties entered into the contract: Lingard, para 9.9, citing *Wiltshire Iron Co Ltd v Great Western Railway Co* [1910] 2 KB 979 (CA); *George Barker (Transport) Ltd v Eynon* [1925] 1 KB 655 and *Mac-Jordan Construction Ltd v Brookmount Erostin Ltd* [1992] BCLC 350 (CA).

[54] On the identification of this date, see paras 28.11–28.13 above.

[55] *Evans v Rival Granite Quarries Ltd* [1910] 2 KB 979; *Heaton & Dugard Ltd v Cutting Bros Ltd* [1925] 1 KB 655.

[56] *Re Opera Ltd* [1891] 3 Ch 260 (CA).

28.34   A third party debt order does not have the effect of transferring ownership of the debt to the judgment creditor. It follows that the chargee takes priority over the applicant for the order unless the debtor has actually made payment to the judgment creditor before crystallization occurs.[57]

Distress for Rent

28.35   Consistently with the rules discussed above, the landlord who levies distress by seizing goods prior to crystallization will have priority over the charge.[58] In some cases, it seems that the landlord may enjoy priority even if distress is completed after crystallization.[59]

---

[57] *Cairney v Back* [1906] 2 KB 746.

[58] *Re Roundwood Colliery Co Ltd* [1897] 1 Ch 373. For an exceptional case, see *Herbert Barry Associates v Inland Revenue Commissioners* [1977] 1 WLR 1437 (noting that the landlord may be deprived of priority if he has been guilty of fraud or unfair dealing).

[59] On this point, see *Rhodes v Allied Dunbar Pension Services Ltd* [1989] 1 All ER 1161, discussed by Lingard at para 9.11.

29

CHARGES OVER SHARES AND OTHER SECURITIES

Introduction

A charge over shares may be taken for a variety of reasons. **29.01**

Where the security consists of a portfolio of listed securities, they will have their own ascer- **29.02** tainable value and there will be a ready market for them in the event that the bank wishes to realize its security. The merit of taking such security will be obvious.

But a bank may also wish to take a charge over shares for other, less obvious reasons. For **29.03** example, if it funds the acquisition of a commercial property by a company specifically incorporated for that purpose, it may also wish to take a charge over shares from the equity investors. It may do so partly in order to secure its control over the entire investment package in the event of a default, and to prevent a transfer of the shares without the knowledge of the lender. It may also have in mind that it wishes to preserve the widest possible range of options in an enforcement situation. For example, for its own reasons, a purchaser might find it more advantageous to acquire the shares in the owning vehicle, rather than the underlying property itself.

There are various means of taking security over shares in a company.[1] **29.04**

---

[1] It will be assumed throughout that the share certificate and transfer documents presented to the bank in connection with such a charge are genuine. It should be noted in particular that: (i) a share certificate issued by a company is *evidence* of title, but is not *conclusive*, and (ii) the bank may incur various liabilities to the issuing company if it presents forged documentation to the company, even if it was not complicit in the fraud: see in particular *Sheffield Corporation v Barclay* [1905] AC 392 (HL).

Legal Charge

29.05 A bank may take security over shares by way of a legal charge.[2] This involves three main steps namely:

(a) the execution of a charge document creating security over the shares;[3]
(b) the transfer of title to the shares to the bank or its nominee;[4] and
(c) the registration of the lender or its nominee as a member in the books of the company.

29.06 A legal charge becomes effective when the transfers in its favour are registered in the books of the issuing company.[5] This form of security offers various advantages to the chargee. In particular, he will be well placed to take control of the shares and to exercise his power of sale should the need arise and, as the registered member, he will receive payment of dividends direct from the company, together with notices of meetings and other documents. The security document will usually require the lender to account for dividends received and to exercise voting rights in accordance with the directions of the chargor, provided that the relevant facility is not in default.[6]

29.07 In addition, it must be remembered that shares constitute choses in action, and that security over them is thus subject to the contractual terms which govern the chose itself. In the case of a share, the bank or its nominee (as registered holder of the shares) will be bound by the terms of the memorandum and articles of association of the issuing company. Whilst this means that the bank will be bound by any pre-emption rights and other restrictions contained in those documents,[7] it will also mean that it can take the benefit of those provisions. Thus, for example, if the directors refuse to provide any consent required for the transfer of the shares to a buyer, then—assuming that the charged shareholding is at a sufficient level for these purposes—the bank could exercise such rights as the member may

---

[2] 'Legal mortgage' would perhaps be the more accurate term: on the whole subject, see Fisher & Lightwood, paras 17.21–17.25.

[3] In drafting the security, it is necessary to pay close attention to the precise scope of the security. For example, it should extend to the benefit of bonus issues, and to shares issued to the chargor on completion of a share for share takeover offer. The security should also extend to dividends, although the bank will often agree to release these back to the chargor so long as the facility is not in default. In other words, the security should cover any assets or benefits which are derived from the shares which are initially provided as security. If the charge receives details of rights issues, it appears that it is not entitled to take up the rights shares at its own expense and add the cost to the mortgage debt: see Fisher & Lightwood, para 17.23.

[4] This involves the execution of a form of transfer and the registration of the bank/nominee in the register of members of the company. The charge document should include a provision for the re-transfer of the shares to the chargor on redemption but, if it is absent, such a term would readily be implied.

[5] *Rose v Inland Revenue Commissioners* [1952] 1 Ch D 499.

[6] The court may order the charge to vote in accordance with the chargor's wishes: *Musselwhite v C H Musselwhite & Co Ltd* [1962] Ch 964.

[7] This point applies with even more force in the context of an equitable charge, and is thus discussed in more detail below. It should be appreciated that the articles of association of a private company may contain restrictions on the transfer of shares, but no such restrictions will generally be applied in the articles of a public company.

have to convene a meeting, to alter the articles or to remove the directors.[8] A legal charge thus confers a significant and effective degree of control over the shares. Of course, whether there is a market for those shares is another matter. In particular, a minority stake in a private company confers very limited influence over the conduct of its affairs, and may thus be effectively valueless.

On the other hand, a degree of care is required in certain contexts. For example, the registered member is liable for any amounts which may be called up on the shares, with the result that a legal charge will not usually be appropriate where the relevant shares are partly paid. Equally, if a winding-up petition has been presented against the issuing company, then the bank's security over the shares will be void if a winding-up order is subsequently made on that petition.[9] Finally, it may be necessary to examine whether the issuing company operates a 'defined benefit' pension scheme for, if it does, the charge as a registered member may become liable to provide financial support or contribute to shortfalls under the provisions of the Pensions Act 2004. This could be a very significant liability and obviously requires careful investigation.[10]   **29.08**

Equitable Charge

An equitable charge over shares involves, as a minimum, the deposit of the relevant share certificate[11] with the intention of creating security for the shareholder's indebtedness to the bank.[12] In such a situation, it is incumbent on the bank to show that the deposit was intended to create security, and was not merely by way of safe custody. In practice, however, a bank accepting such a security will also require the deposit of a blank, executed form of transfer[13] in order to facilitate any eventual enforcement, and this will provide the requisite evidence of intention.[14] The bank will additionally often require a standard form of charge   **29.09**

---

[8] These comments will apply principally to shares in private companies. Where the shares are listed, they will usually be settled through CREST and the considerations noted at paras 29.15–29.21 below will apply.

[9] This would seem to be the effect of s 88 of the Insolvency Act 1986, because the security depends for its validity upon the transfer of the shares.

[10] Banks providing finance for takeovers can apply for advance clearances for this purpose.

[11] If the chargor wishes to create security over part only of his shareholding, then it may be necessary to request the company to issue split certificates as required. If the shares are held by a nominee on behalf of the chargor, they are effectively regarded as fungible, so that an equitable charge over a holding of 100 out of a holding of 1,000 shares will not be void on the basis that the precise shares intended to be subject to the security cannot be identified: *Hunter v Moss* [1994] 3 All ER 215 (CA), followed in *Re Harvard Securities Ltd (in liquidation)* [1997] 2 BCLC 369.

[12] *Harold v Plenty* [1901] 2 Ch 314.

[13] See *Barclay v Prospect Mortgages Ltd* [1974] 2 All ER 672. A transfer under hand will suffice unless: (i) the chargor is a company, or (ii) the articles of association of the issuing company require the execution of the transfer as a deed. It is important that the charge observe these formalities and obtain any power of attorney which may be necessary to ensure that the transfer is duly executed: see the Stock Transfer Act 1963 and the decision in *Powell v London and Provincial Bank* [1893] 2 Ch 555(CA), discussed in Lingard, paras 15.2–15.5. In the ordinary case, however, the delivery of the blank transfer to the charge will carry the implication that the lender is appointed as the chargor's agent to complete and deliver the form to an intending purchaser: *Colonial Bank Ltd v Cady* (1890) 15 App Cas 267 (HL).

[14] See, for example, *Stubbs v Slater* [1910] 1 Ch 632 (CA). An equitable charge is nevertheless a valid and effective security interest even if the blank transfer is not delivered: *Pennington v Waine* [2002] EWCA Civ 227.

document in order to place the matter beyond any doubt, although there is no formal requirement that it must do so.[15]

29.10 The main disadvantages of an equitable charge include the following:

(a) competing equitable interests rank according to the date of their creation.[16] Consequently, if the chargor is in fact a trustee of the relevant shares, the title of the beneficiaries will rank ahead of any equitable charge created in favour of the bank;[17] and

(b) whilst the chargor remains the registered owner, he will continue to receive any allotment of bonus shares and these would likewise be registered in his name. Since these would be 'derived' from the original security package, the bank would often stipulate that its security extends to such bonus shares but it would have no immediate or effective control over them.

29.11 In other words, an equitable charge is in some respects a weaker form of security because no legal relationship is established between the issuing company and the charge.[18] It is well established that a company is not required to recognize equitable interests in its shares, and that it is required to continue to deal solely with its own registered members who are parties to the contract created by the articles of association. As a result, a company cannot accept notice of any equitable interest in its shares, with the necessary result that the normal rule as to the priority of competing assignments[19] cannot apply to security over shares.[20] By way of exception, a person who claims an equitable interest in shares may file at court and serve on the issuing company a 'stop notice', which requires the company to give notice before registering a transfer of the relevant shares. This is, however, in the nature of a 'caution' and

---

[15] Section 2 of the Law Reform (Miscellaneous Provisions) Act 1989 creates a requirement for security documents to be signed by both parties, but this applies only where the security consists of land or any interest in it.

[16] This rule is subject to any estoppel which may arise as against prior beneficiaries on the basis of their own fraud or negligence.

[17] See, for example, the decision in *Coleman v London County and Westminster Bank Ltd* [1916] 2 Ch 353 (noted by Lingard at para 15.10), where precisely such a situation arose. The bank perfected a legal charge over the shares as soon as it became aware that the chargor was in fact a trustee, but it was by then too late because the bank had acquired notice of the prior equitable interest.

[18] In contrast, as noted above, a legal charge involves the registration of the bank (or its nominee) as a member of the issuing company.

[19] Namely, that they take priority according to the date on which notice is given to the relevant obligor. This is the rule in *Dearle v Hall* (1828) 3 Russ 1, which is discussed in more depth at paras 30.09–30.11 below. That the rule in *Dearle v Hall* is inapplicable to security over shares is conformed by the decision in *Macmillan Inc v Bishopsgate Investment Trust plc (No 3)* [1996] 1 All ER 585.

[20] The point is confirmed by the decision in *Societe Generale de Paris v Walker* (1885) 11 App Cas 20 (HL). The same principle is extended to shares in paperless form: see the Uncertificated Securities Regulations 2001 (SI 2001/3755), reg 23(3). Nevertheless, it is often recommended that notice of an equitable security should be given to the issuer company: see Fisher & Lightwood, para 17.25. There may be various advantages in adopting this procedure. For example, if the directors allow the registration of a fraudulent transfer of the shares so as to defeat the security interest, they may incur personal liability to the charge: *Societe Generale de Paris*, above. In addition, notice may prevent the company from exercising a lien over the shares in relation to any future transactions: see *Bradford Banking Co v Briggs Son & Co Ltd* (1886) 12 App Cas 29 (HL); *Champagne Perrier-Jouet SA v HH Finch Ltd* [1982] 3 All ER 713.

does not oblige the company itself to recognize or give effect to any such equitable interest.

Foreign Shares

The validity of a security interest created over shares in a foreign company requires separate **29.12** consideration.[21]

It is submitted that the correct starting point appears to be that the validity of a security **29.13** interest over foreign shares is governed by the law of the place of incorporation of the issuing entity concerned. This follows from a decision to the effect that, where shares in a New York company had been sold fraudulently, the ability of the buyer to rely on a 'bona fide purchaser' or similar doctrine to preserve his title against prior equitable interests would be a matter of New York (rather than English) law.[22] It seems that this rule would govern all issues relating to the transfer of, and security over, foreign shares.[23] There is a question whether it is in fact the law of the place of incorporation or the law of the country in which the share register is kept which governs this particular issue. In many cases, of course, this will be the same country in any event and the distinction will accordingly be immaterial. However, should the issue arise, it is submitted that it is the law of the place of incorporation which is relevant, since that law is the source of the rights which constitute the chose in action concerned. In addition, many companies are permitted to maintain branch registers in different countries, with the result that the 'location of the branch register' test may lead to confusion.[24]

Reference should also be made to the decision in *Re Harvard Securities Ltd*,[25] where a secu- **29.14** rities dealer based in England had gone into liquidation. It held shares in various US and Australian companies, and the question arose whether clients of the firm had a beneficial interest in those securities. The US shares were held by nominees in London, whilst the Australian shares were held through a local bank in that country. It was decided that, in view of the location of the nominees, the existence of any such equitable interest was determined (i) in the case of the US shares, by English law and (ii) in the case of the Australian shares, by Australian law. It is respectfully submitted that this decision is doubtful. In particular, it is not clear why the validity of the beneficial interest should be governed by the location of the nominees, since it is quite likely that those nominees will have been selected

---

[21] It should, however, be appreciated that the points about to be made will apply principally where the securities concerned are in paper form. On uncertificated securities, see paras 29.15–29.21 below.

[22] *Macmillan Inc v Bishopsgate Investment Trust plc (No 3)* [1996] 1 All ER 585.

[23] Dicey Morris, & Collins, para 24-060.

[24] It should be said, however, that there are a series of cases which focus on the notion that shares should be deemed to be situate in the location in which the owner would normally have dealt with them, that is, where the relevant main or branch register is kept. See, in particular, *R v Eva Mary Williams* [1942] AC 541 (PC), *Re Kettle's Gift* [1968] 3 All ER 88 and *Standard Chartered Bank v IRC* [1978] 3 All ER 644. However, all of these cases deal with liability for estate or death duties, and it may be that they are to be distinguished on the basis that they address specific statutory provisions in a context rather different from that considered in the text.

[25] [1997] 2 BCLC 369.

unilaterally by the dealer without reference to the client. Why, then, should third party rights and interests be affected by such a matter? In addition, the clients had no doubt entered into transactions with the dealer on the basis that English law applied to their relationship. If the arrangements created an equitable interest in the shares, then the court should have enforced that interest against the dealer *in personam*, regardless of the place of incorporation of the issuer, the location of the nominees or any other matter.[26]

Charges over Uncertificated Securities

29.15 The above discussion has dealt with the taking of security over shares in paper form. This was, of course, the traditional mode of settling transactions in, and taking security over, such assets. But both markets and technology move on. Shares listed on stock exchanges are now generally traded in scriptless, or paperless, form. Debt instruments are likewise held through clearing systems.[27] It is necessary briefly to review these developments in the context of security offered to banks over assets of this kind.

29.16 The validity and effectiveness of a security interest obviously depends in large measure upon the nature of the underlying asset. In principle, at least, the economic and security value of a charge over a share should not change merely because the share is transformed from a certificated into a dematerialized asset. The lender should retain the same effective rights and remedies, including the same power of sale and right to receive dividends and other benefits flowing from the asset. How and to what extent is this position achieved?

29.17 In part, this objective has to be achieved despite the inter-position of additional parties between the issuer of the securities and their ultimate owner. In the United Kingdom, most uncertificated settlement in listed shares is achieved through the CREST system.[28] Equities, debt instruments, and certain other types of securities can be settled through CREST. Only securities issued by companies incorporated in the United Kingdom and certain other jurisdictions[29] can be settled through CREST, but shares issued by companies in other countries can be indirectly settled through a depositary receipt structure.[30]

29.18 Securities which are settled through CREST are referred to as 'uncertificated securities', with the consequences that (i) no physical share certificates are issued in respect of them and (ii) no paper transfers are needed to effect dealings in them.[31]

---

[26] Compare the discussion of the *British South Africa* case, at para 27.28 above.

[27] For an early discussion of some of the consequences of these developments, see Goode, 'The Nature and Transfer of Rights in Dematerialised and Immobilised Securities' (1996) 4 JIBFL 167. For more recent and detailed discussions, see Benjamin, *Interests in Securities* (Oxford University Press, 2000), *Goode on Legal Problems of Credit and Security* (4th edn, Louise Gullifer, 2008) ch VI, and Financial Markets Law Committee, 'Property Interests in Investment Securities', July 2004.

[28] The system is operated by Euroclear UK & Ireland Ltd, formerly known as CRESTCO Ltd. On initiatives to create a harmonized system of rules in this area, see UNIDROIT Convention on Substantive Rules for Intermediated Securities (UNIDROIT, 9 October 2009).

[29] Currently including Ireland and various other jurisdictions.

[30] The depositary receipt structure is described in the CREST Manual.

[31] The amendments to generally applicable company law required to achieve this position are to be found in the Uncertificated Securities Regulations 2001 (above).

Members of CREST have access to its computer system and CREST will record transac- **29.19** tions in shares provided that matching instructions are received from both buyer and seller and the buyer has sufficient credit to complete the transaction.[32] It should be appreciated that CREST does not hold the underlying shares as intermediary or custodian; it merely maintains a register of entitlement in parallel with that which the issuer company itself is required to maintain. The two sets of records should, of course, correspond but, in the event of a discrepancy, the register maintained by CREST will prevail.[33] As a result, CREST may perhaps be most accurately described as a settlement system, rather than a custodian.

But—to return to the main question—what is the nature of the rights of an owner of such **29.20** securities and, by extension, what is the nature of the corresponding rights acquired by a chargee of such securities? At the risk of over-simplification, the following comparison may be helpful:

(a) the holder of *directly held* securities will be a member or creditor of the issuing company itself, and will usually appear on a register maintained for that purpose by or on behalf of the issuer itself;

(b) in contrast, a holder of *indirectly held* securities will not personally appear on any such register. The holding is likely to be registered in the name of a custodian and—possibly via intermediate or sub-custodians—held in an account maintained by a financial institution for the ultimate client. The client will thus enjoy a contractual right to direct the institution to dispose of those securities in accordance with his directions. In addition, and whilst the client will not enjoy the right to delivery of *specific* securities, all securities of that class held by that institution for its own clients will be held on trust for the customers noted in its own records, according to their respective entitlements. Each of those clients will thus have a pro rata beneficial interest in the 'pool' of identical securities held by the institution concerned.[34] It is this feature which will generally protect the client in the event of the insolvency of the institution concerned, for the pool of securities will be separate from its own assets and will thus not be available to its creditors. A charge over such securities thus in substance amounts to a charge over the contractual and beneficial rights and interests just described;[35]

(c) it will therefore be apparent that the pooling of the securities and the use of one or more intermediaries does have substantive effects and alters the nature of the rights at issue.

---

[32] Note that CREST does not itself hold cash on behalf of members, but each member is required to nominate a settlement bank which provides an irrevocable undertaking to make payments up to a set limit.

[33] Uncertificated Securities Regulations 2001, reg 24.

[34] As noted earlier, a trust over a portion of securities held in a pooled account is not to be treated as void on the basis that the subject matter of the trust is uncertain or is inadequately identified: *Hunter v Moss* [1994] 3 All ER 215 (CA), followed in *Re Harvard Securities Ltd (in liquidation)* [1997] 2 BCLC 369. For a decision to similar effect in the specific context of an immobilized securities system, see the decision of the Court of First Instance, Hong Kong SAR, in *Re CA Pacific Finance Ltd* [2000] 1 BCLC 494.

[35] In contrast to the position in relation to paper securities (see para 29.11 above), it is submitted that a charge of this kind should be perfected by giving notice to the institution which holds the shares for the account of the client, since the charge does not directly relate to the shares themselves, but relates to contractual obligations of the institution and a beneficial interest in respect of which it is the trustee. Under these circumstances, the priority of competing charges over uncertificated securities would appear to be determined by the respective dates on which notice is given to the institution concerned, in accordance with the rule in *Dearle v Hall* (1828) 3 Russ 1.

For example, a holder of indirectly held securities has no direct rights against the issuing company at all, for he has no contractual or other relationship with it. Generally speaking, his rights and recourse in respect of the securities will be limited to his account-holding intermediary.[36] This also means that the focus of the client's rights shifts from the place of incorporation of the issuing company to the place in which the intermediary maintains the client's securities account. This has significant consequences in the sense that it changes the location of the asset to which the client is entitled and—hence—has an impact on the effect of such arrangements for private international law purposes.[37]

29.21 There are two possible means of perfecting a security interest[38] over uncertificated securities:

(a) the relevant shares can be transferred to the CREST securities account of the charge, thus giving it control over subsequent dealings. This may be equated to the registration process for the perfection of a legal charge;[39] or

(b) the shares can be transferred to a sub-account of the chargor as an escrow balance under the control of the chargee or its nominee (which must itself be a CREST member). This may legitimately be regarded as equivalent to an equitable charge over paper securities.[40]

Registration Formalities

29.22 In principle, a charge over shares executed by a corporate chargor[41] does not require registration at Companies House, because it does not fall within any of the categories of security listed in section 860(7) of the Companies Act 2006.[42] Three reservations may be noted in this context:

(a) In practice, a charge over shares is frequently delivered to the Registrar under these provisions, and the Registrar issues certificates of registration in respect of such security. This may follow in part from the fact that standard forms of security will extend to dividends declared in respect of the shares, and this may be regarded as a charge over book debts, which is thus registrable under that separate heading.[43] This view may be excessively cautious, because a dividend does not constitute a debt of any kind until it

---

[36] For example, the issuer company will obtain a good discharge by paying dividends to the registered holder (ie the custodian or other intermediary). The client thus has to rely on the intermediary to account to him for that payment.

[37] See the discussion of the PRIMA approach at para 36.18 below.

[38] It should be appreciated that this discussion deals with the *perfection* of the security interest. The *creation* of that interest should be evidenced by a charge agreement in the usual way.

[39] On this subject, see paras 29.05–29.08 above.

[40] On charges of this kind, see paras 29.09–29.11 above.

[41] There are no relevant registration requirements where the chargor is an individual.

[42] For the listing, see para 27.23(e) above.

[43] A charge over book debts owing to the company is subject to registration under s 860(7)(f) of the Companies Act 2006: see para 30.07 below.

has been declared[44] and, even when it has, it must be doubtful whether the dividend constitutes a 'book debt' in the accepted meaning of that term.[45]

(b) Where the charge provides for further security to be delivered[46] or for the substitution of the security package, then it may be argued that this amounts to '... a floating charge over the company's undertaking or property ...' within section 860(7)(g), and thus subject to registration on that ground. This point may, again, be debateable, because it is thought that provisions of the kind just described will not operate to convert a fixed security into a floating charge;[47] and

(c) Unless the chargor company is in the business of trading in shares, it will generally be difficult to argue that a charge over shares should be characterized as a floating charge. Especially where the charge relates to shares in a subsidiary, of the chargor, the assets concerned will not be circulating capital and will not be traded in the ordinary course of business. In the absence of particularly unusual circumstances, such a charge should accordingly be characterized as a fixed charge.[48]

29.23 In practice, no doubt, the cautious practitioner will elect to deliver the security for registration in cases of doubt. These issues will thus only arise for discussion where the matter is overlooked and the chargor subsequently encounters financial difficulties.

29.24 Where the relevant security is created by an overseas company, it will only require registration in the UK if the relevant shares have been issued by a UK company.[49] Where the security document provides for substitution of the collateral, it may be argued that this should be registered on the footing that securities issued by a UK entity may be brought within the scope of the security package at a later date. However, this should not be necessary because the need to comply with the registration requirement is determined by reference to the circumstances subsisting as *at the date on which the charge is created*.[50]

Priorities

29.25 The position as to priorities of competing mortgages over shares may be stated as follows:

(a) as noted above, a bank which takes a legal charge over shares will become the registered owner of those securities in the books of the company.[51] Since this constitutes a legal

---

[44] ie there is no obligation on the company to pay anything unless and until the dividend has been confirmed in accordance with the terms of the company's articles of association.

[45] A book debt is a debt which arises in the ordinary course of business and which would be entered in the books of the creditor company in the ordinary course: see *Independent Automatic Sales Ltd v Knowles and Foster* [1967] 3 All ER 27; *Paul & Frank Ltd v Discount Bank (Overseas) Ltd* [1967] Ch 348. The whole subject of security over book debts is discussed in Chapter 30 below.

[46] eg so as to 'top-up' the value of the security if the market value of the relevant shares has been in decline.

[47] See the discussion of the decision in *Re Queen's Moat Houses plc* [2004] NPC 67, at para 28.05 above.

[48] See, for example, *Arthur D Little Ltd (in administration) v Ableco Finance LLC* [2002] BCLC 799.

[49] See reg 9(1)(b) of the Overseas Companies Charges Regulations 2009, discussed at para 27.37(b) above.

[50] See the discussion on this subject at para 27.37 above.

[51] Or, in the case of a charge over uncertificated securities, the shares will be transferred to a securities account in its name or under its control.

interest in the shares, the charge will enjoy priority over both pre-existing and subsequent charges over the same shares since, by their very nature, those arrangements must have amounted to equitable charges only. The customary exception will apply, in that the legal chargee's interest will be subject to any prior equitable interest of which it had actual or constructive notice at the time of taking the charge;[52]

(b) where the competing security interests are of an equitable nature only, then they will generally rank according to their respective dates of creation. However, since the security takes effect in equity, the interests of a prior claimant may be postponed to a later interest if his conduct disentitles him to the priority—for example, because he represented to the later charge that he had no security interest, or because he failed to obtain possession of the share certificate, thus enabling the chargor fraudulently to raise money on the basis of the same security;[53]

(c) unlike other choses in action, priority between competing charges is not determined by notice to the company as issue or obligor in respect of the chose, since a company is not generally affected by notice of equitable interests in its shares.[54]

---

[52] Authority for this proposition is provided by *Earl of Sheffield v London Joint Stock Bank* (1888) 13 App Cas 333 (HL). For the purposes of this paragraph it is assumed that the bank has given value for the security (eg by providing new facilities or extending the maturity date of existing loans).

[53] *Moore v North Western Bank* [1891] 2 Ch 599; *Societe Generale de Paris v Walker* (1885) 11 App Cas 20.

[54] *Societe Generale de Paris v Walker* (1885) 11 App Cas 20. There may, nevertheless, be advantages in giving such notice: see the discussion at para 29.11 above.

30

CHARGES OVER RECEIVABLES

Introduction

A lender may wish to take security over debts owing, or to become owing, to its borrower. **30.01** Occasionally, this may involve *specific* debts owing by *particular* customers of the borrower. This may be especially advantageous where the credit standing of the underlying customer is superior to that of the borrower itself. Frequently, however, a charge over the benefit of book debts owing to the borrower will simply form a part of the standard security package, and will be included as a part of a fixed and floating charge over the entire assets and undertaking of the borrower.

Essential Validity

The essential validity of security over book debts—including the fixed or floating nature of **30.02** the charge—has been the subject of a certain amount of recent case law.

It is common for standard bank debentures to contain a purported fixed charge over book **30.03** debts as part of the normal security package. Lenders in the asset-based lending or receivables financing market take a similar form of security over receivables and, in this context, the precise nature of the security assumes a greater importance. The amount available for drawdown will usually be adjusted from time to time and will reflect a set percentage of the face value of those receivables. Clearly, if the security amounts only to a floating charge, then the available percentage should be lowered to reflect the possible intrusion of the preferential creditors and the 'prescribed part' into the security pool.[1] This state of affairs has obvious implications for lenders and borrowers alike; it is clearly in the interests of the

---

[1] On this subject and associated issues, see para 28.20 above.

borrower to maximize the financing value of the receivables by ensuring that a fixed charge is created. But how can this be done?

30.04 The following points may be noted in this regard:

(a) There is no doubt that a lender can take a *floating* charge over book debts and that a charge will be characterized as such if it is intended that the borrower will have the use of the proceeds of those receivables in the ordinary course of its business.[2] This is much as one would expect, given that it is generally accepted that a floating charge can be created over the entirety of the assets and undertaking of a company.

(b) A purported *fixed* charge over book debts may be valid as between the chargor and the chargee even though notice of the charge is not (or is not immediately) given to the underlying debtor.[3] This is so even though the absence of such notice means that the security is rendered tenuous in some respects. For example, the debtor will still obtain a good discharge by paying the chargor himself or by entering into some form of settlement with him,[4] and he may acquire further rights of set-off against the receivable concerned.[5] Furthermore, a subsequent chargee who does give notice to the debtor will thereby become the first-ranking security-holder in accordance with the principle in *Dearle v Hall*,[6] to the effect that the priority of competing assignments is determined by reference to the date on which the notice of assignment is given to the debtor.[7] The security may be tenuous but it nevertheless remains valid and effective until one of these prejudicial events actually occurs.

(c) Once notice of the assignment is given to the debtor, the debtor cannot acquire further rights of set-off as against the creditor in respect of that debt by entering into future transactions with him, since he deals with the creditor in the knowledge of the assignee's interest. Yet debt claims are naturally very susceptible to assertions of set-off rights and it becomes necessary for the lender to have a close appreciation of the vulnerability of its security. In essence, as was explained in *Business Computers Ltd v Anglo-African Leasing Ltd*,[8] a debtor who receives a notice of assignment can nevertheless continue to exercise a right of set-off against that debt—to the detriment of the assignee—in three cases, namely (i) in relation to debts which have accrued before the notice is

---

[2] See, for example, *Illingworth v Houldsworth* [1904] AC 355 (HL).

[3] *Holt v Heatherfield Trust Ltd* [1942] 2 KB 1. Such a charge necessarily takes effect as an *equitable* security, since notice to the debtor is one of the necessary ingredients of a *legal* charge over debts: s 136 of the Law of Property Act 1925 and *Holroyd v Marshall* (1862) 10 HL Cas 191. In practice, notice is often not given to debtors whilst the facility is functioning satisfactorily. The borrower may not wish the market to know that it has given security over its debts. In addition, the number of customers involved may also make this inconvenient from the lender's perspective. Of course, notice will often be given if the facility goes into default.

[4] *Stocks v Dobson* (1853) 4 De GM & G 11.

[5] See, for example, the situation which arose in *Biggerstaff v Rowatt's Wharf Ltd* [1896] 2 Ch 93 (CA).

[6] (1828) 3 Russ 1. On this principle, see paras 30.09–30.12 below.

[7] It should be appreciated that this means *actual* notice to the debtor himself. Registration of the relevant charge at Companies House will not constitute notice to the debtor for this purpose.

[8] [1977] 2 All ER 741.

given,[9] (ii) in relation to a debt which arises out of the same contract,[10] and (iii) in rela-tion to a debt which does not arise out of the contract relating to the assigned debt but is nevertheless closely connected with it.[11]

(d) For many years, and in reliance on the decision in *Siebe Gorman & Co Ltd v Barclays Bank Ltd*,[12] it had been thought that a security interest over receivables would amount to a valid, fixed charge if it was supported by (i) an undertaking to credit all proceeds to an account of the chargor with the lender and (ii) an undertaking not to charge or assign those debts in favour of any third party. In other words, these provisions were sufficient to negative the inference that the chargor could deal with the receivables in the ordinary course of business, so that the charge could not be characterized as 'floating'.[13] On the other hand, if the document merely created a charge without oth-erwise restricting the borrower's dealings with its book debts and their proceeds, then this would amount to a floating charge only.[14]

(e) The law in this area took a further, curious turn as a result of the Court of Appeal's decision in *Re New Bullas Trading Ltd*.[15] In that case, the court held that it was concep-tually possible to distinguish between a book debt and its proceeds, with the result that a charge over the receivable could be categorized as fixed, whilst the proceeds were regarded as subject to a floating charge and thus available to the chargor in the ordinary course of its business. The result may well be conceptually possible and, in many respects, was seen as highly convenient for lenders, but the distinction between a debt and its proceeds seems to be both artificial and commercially unrealistic.

(f) Matters have now been placed on a somewhat clearer footing by the decision of the Privy Council in *Agnew v Commissioner of Inland Revenue*[16] and the decision of the House of Lords in *Re Spectrum Plus Ltd*.[17] These decisions disposed of the notion that a fixed charge over book debts could be created merely by using language of the type employed in the *Siebe Gorman* or *New Bullas Trading* security documents. Both the Privy Council and the House of Lords emphasized the need for a sufficient degree of

---

[9] 'Accrued' means that the debt must have become unconditionally payable, but it does not matter that the debt has not become due for payment when the notice of assignment is received by the debtor: *Christie v Taunton, Delmard, Lane & Co* [1893] 2 Ch 175.

[10] Thus, if a contractor gives notice of assignment of the monies payable to it under the contract, the debtor can nevertheless plead a right of set-off if the contractor fails to complete the work for which payment is due, for the assignee cannot compel the debtor to pay for work which has not been done: *Newfoundland Government v Newfoundland Railway Co* (1888) 13 App Cas 199 (PC). In large scale projects, the debtor may occasionally give an unconditional undertaking to make the payments due under the assigned agree-ment, regardless of the contractor's performance (a so-called 'hell and high water' clause), in order to assist his contractor to obtain the necessary finance. But this goes beyond the formal assignment and is a matter for separate negotiation.

[11] eg because the contracts, whilst formally separate, were nevertheless entered into in the same context or venture.

[12] [1979] 2 Lloyd's Rep 142.

[13] See the third criterion noted in *Re Yorkshire Woolcombers Ltd*, at para 28.06 above.

[14] For an example, see *Re Brightlife Ltd* [1987] Ch 200.

[15] [1994] 1 BCLC 485 (CA).

[16] [2001] 2 AC 714 (PC), an appeal from the New Zealand Court of Appeal.

[17] [2005] 2 AC 680 (HL), followed in *Russell Cooke Trust Company Ltd v Elliott* [2007] EWHC 1443 (Ch). For a clear and helpful analysis of the *Spectrum* decision, see Anderson, 'The Spectrum Plus Case' (2005) 16(10) ICCLR 405.

control over both the charged receivables and their proceeds.[18] The difficulty with the *Siebe Gorman* approach was that the lender had insufficient control over the proceeds—once they had been paid into the relevant bank account, the chargor had the free use of those proceeds without any requirement for the consent of the chargee.

(g) As a result of these decisions, it is now accepted that the proceeds of the receivables must be paid into a blocked account under the exclusive control of the lender.[19] Thus, in the asset-based lending or receivables financing market, the borrower is required to ensure that the proceeds of invoices are credited to a specific, blocked account,[20] and the debtor will be prohibited from entering into any other factoring or other arrangements involving a disposal of the debts. These proceeds will be applied in reducing the outstanding indebtedness and the borrower will be left to make fresh drawings on the main facility, subject to availability of sufficient eligible receivables or other assets required to support such a utilization, the absence of any event of default, and other relevant conditions precedent. It is submitted that these arrangements justify the conclusion that the charge over receivables constitutes a *fixed* security. In most other cases, however, the security is likely to be characterized as a floating charge.[21]

(h) All of this is reasonably clear but it would be of limited value unless it is likewise affirmed that a *fixed* charge can also extend to *future* receivables. The prosperity of the underlying business plainly rests on the due payment of current receivables and the creation of new ones in the ordinary course. In *Tailby v Official Receiver,*[22] it was decided—contrary to earlier views—that it was indeed possible to take a charge over future book debts. It is true that the House of Lords referred to this as a *floating* charge, but it was not pressed to reach any further conclusion. More recent case law suggests that the courts should have no difficulty with the concept of a fixed charge over future receivables.[23]

30.05 It follows that it is perfectly possible to create a fixed charge over both present and future receivables, but a relatively sophisticated blocked account and security structure will be required, and the lender will be required to engage in a certain amount of monitoring and supervision.

---

[18] As a result, it is necessary to look at the substance of the arrangements implemented by the parties, rather than their mere form. Usually, of course, the lender's documentation will describe the arrangement as a fixed charge but, in the absence of the necessary degree of control such that the chargor is free to deal with the book debts in the ordinary course, the court will characterize the arrangement as a floating security. For earlier decisions on this subject, see the decisions in *Re ASRS Establishment Ltd* [2000] 2 BCLC 631 (CA); *Chalk v Khan* [2000] 2 BCLC. For an unusual decision to the opposite effect, where the security was described as floating but was in fact held to be a fixed charge, see *Russell Cooke Trust Company Ltd v Elliott* [2007] EWHC 1443 (Ch).

[19] See in particular the judgment of Lord Walker of Gestingthorpe in *Re Spectrum Plus Ltd* [2005] 2 AC 680.

[20] This may be achieved by an appropriate statement to that effect on the invoices, even though no formal notice of the charge is given to the underlying debtor.

[21] See, for example, *Fanshaw v Amav Industries Ltd* [2006] All ER (D) 246 (Feb).

[22] (1888) 13 App Cas 523 (HL).

[23] See, for example, *Re Permanent Homes (Holdings) Ltd* [1988] BCLC 563 and *Welsh Development Agency v Export Finance Co Ltd* [1992] BCLC 148 (CA).

Foreign Receivables

Where a charge created by a UK company extends to foreign receivables, this will be a valid **30.06** security as far as the English courts are concerned. If formalities associated with the security in the foreign country were not completed, then the lender will have to await the repatriation of the proceeds of those debts by the liquidator or administrator. Action taken by creditors—even if unsecured—in the country of the relevant debtor may diminish the amount of the proceeds which may become available to the secured creditor.[24]

Registration Formalities

A charge over receivables will require registration under section 860(7)(f) of the 2006 Act **30.07** if it constitutes a charge over 'book debts' owing to the company. This expression clearly does not include every form of debt which may be owing to a company. It extends only to debts which, in the ordinary course of a well-run business, would be entered into the books of the company.[25] In cases of dispute, accountancy evidence could be admitted to resolve the matter. But a 'book debt' will usually be a fixed and ascertained debt arising as a result of trading in the ordinary course of business. A purely contingent debt arising as a result of a possible claim under an insurance policy will generally not be quantified and would thus not normally constitute a book debt for these purposes.[26] In contrast, a charge over future book debts will require registration under this heading.[27]

The deposit of a promissory note or other negotiable instrument given to secure the pay- **30.08** ment of book debts is not treated as a charge over the book debts themselves.[28] Hence, if the customer gives time for the payment of a debt on the basis that the obligor provides to it a bill of exchange accepted by a bank, no registration requirement applies if the customer in turn deposits that bill of exchange with his own bank by way of security for his own overdraft. However, this exemption only applies where the arrangement has been completed by actual delivery of the negotiable instrument to the lender. Registration will thus be required if those formalities have not been fully completed.[29]

Priorities

In contrast to many other forms of security, the priority of successive charges over receiv- **30.09** ables is governed neither by the date of the creation of the charge nor by the date of its registration (if applicable).

---

[24] In other words, the principles derived from the *British South Africa* case will again apply in this context: see para 27.78 above.

[25] Note that this is an objective test. Thus, the fact that the chargor itself does not enter the relevant debt in its books is not conclusive. Likewise, the fact that the company elects to enter a particular item in its books does not necessarily make that item a 'book debt' for these purposes.

[26] *Paul & Frank Ltd v Discount Bank (Overseas) Ltd* [1967] Ch 348.

[27] *Independent Automatic Sales Ltd v Knowles and Foster* [1962] 3 All ER 27.

[28] Section 861(3) of the Companies Act 2006.

[29] *Chase Manhattan Asia Ltd v Official Receiver and Liquidator of First Bangkok City Finance Ltd* [1990] BCC 514 (PC).

30.10 Instead, the priority of competing assignments is governed by the date on which notice of the assignment is given to the debtor or obligor.[30] This rule has a sound basis in common sense because:

(a) the debtor needs to know the identity of the person whom he has to pay in order to obtain a good discharge of his obligation; and

(b) if an assignee fails to give notice, then the debtor will know nothing of the arrangement and may confirm to a subsequent assignee that the debt is unencumbered. Under these circumstances, the second assignee should have priority as a matter of fairness and because due inquiry by him will not reveal the existence of the prior security.[31]

30.11 In spite of the 'notice' rule, a second assignee who knows of the prior security interest will rank after it even if the first chargee had not given any notice to the debtor.[32] In the unlikely event that two lenders take a competing assignment of the same debt—a situation which will usually imply fraud on the part of the customer/assignor—and the lenders give contemporaneous notices to the debtor, then priority will be governed by the dates on which the respective security interests were created.[33]

30.12 As a further exception to the 'priority by order of notice' rule, where the charge over the receivable arises as a result of a charging order (as opposed to a voluntary assignment), the charge is not treated as having been given for value, with the result that the charge will rank after a prior assignee even though he may have omitted to give notice to the debtor.[34]

---

[30] ie under the well-known rule in *Dearle v Hall* (1828) 3 Russ 1.

[31] Although it should be said that it is the fact that notice is given which governs priority, and not the nature or extent of any inquiries made by the later assignee: *Ward v Duncombe* [1893] AC 369.

[32] This does, of course, assume that the first charge is intrinsically valid and has been duly registered where required. If the second charge is a bank, it is reasonable to expect it to make appropriate searches at Companies House, and it may acquire actual or constructive notice of the prior security via that route. On the points made in the text, see *Re Holmes* (1885) 29 Ch D 786; *Rhodes v Allied Dunbar Pension Services Ltd* [1988] 1 All ER 524.

[33] *Callisher v Forbes* (1871) 7 Ch App 109 (CA).

[34] *United Bank of Kuwait v Sahib* [1995] 2 All ER 973, affirmed on different grounds, [1996] 3 All ER 215 (CA).

31

CHARGES OVER BANK BALANCES

Introduction

It will be recalled that a bank deposit constitutes a simple debt repayable by the bank on **31.01** demand or otherwise in accordance with the terms of the deposit contract.[1] As a result, aspects of this type of security rest on principles similar to those discussed above in the context of a charge over book debts. Nevertheless, the circumstances under which this type of security is usually given and the particular nature of bank deposits mean that separate consideration is required.

Features of the Security

In what respects does a charge over a bank deposit differ from a charge over an ordinary **31.02** book debt? In very general terms, the main areas of difference are likely to be as follows:

(a) A charge over a bank deposit will usually be specific to an identified deposit account and, in view of the steps described below, there is usually little doubt that the charge will be of a fixed (rather than floating) nature.[2]

(b) A charge over a bank deposit will often be taken by way of security for the customer's obligation to indemnify the bank against a call under a guarantee, bond, documentary credit, or other instrument issued by the bank for the account of the customer.

---

[1] See the discussion of *Foley v Hill* (1848) 2 HL Cas 28 (HL) at para 15.10 above.

[2] It should, however, be borne in mind that a typical form of debenture will purport to create a fixed charge over bank deposits and other credit balances with banks. This standard language, shorn of the additional steps about to be considered, will not involve any real degree of control over the accounts so far as the chargee is concerned. Consequently, for the reasons discussed in the context of receivables (above), security of this kind will constitute a floating charge. For an illustration of this type of situation, see *Re ASRS Establishment Ltd (in administrative receivership and liquidation)* [2002] BCLC 631.

(c) Where the deposit-holding bank and the issuer of the relevant obligation are the same institution, then the bank will block the account via its normal internal procedures for that purpose. The bank will thus enjoy the necessary degree of control over the operation of the account to justify the conclusion that the security constitutes a fixed charge. It was for some time doubted whether a bank could, in conceptual terms take a charge over its own indebtedness to the chargor, on the basis that (i) a debt is a chose in action, (ii) a chose in action is enforced by means of legal proceedings, and (iii) the bank cannot sue itself.[3] This view was subsequently doubted,[4] and eventually overruled by the House of Lords.[5] Whilst the subject generated significant debate at the time, it is not now necessary to pursue the subject.[6]

(d) Where the cash deposit is held by an institution other than the bank which is taking the security, then a greater degree of formality is required. In particular, it is necessary to give notice of the assignment or charge to the account-holding bank.[7] The bank will also be asked to provide various confirmations for the benefit of the chargee. In particular, (i) the bank should be asked to confirm that it has not received notice of any prior charge over the same deposit,[8] (ii) the bank must be asked to confirm that it will not exercise any right of set-off over the deposit, and (iii) the bank must be asked to confirm that it will operate the account on the instructions of the chargee, so that the security is capable of prompt and effective enforcement.

Registration Formalities

31.03 A charge over a bank deposit is only subject to registration under section 860 of the Companies Act 2006 if it constitutes a charge over a book debt.[9]

31.04 The question, therefore, is whether a bank deposit is a debt which arises in the course of business and would be entered into the books of the company in the ordinary way. Instinctively, one feels that this question should be answered in the negative, because the

---

[3] *Re Charge Card Services Ltd* [1987] Ch 150. It is submitted that the concentration on the ability to sue on the debt led the court into an analytical error. For example, a share in a company is a chose in action, but enforcement will usually be enforced by means of a sale, rather than by means of legal proceedings.

[4] *Welsh Development Agency v Export Finance Co Ltd* [1992] BCLC 148.

[5] See *Re Bank of Credit and Commerce International SA (No 8)* [1997] 4 All ER 568, (HL).

[6] The debate often took place in conjunction with a discussion of the rules on set-off and r 4.90 of the Insolvency Rules 1986. That aspect of the subject is considered in Chapter 36 below. It may be added that the decision in *Re Charge Card Services Ltd* did not meet with approval in a number of common law jurisdictions, and was reversed by legislation in a number of cases: see, for example, s 15A of the Hong Kong Law Amendment and Reform (Consolidation) Ordinance (Cap 23); s 9A of the Civil Law Act of Singapore (Cap 43).

[7] Under the general law, notice can be given by any party. In practice, however, the bank would require a notice signed by an authorized signatory of the account holder.

[8] The point is important because the chargee will wish to ensure that he has a first-ranking security, and the priority of successive charges over bank deposits (or any other debts) is governed by the date on which notice of the respective assignments is received by the account-holding bank (or debtor): see the discussion of the rule in *Dearle v Hall* (1828) 3 Russ 1, at paras 30.09–30.11 above.

[9] See s 860(7)(f) of the Companies Act 2006, discussed in the context of receivables (above). It should be emphasized again that the registration requirements apply only to companies and to limited liability partnerships.

bank deposit simply represents an application of surplus funds by the company itself. This view draws support from various decisions, although the point does not appear to have been conclusively decided.[10] Until it is, it will no doubt remain the general practice to register security of this kind.[11]

Priorities

As noted above, a bank deposit is in the nature of a debt owed by the recipient bank. As a result, the rules governing the priority of competing fixed charges over book debts will apply equally to consecutive charges over bank deposits.[12]   **31.05**

---

[10] *Northern Bank Ltd v Ross* [1990] BCC 883, referred to with apparent approval in *Re Bank of Credit and Commerce International SA (No 8)* [1997] 4 All ER 568 (HL).

[11] Note also, however, that the exemptions created by the Financial Collateral Regulations may also be relevant in this context: see paras 35.22–35.31 below.

[12] See the priorities discussion at paras 30.09–30.12 above.

32

CHARGES OVER REAL ESTATE

Introduction

English law generally enjoys a positive reputation in the spheres of commercial and bank- **32.01** ing law, usually producing outcomes which are seen as appropriate by the business and financial communities.

Sadly, the same comment cannot be extended to land law in England, which can often **32.02** appear opaque and is made even more complex by its somewhat tortuous historical development, often mired in the conflict between the common law and equity. This is not the place to attempt a detailed description of that subject.[1]

For centuries, the process of transferring and mortgaging land had necessarily to be under- **32.03** taken through paper means. The investigation and verification of title to land was therefore not always a straightforward process. Thankfully, however, more modern developments have streamlined the process and most land—and transactions relating to it—is now registered on a central registry, known as the Land Registry.[2] It is therefore proposed to concentrate on registered land for the purposes of the present discussion, which is intended to be of an illustrative and practical nature only and, hence, of relatively limited scope.[3]

---

[1] See generally Megarry & Wade, *The Law of Real Property* (7th edn, Sweet & Maxwell, 2008).
[2] It may be noted that the State, through the Chief Land Registrar, effectively guarantees title to registered land by providing indemnities to those who suffer loss as a result of relying on any inaccuracies in the register: see s 103, read together with Sch 8 to the Land Registration Act 2002.
[3] For the definitive work in this area, see Fisher & Lightwood.

32.04 As is the case with any security interest, the lender is principally concerned with three questions, namely:

(a) What is the nature of the asset over which security is to be taken? This will frequently be obvious,[4] but a certain amount of discussion is required in relation to real estate.

(b) What is the nature of the security to be given to the lender, and what rights and remedies does it confer?

(c) On what grounds may the validity of the security later be challenged?

Nature of the Asset

32.05 As with any asset proffered to it as security, the bank will need to ensure that the borrower (or 'mortgagor') owns the asset and is entitled to take security over it and that the asset creates or implies the monetary value which the borrower seeks to ascribe to it. This can be a complex process in relation to land in England because different interests in the same piece of real estate may have differing values. For example:

(a) a 'freehold' interest connotes a permanent and indefeasible interest in land. In principle, this should be the most valuable interest, but this can be diminished by the existence of leases or other third party interests;

(b) a 'long leasehold' interest implies the right to occupy the property for a set term of years from the date of the lease.[5] This type of lease will carry a very nominal annual rent (usually described as a 'ground rent') and the real value for the lease will have been paid by way of premium on the commencement date. Possession and occupation of the property reverts to the freeholder on the expiry of the stated lease term.[6] Leases of 99 or even 999 years are commonly seen in the market, and will be freely transferable by the leaseholder. The result will be that the real value of such a property resides in the leasehold interest, rather than the freehold. The value of the underlying freehold interest in such a case will often be relatively small.[7]

32.06 As will be seen,[8] both forms of title may be impaired by other forms of interest in property, some of which may not even appear on the title register. It follows that a degree of investigation may be required even in the apparently most straightforward of cases.

32.07 On the footing that the relevant interest—freehold or leasehold—is registered at the Land Registry and the intending mortgagor is shown as the owner of that interest, what are the factors which the prospective lender must take into account in determining the value of the security offered to it? These would appear to fall into three categories.

---

[4] eg as in the case of security taken over listed shares, bonds, or similar instruments.

[5] A long leasehold interest of the type now under discussion must be distinguished from an ordinary commercial (or 'rack rent') lease, where the rent will be paid periodically throughout the term of the lease and no premium is paid for the grant of the lease at the outset.

[6] In practice, there are a number of statutory exceptions to this principle, allowing the owner to require the grant of an extended lease or, in some cases, to purchase the freehold. The relevant provisions are detailed and beyond the scope of this work.

[7] The exact value will often depend principally on the cash flow represented by the ground rents.

[8] See paras 32.09 and 32.10 below.

First of all, the proprietary interest will be subject to any adverse rights or interests **32.08** which appear on the register itself—for example, leases, sub-leases, and any pre-existing mortgages.

Secondly, the value of any property may be affected by extrinsic factors, such as planning **32.09** permissions granted for the construction or development of other projects in the vicinity. These are not matters which go directly to the formal title to the property, and they will accordingly not be disclosed on the register. It will be necessary for the lender to make separate enquiries of the relevant local authority in order to ascertain matters of this kind.[9]

Finally, certain interests in the property may remain valid and binding as against a mort- **32.10** gagee even though they are not recorded on the register. These are known as 'overriding interests' and, most significantly for the intending lender, these include the interests of any person in actual occupation of the property.[10] This has proved problematical for banks when taking a mortgage from a husband, and it subsequently transpires that the wife has contributed to the cost or maintenance of the property and has thereby acquired a beneficial interest in it. Since she will be in actual occupation of the property, her claim will be an 'overriding interest' for these purposes.[11] Banks must therefore ensure that the spouse or partner of the registered owner agrees to postpone any beneficial interest to the security position of the bank. In principle, arrangements of this kind are valid and effective[12] but, like any other contract entered into in this type of situation, it is vulnerable to attack on the basis that it was procured through duress or undue influence.[13]

Nature of the Security

The bank will usually require that it is granted a full legal mortgage over the property which **32.11** is registered in the charges section of the register.[14] This will ensure that the bank's interest is protected and prioritized against parties to any subsequent transactions.[15] Upon completion of the registration process in relation to the security, the lender has all the powers of enforcement and sale attributable to a legal mortgage.[16] A charge which is registered in this way will take priority over any security *registered* at a later date, even though it may have been *executed* at an earlier date.[17]

---

[9] Information of this kind will of course be relevant to the surveyor who is instructed to prepare a valuation of the property for mortgage purposes.

[10] This provision, formerly s 70(1)(g) of the Land Registration Act 1925, is now to be found in ss 11 and 12, and Schedule 1 to the Land Registration Act 2002.

[11] The problem really came to notice as a result of the decision in *Williams & Glyn's Bank Ltd v Boland* [1981] AC 487 (HL) but, inevitably, a series of similar cases have followed.

[12] See, for example, *Nationwide Anglia Building Society v Ahmed* (1995) 70 P&CR 390; *Le Foe v Woolwich plc* [2001] 2 FLR 970.

[13] Compare the situation which arose in *Royal Bank of Scotland v Etridge (No 2)* [2002] 2 AC 773 (HL), discussed at paras 32.39–32.48 below. The lender would be well advised to adopt the procedures there discussed (including the requirement for independent legal advice) in the present context.

[14] See s 27 of the Land Registration Act 2002.

[15] Section 30(2) of the Land Registration Act 2002.

[16] See ss 51 and 52 of the Land Registration Act 2002.

[17] Section 48 of the Land Registration Act 2002. It is possible to obtain a priority period, which means that the lender will obtain his priority by reference to the date of his priority search, rather than the later date of actual registration: see s 72 of the 2002 Act.

32.12   The detailed processes involved in the registration of mortgages and other interests in land are set out in the Land Registry Practice Guide. The application is made in a prescribed format (Form AP1) and must be accompanied by both the charge itself and the appropriate registration fee.

32.13   It should be appreciated that the registration of a mortgage at the Land Registry is not exclusive of any other statutory requirements. Thus, even if a mortgage is recorded at the Land Registry, it will nevertheless be void against the liquidator, administrator, and creditors of a company incorporated in the UK unless it has also been delivered for registration in accordance with section 860 of the Companies Act 2006.[18] Thus, the applicant for registration of a mortgage must produce the appropriate certificate of registration issued by the Registrar of Companies; if he fails to do so, then the title register must include a note to that effect.[19]

32.14   Finally, in the absence of any contrary intention of the parties, a mortgage over land will extend to items annexed to the land, whether as at the date of the mortgage or at any subsequent time ('fixtures'). Whether or not a particular item has become a fixture may involve difficult factual questions. However, if the structure has been specifically designed and annexed for use at that particular site, then it is likely to be a fixture for these purposes.[20] By the same token, if an item can readily be detached and is easily usable in other locations, then it will probably not be treated as a fixture. The point is obviously important in the sense that a fixture will form part of the lender's security package, whilst an item which can be removed will be available to creditors generally.[21]

Extent of the Security

32.15   A lender needs to take some care over the precise extent of his security, especially where second or subsequent mortgages may come into the picture. In particular, precisely how much of his facility will enjoy priority if he advances funds *after* receiving notice of a second charge?

32.16   The position is that additional advances made by the first lender[22] will continue to enjoy first priority provided that one of the following conditions is satisfied:[23]

   (a)   the lender had not received notice of the creation of the second mortgage;[24]

---

   [18] On these requirements, see para 27.23 above.
   [19] Land Registration Rules 2003, r 111. As noted at para 27.23(g) above, it should be appreciated that such a security interest remains enforceable against the company itself. In theory, it may thus be advisable to register the mortgage at the Land Registry even if the lender has failed to register the security at Companies House and the situation cannot be remedied for some reason.
   [20] *Elitestone Ltd v Morris* [1997] 2 All ER 513 (HL).
   [21] For further details and case law, see Fisher & Lightwood, para 8.2.
   [22] The commentary does, of course, assume that the relevant advances are within the scope of the obligations secured by the mortgage. There will be no difficulty where the mortgage is expressed to secure all monies owing by the borrower to the lender.
   [23] On the points about to be made, see s 94 of the Land Registration Act 2002. Since these provisions are concerned with the 'tacking' of further advances, it will be appreciated that they will be of no real relevance where the facility is to be drawn down in a single amount at the outset (eg to assist in the purchase of the property in the first instance).
   [24] The notice must emanate from the second mortgagee, since registration of the second charge is not of itself notice to the first lender. The rules provide for 'deemed receipt' of such a notice, which means that the

(b) the second mortgagee consents to the continuing priority of the first lender;[25]
(c) the lender is contractually obliged to make further advances and that fact is noted on the land register;[26] or
(d) the first lender's mortgage stated the maximum amount secured by the charge and that limit has not been exceeded.[27] This provision may be helpful for overdrafts and revolving credits, where the facility can be repaid and redrawn at a later date, up to the stipulated limit.

The lender should appreciate that—unless one of the provisions in paragraphs (a)–(d) above applies[28]—it is vulnerable to the postponement of its security as a result of the application of the rule derived from *Clayton's Case*.[29] Under this rule, payments into a current account are deemed to reduce the earliest debts incurred on the account. Thus, unless one of the above exceptions applies, payments into the account by the borrower will reduce the amounts entitled to priority under the mortgage. On the other hand, further drawings from the account—whilst still secured by the mortgage—will rank *after* the subsequent security. As a result, the normal utilization of an overdraft account or revolving credit facility will have the effect of progressively subordinating the lending bank's mortgage to the security created in favour of the second charge.[30] **32.17**

What action should a bank take if it receives notice of a second charge[31] under circumstances in which none of the exceptions listed in paragraphs (a)–(d) above applies, with the result that the application of the rule in *Clayton's Case* will subordinate its security in respect of further advances? The lender has the following options: **32.18**

(a) in the case of an overdraft, the bank should 'rule off' the account so that older debts—which would otherwise be discharged—are preserved, and a new account should be opened for subsequent debits and credits. This ensures that first priority is preserved for the existing indebtedness;

---

first lender may lose its priority even though it has no *actual* knowledge of the second security. For the details, see Fisher & Lightwood, para 38.19.

[25] It is always open to multiple mortgagees to enter into agreements regulating their respective priorities and other matters (eg such as the circumstances under which the second mortgagee may enforce his security against the wishes of the first lender). There is no policy reason to strike down such an agreement since it does not operate in a manner detrimental to the unsecured creditors of the mortgagor.
[26] Note however that the obligation to make further advances can be contained in the associated facility agreement. It does not need to be stated in the mortgage document itself.
[27] The maximum amount so stated must include principal and interest and must be recorded on the register: Fisher & Lightwood, para 38.21.
[28] It should also be appreciated that, even where one of the exceptions does apply, they are only available to a mortgagee who has completed the registration of his mortgage at the Land Registry.
[29] *Devaynes v Noble, Clayton's Case* (1816) 1 Mer 572.
[30] For applications of this rule, see *Deeley v Lloyds Bank Ltd* [1912] AC 756 (HL) and *Siebe Gorman & Co Ltd v Barclays Bank Ltd* [1979] 2 Lloyd's Rep 142.
[31] A restriction entered on the register will frequently prohibit the *registration* of a second or subsequent charge. But this would not prevent a second charge from accepting an equitable security. An equitable charge does not require registration to be effective. Section 27(2)(f) of the Land Registration Act 2002 provides that only a legal charge is a registrable disposition, although an equitable charge should be protected by the entry of a notice: ss 32–39 of the 2002 Act.

(b) this does, however, presuppose that the bank is prepared to accept a second ranking or subordinated security position in respect of further advances. It almost certainly will not have contracted to do so;

(c) where the underlying facility agreement is a detailed document, the creation of the second charge without the lender's prior approval will almost certainly constitute a breach of the negative pledge undertaking.[32] Since the breach of the negative pledge will amount to an event of default, the lender will be entitled to suspend further advances until the situation is remedied to its satisfaction; and

(d) where the facility is made available by way of overdraft, the facility letter is unlikely to contain a detailed negative pledge provision.[33] However, it will almost certainly be an implied term of the contract that (i) all advances are to be secured by a first ranking mortgage over the property and (ii) the bank is entitled to suspend advances if this condition is not met.[34] In practice, the bank will generally have the right to cancel the overdraft, and it may simply elect to take that route.

Registration of the Security

32.19 Security created over registered land will require registration:

(a) at the Land Registry;[35] and

(b) if created by a company, at Companies House.[36]

32.20 Registration is not required merely because a person holds debentures which entitle him to the benefit of a charge over land.[37] Thus, where security over land is given in favour of a trustee or security agent for debenture holders or participants in a syndicated loan, the mortgage must be registered in favour of the trustee or security agent (as the case may be). But it is not necessary for individual debenture holders or lenders to effect further registration.

Remedies of the Mortgagee

32.21 As with any other security interest, the object of the arrangement is to insulate the lender against the consequences of the default or insolvency of his borrower. What is the nature of the remedies available to a mortgagee in this situation, and what are the constraints on the exercise of those remedies?

---

[32] On the negative pledge undertaking, see para 20.37(b) above.

[33] Although the bank may have sent a set of standard terms and conditions which might include such a clause.

[34] The second part of this formulation is necessary to make the implied term effective. It would be insufficient for the bank merely to have an action for damages in respect of the creation of the second security.

[35] See para 32.11 above.

[36] In the case of a UK company and a foreign company with a registered establishment in the UK, see generally Chapter 27 above. No Companies House filing will be required in the case of a foreign company which has not registered any establishment in this country.

[37] The point is confirmed by s 861(1) of the Companies Act 2006.

It should be noted at the outset that a mortgage which has been registered at the Land **32.22**
Registry takes effect as a charge by deed by way of legal mortgage.[38] As a result, the powers
available to the mortgagee are governed by the provisions of the Law of Property Act 1925
('the 1925 Act').

Power of sale

Apart from any specific powers which may be conferred by the mortgage deed itself,[39] the **32.23**
mortgagee enjoys a statutory power of sale.[40] In one of those curiosities which plagues
English land law, there is a distinction between the point of time at which the power of sale
arises and the time at which it becomes *exercisable*. The power of sale is said to arise if the
mortgage is by deed, the secured monies are due and the mortgage does not suggest a contrary intention.[41] However, that power will only become exercisable if (i) a part of the
mortgage money has been outstanding for three months after notice of demand, (ii) interest is two months overdue, or (iii) there has been some other breach of an obligation of
the mortgagor under the mortgage itself or under the terms of the Law of Property Act.[42]
The 1925 Act allows that the mortgage may vary the terms applicable to these powers[43]
and, unsurprisingly, mortgages usually take advantage of this power by eliminating or
reducing the notice or grace periods. Accordingly, if the mortgage provides a list of events
which will trigger the right to exercise the power of sale, it may be inferred that the list is
intended to be exhaustive of the situations in which that power can be exercised.[44]

Depending on the nature of the property, it may be necessary to obtain possession of the **32.24**
property as a necessary precursor to the sale.[45]

Appointment of Receiver

The Law of Property Act 1925 also provides a statutory right for the mortgagee to appoint **32.25**
a receiver.[46] As the name implies, this option will usually be of interest to the bank only
where all or part of the mortgaged property is let and, hence, income-producing. This may
be particularly advantageous if, for example, the income is likely to be sufficient to cover
the interest but capital values are depressed in the prevailing market conditions.

The power to appoint a receiver is subject to the same terms and conditions as those **32.26**
applicable to the power of sale (see above).

The mortgage will usually provide that any receiver is the agent of the mortgagor, so that **32.27**
the mortgagee will not be personally responsible for his actions. Nevertheless, the receiver
must preserve the property and is generally subject to the same obligations as the mortgagee

---

[38] Section 51 of the Land Registration Act 2002.
[39] An express power of sale will normally include an obligation to give notice before the power of sale is
exercised. On this subject, see Fisher & Lightwood, para 30.11.
[40] Section 101(1)(i) of the Law of Property Act 1925.
[41] Section 101(1) of the Law of Property Act 1925.
[42] Section 103 of the Law of Property Act 1925; Fisher & Lightwood, para 30.12.
[43] Section 103(3) of the Law of Property Act 1925.
[44] *West Bromwich Building Society v Wilkinson* [2005] 1 WLR 2303.
[45] On this process, see para 32.27 below.
[46] Section 101(1)(iii) of the Law of Property Act 1925.

itself in exercising the power of sale.[47] The duties of a receiver include a duty to actively manage and preserve the property with due diligence, and to deal with it in a manner which is fair and equitable as between his appointor and the other parties interested in the equity of redemption.[48]

Taking Possession

32.28 In theory, a mortgagee has the power to take possession of the land even if the borrower has not defaulted on its obligations.[49]

32.29 In practice, banks will only wish to seek possession of the mortgaged property as a prelude to exercising the power of sale following a default. At least in residential cases, this will usually be achieved by means of a court order, to avoid any later allegation that the bank or its agents have acted unlawfully in removing the mortgagor from his property.[50] The court has a general power to adjourn or suspend possession proceedings if it appears likely that the debtor may be able to remedy his payment default or achieve a sale of the property.[51]

Restrictions on the Exercise of the Mortgagee's Powers

32.30 What are the terms and conditions upon and subject to which the various powers just described may be exercised?

32.31 As a general rule, the mortgagee is allowed both to select the remedy which he wishes to adopt and to control the manner and timing of its exercise.[52] Although the mortgagee must exercise his powers in good faith and for the purposes for which they were conferred,[53] this does not imply any obligation on the mortgagee to select the remedy which is most likely to prove beneficial to the mortgagor,[54] nor does he owe him any form of fiduciary duty in exercising those powers. The mortgagee is thus entitled to act in his own interests in this respect. The main obligation of the mortgagee is to obtain the best price reasonably obtainable in the circumstances.[55]

---

[47] On this subject, see para 32.31 below.

[48] For analysis, see *Downsview Nominees Ltd v First City Corp Ltd* [1993] AC 295 (PC) and *Silven Properties Ltd v Royal Bank of Scotland plc* [2004] 4 All ER 484.

[49] *Four-Maids Ltd v Dudley Marshall Properties Ltd* [1957] Ch 317. Once again, this is something of a curiosity of English land law. The bank is in the business of lending money to customers so that they can acquire property; it will not usually wish to enter into possession itself.

[50] For completeness, it should be noted that the mortgagee also has a right of foreclosure, which has the effect of vesting the property in the mortgagee, thus cancelling the mortgage debt. This remedy is now rarely used and is therefore not considered here. On the whole subject, see Fisher & Lightwood, ch 32.

[51] Section 36 of the Administration of Justice Act 1970. For a more detailed discussion, see Halsbury's Laws of England, *Mortgages*, paras 755–759.

[52] *Medforth v Blake* [2000] Ch 86.

[53] ie obtaining repayment of the mortgage debt.

[54] *Downsville Nominees Ltd v First City Corp Ltd* [1993] AC 295.

[55] *Cuckmere Brick Co Ltd v Mutual Finance Ltd* [1971] Ch 948; *Downside Nominees Ltd v First City Corp Ltd* [1993] AC 295 (PC).

Consolidation

A slightly different form of remedy for the mortgagee is the right of consolidation. In many **32.32** senses, consolidation is more in the nature of a right to *preserve* security, rather than a remedy to *enforce* it.

The starting point for this discussion is offered by section 93(1) of the Law of Property **32.33** Act 1925, which allows a mortgagor to redeem a mortgage without paying off other mortgages owing to the same lender. This provision accordingly excludes any right for the lender to consolidate two or more mortgages, but the section only applies subject to any contrary provision in the mortgage itself. Inevitably, given that the right of consolidation favours the lender, standard form mortgages will invariably contain a provision excluding the application of section 93, with the result that the bank will continue to enjoy its rights of consolidation.

The substance of the mortgagee's right of consolidation is that the lender may effectively **32.34** treat a series of outstanding mortgages from the same debtor as a single mortgage, and thus refuse redemption of one of them unless all are contemporaneously redeemed. This curious right apparently flows from the fact that (i) the right to redeem following a default is of an equitable nature and (ii) he who seeks equity must do equity.[56] It is thus apparently regarded as inequitable for a mortgagor to be entitled to redeem a single mortgage from the series. The right for the mortgagee to insist on consolidation does, however, apparently only arise after the debtor has gone into default.[57]

It seems that the right to consolidate mortgages will in practice be of limited importance, **32.35** at least in relation to corporate security. Usually, all properties charged by a company will each secure the entirety of the debt, with the result that the borrower has no right to redeem any of the properties until the whole of the indebtedness is repaid.

It is also suggested that the courts should readily infer an intention to exclude the right of **32.36** consolidation where security is given over a portfolio of properties and—as is commonly the case—the borrower is required to maintain a particular security ration (that is, to ensure that outstanding amount of the loan does not exceed a set percentage of the value of the properties). This implies that the borrower should be entitled to withdraw individual properties from the security package so long as the resultant proceeds are paid to the lender in reduction of the overall debt and the loan to value ratio is still met.

Priorities

Some aspects of the rules governing the priority of successive mortgages over land have **32.37** already been noted above.[58]

---

[56] *Chesworth v Hunt* (1880) 5 CPD 266, noted by Halsbury, *Mortgages*, para 699.
[57] See in particular *Cummins v Fletcher* (1880) 14 Ch D 699 (CA) and *Jennings v Jordan* (1881) 6 App Cas 698 (HL).
[58] See 'Extent of the Security', at paras 32.15–32.18 above.

32.38 Subject to that discussion, mortgages over registered land will rank in the order in which they are shown on the register.[59] The result is that a mortgagee who is tardy in registering his security may find himself postponed to another charge whose security in fact bears a later date. This rule is, however, subject to various exceptions:

(a) The applicable legislation provides for a system of priority notices, under which a person intending to take a charge over a property may apply for a notice to be entered on the register to that effect. If the intended mortgage is then in fact registered within the priority period, then its priority will relate back to the date on which the original notice was given, rather than the date of the mortgage document itself. This system is designed for the protection of pending transactions, so that there will be a clear period for the completion of the security and during which no competing transaction can obtain priority.

(b) Successive mortgagees may enter into a priorities or intercreditor agreement which alters the order of priority which would otherwise apply. The alteration is completed by an appropriate entry on the register.[60] In practice, the borrower would itself be made a party to the necessary agreement, but this does not appear to be a necessary condition.[61]

(c) If a mortgagee makes an incorrect representation about the priority of his security to another lender and the latter relies on that statement to his detriment, then the first mortgagee may be estopped from pleading or relying upon his true statutory priority.[62]

Grounds of Challenge

32.39 The taking of security over residential property which is jointly-owned by the sole borrower and his spouse/partner has given rise to particular difficulty over recent years.

32.40 There should be no special problem if the loan is made to finance or refinance the acquisition of a home in joint names, but issues may arise if the security is given in respect of the separate debts of one party only—for example, as is commonly the case, where the security is given to secure an overdraft facility provided to the husband's business.

32.41 As a general rule, a bank which is requested to finance a transaction owes no duty to advise the borrower, any guarantor, or any other party on the viability or wisdom of that transaction.[63] In the absence of special circumstances, the bank does not stand in a fiduciary or advisory relationship so far as borrowers or guarantors are concerned.

---

[59] Section 48(1) of the Land Registration Act 2002.
[60] Rule 102(3) of the Land Registration Rules 2003.
[61] *Cheah Theam Swee v Equiticorp Finance Group Ltd* [1992] 1 AC 472 (PC).
[62] *Nationwide Anglia Building Society v Ahmed* (1995) 70 P&CR 381. The decision is noted by Fisher & Lightwood, para 36.1.
[63] *National Commercial Bank (Jamaica) Ltd v Hew* [2003] UKPC 51. This case has been noted at para 25.09 above.

The difficulty is that, in a tripartite relationship, there may be a possibility that the bor- **32.42** rower may mislead or otherwise take advantage of the surety, and the circumstances may mean that the bank should be aware of that danger. This, in turn, may mean that any guarantee or third party security given by the surety may be vulnerable to attack on various grounds. For example, if the bank delegates to the borrower the task of procuring the execution of the guarantee, then (i) the borrower may be regarded as the agent of the bank for that purpose and (ii) as a result, any misrepresentation made by the borrower to the guarantor may be treated as that of the bank, and (iii) the guarantor may therefore be entitled to rescind the guarantee or security on that footing.[64] Cases of this kind will, however, necessarily be out of the ordinary partly because the borrower will not normally have any authority to represent the bank and partly because of the processes put in place by banks to deal with the 'undue influence' decisions discussed below.

The circumstances of the case and the relationship between the borrower and the guaran- **32.43** tor may be suggestive of other difficulties, such as the exercise of duress or undue influence over the surety. 'Undue influence' involves the exercise of influence over the surety in a manner which is *unconscionable*,[65] and will generally entitle the victim of that influence to rescind the transaction. Alternatively, the borrower may have misrepresented the nature and substance of the transaction to the guarantor.[66]

These issues came to the fore in two House of Lords decisions namely *Barclays Bank plc v* **32.44** *O'Brien*[67] as more recently considered and refined in *Royal Bank of Scotland* plc *v Etridge (No 2)*.[68] Both cases involved a charge executed by a wife to support bank facilities provided to her husband's business.[69] In these situations, the House of Lords in *Etridge* held that a *presumption* of undue influence will arise if:

(a) the relationship between the parties was one of husband/wife or similar relationship in which the surety would repose significant trust and confidence in the borrower in the conduct of financial affairs;[70] and

(b) the transaction calls for an explanation, in the sense that it is not obvious why the surety should have agreed to it in the absence of persuasion.[71]

It should be appreciated that *both* of these tests must be met if any presumption of undue **32.45** influence is to arise. For example, if the transaction to be financed is clearly of benefit to

---

[64] See, for example, *King's North Trust Ltd v Bell* [1986] 1 WLR 119 (CA).

[65] On the subject of undue influence generally, see Chitty, ch 7.

[66] This was the situation in the *O'Brien* case, discussed below.

[67] [1994] 1 AC 180 (HL).

[68] [2002] 2 AC 773 (HL).

[69] This has tended to be the common situation although, as noted above, the issues now under discussion can arise in any non-commercial relationship, including sexual and family relationships.

[70] Note that the 'trust and confidence' point is not itself a matter of presumption and the wife has to demonstrate that she did in fact entrust the running of finances to the husband. For a case in which the wife was unable to meet this test, see *MacKenzie v Royal Bank of Canada* [1934] AC 469 (PC), noted by Lingard at para 13.38. However, the mere fact that a group of business partners also happen to be close friends does not by itself give rise to any presumption of undue influence: *Bank of Scotland plc v Makris and O'Sullivan* Ch D (15 May 2009).

[71] As the House of Lords noted in *Etridge*, the bank will in practice be placed on enquiry whenever a wife acts as surety for her husband's debts.

both husband and wife, then no such presumption can arise.[72] In such a situation, the transaction does not require explanation for the purposes of (b) above and no presumption of undue influence will arise.[73]

32.46   Nevertheless, situations of this kind pose significant practical difficulties for banks. It is true that the presumption that the husband has applied undue influence in relation to a transaction requiring explanation is a rebuttable one; it is perfectly conceivable that the wife fully understood the risks involved but elected to support her husband's business venture in any event. But the problem for the bank is one of evidence; the husband is unlikely to provide evidence which will undermine the case which his wife seeks to establish. In any event, the bank does not wish to face defences of this kind at the point of enforcement. If at all possible, it needs to close off such potential challenges before it advances the facility in the first instance, because the necessary evidence will not be available at a later date. The question is: what can the bank do to acquire the necessary evidence at the point of arranging the facility?

32.47   In *O'Brien*, the House of Lords had suggested that the surety should receive independent legal advice and confirm to the bank that the surety understood the risks involved in the proposed transaction. Yet this does not really seem to address the issue. The surety may well fully understand the nature of the guarantee or security, but may still have been coerced into entering into it. This guidance was therefore considerably refined in *Etridge*, as follows:[74]

    (a)   the bank should communicate directly with the wife (i) to ascertain the identity of the solicitor whom she wishes to advise her on the arrangements,[75] (ii) to explain that, for its own protection, the bank will require written confirmation from the solicitor that he has explained the nature and effect of the documents and their practical consequences,[76] and (iii) to explain that the solicitor's confirmation is required so that she cannot dispute the validity of the guarantee/security at a later date;

    (b)   the bank should disclose—either to the wife herself or to the solicitors instructed by her—details of the existing indebtedness of the husband and of any new facility;[77]

    (c)   if the bank suspects that the husband has misrepresented the nature of the transaction, believes that the wife is being pressurized to enter into it, then the bank should disclose the relevant circumstances to the wife's solicitors; and

---

[72]   This point was expressly recognized in *Barclays Bank v O'Brien* [1994] 1 AC 180 (HL).

[73]   See *CIBC Mortgages Ltd v Pitt* [1994] 1 AC 200 (HL) and contrast *Northern Rock Building Society v Archer* [1997] Lloyd's Rep Bank 32 (CA).

[74]   See in particular the judgments of Lord Nicholls at 811–812 and Lord Scott at 849.

[75]   According to *Etridge*, this may be the solicitor who is already advising the borrower, provided that no conflict of interest arises.

[76]   The bank cannot reasonably rely on the solicitor's certificate unless it expressly states that he has advised on the nature and effect of the transaction: see *Yorkshire Bank plc v Tinsley* [2004] EWCA 816 (Civ). However, it should be noted that this does not mean that the solicitor has to state that he has positively advised the surety to enter into the transaction.

[77]   The provision of this information would require the consent of the husband in order to avoid any breach of the duty of confidentiality owed to him.

(d) the required confirmation should be obtained from the wife's solicitor before the facility is drawn.

It remains to note a few general points in this area:

32.48

(a) whilst the preponderance of recent cases have involved assertions of undue influence made by wives, it should be appreciated that presumptions of undue influence may arise in the context of cohabitees or other family relationships—for example, where a child signs a guarantee for his parents [78] or where aging parents give guarantees for the obligations of their grown up children;[79]
(b) where a bank refinances an earlier transaction and that transaction was effected under circumstances giving rise to a presumption of undue influence, the bank cannot simply assume that the first transaction was regular. It should apply the processes outlined in *Etridge* on the same basis;[80] and
(c) the bank may be placed in a difficult position if the presumed 'victim' of undue influence refuses to seek the requested legal advice. The Banking Code and the Business Banking Code[81] both suggested that the individual concerned should provide a written declaration to the bank to that effect. This is perhaps the best that can be done under such circumstances, yet it is difficult to see how such a declaration would rebut any presumption of undue influence which may have arisen. To the contrary, the refusal to seek advice may tend to suggest that *actual* undue influence is being applied by the borrower; and
(d) it may be noted that courts in Canada have allowed that the presumption of undue influence may be rebutted by other means, for example, by demonstrating the financial sophistication of the spouse and the probability that she did not rely on the husband.[82] They have also held that it is sufficient to advise the spouse that legal advice should be taken, and that the bank should not be affected if that suggestion is rejected.[83] It is fair to say that the *Etridge* decision has received a mixed reception in Canada, and the courts have declined to follow it on at least one occasion.[84]

Security Over Foreign Land

Questions of title to foreign land are necessarily governed by the law of the country in which that land is situate. As a result, the validity of any mortgage or security interest over that land—and any remedies available for its enforcement—are likewise governed by that system of law.[85] A lender taking security over such an asset should therefore ensure that all registration and other steps are taken under the local law in order to ensure the perfection, validity, and priority of the charge in accordance with that law.

32.49

---

[78] *Lancashire Loans Ltd v Black* [1934] 1 KB 380 (CA).
[79] *Avon Finance Co Ltd v Bridger* [1985] 2 All ER 281 (CA).
[80] *Yorkshire Bank plc v Tinsley* [2004] EWHC 816 (Civ).
[81] See para 13 of both Codes. These Codes are no longer in force: see the discussion of the BCOBS section of the FSA Handbook in Chapter 3 above.
[82] *Bank of Montreal v Duguid* (2000) 185 DLR (4th) 458 (Ontario Court of Appeal).
[83] *CIBC Mortgage Corporation v Rowatt* (2002) DLR (4th) 139 (Ontario Court of Appeal).
[84] *Bank of Montreal v Courtenay* (2005) 261 DLR (4th) 665 (Nova Scotia Court of Appeal).
[85] See Fisher & Lightwood, para 1.24.

32.50   Yet matters are not always so straightforward. If a bank takes a standard form of debenture[86] from an English company, this will (at least so far as English law is concerned) extend to all land owned by the company, *wherever situate*. The bank may therefore seek to argue that it has a recognizable and effective security interest against that asset—even though local registration or other formalities have not been met. This may occur because the relevant asset only comes to the attention of the bank once insolvency proceedings have been started, or because the bank originally (and, in the events which happen, erroneously) believed that the security available to it in the United Kingdom would be sufficient to cover its facility in the event of a default.

32.51   As noted above, there are limited circumstances under which an English court can concern itself directly with issues touching the title to foreign land. But there may be limited cases in which the court can lend some assistance to the secured lender. In particular:

(a) if by chance the borrower remains solvent and otherwise able to manage its affairs at the point of time at which the bank becomes aware of the foreign asset, then the court might order the borrower to take such steps as may be necessary to perfect the security under the local law. There are two possible bases for such an order. First of all, since the debenture extends to foreign land, it may be an implied term of the contract that the borrower will perfect the security in accordance with the local law on request.[87] Alternatively, the standard form debenture will usually contain a standard 'further assurance' clause under which the chargor undertakes to take any steps and execute any documents required in order to perfect the security intended to be created pursuant to the debenture. In such a case, the court is not making an order which directly affects the title to foreign land. Rather, it is simply exercising an equitable jurisdiction *in personam*, ordering the company to perform the obligation which it has expressly or impliedly undertaken.[88] An English court has recently refused to order a chargor to execute a security document over Dutch assets pursuant to the further assurance clause in an English charge, although it accepted that such a remedy ought in principle to be available in this type of case.[89] It may be objected that, in practice, any such further security document is likely to be requested and executed when the company is on the threshold of insolvency and that, since the loan will have been advanced long ago, the resultant security will be amenable to challenge as a preference or as a transaction at an undervalue.[90] Although the point is eminently arguable, it is submitted that such challenges should not succeed, in part because the security created in the original debenture is valid as against the company, at least so far as English law is concerned;[91]

---

[86]   The expression 'debenture' is used here to connote a document creating a fixed and floating charge over the entire assets and undertaking of the company.

[87]   Such an implied term would be necessary to give full effect to the intended security package, and could thus be justified on 'business efficacy' grounds.

[88]   On this principle as it applies to foreign land, see *Penn v Lord Baltimore* (1750) Ves Sen 444.

[89]   *Ford v Polymer Vision Ltd* [2009] EWHC 945 (Ch).

[90]   On preferences and transactions at an undervalue, see ss 238 and 239 of the Insolvency Act 1986, considered in Chapter 39 below.

[91]   The validity of the security under English law is developed in (b), below. Briefly, the execution of the foreign security document would not be a 'transaction at an undervalue' because the company is executing

(b) although the security interest created by the debenture is not enforceable in the foreign jurisdiction concerned, it is submitted that it remains valid and effective as between the lender and the English company *so far as English law is concerned*. The English courts will treat the security document as a valid equitable charge over the foreign property, and the fact that such a form of security is unregistered in the foreign jurisdiction will be irrelevant.[92] As a result, any proceeds of sale of the property received by the administrator or liquidator would be subject to the security interest created by the original debenture over that property, and should thus be paid to the lender in priority to the unsecured creditors.[93] However, since the charge is not valid by the law of the country in which the land is situate, he will not be able to prevent other creditors from taking action against the property under the law of that country.[94] The general point is nevertheless worth keeping in mind for a creditor in this situation, although it will only have substance if proceeds remain available to the liquidator or administrator following any local enforcement action taken by other creditors;[95] and

(c) there may be a question mark as to the characterization of the charge as fixed or floating. The failure of the lender to perfect its security under the local law will probably mean that—so far as English law is concerned—the lender has not taken sufficient control over the asset to establish a fixed charge.[96] The security would thus take effect as a floating charge.

---

the charge in compliance with a pre-existing obligation. The company has thus not 'entered into a transaction' for the purposes of s 238 of the Insolvency Act 1986, since that expression connotes a voluntary action on the part of the company or (alternatively) it is executing the document pursuant to the earlier debenture, for which it has received full value. Likewise, the creation of the foreign charge is not a 'preference' because it does not have 'the effect of putting [the lender] into a position which, in the event of the company going into insolvent liquidation, will be better than the position he would have been in if the thing had not been done' for the purposes of s 239(4)(b) of the 1986 Act. Again, this follows from the fact that English law should treat the security created by the original debenture as valid, with the result that the foreign security document does not operate to the detriment of the general body of creditors.

[92] ie because equity acts *in personam* and does not act directly against the foreign property.

[93] This does, of course, pre-suppose that the debenture was registered in accordance with s 860(7)(g) of the Companies Act 2006, on which see para 27.23 above, and that the debenture is otherwise valid as a matter of English law.

[94] *Re Maudslay, Sons & Field* [1900] 1 Ch 602.

[95] ie as happened in the *Maudslay* case, above.

[96] On the degree of control as an indicator of a fixed charge, see para 30.04 above.

33

CHARGES OVER AIRCRAFT

Introduction

Aircraft are complicated pieces of equipment and it is perhaps unsurprising that the processes involved in their registration and operation are likewise fairly involved. At least for larger aircraft flown internationally by recognized airlines, the sums involved can also be very significant.   **33.01**

For these reasons, aircraft finance and security is a relatively specialized subject and it is proposed here to consider the topic in general outline only. For obvious reasons, this chapter is principally aimed at aircraft registered in the United Kingdom, but a brief consideration of security over foreign aircraft will also be included.   **33.02**

UK Aircraft

At the outset, it should be appreciated that provision is made for the registration of UK aircraft on the national register by the terms of the Air Navigation Order 2005.[1]   **33.03**

For present purposes, the key provision is article 4 of the 2005 Order. This provides for the Civil Aviation Authority to maintain a register of UK aircraft, and that an aircraft can only be entered or remain on the UK register if it is owned by a 'qualified person'. This term includes (i) the UK Government, (ii) Commonwealth citizens and corporations,[2] and (iii) EEA citizens and companies. In addition, the aircraft may be registered in the United Kingdom if it is chartered by demise to a qualified person, even though the owner would   **33.04**

---

[1] SI 2005/1970. The Order also makes extensive provision for other matters, including airworthiness, aircraft crew and licensing, aircraft operation, air traffic services, and similar issues.

[2] This expression would of course include citizens of, and companies incorporated within, the UK.

not itself be so qualified. However, the duration of the registration is limited to that of the demise charter,[3] so the aircraft would have to be re-registered elsewhere upon expiry.

33.05 The main legislation of interest to finance lawyers in this field is the Mortgaging of Aircraft Order 1972.[4] The main provisions of this Order include the following:

(a) An aircraft which is registered in the United Kingdom nationality register (including any store of spare parts for that aircraft) may be charged by way of security for a loan or other good consideration.[5]

(b) A mortgage against such an aircraft may be registered against it by delivery of a certified copy of the mortgage[6] and a registration form as set out in Part I of schedule 1 to the Order.

(c) Where it is intended to create a mortgage over an aircraft, it is possible to lodge a 'priority notice', which secures priority for that mortgage if registered within the ensuing 14 days even though another mortgage is registered within the intervening period.[7]

(d) All persons are at all times deemed to have express notice of all information which appears on the register, so that any person taking a mortgage over an aircraft is taken to have notice of any prior charge over the asset. However, registration of an aircraft mortgage is not evidence of its validity.[8]

(e) It is specifically provided that the Bills of Sale Acts 1878 and 1882 do not apply to any mortgage over an aircraft on the UK register. This confirmation is helpful in the sense that the excessive formalities of the Bills of Sale Acts are not readily applied to security over an aircraft. In practice, however, the point is only material where the mortgagor is an *individual*, since it has been decided that the Bills of Sale Acts do not apply to bills of sale executed by way of security by a body corporate.[9]

33.06 From a security perspective, it should also be borne in mind that:

(a) if the owner is a company incorporated in the United Kingdom, then the relevant charge will also require registration at Companies House within 21 days after the date of its creation;[10] and

(b) if the owner is an entity incorporated outside the United Kingdom, the charge will also require registration at Companies House if—but only if—that entity has registered a branch or established place of business in the United Kingdom.[11]

---

[3] ie a charter under which the charterer assumes full responsibility for the maintenance, operation, and control of the aircraft. This means that an aircraft owned by (say) a non-qualified finance company can still be registered in the UK if the charterer itself is a qualified person.

[4] SI 1972/1268.

[5] Article 3 of the 1972 Order.

[6] Note that, in contrast to the position for ships, there is no prescribed form of aircraft mortgage and its contents is therefore a matter for negotiation between the parties.

[7] See art 5 of the Order. This procedure is in some respects similar to that applicable to registered land, discussed in Chapter 32 above.

[8] On these provisions, see art 13 of the Order. As in the case of registration at Companies House, the registration process does not have the effect of validating an invalid charge: see para 27.23(k) above.

[9] On this point, see *Slavenberg's Bank NV v Intercontinental Natural Resources Ltd* [1980] 1 All ER 955.

[10] See s 860(7)(h) of the Companies Act 2006, noted at para 27.23 above.

[11] See reg 9 of the Overseas Companies Charges Regulations 2009, considered at para 27.37 above.

As noted above, there is no statutorily prescribed form of aircraft mortgage. In practice, **33.07** these may be quite detailed documents and may include the following:

(a) warranties that the aircraft is free of encumbrances or other third party interests;
(b) an extension of the security not only to the aircraft itself but also to spare parts and other equipment;
(c) detailed obligations as to the insurance of the aircraft and (except in the case of liability insurance), an assignment of the relevant policies in favour of the bank;
(d) if the aircraft is to be chartered, an assignment of the hire or other resultant income;[12] and
(e) numerous other undertakings will be imposed as to the repair, condition, servicing, and maintenance of the aircraft.[13]

Finally, it should be appreciated that an aircraft is not a single chattel but several, compris- **33.08** ing the airframe, the engines, and other spare or removable parts.[14] This can give rise to practical difficulties, in that the original engines may be removed or replaced for servicing, or under engine pooling arrangements. If engines are replaced, then the lender needs to ensure that it obtains valid and effective security over the replacement parts.

Priorities

In terms of the priority of competing mortgages and security interests over aircraft, (i) a **33.09** registered mortgage always takes priority over an unregistered mortgage, even if the holder of the registered security was in fact aware of the prior interest, (ii) registered mortgages rank according to the dates on which they are entered on the register, save that a mortgage in respect of which a priority notice was given and which is in fact registered within the 14 day priority period will rank ahead of any other charge registered during that period, and (iii) possessory liens for work done on the aircraft may continue to rank ahead of registered mortgages.[15]

Foreign Aircraft

A transfer or mortgage over a chattel must usually be effective according to the law of the **33.10** place where the relevant asset is situate at the time of the charge. There are exceptions to this rule and it may be argued that an aircraft should be deemed to be situate in the jurisdiction

---

[12] A charge of this kind may be regarded as security over a book debt and would hence require registration under s 860(7)(f) of the Companies Act 2006 or, for a foreign company registered in England, reg 9 of the Overseas Companies Charges Regulations 2009 (although, in the latter case, this may depend on the *situs* of the debt for the reasons discussed at para 27.37 above). In practice, the point is unlikely to cause difficulty because the mortgage will be a single document and will be registered in its entirety.

[13] These are designed to ensure that—in the event of a default and repossession of the aircraft—the mortgagee will acquire an asset in a condition in which it can be sold and without requiring significant additional expenditure.

[14] Although an aircraft may be regarded as a chattel, the creation of security over it does not amount to a bill of sale: see the discussion under 'Foreign Aircraft', below.

[15] On these rules, see art 14 of the 2005 Order. Note that the priority for possessory liens in some respects mirrors the position for maritime liens: see para 34.04 below.

in which it is registered. There is some doubt about this point, however, and it is perhaps prudent to ensure that a charge over an aircraft is valid in both the country of registry and the place of physical location at the time of the charge.[16]

33.11 A mortgage which is valid according to the laws of those two jurisdictions will be recognized by an English court and it will thus allow the exercise of any mortgagee's remedies, such as rights of detention and sale.

33.12 It may be objected that a charge over an aircraft amounts to a bill of sale for the purposes of the Bills of Sale Act 1878 (as amended). A bill of sale is an instrument under which a chattel is charged to a lender but under the terms of which the relevant asset is to remain in the possession of the chargor. Under section 9 of the Bills of Sale Act (1878) Amendment Act 1882, a bill of sale made or given by way of security for the payment of money by the grantor thereof is to be void unless it is made in the form set out in the schedule to that Act. However, the expression 'bill of sale' specifically excludes '... bills of sale of goods in foreign parts or at sea ...'[17] and thus would not apply to a charge over an aircraft which is outside this country as at the date of the creation of the security. Furthermore, and most decisively, it now appears to be accepted that the Bills of Sale Act does not apply to security created by limited companies,[18] which will almost invariably be the relevant category of chargor in this type of case. It follows that this legislation will not generally be of concern when taking security over a foreign aircraft.

International Issues

33.13 It hardly needs to be stated that aircraft are not infrequently physically situate in countries other than their State of registration. This has consequences for the recognition and enforcement of proprietary interests in—including mortgages over—aircraft.

33.14 The Convention on International Recognition of Rights in Aircraft, 1948 (the Geneva Convention) was designed to protect proprietary and security interests in aircraft according to the law of the State of registration. Whilst the United Kingdom signed the Geneva Convention, it never ratified it.[19] The Geneva Convention was in any event regarded as inadequate in many respects. In particular, whilst it provided for the recognition of rights created by the State of registration, this merely created a rule of private international law and did not create a uniform system of registration, recognition or enforcement.

---

[16] On this subject, see Dicey, Morris & Collins, para 22E-060. In principle, however, it should be sufficient if the mortgage conforms to the law of the State of registration, since an aircraft has the nationality of that State, cannot simultaneously be registered in more than one State and the validity of dealings with an aircraft are generally governed by the laws of the State of registration: see Arts 17–19 of the Chicago Convention on International Civil Aviation (1944).

[17] See s 4 of the 1878 Act.

[18] In *NV Slavenberg's Bank v Intercontinental Natural Resources Ltd* [1980] 1 All ER 955, the court decided that the security provisions of the Act were aimed at charges over chattels which remained in the possession of an *individual* debtor.

[19] Section 90 of the Civil Aviation Act 1982 (as amended) provides for an Order in Council to implement the Convention, but no such Order has been made.

The Geneva Convention is, in any event, in the process of being superseded by the Convention on International Interests in Mobile Equipment 2001 (the Cape Town Convention) and the associated Protocol on Matters Specific to Aircraft Equipment.[20]

The Cape Town Convention creates the framework for an 'international interest' in aircraft **33.15** and related equipment, and a charge over an aircraft is classified as an international interest for the purposes of the Convention if the agreement creating the security:

(a) is in writing;
(b) relates to an aircraft over which the chargor has power to create security;
(c) enables the aircraft to be identified in accordance with the Protocol; and
(d) provides for the identification of the secured obligations (although without any necessary requirement to state a maximum secured amount).

If a security amounts to an 'international interest' within these relatively unchallenging **33.16** parameters, then two essential consequences will follow. First of all, that interest may be registered with the International Registry. Secondly, a uniform menu of default rights must be recognized and applied throughout Contracting States.

The International Register[21] is established to record international interests and certain **33.17** other rights.[22] There are various formal requirements as to the validity and time periods allowed for registration[23] and the International Register is searchable by electronic means.[24] Competing, registered international interests (whether by way of security or otherwise) rank according to their date of registration, and any registered interest ranks ahead of an unregistered interest, regardless of the respective dates of creation.[25] The effect of a registered international interest must be recognized in any subsequent insolvency proceedings affecting the chargor.[26]

The regime of default remedies applicable to an international interest are set out in chapter **33.18** III (Articles 8–15) of the Cape Town Convention, as varied and extended by Article XI of the Protocol. These provide that, following a default by the debtor, the creditor may exercise a number of remedies including (i) taking possession of the aircraft, (ii) selling or granting a lease in respect of it, or (iii) collecting hire or other income. Article XI of the Protocol

---

[20] The Cape Town Convention was sponsored and promoted by the International Civil Aviation Organisation (ICAO) and the International Institute for the Unification of Private Law (UNIDROIT). It may be added that the Cape Town Convention also applies to security over railway rolling stock and space assets. However, these specialist areas are felt to lie beyond the scope of this work.

[21] The International Register is operated and maintained by Avarieto Ltd, a company based in Shannon, Ireland, under the supervision of the ICAO in accordance with Art 17 of the Convention.

[22] See Art 16 of the Cape Town Convention.

[23] See in particular Arts 19–21 of the Cape Town Convention.

[24] Article 22 of the Cape Town Convention.

[25] Article 29 of the Cape Town Convention.

[26] Article 30 of the Cape Town Convention. This is an obvious requirement if the Convention is to be effective. However, Art 30 acknowledges that an international interest created as a preference or in fraud of creditors can be set aside under national law, and that enforcement may be subject to procedural protections in favour of the relevant insolvency official.

adds to these remedies by allowing the charge to deregister the aircraft and to remove it from the territory in which it is physically situate.

33.19 The Cape Town Convention has come into force, having been ratified by the United States and various other countries.[27] Pending ratification by the United Kingdom, the recognition and enforcement of mortgages over foreign aircraft will continue to depend on the ordinary rules of private international law.[28]

---

[27] Although the UK is a signatory, it had not ratified the Convention at the time of writing.
[28] See the discussion on 'Foreign Aircraft', at para 33.10 above.

34

CHARGES OVER SHIPS

Introduction

Ships, like aircraft, are by their nature international pieces of equipment which will peri-odically be found in different parts of the world. However, and in contrast to the position for aircraft,[1] there is no international convention which seeks to deal with the recognition and enforcement of ship mortgages created under foreign systems of law.   **34.01**

With this point in mind, it is proposed to consider: **34.02**

(a) the regime for the creation of ship mortgages in England; and
(b) the rules of private international law applied by the English courts when considering a mortgage over a foreign vessel.

English Ship Mortgages

Before considering the specific provisions applicable to ship mortgages, it is necessary briefly to outline the rules dealing with the registration of ships in the United Kingdom. In summary: **34.03**

(a) the Registrar General of Shipping and Seamen is required to maintain a register of British ships;[2]

---

[1] See the discussion in Chapter 33 above.
[2] Section 8 of the Merchant Shipping Act 1995 ('the 1995 Act').

(b) entries in the register must reflect the requirement that property in a ship is divided into 64 shares.[3] Ownership can therefore be divided by shares, but this is only rarely encountered in practice;

(c) the register is maintained in four parts. Parts II, III and IV consist of fishing vessels, small ships, and vessels registered under the bareboat charter provisions contained in section 7 of the 1995 Act.[4] Part I of the register will therefore include larger, cargo vessels,[5] and the present section accordingly focuses on Part I;[6]

(d) a vessel may only be entered on Part I of the register if its owners are British citizens or subjects, or companies incorporated in the United Kingdom or any British possession. Persons or companies from the EEA are also eligible for these purposes;[7]

(e) where the Registrar is satisfied that a ship qualifies for registration and all appropriate documentation has been provided to him, then he is required to register it and to issue a certificate of registry.[8] Registration is generally for a period of five years, but may be renewed;[9] and

(f) a transfer of title to a registered vessel must be effected by means of a bill of sale in a prescribed form.[10] The transferee must, of course, be a person eligible to own a British ship.[11]

34.04   Schedule 1 of the 1995 Act and Part VII of the 1993 Regulations deal with the registration of ship mortgages. In particular:

(a) a ship or a share in it may be made a security for the repayment of a loan or the discharge of any other obligation;[12]

(b) the mortgage must be in a prescribed form;[13]

(c) the Registrar must enter the mortgage on the ship's register, including the date and time of registration;[14]

(d) as noted above, the registration of a vessel may expire after five years, and it would then be removed from the register. However, this does not affect the validity of any undischarged mortgage which remains on the register;[15]

---

[3] Regulation 2(5) of the Merchant Shipping (Registration of Ships) Regulations 1993 (SI 1993/3138) ('the 1993 Regulations').

[4] Section 7 provides for the registration of vessels which would not otherwise be eligible for registration but are bareboat chartered to a person who is so eligible.

[5] It will also include pleasure vessels/boats.

[6] Note that fishing vessels entered on Part II of the register can only be mortgaged if they have full registration, and small ships on Part III are outside the regime for registration of ship mortgages.

[7] For the complete list, see reg 7 of the 1993 Regulations.

[8] Regulations 36 and 37 of the 1993 Regulations.

[9] Regulations 39 and 42 of the 1993 Regulations.

[10] Regulations 43 and 44 of the 1993 Regulations. Note that this instrument is not a 'bill of sale' within the scope of the Bills of Sale Act 1878, since the definition of that expression specifically excludes 'transfers or assignments of any ship or vessel or any share thereof'. The more general effect of this legislation has been noted in relation to foreign aircraft: see para 33.12 above.

[11] See para 2, Sch 1 to the 1995 Act.

[12] See para 7(1), Sch 1 to the 1995 Act.

[13] See para 7(2), Sch 1 to the 1995 Act; reg 57 of the 1993 Regulations.

[14] See para 7(3), Sch 1 to the 1995 Act; reg 58 of the 1993 Regulations.

[15] Regulation 63 of the 1993 Regulations.

(e) in order to protect lenders from environmental liabilities, it is specifically provided that a mortgagee is not to be treated as an owner of the vessel;[16]

(f) it should be appreciated that a ship mortgage must also be lodged at Companies House within 21 days after the date of its creation, if it is created by a United Kingdom company or a foreign company which has registered a place of business in the UK;[17]

(g) the holder of a registered mortgage has power to sell the ship to recover overdue monies, but a second or subsequent mortgagee may only do so with a court order;[18]

(h) although it is not proposed to deal with the subject in detail, it should be appreciated that the security offered by a registered ship mortgage may be significantly impaired by the existence of maritime liens. These do not require registration and constitute valid, preferential claims against the vessel regardless of notice or any other matter.[19] Maritime liens include (i) wages and other amounts contractually due to the master and the crew,[20] (ii) costs incurred by the master for the benefit of the vessel and within the scope of his authority, (iii) liens for salvage, and (iv) liens covering damage for collisions.[21] There may thus be significant claims which will enjoy priority over a registered mortgage. However, the holder of a lien may lose his rights if he fails to assert them in the context of a judicial sale of the vessel[22] or if he fails to pursue them with reasonable diligence.[23] It may be noted that, so far as the English courts are concerned, whether a particular claim can be characterized as a 'maritime lien' and thus enjoys priority is determined by the law of the place of arrest of the vessel.[24]

Until the mortgagor defaults on the loan, he is entitled to exclusive possession of the vessel **34.05** and to enter into contracts relating to its use. He can do so even though these engagements will result in the creation of maritime liens which will rank in priority to the mortgage,[25] although the mortgagee may intervene if the mortgagor has no reasonable prospect of discharging those liabilities,[26] or if the action taken by the mortgagor is otherwise detrimental to the security.[27] If the mortgagee is aware of, and acquiesces in, the engagements entered into by his borrower, he does not thereby become liable for the obligations thereby assumed.[28]

---

[16] See para 10, Sch 1 to the 1995 Act. See also *Law Guarantee and Trust Society v Russian Bank for Foreign Trade* [1905] 1 KB 815 (CA); *The St George* [1926] P 217.

[17] Section 860(7)(h) of the Companies Act 2006 and reg 9(3)(h) of the Overseas Companies Charges Regulations 2009. These provisions have already been discussed at paras 27.23–27.44 above.

[18] See para 9, Sch 1 to the 1995 Act.

[19] Such liens thus remain effective even as against a bona fide purchaser of the vessel who is unaware of the lien: see *The Bold Buccleugh* (1851) 7 Moo PC 257.

[20] See generally s 41 of the 1995 Act; *The Halcyon Skies* [1977] 1 QB 14; *The Ever Success* [1999] 1 Lloyd's Rep 824; *The Turridu* [1999] 2 Lloyd's Rep 401.

[21] On the scope of this lien, see *The Rama* [1996] 2 Lloyd's Rep 281 and, in relation to oil pollution, see Part VI of the 1995 Act.

[22] *The Cerro Colorado* [1993] 1 Lloyd's Rep 58.

[23] *The Kong Magnus* [1891] P 223.

[24] ie English law, in most cases with which the English courts will be concerned: *The Halcyon Isle* [1980] 1 Lloyd's Rep 325 (PC).

[25] *Keith v Burrows* (1877) 2 App Cas 636 (HL).

[26] *The Manor* [1903] P 339.

[27] *The Heather Bell* [1901] P 272 (CA); *The Myrto* [1977] 2 Lloyd's Rep 243.

[28] *Tyne Dock Engineering Co Ltd v Royal Bank of Scotland* 1974 SLT 57.

34.06   It should be appreciated that these rules apply to security *over the vessel itself,* since the prescribed form of ship mortgage is similarly so limited. This, of itself, will not be sufficient, and a lender will also require security over:

(a) the proceeds of any insurance policies in the event of serious damage or loss;

(b) the benefit of any charter hire (or rental income); and

(c) any requisition compensation payable in the event that the vessel is appropriated for public use (eg in time of war or unrest).

34.07   This aspect of the security is usually created by means of a deed of covenant, creating security over the items just described. Since these will usually amount to assignments of payment or monetary obligations, it is important to ensure that the security is properly perfected. There are various aspects to this process:

(a) the priority of successive assignments of a chose in action is governed by the date on which notice of the security is given to the relevant obligor.[29] It is thus important that notice is given as soon as the security is taken or, at least, as soon as it becomes apparent who is obliged to make the payments concerned; and

(b) it must also be recalled that insurances may expire and may be replaced. It is therefore important for the lenders to obtain appropriate undertakings from the owner's insurance brokers to ensure that their interest is at all times noted on the applicable policies.

Priorities

34.08   A lender intending to take a mortgage over a registered vessel may lodge a 30 day priority notice with the Registrar and, if he does register a mortgage within that period, then the priority of the mortgage operates from the date of the notice (rather than that of the mortgage itself), so that it will rank ahead of any other mortgage registered on an intervening date.[30]

34.09   Subject to the procedure noted above, the priority of competing mortgages will be determined by reference to their respective dates of registration.[31]

Foreign Ship Mortgages

34.10   In general terms, an English court will only be concerned with the validity and effect of a mortgage over a foreign ship if an attempt is made to arrest and sell the vessel on its arrival into a British port.

34.11   It is not necessarily easy to reconcile the rules of private international law with some of the practicalities in this sphere. In particular, physical assets are treated as situate in the country in which they are found at any relevant time, and the validity of any transfer, mortgage, or

---

[29] ie in accordance with the rule in *Dearle v Hall* (1828) 3 Russ 1. That rule has been discussed at paras 30.09–30.12 above.

[30] Regulation 59 of the 1993 Regulations.

[31] See para 8, Sch 1 to the 1995 Act.

other dealing with that asset will be governed by the law of that place,[32] but it does not really seem to prescribe an appropriate, alternative rule for this particular class of asset. It has been suggested that a merchant ship may *at some times* be deemed to be situate at her port of registry,[33] but that this would only apply when the ship is on the high seas. The actual *situs* would apply when the vessel is in territorial waters. This may be satisfactory for some purposes, but it is not acceptable in the case of transfers of, or security over, a vessel, which will invariably be achieved at the port of registry through procedures broadly similar to those described above in relation to British ships. Thus, even if the ship is in British waters at the point of time at which a mortgage is filed in her home registry, it is submitted that the validity of the security should be determined by reference to the law of the home registry (ie and not by reference to English law as the physical *lex situs*).

This would be consistent with the corresponding position for aircraft, where nationality is governed by the law of the State of registration.[34] Despite this slight theoretical difficulty, it appears that the English courts do work by reference to the law of the place of registration in such matters. In any event, the owner/mortgagor itself, having signed the security documents, may perhaps be estopped from denying their validity and effect before the English courts.[35]   **34.12**

Enforcement of Ship Mortgages

The mortgagee has the usual duties of a secured lender when taking enforcement proceedings and seeking to realize its security.[36]   **34.13**

Nevertheless, a sale will often have to be preceded by the arrest of the vessel, and the sale will then take place under the supervision of the court (eg by means of an auction). In that event, the proceeds of sale are paid into court and the mortgagee's interest in the vessel is replaced by a corresponding charge over, or interest in, those proceeds.[37] Accordingly, subject to the prior payment of any maritime liens for which judgment may have been obtained,[38] the lender would be entitled to redeem his own mortgage and would then have to account for the surplus to subsequent mortgagees or the borrower (as the case may be). Although the sale by the court deprives the mortgagee of a degree of control over the realization process, it nevertheless has certain benefits. Since the purchaser acquires title through a court order, that title will be unimpeachable.[39] Furthermore, the mortgagee   **34.14**

---

[32] See generally Dicey, Morris & Collins, para 22-058.
[33] See preceding footnote.
[34] See Art 17 of the Chicago Convention on International Civil Aviation, noted in relation to aircraft at para 33.10 above.
[35] Although, of course, such estoppel would not apply as against an insolvency official or other creditor of the owner.
[36] On this principle, see Fisher & Lightwood, para 30.32, citing *Gulf and Fraser Fisherman's Union v Calm C Fish Ltd* [1975] 1 Lloyd's Rep 188; *Den Norske Bank AS v Acemex Management Ltd* [2003] EWCA Civ 1559.
[37] *The Queen of the South* [1968] 1 Lloyd's Rep 182.
[38] On this point, see Fisher & Lightwood, para 16.10.
[39] *The Acrux* [1962] 1 Lloyd's Rep 405.

cannot be answerable to the owner for the adequacy of the price realized as a result of the court-driven process.[40]

34.15 Recognizing the international nature of the market for assets of this kind, the court may order the sale of the vessel for a price expressed in a foreign currency[41] although, in fairness to all of the parties who may have a claim against the proceeds, this should presumably be a freely transferable and convertible currency.

34.16 As already noted, the holder of a registered ship mortgage enjoys certain powers of sale.[42] But a mortgagee who takes possession is not obliged to exercise that power at any particular point of time, especially in a depressed market which would not realize sufficient funds to redeem the mortgage in full. The mortgagee accordingly enjoys various other rights pending the sale:

(a) The lender can take control of the vessel by dismissing/appointing the master.[43]

(b) The lender is entitled to receive the payment of freight/charter hire, and to apply the proceeds in payment of expenses and the repayment of the secured debt.[44] In practice, as noted earlier,[45] the benefit of the ship's earnings will have been specifically assigned to the lender under the terms of a deed of covenant. It will therefore be necessary to give notice to the relevant obligors, if this has not already been done.

(c) The mortgagee may manage the vessel by entering into new charters and other income-earning arrangements, but must do so on a conservative basis so as not to put the asset at risk, for example, by sending it into a war zone.[46]

(d) The mortgagee will become responsible for expenses arising from the future use of the vessel,[47] although these would usually be added to the secured debt.

---

[40] As noted in other contexts, the mortgagee generally has a duty to obtain the best price reasonably obtainable when exercising his power of sale.

[41] *The Halcyon the Great* [1975] 1 WLR 515.

[42] See para 9, Sch 1 to the 1995 Act, noted at para 34.04(g) above.

[43] Fisher & Lightwood, para 29.94.

[44] Fisher & Lightwood, para 29.95, citing *The Span Terra (No 2)* [1984] 1 WLR 27.

[45] See para 34.06 above.

[46] *European and Australian Royal Mail Co v Royal Mail Steam Packet Co* (1858) 4 K&J 667, and other cases noted by Fisher & Lightwood, para 29.97.

[47] Fisher & Lightwood, para 29.96.

35

FINANCIAL COLLATERAL ARRANGEMENTS

Introduction

The preceding chapter discussed the formalities of taking security over a variety of financial **35.01** assets, including cash, shares, and bonds.

But, insofar as a charge is taken over cash or securities transferred or held in a recognized **35.02** clearing and settlement system, the security position of the charge is in some respects reinforced. As others have noted,[1] the European Commission has been concerned to manage systemic risk in such settlement systems. 'Systemic risk' refers to the fact that the insolvency of a single institution could infect the rest of the market and bring down additional institutions which, otherwise, would remain sound. This might occur, for example, if transactions settled through such systems shortly prior to a collapse could be challenged and unwound on the basis that they constituted preferences or transactions at an undervalue,[2] or under similar principles applicable in the home jurisdiction of the institution concerned. Official concerns with settlement finality may be traced back to 1974, when a German institution, Bankhaus Herstatt, collapsed after the Deutsche mark leg of a foreign exchange transaction had been completed in the morning but where, due to time differences, the US dollar payment had not gone through at the point of time at which Herstatt became insolvent and was closed.[3]

---

[1] See, for example, the very useful discussion in Goode, *Legal Problems of Credit and Security* (4th edn, Louise Gullifer, 2008), paras 6.34–6.44.

[2] On these issues, see generally Chapter 39 below.

[3] On the whole subject, see 'Settlement Finality as a Public Good in Large Value Payment Systems', ECB Working Paper Series no 506, July 2005.

35.03   The present chapter examines the two key measures introduced by the Community and which are designed to support the stability of such systems.[4]

Settlement Finality Directive

35.04   The Directive on Settlement finality in Payment and Securities Systems[5] was implemented in the United Kingdom by means of the Financial Markets and Insolvency (Settlement Finality) Regulations 1999.[6] This was the first major step in seeking to reinforce the security of payment and settlement systems. Recitals (1) and (2) of the Directive succinctly state the objectives of legislation of this kind:

(1) ... whereas the reduction of legal risks associated with participation in real time gross settlement systems is of paramount importance, given the increasing development of these systems;

(2) Whereas it is also of the utmost importance to reduce the risk associated with participation in securities settlement systems, in particular where there is a close connection between such systems and payment systems;

35.05   There is, of course, frequently a close connection between payment and securities settlement systems. In order to eliminate counterparty risk, the transfer of the securities and the cash must occur simultaneously, and must be irrevocable.[7]

Structure of the Settlement Finality Regulations

35.06   Although the present section is concerned principally with the impact of the Settlement Finality Regulations on security arrangements, it is nevertheless necessary to have an understanding of the general scope of the Regulations.

35.07   Since the Regulations are designed with a view to preserving systemic stability, it is perhaps unsurprising that the provisions of the Regulations are targeted specifically at transactions effected through systems which are regarded as important from a systemic perspective. The systems which have been designated for the purposes of the Regulations include CREST for securities settlement and CHAPS for payments.

35.08   The payment systems are considered elsewhere in this work.[8] The taking of a charge over securities in CREST has already been discussed in an earlier chapter.[9] From the perspective of a bank taking a charge over securities within CREST, Part III (Transfer Order Effected Through A Designated System and Collateral Security) is the most relevant part of the Regulations.

---

[4]   It should be appreciated that the legislation about to be discussed is both detailed and complex, and that the below commentary provides an overview only. It should be noted that an amending Directive 2009/49/EC, OJ L 146/37, 10.06.2009 extends the Settlement Finality Directive to cover the taking of collateral over receivables on loans made by banks. This reflects the wider range of collateral provided to central banks during the current financial crisis. The Directive is to be implemented into national law by 30 December 2010.
[5]   Directive 98/26, OJ L 166/45, 1998.
[6]   SI 1999/2979, as amended.
[7]   This is referred to as 'delivery versus payment' (DVP).
[8]   See generally Chapter 19 above.
[9]   See the discussion in Chapter 29 above.

Regulation 13(1) provides that the general law on insolvency applies in relation to: **35.09**

(a) transfer orders[10] effected through a designated system and action taken under the rules of a designated system with respect to such order; and

(b) collateral security.[11]

but the application of those rules is subject to, and is limited by, the other provisions of Part III.

Regulation 13(2) then states that, to the extent that Part III disapplies generally applicable **35.10** insolvency law, that disapplication extends only to:

(a) insolvency proceedings in respect of a participant in a designated system; and

(b) insolvency proceedings in respect of a provider of collateral security to a central bank in connection with its functions, insofar as the relevant proceedings affect its right to the collateral.

However, general insolvency law will apply to all issues which fall outside the scope of **35.11** (a) and (b) above, even though any other question relating to transfer orders or collateral security may arise in the course of the relevant proceedings.

These provisions do not make for easy reading but their overall objective seems to be rea- **35.12** sonably clear; a transfer of, or charge over, securities or financial collateral is to be secure in favour of the transferee or chargee, regardless of any provision of insolvency law under which it may be challenged or which might detract from its validity or value. This broad position is reinforced by the ensuing provisions of Part III of the Regulations.

Regulation 14 provides for certain rules of designated systems to prevail over general insol- **35.13** vency law. These provisions are necessary because, for example, the netting and settlement arrangements which are contractually applicable following the occurrence of insolvency might otherwise be void on public policy grounds.[12] Thus, the following matters are to be treated as valid notwithstanding any contrary rules relating to the distribution or administration of an insolvent estate:

(a) a transfer order;[13] rules of a designated system intended to limit systemic risk flowing from the insolvency or default of a participant, including rules dealing with (i) bilateral

---

[10] Insofar as it relates to securities, a 'transfer order' is an instruction by a participant in a designated system to transfer the title to, or an interest in, securities by means of a book entry in a register or otherwise: see the definition of that expression in reg 2.

[11] The expression is defined in reg 2 to include any realisable assets (including cash or securities) provided under a charge or repurchase agreement: (i) for the purpose of securing rights and obligations potentially arising in connection with a designated system; or (ii) to a central bank for the purpose of securing rights and obligations in connection with its operations in carrying out its functions as a central bank.

[12] See the decisions in *British Eagle International Airlines Ltd v Compagnie Nationale Air France* [1975] WLR 758 (HL) and the different conclusion reached by the High Court of Australia in *International Air Transport Association v Ansett Australia Holdings Ltd* [2008] HCA 3.

[13] This refers to transfer orders given prior to the onset of insolvency. Transfer orders given on the day of insolvency itself may also attract the benefit of these protections if the relevant settlement agent, central counterparty or clearing house can demonstrate that it did not have knowledge of the relevant order or other action at the time of settlement of the transfer order: see reg 20.

or multilateral netting, (ii) the closing out of open positions, (iii) the application or transfer of collateral, and (iv) the provisions of a contract for the purpose of realizing collateral in connection with the functions of a central bank;

(b) as is well known, the appointment of an administrator results in a moratorium on the enforcement of security.[14] However, these rules do not apply to the transfer or enforcement of collateral in accordance with the rules of a designated system;[15] and

(c) the claim of the participant or central bank to the relevant collateral takes priority over both the expenses of the winding up/administration and other preferential debts.[16] As a result, it should not matter whether any collateral agreement is classified as a floating charge. The effect of this provision is to ensure that the collateral arrangement is given the same priority as a fixed charge in any event.

35.14 The ensuing provisions of Part III of the Settlement Finality Regulations deal with other, important matters of detail:

(a) where collateral has been realized and any netting processes have been completed, any remaining balance can be proved in the liquidation of the obligor;[17]

(b) a liquidator is barred from disclaiming a transfer order or contract for the purpose of realizing collateral security on the basis that it constitutes onerous property;[18]

(c) the court may not make an order to adjust a transfer order or other action relating to collateral security on the basis that (i) the relevant transaction was entered into at an undervalue,[19] (ii) the transaction was a preference,[20] or (iii) the transaction defrauded creditors;[21] and

(d) various other rules applicable to the administration procedure will not apply to collateral security charges.[22]

Private International Law Issues

35.15 As is always the case, difficult legal subjects always assume an even greater degree of complexity when a cross-border angle is introduced into the equation.[23] The present topic is no exception to that rule.

35.16 For example, it has been shown that English law will allow for the enforcement of collateral held through a designated system and for the exercise of certain other rights. But what is to

---

[14] See Insolvency Act 1986, Sch B1 (as amended), paras 42–44.

[15] For the details, see reg 14(2) and Part VII of the Companies Act 1989 (applicable to market charges and system charges, the effect of which is specifically preserved by reg 13(3) of the Settlement Finality Regulations). Note, however, that the underlying debt cannot be proved in the insolvency or be subjected to insolvency set-off until the realization of the collateral or other action has been completed: reg 14(4).

[16] Regulation 14(6).

[17] Regulation 15.

[18] Regulation 16. On the liquidator's power to disclaim onerous property, see Insolvency Act 1986, s 178.

[19] ie under s 238 of the Insolvency Act 1986, on which see para 39.05 below.

[20] ie under s 239 of the Insolvency Act 1986, on which see para 39.06 below.

[21] ie under s 423 of the Insolvency Act 1986, on which see para 39.12 below.

[22] Regulations 18 and 19.

[23] For a broader discussion of the whole subject, see Ooi, *Shares and Other Securities in the Conflict of Laws* (Oxford University Press, 2003).

be the position where, for example, a UK institution provides security over collateral held in a foreign settlement system, or where a foreign institution provides a charge over securities held within CREST? It is one thing to disapply the relevant provisions of insolvency law in this type of situation, but how does one determine whether the security is intrinsically valid in the first place? As has been seen,[24] certain aspects of such matters will often be referred to the law of the place of incorporation of the entity which issued the securities in the first place, and this can be a highly inconvenient result. Systemic stability would not be aided if a multiplicity of laws had to be applied in determining whether all elements of a particular security package are valid and binding in the first instance. Happily, this issue is also addressed by the Settlement Finality Regulations.

Regulation 23 provides that, where collateral has been provided to a system participant or to a central bank and the chargor's entitlement to the securities concerned is recorded on a register, account, or centralized depositary system located in an EEA State, then the rights[25] of the system participant or central bank as holder of the collateral are governed by the law of that EEA State. A few points may be made about this provision. **35.17**

First of all, regulation 23 adopts the so-called PRIMA[26] principle, which holds that a charge over shares held in a securities account should be governed by the law of the place in which the account is maintained and—hence—where the relevant intermediary carries on business. This is consistent with general principles of private international law because, as noted earlier,[27] the source of the rights and, thus, the *situs* of the assets is the account, and not the underlying securities themselves. **35.18**

Secondly, regulation 23 provides a mandatory choice of law which is not capable of being derogated from by a contractual selection by the parties. This is logical because the regulation deals with proprietary issues and may thus affect the rights of third parties. Parties can select the law applicable to their *contractual* obligations,[28] but—given the potential impact on third parties—the law governing *proprietary* or *security* rights is generally ascertained by more objective criteria. It is, however, appropriate to note the terms of the Hague Convention on the law applicable to indirectly held securities (2002). This would, likewise, adopt the PRIMA test but would allow the parties to select the governing law provided that it has a genuine nexus with the business carried on by the intermediary.[29] It is not entirely clear whether party autonomy as to the choice of law is desirable in the field of proprietary rights, but it should be said that this mirrors the approach adopted by article 8 of the US Uniform Commercial Code.[30] It may be valuable to reproduce the relevant provisions of article 8-110 because subsection (a) deals with the law governing *directly held* securities and generally provides for the law of the State of the *issuing entity's* incorporation **35.19**

---

[24] See paras 29.12–29.14 above.
[25] This would include the essential validity of the security, the steps which may be taken on enforcement and similar matters.
[26] Place of Relevant Intermediary Approach.
[27] See para 29.20 above.
[28] On the whole subject, see Chapter 40 below.
[29] See Arts 4 and 5 of the Convention.
[30] Article 8 of the UCC was influential in the preparation of the Hague Convention, above.

to govern the rights and obligations of the parties whilst, in the case of *indirectly held* securities, subsection (b) provides for the law of the securities intermediary's jurisdiction to apply:[31]

    (a) The local law of the issuer's jurisdiction ... governs:
        (1) the validity of a security;
        (2) the rights and duties of the issuer with respect to registration of transfer;
        (3) the effectiveness of registration of transfer by the issuer;
        (4) whether the issuer owes any duties to an adverse claimant to a security; and
        (5) whether an adverse claim can be asserted against a person to whom transfer of a certificated or uncertificated security is registered or a person who obtains control of an uncertificated security.
    (b) The local law of the securities intermediary's jurisdiction ... governs:
        (1) acquisition of a securities entitlement from the securities intermediary;
        (2) the rights and duties of the securities intermediary and holder arising out of a securities entitlement;
        (3) whether the securities intermediary owes any duties to an adverse claimant to the security entitlement; and
        (4) whether an adverse claim can be asserted against a person who acquires a securities entitlement from the securities intermediary or a person who purchases a securities entitlement or interest therein from an entitlement holder.

35.20 These two subsections neatly illustrate the distinction between directly and indirectly held securities and the differing rights and obligations to which they may give rise.

35.21 The Settlement Finality Regulations also make various supplemental provisions in relation to insolvency proceedings which are designed to reinforce the rules just discussed. In particular:

    (a) where insolvency proceedings are brought in any jurisdiction in relation to a system participant, any question which falls to be determined in England in relation to that participant is to be determined in accordance with the law applicable to the system concerned.[32] In other words, the primacy of the rules created by the Settlement Finality Directive in the spheres of collateral, netting, default, and similar matters must be respected, regardless of any rule of insolvency law or other provision which might otherwise be applicable to the insolvency proceedings (eg such as the winding-up procedures in effect in the company's jurisdiction of incorporation);
    (b) various statutory provisions[33] provide for cooperation between courts and may provide for the application of insolvency law. It is specifically provided[34] that, for these purposes, 'insolvency law' includes a reference to the rules created by Part III of the Settlement Finality Regulations themselves. As a result, an English court may not give effect to a foreign rule which would operate inconsistently with the terms of Part III of the Regulations. Once again, this ensures that the provisions of the regulations are of

---

[31] The identification of the 'securities intermediary's jurisdiction' is governed by subsection (e) of Art 8-110. This allows for a degree of party selection or autonomy, but otherwise focuses on the law of the place in which the account is held or in which the intermediary carries on its business.

[32] Regulation 24.

[33] Including, in particular, s 426 of the Insolvency Act 1986.

[34] Regulation 25(1).

mandatory application, regardless of any contrary provision of any relevant foreign system of law; and

(c) provision is made for recognition by the English courts of any equivalent legislation introduced in other EEA States with a view to the implementation of the Settlement Finality Directive.[35]

Financial Collateral Regulations

The process of enhancing settlement finality was taken further by the EC Directive on financial collateral arrangements.[36] This, in turn, was implemented in the United Kingdom by the Financial Collateral Arrangements (No 2) Regulations 2003.[37] **35.22**

As has been seen, the Settlement Finality Directive was concerned principally with *systemic* risk arising from the use of payment and securities settlement systems. The Financial Collateral Regulations go further in seeking to reinforce the validity and security of collateral provided under purely bilateral arrangements, without reference to the use of any particular form of settlement system. The regulations seek to preserve and reinforce such arrangements by: **35.23**

(a) disapplying various formalities which would otherwise vitiate the security in the event of non-compliance; and

(b) disapplying various provisions of insolvency law.

The regulations apply to 'financial collateral arrangements' entered into between bodies corporate.[38] The expression 'financial collateral arrangement' includes: **35.24**

(a) a 'title transfer financial collateral arrangement' under which a collateral provider transfers to a collateral taker the legal and beneficial title to financial collateral[39] by way of security for an obligation owed to the collateral taker, on the footing that equivalent securities will be re-transferred after the obligation has been performed; and

(b) a 'security financial collateral arrangement', under which financial collateral is delivered into the possession or control the collateral taker under a security interest to secure an obligation of the collateral provider to the collateral-taker.[40]

---

[35] Regulation 25.

[36] Directive 2002/47/EC of the European Parliament and of the Council of 6 June 2002 on financial collateral arrangements, OJ L 168, 27.06.2002, p 43.

[37] SI 2003/3226, hereafter the 'Financial Collateral Regulations'. An attempt was made to challenge these regulations by means of judicial review, on the grounds that they fell beyond the scope of s 2(2) of the European Communities Act 1972, under which they were made. However, leave was refused: *R (on the application of Cukurova Finance International Ltd and another) v HM Treasury* [2008] All ER (D) 102.

[38] This requirement should be carefully noted. The regulations thus do not apply to security given by individuals or general partnerships.

[39] 'Financial collateral' includes both cash and securities: see the definition of that term in reg 3. However, under an amending Directive 2002/47/EC, OJ L 168/43, 10.06.2009, the definition will be extended to cover collateral consisting of receivables under bank loans. Member States are required to implement the Directive by 30 December 2010.

[40] Financial collateral remains in the possession or control of the collateral-taker for these purposes even though the provider has the right to substitute the collateral or withdraw any excess: see para (c) of the definition of 'security financial collateral arrangement' in reg 3. This provision ensures that an arrangement

35.25   The reference to a 'security financial collateral arrangement' probably requires no further explanation; it is a familiar form of security under which the chargor has an equity of redemption and is entitled to the return of the collateral upon the fulfilment of the underlying obligation. However, the expression 'title transfer financial collateral arrangement' perhaps requires some discussion. This refers to repurchase agreements (or 'repos') under which securities are sold on the basis that the seller will repurchase equivalent securities at a later date and at a pre-set price. The financial effect is similar to a borrowing on security although, since the purchaser acquires legal and beneficial title to the securities and can deal with them as it wishes, the seller is exposed to the risk that the purchaser may become insolvent or otherwise unable to redeliver equivalent securities.[41] Although a 'title transfer' arrangement has an effect similar to the creation of security, it would not generally be re-characterized as such.[42] In any event, this so-called 're-characterization risk' will now be of lesser importance in the specific field of financial collateral, because the regulations place both security and title transfer arrangements on the same footing.

35.26   What, then, is the effect of the Financial Collateral Regulations?

First of all, certain formalities which would otherwise operate to vitiate the financial collateral are rendered inapplicable. Specifically:[43]

(a)   where the financial collateral is given by way of guarantee, this will remain effective even though there is no memorandum of the guarantee signed by or on behalf of the guarantor;[44]

(b)   likewise, the usual requirements for the transfer of an equitable interest[45] or for a legal assignment of a chose in action[46] to be in writing and signed do not apply to financial collateral arrangements; and

(c)   the requirement for a financial collateral arrangement to be registered at Companies House is likewise stated to be inapplicable.[47]

35.27   Secondly, a financial collateral arrangement is insulated from various statutory provisions applicable to the insolvency process. In particular:[48]

---

remains within the definition even though the collateral-provider has the right to the return of his securities in return for others (which must usually have an equivalent rating and/or meet other criteria), or is entitled to withdraw some of the security, for example, on the basis that the amount of the secured obligation has fallen or the value of the securities themselves has increased. Rights of this kind are commonly seen in this type of security documentation.

[41]   In the case of a *secured* transaction, the charge should remain in possession of the relevant securities and, subject to payment, these would remain available to the chargor even though the charge became insolvent.

[42]   *Lloyds & Scottish Finance Ltd v Cyril Lord Carpet Sales Ltd* [1982] BCLC 609.

[43]   On the points about to be made, see reg 4.

[44]   The formal requirements of s 4 of the Statute of Frauds 1677 are thus rendered inapplicable. On s 4 generally, see para 26.19 above.

[45]   See s 53(1)(c) of the Law of Property Act 1925.

[46]   Section 136 of the Law of Property Act 1925.

[47]   On this requirement, see generally para 27.23 above. For the reasons given above, a 'title transfer' arrangement would not generally amount to a security interest and would thus not require registration in any event. However, in view of the point made in the text, the issue is no longer of practical importance in relation to financial collateral arrangements.

[48]   On the points about to be made, see reg 8.

(a) the moratorium against enforcement of security during administration does not apply to financial collateral arrangements;[49]

(b) a receiver appointed in respect of financial collateral may remain in office and continue managing and realizing the collateral notwithstanding the appointment of an administrator;[50] and

(c) correspondingly, the administrator's usual power to deal with charged property[51] does not apply to financial collateral.

Thirdly, various provisions allowing for the avoidance of antecedent transactions are also disapplied. Specifically: **35.28**

(a) the power of the court to avoid dispositions of property do not apply to a proprietary or security interest arising under a financial collateral arrangement, nor will it prevent the application of any close out netting arrangements provided for by the terms of the contract;[52]

(b) the Insolvency Act provision vitiating a transfer of shares effected after the commencement of a winding up does not apply where those shares are transferred under a financial collateral arrangement;[53]

(c) even if the financial collateral arrangement constitutes a floating charge over the assets of the collateral provider, the security concerned cannot be diluted by the obligation to provide a prescribed part of the floating charge assets for the benefit of unsecured creditors[54]. Likewise, the security is not available for payment of preferential debts which would otherwise enjoy priority over a floating charge;[55]

(d) a financial collateral arrangement cannot be disclaimed by a liquidator of either the collateral taker or the collateral provider;[56] and

(e) floating charges may be set aside if they are given in the period prior to insolvency for inadequate consideration. Again, however, this power cannot now be exercised in relation to a financial collateral arrangement, even if it would otherwise be categorized as a floating charge.[57]

---

[49] On this moratorium, see Insolvency Act 1986, Sch 1, paras 42–44.

[50] Such a receiver normally has to vacate office in such a situation: para 41(2) of Sch B1 to the Insolvency Act 1986.

[51] ie under the Insolvency Act 1986, Sch 1, para 2.

[52] Regulation 10(1) of the regulations, disapplying s 127, of the Insolvency Act 1986.

[53] See s 88 of the Insolvency Act 1986, disapplied in this context by reg 10(2). In practice, it is difficult to see how this provision will often need to be used. Shares offered as security in this type of arrangement will usually be dematerialized securities held in CREST or a similar system, and there will thus be no 'transfer' of the shares so far as the issuing company is concerned. On securities held via CREST, see paras 29.15–29.21 above.

[54] On this provision, see s 176A of the Insolvency Act 1986. The provision does not apply to financial collateral arrangements by virtue of reg 10(3).

[55] Section 754 of the Companies Act 2006 and reg 10(6).

[56] On the power of liquidators to disclaim onerous property, see s 178 of the Insolvency Act 1986. On its disapplication, see reg 10(4).

[57] The power of the court is contained in s 245 of the Insolvency Act 1986, on which see para 39.09 below. It is disapplied by reg 10(5).

35.29   Fourthly, close-out netting provisions[58] and the taking of collateral are to be effective against third parties provided that the party relying on such provisions or taking the security was not (and should not have been) aware of the insolvency of the collateral provider at the relevant time.[59]

35.30   The final set of provisions allows for the use and appropriation of financial collateral by the collateral taker:

(a)   under a *title transfer* financial collateral arrangement, the recipient of the collateral obtains the right to use the collateral for the purposes of its own business and at its own discretion. This necessarily follows from the fact that absolute title vests in the collateral taker. However, it had become the practice for *security* financial collateral arrangements to include a provision allowing the recipient to deal with the security in the same way. There may have been a question mark over the validity of such a provision since it may operate in a manner inconsistent with the equity of redemption. It is now specifically provided that such a provision is valid in accordance with its terms, and the collateral taker is then obliged to return equivalent securities or otherwise to provide equivalent value in accordance with the terms of the arrangement.[60] Such provisions necessarily involve a risk for the collateral provider in the event that the collateral taker becomes insolvent before returning equivalent securities;

(b)   the collateral taker can appropriate and sell financial collateral without any need to apply to court, but he must value the collateral in accordance with the terms of the arrangement and in a commercially reasonable manner, giving credit to the collateral provider as necessary.[61] The expression 'appropriate' has already received judicial consideration. Oddly, given the European origin of the regulations, this was at the hands of the Judicial Committee of the Privy Council on an appeal from the British Virgin Islands in *Cukurova Finance International Ltd v Alfa Telecom Turkey Ltd.*[62] The issue arose because security over shares of companies incorporated in that jurisdiction was expressed to be governed by English law and to be subject to the regulations. As the Privy Council observed, the regulations appear to have presupposed that a right of 'appropriation' was a pre-existing remedy under English law, whereas this was not in fact the case. The Privy Council noted that the concept of appropriation was closer to a sale than a foreclosure, in part because the regulations required the collateral taker to account for any surplus. Nevertheless, it was effectively a sale to the collateral taker

---

[58] A 'close-out netting provision' is a term of a financial collateral arrangement under which, following a default, the parties' obligations are accelerated and replaced by an obligation to pay the current value of the outstanding contracts: see the definition of the expression in reg 3. Provisions of this kind are commonly found in swap, repurchase, and similar agreements. If there is an event of default before the due date for performance, the non-defaulting party will need to enter into appropriate replacement arrangements with a third party, and the close-out provisions are designed to calculate that sum. It was necessary to provide for clauses of this kind to be effective since, otherwise, they may have the effect of re-organizing priorities of payment in insolvency, a result precluded by the decision in *British Eagle International Airlines Ltd v Cie Nationale Air France* [1975] 2 All ER 390 (HL).

[59] Regulations 12 and 13.

[60] For the details, see reg 16.

[61] On these points, see regs 17 and 18.

[62] Privy Council Appeal no 60 of 2008.

itself, based on the valuation provisions contained in the agreement. It was agreed that the act of appropriation involved the collateral taker in becoming the absolute owner of the shares in question. The issue was—had this process of appropriation been completed in the present case, given that the shares were in registered form and the collateral taker had not procured its registration in the register of members at the relevant time? Having regard to the purposes of the EU Directive from which the regulations were derived (which contemplates 'rapid and non-formalistic enforcement' of financial collateral), the Privy council held that the necessary appropriation of the shares was completed when the collateral taker gave notice of enforcement of the security to the collateral provider. No further steps were necessary to complete that process.[63]

Finally, where the financial collateral consists of book entry securities held through one or more intermediaries, the validity of those arrangements, the formalities required to perfect them and any questions relating to priorities or competing interests are to be decided by reference to the domestic law of the country in which the relevant account is maintained.[64]   **35.31**

---

[63] The time of completion of the process was important because it was necessary to determine whether this had occurred before or after an injunction had been obtained.

[64] On this point, see reg 19.

36

LIEN AND SET-OFF

Introduction

The banker's rights of lien and set-off do not generally involve a taking of security in the **36.01** manner contemplated by other chapters within this section. Yet those rights can in practice operate as a valuable form of security in the event of the customer's insolvency, and it is thus appropriate to consider them here.

Right of Lien

It is generally accepted that a bank has a lien over all securities deposited with it by its cus- **36.02** tomer.[1] It appears that the lien arises by operation of law and it will accordingly apply in every case unless the circumstances imply a contrary intention on the part of both the banker and the customer. This may be contrasted with a pledge, where a positive intention to create the security interest must exist or be apparent from the circumstances of the case.[2] In view of the distinction, it is necessary to ask whether the bank's lien implies a power of sale in relation to the shares or other securities deposited with it? It is submitted that it does not, because a power of sale should not be implied where no security interest was intended by the parties in the first instance. The point may often be theoretical in any event.

---

[1] See Paget, para 29.2, citing *Davis v Bowsher* (1794) 5 Term Rep 448 and *Brandao v Burnett* (1846) 12 Cl & Fin 787.

[2] This distinction was highlighted in *Re Cosslett (Contractors) Ltd* [1998] Ch 495 (CA), where it was noted that both a pledge and a lien involve the physical delivery of goods or securities, but a pledge involves a positive intention to create security, whilst a lien merely implies a right to retain assets originally delivered for some other purpose.

For example, if the bank is seeking to exercise a lien over share certificates, it may need a court order in order to achieve that objective since it will not hold the executed forms of transfer necessary to complete the sale.[3] In addition, the bank may have a lien over payment instruments delivered to it for collection. However, in that instance, the point will again be largely academic. Whether or not the bank has a lien over such an instrument, it will be under an obligation to collect items presented for credit to the account. Once it has undertaken that task, its lien over the instrument will mutate into a right of set-off over its proceeds (see below). It has been decided that a possessory lien may be combined with a contractual power of sale at the time when goods or securities are deposited, and that such an arrangement does not constitute a charge; rather, it remains a lien because its efficacy rests on possession and, if the bank parts with possession, the 'security' is lost.[4] Nevertheless, since the lien coupled with a power of sale does not amount to a charge, it does not require registration under section 860 of the Companies Act 2006.[5]

36.03   The general lien may be excluded either by an express agreement or by the intention of the parties as inferred from the circumstances of the case. Thus, if documents are delivered specifically for safe custody, it may be possible to infer that the lien has been excluded. However, if this is coupled with a duty for the bank to collect payments on financial securities, then it is likely that the lien will apply.[6] Likewise, if securities are deposited to cover a *specific* loan facility, it may be implicit in that arrangement that the securities are not intended to cover a *general* overdraft facility.[7] However, if the customer does not reclaim the securities following repayment of the specific facility, then it may be possible to infer that the bank's ordinary lien is again intended to apply.[8]

36.04   As a general rule, of course, the lien can only extend to property which is beneficially owned by the customer himself. Thus, if the bank knows of a third party interest in the securities at the time it receives them, then its lien will necessarily be subordinated to that interest. On the other hand, if the bank receives securities in good faith and without notice of a third party interest, then the lien will remain effective.[9]

---

[3] Contrast the position where the bank takes a charge over such instruments: see generally Chapter 29 above. The bank's lien may apply to instruments which are not readily and freely negotiable or transferable. Thus, both share certificates and deposit receipts may be subject to the lien: see respectively *Re United Services Co, Johnston's Claim* (1870) 6 Ch App 232 and *Jeffryes v Agra and Masterman's Bank* (1866) LR 2 Eq 674. In relation to title deeds to real property, the bank may retain those deeds until the outstanding obligations are paid, since that is the essence of a lien. Once again, however, it is submitted that it has no general power of sale. Apart from other considerations, the existence of such a power would be inconsistent with the provisions of s 2(1) of the Law of Property (Miscellaneous Provisions) Act 1989.

[4] See Paget, para 29.3, citing *Great Eastern Rly Co v Lord's Trustee* [1909] AC 109, *Re Cosslett (Contractors) Ltd* [1998] Ch 495 (CA) and *Re Hamlet International plc* [1999] 2 BCLC 506 (CA). The decision in *Lord's Trustee* has been approved and applied in New Zealand: see *Waitomo Wools (NZ) Ltd v Nelsons (NZ) Ltd* [1974] 1 NZLR 484.

[5] *Re Hamlet International plc* [1999] 2 BCLC 506 (CA). On registration of company charges, see para 27.23 above.

[6] *Sutters v Briggs* [1922] 1 AC 1 (HL); Paget, para 29.9.

[7] *Re Bowes, Earl of Strathmore v Vane* (1886) 33 Ch D 586.

[8] *Re London and Globe Finance Corp* [1902] Ch 416, considered by Paget at para 29.10.

[9] *Brandao v Barnett* (1846) 12 Cl & Fin 787 and *Jones v Peppercorne* (1858) John 430, noted by Paget, para 29.22.

Bank's Right of Set-off

The bank's lien applies to securities and payment instruments deposited with it for collec-   **36.05**
tion. In contrast, the right of set-off applies to credit balances on the customer's account
with the bank. In the past, it was common to refer to a bank's 'lien' over the customer's
deposits, but it is now clear that deposits are subject to a right of set-off, rather than to any
form of lien, and it is thus necessary to draw a careful distinction between the two rights.[10]
The following points may be noted in relation to the right of set-off:

(a) a bank may, without any requirement to notify the customer, combine two current
     accounts so that a credit balance on the first account extinguishes or reduces the debit
     balance on the second;[11]

(b) the usual right of set-off can be varied by the express or implied intent of the parties.[12]
     Consequently, if (for example) the bank has made a term loan to the customer to assist
     it in buying a property, and credit balances on the current account are used for the daily
     operation of the business, it will generally be an implied term that the bank will not
     combine the loan account with the current account since this will defeat the arrange-
     ments which the parties originally had in mind;[13]

(c) it has been said that the fact that the accounts are maintained in different currencies
     may be sufficient to imply an agreement excluding the general right of set-off.[14] Yet the
     fact that a multinational company needs accounts in a variety of different currencies
     does not appear sufficient to justify this conclusion. If, however, the foreign currency
     accounts are held with branches of the bank in the other countries concerned, then the
     right of set-off probably is excluded because of the attenuated nexus between the
     accounts and because the foreign accounts will be governed by different systems of law
     which may not recognize the existence of such a right;

(d) the right of set-off cannot apply where one of the accounts is held by the customer as a
     trustee and the bank is aware of that fact.[15] This point may seem obvious, but practical
     difficulties may arise. For example, the bank may be unaware of the third party interest
     when it accepts the deposit, but may only be advised of it at a later stage. Under these
     circumstances, it is submitted that the bank should be able to exercise its right of set-off
     up to the amount owing as at the date on which such notice is received;

---

[10] *Halesowen Presswork and Assemblies Ltd v National Westminster Bank Ltd* [1972] AC 785 (HL).
[11] *Garnett v McKeown* (1872) LR 8 Exch 10; *Prince v Oriental Credit Bank Corp* (1878) 3 App Cas 325
(PC); *Halesowen Presswork*, above.
[12] The same position applies in Australia: see *Inglis v Commonwealth Trading Bank of Australia* (1974) 3
ALR 19 (High Court of Australia).
[13] *Bradford Old Bank Ltd v Sutcliffe* [1918] 2 KB 833 (CA), followed in *Re EJ Morel (1934) Ltd* [1962]
Ch 21 and approved in the *Halesowen Presswork* case, above.
[14] Paget, para 29.4.
[15] *Re Gross, ex p Kingston* (1871) 6 Ch App 632; *Bank of New South Wales v Goulburn Valley Butter Co Pty
Ltd* [1902] AC 543 (PC).

(e) if the right of set-off is excluded, whether expressly or by virtue of the types of arrangements described above, then it will come to an end on the liquidation of the customer or other termination of the relationship;[16]

(f) if the bank wishes to resume its rights of set-off, then it must give notice to that effect to the customer. The bank must continue to honour cheques on the overdrawn account but it may cease to do so as soon as the notice is received by the customer. If a period of notice had to be given, then the result would be that the customer would transfer the entire credit balance to another bank, thus entirely defeating the object of the exercise;[17] and

(g) under the terms of its general right of set-off, the bank can only apply a credit balance against a debit balance which is due and payable. A bank must therefore repay an ordinary credit balance on demand and cannot retain it against a future or contingent liability of the customer.[18]

Other Rights of Set-off

36.06 Although a bank may enjoy the special rights of set-off noted above, this is not exclusive of more general rights which might be available to it. For example, a legal right of set-off may apply as between two fixed and matured debts which have arisen as between the bank and its creditor.[19] As a result, a bank which is owed money by the beneficiary of a letter of credit issued by it may be able to exercise a legal right of set-off when documents are presented under the credit for payment, at least if there is a sufficiently close connection between the credit and the beneficiary's indebtedness.[20] However, a bank is generally obliged to repay its customer on demand, and cannot refuse payment on the basis that there is an arguable case that it has a right of set-off on the basis that a person other than the account holder is the beneficial owner of the credit balance and that the bank has valid cross-claims against that person.[21] Set-off will only be permitted in this type of situation where the existence of the nominee or trust arrangements is very clear from the evidence; it will not be sufficient merely to prove that the account holder is acting as nominee for some third party, it must be shown that he is the nominee of the bank's debtor in respect of which the set-off is claimed.[22]

---

[16] *Halesowen Presswork*, above.

[17] *Halesowen Presswork*, above.

[18] *Jeffryes v Agra and Masterman's Bank* (1866) LR 2 Eq 674. The position will change in the event of insolvency: see the discussion of r 4.90 of the Insolvency Rules 1986, at para 36.07 below.

[19] *Stein v Blake* [1996] AC 243 (HL).

[20] *Hong Kong and Shanghai Banking Corp v Kloeckner & Co AG* [1989] 2 QB 514, noted by Paget, para 29.26. The bank's general right of set-off plainly could not apply in this situation, since the debt was owing by the beneficiary of the credit and not by the bank's customer (ie the applicant for the credit).

[21] *Bhogal v Punjab National Bank* [1988] 2 All ER 296 (CA) and *Uttamchandani v Central Bank of India* [1989] 133 Sol Jo 262 (CA). The two cases are discussed by Paget, para 29.27.

[22] On these points, see *Re Hett Maylor & Co Ltd* (1894) 10 TLR 412; *Saudi Arabian Monetary Authority v Dresdner Bank AG* [2004] EWCA Civ 1074 (CA).

The bank may also enjoy statutory rights of set-off in the event of the customer's insolvency. **36.07**
Rule 4.90 of the Insolvency Rules 1986[23] provides for the set-off of '… mutual credits,
mutual debts or other mutual dealings …' which occurred between the parties prior to
insolvency. The application of rule 4.90 is mandatory once the customer has gone into
insolvency proceedings[24] and, if the parties have agreed wider rights of set-off under a contractual arrangement (eg allowing set-off against liabilities of a third party), those rights will
not be enforceable in the insolvency. They would have the effect of widening the rights to
which the bank would be entitled, to the detriment of the general body of creditors, and
this would be contrary to public policy.[25] Nevertheless, that statutory right of set-off is itself
relatively broad, and extends to the rights to value and set-off against liabilities which are
merely contingent as at the date of the insolvency.[26] Thus, a bank which has issued a guarantee or documentary credit at the behest of the insolvent customer will usually be entitled
to retain the funds in the customer's account and exercise a right of set-off representing the
likely level of any demand.

Where the bank itself has become insolvent, then a guarantor of a customer's debt— **36.08**
usually, a controlling shareholder of the borrower company—whose guarantee is expressed
to be a primary obligation will be entitled to set off his obligation in that capacity against
any deposits which the bank holds from the guarantor, because the obligation under the
guarantee and the deposit will constitute 'mutual dealings' for the purposes of rule 4.90 of
the Insolvency Rules 1986.[27] If, however, the depositor has merely deposited cash with the
bank by way of third party security (ie without a personal obligation to pay), then there will
be no mutual obligations which are capable of set-off in the bank's insolvency.[28] The result
will be that the bank can instead sue the borrower itself and recover on any security which
may be available to it. It can later have recourse to so much of the charged deposit as may
be necessary but, subject to that, the guarantor has no particular right or remedy against the
bank by virtue of his status, and must prove for his deposit in the liquidation.[29] In other
words, the controlling shareholder will effectively suffer a 'double loss', in that he will lose
both the assets of his company and his charged deposit.[30]

[23] SI 1986/1925.
[24] See the decision in *Halesowen Presswork*, n 10 above.
[25] *British Eagle International Airlines Ltd v Cie Nationale Air France* [1975] 2 All ER 390 (HL).
[26] *Re Charge Card Services Ltd* [1987] Ch 150; *Stein v Blake* [1996] AC 243 (HL).
[27] *MS Fashions v Bank of Credit and Commerce International SA* [1993] Ch 425.
[28] The mere deposit of money with a bank by way of charge for a third party's obligations has the effect of
creating security in favour of the bank but, in the absence of express terms, does not impose a personal payment obligation on the depositor himself: see *Tam Wing Chuen v Bank of Credit and Commerce Hong Kong Ltd
(in liquidation)* [1996] BCLC 69 (PC).
[29] This follows from the fact that a creditor is generally entitled to exercise his remedies in such order and
manner, and at such times, as he sees fit: see *China and South Sea Bank Ltd v Tan* [1990] 1 AC 536 (PC).
[30] *Re Bank of Credit and Commerce International SA (in liquidation) (No 8)* [1998] 1 BCLC 68 (HL).

37

VITIATING FACTORS—'FINANCIAL ASSISTANCE'

Introduction

The present and the ensuing chapters consider certain company law issues which may be **37.01** relevant to a transaction involving either (i) an acquisition of shares in a company or (ii) a dealing between a company and a party related to it. The present chapter considers the rules preventing a company from financing an acquisition of its own shares, whilst Chapter 38 considers the impact of the statutory rules on dealings with directors.

Financial Assistance

Section 678(1) of the Companies Act 2006 prohibits a public company or any of its sub- **37.02** sidiaries from giving financial assistance for the purpose of the acquisition of its shares. Section 687(3) likewise prohibits the giving of such assistance after the acquisition has been completed.

The provision is often said to be related to the rules requiring the maintenance of a com- **37.03** pany's capital base for the protection of its creditors. If a company is not generally permit- ted to reduce its share capital, then it should not be permitted to circumvent that requirement by providing assistance to others for the purpose of buying its shares.[1]

---

[1] cf the rule in *Trevor v Whitworth* (1887) 12 App Cas 409; Roberts, *Financial Assistance for the Acquisition of Shares* (Oxford University Press, 2005), para 1.01. For a different approach to the subject, see *Tallglen Pty Ltd v Optus Communications Pty Ltd* [1998] NSWC 421.

37.04   The financial assistance prohibition has its origins in section 45 of the Companies Act 1929.[2] The rules have enjoyed something of a mixed press over the years, with a perception that they catch entirely unobjectionable transactions whilst, at the same time, allow scope for abuse.[3] This is not the place to attempt a wide-ranging commentary on the prohibition,[4] but it may suffice to note that those opposed to the financial assistance rules received a measure of satisfaction when their scope was significantly cut back by the terms of the Companies Act 2006.[5] The present section is naturally limited to those aspects of the financial assistance rules which may be of relevance to banks in structuring and financing transactions designed to assist in an acquisition of shares.

Scope of the Prohibition

37.05   At the outset, it is necessary to consider the precise scope of the financial assistance prohibition.

There are essentially four 'limbs' to the prohibition. The first two limbs are to be found in section 678, which deals with the acquisition of shares in *public* companies. The first two subsections read as follows:

> (1) Where a person is acquiring or is proposing to acquire shares in a public company, it is not lawful for that company, or a company that is a subsidiary of that company, to give financial assistance directly or indirectly for the purpose of the acquisition before or at the same time as the acquisition takes place.
> (2) Subsection (1) does not prohibit a company from giving financial assistance for the acquisition of shares in it or its holding company if:
>   (a) the company's principal purpose in giving the assistance is not to give it for the purpose of any such acquisition, or
>   (b) the giving of the assistance for that purpose is only an incidental part of some larger purpose of the company,
> and the assistance is given in good faith in the interests of the company.

37.06   Subsection (1) accordingly deals with the provision of assistance before or at the time of the acquisition. For convenience, this is referred to as the *'pre-acquisition prohibition'*. Subsection (2) creates an exception where the company has some other objective in view, and this will be referred to as the *'pre-acquisition exception'*.

37.07   The ensuing subsections of section 678 then provide:

> (3) Where:
>   (a) a person has acquired shares in a company, and

---

[2] The Act itself was the result of the work of the Company Law Amendment Committee (The Greene Committee, Cmnd 2657).

[3] The Jenkins Company Law Committee (1962) observed that the rules 'proved to be an occasional embarrassment for the honest without being a serious inconvenience to the unscrupulous'.

[4] For a broader discussion prepared while the Companies Bill was under debate, see Proctor, 'Financial Assistance: New Proposals and New Perspectives?' (2007) 28(1) *Company Lawyer* 3.

[5] As will be seen, the financial assistance prohibition now applies essentially to transactions involving public companies. This aspect of the prohibition had to be maintained for consistency with Art 23 of the Second Company Law Directive, 1992 OJ L 347/64.

(b) a liability has been incurred (by that or any other person) for the purpose of the acquisition,

it is not lawful for that company, or a company that is a subsidiary of that company, to give financial assistance directly or indirectly for the purpose of reducing or discharging the liability if, at the time the assistance is given, the company in which the shares were acquired is a public company.

(1) Subsection (3) does not prohibit a company from giving financial assistance if:

(a) the company's principal purpose in giving the assistance is not to reduce or discharge any liability incurred by a person for the purpose of the acquisition of shares in the company or its holding company, or

(b) the reduction or discharge of any such liability is only an incidental part of some larger purpose of the company,

and the assistance is given in good faith in the interests of the company.

Subsection (3) therefore bars the provision of financial assistance after the acquisition of **37.08** shares has taken place. This will accordingly be referred to as the '*post-acquisition prohibition*'. In parallel, subsection (4) will be referred to as the '*post-acquisition exception*.'

These two prohibitions—and the corresponding exceptions—are then mirrored in section **37.09** 679. That section prohibits both pre-and post-acquisition financial assistance given by a *public company subsidiary* for the acquisition of shares in its *private* holding company. It should be carefully noted that this provision only prohibits the provision of assistance by the subsidiary which is a public company; it does not prohibit the provision of assistance *by the private holding company itself.*[6] It is often stated that the financial assistance rules contained in the Companies Act 2006 are now restricted to public companies. This is true up to a point, but the statement risks over-simplification. An acquisition of shares in a private company can still engage the financial assistance rules if a public company subsidiary is to provide guarantees or other security for the purposes of it. Likewise, the giving of guarantees or security by a private company may conceivably have financial assistance implications if the ultimate parent is a public company. As a result, banks and their advisers must be alert to the overall group structure even where primarily concerned with an acquisition of shares in a private company.[7]

Before moving on to matters of detail, it may be appropriate to make a few general remarks **37.10** about the scope of the prohibitions reproduced and described above. In particular:

(a) the prohibitions apply only to shares. A company may thus lawfully give financial assistance to enable a purchaser to acquire assets from, or debentures issued by, the company;

(b) the prohibition in section 678 extends to the provision of financial assistance by a public company or any of its subsidiaries for an acquisition of shares in the public

---

[6] Whilst this appears at first sight to be an odd situation, it is consistent with the intention to abolish the financial assistance rules in relation to private companies, as discussed at para 37.04 above. Of course, if the parent entity were itself a public company, then the proposed assistance would fall within the scope of the prohibition in s 678.

[7] Unless the subsidiary is listed or there are other reasons why it needs to be maintained as a public company, it may be possible to avoid financial assistance problems altogether by converting the entity into a private company before any assistance is given for the purposes of an acquisition.

company. The reference to a 'public company' plainly means a public company incorporated in the UK.[8] In principle, references to a 'subsidiary' include any body corporate—domestic or foreign—over which the public company has control.[9] However, it has been decided that, in this particular context, the expression is confined to entities incorporated in the United Kingdom. This follows from the fact that matters such as corporate governance, capital maintenance and similar issues are governed by the law of the country of incorporation, and there is a presumption against legislation having extra-territorial effect;[10]

(c) whether assistance is being given '… for the purposes of …' a share acquisition is a question which must involve an inquiry into the subjective intentions of the directors, and it is obviously necessary to establish a nexus between the financial assistance and the acquisition.[11] The prohibition will apply if the directors intend to assist the acquisition, even though they may have several other objectives in view.[12] However, the prohibition will not apply where the company is entering into a transaction or incurring a liability for a bona fide purpose unconnected with an acquisition of its own shares;[13] and

(d) it has been said that financial assistance will contravene the prohibition if it has the effect of '… smoothing the path …' for the purchaser to complete the transaction,[14] that is, it will then be treated as given '… for the purpose of …' the acquisition.

37.11 It must nevertheless be said that, on a plain reading, the basic financial assistance prohibitions are not easy to follow. It may help to put some flesh on the bones if the meaning of the expression 'financial assistance' is explored in more depth. It will then be possible to move on to exemptions and other matters.

---

[8] See the definition in s 4(2) of the 2006 Act.

[9] See the definition in s 1159 of the 2006 Act. Curiously, it seems that an entity may not be regarded as a 'subsidiary' for these purposes if its shares have been charged to a lender by way of a legal mortgage, such that the shares have been registered in the name of the bank or its nominee, since the chargor no longer has the requisite degree of control. On the mechanics for the creation of a legal charge over shares, see Chapter 29 above and, for the wider point just made, see *Enviroco Ltd v Farstad Supply A/S* [2009] EWCA Civ 1399 (CA).

[10] See *Arab Bank plc v Mercantile Holdings Ltd* [1994] Ch 71; *AMG Global Nominees (Private) Ltd v SMM Holdings Ltd* [2009] EWHC 221 (Ch). It should however, be appreciated that the public company or relevant subsidiary could not 'downstream' cash or assets to the foreign subsidiary in order to enable it to provide the assistance, for the UK entity would thereby provide financial assistance indirectly for the purposes of the acquisition.

[11] See *Rockyana Lodge Ltd v Sternberg* [1999] NZCA 294 at para 29 (New Zealand Court of Appeal); *Dyment v Boydon* [2005] 1 BCLC 163 (CA).

[12] *Robert Chaston v SWP Group plc* [2002] EWCA Civ 1999 (CA).

[13] The point was made in *Belmont Finance Corp v Williams Furniture Ltd* [1980] 1 All ER 380. See also the decision of the Singapore Court of Appeal in *Intraco Ltd v Multi Pak Singapore Ltd* [1995] 1 SLR 313 and the Australian decision in *Sterileair Pty Ltd v Papallo* (1998) 29 ASCR 461 (Federal Court of Australia).

[14] *Robert Chaston v SWP Group plc* [2002] EWCA Civ 1999 (CA). For similar remarks, see also the 'facilitation' test referred to in *Re National Mutual Royal Bank* (1990) 3 ASCR 94.

'Financial Assistance'

The expression 'financial assistance' is given a fairly detailed definition.[15] The term **37.12** includes:

(a) financial assistance given by way of gift;[16]

(b) financial assistance given by way of guarantee, security, or indemnity;

(c) financial assistance given by way of a loan or other agreement under which any of the obligations of the person giving the assistance are to be fulfilled at a time when any obligation of the other party to the agreement remains unfulfilled; and

(d) any other financial assistance given by a company which has no net assets or whose net assets are reduced to a material extent as a result of providing the assistance.

It may be noted at the outset that each aspect of the definition has two 'heads'. For example, **37.13** under the provision noted in (c) above, an act only constitutes 'financial assistance' for the purposes of the Act if it is both:

(a) financial assistance; *and*

(b) given by way of a loan or similar agreement.

It will generally be relatively easy for the lawyer to determine whether a particular arrange- **37.14** ment amounts to a 'loan agreement.' But does that arrangement also amount to 'financial assistance' for the purpose of the definition? In *Charterhouse Investment Trust Ltd v Tempest Diesels Ltd*,[17] the court noted that the expression 'financial assistance' was a commercial expression which had no defined commercial meaning,[18] but that financial assistance would normally fall into one of two categories:

(a) in the first category are transactions which have the effect of placing funds in the hands of the purchaser to enable him to complete the acquisition. Thus, in relation to paragraph (c) above, a loan made by the company[19] to assist the purchaser will amount to 'financial assistance' even though the loan may have been made on terms favourable to the company itself. On the other hand, it is also clear that a purchase of assets by the company designed to enable the vendor of those assets to acquire shares in the

---

[15] See s 677 of the 2006 Act. It should be emphasized that the summary which follows is not complete, and has been edited to highlight only those aspects which are likely to be relevant to banking transactions.

[16] A transaction effected at a discount may be a gift by the company to the extent of the shortfall in the consideration: *Gradwell Pty Ltd v Rostra Printers Ltd* 1954 4 SA 419(A).

[17] [1986] BCLC 1.

[18] The decision in *Charterhouse* has been approved on a number of subsequent occasions; see, for example, *Robert Chaston v SWP Group plc* [2002] EWCA Civ 1999 (CA), *British & Commonwealth Holdings plc v Barclays Bank plc* [1996] 1 BCLC 1 (CA), *MacNiven (Inspector of Taxes) v Westmoreland Investments Ltd* [2003] 1 AC 311 (HL) and *TFB (Mortgages) Ltd v Anglo Petroleum Ltd* [2006] EWHC 258. For a recent decision which also applies *Charterhouse* and demonstrates a pragmatic approach to the whole subject, see *Corporate Development Partners LLC v E-Relationship Marketing Ltd* [2007] EWHC 436 (Ch).

[19] The language reproduced in (c) above is apt to embrace a loan made *by* the company. A loan made *to* a company in conjunction with a transaction involving the acquisition of its shares does not involve the giving of financial assistance even though the company has to repay the loan, with interest, at a later date: *Sterileair Pty Ltd v Papallo* (1998) 29 ASCR 461 (Federal Court of Australia), approved in *MT Realisations Ltd v Digital Equipment Co Ltd* [2003] BCC 415 (CA).

company is 'financial assistance' in the general sense, even though effected at fair value.[20] However, since 'financial assistance' is now more closely in an overall sense,[21] it would seem that such a transaction could only infringe the prohibition if it resulted in a reduction in the net assets of the company—that is to say, it is effected at a price which exceeds the fair value of the assets concerned;[22]

(b) in the second category are transactions not involving the provision of cash by the company direct to the purchaser. In such a case, the company may only be said to provide financial assistance if it has made a 'net transfer of value' which will have the effect of reducing the overall purchase price payable by the buyer.[23]

37.15 At the risk of stating the very obvious, it should also be appreciated that a transaction only amounts to financial assistance if (i) it constitutes 'assistance' and (ii) that assistance is of a 'financial' character. A few points may perhaps be derived from these obvious propositions:

(a) 'assistance' connotes a voluntary act on the part of the company. Thus, if the company owes a debt which is due and payable, the repayment of that money to enable the creditor to buy shares in the company does not amount to 'assistance' because the company is obliged to make the payment in any event;[24]

(b) assistance is only likely to be 'financial' if it involves some form of monetary cost to the company.[25] Thus, if a target company acting in good faith gives representations as to its business condition to the intending purchaser or to his financier, those representations may be said to *induce* the purchaser to enter into the transaction but they do not *financially assist* the deal;[26] and

(c) there is no requirement that the purchaser of the shares must himself be the recipient of the assistance. For example, the financing bank may be the recipient of security

---

[20] A point affirmed by decisions on earlier forms of the prohibition: see, for example, *Belmont Finance Corp v Williams Furniture Ltd* [1980] 1 All ER 380; and the Australian decisions in *Saltergate Insurance Co v Knight* [1982] 1 NSWLR 369; *Independent Steels Pty Ltd v Ryan* [1990] VR 247; *Wambo Mining Corporation v Wall Street (Holdings) Pty Ltd* [1998] NSWSC 448.

[21] See the categories defined in (a)–(d) in para 37.12 above.

[22] Compare the decision of the Singapore Court of Appeal in *Intraco Ltd v Multi Pak Singapore Ltd* [1995] 1 SLR 313, holding that a transaction effected by the company in good faith did not infringe the prohibition even though the counterparty used the proceeds to purchase shares in the company.

[23] Usually, this will occur by the company making a transfer of assets to the vendor, so that the price payable by the purchaser is thereby reduced. Even here, however, some care is necessary, since it may be legitimate to reorganize the business so that it is in a shape acceptable to the purchaser: see *Gradwell Pty Ltd v Rostra Printers Ltd* 1954 4 SA 419(A).

[24] See the discussions in *Armour Hick Northern Ltd v Whitehouse* [1980] 1 WLR 1520 and *Gradwell Pty Ltd v Rostra Printers Ltd* 1959 (4) SA 419(A) (South African Appellate Division), especially at 426 and, for a decision to similar effect, see *MT Realisations Ltd v Digital Equipment Co Ltd* [2003] BCC 415 (CA). Of course, if the relevant debt is not currently due and payable, then the company may be said to give 'assistance' if it agrees to the voluntary acceleration of the maturity date under circumstances where it is not obliged to do so.

[25] *Catley v Herbert* [1988] 1 NZLR 606 (New Zealand Court of Appeal).

[26] This is so even though any breach of the representations may result in a financial liability on the part of the target company to the purchaser: see *British & Commonwealth Holdings plc v Barclays Bank plc* [1996] 1 All ER 381; *Burton v Palmer* [1980] 2 NSWLR 878. This case law perhaps needs to be treated with some caution in the light of the subsequent decision in *Robert Chaston v SWP Group plc* [2002] EWCA Civ 1999 (CA); see in particular para 44.

granted by the target company to support the acquisition by the purchaser but the creation of that security will still engage the financial assistance prohibition.[27]

'Larger Purpose' Exemption

Having considered the general scope of the financial assistance rules, it is now possible to consider the relevant exemptions. **37.16**

The terms of the pre-acquisition exemption and the post-acquisition exemption have already been set out.[28] In summary, these exceptions will apply if (i) in giving the assistance, the company has a wider purpose in view or the assistance is an incidental part of some larger purpose of the company and (ii) the assistance is given in good faith in the interests of the company. **37.17**

In either case, there must be a purpose in view which goes beyond the mere acquisition of the shares themselves. Thus, if the company gives assistance to enable one joint venture partner to buy out another in order to resolve a deadlock between them, this will be unlawful because the *purpose* of the assistance is to facilitate an acquisition of shares in the company itself. The fact that there is a perfectly valid *reason* for providing the assistance is not sufficient to bring the exceptions into operation.[29] Some of the circumstances under which the pre-and post-acquisition exceptions may be relevant are illustrated by the examples given later in this section.[30] **37.18**

The requirement that the assistance must be given in good faith in the interests of the company must not be overlooked. Given the reference to the 'interests of the *company*', it must be shown that the company giving the assistance has some interest in the transaction at hand; it is not sufficient that the transaction suits the interests of its parent company or other members of the same group. Whether or not the assistance is given in good faith involves an inquiry into the motives and intentions of the directors,[31] but it is difficult to see how the test can be satisfied if the transaction has an adverse impact on the solvency of the company.[32] **37.19**

Other Exemptions

Aside from the 'larger purpose' exemption, the 2006 Act creates various other exceptions to the financial assistance prohibition. The main exceptions likely to be of relevance to a lending bank include: **37.20**

---

[27] For examples, see *EH Dey Pty Ltd v Dey* (1966) VR 464; *Evrard v Ross* 1977 (2) SA 311; *R v Herholdt* 1957 (3) SA 236; *Robert Chaston v SWP Group plc* [2002] EWCA Civ 1999 (CA).
[28] See paras 37.05–37.08 above.
[29] This important distinction between the purpose of financial assistance and the reason for it lie at the heart of the decision in *Brady v Brady* [1989] AC 755 (HL).
[30] See the illustrations given at paras 37.25–37.27 below.
[31] *Brady v Brady* [1989] AC 755 (HL).
[32] *Plaut v Steiner* (1989) 5 BCC 352.

(a) The payment of a lawful dividend[33]—that is to say, a dividend lawfully paid out of profits available for that purpose.[34] It will often be the case that a company has sufficient distributable profits to pay a dividend, but does not have sufficient ready cash for that purpose. It will accordingly need to draw on bank facilities for that purpose.[35] If the company has to give a charge over its assets to the lender for that purpose and the company is aware that one of the recipients will use the proceeds to acquire shares in the company from a third party, does this constitute financial assistance under the 'guarantee, security, or indemnity' heading?[36] It is submitted that this question must be answered in the negative. If the primary transaction—the payment of the dividend—is lawful, then a secondary transaction designed to raise the finance for it must likewise be lawful and cannot contravene the financial assistance prohibition. Thus, in *Re Wellington Publishing Co Ltd*,[37] a dividend payment was financed by means of security arrangements of this type, and that aspect of the matter appears to have gone unchallenged.[38]

(b) A payment made by a company to effect a reduction of capital or to complete a redemption or purchase of shares in the manner allowed by the 2006 Act does not contravene the financial assistance prohibition.[39] Once again, a bank could be called upon to finance a transaction of this nature and may require security for it. It would appear that the principles discussed in (a) above would apply equally to the funding of such a transaction, again with the result that neither the provision of the loan nor the taking of the security would be taken to contravene the prohibition.

(c) Finally, a company whose ordinary business includes money lending does not contravene the prohibition if it lends money in the ordinary course of business and the

---

[33] Section 681(2)(a) of the 2006 Act.

[34] If there are any circumstances in which a dividend is paid out of non-distributable or fictitious profits, then it is submitted that the company only contravenes the prohibition when the dividend is paid, and not merely when it is declared: see the South African decision in *Novick v Comair Holdings* [1979] (2) SA 116.

[35] For present purposes, it is assumed that the company negotiates a facility for the specific purpose of the dividend. If, however, it merely draws on a secured facility previously made available to it by its bank for general business purposes, the existence of the security will not lead to a breach of the financial assistance prohibition because it will not have been given 'for the purpose of' the acquisition of its shares.

[36] See part (b) in para 37.12 above.

[37] [1971] NZLR 133.

[38] Further support for the view that secondary transactions or funding arrangements of this nature do not contravene the financial assistance prohibition may be derived from *Gradwell Pty Ltd v Rostra Printers Ltd* 1959 (4) SA 419(A) (raising funds and giving security to fund an immediately repayable debt do not constitute financial assistance) and *TFB (Mortgages) Ltd v Anglo Petroleum Ltd* [2006] EWHC 258, where the court observed that 'if it is lawful for the company to repay its own indebtedness and there is a genuine commercial justification, it must also be lawful for the company to assist that repayment by providing security'. To the contrary effect, see *Re Hill & Tyler Ltd (in administration)* [2005] 1 BCLC 41, where the court held that, whilst a loan raised by a company did not constitute financial assistance, security given for that loan could breach the prohibition. But in creating the security, the company is raising funds for its own use and, notwithstanding comments to the contrary in the *Robert Chaston* case (n 12 above), it is a misuse of language to suggest that a company can give financial assistance to itself. By its very nature, assistance is something which one gives to another person. It is respectfully submitted that the views expressed in *Gradwell* and *TFB* are to be preferred.

[39] See s 681(2)(c) and (d) of the 2006 Act.

borrower happens to use those funds to acquire shares in the company.[40] There is an element of conditionality to the exemption, in the sense that a lender which is a public company[41] must have net assets[42] which are not reduced by the provision of the assistance or, to the extent to which they are so reduced, the assistance is provided out of distributable profits. This particular provision is problematic. It is difficult to see how a loan is made in the 'ordinary course' of the lender's business if it is designed specifically to finance an acquisition of shares in the lender itself.[43] The exception may perhaps be taken to confirm that a bank which makes available a general overdraft facility does not infringe the financial assistance prohibition merely because the borrower happens to use a part of the proceeds to buy shares in the bank itself, but this would not amount to a contravention in any event since the facility is not made available '… for the purpose of …' the acquisition.[44] In view of these difficulties, a bank should not rely on this exemption in providing finance to its customers.

Consequences of Breach

Having provided a brief overview of the financial assistance rules, it is necessary to examine their practical relevance in banking transactions. Why should a bank be concerned with the financial assistance prohibition in relation to transactions funded by it? It is suggested that there are three main reasons. **37.21**

First of all, for general and reputational reasons, the bank would not wish to become involved in funding a transaction which may be tainted with illegality. **37.22**

Secondly, contravention of the financial assistance prohibition involves the commission of a criminal offence, principally on the part of the company and any of its officials involved in the transaction.[45] However, bank officials who knowingly assist in the financing of an unlawful transaction may be guilty of associated offences such as conspiracy, or aiding and abetting. It hardly needs to be stated that this type of consequence is to be avoided. **37.23**

Finally, a breach of the prohibition may have an adverse impact on the legality and enforceability of the bank's facility and security arrangements. This has in practice proved to be the major issue for lenders, and it may be helpful to note the following points: **37.24**

---

[40] Section 682(2)(a) of the 2006 Act. It should be added that s 682(2) creates a number of other exceptions relating to employee share schemes and similar arrangements. These will not normally be of relevance in a banking context and they are thus left out of account for present purposes.

[41] That is to say, a public company whose own shares are being acquired for the purposes of s 678, or a public company assisting an acquisition of shares in its private holding company for the purposes of s 679. If the lender is a private company, the exemption is only relevant if it is assisting an acquisition of shares in its public company parent for the purposes of s 678 since, otherwise, the prohibition would not be applicable at all.

[42] On the meaning of 'net assets' for these purposes, see s 682(3) and (4) of the 2006 Act. In assessing the impact of a transaction on the net assets of a company, it is necessary to take into account not only the costs of the transaction but also any benefits derived from it: *Parlett v Guppys (Bridport) Ltd* [1996] 2 BCLC 34 (CA). In the normal course, a lending transaction would have no impact on net assets on the date it is made, since the outgoing cash is replaced by a loan asset of equivalent value.

[43] See *Steen v Law* [1964] AC 287 (PC).

[44] ie the facility would not be caught by s 678 (1) in the first instance.

[45] Section 680 of the 2006 Act.

(a) As noted above, a contravention of the financial assistance rules constitutes a criminal offence. However, the 2006 Act is silent as to the civil consequences of such a contravention.

(b) After some initial uncertainty on the subject,[46] it was established that a transaction effected in contravention of the financial assistance prohibition was void and unenforceable.[47] Thus, in *Heald v O'Connor*,[48] the claimant sold its shares in a company to the defendant. Part of the purchase price was left outstanding as a loan and the company gave a debenture to the claimant by way of security for the repayments. This arrangement transparently contravened the prohibition and was held to be void as a consequence. This decision has been assumed to be correct in two subsequent cases in the House of Lords,[49] and must therefore be taken to be definitive notwithstanding the earlier decisions to contrary effect.

(c) In *Heald v O'Connor*, it was plain that the lender knew of the factual circumstances[50] of the transaction—it was not only the lender but also the vendor shareholder. That it was aware of the facts giving rise to the contravention was beyond dispute and the point is not even mentioned in the judgment. The position of a bank lender would normally be the same if it is providing facilities and taking security in full knowledge of the relevant background and intended share acquisition. But a bank which provides a general overdraft facility and takes security will remain entitled to enforce its rights if—unknown to the bank—the company unlawfully lends part of the proceeds to a third party to enable it to purchase shares in the company itself.[51]

(d) It may be noted that the courts may under some circumstances enforce parts of the commercial arrangements even though other aspects may infringe the financial assistance prohibition.[52]

---

[46] See, for example, the decisions in *Spink (Bournemouth) Ltd v Spink* [1936] Ch 544 and *Victor Battery Co Ltd v Currys Ltd* [1946] 2 Ch 242.

[47] *Selangor United Rubber Estates Ltd v Cradock (No 3)* [1968] 2 All ER 1073, which also established that the directors who sanctioned the transaction will generally have acted in breach of fiduciary duty and may be made personally liable for any resultant losses. See also the decision of the Malaysian Supreme Court in *Kidurong Land Sdn Bhd v Lim Gaik Hua* [1990] 1 MLJ 485.

[48] [1971] 2 All ER 1105.

[49] *Brady v Brady* [1989] AC 755; *Neilson v Stuart* 1991 SC (HL) 22. See also the decision to similar effect in *Re Hill & Tyler (in administration)* [2005] 1 BCLC 41. Courts in other countries have likewise concluded that contracts entered into in breach of the prohibition are void: see, for example, the South African decisions in *Vernon v Schoeman* 1978 (2) SA 305 and *Lipschitz v UDC Bank Ltd* 1979 SA (1) 789. Even if neither of the parties plead the illegality, it would appear to be incumbent on the court to raise the issue of its own motion if necessary, since the court cannot allow its process to be used for the enforcement of illegal contracts.

[50] In dealing with the contractual consequences of illegality, it should be appreciated that it is the parties' knowledge of the factual circumstances giving rise to the contravention which is relevant—not their knowledge of the precise legal position: see Chitty, para 16-012.

[51] In other words, an apparently lawful facility granted by the bank does not become unenforceable merely because the borrower intends covertly to use it for an unlawful purpose: see Chitty, para 16-011, citing *Bank fur Gemeinwirtschaft AG v City of London Garages Ltd* [1971] 1 WLR 149 and *Credit Lyonnais v PT Barnard Associates* [1976] 1 Lloyd's Rep 557, both cases involving a unilateral breach of UK exchange control regulations by one party.

[52] ie by application of the doctrine of severance: see *Carney v Herbert* [1985] 1 All ER 438; *Neilson v Stuart* 1991 SC (HL) 22. It is, however, difficult to see how this principle could protect a bank which had accepted guarantees and security when it knew of the factual circumstances giving rise to the breach.

Illustrative Transactions

The above discussion has noted certain types of transactions which may—or may not— **37.25** contravene the financial assistance prohibition. Yet the occasionally obscure nature of the statutory provisions does mean that prohibited transactions may sometimes be difficult to identify in practice. Nevertheless, for the reasons given in the preceding section, banks must exercise vigilance in this area.

In an effort to illustrate the possible pitfalls and the operation of selected exemptions, it is **37.26** proposed to offer and to analyse an admittedly rather artificial factual scenario, as follows:

(a) Bidco, a private company, is a wholly-owned subsidiary of Parentco, a public company whose shares are listed on the London Stock Exchange;
(b) Bidco has launched a takeover offer for another company, Targetco, which is likewise a public company listed on the London Stock Exchange;
(c) Targetco has encountered serious financial problems, and the takeover offer is thus in the nature of a rescue operation which has been approved by the Targetco board and recommended to its shareholders;
(d) if they accept the takeover offer, Targetco shareholders will receive, for each Targetco share, a combined consideration of (i) 10 pence and (ii) two Parentco shares;
(e) in order to fund the cash consideration, Bidco has arranged a facility with Z Bank. It has been agreed that the facility will be secured by (i) a guarantee by Parentco, (ii) a charge by Bidco over the acquired shares in Targetco, and (iii) a fixed and floating charge to be granted by Targetco over its entire assets and undertaking following completion of the acquisition;
(f) one year following the acquisition, Bidco wishes to dispose of 20 per cent of the Targetco shares to a prospective joint venture partner, but without repaying any of the funding associated with the original acquisition. Z bank agrees to this on condition that Bidco provides a fixed charge over commercial premises owned by it;
(g) six months later, X bank offers to refinance the Z Bank debt on cheaper terms, but will require an identical security package.

What are the financial assistance implications of each of these steps, both for the companies **37.27** involved and for the funding banks? The following points may be noted:

i. The Parentco guarantee is given to enable Bidco to mount its takeover offer for Targetco. Under the terms of that offer, accepting shareholders will acquire shares in Targetco itself. It has already been shown that the granting of such security can constitute financial assistance even if it is given to a person other than the purchaser.[53] It is therefore pertinent to enquire whether the guarantee infringes the prohibition. It is submitted that it does not, because the assistance is but an incidental part of Parentco's larger purpose in ensuring the acquisition of Targetco by its own subsidiary, Bidco. As a result, the pre-acquisition

---

[53] See para 37.15(c) above.

exception[54] will apply to the Parentco guarantee.[55] That document will therefore remain enforceable by Z Bank notwithstanding that it did indirectly facilitate the acquisition of Parentco shares by accepting Targetco shareholders.

ii. Bidco is itself a private company but it is a subsidiary of Parentco—a public company. It is also engaging in transactions which will indirectly assist accepting Targetco shareholders to acquire Parentco shares pursuant to the offer. The two main activities of Bidco in this context are (a) the raising of finance from Z Bank and (b) the creation of security over the acquired Targetco shares. It has already been shown that the raising of a loan by Bidco itself does not engage the financial assistance prohibition.[56] In addition, the creation of security over Targetco shares should not engage the prohibition, because the security is given in respect of Bidco's own liability. But even if the prohibition does apply in principle, the pre-acquisition exemption will preserve the validity of the security because it is given in the context of Bidco's larger objective of acquiring Targetco.[57]

iii. Upon successful completion of the takeover offer, Z Bank seeks a debenture from Targetco, in accordance with the agreed financing terms.

iv. Targetco remains a public company at this point, and its shares have just been acquired by Bidco. The requested security would have the effect of providing financial assistance for the purpose of reducing or discharging a liability associated with the acquisition of Targetco's own shares. Even though the *reason* for the acquisition was to rescue Targetco from its own financial difficulties, the overall *purpose* remains the acquisition of Targetco shares. Accordingly, and by parity of reasoning with the decision in *Brady v Brady*,[58] the post-acquisition exception cannot apply at this point. It accordingly remains unlawful for Targetco to provide the requested security at this juncture.

v. In due course, Targetco is de-listed from the Stock Exchange and converted into a private company.[59] At that point, it will become lawful for Targetco to provide the required security to reduce the liabilities associated with the original acquisition of its shares, since the prohibition against the provision of post-acquisition financial assistance[60] only applies '… if, at the time the assistance is given, the company in which the shares were acquired is a public company…'. Since Targetco is now a private company, the post-acquisition prohibition no longer applies.

vi. There is, however, a slight twist in this story, in that the Targetco security may also be said to reduce or discharge liabilities associated with an acquisition of Parentco—now

---

[54] See para 37.06 above.

[55] This does, of course, assume that the second part of the test—that the assistance is given in good faith in the interests of the Parentco—is also met. But this should not prove to be controversial once it has been decided that the acquisition of Targetco is in the best interests of Parentco itself.

[56] See para 37.14(a) above.

[57] In other words, the considerations outlined in (i) above will again apply in this context.

[58] [1989] AC 755 (HL). The decision has been noted at para 37.18 above.

[59] This conversion process inevitably takes some time, because some shareholders may not accept the offer and it will be necessary compulsorily to acquire their Targetco shares under the 'squeeze out' procedure set out in ss 979–982 of the 2006 Act. A special resolution is in any event required to achieve the conversion of Targetco to a private company (see the conversion procedure set out in s 97 of the 2006 Act) and a period of notice will thus be required whilst minority Targetco shareholders remain in place.

[60] See s 678(3) of the 2006 Act, reproduced at para 37.07 above.

Targetco's own parent—and not merely liabilities associated with the acquisition of shares in Targetco itself. Parentco remains a public company, and any security given by Targetco as a subsidiary may thus in principle be caught by the post-acquisition prohibition. Although the argument appears strange, it is submitted that the creation of the security by Targetco is for the principal purpose of securing the debt incurred by Bidco for the purpose of acquiring Targetco, and any assistance which may be said to be given with respect to the acquisition of Parentco shares by Targetco shareholders is but an incidental part of Targetco's larger purpose. In other words, the post-acquisition exception is again applicable in this context.

vii. Bidco later wishes to give further security to Z Bank in return for a release of the charge over 20 per cent of its Targetco stake, which it now wishes to sell. In order to induce Z Bank to release that security, Bidco executes a charge over a commercial property in favour of Z Bank. The execution of the new security may be said to reduce or discharge liabilities associated with the acquisition of Parentco shares by Targetco shareholders pursuant to the offer. However, Bidco's principal purpose in creating that security is to arrange the release of the share security to enable Bidco to realize the value of 20 per cent of its Targetco stake. This represents a larger purpose of Bidco, with the result that the post-acquisition exception will again apply.

viii. What is the position when X Bank offer to refinance the facility at a reduced price and Parentco, Bidco, and Targetco wish to replicate the security package in favour of X Bank? As has been shown, the principal purpose of the Z Bank financing was to enable the acquisition of the shares in Targetco, not to facilitate the acquisition of shares in Parentco by accepting Targetco shareholders. Given the objectives of the original Z Bank financing, it is submitted that the same principles (including the post-acquisition exception) would apply equally to the replacement arrangements made by the three group entities involved. Once again, therefore, the revised financing arrangements would not infringe the financial assistance prohibition.

38

TRANSACTIONS BETWEEN COMPANIES AND THEIR DIRECTORS

Introduction	38.01
Substantial Property Transactions	38.03
Transactions involving Directors	38.06

Introduction

Banks must exercise some care when invited to fund transactions between a company and one of its directors, or a person connected with such a director. **38.01**

The Companies Act 2006 contains a number of provisions designed to enforce the principle of fair dealing as between a company and its directors. Many of these provisions will have only limited relevance to a bank which is called upon to finance a transaction, and they are thus ignored for present purposes.[1] Two aspects do, however, require brief consideration. **38.02**

Substantial Property Transactions

Section 190(1) of the 2006 Act prohibits a company[2] from entering into an arrangement under which it is to sell to, or acquire from, a director of the company or a holding company, or any connected person any substantial non-cash asset.[3] For these purposes, a 'substantial non-cash asset' is an asset the value of which (i) exceeds £100,000 or (ii) exceeds £5,000 *and* represents more than 10 per cent of the company's asset value.[4] The company **38.03**

---

[1] It will, however, always be necessary to take account of the directors' fiduciary duties. Some relevant aspects of these duties have already been considered at paras 26.49–26.53 above.

[2] Note that the section only applies to companies incorporated in the UK—a point confirmed by s 190(4)(a) of the 2006 Act.

[3] Note that the section deals with the acquisition of '*non-cash assets*'. Consequently, where a bank lends money to a director to enable him to subscribe shares in the company, the section does not apply. The director acquires shares in the company, but these represent a *liability* of the company, rather than an *asset*. Likewise, the company acquires an asset from the director, but this will be a *cash* asset.

[4] On the valuation of a company's assets, see s 191(3) of the 2006 Act. The classification and valuation of non-cash assets is not always a straightforward matter: see *Micro Leisure Ltd v County Properties and Developments Ltd (No 2)* 1999 SLT 1428 and *Ultraframe (UK) Ltd v Fielding* [2005] EWHC 1638 (Ch).

can only enter into such an arrangement if it has been approved by a resolution of the members or is conditional on such approval being obtained.[5]

38.04   A few points may be made about this section:[6]

(a)   Section 190(1) prohibits both direct and indirect transactions between a company and its directors and directors of its holding company. It also prohibits transactions with persons connected with such directors.[7] Some care is therefore necessary in this area since it may not always be immediately apparent—at least to a bank approached for finance—that the proposed transaction may fall within the scope of section 190.

(b)   Where the proposed transaction involves a director of the holding company, approval of the members of that company is also required, at least if the company is incorporated in the United Kingdom.[8]

(c)   No approval is required on the part of an entity which is a wholly-owned subsidiary of another body corporate.[9] Consequently, where the company entering into the arrangement is a wholly-owned subsidiary, no shareholder approval is required at that level. However, if it is entering into a transaction with a director of its holding company (or a person connected with such a director), then shareholder approval will be required at the holding company level—unless, of course, that holding company is itself a wholly-owned subsidiary of an entity further up the corporate chain.

(d)   Shareholder approval is not required for certain transactions among group companies,[10] involving companies in administration[11] or effected on a recognized investment exchange.[12]

(e)   As is the case for any transaction, an approval given by the shareholders of a company will only be effective if the price and other key terms have been properly disclosed to them.[13]

38.05   Why are these provisions important to a bank providing finance for the acquisition of an asset from the company? In general terms, a transaction which infringes section 190 is voidable at the instance of the company.[14] Thus, if the lender has financed an offending acquisition and has taken security over the asset acquired from the company, it may find that the avoidance of the transaction at the instance of the company involves the loss of its security.[15] It is true that the company's right to avoid the transaction is lost if this

---

In cases of doubt, the proper course for the lending bank would be to insist on the passing of a members' resolution in any event.

    [5]   In the latter case, the company cannot be subjected to any liability if the approval is withheld: s 190(3) of the 2006 Act.
    [6]   For a recent discussion and analysis of the case law in this area, see *NBH Ltd v Hoare* [2006] EWHC 73 (Ch).
    [7]   Persons 'connected' with a director include certain family members and companies which he controls or with which he is associated. For full details, see the definitions in ss 252–257 of the 2006 Act.
    [8]   See s 190(2), read together with s 190(4)(a) of the 2006 Act.
    [9]   See s 190(4)(b) of the 2006 Act.
    [10]   See s 192 of the 2006 Act.
    [11]   See s 193 of the 2006 Act.
    [12]   See s 194 of the 2006 Act.
    [13]   See *Demite Ltd v Protec Health Ltd* [1998] BCC 638.
    [14]   See s 195 of the 2006 Act.
    [15]   The obligation of the director or connected person to repay the loan would remain enforceable, but the transaction would become unsecured as a result of the avoidance of the main transaction.

would prejudice the rights of a third party which had been acquired '… in good faith, for value and without actual notice of the contravention …', but a lending bank will usually have inquired into the transaction and will be aware of the relationship between the parties.[16] It will thus have notice of the facts which give rise to the contravention of section 190.[17] If a bank discovers after the fact that it has financed a transaction which infringes section 190, then it should endeavour to persuade the company to affirm the transaction as soon as possible.[18]

Transactions involving Directors

Section 41 of the 2006 Act is both broader and narrower than section 190. It is broader in the sense that it applies to *any* transaction between a company and its directors or connected persons.[19] Yet it is narrower in that it only applies where the directors have exceeded any limitation imposed upon them by the company's constitution and the validity of the transaction depends on the application of section 40(1) of the 2006 Act.[20] **38.06**

Section 41(2) provides that any such transaction entered into by a company and the parties to which include a director of the company or its holding company[21] will be voidable at the instance of the company itself. **38.07**

Once again, the transaction cannot be avoided as against a lending bank which has taken security over the asset concerned in good faith and without actual notice of the fact that the directors had exceeded their powers.[22] It may, however, be difficult for a lender to rely on this provision where it has financed the acquisition of an asset by the company from a director, for the bank may well be familiar both with the identities of the various parties involved and with the terms of the company's constitution. The application of the statutory provisions at this point becomes somewhat complex. For example: **38.08**

(a) The bank might seek to argue that, as an 'outsider' it is entitled to hold the company to the loan and security arrangements by virtue of section 40(1) of the 2006 Act,[23] but

---

[16] See s 195(2)(c) of the 2006 Act.

[17] In accordance with general principle, it is only necessary that the bank have notice of the facts giving rise to the application of s 190. It is not necessary for the bank to be aware of the legal effect of that provision: see the corresponding discussion in para 37.24 above, in the context of the financial assistance prohibition.

[18] A transaction of this kind may be affirmed by the company in general meeting, but this must be done within a reasonable period after the date of the transaction: see s 196.

[19] ie there are no *de minimis* financial limits, as there are for s 190, nor is s 41 confined to property transactions.

[20] Transactions entered into by the directors in excess of their powers are generally binding as far as third parties are concerned by virtue of s 40(1) of the 2006 Act. That section has been separately considered at para 26.50 above. Section 41 is dealt with here since it may have the ultimate effect of vitiating security taken by the bank. But it is pertinent to note that the section effectively 'claws back' transactions involving insiders which would otherwise be validated or protected by s 40.

[21] Once again, the section extends to certain persons connected or associated with the director concerned.

[22] See s 41(4)(c) of the 2006 Act.

[23] On s 40(1), see para 26.50 above.

can the bank be said to have acted in good faith for the purposes of that provision if it has knowingly funded an 'insider' transaction?

(b) Section 41(6) provides that nothing in the section '… affects the rights of any party to the transaction …' who is not a director of the company, the holding company or a connected person. But this does not assist the bank because it is has provided a separate loan facility and is thus not a '… party to the transaction …' referred to in section 41(6).

38.09 Matters may become even more challenging for the bank in the converse case, that is to say, where it provides finance to a director or connected person to acquire an asset from the company. Section 40 will have no application or relevance to the bank since it will be entering into a financing transaction with the director or connected person himself; the bank will not be entering into a contract with the company to which section 40 could potentially apply. It may again be said that the bank has notice of the irregularities and the transfer of the relevant assets remains voidable at the instance of the company. The avoidance of the transaction may involve the loss of the bank's security.[24]

38.10 In view of these doubts and difficulties, a bank must take special care when financing a transaction between a company and an 'insider'. In particular, the bank should ensure that the transaction is within the powers of the company, and verify the authority of the directors to enter into it. It would usually be advisable to insist on shareholder approval, thus ensuring that all corporate stakeholders are aware of and approve the transaction.

---

[24] See s 41(3)(c) of the 2006 Act.

39

AVOIDANCE OF SECURITY IN INSOLVENCY

Introduction

It often happens that, as a company's financial circumstances deteriorate, the directors will **39.01** approach the bank with a view to additional funding or the extension of existing facilities. The bank may be willing to accede to that request, but on the basis that security (or additional security) is provided for that purpose. Not infrequently, the bank will seek security not only from the company itself; it will also seek guarantees and security from affiliated entities.

As the company nears the abyss, however, the law requires the company and its directors to **39.02** have regard to the interests of the creditors as a whole. This concern is reflected in various statutory provisions which allow the court to adjust or reverse transactions which are entered into during this period, and which are to the detriment of unsecured creditors.[1] At the risk of an over-simplification, these provisions may be seen as an attempt to hold a fair balance between the various categories of creditors involved during the period leading up to the company's failure. Lenders (such as banks) which are in a position to take security are likely to have more information about the company's situation than is available to the general body of trade creditors. It is thus appropriate that there should be some effective constraint against the bank's ability to prop up the company in a manner which, in the final analysis, may be detrimental to the interests of the unsecured creditors.[2]

---

[1] These rules are supplemented by provisions for the personal liability of the directors if they have been responsible for fraudulent or wrongful trading: see Insolvency Act 1986, ss 213 and 214. A discussion of these provisions is beyond the scope of the present work.

[2] It has already been seen that guarantees and security given by subsidiaries of a borrower on an 'upstream' basis are vulnerable to attack on the grounds that they may have been given in breach of fiduciary duty: see the discussion at para 26.50 above.

39.03 Against this background, it is proposed to consider the following matters:[3]

(a) transactions at an undervalue;
(b) preferences;
(c) extortionate credit transactions;
(d) floating charges; and
(e) transactions defrauding creditors.

Transactions at an Undervalue

39.04 Where a company goes into administration or liquidation, the office holder[4] may apply to the court for an order to restore the position if '… the company has at a relevant time … entered into a transaction with any person at an undervalue …'.[5]

39.05 This provision raises a number of issues of definition, as follows:

(a) When does a company 'enter into a transaction with any person'? There may be cases in which this fundamental requirement is by no means easy to apply. It is true that 'transaction' is broadly defined to include '… a gift, agreement or arrangement …' and that references to '… entering into a transaction …' must be construed accordingly.[6] It seems to follow that any arrangement—whether or not legally binding—under which the third party derives a benefit may be susceptible to challenge under this provision. Nevertheless, the section requires that the 'transaction' be entered into 'with' another person. This may have the effect of limiting the scope of the section in certain cases. For example, suppose that a parent company voluntarily instructs its bank to make payment in respect of invoices outstanding to a creditor of one of its subsidiaries. It does so in order to preserve the subsidiary's access to trade credit, and does so without reference to the creditor.[7] When the parent itself becomes insolvent, could the payments be challenged under this section? It is submitted that they could not. The payment is not a 'gift', for the parent derives a tangible commercial benefit from the continued availability of trade credit to the subsidiary. Furthermore, the instruction to the parent's bank to transfer the necessary funds cannot be seen as the conclusion of a

---

[3] As will be apparent, the discussion is centred on the insolvency of companies. However, it should be appreciated that the statutory provisions applicable to corporate insolvency are also applicable to individuals with appropriate modifications: see Insolvency Act 1986, ss 339–343.

[4] This expression refers to the administrator or liquidator, as the case may be.

[5] Insolvency Act 1986, s 238. For the provisions applicable to companies in Scotland, see s 242 of that Act (Gratuitous Alienations).

[6] Insolvency Act 1986, s 436. It is true that the definition is not exclusive, and that other arrangements could thus constitute a 'transaction' for these purposes. Nevertheless, one cannot escape the view that 'transaction' (especially when linked with the words 'with any person' in s 238(2)) connotes an element of mutual dealing, rather than a merely unilateral and unsolicited act of payment from the company concerned. This view is supported in *Clarkson v Clarkson* [1994] BCC 921, aff'd by the Court of Appeal but without specific discussion of this point: [1994] BCC 929.

[7] In such a case, the parent is unlikely to disclose the subsidiary's difficulties to the creditor; in some respects, the very purpose of making the payment is to conceal those difficulties.

'transaction' with the 'person' concerned.[8] Equally, the expression 'transaction' connotes an arrangement *pursuant to which* a payment is to be made. As a consequence, the mere receipt of a payment itself (without more) cannot therefore amount to a 'transaction' within the scope of the section. This view of the subject is supported by the decision in *Re Taylor Sinclair (Capital) Ltd*[9] and, it is submitted, the decision is appropriate. It is not uncommon that an invoice rendered to one group company is paid by another member of the same group, and (without more) there is no obvious reason why a creditor who receives payment in this way should be at the risk of prejudice under section 238 of the Insolvency Act 1986.

(b) If the company is found to have entered into a transaction with a person for these purposes, was that transaction at an 'undervalue'? The statutory provisions confirm[10] that an undervalue transaction involves either (i) a gift or other arrangement under which the company receives no consideration or (ii) a transaction '… for a consideration the value of which, in money or money's worth, is significantly less than the value, in money or money's worth, of the consideration provided by the company …'. So far as the borrowing company is concerned, this provision should pose no threat to the lending bank which takes security for new funding. The company plainly receives consideration, and the security provided by the company itself will clearly have no greater value than the loan plus funding costs.[11] The position becomes more obscure where—as will usually be the case—the bank requires that the security extends to *past* borrowings or requires new guarantees and security from subsidiaries.[12] In such cases, it may well be that the value of the security provided to the bank will be of significantly greater value to it than the injection of new funds received by the company itself.[13]

---

[8] For reasons given below, it is submitted that a transaction of this kind likewise cannot be challenged under the 'preference' rules in s 239 of the Act.

[9] [2001] BCLC 176. It should, however, be noted that Paget (para 14.23, note 2) expresses a different view of this decision.

[10] Insolvency Act 1986, s 238(4).

[11] For example, if a company borrows £1,000 but provides security over a property worth £10,000, no question of an 'undervalue' arises because, after realizing the security, the bank would have to return the surplus funds to the borrower.

[12] Viewed in isolation, the issue of a guarantee to a bank will inevitably be a transaction at an undervalue for the purposes of s 239(4)(a). Although the making or continuation of advances to the borrower is sufficient consideration to support the guarantee (see para 26.14 above), this would not constitute consideration which is *received by the guarantor company* for the purposes of that section. Alternatively, any consideration received by the guarantor company is likely to be significantly less than the value of the guarantee to the bank, with the result that the guarantee would be an undervalue transaction within s 239(4)(b): see Paget, para 14.23.

[13] In *Re MC Bacon Ltd* [1990] BCLC 324 at p 340, the court held that the creation by a company of security for its own borrowings could not be caught by the 'undervalue' rules, since the company's assets were not thereby depleted and the company did not thereby provide consideration which could be measured in money or money's worth. However, for the reasons given by Paget (para 14.23) this analysis cannot apply where the company is providing security for past borrowings, a view confirmed by *Hill (as Trustee in Bankruptcy of Nurkowski) v Spread Trustee Co Ltd* [2001] BCC 646. In terms of s 239(4), the security may be an undervalue transaction because the company will 'receive no consideration' for the security. If some new money is advanced, then it would be necessary to determine whether the new money is 'a consideration the value of which, in money … is significantly less than the value, in money or money's worth of the consideration provided by the company'. For a case which illustrates the circumstances under which consideration received by a person may be 'significantly less' than that received by it, see *Re Kumar (A Bankrupt)* [1993] 2 All ER 700. The decisions made under s 423 of the Act (discussed at paras 39.12–39.14 below) may also be of relevance in the present context.

Such transactions may, however, be 'saved' pursuant to some of the provisions discussed in subparagraphs (e) and (f) below. Furthermore, the court must not take a narrow view in examining the consideration received by the company. Instead, it must take a view of the entire circumstances of the transaction, including the benefit of any collateral arrangements with others who may be involved.[14]

(c) If the company is found to have entered into a transaction with a person at an undervalue for the purposes of the section, was that transaction entered into at a 'relevant time'? In the present context, this refers to the period of two years leading up to the onset of insolvency.[15] There are various exceptions to this rule but it seemed more convenient to discuss these under the 'saving' provisions considered in subparagraphs (e) and (f) below.

(d) There are various important provisions which, in favour of the lender, may save certain guarantees and security transactions which might otherwise be subject to a successful challenge pursuant to the 'undervalue' rules.

(e) In particular, a transaction cannot be adjusted under these rules unless either (i) at the time of the transaction, the company was already insolvent[16] or (ii) it was rendered insolvent as a result of entering into the transaction concerned.[17] This provision may be of particular value to the bank where the company's insolvency results from a sudden misfortune, rather than a gradual deterioration of its prospects. In effect, the provision is designed to save transactions where insolvency was not believed to be an imminent prospect. It may also be of assistance where the bank takes guarantees and security for a parent's borrowings where the parent is in difficulty but the subsidiary providing the security is itself solvent.[18]

(f) Furthermore, a court may not make an order under section 238 if it is satisfied that (i) the company entered into the transaction in good faith[19] and for the purpose of carrying on its business and (ii) at the time of the transaction, there were reasonable grounds for believing that the transaction would benefit the company.[20]

(g) If the court finds that the relevant arrangement was indeed a 'transaction at an undervalue' for these purposes, then it must[21] make '... such order as it thinks fit for restoring

---

[14] *Phillips v Brewin Dolphin Bell Lawrie Ltd* [2001] 1 WLR 143 (HL).

[15] Section 240(1) of the Insolvency Act. Broadly speaking, means either (i) the date on which an application for the appointment of an administrator is made or (ii) the date of commencement of the winding up: s 240(3), Insolvency Act.

[16] That is to say, it was unable to pay its debts within the meaning of s 123 of the Act.

[17] Section 240(2) of the Insolvency Act. If these conditions are not met, then the transaction was not entered into at a 'relevant time' for the purposes of s 239(2). Where the beneficiary of the transaction is connected to the company, there is a presumption that the company was indeed insolvent or was rendered insolvent as a result of the transaction at hand. This point is, however, unlikely to be of concern in the context of a banking transaction in the normal course of business.

[18] For other possible grounds of challenge to such an arrangement, see para 26.50 above.

[19] In the context of insolvency legislation, 'good faith' will often require that the company receives a tangible element of consideration: see *Re Windle* [1975] 1 WLR 1628.

[20] In practice, the court may be reluctant to find that this test is satisfied where the relevant transactions have been entered into with relatives or close associates: *Re Barton Manufacturing Co Ltd* [1999] 1 BCLC 740.

[21] Section 238(3). Note that, if the court is satisfied that the conditions of the section are met, then it must make an order to restore the position; the section is not merely discretionary in that sense, although the type of order to be made in each case will obviously depend on the particular circumstances of each case.

the position to what it would have been if the company had not entered into that transaction …'. Without restricting the breadth of this general power, the Act specifically allows the court to order (i) the re-transfer to the company of any property transferred pursuant to the transaction in question, (ii) the release of any security given by the company as part of the transaction, (iii) the payment of compensation by any person who received the benefit of the transaction, and (iv) the revival of any guarantees which were discharged as a result of the transaction concerned.[22] An order may be made against any person,[23] whether or not he was a party to the relevant transaction, but a party who acted in good faith and provided value is entitled to certain protections.[24]

Preferences

Where a company has gone into administration or liquidation, and has given a preference to any person at any relevant time, the office holder may apply to the court for an order which restores the position to what it would have been had the company not given that preference.[25] The provision may be dissected as follows: **39.06**

(a) The expression 'preference' requires explanation. A company gives a preference to a person if (i) that person is one of the company's creditors, or is a surety or guarantor for any of the company's obligations and (ii) the company does anything, or permits anything to be done, which has the effect of putting that person into a better position than he would otherwise have enjoyed if the company goes into insolvent liquidation.[26]

(b) Whether or not a person is a 'creditor' will not usually pose particular problems in this type of case. A creditor is any person who would be entitled to prove in the liquidation of the company, and thus includes a guarantor or any other person entitled to a right of indemnity against the company.[27] However, the clear consequence is that there must be a pre-existing transaction between the company and the creditor under which the company has incurred a liability. The preference is a subsequent act on behalf of the company which is designed to enhance that creditor's position.[28]

(c) Although not specifically defined, the 'preference' must therefore connote the making of a payment which reduces the amount owing to the creditor[29] or the amount covered

---

[22] For the complete list, see s 241 of the Act.

[23] Including a person resident overseas: *Re Paramount Airways Ltd* [1993] Ch 223 and the discussion at para 39.14 below.

[24] See s 241(2) of the Act. The remainder of s 241 deals with the question of 'good faith' in some depth.

[25] Section 239 of the Act. For the corresponding provisions in Scotland, see s 243 (Unfair Preferences (Scotland)).

[26] Section 239(4) of the Act. Note that a particular payment or other act may constitute a preference even though effected pursuant to a court order: s 239(7).

[27] *Re Blackpool Motor Car Co Ltd* [1901] Ch 77; *Re Beacon Leisure Ltd* [1992] BCLC 565.

[28] As a result, a subsidiary which provides a guarantee to cover the overdraft of its troubled parent does not thereby give a 'preference', because the bank is not a creditor of the subsidiary until the guarantee is actually given. Of course, the giving of such a guarantee may constitute a transaction at an undervalue on the part of the subsidiary.

[29] *Re Cohen* [1924] 2 Ch 515.

by the guarantor,[30] or the giving of security which provides the creditor with an enhanced prospect of repayment as compared to the general body of creditors.

(d) It is, however, obvious that, whilst every payment made to a creditor has the effect of discharging a debt (and thus improving the creditor's position in the event of a later insolvency), not every such payment can constitute a preference. There are, therefore, various limiting factors.

(e) It should be appreciated that the court can only make an order '... in respect of a preference given to any person unless the company which gave the preference was influenced in deciding to give it by a desire to produce in relation that person the effect of ...' a preference. It seems that the company's intention, or one of its intentions,[31] must be to improve the creditor's position in the event of insolvency.[32] Thus, if a company pays a particular creditor because it needs him to continue to provide supplies, the payment cannot later be set aside as a preference. Likewise, if security is given to an existing creditor to induce him to provide additional funding,[33] or to a bank with a view to ensuring the company's survival[34] then this, likewise may not constitute a preference.

(f) Where the recipient of the preference is a person connected with the company, it is presumed that the requisite intention is present.[35] Thus, where the directors sanction the repayment of their own personal loans to the company, it will be presumed that they intended to prefer themselves.[36] Likewise, if the company pays off a creditor whose debt had been personally guaranteed by a director, the same presumption will apply.[37] Although the bank will not usually be a person connected with the company, it may nevertheless be affected in the type of situation just described.[38]

(g) Once again, the court cannot make an order under these provisions unless the company is insolvent at the time of the preference or is rendered insolvent as a result of giving it, although this requirement is presumed to be satisfied where the recipient of the preference is connected with the company.[39]

---

[30] *Re Kushler Ltd* [1943] Ch 248; *Re FP and CH Matthews Ltd* [1982] Ch 257.

[31] In practice, the intention must be that of the director or manager who sanctions the relevant payment or other transaction.

[32] *Re MC Bacon Ltd* [1990] BCLC 324. Thus, if the transaction is motivated purely by proper commercial considerations, it cannot be set aside as a preference: *Re Conegrade Ltd* [2003] BIPR 358.

[33] *Re MC Bacon Ltd* (above); *Re Fairway Magazines Ltd* [1993] BCLC 643.

[34] *Re FLE Holdings Ltd* [1967] 3 All ER 533; *Re Fairway Magazines Ltd* [1993] BCLC 6423.

[35] Section 239(6). References to persons 'connected' with the company will occur frequently in this chapter. They are essentially designed as an anti-avoidance provision. A person is 'connected' with the company if he is a director or shadow director of the company, or is an associate of such a director or of the company itself: s 249. The term 'associate' is very widely defined in s 435 of the Act, and includes (among others): (i) spouses and certain other relatives, (ii) business partners, (iii) employers and employees, (iv) trustees, and (v) companies under common control.

[36] *Wills v Corfe Joinery Ltd* [1998] 2 BCLC 75. For a case in which the connected parties managed, at least to a limited extent, to rebut this presumption, see *Re Fairway Magazines Ltd* [1993] BCLC 643.

[37] *Re Agriplant Services Ltd* [1997] 2 BCLC 598. The presumption may be rebutted if the bank is fully secured by a charge over the assets of the company and could recover its loans in full from that source (or, alternatively, the director would be subrogated to that security: see *Re Hawkes Hill Publishing Ltd* [2007] BIPR 1305; *Re Oxford Pharmaceuticals Ltd* [2009] EWHC 1752 (Ch).

[38] In such a case, the bank may have to refund the payment made by the company, but would then be able to claim payment under the director's guarantee.

[39] This follows from the 'relevant time' provisions: see s 240(2).

(h) A transaction can only be set aside as a preference if it was given during the six month period prior to insolvency.[40]

(i) The orders which the court may make to restore the position mirror those available in the context of a transaction at an undervalue.[41]

(j) It should be appreciated that, if a transaction is set aside as a preference, this does not invalidate the underlying transaction to which the preferential transaction related. Consequently, the creditor will still be entitled to prove in the liquidation for the monies which are owing to him.[42]

Extortionate Credit Transactions

Companies encountering financial difficulties may be driven to desperate measures and may borrow from lenders seeking to exploit their situation. Transactions of that type may be detrimental to the unsecured creditors and, although not constituting a preference for the purposes of section 239 of the Insolvency Act 1986,[43] the effect is similar. **39.07**

As a result, section 244 of the Act allows the administrator or liquidator to apply for an order declaring that the credit transaction was extortionate. The following comments may be made in this regard: **39.08**

(a) A credit transaction is extortionate[44] if, having regard to the risk accepted by the person providing the credit, (i) the terms of the credit required '... grossly exorbitant payments to be made in respect of the provision of the credit or (ii) the terms otherwise grossly contravened ordinary principles of fair dealing …'.

(b) If the office holder makes an application with respect to a particular credit transaction, it is presumed to be extortionate unless the creditor proves otherwise.

(c) The court can, however, only make an order with respect to a credit transaction entered into during the three year period prior to the onset of insolvency and, in this respect, the burden of proof appears to rest on the administrator or liquidator.[45]

(d) If the court finds that the credit transaction was exorbitant, then the court may make a variety of orders to set aside or vary the terms of the transaction, and to require the creditor to refund payments or surrender security.[46]

---

[40] Section 240(1). The period is extended to two years where the beneficiary of the preference is connected with the company.

[41] See s 241 of the Act and the discussion at para 39.05(g) above.

[42] Any reader with particular stamina is invited to review the decision of the Supreme Court of Western Australia in *The Bell Group Ltd (in liquidation) v Westpac Banking Corporation (No 9)* [2008] WASC 239. The judgments—excluding annexes—runs to some 2,500 pages and addresses numerous issues which arose when a large number of banks sought to obtain security as the Bell Group approached insolvency.

[43] It is, however, clear that a credit transaction could also constitute a transaction at an undervalue for the purposes of s 238. Consequently, orders under ss 238 and 244 may be made in relation to the same transaction: see s 244(5).

[44] See s 244(3).

[45] See s 244(2).

[46] See s 244(4).

Avoidance of Floating Charges

39.09   When it sees that its customer is running into financial difficulty, a bank may be tempted to demand the execution of a general floating charge over the assets of a company and its subsidiaries. The bank may also advance new money at that time, but the security will also cover pre-existing liabilities.

39.10   Once again, arrangements of this kind may run to the disadvantage of the general body of unsecured creditors, and section 245 of the Insolvency Act allows for such security to be challenged in stated circumstances. Where it is clear that the stated security does consist of a floating charge,[47] a liquidator is likely to invoke section 245 in priority to the 'undervalue' and 'preference' provisions which were considered above.[48]

39.11   The main issues are as follows:

(a) If a company creates a floating charge[49] during the 12 month period prior to the onset of insolvency,[50] then it is invalid except to the extent of (i) moneys advanced[51] at the same time as, or following, the creation of the charge,[52] (ii) the value of consideration that consists of the reduction, at the same time as, or after the creation of the charge of

---

[47] On the distinction between fixed and floating security, see paras 28.03–28.10 above.

[48] The 'undervalue' provisions set out in s 238 require the office holder to prove that the transaction was indeed at an undervalue so far as the company is concerned, and the beneficiary of the transaction may have a defence if the company entered into the transaction in good faith and there were reasonable grounds for believing that the transaction would benefit the company. Likewise, in the case of the 'preference' rules, the office holder has to prove that the company intended to prefer the particular creditor. These obstacles do not apply if the office holder is able to proceed under s 245.

[49] Although the point will only rarely arise in practice, s 245 is only expressed to apply to 'a floating charge on the company's undertaking or property'. Although the point is by no means clear, this seems to suggest that the section only applies where the company creates a floating charge over the entirety of its undertaking. On that basis, a floating charge limited to a *particular class* of assets would not fall within the scope of s 245. Any challenge to such a security would therefore have to be based on the 'undervalue' or 'preference' rules described earlier in this chapter.

[50] Section 245(3). The period is extended to two years if the chargee is a person connected with the company. The 'onset of insolvency' is the date of the application or other step leading up to the appointment of an administrator, or the commencement of the winding up, as the case may be: s 245(5) of the 1986 Act. The time which follows the onset of insolvency is accordingly left out of account in calculating the necessary 12 month period: see *Power v Sharp Investments Ltd* [1994] BCLC 111 (CA).

[51] The section also deals with security which has been provided in consideration of the supply of goods and services. However, these will rarely be of direct relevance in the present context, and the discussion is therefore limited to the provision of financial accommodation.

[52] The lender needs to take particular care to ensure that the security has been executed by the time the money has been advanced. If the lender makes an advance on the faith of a promise that security will be given, then he takes the risk that his floating charge will be invalidated under s 245: see *Power v Sharp Investments Ltd* [1994] BCLC 111 (CA). However, where the borrower has undertaken to provide a floating charge, equity may regard the floating charge as given as at the date of the undertaking (ie because equity regards as done that which ought to have been done), with the result that the time delay would not prejudice the lender in such a case: *Power v Sharp Investments Ltd* (above). However, the lender must press for the security to be given promptly. If he is complicit in any delay, then equity may no longer assist him: see *Re F and E Stanton Ltd* [1929] Ch 180. Where a lender made cash advances in April, May, and June but the promised debenture was not executed until 24 July, the security was not given 'at the same time as' the security, which was accordingly void under s 245: *Re Shoe Lace Ltd* [1992] BCLC 636.

any of the company's indebtedness, and (iii) interest on the amounts specified in (i) and (ii).

(b) There is a certain amount of case law derived from section 245 and its predecessors. Much of this revolves around the extent to which consideration for the charge may be said to have been advanced at the time of, or following, its creation, and has already been noted in connection with paragraph (a), above. The available authorities have, however, also decided various other points. For example, if the company has created a floating charge which would otherwise be vulnerable to attack under section 245, a payment later made by the company to redeem that charge cannot itself be challenged under section 245 on the basis that the floating charge could have been set aside, had it still subsisted.[53] There no longer exists a floating charge to which the section could apply and it is inappropriate to speculate on what the position might have been. The office holder would thus have to challenge the payment itself, on the grounds that it was a preference, if the circumstances of the case entitled him to do so.

(c) The courts have also had to assess whether the consideration provided in particular cases has been sufficient to take the security outside the ambit of section 245. For example, it has been decided that the lender can insist that the funds are applied to a particular purpose (eg in discharging a specified liability of the company), and it is thus not necessary that the new money should be placed at the unconditional disposal of the company.[54] But the company must derive some tangible benefit from the transaction since, otherwise, the consideration may effectively be non-existent and will not prevent a challenge to the floating charge under section 243.[55]

(d) As in the case of undervalue transactions and preferences, a floating charge cannot be invalidated under section 245 if the company was solvent at the time of its creation and is not rendered insolvent as a result of the transaction to which the charge relates.[56]

(e) Once again, it should be emphasized that the invalidity of a floating charge under section 245 does not lead to the unenforceability of the underlying loan or other credit transaction to which it was intended to relate. The lender or other creditor will thus remain entitled to prove in the liquidation for the sums owing to him.

(f) The application of section 245 is not prejudiced by the fact that the floating charge may have crystallized[57] before the onset of insolvency, since the section applies to '... a charge which, *as created*, was a floating charge ...'.[58]

---

[53] See *Mace Builders (Glasgow) Ltd v Munn* [1987] Ch 191 (CA).

[54] *Re Matthew Ellis Ltd* [1993] Ch 458 (CA).

[55] *Re Fairway Magazines Ltd* [1993] BCLC 643, where the floating charge was held to be void in so far as it related to an advance which merely served to reduce a director's liability under a personal guarantee given to the bank.

[56] Section 245(4).

[57] On crystallization of floating charges, see paras 28.11–28.13 above.

[58] See the definition of 'floating charge' in s 251 of the 1986 Act.

Transactions Defrauding Creditors

39.12   The marginal note to section 423 of the Insolvency Act states that it deals with 'Transactions defrauding creditors'. The section appears immediately under the heading to Part XVI of the Act, 'Provisions against Debt Avoidance'. In spite of this apparent concern with the evasion of creditors,[59] the section bears a number of similarities to the rules on transactions at an undervalue, which have been discussed earlier in this chapter.

39.13   Insofar as it relates to companies,[60] the key provisions of the section are as follows:

(a)   The section is stated to relate to transactions at an undervalue, and provides that a company enters into such a transaction if (i) it makes a gift to any person, (ii) it enters into a transaction under which it receives no consideration, or (iii) it enters into a transaction where the value of the consideration received by the company is significantly less than the value of the consideration provided by it.[61]

(b)   Where a company has entered into such a transaction, the court may make an order to restore the position including, without limitation, (i) the retransfer of property to the company, (ii) the release of any security given by the company, (iii) the payment of compensation by a party who received a benefit from the transaction, and (iv) the revival of any guarantees discharged as a result of the transaction. There are also provisions for the protection of those who have acquired an interest in the company's property for value and in good faith.[62]

(c)   Thus far, these provisions are essentially identical to those discussed earlier in relation to a transaction at an undervalue.[63] At this point, however, the two sets of provisions begin to diverge, and more emphasis is placed upon the potentially dishonest aspects of the transaction at issue.

(d)   An order may only be made if the court is satisfied that the company entered into the transaction for the purpose of putting assets beyond the reach of a person who is making a claim against him or may do so at some future time, or otherwise for the purpose of prejudicing the interests of such a person in relation to any such claim.[64] It will not always be easy for the victim or applicant for the order to satisfy this test, because the purpose of the transaction must be to put assets beyond the reach of the creditor, but the debtor may have had a number of different objectives in view.[65]

---

[59]   This emphasis explains why the section is to be found in an entirely separate part of the Act than the provisions discussed earlier in this chapter. Nevertheless, it was felt convenient to deal with s 423 in the present context.

[60]   The section also applies to transactions by individuals. This provision may therefore be relevant to a bank when a personal customer or guarantor seeks to place assets beyond the reach of his creditors.

[61]   The true value of an asset is of course a matter of evidence and it may be necessary to take account of tenancies and other encumbrances affecting the property: see *Delaney v Can Chen* [2010] EWHC 6 (Ch).

[62]   On the points made in this paragraph, see s 423(2) read together with s 425.

[63]   See the discussion of ss 238 and 240 of the Act, above.

[64]   See s 423(3).

[65]   On this point, see *IRC v Hashmi* [2002] 2 BCLC 489.

(e) Since the emphasis is placed on the (fraudulent) intention of the company, there is no time limit for making a claim under this section.[66] Furthermore, there is no explicit saving for transactions effected at a time when the company can be shown to have been solvent.[67]

(f) Once again, an application under section 423 may be made by an administrator or liquidator of the company. However, and again in contrast to the provisions discussed earlier in this chapter, there is no requirement that the company should have gone into formal insolvency proceedings. Consequently, an application may also be made by the person (referred to as the 'victim') whose claim against the company has been impeded by the transaction at issue.[68]

(g) It is perhaps fair to say that the provisions discussed earlier in this chapter dealing with transactions at an undervalue, preferences, and extortionate credit transactions are most likely to be raised to the detriment of a lending bank with a view to challenging the benefit of transactions entered into shortly before the customer's insolvency. In contrast, section 423 is perhaps more likely to be invoked on behalf of the bank when it is discovered[69] that the customer or its guarantors have attempted to place assets beyond the reach of the bank.[70]

It may be noted that section 423 is not subject to any explicit territorial limitation, with the **39.14** result that an order may be made against any debtor, regardless of its place of incorporation. It has been decided that the matter or transaction must have at least some nexus with England if an order is to be made under section 423.[71] However, the more tenuous the connection with England the more cautious the court should be in exercising its discretion to make an order. A recent illustration of these points is offered by the decision in *Donoch Ltd v Westminster International BV*,[72] where a foreign company which owned a foreign-registered vessel physically situate outside England, sold it to another foreign affiliate for a nominal sum. The vessel had been involved in a collision and suffered considerable damage. This was the subject of a dispute with the insurers, and the vessel had been transferred to the affiliate with a view to preventing the disposal of the vessel by the underwriters in

---

[66] Contrast the specific time limits imposed in relation to transactions at an undervalue and preferences.

[67] Although if it can be shown that the company was financially sound at the time of the transaction, this evidence may presumably be used to negative the necessary intention to defeat creditors. That the insolvency of the company is not a necessary prerequisite for an order under s 423 was recently confirmed in *Dornoch Ltd v Westminster International BV* [2009] EWHC 1782 (Admiralty).

[68] See s 424.

[69] It appears that the limitation period only begins to run in respect of a claim under s 423 when the creditor discovers the fraudulent transfer or could have done so with reasonable diligence: see *Giles v Rhind* [2008] Civ 118.

[70] There may, however, be exceptions to this observation. If, for example, a bank knew that a husband was in serious financial difficulty but granted facilities which assisted in the transfer of assets to his wife (eg by providing a deposit on a property to be purchased in the wife's sole name), then it may be that the court could order that the proceeds of sale should be applied firstly in repaying the deposit to the husband's creditors and thereafter in repayment to the bank. The bank would suffer a loss if the property had fallen in value in the interim period. The bank would be unable to claim the protection afforded to third parties by s 425(2), because its knowledge of the husband's financial position may be sufficient to show that the bank had not acted in good faith.

[71] *Re Paramount Airways* [1993] Ch 223.

[72] [2009] EWHC 1782 (Admiralty).

accordance with the terms of the policy. Since the objective of the transaction was to deprive the insurers of their contractual rights, and given that the insurers were based in London, it was appropriate to order the re-transfer of the vessel to preserve the insurer's position. The court indicated that it would have power to make a section 423 order if the 'real and substantial purpose' of the transfer was to place the vessel beyond the reach of the insurers; it did not have to be the *sole* purpose.

PART F

SELECTED CROSS-BORDER ISSUES

Introduction

This section deals with a number of issues which may arise in a cross-border context and which may thus be of special concern to international banks or banks dealing with customers outside the bank's home country.

The subject matter is arranged as follows:

(a) Chapter 40 considers a series of private international law questions which may arise in the context of a cross-border banking relationship;

(b) Chapter 41 considers consumer protection laws in a cross-border context;

(c) Chapter 42 considers conflicting obligations of confidentiality and disclosure;

(d) Chapter 43 considers the impact of worldwide freezing injunctions on international banks;

(e) Chapter 44 considers the impact of execution proceedings on deposits held outside England;

(f) Chapter 45 examines the extent to which a bank based in England is liable to meet the deposit obligations of its foreign branches if, for some reason, they are prevented from doing so directly;

(g) Chapter 46 considers the impact of economic sanctions on the banker-customer relationship;

(h) Chapter 47 considers the extent to which considerations of foreign law (such as moratoria or exchange controls) may affect the customer's obligations to the bank.

40

THE BANKER-CUSTOMER CONTRACT IN PRIVATE INTERNATIONAL LAW

Introduction

The contractual nature of the relationship between the bank and its customer has been considered earlier in this work.[1] In that context, the discussion concentrated on the relationship as it operates under English law; in general terms, it was assumed that the bank was established in England, and that its customer was likewise resident in the same country. **40.01**

Whilst that analysis will, of course, be appropriate to the vast majority of accounts held in England, it is by no means of universal application. Multinational companies may need to have bank accounts in a number of different countries; wealthy individuals may choose to maintain accounts with banks in more advanced jurisdictions, so that they may also have access to portfolio management or other services. Business of this kind has grown as exchange controls have receded over recent decades.[2] Banks, for their part, may promote their services to overseas customers. They may also wish to take security over assets situate outside England.[3] **40.02**

It hardly needs to be stated that business of this kind raises more complex issues than those encountered in the purely domestic sphere, for the laws of at least two jurisdictions will be **40.03**

---

[1] See generally Chapter 15 above.

[2] The holding of accounts with foreign institutions is generally prohibited under most forms of exchange control. Legislation of this kind has, however, been in retreat over recent decades. In general terms, its reintroduction by an EU Member State would not generally be permissible in view of the 'free movement of capital' provisions in the EC Treaty.

[3] For the most part, the issues raised by taking security over foreign assets have been considered in Chapters 27–35 above.

involved in such cases. How does this affect the legal nature of the banker-customer relationship?

40.04 In order to address these issues, the subject matter of the present chapter is organized as follows:

(a) the governing law of the banker-customer relationship will be considered;
(b) the effect and consequences of the applicable law will be outlined;
(c) the law governing capacity and authority will be described; and
(d) the *situs* of deposit obligations will be discussed.

40.05 It should be appreciated that questions of private international law do not merely arise in the context of the direct contractual relationship between a bank and its customer. They will also arise, for example, in the context of documentary credits, and may be highly significant where the bank itself is contemplating a cross-border merger; the taking of security in other countries will also plainly involve questions of foreign law. However, it was felt more convenient to deal with the private international law issues in those specific contexts.[4]

The Governing Law of the Relationship

40.06 How does one ascertain the law applicable to a contractual relationship? In a purely domestic context, the question does not really arise at all. Where an English bank opens an account for a customer resident in England, it is clear that English law will apply; the point will not even arise for discussion.

40.07 But where the customer is resident abroad, the question does arise. Is the account relationship governed by the law of the place where the bank branch is situate, or the law of the customer's place of abode? At this point, it is necessary to have recourse to the regulation of the European Parliament and the Council on the law applicable to contractual obligations (Rome I)[5] which, in accordance with the terms of Article 1(1), becomes relevant

---

[4] On documentary credits, see Chapter 24 above; on bank mergers, see Chapters 9–11 above; on security, see Chapters 27–35 above.

[5] Regulation (EC) 593/2008, OJ L 177, 4.07.2008, p 6. The regulation is generally referred to as 'Rome I', in part because it replaced the Rome Convention on the law applicable to contractual obligations, which had been in effect in the United Kingdom since 1 April 1991: see the Contracts (Applicable Law) Act 1990 and the Contracts (Applicable Law) (Commencement No 1) Order 1991 (SI 1991/707). The Giuliano-Lagarde Report on the Convention (OL 1980 C 282/1) was to be taken into account in the interpretation of the Convention: s 3(3) of the 1991 Act. The new Rome I does not specifically refer to the Giuliano-Lagarde Report but it will be referred to where the relevant provisions are similar. Without wishing to address the matter in any great depth, it may be noted in passing that Rome I originally attracted significant opposition in the UK, both in financial circles and in the wider business community. Some of the difficulties flowed from the fact that Rome I was presented as a measure which reflected the provisions of the earlier Convention, but in fact significant changes had been made in important areas without sufficient consultation. So strong was the reaction that the UK originally exercised its right to opt out of the regulation—a state of affairs recorded in recital (45) to that document. The main concerns revolved around areas of perceived legal uncertainty, but these were resolved in subsequent negotiations. The UK accordingly opted back into the regulation. On the whole subject, see the Ministry of Justice Consultation Paper 'Should the UK Opt in?' (2 April 2008).

in '… situations involving a conflict of laws, to contractual obligations in civil and commercial matters …'.

In broad terms, Rome I preserves the right of the parties to choose the system of law which **40.08** is to govern their contractual relationship. Article 3(1) thus provides that the parties' choice is binding, provided that it is expressly stated or is demonstrated with reasonable certainty by the terms of the contract or the circumstances of the case.[6] If the account opening documentation which forms the basis of the contract stipulates that English law is to be applicable, then that will generally be conclusive.

Article 3 will thus satisfactorily cover cross-border cases where the banking contract or **40.09** mandate stipulates for English law. However, it must be said that banks frequently prefer simplicity and clarity over legal minutiae, and an express choice of law will not always be found.[7] In such a case, it is necessary to have recourse to Article 4 of Rome I.[8] The provisions of this Article depart in some respects from the former, corresponding provisions in the Rome Convention, and some explanation is therefore required:

(a) Article 4 of Rome I lists a series of particular types or classes of contracts where the governing law is to be ascertained by the application of a specific rule. Specifically, Article 4(1)(b) states that '… a contract for the provision of services shall be governed by the law of the country where the service provider has his habitual residence …'.

(b) A contract for the provision of a current account is plainly a 'services' contract for these purposes. It will thus be governed by the law of the habitual residence of the bank.

(c) The 'habitual residence' of a body corporate will be the place of its central administration (ie its head office). However, where the contract is concluded in the course of the operation of a branch, agency or other establishment or if, under the terms of the contract, performance is the responsibility of a particular branch, agency or establishment, the country in which that branch (etc) is located shall be treated as the 'habitual residence' of the service provider.[9] Since the customer will open an account with a particular branch because he is looking for services in that particular location, this proviso will invariably apply in the context of the banker-customer relationship. It follows that, where a French customer opens an account with the London branch of a German bank, the relationship will be governed by English law.

(d) It is thought that this provision would cover virtually all of the account arrangements which may subsist between a bank and its customer. For example, it is submitted that a bank is still providing a 'service' on an account even though it may become

---

[6] It may be added that Art 3 of Rome I allows the parties to agree that different systems of law shall apply to different aspects of their contract.

[7] Where such a choice is made, it will almost invariably refer to the law of the country where the relevant branch is situated. For an exceptional case in which correspondence between the parties and other evidence suggested that an account maintained in London was intended to be governed by New York law, see *Libyan Arab Foreign Bank v Manufacturers Hanover Trust Co (No 1)* [1988] 2 Lloyd's Rep 494. That contention was, however, ultimately rejected: see *Libyan Arab Foreign Bank v Manufacturers Hanover Trust Co (No 2)* [1989] Lloyd's Rep 608.

[8] Article 4 is also considered in Chapter 41 below.

[9] On these points, see Art 19 of Rome I. 'Habitual residence' is tested as at the time when the contract is made: see Art 19(3).

overdrawn.[10] There may, however, be cases in which it might be argued that the bank is not providing a 'service' as such. For example, it might be argued that a term facility should be categorized as a contract for a loan (rather than a contract for services).[11] On that basis, it becomes necessary to consider the alternative formulations.

(e) Subject to various exceptions which will generally have no application in the present context,[12] a contract which does not fall within the ambit of the 'services' rule or any of the other categories listed in Article 4(1) will be '… governed by the law of the country where the party required to effect the characteristic performance of the contract has his habitual residence…'.[13]

(f) In such a case, the question is—whose obligations characterize the contract? Those of the bank? Or those of the customer? In the present context, this point almost goes by default. Once the account is opened, the customer has very few obligations at all. He may pay money into the account and may draw it out but, as against the bank, he is under no obligation to do so. If he draws cheques or gives other instructions to the bank, then certain obligations may arise,[14] but these are of a very limited nature and certainly do not go to the 'core' of the contract. By contrast, the bank is providing services in the normal course of its business. Its obligations are central to the contract and typify the services which lie at the heart of the arrangements between the parties. Likewise, if it is argued that some of the bank's activities—such as fixed term loan agreements—do not constitute a 'service' for the purposes of Article 4(1), then it is submitted that it is the provision of the facility and the advance of the loan which 'characterize' the agreement.[15] There can, therefore, be little doubt that it is the obligations of the bank which 'characterize' the contract for these purposes.[16]

(g) It follows that, whether one classifies a particular banking activity as a 'service' or not, the arrangements which subsist between a bank and its customer should always be governed by the law of the country in which the relevant bank branch is located.

(h) This result is in many respects convenient because English courts had reached the same conclusion in relation to cases arising in the pre-Rome Convention and

---

[10] It would, in any event, be highly undesirable if the governing law of the relationship changed as the account went into and out of overdraft: see the discussion at subpara (j) below.

[11] The writer would, however, argue that the arrangement should still be classified as one of the 'services' provided by the branch.

[12] The exceptions deal with contracts relating to consumer contracts, insurance contracts, employment contracts, and contracts for the carriage of goods: see Arts 5–8 of Rome I. The proviso relating to consumer contracts is plainly relevant in the present context, but this area is addressed separately in Chapter 41 below.

[13] The meaning of 'habitual residence' has already been noted at subpara (c) above. Note that, where the contract is manifestly more closely connected with another country, then the law of that country shall apply instead (Art 4(3)) and, where the applicable law cannot be ascertained under Art 4(1) or (2), then the contract is governed by the law of the country with which it is most closely connected (Art 4(4)). However, resort to these provisions will not generally be necessary in the context of an ordinary banking relationship.

[14] On these obligations, see paras 15.23–15.37 above.

[15] ie as opposed to the obligations of the customer, which merely involve the repayment of the loan.

[16] This is also the conclusion reached by the Giuliano-Lagarde Report in its commentary on Art 4(2) of the Rome Convention, where it notes that it is the provision of services by the bank which 'usually constitutes the centre of gravity and the socio-economic function of the contractual obligation'.

pre-Rome I era, and it thus remains possible to draw upon that case law in the modern context.[17]

(i) In the modern era, however, this perhaps presents an excessively simplified view, because many customers may have accounts with different branches of the bank throughout the world. Where these accounts are separate and independent arrangements, then the analysis provided above will apply separately to each individual contract. Where, however, there is a clear link between accounts in different jurisdictions, a degree of complexity may arise. In one leading case,[18] the customer had an arrangement under which funds were automatically switched between accounts in London and New York under defined circumstances. Under these circumstances, the court held that there was a single contract, governed partly by English law and partly by New York law. It was still open to a court to reach such a conclusion under the terms of the Rome Convention, because Article 4(2) allowed that—even in the case of an implied choice of law—a 'severable part' of the contract could be governed by a different system of law.[19] However, such a decision may now be a little more difficult to rationalize because Article 4 (Applicable law in the absence of choice) of Rome I does not contain any corresponding provision for the splitting of the applicable law in this fashion.

(j) It may be added for completeness that the relationship with a bank in this country should continue to be governed by English law even though the account is overdrawn. There is no reason to change the applicable law merely because the customer overdraws his account. If the overdraft is agreed by the bank, then the same analysis should continue to apply, either on the basis that the overdraft arises on an account which is itself subject to English law, or because the overdraft arrangement constitutes a separate contract but it is the obligations of the bank which 'characterize' that contract for the purposes of Article 4(2) of Rome I.[20]

This analysis leads to the conclusion that, in the absence of some other, express choice, the relationship between the bank and its customer will generally be governed by the law of the country in which the account-holding branch is situate. Where the relevant bank branch is **40.10**

---

[17] For examples, see *Joachimson v Swiss Bank Corporation* [1921] 3 KB 110 (CA); *Arab Bank Ltd v Barclays Bank (DCO)* [1954] AC 495 (HL); *XAG v A Bank* [1983] 2 All ER 464; *MacKinnon v Donaldson Lufkin Jenrette Securities Corporation* [1986] Ch 482; *Libyan Arab Foreign Bank v Bankers Trust Co* [1989] QB 728; *Libyan Arab Foreign Bank v Manufacturers Hanover Trust Co (No 2)* [1989] 1 Lloyd's Rep 608; *Attock Cement Co Ltd v Romanian Bank for Foreign Trade* [1989] 1 All ER 1189 (CA). Courts in the United States have likewise concluded that the governing law of the relationship is the law of the country in which the account-holding branch is situate: see *American Training Services Inc v Commerce Union Bank* 415 F Supp 1101 (1976) aff'd 612 F 2d 580 (1979).

[18] *Libyan Arab Foreign Bank v Bankers Trust Co* [1987] QB 728.

[19] See also the decision in *Sierra Leone Telecommunications Co Ltd v Barclays Bank plc* [1998] 2 All ER 821.

[20] This was the view adopted in *Libyan Arab Foreign Bank v Bankers Trust Co* [1987] QB 728 and, it is submitted, this is reinforced by the terms of Rome I. For a discussion of some of the difficulties which formerly arose in this area, see Pennington, 'Court Orders Affecting Foreign Bank Deposits' in *Legal Issues of Cross-Border Banking* (Chartered Institute of Bankers, 1989), pp 53–55. Courts in the United States have held that loan contracts are governed by the law of the place in which repayment is due. This will, of course, usually coincide with the place in which the relevant bank branch is situate, whether the account is in credit or overdrawn: see, for example, *Sokoloff v National City Bank* 164 NE 745 (1928); *Tuition Plan Inc v Zicari* 335 NYS 2d 95 (1972); *Residential Industrial Loan Co v Brown* 559 F 2d 438 (1977).

situate in England, this will mean that the relationship will be governed by English law and it will accordingly be subject to the rules which have been discussed earlier in this work.[21]

The Effect of the Applicable Law

40.11   It must not be forgotten that the resolution of questions of *private international law* does not itself deal with the substantive issue which has arisen between the parties. Instead, it will merely enable the court to determine which system of *domestic law* should be applied for that purpose.[22] Even then, a degree of care is required, because the law applicable to a contract does not necessarily govern every issue which may be disputed. It is therefore necessary to consider, in relatively abstract terms, the scope and effect of the applicable law, and to seek to apply those rules to the particular legal relationship with which the present discussion is concerned.

40.12   In general terms, the law applicable to the banker-customer relationship—assumed to be English law for these purposes—will govern the following matters:[23]

(a) *The material validity of the contract.* Whether or not a contract has come into existence between the parties, and whether or not particular terms of the contract are intrinsically valid, is to be determined by reference to the law which would govern the contract, were it found to be valid.[24] In the present context, therefore, English law will be applied to determine whether the banker-customer contract has come into being, or whether matters had not passed beyond the mere negotiation stage.[25] English law will also determine whether the contract can be set aside, whether by reason of misrepresentation or on any other ground. No other law—such as the law of the customer's country of residence—is to be applied in determining these matters.[26]

(b) *The formal validity of the contract.* The 'formal validity' of a contract refers to any particular formalities which must be met in order to ensure that the contract is valid. Examples include any requirement for the contract to be under seal or to be subject

---

[21]   See Chapter 15 above.

[22]   It should be noted that, once the law applicable to the contract has been identified, the court must apply only those rules which form part of the domestic law of the country concerned; that country's rules of private international law are specifically excluded from the analysis, with the result that there is no room for the operation of the doctrine of renvoi in the field of contracts. On this subject, see Art 20 of Rome I.

[23]   It should be appreciated that the following description is very much an overview.

[24]   There is a certain lack of logic in this approach to the issue where the very existence of the contract is disputed by one of the parties. An ideal solution to this problem may perhaps prove elusive and, in view of the clear terms of Art 10, it is unnecessary to pursue the issue in the present context.

[25]   ie so that the parties cannot be said to have formed the necessary intention to enter into a legally binding relationship. It is difficult to see how the issue can arise in the ordinary course. A dispute over an account will only arise if funds have been passed through it and, at that point, it will be obvious that a banker-customer contract has come into being. It should be noted that, in very limited circumstances, the question whether the customer had given the consent necessary to the contractual relationship may be governed by the law of the country in which the customer is habitually resident: see Art 10(2) of Rome I, although it is difficult to see how this exception could arise in practice: see the commentary on in the Giuliano-Lagarde Report on the corresponding provision in Art 8(2) of the Rome Convention.

[26]   For possible reservations in the context of consumer protection, see generally the discussion in Chapter 41 below.

to notarization. If the banker-customer contract is valid in point of form under English law, then it will likewise be treated as valid for the purposes of Rome I.[27] English law leans against excessively formal requirements and, in any event, the completed mandate form will usually be a sufficient record that the contract is formally valid. It is therefore unnecessary to dwell on this aspect.

(c) *Interpretation of the contract*. The interpretation (meaning) of a contract is governed by the law applicable to it.[28] In the present context, the result is that English law principles must be applied in determining (i) the meaning to be ascribed to the express terms contained within the parties' agreement and (ii) the nature of any terms which are to be implied into the contract.[29]

(d) *Performance of the contract*. Questions touching the performance of the contract will likewise be governed by English law as the law applicable to the contract as a whole.[30] By way of examples, English law will therefore determine (i) whether or not the customer has made a valid payment to the bank in reduction of his overdraft,[31] (ii) whether or not the bank has irrevocably credited an amount to the customer's account,[32] (iii) whether or not the bank is entitled to debit the customer's account and/or remit a

---

[27] Article 11 of Rome I. Under the terms of that provision, the contract will also be formally valid if it satisfies the formal requirements of the laws of the country in which it is made, or the laws of the countries in which either of the parties are present when the contract is made. In view of the range of choice, it will be apparent that Rome I seeks to avoid the vitiation of contracts on the basis of a failure to comply with formal requirements.

[28] Article 12(1)(a) of Rome I.

[29] The latter point is important in the context of the banker-customer contract for, as has been seen, many of the most important aspects of the relationship are based upon implied terms: see *Joachimson v Swiss Bank Corporation* [1921] 3 KB 110, discussed in detail at para 15.20 above.

[30] Article 12(1)(b) of Rome I. Note, however that, in relation to questions touching the manner of performance, and the steps to be taken in the event of defective performance, regard is to be had to the law of the country in which performance takes place: Art 12(2) of Rome I. The distinction which has to be made between the *substance* and the *manner* of performance for these purposes may not always be an easy one. Where an obligation arising pursuant to the banker-customer contract is governed by English law and payment is to be made in this country then, of course, the question will not arise. Where, however, the customer is to make a payment in US dollars by credit to a New York bank but pursuant to an obligation governed by English law, Art 12(2) may potentially come into effect. Thus, if the due date is not a business day and, under New York law, payment on the following day is a sufficient discharge of the obligation, then the English court may 'have regard' to the New York rule and likewise hold that the obligation has been validly performed under those circumstances. However, this analysis is not without its difficulties. The place of performance (or payment) strictly remains the London branch, even though settlement of that obligation may occur through a correspondent bank in New York.

[31] This point may seem to be obvious, and to be incapable of dispute in most cases. Yet difficulties may arise in a cross-border context. Suppose that the customer is due to make a payment of interest to the bank, but his country of residence requires him to make a 10 per cent deduction on account of taxation, and to pay the amount of that deduction to the local revenue authorities. Bearing in mind that such arrangements are designed to collect tax chargeable against the bank which has a source in the collecting country, does the customer obtain a complete discharge by paying 90 per cent of the interest to the bank, and 10 per cent to the revenue authority? This question must be answered in the negative, because matters touching the substance of performance are governed (exclusively) by English law. On that basis, the bank has received 90 per cent of the interest due and is entitled to a direct payment equal to the additional 10 per cent. The fact that a separate payment of 10 per cent has been made under the terms of a foreign law cannot be taken into account, having regard to the express terms of Art 12(1)(b). For a clear illustration of this point in the context of an interest payment, see *Indian and General Investment Trust Ltd v Borax Consolidated Ltd* [1920] 1 KB 539.

[32] For a case which illustrates the problem, see *Momm v Barclays Bank International Ltd* [1977] QB 790.

payment back to the original sender,[33] (iv) whether or not the bank has wrongfully dishonoured the customer's cheques, and (v) whether or not the bank has breached its obligation of confidentiality to the customer.

(e) *The consequences of breach.* In a slightly confusing provision,[34] Rome I provides that the applicable law governs '… within the limits of the powers conferred on the court by its procedural law, the consequences of a total or partial breach of obligations, including the assessment of damages in so far as it is governed by rules of law …'. The expression 'consequences of a breach' plainly embraces any right to damages, any right of termination or any similar right flowing from the contractual breach of the other party. Thus, where the banker-customer contract is governed by English law, the customer's right to damages for a breach of the duty of confidentiality will likewise be governed by English law.[35] If, however, the court is dealing with a breach of a banker-customer contract governed by a foreign system of law, then (i) the right to receive damages, the existence of a duty to mitigate, and similar matters of substance will be governed by the law applicable to the contract but (ii) the quantification of damages is a procedural matter and would thus be governed by English law in the context of proceedings in England. The award of damages must be made in compliance with English rules,[36] with the result that an award must usually consist of a single lump sum, even though the law applicable to the contract provides for payment by instalments and other types of remedy.

(f) *Extinguishing obligations, prescription, and limitation.* As has been seen, the law applicable to the banker-customer contract determines whether an obligation has been discharged by performance.[37] The same system of law must be applied in determining whether a contract has been discharged otherwise than by performance, for example, by frustration or by the lapse of a limitation period.[38] Thus, where the contract is governed by English law, the limitation periods applicable to claims in respect of credit balances or overdrafts will be determined in accordance with the rules which have already been discussed in that context.[39]

(g) *The consequences of nullity of the contract.* If the banker-customer contract proves to be void for some reason, then the consequences of that state of affairs will fall to be determined by reference to the putative applicable law—that is, the law which would have

---

[33] See the difficulties which arose in *Tayeb v HSBC Bank plc* [2004] 4 All ER 1024. The case is considered at paras 7.87–7.89 above.

[34] Article 12(1)(c) of Rome I.

[35] On the subject of damages in the event of a breach of the duty of confidentiality, see para 42.63 below. Equally, if an applicant in England seeks damages for the dishonour of cheques drawn on a bank in Iran, then the right to damages and their calculation will be a matter of Iranian law: see *Karafarin Bank v Gholam Reza Mansoury Dara* [2009] EWHC 3265 (Comm).

[36] Note the words 'within the limits of the powers conferred on the court by its procedural law' at the beginning of the provision.

[37] See subpara (d) above.

[38] Article 12(1)(d) of Rome I. The rule is consistent with the provisions of the Foreign Limitation Periods Act 1984.

[39] In the case of an ordinary current account, time will only begin to run when the customer makes a demand for payment.

governed the contract, had it been valid and effective.[40] This would mean that the court should apply English rules on restitution if a contract between an English bank and its customer proved to be void. It is very difficult to envisage the circumstances in which this could arise in practice in the context of the ordinary banker-customer contract and, in any event the customer's simple remedy would be to draw out his money and close the account. It is accordingly not proposed to consider this point in any further depth.

The above discussion thus provides a brief overview of the rules of private international law as they apply to the formation, validity, interpretation, performance, and discharge of the banker-customer contract. The applicable law may thus be described as dominant in most of the major aspects of the relationship. From the perspective of the bank, these rules are for the most part highly convenient from a commercial viewpoint; the essential features of the bank's relationships with all of the customers at a particular branch will be governed by the same system of law, wherever those customers happen to be resident or incorporated. The practical consequence is that it is usually unnecessary for the bank to enquire into the laws of the customer's 'home' jurisdiction.[41] Consequently, for example, the ability of an English bank to enforce the customer's obligations in England will be unaffected by any exchange controls or other laws in force in that jurisdiction which render it unlawful for the customer to enter into the relationship.[42] It is submitted that this position is effectively preserved by Article 9(3) of Rome I which provides that '... Effect may be given to the overriding mandatory provisions of the law of the country where the obligations arising out of the contract have to be or have been performed, in so far as those overriding mandatory provisions render the performance of the contract unlawful'. Whilst the concept of performance for these purposes should no doubt be given an autonomous meaning for the purposes of Rome I,[43] it seems reasonable to infer that the place of performance is the place in which the bank is entitled to receive the benefit of that performance or (as the case may be), the country in which the bank is required to meet cheques and carry out its other obligations. In each case, England will be the place of performance where the branch is located **40.13**

---

[40] Article 12(1)(e) of Rome I. The corresponding provision in Art 10(1)(e) of the Rome Convention did not apply because of an opt out exercised by the UK and certain other Member States. However, the provisions of Rome I apply on a uniform basis.

[41] The only real exception to this may be offered when a new corporate customer opens an account with the bank. However, this relates to questions of capacity and authority, and does not affect questions touching the law applicable to the contract.

[42] A very clear illustration of the application of this rule is offered by the decision in *Kleinwort Sons & Co v Ungarische Baumwolle Industrie AG* [1939] 2 KB 678 (CA), applied in context of an obligation to open a letter of credit in *Toprak Mahsulleri Ofisi v Finagrain Compagnie Commerciale Agricole et Financiere SA* [1979] 2 Lloyd's Rep 98 (CA). See also *British Nylon Spinners v ICI Ltd* [1955] Ch 37. Accordingly, the bank can debit the necessary amounts to the customer's accounts in England without any reference to the effect of such laws. Of course, if the bank needed to enforce its claim in the customer's home jurisdiction, then it may face very considerable difficulty in doing so, since the application of such laws will be mandatory in proceedings in that country.

[43] ie as opposed to a meaning derived purely from an English law analysis.

here and there will therefore be no scope for the application of any 'overriding mandatory provisions' of another country for the purposes of Article 9(3).[44]

40.14 But all rules have exceptions, and it is necessary to discuss the scope and application of those which may be relevant in the banker-customer context. One of the principal areas of concern in this sphere is the position of consumers. However, this is a relatively detailed subject which will be considered separately in the next chapter. It accordingly remains to consider the specific area of capacity and authority, which will plainly be an area of concern to a bank and which will not be governed by the applicable law.

Capacity and Authority

40.15 The foregoing sections have demonstrated that, subject to various exceptions, all matters which are essentially 'internal' to the contract are governed by the applicable law. But not all matters are 'internal' to the contract. Some matters affect, or are internal to, the individual parties, rather than the contract itself. These include matters such as the contractual capacity of both individual and corporate customers. As will be shown, issues of this kind generally fall outside the scope of Rome I.

40.16 It is thus proposed briefly to discuss some of the issues which may arise in dealings with individuals resident, and companies incorporated, outside England and Wales. Of course, a bank may deal with other customers such as foreign States and their regional authorities, and international organizations. Matters of this kind are too detailed for discussion here but the essential questions will remain the same, namely, (i) does the customer have the necessary capacity to enter into the proposed arrangements and (ii) if so, has it taken all necessary corporate steps to ensure that the arrangement is properly authorized and binding?

Foreign Nationals/Individuals Resident Abroad

40.17 An individual who can show that he lacked the necessary capacity to enter into a contract may avoid the contract concerned.[45] The point is important in the present context because a bank which has made facilities available would not wish to have to meet the defence that the customer lacked the capacity to enter into the arrangements.

40.18 In the context of a relationship between a bank and a foreign customer, however, which law is to govern the question of capacity? Subject to one exception which can be of particular relevance in the present context, Rome I does not apply to questions of contractual capacity.[46]

40.19 According to the leading text in this field, an individual should be treated as having contractual capacity if he has such capacity either (i) under the law of his domicile or (ii) under the

---

[44] ie the application of foreign law will be excluded from the analysis, as occurred in *Libyan Arab Foreign Bank v Bankers Trust Co* [1987] QB 728.

[45] Note that, as a starting point, every individual is presumed to have the capacity to enter into contracts. Consequently, the onus of proof is on the party alleging the incapacity.

[46] See Art 1(2)(a) of Rome I. The exception is provided by Art 13, and is considered below.

laws of the country with which the contract is most closely connected.[47] Leaving aside the domicile test, it is submitted that the contract between a banker and its customer is most closely connected with the country in which the relevant bank branch is situate.[48] As a result, so far as the English courts are concerned, the customer should be treated as having capacity to enter into the relationship if he has that capacity according to English law, regardless of his domicile, country of residence, or other factor of that kind. Consequently, any individual who is over the age of 18 and not suffering from any mental or other incapacity[49] will be regarded as having capacity to enter into a banking relationship.

Perhaps curiously, this position is in some respects reinforced by the one exception to which reference has already been made. If the foreign customer opens his account on a visit to London and the contract is thus made whilst both parties are in the same country, then the customer cannot plead his own incapacity under the laws of another jurisdiction[50] unless the bank was aware of that incapacity at the time the contract was made or would have been so aware, but for its own negligence.[51] Thus, to take an obvious example, it is well known that the age of majority in England and in many other countries is 18, and an individual can thus open a bank account under his own control once he has attained that age. If an individual visiting London produces documentation showing that he is 20 years of age, the bank may usually assume that he has the necessary capacity to enter into the relationship and he would be unable subsequently to rely on the fact that the age of majority in his home country is, in fact, 21. **40.20**

As a result, a bank would not normally have to make inquiries into the laws of the prospective customer's home country before agreeing to open an account for him. Once again, from the bank's perspective, this is a commercially very convenient result. **40.21**

Foreign Companies

Once again, Rome I does not apply to questions governed by company law, such as the incorporation, corporate capacity, and internal organization of such an entity.[52] Nor does it deal with the ability of a board of directors or similar governing body to bind a corporate entity to contracts.[53] Logically enough, such matters are governed by the law of the country **40.22**

---

[47] The domicile test may be difficult to apply in practice, since banks will seek to identify where the customer is resident but will be less concerned with the country which he may regard as his domicile (ie his permanent or ultimate home).

[48] The reasons for this conclusion are essentially similar to those offered in relation to the application (if and wherever necessary) of Art 4 of Rome I in relation to the banker-customer relationship: see para 4.09 above.

[49] That is to say, someone who has contractual capacity according to English domestic law.

[50] In the present case, a jurisdiction other than England.

[51] This is the effect of Art 13 of Rome I. Note that the provision applies if the two parties are '… in the same country…' at the time when the contract is made. It is not necessary that the parties should have met face to face for these purposes.

[52] This is the effect of Art 1(2)(f) of Rome I.

[53] Article 1(2)(g) of Rome I.

in which the company is incorporated,[54] since that is the system of law from which the company derives its constitution and its very existence.

40.23 When dealing with an English company, a bank is well advised to obtain copies of incorporation documents, board resolutions, and any other paperwork necessary to demonstrate both that (i) the company exists as a legal entity and (ii) all necessary internal action has been taken to sanction the opening of the account or other transaction at hand.[55] How should the bank proceed if seeking to open an account for a foreign company? The following points are suggested in this regard:

(a) The bank must obtain an official document (or, possibly, a legal opinion) confirming that the entity is validly incorporated and existing under the laws of the relevant jurisdiction. Of all issues which are crucial to the existence of the banker-customer relationship, the actual existence of the customer as a contracting party is surely among the most important. There would seem to be no satisfactory way of avoiding the need to obtain some satisfactory evidence in this regard.[56] However, once the validity of the *initial* mandate has been verified in this way, the ability of the individual signatories to operate the account will be governed by English law, and not by the law of the place of incorporation.[57] Consequently, if the mandate allows that authorized signatories may nominate additional or substitute signatories, then the bank may accept new signatories in accordance with the mandate and is not obliged to enquire whether the customer has completed any necessary internal corporate processes for that purpose.

(b) It will be necessary to obtain evidence to demonstrate that the establishment of the account has been duly authorized by the board or equivalent governing body of the corporation. This will consist of an appropriate resolution and, once again, the confirmation of a legal opinion may be desirable.[58]

40.24 It should be appreciated, however, that a failure to follow these procedures is not *necessarily* fatal to the bank's ability to enforce the customer's obligations in respect of the account.

---

[54] It may be possible to open an account for a corporation established in a State which is not recognized by the UK, provided that the territory concerned has a system of law which is being administered by a settled court system: see generally the Foreign Corporations Act 1991.

[55] Although, as noted at paras 26.49–26.53 above, the bank benefits from a number of statutory protections in this context if it is dealing with the directors of a company in good faith.

[56] If the customer does not exist as an independent legal entity, then it cannot incur any liability or be made party to any legal proceedings: see, for example, *International Bulk Shipping and Services Ltd v Minerals and Metals Trading Corporation of India* [1996] 1 All ER 1017; *The Kommunar (No 2)* [1997] 1 Lloyd's Rep 8. Of course, if the principal does not in fact exist, then those who have purported to act on its behalf may incur liability for breach of warranty of authority, but in practice this may be of limited assistance to the bank.

[57] See, for example, the situation which arose in *Sierra Leone Telecommunications Co Ltd v Barclays Bank plc* [1998] 2 All ER 821.

[58] It may be noted at this point that the Foreign Companies (Execution of Documents) Regulations 1994 (as amended) provide that a document or contract is to be regarded as duly executed by a foreign company if it has been executed: (i) in any manner allowed by the law of the country of incorporation for documents of that type, or (ii) by any person who has the express or implied authority of the company in accordance with the laws of the place of incorporation. These rules are continued in force by art 7 of the Companies (Consequential Amendments etc) Order 2008 (SI 2008/948). However, they appear to deal only with the validity of contracts in point of form, and would not cure defects which relate either to the corporate capacity of the company or the authority of its agents.

This conclusion may at first sight appear to be surprising, but other principles of English law may come to the bank's aid.

For example, let it be supposed that a foreign customer established an account some months ago, and the directors provided the usual mandate for named individuals to operate that account on behalf of the company, and to incur overdrafts if necessary. The signatories negotiate and utilize the overdraft, but the company[59] later claims that the facility had not been properly sanctioned by the governing body, or some other formality had not been observed. It thus seeks to avoid liability for the overdraft. Under these circumstances, it is submitted that the company should fail in that endeavour, because the delivery of the mandate by the directors is intended to clothe the signatories with the necessary authority. As a result, the company is estopped from denying the authority of the signatories to operate the account in accordance with the mandate. It is true that questions touching the authority of the company are, in the first instance, questions for the law of the place of incorporation and that, by contrast, estoppel is very much an English law concept. The English court can nevertheless apply the estoppel because (i) estoppel is a procedural rule and (ii) questions of procedure are governed by the law of the forum.[60] In effect, the company is prevented by its own conduct from raising the issue of foreign law on which it wishes to rely in order to defeat the bank's claim.[61]. Alternatively, where the relevant contract is governed by English law, the authority of agents to bind the foreign company may itself be governed by English law, and it may thus be possible to rely on the ostensible authority of the officials concerned.[62]   **40.25**

Situs of Deposit Obligations

Thus far, this chapter has principally been concerned with *contractual* questions touching the banker-customer contract in private international law.   **40.26**

It must not, however, be forgotten that the balance as between banker and customer constitutes a debt in favour of the party who is in credit.[63] The balance thus constitutes a form of property, which may be capable of being transferred or made subject to a   **40.27**

---

[59] Or, perhaps more likely, its liquidator or other insolvency official.

[60] It is submitted that estoppel, at least in the form described in the text, is of a procedural character. In *Janred Properties Ltd v ENIT* [1989] 2 All ER 444 (CA), the court appears to have applied an estoppel on the basis that it formed part of the law applicable to the contract (ie as opposed to a part of the procedural law of the forum). In the present context, the distinction is unlikely to be of great practical significance because, as already shown, the contract between a foreign customer and an English bank will almost invariably be governed by English law. In this type of case, however, it would be important to note that the signatory on the account must be held out as having the requisite authority by another director of the company; one cannot acquire any form of apparent authority by holding oneself out as an authorized person: see *Cleveland Manufacturing Co Ltd v Muslim Commercial Bank Ltd* [1981] 2 Lloyd's Rep 646.

[61] It is accepted that there may be other grounds on which the bank may be able to recover the overdraft, for example, by way of an action for money had and received. As noted at para 40.12 above, a restitutionary claim of this kind would be governed by English law in accordance with Art 12(1)(e) of Rome I.

[62] See *Rimpacific Navigation Inc v Daehan Shipbuilding Co Ltd* [2009] EWHC 2941 (Comm).

[63] See the discussion of *Foley v Hill* (1848) 9 ER 1002, at para 15.10 above.

security interest.[64] The point is important because, for private international law purposes, an item of property must have a *situs* ascribed to it for various purposes—for example, in determining whether title to that property has passed to another person, whether a security interest has been created, or whether it has been validly expropriated by governmental action. It will thus be seen that the situs of a deposit will be of importance in some of the ensuing chapters.[65] How, then, is the *situs* of a bank deposit determined? This is plainly a matter of private international law.

40.28　Whilst it is generally a relatively easy task to determine the *situs* of land or other tangible assets for private international law purposes, it is less easy to do so in relation to bank deposits or other debts, which can naturally have no *physical* location as such.[66] Nevertheless, private international law has evolved rules to deal with this difficulty.

40.29　The starting point is that a debt or other chose in action is generally situate in the country in which it can properly be recovered or enforced;[67] this usually means that the debt is legally situate in the country in which the debtor resides, for the creditor would normally take enforcement proceedings in that country.[68] In many respects, the application of this rule may be inconvenient in the case of a current account, where the *situs* of the obligations on the account might vary frequently, depending upon the credit or debit balance on the account.[69] A 'residence' test is also not easy to apply to a multinational bank; case law has frequently determined that a company is resident in the country in which its affairs are controlled.[70]

40.30　Perhaps in view of these difficulties, the 'residence of the debtor' test was disregarded by the court in *Libyan Arab Foreign Bank v Bankers Trust Co*,[71] where it was decided that the debtor-creditor relationship arising on a bank account is situate in the country in which

---

[64] In other words, the difficulties which may arise in relation to a bank deposit are not restricted to matters of a *contractual* character; questions of a *proprietary* or a *security* nature may also arise. The processes involved in taking security over a bank account in England have already been discussed at in Chapter 31 above.

[65] See in particular Chapters 44 and 45 below.

[66] In *Re Helbert Wagg & Co Ltd* [1956] Ch 323, it was stated that a debt could have no *situs* until it fell due for payment. However, it is submitted that this is incorrect; a debt is an asset which can be sold or dealt with prior to maturity, and a *situs* must thus be attributed to it even before its due date for repayment. Both earlier and later authorities confirm this point: see, for example *English, Scottish and Australian Bank Ltd v Commissioner of Inland Revenue* [1932] AC 238 (HL); *Kwok Chi Leung Karl v Commissioner of Estate Duty* [1988] 1 WLR 1035 (PC).

[67] See *New York Life Insurance Co v Public Trustee* [1924] Ch 101, 109 (CA) and *Kwok Chi Leung Karl v Commissioner of Estate Duty* [1988] 1 WLR 1035 (PC). A number of cases could be cited by way of additional authority; see, for example, *Arab Bank Ltd v Barclays Bank (DC&O)* [1954] AC 495 (HL); *Societe Eram Shipping Co Ltd v Compagnie Internationale de Navigation* [2003] 3 WLR 21 (HL). For US case law, see *Pervez v Chase Manhattan Bank NA*, 463 NE 2nd 5 (1984), *Callejo v Bancomer SA* 764 F2d 1101 (1985, US Court of Appeals, Fifth Cir) and *Citibank NA v Wells Fargo Asia Ltd* 495 US 600 (1990). Recent Australian authority is provided by *European Bank Ltd v Citibank Ltd* [2004] NSWCA, 76. These cases are discussed in specific contexts later in this section.

[68] For authority to this effect, see *English, Scottish and Australian Bank Ltd v Commissioner of Inland Revenue* [1932] AC 238 (HL). For the reasons given below, this decision may no longer be authoritative in the specific context of a bank account.

[69] ie if the account was in credit, then the debt would be situate in the country in which the bank branch is located; in the case of a debit balance, the debt would be situate in the customer's country of residence.

[70] *Unit Construction Co v Bullock* [1960] AC 351 (HL).

[71] [1989] QB 728.

the relevant branch is located.[72] Whilst it remains open to parties to argue that the more traditional, 'residence' test should be applied, it is submitted that the approach adopted in the *Libyan Arab Bank* case is both convenient and commercially realistic. It is particularly convenient from the commercial perspective because both the governing law of the account relationship (that is, the law which governs the rights and obligations arising from the account) and its *lex situs* will be identical. The present work will therefore proceed on the same basis, that is to say, that the *situs* of the debt will always be the country in which the account-holding branch is situate.

In most cases, the identity of the branch at which the account is maintained will be obvious.[73] But the occasional difficulty may arise. In one case affected by the outbreak of the Second World War, American depositors had paid US dollar amounts to a California branch of Sumitomo Bank. However, the evidence demonstrated that these sums were intended to be converted into yen and repayment would accordingly be effected through a branch in Japan. As a result, Japan (rather than California) was the *situs* of the deposit obligation.[74] It is possible to envisage similar cases arising in a more modern context, for it is not uncommon for banks to arrange for the opening of accounts with overseas branches or subsidiaries, In the final analysis—as in the example just given—the result must depend upon the intention of the parties. Where was the account relationship intended to be located? **40.31**

As noted earlier, the identification of the *situs* of a bank deposit can be of importance in a variety of contexts. For present purposes, the main point is that title to (or ownership of) a bank deposit can—in the absence of action on the part of the customer himself—only be changed by virtue of legislation or court orders which form a part of the law of the *situs*. As a matter of private international law, rules forming part of another system cannot affect title to such a deposit.[75] As noted earlier, the legal consequences of this state of affairs will be considered in more depth in the ensuing chapters. **40.32**

But the issue may also arise in other contexts. For example, since a bank account is a species of property, the question of entitlement to a joint account on the death of one party will be governed by the *lex situs*, that is, the place in which the account-holding branch is situate. The rule is logical because the bank will need to be able to obtain a discharge of its obligations under the law applicable to the account and, as noted, these two systems of law will coincide.[76] **40.33**

---

[72] So far as English law is concerned, it is an implied term of the contract that the obligation to repay is 'localized' at the branch at which the account is kept: *Joachimson v Swiss Bank Corporation* [1921] 3 KB 110 at 129.

[73] For example, printed forms of cheques usually state the address of the account holding branch.

[74] *Aratini v Kennedy* 317 F 2d 161, motion denied, 323 F 2d 427 (1963). In other words, the California branch did not accept the funds as a deposit on its own account; it accepted them as agent for its Head Office in Japan.

[75] As a matter of principle, title to property situate in England can only be changed or varied by English law, and questions of foreign law would be irrelevant: see *Banco de Vizcaya v Don Alfonso de Borbon y Austria* [1934] All ER 555. See also *Zwack & Co v Kraus Bros & Co* 237 F 2d 235 (1956).

[76] See *Berbaum Estate v Silver* 192 NSR 2d 30 (Nova Scotia).

Conclusions

40.34 Is it possible to draw any general conclusions from the various issues of private international law considered in this chapter?

40.35 Perhaps at the risk of overgeneralization, it is possible to say that in the vast majority of cases, the law applicable to the account—which governs contractual matters—and the law of the country in which the relationship is deemed to be situate—which governs proprietary questions—will coincide.

40.36 This is a commercially convenient result—at least from the bank's perspective. The customer business which it maintains at a particular branch will be subject to the laws of the country in which that branch is to be found, and it will only be concerned with questions of foreign law in relatively limited cases. The ability to run customer relationships solely within the single legal framework applicable to the bank branch will, of course, also enhance the speed with which the bank is able to respond to its customers' instructions.

41

CROSS-BORDER FINANCIAL SERVICES, CONSUMER PROTECTION, AND UNFAIR CONTRACT TERMS

Introduction

It was noted in the last chapter that most of the incidents of the banker-customer relationship will be governed by the law of the country in which the account-holding branch is located. **41.01**

From a banking perspective, this is satisfactory as far as it goes, but banks now do more than simply provide current and deposit accounts. They may undertake wider dealings in the financial markets on behalf of their customers. In such instances, will they again be entitled to assume that English law will govern the contractual relationship? **41.02**

Banks may, in addition, provide services to high net worth individuals—often resident abroad—who are 'consumers' in the technical sense of that term but that will not in practice reflect the reality of the relationship. Banks may therefore wish to know whether arrangements entered into with such customers are amenable to challenge on the basis of legislation directed towards the protection of the weaker contracting party. **41.03**

It is also fair to observe that—whilst Rome I preserves many of the features of its predecessor Convention—many of the new provisions which have been introduced deal specifically with financial instruments and contracts for the provision of financial services. The recent **41.04** introduction of Rome I thus means that it is an opportune time to consider the effect of these provisions.

41.05 Against this general background, this chapter considers the following subject matter:

1. the background to Rome I and its consumer protection rules;
2. the meaning of 'financial instruments' for Rome I purposes;
3. contracts concluded within a multilateral trading system (Articles 4(1)(h) and 6(4)(e));
4. various consumer law exemptions applicable to financial instruments, rights issues and takeover offers (Article 6(4)(d));
5. the consumer law exemption relating to foreign services (Article 6(4)(a));
6. the banker-customer relationship;
7. the impact of domestic consumer laws; and
8. the conclusions to be drawn from the various provisions discussed above.

Choice of Law under Rome I

41.06 As noted in the previous chapter,[1] and to respect party autonomy, an express choice of law is to be applied by the courts. Accordingly, a contract is governed by the law chosen by the parties. This choice can be made expressly or must be clearly demonstrated by the terms of the contract or the circumstances of the case.[2] As before, parties to a contract can therefore avoid uncertainty by inserting an express choice of law clause.

41.07 In practice, most problem cases arise in the absence of an express choice of law. Rome I provides a series of rules designed to identify the country that will provide the governing law of specific types of contract.[3] For example, and insofar as potentially relevant to financial market contracts, Rome I provides that:

(a) contracts for the sale of goods or services will be governed by the law of the country in which the seller of goods/provider of services has his habitual residence;[4] and
(b) contracts concluded within a multilateral trading system governed by a single law will be governed by that system of law.[5]

41.08 Contracts of a kind not listed in Article 4(1) will generally be governed by '... the law of the country in where the party required to effect the characteristic performance of the contract has his habitual residence ...' in accordance with Article 4(2). In the case of a corporation, its 'habitual residence' is the place of its central administration or the branch or agency through which the contract is concluded or is to be performed.[6]

---

[1] See para 40.08 above.
[2] Article 3 of Rome I.
[3] Article 4(1) of Rome I.
[4] This rule, which is of importance in the context of the contract between a bank and an account holder, has already been discussed in some depth in Chapter 40 above.
[5] On this subject see 'Multilateral Trading Systems', below.
[6] For the details, see Art 19 of Rome I.

Provisions Relating to Consumer Contracts

Contracts between consumers and professionals create a further layer of complexity, in **41.09** view of the long-perceived need to protect consumers against contracting parties who are seen to enjoy significantly greater bargaining power and/or knowledge of the subject matter. Consumers are defined as those individuals[7] who conclude a contract for a purpose that is outside their trade or profession; conversely, and unsurprisingly, professionals[8] are those acting in the exercise of their trade or profession.

Rome I—like the Rome Convention before it—accepts that a consumer contract can **41.10** include an express choice of law[9] but this cannot detract from protections afforded to the consumer from which it is not possible to derogate under the laws of his country of habitual residence.[10]

In the absence of an express choice of law in a contract between a consumer and a profes- **41.11** sional, the contract *as a whole* will be governed by the laws of the consumer's habitual residence as long as the professional either carries on his commercial or professional activities in that country, or otherwise directs such activities to that country.[11]

The practical effect of these two provisions is that a consumer cannot be deprived of the **41.12** benefit of his local law on implied warranties as to fitness/quality, unfair contract terms, and similar matters merely because the supplier's standard terms of business select a different governing law for the contract.

Yet, having extended to the consumer a number of special protections to compensate for **41.13** his limited bargaining power, Article 6(4) then backtracks, and strips away that protection in specific cases which have relevance in the fields of financial and investment services.[12] But before seeking to address the details, it is necessary at the outset to address certain matters of definition.

---

[7] A 'natural person' as opposed to a company: see Art 6(1) of Rome I.

[8] Including individuals and bodies corporate.

[9] This state of affairs was not, however, achieved without some difficulty. An earlier version of Rome I provided for consumer contracts to be governed, in their entirety by the laws of the consumer's home state; happily, their proposal was dropped. For discussion, see Financial Markets Law Committee, 'Legal Assessment of the conversion of the Rome Convention to a Community Instrument and the Provisions of the Proposed Rome I Regulation', Issue 121, April 2006, section 7, and the Ministry of Justice Consultation Paper, 'Rome I—Should the UK Opt in?' (2 April 2008).

[10] Article 6(2) of Rome I. For convenience, these laws are referred to in this article as the 'home State consumer protection laws'. However, whilst this is a convenient tag, it should be appreciated that Art 6(2) is not in terms confined to laws which are specifically intended for the protection of consumers. The provision merely states that, where one party is a consumer, the governing law cannot detract from rules which cannot be diluted under the consumer's home law, regardless of the identity or terms of the applicable law itself.

[11] Article 6(1) of Rome I.

[12] As will be seen, we are here concerned specifically with Art 6(4)(a), (d) and (e). The other sub-paragraphs of Art 6(4) deal with contracts of carriage and contracts related to real estate, which are not relevant in the present context.

Financial Instruments

41.14 The expression 'financial instruments' runs through the Rome I provisions about to be discussed. Financial instruments are those instruments specified in Article 4(1), point 17 of the Markets in Financial Instruments Directive 2004/39/EC (MiFID)[13] and accordingly includes:

(a) transferable securities (including shares and debt instruments traded on the capital markets);

(b) money market instruments;[14]

(c) units in collective investment schemes;

(d) options, futures, swaps, forward rate, and other derivative contracts relating to securities, currencies, interest rates, or financial indices;

(e) options, swaps, and other derivative contracts relating to commodities;

(f) credit default swaps;

(g) financial contracts for differences; and

(h) certain arrangements relating to climatic variables.

41.15 This covers most, if not all of the financial instruments which may be relevant in the context of takeover offers or rights issues and those that may exist within the multilateral trading systems covered by the bespoke provisions of Rome I. Banks or their affiliates may be involved in the arrangement of dealings for their clients in instruments of this kind, and it is thus appropriate to consider the system of law which governs such arrangements and thus determines the respective rights and obligations of the parties in each case. It is thus now possible to turn to the substantive provisions.

Multilateral Trading Systems

41.16 Reference has already been made to Article 4(1)(h) of Rome I.[15] The provision applies in the absence of an express choice of law. The relevant text reads as follows:

> To the extent that the law applicable to the contract has not been chosen in accordance with Article 3 ... the law governing the contract shall be determined as follows ...
>
> (a) a contract concluded within a multilateral system which brings together or facilitates the bringing together of multiple third-party buying and selling interests in financial instruments .... in accordance with non-discretionary rules and governed by a single law, shall be governed by that law ...

---

[13] This point is confirmed by Recital (30) to Rome I. The actual list is set out in Section C of Annex I to MiFID. There are certain questions of detail which arise from the individual items, but issues of this kind go beyond the scope of the present chapter.

[14] The expression 'money market instrument' is generally taken to refer to short-term, fixed income securities representing obligations of high grade issuers.

[15] See 'Choice of Law under Rome I', above.

Article 4(1)(h) is new law, in the sense that it has no predecessor in the Rome Convention. **41.17** Multilateral trading systems receive further attention in Article 6(4)(e), which provides that the home State consumer protection laws '... shall not apply to ... a contract concluded within the type of system falling within the scope of Article 4(1)(h) ...'. The rationale behind these new rules can be deduced from recital (28) of Rome I, which reads:

> It is important to ensure that rights and obligations which constitute a financial instrument are not covered by the general rule applicable to consumer contracts, as that could lead to different laws being applicable to each of the instruments issued, therefore changing their nature and preventing their fungible trading and offering. Likewise, whenever such instruments are issued or offered, the contractual relationship established between the issuer or the offeror and the consumer should not necessarily be subject to the mandatory application of the law of the country of habitual residence of the consumer, as there is a need to ensure uniformity in the terms and conditions of an issuance or an offer. The same rationale should apply with regard to the multilateral systems covered by Article 4(1)(h) in respect of which it should be ensured that the law of the country of habitual residence of the consumer will not interfere with the rules applicable to contracts included within those systems or with the operator of such systems.

The combined effect of these provisions in relation to a contract concluded within a **41.18** multilateral trading system may be summarized as follows:

(a) it remains open to the parties to select the law applicable to their contract in accordance with the 'freedom of choice' provisions in Article 3 of Rome I. It is however likely that any choice would be contained in the professional's standard terms of business and would refer to the law under which the system operates;

(b) in the absence of any express choice, the contract will in any event be governed by the law applicable to the system itself; and

(c) in either case, where one party to the contract is a consumer,[16] the home State consumer protection laws will not be applied in order to detract from the effectiveness or scope of the law applicable to the contract as a whole.

It is now necessary to move to more detailed matters of definition. It has already been **41.19** shown[17] that the expression 'financial instruments' has a broad definition. But what of the expression 'multilateral system'? The use of the term 'financial market' was avoided on the grounds that a lack of a settled definition of this term in European law would cause considerable legal uncertainty.[18] Instead, Article (4)(1)(h) itself provides a functional definition. It states that a multilateral system is a system which facilitates the mutual introduction of buying and selling interests in financial instruments. The system must also have a set rule book and must be governed by a single system of law. This does, of course, connote a sale and purchase of shares, debentures or other securities through a stock exchange or other form of multilateral trading facility.

---

[16] As to the likelihood of a consumer being a party to such a contract, see below.
[17] See the discussion under 'Financial Instruments', above.
[18] Doc no 7418/07 of 15 March 2007 from the Services of the Commission to the Council's Committee on Civil Law Matters on Certain Financial Aspects relating to the application of Articles 4 and 5, p 3.

41.20 The language does, however, require further examination. The '… contract concluded *within* a multilateral system …' would usually be the contract between the brokers representing the buyer and the seller. As a general rule, only brokers can trade through such systems because settlement is guaranteed via the relevant clearing house. As against each other and the exchange, brokers will therefore invariably act as principals. It follows that, for example, all contracts for the sale and purchase of securities as concluded through the London Stock Exchange would be governed by English law in any event,[19] regardless of factors such as the identity of the brokers, the nationality of the issuer of the securities, the location of the respective clients/consumers, or any other matter.

41.21 This rule is convenient and no doubt reflects the commercial expectations of the parties concerned. But Article 4(1)(h) applies only to the contract between the 'professionals' or brokers since, under the rules of any exchange, they will be the only parties between whom '… a contract [may be] concluded *within* a multilateral system …'. This position is, however, difficult to reconcile with recital (28), in which it is stated that '… the country of residence of the consumer [should] not interfere with the rules applicable to contracts concluded *within* those systems …'. But the consumer will not be party to those contracts in any event—they will be concluded between professionals, acting between themselves as principals and not as agent for their respective clients.[20] On that basis, it is a little difficult to see how consumers and their special rights could intervene in such contracts; the home State consumer protection laws cannot apply to agreements to which no consumer is a party. It is thus hard to see how Article 6(4)(e)—which disapplies those rules in relation to contracts concluded within such a system—can have any practical effect.[21] The consumer would be contracting with his broker, and his entitlement to the benefit of his home State consumer protection laws in the context of that particular contract would be determined by reference to other provisions of Rome I.[22]

Financial Instruments/Rights Issues/Takeover Offers

41.22 Article 6(4)(d) excludes from the scope of the home State consumer protection laws:

(a) rights and obligations which constitute a financial instrument;

(b) rights and obligations constituting the terms and conditions of a public offer of securities;

(c) rights and obligations governing public takeover bids for shares or other transferable securities; and

---

[19] ie even apart from the provisions of Art 4(1)(h), either because the parties would have expressly selected that law, or because the selling broker—who performs the obligations which are 'characteristic' of the contract for the purposes of Art 4(2) of Rome I—would be acting through a branch or office in England.

[20] The point is confirmed by the 15 March 2007 paper referred to in n 18 above, which rightly observes that: 'Contracts for the provision of services between a financial intermediary and a client are not concluded within these systems …'

[21] The provision does not appear to do any positive harm, but it is difficult to envisage any circumstances under which it might apply.

[22] In relation to this issue, see 'Foreign Services', below.

(d) rights and obligations governing the subscription and redemption of units in collective investment schemes (to the extent to which these activities do not themselves amount to the provision of a financial service).

These exceptions will be considered in that order.

Financial Instruments

It is important to note that the 'financial instruments' exclusion applies only to the rights **41.23** and obligations which *constitute* the financial instrument. This means, for example, that a foreign holder of a traded option[23] cannot challenge the terms of that option on the basis that it is in some way inconsistent with his home State consumer protection laws. Likewise, such rules could not be invoked to the detriment of the law governing shares or debentures issued by a company.[24]

In the writer's view, the exclusion of home State consumer protection laws in this context **41.24** is clearly appropriate. The respective rights and obligations of a company vis á vis its shareholders or bondholders should clearly be governed by a single system of law. The fungibility of financial instruments is essential to the ability to trade them, and this depends upon each instrument conferring identical rights on the holders irrespective of their 'home' countries or whether they are acting as consumers. This view is reinforced by the fact that financial instruments of a particular class (i) will invariably be intended to rank *pari passu* among themselves and (ii) will often create rights and obligations among the holders *inter se*, and not merely as against the issuer.[25] It would thus plainly be inappropriate that some investors should have greater rights than others in respect of financial instruments intended to be issued on identical terms.

In practice, consumer-related claims are more likely to arise under the *contract for the sub-* **41.25** *scription or purchase* of the financial instrument for example, on the footing that the consumer had contracted to purchase the instrument on the faith of representations which are later shown to be false. But, as will be shown below, the protection of home State consumer protection laws is once again withdrawn where the relevant contract results from an offer made to the public.

Terms and Conditions of Public Share Offers

The preceding section dealt with the terms of the financial instrument itself. However, **41.26** Article 6(4)(d) also deals with the contract which leads up to the acquisition of such an instrument.

---

[23] A traded option would constitute a 'financial instrument' for the purposes of the definition given above.

[24] Once again, shares and debentures are 'financial instruments' for the purposes of the definition given above. The point is made for convenience of illustration but it should be appreciated that instruments of this kind would frequently fall outside the scope of Rome I in any event. In relation to shares, it appears that any issues would be 'questions governed by the law of companies' which are excluded from Rome I by Art 1(2)(f). Likewise, debentures will often be negotiable instruments which are excluded by Art 1(2)(d).

[25] For example, a trust deed entered into in connection with an issue of debentures will contain clauses dealing with meetings, voting, enforcement action, and other matters which will be binding as between the holders themselves and the trustee.

41.27   It should be noted that the share offers exclusion applies only to *public* offers,[26] but, subject to that consideration, it applies equally to an offer of new shares by the issuing company and a vendor placing.[27] This is a justifiable exception, because:

(a)   subscribers or purchasers may be resident in a number of different countries and it is unreasonable to expect the issuer or vendor to acquaint itself with their respective consumer laws;

(b)   rights created by such an issue should be non-discriminatory, in the sense that no subscriber/purchaser should have *greater* rights against the issuer/vendor merely because he is resident in a particular country; and

(c)   it is likely that subscribers/purchasers will be adequately protected by the laws applicable to the issue (eg remedies for misleading listing particulars,[28] misrepresentation, and similar claims).

Public Takeover Offers

41.28   Once again, the takeover bids exclusion applies only to *public* takeover offers, and not to private acquisitions.[29]

41.29   It will often be difficult to apply home State consumer protection laws to public takeover offers in any event, because the formal recipient of the offer will frequently be the custodian which will appear on the target company's register of shareholders.[30] The offeror will thus not know the identity of the underlying owner, still less whether or not he is a 'consumer' and, if so, in which country he has his habitual residence. As a practical matter, it would therefore be unreasonable to impose home State consumer protection laws on the contract resulting from the acceptance of the bidder's offer.

41.30   It is, in any event, doubtful whether the offeror company can be said to be contracting with the ultimate consumer. The offer is made to registered members of the target, and not to the underlying, beneficial owners.

Collective Investment Schemes

41.31   This exemption disapplies home State consumer protection laws in the context of contracts for the *subscription and redemption* of units in a collective investment scheme. Once again, the exemption is justifiable largely for the reasons given above in relation to share issues and takeover offers. Following their issue, the units will constitute 'financial instruments' to which home State consumer protection laws will, again, be inapplicable.

---

[26]   The exclusion would not be appropriate in relation to offers of a *private* character, where the issuer or vendor has a greater degree of control over the identity of the recipients of the offer.

[27]   This conclusion appears to be justified by the terms of Art 6(4)(d), which refers to 'the issuance *or offer* to the public ... of transferable securities' (emphasis supplied).

[28]   This point is reinforced by the fact that the available remedies in such cases have been harmonized pursuant to the Prospectus Directive (2003/71/EC) on the prospectus to be published when securities are offered to the public or admitted to trading on a regulated market.

[29]   This state of affairs would again seem to be justified, largely for the reasons given in n 26 above.

[30]   In order to facilitate trading in listed, uncertificated securities, they will be registered in the name of a custodian for the relevant clearing system and the identity of the 'real' owner will not appear.

Foreign Services

The above discussion has demonstrated that home State consumer protection laws will not   **41.32**
apply to contracts which *constitute* a financial instrument or involve a *public* offer of or for
such instruments. But many transactions involving financial instruments or services provided by banks in relation to them will be of a *private* character. How does Rome I deal with
contracts of this kind?

Although the provision is not directly or specifically aimed at the financial markets, it   **41.33**
should be noted that Article 6(4)(a) of Rome I[31] disapplies the home State consumer protection rules in relation to '… a contract for the supply of services where the services are to
be supplied to the consumer exclusively in a country other than that in which he has his
principal residence …'.

A contractual choice of law would therefore be binding in its entirety on the consumer in   **41.34**
this type of case, and his home State consumer protection laws will accordingly be inapplicable. The question, of course, is when are services provided 'exclusively' outside the
consumer's home State?

Plainly, the provision of any part of the services within the consumer's home State will   **41.35**
deprive the supplier of the protection of Article 6(4)(a)—the use of the word 'exclusively'
does not admit of any form of materiality or similar test or any 'balancing' between the
levels of services provided within or outside the consumer's home State. This, in turn,
means that two questions will require particular focus, namely:

(a) what type of activity constitutes a part of the 'service'; and
(b) where is that activity carried out?

As to the first question, suppose that a bank in London receives instructions from a foreign   **41.36**
client to execute a transaction involving financial instruments. It may advise the client on
pricing and other matters. It will then carry out those instructions and send a confirmation
to the client. It may also arrange to have the securities held by a bank or other custodian on
behalf of the client. All of these activities would appear to form a part of the 'service' offered
by the bank to its client pursuant to the contract between them.

In relation to the second question, the services just described will involve contact with the   **41.37**
client, who will receive and act upon his bank's advice in his own home State. Nevertheless,
the bank provides the relevant advice and despatches the necessary communications from
its London office, and it seems clear that such services are provided exclusively outside the
consumer's home State.[32] In such a case, the result is that Article 6(4)(a) deprives the client
of the benefit of his home State consumer protection laws.

---

[31] The provision mirrors the terms of Art 5(4) of the Rome Convention.
[32] In other words, the fact that the consumer receives and acts upon advice within his home State does not
prejudice the conclusion that the services are provided exclusively outside that State. It is difficult to provide a
professional or business service without communicating with the client at some point of the process!

41.38   Although not specifically directed towards the provision of *financial* services, the above example makes it clear that Article 6(4)(a) has significance for banks and other service providers in the UK's financial and securities markets. In particular, and as a very general rule, the application of this provision means that overseas consumers who use the services of UK financial institutions will not be entitled to the protection of their home State consumer protection laws. The result is that the institutions providing such services are not required to inquire into any such laws which may be in effect in the home States of their respective customers.

The Banker-Customer Contract

41.39   The identification of the system of law applicable to the banker-customer relationship has already been discussed in depth in the last chapter. It was concluded that the contract will in the ordinary course be governed by English law where the bank is located in England. Once again, however, it is necessary to consider whether the customer's home State consumer protection laws will be imported into the contract, thus perhaps creating rights and obligations which the bank had not anticipated.

41.40   Once again, it is suggested that the application of any protections afforded by the customer's home State consumer protection laws will be precluded by the provisions of Article 6(4)(a) of Rome I, because the services to be rendered under the contract will be '… supplied to the consumer exclusively in a country other than that in which he has his habitual residence …'. The services to be provided by the English bank will consist of the collection and payment of cheques, money transfers, the provision of deposit account facilities, and the like. All of these services will be operated in the normal way out of the account-holding branch. Although the customer will perhaps receive the effective economic benefit of these services in the place of his habitual residence, the services themselves are provided in England.

41.41   In the writer's view, this position does not change merely because representatives of the bank visit the customer in his home State in order to procure the signature of mandates, the execution of overdraft, or other facility agreements, and the like. These documents are important but they are of an essentially *preparatory* nature; it remains the case that the actual services are provided from the bank branch in England.

41.42   Save under unusual circumstances, it will therefore follow that a bank providing its ordinary services out of an English branch will not have to concern itself with the customer's home State consumer protection laws, since there are no situations under which these could become applicable to the contractual arrangements.[33]

---

[33] For a slightly different approach to this subject, see Dicey, Morris, & Collins, para 33-298.

The Impact of Domestic Consumer Protection Laws

The foregoing discussion has established that the consumer protection laws of a customer's **41.43** home State will not generally apply in the context of a number of cross-border financial services contracts. As noted above, from the perspective of the provider, this is no doubt a satisfactory outcome. He is relieved of the burden of investigating the laws of the customer's country of residence and, in any event, such laws are by their very nature invariably designed to operate to the advantage of the consumer and to the detriment of the service provider.

But what of the consumer protection laws of the country in which the bank or other service **41.44** provider is located or which form a part of the law applicable to the contract? Where the contract is governed by English law, the United Kingdom's consumer protection laws will form a part of the law applicable to the financial services contract itself.[34] Should those laws be applied in cross-border cases of this kind?

In principle, it might be thought that the answer to this question is straightforward. If the **41.45** contract is governed by English law, then English consumer protection laws will form a part of the system of law which governs the contract and, accordingly, the foreign customer will be entitled to the benefit of such rules.[35] Up to a point, this is true but the question will be—are those laws applicable in the particular circumstances of the case? This, in turn, raises the perennially difficult question of territoriality—in this context, do the relevant rules apply for the protection of consumers resident outside the United Kingdom? The question is frequently left unanswered by the legislation at issue.[36]

It is proposed to consider three pieces of United Kingdom legislation in this context.[37]   **41.46**

Unfair Contract Terms Act 1977

The terms of the Unfair Contract Terms Act 1977 ('the 1977 Act') have already been **41.47** discussed.[38] However, for present purposes, it may be helpful briefly to note that the 1977 Act is designed for the protection of:

(a) consumers; and
(b) other persons who may be dealing in the course of a business but who have no realistic opportunity to influence the terms of the contract.

Viewed from the other angle, the 1977 Act was intended to prevent the stronger party from **41.48** exploiting its position in order to deprive the other party of rights or remedies which ought otherwise be available to it. In such cases, the stronger party cannot, by reference to any

---

[34] ie in accordance with Art 20 of Rome I. It is therefore unnecessary to have regard to provisions such as Art 3(3) or 9 dealing with the application of mandatory rules in various situations. They form a part of the governing law in any event.

[35] Compare the situation which arose in *Centrax Ltd v Citibank NA*, discussed at para 41.51 below.

[36] For a discussion of the whole subject, see Dicey, Morris, & Collins, paras 1-032 *et seq*.

[37] On some of the issues about to be discussed, see Dicey, Morris, & Collins, paras 33-027–33-043.

[38] See paras 15.38–15.44 above.

contract term, exclude or restrict his liability for breach of the agreement, unless he can demonstrate that the relevant term is reasonable.

41.49 It is not necessary to repeat the relevant provisions here because, in a cross-border context, the key question will be: does the 1977 Act apply at all? Plainly, if the Act is inapplicable in the first instance, then questions of 'reasonableness' and other matters derived from the 1977 Act will not arise.

41.50 In this context, it is proposed to examine the decision of the Court of Appeal in *Centrax Ltd v Citibank NA*,[39] which provides an interesting example of the vital role which the identification of the applicable law can play in determining the outcome of litigation. The relevant factual background may be summarized as follows:

(a) in 1991, Centrax had subscribed to the 'Worldlink' system operated by Citibank. The system allowed Centrax and other subscribing customers to the facility to write cheques in numerous different currencies in different parts of the world, thus avoiding or mitigating some of the costs and delays otherwise involved in making such payments. The use of this service obviously relied on access to Citibank's extensive international network;

(b) in order to participate in Worldlink, Centrax executed a standard form document prepared by Citibank and titled the 'World International Client Service Agreement';

(c) the Worldlink Agreement governed the use of the system and provided a number of protections for Citibank. In particular, clause 7(b) required Centrax to indemnify Citibank against any losses which Citibank might suffer as a result of the '... loss, theft, destruction *or unauthorised use* of any payment instrument ...';

(d) clause 11 of the Worldlink Agreement provided that '... This Agreement and all agreements and instruments related to this Agreement shall be governed and interpreted according to the laws of the State of New York, United States of America, provided that any action or dispute between the parties regarding any payment instrument shall be governed by the laws of the country or State in which the drawee of such payment instrument is located ...';

(e) for good measure, and lest there be any doubt on the subject, clause 17(d) of the Agreement confirmed that document was to be understood '... in the English language as used in the United States of America...'.

41.51 Against this contractual background, 66 Centrax cheques totalling some £403.650.93 were paid by Citibank's branch in London notwithstanding that—according to Centrax—the signatures on those cheques had been forged.[40] Now, if the cheques were indeed forged, Citibank would not normally have been entitled to debit the account of Centrax with the value of those cheques. The banker-customer relationship would have been governed by English law and, subject to very limited exceptions, the paying bank takes the risk of forgery.[41] However, as noted above, clause 11 of the Worldlink Agreement contained an

---

[39] [1999] All ER (D) 221 (CA).

[40] This question was not decided on the evidence because the hearing before the Court of Appeal was concerned solely with the application (or otherwise) of the 1977 Act.

[41] On this subject, see the discussion at para 15.24 above.

express choice of the laws of the State of New York as the governing law of the contract. This, however, did not finally resolve matters because the provision allowed for English law to govern disputes concerning a particular payment instrument. In view of the terms of clause 7(b) of the Agreement (reproduced above), the application of New York law would provide Citibank with an indemnity, whilst the application of English law would impose on it an uncovered liability. The crucial question therefore was: which system of law applied under the particular circumstances which had arisen?

The Court of Appeal noted that (i) the general rule was that the arrangements between the parties were governed by New York law but (ii) by way of exception, the issue would be governed by English law if the contract related to a 'payment instrument' because, in the present case, Citibank London was the drawee of the cheques for the purposes of clause 11 of the Worldlink Agreement. **41.52**

Now, in a loose sense, it may be said that virtually *every* dispute arising from the Worldlink Agreement would in some way relate to a payment instrument, since the whole function of the Agreement was to facilitate the drawing of cheques in a multiplicity of currencies. But to apply the law of the drawee's location in every such case would plainly subvert the general rule in clause 11, since in practice New York law would then only apply if the cheque was drawn on Citibank New York. For these reasons, the Court of Appeal held that the proviso governed only those cases where the dispute arose directly from the payment instrument itself—for example, where the dispute concerned the respective obligations of the parties in their capacities of drawer and drawee of a particular cheque. The court accordingly held that New York law applied to the issue which had arisen in relation to the scope and effect of the indemnity clause, with the result that the validity of that provision could not be challenged under the terms of the 1977 Act.[42] **41.53**

The value of this decision to Citibank is immediately obvious, since the choice of New York law had the effect of excluding the operation of the 1977 Act. As a result, the indemnity against unauthorized payments could not be challenged on the basis of this legislation. Had the clause been governed by English law, then it may have been very difficult to defend it against an attack on 'reasonableness' grounds, since the bank would be protected even in situations where it had paid without a valid authority from the customer. Although the agreement at issue dealt with the use of cheques, which are now less frequently used as a means of payment in international transactions, it is quite conceivable that global 'framework' agreements of this type are still in use. On this basis, the *Centrax* decision may remain relevant for the future. **41.54**

---

[42] It is true that the English courts will not apply a selection of a foreign governing law if it was made 'wholly or mainly for the purpose of enabling the party imposing it to evade the operation of this Act': see s 27(2)(a) of the 1977 Act. But the contract was an 'international' contract in the sense that it gave the customer access to Citibank's branches on a worldwide basis. It thus could not seriously be argued that the 'anti-evasion' provision had any relevance to the circumstances of this particular case.

Unfair Terms in Consumer Contracts Regulations

41.55 The Unfair Terms in Consumer Contracts Regulations 1999 ('the 1999 Regulations')[43] are designed to protect consumers against unfair terms in standard contracts which have not been individually negotiated. The European origin of the regulations suggests that they are designed solely for the protection of consumers resident in an EU Member State. However, it is tentatively suggested that the regulations are intended to apply regardless of the consumer's location. There are various indications that the application of the regulations cannot be avoided by selecting the law of a non-Member State to govern the contract. For example, regulation 9 states that, where such a law has been selected, the regulations should nevertheless be applied 'if the contract has a close connection with the territory of the Member States …'. The inference must be that the 1999 Regulations—where they apply as a part of the system of law applicable to the contract—must be applied *regardless* of the nature or extent of any connecting factor with a Member State. In this context, it may be observed that the Supreme Court has recently confirmed that certain standard contractual provisions for the payment of bank charges are not amenable to challenge by the Office of Fair Trading under the 1999 Regulations, but it does not appear to have been suggested that consumers resident outside the European Union should be treated less favourably in the context of any review which might otherwise take place.[44] It may be that the point did not arise, was not regarded as material, or was marginal in the context of the main issues in dispute. Or the point may have been regarded as obvious. At all events, it seems appropriate to proceed on the basis that any consumer—wherever resident—is entitled to the benefit of the 1999 Regulations in relation to any contract governed by English law.[45]

Consumer Credit Act 1974

41.56 The Consumer Credit Act 1974 ('the 1974 Act')[46] poses a similar set of problems, although the approach to interpretation must perhaps be different since the legislation lacks a European origin.[47]

41.57 Certain provisions of the 1974 Act do contain indications as to their territorial scope. Furthermore, the Secretary of State has power to exempt consumer credit agreements from the terms of the 1974 Act where they have '… a connection with a country outside the United Kingdom …'. That power has been exercised in relation to agreements made '… in connection with trade in goods and services between the United Kingdom and a country outside the United Kingdom or within a country or between countries outside the

---

[43] SI 1999/2083, implementing the Council Directive of 5 April 1993 on unfair terms in consumer contracts, [1993] OJ L 95/29.

[44] See *Office of Fair Trading v Abbey National plc* [2010] 1 All ER 667 (Supreme Court). The decision is considered at para 15.48 above.

[45] The point is not as remote as it may at first appear. Many London banks pursue business from high net worth individuals based in the Middle and Far East who, despite the scale of their personal resources, would still be regarded as consumers for the purposes of legislation of this kind.

[46] As amended by the Consumer Credit Act 2006. The Act has been discussed in Chapter 4 above.

[47] Recast European initiatives in the field of consumer credit have already been discussed at paras 4.40–4.42 above.

United Kingdom, being an agreement under which credit is to be provided to the debtor in the course of a business carried on by him ...'.[48]

But these matters of detail do not really assist on the broader questions. The problem can **41.58** perhaps best be illustrated by a practical example. Section 173(1) of the 1974 Act provides that:

> A term contained in a *regulated agreement* ... is void if, and to the extent that, it is inconsistent with a provision for the protection of the debtor ... contained in this Act or in any regulation made under this Act ...'

The expression 'regulated agreement' includes a consumer credit agreement[49] and 'con- **41.59** sumer credit agreement' is defined as[50] '... an agreement between an individual (the "debtor") and any other person (the "creditor") by which the creditor provides the debtor with credit of any amount ...'.

The status of a particular contract as a 'regulated agreement' is therefore in many respects a **41.60** matter of statutory interpretation (ie as opposed to a question of private international law). In this context, it will be noted that the statutory language reproduced above has no territorial limitation.[51] Nevertheless, it is tempting to conclude that section 173(1) can have no application to an agreement entered into abroad and which had no connection with the United Kingdom at the time when it was made.[52] So what is to be the position if a German law contract is made between a bank in Germany and a debtor in France, but the debtor subsequently takes up residence in England. If the German bank then finds it necessary to pursue proceedings in England, can the debtor resist the claim on the basis of any non-compliance with the 1974 Act? It is submitted that the position is as follows:

(a) Section 173(1) contains a rule of substantive law, as opposed to a rule of procedure.[53] On this basis, section 173 could only be applied by the English courts if (i) it forms a

---

[48] On these points, see s 16(5)(c) of the 1974 Act and art 5 of the Consumer Credit (Exempt Agreements) Order 1989 (SI 1989/869).

[49] See the definition of 'regulated agreement' in s 189 of the 1974 Act.

[50] See s 8(1) of the 1974 Act.

[51] Although arising in a slightly different context, it should be noted that territorial issues affecting the 1974 Act were the subject of the recent House of Lords decision in *Office of Fair Trading v Lloyds TSB Bank plc* [2007] UKHL 48. Under s 75 of the Act, a card issuer is jointly and severally liable to the debtor for any misrepresentation or breach of contract by the supplier in relation to the underlying commercial transaction. The bank argued that this did not apply to overseas supply transactions effected outside the UK. However, the House of Lords held that no such limitation could be read into s 75 and that no extra-territoriality was involved in the application of the section. It merely imposed certain obligations on card issuers operating within the UK credit markets. Although the point was not specifically addressed, it may perhaps be inferred that s 75 would apply even though the cardholder himself is resident abroad.

[52] There is a presumption to the effect that UK legislation is not intended to have extra-territorial effect: *Re Sawers, ex p Blain* (1879) 12 Ch D 522.

[53] Note the use of language to the effect that an offending term of any contract 'is void'. Where a statute uses the word 'unenforceable' or similar formulation, this may tend to suggest that the rule is one of procedure which is, hence, applicable in English courts regardless of the law which governs the contract. For an illustration of this position in relation to s 4 of the Statute of Frauds 1677 and guarantees governed by a foreign system of law, see *Leroux v Brown* (1852) 12 CB 801.

part of the system of law applicable to the contract[54] or (ii) it is an overriding mandatory provision of the forum which must be applied regardless of the law applicable to the contract.[55]

(b) In either such case, however, one is driven back to the fundamental question of statutory interpretation—do the provisions of section 173(1) apply to a contract made outside the United Kingdom and which has no connection with that jurisdiction or merely has the limited connection that the parties have chosen English law to govern their relationship?

(c) In the writer's view, section 173(1) should not apply in either of these cases. In the absence of any statutory guidance on territorial scope, one has to look to the objectives and purpose of the legislation. The 1974 Act was derived from the Report of the Crowther Committee (1971),[56] which examined the state of the credit markets *in the United Kingdom*. It is thus reasonable to infer that the 1974 Act was designed to regulate credit providers in that market.[57] It seems bizarre to suggest that the 1974 Act should apply to an agreement entered into in a foreign market, simply because the debtor moves to England at a later date,[58] or merely because the contract is subject to English law as a result of an express selection of that law as contained in the document itself. Furthermore, an agreement should only be regarded as a regulated agreement for these purposes if it was regulated when originally made. It plainly should not become regulated on a retrospective basis.

41.61 If this analysis is correct then a debtor in the example scenario described above is deprived of the benefit both of his home State consumer protection laws and the consumer protection laws forming a part of the applicable law. In the first case, this follows from the 'foreign services' exception; in the second case, the relevant consumer laws were not intended for his protection and thus do not apply. It may be thought that this is not an unreasonable result, since a degree of sophistication can perhaps be attributed to a consumer who goes to a foreign market to raise finance. Yet this may not necessarily be so; the creation of the euro and rules on free movement of capital were designed to act as a spur to cross-border financial services, and it may thus be inferred that individuals may more frequently borrow in other markets than was formerly the case.

---

[54] Given that the present example works on the basis that neither the debtor nor the creditor was resident in the UK when the contract was made, this could only arise if the contract contained an express choice of English law.

[55] On mandatory rules of this kind, see Art 9(2) of Rome I.

[56] Cmnd 4596.

[57] It is submitted that this view of the matter is entirely consistent with the overall structure of the 1974 Act, which provides for the licensing of suppliers of credit and regulates the content and enforcement of consumer credit agreements.

[58] In any event, such an argument is foreclosed by Art 19(3) of Rome I, which provides that habitual residence is determined as at the time the contract is made (ie and not as at the date of the proceedings). This must be correct since certainty requires that the legal content and effect of the contract must be ascertainable as at the date on which it is made. The result is that any home State consumer protection laws to be applied pursuant to Rome I must be those of the country in which the consumer is habitually resident at the time of the contract (ie and not the consumer laws of the UK).

Of course, if the creditor is based in the United Kingdom at the time of the contract, then **41.62** the connecting factor is far more evident and, in such a case, the contract should be treated as a 'regulated agreement' for the purposes of section 173(1).[59] In other words, the fact that the creditor operates in the United Kingdom is a sufficient connecting factor to characterize the contract as a 'regulated agreement' for the purposes of section 173(1). The provisions of that section will then be applied either on the basis that the contract is governed by English law or on the footing that section 173(1) is an overriding rule of the forum to be applied regardless of the applicable law.[60] This appears to be so even though the debtor is not resident here, because the 1974 Act was designed for the protection of consumers dealing in the UK markets, regardless of their own place of abode.[61] This vital connecting factor was absent from the hypothetical case discussed earlier in this section.

It may be added that these questions are likely to acquire a greater importance following the **41.63** Consumer Credit Act 2006 ('the 2006 Act'). Before that Act, an agreement would not be a 'regulated agreement' unless it involved the provision of credit in excess of £25,000,[62] and a consumer would rarely bother to go to a foreign market to raise such a relatively nominal amount. However, the removal of this limit means that even very substantial loans made to individuals can potentially constitute 'regulated agreements'. It is true that the 2006 Act creates an exemption for credit provided to high net worth debtors, but that exemption is subject to certification and other requirements.[63] It is thus possible to envisage that wealthy borrowers from outside the United Kingdom might seek to challenge the enforceability of such arrangements made with London banks. This may be especially likely if such borrowers begin to encounter difficulties as a result of the current crisis in the financial markets.[64]

---

[59] See the comments made above on the focus of the Crowther Report.

[60] On mandatory rules, see Art 9(2) of Rome I, to which reference has already been made. In two cases, mandatory hire purchase laws were applied in cases in which the contract was entered into within the jurisdiction and the debtor was resident there: see *English v Donnelly* 1958 SC 494, *Kay's Leasing Corp Pty Ltd v Fletcher* (1964) 116 CLR 124 and Dicey, Morris, & Collins, para 32-074.

[61] Although the decision is not directly relevant in the present context, Lord Hoffman has observed that s 75(1) of the 1974 Act is a 'consumer protection legislation for the benefit of customers of United Kingdom creditors': *Office of Fair Trading v Lloyds TSB Bank plc* [2007] UKHL 48, para 7. This at least suggests that the Act extends to foreign consumers, provided that they are dealing with a UK-based creditor.

[62] Section 8(2) of the 1974 Act, now repealed by s 2(1)(b) of the 2006 Act.

[63] See s 16A of the Consumer Credit Act 2006 and the Consumer Credit (Exempt Agreements) Order 2007 (SI 2007/1168). The £25,000 limit now applies only if the relevant agreement 'is entered into by the debtor wholly or predominantly for the purposes of a business carried on, or intended to be carried on, by him': see s 16B(1) of the 2006 Act. Another exemption may be available where the credit is used to fund the acquisition of an investment property: see s 16C of the 2006 Act. On consumer credit legislation generally, see Chapter 4 above.

[64] It may be noted for completeness that a consumer resident in another EU Member State may enjoy certain rights under the Financial Services (Distance Marketing) Regulations 2005 (SI 2005/2095). The regulations apply to distance contracts entered into without face-to-face contact (eg via the internet) pursuant to organized distance-selling arrangements. They require the provision of certain pre-contractual documentation and provide for a cancellation (or 'cooling off') period. The subject matter of the regulations coupled with their origin in the Directive on the distance selling of financial services (Directive 2002/65/EC), make it clear that the regulations are intended to benefit consumers both within and outside the UK.

Conclusions

41.64 Although they obviously remain to be tested in the heat of battle, the various provisions of Rome I discussed in this chapter generally deserve a cautious welcome.

41.65 The new rules ensure that financial instruments will be subject to a single system of law, thus ensuring both their fungibility and fairness as between investors. The same logic properly applies to public offers relating to such instruments, and Rome I follows this logic in a clear and coherent way.

41.66 The exclusion of home State consumer protection laws in relation to ordinary banking arrangements is also appropriate. Such services are in any event provided by authorized institutions, so the consumer will usually enjoy avenues of complaint and redress in the event that he has been unfairly treated.

41.67 It therefore appears that the exclusion of the home State consumer protection laws in the instances described above is both justifiable and proportionate. The regulated nature of the financial services industry means that the loss of 'home' consumer laws is unlikely to be seriously detrimental to the customer in practical terms.

42

THE BANKER'S DUTY OF CONFIDENTIALITY

Introduction

The existence of a legal obligation on a bank to maintain the confidentiality of its customer's affairs is well established. Yet it is easy to forget that the obligation has its limits. It is also fair to say that the well-known exceptions to the duty are not always clear, and may sometimes require re-interpretation in the light of rapidly changing conditions affecting the banking industry. **42.01**

Given the importance attached to confidentiality in modern business affairs,[1] it is perhaps surprising that the case law on the present subject is relatively limited. Perhaps this reflects the fact that banks are so keenly aware of the obligation that breaches of the duty **42.02**

---

[1] It should be appreciated that banks may be subject to obligations of confidentiality beyond the implied terms which are discussed in this chapter. For example, they may undertake express contractual obligations of secrecy when they are provided with information about a company for which one of the bank's customers proposes to make a takeover bid. The target company—if it knows about the intended bid and is prepared to provide information—will frequently insist on a confidentiality undertaking as part of the process of disclosure. Express confidentiality undertakings will require interpretation in accordance with normal principles and call for no special comment in the present context. Equally, a bank may receive information under circumstances which imply a duty of confidentiality which is binding upon it, and duties of confidentiality may be imposed in favour of persons who are not even customers of the bank. Additional duties of this kind are considered at paras 42.68–42.80 below.

occur only rarely. Apart from the possible legal consequences, a breach of the duty may also be seriously damaging to the bank's business reputation. Banks do, therefore, perhaps take special care in this sphere.

42.03   But it must also be said that there may be many occasions where information is disclosed without the knowledge of the customer, for example in response to inquiries made pursuant to a statutory and investigatory power. Internally, a bank will have to consider carefully whether disclosure is justified by reference to one of the exceptions which will be discussed below. But proceedings by the customer will rarely ensue. In many cases, no doubt, this is again because the bank will have exercised great care in making the decision to disclose. As a practical matter, it may often be that case that the customer will not even discover that a disclosure has been made. If the customer does become aware of the disclosure, this is likely to occur in the context of a wider investigation into his affairs, and it is perhaps unlikely that he will seek to take action against the bank under these circumstances.

42.04   The nature and scope of the bank's duty, and of the exceptions to it, are considered in this chapter.[2] Whilst it is necessary to discuss the duty in general terms, it is proposed to examine in detail the difficulties which may confront a bank with branches in a number of different countries and whose business may therefore be subjected to several different systems of law.

42.05   Against this background, it is proposed to consider the subject under the following headings:

(a) the system of law applicable to the duty;
(b) the general nature and scope of the duty;
(c) disclosure under compulsion of law;
(d) disclosure in the interests of the bank itself;
(e) disclosure in the public interest;
(f) disclosure with the consent of the customer;
(g) damages for breach of the duty;
(h) the Data Protection Act 1998;
(i) wider duties of confidence;
(j) duties of confidentiality to third parties;
(k) other duties of confidentiality; and
(l) conclusions.

The Applicable Law

42.06   It is, perhaps, unusual to begin a discussion of this subject with an outline of the relevant conflict of law principles.[3] Yet, in a text which seeks to provide an international perspective,

---

[2] For another treatment of the subject, see Paget, ch 8.
[3] The principles of private international law which are likely to be relevant in the context of the banker-customer relationship have been considered in general terms in Chapter 40 above.

this does provide a logical starting point. One cannot begin to discuss the content of a bank's legal duty unless one has identified the system of law which governs the existence, nature and content of that duty. Of course, the question does not really arise in the context of a purely 'domestic' account, but it may be of importance where the customer resides in one country and the relevant bank branch is situate in another.[4]

As has been seen,[5] a contract is governed by the system of law expressly selected by the parties for that purpose. If the contractual documentation entered into with the customer includes such a choice, it should almost invariably select the law of the jurisdiction through which the relevant branch of the bank is to maintain the relationship. Apart from other considerations, the branch will have to administer numerous such relationships, and it would clearly be inconvenient and confusing if the legal content of those relationships were governed by different systems of law. Even in an increasingly formalistic world, however, standard account documentation frequently contains no explicit selection of the law which is to govern the relationship. Under these circumstances, how is the applicable law to be identified? **42.07**

In such a case, the law which governs the contract will generally be the law of the country in which the account-holding branch is located.[6] The commentary on the content and effect of the duty of confidentiality set out below thus applies whenever the account is held with a bank branch located in England, regardless of the place of residence or incorporation of the customer. **42.08**

Correspondingly, where the account is maintained by a branch outside England, then the nature, scope, and extent of the duty of confidentiality will—in the absence of any express and contrary choice of law—be governed by the law of that place. **42.09**

Nature and Scope of the Duty of Confidentiality

It is frequently merely stated that a bank[7] owes a contractual[8] duty of confidentiality to its customers, and that there are certain well-established exceptions to the general rule. Authority for both of these propositions is derived from the well-known decision in **42.10**

---

[4] It will be recalled that some form of cross-border element is required before Rome I can assume any relevance to the matter before the court: see Art 1(1) of Rome I, discussed at para 40.07 above.

[5] See the discussion of Art 3 of Rome I, at para 40.08 above.

[6] This is the result of the application of Art 4(1)(b) of Rome I, as discussed at para 40.09 above.

[7] The present discussion is principally concerned with commercial banks. However, similar duties may be owed by investment banks, building societies, credit unions, and similar institutions: see *Winterton Construction Pty Ltd v Hambros Australia Ltd* (1993) ATPR 41-205 and *Bodnar v Townsend* [2003] TASCC 148 (Tasmanian Supreme Court).

[8] So far as English law is concerned, both the duty itself and the exceptions to it are formulated as implied terms of the banker-customer contract. In other jurisdictions, however, banking secrecy may have been codified and the subject may thus take on a more political dimension. See, for example, the discussion of the history of Swiss banking secrecy under s 47 of the Banking Act in Webster, 'Swiss Banking Secrecy in Evolution' (2002) 18 BFLR 317.

Tournier v National Provincial and Union Bank of England,[9] but the discussions tend to focus on the nature of the exceptions, rather than the scope of the rule itself.[10] As a practical matter, this approach may well be justified on the basis that, regardless of the scope of the rule in technical terms, banks will in practice take great care to preserve the confidentiality of their customers' affairs, whether or not particular pieces of information are strictly or technically covered by the duty. As noted above, there are reputational reasons for this approach.

42.11 Yet this seems to be an unsatisfactory approach to the subject.[11] Just as one must define the meaning of the expression 'customer' in order to decide whether a banker-customer relationship has come into existence,[12] likewise it should be possible to define the legal content of the relationship, and to describe the types of information to which a duty of confidentiality will attach. The following propositions are suggested in this regard:

(a) It should be borne in mind that the duty of confidentiality is owed to the account holding customer itself (and not, for example, to its shareholders or directors).[13]

(b) Not all information provided by a customer to his bank can be subjected to a duty of confidentiality. The duty clearly extends to the state of the customer's account (including transactions taking place on it and any security held with respect to it), and it should also extend to other information which is itself in some way referable to the contractual relationship even if it is received from persons other than the customer himself[14]—at least provided that the information is received by the bank in its capacity as banker to the customer.[15]

---

[9] [1924] 1 KB 461 (CA). Whilst *Tournier* is regarded as the *locus classicus* in this area because of its comprehensive approach to the subject, it should be appreciated that the existence of the bank's duty of confidentiality had been recognized at a much earlier stage: see, for example, *Tassel v Cooper* (1850) 9 CB 509, *Foster v Bank of London* (1862) 3 F&F 214 and *Hardy v Veasey* (1868) LR 3 Ex 107.

[10] It is noteworthy that, in the *Tournier* case itself, Bankes LJ observed (at 472) that 'it is necessary in a case like the present to direct the jury what are the limits and what are the qualifications of the contractual duty of secrecy implied in the relationship of banker and customer'. Yet he then proceeded to examine the qualifications (or exceptions) to the duty, without examining the limits of the basic duty itself. As will be seen, however, the other members of the Court of Appeal did attempt to deal with this subject, albeit briefly.

[11] In the writer's experience, it is often dangerous to seek to define an obligation by reference to its exceptions.

[12] On the meaning of 'customer', see paras 15.05–15.08 above.

[13] For an illustration of this point, see the Northern Irish decision in *Jeffers v Northern Bank Ltd* [2004] NIQB 81.

[14] Paget, para 8.2, quoting the remarks of Atkin LJ in *Tournier*, at 485. The same formulation was adopted in *Christofi v Barclays Bank plc* [1998] 2 All ER 484 at 489 (upheld on appeal, [1999] 4 All ER 437).

[15] *Barclays Bank plc v Taylor* [1989] 1 WLR 1066, 1070, where Lord Donaldson MR remarked that the relationship creates 'a duty of confidentiality in relation to information concerning the customer and his affairs *which it acquires in the character of his banker*...' (emphasis supplied). See also *Royal Bank of Canada v IRC* [1972] 1 Ch 665 (at 660), where Megarry J observed that the duty of secrecy 'is not confined to ordinary banking transactions but would extend to any banking transaction which is effected for a customer, whether ordinary or extraordinary...'

(c) Accordingly, information pertaining to the customer's account (including its credit or debit balance[16]) and to transactions undertaken at his request or on his behalf are covered by the duty of confidentiality.[17]

(d) By the same token, information provided by the customer in connection with a venture for which the customer has requested funding must also be covered by the duty, whether or not the bank agrees to finance the customer's plans.

(e) Similarly, if the bank acquires information about the general business strategy of the customer in the course of arranging loans to it, that information is likewise impressed with the duty of confidentiality.[18]

(f) On the other hand, information provided by the customer and which is already in the public domain cannot be covered by the duty, for it cannot have been communicated with any implication of confidentiality.[19] Yet care must be taken in this regard, for customer information remains confidential even though the recipient could readily have obtained that information through enquiries with other sources such as a credit reference agency.[20]

(g) Likewise, where the bank has to enter into discussions relating to the account with a third party (such as a trustee in bankruptcy), the bank is not obliged to refrain from discussing information which it might reasonably expect to be in the possession of that person.[21]

(h) It would also seem that information held by the bank before the customer approaches the bank with a view to establishing a relationship cannot become subject to a duty of confidentiality when that relationship comes into being, for the information concerned has not been derived from the account relationship.[22] The obligation does, however, continue to apply even though the account has become dormant or has been closed.[23]

(i) In New York, two cases suggest that the duty of confidentiality does not extend to the fact that a borrower has defaulted in respect of outstanding loans.[24] So far as English

---

[16] For a case in which a bank improperly disclosed credit balances on a deposit account and thus allowed the customer's creditors to obtain freezing orders, see *Milohnich v First National Bank of Miami Springs* 224 So 2d 759 (1969).

[17] A review commissioned jointly by the Treasury and the Bank of England recommended that the banker's duty of confidentiality should be codified, and that it should extend to all information which the bank has acquired about the customer in the course of providing banking services to him: see 'Banking Services: Law and Practice, Report by the Review Committee' (1989) Cm 622, Chairman, Professor RB Jack (hereafter the 'Jack Report'). The Committee's recommendation that the duty should be placed on a statutory footing has not been pursued.

[18] See the situation which arose in *United Pan-Europe Communications NV v Deutsche Bank AG* [2000] All ER (D) 701.

[19] Even if it could be said that the duty did apply in this type of case, it would be very difficult for the customer to prove that he had suffered any loss as a result of a breach.

[20] That information remains subject to the duty of confidentiality in such a case is apparent from the decision in *Jackson v Royal Bank of Scotland plc* [2005] 2 All ER 71 (HL); see in particular para 34 of the judgment.

[21] This is the effect of the decision in *Christofi v Barclays Bank plc* [1999] 4 All ER 437 (CA).

[22] See the remarks of Scrutton LJ in *Tournier*, at 481.

[23] *Tournier*, at 473 and 485.

[24] See *Graney Development Corporation v Taksen* 400 NYS 2d 717 (1978), aff'd 411 NYS 2d 756 (1978) and *Sharma v Skaarup Ship Management Corporation* 699 F Supp 440 (SDNY, 1988). In *Taksen*, the court

law is concerned, it is very doubtful whether the existence of a default of itself releases the bank from the duty of confidence.[25]

(j) The duty of confidentiality applies to specific information which is, expressly or impliedly, referable to the customer.[26] Thus, for example, a general announcement that the bank has had to make certain provisions for bad debts does not contravene the duty, because none of the relevant customers would thereby be identified.

(k) It appears that a breach of the duty may occur even if the recipient of the information is a subsidiary of the customer itself.[27]

42.12 As indicated above, however, banks rarely seek to rely on arguments to the effect that the duty of confidentiality does not apply to particular types of information. In many cases, such arguments would appear narrow and technical,[28] and the very fact that such an argument is invoked may send a negative signal to present and prospective customers.

42.13 As a result, banks prefer to justify their action on the basis that disclosure[29] was permitted by virtue of a specific and identifiable exception to the duty. But what are those exceptions? The traditional starting point is provided by the *Tournier* case, where Bankes LJ noted that[30] '... the qualifications can be classified under four heads: (a) where there is disclosure under compulsion of law; (b) where there is a duty to the public to disclose; (c) where the interests of the bank require disclosure; (d) where the disclosure is made by the express or implied consent of the customer'.

---

felt that information about a default would not normally expect to be kept confidential. In *Sharma*, however, the court held that New York law implies a duty of confidentiality in favour of depositors, but not in favour of borrowers.

[25] Such a default may however justify disclosures under exceptions to the duty. For example, if the bank needs to take legal proceedings to recover the debt, it may do so because the bank's own interests so dictate: on this exception, see paras 42.42–42.46 below. However, the essential duty would remain in place and disclosures would therefore have to fit strictly within the scope of the exception.

[26] It may be noted that, in the context of statutory provisions to protect bank confidentiality in s 47 of the Singapore Banking Act, s 40A of the Act defines 'customer information' as 'any information relating to, or any particulars of, an account of a customer of the bank, whether the account is in respect of a loan, investment or any other type of transaction, but does not include any information that is not referable to any customer or group of named customers...'. For a discussion of some of the issues raised by this legislation, see Ellinger, 'Disclosure of Customer Information to a Bank's other Branches and Affiliates' (2006) 20 BFLR 137.

[27] *Bank of Tokyo Ltd v Karoon* [1987] AC 45 (CA).

[28] In addition, reliance on such narrow arguments may overlook the fact that any person (including a bank) may be under a more general duty to maintain the secrecy of information communicated to him under circumstances which imply an obligation of confidentiality—see paras 42.68–42.72 below.

[29] In an action for damages, it will of course be incumbent on the claimant to demonstrate that confidential information had been released in breach of that duty. It may, however, be sufficient to prove that the recipient was an affiliate of the bank itself: see *Bank of Tokyo Ltd v Karoon* [1987] AC 45 (CA), where the point was held to be arguable but was not finally decided. In principle, it seems right that a disclosure to an affiliate of the bank could well breach the duty given that the subsidiary is a separate legal entity. It would then be incumbent on the bank to demonstrate that disclosure was justified by reference to one of the exceptions to the duty.

[30] At 472. This statement of the exceptions has been approved on numerous occasions. See, for example, *Turner v Royal Bank of Scotland plc* [1999] 2 All ER (Comm) 664. Many common law countries have introduced specific legislation on the scope of the duty of confidentiality owed by banks to their customers. See, for example, the Singapore legislation mentioned in n 26 above). In such a case, it is quite likely that a bank can no longer rely on the *Tournier* exceptions but is confined to the terms of the statute: see *Susilwati v American Express Bank Ltd* [2009] SGCA 8 (Singapore Court of Appeal).

It is fair to say that this remains an authoritative statement.[31] Nevertheless, the growth of **42.14** international banking and other developments have served significantly to expand the nature and scope of the disclosures which may be requested. The question is, can such disclosures be justified under any of these four headings?

It is proposed to examine each of these exceptions in turn.[32]   **42.15**

Compulsion of Law

Introductory Remarks

A bank may be legally compelled to disclose information about its customer in a variety of **42.16** circumstances. The most obvious cases are:

(a) where a request for information is made by a public authority pursuant to some statutory authority, or legislation imposes a duty on the bank to make a disclosure on its own initiative. Obvious examples falling within the first, 'response' category include section 20 of the Taxes Management Act 1970, under which the bank may be required to assist the Inland Revenue by providing information about the customer's financial position. In the second 'own initiative' category, one could include the bank's duty to disclose suspicions of money laundering under the provisions of the Proceeds of Crime Act;[33]

(b) where the bank is obliged to provide information pursuant to a court order made in the context of civil proceedings involving its customer and third parties (and to which the bank itself will not normally be a party).

On the face of it, this exception appears to be fairly self-contained; a bank does not breach **42.17** its duty of confidentiality if it discloses information pursuant to a legal requirement— whatever its actual source—which is binding upon it.[34] Inevitably, however, matters are less

---

[31] For a similar formulation of these exceptions in a US decision, see *Peterson v Idaho First National Bank* 367 P 2d 294 (Idaho, 1961).

[32] Following a review of the scope of these exceptions, one can only agree with Professor Ogilvie's remark that, in modern banking law, 'secrecy has become the incredibly shrinking concept …': see Ogilvie, 'From Secrecy to Confidence to the Demise of the Banker and Customer Relationship: Rodaro v Royal Bank of Canada' (1997) 19 BFLR 103.

[33] The bank's duties in relation to money laundering and terrorist finance have been discussed in detail in Chapter 7 above.

[34] Three points should be noted in this context. First of all, the information must be disclosed under *compulsion* of law; a bank may still be in breach of its duty if it releases information under a statutory provision which merely *permits* such disclosure. Secondly, the bank must take care to disclose only that information which is *required* to be disclosed by the relevant provision or order; it could still commit a breach of the duty if it provided information in excess of the essential requirements. Thirdly, in strict terms, it will be necessary to construe the legislation at issue to ascertain whether it is intended to override the duty of confidentiality. It has in the past been held that statutory disclosure obligations do not generally override *legal professional privilege*, at least in the absence of very clear wording: see *R (on the application of Morgan Grenfell & Co Ltd v Special Commissioners of Income Tax* [2003] 1 AC 563 and, for a similar decision in New Zealand, see *Commissioner of Inland Revenue v West-Walker* [1954] NZLR 191. However, as a matter of construction, the statutory obligation will usually override a duty of confidentiality which is of a purely contractual nature. For discussions of this point in relation to an Australian revenue statute, see *Smorgon v Australian and New Zealand Bank Group Limited* (1976) 134 CLR 475 (High Court of Australia), *O'Reilly v The Commissioners of the State of Victoria*

straightforward in the modern era, not least because a request for information may be directed to branches of a bank established in jurisdictions other than that in which the account is held or customer relationship is maintained. Equally, a foreign court may seek disclosure of information from a local branch, but the information may be held by a branch in England. In order to deal with this range of complexity, it is proposed to deal with the subject matter as follows:

(a) it is proposed to provide some examples of those cases in which a statute may compel disclosure;

(b) it is proposed to examine those cases in which an English court has sought disclosure from a foreign branch or subsidiary; and

(c) the response of the English courts to disclosure orders from foreign courts will be considered.

Statutory Obligations of Disclosure

42.18 For present purposes, it will be sufficient to provide a brief explanation of some of the better-known statutory provisions which may compel a bank to provide information about a customer's account without his consent:[35]

(a) Statutes dealing with the investigation of crime occasionally empower the relevant authorities to demand from financial institutions information which they hold concerning their customers. The Serious Fraud Office has power to require any person (including a bank) to produce documents if there is reason to believe that they may be relevant to the investigation.[36] If the bank's duty of confidentiality is to be overridden, then the disclosure order must have been authorized at a very senior level within the Office[37] but, subject thereto, the bank must comply with the terms of the request. Some statutory powers are directed specifically towards banks and financial institutions. A particular example is offered by sections 363–375 of the Proceeds of Crime Act, which allows the court to make 'customer information orders' and 'account monitoring orders'. A customer information order[38] may be made in the context of a money laundering investigation and may be directed to a particular institution or to financial institutions generally. Such an order requires the disclosure of the information specified in the application. In contrast, an account monitoring order[39] must be directed to a single institution and may require the bank to provide to the authorities specified

---

(1982) 153 CLR 1 (High Court of Australia) and *Citibank Ltd v Federal Commissioner of Taxation* (1988) 83 ALR 144 (High Court of Australia).

[35] As will be seen, the provisions concerned are mainly related to taxation and the investigation of crime, although these categories are by no means exclusive. For another discussion of this subject, see Paget, paras 27.16–27.17. The Jack Committee on Banking Services Law (1989) suggested that the exception should be clarified by statute, so as to provide a list of those statutory provisions which could form a basis for disclosure.

[36] Section 2 of the Criminal Justice Act 1987.

[37] Section 2(10) of the Criminal Justice Act 1987. The subsection also contemplates that the customer may consent to disclosure, but the authorities would naturally object to an approach for such consent if the account holder is himself the subject of the investigation.

[38] For the details, see s 363 of the Act.

[39] For the details, see s 370 of the Act.

information regarding the account for a period of up to 90 days. It is specifically provided that these orders are effective notwithstanding any duty of confidentiality owed by the recipient of the order,[40] with the result that the *Tournier* duty is specifically overridden.

(b) Whilst most statutes falling within this category will require a bank to disclose information only in response to a request from a relevant authority, some go even further and require financial institutions to disclose information to the police on their own initiative. The most obvious example is offered by the duties imposed on employees of these institutions to disclose suspicions of money laundering or terrorist funding which come to their attention in the course of their work. The substance of these provisions is discussed elsewhere.[41] For present purposes, it is merely necessary to note that the Act specifically confirms that a disclosure in accordance with its terms is not to be treated as a breach of any obligation of confidentiality.[42]

(c) Section 7 of the Bankers' Books Evidence Act 1879[43] ('the 1879 Act') permits a party to any legal proceedings to apply for an order allowing that party to inspect and take copies of any entries in a banker's books for the purpose of those proceedings.[44] An order may be made under this section even though the bank is not alleged to be at fault in any way[45] but, it seems, an order should only be made if there is a real prospect that it will assist in locating or preserving the defendant's assets.[46] A court would normally exercise this power only in relation to an account held by a party to the proceedings, but an order may be made against a third party if his account was in fact being used for transactions effected by the claimant or defendant.[47] The court's order should apply only to the transactions or periods which are relevant to the proceedings concerned, and the court should refuse to make the order if the primary purpose of the

---

[40] See s 368 (customer information orders) and s 370 (account monitoring orders). In view of the Australian decision in *Smorgon v Australia and New Zealand Banking Group Ltd* (1976) CLR 475 (High Court of Australia), provisions of this kind may be helpful but are not strictly necessary.

[41] See the discussion of s 330 of the Proceeds of Crime Act 2002 and s 21A of the Terrorism Act 2000, at paras 7.67 and 7.78 above.

[42] Section 337 of the Proceeds of Crime Act 2002; s 21B of the Terrorism Act 2000. For an essentially similar framework of statutory disclosure and protection provisions, and for the conclusion that those provisions overrode the *Tournier* duty of confidentiality, see *Australian Securities Commission v Zarro* [1991] FCA 574 (Federal Court of Australia).

[43] It should be noted that s 7 may also be invoked in relation to criminal proceedings.

[44] The 1879 Act was intended for the convenience of the banking community; it was clearly inconvenient for a bank to have to produce its ledgers in court proceedings, when they were required for the daily business of the bank. The Act must be interpreted and applied in that light: see *Douglas v Pindling* [1996] AC 890 (PC). The reference to 'bankers' books' must be construed in the light of modern banking conditions; the expression has been held to include microfilm and would clearly include more modern forms of data storage: *Barker v Wilson* [1980] 2 All ER 81. The expression does not, however, extend to paid cheques or paying-in slips, since these are not entries in the permanent records of the bank: see *Williams v Williams* [1988] QB 161.

[45] *Bankers Trust Co v Shapira* [1980] 3 All ER 353 (CA).

[46] *Arab Monetary Fund v Hashim (No 5)* [1992] 2 All ER 911. It should, however, be said that this case did not directly involve the 1879 Act.

[47] *South Staffordshire Tramways Co v Ebbsmith* [1895] 2 QB 669. Thus, an order may be made in respect of a husband's account if there is evidence that his wife (a party to the proceedings) was using his account to effect transactions which form the subject matter of the suit: *Ironmonger & Co v Dyne* (1928) 44 TLR 579. Similar principles were applied by the Court of Appeal in *DB Deniz Nakilyati v Yugopetrol* [1992] 1 All ER 205.

proceedings as a whole is to obtain access to bank account details.[48] Nevertheless, once an order has been directed to a bank, it will not be found to be in breach of its duty of confidentiality to the customer, provided that it complies strictly with the terms of the order and the 1879 Act itself.[49]

(d) In the interests of international comity,[50] the English courts may assist foreign courts by making an order to assist in the gathering of evidence in England which is relevant to proceedings pending before that foreign court.[51] The English courts must exercise this power with some care where evidence is sought from a bank, and there is a need to balance between (on the one hand) the desire to assist the requesting court and (on the other) the need to respect the bank's obligations of confidentiality. A wide-ranging request which amounts to no more than a 'fishing expedition' may be refused[52] although, provided that the inquiries appear to be relevant, the court may allow even wide-ranging questions to be put where the litigation relates to a major international fraud.[53] The court should also decline a request which may be oppressive, for example, because the bank on which the order is to be served may later be made a party to the proceedings as a defendant.[54]

(e) Under the provisions of the Taxes Management Act 1970[55] and other legislation, the Inland Revenue Commissioners enjoy extensive powers to require banks to provide information in connection with their investigations into the tax liabilities of the customers of those banks. It should be appreciated that disclosure provisions of this kind

---

[48] On these points, see *Perry v Phosphor Bronze Co Ltd* (1894) 71 LT 854; *Williams v Summerfield* [1972] 2 QB 512. In general terms, the court will only make an order under s 7 in civil proceedings if the relevant documents ought to be subject to discovery in any event: *Re Bankers' Books Evidence Act 1879, R v Bono* (1913) TLR 635. In other words, the 1879 Act offers a convenient means of producing evidence; it does not create a right to the production of evidence which would not otherwise be available.

[49] *Emmott v Star Newspaper Co* (1892) LJQB 77. The same point was made in *Bankers Trust Co v Shapira* [1980] 3 All ER 353 (CA).

[50] It must be said that this expression, whilst frequently used, is not often explained. A discussion of the subject perhaps goes beyond the scope of the present work, but see Mann, *Foreign Affairs in English Courts* (Clarendon, 1986), ch 7.

[51] The power is provided by the Evidence (Proceedings in Other Jurisdictions) Act 1975. The Act follows from the Hague Convention on the Taking of Evidence Abroad in Civil or Commercial Matters, which allows for the issue of 'letters rogatory' or 'letters of request' to the State in which relevant documents or information is held. It should be said that the 1975 Act extends to criminal (as well as civil) proceedings. The court must, however, take care to ensure that criminal proceedings have actually commenced: on this point, see the decision in *Re Westinghouse Uranium Contract* [1978] 2 WLR 81. The court cannot make an order for disclosure if the request infringes, or is prejudicial to, the sovereignty of the UK: see s 2 of the Protection of Trading Interests Act 1980. It may also be observed in passing that courts in the US have held that the Hague Convention offers only one means of obtaining evidence from outside the jurisdiction, and that those courts can thus still issue a subpoena to compel the production of materials situate abroad: *Societe Nationale Industrielle Aerospatiale v US District Court for the Southern District of Iowa* 482 US 522 (1987, US Supreme Court). The decision in this case has been criticized but it continues to be applied: see, for example, *In re Automative Refinishing Paint Antitrust Litigation, BASF and BASF Coatings AG* 358 F 3d 288 (2004).

[52] Contrast the decisions of the Court of Appeal in *Re State of Norway's Application* [1987] QB 433 (which rejected a request which might have involved the private financial affairs of unnamed individuals) and the House of Lords in *Re State of Norway's Application (No 2)* [1990] 1 AC 723 (which upheld a more narrowly drafted request).

[53] *First American Corporation v Sheikh Al-Nahyan* [1998] 4 All ER 439.

[54] See the decision in *First American Corporation v Sheikh Zayed Al-Nahyan* [1998] 4 All ER 439.

[55] See in particular ss 17, 20 and 24.

must be applied in accordance with their terms; there is no presumption that the legislature intends such provisions to be applied subject to the bank's duty of confidentiality;[56] if the statutory provision is intended to take effect subject to that duty, then express words must be used for that purpose.[57] Once again, the bank cannot incur liability to the customer for breach of the *Tournier* duty, provided that it has disclosed only the information which it is required to disclose in accordance with the terms of the statute concerned.[58]

(f) A bank may also be required to disclose information about its dealings with a company, whether as part of an investigation into its affairs[59] or as part of an inquiry into the circumstances leading up to its insolvency.[60] The powers of the court under these sections are very wide, since they are designed to assist the liquidator or administrator in performing his functions; the court must balance the need for information against the burdens imposed on the person requesting it.[61]

(g) It may be added that statutory provisions of the kind discussed above will usually render the bank liable to a fine or similar penalty in the event of non-compliance.[62] However, it seems that continued refusal to comply could be met by an application for an injunction to compel compliance, with the ultimate sanction of imprisonment for contempt of court.[63]

(h) Separately, a court should perhaps be reluctant to order disclosure of bank information against individuals who are not party to the litigation before it, since this may be regarded as a 'fishing expedition'.[64]

Limitations on the 'Compulsion of Law' Exception

Even in this modern era of international banking, where bank branches are linked **42.19** together through their computer systems, it has been shown that the particular branch with which the customer maintains his account continues to have some relevance to the legal

---

[56] This is the effect of the decision in *Smorgon v Australia and New Zealand Banking Group Ltd* (1976) 134 CLR 475 (High Court of Australia), considering a disclosure made to the Commissioner of Taxation under the terms of the Income Tax Assessment Act 1936.

[57] English law does offer some examples of such provisions. See, for example, ss 452(1A) and 452(3) of the Companies Act 1985.

[58] Whether or not a statutory provision of this kind enables the revenue authorities to require details of customers who are not themselves under investigation must be a matter of construction: see the decision of the Supreme Court of Canada in *Canadian Imperial Bank of Commerce v A-G of Canada* (1962) DLR (2nd) 49.

[59] See, for example, ss 431-453 of the Companies Act 1985.

[60] See s 236 of the Insolvency Act 1986.

[61] For examples arising in the context of s 236 of the Insolvency Act 1986, see *British and Commonwealth Holdings plc (joint administrators) v Spicer & Oppenheim* [1993] AC 426 (HL); *In re Galileo Group Ltd* [1998] 1 All ER 545. Where the inquiry relates to a foreign company the court may make an order under s 236 with respect to documentation held outside the jurisdiction: *Re Mid East Trading Ltd* [1998] 1 All ER 577 (CA).

[62] See, for example, the penalties imposed by s 334 of the Proceeds of Crime Act 2002.

[63] See the Australian decision in *Attorney General v Thomas* (1983) 13 ATR 859 (a case relating to disclosure under a taxing statute).

[64] See the Canadian decision in *Royal Bank of Scotland plc v 'The Golden Trinity'* 2001 FCT 427. This point naturally applies only in the context of civil proceedings.

relationship between the parties. In particular, the law which governs the banker-customer contract will be the law of the country in which the relevant bank branch is located.[65]

42.20 This rule has a particular consequence in the context of the 'compulsion of law' exception in that the law which compels the disclosure must form a part of the system of law which governs the account.[66] In spite of the growth of multinational banking, the customer continues to deal with a particular branch in a particular country. It is reasonable to expect that information relating to his account will remain confidential to the bank within that jurisdiction.[67]

42.21 It should also be appreciated that, where a disclosure is to be made in reliance on the 'compulsion of law' exception, it is necessary to ensure that the disclosure is limited to materials which are relevant to the purpose at hand. The exception does not provide *carte blanche* in relation to the entirety of the information available in relation to that particular customer.[68]

Disclosure Orders made by an English Court in relation to Materials in England

42.22 Clearly, where a bank in England receives a subpoena to produce information about a customer's account, it must comply with that order in any event.[69] The customer's consent is not in principle required, because the 'compulsion of law' exception clearly applies where information is required pursuant to an English court order or proceeding.

42.23 Although this proposition appears to be straightforward, it is nevertheless pertinent to ask whether the customer has any rights in this situation. For example, is the bank obliged to notify the customer of its receipt of the order, so that he can apply to court to challenge that order before the bank complies with it? Where the order involves a *criminal* investigation, the answer must surely be in the negative, since disclosure might have the effect of

---

[65] This rule can even be applied to a bank which runs its business via the internet, and has no branches in the traditional sense, because the business must be authorized and operate its internet facilities from a given location.

[66] See the decision of the Hong Kong Court of Appeal in *FDC Co Ltd v Chase Manhattan Bank NA* (1984), discussed at para 42.39 below. The US Court of Appeals for the Second Circuit *seems* to have decided that a 'compulsion of law' exception in the Panamanian Constitution allowed a Panamanian branch to disclose information in response to a subpoena issued by the US courts: see *First National City Bank of New York v Internal Revenue Service* 271 F 2d 616 (2nd Circuit, 1959), see in particular the discussion at 619–620. Although the detailed question would strictly be a matter of Panamanian law, it is submitted that the decision is wrong in principle.

[67] This view is in part derived from the decision in *R v Grossman* (1981) 73 Cr App Rep 302, to the effect that bank branches in different jurisdictions should be treated as separate entities for these purposes. The decision is considered later in this section.

[68] For a cautionary note to this effect, albeit in a slightly different context, see *R (on the application of Amro International SA) v Financial Services Authority* (QBD) Admin, 26 August 2009.

[69] There are many bases on which such an order may be made in proceedings to which the bank is not itself a party. For example, a bank may have received a credit for the account of a customer which represents the proceeds of a fraud. Although the bank may be wholly innocent of any wrongdoing and is thus not under any obligation to compensate the victim for his loss, it may nevertheless be required to assist the victim in the investigation of the fraud and the recovery of his money. A discovery order may therefore be made against the bank, requiring it to provide details of the customer and his account: see *Bankers Trust Co v Shapira* [1980] 3 All ER 353 (CA), applying the decision in *Norwich Pharmacal Co v Customs & Excise Commissioners* [1974] AC 133 (HL).

prejudicing the investigation.[70] In some cases, the point is made clear by the relevant legislation,[71] but the principle would seem to be of general application. Consistently with this view, it has been decided that a bank is not obliged to resist a disclosure order made under the Police and Criminal Evidence Act, nor is it obliged to notify the customer of this development. The required disclosures would be covered by the 'compulsion of law' exception, at least provided that the orders appeared to be valid on their face.[72]

The position may be different in the case of *civil* proceedings. It has been held that there is **42.24** nothing to *prevent* the bank from notifying the customer that it has received the order, but it is less clear whether it is under a positive *obligation* to notify, or to use its best endeavours to notify, the customer prior to compliance.[73] It is, however, submitted that the court should not imply a notification requirement of this kind into the banker-customer contract in this type of case. It is doubtful that such a term would pass the 'business efficacy' test applied for these purposes.

As a final point, an English court can clearly demand the production of information or **42.25** documents which are available in England; but where is information deemed to be located for these purposes? This issue assumed a certain relevance when the UK tax authorities decided to seek information about undeclared income held in offshore accounts held by UK residents.[74] The Revenue relied on section 20 of the Taxes Management Act 1970, which provides that '… an inspector may, for the purposes of enquiring into the tax liability of any person (the "taxpayer"), by notice in writing require any other person to deliver to the inspector such documents as are in his *possession or power* and as … contain, or may contain, information relevant to any tax liability to which the taxpayer is, or may be, subject …'. The Revenue obtained the consent of the Special Commissioner for Taxation for the service of a section 20 notice in relation to information concerning the offshore subsidiaries of UK banks.[75] It happened that the processing of their customer information was undertaken centrally by the head office of the bank and, although access to that information was heavily restricted by confidentiality agreements, nevertheless certain employees in the UK did hold the necessary access codes. The Special Commissioner accordingly

---

[70] *Barclays Bank plc (t/a Barclaycard) v Taylor* [1989] 3 All ER 56, where it was held that it was not necessary to give business efficacy to the banker-customer relationship that a term should be implied requiring the bank to contest an order for disclosure under the Police and Criminal Evidence Act 1984.

[71] For example, the Proceeds of Crime Act 2002 creates a 'tipping off' offence: see para 7.70 above.

[72] *Barclays Bank plc v Taylor* [1989] 1 WLR 1066.

[73] See *Robertson v Canadian Imperial Bank of Commerce* [1995] 1 All ER 824 (PC).

[74] Individuals resident in the UK are in principle liable to UK tax on all of their income, whether arising in this country or abroad.

[75] For the main decision, see *HMRC v Barclays Bank plc* [2006] SPC 526 (13 February 2006). This is one of a series of rulings which have required the disclosure of customer information from overseas branches of banks. A more recent ruling will apparently give access to information held in various tax havens: see 'Taxman wins right to see details of 500,000 offshore bank accounts', *The Times*, 13 August 2009. A series of disclosure orders have now been made in cases of this kind: see, for example, Special Commissioners for Taxation, *Application to Serve a TMA s20 Notice on Financial Institution No 8* (26 March 2009). For a much earlier decision on tax disclosure provisions of this kind, see *Royal Bank of Canada v IRC* [1972] 1 All ER 225. Courts in the US have long felt able to issue subpoenas to domestic branches requiring production of documentation held abroad, on the basis that those materials are within the control of the head office: see *First National City Bank of New York v Internal Revenue Service* 217 F 2d 616 (1959).

decided that the required information was in the 'possession or power' of the UK bank and that a section 20 order could accordingly be made in respect of it. Disclosure would, of course, result in a breach of the duty of confidentiality owed by the subsidiaries to their customers, but it seems that this was only faintly argued as a ground for declining production. This approach avoided some of the difficulties which might have arisen if the materials were deemed to be held abroad (see below). It may also reflect the specific terms of the legislation at issue in that case. Nevertheless, the decision demonstrates that information held on a computer may be subject to disclosure orders in all of the jurisdictions in which it is accessible, even if only by a very limited number of employees. This has obvious, and negative, consequences for the scope of customer confidentiality.[76]

Disclosure Orders made by an English Court in relation to Materials held Abroad

42.26 Matters may become more complex where an English court is asked to make an order for production of documents held by a bank at a branch outside England. In principle, it seems that the English courts are reluctant to order the production of documents held outside the jurisdiction. This follows partly from their view that overseas branches should *for some purposes* effectively be viewed as separate entities,[77] and partly from the desire to avoid conflict with the courts of other jurisdictions which may be called upon to enforce the bank's duty of confidence.[78] Even where there is no conflict with the banking secrecy laws of another jurisdiction, the court will not generally make an order for disclosure because this will infringe the sovereignty of the other State involved.[79] There may be exceptional circumstances where an order may be made—for example, where the case involves major fraud or crime and the order is necessary to prevent the disappearance of evidence or the removal of the fruits of the crime.[80]

---

[76] A similar difficulty affected the Society for Worldwide Financial Telecommunications (SWIFT), a Belgian-based entity whose information on funds transfers was also accessible in the US. The US Treasury issued subpoenas to SWIFT requiring it to provide access to some of that information for the purposes of its Terrorist Finance Tracking Programme. SWIFT was thus placed in a position in which compliance with the US subpoenas may have involved a breach of the EU Data Protection Directive. For further discussion of these episodes, see Proctor, 'Terrorism, Tax and Bank Secrecy' (2006) 11 JIBFL 477 and 'Terrorism, Tax and Bank Secrecy: A Continuing Saga' (2007) 10 JIBFL 585.

[77] *R v Grossman* (1981) 73 Cr App Rep 302 (CA); *Pan-American Bank & Trust Co v National City Bank* 6 F 2d 762 (2nd Circuit) cert denied, 269 US 554. US courts will, however, treat a bank (including its foreign branches) as a single corporate entity for the purpose of securing compliance with a subpoena: see *First National City Bank of New York v Internal Revenue Service* 271 F 2d 616 (2nd Circuit, 1959).

[78] *R v Grossman*, above.

[79] *MacKinnon v Donaldson Lufkin and Jenrette Securities Corp* [1986] 1 All ER 653 (a case in which the victim of an 'advance fee fraud' was seeking to recover his money). In that case, the court declined to make an order on the basis that this would result in an infringement of the sovereignty of the US. As will be seen, this sensitivity to questions of national sovereignty has not always been reciprocated. The rationale of the decision in *MacKinnon* has been accepted and followed in Australia: see *Arhill Pty Ltd v General Terminal Co Pty Ltd* (1991) 23 NSWLR 545 (New South Wales Supreme Court). For a case in which an Australian court found a Swiss company to be in breach of an Australian production order even though compliance would have resulted in a breach of Swiss banking secrecy laws, but then invoked international comity as a ground for declining to impose penalties, see *Australian Securities Commission v Bank Leumi and EBC Zurich AG* [1995] FCA 1744 (Federal Court of Australia).

[80] This was the position in *London & County Securities v Caplan*, 26 May 1978 (unreported but referred to in the *MacKinnon* case, above), where an order was made to produce documents from overseas branches

It may be noted at this point that the practice of courts in the United States in this sphere **42.27**
has developed in a very different direction. It has already been noted that US courts do
not regard themselves as confined to the Hague Convention when seeking to gather evidence from outside their jurisdiction.[81] The point is of obvious importance in the present
context, given the worldwide presence of many US banks.

US courts have held that an order of this kind can be made against a bank over which the **42.28**
court has personal jurisdiction and, if it can be shown that it has control over the documents concerned, it can be required to produce them even though they are physically situate abroad,[82] and even though the bank branch within the United States has no connection
with the dispute giving rise to the order.[83]

Although the jurisdiction is therefore very wide, early cases suggested a certain appreciation **42.29**
of foreign laws designed to preserve bank secrecy, of the difficulties which they could pose
in complying with orders made against the head office of the bank in the US and of the
need to respect the sovereignty of other States. The power to make such orders was therefore exercised with a degree of restraint. In two cases, the courts refused to make orders for
production in respect of materials held in foreign branches where the local law prohibited
such disclosure.[84] In another case involving a Canadian bank, the court refused to order
officers of the New York branch to produce information held in Quebec, on the basis that
the 'letters rogatory' procedure could be used and it was not appropriate for a US court to
order a violation of the laws of a friendly State.[85]

Thereafter, the climate appears to have changed. There may be a variety of reasons for this, **42.30**
but one is offered by section 40 of the Restatement (Second) of Foreign Relations Law,
1965. The provision states that a court should, in determining the scope of its enforcement
jurisdiction, balance a number of competing factors, including (i) the vital national interests of the United States and of the foreign State concerned, (ii) the hardship which an order
would impose on the party concerned, (iii) the extent to which the order requires action
to be taken in the foreign State, (iv) the nationality of the party subject to the order, and
(v) the extent to which the order may be likely to achieve compliance. This provision
became relevant in a series of subsequent cases, and the result seems to depend upon the
relative weight which the court places on each of the factors just described.

---

of the bank in aid of a tracing claim to recover assets allegedly embezzled by Mr Caplan. The case was thus
exceptional and described as one of 'hot pursuit'.

[81] See n 51 above and the decision in *Societe Nationale Industrielle Aerospatiale v US District Court for the
Southern District of Iowa* 482 US 522 (1987, US Supreme Court).

[82] See, for example, *In re Marc Rich & Co AG* 707 F 2d 663 (2nd Cir, 1982), cert den 463 US 1215 (1983)
and *In re Grand Jury Subpoena Addressed to First National City Bank* 396 F 2d 897.

[83] See, for example, *Metro Life Insurance Co v Robertson-Ceco Corporation* 84 F 3d 560 (2nd Cir, 1996);
Financial Trust Co Inc v Citibank NA 268 F Supp 561 (1996).

[84] See *Societe Internationale pour Participations Industrielles et Commerciales SA v Rogers* 357 US 197 (1958),
where the production of the documentation would have resulted in an offence under Swiss law; *First National
City Bank of New York v Internal Revenue Service* 271 F2d 616 (1959).

[85] See *Ings v Ferguson* 282 F 2d 149 (1960). This decision may no longer be followed in light of the later
decision of the Supreme Court in the *Aerospatiale* case, see n 51 above. For a similar Canadian decision, see
Frischke v Royal Bank of Canada (1977) 80 DLR (3d) 393, where the court refused to order the disclosure of
information held by the Panamanian branch of the Royal Bank, in breach of that country's secrecy laws.

42.31   Most cases seem to have concentrated primarily on the first issue namely, the competing national interests of the United States and the other country involved. Applying this test, US courts have ordered disclosure of information held at foreign branches of banks on the basis that the vital interests of the United States in enforcing its insider trading laws,[86] its tax laws,[87] its narcotics laws,[88] its anti-money laundering laws,[89] and its criminal law generally[90] outweigh the interests of the foreign jurisdiction in preserving the effect of their bank secrecy laws.[91] Orders for disclosure were thus made in each case, even though, in some cases, disclosure necessarily involved the commission of a criminal offence in the jurisdiction in which the relevant records were held.[92] Under similar circumstances, the Supreme Court of Canada has ordered a bank employee to provide evidence in contravention of bank secrecy laws in the Bahamas, on the basis that a foreign law could not be invoked to frustrate the administration of justice in Canada.[93]

42.32   A minority of cases have, however, focused on different aspects of the 'balancing' test and have come to a different conclusion. In one case, the court noted the hardship which would be caused to the bank as a result of inconsistent orders made by courts in the United States and Greece (where the requested information was held), and thus decided not to enforce a summons requiring a US bank to produce materials held by its branch in Athens.[94] In another case which has already been noted, the court felt that enforcement of the

---

[86] *Securities and Exchange Commission v Banca Della Svizzera Italiana* 92 FRD 111 (1981).

[87] *Garpeg Ltd v United States* 583 F Supp 789 (SDNY 1984); this is the 'companion' case to the decision of the Hong Kong Court of Appeal discussed at para 42.39 below. See also *United States v Field* 532 F. 2d 404 (5th Cir, 1976) and *First National City Bank v Internal Revenue Service* 271 F. 2d 616 (2nd Cir, 1959), cert den, 361 US 948 (1960), where the court required production of information held by the Panamanian branch of a New York bank. It must be said, however, that the evidence on Panamanian law as to the criminal nature of any disclosure was not especially strong, and the decision appears to be significantly affected by this factor.

[88] *In re Grand Jury Proceedings Bank of Nova Scotia* 740 F 2d 817 (11th Cir, 1984), cert den, *Bank of Nova Scotia v United States* 469 US 1106 (1985).

[89] *In re Sealed Case* 825 F 2d 494 (DC Cir, 1987), cert den. *Roe v United States* 108 SC 451 (1987).

[90] *United States v Davis* 767 F 2d 1025, at 1035.

[91] In making this type of order, the US courts have taken into account the record of the relevant foreign State in prosecuting bank officers for a breach of the local bank secrecy laws and the likelihood that they would do so in the particular circumstances of the case: see, for example, *United States v Vetco* 691 F 2d 1281 (9th, Cir 1981), *In re Grand Jury Subpoena dated August 9, 2000*, 218 F Supp 2d 544 (SDNY, 2000) and *Bodner v Banque Paribas* 202 F2d 370 (SDNY, 2000). Considerations of this kind can, of course, only be relevant if disclosure constitutes a criminal offence in the jurisdiction in the required information is held. It follows that the US court is more likely to make the order if—as is the case in England—the customer's right to confidentiality enjoys only contractual protection.

[92] Nevertheless, the courts have stated that they must have regard to any special problems confronting the bank in the jurisdiction in which the information is held, and the terms of any intervention by that foreign State on behalf of the bank: see *Societe Nationalle Industrielle Aerospatiale v US District Court for the Southern District of Iowa* 482 US 522 (1987, US Supreme Court), to which reference has already been made. The decision in this case remains controversial: see Bergmann, 'The Hague Evidence Convention in the Supreme Court: A Critique of the *Aerospatiale* Decision' (1989) 63 *Tulane Law Review* 532 and Buxbaum, 'Assessing Sovereign Interests in Cross-Border Discovery Disputes: Lessons from Aerospatiale' (2003) 38 *Texas International Law Journal*. The failure of the foreign government concerned to object to the subpoena has occasionally influenced the court in favour of making the order: see *In re Grand Jury Proceedings* 691 F 2d 1384 (11th Cir, 1982) and *United States v Chase Manhattan Bank NA* 584 F Supp 1080 (SDNY, 1984).

[93] *Re Spencer and the Queen* (1985) 21 DLR (4th) 756.

[94] *United States v First National Bank of Chicago* 699 F 2d 341 (7th Cir, 1983). In this case, the court looked to the second head of the balancing test.

subpoena would compel the bank to violate the laws of its own country, and that this outweighed the need for the requested materials.[95] The court may decline to enforce a subpoena if the bank has acted in good faith and has used its best efforts to comply with the subpoena (eg in seeking to obtain any necessary consent from the foreign government concerned) before indicating its refusal.[96]

The Canadian practice appears to mirror that of the US courts. The fact that information **42.33** may be held subject to a duty of secrecy under a foreign banking law is not of itself a reason for refusing a disclosure order, but the court will take into account the extent to which the relevant foreign authority is likely to take proceedings. Other relevant factors include the importance of the documents, the existence of a national interest, and the good faith of the bank in resisting disclosure.[97]

Disclosure Orders made by a Foreign Court

As noted above, courts in the United States do not believe that they are compelled to **42.34** use the 'letter of request' procedure prescribed by the Hague Convention.[98] In a banking context, they will sanction the issue of a subpoena to a branch of the bank within the United States, requiring it to produce information or documents held by a foreign branch and which are subject to a duty of confidentiality under the laws of the jurisdiction concerned.[99]

It has already been seen in a slightly different context that this type of order places the bank **42.35** in a difficult position. It must either comply with the order and thus breach the duty of confidentiality owed to the customer, or it must ignore the order and risk a finding of contempt by the court making the order. As already pointed out, the 'compulsion of law' exception applies only where the law requiring disclosure forms a part of the law applicable to the contract.

In practice, a bank in England should seek to notify its customer that the request for **42.36** information has been received, and seek his written consent to comply with that request.[100] This may afford to the customer an opportunity to apply to the English court for an injunction preventing the English branch from complying with the foreign court order. If the

---

[95] See *In re Sealed Case* (n 89 above). The court thus concentrated on the third head of the balancing test. It should be noted that compliance was not enforced as against the bank, but an individual officer was held in contempt of court for refusing to give evidence.

[96] See *Matter of Two Grand Jury Subpoenas Duces Tecum Served Upon Union Bank of Switzerland* 601 NYS 2d 253 (New York Supreme Court, 1993). Contrast *In re Grand Jury Subpoena dated August 9 2000*, 218 F Supp 2d 544 (SDNY, 2000), where the recipient had sought assistance from the foreign government to resist the subpoenas, and *Matter of Grand Jury Subpoena (Continental Illinois National Bank and Trust Company of Chicago)* 464 NYS 2d 792 (1983).

[97] *Comalpex Resources International Ltd v Schaffhauser Kantonalbank* (1990) 42 CPC (2d) 330.The case is noted by Crerar, 'Mareva Freezing Orders and Non-party Financial Institutions; A Practical Guide' (2005) 21 BFLR 169.

[98] The Hague Convention on the Taking of Evidence Abroad in Civil or Commercial Matters (1970), and the attitude of the US Supreme Court, has already been noted at n 92 above.

[99] Although the leading case law in this area flows from orders made by courts in the US, the principles about to be discussed would apply equally to orders emanating from other jurisdictions.

[100] See *Robertson v Canadian Imperial Bank of Commerce* [1995] 1 All ER 824 (PC), noted above.

customer fails to take that step within a reasonable time, then it may be that the bank can respond to the request for disclosure and, in the event of a subsequent claim for breach of the duty, the court would no doubt have regard to the customer's failure to act in determining whether any breach of the duty had occurred and (if so) in calculating any damages which the court may see fit to award.[101]

42.37 This process will afford to the customer the opportunity to apply for an injunction to prohibit the disclosure. But how is the court to respond if the customer does indeed decide to seek an injunction against the bank? The bank faces a clear difficulty, in that an order made in one jurisdiction compels it to breach an obligation owed under English law.

42.38 The problem arose in a very clear form in *XAG v A Bank*,[102] where the defendant was the London branch of a US bank. The US Department of Justice served a subpoena on the head office of the bank, requiring the production of information held by the London branch. The court decided to grant the injunctions, holding that the balance of convenience lay with the customer in maintaining the confidentiality to which he was entitled under English law and by which its accounts were, of course, governed.[103] The court's decision was influenced by a number of factors, including (i) the order requiring the production of documents held in a different country was, by English standards, territorially excessive, (ii) if the court did not grant the injunction, then it would effectively be allowing a foreign State to enforce one of its public laws in England, in contravention of well-established principles, and (iii) the available expert evidence suggested that the US doctrine of 'foreign government compulsion' would prevent the US court from holding the head office to be in contempt of its order; the documents were located in England and the order of a local court would be seen as an adequate reason for their non-availability). The expert evidence in that case asserted that '… no United States court has ever held a bank or other party in contempt in such circumstances …'.

42.39 It may also be helpful to compare the approach adopted by the Court of Appeal in Hong Kong in *FDC Co Ltd v The Chase Manhattan Bank, NA*.[104] In that case, the US Internal Revenue Service was conducting an investigation into the affairs of a company within the United States. A summons was issued to the New York head office of Chase, requiring it to produce information held at its Hong Kong branch, and non-compliance was penalized by a daily fine of US$15,000. Nevertheless, the Court upheld injunctions granted at the behest of the customer to prevent the transmission of the required information to the United States. The court simply noted that anyone opening an account with a bank in Hong Kong was entitled to expect the local courts to enforce the duty of confidentiality which was an integral part of the banker-customer relationship.

---

[101] On damages for breach of the duty, see paras 42.63–42.64 below. There is, of course, no perfect solution for the bank when confronted with conflicting obligations of this kind. The approach suggested in the text may be appropriate in civil proceedings but, for obvious reasons, an approach to the customer may be more problematical where the foreign court order is made in the context of a criminal prosecution and confidentiality may be of the essence.

[102] [1983] 2 All ER 464.

[103] On the law applicable to the banker-customer relationship, see Chapter 40 above.

[104] [1990] 1 HKLR 277. The decision is discussed by White, Principles of Confidentiality in Cross-Border Banking in Cranston (ed.), *Legal Issues of Cross-Border Banking* (Chartered Institute of Bankers, 1989), p 19.

Although the tone and approach of these two decisions is different, it is nevertheless clear **42.40** that the courts were keen to protect the customer's right to confidentiality in each jurisdiction. Whether this line will continue to hold is another matter. As noted elsewhere, the customer's right to confidentiality has been steadily eroded by legislation over the years, and there is now a general acceptance that bank secrecy should not be used as a cloak for tax evasion or crime. Again, as has been seen, the UK revenue authorities are becoming more aggressive in seeking information relating to offshore accounts. It may therefore be that the English courts will become more willing to order the production of information held by foreign branches of banks in England and, by the same token, they may become less resistant to the disclosure to foreign authorities of information held in this country.[105]

Thus far, the present section has worked on the basis that an order is made against a branch **42.41** of a bank in one country, directed to information held by a branch of the same bank in another country. In some respects, the position becomes clearer where the business is organized through separate companies (rather than branches). Thus, if a US incorporated parent company is involved in litigation in New York, a UK subsidiary of that entity may breach its obligation of confidentiality if it discloses information to its parent for the purposes of the litigation.[106] Nevertheless, it may remain open to the courts to direct a parent company to produce materials from its subsidiaries, on the footing that it has control over their affairs. The principles discussed in this section are thus likely to be equally applicable in such a situation.

Interests of the Bank

There seems to be very little authority on this particular exception to the duty of confiden- **42.42** tiality. There are, however, some obvious cases:

(a) Where a customer has failed to respond to a demand in respect of his overdraft, the bank must issue proceedings stating that the defendant is a customer and stating the amount claimed (ie giving particulars of the state of his account). These details will thereby come into the public domain, but it is clearly in the interests of the bank to disclose these details in order to recover the moneys owing to it. The issue and conduct of the proceedings is therefore clearly covered by the 'bank's interest' exception.[107]

(b) Likewise, a bank may need to disclose the state of the account to a guarantor of the overdraft, in order to make demand against him. Once again, it seems clear that such a disclosure is covered by the present exception.[108]

---

[105] In the case of revenue and some other public claims, there remains the objection that a foreign State cannot enforce its sovereign rights within the UK without the latter's consent. The leading authority in this area is *Government of India v Taylor* [1955] AC 491 (HL). On this case and later decisions in this area, see Proctor: 'Foreign Taxes in English Proceedings' (1999) 7 JIBFL 292.

[106] See *Bank of Tokyo Ltd v Karoon* [1987] AC 45.

[107] This exception was noted in the *Tournier* case itself.

[108] Alternatively, it may be argued that the customer, in arranging for the issue of the guarantee, has impliedly consented to the bank disclosing the state of the account to the guarantor for the purposes of effecting a recovery. The court in *Ross v Bank of New South Wales* (1928) 28 SR (NSW) 539, however, proceeded on the basis of the 'bank's interest' exception, holding that the bank could disclose to a guarantor details of

(c) If the bank suspects that the customer has been guilty of fraud and that the account may include the proceeds of that activity, then the bank may apply to court for guidance as to the proper method of dealing with the assets. The disclosures to the court and others which are necessary for that purpose would again be protected by the 'bank's interest' exception.[109]

(d) Where a third party, at the request of the customer, lodges a complaint in respect of the conduct of the account, it is in the interests of the bank to respond to that complaint, and it may disclose to the third party such information as may be necessary for that purpose.[110]

(e) Where a loan has gone into default and the bank wishes to dispose of the loan and associated security package to a third party, it seems that the bank cannot rely on this exception because the sale is not *necessary* to protect its interests.[111]

42.43 It should, however, be noted from the above examples that the 'interests of the bank' exception deals with those cases which intimately affect the relationship of the bank and its customer. In many respects, the exception is a necessary consequence of the fact that the relationship is of a legal character, with the result that enforcement or other steps may be required at some point. It would therefore seem that the exception can only be invoked in the context of a disclosure relating to the *private law* relationship between the parties themselves.

42.44 At all events, it has been held that the exception cannot be invoked merely because a foreign court has directed an order to the bank requiring production of documents held by the London branch, and that non-disclosure might result in the bank being held in contempt of the foreign court.[112] This ruling appears to be consistent with the principles outlined above.

---

the current balance owing, the rate of interest and the progress made by the bank in realizing other security held by it. In other words, the disclosure is limited to that which is relevant to the guarantor; the bank cannot simply provide copies of all information held on the customer's file.

[109] Compare the situation which arose in *Finers v Miro* [1991] 1 All ER 182. A bank does, however, need to exercise a certain degree of care. In one case, a bank which received a cheque for collection was later notified by the paying bank that the cheque had been fraudulently altered and, as a result, the collecting bank froze the customer's account. However, the customer succeeded in obtaining damages for breach of confidentiality when his bank entered into correspondence with the paying bank: *BMP Global Distribution Inc v Bank of Nova Scotia* 2005 BCSC 1091 (Supreme Court, British Columbia). The decision to some extent turns on the account operating conditions. Subject to that, however, it is submitted that the 'bank's interest' exception should have permitted such disclosures as may be reasonably necessary to investigate an alleged fraud.

[110] This conclusion may be drawn from the decision in *Sunderland v Barclays Bank Ltd* (1938) LDAB 163, where information was disclosed to a husband who had been instructed by his wife to lodge such a complaint, and the bank disclosed that she was writing cheques in favour of bookmakers. The case may also be explained on the basis of the customer's implied consent—see paras 42.60–42.61 below. For a more recent case in which the 'bank's interest' exception was discussed, see *Christofi v Barclays Bank plc* [1999] 4 All ER 437. The case was, however, decided on different grounds which have already been discussed above.

[111] *Rodaro v Royal Bank of Canada* (2002) 59 OR (3d) 74 (Ontario Court of Appeal). As in that case, however, the point will rarely arise because, in practice, the bank's standard facility documentation will specifically authorize disclosure in such a case.

[112] See the decisions in *XAG v A Bank* and *FDC & Co Ltd v Chase Manhattan Bank NA*, discussed above.

If a bank legitimately decides to disclose information in reliance on the 'own interest' **42.45** exception, it does not thereby come under a duty to notify the customer that the disclosure has been made.[113]

It follows that the 'interests of the bank' exception is confined to matters affecting the bank **42.46** *directly in the context of its contractual relationship with the customer.*[114] The exception has no broader or wider application.[115] As a result, this exception cannot be invoked to justify the provision of information to a third party who may be considering the acquisition of the bank or part of its business.[116] In practice therefore, such transactions must proceed either on the basis that (i) no customer-specific information is disclosed or (ii) any disclosures which are made, whilst perhaps constituting a breach of the duty, will not result in any loss to the customer which may form the basis of a damages claim.[117]

Public Interest

It has been argued by some that the 'public duty' exception should now be seen as redun- **42.47** dant, or should be abolished. For example, the Jack Report felt that, in the years since *Tournier*, '... statutory specification of this type of disclosure has now been carried so far that it is hard to see in what circumstances the generalised provision, with its uncertainty of application, could any longer be needed, given that emergency legislation could always be enacted in time of war ...'.

That recommendation has not been pursued, and it is submitted that the 'public interest' **42.48** exception may now be assuming a renewed importance. The comment of the Jack Committee (reproduced above) is no doubt justifiable in a domestic context. As has been shown, there are now a large number of statutory provisions which enable various authorities to intrude upon the privacy of the banker-customer relationship, and virtually all of these have been enacted since the *Tournier* decision was handed down. But, as has been shown, the 'compulsion of law' exception applies only where disclosure is required by

---

[113] *Jawhary v Bank of Credit and Commerce International SA* [1993] BCLC 396.

[114] This may be contrasted with the 'public duty' exception, which is about to be discussed. The 'private interests' exception is essentially invoked to deal with cases in which the obligations of the customer in relation to his account fall to be enforced; by contrast, the 'public interest' exception affects the relationship of the bank with the public, and may be invoked regardless of any default by the customer in the context of his contractual relationship with the bank.

[115] Indeed, it may be noted that the Jack Report recommended that the 'interests of the bank' exception should be limited to (i) disclosure to a court in the event of legal proceedings to which the bank is a party, (ii) disclosure among members of the same banking group solely for the purpose of protecting the group against loss, and (iii) disclosure made for the purposes of the sale of the bank or a substantial part of its business. Whilst the first two categories would tend to limit the scope of the exception, the third category would, for reasons about to be given, operate to broaden the scope of the exception.

[116] Equally, a disclosure designed to protect the bank's own general business reputation could not usually be justified under the 'bank's interest' exception.

[117] ie because the buyer itself will usually be a bank which will understand the need for confidentiality and which will, in any event, usually give undertakings to the prospective seller in that regard. On damages for breach of the duty, see paras 42.63–42.64 below.

English law.[118] This limitation is a serious one under current conditions, where serious offences such as major frauds, corruption, money laundering, and terrorist activity frequently have an international dimension and may be under investigation by authorities or courts outside the United Kingdom.

42.49 Whilst the 'public interest' exception must be handled with great care and no doubt poses the greatest difficulty,[119] it is submitted that it may now be invoked to deal with a number of situations arising in a cross-border context and to which the 'compulsion of law' exception does not apply. Whilst the 'public interest' exception may have been thought to have a relatively narrow compass when originally formulated in *Tournier,* it is open to the courts to approach the exception afresh, having regard to changes in banking practice[120] and modern conditions.

42.50 In order to pursue this discussion, it is necessary to begin with a review of the exception as originally formulated, and to discuss such authorities as currently exist in this field. It will then be possible to review those conditions which, in the writer's view, would justify a broader approach to this particular exception.

42.51 Dealing firstly with the existing case law:

(a) in *Tournier* itself, the Court of Appeal observed that the bank has the right to disclose information '… to the extent to which it is reasonably necessary … to protect the Bank, or persons interested, or the public, against fraud or crime …';[121]

(b) in the same case, the Court indicated that danger to the State or public duty may supersede the banker's duty of confidentiality;[122]

(c) it appears that the 'public duty' exception may apply where a bank provides information to its regulator in order to enable the latter to carry out its functions as supervisor of the financial system;[123]

---

[118] See the discussion (above) of the decision of the Hong Kong Court of Appeal in *FDC & Co Ltd v Chase Manhattan Bank.*

[119] The point is made by Paget, para 8.4.

[120] Not least the internationalization of banking business which has occurred in the intervening years.

[121] Of course, consistently with points made earlier in this chapter, the information which forms the subject matter of the disclosure must be limited to that which is necessary to serve the relevant public interest. Of equal importance, however, is the obvious point that disclosure must be limited to those persons to whom disclosure is reasonably necessary to further that public interest. For a Canadian case in which the public interest exception was invoked under unusual circumstances, see *Canada Deposit Insurance Corporation v Canadian Commercial Bank* [1989] AJ No 44, No 8503. A suspicion of crime such as drug smuggling might also justify a 'public interest' disclosure to the authorities: see the Canadian decision in *Lesser Antilles Trading Co Ltd v Bank of Nova Scotia* [1985] LRC (Comm) 39 (where, however, the requisite evidence was absent). As noted below, this point may now be academic, at least in the UK, because of the bank's duty to make relevant disclosures under the Proceeds of Crime Act.

[122] See in particular the judgment of Bankes LJ. He quoted comments to that effect in *Weld Blundell v Stephens* [1920] AC 956 at 965.

[123] See *Libyan Arab Foreign Bank v Bankers Trust Co* [1989] QB 728 at p771. It may be noted that the Court specifically rejected the arguments that such disclosure could be justified either by reference to the interests of the bank or the implied consent of the customer. In many cases, of course, the obligation to assist the regulator will have a statutory source: see, for example, s 165 of FSMA. In such cases the bank will, of course, be able to rely on the 'compulsion of law' exception. On the effect of the duty of the regulator itself to maintain the confidentiality of information so provided to it, see *Barings plc (in liquidation) v Coopers & Lybrand* [2000] 3 All ER 910 (CA).

(d) it may be that the 'public interest' exception would justify disclosure of defaulting customers to credit reference agencies, so as to prevent them from seeking to obtain credit from other sources without disclosing existing obligations. However, this point can by no means be regarded as clear;

(e) there may be cases in which a bank is justified in making a disclosure to *prevent* the possible perpetration of a fraud. In one case, a trustee company proposed to make a loan to a customer and made enquiries with the borrower's bank. In the course of those discussions, it became apparent that the borrower had not disclosed to the trustee company a default on a facility owing to the bank itself. The bank disclosed the issue to the trustee company. When sued by the bank for the outstanding loan, the borrower counterclaimed for damages for breach of confidentiality on the basis that—had the bank remained silent—it would thereby have assisted the customer in obtaining a loan from the trustee company by deception. The public interest exception was accordingly applied.[124] Nevertheless, the issue is one of some difficulty. If the bank knows that the customer is selling an unprofitable business and may not have disclosed that fact to the purchaser, the bank will not be justified in unilaterally disclosing that information to the buyer under the 'public interest' exception because the principle of *caveat emptor* applies and the circumstances do not necessarily point to fraud;[125]

(f) in the context of the collapse of the Bank of Credit and Commerce International, it has been held that the public interest in investigating fraud affecting an international financial institution overrides the bank's duty of confidentiality, at least where the documents concerned may be relevant to the alleged fraud.[126] It may be noted that the 'public interest' exception was applied in this case even though the request for disclosure arose in the context of *foreign* proceedings between *private* parties.

What can be said of this, admittedly scanty, body of authority? Consistently with the observations of the Jack Report (noted above), it must be said that some of these categories are now likely in practice to be covered by statutory obligations of disclosure. For example, if employees of a bank become aware that a customer is engaged in financial fraud—whether within the United Kingdom or elsewhere—then it is very likely that they will also suspect him of a money laundering offence. In such a case, a duty to disclose the relevant information to the Serious Organised Crime Agency will usually arise by statute,[127] and the need to invoke the 'public interest' exception will not normally arise.

42.52

But, as noted above, difficulties may arise where the bank receives a request for information from a foreign authority investigating major international crimes such as bank fraud, drug

42.53

---

[124] See the Canadian decision in *Canadian Imperial Bank of Commerce v Sayani* [1994] WWR 260. For a further Canadian case in which the public interest was found to justify disclosure, see *Bank of China v Fan* (2003) 22 BCLR (4th) 152.

[125] *Kabwand Pty Ltd v National Australian Bank Ltd* (1989) ATER 40-950. The position may change if, for example, the bank is aware that the seller has provided a fraudulent set of accounts to the buyer.

[126] *Pharaon v Bank of Credit and Commerce International SA (in liquidation)* [1998] 4 All ER 455. The documents to be provided in that case were subject to redaction, but this merely reflects the (now familiar) proviso that the relevant disclosure should not go beyond that which is necessary to serve the objective by reference to which the disclosure is justified.

[127] See s 330 of the Proceeds of Crime Act 2002. The provision is discussed at paras 7.47–7.58 above.

dealing, money laundering, corruption, or similar activities. It is true that those authorities may apply for information under mutual assistance arrangements,[128] but participants in crimes of this kind will generally be fleet of foot and investigatory opportunities may be lost whilst these procedures are being followed. In the context of very serious crime, is a bank bound to remain silent merely because an investigation is being conducted by a foreign authority, which lacks the necessary powers under English law which would enable the bank to rely on the compulsion of law exception?

42.54 Whilst the foreign authority cannot *compel* disclosure under these circumstances, it is submitted that, in an appropriate case, the bank may *voluntarily* disclose information to that authority. The difficulty, of course, is to determine which type of case would be *appropriate* for these purposes.[129] For the bank which receives such a request, the dilemma is especially acute, for it cannot know the full details of the investigation at hand and it has no investigatory powers of its own. It is impossible to generalize, for each situation will be different and would have to be viewed on its own merits. Nevertheless, a few broad propositions may be stated:

(a) the use of the 'public interest' exception in this context could only begin to be justified in cases involving major crimes which are subject to international condemnation;[130]

(b) crimes within this category would include massive frauds perpetrated against the public in a number of countries. As a result, banks holding information relating to the BCCI collapse would have been justified in disclosing that information to investigating authorities in relevant jurisdictions;[131]

(c) corruption, terrorism, and money laundering are all condemned by international treaties or international law, and it is submitted that the 'public interest' exception would justify disclosure of relevant customer information in major[132] cases;

(d) this view may be justified by various considerations. For example, major acts of corruption will frequently rely on the international financial system to enable the recipient to

---

[128] See, for example, the Evidence (Proceedings in other Jurisdictions) Act 1975.

[129] It is interesting briefly to note the US case law in this area. The Maryland court in *Suburban Trust Co v Waller* 408 A 2d 758 (1979) held that there was no 'public interest' exception to the duty of confidentiality, largely on the basis that this would confer a broad discretion on the bank and substantially erode the duty of confidentiality; it is submitted that this approach is excessively simplistic. On the other hand, the Indiana Court of Appeals in *Indiana National Bank v Chapman* 482 NE 2d 474 (1985) dismissed a claim against a bank which had provided information about the customer in response to a police request in the context of a criminal investigation. The charges against the customer were later dismissed, but it was held that the bank could rely on the public interest defence because of the context in which the request arose. The decision illustrates a further point, namely that the conduct of the bank in the context of its contractual obligations must be viewed at the time the disclosure is made, and not in the light of any subsequent events.

[130] In this context, it is probably fair to observe that the 'public' in whose 'interest' the disclosure is made must be the public in the jurisdiction in which the relevant bank branch is located. But the public may be taken to have an interest in the suppression of crimes such as major international fraud and corruption, wherever they occur. In other words, whilst the foreign State seeking information must have a clear connection with the crimes under investigation, those crimes must also be of a nature which are a concern to the international community.

[131] This statement must be read subject to subpara (f) below. An example of the use of the public interest disclosure in this type of case is offered by the decision in *Pharaon v Bank of Credit & Commerce International SA (in liquidation)*, to which reference has already been made.

[132] This qualification should be carefully noted.

enjoy the fruits of his activity. Major acts of terrorism will have to be financed and funds may pass through the international banking system. Disclosure is plainly in the public interest in such cases, and the cloak of banking confidentiality should not be invoked to protect those involved in crimes of this nature;

(e) disclosure may perhaps be more easily justified where the foreign authority concerned has a clear interest in pursuing the investigation (eg because the crime took place on its territory and involved its own nationals—whether as perpetrators or victims—or there is some other clear and compelling connection between the requesting State and the criminal conduct at issue);

(f) nevertheless, there must be a degree of protection for the customer in such cases. Whilst the bank plainly cannot investigate the merits of the case, it should endeavour to satisfy itself that the requesting authority is involved in a proper investigation[133] and that the information sought appears to have a legitimate connection to that investigation;

(g) it may be asked why a bank should elect to disclose information in such cases when, as noted above, it is under no positive *obligation* to do so? The answer, perhaps, lies in the fact that a reputable bank may not wish to be seen to withhold information which may be relevant to crimes of the type and magnitude discussed in this section. The more cynical observer might note that an international bank would not wish to upset the authorities in other countries in which it may also do business and where it is reliant on the government for the necessary licences or authorities. That may well be so, but that point should not be relevant to the 'public interest' analysis.

It should be said that cases of this kind will not arise with any great frequency. In most **42.55** major cases, the authorities in the United Kingdom would usually be involved, and it will thus often be possible to provide information under the 'compulsion of law' exception. Nevertheless, and whilst banks would obviously wish to proceed with great caution in this area,[134] it is submitted that the 'public interest' exception could be invoked in the categories of cases which have been described above. Whilst a customer who is ultimately found to be innocent of any wrongdoing might feel aggrieved that account information has been disclosed, it is submitted that a court should take a sympathetic attitude towards the bank's actions, bearing in mind the nature of the crimes which have been discussed. The application of the 'public interest' exception necessarily involves a balancing of private rights against public good. That exercise, and the extent of the exception, may require modification to meet the challenges of a globalizing world, and the threats with which it may from time to time be confronted.

Consent of Customer

Since the duty of confidentiality is a contractual one which is owed solely to the customer, **42.56** it is clear that he can waive that duty in any particular case. Consequently, no breach of the

---

[133] This qualification may likewise cause difficulty, for example where a corruption investigation may have been opened on the grounds of political expediency.

[134] ie because of the potential liability in damages in the event of wrongful disclosure.

Tournier duty occurs if the disclosure is made with the express or implied consent of the customer.

42.57   It is tempting to think that this exception requires no further explanation; yet matters may not be so straightforward. It may be helpful to consider express and implied consent separately for these purposes.

Express Consent

42.58   In most cases, the existence of an express consent will be a matter of evidence. In some cases, the bank may have obtained written consent;[135] in others it may rely on a verbal consent given by telephone. Especially in the latter case, there may be questions about the precise scope of the consent. The customer will rarely give consent for disclosure of any information to anyone; the consent will be limited to the provision of particular information to particular recipients. The court may therefore have to decide on the ambit of the customer's consent, and on the extent to which the disclosure by the bank fell within (or exceeded) the consent actually given. These may be difficult questions, but in the final analysis they will depend largely upon the evidence, rather than any sophisticated legal reasoning.

42.59   More subtle questions can, however, arise when dealing with the circumstances under which the consent is given. Just as a contract is voidable by a party who entered into it under duress,[136] it would seem to be inappropriate for a bank to rely upon a consent for present purposes if it knew that it had been extracted under duress. This may occur where, for example, a foreign court directs a defendant to provide such consent, on pain of penalties or imprisonment in the event of refusal.[137] The Grand Court of the Cayman Islands has ruled that a consent given under such circumstances was not a valid consent for the purposes of a local law designed to preserve confidentiality, and that a local bank ought not to release information in reliance upon it.[138] In the absence of any direct authority in this country, it is submitted that this decision is right as a matter of principle; 'consent' must mean 'free consent'. The decision should therefore be followed in England, should the occasion arise.

Implied Consent

42.60   The circumstances surrounding the disclosure may be sufficient to imply the customer's consent to a disclosure. For example, if a wife visits her bank manager to complain about transactions affecting her account, and takes her husband to the meeting, it may be inferred that she consents to disclosure of details of her account to her husband, at least so far as they are relevant to the matter under discussion.[139] Likewise, if a customer asks his bank to confirm to a third party that it has been authorized to make certain payments, then the

---

[135] The Jack Report considered that the 'customer consent' exception should only be available where the customer had given written consent which stated the purpose for which the consent is given.

[136] See Chitty, para 7-045.

[137] The US Supreme Court has decided that courts in that country can be compelled by a court order to sign such a consent, without thereby infringing his constitutional rights: *John Doe v United States* 487 US 201 (1988).

[138] *In the matter of ABC Ltd* [1985] FLR 159.

[139] A similar situation arose in *Sunderland v Barclays Bank Limited* (1938) 5 LDAB 163.

customer thereby impliedly authorizes the bank to advise the third party in the event that its instructions are revoked.[140]

In contrast, it was for many years the practice of banks to provide customer references at the request of other banks. Frequently, the requesting bank would be seeking information on behalf of one of its own customers, rather than for itself.[141] It was eventually decided that, whilst banks were well aware of this practice, their customers generally were not. As a result, it was not possible to imply any consent on the part of the customer, and the provision of a reference without his consent thus constituted a breach of the *Tournier* duty.[142]   **42.61**

Liability to the Recipient

If a bank does decide to disclose customer information to a third party, then it will obviously take care to ensure the accuracy of that information. However, what is the bank's position in the event that (i) due to negligence within the bank, inaccurate information is provided, (ii) the recipient relies on that information, and (iii) he suffers loss as a consequence? Does the bank incur a liability to compensate him for that loss? Much will, of course, depend upon the precise circumstances but the following general propositions are suggested: **42.62**

(a) if the bank provides a customer reference to a third party,[143] then the bank may in principle be liable to compensate the third party for its losses, because (i) the bank will realize that the third party will rely on the information provided to it and (ii) as a consequence, the bank assumes a duty of care to the third party.[144] A bank will usually include an express disclaimer of liability in such cases and, in principle, the courts should give effect to such a provision.[145] It is true that, in cases of this kind, the bank '... cannot ... exclude or restrict his liability for negligence except in so far as the term or notice satisfies the requirement of reasonableness ...'.[146] But, at any rate in the absence of recklessness on the part of the bank, it is submitted that such an exclusion clause should be regarded as reasonable because (i) the bank will not usually receive any fee or other remuneration for the provision of the reference and (ii) it will not usually have any wider involvement in, or knowledge of, the intended transaction between the customer and the recipient of the reference;

---

[140] *Lee Gleeson Pty Ltd v Sterling Estates Pty Ltd* [1992] 1 Bank LR 342 (Supreme Court of New South Wales).

[141] For example, the customer of the first bank might be a prospective tenant of the customer of the second bank, and the landlord wished to know whether the tenant was likely to meet his commitments under the lease.

[142] *Turner v Royal Bank of Scotland plc* [1999] 2 All ER (Comm) 664. For further proceedings in the same case, see [2001] All ER (D) 139 (CA). As Paget points out (para 8.11), it is remarkable that this very long standing practice was not challenged until the *Turner* case.

[143] As noted at para 42.61 above, it is now established that such references should only be given with the explicit consent of the customer.

[144] This is the effect of the well-known decision in *Hedley Byrne & Co Ltd v Heller & Partners Ltd* [1964] AC 465.

[145] *Hedley Byrne*, above.

[146] Section 2(2) of the Unfair Contract Terms Act 1977. On the whole subject and for the relevant case law, see Chitty, ch 14.

(b) where the bank is compelled to disclose information pursuant to a statutory obligation, it cannot be said *voluntarily* to have assumed any responsibility as regards the
recipient. Consequently, if an investigating authority relies on that information to its
detriment, it cannot recover damages in tort in respect of any losses which flow from
any inaccuracies;[147]

(c) where the disclosure is made in the public interest,[148] it is true that the disclosure is
made voluntarily and, at least in theory, it is possible that the bank could incur liability
to the third party recipient who has relied on that information to his detriment.
However, it is submitted that it would not be 'fair, just and reasonable' to impose a duty
of care on a bank which makes a disclosure for public interest reasons; and

(d) it would more obviously be reasonable to impose a duty of care where the bank makes
a disclosure in pursuit of its own interests. However, it is difficult to envisage the circumstances under which a third party recipient could actually suffer loss. For example,
if information is disclosed to enable a bank to sue for an overdraft, its legal advisers may
rely on that information in preparing the necessary court proceedings. But even if that
information later proves to be inaccurate, it is hard to see how those legal advisers—or
anyone else involved in the proceedings—could suffer any loss as a consequence.

Damages for Breach

42.63 As noted previously in this chapter, banks tend to take their duty of confidentiality very
seriously. As a result, cases which consider the consequences of a breach of the duty tend to
be rare. Nevertheless, it is possible to state a few general principles:

(a) there is very limited case law on the assessment of damages for a breach of the bank's
duty of confidentiality. Case law dealing with assessments in other cases where a duty
of confidentiality is imposed is not directly comparable to the subject at hand, and
must therefore be treated with some caution.[149] It is therefore necessary to work from
first principles;

(b) the customer must establish that he has suffered loss as a result of the breach of the duty
of confidentiality;[150]

---

[147] Compare the situation which arose in *Customs and Excise Commissioners v Barclays Bank plc*, discussed
at paras 43.31–43.38 below.

[148] eg with a view to preventing crime or fraud: see para 42.54 above.

[149] See *McGregor on Damages* (17th edn, Sweet & Maxwell, 2003), paras 28-032 (contract) and 40-025
(tort).

[150] That this general requirement applies in this context is confirmed by the decision in *Robertson v
Canadian Imperial Bank of Commerce* [1995] 1 All ER 824 (PC). This is a point of great significance in practice; whilst a customer may be dismayed to find that information has been disclosed, he will frequently have
difficulty in demonstrating any identifiable loss. The requirement for proof of actual loss in this context may
be contrasted with the position where a bank wrongfully dishonours a customer's cheques: see *Wilson v United
Counties Bank* [1920] AC 102 (noted at para 17.11 above). In Canada, it has been stated that a breach of the
duty of confidentiality is actionable if the customer suffers loss or if the bank makes a wrongful gain as a result
of the disclosure. It appears that damages may also be awarded in respect of a potential business opportunity
which is lost as a result of the breach (although no such award was made on the facts of the case): see *Rodaro v
Royal Bank of Canada* (2002) 59 OR (3d) 74 (Ontario Court of Appeal).

(c) how should such damages be assessed? Whilst there is limited direct authority on damages for breach of the *Tournier* duty, the decision of the House of Lords in *Jackson v Royal Bank of Scotland plc*[151]—relating to a breach of a duty of confidentiality owed to the beneficiary of a transferable documentary credit—does offer some useful parallels. In that case, the disclosure at issue led to the loss of the beneficiary's main customer, and his business was ultimately forced to close as a result. The House of Lords held that, in cases of this kind, it was usually necessary to have recourse to the first 'limb' of the rule in *Hadley v Baxendale*.[152] In the circumstances of the *Jackson* case, the loss of the middleman's business relationship with his customer was a natural consequence of the disclosure of his profit margin to the ultimate buyer; both parties must have had this in mind as a natural and probable consequence of the breach.[153] Damages for loss of that relationship were thus not too remote from the breach and were, therefore, in principle recoverable[154] although, as a matter of causation, the claimant must show that he had a real and substantial chance of further business, as opposed to a merely speculative prospect.[155] Whilst the calculation at issue in that case was, for many reasons, accepted to be unsatisfactory, a few general points may be drawn from that case. In essence, the court has to examine the nature and stability of the business relationship at issue,[156] the period for which it would probably have continued to subsist, and the likely levels of profit which would have been derived from it over that period. The nature of the assessment only has to be stated to realize that the exercise is a difficult and hazardous one. It is, however, submitted that the court should adopt a conservative approach to the award of damages in such cases, not least because (i) modern market conditions mean that business relationships are constantly under review with reference to cost and other factors, and may thus change with relative frequency and (ii) even in the context of continuing relationships, buyers are constantly seeking to

---

[151] [2005] 2 All ER 71 (HL).

[152] (1854) 9 Exch 341. At the risk of repeating a well-known formulation, the relevant passage reads: 'Where two parties have made a contract which one of them has broken, the damages which the other party ought to receive in respect of such breach of contract should be such as may fairly and reasonably be considered either arising naturally, ie according to the usual course of things, from such breach of contract itself, or such as may reasonably be supposed to have been in the contemplation of the parties at the time they made the contract, as the probable result of the breach of it'. It should, however, be added that the House of Lords reliance on the first limb of this rule arose in the context of a duty of confidentiality owed to the beneficiary of a credit where, it seems, there had been no specific negotiation of the terms of the credit between the bank and the beneficiary. The second limb of the rule is much more likely to come into operation in the context of the *Tournier* duty, because the bank is much more likely to have a closer knowledge of the circumstances peculiar to its own customer.

[153] As the court noted in *Kpohraror v Woolwich Building Society* [1996] 4 All ER 119, the starting point for any application of the rule in *Hadley v Baxendale* is to examine the extent of the shared knowledge of the parties. Armed with that knowledge, the court can then determine which losses may be said to flow naturally from the breach, and those which the parties may have specifically had in contemplation.

[154] In other words, the loss of a chance of repeat business is not too remote and thus an award of damages may be made in respect of that loss. In this context, see *Victoria Laundry (Windsor) Ltd v Newman Industries Ltd* [1949] 2 KB 528, *Rodaro v Royal Bank of Canada* (above) and, more generally, *McGregor on Damages*, ch 8.

[155] See *Allied Maples Group Ltd v Simmons & Simmons* [1995] 1 WLR 1602.

[156] This factor was of some importance in *Jackson* itself, where the claimant was a middleman, his customer knew the identity of the ultimate supplier and could easily have decided to place orders direct. The position of the middleman and his relationship with his customer was thus rightly described as 'precarious'.

reduce their purchasing costs. Factors of this kind should operate to limit the appropriate level of the award in most cases;

(d) it is noteworthy that, in the *Jackson* case, the loss of the business relationship at issue led to the loss of the claimant's major source of income and, ultimately, to the closure of his business. It does not seem to have been suggested that the resultant loss of the claimant's business *as a whole* should form the basis for a separate award. In general terms, and applying the first test in *Hadley v Baxendale*, it may be that the loss of the particular business relationship flows naturally from the breach of duty, but the loss of the customer's entire business does not. It is submitted that this line of reasoning should apply not only in the context of a breach of the specific duty of confidentiality which arose in *Jackson*, but also in relation to a breach of the more general, *Tournier* duty;

(e) as a result of the considerations noted in paragraph (d) above, it is necessary to conclude that damages flowing from a disclosure of information in this type of case must reflect the loss of profit from existing business relationships over the period for which they may have been expected to endure. This may, of course, be a very substantial figure in the case of a large business with multiple business relationships. However, it seems that the corporate customer (or its liquidator) cannot make any separate recovery in respect of the loss of the business if insolvency proves to be the consequence of the disclosure. This is because, in the final analysis, the business itself consists of its existing customer relationships and damages have already been assessed in that regard. Losses resulting from the loss of the opportunity to develop new and profitable business relationships at a future date would be too speculative or remote, and no damages could therefore be awarded under that heading;

(f) of course, in a situation of the kind described in paragraph (e) above, it is likely that the shareholders of the borrower will lose the market value of their investment. Harsh though it may, from their perspective, appear, it is submitted that they would have no cause of action against the bank in this type of situation. The shareholders are not customers of the bank, and there is thus no contractual duty of confidentiality. Furthermore, the information confided to the bank and which forms the subject matter of the breach was provided to it by the customer, and not by its shareholders. Consequently, the equitable duty of confidentiality[157] is owed to the company alone;

(g) matters are complicated by the fact that the outright loss of existing customer relationships is not necessarily the only type of loss which the customer may suffer. It is quite foreseeable that suppliers to the customer may be unnerved by information which the bank wrongfully allows to slip into the public domain. They may decline to continue supply, thus prejudicing the customer's ability to fulfil orders which have been placed with it, or they may continue to supply but withdraw credit terms which they previously allowed. Either eventuality can have serious consequences for the customer's business. It seems clear that the customer could recover damages for the loss of its credit under these circumstances, for these consequences would flow naturally from the

---

[157] ie the duty described in *Seager Ltd v Copydex Ltd,* on which see the discussion at para 42.70 below.

bank's breach of duty.[158] The duty of confidentiality exists in part to sustain the customer's credit, and damages may be awarded to compensate for any loss suffered in that respect.[159] If the customer remains in business, then it seems likely that it could recover from the bank the (essentially 'one-off') costs which it incurs in securing alternative sources of supply, or the cost of funding the necessary advance payments to its suppliers.[160] If, however, the customer is forced into insolvency as a result of the disclosure, then a different analysis must apply, for the customer will no longer need its sources of supply. Under those circumstances, the court must assess the profits which the customer might have expected to make from its existing business relationships over a period equal to their likely duration. No separate award of damages could generally be made in respect of the loss of the business itself;[161]

(h) It seems that a corporate customer which has gone into liquidation for reasons unconnected with the breach of duty[162] should be able to recover only general damages,[163] which will be relatively insubstantial. Since the customer will no longer be able to use its credit standing for any purpose, it is difficult to see how it could establish any material loss under such circumstances.

In view of the importance attached to the duty of confidentiality, the Jack Report recom- **42.64** mended that damages for breach on the part of the bank should include compensation for distress, embarrassment, and inconvenience, even if no actual financial loss could be proved.[164] That recommendation has not, however, found its way onto the statute book, and it thus remains the case that ordinary rules as to the assessment of damages, as discussed above, continue to apply in this context.

Data Protection Act 1998

In determining whether customer information should be released to a third party, a bank **42.65** must also be mindful of the statutory duties imposed upon it by the Data Protection Act 1998 ('the 1998 Act').

---

[158] ie these losses would be recoverable under the first 'limb' of the rule in *Hadley v Baxendale* (above). See, however, *McGregor on Damages*, para 2-028, where it is suggested that such damages would only be available if they were within the contemplation of the parties for the purposes of the second 'limb' of that rule.

[159] See *Wilson v United Counties Bank* [1920] AC 102 (HL); *Kpohraror v Woolwich Building Society* [1996] 4 All ER 119 (CA), although the latter case deals with loss of reputation following the dishonour of a cheque, rather than a breach of the duty of confidentiality.

[160] The customer must, of course, seek to mitigate its claim in either case. In the latter case, it is submitted that the customer could recover the additional funding cost until the date on which, with reasonable business efforts, it should have re-established its credit standing with its suppliers.

[161] In other words, the analysis noted in para (e) above would again apply in this context.

[162] This should be carefully contrasted with the situation which arose in *Jackson v Royal Bank of Scotland* [2005] 2 All ER 71 (HL), where the breach of a duty of confidentiality led to the failure of the business concerned.

[163] The point was made in the *Jackson* case, above.

[164] In favour of the customer, this would, of course, represent a departure from the normal rules as to the recoverable heads of damage in breach of contract claims.

42.66 The essential starting point under the 1998 Act is that 'personal data' should not be pro-cessed[165] unless this is done fairly and lawfully in accordance with the 'Data Protection Principles' set out in Schedule 1 to the Act. Processing of personal data must be adequate, relevant, and proportionate to the underlying purpose of the processing.[166]

42.67 Whilst it is not intended to review the provisions of the 1998 Act in depth, the follow-ing points may be relevant to a bank which is considering disclosure of customer information:

(a) the 1998 Act applies only to data relating to *individuals*.[167] Information relating solely to the business affairs of a *corporation* will thus not generally fall within the scope of the Act;[168]

(b) the 1998 Act applies only to data held within a 'relevant filing system' which is struc-tured so as to make specific information readily accessible.[169] Searchable information held on a computer system will generally fall within the scope of this definition, but a paper file of correspondence and documents may not;[170] and

(c) if particular personal data is found to fall within the scope of the 1998 Act, then it is necessary to consider whether its disclosure would be covered by an exception. Although the available exemptions do not precisely mirror those discussed in the con-text of *Tournier* (above), they are in practice likely to be available in similar circum-stances. For example, the processing of personal data with a view to the prevention, detection, or prosecution of crime is exempt from the non-disclosure provisions of the 1998 Act.[171] Likewise, the non-disclosure provisions are inapplicable where the rele-vant disclosure is required by law or by a court order, or is necessary for the purpose of legal proceedings or otherwise in connection with the exercise of legal rights.[172]

The Wider Duty of Confidence

42.68 For reasons which are entirely understandable, text books dealing with the bankers' duty of confidentiality tend to focus on the decision in the *Tournier* case and the exceptions to the duty which it established.

42.69 Yet this approach may encourage an unduly narrow mindset, partly because it may suggest that *Tournier* provides an exclusive definition of the scope of the duty of secrecy owed by a bank, and partly because the notion of 'confidentiality' suggests that a breach of the duty occurs only where customer information is divulged to a third party—that is to say, to a

---

[165] References to the processing of data include its retrieval, use or disclosure: see s 1(1) of the 1998 Act.
[166] See Sch 1, para 3 of the 1998 Act.
[167] See the definition of 'data subject' in s 1(1) of the 1998 Act.
[168] See *Smith v Lloyds TSB Bank plc* [2005] All ER (D) 358. However, some care may be necessary if any of the information to be disclosed relates to individual directors or managers of the corporation.
[169] See the definition of 'relevant filing system' in s 1(1) of the 1998 Act.
[170] *Durant v Financial Services Authority* [2004] IP &T 814. It may be that this restrictive approach to the definition of 'relevant filing system' is inconsistent with the EU Data Protection Directive, from which the 1998 Act is derived. However, this issue goes beyond the scope of the present discussion.
[171] See s 29(1), read together with s 29(3) of the 1998 Act.
[172] See s 35 of the 1998 Act.

person outside the bank. For the reasons given below, it is submitted that neither of these propositions can be sustained.

It must not be forgotten that equity imposes a fairly broadly based duty of confidence. This **42.70** is more extensive that a mere duty of secrecy or non-disclosure, in the sense in which those expressions would normally be understood. Rather, as stated in *Seager Ltd v Copydex Ltd,*[173] the duty implies that '... he who has received information in confidence shall not take unfair advantage of it. He must not make use of it to the prejudice of him who gave it without obtaining his consent ...'. The rule is in some respects linked with the difficulties posed by conflicts of interest, and the problems are well illustrated by the decision in *United Pan-Europe Communications NV v Deutsche Bank AG.*[174] In that case, the bank had participated in syndicated loans for UPC and had also participated in its initial public offering of shares. In these capacities, it had received information about UPC's finances and acquisition strategy on a confidential basis. The bank subsequently made a bid for, and acquired, a company in Germany under circumstances where UPC had an interest in launching a bid for the same entity. It was alleged that, in formulating its bid, the bank might have made use of the confidential information supplied by UPC. On the facts, it was held that a fiduciary duty had come into existence and that the onus accordingly fell on the bank to demonstrate that it had not misused that information. It must be emphasized that the case does not appear to have gone to a full trial and that the allegations were thus not tested. Nevertheless, the factual matrix demonstrates the type of difficulties which a bank may face where it receives confidential information for use only in specific capacities.

As a result, it seems that a bank must ensure that information held by it with respect to **42.71** customer A cannot come into the hands of those dealing with customer B or otherwise used to the advantage of customer B, where interests may come into conflict and the information about customer A may be used to its disadvantage (eg because B is contemplating a takeover offer for A). Whilst a bank does not generally owe a fiduciary duty to avoid conflicts between its relationships with customer A and customer B,[175] it must ensure that information held with respect to either customer is not misused in a takeover situation of this kind.[176]

Difficulties of this kind have been recognized by various regulatory bodies. For example, **42.72** the FSA requires that 'Chinese Walls' must be established between different functions

---

[173] [1967] 1 WLR, 923, 931. See also *Seager Ltd v Copydex Ltd (No 2)* [1969] 2 All ER 718, *Parry-Jones v Law Society* [1969] 1 Ch 7 and the Australian decision in *Crowley v Murphy* (1981) 34 ALR 496. Although these cases arose in the context of a professional relationship there seems no reason to doubt that the principle should apply equally to the bank and its customer. Although the relationship is essentially contractual, it is also of a fiduciary character and it thus seems appropriate to impose equitable duties of this kind. The *Seager* decision has won general approval: see, for example, *FBI Foods Ltd v Cadbury Schweppes Inc* [1999] 1 SCR 142 (Supreme Court of Canada).
[174] [2000] BCLC 461 (CA).
[175] For a case involving a takeover bid in which the court held that a fiduciary duty had, in fact, come into existence, see the decision of the Ontario Court of Appeal in *Standard Investment Ltd v Canadian Imperial Bank of Commerce* (1985) 52 OR 473.
[176] See *American Medicorp Inc v Continental Illinois National Bank* 475 F Supp 5 (1977) and *Washington Steel Corporation v TW Corporation* 602 F 2d 594 (1979).

within an institution;[177] similar provisions are to be found in the Takeover Code.[178] But a party seeking an award of damages in respect of these duties may well have to ground his action in breach of confidence; he may not be able to rely upon a breach of the *Tournier* duty of confidentiality, for he may be unable to show that the information concerned was actually disclosed to anyone outside the bank itself.[179]

Duties of Confidentiality to Third Parties

42.73 It is perhaps implicit in the *Seager* decision (noted above) that the bank may owe duties of confidentiality to third parties (non-customers) who communicate information to it under circumstances which imply a duty of confidentiality.

42.74 This point is well illustrated by the decision of the House of Lords in *Jackson v Royal Bank of Scotland plc*.[180] In that case, the bank issued a transferable letter of credit to a supplier of goods, who in turn transferred the benefit of a part of the credit to the ultimate supplier. A number of transactions were effected between the supplier and the ultimate buyer on this basis, but the relationship came to an abrupt end when the bank mistakenly sent to the buyer a copy of the invoices issued by the ultimate supplier, thus revealing the profits earned by the middleman in the deal. In the House of Lords, it was not disputed that the bank owed an implied duty of confidentiality to the beneficiary of a transferable letter of credit,[181] because the beneficiary clearly had good commercial reasons for preserving the secrecy of his mark up on the sale.[182]

42.75 It is fair to say that, in view of the breadth of the *Copydex* principle, there is no limit to the category of persons to whom a bank may owe a duty of confidentiality, if the circumstances justify it. Corporate transactions will offer many obvious cases. For example, if a customer of the bank receives business-sensitive information from a company which it proposes to acquire, it may provide that information to its bank with a view to seeking funding for the acquisition. In this situation, the bank does, of course, owe its usual *Tournier* duty to its own customer. In addition, however, the circumstances also imply a duty of confidentiality in favour of the target company, even though the bank may have had no direct dealings with it.

---

[177] On this subject see, for example, the FSA Handbook, SYSC 10 and MAR 1.3.5E.

[178] On the use of information barriers in the context of acquisition finance, see 'Debt Syndication during Offer Periods' (Takeover Panel Practice Statement No 25, 17 June 2009).

[179] In the example given above, the advice given by the corporate finance advisers to B could be tailored to take account of information held with respect to A, even though the information is not actually disclosed to B itself.

[180] [2005] 2 All ER 71 (HL). The case has been noted at para 42.63 above.

[181] It may be added that the issue of a letter of credit constitutes a contract between the issuing bank and the beneficiary: see para 24.19(a) above. As a result, there exists a contractual framework into which terms can be implied. Even in the absence of a contract, however, a duty of confidentiality would presumably arise in accordance with the *Copydex* principle, which has already been discussed.

[182] It happens that the middleman was also a customer of the same bank, but it is clear that the House of Lords affirmed the existence of the duty in his capacity as a beneficiary of a transferable credit: see para 19 of the judgment.

Whilst there may be no explicit limit to the categories of persons in whose favour a duty of **42.76** confidentiality may be owed, there must, of course, be some limit to the nature or legal content of the duty itself. The duty may not apply to information which is already in the public domain and, in addition, it is submitted that this particular obligation of confidentiality must operate in a manner which is commercially realistic; as a result, it seems that it must be subject to exceptions which are similar to those already discussed in the context of the *Tournier* duty itself. Likewise, in the event of a breach of this particular duty, it would appear that damages should be calculated on a basis similar to that to be adopted in the context of a breach of the *Tournier* duty.[183]

Other Duties of Confidentiality

The various duties of confidentiality discussed thus far have centred around duties owed to **42.77** particular parties. But there may be occasions where the release and/or misuse of information may have regulatory consequences or may even constitute a criminal offence.

A particular example of this is offered by the EU's Market Abuse Directive[184] which was **42.78** implemented into the United Kingdom in part by sections 118–131A of the Financial Services and Markets Act 2000[185] and partly by revisions to the FSA's Handbook.

In essence, the legislation creates seven types of conduct which may amount to 'market **42.79** abuse' in relation to prescribed securities.[186] Conduct amounting to 'market abuse' includes (i) dealing in prescribed securities on the basis of inside information[187] and (ii) the improper disclosure of inside information.[188] As will be seen from this non-exhaustive list, the use of inside information[189] may involve a breach of the relevant provisions of the FSMA.

What are the practical difficulties for a bank in this type of situation? The problem is that **42.80** a bank will frequently receive or come into possession of inside information relating to its borrowers which might well have a significant impact on its share price if it became public. This is especially the case where the information relates to the possible occurrence of a default or a request for the rescheduling of bank debt. The result is that the bank must take steps—such as the establishment of information barriers—designed to ensure that the relevant information does not find its way to others within the institution who may trade in those securities for any purpose.[190]

---

[183] The relevant principles have been considered at paras 42.63–42.64 above.

[184] 2003/6/EC.

[185] As inserted by the Financial Services and Markets Act 2000 (Market Abuse) Regulations 2005 (SI 2005/381).

[186] 'Prescribed securities' includes shares and other transferable securities, money market and other instruments which are listed on a regulated market: see the Financial Services and Markets Act 2000 (Prescribed Markets and Qualifying Investments) Order 2001 (SI 2001/996), as revised by the Market Abuse Regulations mentioned in the preceding footnote.

[187] Section 118(2) of the FSMA.

[188] Section 118(3) of the FSMA.

[189] 'Inside information' means any information which is not publicly available but, if it were to become so, would be likely to have a significant effect on the price of relevant securities.

[190] For further guidance on this subject, see section MAR 1 of the FSA Handbook. See also the Loan Market Association's paper, 'Private and Inside Information in the Loan Markets' (August 2007).

Conclusions

42.81   The decision in the *Tournier* case is very well known to the banking community and tends to be the first port of call when questions of confidentiality arise. Since the decision deals specifically with the *banker's* duty of confidence, there is an understandable tendency to regard this as the last word on the subject. However, it must not be overlooked that broader obligations of confidentiality may apply equally to banks as they do to others. Consequently, as has been seen, prospective disclosure of information also requires consideration of the Data Protection Act 1998 and, possibly, the principle in *Seager Ltd v Copydex Ltd*. In addition, broader duties of confidentiality may apply for the protection of the integrity of the financial markets as a whole.

42.82   It is perhaps inevitably the case that the greatest difficulties arise in cross-border situations, where the most acute and direct forms of conflict can arise. The law of the country in which the account-holding branch is located requires confidentiality, whilst the law of another country requires disclosure. The 'compulsion of law' exception—so frequently used in a domestic context—is not available once an international element of this kind is introduced. This chapter has attempted to provide solutions by reference to the 'public interest' exception, but this will necessarily only be of assistance in a limited category of cases. The globalization of banking services will only add to these difficulties, and it may be that further case law will clarify the bank's proper course in this type of situation.

43

FREEZING INJUNCTIONS AND INTERNATIONAL BANKS

Introduction

The last chapter dealt with court orders designed to secure enforcement of a final judgment **43.01** already handed down by the court. It was thus concerned with third party debt orders and other remedies by way of *post-judgment* execution.

However, as is well known, the court also has power to make pre-judgment orders which are **43.02** designed to prevent a respondent from disposing of or dissipating his assets pending trial. The objective is to ensure that any eventual judgment is not rendered nugatory by the respondent moving or concealing assets which might otherwise be available to meet that judgment.[1]

Whilst freezing injunctions will be directed principally at the respondent to the applica- **43.03** tion, they may be served on any third party who is believed to hold assets belonging to him. Experience has shown that the third party will frequently be a bank, and the effectiveness

---

[1] It follows from this statement that a freezing injunction will only be granted where the applicant seeks payment of a debt or damages; it would not usually be appropriate where the proceedings involve an equitable remedy. The application must therefore be incidental to wider proceedings, and the court must have *in personam* jurisdiction over the defendant: *The Siskina* [1979] AC 210 (HL); *Siporex Trade SA v Comdel Commodities Ltd* [1986] 2 Lloyd's Rep 428. Note that the decision in *The Siskina* was questioned in a dissenting judgment in the Privy Council decision in *Mercedes Benz v Leiduck* [1996] AC 284 and has not been followed in Australia: see n 11 below.

of freezing injunctions has depended in large measure upon the blocking of bank accounts.[2] Nevertheless, it must be said that a bank which receives a freezing injunction will not usually be involved in the main proceedings, and it will have independent obligations both to its own customer and to third parties. The position of a bank may be further complicated by the fact that it has overseas branches which may also hold accounts for the customer targeted by the freezing injunction.[3]

43.04 The present chapter accordingly considers the position of a bank which is notified of the existence of a freezing injunction, and examines the scope of its responsibilities and liabilities. More specifically, the following matters will be considered:

(a) the nature and effect of a freezing injunction;
(b) the action to be taken by a bank on receipt of notice of a freezing injunction;
(c) the impact of the injunction on the relationship between the bank and its customer;
(d) the relationship between the bank and the applicant for the injunction;
(e) the relationship between the bank and certain third parties;
(f) the territorial issues raised by orders of this kind; and
(g) finally, certain general conclusions will be stated.

Nature and Effect of a Freezing Injunction

43.05 As noted above, a freezing injunction is a court order designed to prevent the dissipation of assets, which might render a court judgment ineffective.[4] Injunctions of this kind were formerly known as 'Mareva Injunctions', named after one of the early cases which developed the jurisdiction.[5]

---

[2] See *Oceanica Castelana Armadora SA of Panama v Mineralimportexport* [1983] 2 All ER 65. However, as noted by Paget (para 26.1), the freezing injunction imposes burdens on banks but they have also benefited from it, especially when seeking to trace moneys of which the bank itself has been defrauded.

[3] As in the case of the last chapter, it will be necessary to outline a number of domestic law issues relating to freezing injunctions. However, since there will be a significant emphasis on cross-border and territorial issues, it seemed best to deal with the entire subject matter in a single chapter forming a part of this section of the book.

[4] See *The Siskina* [1979] AC 210; *Iraqi Ministry of Defence v Arcepey Shipping Co SA, The Angel Bell* [1981] QB 65; *Ninemia Maritime Corp v Trave Schiffahrts GmbH & Co KG, The Niedersachsen* [1984] 1 All ER 398. The jurisdiction to grant orders of this kind was placed on a statutory footing by s 37 of the Supreme Court Act 1981, discussed below. Although reference will be made throughout to court judgments, it may be noted that freezing injunctions may also be made in support of arbitration proceedings: see s 44(2)(e) of the Arbitration Act 1996.

[5] *Mareva Compania Naviera SA v International Bulk Carriers, The Mareva* [1980] 1 All ER 213, although the first such order was granted in *Nippon Yusen Kaisha v Karageorgis* [1975] 3 All ER 282. The term 'freezing injunction' has been used since the introduction of the Civil Court Practice (see below). It is of some interest to note in passing that the US Supreme Court has specifically declined to adopt a procedure similar to the Mareva injunction, even in relation to assets held within the US itself. In *Grupo Mexicano de Desarrollo v Alliance Bond Fund* 527 US 308 (1999), it was decided that a federal district court lacked jurisdiction to grant a preliminary injunction to prevent a debtor from disposing of its assets pending judgment—at least where no equitable or security interest in the asset was asserted. The decision rests partly on the ground that, in the US, equity jurisdiction is derived from the Judiciary Act 1789, and it was not open to a US court to adopt an equitable device which had only been invented by the English courts as late as 1975. It thus remains the case that US courts can only grant protective injunctions of this kind *after* judgment has been obtained. Once such a judgment has been obtained, then the court has power to order the judgment debtor to turn over 'out of State' assets, since the order operates *in personam*, rather than *in rem*: see *Gryphon Domestic VI LLC v APP International Finance Co BV* 836 NYS 2d (NY App Div, 1995).

Although the freezing injunction may cause considerable inconvenience to the debtor— **43.06**
and applicants will inevitably seek to obtain such an injunction with that objective in
mind[6]—it should be appreciated that the order does not have the effect of creating a security
interest over the assets concerned. An early suggestion that a freezing injunction operated *in
rem* or by way of attachment[7] can no longer stand in the light of subsequent authority.[8]

The power to grant freezing injunctions is now derived from section 37 of the Supreme **43.07**
Court Act 1981,[9] which reads as follows:

(1) The High Court may by order (whether interlocutory or final) grant an injunction or
appoint a receiver in all cases in which it appears to the court to be just and convenient
to do so.
(2) Any such order may be made either unconditionally or on such terms and conditions as
the court thinks just.
(3) The power of the High Court under subsection (1) to grant an interlocutory injunction
restraining a party from removing from the jurisdiction of the High Court, or otherwise
dealing with, assets located within that jurisdiction shall be exercisable in cases where
that party is, as well as in cases in which he is not domiciled, resident or present within
that jurisdiction.

These statutory provisions are reinforced by Part 25 *(Interim Remedies and Security for* **43.08**
Costs) of the Civil Procedure Rules (CPR),[10] which contemplate orders prohibiting the
removal of assets from England and Wales and, in appropriate cases, preventing dealings
with other assets, whether located within the jurisdiction or not.

The circumstances under which an applicant can seek and obtain a freezing injunction **43.09**
(whether with or without notice to the respondent) are the subject of detailed rules and
extensive case law.[11] But the present work is not concerned with such matters, for the bank

---

[6] Although freezing injunctions should only be granted where (i) the applicant is likely to recover a money
judgment and (ii) there are reasons to believe that the respondent may seek to defeat the judgment by moving his assets abroad. They should not be used simply as a means of pressurizing the defendant or seeking to
extract a settlement: *Z Ltd v A-Z and AA-LL* [1982] QB 558 (Kerr LJ).
[7] See *Z Ltd v A-Z and AA-LL* [1982] QB 558; *Admiral Shipping Ltd v Portlink Ferries Ltd* [1984] 2 Lloyd's
Rep 166 (CA).
[8] The point was most recently noted by the House of Lords in *Fourie v Le Roux* [2007] UKHL 1. For
other authorities, see *Babanaft International Co SA v Bassatne* [1990] Ch 13 (CA); *Derby & Co Ltd v Weldon
(Nos 3 and 4)* [1990] Ch 65.
[9] To be cited as the Senior Courts Act 1981: see the Constitutional Reform Act 2005, Sch 11, para 1.
[10] CPR, r 25.1(1)(f).
[11] For detailed discussions, see Gee, *Commercial Injunctions* (5th edn, Sweet & Maxwell, 2005); Hoyle, *Freezing
and Search Orders* (4th edn, informa, 2006). By way of examples, it must generally be shown that the claimant has
a 'good arguable case' in the substantive proceedings, and the injunction must be served in anticipation of proceedings in England: *The Siskina* [1979] AC 210, although the Australian courts have extended this approach to cover
a pending foreign suit: see *Davis v Turning Properties Pty Ltd and Turner* (2005) 222 ALR 676 (New South Wales
Supreme Court) and the further Australian cases noted by Paget, para 26.4, note 8. By way of exception to the basic
principle, an English court may grant a freezing injunction (including, in an appropriate case, a worldwide injunction) in support of proceedings pending in another EEA State in accordance with s 25 of the Civil Jurisdiction
and Judgments Act 1982 (as amended). A worldwide order was granted in support of Swiss proceedings in *Credit
Suisse Fides Trust SA v Cuoghi* [1998] QB 818 (CA). The decision has been followed on various occasions: see, for
example, *Indosuez International Finance BV v National Reserve Bank* [2002] All ER (D) 266 (Apr); *Banco Nacional
de Comercio Exterior SNC v Empresa de Telecommunicationes de Cuba SA* [2007] EWCA Civ 662.

will not be party to the underlying proceedings.[12] It may have some general, background knowledge of the underlying dispute as a result of the banker-customer relationship but, equally, it may know nothing at all of the situation until it receives a copy of the freezing injunction. At all events, the bank must comply with the terms of the injunction and, in so doing, it must be guided solely by the terms of the injunction itself.[13] It cannot become involved in the substantive dispute between the parties to the litigation.

43.10 It may be noted that a freezing injunction may be limited to assets in England and Wales, or it may be expressed to have worldwide effect.[14] Whilst special guidelines apply to the grant of such an injunction in the first instance,[15] once again the background to the order and the events leading up to it will be of no interest to the bank; it is concerned only to comply with the terms of the order itself.

43.11 Since the present section of this work is principally concerned with cross-border issues, this chapter proceeds on the basis that a bank is concerned with a *worldwide* freezing order, although some of the points made below would apply equally to an order confined to assets within England and Wales.[16] The present chapter also proceeds on the basis that the injunction will be made substantially in the applicable form[17] set out in the Annex to the Practice Direction which supplements CPR Part 25.

43.12 Against this background, it seems appropriate to consider two aspects of worldwide freezing injunctions, as relevant to the recipient bank:

(a) what action should a bank take when it receives a worldwide freezing injunction; and

(b) how does such an order affect the bank's relationship with the customer (eg in terms of the duty to comply with the mandate, the exercise of rights of set-off and the enforcement of security)?

---

[12] The present chapter is concerned only with cases in which the bank becomes involved as a result of holding an account or other assets for the respondent in the proceedings. Whilst it will be very common for a bank to be served with notice of a Mareva injunction, it will be very unusual for such an order to be made against a bank itself, largely because money is a bank's stock in trade and the making of such an order would render it impossible to run its business: see Paget, para 26.9, discussing *Polly Peck International plc v Nadir (No 2)* [1992] 4 All ER 769 and *Camdex International Ltd v Bank of Zambia (No 2)* [1997] 1 All ER 728. However, for a case in which a freezing injunction was granted in respect of the English assets of a foreign bank, see *Z Bank v D1 and others* [1994] 1 Lloyd's Rep 656.

[13] For this reason, it will become necessary to examine some of the detailed provisions usually found in such a document: see para 43.11 below.

[14] That a worldwide order could be made against a respondent was originally established in *Babanaft International Co SA v Bassatne* [1990] Ch 13.

[15] For the relevant guidelines, see *Third Chandris Shipping Corp v Unimarine* [1979] QB 654.

[16] There is, of course, a *territorial* distinction between such orders but, subject to that, both forms of order are similar in that they prohibit disposals of, and other dealings with, the respondent's assets. As to the circumstances under which the court will allow the enforcement of a worldwide freezing order, see *Dadourian Group International Ltd v Simms* [2006] 3 All ER 48. Once again, however, the guidelines set out in that case and the manner in which they are applied will not be of direct relevance to the bank since it is not a party to the proceedings. It will merely be concerned to comply with the terms of any order served upon it.

[17] Henceforth referred to as 'the standard order'.

Action to be taken by the Bank

How should a bank respond to the receipt of a worldwide freezing injunction?　　**43.13**

Necessity for Compliance

It is important at the outset to emphasize the need for banks to comply with the terms of　**43.14**
the injunction. Any breach of the injunction could place the bank itself in contempt of
court.

This point does, however, require some development, because, on a first reading, the stan-　**43.15**
dard order may tend to mislead the recipient bank as to the scope of its liability in this
sphere. The following points may be noted in this context:

(a) The Penal Notice endorsed on the standard order refers to parties other than the
respondent (ie such as the recipient bank) and states that '... Any other person who
knows of this Order and does anything which helps or permits the respondent to
breach the terms of this Order may also be held in contempt of court and may be
imprisoned, fined or have their assets seized ...'.

(b) This is, perhaps, an obvious point. Once a bank knows of the Order, it must not accede
to customer instructions to pay or transfer funds in breach of the Order,[18] for it may
thereby '... help or permit ...' (or, to use language which is frequently adopted, aid or
abet) the customer to breach the terms of the order.[19]

(c) Yet the Penal Notice does not state the full extent of the bank's potential liability for
contempt. As the House of Lords has recently pointed out,[20] it is an *independent* contempt of court for any person '... to do an act which deliberately interferes with the
course of justice by frustrating the purpose for which the order was made ...'. As a
result, even action taken unilaterally by the bank may involve a breach of the order,
even in the absence of any intention to assist the customer to breach the order. It is true
that a criminal standard of proof applies,[21] yet this formulation nevertheless poses
difficulties for a bank in relation to the enforcement of security arrangements.[22]
The courts have shown themselves willing to punish banks for contempt in relation to

---

[18] Whether or not a particular payment or transfer constitutes a breach of the order will obviously depend
on the terms of the order itself. However, the injunction will usually be issued in terms which are very close to
the standard order, and the present discussion proceeds on that basis.

[19] The order applies to any instructions which the bank has not actioned before it receives notice of the
order, and even if the instructions pre-date the order itself: see *Z Ltd v A-Z and AA-LL* [1982] QB 558 240
(CA).

[20] See *Customs and Excise Commissioners v Barclays Bank plc* [2007] 1 AC 181, para 29 (Lord Hoffman), noting the earlier discussion of contempt in relation to Mareva injunctions in *Z Ltd v A-Z and AA-LL* (above).

[21] See the cases noted in the previous footnote.

[22] This aspect of the matter is discussed at paras 43.29–43.30 below.

their management of freezing injunctions,[23] although a bank will not be in contempt if payment is made by mistake and without intending to defeat the order.[24]

Steps to be taken

43.16 The applicant should specify in as much detail as possible the assets—usually, the bank account—which the respondent is believed to hold with the recipient bank (eg branch, account number, etc).[25] Frequently, of course, the applicant will not know the precise details and the bank will be obliged to make a search in order to enable itself to comply with the order.[26] In this context:

(a) the cost of carrying out the search must usually be met by the applicant;[27]

(b) if any accounts[28] are discovered, they must immediately be frozen, so that no further payments may be effected[29] beyond any limit stated in the order,[30] although payments into the account may continue to be accepted and will become subject to the freeze;[31]

---

[23] One such instance is *Z Bank v D1 and others* [1994] 1 Lloyd's Rep 656, although the case is not really in point since the bank was itself the respondent in the relevant proceedings. A more relevant case is *R ex p Revenue & Customs Prosecution Office v R and Lloyds TSB plc* [2007] EWHC 2393 (Admin), where a bank was held in contempt because it moved blocked funds to a deposit account in order to facilitate compliance with the freezing order. It was found to be in contempt as a result, although it is respectfully suggested that this decision was erroneous. As noted at para 15.10 above, a bank account is simply a debt owed by a bank to its customer, and the bank should not be in contempt merely on the grounds that it has re-designated the account. This action does not assist in the disposal of the asset, nor does it constitute a 'dealing' with the asset in any meaningful sense. It should be said, however, that the court specifically rejected submissions to this effect.

[24] *Customs & Excise Commissioners v Barclays Bank plc* [2006] 4 All ER 256, discussed at para 43.34 below.

[25] *Searose Ltd v Seatrain (UK) Ltd* [1981] 1 All ER 806. Specification of these details will help to contain the costs incurred by the bank for the purposes of the search.

[26] This point was made by Kerr LJ in *Z Ltd v A-Z Ltd and AA-LL* [1982] QB 588. He indicated that a search would have to be made at all bank branches but it seems unlikely that he intended to include branches outside the jurisdiction.

[27] *Searose Ltd v Seatrain (UK) Ltd* [1981] 1 All ER 806; *Clipper Maritime Co of Monrovia v Mineralimportexport* [1981] 1 WLR 1262. Paragraph (7) of Sch B to the standard order states that 'the Applicant will pay the reasonable costs of anyone other than the Respondent which have been incurred as a result of this order including the costs of finding out whether that person holds any of the Respondent's assets …'.

[28] Accounts in the joint name of the respondent and another party should not normally be subjected to the freezing order: see *Z Ltd v A-Z and AA-LL* [1982] QB 558, but the bank will obviously need to examine the precise terms of the order in each case. There may be cases in which the applicant seeks to bring within the scope of the order bank accounts wholly in the name of a third party (eg on the footing that the holder is a trustee for the respondent). This will usually have to be demonstrated to the court's satisfaction: see *SCF Finance Co Ltd v Masri* [1985] 2 All ER 747; *Allied Arab Bank Ltd v Hajjar* [1989] Fam Law 68 (CA). It is submitted that the order would have to make express reference to the identity of the third party account holder concerned, since it cannot be reasonable to expect a bank to make its own enquiries in that respect. By the same token, accounts held by the respondent as bare trustee for third parties will fall outside the scope of the order, since they are not his 'assets' and, in any event, are not available to meet any judgment which the applicant might obtain: see *Federal Bank of the Middle East Ltd v Hadkinson* [2000] 2 All ER 395 (CA).

[29] In order to avoid a possible finding of contempt on the part of the bank itself, the bank must revoke the authority of any of its employees in relation to the operation of the account: see *Z Bank v D1 and Others* [1994] 1 Lloyd's Rep 656. Since the block applies with immediate effect, the bank must dishonour any cheque which has not then been cleared: see para 7(c) of the standard order.

[30] Freezing injunctions usually state that the respondent is required to maintain assets of a stated value within the jurisdiction (a 'maximum sum' order). If the bank holds funds in excess of the stated amount, then it may obviously continue to operate the account, subject to the preservation of that sum. Otherwise, it will have to freeze the entire account because it cannot know or police the value of other assets which the respondent holds within the jurisdiction: see *Z Ltd v A-Z and AA-LL* [1982] QB 588.

[31] The freezing injunction applies both to assets in the hands of the bank at the time the order is served and at any later time: *TDK Tape Distributors (UK) Ltd v Videochoice Ltd* [1985] 3 All ER 345. In *Z Ltd v A-Z*

(c) it appears that a bank should not transfer funds to a fixed or time deposit account even though this may assist the bank in monitoring compliance with the order[32] although in practice the applicant's advisers would no doubt readily agree to such a course;

(d) the standard order requires the bank to freeze the defendant's accounts '… whether or not they are in his own name and whether or not they are solely or jointly owned …'. If it is alleged that an account is held by a third party as nominee for the defendant, then it must be for the claimant to demonstrate that this is the case and to persuade the court that the account should be specifically named in the order;[33]

(e) when served with the order, the bank will often be asked to confirm that it will comply with the terms of the order. It will often wish to reply to the effect that it will do so, but it should be appreciated that the bank continues to owe a duty of confidentiality to the customer,[34] and that duty extends to the very fact that a banking relationship even exists. Consequently, the bank must take care not to confirm the existence of any account;[35]

(f) the bank should seek a variation of the order for any transactions which it wishes to effect and which do not clearly fall within the exemptions set out in the order itself;[36] and

(g) if the freezing injunction is expressed in sterling but the bank discovers that it holds accounts in foreign currencies, then it should convert the credit balances into sterling at the prevailing exchange rate.[37]

For a multinational bank, however, the question arises: how far must the required search **43.17** extend? Notwithstanding some of the difficulties of territoriality which are discussed below,[38] it is suggested that:

(a) there is no obligation on the bank to search for accounts held with *branches* outside the United Kingdom. This would be an excessively onerous obligation and, in any event,

---

and AA-LL [1982] QB 558, it was suggested that assets coming into the hands of the bank after service of the order should fall outside its scope. However, this statement does not sit well with the operation of a current or running account and, in the absence of specific exclusions in the order, it would be unsafe to rely on it.

[32] *R ex p Revenue & Customs Prosecution Office v R and Lloyds TSB plc* [2007] EWHC 2393 (Admin). It is submitted that this decision is mistaken. The bank had received a freezing order over a current account. Its systems made it much easier to monitor the necessary block if the funds were credited to a deposit account, and this would have the added benefit that interest would accrue. The court held that the transfer of the funds and its re-designation as a deposit account amounted to a contempt of the order. Yet, whether a current or a deposit arrangement, the account simply represents a payment obligation of the bank, and neither a change in its designation nor the bank's unilateral decision to credit interest to the blocked sums in any way affected the creditor's position. The bank's action did not assist the defendant in breaching the order nor, apart from some very minor inconvenience, did the bank's action impede or defeat the object of the order.

[33] *SCF Finance Co v Masri* [1985] 2 All ER 747, approved in *Allied Arab Bank Ltd v Hajjar* [1989] Fam Law 68 (CA) and discussed by Paget, para 26.11. The bank can clearly only search for the names which it is given. Equally, the terms of the standard order will require the freezing of a *joint* account, even though this was contrary to the practice formerly recommended by the Court of Appeal in *Z Ltd v A-Z and AA-LL* [1982] QB 558 (CA).

[34] On this subject, see generally Chapter 42 above.

[35] The applicant may seek this information from other sources. For example, para 9 of the standard order requires the respondent to provide details of his assets to the applicant.

[36] On variation, see para 13 of the standard order. It may often be appropriate for the customer itself to make the application. A variation should be sought in cases of doubt because 'parties should not lightly take upon themselves the decision as to how best a Mareva should be policed…': *R ex p Revenue & Customs Prosecution Office v R and Lloyds TSB plc* [2007] EWHC 2393 (Admin). This is, of course, true, but see the comment on this case in n 32 above.

[37] *Z Ltd v A-Z and AA-LL* [1982] QB 588 (CA), applying the decision in *Choice Investments Ltd v Jeromnimon* [1981] 2 WLR 80.

[38] See paras 43.42–43.47 below.

the disclosure of that information—even to the head office of the bank itself—may be an offence for branches in some countries;[39] and

(b) there is no obligation on banks to enquire whether the respondent has relationships with any of its *subsidiaries* since, once again, this would be an excessively onerous requirement. However, if the applicant provides information which suggests such a link with a particular subsidiary, then it may be incumbent on the bank to investigate it.[40]

The Extent of Compliance

43.18 Of course, it is easy to state that the bank must comply with the freezing injunction. But what exactly does this mean? The point is of some practical importance, because the order may contain exclusions which allow payments to be made in particular cases. If the bank refuses to sanction payments falling within the scope of those exceptions, then it may be liable to the customer for breach of its mandate. In cases of genuine doubt, the bank is allowed to defer complying with customer instructions for a reasonable time whilst any difficulties are clarified and any necessary application to court is made.[41] Nevertheless, it is necessary to examine those cases in which the bank may be justified in meeting the customer's instructions, notwithstanding the terms of the freezing injunction.[42]

43.19 Paragraph 11 of the standard order contains various provisions which may be relevant in this respect:

(a) Paragraph 11(1) provides that the order does not prohibit the respondent from spending a stated amount on ordinary living expenses and legal expenses. However, it may on occasion be quite difficult for a bank to release funds from the account on this basis because it does not know whether the customer has other sources of funds and is complying with the terms of the limit set out in the order. Paragraph 18 of the standard order does, however, allow that a bank may release funds up to the specific amounts stated in the order, provided that withdrawal from the account *appears* to be permitted by the order. Payments up to the set limits will therefore generally be permissible.

(b) Paragraph 11(2) states that the order '... does not prohibit the Respondent from dealing with or disposing of any of his assets in the ordinary and proper course of business ...'. In principle, this provision should be included in any order which is made against a commercial organization. This provision, especially when read together with paragraph 18 (reproduced above), should enable the bank to allow 'normal course' payments which the customer has previously made from the account—for example,

---

[39] When acknowledging receipt of the order, the bank may wish to confirm that it has only searched at branches in England and Wales.

[40] In such a case the applicant might be expected to serve the order directly on the subsidiary, if it understands the import of the information which it has provided.

[41] The banker-customer contract includes an implied term to this effect: see the discussion of the decision in *Sierra Leone Telecommunications Ltd v Barclays Bank plc* [1998] 2 All ER 821 at para 15.22 above. Note that a bank or other third party is entitled to apply to court for a variation of a freezing injunction: see para 13 of the standard order.

[42] The cases in which the bank may take unilateral action to preserve its own position as against the customer are discussed at paras 43.27–43.30 below.

payments to suppliers of gas and electricity, landlords of commercial premises, etc,[43] although the expression has also been more broadly defined to include any payments to be made in good faith and in the ordinary course of business.[44] However, if the bank has a continuous trading relationship with the customer (eg in commodities, derivatives, or similar instruments), then it seems that the continuation of that relationship requires a variation of the order, so that the court can ensure that this does not cut across the purpose of the injunction.[45]

It follows that the bank may have to undertake a certain amount of supervision to ensure that its duties to the court (as a result of the freezing order) and to the customer (under the mandate) are properly reconciled. In cases of doubt, clarification with the applicant's solicitors or an application to court for a variation of the order should be made. Of course, either step will involve the disclosure of the fact that an account exists,[46] and so it would sometimes be necessary to seek the customer's consent before taking such a step.[47] **43.20**

The bank should also note that paragraph 9 of the standard order allows for a request for disclosure of further information about the defendant's assets.[48] Such an order may be made against the bank itself and, if so, it must of course comply with it. As in any other case, however, the bank must exercise care and ensure that it does not disclose material which goes beyond the scope of the order. **43.21**

Impact on Banker-Customer Relationship

The preceding paragraphs dealt with the steps which a bank is required to take when presented with a freezing order. **43.22**

But what of the relationship between the bank and its customer? As noted above, the bank must comply with the terms of the order, and failure to do so is punishable as a contempt **43.23**

---

[43] It appears that the expression 'ordinary and proper course of business' is to be given a broad meaning, and is not necessarily restricted to transactions of a purely trading nature: see *Normid Housing Association v Ralphs* [1989] 1 Lloyd's Rep 275. The rationale for this exception is that the injunction is designed to prevent the dissipation of assets but is not intended to impede or interfere with the defendant's ordinary business transactions: see *Customs & Excise Commissioners v Anchor Food Ltd* [1999] 2 All ER 268. Thus, the payment of dividends in the ordinary course of business should not be restrained by the order: see the decision of the Grand Court of the Cayman Islands in *JP Morgan Multi-Strategy LP v Macro Funds Ltd* [2002] CILR 569. However, if the dividend is intended to distribute substantially all of the defendant's assets to the company's shareholders, then this will not be 'ordinary course' and hence will be caught by the injunction: see *Consolidated Constructions Pty Ltd v Bellenville Pty Ltd* [2002] FCA 1513 (Federal Court of Australia).
[44] *Iraqi Ministry of Defence v Arcepy Shipping Co SA* [1981] QB 65.
[45] *Avant Petroleum Inc v Gatoil Overseas Inc* [1986] 2 Lloyd's Rep 235 (CA), where the court allowed for the continued issue of letters of credit for the purchase of oil, but on condition that any surpluses were subjected to the freezing injunction. It may also be inferred from this decision that a right to draw on an overdraft constitutes an 'asset' of the customer which falls within the scope of a freezing injunction. On that basis, a variation of the freezing injunction would be required to allow the continuation of such a facility, unless it appeared that the funds are to be applied in the ordinary course of the customer's business.
[46] Where a bank seeks a variation of the freezing injunction, it must do so on notice to the applicant's solicitors and provide appropriate details: see para 13 of the standard order.
[47] It may be otherwise where the application is made to protect the bank's own interests: see paras 43.29–43.30 below.
[48] CPR, r 25.1(1)(g).

of court. It must follow that (i) obedience to the customer's cheques or payment instructions would be unlawful and (ii) any action against the bank for breach of mandate under these circumstances must necessarily fail, since there cannot be default in failing to do that which the law forbids to be done.[49]

43.24 Furthermore, whilst banks will naturally be most concerned with current or deposit accounts, they may hold other assets such as shares or bonds,[50] or other physical materials held for safe custody. The standard order appears to apply to such assets, notwithstanding a suggestion that this was impracticable and that they should accordingly be excluded from the scope of the order.[51]

43.25 This much is clear and, perhaps, obvious. Yet it only deals with the traditional banking service of providing current accounts and associated payment facilities. The bank may have provided overdrafts or other facilities; it may hold security over some or all of the assets of the customer and, to that extent, could be seen as a party whose interests conflict with those of the applicant for the freezing injunction.

43.26 There are two main situations in which a bank may have to look to its own interests where a freezing injunction has been served namely, (i) where it wishes to exercise a right of set-off and (ii) where it wishes to enforce its security over assets which may fall within the scope of the order.

Set off

43.27 Freezing injunctions which are to be served on banks should contain paragraph 17 of the standard order, which provides that '… this injunction does not prevent any bank from exercising any right of set off it may have in respect of any facility which it gave to the respondent before it was notified of this order …'. The exercise of such a right therefore does not involve an application to court for the variation of the freezing injunction. It is, of course, reasonable that the bank should not acquire additional rights of set-off by extending additional facilities after receiving notice of the order, for it does so in full knowledge of the situation and, hence, at its own risk.

43.28 Nevertheless, there are various points which should be made in this regard:

(a) subject to the various limitations described below, and although paragraph 17 only applies to facilities granted *before* the bank has notice of the order, it is submitted that the right of set-off can be exercised in relation to items presented for the credit of the relevant account even after the bank has received notice of the order. Otherwise, paragraph 17 would have a very limited effect in practice;

(b) the language of paragraph 17 seems to contemplate only the bank's ordinary rights of set-off, for example, between different accounts of the same customer, or the right to apply items paid in against an existing overdraft balance. Furthermore, it contemplates only *bilateral* arrangements between the bank and a single customer. Consequently, the

---

[49] See *Z Ltd v A-Z and AA-LL* [1982] 1 Lloyd's Rep 240 (CA), citing the decision in *Denny Mott & Dickson Ltd v Fraser & Co Ltd* [1944] AC 265 (HL).

[50] Many such securities may now be held in paperless form, but they would remain under the control of the bank through the relevant custody or similar agreement put in place to evidence such arrangements.

[51] *Z Ltd v A-Z Ltd and AA-LL* [1982] QB 558 (CA).

provision may not be available for group cash management or treasury arrangements involving multilateral set-off among the balances of several entities within the same group;

(c) for essentially the same reason, the set-off provision cannot apply where the respondent is a *guarantor* who has deposited cash into an account as security for the obligations of a principal borrower. This will be a trilateral relationship and, in any event, the indebtedness does not flow from '… any facility which [the bank] gave to the respondent …'; it will have been granted to the principal borrower;[52] and

(d) it has been said that, in the absence of the set-off provision, the exercise of a right of set-off by a bank would require a variation of the order.[53] The point should now be academic, given that paragraph 17 is to be seen as an integral part of the standard order. Nevertheless, as a matter of principle, it is suggested that this view of the matter should not go unchallenged.[54] First of all, the freezing injunction is designed to preserve assets which the respondent might have available to meet a judgment and which, in the absence of such an order, he may seek to conceal or dissipate. Referring back to the two 'heads' of contempt of court,[55] a bank which exercises a right of set-off will do so for its own protection, and not for the purpose of 'aiding and abetting' the respondent in a breach of the order. Furthermore, it is hard to see how the bank can be said to be frustrating the purpose of the order, given that the order seeks to preserve 'free' assets available to meet the judgment. Funds received by the bank into the account are subject to the right of set-off and, hence, not available to meet a judgment in any event. As noted earlier, a freezing injunction operates *in personam* against the respondent and it should not therefore have any impact on prior rights of set-off, which are closer to proprietary rights. Even in the absence of paragraph 17, therefore, the exercise of a right of set-off does not have the effect of frustrating the purpose of the court's order.

Enforcement of Security

It will, of course, frequently be the case that the bank which maintains accounts for the respondent will also be its chief provider of finance.[56] It will often hold security over some or all of its assets. Under these circumstances, there is potential for conflict between the interests of the applicant and those of the bank, since the freezing injunction may apply to assets which fall within the scope of the bank's charge. **43.29**

What is the position of a bank which wishes to take steps to enforce its security after it has received notice of the freezing injunction? The following points may be noted: **43.30**

(a) the Court of Appeal has held that a freezing injunction does not operate to the prejudice of a lender which holds a floating charge over the assets of the respondent. This is

---

[52] An application to court for a variation of the order would therefore be required before the bank could exercise rights of this description.

[53] See the discussion in *Oceanica Castelana Armadora SA of Panama v Mineralimportexport* [1983] 2 All ER 65.

[54] An essentially similar point arises in relation to the enforcement of a lending bank's security (see below). The issue is of greater importance there because the standard order does not deal with that type of situation.

[55] See para 43.15 above.

[56] It should be repeated that we are here concerned only with facilities provided and security taken *before* the bank receives notice of the freezing injunction. The bank must assume the risk of any facilities it provides after that date.

an effective equitable charge at the point of time at which it is created. Consequently, it is not affected by the freezing injunction even if crystallization of the floating charge occurs only after the bank has received notice of the order.[57] This must, of course, be correct given that the freezing injunction operates *in personam* whilst the security interest obviously operates *in rem*;

(b) nevertheless, it has been held[58] that a bank which wished to enforce its security over assets of the customer/respondent '… had adopted exactly the right course in coming to court to get the order varied so as to permit it to realise its security interest in the properties …', but that '… it was entitled to exercise its rights in accordance with its own commercial judgment provided always that it did nothing inconsistent with the underlying purpose of the injunction …'. The court refused to impose conditions on the bank's right to realize its security, concluding that '… its duty in relation to disposal is no higher than to act in good faith in the ordinary course of its business …';

(c) it is submitted that it is unsatisfactory to require a bank to apply to court for a variation of the order under these circumstances. Subject to the proviso that the bank is acting in good faith in realizing the security—and that can, of course, generally be assumed— the court application seems to serve no obvious purpose. Even if the bank's action is inconsistent with the order or detrimental to the applicant, this should not be an obstacle to the bank's ability to exercise its pre-existing rights;

(d) it may of course be that the need to make an application will not be especially prob- lematical and the necessary hearing can be organized at short notice. This may be perfectly satisfactory where the security consists of real estate and is not likely to suf- fer very short-term fluctuations in value. But there may be cases in which time may be of the essence—for example, where the security consists of listed shares or for- eign currency deposits held with third party banks,[59] where values may change not merely from day to day but even intra-day.[60] In any event, for the reasons given above, it seems wrong in principle to require a bank to apply to court under these circumstances;

(e) it may be that the matter could be addressed by adding to the standard order a further provision allowing a bank or financial institution to enforce any pre-existing secu- rity interest in the ordinary course of business. If banks are allowed to exercise rights of set-off,[61] then there seems to be no reason why they should be inhibited in the

---

[57] *Cretanor Maritime Co Ltd v Irish Marine Management Ltd* [1978] 1 WLR 966. On crystallization of floating charges, see paras 28.11–28.13 above.

[58] See *Gangway Ltd v Caledonian Park Investments (Jersey) Ltd and another* [2001] 2 Lloyd's Rep 715.

[59] Where a foreign currency deposit is held with the bank itself, then the bank will usually be able to rely on the set-off exception (above), even though there may be a mis-match between the currency of the deposit and the currency of obligation. However, where the security consists of a charge over deposits with another bank, then this does not naturally fall within the type of bilateral set-off contemplated by the standard order. Consequently, enforcement of that type of security would involve a variation of the order.

[60] The point can assume a particular importance in the context of swap transactions, where any collateral is intended to be highly liquid and readily convertible into cash. The need to apply to court to enforce the collateral in such circumstances may have other consequences. If the mark to market value of the transaction is moving against the respondent, then the necessary delay in enforcing the security may result in an increase in his overall financial liability.

[61] See para 17 of the standard order, which has been considered at paras 43.27–43.28 above.

realization of other forms of security. Furthermore, the addition of such a provision would be consistent with the court's often-repeated approach to freezing injunctions, namely that they should not affect the normal conduct of business and third parties should be given as much protection as circumstances allow.[62] Given that the bank in *Gangway* was allowed to enforce its security in the normal way, it is hard to see how the need for an application to court provided any meaningful assistance to the applicant for the order; and

(f) for the present, however, a bank seeking to enforce its security over the customer's assets must seek an appropriate variation of the order for that purpose.[63]

Relationship between the Bank and the Applicant

The earlier part of this chapter has considered the obligations of the bank when it has been served with a freezing injunction. That review has been undertaken in the context of possible liability for contempt of court if steps are taken by the bank to assist the respondent in breaching the injunction, or which might otherwise frustrate it. But it is pertinent to inquire whether the service of the freezing injunction has any wider implications in terms of the creation of obligations as between the bank and the applicant for the order.   **43.31**

Obligations of the Bank

Quite apart from its potential liability for contempt of court,[64] does the bank incur any further obligation to the applicant for the order? In particular, if funds are released to the customer as a result of an error, can the bank be made to compensate the applicant for the loss which it may suffer?   **43.32**

It would, of course, be obvious to the bank that, if it failed to give proper effect to the freezing order, the applicant (creditor) may suffer loss because assets may no longer be available to meet any eventual judgment. But negligence on its own does not create a liability; there must be a duty of care in the first place. Does the bank owe such a duty in this type of situation?   **43.33**

This very subject has recently been considered by the House of Lords in *Customs and Excise Commissioners v Barclays Bank plc*.[65] Barclays received notice of two freezing orders against named defendants in relation to specified accounts but, due to an error, funds were released   **43.34**

---

[62] See, for example, *Galaxia Maritima SA v Mineralimportexport* [1982] 1 WLR 539 (CA).

[63] Paragraph 13 of the standard order allows the bank to make the necessary application without the consent of the customer. It is true that the making of such an application will inevitably mean that information about the customer relationship is disclosed both to the applicant and to the court. However, this should not usually involve a breach of the bank's duty of confidentiality, since disclosure is necessary to protect the bank's interests: see the discussion of this exemption from the duty at paras 42.42–42.46 above.

[64] It may be noted in passing that, since contempt proceedings are punitive, the intention to frustrate the order must be proved beyond reasonable doubt: see *A-G v Punch Ltd* [2003] 1 AC 1046.

[65] [2006] 4 All ER 256 (HL). For discussions of this case, see Gee, 'The Remedies carried by a Freezing Injunction' (2006) 122 LQR 535 and Huang 'The House of Lords concludes that Bank owes no Duty of Care to the Beneficiary of Freezing Orders' (2006) 22 BFLR 449. The refusal to impose a duty of care in this type

from the accounts a few hours later. The Commissioners were subsequently unable to recover the funds owing by the respondent companies, and they accordingly sought recourse against Barclays.

43.35   Since the Commissioners were seeking to recover economic loss, it was necessary to demonstrate that Barclays had in some way assumed responsibility[66] to the Commissioners to ensure that the accounts were not operated. However, the circumstances do not justify any inference that Barclays had voluntarily accepted responsibility. To the contrary, they were recipients of a court order which had been obtained and served by the Commissioners; any duties they had were imposed upon them, not voluntarily assumed. Furthermore, the court order carried its own remedies and it was not appropriate to imply any further or additional obligations on the recipient bank. Under these circumstances, it was not fair, just and reasonable to impose a duty of care. The freezing injunction carried its own sanction in the form of proceedings for contempt, where appropriate. Receipt of the order thus created duties to the court in the context of the administration of justice, but there was no basis for implying a further duty in favour of the creditor. The Commissioners' claim accordingly failed.

Obligations of the Applicant

43.36   Does the applicant for a freezing injunction incur any liability to the recipient bank? Unlike the bank, the applicant is a willing participant in the process and is seeking the assistance of the bank in the implementation of the freezing injunction.

43.37   It is generally accepted that, in serving a copy of the injunction, the applicant agrees to indemnify the bank against any expenses which it may incur in complying with the order. Indeed, paragraph 7 of Schedule B to the standard order provides that:

> The Applicant will pay the reasonable costs of anyone other than the Respondent which have been incurred as a result of this order including the costs of finding out whether that person holds any of the Respondent's assets and if the court later finds that this order has caused such person loss, and decides that such person should be compensated for that loss, the Applicant will comply with any order the court may make.

43.38   It is suggested that this indemnity should extend to the cost of any application to vary the freezing injunction where this is necessary to protect the bank's own position (eg where it wishes to enforce security for facilities provided to the customer), not least because it would usually be open to the applicant to agree that course without the need for an application to court. However, the indemnity would probably not cover any further costs which the bank might incur for its own protection—for example, in obtaining advice as to whether it may exercise a particular set-off right following receipt of the order.

---

of case appears to be consistent with the decision of the Canadian Supreme Court in *Cooper v Hobart* [2001] 3 SCR 537, which has already been considered in a different context at para 14.30 above.

[66]   eg in the way that a bank providing a reference may incur liability: *Hedley Byrne & Co Ltd v Heller & Partners Ltd* [1964] AC 465.

Relationship between the Bank and Third Parties

Freezing injunctions will, of course, usually be directed to the freezing of monies standing **43.39**
to the credit of a bank account.

However, the bank may also have incurred obligations to third parties for the account of **43.40**
the customer, for example, by issuing guarantees or documentary credits. Since these will
constitute obligations of the bank itself, it hardly needs to be stated that their performance
is entirely unaffected by the service of a freezing order against the customer's account. It will
commonly be the case that the bank will have taken cash security in respect of the customer's counter-indemnity obligations and the bank would be able to exercise its set-off
rights over such cash by virtue of the proviso in paragraph 17 of the standard order.[67]

Where the customer is a *beneficiary* of a guarantee or letter of credit, the bank may be **43.41**
involved in collecting the relevant payment on the customer's behalf. Although the right to
draw under such a document is an 'asset' of the customer, the freezing injunction should
not normally prevent a drawing under such a document since the courts regard them as the
'lifeblood of commerce'. However, on payment, the proceeds of the credit may fall within
the scope of the injunction.[68]

Territorial Issues

It has been noted above that a court may make a *worldwide* freezing order.[69] This means **43.42**
that the respondent (or respondent in the action) is restrained from dealing with any of his
assets, wherever they may be held. This does not involve any territorial excess on the part of
the English court,[70] since the freezing injunction operates *in personam* against a party who
is amenable to the jurisdiction of the English court.[71]

But how do such injunctions affect banks and their international dealings? Here are really **43.43**
two aspects of this question namely, (i) what consequences does a worldwide freezing
injunction have for a foreign branch[72] and (ii) how does the order affect assets held by the
bank outside England for the account of the customer?

---

[67] See the discussion at paras 43.27–43.29 above.

[68] *Intraco Ltd v Notis Shipping Corporation (The Bhoja Trader)* [1981] 1 Lloyd's Rep 256 (CA); *Power Curber International Ltd v National Bank of Kuwait SAK* [1981] 3 All ER 607 (CA).

[69] The English courts originally took the view that freezing injunctions could only be made in relation to assets held within the jurisdiction of the court: see *Ashtiani v Kashi* [1987] QB 888 (CA). Matters have now moved on and a detailed historical analysis is beyond the scope of this work. For the development of the jurisdiction, see Collins, 'The Territorial Reach of Mareva Injunctions' (1989) 105 LQR 262.

[70] *Derby & Co Ltd and others v Weldon and others (Nos 3 and 4)* [1990] Ch 65 (CA).

[71] Freezing injunctions have thus been issued with respect to bank accounts outside England: see, for example, *Republic of Haiti v Duvalier* [1990] 1 QB 202; *Babanaft International Co SA v Bassatne* [1990] Ch 13. The respondent is obviously obliged to comply with such orders; the extent to which they affect the account-holding bank is discussed in the remainder of this chapter.

[72] It will be seen that the courts have developed various provisos which are intended to form a part of the standard order and which should usually be included as a matter of course. This reflects the courts con-cern to safeguard the position of third parties who may be affected by the order but who are not parties to the

Foreign Branches

43.44 Banks are frequently multinational entities which may have relationships with a customer through a number of different branches, both within England and abroad. Overseas branches may become aware of a freezing injunction, either because they are advised of it by the London branch which has received it,[73] or because it is sent to them directly by the applicant's advisers. At this point, matters become complex. The London branch may clearly be held in contempt if it releases assets in breach of the order; but what of branches outside the jurisdiction? May they, likewise, be guilty of contempt merely because they have become aware of the order and the London branch provides a jurisdictional nexus with England?

43.45 This point received careful and detailed consideration in *Babanaft International Co SA v Bassatne*.[74] In that case, Nicholls LJ observed that:

> ... if it is to be free of extra-territorial vice, the order must not attempt to regulate the conduct abroad of persons who are not duly-joined parties to the English action in respect of property outside the jurisdiction. The actual residence or domicile of such persons, or their presence within the jurisdiction, is essentially irrelevant. For instance, Banque Nationale de Paris should not be affected by this order in respect of any money it holds for the defendants abroad. This should be so whether or not it has a branch in London. Likewise with Lloyds Bank. It is resident here, but it should not be affected by the order in respect of any money it holds for the defendants abroad ...

43.46 It might have been best if matters had been allowed to rest there; it is unreasonable to expect foreign bank branches to observe orders made in proceedings to which they are not even party. An attempt to hold a foreign bank in contempt would involve an obvious excess of jurisdiction. However, in *Derby & Co Ltd v Weldon and others (Nos 3 and 4)*,[75] the Court of Appeal noted that a person wholly outside the jurisdiction could not be punished for contempt, either because he is not to be regarded as in contempt or because it would involve an excess of jurisdiction to punish him for it. Nevertheless, the court offered various reasons why the form of order adopted in *Babanaft* was inadequate.[76] The court reformulated the provision and, following further refinement, it now appears as paragraph 19 of the standard order, reading as follows:

> (1) Except as provided in paragraph (2) below, the terms of this order do not affect or concern anyone outside the jurisdiction of this court.
> (2) The terms of this order will affect the following persons in a country or state outside the jurisdiction of this court—
>   (a) the Respondent or his officer or agent appointed under a power of attorney;

---

litigation and who will not be before the court when the order is granted: see, for example, *Bank of China v NBM LLC* [2002] 1 WLR 844 (CA), discussing and applying the *Babanaft* proviso.

[73] As mentioned in para 43.17 above, there is no positive *obligation* on a bank to search for accounts with overseas branches. However, it may be that individuals in the London branch happen to know of such relationships with other parts of the bank and the information is passed on through that means.

[74] [1990] Ch 13 (CA).

[75] [1990] Ch 65 (CA).

[76] See the judgment of Lord Donaldson of Lymington MR, at 83–84. It is submitted that the objections raised by the Court of Appeal are not especially convincing.

  (b) any person who—
    I. is subject to the jurisdiction of this court;
    II. has been given written notice of this order at his residence or place of business within the jurisdiction of this court; and
    III. is able to prevent acts or omissions outside the jurisdiction of this court which constitute or assist in a breach of the terms of this order; and
  (c) any other person, only to the extent that this order is declared enforceable or is enforced by a court in that country or state.'

It is, of course, part (b) of this formulation which may be relevant to a bank which has a   **43.47**
branch in England. The provision is not free of difficulty. In particular:

(a) it is implicit in paragraph (b) that a bank is to be treated as a single corporate entity. Thus, if a bank has a branch in London, then the starting point is that the bank *as a whole* is subject to English jurisdiction. This is unfortunate and it is submitted that, for these purposes, the London branch should be treated as a separate entity which is alone subject to the jurisdiction. This approach has not infrequently been adopted in similar contexts;[77]

(b) alternatively, it should be recognized that, whilst a bank may be subject to the jurisdiction, that does confer upon the court power to require the bank to take steps in another jurisdiction. In other words, whilst the court may have *personal* jurisdiction over the bank, it may lack *subject matter* jurisdiction in relation to its overseas activities;[78]

(c) leaving aside these preliminary criticisms, it is of course necessary to determine the position of an international bank which receives an order of this kind via its London branch. This does, of course, presuppose that the conditions in paragraphs (b)(i) and (ii) have been met, with the result that the spotlight must fall on paragraph (b)(iii);

(d) the effect of that sub-paragraph is that the order will apply if the bank *as a whole*[79] is 'able to prevent' acts or omissions outside England which would constitute a breach of the order. Of course, the difficulty is that the bank as a corporate entity will always be able to prevent dealings between the bank and the customer, anywhere in the world; indeed, whilst an English court order plainly could not compel disobedience of the *criminal* law in a foreign jurisdiction, it has been argued that the 'able to prevent' language may compel a bank to breach contractual obligations in another country, where that is necessary in order to give effect to the freezing injunction.[80] This would mean that any international bank served with a freezing injunction in London would have

---

[77] See, for example, *R v Grossman* (1981) Cr App Rep 301 (CA), and remarks to this effect in *Libyan Arab Foreign Bank v Bankers Trust Co* [1989] QB 728. Courts in the US have occasionally held that transactions between a branch of a bank and its head office should be viewed as arms' length transactions between independent entities: see *Pan-American Bank & Trust Co v National City Bank* 6 F 2d 762 (2nd Cir), cert denied 269 US 554.

[78] The point is made by Collins, 'The Territorial Reach of Mareva Injunctions' (1989) 105 LQR 262 in reliance on the decision in *Mackinnon v Donaldson, Lufkin & Jenrette Securities Corp* [1986] Ch 482. This approach to the matter also derives implicit support from the decision of the Court of Appeal in *Bank of China v NBM LLC* [2002] 1 WLR 844.

[79] It may be repeated that para (b) treats the *entire* bank as a single corporate entity.

[80] See *Bank of China v NBM LLC* [2002] 1 All ER 717 (CA). The argument was rejected but, in view of the practical difficulties which had been experienced with the *Derby v Weldon* proviso, the Court of Appeal decided that the proviso established in the *Baltic* case (see below) should be a standard provision.

to give effect to it via all of its international branches.[81] It would also mean that, for example, a foreign branch of the bank would have to seek a variation of the order before it could safely enforce any security provided to it, even though that security is outside England.[82] It hardly needs to be stated that this involves an exorbitant exercise of jurisdiction. Ultimately, an English court would surely have to hold that it lacked subject matter jurisdiction over such issues, so that the bank could not be held in contempt.[83] But this is not a satisfactory position and paragraph 19 of the standard order would benefit from further consideration; and

(e) it may be that some of these difficulties are recognized—and, to some extent, mitigated—by paragraph 10 of Schedule B to the standard order, which provides that the applicant may not seek to enforce the order outside England without the consent of the court.

Assets held Abroad

43.48 Some—although by no means all—of the difficulties considered above are mitigated by paragraph 20 of the standard order, which provides that:

> Nothing in this order shall, in respect of assets located outside England and Wales, prevent any third party from complying with—
> (1) what it reasonably believes to be its obligations, contractual or otherwise, under the laws and obligations of the country or state in which those assets are situated or under the proper law of any contract between itself and the Respondent; and
> (2) any orders of the court of that country or state, provided that reasonable notice of any application for such an order is given to the Applicant's solicitors'.

43.49 Paragraph 20 found its way into the standard order following the decision in *Baltic Shipping Co v Translink Shipping Ltd and Translink Pacific Shipping Ltd.*[84] In that case, the London branch of a French bank had been notified of a worldwide freezing injunction. It was concerned that it might be guilty of a contempt of court if its New Caledonian subsidiary released funds to the respondent, on the basis that the bank was '... able to prevent ...' such payments[85] by virtue of the parent-subsidiary relationship.[86] The court decided that it was not reasonable to place the bank or its subsidiary in a position where—in order to avoid a

---

[81] This appears to have been the view of the court in *Securities and Investment Board v Pantell SA* [1990] Ch 426, at 432 (1989)433 where it is said that (on the one hand) the *Derby v Weldon* proviso meant that the freezing injunction had no effect in the Channel Islands but (on the other hand) the Guernsey branch of the UK bank concerned would have to freeze any accounts of the respondent which were maintained there. However, this approach to the matter did not find favour with the Court of Appeal in *Bank of China v NBM LLC* [2002] 1 All ER 717.

[82] See the discussion of the decision in the *Gangway* case, at para 43.30 above.

[83] Of course, if officials of the London branch were themselves involved in arrangements for the movement of assets by foreign branches in breach of the order binding on the respondent, then they may be personally liable in contempt.

[84] [1995] 1 Lloyd's Rep 673.

[85] See the language of para 19 of the standard order, discussed above.

[86] Whether or not payment by the New Caledonian subsidiary would in fact have constituted a contempt of court was not really considered. This is perhaps inevitable in that such matters tend to come before the court as an application for a variation of the order, and there is little incentive to consider whether the proposed course of action is consistent with the original order or not.

contempt of the English court—it might have to break a contract made by a foreign branch and subject to the local law.[87] This was especially the case given that the bank was not itself a party to the main proceedings, and was consistent with the court's approach to the protection of third parties who may be affected by freezing injunctions. Paragraph 20 was thus inserted into the standard order to deal with this situation.

Paragraph 20 allows that the bank may comply with its obligations under a foreign system **43.50** of law. This would usually allow a foreign branch to run the customer's local account in the usual way, because that account relationship will almost invariably be governed by the law of the place where the relevant bank branch is located.[88] Yet, again, this is unsatisfactory. The provision appears only to apply to contractual obligations subsisting at the time the order is served, and thus seems to imply that the foreign branch should not enter into new arrangements with the customer (eg for the provision of new facilities).

Conclusions

It is difficult to say much by way of general conclusions, except perhaps to note that: **43.51**

(a) freezing injunctions have clearly been a useful weapon in the armoury of creditors who fear that their debtors might prove to be elusive;
(b) the courts have developed standard provisions designed for the protection of banks which receive notice of these injunctions (eg allowing for the exercise of rights of set-off), but it is suggested that further work could be done in relation to the exercise of security and collateral rights. A bank exercising its enforcement and realization rights in the ordinary course should not be taken to be in contempt of court; and
(c) it should be more clearly recognized that, whilst a freezing injunction can bind the respondent on a worldwide basis, it can generally have no application to the ordinary conduct of business by bank branches outside the jurisdiction.

---

[87] It is not reasonable to force a bank or other third party to accept the risk of litigation merely because an indemnity is offered: see, for example, *Galaxia Maritima SA v Mineralimportexport (The Eleftherios)* [1982] 1 WLR 539.
[88] On this subject, see generally Chapter 40 above.

44

EXECUTION PROCEEDINGS AND FOREIGN DEPOSITS

Introduction

It has been shown that, in general terms, the banker-customer relationship is governed by **44.01** the law of the country in which the account-holding branch is located. As a necessary consequence, it will follow that action taken by a foreign court or government cannot have an impact upon either the ownership of, or the contractual terms applicable to, a deposit placed with a bank branch situate in England.[1]

For completeness, it remains to examine the extent to which the English courts have **44.02** attempted to make orders which may have extra-territorial effect, in the sense that they seek to affect the rights and obligations of banks with respect to deposits placed with branches outside the jurisdiction.[2]

It is proposed to consider the subject matter as follows: **44.03**

(a) third party debt orders;
(b) the attitude of the English courts in extra-territorial cases;
(c) the case law;
(d) special cases; and
(e) conclusions.

---

[1] See the discussion in Chapter 40 above. Certain aspects of foreign governmental action and the obligations of an English bank and its customer are also considered in Chapter 47 below.
[2] For another discussion of this subject, see Paget, ch 25.

Third Party Debt Orders

44.04   At the outset, it is necessary briefly to describe the context of the present chapter.

As in other cases,[3] this chapter is concerned with disputes to which the bank itself is not a party. The bank happens to hold funds belonging to a judgment debtor, and the judgment creditor is seeking access to those funds as a means of satisfying some or all of the judgment.[4] There is a certain amount of case law which explains the nature of a third party debt order,[5] and when it should properly be made.[6] It is also necessary carefully to distinguish between interim and final orders.

44.05   An interim third party debt order[7] operates as an injunction[8] against the account-holding bank and requires it to ensure that the minimum amount stated in the order remains credited to the account for the time being.[9] Unless the interim order identifies the relevant account, the bank must undertake a search to identify any accounts held for the debtor, and must give details of the accounts and their balances to the creditor within seven days of service of the order.[10]

44.06   If the order is made final,[11] then the bank must make payment[12] of the requisite amount to the judgment creditor; in doing so, it will obtain a corresponding discharge of its

---

    [3] See, for example, Chapter 43 (Freezing Injunctions) above.

    [4] This should be contrasted with the position discussed in Chapter 43 above. A freezing injunction is granted *in anticipation* of a judgment, whilst a third party debt order is granted *post-judgment* and in aid of its execution.

    [5] It may be noted that the expression 'third party debt order' is derived from CPR, Part 72. The order was formerly known as a 'garnishee order'. It seems that Part 72 was not intended to make any substantive changes to the procedure (although see nn 8 and 9 below). As a result, reference to the older case law still remains pertinent.

    [6] As is the case with many remedies by way of execution, the court has a discretion (and not an obligation) to grant a third party debt order: CPR, r 72.8.3.

    [7] Formerly known as a 'garnishee order nisi'. An interim order will be made without a hearing. It is designed to prevent dissipation of the deposit until a full hearing can take place.

    [8] A garnishee order operated by way of attachment and thus had *proprietary* consequences, whilst an interim third party debt order operates as an injunction and, hence, *in personam*. The replacement of the former equitable charge with a personal remedy has not escaped criticism: see the judgment of Lord Millett in *Societe Eram Shipping Co Ltd v Compagnie Internationale de Navigation* [2003] 3 All ER 465 (HL).

    [9] See *Choice Investments Ltd v Jeromnimon* [1981] QB 149 and CPR, r 72.4. A bank which pays the customer under such circumstances runs the risk of having to pay the judgment creditor as well: *Crantrave Ltd v Lloyds Bank plc* [2000] QB 917, where the bank mistakenly released funds to the judgment creditor against receipt of an *interim* third party debt order, when it should merely have blocked the account and awaited the *final* order. However, given that a third party debt order now operates as an injunction and does not create an equitable charge, it may be that this decision should be reconsidered in the light of the House of Lords decision in *Customs & Excise Commissioners v Barclays Bank plc* [2006] 4 All ER 256. That decision is considered at para 43.34 above.

    [10] CPR, r 72.6. This may be contrasted with the bank's position in relation to a freezing injunction (see para 43.16 above), where the bank must search for accounts but, in the absence of any further order, its duty of confidentiality continues to apply in relation to the state of the account.

    [11] The order may not be made final if, for example, the judgment creditor would thereby obtain an unfair advantage over other creditors: *Rainbow v Moorgate Properties Ltd* [1975] 2 All ER 821; *Pritchard v Westminster Bank* [1969] 1 All ER 999. The bank will not, however, be concerned with such matters since it will not usually be a party to the proceedings. It will merely be concerned to comply with the terms of the order served upon it.

    [12] Note that a final third party debt order creates a payment obligation which is enforceable against the bank itself. This was not always the case: see the discussion in Paget, para 25.5.

obligations to its own customer, the judgment debtor.[13] The order can only apply to amounts owing to the judgment debtor. Consequently, if the bank has pre-existing set-off or security rights over the account, these will take priority over the claimant and the order which he has obtained.[14]

Although the bank will normally be concerned only with the strict compliance with the terms of the order, it will nevertheless wish to look to its own interests in certain respects. In principle, the bank is only required to give to the judgment creditor that which it is obliged to give to the customer.[15] For example, the bank is only obliged to pay that which is actually *due*. Consequently, a third party debt order does not accelerate the due date for a time deposit.[16] Likewise, it appears that there will be no debt due to the customer if the account is subject to a prior security interest.[17]   **44.07**

All of these rules operate satisfactorily in a purely domestic context, where all of the relevant relationships are governed by English law and it is thus plain that the bank will obtain a good discharge when it makes payment to a judgment creditor pursuant to a final third party debt order. But complexities will inevitably arise when the circumstances of the case introduce a multi-jurisdictional aspect.   **44.08**

Attitude of the English Courts in Extra-Territorial Cases

The jurisdictional difficulties which may arise in this sphere are to some extent acknowledged by the introduction to Part 72 of the CPR, which states that 'This Part contains rules which provide for a judgment creditor to obtain an order for the payment to him of money which a third party *who is within the jurisdiction* owes to the judgment creditor'.[18] As has been seen, the court has a discretion to make a third party debt order and, in a domestic case, the bank will usually not be concerned with the exercise of that discretion. However, it may need to challenge an order which may result in a conflict between (i) its obligations under the English court order and (ii) any duties owed to customers and others under foreign systems of law.   **44.09**

In England, various attempts have been made over the years to enforce judgment or other debts against deposits held abroad. In general terms, actions of this kind have failed, in large measure because: **44.10**

(a) the obligation to repay the deposit will be governed by the law of the place where the relevant bank branch is situate;

---

[13] CPR, r 72.9. In deciding whether the debt is capable of attachment, conditions requiring a period of notice of withdrawal or a personal request by the account holder are to be disregarded: s 40 of the Supreme Court Act 1983.

[14] This appears to be the effect of *Hutt v Shaw* (1887) 3 TLR 354, noted by Paget, para 25.11. Note, however, that (i) the right of set-off will not apply to customer liabilities incurred *after* the date on which the bank is served with the order (*Tapp v Jones* (1875) LR 10 QB 591) and (ii) any right of set-off which the bank proposes to assert must be notified to the court within seven days after the receipt of the order: CPR, r 72.6.2. See also Paget, para 25.19.

[15] See *Re General Horticultural Co ex p Whitehouse* (1886) 32 Ch D 512.

[16] See, for example, *Webb v Stanton* (1883) 11 QBD 518; *Re Greenwood* [1901] 1 Ch 887.

[17] *Holt v Heatherfield Trust Ltd* [1942] 2 KB 1; *Rekstin v Severo Sibirsko Gosudarstvennoe Akcionare Obschestro* [1933] 1 KB 47; *ED&F Man (Coffee) Ltd v Miyazaki SA* [1991] 1 Lloyd's Rep 154.

[18] CPR, r 72.1 (emphasis added).

(b) questions touching the ownership of the deposit are likewise governed by the same system of law;

(c) English law can therefore neither (i) dictate that the obligation shall be treated as discharged by payment to a person other than the account holder or (ii) demand that the deposit be treated as the property of the judgment creditor in the proceedings; and

(d) it would therefore be wrong for an English court to make such an order, because the account-holding bank would not, by complying with it, obtain a good discharge as against its own customer.[19]

Against this background, a brief survey of the relevant case law is appropriate.

The Case Law

44.11 An excellent illustration of these principles is afforded by the decision of the Court of Appeal in *Martin v Nadel (Dresdner Bank, Garnishee)*.[20] In that case, Martin had obtained a monetary judgment against Nadel. Martin knew that Nadel held funds with the Berlin branch of Dresdner Bank; Martin therefore instituted garnishee proceedings against the London branch of Dresdner Bank with a view to securing payment from that source.

44.12 Martin failed to obtain the requested order on two, related grounds:

(a) third party debt orders are made to enforce judgment debts and thus form a part of English procedural law. Of course, the German courts would apply their own procedural law in any case before them, and would disregard matters of English procedure;[21] and

(b) a garnishee order is a form of execution which deprives the debtor of ownership of his own property by requiring the bank to pay the judgment creditor, rather than the judgment debtor.[22] Where the debt is governed by English law or is situate in England, this amounts to a good discharge of the bank to the extent of the payment.[23] In the present case, however, the bank would not enjoy that protection because the deposit was located in Germany. The German courts would therefore disregard any English court order which purported to vest ownership of those sums in the judgment creditor.

---

[19] These general principles of private international law have already been considered in Chapter 40 above. In the light of these principles, the creditor may have to commence proceedings for the recognition or registration of his judgment in the foreign country in which the account is held.

[20] [1906] 2 KB 26 (CA). For other examples, see *SCF Finance Co Ltd v Masri (No 3)* [1987] QB 1028; *Interpool Ltd v Galani* [1988] QB 738; *Deutsche Schachtbau- und Tiefbohr GmbH R'As al-Khaimah National Oil Co* [1990] 1 AC 295.

[21] This remains the position under the terms of Rome I: see Art 1(3).

[22] This is a rather brief explanation which is perhaps sufficient for present purposes, but a full explanation of the history, nature, and effect of such orders is given in the judgment of Lord Bingham in the *Societe Eram* case (below). It is, however, clear that a third party debt order is intended to constitute a form of enforcement against the debt itself in the place in which it is situate (ie *in rem*), rather than against the third party debtor personally in the country in which he may happen to be found (*in personam*), with the result that one is concerned with the situs of the third party debt, rather than the law applicable to it: see the *Kuwait Oil Tanker* decision (below).

[23] This point has already been noted, above.

As a result, and regardless of any order which the English court might make, Nadel would **44.13**
be able to recover his deposit from the Berlin branch by proceedings in Germany.
An English court order could not protect Dresdner from this 'double liability', and it was
thus inappropriate for the court to make an order of this kind.[24]

Likewise, in *Richardson v Richardson (National Bank of India Ltd, Garnishee)*,[25] a divorcee **44.14**
sought to recover costs from her former husband by applying for garnishee orders against
the London branch of his bank, even though his accounts were held at branches of that
bank in Kenya and Tanganyika. The court found that it had no jurisdiction to make such
an order because the debts represented by the deposits were not recoverable by action in
England.[26]

In spite of doubts which had been expressed in the intervening decades, these two decisions **44.15**
were held to be correct in *Societe Eram Shipping Co Ltd v Compagnie Internationale de
Navigation*.[27] In that case, a Romanian shipping company had obtained a judgment for
demurrage in France. It subsequently registered the judgment in England for enforcement
purposes, and attempted to obtain a third party debt order form the court against a member of the HSBC Group. Whilst that company had a branch in London, the accounts of
the judgment debtors were held at the bank's head office in Hong Kong. The House of
Lords applied the decision in *Martin v Nadel* and held that the court had no jurisdiction to
make a third party debt order in respect of debts situate abroad where the order of the
English court would not constitute a discharge of the obligations of the third party debtor
vis-à-vis the judgment debtor himself. It may be emphasized that, whilst the court has
discretion to make a third party debt order in respect of a debt situate in England,[28] it has
no jurisdiction at all to make such an order in respect of debts located elsewhere.[29] As a
matter of principle, it is submitted that this should be correct; the third party debtor was
not a party to the original litigation and has only been drawn into it because he happens to
owe money to the judgment debtor. An English court should have no jurisdiction to expose
such a person to the possibility of double jeopardy (or double payment).

---

[24] The decision was in part motivated by consistency and reciprocity, for the Court of Appeal noted that:
'If we consider the converse case it is clear, to my mind, that we should take that view of a similar transaction
occurring abroad....' (per Vaughan Williams LJ at 29).

[25] [1927] P 228.

[26] A third party debt order can only apply to a *debt* and, clearly, this point will not usually be disputed in
relation to a bank account. It has often been said that the debt must be recoverable by English proceedings,
but it seems that this should not be regarded as an 'infallible test', see CPR, r 72.2.1.

[27] [2003] 3 All ER 465 (HL). On the point just made in the text, see paras 104 (1989)106 of the
judgment.

[28] As noted above, nearly all remedies by way of execution are at the discretion of the court.

[29] Earlier cases suggested that the discretion did exist in relation to foreign debts, but that it would hardly
ever be exercised; it would be inequitable to do so because of the obvious prejudice to the third party debtor.
It was, nevertheless, held to be incumbent on the bank to demonstrate that it was likely to be obliged to pay
under the relevant foreign law and was thus exposed to 'double jeopardy': *Swiss Bank Corporation v Boehmische
Industrial Bank* [1923] 1 KB 673. In the light of the decision in *Societe Eram*, it is doubtful whether the bank
should now be put to proof on such matters.

44.16 An essentially identical point is made by the contemporaneous decision of the House of Lords in *Kuwait Oil Tanker Co SAK v Qabazard.*[30] Since that case involved debts situate in Switzerland, it was merely necessary for the House of Lords to add that the Lugano Convention on Jurisdiction and the Enforcement of Judgments in Civil and Commercial Matters did not confer upon the English court the right to make third party debt orders against debtors resident in Switzerland. Once that point had been disposed of, the case was governed by principles identical to those discussed in the *Societe Eram* decision.[31]

44.17 A broadly similar issue has recently arisen before the New York Court of Appeals in *Koehler v The Bank of Bermuda.*[32] In that case, the Bank of Bermuda had submitted to the personal jurisdiction of the New York courts. It was not itself a judgment debtor, but held assets belonging to a debtor under a New York judgment. Relying on an earlier New York decision,[33] the Court of Appeals held that it had power to require a garnishee to turn over assets held abroad (ie because that power depends on personal jurisdiction over the garnishee, rather than jurisdiction over the asset which forms the subject matter of the order). It appears that the court has no discretion in the matter, since the relevant statutory provisions (as reproduced in *Koehler*) state that '… where it is shown that the judgment debtor is entitled to the possession of such property, the court *shall* require such person to pay the money, or so much of it as is sufficient to satisfy the judgment, to the judgment creditor …'. Where the asset is situate outside the United States, the account holding bank may thus be placed in a situation in which it has to pay twice (ie the very situation which the House of Lords sought to avoid in *Societe Eram*).

Special Cases

44.18 It has been emphasized on a number of occasions that the bank's primary concern is to secure compliance with the order served on it. Nevertheless, it should be alert to a few special considerations:

(a) Accounts held for foreign governments or their departments, or for foreign central banks, may be immune from execution proceedings.[34] The bank will usually have no means of knowing whether this is the case, since it is not party to the underlying dispute and, in any event, the extent of immunity can be varied by contracts which the bank may not have seen.[35] The bank may therefore wish to proceed with caution when it receives a third party debt order in relation to such an account, although in principle

---

[30] [2003] 3 All ER 501 (HL).

[31] In addition, however, the House of Lords held that the Swiss courts had exclusive jurisdiction under Art 16(5) of the Lugano Convention.

[32] 4 June 2009.

[33] *Morgenthau v Avion Resources Ltd* 49 AD 3d 50, modified on other grounds, 11 NY 3d 382 (2008).

[34] On the whole subject, see Fox, *The Law of State Immunity* (Oxford University Press, 2004) ch 9. For a case dealing with the immunity of foreign embassy accounts, see *Alcom Ltd v Republic of Colombia* [1984] AC 580 (HL). In the absence of written agreement to the contrary, accounts held by central banks will be immune from execution proceedings irrespective of the intended use of the funds: *AIC Ltd v Federal Republic of Nigeria* [2003] EWHC 1357; *AIG Capital Partners Inc v Republic of Kazakhstan* [2006] 1 All ER (Comm) 1.

[35] See ss 13 and 14 of the State Immunity Act 1976.

it should still receive a good discharge if it makes payment out of an English account in compliance with a final order.[36]

(b) The bank must also proceed with care if it believes that the monies held within the account are subject to a trust and thus beneficially owned by third parties, for the bank should not facilitate the mis-application of trust funds.[37] However, it seems that the trust arrangement must be one which would be recognized and enforced in England. In one case, it was argued that development aid paid by the European Community to Sierra Leone should not be subject to third party debt proceedings because the funds had been paid on trust for particular purposes. However, the payment had been made under a treaty which did not create rights capable of enforcement before the English courts. The trust therefore had to be disregarded and the third party debt order was made in the ordinary way.[38]

Conclusions

This chapter has again demonstrated the importance of the *situs* of bank accounts and **44.19** deposit obligations, and has highlighted some of the attempts which have been made to attach foreign deposits by serving a third party debt order on the London branch of the account-holding branch.

From the perspective of the banking industry, the House of Lords' decision in *Societe Eram* **44.20** (above) reaches the entirely satisfactory conclusion that such applications should no longer be entertained. Judgment creditors must thus have recourse to enforcement proceedings in the country in which the relevant account-holding branch is situate.

---

[36] It is for the defendant, rather than the bank, to raise questions of sovereign immunity.
[37] An application to court on the part of the bank would usually be necessary in such a case.
[38] *Philipp Bros v Republic of Sierra Leone* [1995] 1 Lloyd's Rep 289 (CA).

45

LIABILITY FOR BRANCH DEPOSITS AND THE IMPACT OF FOREIGN LAW

Introduction

Multinational banking gives rise to a number of difficult legal issues.[1] Whilst banks may be **45.01** truly international in nature, the countries in which they do business operate by reference to their differing legal frameworks. The harmonization of requirements in the field of bank supervision and regulation no doubt mitigates some of these problems[2] but, as will be seen, a political or economic crisis in one country may have awkward consequences for banks.[3]

---

[1] It should be appreciated that the discussion in the present chapter is directed towards the bank which carries on business in a number of countries through a branch network. Where, instead, the parent bank has established subsidiaries in the different countries, then in principle the parent is not liable for the debts of the subsidiaries, since they are separate corporate entities. In practice, supervisors in some jurisdictions may require the parent to guarantee the liabilities of the subsidiaries, but in such a case the liability of the parent will flow from the contractual terms of the guarantee, rather than from the rules discussed in this chapter. It should equally be appreciated that this chapter is directed to difficulties associated with a particular *branch* of a bank and does not seek to consider the issues which may arise where the bank *as a whole* has become insolvent. For another discussion of this subject, see Blair, 'Liability for Foreign Branch Deposits in English Law' in Cranston (ed), *Making English Commercial Law: Essays in Honour of Roy Goode* (Clarendon, 1997).

[2] Some of these developments have been discussed in Chapter 2 above. However, the fact remains that regulatory frameworks are essentially domestic in nature, and the supervision of multi-national institutions is inevitably complicated by that inescapable fact.

[3] Unsurprisingly, most of the cases about to be discussed arise from cataclysmic events, such as the Russian and Cuban Revolutions, and other episodes. It might be hoped that issues of the kind considered in this chapter will not recur, since governments are now more likely—whether through the International Monetary Fund or otherwise—to seek a negotiated international solution to their problems, rather than to resort to a simple and unilateral seizure or blocking of foreign-owned assets. Nevertheless, wars and crises often appear from unexpected directions, and Venezuela's recent expropriation of oil assets demonstrates that situations of this kind may still recur.

In some respects, the issues about to be discussed are related to the credit risks inherent in lending to the bank itself;[4] but, quite apart from the usual risks associated with lending to any entity, the depositor or creditor takes the additional risk that the government in the country in which the bank branch is located may take steps to prevent the local branch from meeting its obligations.[5] There is, therefore, an element of sovereign or transfer risk involved in dealing with branches of this kind. The consequences for the bank as a wider corporate entity are also potentially serious. The head office would doubtless come under pressure to meet deposits which have been blocked in this way. But is it under any positive, legal obligation to do so?

45.02 It is thus proposed to consider the difficulties which may arise when the head office of a bank is called upon to meet obligations incurred by a branch situate in another jurisdiction.[6] Of course, this type of issue does not generally arise, because banks must meet their obligations in the normal course in order to preserve their reputations and market credibility. It is therefore unsurprising that many of the cases to be discussed in this context arose out of crises of international proportions, including the First and Second World Wars, the Cuban expropriation, the Vietnam War and an economic crisis which afflicted the Philippines in the early 1980s.

45.03 In an effort to bring some order to this difficult subject, the discussion is organized as follows:

(a) a few general principles will be outlined;
(b) the impact of a foreign branch will be considered;
(c) the consequences of an outbreak of war will be noted;
(d) the effect of a foreign expropriation law will be considered;
(e) the effect of other forms of seizure will be discussed;
(f) exchange control laws will be considered;
(g) the effect of a foreign moratorium will be discussed;
(h) blocking orders will be considered; and
(i) a few conclusions will be stated.

As will be apparent, the material is therefore organized around the underlying reasons for non-payment in particular cases.

---

[4] As has been seen, the placing of a deposit with a bank is equivalent to the making of a loan: see the discussion of *Foley v Hill* (1848) 2 HL Cas 28 (HL), at para 15.10 above.

[5] This may happen for a variety of reasons. The government concerned may be facing an economic crisis and thus wishes to conserve resources within the country; or it may be involved in a political dispute which leads to the imposition of sanctions of the kind discussed in Chapter 46 below.

[6] It has been said that, where a foreign branch wrongfully refuses to repay a deposit, the ensuing action against the head office should be regarded as an action for breach of contract, rather than a simple claim in debt: see *United States v First National City Bank* 379 US 378, 405, noted in *Citibank, NA v Wells Fargo Asia Ltd* 505 US 1204 (1990). It is submitted that there is no justification for changing the nature or character of the claim merely because it has to be asserted against a different part of the same corporate entity. If the claim has to sound in damages, then the depositor has to take steps to mitigate his loss, and it is far from obvious why this should be so.

The General Principles

As noted previously,[7] the separate branches of a bank are for certain limited purposes **45.04**
regarded as separate entities.[8] However, at least so far as English law is concerned, a deposit
or other obligation undertaken by one branch of a bank can be enforced against every
branch, for the corporation as a whole is liable for all of the debts incurred on its behalf.[9]

This rule reflects the fact that a company is to be regarded as a single corporate entity,[10] and **45.05**
the fact that, otherwise, a company could avoid liabilities by closing the branch which
incurred them.[11]

Nevertheless, English law imposes certain preconditions before a branch of a bank can **45.06**
be made liable to meet an obligation incurred by another branch. In particular, it is an
implied term of the banker-customer contract that the bank will operate the account from
the branch at which it is held; as a result, demand for payment must, at least initially, be
made at that branch; in other words, the obligation to repay is, at least in the first instance,

---

[7] See, for example, the discussion of *R v Grossman* (1981) 73 Cr App Rep 302 (CA) in the context of
banking confidentiality (para 42.26 above). In the US, the courts recognize that, while bank branches may
effectively operate independently of each other, each branch of a single bank must be viewed as part of the
parent bank, and not as a separate entity. In *Sokoloff v National City Bank of New York* 224 NYS 102 (1927)
aff'd 164 NE 745 (1928), the New York Supreme Court observed that 'when considered with relation to the
parent bank, they are not independent agencies; they are what their name imports, namely branches, and
are subject to the supervision and control of the parent bank, and are instrumentalities whereby the parent
bank carries on its business, and are established for its own particular purposes, and their business conduct
and policies are controlled by the parent bank, and their property and assets belong to the parent bank,
although nominally held in the names of the particular branches. Ultimate liability for a debt of a branch
would rest upon the parent bank…'. As the US Court of Appeals has observed, the formulation in *Sokoloff*
has become a part of the federal common law and has been applied on numerous occasions: see *United States
v BCCI (Luxembourg) SA* 48 F 3d 551 (1995). The decision in *Sokoloff* effectively established that the Soviet
nationalization of the banks following the Revolution did not prevent customers from seeking repayment of
their deposits out of assets held by those banks in New York, even though those deposits had been made in
roubles at a branch within Russia. Although not directly relevant in the present context actions by depositors
in this situation ceased to be maintainable after the US recognized the Soviet Union in 1933 and, as part of
that arrangement, any outstanding assets of the former Russian Government within the US were transferred
to the US Government under the so-called Litvinov Assignment. Thereafter, claims against such assets had to
be pursued via a Foreign Claims Settlement Commission. It was for this reason that a much later claim similar
to that in *Sokoloff* failed in *First National City Bank of New York v Gillilland* 257 F 2d 233 (1958, District of
Columbia Court of Appeals).
[8] Especially in the modern era, the treatment of international branches as separate entities is in many
respects justifiable. The formulation in *Sokoloff* (above) is of course true, but banks are now heavily regulated
in each of the jurisdictions in which they are present, and the wishes of Head Office are thus not wholly determinative of the conduct of such branches.
[9] This is so even though the *primary* recourse for the deposit is confined to the branch concerned: *R v
Lovitt* [1912] AC 212 (PC). But this merely means that, in the first instance, a demand for payment must
be made at the account-holding branch. The claim may thereafter be enforced against the bank as a whole,
if necessary.
[10] This rule is universally accepted. In this country, it finds voice in s 16 of the Companies Act 2006.
See also *Harrods Ltd v Lemon* [1931] 2 KB 157 (CA), where the court emphasized the single corporate person-
ality of a company even though it carried on distinct businesses through separate departments. A company's
internal organization cannot affect the nature or extent of its external obligations to third parties.
[11] See the decision in *New York Life Insurance Co v Public Trustee* [1924] 2 Ch 101 (CA).

attributed to the account-holding branch.[12] However, once a demand has been made at that branch and payment has not been made, then proceedings may be taken against other branches of the bank or, perhaps more accurately, against the bank as a whole.[13] In other words, once the demand is made and not met, this serves to crystallize a claim against the bank which can be enforced wherever it can be found.[14]

45.07 It is true that, in the UK, banks will frequently allow customers to make use of other branches without demur; modern technology means that every branch in the UK will usually be able to access account details of all customers, and can thus check that adequate funds or facilities are available for the purpose of the requested drawing or other transaction. In an international context, however, it remains appropriate to apply the rule which requires demand to be made at the account-holding branch in the first instance.[15] It would be unreasonable, without more, to require an overseas branch to meet a demand made in respect of an account held in the United Kingdom. Time differences may make it difficult to discuss the requested transaction with the account-holding branch, and it may be necessary to complete an exchange transaction in order to accommodate the request.[16] Whilst an overseas branch *may* meet such a request to accommodate its customer, it is certainly under no *obligation* to do so.[17]

45.08 The position may, however, change if the account-holding branch is unable or refuses to meet its obligations for some reason. The precise legal position may depend upon the reason for non-payment at that branch.[18]

45.09 Before moving on to the more general discussion, it is appropriate to note that courts in the United States have tended to hold that the US head office of a bank is strictly liable for

---

[12] Compare the rule (noted at paras 40.26–40.33 above) that the *situs* of a bank deposit is the place in which the relevant account is maintained. See the decisions in *Clare & Co v Dresdner Bank* [1915] 2 KB 576 and *Joachimson v Swiss Bank Corporation* [1921] 3 KB 110 (CA), and the general discussion of this subject at para 15.20 above. The requirement for demand at the account-holding branch is perhaps subject to the proviso that no such demand is required if it has become impossible as a result of a change in circumstances, such as the outbreak of war. Nevertheless, in *Clare & Co v Dresdner Bank* [1915] 2 KB 576, it was held that a demand on the account-holding branch in Berlin was a necessary pre-condition to liability on the part of the London branch of a German bank; the decision in *Joachimson v Swiss Bank Corporation* [1921] 3 KB 110 (CA) is to similar effect. By way of comparison, see s 46(2) of the Bills of Exchange Act 1882 and the decision in *Cornelius v Banque Franco-Serbe* [1942] 1 KB 29.
[13] For an example, see *Leader v Direktion der Disconto Gesellschaft* (1914) 31 TLR 83. For later proceedings, see [1915] 3 KB 154. Days before the outbreak of the First World War, the claimants demanded payment of moneys owing by the Berlin branch of the defendant bank. When payment was not made, the account holder was entitled to judgment against the London branch. In contrast, where no demand had actually been lodged against the Berlin branch, the account holder could not require payment from the London branch because there was no breach of a contractual obligation on which such claim could be founded: see *Clare & Co v Dresdner Bank* [1915] 2 KB 576. The US decisions to similar effect (beginning with *Sokoloff*) have already been noted above.
[14] *Clare & Co v Dresdner Bank*, above.
[15] This is so notwithstanding remarks to the contrary in *Gavilanes v Matavosian* 475 NYS 2d 987 (1984).
[16] These reasons were noted in *R v Lovitt* [1912] AC 212 (PC). The broad thrust of this reasoning still remains relevant.
[17] For confirmation of this point, see *Clare & Co v Dresdner Bank* [1915] 2 KB 576.
[18] For a text which contains several chapters relevant to the present subject matter, see Cranston (ed), *Legal Issues of Cross Border Banking* (Chartered Institute of Bankers, 1989).

the obligations of its worldwide branches.[19] The English courts have adopted the same general principle but have then looked more closely at the reason for non-payment at the account-holding branch and, if payment is prohibited under the law applicable to the relationship, then payment will not be enforced in England. But however that may be, references to the US case law must now be read in the light of amendments to the New York Banking Law and corresponding amendments to the Federal Reserve Act. These legislative changes were a direct response to decisions[20] which held a New York head office to be liable for deposits expropriated by foreign governments. These amendments are to the effect that—in the absence of an express written agreement to the contrary—the US head office of a bank will not be required to repay a deposit made at a foreign branch if that branch is unable to repay due to an act of war, insurrection or civil strife, or as a result of action taken by the government of the country in which the branch is located. This legislation therefore in some respects places US banks on a similar footing to their English counterparts in this area, although the result is achieved via a rather different route.[21]

Closure of a Branch

If the account-holding branch is voluntarily closed by the bank, then another branch of the **45.10** bank in the United Kingdom may be called upon to meet the demand. In such a case, the requirement for a demand at the account-holding branch must clearly cease to apply, for the bank's action has put it beyond the customer's power to comply with this formality. In a cross-border context, the point is illustrated by two decisions involving a bank's voluntary decision to close a foreign branch (although, in each case, it must be said that pressures of a fairly extreme political nature must have motivated these decisions). In the first case,[22] a company had placed deposits in piasters with the Saigon branch of an American bank. In April 1975, the branch was closed because of the rapidly deteriorating situation in Vietnam. The New York court held that the deposits could be recovered in New York, because they were liabilities of the bank as a whole;[23] judgment could be given even though no demand had actually been made against the Saigon branch.[24] In the second case, the

---

[19] See the discussion of *Sokoloff* (above) and the decisions in *Wells Fargo, Trinh* and *Garcia* (below).

[20] See the decisions mentioned in the preceding footnote.

[21] The legislation is discussed at para 45.30 below.

[22] *Vishipco Line v Chase Manhattan Bank* 660 F 2d 854 (1981). For an earlier decision to similar effect, see *Sokoloff v National City Bank of New York* (1928) 164 NE 745. See also Heiniger, 'Liability of US Banks for Deposits placed in their Foreign Branches' (1979) 11 Law & Pol Int'l Bus 903. It should be noted that cases of this kind arising in the US may now be decided differently: see the legislation described in para 45.30 below.

[23] The court held that, upon closure of the Saigon branch, the deposit could be recovered from the head office because it 'sprang back' to it. But there was no need to invent such a doctrine because the deposit obligation was a liability of Citibank *as a whole*.

[24] The decision in this case was applied by the US Court of Appeals (Sixth Cir), in *Trinh v Citibank, NA* 850 F2d 1164 (1988). In that case, Citibank sought to argue that the deposit liabilities had been assumed by the incoming revolutionary government. However, whilst the government had confiscated the *assets* of the bank, there was insufficient evidence to suggest that they had also assumed its *liabilities*. It may be safe to assume that a government taking power in the circumstances of South Vietnam in 1975 did not intend to make itself responsible for liabilities of this kind. It may be noted that the account forms in *Trinh* allocated political risk to the customer, but the court disregarded this provision on the basis that the customer had a 'legitimate expectation' that a bank with Citibank's worldwide reputation would honour its obligations.

Indian Supreme Court held that an Indian bank remained liable for the obligations of branches located in Pakistan, even though those branches had been closed shortly following the partition of the two countries, partly because there was no evidence that local deposits had been expropriated by the Government of Pakistan.[25]

45.11 Problems of a slightly different order may arise where the bank concerned is established abroad and is withdrawing from the United Kingdom altogether. In such a case, the customer may direct his demand to the head office of the bank, wherever it may be. However, what is to be the position if interest has accrued on the account in the meantime, but the law of the bank's home jurisdiction requires it to withhold on account of local taxation, because the interest now has its source in that country?

45.12 In such a case, it is submitted that the bank would have to pay interest gross to the customer, and itself bear any taxes imposed on the interest in its home jurisdiction. The reason is that the action of the bank in closing its London branch does not alter the fact that the banker-customer contract is governed by English law.[26] Consequently, payment of interest under deduction of the local tax would not amount to full performance of the obligation.[27]

45.13 In practice, problems of this kind tend not to arise. When an institution proposes to withdraw from this country, it must surrender its authorization to accept deposits.[28] That surrender can, however, only become effective when depositors have either been repaid[29] or, where accounts are dormant, adequate provision has been made to secure the position of those depositors.[30]

Outbreak of War

45.14 An outbreak of hostilities will often be accompanied by emergency legislation prohibiting trade or economic contacts with the enemy.[31] It is proposed briefly to consider the position in the event that the United Kingdom is party to the conflict, and the bank and its customer find themselves on opposite sides of the line.

---

[25] *United Commercial Bank Ltd v Okara Grain Buyers Syndicate Ltd* AIR 1968 SC 1115. This seems to be a case in which the decision to close the branch was taken voluntarily although the decision followed from inter-communal riots resulting from the division of India and Pakistan.

[26] A change in the governing law of the contract can obviously only be made with the consent of the customer.

[27] By way of illustration of this point, see *Indian and General Investment Trust v Borax Consolidated Ltd* [1920] 1 KB 539. Since unilateral closure of the London branch could not by itself result in a variation of the terms of the contract, the head office would have to honour the obligations arising with respect to the account in accordance with its original terms.

[28] On the subject of authorization, see generally Chapter 1 above.

[29] It will be recalled that the bank has the unilateral right to terminate the customer relationship by payment of the monies owing to the customer: see para 15.20 above.

[30] The British Bankers Association runs a scheme to assist individuals in tracing dormant accounts.

[31] See, in the case of the UK, the Trading with the Enemy Act 1914, as amended. Similar measures may be taken even though war is not formally declared.

Foreign Customers of UK Banks

It is established that a state of war does not have the effect of terminating contracts between **45.15**
a UK bank and an enemy alien, and that '... accrued rights are not affected although the
right of suing in respect thereof is suspended ...'.[32] The right to a credit balance in a bank
account must be treated as an 'accrued right' for these purposes. As a consequence, the right
to repayment is preserved both in the case of a deposit account where no demand for repayment is required[33] and even in the case of a current account, where a demand is a necessary
precondition to payment.[34] Performance of the obligation is, however, suspended until the
termination of hostilities.[35] The bank is not generally obliged to pay interest for the period
of the delay, because non-payment does not flow from any breach of contract on behalf of
the bank.[36]

UK Customers of Foreign Banks

What is the position where the roles are reversed, and a UK national has an account with a **45.16**
foreign bank on the other side of the line?

Perhaps unsurprisingly, the English courts have held that the English depositor can recover **45.17**
his funds from the assets of the bank's London branch, at least provided that a demand has
been made against the account-holding branch.[37]

Expropriation

Expropriation or forfeiture of deposits involves their mandatory transfer into public own- **45.18**
ership—whether with or without compensation.[38] Whether or not particular government
action amounts to the 'expropriation' of a deposit is a matter of substance to be determined
by reference to all of the surrounding circumstances. For example, the courts are not likely
to condemn arrangements involving the transfer of deposits to a new entity as part of its
efforts to deal with a genuine banking crisis.[39]

How should the English courts respond if a customer seeks to recover an allegedly expropri- **45.19**
ated deposit by means of proceedings against the London branch of the bank concerned?

---

[32] *Ertel Bieber & Co v Rio Tinto Co Ltd* [1918] AC 260 (HL) at 269, per Lord Dunedin.
[33] *Schering v Stockholms Enskilda Bank* [1946] AC 219.
[34] *Arab Bank Ltd v Barclays Bank (DC&O) Ltd* [1954] AC 495 (HL).
[35] *Arab Bank*, above.
[36] The same principle should apply to sums placed on interest-bearing deposit, at least once the initial
maturity period has expired because, whilst the bank will have retained the funds, it would not otherwise have
been compelled to accept a renewal of the deposit.
[37] *Leader v Direction der Disconto Gesellschaft* (1914) 31 TLR 83.
[38] This should be carefully distinguished from the substitution of a local currency obligation. That issue is
considered under 'Exchange Controls', below.
[39] See, for example, the discussion of Bangladesh's measures to deal with the local consequences of the
BCCI collapse in *Wright v Eckhardt Marine GmbH* (above).

45.20 This subject is by no means straightforward. It seems, however, that the English court must review and classify the terms of the foreign law at issue. If the law amounts to an outright expropriation,[40] then the relevant considerations appear to be as follows:

(a) Title to a bank deposit is governed by the law of the country in which the debt is situate. Since a bank deposit is primarily recoverable at the branch where the relevant account is held,[41] title to the deposit will thus be determined by reference to the laws of the expropriating State (including the expropriation law itself).

(b) English law will recognize the effect of foreign expropriation laws, even where the affected foreign depositors are offered no compensation at all and the expropriation is a clear breach of international law. The English courts will not consider the merits of the foreign law at issue, nor will they disregard it on public policy grounds.[42]

(c) In such a case, the depositor is no longer the 'owner' of the deposit, for English law recognizes the transfer of title effected by the expropriation law. As a result, any claim by the depositor against the London branch of the bank must necessarily fail. Thus, where a deposit was held to be situate in Israel, the English courts recognized and gave effect to Israeli legislation which vested title to that deposit in the Custodian of the Property of Absentees. The original depositor therefore had no title to the deposit, and could not enforce payment against the head office of the bank in London.[43]

---

[40] As the Privy Council noted in *Wright v Eckhardt Marine GmbH* (above), it will often be necessary to distinguish between an expropriation, where the validity of that action falls to be determined by reference to the *lex situs*, and cases in which the legislation merely varies the terms of the deposit, in which case the law applicable to the contract governs the issue. The point posed some difficulty in *Re United Railways of the Havana and Regla Warehouses Ltd* [1960] AC 1007 (HL), where the *situs* was Cuba but the contract was governed by the laws of Pennsylvania. Fortunately, this type of difficulty will not normally arise in the case of bank deposits; as has been shown, the place in which the bank branch is located will usually provide both the *lex situs* and the law applicable to the contract. Thus, for example, the Russian bank nationalizations technically involved the discharge of existing obligations and the creation of corresponding obligations on the part of a State bank, but in practice they amounted to an expropriation. But the point did not much matter, because the *lex situs* and the governing law would usually coincide: see *In re Russian Bank for Foreign Trade* [1933] Ch 745, *Re Banque des Marchands de Moscou (Koupetschesky)* [1952] 1 All ER 1269 and *In re Banque des Marchands de Moscou (Koupeteschesky) (No 2)* [1954] 1 WLR 1108, as explained in *Wright v Eckhardt Marine GmbH* (above). The distinction between the suspension or discharge of an obligation (on the one hand) and its expropriation or confiscation (on the other hand) may be of particular importance in the US because the Second Hickenlooper Amendment (22 USC Sec 2370(e)(2) (1982)) applies to the second category of foreign governmental action, but not to the first: see the discussion of the decision in *West v Multibanco Comermex SA* 807 F 2d 820 (1986), at para 45.27(h) below.

[41] See *Joachimson v Swiss Bank Corporation* [1921] 3 KB 110 (CA) and other cases discussed at para 15.20 above.

[42] See, for example, *Williams and Humbert v W and H Trademarks (Jersey) Ltd* [1986] AC 368 (HL). The position may, however, be different where the expropriation law forms a part of some wider programme whose recognition would be repugnant to central norms of international law and, hence, contrary to public policy in England. A well-known example of this principle is offered by the decision in *Oppenheimer v Cattermole (Inspector of Taxes)* [1976] AC 249 (HL).

[43] *Arab Bank Ltd v Barclays Bank (DCO) Ltd* [1954] AC 495 (HL). Any other decision would have involved the bank in a 'double liability' to the depositor and the custodian. The *Barclays* case is one of some interest on the facts, since it arises out of the foundation of Israel in 1948. Arab Bank was a Jordanian bank which held an account with Barclays in Jerusalem, which was then within Palestine under the British Mandate. The Barclays branch closed because of fighting in the area and, by the time it re-opened, it was within the State of Israel. Repayment of the deposit was made unlawful under regulations introduced by the new government because of tensions with Jordan and other neighbouring States. Subsequently, Israeli legislation required the payment of the funds to the custodian. The transfer of the deposit to the custodian under Israeli law was recognized

Likewise, where a Cuban law expropriated deposits placed by certain officials of a previous government, the depositors could not obtain judgment against the New York head office of the bank because they no longer had title according to the law of the *situs;* payment of the deposit to the Cuban authorities thus had the effect of discharging the bank's obligation to repay the deposit.[44]

(d) It should, however, be emphasized that, so far as the English courts are concerned, the effect of laws of this kind will be confined to deposits which are situate within the territory of the legislating State in question. In other words, so far as English private international law is concerned, a law passed within that country can only affect title to assets which are located there.[45] Thus, where a Spanish decree confiscated the assets of a former king, the English courts could not give effect to that decree in relation to assets held with a London bank.[46] Likewise, Iraqi legislation expropriating the assets of the King of Iraq could not be applied by the New York courts in relation to deposits held outside Iraq.[47]

(e) It will be appreciated that, in accordance with well-established principles, the English courts will not enforce foreign laws of a penal, revenue, or public nature, for this would enable the foreign State concerned to enforce its sovereign rights within the United Kingdom.[48] However, this principle has no application in the present context, because the English court is merely *recognizing* the effect of a foreign law within its own jurisdiction. It is not lending its process to the active *enforcement* of that law.[49]

(f) It should, however, be appreciated that these principles apply where the deposit obligation is 'localized' to a particular branch of the bank. As has been noted previously,[50] localization of the deposit will be the general rule but, since that principle may flow from an *implied* term of the contract, it can necessarily be overridden by an *express* term.[51] Consequently, if a deposit is placed in Cuba but the corresponding certificate of deposit states that the corresponding funds are repayable at any branch in the world, then recovery is not barred by expropriation in Cuba.[52] The same result may follow if

---

by the English courts, because Israel was the *situs* of the deposit. If, however, a valid demand for repayment had been made at the branch before payment was rendered unlawful by the actions of the new Israeli Government, then it seems likely that the claim against the head office of Barclays in London would have succeeded: compare the situation in the *Sokoloff* case, above.

[44] *Perez v Chase Manhattan Bank* 463 NYS 2d 764 (1983). The court further held that the deposit was situate in Cuba and that the Cuban expropriation amounted to an act of State which had the effect of exonerating the bank from its obligations to the customer. This decision is directly contrary to that in *Garcia v Chase Manhattan Bank NA* 735 F 2d 645 (1984) (see subpara (f) below), although the difference between the cases perhaps lies in the oral representations made by the Cuban officials of the bank in *Garcia*.

[45] *Bank voor Handel en Scheepvaart NV v Slatford* [1953] 1 QB 248.

[46] *Banco de Vizcaya v Don Alfonso de Borbon y Austria* [1935] 1 KB 140.

[47] *Republic of Iraq v First National City Bank* 353 F 2d 47 (1965) cert den 392 US 1027 (1966).

[48] On this principle, see *Government of India, Ministry of Finance (Revenue Division) v Taylor* [1955] AC 491 (HL).

[49] It may be added that a law which expropriates assets in the national interest is probably not a law of a 'revenue or penal' nature, but it may perhaps fall within the residual category of 'public laws' to which the principle applies.

[50] See the discussion of *Joachimson v Swiss Bank Corporation* [1921] 3 KB 110 (CA) at para 15.20 above.

[51] *Richardson v Richardson* [1927] P 228.

[52] *Manos y Pineiro v Chase Manhattan Bank NA* 443 F Supp 418 (1978).

the relevant bank officials gave an oral assurance in similar terms,[53] or if the parties subsequently varied their contract to that effect.[54]

(g) Of course, a court will usually recognize and give effect to the forfeiture of any property effected by the State in which it is situate. Thus, if the US Government has made a valid forfeiture order with respect to deposits owing by a bank located within its jurisdiction, then any action by foreign customers to recover deposits within the United States must necessarily fail.[55]

Other Forms of Seizure

45.21   The term 'expropriation' connotes an appropriation of an asset in the interests of the State concerned. But deposits may be subject to seizure or confiscation for more specific reasons, for example, in pursuit of the fight against terrorism or other crimes.

45.22   A good, if perhaps rather extreme, example of this type of law is offered by the US Patriot Act.[56] Section 319 provides that:

> ... For the purposes of a forfeiture under this section, if funds are deposited into an account at a foreign bank, and that foreign bank has an interbank account in the United States ... the funds shall be deemed to have been deposited in the interbank account in the United States, and any restraining order, seizure warrant or arrest warrant in rem regarding the funds may be served on the [United States] financial institution, and funds in the interbank account, up to the value of the funds deposited into the account at the foreign bank, may be restrained, seized or arrested ...

In other words, if a suspected terrorist organization has deposited funds with a bank outside the United States, then the US authorities may seize a corresponding amount from an account of that foreign bank in the US. This is, of course, a significant power because all banks will need to have US dollar correspondent accounts within the United States.

45.23   It was presumably action taken under the US PATRIOT Act (or legislation to similar effect) which gave rise to the decision of the New South Wales Court of Appeal in *European Bank Ltd v Citibank Ltd*.[57] The factual background to this case is relatively straightforward. European Bank Ltd (EBL) placed a deposit of some US$8 million with Citibank Ltd in Sydney (Citibank Australia), an Australian incorporated subsidiary of the Citibank Group.

---

[53]   *Garcia v Chase Manhattan Bank NA* 735 F 2d 645 (1984). In this case, the US Court of Appeals for the Second Circuit also held that the Cuban expropriation of deposits did not amount to an act of State which would have enabled the New York branch of the bank to avoid liability for repayment of the deposits. For a similar approach, see the decision of the US Court of Appeals in *Edelmann v Chase Manhattan Bank NA* 861 F 2d 1291 (1st Cir).

[54]   *Isaacs v Barclays Bank Ltd* [1943] 2 All ER 682.

[55]   For an example, see *United States v BCCI (Holdings) (Luxembourg) SA* 48 F 3d 551 (1995, District of Columbia Court of Appeals). This does, of course, pre-suppose that the forfeiture is valid and does not infringe any constitutional or other guarantee of property rights which forms a part of the domestic system of law in question.

[56]   Or, to provide its official short title, 'Uniting and Strengthening America by Providing Appropriate Tools to Intercept and Obstruct Terrorism (USA PATRIOT ACT) Act of 2001.'

[57]   [2004] NSWCA 76. It should be added that the claim was also defended with reference to a specific contract term dealing with *force majeure*, but it is not necessary to consider that aspect of the decision in the present context.

Since the deposit was made in US dollars, payment was made to Citibank NA, which acted as Citibank Australia's correspondent bank in New York. A warrant was then issued by the US District Court requiring the seizure of EBL's funds with Citibank Australia's correspondent bank in New York. The correspondent bank paid over the funds to the US Marshall and debited Citibank Australia, which in turn debited the Sydney account of EBL.

When EBL sued for repayment of the deposit, Citibank Australia, the latter seems to have argued that the debt had been discharged because US dollar deposits always have to be placed via correspondent arrangements in New York.[58] Yet, as the court pointed out,[59] this factor did not affect the fact that the deposits were represented by credits to accounts held in Australia; both contractual and proprietary questions arising from the Sydney account thus fell to be determined by the laws of New South Wales, as the governing law of the contract and the law of the *situs*. **45.24**

It was also argued that it was EBL's money which had been seized pursuant to the US warrant, and that Citibank Australia was thus discharged from the obligation to repay. Once again, this argument could not succeed because the credit made by EBL with Citibank as correspondent bank resulted in that money becoming the absolute property of Citibank Australia.[60] EBL did not have any money in New York at all; the payment to the correspondent bank had the effect of making Citibank Australia a debtor to EBL in the amount concerned.[61] That debt was governed by the laws of, and was situate in, New South Wales. In the instant case, the US warrant sought to transfer title to the deposit and was thus of a proprietary character,[62] and the effect of the warrant thus fell to be judged by reference to the law of the *situs*.[63] Since New York law could not operate to deprive EBL of its title to a debt situate in New South Wales, it followed that EBL was entitled to judgment.[64] **45.25**

---

[58] See paras 36–38 of the judgment.

[59] Paragraphs 50–59 of the judgment. As the court had previously observed, it is necessary to distinguish between mutual expectations and common intentions. It was true that both parties expected that correspondent banks in New York would have to be used to effect the transaction; it is quite another thing to impose a condition that the bank would only be required to repay if the necessary funds were still available at that correspondent bank (see paras 9–11 of the judgment).

[60] Paragraphs 60–61 of the judgment, citing *Foley v Hill* (1848) 9 ER 1002 and *Foskett v McKeown* [2001] 1 AC 102 at 127.

[61] Again, as the court pointed out, the account relationship in New York involved a credit on Citibank Australia's correspondent account with Citibank. Matters affecting that account could not have any impact on the obligations owed by Citibank Australia to EBL. The duty to repay the deposit to EBL was a general obligation of Citibank Australia, and was not limited to the credit on the correspondent account or to any other particular source of funds: see para 64 of the judgment. The debt obligation which arose in New York arose only as between Citibank and Citibank Australia.

[62] On the proprietary nature of garnishee or third party debt orders, see the remarks of Lord Bingham in *Societe Eram Shipping Co Ltd v Compagnie Internationale de Navigation* [2003] 3 WLR 21 at 33. This case has already been noted more generally at para 44.15 above.

[63] The respective roles of the law applicable to the contract and the law of the *situs* have been discussed in Chapter 40 above.

[64] It may be added that the US warrant at issue in this case was apparently of a penal character and the court felt that it should not be enforced in Australia on that ground, given the well-known principles which prohibit the enforcement of the sovereign authority of a foreign State: see *Huntington v Attrill* [1893] AC 150 (HL) and *Government of India v Taylor* [1955] AC 491 (HL). It is submitted that this approach to the matter would be open to question, because the court was not asked to *enforce* a foreign penal law; it was merely being asked to *recognize* the effect of certain actions taken by a foreign authority within its own jurisdiction.

The argument seems to have been confined solely to the question whether the deposit remained owing to EBL, and the potential difficulties in complying with the order do not appear to have been raised. Nevertheless, and notwithstanding certain difficulties in the manner in which the case appears to have been presented,[65] it is submitted that the outcome of these proceedings is plainly correct.

45.26 It follows that the seizure of funds effected pursuant to the PATRIOT Act will not be recognized in the country in which the relevant foreign bank branch is situate.

Exchange Controls

45.27 If, on the other hand, the debt is not subjected to outright expropriation or seizure but the bank is instead required to repay in the local currency (rather than the foreign currency in which the deposit was originally made) then problems of a different order will arise. Laws of this kind fall under the general heading of 'exchange control' regulations.[66] It must be appreciated that, whilst the above section dealt with questions of a *proprietary* nature, the present section is concerned with *contractual* issues, in the sense that they affect the identity of the currency in which repayment must be made. If the depositor subsequently sues the London branch of the relevant bank for the foreign currency deposit, how should the English courts respond? Should they enforce the contract in accordance with its original terms, or should they accept and give effect to the foreign currency substitution? It is suggested that the following process should be applied:

(a) The claim for the repayment of the deposit is essentially a claim for the repayment of a contractual debt. Consequently, it becomes necessary to examine the terms of the obligation.

(b) This process must begin with the identification of the law applicable to the contract, because the analysis of obligations can only be undertaken once the appropriate legal matrix has been established.[67]

(c) It has been shown that the law which governs the banker-customer relationship will usually be the law of the country in which the account-holding branch is located.[68]

(d) Consequently, the law which effects the change in contractual terms will form a part of the law applicable to the banker-customer contract;

It should, however, be said that the point was not explored in depth and the case was decided largely on the grounds described in the text. The court also added (at para 82) that 'decision in favour of Citibank Australia would recognise an exorbitant jurisdiction in the United States to attach US dollar deposits outside that country'. The court did not pursue the point further but was clearly of the view that such recognition should not be extended.

[65] Remarkably, the decision in the *Libyan Arab Foreign Bank* case is not even mentioned, and (notwithstanding the identity of the parties before the court) the decisions in *Citibank NA v Wells Fargo Asia* 495 US 660 (1990) and 936 F 2d 723 were only drawn to the court's attention after the hearing had concluded (see para 76 of the judgment). The *Wells Fargo* litigation is noted at para 45.36 below.

[66] For a full treatment of laws of this kind, see Mann, *Money*, chs 14–16.

[67] See, for example, the discussion of this subject in *Amin Rasheed Shipping Corporation v Kuwait Insurance Co* [1984] AC 50 (HL).

[68] See Chapter 40 above.

(e) As a result, the English court will recognize that the bank's obligation has indeed been varied by the law concerned and that, as a consequence, the obligation is validly performed by payment in the local currency in accordance with the new law.[69] This rule may only be overridden if the application of the foreign law at issue would be manifestly contrary to public policy in England,[70] but this will only very rarely be the case.[71]

(f) These rules are well illustrated by the decision in *Re Helbert Wagg & Co Ltd's Claim.*[72] In that case, an English company had advanced £350,000 to a German company. The loan was expressed to be repayable in sterling and the contract was governed by German law. Subsequently, a German law was introduced which required that foreign debts should be converted into Reichsmarks and paid to a German agency. Since the law formed a part of the law applicable to the contract, the English court had to give effect to the relevant law and thus held that the debt had been discharged by payment according to that law. The court found that the law had been introduced in a genuine effort to resolve Germany's prevailing economic problems and there were thus no public policy grounds upon which the court should disregard the effect of that law.[73]

(g) There have been various instances where governments have converted US dollar deposits into the local currency with a view to resolving economic crises and preserving dollar resources. The rate of exchange which is applied for these purposes is invariably significantly below the prevailing market rate, thus leaving depositors out of pocket. The main examples in recent times have been Mexico, which in 1981 converted US dollar deposits into pesos during an economic crisis resulting from a collapse in oil prices, and Argentina, which took similar steps in 2001. Cases brought in US courts against Mexican banks seeking judgment in US dollars tended to fail, either on the basis that (i) the introduction of exchange controls was a sovereign act which was not reviewable by the US courts in consequence of the Foreign Sovereign Immunities Act[74] or (ii) the suit was barred by the US act of State doctrine.[75] To the English mind, it is a little surprising that international concepts such as act of State and sovereign immunity

---

[69] This conclusion follows from the fact that questions touching the substance of performance are subjected to the applicable law in accordance with Art 12(1)(b) of Rome I. However, the currency in which payment may be made may also be treated as relating to the mode of performance, where Art 12(2) allows the court to have regard to the law of the place of performance.

[70] Article 21 of Rome I. The applicable law of the contract may also be overridden by the mandatory laws of the forum in accordance with Art 9(2) of Rome I, but that point is perhaps unlikely to arise.

[71] See *Oppenheimer v Cattermole (Inspector of Taxes)* [1976] AC 249 (HL).

[72] [1956] Ch 323.

[73] For the purposes of Art 21 of Rome I, the application of a law of this kind might be disregarded on public policy grounds if it was intended to be discriminatory: for an example, see *Re Friedrich Krupp AG* [1917] 2 Ch 188.

[74] For examples in this category, see *Braka v Nacional Financiera* No 83-4169 (SDNY, 9 July 1984) and *Frankel v Banco Nacional de Mexico* 82-6457 (SDNY, 31 May 1983).

[75] For examples in this category, see *Braker v Bancomer SA* 589 F Supp 1465 (SDNY, 1984), aff'd 762 F 2d 222 (2nd Cir, 1985); *Braker v Multibanco Comermex* 589 F Supp 802 (SDNY, 1984); *Callejo v Bancomer SA* 764 F 1101 (5th Cir, 1985, US Court of Appeals). The US Act of State doctrine recognizes that: 'Every sovereign State is bound to respect the independence of every other sovereign State, and the courts of one country will not sit in judgment on the acts of the government of another, done within its own territory. Redress of grievances by reason of such acts must be obtained through the means open to be availed of by sovereign powers as between themselves...': *Underhill v Hernandez* 168 US 250 (1897). The doctrine is thus

have to be invoked to deal with a dispute of this nature. Once it has been determined that the deposit is governed by the law of Mexico and there is no public policy reason for disregarding the effect of the exchange control regulations, then the deposit would be repayable in pesos in accordance with the law applicable to the contract.[76] Nevertheless, if the route is rather different, the journey appears to lead to the same destination.[77]

(h) Finally, it may be noted that the imposition of exchange controls in this way may well diminish the value of the depositor's claim, but it is not equivalent to an expropriation of that claim. As a result, the two issues must be clearly distinguished. The point is of some importance in the US case law, because as a result of the Second Hickenlooper Amendment:[78]

> ... no court in the United States shall decline on the ground of the federal act of State doctrine to make a determination on the merits of giving effect to the principles of international law in a case in which a claim of title or other rights to property is asserted by any party based upon (or traced through) a confiscation or other taking ... by an act of that State in violation of the principles of international law ... including the principles of compensation ...

As a result, in *West v Multibanco Comermex SA*,[79] the Second Hickenlooper Amendment could not be applied because the imposition of exchange controls was not a 'confiscation or other taking' for the purposes of the Amendment. Consequently, the act of State doctrine could be applied, with the result that the plaintiff's claim for repayment of his deposit in US dollars had to fail.

Moratoria

45.28 Occasionally, a foreign law may seek neither to expropriate the deposit nor to vary the currency in which it is payable. Instead, it may simply delay payment for a period, by the imposition of a moratorium. This will usually occur where a State is suffering severe balance of payment difficulties and wishes to conserve foreign exchange resources.[80] In such a case, what is the position if a customer whose funds have been blocked at a foreign branch seeks repayment from the London branch of the bank concerned, notwithstanding that the foreign moratorium remains in force? The position under English law can be shortly stated:

(a) A moratorium seeks to vary the terms on which a deposit is repayable. Since this goes to substantive questions of performance, a moratorium can only validly defer the repayment date if it forms a part of the law applicable to the contract.[81]

---

in some respects similar to the theory of 'judicial restraint' adopted by the House of Lords in *Buttes Gas & Oil Co v Hammer (Nos 2 & 3)* [1982] AC 888.

[76] See Art 12(1)(b) of Rome I and *Re Helbert Wagg*, n 72 above.

[77] The reader of these cases can only empathize with the court's remark in *Callejo*, that 'if the Foreign Sovereign Immunities Act is a tangled web of statutory ambiguities, the act of State doctrine is an airy castle ...'.

[78] 22 USC Sec 2370(e)(2) (1982). The amendment was designed to reverse the effect of the decision in *Banco Nacional de Cuba v Sabbatino* 376 US 398 (1984).

[79] 807 F 2d 820 (1981). The factual background is very similar to *Callejo*, above.

[80] A moratorium is therefore usually designed to preserve such resources for urgently needed imports, so that future suppliers may effectively gain preference over existing creditors.

[81] See Art 12(1)(b) of Rome I.

(b) This requirement will, however, usually be satisfied because, as has been seen,[82] the contract between the banker and the customer will usually be governed by the law of the country in which the account-holding branch is situate, and this will coincide with the law of the country which has imposed the moratorium.

(c) As a result, the English court will give effect to the moratorium, and the depositor will be unable to recover his deposit from the London branch.

(d) Once again, however, the effect of the moratorium is confined to deposits which are governed by the law of the legislating State and, in practice, this will refer to deposits held at branches within the territory of that State. Thus, if the relevant law seeks to impose a moratorium on deposits held with the London branch of its national banks, the English courts will not give effect to it. In such a case, the banker-customer contract is governed by English law, and its terms cannot be varied or discharged under the provisions of any other system of law.[83] By way of example, in *National Bank of Greece and Athens SA v Metliss*,[84] a Greek bank issued bonds governed by English law. It ceased to make payments but, given that the bank had no presence in England, no action was taken for an extended period. Greece had imposed a moratorium on payments under the bonds, and the relevant regulations remained in force. However, the issuer subsequently merged with another bank which did have a London branch. Under the terms of the Greek law effecting the merger, the new entity succeeded to all of the rights and obligations of the issuer, and this would have included the English law bonds. The bondholders accordingly started proceedings and obtained judgment, on the essentially straightforward bases that (i) the new bank was created under Greek law, with the result that the English courts would recognize its status as an obligor in respect of the bonds[85] and (ii) bonds governed by English law had to be repaid in accordance with their contractual terms and a Greek moratorium law could not operate to defer the required repayment date.[86]

The position under New York law, in contrast, appears to be a little confused but it seems **45.29** that the courts adopt a different approach. In *Citibank NA v Wells Fargo Asia Ltd*,[87] Wells Fargo Asia (a bank established in Singapore) placed a deposit with the Manila branch

---

[82] See generally the discussion in Chapter 40 above.

[83] See generally Art 12 of Rome I.

[84] [1958] AC 509 (HL).

[85] See the discussion on corporate issues in private international law at paras 40.22–40.25 above.

[86] The Greek Government subsequently introduced legislation which retrospectively excluded the relevant English law bonds from the scope of the merger and argued that, since this went to the corporate terms of the merger, the English courts had likewise to recognize the effect of that law and hold that the bank was no longer liable under the terms of the bonds. Whilst it is true that questions of corporate existence and capacity are governed by the law of the place of incorporation, it remains necessary to determine the question of characterization—in other words, is the relevant law genuinely a law which addresses corporate issues? Notwithstanding the apparent effect of the new Greek law, its effect was to discharge an obligation to which the bank was already subject. However, the discharge of an obligation can only be achieved by the terms of the law applicable to it and, hence, the Greek law was ineffective to discharge the bank from bond obligations governed by English law: see *Adams v National Bank of Greece* [1961] AC 255 (HL). See now Art 12(1)(d) of Rome I.

[87] For the various decisions in this litigation, see 852 F 2d 657 (1988); 495 US 660 (1990); 926 F 2d 273 (2nd Cir), cert den 505 US 1204.

of Citibank; repayment was then delayed as a result of the imposition of exchange controls and a moratorium by the Philippine Government. Applying the principles discussed elsewhere,[88] it is submitted that (i) the deposit contract was governed by the laws of the Philippines, (ii) the Philippine moratorium could thus validly vary the obligation contracted by Citibank, and (iii) the US court should have respected that position and held that the obligation to repay was suspended for the period of the moratorium.[89] Ultimately, however, the New York courts appear to have held that the contract was governed by New York law, on the basis that payment was ultimately to be made via the New York clearing system for US dollars; Wells Fargo was thus entitled to collect payment from Citibank in New York.[90]

45.30 As a result of cases of this kind, legislation[91] was introduced which relieves the head offices of US banks from liability for the blocked deposit obligations of overseas branches if '... the branch cannot repay the deposit due to (1) an act of war, insurrection or civil strife or (2) an action by a foreign government or instrumentality (whether de jure or de facto) in the country in which the branch is located ...'. In other words, in the limited circumstances just described, the relevant foreign branch is effectively to be regarded as an entity which is legally separate from the head office of the bank. Subject to that, however, a US bank will remain liable if a foreign branch is unable to repay on other grounds (eg insolvency).

Blocking Orders

45.31 A foreign government might seek to influence the terms applicable to the repayment of a deposit held in London in a variety of ways. This may occur where a foreign government introduces legislation designed to prevent named individuals (often a former ruler or his associates) from obtaining access to funds allegedly acquired corruptly or which might otherwise be viewed as property of the State. Alternatively, a foreign State may have imposed sanctions against another State and, as part of those sanctions, requires foreign branches and subsidiaries to adhere to those sanctions.[92]

---

[88] See the discussion of the law applicable to deposit contracts, in Chapter 40 above.

[89] Such a finding would have been consistent with the so-called 'separate entity doctrine' discussed in the Supreme Court's judgment. That doctrine recognizes that foreign branches are subject to banking laws and the sovereign authority of each country in which it does business, and should be treated accordingly.

[90] It is submitted that this reasoning confuses two issues. New York was the place of *settlement*, but this should have relatively limited legal consequences. Manila was the place of *payment*, and the US court should thus have had regard to the effect of the moratorium law.

[91] See US Code Title 12, s 633. The bank can contract out of this provision in relation to particular obligations, if it wishes to do so.

[92] As will be seen, this was the position in the *Libyan Arab Foreign Bank* litigation, considered below.

The most well-known decision in England in this arena is the decision of Staughton J in **45.32**
Libyan Arab Foreign Bank v Bankers Trust Co,[93] and it is necessary to consider the factual
background to this case insofar as it is relevant in the present context.[94]

On 8 January 1986, the President of the United States signed an Executive Order which **45.33**
froze Libyan assets in the United States. The Order was expressed to extend to deposits held
by overseas branches of US banks (including Bankers Trust). At that time, LAFB had some
US$131 million on deposit with the London branch of Bankers Trust. When LAFB sued
for non-payment of the deposit, Bankers Trust naturally argued that payment was rendered
unlawful by the Executive Order.

The Executive Order sought to prevent payment and it was thus necessary to decide whether **45.34**
the English courts could give effect to this provision. Now, it will be obvious that a law
which seeks to defer the repayment date of a deposit must be characterized as a rule affecting the *performance* of the bank's contractual obligations. As has been shown, questions
touching the substantive performance of such obligations are to be determined by reference to the applicable law.[95] Once the court had decided that the deposit contract between
Bankers Trust (London branch) and LAFB was governed by English law,[96] it was plain that
the Executive Order could not, on that ground, afford a defence to LAFB's claim.

At this point, however, it becomes necessary to consider precisely what steps English law **45.35**
required the bank to take in order to perform its obligation of payment? It is necessary to
recall that currencies are usually cleared through the principal financial centre in the currency of issue;[97] this is especially so in relation to large, Eurodollar transactions of the type
at issue in this case.[98] If English law required the deposit to be settled by means of a transfer
to another bank in New York, then an immediate difficulty arose in that it would presumably be unlawful for the necessary transfers to be made between accounts located within the
United States. Bankers Trust accordingly argued that:

(a) it was an implied term of the contract that a Eurodollar deposit was not required to be
    paid in cash or by other means, and that the customer's rights were limited to repay-
    ment by means of a transfer to another bank account;
(b) since such a transfer involved a movement of funds between accounts located in
    New York, performance was required to be effected in that place; and

---

[93] [1989] QB 728. On this case, see Smedresman and Lowenfeld, 'Eurodollars, Multinational Banks and
National Laws' (1989) New York University LR 733. See also the essentially comparable decision of Hirst J in
Libyan Arab Foreign Bank v Manufacturers Hanover Trust Co (No 2) [1989] 1 Lloyd's Rep 608.
[94] The actual decision is complicated by the existence of other, related arrangements with the bank's
New York branch, but these are disregarded for present purposes.
[95] See Art 12(1)(b) of Rome I, discussed at para 40.12 above.
[96] In fact, the court held that there was a single contract between Bankers Trust and LAFB which was in
part governed by English law and in part governed by New York law. However, the deposit arrangements with
the London branch fell within the English law segment of the contract.
[97] On this point, see the discussion at para 19.24 above.
[98] Note that the US Supreme Court has defined Eurodollars as 'United States dollars that have been deposited with a banking institution outside the US with a corresponding obligation on the part of the banking
institution to repay the deposit in US dollars': *Citibank NA v Wells Fargo Asia* 495 US 660 (1990).

(c) an English court would not enforce a contract if this involved the commission of an unlawful act in the place of performance.[99]

45.36 Despite the existence of considerable legal and economic authority which supported the existence of the implied term, the court held that, since the obligation was expressed in monetary terms, the creditor was entitled to payment in cash in London, that is to say, at the branch at which the account was held. It had not become unlawful to perform the payment obligation in the place of performance, which the court found to be England. The fact that performance might incidentally involve an unlawful transfer within New York could not affect the customer's right to repayment of his money.[100]

45.37 The case law accordingly establishes that the unilateral imposition of sanctions by a foreign State cannot affect the obligation of a London branch to repay a deposit governed by English law, even if the relevant obligation is denominated in the currency of the country which has imposed the sanctions concerned.

Conclusions

45.38 In very broad terms, it is possible to conclude that:

(a) an English branch of a bank may be made responsible for the payment of obligations incurred by branches in other parts of the world, but only to the extent to which the relevant obligation is required to be performed under the law applicable to the contract which created it; and

(b) blocking and other action taken by foreign governments cannot affect or detract from obligations due to be performed in England and governed by English law. This remains the case even though (i) the head office of the bank is established in the country which initiates the blocking action and/or (ii) the deposit was originally placed in the currency of that country.

---

[99] This is the effect of the rule in *Ralli Bros v Compania Naviera Sota y Aznar* [1920] 2 KB 287. The rule appears to be a part of English domestic law (rather than private international law); it would have to be so if it were to apply in the present context. However, it seems that the rule is also now effectively a part of English private international law: see Art 9(3) of Rome I. For a criticism of the rule in *Ralli Bros* insofar as it applies to monetary obligation, see Mann, *Money*, para 16.38.

[100] Compare, for these purposes the decision of the US Supreme Court in *Citibank NA v Wells Fargo Asia* 495 US 660, where a distinction was drawn between the place of settlement in US dollar transactions (New York) and the place of payment (the place where the relevant deposit holding branch was situate). Further support for this distinction may also be drawn from other cases: see, for example, *Callejo v Bancomer SA* 764 F 2d 1101 (5th Cir, 1985, US Court of Appeals), where it was held that the *situs* of an obligation represented by a certificate of deposit issued by a Mexican bank was Mexico, even though payment would be remitted to the holder in Texas.

46

ECONOMIC SANCTIONS

Introduction

The imposition of sanctions against countries or territories deemed to have committed a **46.01** particularly heinous international sin has become a familiar feature of the modern political landscape.

In earlier times, sanctions tended to be aimed at particular countries. Some—such as the **46.02** regime of sanctions enforced against South Africa during the apartheid era—were multilateral initiatives. Others—such as the UK's sanctions against Argentina immediately following the Falklands invasion in 1982—were unilateral measures which were not immediately replicated by the international community as a whole. In more recent years, there has been a tendency to impose sanctions against high ranking officials in a particular country, rather than against the country as a whole; the measures taken over recent years against named officials in Zimbabwe offer an example of this trend.

In either case, the broad objective is the same. Future dealings with the targeted State or **46.03** individuals are to be prohibited whilst the sanctions remain in force. Furthermore, the existing assets of the target are to be blocked, so that the target is deprived of the effective benefit of them. Both of these restrictions will be binding on banks with branches in England, although it is the freeze on existing assets which is most likely to be of concern to banks.

The present chapter considers the consequences for banks in England which may follow **46.04** from the implementation of sanctions by the United Kingdom.[1]

---

[1] This qualification should be carefully noted. For the—now quite rare—situation in which the English courts have to consider sanctions imposed unilaterally by foreign States, see the discussion of the decision in *Libyan Arab Foreign Bank v Bankers Trust Company* [1989] QB 728, at paras 45.32–45.37 above.

46.05 The present chapter is arranged under the following headings:

(a) the sources of sanctions legislation;

(b) the effect of sanctions; and

(c) conclusions.

The Sources of Sanctions Legislation

46.06 Banks will not usually be concerned with the underlying political objectives or legislative basis for a particular sanctions regime; they will be principally focused on the need for compliance. Nevertheless, a brief description of the relevant sources may help to inform the interpretation of particular regulations.

46.07 So far as the United Kingdom is concerned, there are three principal sources:

(a) the Security Council of the United Nations may make recommendations to deal with any act of aggression or threat to international peace or security. It may also call on member countries to implement associated measures, including '… complete or partial interruption of economic relations …',[2] and the necessary authority for the implementation of those measures in the United Kingdom is the United Nations Act 1946. Orders may be made under that Act which will mirror the steps required to be taken by the Security Council resolution;

(b) the European Union may introduce sanctions in particular cases—often in parallel with UN initiatives. These will usually be made by way of a regulation, which will be directly binding in individual Member States without the need for further, implementing action at the national level;[3] and

(c) at a purely domestic level, section 4 of the Anti-Terrorism, Crime and Security Act 2001 applies if the Treasury is satisfied that a foreign State is or is likely to take steps which are detrimental to the economic position of the United Kingdom. In such a case, the Treasury can make orders prohibiting the transfer of funds or other financial

---

[2] On these points, see Arts 39–41 of the UN Charter.

[3] See Arts 60 and 301 of the EC Treaty, which provides the basis for a sanctions regime. The article provides for joint action to limit economic relations with third countries as part of the common foreign and security policy. It should be said that Community case law boasts a considerable body of decisions dealing with the imposition and administration of such sanctions, including their essential validity and matters such as procedural fairness. Purely by way of examples, see Case C-84/95, *Bosphorous Hava Yollari Ticaret AS v Minister for Transport* [1996] 3 CMLR 257 (ECJ) and Case C-177/95, *Ebony Maritime SA v Prefetto della Provincia di Brindisi* [1997] 2 CMLR 24 (ECJ), both dealing with sanctions against Serbia and Montenegro. There have also been a number of more recent cases involving sanctions against organizations suspected of involvement in terrorist activity. The relationship between sanctions imposed by the United Nations and corresponding measures adopted at a European Union level was considered in Joined Cases C-402/05 P and C-415/05 P, *Yassin Abdullah Kadi and Al Bakaraat International Foundation v Council and Commission* (3 September 2008). Important though these issues are, they will usually be of limited concern to banks which—in this, as in many other contexts—are in the position of a 'middleman'. A bank will be holding funds belonging to a targeted State, individual or organization and will merely wish to ensure that it acts lawfully in relation to them. It will usually have no direct financial interest of its own in that context. The bank will therefore not usually be seeking to challenge the essential validity of the sanctions regulations themselves, nor would it be reasonable to expect a bank to form a view about the validity of sanctions against a framework of EU law.

assets or economic benefits at the request or direction of that foreign State or anyone resident within it.[4]

It will, of course, always be necessary for banks to scrutinize the details of any regulations which are made. They may not prohibit every form of payment or transaction, and they will frequently allow the Treasury or other relevant authority to grant waivers in appropriate cases. Measures of this kind tend to be matters of high policy, and banks must therefore exercise great care in their dealings with the targeted State and its nationals. If they were to decline a payment or transfer which was not, in fact, caught by the relevant regulations, then they may be liable in damages for any resultant losses suffered by the customer.   **46.08**

It should not be overlooked that other States may occasionally impose unilateral sanctions with which the United Kingdom is not directly concerned,[5] and situations of this kind, though rare, will raise their own specific set of difficulties.   **46.09**

Effect of Sanctions

In practice, an English court is likely to be confronted with sanctions legislation in two distinct types of cases namely, (i) where the sanctions form a part of English law and (ii) those cases in which the sanctions have been imposed unilaterally by a foreign State, and the United Kingdom is not party to them.   **46.10**

Where the sanctions form a part of English law, their application in this country will be mandatory regardless of the governing law of the contract, the extent of any nexus between the contract and the United Kingdom, or any other matter.[6] An English court will thus not under any circumstances order the performance of a contractual obligation—or award damages for its non-performance—to the extent to which the required actions would infringe the relevant regulations. It should be noted that the regulations may not merely prohibit future dealings; they may also have the effect of expropriating funds belonging to targeted individuals. In the case of Iraq, banks and others who held funds belonging to designated persons deemed to have been in some way responsible for the government of Iraq were required (i) to notify HM Treasury and (ii) to transfer those funds to the Development Fund for Iraq via an account at the New York Federal Reserve.[7] In the case of an English bank account, payment to the Development Fund would constitute a valid discharge of the bank's debt since the regulations form a part of English law.[8] To the extent to which this may be regarded as an expropriation of the depositor's property, this should   **46.11**

---

[4] On the meaning of 'funds' for these purposes, see s 5(b) of the 2001 Act. As has been seen, however, this is not the only weapon at the government's disposal. The use of this provision in relation to Iceland has already been discussed at paras 13.13–13.15 above. The section replaced earlier rules to similar effect in the Emergency Laws (Re-Enactment and Repeals) Act 1964.

[5] The situation which arose in the two *Libyan Arab Foreign Bank* cases, discussed in the previous chapter, appears to be the only instances in which the English courts have had to consider this particular issue.

[6] ie the sanctions regime will constitute 'overriding mandatory rules' for the purposes of Art 9(2) of Rome I.

[7] See art 5A of Iraq (United Nations Sanctions) Order 2000 (SI 2000/3241) as inserted by Sch 1 of Iraq (United Nations Sanctions) Order 2003 (SI 2003/1519).

[8] Article 12(1)(b) of Rome I.

likewise be regarded as valid as a matter of private international law because (i) England is the *situs* of the deposit and (ii) the expropriation is effected by English law.[9] At all events, the bank should not be under an obligation to pay twice; payment to the Development Fund would fully discharge the bank's payment obligations.[10]

46.12   Two final points should be noted:

(a) the position is, of course, different where sanctions have been imposed by a foreign State and do not have a counterpart in English law.[11] Sanctions of this kind will generally have no impact on obligations owed by an English branch and governed by English law;[12] and

(b) it should be appreciated that sanctions imposed by the United Kingdom prohibit the performance of obligations owed by persons in the United Kingdom to targeted States or individuals. However, they do not affect any obligations which the targeted State or individual may owe to a London bank. So far as the English courts are concerned, those obligations would remain enforceable in accordance with their terms.

Conclusions

46.13   A regime of economic sanctions imposed by the United Kingdom will invariably be a matter of high policy. It is therefore unsurprising that compliance is mandatory for UK entities under all circumstances, regardless of the law applicable to any relevant contracts or any other matter.

46.14   It will remain important for the bank both to ensure compliance and to take whatever steps may be necessary to ensure that it does not incur any liability to affected customers.

---

[9] On the governing law and the discharge of obligations, see Chapter 40 above, and, on the expropriation of deposits, see paras 45.18–45.20 above. It is beyond the scope of this work to consider whether such an expropriation could be challenged by reference to the rights of property guaranteed by the European Convention on Human Rights, or the Human Rights Act 1998.

[10] In practice, matters may be more complex and a certain amount of due diligence would be required to ensure that the customer is indeed the person intended to be named on the designated list.

[11] As in the *Libyan Arab Foreign Bank* case discussed in the previous chapter, this may occur where sanctions are imposed in the context of a bilateral dispute which has not justified coordinated action at the United Nations level. In the rare cases in which the payment obligation is not governed by English law, the bank might be placed in some difficulty. It would still be under an obligation to make payment to the Development Council, and an English court would probably still regard this as a valid performance of the obligation by virtue of the 'mandatory rules' provision in Art 9(2) of Rome I. However, the bank would not have discharged the payment obligation according to the law applicable to the contract, and an element of double jeopardy may therefore arise if proceedings are taken in another jurisdiction.

[12] See the discussion in the previous chapter.

47

CUSTOMER OBLIGATIONS AND
FOREIGN LAW

Introduction

The foregoing chapters have considered a variety of private international law issues which **47.01** may affect the banker-customer relationship or the obligation of the bank to repay deposits.

By way of further refinement, the present chapter will examine the effect of foreign law on **47.02** the obligations of the customer to the bank in respect of any facilities extended to it. Laws which may become relevant in this context will again frequently take the form of moratoria or exchange controls.

The subject is addressed because, of course, the enforceability of obligations owed by **47.03** customers is a matter of considerable and obvious importance to English banks. However, the subject matter can be considered relatively briefly because much of the private international groundwork has been laid in the preceding chapters. It will be assumed throughout that the arrangements between the bank and the customer will be governed by English law.[1]

Why are these issues important? Exchange controls and similar laws will be of mandatory **47.04** application in the country concerned, and the borrower will have no choice but to comply with them. It may therefore be impossible for the borrower to instruct its bank to make the necessary payments. It is thus fairly important not to lose sight of this very important

---

[1] This will almost invariably be the case either because (i) the facility agreement will contain an express choice of English law or (ii) English law otherwise applies to the relationship for the reasons given in Chapter 40 above.

practical constraint. It nevertheless remains important to know whether the English courts will continue to regard the debt obligation as valid, because:

(a) The borrower may have given security over assets in England. Can that security still be enforced even though, according to a foreign moratorium law, the underlying debt is not yet due?

(b) Likewise, can the bank exercise a right of set-off over deposits held at the London branch, notwithstanding the moratorium on the payment of the borrower's debts?

(c) What will be the impact of foreign exchange controls so far as the English courts are concerned?

47.05 Against that background, the present chapter considers the following matters:

(a) moratoria,

(b) exchange controls; and

(c) conclusions.

Moratoria

47.06 Occasionally, a State will announce a unilateral moratorium on its foreign debt obligations. This will usually occur in times of serious balance of payments difficulties and will be achieved by legislation or official order, decree, or similar ruling.[2] Obviously, the measures will form a part of the body of law of the State concerned, and would be given effect by its courts in the event of local proceedings.

47.07 In view of the principles discussed earlier in this section, it hardly needs to be stated that such a moratorium cannot vary or discharge an obligation governed by English law.[3] As a result, the English courts would continue to enforce such an obligation according to its original terms.[4]

47.08 The English courts will accordingly treat the debt as due in compliance with the original contractual terms. Assuming that the loan has become due, then:

(a) the bank will be able to exercise any right of set-off in respect of deposits held by it from the borrower; and

(b) the bank may also enforce any security which it may hold over real estate or other assets situate in this country.

47.09 The imposition of the local moratorium will clearly be a significant impediment in obtaining access to the 'home State' assets of the borrower, but it should be possible to obtain an English judgment and to enforce it against assets situate in this country and (possibly) elsewhere.

---

[2] See, for example, the Philippine legislation at issue in the *Wells Fargo* litigation, discussed at para 45.29 above.

[3] Article 12(1)(a) of Rome I, considered at para 40.12 above.

[4] For cases in which the English courts refused to give effect to a foreign moratorium, see *National Bank of Greece and Athens SA v Metliss* [1961] AC 255 (HL) and *Adams v National Bank of Greece SA* [1961] AC 255 (HL). These cases have already been noted at para 45.28 above.

Exchange Controls

It may occasionally be the case that the State in which a borrower is resident will impose **47.10** exchange controls during the period of the loan contract.[5] This will usually require the borrower to obtain official approval in order to make the necessary payment to the lender and/or to purchase the necessary currency at an official (and less favourable) rate.

On the basis that the loan agreement is governed by English law, how should the English **47.11** courts respond to the borrower's arguments that (i) payment should be excused (or at least suspended) because it has been unable to obtain the necessary consent and/or (ii) the contract should be regarded as frustrated or otherwise terminated because the cost of servicing the loan has—in terms of the borrower's home currency—been greatly increased by the need to purchase the relevant foreign currency at the official rate?

Dealing firstly with the effect of the supervening exchange control regime and the need for **47.12** consent:

(a) It has been seen that questions touching the substance of a monetary obligation and its performance are governed by the law applicable to the contract.[6] Since the loan contract is governed by English law, the foreign exchange control regulations do not in principle detract from or otherwise affect the borrower's duty to make payments due under the agreement.

(b) It is true that the English courts may take account of a foreign law which renders payment unlawful in the country in which payment is required to be effected.[7] However, as has been seen, the place of performance of a monetary obligation owed to a bank is the country in which the lending branch is situate. This remains the case even though the loan was made in a foreign currency and the funds necessarily have to be remitted through the clearing system in the issuing State.[8]

(c) Although, of course, the borrower may have to take preparatory steps in its own country in order to make the payment (ie by instructing its local bank to make the necessary transfer), its home country does not thereby become a (or the) place of performance for the purposes of paragraph (b) above.[9] In principle, therefore, the imposition of exchange controls in the borrower's home country does not affect the borrower's obligations under a contract governed by English law.[10] It maybe noted in passing that

---

[5] The present section deals only with supervening exchange controls, on the basis that the parties will have complied with any requirements in effect as at the date on which the contract was originally made.

[6] See para 40.12 above.

[7] See Art 9(3) of Rome I and *Ralli Bros v Compania Naviera Sota y Aznar* [1920] 2 KB 287 (CA).

[8] See the discussion at paras 45.32–45.37 above, noting the decisions in *Libyan Arab Foreign Bank v Bankers Trust Company* [1989] QB 728 and *Citibank, NA v Wells Fargo Asia Ltd* 495 US 660 (1990), and the important distinction between the *place of payment* and the *place of settlement*.

[9] This point was noted in the *Libyan Arab Foreign Bank* case, above.

[10] This conclusion is consistent with the decision in *Kleinwort Sons & Co v Ungarische Baumwolle Industrie AG* [1939] 2 KB 678 (CA). In that case, the defendant was obliged to provide cash cover for bills in London, but Hungarian exchange controls were introduced which prevented it from doing so. It was true that, under the rule in *Ralli Bros v Compania Naviera Sota y Anzar* [1920] 2 KB 287 (CA), payment could not be enforced if this necessarily involved an act which was unlawful in the place of performance. But payment did not

courts in the United States have tended to hold that matters touching the repayment of a bank deposit, or of a loan owing to a bank, are governed by the law of the *situs* of the deposit or obligation, rather than by the law which governs the contract.[11] This point will clearly only be material where the *lex situs* differs from the law applicable to the debt.

47.13 As a secondary matter, can the borrower assert that the English law contract has been frustrated or otherwise terminated as a result of the supervening legislation, which has the effect of significantly increasing its cost of funding the necessary foreign currency payments? This question must be answered in the negative, because:

(a) increased expense is not of itself a ground on which a contract may be said to be frustrated;[12]

(b) a borrower must be held to be absolutely responsible for his own solvency and the unexpected difficulty in acquiring or accessing funds cannot preclude the creditor from obtaining judgment;[13] and

(c) courts in the United States have rightly held that official action which results in a deteriorating exchange rate position does not afford a defence to a creditor's claim.[14]

Conclusions

47.14 It appears safe to conclude that the imposition of a moratorium or the introduction of exchange controls in a foreign borrower's home jurisdiction will not adversely affect the validity of any payment or other obligations which may be governed by English law.

47.15 So far as the English courts are concerned, both the loan agreement itself and any security or guarantee given in respect of that agreement would thus remain enforceable in accordance with the terms of the original documentation. As a result, the main consequences of such legislation are the difficulties of pursuing the borrower for payment within its jurisdiction of incorporation. However, such measures should not in principle affect any attempts at enforcement against assets which are located in another country.

---

necessarily involve any act in Hungary; payment could be made from an account in England or any other jurisdiction.

[11] See *Callejo v Bancomer SA* 764 F 2d 1101 (5th Cir, 1985) and contrast *Allied Bank International v Banco Credito Agricola de Cartago* 757 F 2d 516 (2nd Cir), cert den, 473 US 934 (1985).

[12] The most frequently cited authority for this proposition is *Davis Contractors Ltd v Fareham UDC* [1956] AC 696 (HL).

[13] *Universal Corporation v Five Ways Properties Ltd* [1979] 1 All ER 552 (CA), where a change in Nigerian exchange control regulations caused difficulty for the buyer of a property in completing the purchase when due, because monies held within that country had been its sole source of funding for the transaction. Although the Court of Appeal reversed the first instance judgment on other grounds, it approved the judge's statement that 'quite emphatically, the doctrine of frustration cannot be brought into play merely because the purchaser finds, for whatever reason, that he has not got the money to complete the contract …'.

[14] *Bank of America NT &SA v Envases Venezolanos* 740 F Supp 260 (1990) aff'd 923 F 2d 843 (1990).

PART G

ISLAMIC FINANCE

Introduction

The present section is designed to provide a general description of some of the key features of Islamic Finance.

It is proposed to deal with the subject matter as follows:

(a) Chapter 48 will consider the essential foundations of Islamic finance (eg the well-known prohibition against interest) and some of the product structures which have been developed with a view to Shariah compliance;

(b) Chapter 49 will examine the case law which has thus far become available in the context of transactions which are designed to be Shariah-compliant;

(c) Chapter 50 will consider a variety of corporate and regulatory issues which are specific to the field of Islamic finance; and

(d) Chapter 51 will consider some of the challenges confronting the growth of a truly *international* market in Shariah-compliant finance.

It may be objected that some of these issues should more properly have been dealt with separately in the various chapters dealing with transactional structures and bank regulation. There would be some merit in that view, but it seemed more convenient to seek to provide an overview of the whole subject in a single chapter, especially since the whole subject flows essentially from Shariah principles which need to be described in a cohesive way.

48

ISLAMIC FINANCE—PRINCIPLES AND STRUCTURES

Introduction

As practitioners and others will be aware, the field of Islamic finance has been of growing **48.01** importance in recent years. The desire of Muslim investors to structure their transactions in a manner which appears to be consistent with their faith and Islamic law (in Arabic, the 'Shariah') has been readily embraced by the financial markets. This development is most obviously noted in Muslim countries in the Middle and Far East, but markets based in secular countries have likewise followed this trend.[1]

It should be appreciated that Islamic financial transactions are not, in practice, the sole **48.02** concern of the Muslim community. Banks generally providing 'conventional' loans and other facilities have endeavoured to structure Islamic-compliant products for their Muslim customers, no doubt partly to satisfy demand and partly to forestall the possible loss of business to other institutions. Equally, on the borrower side, non-Muslim entities may

---

[1] London offers a notable example of this trend. This is in part attributable to London's position as a leading international financial centre and in part to the presence of a substantial Muslim population.

structure their funding arrangements in an Islamic compliant manner in order to access the pools of capital controlled by Muslim investors.[2]

48.03 The present chapter considers the foundations of Islamic finance and the product structures which are most frequently encountered in practice.[3]

The Foundations of Islamic Finance

48.04 In the words of an expert witness in an English case,[4] Shariah law is:

> ... the law laid down by the Qu'ran, which is the holy book of Islam, and the Sunnah (the sayings, teachings and actions of Prophet Mohammad (pbuh)). These are the principal sources of the Shariah. The Sunnah is the most important source of the Islamic faith after the Qu'ran and refers essentially to the Prophet's example as indicated by the practice of the faith. The only way to know the Sunnah is through the collection of Ahadith, which consists of reports about the sayings, deeds and reactions of the Prophet ...

48.05 Thus, the principal source of Shariah law is the Qu'ran itself, that is, divine law as revealed to the Prophet. This is supplemented by the Sunnah, which describes the actions of the Prophet, whether by act, word or deed, or by tacit or implicit approval. These matters are known through the Hadith, which are reports of the Prophet's conduct. These are in turn supplemented by secondary sources, namely:

(a) *Ijma'a*, which represents rules reflecting the general consensus of the Islamic community;

(b) *Qiyas*, which refers to the application of previously accepted principles to modern situations; and

(c) *Ijtihad*, which refers to the opinions of Islamic jurists on particular subjects.

48.06 To the lawyer, the difficulty with these formulations is that the Shariah consists of religious rules or concepts on which Muslims are required to base their conduct. It does not create a system of law in the sense of legally valid and binding obligations. This obviously creates difficulties in a purely financial context, since the validity and enforceability of obligations is crucial to both parties. In practice, questions of Shariah law have not generally prevented the enforcement of financial bargains by the courts, although they have given rise to defences which may have delayed the enforcement process.[5] Yet the parties do not enter

---

[2] A prominent example is offered by the *sukuk* bond issue launched by the Government of Japan in 2007.

[3] It should be noted that the literature in this field has naturally grown over the last few years as the market has flourished. Mahmoud A El-Gamal, *Islamic Finance: Law, Economics and Practice* (Cambridge University Press, 2005), hereafter 'El-Gamal', is a very useful and accessible text. It offers an explanation of the key prohibitions and transaction structures. It also deals with insurance and other matters which are essentially outside the scope of the present chapter. For a purely legal text, see *The Encyclopaedia of Banking Law (Islamic Financial Institutions and Islamic Finance)* (LexisNexis, looseleaf) which provides a very valuable guide to the whole subject.

[4] *Beximco Pharmaceuticals Ltd v Shamil Bank of Bahrain EC* [2004] 4 All ER 1072 (CA). The quoted words are taken from para 2 of the judgment, and the case is discussed in more depth at paras 49.08–49.11 below.

[5] See the discussion of the English and Malaysian case law in Chapter 49 below.

into transactions with a view to enforcement proceedings. The starting point for parties to an Islamic finance transaction is that the structure of their arrangements must be Shariah-compliant. The transaction will thus not even come into being unless the Islamic bank and/or the customer are satisfied that the arrangements are indeed compliant in this way.

Turning now to more specific matters, the forbidden forms of financial transaction are essentially driven by four main forms of prohibition, namely, *riba, maisir, gharar,* and unjust enrichment. It is necessary to provide a brief description of these four concepts.[6]   **48.07**

Riba

The prohibition against *riba* is often regarded as one of the cornerstone principles which dictates the forms of structures which are (and which are not) acceptable within the sphere of Islamic finance.   **48.08**

Riba is usually associated with a prohibition against the charging of *interest*, on the basis that money is a medium of exchange; it thus has no independent value and should not be a tradable commodity which is itself capable of being exploited for profit. Thus, it has been explained that money:[7]   **48.09**

> … only reflects the value of goods … money should not be created just because its very existence should create a demand for it, but rather it should be used for the procurement of other goods …
>
> Money has been created so as to be a measure of value and an instrument for exchange. Money itself has no intrinsic value. Had it an intrinsic value, it could not have played its role as money and would have become like other commodities …
>
> Hoarding of money, as well as collecting riba on money, means man has turned money into something desirable for its own sake. 'Riba' denotes that man is trying to 'create' money through the medium of money itself, to earn more money with less money …

In other words, since money has no independent value and has a limited role in society, it is unacceptable to use it as a self-standing means of money-making. Yet it seems to be at least arguable that *riba* and (prohibited) interest are not entirely synonymous.[8]   **48.10**

The word *riba* is derived from an Arabic word which means 'to increase'.[9] Jurists thus originally seem to have applied the term to trading in goods, where the resale price was excessive and did not represent a fair compensation for the trader's efforts. In other words, it may be said that a fair and honourable reward for one's work is permitted (or *halal*) but an excessive return is prohibited (or *haram*). Of course, this distinction may be difficult to draw in practice.   **48.11**

---

[6] It should be noted that the prohibitions laid down by Islamic law may be viewed as paternalistic, shielding adherents from potentially damaging and addictive behaviour. It is, for example, well known that pork, alcohol, and gambling are prohibited; these are absolute since neither can be viewed as one of life's necessities. The prohibition against *riba* is likewise paternalistic, in the sense that it prevents an individual from living beyond his means; yet this prohibition is more complex, since contact with the financial markets cannot be avoided in the modern world. See El-Gamal, p 46.

[7] See Thomas, Cox, and Bryan, *Structuring Islamic Finance Transactions* (Euromoney, 2005) p 8, quoting earlier sources.

[8] The discussion in the present paragraph relies heavily on El-Gamal, pp 49–57.

[9] The expression is alternatively translated as 'excess'.

48.12   The first references in the Qur'an itself discouraged *riba;* the text reads,[10] 'That which you lend to increase in the property of others will not increase with God, but that which you give out in charity, seeking God's pleasure, it will surely multiply'. Two points may be noted here. First of all, the prohibition does not seem to be restricted to the charging of interest (the rule most closely associated with *riba*), but appears to address any form of exploitation of others. Secondly, there is clear disapproval but no explicit prohibition. Later verses[11] deal specifically with interest but it may be argued that this only prohibits the charging of interest on debts which are overdue, and to the subsequent compounding of that interest; this would not ban the collection of 'ordinary' interest. Some of the final verses[12] do explicitly prohibit *riba* and require Muslims to abandon the practice. However, it is not totally clear whether the explicit prohibition refers to the wider, 'exploitative' form of the practice or to the narrower form which is perhaps closer to an interest prohibition.[13] Nevertheless, the modern approach seems to be to prohibit all forms of interest-bearing loans as *riba*,[14] even though some of the products which are accepted to be Islamic-compliant necessarily include a mark-up element which some may regard as equivalent to interest.[15] It may be noted that, in a 1999 judgment frequently described as 'historic', the Shariah Appellate Bench of the Supreme Court of Pakistan adopted a very wide-ranging definition of *riba*, remarking that '… any additional amount over the principal in a contract of loan or debt is *Riba*, prohibited by the Holy Qur'an in several verses. The Holy Prophet (PBUH) has also termed the following transactions as *Riba* … A transaction of money for money of the same denomination where the quantity on both sides is not equal, either in a spot transaction or in a transaction based on deferred payment …' Such a transaction would be *riba* '… whether the additional amount stipulated over the principal amount of the loan or debt is large or small …'.[16] The result of this decision was that all legislation in Pakistan allowing

---

[10]   Makka, 30,39.

[11]   Sura, 3:130. The translation referred to in the *Shamil Bank* case (para 3), reads: 'O Ye who believe, devour not interest, for it goes on multiplying itself; and be mindful of your obligation to Allah that you may prosper.'

[12]   Sura, 2:275–9.

[13]   It is noteworthy that a conference of the Islamic Research Institute (Cairo, 1965), recorded that 'Interest on any type of loan is considered forbidden *riba*': El-Gamal, p 145. The statement suggests that interest is merely considered as one form of *riba*, so that the concept must have a greater width.

[14]   In line with the issues discussed in this section, it should be noted that Islamic principles reject the notion of interest in the sense that it must be calculated and paid at a pre-determined rate regardless of the customer's success in the business venture concerned. However, it does not totally reject the idea that money may have a time value; a financier may stipulate for a return which will be calculated at a later date by reference to the success of the venture. In other words, it is legitimate to *invest*, but not to *lend*. On the whole subject, see Thani et al, 'Law and Practice of Islamic Banking and Finance' (Sweet & Maxwell, 2003) p 35. In very broad terms, it follows that conventional *debt* financing is incompatible with Islamic principles. On the other hand, scholars appear to have little difficulty with *equity* funding, where the financier does not take a pre-determined return but instead shares in the hazards and rewards of the venture.

[15]   See in particular the discussion of the *murabaha* (credit sale) and *ijara* (lease financing), considered at paras 48.26–48.31 and paras 48.38–48.40 below. The distinction between a trading profit and interest is sometimes difficult to draw, with the result that some scholars have condemned certain structures as involving *riba*, whilst others have approved the same transactions.

[16]   *M Islam Khaki & Others v Syed Muhammad Hashim & Others* PLD 2000 (Supreme Court 225) at paras 242 and 245. The court also rejected (at para 245) an attempt to uphold the validity of interest-bearing loans on the basis that they were a necessity in modern financial systems. The decision is discussed by Blair, Walker, and Purves, para 19.25.

for conventional banking and the payment of interest was declared unconstitutional. This judgment remains influential in the development of an Islamic banking system and is often quoted, even though the formal decision was later quashed by the same court and remitted for rehearing by the Federal Shariah Court—in part on the basis that some of the interpretations of the Qu'ran adopted in the original decision were controversial.[17]

As noted above, *riba* is generally associated with a prohibition against interest. But it should **48.13** not be thought that the principle is necessarily limited to that sphere. For example, commitment commissions are often charged by conventional banks[18] as the price of keeping open a line of credit for a pre-agreed period. This cannot be regarded as interest in a conventional sense, since this involves no payment by reference to the time value of money; to the contrary, it is an *availability* charge, rather than a *usage* charge. Nevertheless, such a commission must be regarded as *riba,* since the charge is designed purely to secure the availability of money. Equally, banks will often charge up-front arrangement fees for the provision of a facility. These may pose slightly more difficulty in the present context. To the extent to which the arrangement fee represents a charge for providing money, it seems clear that this, too, would have to be treated as *riba.* However, there is no objection to a bank receiving payment for *services* which it has provided to the customer. Thus, the fee would be acceptable to the extent to which it represents the work actually done by the bank in bringing the facility to fruition, for example, by developing an appropriate transaction structure and selling the transaction to other syndicate members, where applicable. Likewise, penalties or other charges linked to late payment by the customer will often be regarded as *riba,* at least to the extent to which they exceed the *actual* losses and costs suffered by the bank as a consequence of the default. The prohibition thus has a wider impact than a ban on interest in its simplest sense.

The inability of an Islamic institution to charge for the use of money means that particular **48.14** structures have had to be developed to accommodate this principle. These are discussed below but, in very broad terms, it will be seen that the bank has to have a more intimate involvement in, and exposure to, the underlying transaction than would be the case for a conventional institution, where the contractual obligation to repay and to pay interest will be entirely divorced from the success of the underlying transaction or project.[19]

Gharar

The concept of *gharar* connotes a transaction based on incomplete information (or decep- **48.15** tion) and which incorporates an unnecessary degree of risk and/or uncertainty.[20] The rule

---

[17] *United Bank Ltd v Farooq Brothers* (24 June 2002, Civil Shariah Review No 1 of 2001).
[18] Commitment commission is generally chargeable on the undrawn balance of a facility and is designed to compensate a bank for: (i) the capital cost involved in a committed facility; and (ii) the fact that it is obliged to forego other opportunities because funding is earmarked for the borrower. On commitment commission, see generally para 20.28 above.
[19] The most obvious example is offered by the *ijara* lease, where the bank provides property in return for a rental income, rather than a loan at interest. The latter is plainly *haram,* but the former is *halal* because the bank is receiving payment in return for the provision of a service. On *ijara* leasing structures, see paras 48.38–48.40 below.
[20] *Gharar* is usually translated as 'uncertainty'.

applies to commercial transactions involving unquantifiable risks.[21] Thus, whilst *riba* prevents an individual from borrowing beyond his means, *gharar* ensures that he will not use his resources to pay for products which are unnecessary and which may have an uncertain value. The rule appears to have its philosophical basis in justice and fair dealing.[22] Contractual uncertainty is not permitted because the outcome of the uncertain event—or its occurrence or non-occurrence—may result in the unjust enrichment of one party to the unfair detriment of the other.[23]

48.16　However, not everything in life is certain and, in particular, the future is almost by definition uncertain. Consequently, there must be some boundaries to the application of this principle. Thus, it would appear that *gharar* will only invalidate[24] a contract if (i) the risk or uncertainty is significant, (ii) the risk affects the price or the principal objective of the contract (and not merely some minor or ancillary aspect), and (iii) the risk cannot be satisfactorily addressed through other available products which are Islamic-compliant.

48.17　It is thus perhaps understandable that the principle of *gharar* has been found to invalidate commercial insurance contracts, where a premium is paid against an event which is uncertain and (even if it occurs) may cause a loss which is not ascertainable at the outset.[25] Derivatives and options trading have been found to be objectionable on the same basis. Nevertheless, the market continues to break new ground, and a joint effort between the International Islamic Financial Market and the International Swaps and Derivatives Association (ISDA) has resulted in the production of Shariah-compliant derivatives documentation.[26] It may be argued that a derivatives contract used for genuine hedging purposes should not offend this principle, on the basis that such a contract is designed to *reduce or manage* future uncertainty in relation to other contracts (eg relating to the price of commodities).

48.18　Contracts of luck or chance are also prohibited under this heading. Thus, the Court of Cassation in Abu Dhabi held spot and forward foreign exchange contracts to be invalid, in part on the basis that the contracts where *gharar* and, hence, contrary to Shariah law. The court noted that 'the intention of both parties was to generate profit from the fluctuation of the various currencies. They would not know the result of their speculation until the contracts were closed. When the subject of a transaction is not assessed or known to

---

[21] The present discussion draws on El-Gamal, pp 58–63.

[22] 'Do not consume one another's wealth unjustly, and be aware that lawful gain should be only through business based on mutual consent among you, and to not destroy one another': Sura, 4:29.

[23] On unjust enrichment as an independent concept, see para 48.20 below.

[24] It should be appreciated that references to 'invalidate' and similar expressions used in this context refer to the position under Shariah law. The same consequences would generally not follow in the case of court proceedings, where the transaction will be enforced according to the national law applicable to it. On this subject, see Chapter 49 below.

[25] Shariah-compliant insurance has been developed through a cooperative structure known as *takaful*. Insurance products are, however, beyond the scope of this text and the point is mentioned purely for the sake of completeness.

[26] See the ISDA/IIMF Ta' Hawwat Master Agreement, published on the ISDA website (www.isda.org).

either party and is based partially on luck, it is very misleading. They become … illegal bets …'.[27]

Maisir

Maisir[28] refers to speculative or gambling contracts, which are to be regarded as unenforce- **48.19** able. Whilst any commercial contract inevitably involves a degree of speculation, the prohibition applies to contracts where the *outcome* depends on luck or chance. Islamic law thus prohibits gambling contracts under this heading.[29] The expression 'speculation' must not, however, be read too widely for these purposes. Any business venture involves a degree of speculation, but the outcome is not governed purely by luck. In the financial markets, swap and derivative transactions would again clearly require consideration against this principle.[30]

Unjust Enrichment

A person must not unjustly enrich himself at the expense of another person. As a result, a **48.20** contract which is unfair or which is imposed (eg under duress) on a weaker counterparty to his detriment will not be Shariah-compliant. The authority usually quoted reads,[31]'Deal not unjustly and you shall not be dealt with unjustly'.

Thus, for example, a fee or penalty imposed for late payment will often constitute unjust **48.21** enrichment, since it is exploitative of the debtor's difficulties. In practice, such penalties may be imposed in order to provide an incentive to the debtor for timely performance, but on the basis that the creditor may only recoup actual losses flowing from late payment, and any excess will be donated to a suitable charity.

Rules Governing Islamic Finance Transactions

It will be appreciated from the foregoing discussion that Islamic principles are not a system **48.22** of law, in the sense which the common lawyer would understand that term. Rather, they are a set of principles drawn from the Qu'ran and other sources. There is no single, high authority which has the power to give binding rulings on the effect of these principles in particular cases. The process involves the sometimes difficult task of applying principles formulated many centuries ago to the modern economy and its financial markets. For these reasons, there is naturally scope for disagreement between different scholars and different schools; attitudes may also vary from country to country.[32]

---

[27] Abu Dhabi Court of Cassation judgment no 158 & 208/18, reported in Price and Tamimi, *United Arab Emirates Court of Cassation Judgments 1989–1997* (Kluwer Law International, 1998), p 23, noted by Blair, Walker, and Purves, para 19.28. It should be said that gambling contracts are more frequently categorized as *maisir* (below).

[28] The expression *Qimar* is also sometimes used and appears to have an identical meaning.

[29] They may also be regarded as prohibited on the basis that they are uncertain or *gharar* (see above).

[30] See the preceding footnote.

[31] Sura, 279.

[32] El-Gamal, p 198, notes eight main schools of jurisprudence and their geographical dominance as follows: (i) the Hanafi school (India, Pakistan, Afghanistan), (ii) the Maliki school (upper Egypt and Africa), (iii) the Shafi'i school (lower Egypt, the Levant, Malaysia), (iv) the Hanbali school (countries within the Gulf

48.23 In practice, therefore, a bank which offers Islamic-compliant products will establish its own Religious Board or Committee which will advise management on Shariah issues associated with the products which it offers to its customers.[33] This state of affairs inevitably limits the ability of a court to issue rulings on products which are intended to be Shariah compliant.[34] However, this is not to imply that no efforts have been made, and the leads given by certain organizations may, in the longer run, help to produce a degree of harmony and coordination. For example, the Shariah Advisory Council of the Central Bank of Malaysia (Bank Negara Malaysia) has addressed this issue by publishing centrally approved Shariah standards for Islamic financial transactions.[35] In terms of any legal proceedings which have an Islamic financial aspect, the court or arbitrator is required to take account of the published rulings of the Council, and may refer the relevant question to the Shariah Advisory Council for a ruling.[36] Likewise, the State Bank of Pakistan has established a Shariah Board which has issued both guidelines and required forms of contractual documentation. In addition, the Accounting and Auditing Organisation for Islamic Financial Institutions (AAOIFI) has published the rulings of its own Shariah Board on various products.[37] The Islamic Financial Services Board (IFSB) is headquartered in Kuala Lumpur, Malaysia. It has not generally sought to publish Shariah standards but has rather tended to focus on issues such as the application of capital adequacy standards to Islamic institutions, transparency, governance, and similar matters.[38]

48.24 It is necessary to consider one final point of a general nature before moving on to consider more detailed matters. A conventional bank makes money by providing funds and thus

---

Cooperation Council), (v) the Zahiri school (relatively few modern adherents), (vi) the Ja'fari school (Iraq, Iran), (vii) the Zaydi school (no particular geographical dominance), and (viii) the Ibadi school (Oman, north/east Africa).

[33] Individual products or transactions may be approved by the issue of a certificate or *fatwa* (plural, *fatawa*). The financial statements of an Islamic financial institution may include a statement by this Board to confirm that its business has been conducted in compliance with Islamic principles. For further discussion of Shariah boards of this kind, see paras 50.08–50.12 below.

[34] Indeed, this approach to the matter was one of the grounds for the decision in *Beximco Pharmaceuticals Ltd v Shamil Bank of Bahrain EC* [2004] 4 All ER 1079; see paras 7 and 41 of the judgment. This and other case law is discussed in further detail in Chapter 49 below.

[35] The Central Bank of Malaysia Act 1958 was amended in 2003 in order to confer on the Shariah Advisory Council the status of the sole authoritative body on questions touching the Islamic financial markets in Malaysia. The position, status, and role of the Shariah Advisory Council are now governed by ss 51–58 of the Central Bank of Malaysia Act 2009. The Council is described as 'the authority for the ascertainment of Islamic law for the purpose of Islamic financial business ...' and, accordingly, its rulings prevail over any inconsistent decisions by the Shariah board or committee of an individual Islamic financial institution (see ss 51 and 58 of the 2009 Act). The Central Bank itself is obliged to consult the Council on matters relating to Islamic finance business, and any Islamic financial institution can also seek guidance or a ruling from the Council: see s 55 of the 2009 Act. It may be noted that other countries have sought to adopt a similar approach. For example, the Indonesian National Shariah Board was established in 1999. It is recognized by Bank Indonesia and has issued rulings on a number of products.

[36] Section 56 of the Central Bank of Malaysia Act 2009. Any such ruling is binding on the court or arbitrator by virtue of s 57 of that Act.

[37] See 'Shari'a Standards' published by AAOIFI as at May 2003 (hereafter 'Shariah Standards'). Some countries (including Bahrain, Sudan, and Syria) have adopted AAOIFI rulings as part of their own regulations, whilst other countries have used them as a guideline in formulating their own regulatory frameworks.

[38] In the writer's view, this is one of the factors which inhibits the emergence of a truly *international* market in *Shariah*-compliant products: see the discussion in Chapter 51 below.

makes 'money on money'. This type of arrangement is, of course, prohibited as *riba* on the basis of the principles discussed earlier. So how does an Islamic bank justify its income and profits? In essence, it does so by providing assets or services, and/or by taking a risk on assets. The Shariah allows profit for labour or for the taking of risk, but not merely for the use of money. As a result, it will be seen that Shariah-compliant products depend for their validity on the sale of assets or the receipt of rent for the use or occupation of property or other assets. These are the core features which shape the structures of the Shariah-compliant products which are about to be considered.

Product Structures—Customer Funding

Against this background, it is possible to examine some of the structures which have been developed for Islamic-compliant financial products.[39] They depend essentially on the Qur'anic verse to the effect that, whilst God has prohibited *riba*, trade remains permissible.[40] In other words, whilst the charging of interest for the use of money is prohibited,[41] the realization of profits is allowed *in the context of a wider trading transaction or venture.*[42] Islamic-compliant financial products thus tend to rely upon the use of physical assets and/or may involve the lender in a degree of responsibility or risk in the transaction concerned.[43] In essence, a compliant product will involve one of the following characteristics: **48.25**

(a) the sale of an asset on deferred terms, with a pre-agreed profit mark-up;[44]
(b) the provision of assets for use by the customer at a rental charge;[45] or
(c) the sharing of profits from a joint venture or similar arrangement.[46]

Murabaha

In a *murabaha* transaction, the parties agree to trade an asset or assets at a price equal to the original acquisition cost plus a mark-up. **48.26**

---

[39] It should be emphasized that the discussion below is selective and is designed only to provide an overview of some of the more common structures, using them to describe the features which render a product Islamic-compliant.

[40] Sura, 2:275.

[41] This simplified expression of the principle should be read in the light of the discussion of *riba*, above.

[42] It should be added that Islamic-compliant structures may not be used to finance business activities which are themselves incompatible with Islam (eg the manufacture or sale of alcohol, pork products, the provision of conventional banking products, gambling, and pornography, amongst others).

[43] That is to say, a degree of risk going beyond the loss of the principal and charges involved in the transaction. Since transactions may involve ownership of the relevant assets by the financier and given the risks which may be associated with ownership, the assets concerned are often acquired and held through the medium of a special purpose vehicle (ie in order to insulate the bank itself from some of the wider risks which may be involved). This is consistent with the Prophet's statement that 'profits are justified for the one bearing liability for losses...': El-Gamal, p 145. According to the expert evidence placed before the court in the *Symphony Gems* case (see para 49.04 below), the financier must accept responsibility for any subsequent defect discovered in the goods, and for their loss.

[44] See, for example, the discussions below in relation to the *murabah, tawarruq, bai' salam* and *Bai' al 'ina* products.

[45] See, for example, the discussion of the *ijara* and *istisna'a* products, below.

[46] See the discussion of the *musharaka* and *mudaraba* products, below.

48.27   In a typical case,[47] the bank or lender will agree to sell an asset to its customer at a set price plus a mark-up. Thus, the bank may purchase an asset from the intending supplier and agree to sell it to its customer by instalment payments over an extended period. Prevailing opinion requires that the bank must be the owner of the asset before it can agree to resell it. Although the rate of return may be linked to interest rates, the rate of return earned by the bank is not purely an interest return, since it runs the risks involved in ownership of the asset (even if only for a brief period), for example, the risk of loss or destruction and the risk that the customer may return the asset and claim a refund if the assets are defective in any way.[48] These risks effectively flow from the 'trading' relationship as buyer/seller of the assets, as opposed to the conventional structure of the secured lender/borrower relationship.[49] In practice, however, these risks are minimized because the purchase of the assets by the bank and their resale to the customer will occur almost simultaneously.

48.28   The structure is accordingly in popular use for the financing of import transactions. Various detailed criteria must be met in order to validate the transaction from a Shariah perspective. In particular, (i) the object of the sale must exist at the time of the transaction,[50] (ii) the seller must have a valid title to, and possession of,[51] that object, (iii) there must be certainty of price,[52] and (iv) the object must be permissible (or *halal*) in Shariah terms.[53]

48.29   How does this structure translate into a financing context? Of course, the bank will not generally be in the business of buying and selling goods. It will not possess the necessary expertise and may have only limited familiarity with the customer's business. Consequently, the bank will usually appoint the customer as its agent for the purpose of selecting, inspecting, ordering, and taking possession of the goods. For reasons which will become apparent later,[54] it may be helpful to note that another product—*al bai bithaman ajil*—also works on the basis of a deferred sale price and displays features which are in many respects essentially similar to the *murabaha*.

---

[47]   In a retail banking context, the structure is frequently used as a substitute for conventional mortgage lending.

[48]   In practice, the documentation will seek to restrict or disclaim any warranties on the part of the bank in relation to the goods; this was the situation in the *Beximco* case, discussed at para 49.08 below. It is not easy to reconcile provisions of this kind with the requirement that the financier must take some real risk or interest in the goods which form the subject matter of the arrangements.

[49]   Since a secured lender does not become the owner of the assets, he does not run the ownership risks described in the text. For a discussion of the merits of this approach to the matter, see El-Gamal, pp 67–8.

[50]   Otherwise, the transaction is uncertain or *gharar*.

[51]   The requirement for certainty of object includes a requirement that the seller must have it in his power to deliver the goods. It is generally thought (although not universally accepted) that both actual and constructive possession are sufficient for these purposes. On the subject generally, see Shariah Standard No 18, Possession (*Qabd*).

[52]   It appears that there is sufficient certainty if the mode of calculation is clear, even if the actual amount is not. This is necessary to accommodate the cases—frequently encountered in practice—where the periodic instalments vary by reference to LIBOR or a selected index. The reference to LIBOR may seem odd in the context of a transaction which is intended to be Shariah-compliant. But the use of an interest-based index or benchmark for *calculation* purposes appears to be unobjectionable provided that the transaction does not itself involve the *payment* of interest.

[53]   On items which are prohibited (or *haram*), see n 6 above.

[54]   See the discussion of the Malaysian case law at paras 49.21–49.38 below.

One of the difficulties with this type of transaction is the possible duplication of transfer **48.30** taxes, since the structure involves sequential transfers of the same asset. Obviously, this issue depends both upon the type of asset involved and the jurisdiction in which it occurs, since the tax laws of that country will determine any relevant duties or charges. So far as the United Kingdom is concerned, the potential double stamp duty charge in relation to a real estate transaction is eliminated by section 73 of the Finance Act 2003. This was in line with this country's policy of placing conventional and Islamic structures on the same footing in terms of cost.

In order to ensure that conventional and Islamic structures can compete on the same foot- **48.31** ing, the tax treatment of the financier's profit or mark-up is generally placed on the same footing as an interest receipt.[55]

Tawarruq

The *tawarruq* is a variation on the *murabaha* structure.[56] This is an essentially tripartite **48.32** arrangement which enables a customer to raise Shariah-compliant funding even though it has no immediate need to acquire particular assets.

As in a *murabaha* transaction, the financier will purchase an asset from the supplier and **48.33** immediately resell it to the customer on deferred payment terms. The customer will then resell the asset to a third party who has need of it and is able to pay in full on delivery. The customer will thus be in possession of the capital sum which it required, and will owe the deferred instalments to the financier.

The *tawarruq* structure is a popular means of providing interbank funding as between **48.34** Islamic financial institutions. To aid that process, the International Islamic Financial Market published standard, commodity *murabaha* documentation in January 2009.[57]

Bai' Salam

A *bai' salam* (or, simply, *salam*) involves the purchase of goods for future delivery, where **48.35** payment is made in advance. The bank will thus pay a discounted price for goods and, when they are delivered at a later date, will resell them either to the customer or to a third party. It appears to be permissible for the bank to enter into 'back to back' contracts for these purposes, at least provided that they are not each conditional on the execution of the other agreement. This structure is unusual in the sense that a seller may not normally sell goods which do not exist and must also be in possession of the goods at the time of the contract. Under a *bai' salam*, it is sufficient if the goods are fungible and readily available in the market.[58]

---

[55] Sections 47–50 of the Finance Act 2005.
[56] It is often referred to as a 'reverse *murabaha*' or 'commodity *murabaha*'.
[57] The standard documents are available on IIFM's website (www.iifm.net) and include: (i) a structure memorandum, (ii) a master murabaha agreement, (iii) a master agency agreement for the purchase of commodities, and (iv) a commodity purchase letter of understanding.
[58] For the rules applicable to this type of structure, see Shariah Standard No 10.

Bai' al 'ina

48.36 A *bai' al 'ina* is a structure that involves the sale of an asset by the customer to the bank for immediate payment. The customer then agrees to repurchase the asset at a later date and at a higher price, possibly payable by instalments. The differential represents the bank's profit on the transaction.

48.37 The net result of such an arrangement is that the customer receives a cash sum on the date on which the contract is made, with an obligation to pay a higher sum to the bank at a later date. As a result, the structure is the subject of some controversy. The *bai' al 'ina* finds favour in Malaysia,[59] but is generally disapproved by scholars in the Middle East.

Ijara

48.38 *Ijara* is a form of leasing structure.[60] The lease rental payments for the asset concerned will include the financier's required margin of profit.

48.39 Whilst in some respects comparable to a traditional form of finance lease, it should be noted that payments under an *ijara* can only continue whilst the customer has the use of the asset. Consequently, if the asset is lost, stolen, or destroyed, then the obligation to pay rent must terminate. An *ijara* contract must terminate on destruction of the subject matter, and the contract may not validly stipulate that the rental payments must continue under such circumstances.[61] This follows from the fact that the lessor cannot pass the entire risk of the asset to the lessee. The financier may thus have to rely on receipt of insurance proceeds in this type of situation, but that is perhaps consistent with the requirement that the financier must take a broader asset-based risk than may be the case in conventional forms of finance.[62] In spite of these principles, the rental may continue if the loss of the asset is due to the negligence of the lessee, and he may be made liable to compensate the lessor under those circumstances.[63]

48.40 A variety of other issues may arise in the context of an *ijara* lease:

(a) Where the relevant asset is expected to have a residual value at the end of the lease term,[64] it will be necessary both for the bank to know that the customer is obliged to re-take the asset, and for the customer to know that he is entitled to it. This will usually be achieved through the means of a put and call option. In general terms, the customer will have the right to call for the transfer of the asset to it at the end of the lease term,

---

[59] See the rulings of the National Shariah Advisory Council established by bank Negara Malaysia under s 51 of the Central Bank of Malaysia Act 2009 and predecessor legislation (see para 48.23 above).

[60] If title is to pass to the customer at the end of the transaction, then it is known as *ijara wa-iktina* and is in many respects similar to a conventional hire purchase transaction.

[61] Shariah Standard No 9, para 7.1.3.

[62] In a conventional form of finance lease, the risk in the asset is passed to the customer by means of 'hell and high water' clauses, which require the customer to continue paying the rent even though the asset may have become a total loss—at least until the insurance proceeds are settled and the transaction can be fully closed out of the proceeds.

[63] On these points, see Shariah Standard No 9, paras 5.1.4, 5.1.6, and 7.1.4.

[64] This will obviously be the case in the context of real estate, but may also be the case for equipment and other leases.

subject to payment of the pre-agreed price. The bank will have a corresponding right to put the asset to the customer, both at the end of the lease term and in the event of the occurrence of an earlier default. A failure to pay in any on any of these eventualities will entitle the bank to sell the property to recover its initial outlay in purchasing the property.[65] If, for any reason, the bank is tardy in performing its own obligations to the customer pursuant to the put and call agreement, it appears that the bank cannot charge rent during the period of the delay even thought the borrower has had physical possession of the property throughout the period of delay.[66]

(b) It is permissible to use the *ijara* structure for a sale and leaseback transaction, where the customer is the initial owner of the asset in question. However, some additional care is necessary in such transactions to ensure that the bank is not seen merely to be purchasing the benefit of the cash flow arising from the lease.[67] In particular, the lease itself should not be executed until the bank has become the owner of the asset, and it is not permissible for the two transactions to be contractually linked. In other words, the execution of the lease cannot be a condition of the sale and purchase agreement.[68]

(c) It is recognized that the cost of funding the facility may vary from time to time. Accordingly, whilst the amount of the rental instalment for the first period should generally be stipulated in the lease itself, it is permissible for subsequent instalments to vary by reference to a clear and indisputable formula.[69] In such a case, the rental should be stated to be subject to maximum and minimum levels.[70] It is thus not uncommon to find that the rental under an *ijara* lease is variable by reference to LIBOR or a similar benchmark.

(d) The lessor may not stipulate for an increased payment as a result of late payment of the rent. This would amount to *riba*, and would hence be prohibited. In practice, these contracts do occasionally provide some form of penalty for late payment, on the footing that the lessor will retain compensation for his actual loss flowing from the breach and donate any balance to an appropriate charitable cause.[71]

---

[65] In conventional terms, this is equivalent to acceleration of the facility and enforcement of the security. So far as English law is concerned, there seems to be little doubt that such arrangements would be enforceable, especially in view of the case law discussed at paras 49.04–49.19 below. However, the difficulty with the put and call arrangements is that the entire structure does begin to look closer to a secured loan. For this reason, some scholars prefer that there should be a put option or a call option, but not both. At least, it is common for the put and call options to be documented by means of separate and independent agreements.

[66] Likewise, if the lessor delays in handing over possession at the start of the lease, no rent can be charged until possession is given, regardless of the terms of the lease itself: see Shariah Standard No 9, para 4.1.3.

[67] As a dealing in 'money', this would not be permissible. Indeed, some Shariah scholars object to *ijara* contracts concluded on a 'master' basis and intended to be used for a series of assets up to a facility limit, since this suggests a disconnection from the underlying assets and, hence, a transaction concerned principally with monetary obligations.

[68] See Shariah Standard No 9, paras 3.1 and 3.2.

[69] If the variations are at the discretion of the lessor or were otherwise uncertain, then this might infringe the principle discussed at para 48.15 above (*gharar*).

[70] Shariah Standard No 9, para 5.2.3.

[71] On these rules, see Shariah Standard No 9, paras 6.3 and 6.4. The general prohibition against late payment penalties (*riba*) will of course apply equally to other products. The 'actual loss' referred to in the text would include collection costs and similar expenses, but would not include funding costs.

(e) Although payment penalties are of doubtful validity, the lessor may retain other, non-monetary remedies in the event of a payment default or other breaches of the agreement, for example, the right to terminate the *ijara* lease[72] and to enforce any other security provided in connection with the rental payment obligation.[73]

(f) There appears to be no, Shariah-based objection to the taking of additional cover by means of (i) guarantees from companies affiliated to the customer or (ii) other forms of security such as an assignment of income or a charge over a bank account.[74]

(g) Although enforcement is permitted by the sale of the asset, the lessor can only recover past due rent. It cannot recover instalments falling due at a later date. However, the lessor can also recover any '… legitimate compensations …' necessitated by the lessee's breach of contract …'. This would seem to mean that, if rental values have fallen the lessor would be entitled to recover the shortfall or differential for the remaining period of the lease.[75] This would appear to be appropriate since the calculation must reflect an actual loss, and is not in the nature of a penalty.

(h) Since the lessor cannot pass the entire burden of the property to the lessee, the lessor must retain responsibility for the maintenance of the asset, at least so far as major items are concerned.[76] It is, however, permissible for the lessor to appoint the lessee as its agent for such purposes. The lessee will be entitled to recover the costs involved via an agency agreement, but the lessor in turn may recover the corresponding costs from the lessee.[77]

(i) Since the lessor must retain the risk of the asset concerned, the lessee will not be liable in the event of its loss or destruction, unless this is due to the lessee's own misconduct. The lessor must therefore ensure that the property is adequately insured. It is common practice for the lessor to seek to recover the cost of the premia, either via the agency agreement or through the cost of the financing. It must be doubtful whether this is genuinely permissible, since it merely passes the risk of the property back to the lessee via a different route.[78]

(j) As in the case of other products, the facility must not be used to finance or promote activities which are *haram* or prohibited (eg gambling or the sale of alcohol). This may pose particular problems in the real estate sector where, for example, a hotel provides services which are mostly permitted, but also runs a bar or offers alcohol with meals.[79] This difficulty is often addressed by providing for the profits associated with those activities to be donated to an appropriate charity.

---

[72] Shariah Standard No 9, para 7.2.2.
[73] Shariah Standard No 9, para 6.1.
[74] See Shariah Standard No 9, para 6.1.
[75] On these points, see Shariah Standard No 9, para 6.5.
[76] Shariah Standard No 9, para 5.1.7.
[77] This type of arrangement appears to be consistent with Shariah Standard No 9, paras 5.1.7 and 5.2.4.
[78] On this point, see Jabbar, 'Shariah Compliant Financial Instruments—Principles and Practice' (2009) Company Lawyer 176.
[79] Where the *ijara* facility is provided by an Islamic bank, this rule must be observed even though the lessee is a non-Muslim: see Shariah Standard No 9, paras 5.1.1 and 5.1.3.

(k) In line with the UK policy of placing conventional and Shariah-compliant products on the same footing, the potential double charge to stamp duty arising in relation to *ijara* transactions for real estate has been eliminated.[80]

Istisna'a

An *istisna'a* is the structure generally used for major capital projects or assets (eg for the acquisition of a ship or aircraft), or to finance the manufacture and sale of goods. **48.41**

Generally speaking, the financier will provide finance to the intending supplier in order to enable it to complete the project or manufacture the asset. The financier will then take title on completion and will then sell or lease the asset to the end-user by means of one of the alternative products already described. **48.42**

Musharaka

Once again, the *musharaka* is generally used to finance the acquisition of an asset or a particular project or business venture. **48.43**

In effect, the financier enters into a partnership with the customer[81] under which losses must be borne pro rata to their respective investments but profits may be divided according to agreement. The arrangements will thus entitle the financier to a share of profits representing its original facility plus its mark-up. Although there will be a principal financier, the *musharaka* generally involves some financial contribution from both parties.[82] **48.44**

Musharaka have traditionally been seen in two forms. The first—*sharika mulk*—involves the joint ownership of property (eg such as a house or place of residence) without a view to profit or exploitation. The second—*sharika 'aqd*—connotes a contractual partnership with a view to business profits.[83] However, a relatively new development is the *musharaka muntahia bitamleek*, or diminishing partnership. Under this structure, the financier invests in the customer's business, on the basis that the customer will progressively buy out the financier's share over a period. This has been used in home mortgage finance, where the profit earned by the bank effectively represents rental income,[84] and the customer is required to purchase the bank's share by instalments over a period. The structure thus replicates the effect of a conventional mortgage, but in a Shariah-compliant fashion. **48.45**

---

[80] Sections 71–73 of the Finance Act 2003. The double charge would otherwise arise from the fact that: (i) the bank takes a transfer of the land from the vendor, and (ii) the bank will later execute a transfer of the land to the customer.

[81] Although a partnership in some respects, the customer will usually be solely responsible for the management of the funds so as to produce the necessary returns.

[82] Contrast the position in relation to a *mudaraba*, below, where the manager may be contributing his work and expertise, but not his finance.

[83] On these points, see Jabbar, 'Shariah Compliant Financial Instruments—Principles and Practice' (2009) Company Lawyer 176.

[84] ie it cannot be regarded as *riba*, and hence is not *haram*.

Mudaraba

48.46   A *mudaraba*—variously translated as a 'profit-sharing partnership' or 'equity sharing'—may be compared to an investment fund or similar conventional product.[85] In essence, one or a group of investors (*rab al maal*) pool their resources for a given business venture under the management of a fund administrator or manger (known as the *mudareb*).

48.47   The financier will not generally have any right to be involved in the ongoing management of the venture, but the scope of the administrator's authority and the types of business in which he may invest will be set out in the initial agreement between the parties. The *rab al maal* will also be entitled to accounts and information as to the progress of the underlying business. If the *mudareb* acts contrary to the terms of his remit, then the *rab al maal* thereby acquires the right to terminate the arrangements. The *mudareb* will also be responsible for any losses thereby occasioned. The *mudaraba* must generally have a pre-agreed and limited time span, at the end of which capital is returned to the investors and profits distributed among the parties in accordance with their agreed entitlements. Losses are borne by the investors (*rab al maal*), since the *mudareb* is not a guarantor of the fund and is not liable for losses, except in the case of his own misconduct or negligence.

48.48   The *mudaraba* structure is used as a vehicle for collective investment schemes, where the *mudareb* is a financial institution which manages funds assembled from retail or other investors.

Sukuk

48.49   The *sukuk* is a form of bond which evidences a share in an underlying asset and the revenues which may be derived from it.[86]

48.50   In general terms, the initial owner of the assets will establish a special purpose vehicle (SPV) which sells certificates (known as *sukuk*) for the full amount of the proposed bond issue. The issuer uses those funds to purchase assets (such as real estate) from the primary entity, and leases those assets back to the original owner.[87] The resultant rental income then passes back through the SPV to the holders of the *sukuk*. Upon maturity of the certificates, the assets are sold or transferred back to the primary entity. Once again, the structure is seen to be Islamic-compliant because the *sukuk* holders own an interest in the underlying property and are thus exposed to the risk of loss.[88]

---

[85] The *mudaraba* is also sometimes referred to as *qirad* or *muqarada*. The expression is apparently derived from a reference in the Qu'ran to walking and travelling the earth, since the *mudareb* will go out in search of profitable opportunities.

[86] The *sukuk* (generally translated as 'certificate') is a tradable instrument and may be sold on a secondary market.

[87] This aspect of the transaction must also be Islamic-compliant. The leaseback arrangement may, for example, be structured as an *ijara* (above).

[88] The point just made may, however, be controversial. For a discussion of this point in the context of a 2003 *sukuk* issue by the State of Qatar, see El-Gamal, pp 107–110.

Attitude to Conventional and Ancillary Structures

It will be apparent from the foregoing discussion that many conventional financing struc- **48.51** tures are not acceptable from a Shariah perspective, largely on account of the prohibition against *riba*. As a result, much effort has been expended in developing products which are regarded as Islamic-compliant.

Nevertheless, some conventional structures lie at the margins. It is appropriate to consider **48.52** a few miscellaneous points in this regard:

(a) *Bank Guarantees.* A bank is permitted to issue guarantees for the account of a customer provided that this is done with recourse to the customer itself.[89] Of course, a guarantee issued by an Islamic bank may only cover an underlying obligation which is itself Shariah-compliant and, hence, cannot be used to cover an interest bearing or other prohibited transaction.[90] The bank cannot take remuneration by way of commission which is calculated by reference to the face amount or duration of the guarantee, since this would have the effect of charging 'money for money'. However, the bank may charge administrative and other expenses designed to cover its work and the service provided by it.[91]

(b) *Documentary Credits.* It is permissible for a bank to issue a letter of credit to cover an export import transaction in respect of goods.[92] In this type of case, the bank can charge actual expenses in the issue of the guarantee, and is also permitted to charge a fee by reference to the face amount of the credit.[93] The credit must not relate to goods or transactions which are prohibited by the Shariah[94] and, whilst the bank can take cover for the credit, this must not take the form of interest bearing bonds or similar instruments.[95] A credit issued by an Islamic bank may be subject to the normal terms and conditions applicable to international credits.[96] However, in that event, the issuing bank should specifically state that it will not violate Shariah principles and stipulate that it will not act on clauses relating to interest.[97] In addition, in the light of the prohibition against *riba*, an Islamic institution should not negotiate a credit or discount bills of exchange accepted under a credit at a discount to their face value.[98] Whilst it is thus permissible for an Islamic bank both to issue a credit and to act as an intermediary

---

[89] The whole subject of guarantees—whether issued by the bank itself or issued to it in respect of the obligations of a customer—is addressed in Shariah Standard No 5. On the point made in the text, see para 3.1.3 of that Standard.

[90] Shariah Standard No 5, para 7.1.3.

[91] On these two points, see Shariah Standard No 5, paras 7.1.1 and 7.1.2.

[92] Shariah Standard No 14 is the main Standard dealing with documentary credits: see para 3.2 (the same point is effectively made in Shariah Standard No 5, para 7.2.1). In other words, an Islamic bank can issue an ordinary *commercial* credit. If it is requested to issue a *standby* letter of credit, then this amounts in substance to a guarantee and it is suggested that the points made in the preceding paragraph would apply to that type of instrument.

[93] However, the bank should not 'annualise' the fee or otherwise take its duration into account in calculating the fee: Shariah Standard No 14, para 3.3.1. The point is repeated in Shariah Standard No 5, para 7.2.

[94] Shariah Standard No 14, para 3.1.3.

[95] Shariah Standard No 14, para 3.4.2.

[96] On these rules, see Chapter 24 above.

[97] Shariah Standard No 14, para 3.7.1.

[98] Shariah Standard No 14, paras 3.7.2 and 3.7.3.

bank (eg by advising or confirming the credit), it must negotiate its arrangements with correspondent institutions in such manner as may be necessary to ensure Shariah compliance.[99]

(c) *Customer Guarantees.* In general terms, it is permissible for a bank to accept a guarantee in respect of the obligations of its customer under a Shariah-compliant product.[100] As between the primary customer and the guarantor, the guarantor is not allowed to accept a commission for the provision of the guarantee, but the bank is not obliged to inquire into the underlying arrangements between its customer and the guarantor, or to form a view as to whether those arrangements are, in fact, Shariah-compliant.[101] A guarantee may be given in respect of future debts or debts of an uncertain amount, but the guarantor has a right to revoke such a guarantee before the debt actually comes into existence.[102]

(d) *Security.* It is likewise generally permissible for the bank to require security for the performance of the customer's obligations under a Shariah-compliant product.[103] The charged asset must be one which can be lawfully owned and sold, and must '... be subject to identification by sign, name or description, and capable of being delivered to the creditor ...'. It is not totally clear from this language whether a floating charge over the assets and undertaking of the customer is permissible, although in the writer's experience such security is indeed accepted in practice. A single asset can be made the subject of a series of successive security interests, provided that the situation is disclosed to each party.[104] The chargee has the usual rights of enforcement,[105] and is not liable for any loss of the charged property unless it results from its own negligence or misconduct.[106]

(e) *Set-off.* It is generally permissible to exercise rights of set-off in the manner recognized in conventional banking. Shariah Standard No 4 (Settlement of Debts by way of Set-off) allows for the exercise of set-off rights both as contractually agreed and as may arise under mandatory statutory provisions (eg in the event of insolvency).

---

[99] Shariah Standard No 14, para3.4.1, read together with para 3.7.6.
[100] The whole subject of guarantees is addressed in Shariah Standard No 5. On the general permissibility of guarantees for customer facilities, see Shariah Standard No 5, para 3.1.1. By way of example of the requirement for Shariah compliance of the underlying obligation, the bank as lessor under an *ijara* lease is essentially responsible for the consequences of any loss or destruction of the property. Consequently, any form of guarantee which places that obligation onto a guarantor of the customer will be unenforceable in terms of Shariah law, since the lessee is only responsible for the loss of the property if this is due to its negligence or misconduct: see para 2.3 of the Standard.
[101] Shariah Standard No 5, para 3.1.5.
[102] Shariah Standard No 5, para 3.2. This may be similar to the position under English law where a guarantee is given in respect of an overdraft facility: see para 26.81 above.
[103] This point is confirmed by Shariah Standard No 5, para 4.1.1. That paragraph also appears to confirm that the possession of the security does not prevent the bank from demanding payment when due or otherwise exercising other remedies which may be available to it. It may be noted that this part of Shariah Standard No 5 uses the language of 'pledge', which generally connotes the physical delivery of the charged asset to the bank. However, whilst it is clear that the Standard is directed principally to possessory pledges, it is also stated that the charged asset may 'be left in the possession of the debtor (security or registered pledge) and all rules governing pledges remain applicable to such a pledge...': see para 4.3.2 of the Standard.
[104] On the various points just made, see Shariah Standard No 5, para 4.2.
[105] Shariah Standard No 5, para 4.4.
[106] Shariah Standard No 5, para 4.7.

Product Structures—Deposits

The foregoing section has considered the means by which a customer may access funding **48.53**
facilities from a bank in a manner which is Islamic-compliant, that is, transactions which
will form part of the asset side of the bank's balance sheet. However, some customers will
have spare cash and will be looking to place deposits with the bank. These will appear on
the liabilities side of the balance sheet.

As is well known, a conventional bank deposit is a debt obligation,[107] and it will carry inter- **48.54**
est[108] at a rate agreed between the bank and the customer, regardless of the level of profit
(or loss) made by the bank in employing those funds.[109] In light of comments made earlier
in this chapter, it will be apparent that such interest arrangements would be forbidden as
riba;[110] if the depositor is to earn a return then he must likewise take some degree of risk.
This poses a particular regulatory problem in the United Kingdom which will be considered later in this chapter,[111] but the present section is concerned solely with the structure of
the product.

Mudaraba

As has already been seen, the *mudaraba* is a form of profit sharing arrangement which **48.55**
allows a customer to fund its activities on the basis that both parties share the prospect of
profit and the risk of loss.[112] The same principle is used for deposits. The customer (referred
to in this context as the *rab al maal*) places his funds with the bank as an investment
manager (*mudareb*) to invest the funds on his behalf. In line with the principles discussed
earlier, a guaranteed return would be *riba* and, hence, prohibited; the *rab al maal* must
accept some of the risk of loss. The bank, as *mudareb*, will not generally share in losses but
will be entitled to a proportion of any profits by way of a fee for its services.

The bank will then seek to invest the funds so that a rate of return may be paid on the cus- **48.56**
tomer's investment. The deposit product is thus Islamic-compliant, because (i) the customer takes the risk on his investment, with the result that the return received by him is not
riba and (ii) the funds are entrusted to the *mudareb* for investment but he must not invest
in products which are *haram* (eg companies involved in the brewing or gambling
industries).

---

[107] See the discussion of the decision in *Foley v Hill* at para 15.10 above.
[108] Of course, there will be no Shariah compliance issue with an ordinary current account, because neither
party pays or receives any interest.
[109] The present commentary is concerned with deposit or interest-bearing accounts. Clearly, ordinary
current accounts do not pose any difficulty in this sphere.
[110] This is certainly the current view. For a discussion of some of the conflicting opinions which have been
expressed in relation to deposit interest, see El-Gamal, ch 8.
[111] See 'Regulatory Issues', below.
[112] The *mudaraba* is also sometimes referred to as the *qirad* or *muqarada*.

Wakala

48.57 Again, the *wakala* structure provides for the bank as agent to invest funds on behalf of the customer, with the bank effectively acting as agent or attorney for the customer. The funds will be invested in pool of monies raised by the bank and an agreed profit will be paid at the end of the investment term, with the bank retaining any excess profit made through the employment of the funds. If, however, there is a shortfall below the agreed profit return, then this is borne by the customer, rather than the bank. In many cases, however, the profit will in effect be guaranteed, so that the bank bears the shortfall.[113] It may not be very clear from the documentation whether the bank's obligation is one of payment (debt) or a duty to account (trust). The difference may, of course, be significant where the pool of funds has performed poorly—is the customer's recourse limited to a share of the pool (trust) or is the bank liable to make payment from its other assets (debt)? The issue has been considered recently by the English courts, and they have tended to the view that the repayment obligation is contractual and, hence, a debt of the institution concerned.[114]

Wadi'a

48.58 The *wadi'a* may be characterized as a form of 'fiduciary deposit', under which funds are placed with the bank in trust. The return of the initial sum will be guaranteed by the accepting institution. It may also pay a profit share but this cannot be guaranteed in advance, nor can it be expressed as a percentage of the deposit, which may be regarded as *riba*. The additional payment is therefore generally characterized as a gift (*hibah*) in appreciation for the advance.

Qard

48.59 *Qard* (or *qard hassan*) is a loan or deposit made on a goodwill basis. Since the debtor is only obliged to repay the original sum advanced, no element of *riba* is involved. However, and without any prior commitment on its part, the debtor may in its discretion pay an additional amount—*hibah*—as a token of appreciation for the advance. The voluntary nature of this additional payment ensures that the product is Shariah-compliant.

---

[113] See, for example, the master *wakala* contract discussed in *The Investment DAR Company KSCC v Blom Development Bank SAL* [2009] EWHC 3545 (Ch), where guarantees and indemnities given by the bank meant that the customer was only taking insolvency on the accepting institution, and not investment risk: see the discussion at para 14 of the judgment.

[114] *Blom Development Bank* (n 113 above), at para 18.

49

ISLAMIC FINANCE TRANSACTIONS IN THE COURTS

Introduction

With the benefit of the background provided by the preceding chapter, it seems appropri- **49.01** ate to examine the case law which is so far available in the field of Islamic finance. Inevitably, the writer's emphasis must be on the few English decisions which are available, but refer- ence will also be made to cases decided in other countries. It is of particular interest to examine the developing case law in Malaysia, partly because of its more structured approach to the subject and partly because of the common law tradition which it shares with England and other Commonwealth jurisdictions.[1]

Nevertheless, in reviewing this analysis, some fundamental differences must be borne **49.02** in mind. As is well known, the United Kingdom is an essentially secular society. It has committed itself to the growth of its Islamic financial markets for the benefit of a size- able minority of its population. But, as has been seen, legislative initiatives have been driven largely towards the creation of a non-discriminatory environment, in the sense that Islamic financial products should not be disadvantaged in terms of cost, taxation, or regula- tory treatment. In contrast, of course, Islam occupies a much more significant role in Malaysian life.[2]

---

[1] This is not to undermine the importance of decisions or rulings in other countries, but Kuala Lumpur has a valid claim to be the primary centre for Islamic finance in Asia and the relevant materials are readily accessible to the English writer.

[2] Article 3(1) of the Federal Constitution provides that: 'Islam is the religion of the Federation, but other religions may be practised in peace and harmony in any part of the Federation.'

English Case Law

49.03 The present section therefore provides a brief analysis of the few cases which are so far available in this field and which directly address the enforceability of Islamic products.[3]

Islamic Investment Company of the Gulf (Bahamas) Ltd v Symphony Gems NV

49.04 This case[4] appears to be the first occasion on which the English courts have had to consider the influence of Shariah law on a funding agreement.

49.05 The case concerned an agreement which was expressly intended to take effect as a *murabaha* financing. Symphony Gems wished to acquire a stock of rough diamonds from a company based in Hong Kong. The parties had entered into a master *murabaha* agreement and had expressly agreed that '… this agreement and each purchase agreement shall be governed by and shall be construed in accordance with English law'. The choice of the applicable law was accordingly unequivocal, but the parties nevertheless also stated in their agreement that '… the purchaser wishes to deal with the seller for the purpose of purchasing supplies under this agreement in accordance with the Islamic Shariah …'. It appears that the financier—an entity incorporated in the Bahamas—paid the price to the supplier in accordance with the agreed purchase arrangements. The financier thus became the owner of the gems, and on-sold them to its own customer—on deferred payment terms and subject to an agreed profit or mark-up—in accordance with the *murabaha* financing agreement.[5] Nevertheless, the financier did not take physical possession of the gems; the customer was to accept delivery as its agent. Although the payments were made, delivery of the gems did not occur, and the customer resisted the claim for repayment on that basis. That defence failed, on the grounds that the agreement specifically provided that the repayment obligations were unconditional regardless of delivery or other matters concerning the gems or their quality.[6] In other words, as would be the case with any conventional financing arrangement, the risk of the goods is borne by the customer, and his obligation to repay the bank is unconditional in all respects. As a result, the agreement appeared to lack the essential indicia of a *murabaha* agreement. Nevertheless, this did not affect its validity or enforceability in court proceedings because the agreement was expressed to be governed by English law. As the court observed, the agreement was '… a contract governed by English law. I must simply construe it according to its terms as an English law contract …'. There seems to be little doubt that the agreement would have been unenforceable had Shariah principles been applied.[7]

---

[3] For a discussion of these cases, see Abdul Karim Aldahni, 'The Challenge of Islamic Banking Disputes in the English Courts: The Applied Law' (2009) 6 JIBFL 350.

[4] [2002] WL 346969 (Commercial court), discussed in the *Beximco Chemicals* case, below.

[5] On the details of a *murabaha* agreement, see para 48.26 above.

[6] Provisions of this kind appear to have influenced the view that the financing agreement was not Shariah compliant, because the financier was thereby disclaiming the necessary element of risk sharing or responsibility for the underlying assets.

[7] Indeed, the expert evidence placed before the court was to the effect that 'the agreement in issue does not have the essential characteristics of a Murabaha contract…'.

Having decided that the contract was to be enforced solely in accordance with English law, **49.06** a failure to comply with Shariah principles could therefore only affect the agreement if the performance of the contract would necessarily involve an act which would be unlawful in the country in which it was required to be carried out.[8] For example, Shariah law forms a part of the domestic legal system of Saudi Arabia,[9] and the principle just mentioned could have applied if any relevant acts in performance of the contract had to be taken there. However, there was no relevant nexus with that country or any other jurisdiction in which Shariah law formed a part of the domestic legal system. However, the contract had no relevant nexus with any such jurisdiction; in particular, the contracts contemplated payment to accounts in New York and Zurich.[10]

Finally, the customer sought to avoid liability on the basis that the contract was ultra **49.07** vires the financier, whose memorandum of association provided that it should carry out its business '… in a manner which is consistent with Islamic laws, rules, principles and traditions …'. Arguments of this kind are inherently unattractive but, in any event, the Companies Act of the Bahamas provided for the protection of third parties dealing with the company in good faith,[11] so the court likewise dismissed this line of argument as well.[12]

Beximco Pharmaceuticals Ltd v Shamil Bank of Bahrain EC

The factual background to this case[13] is in some respects similar to that which arose in **49.08** *Symphony Gems*. The *murabaha* agreements executed in this case were stated to involve the sale and purchase of pharmaceuticals. When the bank sued for repayment, the customer argued that (i) the arrangements had been structured as *murabaha* agreements for the benefit of the bank, which was an Islamic financial institution, (ii) they were, in fact, disguised working capital loans involving the payment of interest, and (iii) since the agreements effectively involved the payment of interest, they should be unenforceable under Shariah principles.

It might be thought that the defences should suffer the same fate as those which were **49.09** employed in *Symphony Gems*. However, the *Beximco* agreements contained a governing law clause which read:

> Subject to the principles of the Glorious Shariah, this Agreement shall be governed by and construed in accordance with the laws of England.

---

[8] This principle is derived from the well-known decisions in *Ralli Brothers v Compania Naviera Sota y Aznar* [1920] 2 KB 287 (CA) and *Regazzoni v KC Sethia Ltd* [1958] AC 301 (CA). See also Rome I, Art 9(3).

[9] The law of Saudi Arabia incorporates Shariah law as part of its substantive principles. Consequently, where a particular contract or other issue is governed by the laws of that country, the English court will apply Shariah law based on expert evidence. For an example in the context of the law of succession, see *Al Bassam v Al Bassam* [2004] EWCA Civ 857.

[10] In the context of a monetary obligation, the country in which the creditor's bank account is located will generally be taken as the place of performance: see *Kleinwort Sons & Co v Ungarische Baumwolle Industrie AG* [1939] 2 KB 678.

[11] Compare s 40 of the Companies Act 2006, considered at paras 26.49–26.53 above.

[12] Yet it may be noted that provisions of this kind are generally intended to operate in favour of (rather than against) a third party dealing with a company. They are not generally intended for the protection of the company itself.

[13] [2004] 4 All ER 1079 (CA). The most difficult issue raised by this case is the form of the governing law clause, which differed significantly from that used in *Symphony Gems*.

What was the effect of this provision? The defendants argued that the agreement should only be enforceable if it was valid under both English law and in accordance with Shariah principles.[14] A plain reading of the clause would lend considerable support to this view. Indeed, one could go even further and conclude that Shariah principles were intended to prevail over English law in the event of a conflict. Yet the Court of Appeal found that the parties intended their contract to be governed *exclusively* by English law, for the following reasons:

(a) whilst different parts of a contract can be governed by different systems of law, it is not possible for the same provisions to be governed by the laws of more than one jurisdiction; and

(b) English choice of law rules contemplate that a contract must be governed by the laws of a *country*.[15] Consequently, a set of religious principles can only govern a contractual obligation if they have been formally made a part of the domestic legal system concerned.[16]

(c) Since there is considerable controversy about the application of Shariah principles to financial transactions,[17] the parties cannot have intended that an English court would decide their dispute by reference to religious principles.

(d) The reference to Shariah principles was thus intended to reflect the bank's business model. It was not intended to override the application of English law.[18]

(e) The parties cannot have intended that a secular court would be asked to decide matters of Shariah law, especially since the principles applicable in this area are a matter of some controversy.

---

[14] See para 27 of the judgment.

[15] The Court relied on Art 3(1) of the Rome Convention on the law applicable to contractual obligations. See now the corresponding provisions in Art 3 of Rome I. The same rule has been held to apply to an arbitration agreement, even though such contracts fall outside the scope of the Rome Convention and Rome I: see *Musawi v RE International (UK) Ltd* [2007] EWCA 2981 (Ch).

[16] See *Al Bassam v Al Bassam* [2004] EWCA 857 (CA) and *Al Midani v Al Midani* [1999] 1 Lloyds Rep 923, each to the effect that an English court may be required to recognize and give effect to Shariah law to the extent to which it forms a part of the domestic legal system of Saudi Arabia, and compare *Halpern v Halpern* [2007] EWCA Civ 291 (CA). However, these cases deal with preliminary issues and are of only limited assistance in the present context. But it is of some interest to note that a US Court has applied Shariah law—as part of the domestic law of Saudi Arabian law which governed the contract at issue—in *National Group for Communications and Computers Ltd v Lucent Technologies International Inc* 331 F Supp 2d 290 (2004). In that case, applying the principle of *gharar* as discussed above, the court held that the claimant could only recover losses which were actually and directly attributable to the defendant's breach, and could not recover in respect of 'speculative' losses. In addition, the laws of the Islamic Republic of Iran prohibit the recovery of interest but allow for the recovery of losses resulting from inflation. This rule has been applied where an action was brought in England following the dishonour of a cheque drawn on an Iranian account, with the result that the payee was awarded compensation, rather than interest: see *Karafarin Bank v Gholam Reza Mansoury Dara* [2009] EWHC 3265.

[17] This point has been discussed generally in Chapter 48 above.

[18] This view was reinforced by the fact that matters of Shariah compliance were a matter for the bank's Religious Supervisory Board.

Under these circumstances, the bank was entitled to recover the monies owing to it under **49.10** the *murabaha* agreements. Even if they did include an element of interest or were otherwise non-Shariah-compliant, they would remain enforceable because the rights and obligations of the parties were governed exclusively by English law.

Although the language of the governing law clause differed substantially from that used in **49.11** *Symphony Gems*, the Court of Appeal nevertheless came to an identical conclusion as to the enforceability of the documentation. Whilst the interpretation of that clause in *Beximco* perhaps involves a construction which is not immediately obvious, the outcome in both cases is perhaps satisfactory because (i) given that scholars differ quite sharply over the application of Shariah principles to financial transactions, it would be very difficult for an English court to resolve such matters and (ii) the decisions lean in favour of the enforceability of financial contracts. Once again, however, it should be observed that an application of Shariah principles would very likely have led to a different result, since the financier was not taking any risk on, or responsibility for, the assets which formed the subject matter of the arrangements.

The impression that the parties' attempt to contract in a Shariah-compliant manner will **49.12** not affect or detract from obligations arising under English law is reinforced by the decision in *Riyad Bank and Others v Ahli Bank (UK) plc*,[19] where it was decided that an Islamic investment manager is subject to a duty in tort adequately to value the assets held within a Shariah-compliant fund.

Nevertheless, it should not be thought that references to the Shariah are left without any **49.13** impact or meaning. For example, the fact that the parties were seeking to create a Shariah-compliant structure may give colour or background to some of the terminology employed in the contract, and may assist the court in identifying the intended meaning of particular contractual provisions. However, as has been seen, such references will not affect the essential enforceability of the contract, which will continue to be determined by reference to the domestic system of law applicable to it.

If the contract refers *solely* to Shariah law as the law applicable to the agreement then, based **49.14** upon the principles outlined above, the court would have to endeavour to identify the domestic or national system of law which is to govern its terms. As discussed elsewhere, this will usually be the law of the country in which the relevant bank branch is situate.[20] It must be said, however, that this view may be at odds with a remark in the *Beximco Chemicals* case,[21] to the effect that '... The fact that there may be a general consensus on the proscription of *Riba* and the essentials of a valid *Morabaha* agreement does no more than indicate that that, if the Shariah law proviso were sufficient to incorporate the principles of Shariah law into the parties' agreement, the defendant would have been likely to succeed ...' (ie on the basis that the agreement was not Shariah-compliant). It is respectfully suggested that

---

[19] [2006] EWCA Civ 780 (CA). Indeed, it does not even appear to have been argued that the Shariah-compliant nature of the fund made any difference to the nature or scope of the investment manager's obligations.

[20] On this rule of private international law, see generally Chapter 40 above.

[21] At para 55 of the judgment.

this view cannot be supported. In the final analysis, the rights and obligations of the parties under a contract must be governed by a recognized, domestic system of law.

The Investment DAR Company KSCC v Blom Development Bank SAL

49.15   The *Blom Development Bank* case[22] is the most recent case concerning Islamic financial products to have come before the English courts. In contrast to the two earlier cases which considered *murabaha* facilities, *Blom* involved a *wakala* contract which is in many ways similar to a conventional bank deposit.[23]

49.16   In essence, the depositor in that case was seeking repayment of funds deposited under a master *wakala* agreement and which were intended to be invested to create a fixed return. The bank and the customer were incorporated in Kuwait and the Middle East respectively and the only apparent connection with this country was the choice of English law to govern the contract.

49.17   The incorporation documents of the financial institution stated that all of its business was to be conducted in a Shariah-compliant manner. The bank then sought to defend the customer's claim for repayment on the footing that the *wakala* arrangements were merely a disguised deposit at interest and were, hence, prohibited both as a matter of Shariah law and, hence, in terms of the bank's constitution.[24] In contrast to the earlier cases, the court appeared to be willing to consider the (conflicting) evidence placed before it as to matters of Shariah law although, in this particular case, it may be observed that the Shariah question went to the corporate capacity of the bank, rather than to the intrinsic validity of the contract itself. It is nevertheless clear that the court was reluctant to allow the use of Shariah-based defences when the transaction had been approved by the bank's own Shariah Committee.[25]

49.18   In the result, the court gave the defendant institution permission to defend the claim although clearly considered its prospects of success to be relatively slim. It accordingly gave that permission conditionally on the principal sum being paid, leaving only the profit element or guaranteed sum outstanding. In terms of legal certainty, the decision may be unfortunate and perhaps marks something of a retreat from the more robust approach adopted in the earlier English cases.

English Case Law—Conclusions

49.19   It is perhaps unsurprising that the English courts have sought to avoid decisions which would have involved judgments on questions touching Shariah principles. There are a number of reasons for this view. In particular, and as discussed previously, the Shariah is not a system of law in the sense of a system which the English courts are accustomed to administer. Furthermore, English commercial and banking law are built on the enforceability

---

[22]   [2009] EWHC 3545 (Ch).

[23]   See the discussion of this product at para 48.57 above.

[24]   See para 16 of the judgment.

[25]   See para 10 of the judgment. It may be argued that the ruling of that Committee would have been relied upon by the customer in entering into the transaction in the first instance, and that the bank should accordingly be estopped from re-opening a Shariah point of this kind in later proceedings.

of bargains. In the *Symphony Gems* and *Beximco* cases discussed above, an application of Shariah principles would almost certainly have led to the conclusion that the relevant agreements were unenforceable. The court may have felt that such a conclusion could not be justified. Although the point is not mentioned in the judgments, it may be added that a decision to the effect that the contracts were unenforceable may well have adverse consequences for the Islamic banking industry itself, and may have rendered it less competitive. If it had become clear that the standard products in daily use by that market were of doubtful validity, then Islamic banks might have had to ascribe more capital to their transactions to account for the increased risk of loss.[26] For these reasons, it is suggested that the slightly more reserved approach adopted in the *Blom Development Bank* case should be the exception, rather than the rule.

Accordingly, and although this statement at first sight appears perverse, it is suggested that the English decisions to enforce agreements which may have been doubtful in terms of their Shariah-compliance are, in fact, a positive for the development of the Islamic financial markets in the United Kingdom. **49.20**

Malaysian Case Law

Introduction

The starting point for the Malaysian case law is provided by articles 74 and 121 of the Federal Constitution, 1957. Amongst other things, article 74 provides that the Federation has legislative competence over the various matters noted in List I of the Ninth Schedule to the Constitution. Working along parallel lines, article 121 provides that the Malaysian civil courts have jurisdiction over all Federal and State laws, other than matters falling within the scope of the jurisdiction conferred on the Shariah court. Under the terms of paragraph 1 of List II to the Ninth Schedule to the Constitution, the individual States enjoy legislative authority in relation to certain matters of Shariah law, but this authority is essentially directed towards personal and family matters (including marriage, divorce, succession, and similar matters). On the other hand, List I of that Schedule ascribes legislative authority in other areas to the Federation of Malaysia, and jurisdiction over such matters hence rests with the civil courts. It appears to follow that the Federal Courts have jurisdiction to determine questions of Shariah law insofar as they relate to banking and financial matters.[27] The case law has proceeded on this basis, and the terms of List I to the Ninth Schedule offer substantial support for this approach.[28] **49.21**

---

[26] See the comments on the second pillar of Basel II, at para 51.30 below.

[27] By way of comparison and contrast, it may be noted in passing that, in Pakistan, it has been held by the Supreme Court (Lahore) that the legality of interest-bearing loans and other matters concerning *riba* are allocated to the Shariah courts, rather than the ordinary civil courts: see *Danish Brothers v Federation of Pakistan* (January 2009, reported in *The Nation*, 13 January 2009). As in the case of Malaysia, decisions of this kind will obviously depend upon the terms of the particular national constitution which is under consideration.

[28] For example, paras 4(e)(i) and 7(j) of List I state that questions of mercantile law, banking, and the control of credit fall within the scope of federal authority. In addition, para 4(k) of List I confers similar authority in relation to the 'ascertainment of Islamic law and other personal laws *for the purposes of Federal law* ...' (emphasis supplied). It should be said that the division of jurisdiction between the Federal and the

49.22 In regulatory terms, the infrastructure for Islamic finance in Malaysia is provided by the Islamic Banking Act 1983 and the Banking and Financial Institutions Act 1989. This legislation deals primarily with the regulation and supervision of Islamic banks. Thus, a company can only carry on Islamic banking business in Malaysia if it is licensed for that purpose, and a licensed entity should not conduct any business which is not approved by the Religion of Islam.[29]

49.23 It should be noted that not every civil court in Malaysia will necessarily possess the detailed knowledge of the Shariah which will be necessary to determine these matters. As a result, the Malaysian Central Bank has put in place various structures designed to assist in the establishment of Shariah principles as they are to be applied by courts sitting in that country. In particular, a new section 16B was inserted into the Central Bank of Malaysia Act 1958[30] with a view to establishing a new Shariah Advisory Council. The 1958 Act has been repealed and replaced by a new, Central Bank of Malaysia Act 2009, and the provisions dealing with the Council are now to be found in sections 51–58 of that Act. As noted previously:[31]

(a) the Shariah Advisory Council is established within the Central Bank as the authority on Islamic financial matters;[32]

(b) in view of its position as the central authority, rulings of the Shariah Advisory Council take precedence over rulings of Shariah committees of individual institutions;[33] and

(c) a court or arbitrator must have regard to rulings of the Shariah Advisory Council and, if it elects to refer a matter to the Council for a ruling, it will be bound by the ruling so given.[34]

49.24 Finally, in terms of the system of law applied by the Malaysian courts, it should be noted that:

(a) the law of contract is governed by the Malaysian Contracts Act 1950. Subject to a few reservations, the 1950 Act reflects principles which would be essentially familiar to the English lawyer; and

(b) banking and commercial law in Malaysia are generally based on English law.[35]

Shariah courts has occasionally been a matter of controversy, but there appears to be no dispute in the field of banking and financial matters. For a discussion of the jurisdiction of the Civil courts in this sphere, see *Arab-Malaysian Finance Bhd v Taman Ihsan Jaya Sdn Bhd* (Commercial Division, High Court of Malaya, 2008, Suit No D4-22A-067-2003) and, for analysis of this decision, see Jabbar, 'Islamic Finance: A Question of Approach' (2009) 30(7) Company Lawyer 220. The actual decision in this case has been overruled: see para 49.35 below. Nevertheless, the first instance judgement in *Taman Ihsan Jaya* is one of some interest. It includes a discussion of the Shariah-based authorities prohibiting usury and also sets out, by way of comparison, corresponding extracts from the Old Testament. An argument to the effect that the civil courts lacked jurisdiction in Islamic finance cases was also rejected in *Bank Islam Malaysia v Adnan bin Omar* [1995] CLJ 735.

[29] On these points, see ss 3(1) and 3(5)(a) of the Islamic Banking Act 1983. The expression 'Religion of Islam' as used in s 3(5)(a) is not defined elsewhere in the 1983 Act, nor does it appear to be defined in the Federal Constitution or other relevant legislation. This is entirely understandable but it may be noted that the meaning of this expression gave rise to some difficulty in the case discussed at para 49.34 below.

[30] This was achieved pursuant to the Central Bank of Malaysia (Amendment) Act 2003.

[31] See the discussion at para 48.23 above.

[32] Section 51 of the Central Bank of Malaysia Act 2009.

[33] Section 58 of the Central Bank of Malaysia Act 2009.

[34] Section 56 and 57 of the Central Bank of Malaysia Act 2009.

[35] On this subject, see ss 3 and 5 of the Malaysian Civil Law Act 1956.

It is these features which mean that the English and Malaysian case law offer an interesting basis for comparison.

It is now appropriate to turn to some of the available case law. This discussion should be **49.25** read against the background that most of the recent case law refers to banking product known as the *Al-Bai Bithaman Ajil* (BBA), or credit sale. The BBA may be described as the workhorse of Islamic finance in Malaysia, since it is used for the financing of residential property, vehicles, and consumer goods. It is in some respects an extension of the *murabaha* (cost plus) structure which has been discussed earlier.[36] The Malaysian Securities Commission defines a BBA facility as '… a contract that refers to the sale and purchase transaction for the financing of an asset on a deferred and on an instalment basis with a pre-agreed payment period. The sale price will include a profit margin …'.[37] On the other hand, the same source defines a *murabaha* as '… a contract referring to a sale and purchase transaction for the financing of an asset whereby the cost and profit margin (mark-up) are made known and agreed to by all parties involved. The settlement for the purchase can be settled either on a deferred lump sum basis or on an instalment basis, and is specified in the agreement …'. At the risk of oversimplification, therefore, the two products can be regarded as essentially similar, at least for the purposes of the present discussion.[38]

Thus, in the context of a property financing, the BBA structure might operate as follows: **49.26**

(a) the bank's customer would contract to purchase the relevant property from the vendor;

(b) the three parties would then execute a novation agreement, under the terms of which the bank would become the purchaser of the property;

(c) on completion of the purchase by the bank, it would immediately resell the property to the customer on deferred instalment payment terms; and

(d) the borrower will then execute a charge over the property in favour of the bank to secure the instalments.

Earlier Cases

The earlier cases decided by the Malaysian courts in this context tended not to deal very **49.27** directly with questions of Shariah compliance. As a result, they do bear some similarity to the approach adopted by the English courts, as described earlier in this chapter.

Thus, for example, in *Tinta Press Sdn Bhd v Bank Islam Malaysia Bhd*,[39] the court was con- **49.28** fronted with an *ijara* (lease) contract.[40] It held the structure to be valid apparently on the

---

[36] See para 48.26 above.
[37] Malaysian Securities Commission, 'Glossary of Islamic Capital Market Terms'.
[38] The main differences of detail are: (i) in contrast to a *murabaha*, it does not seem to be necessary for a seller under a BBA contract to have title to the asset before he enters into the contract of sale, and (ii) the BBA contract will usually involve a number of payments over a long period, whilst the consideration for goods supplied under a *murabaha* contract will frequently be paid in a single instalment. On these points, see Jabbar, 'Shariah Compliant Financial Instruments—Principles and Practice' (2009) Company Lawyer 176.
[39] [1987] 1 MLJ 474.
[40] On *ijara* contracts, see para 48.38 above.

basis that the documentation displayed the common law characteristics of a lease. It did not seek to analyse the arrangement from a Shariah law perspective.

49.29   Difficulties started to arise when cases involving defaults under BBA facilities came before the courts, with lenders seeking to enforce mortgages for the full amount of the deferred payment instalments. Thus, in *Bank Islam Malaysia Bhd v Adnan bin Omar*,[41] the defendant took out a RM 265,000 BBA facility to purchase a property in 1984. Over the 15 year repayment period, the deferred instalment payments amounted to RM 583,000. The customer defaulted just one year into the transaction and, as is customary, this entitled the bank to accelerate the facility. Now, had the difference between the original purchase price and the resale price represented interest under a conventional financing arrangement, it is plain that the lender could not have charged interest for any of the period following repayment.[42] But the differential was part of the price for which the customer had agreed to repurchase the property, and the result was that the bank was entitled to judgment for the full amount.[43] The customer was, therefore, significantly disadvantaged in financial terms as a result of having utilized the BBA structure. The decision was followed, and an essentially similar result ensued, in *Bank Islam Malaysia Bhd v Shamsuddin Bin Haji Ahmad*.[44] It may be noted that the court in *Adnan bin Omar* in part justified its decision on the grounds that the customer fully understood the terms of the contract which he had made and should be held to his bargain. In other words, and notwithstanding the Islamic nature of the financing, it applied ordinary common law principles, without reference to the Shariah.

49.30   The same approach was applied—perhaps with more justification—in commercial cases. Thus, in *Arab-Malaysian Merchant Bank Bhd v Silver Concepts Sdn Bhd*,[45] the court ordered the payment of all deferred instalments on a commercial BBA facility following a default. Again, in a development which bears some similarity to the English case discussed earlier, the customer sought to argue that the BBA facility agreement is '... illegal, null and void as it is a scheme to defraud the public and the public authority in that although the loan agreement is disguised and couched as a sale transaction, in fact the [BBA] facility agreement is a loan transaction with a fixed interest charge for the loan granted by the lenders to the defendant ...'.[46] In other words, the arrangements were intended to disguise an element of *riba*, and should be unenforceable on that ground. But, in another interesting encounter between Shariah principles and the common law, the court held that the customer, having agreed to the BBA facility, having signed up the required documentation and having made some of

---

[41] [1994] 3 CLJ 735. See also *Dato' Nik Mahmud Bin Daud v Bank Islam Malaysia Bhd* [1996] 4 MLJ 295.

[42] On this subject, see para 20.27 above.

[43] Unlike interest under a conventional facility, the profit element under the BBA did not represent the time value of money—it could not do so, since this would have amounted to *riba*. Hence, there seemed to be no other basis on which the court could refuse enforcement.

[44] [1999] 1 LNS 275. As the court observed in para 17 of the *Zulkifli* case (see para 49.33 below), the result of these cases was 'all the more shocking when it is further realized that a borrower under a *Riba*-ridden loan is far better off'.

[45] [2008] 6 MLJ 295. The court followed the decision in *Zulkifli*, above. In may be noted in passing that the judgment in *Taman Ihsan Jaya* is one of some interest. It includes a discussion of the Shariah-based authorities prohibiting usury and also sets out, by way of comparison, corresponding extracts from the Old Testament.

[46] See para 16 of the judgment.

the stipulated payments, was now prevented by the principle of estoppel from pleading that the transaction was contrary to public policy in this way.[47] Indeed, the very same issue was apparent to the court in an earlier stage of this litigation, where the court observed that '... this case involves the marriage of two distinctly diverse worlds, namely the Islamic world and the common law-sourced civil law, both protected and enabled by the Federal Constitution. The agreements here have Islam as their foundation whilst the foreclosure proceedings come under the civil law jurisdiction, specifically the National Land Code 1965 and the Rules of the High Court 1980 ...'.[48] Similarly, in 2003 the Malaysian Court of Appeal[49] had resort entirely to common law principles in deciding to enforce a land mortgage, observing that '... the facility is an Islamic banking facility. But that does not mean that the law applicable in this application is different from the law that is applicable if the facility were given under conventional banking. The charge is a charge under the National Land Code. The remedy available and sought is a remedy provided by the National Land Code. The procedure is provided by the Code and the Rules of the High Court 1980 ...'.

Issues arising at the crossroads between the common law and Shariah principles again arose **49.31** in *Bank Kerjasama Rakyat Malaysia Bhd v PSC Naval Dockyard Sdn Bhd.*[50] This case involved a slightly different form of Islamic financing product although, at least for present purposes, its essential features are similar to a BBA. The facility had been used to purchase a portfolio of listed shares. These were, in the first instance, purchased by the bank and then on-sold to the customer. The customer unsuccessfully resisted summary judgment for the full amounts owing under the contract, and the following points arose:

(a) Relying on the decision in *Zulkifli*,[51] the customer sought to argue that the purchase price payable by it under the agreement and the resultant profit element were exorbitant. Yet this argument had to fail since, by the time the proceedings came to court, the financing period had expired, with the result that the entire profit element had already been 'earned' by the bank. In any event, and relying on the decision in *Adnan bin Omar* (above), the court noted that the customer had fully understood the nature of the transaction and entered into the transaction voluntarily. Once again, therefore, a common law approach prevented the full airing of an argument based on Shariah principles.

---

[47] It is, however, right to note that the Court did also deal with certain aspects of the substantive issue, noting that: 'I am unable to acquiesce to any argument that, just because a larger sum is agreed to be paid back founded on a buy back concept, with the defendant openly having requested for deferred payment, and with the differential sum resembling interest, the agreement must be void. I am unable to acquiesce to such a suggestion as there is no clear text that prohibits such a transaction entrenched with all those ingredients. Even the followers of the Shafii and Hanafi Schools and the majority of Muslim scholars find it lawful, calling it "*Shifa al ilal fi hokum ziyadat al-thamam li mujarrad al-alal*" (translated "The reason for increasing the price due to lapse of time", The Lawful and Prohibited in Islam by Yusuf al-Qaradawi). I therefore reject the argument of the defendant that, just because the defendant pays more than what was needed to buy the impugned property, such sum (here called profit) must be interest per se ...'

[48] *Arab-Malaysian Merchant Bank Bhd v Silver Concept Sdn Bhd* [2006] 8 CLJ 9, para 13. The decision also includes a discussion on the issues posed by the expression 'Religion of Islam' in the Islamic Banking Act 1983, focusing in particular on differences of interpretation and approach among the different schools.

[49] *Bank Kerjasama Rakyat Malaysia Bhd v Emcee Corporation* [2003] 1 CLJ 625, followed in *Bank Islam Malaysia Bhd v Pasaraya Peladang Sdn Bhd* [2004] 7 MLJ 355.

[50] [2008] 1 CLJ 784.

[51] See para 49.33 below.

(b) It has also been seen that the Shariah prohibits contracts which suffer from excessive uncertainty (*gharar*).[52] Relying on authority from the *hadith*,[53] the customer argued that the contract was unclear because the certificate numbers of the various shares was not disclosed by the contract. Given that listed shares are fungible in any event, the court rightly described this defence as a 'sham' and held that the customer was estopped from raising it by the very fact that it had chosen to enter into the agreement and had made payments under it. Furthermore, section 30 of the Malaysian Contracts Act 1950 provides that agreements which are not certain or capable of being made certain are void. The court held that the two principles are essentially similar.[54]

Later Cases

49.32 More recent cases have demonstrated a willingness to examine the BBA structure a little more closely, perhaps because of the perception that the arrangement has often acted unfairly against a defaulting customer.

49.33 The starting point for this approach is perhaps offered by the High Court decision in *Affin Bank Bhd v Zulkifli Abdullah*.[55] Once again, a BBA facility had gone into default and the bank sought to recover the full sale price which would otherwise have been payable over the 25 year facility period. The court effectively refused to follow *Adnan bin Omar* and similar authorities and held that the claim for 'unearned profit' over the remaining 22 years of the facility would be inconsistent with the principles of a BBA facility.[56] It may be thought that the ability of the bank to claim this amount would in some respects be a Shariah law question, but the court regarded it as a matter of civil law and declined to refer the matter to the National Shariah Advisory Council.[57] It accordingly undertook a calculation of the resale profit earned by the bank on a per day basis, and calculated a rebate accordingly.[58]

49.34 For the Malaysian financial community, particular concern was engendered by the first instance decision in *Arab-Malaysian Bank Bhd v Taman Ihsan Jaya Sdn Bhd*.[59] In essence,:

(a) the court held that the reference to the need for facilities to comply with the 'Religion of Islam' in the Islamic Banking Act 1983 did not state which school (*mazhab*) of Islam

---

[52] See the discussion at para 48.15 above.

[53] 'The Messenger of Allah forbade me to sell a thing which is not my property or selling something that is not apparent and seen clearly': see para 10 of the judgment.

[54] See para 11 of the judgment.

[55] [2006] 3 MLJ 67.

[56] Expressing matters in a slightly different way, the court observed (at para 29) that 'if the customer is required to pay the profit for the full tenure, he is entitled to have the benefit of the full tenure'. There is an obvious fairness to this approach although it overlooks the fact that the customer had gone into default and was not paying for the tenure. It also tends to treat money as having a time value, which is permissible in conventional banking but may amount to *riba* in the present context: see the discussion at para 48.08 above.

[57] As noted above, a facility for such references for guidance purposes is provided by s 16B of the Central Bank of Malaysia Act.

[58] This decision was specifically approved and applied (in preference to the *Silver Concepts* decision) in *Malayan Banking Bhd v Marilyn Ho Siok Lin* [2006] 7 MLJ 249.

[59] See para 49.30 above. For a very clear and helpful discussion of this decision and some of the antecedent case law, see Zulkifli Hasan, 'Shariah Issues in Al Bay' Bithaman Ajil Facility in the case of Arab Malaysian Finance Bhd v Taman Ihsan Jaya Sdn Bhd', available at www.zulkiflihasan.wordpress.com.

was to govern for these purposes. Consequently, a facility would only be compliant if it was unobjectionable to *every* school;[60] and

(b) the court paid little regard to the fact the BBA facility had been approved by the Shariah Advisory Committee of Bank Negara Malaysia;

(c) the BBA facility was not a bona fide sale but a disguised commercial loan. The arrangement was thus unlawful and contrary to the terms of the Islamic Banking Act 1983;[61] and

(d) since the contract was void under Shariah law, the bank could not recover any profit on the transaction but could only claim back its principal sum, effectively on a restitutionary basis.[62]

Given the primacy of the BBA as a financing structure within the Malaysian Islamic financial market, this decision caused a certain amount of concern, since it seemed to create a legally-based pretext for non-payment of the profit element on a mortgage product widely used throughout Malaysia.[63] The approach adopted in *Taman Ihsan Jaya* was followed by the High Court of Sabah and Sarawak,[64] but the original decision itself was subsequently overturned by the Court of Appeal in a series of joined proceedings involving the use of BBA facilities. In *Bank Islam Malaysia Bhd v Ghazali Shamsuddin and others*.[65] In essence, it was decided that BBA agreements are valid according to their terms. The court should not attempt to rewrite the agreement made between the parties, or to recharacterize a sale transaction as a loan.[66] Consequently, the profit made by the bank on the resale should not have been characterized as interest or *riba*.[67] The court specifically noted that the law applicable to the BBA contracts was no different to that applicable to conventional lending and, as a result, the same general principles should be applied: parties should be held to their agreement in the absence of fraud, coercion or other vitiating factors.[68] The Court of Appeal also held that the official Shariah rulings disregarded by the judge should have been

49.35

[60] This test would clearly set a relatively high benchmark. See the discussion of the various schools at para 48.22 above.
[61] The court would, however, have allowed the bank to recover the amount of the original purchase price in accordance with s 66 of the Malaysian Contracts Act 1950, which reads: 'When an agreement is discovered to be void, or when a contract becomes void, any person who has received any advantage under the agreement or contract is bound to restore it, or to make compensation for it, to the person from whom he received it.' It may be noted that this aspect of the decision was plainly at odds with *Silver Concepts* (see, in particular, the extract reproduced in n 47 above.
[62] See s 66 of the Malaysian Contracts Act 1950, reproduced in the previous footnote.
[63] It may be noted that the same judge had also held *istisna'a* contracts to be void on essentially the same basis: see *Tahan Steel Corporation Sdn Bhd v Bank Islam Malaysia Bhd* [2004] 6 MLJ 1. Once again, however, this decision cannot stand in the light of the Court of Appeal decision about to be noted.
[64] *Majlis Amanah Rakyat v Bass Bin Lai* [2009] CLJ JT(1). Amongst a series of other points, the court observed that the judicial system (rather than Shariah boards) was to be the final arbiter of whether a particular product or structure could be regarded as Shariah-compliant. Again, it seems that the decision in this case will have to be treated with considerable caution in the light of the Court of Appeal's ruling in *Ghazali Shamsuddin*, about to be discussed.
[65] Malaysian Court of Appeal, 26 August 2009.
[66] See para 24 of the judgment of the Court of Appeal. Again, note the reliance on common law principles to support the validity of a Shariah-compliant product.
[67] See para 25 of the judgment.
[68] See para 27 of the Court of Appeal judgment. This seems to mark a return to the straightforward, common law approach which characterized the earlier cases discussed at paras 49.27–49.31 above.

taken into account, and it was wrong to suggest that a facility would only comply with the Religion of Islam for the purposes of the Islamic Banking 1983 Act if it was acceptable to all schools.[69] In the result, the bank was entitled to recover the full amount owing under the BBA agreement on default. The Court of Appeal did not directly address the question whether a rebate (*ibra*) should be granted once full settlement has been achieved,[70] in order to address the perceived inequalities with conventional financing structures noted earlier.[71] However, the judgment implies that the bank was under no obligation to consider such a rebate, since the court noted that a comparison between the two types of financing was not an appropriate process.[72]

Malaysian Case Law—Conclusions

49.36   After the diversions created by *Zulkifli* and the first instance decision in *Taman Ihsan*, it seems that the Court of Appeal decision in the latter case has confirmed the status of BBA facilities as Shariah-compliant arrangements. It seems that the same treatment would also be extended to other products approved by the National Shariah Advisory Board.

49.37   It is perhaps fair to note that the Malaysian case law has adopted a traditional common law approach, in the sense that it has sought to hold parties to their contracts and to enforce them in accordance with their terms. To this extent, the decisions bear some resemblance to the decision in the *Beximco* case[73] although, for obvious reasons, the Malaysian courts have considered the applicable Shariah principles in rather more depth.

49.38   The controversy stirred by the first instance decision in *Taman Ihsan* does, however, illustrate a wider difficulty which inhibits the growth of Islamic finance as an *international* business. How can Islamic banks operate effectively on a cross-border basis when the validity of their products may differ from country to country, depending on the prevalent school and local views? The challenges posed by issues of this kind are considered in the next chapter.

---

[69] See paras 29–33 of the judgment of the Court of Appeal. Compare the approach adopted by the Abu Dhabi Court of Cassation in judgment 9/19 to a provision in the Penal Code that 'Islamic law should be applied to all crimes specified by the Divine Command'. It was noted that the provision did not specify which school of Islamic jurisprudence was to be followed for the purpose of giving effect to this rule. The court accordingly decided that the judge had a discretion to implement the provision in accordance with those principles which were in the best interests of the community in the particular case. The decision is reported in Price and Tamimi, *United Arab Emirates Court of Cassation Judgments 1998-2003* (Brill, 2005), and noted in Blair, Walker, and Purves, para 19.35.

[70] The point about the rebate is, however, by no means free from difficulty. Some cases suggest that the *ibra* must be at the discretion of the bank in order to maintain Shariah compliance. Yet this is plainly unattractive from a legal certainty perspective. The High Court in Sarawak adjourned an application for the enforcement of a charge supporting a BBA facility, asking the bank to put forward its proposals for a 'just and equitable' rebate before it would make a decision on the application: see *Malayan Banking Bhd v Ya'kup bin Oje* [2007] 6 MLJ 389. Again, this procedure is objectionable on legal certainty grounds. But, for the reasons given in the text, it now seems that a court should not require the bank to provide a rebate in any event.

[71] See the discussion of the decisions in *Zulkifli* and *Adnan bin Omar*, above.

[72] In para 24 of its judgment, the Court of Appeal noted that: 'BBA contract is a sale agreement whereas a conventional loan agreement is a money lending transaction. The profit in BBA contract is different from interest arising in a conventional loan transaction. The two transactions are diversely different and indeed diametrically opposed.'

[73] See the discussion at para 49.08 above.

50

CORPORATE AND REGULATORY ISSUES

Introduction

The next chapter will consider the problems confronting the growth of a truly international **50.01** market in the sphere of Islamic banking. In contrast, the present chapter will focus exclusively on the regulatory issues which have arisen within the United Kingdom with respect to the authorization and business of Islamic financial institutions.

The growth of the market for Islamic products in the United Kingdom has posed a variety **50.02** of regulatory challenges, largely because the existing regulatory structures are directed towards conventional products involving, amongst other things, the payment of interest and the taking of security. The present section is designed to provide an overview of selected issues and the manner in which they have been addressed.

Constitutional Structure of Islamic Banks

Overview

The Islamic financial institutions currently operating in the United Kingdom have been **50.03** established as companies incorporated in this country (ie as opposed to branches of foreign institutions).[1]

---

[1] This refers to banks which undertake Shariah-compliant business only. As to conventional banks which operate an Islamic 'window', see paras 50.30–50.32 below.

50.04 There is no special UK regime which is specifically applicable to Islamic banks. The policy of the FSA was to create, so far as possible, a level playing field as between conventional and Islamic institutions. As the FSA put it in describing its approach to the authorization of Islamic banks, there would be 'no obstacles, no special favours'.[2] The FSMA and associated regulations accordingly apply to conventional and Islamic banks on an equal footing.

50.05 Similar considerations apply in the field of corporate law, in the sense that an Islamic bank will be incorporated and adopt constitutional documents in exactly the same way. In addition, the directors of such a bank will be subject to the same fiduciary and other duties applicable to directors of any other company.

Constitutional Issues

50.06 In spite of the factors just outlined, the fact that a company is being formed as an Islamic bank may have consequences for the content of the constitution which is adopted by the shareholders and, as a result, for the rights and obligations of those involved with the bank, whether as 'insiders' or as contracting parties. For example:

(a) The shareholders may include in the memorandum of association a clause to the effect that the bank shall carry on all of its business in a Shariah-compliant fashion.

(b) This requirement is not in itself entirely straightforward since, as has been shown, the precise content and effect of Shariah law in the financial sector is the subject of some controversy. As a result, the constitution will usually provide for the establishment of a Shariah Supervisory Board (SSB), which will advise the main board of directors on matters of Shariah compliance. So far as English law is concerned, it is important that the role is *advisory* only.[3]

50.07 Do these voluntarily adopted structural and constitutional differences have any particular legal implications? It is suggested that the following points may arise:

(a) The memorandum and articles of association of a company constitute a contract between the company itself and its members.[4] Consequently, it would seem that a shareholder could take proceedings against the company if it wrote business which is not Shariah-compliant. In general terms, it is hard to find any form of loss which could legitimately form the subject matter of an award of damages by reason only of the writing of such business. However, the shareholder could perhaps obtain an injunction to prevent the deal, if he found out about the proposed business in advance. In addition, he could perhaps establish a right to damages if his shares depreciated in value following a default on the non-compliant business. In practice, however, such remedies are likely to be very difficult to obtain, not least because the English courts would be very reluctant to rule on whether particular business is, or is not, Shariah-compliant.[5] In addition, the argument may in any event be foreclosed if the memorandum of

---

[2] See 'Islamic Banking in the UK', FSA Briefing Note BN016/06, 9 March 2006.
[3] The role of the SSB is discussed in more detail, below.
[4] Section 33 of the Companies Act 2006.
[5] Compare the discussion of the decision in the *Beximco* case, at para 49.08 above.

association provides for the rulings of the bank's SSB to be conclusive as to matters of Shariah compliance.[6]

(b) An alternative avenue for the shareholder may be to take proceedings against the individual directors of the bank (or at least, against those who authorized the transaction concerned).[7] The directors of a company are obliged to exercise their powers and discretions for the purposes for which they were conferred.[8] In the instant case, they were plainly conferred for the purpose of writing Shariah-compliant business. Nevertheless, the court would probably hold that the SSB was the final arbiter on matters of Shariah compliance for the bank concerned. If the directors had acted on the advice of the SSB, then the court would probably hold that there had been no breach of duty in the first place. Even if it could be shown that the SSB's views were erroneous, the court would again hold that there has been no breach of duty since the directors would have relied on the opinion of the appointed scholars in good faith. Alternatively, if a breach of duty could be established, the court would probably find that the director should be excused from any liability which would otherwise result.[9]

(c) What of the position of a third party dealing with the Islamic bank? Suppose that the bank has contracted with a borrower to provide him with a facility which, to the borrower's knowledge, contains significant elements of *riba*. In spite of this knowledge, can the borrower enforce the facility agreement or obtain damages for the bank's refusal to allow utilization in relation to a non-compliant arrangement? Or is he precluded from that course as a result of his knowledge on this issue? On the whole, it seems quite clear that the agreement would remain legally valid and binding so far as English law is concerned. The bank cannot plead by way of defence its lack of capacity to enter into transactions which are non-Shariah compliant.[10] Furthermore, a borrower dealing in good faith with the directors of the bank is entitled to hold the bank to the transaction even though the directors lacked the necessary power to bind the bank to transactions which were non-compliant.[11] The requirement of good faith will be met, since the *riba* elements of the transaction merely have the result that the directors have exceeded

---

[6] The memorandum of one of the UK's Islamic banks provides that the main object of the company is 'to carry on the business of a Shariah compliant bank … The term "Shariah" shall be as determined by the Supervisory Board of eminent scholars from time to time appointed by the company'. This implies that the rulings of the SSB on matters of Shariah compliance are to be binding on the bank, its directors, and its members. Contractual provisions to similar effect will often be contained in the bank's facility documentation, and it seems that an English court will be reluctant to re-examine the views of the Shariah Committee: see *The Investment DAR Company KSCC v Blom Deveopment Bank SAL* [2009] EWHC 3545 (Ch), para 10.

[7] The right to bring an action against a director for breach of fiduciary or other duties is a right of the company itself. Consequently, if the company were unwilling to bring such proceedings itself, the relevant shareholder would need to bring a derivative action with the leave of the court. On this subject, see ss 260–269 of the Companies Act 2006.

[8] Section 171 of the Companies Act 2006.

[9] A director may be excused from liability if he acted honestly and reasonably and, in all the circumstances, ought to be excused: see s 1157 of the Companies Act 2006.

[10] Section 39 of the Companies Act 2006. On this provision, see paras 26.47–26.51 above.

[11] Section 40 of the Companies Act 2006. On this provision, see paras 26.47–26.51 above. An ultra vires argument of this kind was rejected in *Islamic Investment Company of the Gulf (Bahamas) Ltd v Symphony Gems NV* [2002] WL 346969: see the discussion at para 49.04 above.

their powers under the articles, and knowledge of that fact does not by itself constitute evidence of bad faith for these purposes.[12]

(d) In a similar vein, it may be added that there is no obligation on the third party to verify that his proposed transaction has been approved by the SSB. This involves a matter of internal procedure (or 'indoor management') for the bank, and thus does not affect the position of third parties or outsiders.[13]

(e) The position may differ slightly where the bank is incorporated outside the United Kingdom, since questions touching its powers and capacity will be governed by the laws of its jurisdiction of incorporation. However, at least in relation to the amount originally invested, the point may well be moot in many cases, at least where the contract is subject to English law. The agreement will either be valid and enforceable or, alternatively, it will be void for want of capacity on the part of the bank. In the first case, judgment for the debt will be given in the usual way. In the latter case, the amount of the investment will be recoverable by means of an action for restitution. In terms of the original investment, the net result is thus effectively the same in either case, although the ability to recover the agreed profit element will depend upon the essential validity of the contractual arrangement.[14]

The Shariah Supervisory Board

50.08   Reference has already been made above to the SSB but, given its unique role within an Islamic financial institution, it is perhaps appropriate to discuss its functions in a little more depth.

50.09   It was noted above that the role of the SSB must be of an *advisory* nature. Why should this be so? If the SSB could give directions or otherwise become involved in the main business of the bank, then two consequences would follow. First of all, the individuals concerned could become 'shadow directors', with the result that they would owe fiduciary and other duties to the company in the same way as the members of the main board. Secondly, they would require 'approved person' status from the FSA in order to carry out their management duties.[15] This will only be allowed to those who have appropriate experience in the management of banking business, and the members of the SSB will not always meet this criterion.[16] It will usually thus be important to ensure that the SSB has an advisory role only. Even then, it may be asked whether the role of the SSB involves 'advising on investments' in a manner which could require authorization.[17] It is submitted that it does not,

---

[12] Section 40(2)(b)(iii) of the Companies Act 2006.

[13] See the rule in *Royal British Bank v Turquand* (1856) 6 E&B 327 and *First Energy (UK) Ltd v Hungarian International Bank Ltd* [1993] 2 Lloyd's Rep 194. See also the decision in the *Blom Development Bank* case, para 49.15 above.

[14] See the decision in *Blom Development Bank*, para 49.15 above.

[15] On 'approved person' status, see para 1.22(e) above.

[16] The articles of association of one such bank show an appreciation of this problem, and provide that: 'The bank shall establish a Shariah Supervisory Board, whose responsibility shall be to *provide advice* to the Board ... to ensure that the Company's activities are in compliance with the Shariah ... and to report on Shariah-related matters to the Board ...' (emphasis supplied).

[17] See Blair, Walker, and Purves, para 19.73.

because the SSB is not advising on the financial merits of such investments[18]—it is merely advising on the extent to which their formal structures may be regarded as Shariah-compliant.

Of course, different considerations may apply in other jurisdictions. For example, a **50.10** Malaysian commentator has observed that '... Even the decisions of the board of directors and top management of Islamic financial institutions are subject to SSB's review to ensure they comply with the Shariah ...'.[19] For the reasons given above, the SSB could comment as to whether particular structures are Shariah-compliant but could not otherwise have a role in purely business decisions.

Since the members of the SSB are not directors of the bank, they do not owe fiduciary **50.11** duties in the generally accepted sense of that expression. This, in a sense, leaves a 'governance gap' for the SSB. It has been suggested that this is in some respects mitigated by the fact that the SSB members will be Shariah scholars, who may therefore be expected to act with integrity, but that a more formalized governance framework would nevertheless be highly desirable.[20] In this respect, it may be noted that AAOIFI has published a series of 'Governance Standards for Islamic Financial Institutions', which seek to lay down appropriate guidelines in this area. In particular, in an attempt to secure a degree of independence for the SSB, it is recommended that its members should be elected by the shareholders (and not by the directors) of the bank. The Standards also set out guidelines on ethics, standards, the conduct of the Shariah-compliance review, and other matters.

Whilst the FSA has naturally indicated that it will not become involved in the debate **50.12** between different interpretations of the Shariah, it will—for the reasons given above—wish to know the role and functions of the SSB and the influence it enjoys in the operations of the bank.[21]

General Regulatory Issues

As noted above, from a regulatory perspective the FSA has sought to treat Islamic banks on **50.13** the same basis as conventional banks, with a view to allowing them to compete on the basis of a level playing field. As a result, the UK has not adopted a separate regulatory regime for Islamic banking; it has merely contented itself with a few technical amendments relating to stamp duty[22] and consumer protection[23] designed to ensure that the proverbial playing field is indeed level.

---

[18] Under Art 53 of the Regulated Activities Order, the 'advising on investments' activity connotes 'advice on the merits of ... buying, selling, subscribing for or underwriting a particular investment'. Although not explicitly stated, it is submitted that this must refer to the *financial* merits of an investment. The functions of the SSB do not extend to advice of this kind.

[19] Jabbar, 'The Shariah Supervisory Board of Islamic Financial Institutions: a Case for Governance' (2009) Company Lawyer 243.

[20] See Jabbar, previous footnote.

[21] See the FSA publication 'Islamic Finance in the UK', referred to at n 2 above.

[22] See paras 51.34–51.36 below.

[23] See paras 51.26–51.29 below.

50.14 Whilst the United Kingdom has thus adopted a fairly neutral stance to the regulation of the Islamic financial markets, it should be appreciated that governments in the Middle East and the Far East have adopted a more proactive and strategic approach in establishing and promoting their Islamic financial markets. The steps taken by Malaysia have already been discussed in some depth to provide the backdrop to the comparative case law discussion attempted earlier in this section.[24] In relation to the Middle East:[25]

(a) In the Dubai International Financial Centre, the locally established Financial Services Authority regulates the provision of Islamic financial services under the Law Regulating Islamic Financial Business (DIFC Law No 13 of 2004).

(b) In Bahrain, the Central Bank of Bahrain regulates the Islamic financial markets under the terms of the Central bank of Bahrain and Financial Institutions Law 2006 and its Rulebook for Islamic Banks.

(c) The Qatar Financial Services Regulatory Authority is likewise the regulator of Islamic banks in that country, operating pursuant to the Qatar Financial Services Law and its Islamic Finance Rulebook.

50.15 Reverting to the position in the United Kingdom, the FSA has to date authorized five Islamic banks. This refers to institutions which conduct their business on a *wholly* Islamic basis. Some conventional banks have established 'Islamic windows' to cater specifically for Muslim customers. Arrangements of this kind are considered at a later stage.[26]

Regulatory Standards and Guidelines

50.16 As noted above, British adherence to the level playing field has meant that no special rules have been promulgated for the regulation of the Islamic financial markets in this country. As a result, Islamic banks are subject to a regulatory regime equivalent to that applicable to conventional banks. Nevertheless, when questions of *compliance* with those standards arise, it may be pertinent to have regard to the standards and guidelines issued by AAOIFI and the IFSB.[27] These are, in any event, standards with which the bank's own Shariah Supervisory Board is likely to expect compliance. In this context, it may be noted that Shariah Standard No 6 (which sets out the rules applicable to the conversion of a conventional institution into an Islamic bank) contains the following provisions:

(a) In providing banking services, the Standard makes the fundamental point that '... it is not permissible for the bank to receive interest as compensation for services rendered ... It is a requirement that an Islamic alternative be worked out ... It is not permissible to take a commission for providing a mere facility. However, the commission may be linked to expenses incurred for the execution of the credit facility accordingly ...'. In other words, interest and commissions are forbidden but the bank may charge for work actually undertaken in providing facilities.[28]

---

[24] See Chapter 49 above.

[25] In relation to the points about to be made, see Blair, Walker and Purves, para 19.16.

[26] See paras 50.30–50.32 below.

[27] On these instruments, see para 48.23 above. The point in the text is made by Blair, Walker and Purves, para 19.56.

[28] This point has already been noted at para 48.13 above.

(b) On the other side of the bank's balance sheet, the bank's own funding activities must likewise be confined to permissible structures, including (i) the issue of equity share capital, (ii) the issue of *sukuk*,[29] (iii) the use of *salam* contracts, where the bank acts as a supplier of goods on deferred terms,[30] (iv) the use of *istisna'a* contracts under which the bank takes on the role of manufacturer or builder with the price paid to it in advance,[31] (v) entering into *ijara* leases, under which assets of the bank are sold and leased back to it, thereby raising a capital sum and creating an obligation to pay rent,[32] or (vi) entering into *tawarruq* (or reverse *murabaha*) transactions as commodity sales for deferred payments.[33]

Deposit-taking

As has been seen, the regulatory regime for banking business in the United Kingdom is built around the prohibition against the acceptance of deposits.[34] A deposit is a sum of money which is 'repayable' on demand at a future date, whether with or without interest.[35] A payment thus only constitutes a deposit if the principal sum is repayable *in full*. But, on the other hand, an arrangement designed to avoid the payment of interest—such as a *qard* or *wadi'a*—will still constitute 'deposits' for these purposes, with the result that their acceptance is subject to the authorization regime created by the FSMA. **50.17**

Insofar as this provision relates to the provision of non-interest bearing current accounts, this can apply equally to banks in the Islamic market. However, there is an obvious difficulty in the context of accounts which are intended to yield a return because (i) as noted above,[36] an account of this kind offered by an Islamic institution must generally involve the sharing of profits and losses as between the bank and the customer, and (ii) as a result, the original deposit would not necessarily be repaid *in full*. **50.18**

On this basis, it might be argued that an Islamic institution should not be authorized as a deposit-taking institution at all. Rather, it should be authorized on the basis that it offers investment products carrying a possibility of gain and a risk of loss.[37] Yet this would not reflect the realities of the situation and a regulatory approach of this nature might be perceived to be discriminatory. Consequently, in the case of the Islamic Bank of Britain, it is understood that the bank undertook to repay all of its deposits in full, giving depositors the option to return (or not to claim) any amounts which represented the loss which would have been incurred on a fully Islamic-compliant deposit. In consequence of this undertaking, it was possible to authorize the Bank as a deposit-taker.[38] **50.19**

---

[29] On these instruments, see para 48.49 above.
[30] On *salam* and *bai' salam* contracts, see para 48.35 above.
[31] On *istisna'a* contracts, see para 48.41 above.
[32] On *ijara* lease structures, see para 48.38 above.
[33] On the *tawarruq* structure, see para 48.32 above.
[34] See the discussion at para 50.13 above.
[35] See art 5 of the Regulated Activities Order.
[36] See the discussion of the *mudaraba, wakala, wadi'a* and *qard* products at paras 48.53–48.59 above.
[37] Authorization under this heading might be granted on the basis that the institution is operating a collective investment scheme, involving the pooling of cash from a number of investors:
[38] On the whole subject, see the FSA's Briefing Note (BN016/06) entitled 'Islamic Banking in the UK', n 2 above. The subject is also discussed by Blair, Walker, and Purves, paras 19.81–19.85.

Collective Investment Schemes

50.20 It has been noted earlier that the prohibition against receipt of interest has tended to drive Islamic financial institutions in the direction of structures which involve profit-sharing, where the bank and the customer become parties to a joint venture or are 'partners'.

50.21 This, in turn, takes Islamic finance into another area of regulation, namely that of collective investment schemes. Such schemes are subject to a separate regulatory regime based on sections 235–284 of the FSMA. The key characteristics of such a scheme as set out in section 235 itself are as follows:

(a) the arrangements must relate to property of any description, including money;

(b) the purpose or effect of the arrangements must be to enable the persons taking part in them to participate in profits or income derived from the use of that property;

(c) the arrangements must be such that the participants do not have day-to-day control over the management of the property, whether or not they have the right to be consulted or to give directions; and

(d) the arrangements must involve (i) the pooling of the contributions made by the participants and/or (ii) the property must be managed by the manager of the scheme.

50.22 There are several regulatory considerations which will apply if a proposed arrangement amounts to a collective investment scheme. First of all, it is unlawful even for an FSA authorized person to promote such a scheme to prospective participants, unless specific exemptions apply.[39] Secondly, the person responsible for the establishment and operation of the scheme requires FSA authorization for that purpose.[40]

50.23 On the face of it, it may be said that the structures adopted by Islamic banks in connection with customer deposits do appear to fall within this definition. This is especially the case given the emphasis placed on profit-sharing as a means of developing Shariah-compliant products. It may thus be argued that the funds provided by customers are pooled under the management of the bank with the profits being available to participants in the scheme. Yet, for a variety of reasons, this would not be an acceptable conclusion. For the reasons given above, it would be very difficult for Islamic banks to market their deposit services if these were regarded as units in a collective investment schemes, and would place them at a disadvantage to their conventional competitors. Such case law as is currently available in England does however suggest that the 'pooling' and 'investment' features of Shariah-compliant deposit products do not give rise to a trust but constitute direct payment obligations of the bank concerned.[41] As a result, such arrangements should not be taken to constitute a collective investment scheme for the purposes of the statutory provisions noted above.

---

[39] Section 238 of FSMA. Section 238(3) of FSMA includes exemptions for FSA authorized and recognized schemes, whilst further exemptions for high net worth individuals and sophisticated investors are created pursuant to the Financial Services and Markets Act 2000 (Promotion of Collective Investment Schemes) (Exemptions) Order 2001 (SI 2001/1060), as amended.

[40] Article 51 of the Regulated Activities Order.

[41] *The Investment DAR Company KSCC v Blom Development Bank SAL* [2009] EWHC 3545 (Ch).

Nevertheless, given the acknowledged breadth of the definition of 'collective investment schemes', it is clearly desirable that the issue should be placed beyond doubt. Accordingly, a number of exemptions have been created by statutory instrument,[42] and those exemptions include so-called 'pure deposit based schemes' Under the terms of this exception,[43] arrangements '… do not amount to a collective investment scheme if the whole amount of each participant's contribution is a deposit which is accepted by an authorized person with permission to carry on an activity of the kind specified by article 5 of the Regulated Activities Order (accepting deposits) …'.[44] This exemption applies to institutions which adopt the deposit structure used by the Islamic Bank of Britain because, as discussed earlier in this chapter, they have been granted permission to accept deposits. **50.24**

This discussion nevertheless provides a further illustration of the difficulties involved in applying a legislative framework designed for conventional banking to the new challenges posed by the Islamic financial market. **50.25**

Islamic Home Finance

It was noted earlier that home mortgage finance is now within the scope of FSA regulation.[45] However, the scope of regulation applies to credit arrangements which are *secured* on land.[46] This expression does not really capture the *ijara* and diminishing *musharaka* products which are most commonly used for Shariah-compliant home finance in the United Kingdom,[47] because ownership of the property rests with the financing institution for the duration of the transaction. As a result, so-called 'home purchase plans' were brought within the scope of regulation by an amendment to the Regulated Activities Order.[48] The definition of 'home purchase plan' extends to an arrangement under which the financier (referred to as the 'home purchase provider') acquires property with a customer as beneficial tenants in common and the customer is to buy out the provider's interest over the period of the transaction.[49] **50.26**

Once again, the object of this exercise was to ensure a level playing field in the regulatory treatment of conventional and Shariah-compliant products.[50] **50.27**

Other Regulatory Issues

It has been noted that a number of Shariah-compliant products depend on the purchase and deferred sale of commodities—see in particular the earlier discussion of the *murabaha* and *tawarruq* products.[51] Under these arrangements, several transactions may take place in **50.28**

---

[42] Financial Services and Markets Act 2000 (Collective Investment Schemes) Order 2001 (SI 2001/1062), as amended.
[43] See para 3 of Sch 1 to the Order mentioned in the previous footnote.
[44] On the acceptance of deposits as a regulated activity, see paras 1.09–1.24 above.
[45] See the discussion in relation to conventional mortgage products at paras 4.43–4.54 above.
[46] Article 61 of the Regulated Activities Order.
[47] On these products, see paras 48.38 and 48.43 above.
[48] See now art 63F of the Regulated Activities Order.
[49] For the detailed definition, see art 63F(3) of the Regulated Activities Order.
[50] For further discussion, see Blair, Walker, and Purves, paras 19.86–19.88.
[51] See paras 48.26 and 48.32 above.

commodities on the date of the transaction, and the party requiring finance is left with an obligation to pay the deferred purchase price (including profit or mark-up) on the maturity date of the deal.

50.29 Other structures, such as the *istisna'a* or *bai salam*,[52] involve up front payments for a delivery of assets at a later date. The question which arises is: do any of these arrangements amount to 'futures' for the purposes of the Regulated Activities Order, with the result that the parties might require permission from the FSA in order to enter into transactions of this kind? The Regulated Activities Order defines a 'future' as '... rights under a contract for the sale of a commodity or property of any other description under which delivery is to be made at a future date and at a price agreed on when the contract is made ...'.[53] A few points may be noted:

(a) The *murabaha* and *tawarruq* contracts do not constitute 'futures' within this definition because, although the deferred payment is due at a future date, the underlying commodities are all purchased and sold for immediate delivery on the due date.

(b) However, the *istisna'a* and *bai salam* contracts do involve delivery of property at a later date and hence pose more difficulty. Nevertheless, where the contract involves physical delivery, such a contract may be regarded as made for *commercial* (rather than *investment*) purposes, and it will be taken outside the definition of 'future' on that basis.[54]

Islamic 'Windows'

50.30 It has previously been noted that some conventional banks offer Shariah-compliant services to Muslim customers through a so-called 'Islamic Window'.[55]

50.31 The accounting standards published by AAOIFI[56] make specific provision for institutions which are offering these types of services. The main provisions are contained in Financial Accounting Standard No 18 and may be summarized as follows:

(a) Institutions of this type should produce separate accounts for their Shariah-compliant business and these should be annexed to their standard financial statements.[57]

(b) The assets/liabilities and income/profits contained within the 'window' should be segregated from the conventional side of the business[58]—or at least, if it is not, full disclosure of that fact should be made.[59]

---

[52] See paras 48.35 and 48.41 above.

[53] Article 84(1) of the Regulated Activities Order.

[54] It will be recalled that the parties must intend to take physical delivery of the commodity in order to ensure Shariah compliance. On intent to take delivery, see *CR Sugar Trading (in administration) v China National Sugar and Alcohol Co* [2003] EWHC 79 (Comm).

[55] For a discussion of Islamic windows, see Blair, Walker, and Purves, para 19.64.

[56] Accounting, Auditing and Governance Standards for Islamic Financial Institutions (AAOIFI, 2007).

[57] See para 3 of Accounting Standard No 18.

[58] See paras 6 and 7 of Accounting Standard No 18.

[59] See para 11 of Accounting Standard No 18, requiring disclosure of any commingling of funds between the two sides of the business.

(c) Since a conventional institution offering Islamic financial services must certify that their products are Shariah-compliant, it must (i) appoint a Shariah supervisory board to prepare a report on compliance matters and (ii) implement AAOIFI's governance standards for that board.[60]

(d) The institution must disclose its source and application of funds, demonstrating Shariah compliance.[61]

(e) The institution must disclose any non-Shariah compliant revenues and expenditures and, in the case of revenues, explain how they have been dealt with.[62]

(f) The institution must provide a breakdown of its business in percentage terms as between its Shariah-compliant an its conventional banking business.[63]

(g) Various other detailed disclosure requirements apply.[64]

An institution which provides services via an Islamic window in the United Kingdom will, of course, require the FSA permissions which are necessary to that end. In practice, however, its activities will most likely be covered by the authorizations which it already holds in respect of its conventional business.   **50.32**

---

[60] See para 9 of Accounting Standard No 18. On the governance standards for an SSB, see para 50.11 above.

[61] See para 12 of Accounting Standard No 18.

[62] See para 13 of Accounting Standard No 18. This will usually be by means of an appropriate charitable donation.

[63] See para 15 of Accounting Standard No 18.

[64] See para 16 of Accounting Standard No 18.

51

HARMONIZATION AND THE DEVELOPMENT OF THE INTERNATIONAL ISLAMIC FINANCIAL MARKETS

Introduction

This chapter considers the need for standardization and harmonization within the Islamic financial markets.[1] It is intended to review the obstacles to the growth of truly *international* Islamic financial markets, and the steps which need to be taken in order to drive that process. It is necessarily written from a relatively 'high level' perspective. **51.01**

The chapter considers the following subject matter: **51.02**

(a) the imperatives of standardization;
(b) the *tawarruq* and the *sukuk* as illustrations of the need for a harmonized approach;
(c) enforcement issues;
(d) the nature and scope of harmonization;
(e) standardized documentation;
(f) Shariah rulings;
(g) the regulatory framework;
(h) capital adequacy;
(i) taxation; and
(j) conclusions from the overall discussion.

---

[1] This chapter is based on a paper presented by the writer to a conference of the Islamic Financial Services Board in Amman, Jordan in May 2008.

The Imperatives of Standardization

51.03 At the outset, it is necessary to ask precisely *why* standardization is necessary and whether it would help to fuel the growth of the Islamic financial services market?

The following points may be noted in this regard:

(a) standardized documentation and practices direct market expectations and provide benchmarks for the behaviour of participants;

(b) harmonization provides an accepted legal framework for transactions, enhancing legal certainty and thus reinforcing market confidence in the enforceability of bargains;

(c) agreed forms of documentation would provide a sound basis for the interaction of common law and Shariah principles;[2]

(d) as a result, the costs involved in the structuring and negotiation of individual transactions are reduced;

(e) harmonized documentation can be used internationally, with obvious benefits for the growth of the markets;

(f) harmonization creates an established and clear framework within which institutions and their products can be properly supervised and regulated.

51.04 In other words, the objectives of standardization and harmonization are similar to those which drive any other market and they are necessary to enable the Islamic financial markets to compete on an equal footing with their conventional counterparts.

51.05 Yet harmonization—especially on an international plane—poses particular challenges for Islamic finance. The process demands compromise, which may readily be achieved where the parties' objectives are purely of a *commercial* nature. But where the parties are seeking to comply with a set of principles based on *faith*, a new dimension is introduced and compromise thus inevitably becomes more difficult.

The Tawarruq and the Sukuk—Illustrations of the Difficulties

51.06 The lack of a standardized approach to Islamic financial products can cause genuine difficulties for market participants. Recent controversy surrounding the *tawarruq* (or 'commodity/reverse *murabaha*') offers a prime example of the issues which can arise.

51.07 The *tawarruq* involves the 'monetization' of commodities and is one of the few Islamic products which can be used to provide the equivalent of a working capital facility by placing cash in the hands of the customer.

---

[2] The discussion of the English and the Malaysian cases in the previous chapter has illustrated the fact that the two systems and their differing principles/objectives can occasionally come into conflict.

As noted earlier,[3] the structure essentially involves: **51.08**

(a) the purchase of commodities (other than gold or silver) by the bank at the request of the customer;[4]

(b) the sale of those commodities by the bank to the customer on deferred terms, with a profit mark up;

(c) the sale of the commodities by the customer (or, more usually, by the bank acting on its behalf) to realize an immediate cash sum.

The customer is thus left with funds to meet its working capital requirements and a deferred **51.09**
payment obligation with respect to its purchase of the commodities.

Of course, the structure has been developed so that a physical asset is introduced into the **51.10**
transaction—Shariah principles allow for the financing of assets, but not for transactions
in pure money. Yet the structure has been criticized, on the ground that it is an artificial
construct which provides, in reality, a loan at interest. Interest being *riba* is, of course,
haram (forbidden). The Islamic Fiqh Council of the Muslim World League (December
2003) decided that tawarruq transactions are forbidden if the customer does not genuinely
come into possession of the underlying goods, so that the transaction is in some respects
illusory. This was later repeated in another resolution of the International Council of the
Fiqh Academy published in April 2009,[5] although it noted that the structure may be valid
if the bank genuinely comes into possession of the commodity such that there is a genuine
sale of the commodity concerned.[6]

Whilst much may depend on the precise nature of the transaction, the fact remains that **51.11**
some Shariah scholars permit, and others condemn, the tawarruq structure. Tawarruq is,
for example, approved in the compendium of Shariah rulings published by Bank Negara
Malaysia.[7] Perhaps in part because of its convenience and simplicity, the structure remains
in common use, both for liquidity management and in the context of interbank
relationships.

Similar difficulties have beset the *sukuk* market. At least before the onset of the credit **51.12**
crunch, the *sukuk* market was experiencing significant growth and a number of issues had
been listed in London. As is well known, a *sukuk* is a certificate which represents an ownership interest in an underlying asset. It is the interest in an asset which is relied upon as the
most important Shariah-compliant feature, and which distinguishes the *sukuk* from a conventional bond or simple debt instrument. The *sukuk* would thus represent an interest in
an underlying transaction such as a *musharaka*, a *murabaha* or an *ijara* leasing structure.
However, towards the end of 2007, the Shariah-compliant nature of some *sukuk* structures

---

[3] See the discussion at para 48.32 above.
[4] Gold and silver are regarded as money, and thus cannot be purchased or sold for these purposes. They are a means of exchange, not an object of it.
[5] Resolution No 179.
[6] This was referred to in the resolution as the 'classical' tawarruq (which may be permissible) as opposed to the 'contemporary' tawarruq (which is not). This suggests that it will be important to ensure that the provisions of AAOIFI's Shariah Standard No 8 are met, in the sense that the financier must clearly come into actual or constructive possession of the asset for some period of time prior to the re-sale.
[7] See Resolution of the 51st Meeting (28 July 2005), Resolutions of the Shariah Advisory Council of Bank Negara Malaysia, p 12.

was questioned, partly on the basis that they represented interests in revenue streams, rather than assets. As a result, the Accounting and Auditing Organisation for Islamic Financial Institutions (AAOIFI) issued new guidelines in March 2008. It may therefore be that some of the earlier issues must now be regulated as non-compliant, with obvious difficulties for investors and the market.

51.13 Problems of this kind inevitably undermine the potential for growth in the use of Islamic financial products. Apart from other considerations, standardization of approach will bring a degree of permanence to the product line and, hence, give confidence both to banks and to the investor base.

Enforcement Issues

51.14 It is clearly unhelpful that there remains a debate as to the essential validity of core products from a Shariah-compliance perspective. These difficulties are exacerbated by the fact that views on an identical product may vary from country to country. But the enforceability of bargains is, of course, one of the foundation stones on which a financial market is built. It is important for banks and their investors to know that their contracts are binding; regulators could hardly function if a significant proportion of a bank's asset base was subject to the vagaries of legal uncertainty.

51.15 Happily—at least from a financial market perspective—the courts have not generally allowed such uncertainties to detract from the validity of the contracts.[8] But standardization of contracts would still clearly be advantageous. If, for example, in *Beximco Pharmaceuticals Ltd v Shamil Bank of Bahrain EC*[9] the Court of Appeal had been confronted with a *murabaha* contract which was in a standard form which was in common use throughout the financial markets, then the decision as to the enforceability of the arrangements would have been of much more value to the markets as a whole.

51.16 As will be apparent from the discussion in the previous chapter, failure to adhere fully to Shariah principles will not usually prejudice the transaction, even though the parties intended it to be compliant. This is a satisfactory result from a financial market perspective, but may obviously be less acceptable to those who would wish to see the acceptance of Shariah principles as a determining factor for compliant transactions. The absence of a uniformly accepted set of rulings on Shariah standards plainly inhibits this process.

What Needs to be Harmonized?

51.17 The foregoing discussion has attempted to explain some of the practical difficulties which act as a brake on the growth of the Islamic banking sector. Standardization of documentation and market practices would act as a spur to that business, because of both greater certainty and greater familiarity.

---

[8] See the analysis of some of the relevant case law in the preceding chapter.
[9] [2004] 4 All ER 1079 (CA). The case has been noted at para 49.08 above.

Assuming that harmonization is regarded as a desirable objective, what precisely needs to **51.18** be standardized in order to promote the Islamic financial markets?

It is suggested that the following areas would require attention: **51.19**

(a) facility documentation;
(b) Shariah rulings;
(c) regulatory frameworks;
(d) capital adequacy; and
(e) taxation.

Each of these issues is considered separately in the ensuing sections of this paper.

Documentation

The production of standard documentation for general use by banks should be the respon- **51.20** sibility of the market or market associations. It is not really the function of the regulators to become involved in the drafting process (although particular features of the documentation may have regulatory consequences).

It is not easy to determine who should assume responsibility for this process. The UK's **51.21** Loan Market Association (LMA) has some years' experience in developing and maintaining documentation for *conventional* facilities, and it might therefore be convenient for that Association to take on the task. This view may be reinforced by the fact that much of the documentation currently in use for Shariah-compliant transactions was developed by English firms and is in use in the UK, the Middle East and other areas. The LMA has already published a practice note on Islamic finance including some suggested documentary changes—but it has not yet adopted a comprehensive approach to the subject. If the documentation process could be monitored and approved by appropriate organizations— such as the Islamic Financial Services Board and the AAOIFI—then this would obviously help to secure wider market acceptance.

The publication of standard documentation would have a variety of advantages, especially **51.22** in reducing the cost of completing Shariah-compliant transactions. In particular:

(a) experience shows that the publication of market standard clauses tends to limit both the time and cost in negotiating transactions; and
(b) the wider availability of standard forms will open up the market to a wider range of potential customers, thus increasing competition and driving down costs.[10]

Shariah Rulings

Islamic banks establish Shariah Supervisory Boards (SSBs) whose task it is to confirm that **51.23** the bank's business is being conducted in a compliant fashion. A statement to that effect will be included in the annual audited accounts of the institution concerned.

---

[10] The initiative in relation to standard form hedging documents has already been noted at para 48.17 above.

51.24   The difficulty is that there is no unanimity of view, or harmonized standard, which is internationally accepted as the benchmark for this statement of opinion. This is obviously understandable, since different schools may take different views and, in any event, Shariah principles were not originally formulated exclusively with financial transactions in mind. But it would be unfortunate if the goal of harmonization in this field were driven purely by commercial or competitive pressures. Fortunately, there have been some steps in the right direction:

(a) as previously noted, Bank Negara Malaysia has published a set of 'Shariah Resolutions in Islamic Finance' which provide guidance to Malaysian banks as to acceptable structures;[11]

(b) the AAOIFI has launched a major initiative to streamline Shariah compliance checks for Islamic financial contracts. The certification programme is linked to the Shariah standards published by AAOIFI over recent years;[12]

(c) the Dubai International Financial Centre has announced a research initiative on the standardization of Islamic finance, with particular reference to the need for global (as opposed to purely regional) acceptance.

51.25   Nevertheless, it is clear that the relatively under-developed state of Shariah jurisprudence acts as a brake on the growth of the market,[13] and may in part be held responsible for some of the confusion which has plagued some of the Malaysian case law.[14]

The Regulatory Framework

51.26   One of the core difficulties which has confronted the growth of Islamic banking has been the absence of a regulatory framework tailored to its specific products and needs.

51.27   This has been particularly apparent in the United Kingdom where—notwithstanding a legal and regulatory body aimed specifically at *conventional* banking—the Financial Services Authority (FSA) has authorized a retail bank and a number of wholesale banks. The first licence was granted to the Islamic Bank of Britain in August 2004. The main obstacle sprang from the fact that a bank is an institution which accepts deposits, and a 'deposit' is 'a sum of money paid on terms under which it will be repaid either on demand or in circumstances agreed by the parties ...'. This connotes that the deposit must be repaid *in full.* This was inconsistent with the *mudaraba* product to be offered by the bank and which necessarily involves the acceptance of losses, as well as the sharing of profits. In order to meet the regulatory definition, the bank has to guarantee payment of the full deposit but customers can later agree to accept payment based on a Shariah-compliant formula.[15]

51.28   Regulatory considerations may also potentially intrude on the role of the Shariah Supervisory Board. In particular, it must be clear that the role of the SSB is purely *advisory*

---

[11] On these rulings, see para 48.23 above.

[12] Reference to the AAOIFI Shariah Standards has already been made. See in particular para 48.23 above.

[13] The point is emphasized by Ryder, 'The Virtue of Certainty' (2009) Comp Law 225.

[14] See the discussion of the Malaysian case law at paras 49.21–49.30 above.

[15] For more detailed consideration of the applicable UK regulatory framework, see paras 50.13–50.29 above.

and that it has no functions of an *executive* nature. If members of the SSB were deemed to have executive powers, for example in structuring the bank's product line, then they would have to be 'approved persons' for FSA purposes. But the FSA will only approve individuals who have relevant and significant experience in the management of a bank, and many Shariah scholars may not meet this test.

It may be noted that harmonization has occurred within the EU banking industry, and that **51.29** this may work to the advantage of Islamic banks authorized in London. Using the EU's 'passporting' procedure,[16] these banks may now establish branches or provide services in other EU Member States without the need for a further licence from the other States concerned. It might be thought that UK authorization may therefore have significant benefits for Islamic banks but this may in many respects be illusory since Islamic products cannot compete on an equal footing in all countries.[17]

Capital Adequacy

As discussed elsewhere,[18] the United Kingdom and other countries have recently imple- **51.30** mented the new capital adequacy framework for banks created by Basel II. The new framework was designed to adopt a more risk-sensitive approach and to take account of modern banking practices in the field of risk management.

Basel II rests on three 'pillars', namely: **51.31**

(a) Pillar 1—minimum capital requirements (eg credit, market and operational risk);
(b) Pillar 2—supervisory review and additional risks (eg interest rate, legal and reputational risks); and
(c) Pillar 3—transparency and market discipline.

The FSA has indicated that it is developing its approach to these areas but, if any special **51.32** risks affecting Islamic banks are identified, then capital may have to be ascribed to those risks under Pillar 2. At a general level, this approach seems to be appropriate since every institution has to account for risks attributable to its particular business.

Once again, however, it may not be easy to provide a uniform framework or 'level playing **51.33** field'. For example, the Islamic Financial Services Board has published various papers and standards on the application of Basel II to Islamic financial institutions.[19] But these are not applied by the FSA in the United Kingdom, and the capital adequacy position of Islamic institutions may vary from country to country. By way of illustration, and as noted elsewhere,[20] Islamic banks operating in the United Kingdom may be required to guarantee the repayment of deposits, whereas this constraint may not apply to similar institutions

---

[16] On the 'passporting' procedure, see paras 2.13–2.21 above.
[17] See the discussion at para 51.36 below.
[18] See generally Chapter 6 above.
[19] The main paper is 'Capital Adequacy for Institutions (other than Insurance Institutions) offering only Islamic Financial Services' (December 2005), which deals with the application of Pillar I (credit risk) of Basel II to Islamic financial institutions. In January 2009, the IFSB also published its paper on 'Capital Adequacy Requirements for Sukuk, Securitisations and Real Estate Investment'.
[20] See paras 50.17–50.19 above.

operating in other jurisdictions. Equally, the preference for equity investments over debt instruments creates a different risk profile for capital adequacy purposes.

Taxation

51.34 The objective for taxation must be harmonization at a *national* level—that is to say, that conventional and Islamic financing structures must attract an identical tax treatment so as to compete on equal terms.

51.35 The United Kingdom offers a good example of this approach. The structures used for Shariah-compliant mortgage financing—*ijara*, diminishing *musharaka, mudaraba*— involve the bank in taking initial title to the property; title is transferred to the customer when the funding is repaid. This previously involved a double charge of stamp duty, since two transfers of property were involved. The government introduced new legislation to deal with issues of this kind[21] and, whilst a certain amount of work remains to be done, Islamic financial products now compete on broadly equal terms with conventional products.

51.36 The difficulty is that relatively few countries have gone down this path.[22] This makes it difficult for Islamic banks to sell *cross-border* services, since other countries do not offer a level playing field. Discrimination within the domestic tax system inevitably drives consumers towards conventional products.

Conclusions

51.37 What conclusions may be drawn from this discussion?

51.38 First of all, it seems clear that a much greater degree of harmonization is required to provide an effective, sustainable, and reliable legal framework in order to encourage and enhance a truly international market in Islamic financial products.

51.39 Secondly, market participants need to take the lead in pressing for standard documentation and practices, thus enhancing familiarity with Shariah-compliant products and driving down transaction costs.

51.40 Thirdly, the momentum towards a set of agreed Shariah standards must be maintained.

51.41 Fourthly, regulatory frameworks require review and revision to ensure that Islamic banks are treated on a par with conventional institutions.

51.42 Finally, many tax systems effectively discriminate against the use of Shariah-compliant products. Governments must be encouraged to revise their codes of practice to provide parity of treatment.

---

[21] For some of the relevant legislation, see the discussion at para 48.30 above.
[22] There are, however, signs that attitudes are beginning to change. In early 2009, the French Government introduced changes to its tax code designed to secure equality of treatment for Shariah-compliant products. Hong Kong has indicated that it is considering a similar move.

INDEX

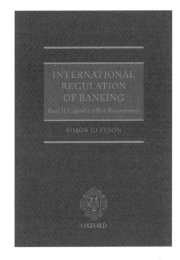

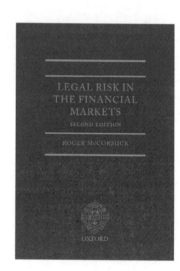
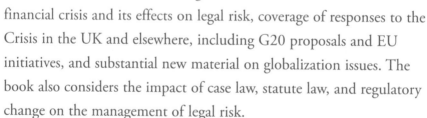
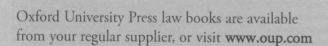